ATTIC RED-FIGURE
VASE-PAINTERS

Oxford University Press, Amen House, London E.C.4

GLASGOW NEW YORK TORONTO MELBOURNE WELLINGTON
BOMBAY CALCUTTA MADRAS KARACHI LAHORE DACCA
CAPE TOWN SALISBURY NAIROBI IBADAN ACCRA
KUALA LUMPUR HONG KONG

ATTIC RED-FIGURE VASE-PAINTERS

BY

J. D. BEAZLEY

SECOND EDITION

VOLUME I

OXFORD
AT THE CLARENDON PRESS
1963

© *Oxford University Press 1963*

PRINTED IN GREAT BRITAIN

UXORI AMATISSIMAE SACRUM

PREFACE TO THE PRESENT EDITION

THE present edition is much enlarged. Great numbers of new vases have come to light in the last twenty years; and I have advanced the lower chronological limit by including the latest phase of Attic red-figure instead of stopping in the earlier part of the fourth century. On the other hand, I have saved some pages by omitting the black-figure work of those red-figure artists who practised both techniques, since it has been dealt with in my *Attic Black-figure Vase-painters* published in 1956; where additions were to be made I have made them, but in general I have been content to refer the reader to the black-figure book.

It need hardly be said that the difference between this edition and the last is not in numbers only; every piece has been reconsidered many times.

In the preface to *Attic Black-figure Vase-painters* I spoke of the help I had received from Dietrich von Bothmer. The red-figure book owes even more to him than the black-figure did. For many years, with the utmost generosity, he has continued to place his notes and photographs at my disposal. Without them many vases would have been less well known to me, and many others would not have been known to me at all: many vases, and indeed whole collections, especially in France, America, and Eastern Europe. He has found time from a busy life to read both the manuscript and the proofs; he has supplied me with countless facts about locations, proveniences, obscure publications, and other matters; and by his patient scrutiny and his acute criticisms he has substantially improved the book.

The thousands of Campana fragments that lay for over eighty years in the magazines and cellars of the Louvre have now been made accessible by Pierre Devambez, and he has recalled to Paris the handfuls that had been distributed all over France. Thanks to his care and kindness I have been able to study the fragments under perfect conditions, and the months I have spent in the Salle Delort de Gléon will always be among my most pleasurable memories.

At Spina the excavations of Valle Pega, begun in 1954 and still continuing, have yielded a quantity of vases even greater than that found in Valle Trebba between 1922 and 1936, with the result that the

Museum of Ferrara has become richer in red-figure pottery of the early classic and classic periods than any other collection. All who care for the past are deeply indebted to the skill, energy, and devotion of the excavator, Nereo Alfieri; and I am particularly grateful to him for the goodwill and true understanding with which he has encouraged my work at Ferrara.

In Athens I remember with special gratitude the welcome I have always had, notwithstanding their many duties, from Christos and Semni Karouzos at the National Museum, and from Homer Thompson, Lucy Talcott, and their colleagues at the Agora.

In 1955 and succeeding years thousands of fragments, nearly all from loutrophoroi, discards from a sanctuary of 'the Nymph', have been found on the south side of the Athenian Acropolis and taken to the Acropolis Museum. To work through these and recompose the vases would take, even if there were room to spread out, many months. In half a dozen mornings during brief visits to Athens I cannot say that I could even skim the material, but I saw many fine things and learned much, and for that I am indebted to the courtesy of the Director, Ioannes Miliadis.

Every summer since 1955 our visits to Naples and Capri have brought us needed repose. I wonder if Mario Astarita realizes how much this book owes not only to the sensitive lover of Greek vases but to the gentle and solicitous friend.

For years Brian Shefton has been faithfully assisting me with accurate information about vases in out-of-the-way places and by sending me photographs.

Brian F. Cook, who has made a special study of the red-figured lekythos, has kindly allowed me to use his photographs and notes.

I am grateful to Herbert A. Cahn for kind acts and for bringing to my notice vases that would otherwise have escaped me. I am grateful to Robert E. Hecht for the same reasons.

Many other friends and acquaintances, some professional scholars, others not, have helped me in many ways. Among those who are no longer with us, I should like to name Paul Jacobsthal, Charles Dugas, Henry Winslow, William Llewellyn Brown, Ernst Buschor; then, of the living, Mrs. Massenet de la Genière, Miss Emilie Haspels, Miss Dorothy Kent Hill, Miss Chrysoula Kardara, Miss Winifred Lamb, Miss Anna Magi, Mrs. Lilly G. Kahil, Miss Hazel Palmer, Miss Anna

Peredolskaya, Miss Barbara Philippaki, Miss Giuliana Riccioni, Miss Gisela M. A. Richter, Miss Erika Simon, Mrs. Annie Dunman Ure, Miss Violette Verhoogen, Mrs. Paola Zancani Montuoro; Giovanni Annibaldi, Bernard Ashmole, Luigi Bernabò Brea, Hansjörg Bloesch, John Boardman, Jacques Bousquet, Niels Breitenstein, Frank Brommer, Alexander Cambitoglou, Arcadio Campi, Giacomo Caputo, Serapheim Charitonides, R. M. Cook, P. E. Corbett, Alfonso de Franciscis, Nevio Degrassi, Antonino Di Vita, Hans Diepolder, Georgios Dontas, Fritz Eichler, Giorgio Fallani, Jiří Frel, Adolf Greifenhagen, Pietro Griffo, Roland Hampe, Herbert Hoffmann, Ernesto Italiano, K. Friis Johansen, Franklin P. Johnson, Caspar Kern, Nicolas Koutoulakis, Emil Kunze, Ernst Langlotz, Reinhard Lullies, Filippo Magi, Amedeo Maiuri, A. H. S. Megaw, Paolino Mingazzini, Hans Möbius, Athos Moretti, Domenico Mustilli, Carlo Navarra, R. V. Nicholls, Piero Orlandini, Venturino Panebianco, Enrico Paribeni, Karl Peters, Vagn Poulsen, Martin Robertson, Andreas Rumpf, Karl Schefold, H. R. W. Smith, E. G. Spencer-Churchill, A. D. Trendall, Vincenzo Tusa, Cornelius Vermeule, François Villard, Humfrey Wakefield, Giovanni Zirretta. To all these my thanks.

A grant from the Leverhulme Trustees enabled me to make a journey which I should scarcely have been able to make without it. The British Academy made me a grant towards the expense of typing. To these also my thanks.

The rule of the Clarendon Press precludes more than a general acknowledgement of indebtedness to the Delegates, the Secretary, the Printer, and their staffs. This I most gladly make; and now that John Johnson, Printer to the University between 1925 and 1946, has passed away, I should like at least to say that he stood by me at a critical moment in 1940 and I do not forget it.

Any day a new vase, or a familiar one seen again, may light up a dark corner; and I have no doubt that if I kept my manuscript longer I could improve it in many places; but I have kept it a long time, and I think that the hour has come to let it go.

The book is dedicated to my wife, who for more than forty years has been my great support. She has helped me in every way, both in front of the vase itself, and at every distance from it: in the outer orbit, by bringing about those conditions without which the work could hardly have been completed: good health, and good spirits.

PREFACE TO THE 1942 EDITION

THIS is a new edition of a work published by the firm of Siebeck in 1925. The first edition contained some 10,000 items; the second has more than half as many again. In these seventeen years hundreds of vases have come to light in excavation; others, lost, have reappeared; many others I did not know in 1925; and I knew all less well than now. Moreover, this edition covers a somewhat larger field: for, first, it includes the white lekythoi, whereas in the old edition I mentioned only those white lekythoi that were by red-figure painters; secondly, I have learned more about the black-figure work of the artists who practised black-figure as well as red; and thirdly, I have advanced my lower chronological limit so as to take in the early fourth century instead of stopping at the end of the fifth.

In the years I have been working at the subject I have received help from so many that it would hardly be possible to give all their names: I beg the living to accept a general expression of gratitude in place of a particular. I am deeply indebted to the Delegates and Staff of the Oxford University Press for undertaking the book, and producing it in spite of difficulties, *patriai tempore iniquo*.

J. D. B.

June 1942

CONTENTS

VOLUME I

BOOK I (Chapters 1–2). EARLY RED-FIGURE POT-PAINTERS

BOOK II (Chapters 3–13). EARLY RED-FIGURE CUP-PAINTERS

BOOK III (Chapters 14–21). LATE ARCHAIC POT-PAINTERS

BOOK V (Chapters 30–36). EARLY CLASSIC PAINTERS OF
LARGE POTS

BOOK VI (Chapters 37–42). EARLY CLASSIC PAINTERS OF
SMALLER POTS

VOLUME II

BOOK VII (Chapters 43–48). EARLY CLASSIC CUP-PAINTERS

BOOK XI (Chapter 64). CLASSIC PAINTERS OF WHITE LEKYTHOI

BOOK XVI (Chapters 72–73). LATE-FIFTH-CENTURY PAIN-
TERS OF SMALL POTS

72. Painters of oinochoai

BOOK XIX (Chapters 77–88). FOURTH-CENTURY POT-PAINTERS

APPENDIX I. THE HEAD VASES

VOLUME III. INDEXES

INSTRUCTIONS FOR USE

THE words 'Group' and 'Class' are used in special senses. 'Class' refers to shape, 'Group' to style of drawing. Thus from the point of view of shape a vase may belong to *Class* X, while from the point of view of drawing it belongs to *Group* Y.

The arrangement of the painters is roughly chronological; but groups of painters are kept together, and naturally it often happens that contemporary vases are widely separated, and a vase described on p. 200 may be earlier than one described on p. 80. I would beg the reader to keep this well in mind. A friend has said that the book is like a map on Mercator's projection: 'everything is there, but some of the distances are rather misleading'.

The arrangement in chapters is rough and ready. One chapter may be homogeneous (treating the work of a single artist or of a few interconnected artists). The next may be much less so, and one chapter is even entitled 'Fourth-century odds and ends'. The ninety chapters are grouped in twenty 'books' under such general titles as 'Late archaic cup-painters'. The later works of an artist who is called 'a late-archaic cup-painter' may belong to the succeeding period, the early classic; and sometimes one hesitates whether to count a painter as belonging to an earlier period or a later, seeing that in truth he straddles both periods. Sometimes I have drawn attention to such facts, but often I have trusted to the good sense of the reader.

Some of the chapter-titles have the form 'Painters of classic oinochoai' or 'Late-fifth-century painters of small pots'. This does not imply that such artists painted nothing but oinochoai, or never painted large vases: only that oinochoai, or small pots, constitute a characteristic part of their output. Nor again does it imply that all oinochoai of the classic period, or all small pots of the late fifth century, will be found in these chapters; on the contrary, it may well be that the best oinochoai or small pots, or most of the best, will be found elsewhere, being the work, for example, of artists whom we are calling 'cup-painters' because cups are the most characteristic part of their production. Most of the vases in the 'oinochoai' chapter, or the chapter 'small pots', may be residual—what is left after the better pieces have been taken out. Sometimes, again, it is hard to decide whether to classify an artist as a painter of oinochoai or as a painter of cups; as a painter of small vases or as a painter of large.

The vases are red-figured, unless otherwise stated; black-figure vases, and white-ground vases, are specified.

The name of a town means the chief collection in it: thus 'London' means 'the British Museum'. Other collections in London are specified: the full title being given in the index of collections.

'London market' means that the vase is or was at one time in the London market. Paris market, Roman market, similarly.

A fragment of a hydria is placed under 'hydria' not under 'fragments'. That heading is only used if the shape of the vase is uncertain, or not known to me. If several fragments join, they are described as 'a fragment', in the singular; the plural, 'fragments', is only used if they do not join.

If the vase is restored I say so: and by 'restored' I do not mean that it has been put together, honestly, from fragments, but that the ancient parts have in places been repainted or retouched, or modern pieces added, or both. It is a warning, and in many cases a reproach.

'Now cleaned' means that the restorations have been removed, either since the publications were made, or since I described the vase as 'restored'. A 'restored' vase may naturally have been cleaned since I saw it; and a vase, clean when I saw it, may have been tampered with since.

Original publications are distinguished from derivative. Thus '*Mon.* 1 pl. 3; *JHS.* 25 pl. 1' means that the vase is figured in *Monumenti dell'Instituto*, and, *from a new drawing or photograph*, in the *Journal of Hellenic Studies.* Had the reproduction in *JHS.* been simply taken from *Monumenti*, I should have written '*Mon.* 1 pl. 3, *whence JHS.* 25 pl. 1'; and in that case, if both *Monumenti* and *JHS.* are available to the reader, he will be well advised to turn up *Monumenti* rather than *JHS.*, since the reproduction in *JHS.* will not be better than that in *Monumenti* and may be decidedly worse. Well advised so far as the picture is concerned: of course he may wish to see what the writer in *JHS.* says in the text.

In references to the *Corpus Vasorum* I save space by omitting the name of the collection and the rubric III I c. Thus I write 'Louvre G 3. *CV.* pl. 27, 1', where the second sentence is short for '*CV.* Louvre III I c pl. 27, 1'. If the rubric is other than III I c, I add either the small letter (*CV.* III I d pl. 5, 1) or if necessary the large and the small (*CV.* H e pl. 5, 1 = *CV.* III H e pl. 5, 1) or even the whole rubric (*CV.* IV Dr pl. 5, 1). When a vase appears on more than one plate of the *Corpus*, I give the full references to all the appearances: except in the case of the Berlin fascicules: these reached me at the last moment, and in order to reduce the number of alterations I give the prime reference only; the others can easily be found in Greifenhagen's text.

References to the first volume of the Florence *Corpus* are in a special case. The many hundreds of fragments figured there were not numbered by the author of the volume and there was no means of referring to them: when I wrote my *Campana Fragments in Florence* I had to give them numbers myself, and these are the numbers I use here. Thus in 'Florence 1 B 8, frr. *CV.* pl. 1,

B 8' the second sentence means 'CV. Florence III I C, the sherds (of a single vase) put together and described under pl. 1, B 8 in my *Campana Fragments*; not only the single fragment figured in the *Corpus* at that place, but all the fragments of the vase, whether they are figured in other parts of the Florence *Corpus*, or elsewhere, or not figured at all'. For particulars *Campana Fragments* must be consulted: otherwise I should have had to reprint great part of that work. Naturally I have often made additions to what was said in *Campana Fragments*, which was published in 1933.

The references to Ferrara vases take the form 'Ferrara, T.' followed by a number, for instance '49'. Here 'T.' stands for 'Tomba'. The Ferrara vases have no individual numbers and so one gives the number of the tomb in which the vase was found. As each tomb usually contained several vases, an oinochoe on p. 100 may be described as 'Ferrara, T. 49' and a krater on p. 200 in the same way: the shape and the subject distinguish one vase from another, so that there is no confusion. The vases from Valle Pega at Spina have the letters 'VP' following the tomb-number; those from Valle Trebba have no letters (it was not necessary to add 'VT'). Valle Pega is excavated in several sections, so that 'VP' has to be followed by another capital letter, A, B, C, D, or E.

The sherds mentioned in the Preface, from the sanctuary of 'the Nymph', in the Acropolis Museum at Athens, have no individual numbers, but with the permission of the Director I pencilled attributions on the backs. In my text I have sometimes described the sherds, but often I have said no more than 'so many by such-and-such a painter'. Since the sherds are nearly all from loutrophoroi, and since the subjects of loutrophoroi are few, to go into more detail would have occupied more space than could be afforded, and the descriptions would be almost meaningless once the vases came to be re-composed. (Here I wish to repeat, although it is stated in the index of collections, that the words 'Athens Acr.' have a different sense from 'Athens, Acropolis Museum'. 'Athens, Acropolis Museum' means that the vase or fragment is in the Museum on the Acropolis of Athens; 'Athens Acr.' that it forms part of the collection of vases found on the Acropolis in the excavations of 1885 to 1890 and previously, which is preserved not on the Acropolis but in the National Museum).

In references to illustrations in the text of an article I give the pages on which the illustrations occur, not the pages of the whole article or the pages on which the vase is discussed.

Subjects are described as briefly as possible. The one word 'athletes', for example, does not imply that all the figures in the picture are athletes: some may be trainers, or onlookers, but the subject is 'athletes', and the single word suffices. Again, 'Triptolemos' is the subject of a vase, and the one word is enough, although there may be several figures besides him in the picture—Demeter, Persephone, and perhaps others. If, however, a vase or a fragment has no museum number, or if it is in less permanent possession—in the market, or in private hands—, it may be described in more detail to assist identification. In a fragment, if there is not enough left to determine the subject, what remains is put in rounded brackets. Thus 'A, lion' means that the subject of A is a lion, but 'A, (lion)' means that while the subject of the whole picture is uncertain, one of the figures is a lion.

A semicolon between the subjects on a vase implies that they are connected in one way or another; otherwise I put a full stop.

Of inscriptions, I give the signatures and the kalos-names, and these as accurately as I can in point of spelling, punctuation, direction (retrograde or not), separation or non-separation of words, and the main forms of letters. Other inscriptions are only occasionally recorded, chiefly for the purpose of identification.

The serial numbers in the lists are often followed by another number, within rounded brackets: this is the number the vase had in the former edition. Sometimes the bracketed number is preceded by the letter 'a' or the letter 'l': 'a', when the vase did not yet appear in the list of the painter's works, but only in a list of vases connected with him ('a' for 'adjunct', including such headings as 'manner', 'near', or other expressions for relationship); 'l' (for 'list') when the vase was in the list of works ascribed to the painter, although it now appears to be related to him rather than from his own hand. In the few cases where other sigla are employed, they are explained in the preamble to the list.

The bibliographies at the heads of the lists are not exhaustive: they refer to the more comprehensive or more pointed accounts of the artist—in which vases are rightly assigned to him, or his style accurately defined. To such accounts the commentaries on single vases, or on parts of them, must be added: these are sometimes cited, but often they must be elicited from the list of publications. If, for example, a vase is set down as figured in Furtwängler and Reichhold, the reader will naturally turn to what Furtwängler, Reichhold, and their collaborators say about it in the text to the plates. References without surname are to my own writings.

My attributions have often been misquoted. In the former edition of *Attic Red-figure Vase-painters* I wrote that in the *Corpus Vasorum* misquotation appeared to be the rule although I did not know that it had been anywhere prescribed in black and white. I thought of omitting this sentence in the present edition (as possibly indicating a certain lack of calm): but recent experience of the *Corpus* has warned me that it would be foolish to do so. I may perhaps be allowed to point out that I make a distinction between a vase by a painter and a vase in his manner; and that 'manner', imitation, following, workshop, school, circle, group, influence, kinship are not, in my vocabulary, synonyms. If I have written that a vase is in the manner of a painter, it pains me to read that I have attributed it to that painter; if I have written that a vase is by a painter, it pains me to read that I have ascribed it to the workshop of that painter; if I have written that a vase is not by a painter, it pains me to read that I have said it was by him. A scholar is free to disagree with what I have said, to ignore it, or to deride it; but if he quotes me, I hope that he will be so good as to quote me correctly.

A list of vases assigned to a good artist sometimes includes pieces that are unworthy of him. It is my experience that Greek vase-painters were not always at their best, differing in this respect from modern artists.

When an attribution has already been made by someone else, I put the name of the originator in square brackets at the end of the entry. I have not recorded attributions made by others unless I have been able to check them and have found them correct.

The section of Addenda is rather long. The subject is one of those on which new material comes in daily. The book has been a good while printing; and the page-proof stage once reached, substantial additions in the text were not possible. There is often an indication in the text that more matter on a vase will be found in the Addenda, but often there was no room even for the words 'See page' and the number.

SHAPES

REFERENCES when possible to Caskey *Geometry of Greek Vases* (C.), to Richter and Milne *Shapes and Names of Greek Vases* (R. and M.), and to *CV*. Oxford. References to Caskey are to *pages* not to figures.

Amphora.
    Type A: C. 60–61; R. and M. figs. 6–8.
    Type B: C. 59; R. and M. figs. 1–5.
    Type C: C. 80; R. and M. fig. 10.
Pointed amphora. R. and M. fig. 28.
Panathenaic amphora. C. 57 and 77–79; R. and M. figs. 24–25.
Neck-amphora. C. 65 and 72; R. and M. figs. 20–23; *CV*. Oxford pll. 15–16.
Nolan amphora (a special kind of small neck-amphora). C. 63–64, 66–71, and 73–74; R. and M. figs. 18–19; *CV*. Oxford pl. 58, 1–2.
Nicosthenic neck-amphora. R. and M. fig. 34.
Loutrophoros. (Loutrophoros-amphora): C. 81; R. and M. figs. 40 and 42.
    (Loutrophoros-hydria): R. and M. fig. 41.
Pelike. C. 84–90; R. and M. figs. 36–39; *CV*. Oxford pl. 19, 3 and pl. 20, 1–8.
Stamnos. C. 93–97 and 100; R. and M. figs. 64–68; *CV*. Oxford pl. 29.
Dinos. C. 117 fig. 71; R. and M. figs. 70–71.
Nuptial lebes.
    Type 1: R. and M. figs 72–73 and 75.
    Type 2: R. and M. fig. 74.
Volute-krater. C. 121 and 123; R. and M. figs. 50–53; *CV*. Oxford pl. 21, 1–2.
Column-krater. C. 122; R. and M. figs. 45–48; *CV*. Oxford pl. 23, 2–4.
Calyx-krater. C. 124–5; R. and M. figs. 55–58; *CV*. Oxford pl. 21, 3–4.
Bell-krater.
    With lugs: C. 127; R. and M. fig. 63.
    With handles: C. 128–30; R. and M. figs. 60–62; *CV*. Oxford pl. 24, 1–3.
Psykter. C. 131; R. and M. fig. 88; *CV*. Oxford pl. 48, 25–26.
Hydria.
    Of bf. type: C. 107 and 109; R. and M. figs. 78–79.
    Of rf. type (kalpis): C. 110–14; R. and M. figs. 81–86; *CV*. Oxford pl. 31, 1–4 and pl. 32, 1–5 and 8–11.
Oinochoe.
    Shape 1: C. 137; R. and M. figs. 125 and 129; *CV*. Oxford pl. 42, 4.

Shape 2: C. 138; R. and M. fig. 126; *CV.* Oxford pl. 42, 1–3 and 5.

Shape 3 (chous): C. 139; R. and M. figs. 118–21; *CV.* Oxford pl. 43, 1–4 and 6–8.

Shape 4: C. 140–3; *CV.* Oxford pl. 43, 5.

Shape 5A: C. 145; R. and M. fig. 117; *CV.* Oxford pl. 43, 14.

   5B: R. and M. fig. 133; *CV.* Oxford pl. 48, 12.

Shape 6: Masner 48; Pfuhl fig. 792. (Later, R. and M. fig. 130.)

Shape 7: R. and M. figs. 131–32.

Shape 8A (mug): R. and M. fig. 186.

   8B (mug): C. 147. *CV.* Oxford pl. 62, 3.

Shape 8C (mug): C. 146; *CV.* Oxford pl. 48, 14.

Shape 9: Pfuhl fig. 787.

Shape 10: R. and M. figs. 127–8; *CV.* Oxford pl. 42, 6.

Lekythos. C. 213–21; R. and M. figs. 96–97; *CV.* Oxford pl. 38.

Squat lekythos. C. 222–4; R. and M. figs. 99–102; *CV.* Oxford pl. 40, 1–2, and 17–20, and pl. 63, 1–5 and 8–9. (Tallboy, Pfuhl fig. 793.)

Acorn-lekythos. C. 225.

Pointed amphoriskos. C. 82; R. and M. figs. 30–31; *CV.* Oxford pl. 40, 3–5.

Round aryballos. R. and M. figs. 104–6; *CV.* pl. 47, 9 and pl. 64, 1–7.

Alabastron. R. and M. figs. 109–11; *CV.* Oxford pl. 41, 1–6.

Columbus alabastron. *CV.* Oxford pl. 47, 10 and 14.

Askos.

 Type 1: R. and M. fig. 112; *CV.* Oxford pl. 45, 1–4 and 6–9 and pl. 48, 28, 31, and 37–38.

 Type 2: *CV.* Oxford pl. 48, 29.

Astragalos. *CV.* London pll. 26–27.

Onos. Pfuhl fig. 769.

Bobbin. Richter and Hall pl. 178, 74.

Pyxis.

 Type A: C. 227 and 229; R. and M. figs. 139 and 141; *CV.* Oxford pl. 65, 12.

 Type B: *CV.* Copenhagen pl. 162, 5.

 Type C: R. and M. fig. 136.

 Type D: R. and M. figs. 143–5; *CV.* Oxford pl. 47, 11–13.

 Nicosthenic type: Hoppin ii, 231.

 Tripod-pyxis. R. and M. fig. 135.

Lekanis. R. and M. fig. 149; *CV.* Oxford pl. 65, 11 and 14.

Plastic vases. These are of various kinds (drinking-vessels, oinochoai, aryballoi, &c.); they are kept together, for convenience, in the museum index, but differentiated in the text.

Kantharos.

   Type A: C. 161–4; R. and M. fig. 167.

   Type B: R. and M. fig. 169.

   Type C: R. and M. fig. 168.

   Type D: *CV*. Munich pl. 93, 3–4; CB. i, 18.

   Sessile. With high handles, *CV*. Oxford pl. 48, 34; *CV*. London pl. 32,
     15; C. 166. With low handles, *CV*. London pl. 32, 17–18.

Czartoryski Class: see p. 982.

Kantharoid, *CV* Pologne pl. 120, 1.

Kyathos. R. and M. figs. 183–4.

Phiale. Lau pl. 27, 3; R. and M. fig. 181.

Skyphos.

   Type A: C. 155–7; R. and M. fig. 174; *CV*. Oxford pl. 65, 15.

   Corinthian type: R. and M. fig. 176; *CV*. Oxford pl. 65, 17 and 24.

   Type B (glaux): *CV*. Oxford pl. 47, 9 and pl. 62, 1–2; (R. and M. fig. 175
     is not typical).

Stemless cups, and cup-skyphoi.

   There are many types. The following are only a few of them.

   Lipped, deep. R. and M. fig. 172.

   Lipped, shallow. C. 207 fig. 161; R. and M. fig. 157.

   Lipless, shallow. C. 208.

   Bolsal. *CV* Oxford pl. 48, 3 and 6 and pl. 65, 21. For the name see *B.S.A.*
     41, 18 note 2.

Cups.

   Type A (AZ and AY). C. 177; R. and M. fig. 161–2. (AZ: Bloesch
     pl. 3, 3–4; pl. 8, 1–3; pl. 17, 1. AY: Bloesch pl. 8, 4; pl. 9; pl. 10;
     pl. 11, 1; C. 177 fig. 134).

   Type B. C. 181 fig. 136; 183 fig. 137; 187–92; 196–203; R. and M.
     figs. 163 and 166; Bloesch pll. 12–16; pl. 17, 3–4; pl. 18; pl. 19, 1–2;
     pll. 20–31.

   Type C. C. 181 fig. 135; 183 fig. 138; R. and M. fig. 156; Bloesch
     pll. 33–34; pl. 35, 2–4; pl. 36. But I do not count a cup as of Type C
     unless it has an offset lip as well as the characteristic stem and foot.

   Conefoot cup. Bloesch pl. 34, 7.

   Eleusis cup. Bloesch pl. 37.

   Vicup. Bloesch pl. 38.

   Acrocup. Bloesch pl. 39.

Plate. R. and M. fig. 191.

Stemmed plate. See p. 1305.

Stemmed dish. *CV*. Oxford pl. 47, 1.

Standlet of Sosian type. R. and M. fig. 190.

ABBREVIATIONS

The letter p. for page is omitted, unless there might be ambiguity.
  Fr., fragment; frr., fragments. If several fragments join up into one, the singular is used.
  Ph., photograph; phs., photographs.
For abbreviated titles not explained in the following list see the index of publications.

AAA.	*Ancient Art in American Private Collections.*
ABC.	*Antiquités du Bosphore cimmérien.*
ABS.	Beazley *Attic Black-figure: a Sketch.*
ABV.	Beazley *Attic Black-figure Vase-painters.*
A.D.	*Antike Denkmäler.*
AEM.	*Archäologisch-epigraphische Mittheilungen aus Oesterreich.*
A.F.	*Archivio fotografico.*
A.I.	Athens, German Institute.
AJA.	*American Journal of Archaeology.*
Al.	Alinari.
Alfieri and Arias	*Spina* (1958).
Alfieri and Arias *S.G.*	*Guida al Museo archeologico di Ferrara* (1960).
AM.	*Mitteilungen des Deutschen Archäologischen Instituts: Athenische Abteilung.*
And.	Anderson.
Angelini	Patroni *Vasi dipinti del Museo Vivenzio disegnati da Costanzo Angelini nel MDCCXCVIII.*
Anz.	*Archäologischer Anzeiger* (supplement to *Jahrbuch*).
Arch. phot.	Archives photographiques.
Arias and Alfieri	*Il Museo Archeologico di Ferrara* (1955).
ARV.[1]	Beazley *Attic Red-figure Vase-painters*, 1st ed. (1942).
ARW.	*Archiv für Religionswissenschaft.*
Att.V.	Beazley *Attische Vasenmaler des rotfigurigen Stils.*
Aurigemma	*Il R. Museo di Spina.*
Aurigemma *N.S.*	*La Necropoli di Spina.*
AWL.	Beazley *Attic White Lekythoi.*
AZ.	*Archäologische Zeitung.*
B.Ap.	Gerhard's Apparatus of drawings, in the Berlin Museum.
BCH.	*Bulletin de correspondance hellénique.*
Berl.	Beazley *Der Berliner Maler.*
Bloesch	*Formen attischer Schalen.*
Bloesch *AKS.*	*Antike Kunst in der Schweiz.*
BMQ.	*British Museum Quarterly.*
Bothmer *Am.*	*Amazons in Greek Art.*
Bothmer *A.N.Y.*	*Ancient Art from New York Private Collections.*

BSA.	*Annual of the British School at Athens.*
BSR.	*Papers of the British School at Rome.*
Bull. It.	*Bullettino Archeologico Italiano.*
Bull. Metr.	*Bulletin of the Metropolitan Museum of Art.*
Bull. Nap.	*Bullettino Archeologico Napolitano.*
Burl. 1888	*Burlington Fine Arts Club: Catalogue of Objects of Greek Ceramic Art (1888).*
Burl. 1903	*Burlington Fine Arts Club: Exhibition of Ancient Greek Art (1903).*
Buschor	*Griechische Vasenmalerei.*
Buschor G. *Vasen*	*Griechische Vasen.*
Caskey G.	*Geometry of Greek Vases.*
CB.	Caskey and Beazley *Attic Vase Paintings in the Museum of Fine Arts, Boston.*
CC.	Collignon and Couve *Catalogue des vases peints du Musée National d'Athènes.*
CF.	Beazley *Campana Fragments in Florence.*
Cl. Rev.	*Classical Review.*
Cl. Rh.	*Clara Rhodos.*
CR. (or *Compte-rendu*)	*Compte-rendu de la Commission Impériale Archéologique.*
CV.	*Corpus Vasorum Antiquorum.* For the system of reference see p. xliv.
Cypr.	Beazley *Some Attic Vases in the Cyprus Museum.*
Delt.	*Arkhaiologikon Deltion.*
Dev.	Beazley *The Development of Attic Black-figure.*
Diepolder	*Griechische Vasen.*
E.A.A.	*Enciclopedia dell'Arte Antica.*
El.	Lenormant and de Witte *Elite des monuments céramographiques.*
Enc. phot.	*Encyclopédie photographique de l'art.*
Eph.	*Ephemeris arkhaiologike.*
EVP.	Beazley *Etruscan Vase-painting.*
F. Benndorf	*Festschrift für Otto Benndorf.*
FD.	*Fouilles de Delphes.*
FR.	Furtwängler and Reichhold *Griechische Vasenmalerei.*
García y Bellido	*Hispania Graeca.*
García y Bellido HG.	*Los hallazgos griegos de España.*
Gardiner, Norman *Athl.*	*Athletics of the Ancient World.*
Gardiner, Norman *G.A.S.*	*Greek Athletic Sports and Festivals.*
Gardner, E.	*Catalogue of the Greek Vases in the Fitzwilliam Museum Cambridge.*
Gardner	*Catalogue of the Greek Vases in the Ashmolean Museum.*

Gerhard	*Auserlesene Vasenbilder.*
Gir.	Giraudon.
GP.	Gorbunova and Peredolskaya *Mastera grecheskikh raspisnykh Vaz.*
Hambidge	*Dynamic Symmetry: the Greek Vase.*
Haspels *ABL.*	*Attic Black-figured Lekythoi.*
Hesp.	*Hesperia.*
Hesp. Art Bull.	*Hesperia Art Bulletin.*
Heydemann	*Griechische Vasenbilder.*
HM.	Harrison and MacColl *Greek Vase Painting.*
Hoppin	*A Handbook of Attic Red-figured Vases signed by or attributed to the various masters of the sixth and fifth centuries B.C.*
Hoppin *Bf.*	*A Handbook of Greek Black-figured Vases.*
Inghirami	*Pitture di vasi etruschi.*
Izv.	*Izvestiya Imperatorskoi arkheologicheskoi kommissii.*
Izv. Blg.	*Izvestiya na Blgarskoto arkheologichesko druzhestvo.*
Jacobsthal *O.*	*Ornamente griechischer Vasen.*
Jb.	*Jahrbuch des Deutschen Archäologischen Instituts.*
Jh.	*Jahreshefte des Oesterreichischen Archäologischen Institutes.*
JHS.	*Journal of Hellenic Studies.*
Kl.	Beazley *Der Kleophrades-Maler.*
Klein *L.*	*Die griechischen Vasen mit Lieblingsinschriften.*
Klein *Meist.*	*Die griechischen Vasen mit Meistersignaturen.*
Kretschmer	*Die griechischen Vaseninschriften.*
Langlotz	*Die antiken Vasen von der Akropolis zu Athen.*
Langlotz	*Griechische Vasen in Würzburg.*
Langlotz *GV.*	*Griechische Vasenbilder.*
LS.	Levi (Attilio) and Stenico (Arturo) *Pittura greca.*
Ma.	Mansell.
Metr. St.	*Metropolitan Museum Studies.*
ML.	*Monumenti antichi pubblicati per cura della Reale Accademia dei Lincei.*
Mo.	Moscioni.
Mon.	*Monumenti inediti pubblicati dall'Instituto di Corrispondenza Archeologica.*
Mon. gr.	*Monuments grecs publiés par l'Association pour l'Encouragement des Études Grecques en France.*
Mon. Piot	*Fondation Eugène Piot. Monuments et Mémoires publiés par l'Académie des Inscriptions et Belles-Lettres.*

Mostra	*Mostra dell'Etruria Padana e della Città di Spina* (Bologna 1960).
Mü. Jb.	*Münchener Jahrbuch.*
Mü. St.	*Münchener archäologische Studien.*
Mus. Borb.	*Real Museo Borbonico.*
Mus. Greg.	*Museum Etruscum Gregorianum.*
Mus. J.	*Museum Journal* (Philadelphia).
Neugebauer	*Führer durch das Antiquarium, ii. Vasen.*
Neugebauer *ADP.*	*Antiken in deutschem Privatbesitz.*
NSc.	*Notizie degli Scavi di Antichità.*
N.Y. Shapes	*Shapes of Greek Vases* (New York).
Overbeck *KM.*	*Atlas der griechischen Kunstmythologie.*
Panm.	Beazley *Der Pan-Maler.*
Pellegrini	*Catalogo dei vasi greci delle necropoli felsinee.*
Pellegrini *VPU.*	*Catalogo dei vasi antichi dipinti delle collezioni Palagi ed Universitaria.*
Pfuhl	*Malerei und Zeichnung der Griechen.*
Pottier	*Vases antiques du Louvre.*
PP.	Beazley *Potter and Painter in Ancient Athens.*
Q. Pal.	*Quarterly of the Department of Antiquities in Palestine.*
RA.	*Revue archéologique.*
REA.	*Revue des études anciennes.*
REG.	*Revue des études grecques.*
RG.	Beazley and Magi *La raccolta Guglielmi nel Museo Gregoriano Etrusco.*
R.I.	Rome, German Institute.
Riv. Ist.	*Rivista dell'Istituto di Archeologia e Storia d'Arte.*
RM.	*Mitteilungen des Deutschen Archäologischen Instituts. Römische Abteilung.*
Rumpf *MZ.*	*Malerei und Zeichnung der Griechen.*
Schefold *KV.*	*Kertscher Vasen.*
Schefold *U.*	*Untersuchungen zu den Kertscher Vasen.*
So.	Sommer.
St. etr.	*Studi etruschi.*
VA.	Beazley *Attic Red-figured Vases in American Museums.*
VDK.	*Verschiedener deutscher Kunstbesitz* (Berlin 1935).
VPol.	Beazley *Greek Vases in Poland.*
Villard	*Les vases grecs.*

BOOK I

(CHAPTERS 1-2)

EARLY RED-FIGURE POT-PAINTERS

CHAPTER 1

THE EARLIEST POT-PAINTERS

(THE ANDOKIDES PAINTER, PSIAX, AND OTHERS)

ANDOKIDES, POTTER

Bloesch *FAS.* 12-15. Bloesch in *JHS.* 71, 29-31 and 35. *ABV.* 253-4 and 715.

The signature of Andokides appears on nine vases, always with ἐπόησεν or the like. The decoration is by four different painters. For the ninth vase see p. 1617.

(i)

(*akin to Group E*)

BRONXVILLE, Bastis, bf. amphora (type B). See *ABV.* 253 and 715; side-views, *AJA.* 1956 pl. 112, 34-35. The modern knob on the lid has now been removed.

(ii)

(*decorated by the Andokides Painter*)

BERLIN 2159.   See p. 3 no. 1.
LOUVRE G 1.   See p. 3 no. 2.
LOUVRE F 203.   See p. 4 no. 13.
PALERMO V 650.   See p. 5 no. 14. (The bf. part is by the Lysippid Painter).

(iii)

(*decorated by Psiax*)

MADRID 11008.   See p. 7 no. 2.
CASTLE ASHBY, Northampton, bf. neck-amphora. See *ABV.* 293, no. 7.

(iv)

(decorated by Epiktetos)

VILLA GIULIA, calyx-krater. See p. 77 no. 90.

Andokides, in concert with the potter Mnesiades, dedicated a bronze statue on the Acropolis of Athens, the inscribed pillar-pedestal of which remains (*I.G.*[2] 627; Raubitschek *Dedications* 213–16 no. 178). The bf. fragment with the signature of Mnesiades (now Basle, Cahn: ex Riaz: see *ABV*. 314) is from a hydria (of normal bf. type, not round-bodied). The eleventh letter of the signature is M not Γ.

THE ANDOKIDES PAINTER

Norton in *AJA*. 1896, 1–41. Hauser in *FR*. ii, 267–71 and iii, 73–76. *VA*. 3–5. Langlotz *Zeitbestimmung* 23–31. Pfuhl 286–9 and 412–16. *Att. V*. 7–9 and 467. *ABS*. 25 and 38–41. Schweitzer in *Jb*. 44, 129–31. Kraiker in *Jb*. 44, 145–50. Technau in *Corolla Curtius* 132–41. Bloesch *FAS*. 12–15. *ARV*.[1] 1–7 and 948. *Dev*. 75–78 and 114. Bloesch in *JHS*. 71, 29–31 and 35. *ABV*. 253–4. *CB*. iii, text.

In *ABS*. 25 and 38–41 I put together a number of *black-figure* vases and called the painter (after a kalos-name on one of them) the Lysippides Painter. Among his works are the *black-figure* pictures on the six bilingual amphorae in the following list (nos. 7–12) and the *black-figure* part of the bilingual cup (no. 14). In *ABS*. I said that he might be the same as the Andokides Painter —the painter of the red-figure portions of these vases—but I would not decide. Later, in *ARV*.[1] and elsewhere, I made up my mind that the two were the same; but in *ABV*. I came to the conclusion that they were not, and I revived the name of 'Lysippides Painter' for the man who painted the black-figure portions and the all-black-figure vases that go with them.

For the Lysippides Painter see *ABV*. 254–65, 671, 691, and 715.[1]

---

[1] Add the bf. amphora (type A)

New York 58.32. A, Athena mounting chariot, with Herakles. B, fight (Achilles and Memnon). [Bothmer].

Add also the bf. cup (type A)

Swiss private. I, gorgoneion; round this, ships. A–B, between eyes. A, Apollo and two goddesses. B, Leda and the Dioskouroi. At each handle, vine.

The subject on the reverse of no. 8 in the list *ABV*. 255 (Moscow, Pushkin Museum, 70) is a wedded pair in a chariot. Nos. 2 and 11 in the list of vases in the manner of the painter, *ABV*. 257–8, are now New York 56. 171. 14 (*Bull. Metr.* March 1957, 174, 3–4) and New York 56. 171. 7 (A, *Archaeology*, Summer 1958, 127). See also p. 1617.

THE ANDOKIDES PAINTER

AMPHORAE

(type A)

(nos. 1–5, red-figure)

1 (1). BERLIN 2159, from Vulci. Gerhard *TG.* pll. 19–20, whence (A) Overbeck *KM.* pl. 24, 2, *AJA.* 1896, 11, (B) *JHS* 25, 270 fig. 8, (B) Norman Gardiner *G.A.S.* 386, (B) Schröder *Sport* pl. 61, above; FR. pl. 133 and iii, 73 and 76 fig. 38, whence Hoppin i, 33, Swindler figs. 294 and 301, (A) Pfuhl fig. 314, (B) Norman Gardiner *Athl.* fig. 154, (A) Pfeiff *Apollon* pl. 12, b; B, Langlotz *GV.* pl. 1, 1, whence Richter *A.G.A.* fig. 212; A, Neugebauer pl. 42, whence Diepolder *G.V.* 27; B, Blümel *Sport u. Spiel* pl. 5; B, Blümel *S.H.* 124; A, Lane pl. 63, b; details of A, and B, *G.V. Celle* 2, 13, and 12; detail of A, *E.A.A.* i, 358; details of A and B, Kraiker *MG.* pl. 25. A, Herakles and Apollo: the struggle for the tripod. B, wrestlers. On the foot, incised, ΑΝΔΟΚΙΔΕΣΕΠΟΕΣΕΝ. For the shape, Bloesch in *JHS.* 71, 30 no. 2. See p. 1617.

2 (2). LOUVRE G 1, from Vulci. *AJA.* 1896, 8–9; FR. pl. 111 and ii, 272 and 282 fig. 100, 2, whence Hoppin i, 41, (B) Pfuhl fig. 313 (= Pfuhl *Mast.* fig. 27), (detail of A, redrawn) Richter *ARVS.* 43 fig. 13, (B) LS. fig. 35; A, Schaal *Rf.* fig. 2; *CV.* pl. 25 and pl. 26, 2; phs. Gir. 25533, 25535, and 37843–4, whence (B) Buschor *G. Vasen* 124 and (part of A) *Marb. Jb.* 15, 69 fig. 50; A, *JHS.* 71 pl. 17, a, and (mouth and foot) 32 fig. 1; A, Villard *GV.* pl. 24; detail of B, Buschor *Bilderwelt* 27; phs. Al. 23710–11. A, fight (with Athena and Hermes watching). B, citharode. On the foot, incised, ΑΝΔΟΚΙΔΕΣΕΠΟΕΣΕΝ. For the shape, Bloesch in *JHS.* 71, 30 no. 1. Bothmer tells me that the lid Louvre S 1263 belongs.

3 (3). LEIPSIC T 635, from Orvieto. *Jb.* 11, 183. A, Herakles and the lion. B, warrior leaving home (warrior and male, horseman, archer). [Hauser].

4. SWISS PRIVATE. A, Herakles and the lion. B, concert (on platform, two standing side by side—a youth playing the flute, and a man about to sing; on the left a youth standing, on the right a youth seated). See p. 1617.

5 (4). ORVIETO, Faina, 64, from Orvieto. Detail of A, Hadaczek *Ohrschmuck* 19; phs. R.I. 1932. 225–30, whence *Corolla Curtius* pll. 44–47 (whence, part of B, Buschor *G. Vasen* 136, part of B, *Fra Nat.* 1954, 36, 35), (A) Bothmer *Am.* pl. 69, 1, (A) *E.A.A.* i, 359, (part of B) Frel *Ř.V.* fig. 140; A, ph. Al. 32492, whence Tarchi pl. 119, 4; phs. Armoni. A, Herakles and the Amazons. B, Dionysos with Ariadne and satyrs. [Furtwängler]. Late. For the shape, Bloesch in *JHS.* 71, 30 no. 8; for the Amazonomachy, Bothmer *Am.* 133–4.

(no. 6: the part remaining is red-figure)

6. TARANTO, two frr., from Locri. The scene was something like that on the Munich amphora (no. 9), but the person reclining, with a phiale in his

hand, need not have been Herakles. One fragment gives his legs and fingers, with part of the couch; the other, the head of the couch, and to right of it part of a woman standing to left. See p. 1617.

(*nos. 7–12: A, red-figure; B, black-figure. The black-figure part by the Lysippides Painter*)

7 (5). BOSTON 01. 8037, from Orvieto. *AJA*. 1896, 40–41; A, Richter *F*. fig. 122; Scheurleer pl. 26, whence Rumpf *MZ*. pl. 16, 1–2; *Bull. MFA*. 44, 46–47; Trendall *Hdbk Nich*.[2] 287; A, Fairbanks and Chase 66 fig. 72; CB. iii pl. 65, 114, and pl. 66; the shape, Caskey *G*. 61. A, rf., Achilles and Ajax playing; (B, bf., the like). Much restored, especially B (CB. iii pl. 66 gives the genuine parts). [Furtwängler]. See CB. iii, text.

8 (7). LONDON B 193, from Etruria. *AJA*. 1896, 10, whence (A) *JHS*. 25, 269; phs. Ma. 3054–5, whence Walters *H.A.P.* pll. 31–32; *CV*. pl. 1; detail of A, Jacobsthal *O*. pl. 37, b; cleaned, CB. iii, suppl. pl. 17. A, rf., Herakles and the lion. (B, bf., Achilles and Ajax playing). [Furtwängler]. For the shape, Bloesch in *JHS*. 71, 30, no. 3.

9 (8). MUNICH 2301 (J. 388), from Vulci. FR. pl. 4 and i pp. 15, 18, and 266, whence Jacobsthal *Gött. V*. 46–47, Pfuhl fig. 315 (= Pfuhl *Mast*. fig. 28) and fig. 265, (A) Buschor *G.V*. 147, (detail of A, redrawn) Richter *ARVS*. 39 fig. 5; Eckstein fig. 1; A, Schaal *Rf*. fig. 11; B, *AM*. 62 pl. 26, 2; Schuchhardt and Technau 143–5; Schnitzler pl. 30; A, *JHS*. 71 pl. 17, b and (mouth and foot) p. 32 fig. 2; Lullies and Hirmer pll. 1–7, whence LS. figs. 36 and 38; *CV*. pll. 155–8, pl. 188, 2, and p. 9; (A) LS. fig. 37; A, *E.A.A*. i. 675 and 897. A, rf., Herakles resting, and Athena; (B, bf., the like). [Furtwängler]. For the shape, Bloesch in *JHS*. 71, 30 no. 5.

10 (9). BOLOGNA 151, from Bologna. *AJA*. 1896, 18–19; Pellegrini 44–46; R.I. xxiii. 9; phs. Poppi 12137–8. A, rf., Dionysos with maenad and satyrs. (B, bf., Herakles and the lion). [Furtwängler]. For the shape, Bloesch in *JHS*. 71, 30 no. 6. See p. 1617.

11 (6). LOUVRE F 204, from Vulci. *AJA*. 1896, 14–15; Pottier pl. 78; Perrot 10 pll. 6–7 and p. 277; *CV*. a pll. 1–2; A, Schaal *Rf*. fig. 1; A, *Enc. phot*. iii, 2; A, ph. Al. 23707, whence Buschor *G. Vasen* 137 and (detail) Richter *ARVS*. fig. 34; phs. Gir. 37841–2. A, rf., Herakles and Cerberus. (B, bf., Dionysos with maenad and satyrs). [Furtwängler]. For the shape, Bloesch in *JHS*. 71, 30 no. 7. See p. 1617.

12 (10). BOSTON 99. 538. Cecil Smith *Forman* pll. 5–6, whence (A) *VA*. 4, (A) Herford, frontispiece, Pfuhl figs. 316 and 266, Seltman pl. 10, (A) Stella 785; A, Fairbanks and Chase 56 fig. 58; Chase *Guide* 52 fig. 62; *Dev*. pll. 34–35, whence Frel *Ř.V*. figs. 138–9; CB. iii pl. 65, 115, and pl. 67; the shape, Caskey *G*. 60. A. rf., Herakles driving a bull to sacrifice; (B, bf., the like). [Cecil Smith]. Late. See CB. iii, text.

(*no. 13, special technique: like rf., but on a white ground*)

13 (11). LOUVRE F 203. *AJA*. 1896, 2–3; Pottier pl. 78; B, Sudhoff i, 67; Hoppin i, 39; phs. Al. 23706 and Gir. 15266–7, whence (A) Seltman pl. 9,

b; B, Neutsch *Sport* fig. 44. A, Amazons making ready. B, women bathing (Bothmer thinks they may be Amazons). On the foot, incised, ΛΝΔΟΚΙΔΕSΕΓΟΕSΕΝ. Now partly cleaned. For the shape, Bloesch in *JHS*. 71, 30 no. 4; for the subjects, Bothmer *Am*. 153–4.

CUP
(part bf., part rf.)

14 (12). PALERMO V 650, from Chiusi. A–B, *Jb*. 4 pl. 4, whence Perrot 10, 275, Hoppin i, 36, Pfuhl figs. 262–3; A–B, cleaned, *CV*. pll. 1–2. I is missing: part of the net border remains, and the design may have been a gorgoneion. A–B, half red-figure (half black-figure): at each handle, half red-figure (half black-figure), fight; (A, black-figure, between eyes, two archers); B, red-figure, between eyes, trumpeter. On A, retr., [ΛΝ]ΔΟΚ[Ι]ΔΕSΕ[Γ]Ο.... For the shape, Bloesch 12 no. 1.

For the black-figure portions of the bilingual vases in the above list see *ABV*. 254–6.

The following fragments recall the Andokides Painter more or less vividly:

FRAGMENTS OF LARGE VASES

1. BONN, Langlotz, fr. (Dionysos and maenad: his head, to right, her face, to left, and arm with krotala in the hand). Attributed by Langlotz to the Andokides Painter.
2. ATHENS Acr. 602, fr., from Athens. Langlotz pl. 45. Unexplained subject (youth—falling?—, column). Attributed by Langlotz to the workshop of the Andokides Painter.
3. ATHENS Acr. 601, fr., from Athens. Langlotz pl. 45. (Middle of a male running). Attributed to the Andokides Painter, as an early work, by Langlotz.
4. ATHENS, Agora, P 18012, fr., from Athens. (Herakles—thighs, running to right).

CHALICE

5. ATHENS Acr. 726, frr., from Athens. Langlotz pl. 56. A, Dionysos mounting chariot, with maenads. B, symposion (one reclining, one approaching). Below, bf., A, lion and lioness attacking bull, B, similar. Attributed to the Andokides Painter by Hartwig, and, as an early work, by Langlotz. For the style of the animals compare the bf. fragment London B 600. 19 (*JHS*. 49 pl. 17, 6), which may be from a vase of the same shape.

MASTOS

6. ATHENS, frr., from Perachora. *Perachora* ii pl. 145. A, sphinx; B, siren. The inscriptions are reserved. On A, ... +ὶ ... On a loose fragment,

...E⸖E... On another, to right of one picture, ... ⸖. Reserved inscriptions also on the fragments, possibly from a neck-amphora of Nicosthenic type, Athens Acr. 697 (Langlotz pl. 54), and on the stemmed dish Louvre CA 3662 (p. 12 no. 11). See p. 1617.

PSIAX

(Formerly known as 'the Menon Painter')

JHS. 33, 143. Buschor *G.V.* 152. *VA.* 6. Langlotz *Zeitbestimmung* 20. Pfuhl 287 and 414–15. *Att. V.* 9–10 and 467. Zahn in FR. iii, 230–7. *JHS.* 47, 91–92 and 233. *BSR* 11, 9–10. *ABS.* 25. *BSA.* 29, 201. H. R.W. Smith *New Aspects of the Menon Painter.* Richter in *AJA.* 1934, 547–54. Haspels *ABL.* 77, 95, 101, and 106. Richter and Hall 14–17. Gross in *Würzburger Festgabe für Bulle* 47–69 (the bf. vase p. 64 fig. 5 is not that which I had assigned to Psiax, but another in Palermo). Richter in *AJA.* 1939, 645 and in *AJA.* 1941, 587–92. *ARV.*¹ 7–11 and 948. Buschor G. *Vasen* 133. *AJA.* 1950, 311–15. *Dev.* 78–79 and 114–15. *ABV.* 292–5 and 850.

The amphora in Philadelphia (no. 3) bears the signature of the potter Menon. Buschor saw that the Madrid amphora with the signature of the potter Andokides (no. 2) was by the same painter.

I had guessed (*JHS.* 33, 143) that the name of the Menon Painter might be Psiax, known from two alabastra painted for Hilinos (nos. 4–5); and this was made good by Miss Richter (*AJA.* 1934, 547–54).

Psiax, therefore, collaborated with at least three potters: Andokides, Menon, Hilinos. One of the vases he painted for Andokides (no. 2) is bilingual; the other, a neck-amphora in Castle Ashby, is all-black-figure (*ABV.* 293 no. 7); and Psiax is largely a black-figure painter. For his black-figure work see *ABV.* 292–5; see also ibid. 609, 674, and 692. A of the Castle Ashby vase is now republished in *Worc. Ann.* 6, 3; A of Copenhagen inv. 4759 (ibid. 293 no. 6) in Breitenstein *G.V.* 19; London B 591 (ibid. 294 no. 20) in Richter *H.G.A.* 325. Add fragments of a bf. neck-amphora: Istanbul, frr., from Xanthos, A 33. 2324: A, Dionysos mounting chariot; B, Herakles and Apollo: the struggle for the tripod: some of these fragments were mentioned, as near Psiax, in *ABV.* 692, but said to be from an amphora.

Psiax is the 'brother' of a prolific black-figure artist, the Antimenes Painter, who is not known to have used the red-figure technique: see *ABV.* 266–91, 391–2, and 715.

There are indications that Psiax may have been a pupil of the Amasis Painter.

AMPHORAE

(type A)

(nos. 1–2: A, rf.; B, bf.)

1 (1). MUNICH 2302 (J. 373), from Vulci. Handle-palmette, Lau pl. 12, 2; shape, and details of A, FR. i, 151 and 266; A, Richter F. fig. 166; part of B, Schaal *Sf.* fig. 49; H. R. W. Smith *New Aspects* 47 and 53 and pl. 5;

detail of A, *AJA*. 1934, 551 fig. 5; cleaned, *CV*. pll. 153–4, pl. 188, 1, and pp. 7–8. A, Dionysos reclining, with maenad and satyr. B, bf., chariot of Herakles. On B, ΗΙΠΟΚΡΑΤΕϟ ΚΑΛΟϟ.

2 (2). MADRID 11008 (L. 63), from Vulci. *AJA*. 1896, 5–6; *Jh*. 3, 70–71, whence Hoppin i, 34; Ossorio pl. 8, 1 and pl. 29, 2; Leroux pll. 5–6; Pfuhl figs. 317 and 264; *CV*. pl. 23, 1, pll. 24–25, and pl. 26, 1, whence (detail of A) Stella 193, (details) LS. figs. 39–40; detail of A, *AJA*. 1934, 551 fig. 7; R.I. ix. 21; B.Ap. xxii. 49, 1. A, rf., Apollo with Artemis, Leto, and Ares. B, bf., Dionysos with satyrs and maenads. On the foot, incised, ΑΝΔΟΚΙΔΕϟΕΠΟΕϟΕΝ. [Buschor]. Restored. For the shape, Bloesch in *JHS*. 71 no. 19. See p. 1618.

(no. 3, rf.)

3 (3). PHILADELPHIA 5399, from Vulci. Noël Des Vergers pl. 9; *AJA*. 1905 pll. 6–7 and pp. 170–7; *Mus.J*. 5, 32–33 and 35–36, whence Hoppin ii, 203 and (A) Pfuhl fig. 318, whence (part) *BCH*. 1936, 63; detail of B, H. R. W. Smith *New Aspects* 39; detail of A, *AJA*. 1934, 551 fig. 6. A, Apollo with Artemis and Leto. B, youth with horses. On the foot, incised, ΜΕΝΟΝΕΠΟΙΕϟΕΝ.

ALABASTRA

4 (4). CARLSRUHE 242 (B 120), from Athens. Creuzer *Altatt. Gefäss* pl. 1; Panofka *Namen* pl. 3, 9–10; *AJA*. 1895, 486, whence Hoppin ii, 397; Welter pl. 8; sides, Jacobsthal O. pl. 63, b–c; *AJA*. 1934, 551 fig. 6; *CV* pl. 28. A, athlete pouring oil into his hand. B, maenad dancing. Incised on A, ΗΙΛΙΝΟΣΕΠΟΙΕϟΕΝ, on B, ΦϟΙΑ+ϟΕΛΡΑΦϟΕΝ.

5 (5). ODESSA. *Zap. Od*. 17 pl. 2, whence *Anz*. 1894, 180, whence Pfuhl fig. 344 and Hoppin ii, 403; *AJA*. 1934 pl. 38 and p. 548, whence LS. figs. 43–44. A, warrior; B, archer. Incised on A, ΗΙΛΙΝΟϟΕΠΟΙΕ, on B, ΦϟΙΑ+ϟΕΛΡΑΦΕ.

ROUND ARYBALLOS

6 (6). Once BOLOGNA PU 322 (stolen from the Museum). Pellegrini *VPU*. 56–57, whence Studniczka *Artemis* 54; B.Ap. xxii. 63. Herakles and the Amazons. On the bottom, palmettes. [Pfuhl]. See *BSA*. 29, 201.

CUPS

7. SWISS PRIVATE. I, palmettes. A, eyes, and fight. B, eyes, and concert. On A, between eyes, warrior fallen on one knee; beyond each eye, warrior running up. On B, between eyes, citharode; beyond each eye, youth listening. Graffito ΙΩΙΙΛΟΣ. Group of Leipsic T 3599 (see p. 38, no. 8). Same scheme of decoration as in the next (see p. 38).

8 (8). MUNICH 2587. *Jb*. 10 pl. 4 (incompletely, but including a few frr. now mislaid), whence H. R. W. Smith *New Aspects* 3 and (detail, redrawn) Richter *ARVS*. 41 fig. 9; I, Jacobsthal O. pl. 109, f; (without the lost frr., but with some new ones) H. R. W. Smith *New Aspects* pl. 1; details,

Wü. Festgabe Bulle 64 figs. 6–7. I, palmettes. A, eyes, and fight: between eyes, hoplite and archer; beyond one eye, light-armed; beyond the other, warrior. B, between eyes, girl dancing and one playing the flute; beyond one eye, warrior; beyond the other, warrior. [Pfuhl; already assigned by Pellegrini to the same hand as Bologna PU 322, no. 6]. Group of Leipsic T 3599 (see p. 38 no. 9). For the scheme of decoration see p. 38.

9 (9). NEW YORK 14. 146. 1. A, *Bull. Metr.* 10, 99, 2; H. R. W. Smith *New Aspects* 9 and 12–13 and pll. 2–3; part of A, *AJA.* 1934, 549, whence LS. fig. 41; Richter and Hall pl. 1, pl. 2, 1, and pl. 179, 1, whence (detail of A) Richter *Gk Ptg* 9, 1 and (I) Rumpf *MZ.* pl. 16, 6; details, Richter *ARVS.* 41 fig. 10, p. 44 fig. 15, and p. 45; A, Richter *A.G.A.* fig. 213; I, Richter *H.* 205, g. I, archer with horse. A, fight; B, warrior mounting chariot. For the shape, Bloesch 42 no. 2. [H. R. W. Smith].

10 (7). LENINGRAD 98 b, fr., from South Russia. *AJA.* 1934, 553 fig. 9. I, fight. [Peredolskaya].

SKYPHOS

11 (10). ATHENS Acr. 457, fr., from Athens. Langlotz pl. 38. Fight. Assigned by Langlotz to the same hand as Munich 2587 (no. 8). Athens Acr. 452 (chariot, [. . . ΕΓΟ]ΙΕΣΕΝ written on one horse) may belong.

PLATE

12 (11). ATHENS Acr. 7, frr., from Athens. Langlotz pl. 1. Athena. Compared by Langlotz with Bologna PU. 322 (no. 6).

VASE WITH ADDED COLOURS (SIX'S TECHNIQUE)
ALABASTRON

13 (12). LONDON 1900. 6–11. 1, from Eretria. *Mél. Perrot* 252. Youths with horses. The pattern-work above and below is on white ground. Incised, ΚΑΛΟΣΚΑΡΥΣΤΙΟΣ, ΣΜΙΚΡΙΟΝΚΑΛΟΣ, ΜΟΡΥΛΟΣ.

The two cups nos. 7 and 8 (Swiss private and Munich 2587) belong to the Group of Leipsic T 3599, the other members of which are connected more or less closely with Psiax: see p. 38.

A fragment in Athens (Acr.) is half the mouth of a very large lekythos. Neatly incised on the topside (which is black) of the mouth, . . . ΡΑΤΕΣΚΑ [ΛΟΣ]. Impossible to say whether the lekythos was bf. or rf., but the great size makes one think of the Agora lekythos-fragments P 5002 by or near Psiax (*Hesp.* 15 pl. 21, 1–3: *ABV.* 295, top) and therefore of Psiax and of the kalos-name Hippokrates (see pp. 6–7, no. 1).

A small vase was attributed to Psiax by Langlotz (*Z.* 32) and H. R. W. Smith (*New Aspects* 59–60); it is certainly like him in several particulars:

MASTOID

(with flat diagonal handle)

LONDON, Victoria and Albert Museum, 275. 64. Klein *L.* 119; *Burl. 1903* pl. 96, I 67; Jacobsthal *O.* pl. 73, b–c; H. R. W. Smith *New Aspects* pl. 6; Lane pl. 63, a. Komos. Incised, BPA+ASKALOS. Munich 2202 (J. 1260) is a black-figure vase of similar type, but ours is of a special model. For the chequers on the lip compare the plates p. 28 no. 18 and p. 30, and, as Bothmer advises, the Charinos vases in Villa Giulia and Tarquinia (p. 1531 nos. 1 and 2). See also p. 77 no. 90.

Two cups bear the name of Psiax without verb. They are contemporary with the alabastra (p. 7, nos. 4 and 5), and connected with them, but not obviously by the same hand as they: see Richter in *AJA.* 1934, 553–4.

CUPS

1 (1). NEW YORK 14. 146. 2, from Bolsena. A–B, *Bull. Metr.* 10, 98; Hoppin ii, 401; B, *N.Y. Shapes* 18, 2 = Richter and Milne fig. 162; I and A, Richter and Hall pl. 8, 2, pl. 2, 2, and pl. 179, 2; A–B, ph. R.I. 41. 296, middle. I, bf., two ravens and a snake. A–B, between eyes. A, Pegasus. B, nose. On B, ΦSIA+S. See also p. 41, no. 38.

2 (2). MUNICH 2603 (J. 1240), from Vulci. *AJA.* 1895 pl. 22 and pp. 487–8, whence Hoppin ii, 398–9; A, *Jb.* 10, 197; part of A–B, Jacobsthal *O.* pl. 70, a; A (cleaned), *AJA.* 1934, 553 fig. 10; B, *Wü. Festgabe Bulle* 64 fig. 4; B and foot, Bloesch *F.A.S.* pl. 11, 2. I, bf., satyr. A–B, between eyes. A, hoplitodromos putting on his shield. B, nose. On B, ΦSIA+S. The satyr somewhat recalls Munich 2302 (p. 6 no. 1). Restored. Foot B, but with the foot-plate profile of type A: for the shape, Bloesch 42 no. 1. See also p. 41 no. 39.

See also p. 12 no. 11, p. 38 nos. 5 and 10; and pp. 1617–18.

THE PAINTER OF OXFORD 1949

LEKYTHOS

1. OXFORD 1949. 751. Eyles *Pottery in the Ancient World* 37; *Ashm. Report* 1949 pl. 4, d. Three women seated. On the shoulder, three rf. palmettes.

OINOCHOE

(exact shape uncertain)

2. OXFORD 1911. 626, frr., from Cervetri. *CV.* pl. 42, 8. Amazonomachy. For the subject see Bothmer *Am.* 144.

CUP

3. BOULOGNE. I is lost. A–B, between eyes. A, discus-thrower. B, woman with flower. Restored. See p. 46 no. 118.

THE GOLUCHOW PAINTER

V.Pol. 11–13. *ARV.*[1] 12. Peters *Pan.* 59. Augusta Bruckner *Palästradarstellungen* 52–53 and 67.

Peters and Miss Bruckner date the painter somewhat later than I did: I keep him in this chapter because of his very primitive technique.

OINOCHOAI

(nos. 1–2, shape 5 A)

1 (1). WARSAW 142463 (ex Goluchow, Czartoryski, 61), from Cervetri. De Witte pl. 23; *V.Pol.* pl. 3, 1, whence Rumpf *MZ.* pl. 21, 4 and Frel *Ř.V.* fig. 136; *CV.* pl. 17, 2. Discus-thrower. See p. 1618.

2 (2). WARSAW 142308 (ex Czartoryski 62), from Cervetri. De Witte pl. 24; *V.Pol.* pl. 3, 2; *CV.* pl. 17, 1. Acontist. ΚΑΛΩΣ ΜΕΛΙΕΥΣ.

(no. 3, shape 2)

3 (3). CAMBRIDGE 163, from Athens. E. Gardner pl. 32; *CV.* pl. 36, 1, whence Wegner *Mus.* pl. 10, a; *E.A.A.* iii, 976 fig. 1246; B. Ap. xxii. 96. Satyr.

(no. 4, shape 2, another model, with high handle)

4 (4). MUNICH 2446 (J. 1324), from Vulci. *Mon.* 1 pl. 27, 31; *CV.* pl. 84, 1, pl. 86, 1, and pl. 92, 1. Citharode.

In point of shape, Cambridge 163 and Munich 2446 both belong to classes the other members of which are all black-figure: Cambridge 163 to the Briachos Class (*ABV.* 432–3 and 697), Munich 2446 to the Class of Vatican G. 47 (*ABV.* 429–31 and 697). Cambridge 163 and Munich 2446 are most probably by one potter.

In *ARV.*[1] 12 I guessed that a lost oinochoe ('olpe'), once Magnoncourt 86, known from a bare mention, might have been by the Goluchow Painter: I think it more likely now that it was Etruscan of the Praxias Group (on which see *EVP.* 195–8, 204, and 306).

SUNDRY VERY EARLY RED-FIGURE POTS, BY VARIOUS PAINTERS

ARV.[1] 12–14. Those fragments in that list which recall the Andokides Painter have been taken out and placed at the end of his section (pp. 5–6).

AMPHORA
(type A)

1 (α). MUNICH 2300 (J. 375), from Vulci. Upper border, Lau pl. 12, 7; *CV.* pll. 159–60 and pl. 188, 3. A, Dionysos and maenads. B, bf., Achilles and Ajax playing. Compare the column-krater Faina 61 (no. 5).

NECK-AMPHORAE
(no. 2, small, with triple handles)

2 (β). BOSTON 03. 790. *RM.* 16 pl. 5 and p. 119; CB. iii suppl. pl. 18, 1. A, Dionysos seated and satyr; B, Dionysos and maenad (Ariadne?), both seated. See CB. iii, text. The handle-areas with their florals, and the patterns below the pictures, are as in black-figure neck-amphorae; and shape and pattern-work somewhat recall the Three-line Group (*ABV.* 320–1, 693–4, and 700; and below, p. 1588).

(nos. 3–4, of Nicosthenic type)

The model is not quite the same as in the two that Pamphaios made for Oltos (p. 53 nos. 1–2). Vienna 3722 has the same shape as two bf. vases, Villa Giulia 47492 (*ABV.* 319 no. 8) and New York 56.171.24 (ex Hearst: *ABV.* 319 no. 7: A, *Bull. Metr.* March 1957, 172, 6); for the handles, compare Vienna 3607 (side, Jacobsthal O. pl. 49, a: *ABV.* 319 no. 10).

3 (γ). VIENNA 3722 (ex Oest. Mus. 319), from Cervetri. A, *Memorie* 2 pl. 4, whence Roscher s.v. Dike 1019; A, Masner 39; side, Jacobsthal O. pl. 43, a; A, ph. R.I, whence *E.A.A.* i, 66; *CV.* pl. 51; R.I. A, Dike and Adikia. B, Ajax with the body of Achilles. On the neck, bf., A, satyr and maenad, B, the like. On the topside of the mouth, bf., lions and boars. Compare the next. For Adikia see D. S. Robertson in *Cl. Rev.* 73, 11–12.

4 (δ). VILLA GIULIA (M. 633). Mingazzini *V.Cast.* pl. 100; side, Jacobsthal O. pl. 43, b; R.I. xvii. 42. A, Amazon. B, woman (maenad?). On the neck, bf., A, Dionysos and maenad, B, the like. On each handle, bf., maenad. On the topside of the mouth, bf., dolphins. Compare the last. See p. 1618.

COLUMN-KRATERS

5 (ε). ORVIETO, Faina, 61, from Orvieto. Peters *Pan.* pl. 6; *Boll. Restauro* 31–32, 126–8. A, Leto (or Artemis) mounting chariot, with Apollo and Artemis (or Leto). B, bf., Herakles and Triton. Compare the amphora Munich 2300 (no. 1).

6 (τ). ATHENS, Agora, P 14948, two frr., from Athens. A, horseman. Tbe second fragment (top of a head to right, the himation covering the back of the head) may be from B. Small.

HYDRIAI
(of bf. type)

7 (ζ). MUNICH 2418 (J. 56), from Vulci. Details, FR. i, 70 figs. 2 and 4; Vorberg *Gloss.* 745. Dionysos and Ariadne with satyrs. On the shoulder, bf., war-chariots wheeling round to meet each other. For the shape of the vase see *ABV.* 342. See also p. 1618.

8 (η). BERLIN 2174. B. Ap. xxii. 20. Dionysos and satyrs. On the shoulder, palmette between eyes. Restored. Recalls somewhat the cup Florence A B 1 (p. 160, Ama Group).

9 (θ). MUNICH 2419 (J. 742), from Vulci. Detail, FR. i, 70 fig. 1. Dionysos with maenad and satyr. On the shoulder, palmettes. See p. 1618.

OINOCHOE
(shape 1, Altenburg Class, see *ABV.* 422, below, no. 6)

10 (ι). CAB. MÉD. 458, from Cervetri. De Ridder 349; *CV.* pl. 96, 4–6, whence Béquignon *Iliade* 165. Fight (Achilles and Hector). Restored.

STEMMED DISH

(The upper part is something like a very shallow cup-bowl, the lower part is a cup-foot of type AZ, see p. 39).

11. LOUVRE CA 3662. Inside, Athena and Giant ([A]OENAAϟ, ENΚELA-ΔOϟ). Outside, a band of neat rf. palmettes. The letters are reserved (see p. 6). The potter-work makes one think of Nikosthenes; the drawing, in some points, of early Psiax.

FRAGMENTS OF POTS

12 (ξ). AMSTERDAM inv. 332, fr., from Athens. (Knee of a male running to right, and the ends of his cloak).

13 (ϟ). ELEUSIS 596(4213), fr., from Eleusis. *Delt.* 9, 3. (One seated, one standing). On the inscriptions, *AJA.* 1929, 363–4.

PLAQUE

14 (ν). ATHENS, Agora, P 9468, fr., from Athens. Dinsmoor *Heph.* 132. Fight.

CHAPTER 2

THE PIONEER GROUP

(EUPHRONIOS, PHINTIAS, EUTHYMIDES, AND OTHERS)

THE PIONEER GROUP

(Euphronios, Phintias, Euthymides, and their companions)

THESE three artists are pioneers of the new drawing; and the Sosias Painter may be named together with them. The other painters described in this chapter, so far as can be judged at present, were followers or adherents.

EUPHRONIOS

Klein *Euphronios*. Furtwängler in FR. i, 102–4, ii, 1–13, ii, 172–8. *VA*. 30–31 and 82–84. *JHS*. 37, 235–6. Pfuhl in *Anz*. 1918, 63–72. Langlotz *Zeitbestimmung* 61–62. *Att.V.* 50–62 and 468. Haspels in *BCH*. 30, 422–51. Johnson in *Art. Bull.* 19, 557–60. *ARV.*¹ 15–20 and 948. *PP*. 21–22. Peters Pan. 56. Villard in *Mon. Piot* 45, 1–13. CB. ii, 1–3 and 102. Villard in *Mon. Piot* 47, 35–46. *ABV*. 403.

The signature of Euphronios is preserved on seventeen vases. On five of these (below, nos. 2, 3, 15, 17, 18) it is followed by ἔγραψεν, on ten by ἐποίησεν. The ἐποίησεν vases are later than the ἔγραψεν and not by the same hand as they. Not quite certain, indeed, that the Euphronios is the same. For the ἐποίησεν vases, which are all cups, see pp. 313–14.

On one vase the name of Euphronios appears without a verb; but the vase is incomplete, and the verb may have followed; the drawing is close to Euphronios (p. 18 no. 3). On two fragmentary cups the verb is missing: one of these goes with the ἐποίησεν cups, and the verb was doubtless ἐποίησεν (p. 330 no. 5); the other is nearer to the ἔγραψεν vases (p. 19 no. 1).

One vase by Euphronios had the painter's signature, but the name is now wanting (p. 15 no. 10).

It was Furtwängler who first saw that the ἔγραψεν vases were not by the same as the ἐποίησεν, although later he recanted (FR. ii, 177–8).

One of Euphronios' vases was painted for the potter Euxitheos (p. 14 no. 4), another—probably two others—for Kachrylion (p. 16 no. 17 and p. 17 no. 21).

CALYX-KRATERS

1 (4). BERLIN 2180, from Capua. *A.Z.* 1879 pl. 4, whence Hoppin *Euth.F.* pl. 21, (B) Norman Gardiner *G.A.S.* 476, (B) Swindler fig. 225; Hoppin

Euth. F. pl. 20; Lücken pll. 5–6, whence (A) Licht ii, 121, (A) Frel *Ř.V.* fig. 151; Pfuhl figs. 396–7; A, Pfuhl *Mast.* fig. 46; FR. pl. 157 and iii, 245, whence (B) Norman Gardiner *Athl.* fig. 44, (B) Stow pl. 2, (B) Diepolder *G.V.* 29; B, Licht i, 100; side, Jacobsthal O. pl. 56; A, Schaal *Rf.* fig. 15; detail, *BSA.* 29, 218, η; B, Neugebauer pl. 44, whence Diepolder *GV.* 28; B, Richter and Milne fig. 55; Blümel *Sport u. Spiel* pl. 8; Blümel *S.H.* 77–81, whence (detail of A) Schnitzler pl. 37, 51; B, Stow pl. 3; B and part of A, Schuchhardt and Technau 146–7; A, Lane pl. 68, a; part of B, *G. V. Celle* 23; A, ph. Marb. 73772. A, athletes; B, athletes. On A, ᒪEAΛPOᛊ[IC]AᒪOᛊ. On B, ᒪEAΛPOᛊICAᒪOᛊ. Slightly restored. See p. 1619.

2 (1). Louvre G 103, from Cervetri. *Mon.* 1855 pl. 5, whence *WV.* 5 pl. 4 and Klein *Euphr.* 118–19; detail of A, *Jh.* 3 pl. 5, 2; FR. pl. 92, pl. 93, 1, and ii, 325, 1, whence Perrot 10, 405 and 409, Hoppin i, 397, Pfuhl figs. 392–3, (A) Buschor *G.V.* 161, (A) Norman Gardiner *Athl.* fig. 201, (A) Swindler fig. 245, (A) Seltman pl. 16, (detail of A) Richter *ARVS.* fig. 43, (details of B), Kraiker *MG.* pl. 27; part of A, and B, Pottier pll. 100–1, whence (detail of A), Rumpf *MZ.* pl. 20, 3; part of A, Perrot 10 pl. 8; *CV.* pll. 4–5, whence (detail of A) Swindler fig. 314, (detail of A) Lane pl. 68, b; A, Schröder *Sport* pl. 69; A, Zadoks-Jitta 77, 6; sides, Jacobsthal O. pl. 46; *Enc. phot.* iii, 4–5, whence (A) Frel. *Ř.V.* fig. 155; part of A, Buschor *G. Vasen* 142; A, ph. Al. 23687, whence Schnitzler pl. 35, Stella 408, (part) *E.A.A.* i, 410; detail of A, Richter *H.G.A.* 326 fig. 440; detail of A, Robertson *G.P.* 93. A, Herakles and Antaios. B, concert (flute-player). On A, EVΦPONIOᛊEΛPAΦᛊEN. On B, ᒪEAΛPOᛊ KAᒪOᛊ (tag-kalos), and on the platform [ME]ᒪAᛊKAᒪOᛊ. [Me]las is the name of the performer. The pictures slightly restored; foot and base of the vase, with the base-tongues, are modern, and the greater part of the handles if not the whole. See p. 1619.

3 (3, a1, +). Louvre G 110, frr. One fragment, Pottier pl. 105; *Mon. Piot* 45, 2–7 and pl. 1, 1; detail of A, including a new fragment, *Mon. Piot* 47, 45; inscriptions, ibid. 44. A, Herakles and the lion. B, komos (*ἀσκωλιασμός*). On B, EVΦPO[NIOᛊ] EΛP[A]ΦᛊEN. Many fragments were added by Villard to the two small original ones; and another by Bousquet. See Villard in *Mon. Piot* 45, 1–10, and 47, 45–46.

4 (2). Louvre G 33, frr. A, Pottier pl. 91, whence Hoppin i, 450; *CV.* pl. 1, 3 and 6, and pl. 2, 4. A, Dionysos with maenads and satyrs; B, (foot, satyr). On A, [EV+ᛊI]ΘEOᛊ [EΓ]OIEᛊEN and, retr., ᒪ[EA]ΛPOᛊ KAᒪOᛊ. Now cleaned: of the figures there remain, on A, the lower halves of the three left-hand ones and the greater part of the two others, on B the lower half of the right-hand figure and one foot of the figure to left of it. The foot of the vase is ancient.

5. Milan 06.590, fr. *AJA.* 1950 pl. 20, c; *CV.* pl. 5, 1. (Herakles). [Albizzati]. For the subject—Amazonomachy?—, Bothmer *Am.* 137.

VOLUTE-KRATER

6 (5). Arezzo 1465, perhaps from Arezzo. Part, Dempster 1 pl. 19, whence Passeri pl. 163 and FR. ii, 1; *Mon.* 8 pl. 6, whence FR. ii, 3; FR. pll. 61–62 and ii, 14, whence (A) Perrot 10, 441–3, (A) *AM.* 30 Beil. p. 388, (A) Pfuhl fig. 395 (= Pfuhl *Mast.* fig. 47), (A) *Jb.* 44, 123, (A) Seltman pl. 17, (palmettes) Jacobsthal *O.* pl. 118, c; A, Stella 827; Bothmer *Am.* pl. 69, 3; phs. Al. 38339–40. A, Herakles and the Amazons; B, Amazons running up. On the neck, komos. On B, ΦΙLLΙΑΔΕϟΚΑLΟϟ and +ϟΕΝΟΚΑLΟΝ. The pertinences of the words in the neck-picture on A are not clear: not certain that the second word, ΚΑLΟϟ, is meant to continue the first, +ϟΕΝΟΝ. [Furtwängler]. See Bothmer *Am.* 135–7.

STAMNOI

7. Louvre C 11070, frr. *Mon. Piot* 45 pl. 1, 2 and pp. 9–11. A, heroes quarrelling. B, komos. [Villard]. The subject and general composition on A was probably the same as in the Florence-Chicago Oltos cup (p. 59 no. 58). See p. 1619.

8 (6). Leipsic T 523, frr. Part, *JHS.* 12 pll. 22–23; detail, Hartwig 185; with further fragments, *Jb.* 11, 185, whence Hoppin *Euth. F.* pl. 34 and *Anz.* 1918 pl. at p. 68; (with a fragment ex Munich added by Diepolder) Schweitzer *Stamnos des Euphronios* 1–2. A, Peleus and Thetis. B, athletes. On A, . . . Α]ΝΤΙΑ (see p. 1563). See CB. ii, 5 note 1. The Freiburg fragment with mouth, flute, and forearms of a flute-player, mentioned in *ARV.*[1] 16, foot, belongs, and has been transferred to Leipsic. See p. 1619.

NECK-AMPHORAE
(no. 9, with twisted handles)

9 (7). Louvre G 30, from Vulci. Pottier pl. 90; A, *VA.* 30; *CV.* pl. 27, 8–9 and pl. 28, 1 and 4, whence (A) Rumpf *MZ.* pl. 20, 4; *Mon. Piot* 37, 70–71; part of A, Villard *VG.* pl. 19, 3. On the neck, symposion: A, youth playing kottabos; B, youth singing and playing the lyre. On A, ΓΑΙϟ retr., and LΕΑΛΡΟϟ ΚΑLΟϟ. On B, LΕΑΛΡΟϟ ΚΑLΟϟ retr. The foot of the vase is missing. See p. 1619.

(no. 10, the handles missing)

10. Louvre C 11071, frr. *Mon. Piot* 47 pl. 3 and pp. 37–39. A, discus-thrower; B, acontist. On A, . . . Ε]ΛΡΑΦϟΕ (there may or may not have been a final nu), also ΑΝΤΙΑϟΚΑLΟΣ and ΚΑLΟϟ. On B, . . . ΑΝ]ΤΙΑ, ends. [Villard].

PELIKAI (NECK-PELIKAI)

11. Villa Giulia, from near Viterbo. A, youth leading a horse. B, man seated, chastising a boy with a sandal. On A, LΕΑΛΡΟϟ ΚΑLΟϟ. On B, LΕΑΛΡΟϟ ΚΑLΟϟ.

12 (10). VILLA GIULIA, and CHICAGO, Univ., from Cervetri. B, *Art. Bull.* 19, 539 figs. 2–3; the underside of the foot, with the graffito, *St. etr.* 5 pl. 15, 2. A, youth seated having his sandal tied by a boy. B, youth seated, playing with a marten. On B, ᒣEΛᐱPOᕒ ᛕΛᒪOϞ. See *JHS.* 51, 40 no. 6 and *CF.* 33 no. 4; and, for the animal on B, CB. iii, text.

HYDRIA
(*kalpis, with picture on the shoulder, framed*)

13 (11). DRESDEN 295 (ZV. 925). *Anz.* 1892, 165, 31; Hoppin *Euth. F.* 73. Acontist and flute-player. [ᛕ]ΛᒪOϞ ᒣEΛᐱPOϞ retr., ΛΝΤΙΛϞ retr., ϞΜ[Ιᛕᕒ]OOϞ [ᛕ]ΛᒪOᏕ. For the palmette-band compare a fragment of a hydria of the same type in the Louvre, C 11051.

PSYKTERS

14 (a5). BOSTON 10. 221 (one fr. ex Freiburg), from Orvieto. *Jb.* 7 pl. 5, whence Roscher s.v. Pentheus 1931; Philippart *Ic. des Bacchantes* pl. 12; with the Freiburg fr., CB. ii pl. 31, below. Death of Pentheus. See CB. ii. 1–3; and below, p. 1619.

15 (12). LENINGRAD 644 (St. 1670), from Cervetri. *CR.* 1869 pl. 5, whence *WV.* 5 pl. 2 and Klein *Euphr.* 105; FR. pl. 63, whence Hoppin i, 405, (part) Buschor *G.V.* 159, (part) Pfuhl fig. 394, (part) Rumpf *Rel.* fig. 200, (part) Cloché *Classes* pl. 5, 4, (part) Buschor G. *Vasen* 141, (detail) Buschor *Bilderwelt* 31, (part) LS. fig. 56; part, Simon *G.A.* 22–23. Symposion (naked women). EᕦᏑPOΝΙOϞEΛPΛᏑϞEΝ. ΤΙΝΤΛΝᐃEᒣΛΤΛϞϞO ᒣEΛᐱPE retr. The name ΛᐱΛᒠE (retr.) disproves the statement in *Glotta* 36, 105 that ἀγάπη is not a classical Greek word.

FRAGMENTS OF A POT

16 (13). HEIDELBERG 51, two frr. Kraiker pl. 9. (Athlete—or athletes, not certain that the two fragments are from the same figure). …ΛΝ]ΤΙΛϞ, need not be complete aft. From a neck-amphora?

CUPS

17 (14). MUNICH 2620 (J. 337), from Vulci. *Mon. nouv. ann.* 1838 pll. 15–16, whence *WV.* 5 pl. 3 and Klein *Euphr.* 82 and 54–55; FR. pl. 22, whence Perrot 10, 399–401, Hoppin i, 391, Pfuhl fig. 391, Swindler figs. 290, 246, and 295, Seltman pl. 18, (A) LS. fig. 55; I, Langlotz *G.V.* pl. 4, left; I, Schaal *Rf.* fig. 13; shield of Athena, *BCH.* 1930 pl. 22, 1; I, Cloché *Classes* pl. 5, 3; I, Zadoks-Jitta 85, 9; A and foot, Bloesch pl. 13, 1; I, Buschor G. *Vasen* 140, whence Frel *Ř.V.* fig. 149; I, Schoenebeck and Kraiker pl. 82, 2; I, Schuchhardt and Technau 148; head of the foremost youth on B (not of Athena), *Marb. Jb.* 15, 235 fig. 173: A–B, Brommer *Herakles* pl. 26; Lullies and Hirmer pll. 12–16, whence (I and B) LS. figs. 52 and 54; A–B, Stella 812; I, Richter *H.G.A.* 327. I, horseman. A–B,

Herakles and Geryon. On I, LEAΛPOΣ KALOΣ. On A, LEA[Λ]POΣ retr. and KALOΣ. On B, HOΠAIΣ KALOΣ retr., LEAΛPOΣ retr. On the foot, +A+PVLIONEΠOIEΣEN EVΦPONIOΣEΛPAΦΣEN. Coral-red used. Restored, I considerably. For the shape, Bloesch 45 no. 13 and p. 46, and compare a cup-foot, signed Kachrylion, in Marzabotto (p. 108 no. 18). See p. 1619.

18 (15). ATHENS Acr. 176 (part ex Chicago, Univ.; Schliemann; and Martin Robertson), frr., from Athens. Part, *Jb.* 3 pl. 2, whence Hoppin i, 379; part, *JHS.* 14, 190–1; part, Langlotz pl. 8; the Schliemann fr., *AM.* 13, 104, assigned to Euphronios by Wolters; Hartwig suggested that it should belong to this cup; the same fr. (given to the Museum by Henri Seyrig), *BCH.* 1930 pl. 20, 1 and pl. 22, 2; joined to one of the Acropolis frr., ibid. pl. 21; the same fr., *Anz.* 1938, 767 fig. 3; a new fr. found by Martin Robertson, seen by him to be from the Acropolis cup, and given by him to the Museum, *BCH.* 1930 pl. 20, 2–3; the Chicago fr. (now given to the Museum), *Art Bull.* 21, 266 fig. 7; A–B, ibid. 268. I, (on the right, the back of a head, probably male, to left). A–B, wedding of Peleus and Thetis. On A, [EVΦPON]IOΣEΛPAΦΣEN retr. Under one handle, LEAΛ[POΣ] KALOΣ. On B, [? KALO]Σ, LE[AΛPOΣ]. See Svatik in *Art Bull.* 21, 264–7; and below, no. 22.

19 (16). TARQUINIA, fr., from Tarquinia. R.I. xxiii. 236. A, Amazonomachy. Inscription TO+ΣAPI[Σ]. See Bothmer *Am.* 137.

(no. 20, decorated inside only?)

20. LENINGRAD Ol. 18181, fr., from Olbia. *Listy fil.* 1957 pl. 3. I, male (shank and foot with part of the himation). On I, LEAΛP[OΣ .... Coral red used. [Peredolskaya].

(no. 21, decorated inside only)

21. LOUVRE C 11981, fr. Bothmer *Am.* pl. 72, 7. I, Amazon. [? +A+PV-LIO]NEΠOIEΣEN: The inscription may have continued after the interpoints. [Bothmer].

SKYPHOS?

22. ATHENS Acr., fr., from Athens. (On the right, Dionysos). [Karouzou]. Mentioned by Mrs. Karouzou in *BCH.* 1947–8, 425, and said by her to be almost certainly from the cup Athens Acr. 176 (no. 18). The style is indeed very like, but I thought the fragment was more probably from a skyphos (with diagonal handles).

PLATE

23. ATHENS, fr., from Brauron. *Jb.* 71, 98. Hyakinthos. [Karouzou].

MANNER OF EUPHRONIOS

ARV.[1] 18–19.

NECK-AMPHORAE

(nos. 1–2, with twisted handles)

1 (2). Louvre G 107. *Mon. Piot* 9, 35, 32, and 37, whence FR. ii, 9, *Neue Beiträge* pl. 27, (A) *AM.* 30, 389; Pottier pl. 105; *CV.* pl. 33, 1–4. A, Herakles; B, Amazon shooting. On the base below the figure on A, ΔOKEI ⠶ ƧMIKOI ⠶ INAI. Now cleaned. Attributed to Euphronios by Furtwängler. See Bothmer *Am.* 137; and below, p. 1619.

2 (18). Leningrad 610, from Vulci. *Marb. Winckelmann-Programm* 1949 pl. 3; A, *Dev.* pl. 40, 1. A, Herakles shooting; B, the Hydra. For the subject of B, Brommer in *Marb. Winck.* 1949, 6–7. Close to Euphronios. See p. 1619.

(no. 3, the handles lost)

3 (3). Louvre G 106. Geffroy 3, 54; Pottier pl. 105; *CV.* pl. 33, 5–7. A, Amazon; B, Amazon. On A, ΑΝΤΟ+ƧΕΝΟƧ. On B, ΕV[Φ]PO-NIOƧ (there may have been more); and above the head ... VƧ, the end of a word, noticed by Bothmer. Now partly cleaned, and the alien mouth, neck, handles, removed. See Bothmer *Am.* 150 and 154.

CUP

4 (6). Athens Acr. 195, fr., from Athens. Langlotz pl. 9. I, naked male. ... Ε]ΛΡΑΦΕΝ.

A small fragment also recalls Euphronios:

CUP

Florence 9 B 56, fr. *CV.* pl. 9, B 56. A, (one in chiton and himation).

Peters (*Pan.* 56) may be right in attributing a fragment of a *black-figured* panathenaic amphora to Euphronios: Athens Acr. 931 (Graef pl. 56).

The Louvre fragment C 11187 is mouth and neck of a neck-amphora with twisted handles. The neck-floral resembles that of Louvre G 107 (above, no. 1); ivy on the upper section of the mouth as in Louvre G 30 (p. 15 no. 9).

Louvre C 11190 is the mouth of another neck-amphora with ivy on the mouth; what little of the neck remains is black; handles missing.

Dresden 288, from Nola, is a neck-amphora, with twisted handles, of the same type as Louvre C 11187 (and, in essentials, Louvre G 30), but the figures are not Euphronian, though contemporary (Gerhard pl. 124; B.Ap. xxi. 2: A, Herakles; B, Kyknos).

———

Cup-fragments in Berlin and the Vatican, with the name of Euphronios, the verb missing, if by Euphronios, would be very late. They are in a bold manner which is as different as possible from that of the signed cup in Athens (p. 17 no. 18) and which already approximates, in general character, to early proto-Panaetian cups like London E 46 or Louvre G 77 (pp. 315–16 nos. 1–2).

ARV.[1] 19–20.

CUP

1 (1). BERLIN 2281, and VATICAN, frr. The Berlin fragments, *AZ.* 1882 pl. 3, whence Klein *Euphr.* 176 and 160, Hoppin i, 383, *AJA.* 1954 pl. 62 fig. 27; all, *Acme* 6 pll. 1–2 and pp. 506–7; all, *Neue Beiträge* pll. 21–26. The Vatican fragments were recognized by Albizzati. Iliupersis: I, death of Priam; A, fight; B, warriors pursuing women. On I, in the exergue, EV[Φ]PONI[Oϟ.... See Stenico in *Acme* 6, 497–508, and Speier in *Neue Beiträge* 113–24.

By the same hand the cup-fragment

2 (2). BERLIN 2280, fr. Hartwig pl. 24, 2 and p. 241. I, young warrior pursuing a woman; A, (woman, warrior).

Compare with these the cup-fragments

FREIBURG S 131 (three frr.), HALLE inv. 95 (KN 61) (one fr.), and GOETTINGEN (two frr.). The Halle fr., Bielefeld *Halle* 124 fig. 3. One Freiburg fr. gives, from A, part of a fight—a warrior down on one knee, and, on the right, outstretched arm and himation-ends of a woman running to right, looking round. A Goettingen fr. joins on the left, adding the left foot of the warrior and the left foot of his opponent. A second fr. in Freiburg has the upper part of a woman running to left, looking round, and probably comes from A rather than from B. The Halle fr. has, from B, an archer running, leading a horse, and a woman running to right, looking round. The third fr. in Freiburg, and the second in Goettingen, have parts of the key border inside and of the net border outside; the Goettingen has has also a leaf (under the handle). The Goettingen frr. are said to be from Orvieto; the Halle, 'from Tarquinia?'.

———

THE GOTHA CUP

The style of the following shows the influence of artists like Euphronios and the Sosias Painter. See Langlotz in *Gnomon* 4, 327.

CUP

GOTHA, from Kolias. *Mon.* 10 pl. 37a, whence FR. iii, 19 and Hoppin ii, 329; A–B, Jacobsthal O. pl. 69, b; Philippart *C.A.B.* pl. 11, b and pl. 12. I, youth courting boy. A–B, white ground: symposion (A, male reclining; B, man reclining). Restored. The inscriptions are hard to read, partly on account of the repainting. I seemed to make out NI[. . . . .]EƧE on A, where the latter part of the inscription may be [EΓOI]EƧE. The . . . AƧIAΔEƧ (retr.) on B may be the drinker's name and not the signature of Pasiades. For the subject of I, *Cypr.* 28, *a* 46.

Another cup may be compared with that in Gotha. It also recalls Euphronios. Little of the picture remains.

ATHENS, Agora, P 7901, frr., from Athens. *Hesp.* 27 pl. 45, c. I, man (or youth) courting boy. On the inside of the rim, in large letters, AΛAƧI-KAT[EƧ]: KAL[O]Ƨ. For the subject, *Cypr.* 29, γ 15.

SMIKROS

Gaspar in *Mon. Piot* 9, 15–41. *JHS.* 37, 236. *Att. V.* 62. *ARV.*¹ 20–21 and 948.

Imitator of Euphronios.

STAMNOI

1 (1). BRUSSELS A 717. A, *Bull. Mus. Roy.* 1903, 52; *Mon. Piot* 9 pll. 2–3, whence Perrot 10, 519–21, Hoppin ii, 417, (A) Perrot 9, 375, (A) Pfuhl fig. 388, (B) *Dedalo* 1, 159; A, Cloché *Classes* pl. 21, 3; side, Jacobsthal O. pl. 92, b; *CV.* pll. 12–13; details of A, Buschor G. *Vasen* 143, whence (detail) Rumpf *MZ.* pl. 20, 8; detail of A, *PP.* pl. 1, 4; details, Verhoogen *C.G.* pl. 11. A, symposion (youths reclining, with women); B, man and youth filling the dinos. On A, ƧMIKPOƧEΛ[P]AⵁƧEN. On B, ANTIAƧKALOƧ and retr. E[V]ALKIAEꞱKALOƧ. See *PP.* 19.

2 (2). LOUVRE G 43, from Cervetri. Pottier pl. 92; *CV.* pl. 1, 2, 5, and 8, and pl. 2, 1–3; A, Langlotz *F.B.* pl. 14, 2; R.I. xx. 7; phs. Gir. 19557 and 19551. A, Dionysos and maenads; B, satyrs and maenad. Now cleaned.

3 (3). LONDON E 438, from Todi. Fröhner *Brant.* pll. 6–9, whence Hoppin ii, 419 and (A) Johansen *Iliaden* fig. 38; side, Jacobsthal O. pl. 92, a; *CV.* pl. 19, 2. A, fight (Ajax and Hector); B, fight. On A, ƧM[I]KPOƧEAPAⵁ-ƧEN and ANTIAƧKALOƧ. On B, [Ⳇ]EI[Δ]IAΔEꞱKALOƧ (other supplements also possible). See p. 1620.

PELIKAI
(with framed pictures)

4 (4). LENINGRAD 616 (St. 1527). *Epit. Haken* pl. 2; A, G.P. 44. A, Peleus and Thetis. B, jumper and trainer.

5 (5). LOUVRE G 65. Pottier pl. 95; *CV.* pl. 32, 7–10. A, Peleus and Thetis. B, fight.

PSYKTER

6 (6). LOUVRE G 58. Emmanuel *Danse,* frontispiece; *CV.* pl. 58, 3, 6, and 9 and pl. 59, 4–5 and 7–8. Komos. Much restored.

The name of Smikros appears on Louvre G 107 (p. 18 no. 1), but the drawing cannot be said to be his. See also pp. 1619–20.

THE SOSIAS PAINTER

Hauser in FR. iii, 13–22. *Att. V.* 59. *ARV.*[1] 21 and 949.

CUP

1 (1). BERLIN 2278, from Vulci. *Mon.* 1 pl. 24–25; Gerhard *Trinkschalen* pll. 6–7; *AD.* 1 pll. 9–10; FR. pl. 123, whence Hoppin ii, 423, (I and A) Perrot 10, 505 and 509, (I and A) Pfuhl fig. 418, (I) Swindler figs. 310 and 315, (detail of I) Richter *ARVS.* fig. 45, (A–B), Stella 103 and 120, (detail of I) LS. fig. 66; I, Bulle pl. 304; I, Buschor *G.V.* frontispiece; I, Langlotz *GV.* pl. 10, whence Rumpf *MZ.* pl. 20, 5; I, Pfuhl *Mast.* fig. 51; I, Schaal *Rf.* fig. 27; I, Neugebauer pl. 48, 2; I, Buschor *G. Vasen* 147; I, Schoenebeck and Kraiker pl. 15. I, Achilles tending Patroklos. A–B, Herakles entering Olympus. Under one handle, the Moon (see p. 119 no. 1: against, Schauenburg *Helios* 14). On the foot, ꙅOꙅIAꙅEΓOIEꙅEN. For the shape, Bloesch 55–56; for the plant held by the second Hora, Jacobsthal *Gk Pins* 185–6 and 199. See also p. 1620.

KANTHAROS

2 (2). ATHENS Acr. 556, frr., from Athens. Langlotz pl. 42. Herakles entering Olympus.

The only other work with the signature of the potter Sosias might be by the same hand as the Berlin cup, but there is not enough to compare:

STANDLET OF SOSIAN TYPE

BERLIN 2315. *Gaz. arch.* 1878 pl. 25, 2; *A.D.* 1 pl. 10, 2, whence Perrot 10, 513, FR. iii, 13, Hoppin ii, 426. Satyr sitting on the ground. ꙅOꙅIAꙅ EΓOIEꙅEN.

A small fragment recalls the Sosias Painter:

CUP

Once OXFORD 1920. 254, fr., from North Italy. Now lost. *CV*. pl. 14, 1 and 20. I, winged goddess (Eos?). A, (chariot).

The name of Sosias occurs, in greetings, on two vases by Euthymides (p. 27 no. 3, and p. 28 no. 10) and one by Phintias (p. 23 no. 1), occurs also on another vase of the Pioneer Group (p. 33 no. 3).

THE PAINTER OF ACROPOLIS 24

Langlotz, *Acr*. 51. *ARV*.[1] 949.

These small pieces are put here because they recall the Sosias Painter.

PLATES

(*small*)

1 (1). ATHENS Acr. 24, fr., from Athens. Langlotz pl. 2, whence *E.A.A.* i, 52 fig. 77. Woman seated. [Langlotz].

2 (2). OXFORD, Beazley (ex Brummer). *Cat. Parke-Bernet June 8–9 1949*, 3, 2 no. 10. Woman, holding wreath, seated at wool-basket.

PYXIDES?

3 (3). ATHENS Acr. 562, fr., from Athens. Langlotz pl. 42. Women. [Langlotz].

4. ATHENS (ex Rhousopoulos), fr., from Attica. (Arms and thighs of a woman seated to right, holding out a wreath or necklace, upper part of a youth in a himation leaning on his stick to left, left arm extended). Might belong to the last?

PHINTIAS

Stuart Jones in *JHS*. 12, 366–80. Hartwig 167–99. Furtwängler in FR. ii, 65–71 and 169–70. Hauser in *Jb*. 10, 108–13 and in FR. ii, 273–6. *VA*. 28–29. Langlotz *Zeitbestimmung* 63–64. *Att. V*. 57–58. *ARV*.[1] 21–24 and 949. *CB*. ii, 3–6.

The name of Phintias appears on nine vases. On six of them he signs as painter, on three as potter. For the ἐποίησεν vases see p. 25. See also p. 1620.

The Munich cup (p. 24 no. 12), which is very early, from the painter's nonage—pre-Pioneer—was painted for the potter Deiniades.

AMPHORAE
(type A)

1 (1). LOUVRE G 42, from Vulci. Gerhard pl. 22, whence (A) *El.* 2 pl. 56, (A) Overbeck *KM.* pl. 23, 4; FR. pl. 112 and ii, 276, whence Hoppin *Euth. F.* pl. 31 and p. 125, (B) Pfuhl fig. 383, (B) Norman Gardiner *Athl.* fig. 123, (A) Pfeiff *Apollon* pl. 14, b; one figure on B, Reichhold *Skizzenbuch* pl. 1, whence Seltman pl. 15; *CV.* pl. 28, 2–3 and 5–8; A, *JHS.* 71 pl. 17, c and (mouth and foot) p. 32 fig. 4. A, Apollo and Tityos. B, athletes. On B, ΣΟΣΤΡΑΤΟΣ ΚΑLΟΣ, ?ΟΤΙΝΟΝ, +ΑΡΕΣ (retr.), ΔΕΜΟΣΤΡΑΤΕ (the last six letters retr.), +ΑΙΡΕ, ΣΟΣΙΑΣ retr. (the pertinences of the καλός and the χαῖρε probably so). [Stuart Jones]. For the shape, Bloesch in *JHS.* 71, 31, Eukleo Class, B. See p. 1620.

2 (2). TARQUINIA RC 6843, from Tarquinia. *Mon.* 11 pll. 27–28, whence (B) Overbeck *KM.* pl. 24, 4; FR. pl. 91 and ii, 167 and 171, whence Hoppin *Euth. F.* pl. 26, Hoppin ii, 357, (A) Perrot 10, 463, (A) Pfuhl fig. 381, (part of A) Seltman pl. 14, (detail of A) Richter *ARVS.* fig. 46, (B) LS. fig. 65; A, *ML.* 36 pl. 8, 3; A, Romanelli *Tarquinia* 127; *CV.* pl. 1; A, ph. Mo. 5854, 1; A, ph. Al. 26038; B, ph. And. 40992; phs. R.I. 1928. 1–7. A, Dionysos with satyrs and maenads. B, Herakles and Apollo: the struggle for the tripod. On A, ΦΙΝΤΙΑΝ ΕΛΡΑΦΣΕΝ retr. On B, ΦΙΝΤΙΣ ΕΛΡΑΦΣΕΝ. See p. 1620.

PELIKE

3. LOUVRE C 10784. A, Dionysos with maenad and satyr. B, athletes. On A, ΕΛΡΑΦΝΕΝ ΦΙΝΤΙΑΝ. The satyr is Phlebodokos (ΦLΕΒΟΔΟΚΟΝ), the maenad Kissine (Κ[Ι]?ΙΝΕ). The fragments were put together by Villard.

VOLUTE-KRATER

4 (3). BERLIN 2181 and VILLA GIULIA, frr. (see *JHS.* 51, 4 no. 7 and *CF.* 33 no. 6). Detail of the Berlin part, *JHS.* 35, 117 fig. 3, a; part, *JHS.* 51, 41 fig. 1. Fight. [Hartwig, the Berlin part].

CALYX-KRATERS

5 (4). LENINGRAD inv. 1843 (St. 1275), frr. *Mon.* 6–7 pl. 34 (with fancy restorations); now cleaned; the genuine parts, *Anz.* 1912, 106–10, whence Hoppin *Euth. F.* 133; A, FR. iii, 234. A, Theseus and (the bull?). B, wounding of Telephos. [Stuart Jones].

6 (a). LIMENAS, fr., from Thasos. CB. ii, suppl. pl. 11, 2. A, Achilles and Memnon. See CB. ii, 15–16; and below, p. 1620.

HYDRIAI
(nos. 7–9 of bf. shape, with framed pictures)

7 (5). MUNICH 2421 (J. 6), from Vulci. *Philologus* 26 (1867) pl. 2, whence (shoulder, reversed) Klein *Euphr.* 110; FR. pl. 71, 1, and ii, 63, 66 fig. 29,

and 72 fig. 34, left, whence Hoppin *Euth. F.* pl. 28, 1–3 and p. 116 and (shoulder) Pfuhl fig. 385; (shoulder) Licht ii, 85; (shoulder) Vorberg *Gloss.* 733; *JHS.* 71 pl. 18, b and (mouth and foot) p. 32 fig. 8; shoulder, Rumpf *MZ.* pl. 20, 1; Lullies and Hirmer pll. 33–35. Music-lesson. On the shoulder, symposion (two women). On the shoulder, KΑLOI retr. (= καλῷ, as Hauser?), ϟOITENΔI EVOVMIΔEI. EVTVMIΔEϟ (retr.) is also the name given to the seated youth in the chief picture. [Hartwig]. For the shape, Bloesch in *JHS.* 35, Ring-foot Potter no. 1.

8 (6). MUNICH 2422 (J. 50), from Vulci. Lau pl. 29; FR. ii, 68–69 and 70 fig. 32, whence Hoppin *Euth. F.* 118–19. Komos. On the shoulder, satyrs molesting a deer. [Hartwig]. For the shape, Bloesch in *JHS.* 71, 35, Potter of the Hypsis Hydria, no. 2. See p. 1620.

9 (7). LONDON E 159, from Vulci. *JHS.* 12 pll. 20–21 and pp. 367–8, whence FR. ii, 67 and 66 fig. 27, Hoppin *Euth. F.* pl. 27 and pp. 105–6, Hoppin ii, 360–1, (the chief picture) Perrot 10, 467, (the chief picture) Pfuhl fig. 382; *CV.* pl. 70, 1 and pl. 72, 1; ph. Ma. 3147. Youths at the fountain. On the shoulder, symposion (man and youth reclining). MEΛΑKLEϟ KΑLOϟ. On the shoulder, ΦITIΑϟ EΛPΑΦϟEN. For the shape, Bloesch in *JHS.* 71, 35, Ring-foot Potter no. 3.

(no. 10, kalpis, with picture on the shoulder)

10. BASLE, Cahn, 8, fr. Symposion (on the left, male reclining, then a naked woman).

PSYKTER

11 (8). BOSTON 01.8019, from Orvieto. *A.D.* 2 pl. 20, whence *JHS.* 27, 259, Norman Gardiner *G.A.S.* 345, Hoppin *Euth. F.* pll. 32–33, Norman Gardiner *Athl.* figs. 51 and 143, (detail) *VA.* 28, (part) Alexander *Gk Athl.* 17, 3, and 21, 3, (detail) Schröder *Sport* 124; part, Hoppin *Euth. F.* pl. 32; CB. ii pl. 31, above, pl. 32, and p. 3; the shape, Hambidge 99 fig. 17 and Caskey G. 131. Athletes. [Hauser]. See CB. ii, 3–6.

CUPS

12 (9). MUNICH 2590 (J. 401), from Vulci. Hartwig 169–71; FR. pl. 32 and i, 171–2, whence Hoppin *Euth. F.* pl. 25, Hoppin ii, 363, (I) Swindler fig. 283; palmettes, Jacobsthal O. pl. 75, b; A, *Eph.* 1942–4, 65; Lullies and Hirmer pl. 9, above, and pl. 10, whence (A–B) LS. figs. 63–64; B, *E.A.A.* i, 201. I, satyr. A, Herakles and Alkyoneus. B, Herakles and Apollo: the struggle for the tripod. On A, ΦILTIΑϟEΛPΑΦϟEN retr., ΔEIN-[IΑ]ΔEϟ [E]ΓOIEϟEN. Very early. For the shape, Bloesch 32 note 65.

13 (10). FLORENCE PD 117, fr., from Populonia. *NSc.* 1921, 313; Minto *Populonia* pl. 53, 2. I, armourer.

14 (11). BALTIMORE, from Chiusi. Hartwig pl. 17, 1, whence HM. 18, Perrot 10, 464, Hoppin *Euth. F.* 100, Hoppin ii, 355, Pfuhl fig. 384; Richter *Craft* 82 fig. 85; Cloché *Classes* pl. 32, 1; *CV.* Robinson ii pl. 3, 2 and pl. 2,

1, whence Schnitzler pl. 39; *Harv. St.* 52 pl. 3; Sparkes, Talcott, and Frantz, fig. 12. I, youth buying a vase. ⏚IN[TI]A𐤎EΛPA⏚𐤎EN, +ΛIPIA𐤎KAⱢO𐤎. Restored.

The following are related to Phintias, and might be late work of his:

LOUTROPHOROS

1 (a). ATHENS Acr. 636, frr., from Athens. Part, *JHS*. 14 pl. 4, 1–2; Langlotz pll. 50–51. On the neck, procession: a sow led to sacrifice. On the upright handle, woman. OⱢVΓIO[ΔOPO𐤎] KA[ⱢO𐤎]. The inscription to right of the flute-player is ⱢV[KO]𐤎 retr. See also *ABV*. 673.

FRAGMENT OF A POT

2 (a). ATHENS Acr. 766, frr., from Athens. Langlotz pl. 67. Unexplained subject (fight?:—chariot, spear—of one in the chariot?—, man—charioteer?—with kentron?). Inscriptions [?KN]OΓIONO𐤎 and retr. ENV . . . Near the last.

PHINTIAS, POTTER

ARV.[1] 24.

The name of Phintias occurs with ἐποίησεν on three vases:

CUP

1 (α). ATHENS 1628 (CC. 1157), from Tanagra. Hartwig pl. 17, 3, whence Hoppin *Euth. F.* 81, Hoppin ii, 354, and Pfuhl fig. 386; *CV.* pl. 2, 1, 3, and 5; A, Bloesch *FAS.* pl. 16, 2; ph. Marb. 134756. I, warrior kneeling, putting on his helmet. ⏚INTIA𐤎EΓOIE𐤎EN. For the shape, Bloesch 61, no. 1. See also Martin Robertson in *AJA*. 1958, 62–63.

ARYBALLOI
(the body in the shape of cockle-shells)

2 (β). ELEUSIS, from Eleusis. *Eph.* 1885 pl. 9, 10, whence Hoppin *Euth. F.* 109 and Hoppin ii, 359. On the topside of the mouth, ⏚INTIA𐤎 : EΓOIE𐤎EN :

3 (γ). ATHENS Acr. 873, frr., from Athens. Langlotz pl. 75 and p. 82. On the topside of the mouth, ⏚IⱢTIA𐤎 : EΓOIE𐤎ENME : OΓAIKAⱢE :

With these cockle-shell aryballoi (in which the mouth is not of one model) compare others:

1. NEW YORK 23.160.33. *Bull. Metr.* 19, 129 fig. 5; Richter and Milne fig. 108. On the topside of the mouth, HOΓAI𐤎 : KAⱢO𐤎NAI

2. TORONTO 352. Robinson and Harcum pl. 56 and p. 159. On the topside of the mouth, HOΓAI𐤎KAⱢO𐤎 :

3. ITALIAN MARKET. The body is of a different model. On the topside of the mouth, HOΓAIⳞ ⁚ KAⳞOⳞ ˙ NAI ⁚

Compare also the fragment Oxford 333 (see p. 1602), which has NAY-ⳞIⳞPATOⳞ ⁚ KAⳞOⳞ ⁚ NAI ⁚ on the topside of the mouth and the same three-dot interpoints as the Phintias aryballoi.

A slighter vase is compared by Greifenhagen with those in New York and Toronto:

BONN 1521, from Athens. *CV.* pl. 39, 8.

EUTHYMIDES

Furtwängler in FR. i, 63–66 and 173–81, and ii, 65. Buschor *G.V.* 153–5. *JHS*. 30, 41. Hoppin *Euth. F.* (see my review in *JHS*. 37, 233–7). *VA*. 32–33. Langlotz *Zeitbestimmung* 62–63. *Att. V.* 63–64 and 468. Talcott in *Hesp.* 5, 59–69. *ARV*.[1] 24–27 and 949. CB. iii, text.

There are seven signed vases. On six of them the name is followed by ἔγραψεν or the like, and three of these add the father's name, probably, as Robert observed, Pollias (in *PW*. vi, 1512). On fragments of a seventh work by Euthymides (p. 28 no. 17) the patronymic alone is preserved; there may have been an ἔγραψεν; the ἐποίησεν is on a loose sherd and may or may not have been preceded by the name of Euthymides. No. 19 has a potter's signature as well as the painter's, but the name is missing.

Euthymides was a friend of Phintias and I dare say of Euphronios, for I read the inscription on the Munich amphora (no. 1) as a gay challenge to a comrade, not (with Pottier, Perrot, and others) as a cry of senile jealousy.

AMPHORAE

(type A)

1 (1). MUNICH 2307 (J. 378), from Vulci. Gerhard pl. 188; details, Hoppin *Euth*. 3, 11–12, and 26; FR. pl. 14 and i, 63, 66, 70 figs. 3 and 5, and 266, whence Perrot 10, 456–7, Hoppin *Euth. F.* pl. 1 and p. 13 fig. 1, Hoppin i, 433, (A) Robert *Herm*. 90, Pfuhl figs. 364–5, (A) Buschor 150, (B) *Jb*. 44, 121, (detail of A) Swindler fig. 317, (detail of B) Richter *ARVS*. fig. 44, (A) Schnitzler pl. 36, 50; Pfuhl *Mast*. figs. 38–39; A, Schnitzler pl. 36, 50a; mouth and foot, *JHS*. 71, 32 fig. 5; cleaned, Lullies and Hirmer pll. 24–31, whence (details of A) LS. figs. 58–60; *CV*. pll. 165–8, pl. 172, 1, pl. 188, 5, and pp. 14–15; B, Richter *HGA*. 328; B, Robertson *G.P.* 91–92. A, Hector arming. B, komos. On A, EΛΡAΦΝEN EVOVMI-ΔEΝ HOΓOⳞIO. On B, HOⳞOVΔEΓOTEEVΦPONIOΝ. For the shape, Bloesch in *JHS*. 71, 31, Eukleo Class, C. See p. 1620.

2 (4). MUNICH 2308 (J. 374), from Vulci. Hoppin *Euth*. pll. 1–2, whence (B) *Jb*. 23, 99, (B) *Jb*. 31, 130; FR. pl. 81 (the left-hand figure on A restored) and ii, 109, whence Hoppin *Euth. F.* pl. 2, Hoppin i, 435, (B) Pfuhl fig.

366, (B) Norman Gardiner *Athl.* fig. 124, (B, reversed) LS. fig. 61; B, Langlotz *G.V.* pl. 1, 2; B, Pfuhl *Mast.* fig. 40; B, Buschor G. *Vasen* 144; *CV.* pll. 169–71, pl. 172, 2–4, pl. 188, 6, and pp. 16–17. A, Thorykion arming. B, athletes and trainer. On A, H[ΟΓΟLΙ]ΟΕ[ΛΡΑ]ΦΜΕΝ-ΕVΟVΜΙΔΕΜΕΜ. On B, ΕVΟVΜΙΔΕ? ΗΟΓΟLΙΟ retr. For the shape, Bloesch in *JHS.* 71, 32, Eukleo Class, C.

3 (2). LOUVRE G 44, from Vulci. A, Gerhard pl. 176, 2; Pottier pl. 92; Hoppin *Euth. F.* pll. 15–16 and p. 61; part of B, *VA.* 32 fig. 17; horse, Morin-Jean 218; *CV.* pl. 29, 1–4 and 6 and pl. 30, 1. A, warrior mounting chariot. B, woman, youth, and man. On A, ΔΑ[Μ]Α?, +ΑΙ[ΡΕ]?Ο-?Ι?, +ΑΡ+Μ. On B, ... Α? retr., and +ΑΙΡΕ retr. followed by ΤΙ .... Much restored. My drawing in Hoppin *Euth. F.* 61 gives B without the restorations. For the shape, Bloesch in *JHS.* 71, 31, Eukleo Class, A.

4 (3). MUNICH 2309 (J. 410), from Vulci. Gerhard pl. 168; details, Hoppin *Euth.* 23–25 and 27; FR. pl. 33 and i, 173 and 180–1, whence Hoppin *Euth. F.* pl. 3 and p. 17 and (reversed) pl. 24, 1, Pfuhl figs. 368–9, Seltman pl. 19, (detail of B) *VA.* 32 fig. 18, (A) Schuchhardt and Technau 201 fig. 168, Stella 541; detail of A, Buschor *G.V.* 151; detail of A, Schaal *Rf.* fig. 9; A, Langlotz *G.V.* pl. 17, 25; Pfuhl *Mast.* figs. 41–42; detail of A, Buschor G. *Vasen* 145, whence Frel *Ř.V.* fig. 154; A, Lane pl. 65 and pl. 66, b; part of A, *Marb. Jb.* 15, 69 fig. 51; B. Rumpf *MZ.* pl. 20, 6; Lullies and Hirmer pll. 17–23, whence (B) LS. fig. 62; *CV.* pll. 161–4, pl. 188, 4, and pp. 12–13. Theseus carrying off Helen. [Klein]. The names of Korone and Helene on A have been interchanged. For the shape, Bloesch in *JHS.* 71, Eukleo Class, A. See p. 1620.

5. PAESTUM, fr., from Paestum. Komos (parts of a woman to right, playing the flute, and of a komast to right, looking round, with krotala).

NECK-AMPHORAE
(nos. 6–7, the handles missing)

6 (6). SYRACUSE 49305, frr., from Monte Casale. A, (Dionysos?). B, Hermes.

7. LOUVRE C 11072. A, satyr; B, satyr. On A, moving to right, bending, with pointed amphora; on B, moving to right, bending, with kantharos and wineskin. As the next.

(no. 8, with twisted handles)

8 (7). WARSAW 142332 (ex Czartoryski 63). *V.Pol.* pll. 4–6, whence Seltman pl. 20, (B) *AJA.* 1936, 104, 9, (B) Buschor G. *Vasen* 146 fig. 166, (B) Schnitzler pl. 38; *CV.* pl. 18. A, youth pouring wine from a pointed amphora. B, satyr. See *V.Pol.* 13–15.

PELIKE

9 (8, +). LOUVRE G 31. One fr. (mispoised and reversed), Hoppin *Euth. F.* 88. A, two acontists; B, jumper and discus-thrower. Many fragments have been added, mostly by Villard, to the two described in *ARV.*[1] 25

no. 8. Doubtful if ... RO⟨, retr., on B is to be restored as [Leag]ros: the other inscriptions seem meaningless.

VOLUTE-KRATER

10. SERRA ORLANDO, from Serra Orlando. A, *New York Times* 30 Sept. 1958; *AJA*. 1959 pl. 43 fig. 24 and pl. 44; detail of A, *Archaeology* 12 (1959), 133. The pictures on the neck. A, Herakles and the Amazons. B, symposion. On A, ⟨O⟨IA, +A⟨A. On B, +A[I]PE, +AIPE, ⟨O⟨IA, [+A]IPE. See p. 1620.

PSYKTER

11 (9). TURIN 4123, from Vulci. *Annali* 1870 pll. O–P; *JHS*. 35 pll. 5–6 and pp. 190–1, whence Hoppin *Euth. F.* pll. 4–5 and pp. 19 and 22, Hoppin i, 436–7, (A) Pfuhl fig. 367, (A) Schröder *Sport* pl. 61, below, (A) Norman Gardiner *Athl*. fig. 159; part of A, Buschor *Bilderwelt* 33; phs. R.I. 30.286 and 290, whence (A) Erika Diehl *Gr. Weinkühler* pl. 2. A, wrestlers (Theseus and Klytos); B, two athletes. On A, EVΘVMIΔE⟨ EΛPAΦ⟨EN HOΓOLIO. On B, EVΘVMIΔE[⟨] EΛPAΦ⟨EN HOΓLIO. For the inscriptions, *AJA*. 1950, 317. The reading kL[VT]O⟨ on A is Philippart's (*It. i*, 9). For the shape, *CB*. ii, 7, B7.

HYDRIAI
(kalpides, with picture on the shoulder, framed)

12 (10). BONN 70, from Nola. *AZ*. 1873 pl. 9, whence Hoppin *Euth. F.* pl. 6 and Hoppin i, 431; *CV*. pl. 16, 1–2. Symposion (two youths reclining). EVΘV[M]IΔ[E⟨] EΛPAΦE. MEΛAkLE⟨ kALO⟨ retr.

13 (11). FRANKFORT, Mus.V.F. Women at fountain, and satyr (two naked women at a laver, a satyr lying on the ground touching one of them; a woman filling her hydria at the lion-head spout). Restored.

14 (12). VATICAN G. 71, from Vulci. *RG*. 3 and pl. 25; ph. And. 42069. Komos.

15 (13). LENINGRAD 624 (St. 1624). Herford pl. 1, e. Dionysos seated, with satyr and maenad.

16 (14). ORVIETO, Faina, 68, from Orvieto. Phs. R.I. 38.260–261. Dionysos seated, and two satyrs.

CYLINDROID

17 (15). ATHENS, Agora, P 4683 and P 4744, frr., from Athens. Part, *Hesp*. 5, 60–62 and 68, whence (part) Pfeiff *Apollon* Beil. 2 at p. 40, 4. Apollo with Artemis, Leto, and another. ... EΓ]OIE⟨N, ... HO]ΓOLIO. [Talcott].

PLATE

18 (16). ADRIA Bc 64.10, frr., from Adria. Schöne pl. 4, 2, whence Hoppin *Euth. F.* 24 and Hoppin i, 438; part (one fr. is mislaid), *CV*. pl. 2, 7. Warrior. On the rim, chequers on a white ground. EVΘVMI[ΔE⟨] EΛPAΦE. See pp. 29–30.

CUPS

19 (17, 18, +). FLORENCE 7 B 2 (part ex Villa Giulia), three frr.; BOSTON
10.203, one fr.; LONDON 1952. 12–2.7, one fr.; NAPLES, Astarita, 121,
two frr. The Florence frr., *CV.* pl. 7, B 2, and *CF.* pl. Y, 9 and 23–24; the
Boston, *VA.* 32 fig. 16, whence Hoppin *Euth. F.* 87; all, CB. iii, suppl.
pl. 19, 1. Outside, deities in Olympus. As the London fragment has the
inscription HILVOVA the subject on one half if not on both halves must
have been the birth of Athena. [EVOVMI]ΔΕ$ [EΛPA]Φ$EN, [. . .
EΓ]OEI. Coral red used. See CB. iii, text.

20. ATHENS Acr. 211, frr., from Athens. Four frr., *Eph.* 1885 pl. 5, 2; a fifth,
Eph. 1886 pl. 7, 2; A–B, Langlotz pl. 10, whence Vian *R.* pl. 34, 331.
A–B, Gigantomachy. On I, [LEA]ΛPO[$ . . . Coral red used. For the
shape, Bloesch 134 no. 2.

MANNER OF EUTHYMIDES

ARV.[1] 27.

HYDRIA

(kalpis, with picture on the shoulder, framed)

1 (1). Lost. B. Ap. xxi. 61. Naked women at fountain (1, to left, filling her
hydria at a lion-head spout; 2, sitting on the ground, frontal, head down
to right; 3, to right, filling her hydria at a lion-head spout). Compare
the Frankfort hydria (p. 28 no. 13).

RHYTON

(donkey)

2 (2). AGRIGENTO, from Agrigento. *Boll. d'Arte* 25, 65–68; part, Griffo *Mus.
Agr.* 26 fig. 4; part, Griffo *Breve Guida* 23. Above, male (Dionysos?)
reclining, with males and ram. Below: A, komast; B, komast. [Haspels].

PLATE

3 (3). BOSTON 13.193, from Cumae. *VA.* 31; CB. i pl. 2, 4, and p. 4. Satyr.
HE$TIAIO$KALO$.

CUP

4 (4). VILLA GIULIA, fr. A, symposion (right breast, thigh, forearm, of a
male reclining to left, holding an aulos; on the left, elbow of another:
large-scale figures).

The following was attributed to Euthymides by Hoppin. The drawing is
certainly like Euthymides in a number of details, but lacks his force: possibly
his, but an early work? In shape the plate bears a distinct resemblance to the
signed one in Adria (p. 28 no. 18), and the two plates share the uncommon
chequer border on a white ground. See p. 1621.

PLATE

BOSTON 00.325, from Tarquinia. Hoppin *Euth. F.* pl. 24, 2; *VA.* 5; CB i. pl. 2, 3 and p. 3 fig. 3. Nereid. The chequer border is on a white ground.

A small fragment, from the rim of a plate, has the same chequer border as the plates in Adria and Boston, and the fashion of the rim is much as there: VILLA GIULIA, fr., from Veii. The chequers are on a white ground.

See also p. 9.

The name of Euthymides occurs, in a greeting, on a hydria by Phintias (p. 23 no. 7), on a hydria by another member of the Pioneer Group (p. 33 no. 8), and perhaps on a second hydria of the same group (p. 34 no. 9). The name is also given to the youth in the middle of the chief picture on the Phintias hydria.

HYPSIS

Furtwängler in FR. ii, 112–16. *ARV.*[1] 30.

Related to Euthymides.

HYDRIAI

(*no. 1, of bf. shape, with framed pictures*)

1 (1). MUNICH 2423 (J. 4), from Vulci. Gerhard pl. 103; FR. pl. 82 and ii, 113, whence Hoppin *Euth. F.* pl. 35 and p. 137, Hoppin ii, 121, (the chief picture) LS. fig. 67; mouth and foot, *JHS.* 71, 32 fig. 9; Lullies and Hirmer pl. 32; the chief picture, Bothmer *Am.* pl. 72, 2. Amazons. On the shoulder, chariot, and two boys on horseback. HVⲞ𝟝Ⲓ𝟝-ＥΛΡΑⲞＳＥN. For the shape, Bloesch in *JHS.* 71, 35, foot, no. 1.

(*no. 2, kalpis, the picture on the shoulder, framed*)

2 (2). ROME, Torlonia, 73, from Vulci. *A.D.* 2 pl. 8, whence FR. ii, 114, Buschor 152, Hoppin *Euth. F.* pl. 36, and Hoppin ii, 123. Women at fountain. HVⲞ𝟝Ｉ𝟝.

See also p. 34 no. 10; and p. 1621.

THE DIKAIOS PAINTER

JHS. 37, 235. *Att. V.* 64–65, i, and 468. *ARV.*[1] 28–29 and 949. *ABV.* 400.

Companion and imitator of Euthymides. Called after the kalos-name on no. 4.

AMPHORAE

(*type A*)

1 (1). VIENNA, Univ., 631 b (one fr. ex Freiburg), frr., from Orvieto. Part of A, *Hesp.* 5, 65; *CV.* pl. 9. A, Apollo with Artemis and Leto. B, arming. His best work. Of the Freiburg fragments mentioned in *CF.* 33 no. 7,

one has been joined to the fragments in Vienna; the other is not that figured in *CV*. 20.

2 (2). LONDON E 255, from Vulci. Hoppin *Euth*. pll. 5–6, whence Hoppin *Euth*. *F*. pl. 8; detail of A, Abrahams *Gk Dress* 93 fig. 35; details, Hoppin *Euth*. *F*. pl. 10, below; *CV*. pl. 3, 1; mouth and foot, *JHS*. 71, 32 fig. 3; *E.A.A.* i, 465 and iii, 97; A, ph. Ma. 3118. A, Herakles and Apollo: the struggle for the tripod. B, warrior leaving home. For the shape, Bloesch in *JHS*. 71, 31, Eukleo Class, A, 3.

3 (3). LONDON E 254, from Vulci. Hoppin *Euth*. pll. 3–4, whence Hoppin *Euth*. *F*. pl. 7; details, ibid. pl. 10, above; *CV*. pl. 2, 2. A, warrior leaving home. B, citharode. For the shape, Bloesch in *JHS*. 71, 31, Eukleo Class, A, 4.

4 (4). LOUVRE G 45. Pottier pll. 92–93, whence (A) *Jb*. 31, 140; *CV*. pl. 30, 2–5, pl. 31, 1, and pl. 29, 5, whence (detail of B) Rumpf *MZ*. pl. 21, 10, (detail of A) Frel. *R.V.* fig. 153; part of A, ph. Gir. 27033. A, youths and boys. B, warriors setting out. On A, ΔΙΚΑΙΟϹ ΚΑLΟ[Ϲ], ΙϹΑLΟϹ, and retr. +ΑΙΡΕ. For the shape, Bloesch in *JHS*. 71, Eukleo Class, A, 5.

KRATER
(bell-krater rather than calyx)

5 (5). CAB. MÉD. 387, fr., from Tarquinia. *Archiv Gesch. Medizin* 3 (1909), 38 fig. 5. Komos (males and naked woman). On the inscription see *AJA*. 1927, 347.

PSYKTER

6 (6). LONDON E 767, from Vulci. Jahn *Dichter* pl. 5; Genick pl. 23, 1; Hoppin *Euth*. *F*. pll. 17–19 and p. 65; A, *N.Y. Shapes* 10, 2 = Richter and Milne fig. 88, whence LS. fig. 15; *CV*. pl. 104, 1; side, Jacobsthal *O*. pl. 47, b; one figure on A, Pickard-Cambridge *D.F.A.* fig. 196 (misdescribed as Dionysos); ph. Ma. 3210. Komos (A, two baldheads preceded by a boy; B, two men, one of them playing the flute). The leader on A, who plays the lyre, is the poet ΚVΔΙΑϹ. The other inscriptions on A are +ΑΙΡΕ twice. On B, ΚΑΡΤΑ, ΔΙΚΑΙΟϹ; and +ΑΡ+ΟΝ, which may or may not be incomplete fore. For the shape, CB. ii, 7–8, B 8.

HYDRIA
(kalpis, with picture on the shoulder, framed)

7 (7). BRUSSELS R 351, from Vulci. Klein *L*. 124, whence *Jb*. 31, 144; FR. pl. 71, 2 and ii, 73 and 70 fig. 33, whence Buschor 153 and Hoppin *Euth*. *F*. pl. 28, 4 and p. 75; *CV*. pl. 16, 3; Licht i, 185, 2; Vorberg *Gloss*. 35. Symposion (love-making).

For the *black-figure* work of the Dikaios Painter see *ABV*. 400, also Bloesch in *JHS*. 71, 31 note 11.

NEAR THE DIKAIOS PAINTER

ARV.[1] 29–30 and 949.

HYDRIAI
(*kalpides, the picture on the shoulder, framed*)

1 (2). Louvre G 51. Pottier pl. 94; *CV.* pl. 53, 1 and 4; R.I. xxi. 1. Komos (woman making water and youth playing the flute). Restored.

2 (3). Munich, fr., from Athens. Sauer *Theseion* 118; Furtwängler *Aegina* 299. (Archer). See Bothmer *Am.* 223; and below, p. 1621.

FRAGMENT OF A POT

3 (a). Athens Acr. 790, fr., from Athens. Langlotz pl. 71. Youth. From a column-krater or a volute-krater?

See also pp. 33–35 nos. 1, 13, 14, and 18.

THE PEZZINO GROUP

These are somewhat akin to the earliest work of the Kleophrades Painter. Named after the former owner of no. 2. See p. 114.

AMPHORA
(*type A*)

1. Leyden PC 85 (xviii h 36), from Vulci. Roulez pl. 13; Hoppin *Euth. F.* pll. 13–14. A, heroes quarrelling. B, Dionysos and maenads.

CALYX-KRATER

2. Agrigento (ex Pezzino), from Agrigento. A, Griffo *Mus. Agr.* fig. 10; A, Griffo *Guida* 26; A, Griffo *Guide* 29, 2; A, Matt 121. A, warriors lifting the body of a dead hero. B, komos.

HYDRIA
(*of bf. shape*)

3. Munich 2420 (J. 377), from Vulci. Detail, *Jh.* 1, 44 fig. 29; Blümel *S.H.* 98–99, whence (part) *Arch. class.* 2 pl. 8, 3; B.Ap. xvi. 2. Athletes. On the shoulder, chariot harnessing. See p. 1621.

CUP

4. Naples Stg. 5, from Etruria. A–B, ph. So. 11090. I, two naked women (one sponging her boot). A, Dionysos with satyrs and maenads. B, komos. Very large. For the shape, Bloesch 44 no. 2 ('perhaps potter Euxitheos').

See also p. 34 no. 15; and p. 1621.

THE PIONEER GROUP: SUNDRY

These vases belong to the Pioneer Group, but cannot be stated to be by any of the painters described hitherto.

CALYX-KRATERS

1. ISTANBUL, frr., from Xanthos, A 34.2628. Men courting boys. Bothmer thinks of the Dikaios Painter.

2. Once Luynes; and BONN 143a: frr., from Tarquinia? or Vulci? The Luynes part, *Annali* 1833 pl. A, whence *CV*. Bonn 19; the Bonn fragment, *CV*. pl. 16, 6. Warrior mounting chariot, with archer and warrior. The drawing in *Annali* is much restored, and one cannot even be sure of the inscriptions. See Greifenhagen in *CV*. Bonn 18. For the style, he thinks of Euphronios and compares Louvre G 106 (p. 18 no. 3).

3. Once NAPLES, Bourguignon; and OXFORD 1928. 504: fr. The Oxford part, *CV*. pl. 66, 1. (Chariot, with the driver's hand, a warrior, and an archer). Inscriptions [Ϟ]ΟϞΙΑϞ, ΧΙΡΟΝΟϞ. The lost part of the fragment is known to me from a rough tracing only. See *CV*. Oxford 119.

4. FLORENCE PD 411, fr. (Frontal face and right breast of a man—satyr?).

5. ATHENS, Agora, P 22208, fr., from Athens. (Head and shoulder of a youth). Looks like an imitation of Euthymides.

6. GELA, fr., from Gela (Villa Garibaldi). Symposion (middle of a male reclining to left).

7. TARANTO, three frr., from Taranto (via R. Helena). White ground. On one fr., on the left of the picture, leg and tail of a satyr running to right; on the second fr., middle of a maenad moving to left; on the third fr., shank, with foot, of a male—a satyr?—to left. The maenad a little recalls Leyden PC 85 (p. 32 no. 1). A fragment in Oxford, from Taranto, is from the upper border of a calyx-krater: ivy-pattern on a white ground: I do not know whether this may be from the same vase or not.

AMPHORA
(*type B*)

7 *bis*. BRUSSELS A 3581. A, wrestlers; B, two athletes. Recalls the Kleophrades Painter in his earliest period. Poorly preserved.

HYDRIAI
(*nos. 8–12, of bf. shape; with framed pictures*)

These go with three by Phintias (pp. 23–24 nos. 7–9), one by Hypsis (p. 30 no. 1), one in the Pezzino Group (p. 32 no. 3), and a very early work by the Kleophrades Painter (p. 188 no. 67). All these hydriai, assigned and not, are the red-figure counterparts of the many black-figure hydriai of the Leagros Group (*ABV*. 360–6, 384–6, 695–6, and 715).

8. LOUVRE G 41, from Vulci. Pottier pl. 92; Hoppin *Euth. F*. pll. 29–30 and p. 122; *CV*. pl. 51. Dionysos with Ariadne, Poseidon with Amphitrite,

Hermes. On the shoulder, chariot, and warriors making ready. Now partly cleaned. Bothmer's new readings of the inscriptions (after the cleaning): On the body, HEPME⳨+A[IPE], ΔIONV (false start), ΔIO-N[V]⳨O⳨, ΓO⳨EIΔ[ON]. On the shoulder, +ARE⳨ retr., OA⳨ (the first sign a small round filled in with black), ⳨O⳨TPATO[⳨] +AIPE +AIPETO EVOVMIΔE⳨ (the first four letters upside down). Compare the next, and New York 21.88.2 (no. 14).

9. PHILADELPHIA MARKET, and FLORENCE 1 B 15. The two Florence frr., CV. pl. 1, B 15. Herakles with Athena and Dionysos. On the shoulder, symposion. On the chief picture, [H]EPAᛕLEN, AΘENIA⳨ retr., EVOV-MON, ΔIONVN complete; on the shoulder, EVOV, +AIPE, +PE (?), TAVTA, all retr. Not clear from the photographs or the description given me (I have not seen the original, except the small fragments in Florence) whether there were letters after the EVOV. The sigmas have the form of nu's, as in several other vases of the Pioneer Group. Compare Louvre G 41 (no. 8). See also p. 35 and p. 1621.

10. TARANTO, fr., from Locri. Warrior leaving home (1, woman to right, with phiale, 2, young boy to right, 3, feet of warrior to left, and his dog). Recalls Hypsis.

11. ROMAN MARKET (Campanari). B.Ap. xxxii. 3. Peleus and Thetis. On the shoulder, komos. Much restored.

12. TARANTO, frr., from Taranto. (Woman, and a youth, at the fountain); on the shoulder, youths at the fountain.

(*nos. 13–17, kalpides, with picture on the shoulder, framed*)

These go with the hydria by Euphronios, p. 16 no. 13, and the fragment compared with it, ibid.; with hydriai by Phintias, p. 24 no. 10, by Hypsis, p. 30 no. 2, by Euthymides, p. 25 nos. 12–16, and near him, p. 29 no. 1, by the Dikaios Painter, p. 31 no. 7, and near him, p. 32 nos. 1–2. The Kleophrades Painter carries on this type of hydria, p. 188 nos. 68–73.

13. ARLESHEIM, Schweizer. *Auction xiv Basle* pl. 18; Schefold *M.* 168, 158. Herakles and the lion. Recalls Euthymides and the Dikaios Painter.

14. NEW YORK 21.88.2. *AJA.* 1922, 64–65; *AJA.* 1923, 266–7; *Bull. Metr.* 18, 255 fig. 3; *N.Y. Shapes* 12, 3–4 = Richter and Milne figs. 81–82, whence (side) LS. fig. 1; Richter and Hall pl. 11, and pl. 172, 11. Pyrrhic. Recalls the Dikaios Painter; compare also Louvre G 41 (no. 8).

15. LOUVRE G 49. Pottier pl. 94; *CV.* pl. 52, 2–3. Komos (man and youth, both dancing, woman playing the flute). A Louvre fragment joins, adding the lower right-hand corner of the picture. Recalls the Pezzino Group. Close to the next.

16. LENINGRAD (St. 1612). Vorberg *Gloss.* 333. Women and a man at the fountain: one woman and the man have hydriai; the other woman, naked, sits on the ground washing herself. Close to the last.

17. VIENNA, Liechtenstein. Three maenads. Recalls Euthymides.

FRAGMENT

(of a large pot)

18. LOUVRE C 11090, fr. (On the right of the picture, arm, waist, buttocks of a woman to left; then the side-border of rf. palmettes, and the spring of the handle). Recalls Euthymides and the Dikaios Painter.

PLATE

19. ATHENS Acr. 9, fr. from Athens. Langlotz pl. 1. A god and a goddess seated side by side. Recalls the cup and kantharos by the Sosias Painter (p. 21, nos. 1 and 2), a cup by Euthymides (p. 29 no. 19).

A small fragment of a pot is very like the hydria in the Philadelphia market and in Florence 1 B 15 (above, no. 9):

FREIBURG S 218, fr. (Chiton-tail). ...E$ retr. (ends?). Freiburg S 211, as Bothmer has seen, probably belongs. Two other fragments in Freiburg may belong: on one of them, legs of a woman in chiton (with mid-band) and himation.

———

One or two amphorae may be said to be of the same type as those of the Pioneer Group, but the style of drawing is not 'Pioneer':

AMPHORAE

(type A)

1. VIENNA, Univ., 631a. By Oltos (see p. 54 no. 3).
2. LONDON E 253, from Vulci. A, Charlotte Fränkel pl. 2; Hoppin *Euth. F.* pl. 37, pl. 11, below, and p. 145, whence (B) Swindler fig. 306; *CV.* pl. 2, 1; A, *E.A.A.* ii, 170. A, Dionysos with satyr and maenad. B, warrior with horse, and archer. Many details recall the Euergides Painter (p. 87). See p. 162$.
3. OXFORD G 138.23, fr., from Naucratis. *JHS.* 25 pl. 7, 2; *CV.* pl. 50, 1. Courting (hand with panther-cub, man with cock). For the subject, Rumpf in *Gnomon* 1930, 66, reported in *CV.* ii p. viii.

———

THE GALES PAINTER

VA. 26. Caskey in CB i, 10–11. Haspels *ABL.* 69–70. *ARV.*[1] 30–31.

The two vases with the signature of the potter Gales were painted by one hand.

LEKYTHOI

1 (1). BOSTON 13.195, from Gela. Hoppin i, 463, whence *Arch. class.* 2 pl. 49, 5, (part) Rumpf *MZ.* pl. 21, 12; CB. i pl. 4, whence Buschor *Grab* 24,

Chase *Guide* 62, (detail) Richter *ARVS.* fig. 41; back, Jacobsthal O. pl. 54, a; the shape, Hambidge 131 and Caskey G. 213. Procession: cows led to sacrifice. On the topside of the mouth, ΛΑLΕϟΕΓΟΙΕϟΕΝ.

2 (2). SYRACUSE 26967, from Gela. *ML.* 19 (Orsi) pl. 3 and p. 96 figs. 9–10, whence Hoppin i, 465, Schefold *Bildnisse* 51, 3, *BCH.* 1942–3, 248. Komos (Anacreon and friends). On the topside of the mouth, ΛΑLΕϟ-ΕΓΟΙΕϟΕΝ retr. See CB. ii, 61; and below, p. 1621.

By the Gales Painter or near him:

CUP

(*a*) YALE 163, from Vulci. Baur pl. 15 and p. 108, whence Licht ii, 47; the shape, Hambidge 122. I, symposion (youth reclining, embracing a flute-girl).

THE PYTHOKLES PAINTER

ARV.[1] 31.

It is with hesitation that I tack him on to the pioneers, and I only do so for want of a more suitable place.

PANATHENAIC AMPHORAE
(*small*)

1 (1). ATHENS 1689 (CC. 1169), from Aegina. Benndorf pl. 31, 2; CC. pl. 42; Raubitschek *Dedications* 361, left, 362, left, and 363. A, Athena; B, boxers. On A, ΓVΟΟΚLΕΕϟ ΟΝ (= ὤν?) ΚΑLϟ. For the drapery compare Acropolis 703 (p. 118 no. 2).

2 (2). ATHENS 1688 (CC. 1170), from Aegina. Cockerell pl. 12, 3; Raubitschek *Dedications* 361, right, and 362, right. A, Athena. B is lost.

A cup, weaker work, recalls these:

CUP

VATICAN, from Cervetri. *Mus. Greg.* 2 pl. 85, 2, whence (B) Overbeck *KM.* pl. 24, 11; A, *Gymnasium* 67 pl. 17, 2; I and B, phs. And. 42117, 1, and 42104. I, symposion (man and woman reclining). A, Aeneas and Anchises. B, Herakles and Apollo: the struggle for the tripod. Restored.

By the same painter as the Vatican cup, the

SKYPHOS
(*type B, but with disparate handles*)

BERLIN 2318, from Vulci. *CV.* pl. 140. A, Eos with the body of Memnon. B, Herakles and Apollo: the struggle for the tripod.

BOOK II

(CHAPTERS 3–13)

EARLY RED-FIGURE CUP-PAINTERS

CHAPTER 3

EYE-CUPS

In *ARV.*[1] 91–94 and 951 a list of 'unassigned eye-cups' was given, while the others—the assigned—appeared only under their several painters. The list in this chapter contains all the eye-cups, the unassigned being described in full, the others by means of cross-references: it thus provides a conspectus of a type of cup that is very important in early red-figure.

Before giving the list of *standard* eye-cups, which form the vast majority, we describe the few

A. ABNORMAL EYE-CUPS

(i)

1. PALERMO V 650. [ΛΝ]ΔΟΚ[Ι]ΔΕ?Ε[Γ]Ο ... retr. The bf. half of the exterior is by the Lysippides Painter, the red-figure half by the Andokides Painter (see p. 5 no. 14, and *ABV.* p. 256 no. 21). Apart from this bi-section, the scheme of decoration is the same as in a good many bf. eye-cups.

(ii)

Two cups by the Painter of the Vatican Horseman (p. 159 nos. 1 and 2):

2. VATICAN, frr.

3. VILLA GIULIA (part ex Florence), CAB. MÉD., and NAPLES, Astarita, 247, frr.

The eyes are small and high up. Flowers instead of palmettes. No ground-line outside. (The inside decoration is missing). See p. 1621.

(iii)

4. FLORENCE A B 1, frr. Ama Group (p. 160).

Nearly normal, but the palmettes, eyes, and figures placed high up in the field, and the palmettes small, with black hearts that have no upper bounding-line.

(iv)

The Group of Leipsic T 3599.

These are connected by the eyes and palmettes. The eyes are small and placed high; the palmettes are smaller than usual, with few petals and reserved hearts. Both palmettes and eyes are drawn in a particular way. The Philadelphia cup (no. 10) is standard, except for the smallness of the palmettes; the eyes are of almost normal size and are not placed high: but the drawing of eyes and palmettes is the same as in the other members of the group. More elaborate, the Swiss private cup and Munich 2587 (nos. 8 and 9), which have a special scheme of decoration: beyond each eye, instead of a palmette, a figure, which in three of the four cases is connected in subject with what is between the eyes.

The Swiss cup and Munich 2587 are by Psiax, and the others are more or less closely connected with him, not so clearly in the figure-work as in the eyes and palmettes.

(In the two eye-cups that bear the name of Psiax inscribed, p. 9 nos. 1 and 2, the palmettes and eyes are not of this type).

5. LEIPSIC T 3599 (part), T 3619, and T 3712, from Cervetri. I, bf., floral. A–B, between eyes. A, athlete (running to right, looking back); B, trainer (in himation, leaning to right), wand in right hand. Might be very early Psiax. A small fragment in Villa Giulia, ill preserved, may belong and give part of the trainer's face and red wand.

6. LEIPSIC T 3620, fr. A, (parts of the right-hand eye and palmette remain).

7 (ξ). FLORENCE 3 B 12 (part ex Villa Giulia). Part of I, *CV.* pl. 3, B 12; I, *Boll. d'Arte* 29, 266 fig. 14. I bf., satyr balancing a kantharos on his foot. A–B, between eyes. A, nose; B, nose. Between the brows a reserved dot.

8. SWISS PRIVATE. By Psiax (p. 7 no. 7). See above, p. 7.

9. MUNICH 2587. By Psiax (p. 7 no. 8). See above, p. 7.

10. PHILADELPHIA 31. 19. 1. *Mus. J.* 23, 23–24 and 26. I, bf., warrior. A–B, between eyes. A, nose; B, nose. For the drawing of the noses cf. Castle Ashby 6 (p. 42, no. 48). The warrior somewhat recalls those of Psiax.

With Florence 3 B 12 (no. 7) compare the fragments

11 (ο). LEIPSIC T 536 and T 537, frr. A, between eyes, nose; between the brows a reserved dot.

12. VILLA GIULIA, fr. A, between eyes, (lost); between the brows a reserved dot.

Abnormal are also, in one point or another, (v) a 'Chalcicup' (p. 51), (vi) the few cups that have the foot of type B or another type instead of the usual type A: this does not affect the decoration, but will be noted, (vii) a class of *late* archaic eye-cups (p. 51), (viii) a few cups that have eyes on one half of the exterior and not on the other (pp. 48–49 nos. 166–8).

B. STANDARD EYE-CUPS

The standard eye-cups may be divided into three classes:

I. Bilinguals: the inside black-figure, the outside red-figure. This is the largest class, more than twice as numerous as II and III together.

II. Red-figure cups that preserve the traditional scheme of decoration, the only difference from Class I being that the inside is red-figure not black-figure.

III. Red-figure cups which alter the traditional scheme by inverting eyes and palmettes, so that in each half the figure is now between two palmettes, the eyes being shifted towards the handles: 'palmette-eye cups'.

(Between I and II we shall describe those fragments or fragmentary cups in which nothing remains of the inside picture, so that one cannot say for certain whether it was black-figure or red-figure).

The foot. The foot is nearly always of Type A. We distinguish Type AZ from Type AY. They differ in the underside. In AZ it is broad and nearly flat, meets the inside of the stem at an angle, and is reserved. In AY the resting-surface is a mere strip, and is set off from the other part of the underside, which curves gradually up towards the bottom of the bowl; the thin resting-surface is reserved, the other part black. Foot AZ: Bloesch pl. 8, 1–3. Foot AY: Bloesch pl. 8, 4 and pll. 9–10.

In Class I the foot is most often of the older type AZ, but in the later examples it is sometimes of type AY. In Classes II and III it is of type AY. In Class I there are two cases of the 'special Nicosthenic' variant of type AZ (see Bloesch *F.A.S.* pl. 6, 1 and pl. 7, 1–2). A few cups in Classes II and III have the more modern type of foot, B.

The eyes. In Class I the tear-gland is (1) nearly always well marked off from the rest of the eye, and has a *teat-like* shape. With time (2) the tear-gland comes to curve gradually into the rest of the eye with an *elegant* line; and in the last stage (3) the tear-gland loses its independence and we have the *straight-fronted eye*, which is especially favoured by the Nikosthenes Painter and his companions (Bowdoin-Eye Painter, Scheurleer Painter, Winchester Painter, &c.). The straight-fronted eye is very rare in Class I, less so in Class II, common in Class III.

As to the *colouring* of the eye: in Class I it nearly always includes a white ring; but some of the late cups have a reserved ring instead. In Class II the white ring is very rare, and it is not found in Class III.

The palmettes are either *shut* or *open*. In Class I they are hardly ever open; in Class II they are usually shut; and in Class III they are always open.

The *heart* of the palmette is usually red in Class I (the red being laid direct on the clay ground); but in the later members the 'late heart' sometimes appears—black except for a reserved dot in the middle, and bounded above by two or three relief lines. This 'late heart' is invariable in Class III; and in Class II there are only two exceptions, in an unusual cup by Oltos (p. 48 no. 166) and when the Euergides Painter, for once decorating an eye-cup, uses his regular palmette with reserved heart (p. 47 no. 155). There are a few palmettes with reserved heart in Class I.

In the early members of Class I the *inside picture* is often quite small. Another early trait is naturally the more sparing use of relief-lines, as when the tear-gland lacks relief contour.

The *nose* often placed between the eyes in Classes I and II does not appear in Class III.

I am not quite sure how I ought to describe a small object frequently seen between the eyes in Class I and once in Class II. It is shaped like a pear-drop and will be called so: it may sometimes be meant for a bud or leaflet, but at other times it may be meant for a nose, and a similar object occasionally serves as a kind of tilka between the brows, as in gorgoneia from of old.

CLASS I OF STANDARD EYE-CUPS: BILINGUAL

(nos. 13–43 have red palmette-hearts)

13 (α). MUNICH 2580 (J. 503), from Vulci. A, Bloesch *FAS*. pl. 3, 4, whence Buschor G. *Vasen* 129. I, bf., hound. A–B, between eyes. A, pear-drop; B, the like. Foot AZ. For the shape, Bloesch 10, Nikosthenes no. 13.

14 (β). BALTIMORE, Walters Art Gallery, 48. 44. *Journ. Walt.* 1, 24–25. I, bf., goat. A–B, between eyes. A, nose. B, nothing. Foot AZ.

15 (γ). LENINGRAD 391 (St. 217). I, bf., Minotaur. A–B, between eyes. A, pear-drop; B, the like. Foot AZ.

16. LOUVRE C 11262, fr. I, bf., (tail—of Minotaur?). A, between eyes, (lost).

17. LOUVRE C 11263, fr. I, bf., (uncertain remains—hair?). A–B, between eyes. A, horse or fawn. B, (lost).

18. NAPLES, Astarita, 491. I, bf., satyr. A–B, between eyes. A, nose; B, the like. Unusual the borders outside: below A, leaves as in London E 17 (p. 62 no. 80); below B, triple net. Foot AZ.

19 (δ). FLORENCE 3931. I, bf., komast (man dancing). A–B, between eyes. A, bud (diamond); B, the like. Compare the Villa Giulia frr. no. 117.

20. NAPLES, Astarita, 145, fr. I, bf., komast (man to right, holding an amis, οὐρῶν). A, between eyes, (lost). Foot AZ.

21 (ε). BOULOGNE 493. I, bf., satyr. A–B, between eyes. A, nose; B, nose. Foot AZ.

22 (ζ). VILLA GIULIA 761, from Falerii. *CV.* H e pl. 45, 3 and pl. 46, 6–7. I, bf., siren. A–B, between eyes. A, nose; B, nose. Foot AZ.

23 (ρ bis). VILLA GIULIA (part ex Florence). Part, *CV.* Fl. pl. 3, B 5. I, bf., woman running. A–B, between eyes. A, swan; B, swan. Foot AZ.

24 (π). COMPIÈGNE 1105. Group of Louvre F 125 (p. 161 no. 2). Special Nicosthenic foot (see p. 39).

25. ARLESHEIM, Schweizer. ΝΙΚΟΣΟΕΝΕΣΕΓΟΙΕϹ. Group of Louvre F 125 (p. 161 no. 3). Foot AZ.

26. LOUVRE F 125. ΚΟΣΟΕΝΕΣΕΓΟΙ. Group of Louvre F 125 (p. 161 no. 1). Foot AZ. For the shape, Bloesch 9, Nikosthenes no. 11.

27. ADOLPHSECK, Landgraf Philipp von Hessen, 30. Group of Louvre F 125 (p. 161 no. 6). Foot AZ. For the shape, Bloesch 9, Nikosthenes no. 7.

28. BONN 390. ΓΑΝΦΑΙΟΣΕΓΟΙΕΣΕΝ. See p. 128 no. 17. Foot AZ. For the shape, Bloesch 62, Pamphaios no. 3.

29. LOUVRE F 127 *ter*. By Oltos (p. 54 no. 9).

30. VILLA GIULIA 5959. By Oltos (p. 55 no. 10). Special Nicosthenic foot (p. 39).

31. MUNICH 2581 (J. 1170). By Oltos (p. 55 n. 11). Foot AZ. For the shape, Bloesch 9, Nikosthenes no. 9.

32. FLORENCE 3 B 3 (part ex Villa Giulia), frr. By Oltos (p. 55 no. 12).

33. VILLA GIULIA 18587. Near Oltos (p. 67 no. 1). Foot AZ.

34. Once MUNICH, Preyss. Near Oltos (p. 67 no. 2). Foot AY.

35. FLORENCE 2 B 30 (part ex Villa Giulia). Near Oltos (p. 67 no. 3). Foot AZ. For the shape, Bloesch 62, Pamphaios no. 4.

36. LOUVRE C 10461, frr. Part, *CV.* b pl. 18, 4 and 9. I, bf., komast. A, between eyes, man or youth. Unpublished Louvre frr. join, and one of them gives back and cloak of the person on A. Recalls early Oltos (p. 68).

37 (ρ). VILLA GIULIA 20800, from Cervetri. I, *St. etr.* 1 pl. 34, b; I and A, *ML.* 42, 279–80. I, bf., two doves. A–B. between eyes. A, nose; B, nose. Foot AZ. For the shape, Bloesch 9, Nikosthenes no. 8.

38. NEW YORK 14.146.2. ΦΣΙΑ+Σ. Near Psiax (p. 9 no. 1). For the shape, Bloesch 42 no. 2. The alien foot has now been removed.

39. MUNICH 2603. ΦΣΙΑ+Σ. Near Psiax (p. 9 no. 2): as New York 14.146.2 (no. 38). Foot of type B, but with the foot-plate profile of type A: see Bloesch 42 no. 1.

40. CAMBRIDGE 37.14. Incised under one handle, ΗΙΣ+ΥＬΟΣ : ΕΓΟΙ-ΕΣΕΝ. See p. 161 no. 1. Foot AZ. For the shape, Bloesch 31, Hischylos no. 2.

41 (φ). CIVITAVECCHIA. I, bf., maenad (running to right, a sprig in each hand). A–B, between eyes. A, nose; B, nose. Foot AZ. The red palmette-heart is bounded above by three relief-lines, as in Munich 2603 and Cambridge 37.14 (nos. 39–40).

42 (λ). BOULOGNE 562 and FLORENCE 6 B 25. By the Painter of the Boulogne Horse (p. 160 no. 1). Foot AZ. For the shape, Bloesch 10, Nikosthenes no. 14. For the special variety of red palmette-heart in this and the next see p. 160.

43 (μ). FLORENCE 1 B 19 (part ex Villa Giulia). By the Painter of the Boulogne Horse (p. 160 no. 2). See the last.

(in nos. 44–48 the palmette-heart is reserved, and bounded above by a pair of relief-lines; for the palmette-heart in no. 48 see there.)

44 (η). COPENHAGEN, Thorvaldsen Museum, 93. I, *Journ. Walt.* 1, 28 fig. 4. I, bf., fawn. A–B, between eyes. A, nose; B, nose. Foot AZ. Cf. the next.

45. BASLE MARKET (M.M.). I, bf., warrior (moving to right with spear). A–B, between eyes. A, nose; B, (lost). Cf. Thorvaldsen 93 (no. 44).

46 (θ). ERLANGEN (ex Munich J. 1236), from Vulci. I, bf., goat. A–B, between eyes. A, leaf (heart-shaped, point up); B, the like. Between the brows, a pear-drop, tilka-wise. Foot AZ. Never attributed by me to the Carpenter Painter as would appear from Grünhagen *Ant. Or.* 49, M 1214.

47. CASTLE ASHBY 193. By the Delos Painter (p. 172 no. 1). Foot AZ.

48 (κ). CASTLE ASHBY 6. I, *BSR.* 11 pl. 3, 5. I, bf., cock on flowers. A–B, between eyes. A, nose; B, nose. For the drawing of the noses cf. Philadelphia 31. 19. 1 (p. 38 no. 10). Foot AZ, but with special features (see *BSR.* 11, 14). For the palmette-heart see p. 160, and compare especially the eye-cup fragment Brunswick 539 (*CV.* pl. 12, 1) and one in Freiburg (p. 47 no. 142).

(no. 49, palmette-heart as in nos. 44–48, but with a red dot in the middle)

49. LOUVRE C 10462, fr. *CV.* b pl. 18, 5–6. I, bf., (a hand remains). A, between eyes, nothing.

(in nos. 50–71 the palmette-hearts are lost or unknown)

50 (ι). CAPUA 191 (111), from Capua. A, *CV.* pl. 5, 4–5. I, bf., (lost). A–B, between eyes. A, leaf (heart-shaped, point down); B, the like. Foot AZ. Restored. The palmette-hearts are repainted.

51. LOUVRE C 10463, fr. *CV.* b pl. 18, 7. I, bf. (what remains is a little of the border and of the figure, with the inscription . . . ΚΟ . . .—part of the signature of Nikosthenes?). See p. 123.

52. FLORENCE (part ex Villa Giulia), fr. By Oltos (p. 56 no. 28).

53. OXFORD G 141. 3, fr. By Oltos (p. 56 no. 29).

54. Once Noël Des Vergers 102. By Oltos? (See p. 68).

55. HEIDELBERG 2 and BOSTON. By Oltos (p. 56 no. 23). Foot AY.

56. HEIDELBERG 1, fr. Near Oltos (p. 67 no. 4).

57. VATICAN, fr. I, bf., warrior (moving to right, with sword and shield).

58. ROME, private. Signature of Hischylos (see p. 162, and p. 1630, top).

59. BERLIN 2100, fr. By Epiktetos (p. 71 no. 7). Foot AY. For the shape, Bloesch 31, Hischylos no. 3.

60. LOUVRE C 10458, part, frr. By Epiktetos (p. 71 no. 11).

61. LOUVRE C 11264, fr. I, bf., male with spears (the back of the head remains, and the spearheads).

62. FLORENCE (part ex Villa Giulia), fr. By the Scheurleer Painter (p. 169 no. 5).

63 (ψ). DRESDEN, fr. I, bf., woman running (to right, looking round, one hand raised: one arm and knee remain, with long locks of hair). A, (part of one palmette-tendril remains). One would have thought that this might belong to the Dresden fragments ZV.1654 (no. 115), but I have no note to that effect.

64 (ω). FLORENCE, fr., from Populonia. I, bf., fawn.

65 (αα). VILLA GIULIA, fr. I, bf., Herakles (part of the lionskin on his head remains, and the top of his bow: evidently moving to right and looking round).

66 (εε). OXFORD 1954.235, fr., from Al Mina. *JHS.* 59, 1, 2. I, bf., centaur.

67. FLORENCE, fr. I, bf., (bare shank and toes of male moving to right). Below, ΚΑ . . .

68 (ββ). FLORENCE, fr. I, bf., acontist (running to right, looking round).

69 (γγ). LONDON 1900.2–14.3, fr., from Naucratis. *JHS.* 49 pl. 17, 9. I, bf., warrior. . . ΕΓ . . .

69 *bis.* BRYN MAWR P. 903, fr. I, bf., warrior. Η[ΟΓΑΙΣΚΑΛ]ΟΣ.

70 (δδ). MUNICH S.L., fr. Sieveking *BTV.* pl. 45, 2. I, bf., komast.

71. Once ROME, Torlonia, from Vulci. Described by Helbig in *Bull.* 1881, 246. I, bf., runner. A–B, between eyes. A, victor. B, youth.

(nos. 72–116, 'late-hearts', see p. 40)

72. LOUVRE F 126. By Oltos (p. 55 no. 13). Foot AZ. For the shape, Bloesch 31, Hischylos no. 5.

73. LOUVRE F 127. By Oltos (p. 55 no. 14). Foot AY. For the shape, Bloesch 33, Hischylos no. 11.

74. VATICAN 498. By Oltos (p. 55 no. 15). Foot AY. For the shape, Bloesch 33, Hischylos no. 12.

75. LEIPSIC T 3371. By Oltos (p. 55 no. 26). Foot AY. For the shape, Bloesch 33, Hischylos no. 15a.

76. ALTENBURG 224. By Oltos (p. 55 no. 17). Foot AY. For the shape, Bloesch 64, Pamphaios no. 8.

77. CASTLE ASHBY 63. By Oltos (p. 55 no. 18). Foot AY.

78. NAPLES, Astarita, 46. By Oltos (p. 55 no. 19). Foot B.

79. LUCERNE MARKET (A.A.). By Oltos (p. 55 no. 20). Foot A.

80. RIEHEN, Gsell. By Oltos (p. 55 no. 21).

81. NAPLES, Astarita, 492. By Oltos (p. 55 no. 22). Foot AY.

82. BASLE, Cahn, 50, fr. By Oltos (p. 56 no. 24).

83. LONDON 1896.6–21.3. By Oltos (p. 56 no. 25). Foot AY.

84. MUNICH 2604. By Oltos (p. 56 no. 26). Foot B (if it belongs).

85. OXFORD 515. By Oltos (p. 56 no. 27). Foot AY. For the shape Bloesch 36, Antimachos Class, no. 1.

86. VILLA GIULIA 8343. Near Oltos (p. 67 no. 5). Foot AY.

87. VILLA GIULIA (part ex Florence). Near Oltos (p. 67 no. 6).

88. LOUVRE C 10460. Near Oltos (p. 67 no. 7). Foot AY.

89. CAB. MÉD. 335. [+]ELISEΠ[OI]ESИ. A–B are by the Thalia Painter (p. 112 no. 1), I is perhaps by Oltos (see p. 67 no. 8). Foot AY. For the shape, Bloesch 35, Chelis no. 1.

90 (v). LONDON E 4, from Vulci. I, Murray no. 1; palmette, *Jb.* 7, 106 fig. 2; I, *Jb.* 44, 153, 4. I, bf., doe. A–B, between eyes. A, petal. B, (lost). Foot AY. For the shape, Bloesch 33, Hischylos no. 7; for the petal, cf. the cup by Pheidippos in Villa Giulia (p. 165 no. 8). The cup was formerly restored with a pair of alien handles bearing the signature of the potter Thypheithides, which belonged to a bf. little-master cup and have now been removed (*JHS.* 52, 193–4; *ABV.* 178).

91. MUNICH 2582. By Pheidippos (p. 165 no. 1). Foot AZ. For the shape, Bloesch 31, Hischylos no. 4.

92. WÜRZBURG 467. By Pheidippos (p. 165 no. 2). Foot AY. For the shape, Bloesch 33, Hischylos no. 13.

93. MUNICH 2583. By Pheidippos (p. 165 no. 3). Foot AY. For the shape, Bloesch 33, Hischylos no. 14.

94. MUNICH 2584. By Pheidippos (p. 165 no. 4). Foot AY. For the shape, Bloesch 33, Hischylos no. 15.

95. LEIPSIC T 486. By Pheidippos (p. 165 no. 5). Foot AY. For the shape, Bloesch 33, Hischylos no. 9.

96. NEW YORK 41.162.8. By Pheidippos (p. 165 no. 6). Foot AY.

97. VILLA GIULIA (part ex Florence) and HEIDELBERG 8. By Pheidippos (p. 165 no. 7).

98. VILLA GIULIA (part ex Florence), frr. By Pheidippos (p. 165 no. 8). The fragment Heidelberg 15 (no. 140) may be from the same cup.

99. NAPLES, Astarita, 583. I, bf., Minotaur. A–B, between eyes. A, donkey-man; B, donkey. Foot AY. Recalls Pheidippos and early Epiktetos. The figures outside are free replicas of those on the cup by Epiktetos in Leningrad (no. 103).

100. ORVIETO, Faina, 97. By Epiktetos (p. 70 no. 1). Foot AY. For the shape, Bloesch 32, Hischylos no. 6.

101. VILLA GIULIA (part ex Florence) and HEIDELBERG 18. By Epiktetos (p. 70 no. 2). Foot AY.

102. LONDON E 3. By Epiktetos (pp. 70–71 no. 3). Foot AY. For the shape, Bloesch 33, Hischylos no. 8.

103. LENINGRAD 645. By Epiktetos (p. 71 no. 4). Foot AY.

104. ROME, Torlonia. Signed Hischylos. Probably by Epiktetos (p. 78).

105. WÜRZBURG 468. By Epiktetos (p. 71 no. 8). For the shape, Bloesch 9, Nikosthenes, B no. 6. Foot AZ.

106. FLORENCE 2 B 4. By Epiktetos (p. 71 no. 12). Foot AY.

107. LEIPSIC T 3626. By the Bowdoin-Eye Painter (p. 166 no. 1). Foot AY. The palmettes on B are open.

108. COPENHAGEN, Thorvaldsen Museum, 92. By the Bowdoin-Eye Painter (p. 166 no. 2). Foot AY.

109. ARLESHEIM, Schweizer. By the Bowdoin-Eye Painter (p. 166 no. 3). Foot AY.

110. ROME, Torlonia, 151. By the Bowdoin-Eye Painter (p. 166 no. 4).

111. NAPLES, Astarita, 569, frr. I, bf., komast (running to right, horn in right hand, left arm extended in cloak). A–B, between eyes. A, (elbow and foot of one running to left). Recalls the Bowdoin-Eye Painter.

112. AMSTERDAM inv. 997. By the Scheurleer Painter (p. 168 no. 1). Foot AY.

113. ROME, Torlonia, 146. By the Scheurleer Painter (p. 169 no. 3).

114. VATICAN 499. By the Scheurleer Painter (p. 169 no. 4).

115 (χ). DRESDEN ZV. 1654. I, bf., one in a long chiton running (foot, part of the skirt, elbow? remain, with ΚΑL . . .). A–B, between eyes. A, naked male (moving to left; one leg remains). B, (lost). See above, no. 63.

116 (τ). CAMBRIDGE 4.1952. A, Bothmer *Am.* pl. 72, 8. I, bf., komast. A–B, between eyes. A, Amazon. B, nose. Foot AY.

INTERLUDE

Nos. 117–50 *bis* (mostly fragments): not known whether bilingual or red-figure: no trace of the inside picture remaining.

(no. 117, red-heart)

117 (ζζ). VILLA GIULIA, frr. A–B, between eyes. A, nose. B, bud (diamond).

Compare Florence 3931 (p. 40 no. 19): it has the same diamond, and the eyes are also like. Compare also the Florence fragment no. 123.

117 *bis*. LOUVRE C 10464. By Oltos (p. 56 no. 30).

(nos. 118–19, reserved hearts)

118 (*oo*). BOULOGNE. By the Painter of Oxford 1949 (p. 10 no. 3).

119 (*θθ*). VILLA GIULIA, frr. A, between eyes, nose (without relief-contour).

(nos. 120–2, 'late-hearts')

120. LOUVRE G 8 and TÜBINGEN E 7. By Epiktetos (p. 71 no. 6).

121. LOUVRE C 10458, part. By Epiktetos (p. 71 no. 10).

122. OXFORD, Beazley, frr. By Pheidippos (p. 166 no. 10).

(nos. 123–50 bis, the palmette-hearts lost)

123. FLORENCE, fr. A, between eyes, nose (without relief-contour). Compare the Villa Giulia frr., no. 117.

124 (*ηη*). VILLA GIULIA, two frr. A, between eyes, bud (peardrop, point downward).

125. NEW YORK 22.139.81, fr. By the Hischylos Painter (p. 162 no. 1).

126 (*ι*). LIVERPOOL, Univ., fr. A, between eyes, nose.

127 (*λλ*). FREIBURG, fr. Group of Louvre F 125 (p. 161 no. 4).

128 (*μμ*). FREIBURG, fr. Group of Louvre F 125 (p. 161 no. 5). From the same as the last?

129. LOUVRE C 11265, fr. Recalls early Oltos (p. 68).

130. BONN 464, 24, fr. By Oltos (p. 56 no. 31).

130 *bis*. ADRIA B 503, fr. By Oltos (p. 56 no. 32).

131. VILLA GIULIA, frr. By Oltos (p. 56 no. 33).

132. NAPLES, Astarita, 632, fr. By Oltos (p. 56 no. 34).

133. OXFORD, Beazley, fr. By Oltos (p. 56 no. 35).

134. LOUVRE S 1393, fr. By Oltos (p. 56 no. 36).

135. LOUVRE S 1396, fr. By Oltos (p. 57 no. 37).

136 (*κκ*). MUNICH, fr. A, between eyes, nose. The nose is drawn as in eye-cups by Oltos or near him (see p. 68).

137. FLORENCE 3 B 10, fr. The figure is near Oltos (p. 67 no. 9), but the eye is not.

138. FLORENCE 1 B 1, frr. Potter-signature of Pamphaios (p. 128 no. 18).

139. VILLA GIULIA, fr. By Epiktetos (p. 71 no. 9).

140. HEIDELBERG 15, fr. By Pheidippos (p. 165 no. 9). Belongs to Villa Giulia (p. 44 no. 98)?

141 (*ρρ*). TÜBINGEN E 3, fr. Watzinger pl. 17. A, between eyes, youth with stick.

142 (νν). FREIBURG, fr. A, between eyes, (feet of one to left). From the attitude this may be a runner at the start. Eckstein has joined a fr. giving more of the right-hand oculus, and, to right of it, the lower half of the palmette, which is of the same type as in Brunswick 539 (*CV*. pl. 12, 1: see p. 42 no. 48).

143. VILLA GIULIA, frr. By the Nikosthenes Painter (p. 124 no. 1).

144 (σσ). OXFORD G 700, fr., from Naucratis. *CV*. pl. 57, 9. A, between eyes, male (dancing?).

145 (ττ, νν). AMSTERDAM inv. 2212 and FREIBURG S 132, fr. A, between eyes, komast. The Freiburg fr. joins the other below.

146 (ξξ). PALERMO, fr., from Selinus. A, between eyes, discus-thrower (hand with discus, and foot, to right).

147 (φφ). OXFORD 1954.232, fr., from Al Mina. *JHS*. 59, 1, 1, left. A, between eyes, (leg).

148. OXFORD 1954.233, fr., from Al Mina. *JHS*. 59, 1, 1, right. Does not certainly belong to the last.

149 (ππ). MUNICH, fr. A, between eyes, athlete (knees, moving to right, with aryballos).

150. ROME, Antiquarium Forense, fr., from Rome. Ryberg pl. 18, 97; *Bull. Arch. Com.* 76 pl. 14, 181. A, between eyes, naked male (probably a victor as Enrico Paribeni suggests).

150 bis. BASLE, Cahn, 54, three frr. A–B, between eyes. A, male, with (sword?) (the right arm remains, with part of one thigh). B, maenad (in chitoniskos, running to right, looking round, with thyrsus and snake). The incised inscriptions seem modern. Probably by the same hand as Louvre G 88 (no. 162).

CLASS II OF STANDARD EYE-CUPS: RED-FIGURED

151. PALERMO V 652. The inside by Oltos (p. 57 no. 38), the outside by another. Foot AY.

152. NAPLES, Astarita, 47. Potter-signature of Kachrylion. By Oltos (p. 57 no. 39). Foot B.

153. BOSTON 13.83 and Florence. By Oltos (p. 57 no. 40). Foot AY. The palmettes on B open.

154. LOUVRE G 19. By Oltos (p. 57 no. 41). Open palmettes.

155. LOUVRE G 16. The inside by Epiktetos (p. 71 no. 13), the outside by the Euergides Painter (p. 94 no. 94). Enough remains of the stem to show that the foot was of type B. Open palmettes.

156. LOUVRE C 10465, fr. Part, *CV*. b pl. 19, 1. I, (part of the line-border remains). A, between eyes, warrior. Other Louvre frr. have been joined, adding the left-hand palmette on A and one handle. See p. 1622.

157. MONTAUBAN 1. By the Nikosthenes Painter (p. 124 no. 2).

158 (χχ). MUNICH 2585 (J. 1316), from Vulci. A, Bloesch *FAS*. pl. 10, 3. I, satyr. A–B, between eyes. A, komast. B, satyr. Restored. Foot AY. For the shape, Bloesch 38 no. 2.

159 (ψψ). LEIPSIC T 502. A, *Jb*. 10, 194. I, warrior (kneeling, light-armed, kidaris, spear, pelta). A–B, between eyes. A, hoplitodromos kneeling. B, nose. Foot AY. For the shape, Bloesch 33, Hischylos no. 16. Not far from the Scheurleer Painter.

160. BOWDOIN. By the Bowdoin-Eye Painter (p. 167 no. 5). Foot AY. For the shape, Bloesch 36, Antimachos Group, no. 1. Open palmettes on B.

160 *bis*. BASLE 1960.28. By the Bowdoin-Eye Painter (p. 167 no. 6). Foot AY.

161. LONDON E 5. Near the Winchester Painter (p. 171 no. 1). Foot AY. For the shape, Bloesch 38 no. 5.

162 (ωω). LOUVRE G 88. Part of I, Pottier pl. 98 (misprinted G 89); incompletely, *CV*. b pl. 19, 4–8. I, satyr. A–B, between eyes. A, komast. B, nose. Louvre frr. join, adding part of the left-hand eye on A, with the handle. For the opprobrious posture of the satyr compare the Phineus cup in Würzburg (164: FR. pl. 41, whence Pfuhl fig. 164; Rumpf *Chalk.* pll. 40–44; Langlotz pll. 26–27). The Cahn fragments no. 150 *bis* are probably by the same hand; and the later cup Bonn 73 (*CV*. pl. 3) may perhaps be compared. For the eyes compare the last. Foot AY.

163 (ααα+). VILLA GIULIA, and NAPLES, Astarita, 296. I, male (bare legs remain, to right). A–B, between eyes. A, athlete (bending, to left); B, athlete (bending, to right). Peculiar style. The head of athlete A is given by a fragment that was formerly embedded in no. 179: the head is seen in ph. GF 7156. Bothmer has pointed out that the head and shoulders of athlete B are almost certainly given by the Astarita fragment 296: sandy hair, wrinkled forehead, spotty neck.

164 (βββ). TORONTO 351. By the Epeleios Painter (p. 146 no. 1). Foot B.

165 (γγγ). Once Magnoncourt 90. I, athlete (running with acontia). A–B, between eyes. Symposion: A, man reclining; B, naked youth carrying a pointed amphora.

_____

RED-FIGURED EYE-CUPS: ABNORMAL

166. ARLESHEIM, Schweizer. By Oltos (p. 57 no. 42). No eyes on A. The palmettes on B are closed, with red hearts; those on A open (the hearts modern).

167. NAPLES 2615. Potter-signature of Chelis. I and A by Oltos (p. 57 no. 43), B and the palmettes by the Chelis Painter (p. 112 no. 2). The palmettes are not those of eye-cups, and on A there are no eyes. Foot AY. For the shape, Bloesch 35, Chelis no. 2.

168. LONDON E 6. Potter-signature of Hischylos, painter-signature of Pheidippos. By Pheidippos (p. 166 no. 11). B is normal, except that the palmette-tendrils are unusual; but on A there are no eyes, and the palmettes are still farther from the norm. Foot AY. For the shape, Bloesch 33, Hischylos no. 17.

CLASS III. PALMETTE-EYE CUPS

(see p. 39, III)

169. PROVIDENCE 25.076. By Oltos (p. 57 no. 44).

170. LOUVRE C 11217 and ERLANGEN 459, frr. By Oltos (p. 58 no. 45).

171. LOUVRE C 11218, fr. By Oltos (p. 58 no. 46). No saying whether this was from an eye-cup or a palmette-eye cup, but put here because it seemed as if it should belong to Louvre C 11217.

172. FLORENCE I B 32 (part ex Villa Giulia), frr. By Oltos (p. 58 no. 47).

173. VILLA GIULIA (part ex Florence), and NAPLES, Astarita, 301. By Oltos (p. 58 no. 48). Ribbed petals as in Louvre G 5 by Epiktetos (no. 175).

174. ROMAN MARKET (Basseggio?). By Oltos (p. 58 no. 49).

175. LOUVRE G 5. Potter-signature of Pamphaios, painter-signature of Epiktetos. By Epiktetos (pp. 71–72 no. 14). Foot AY. For the shape, Bloesch 64, Pamphaios no. 10. Ribbed petals as in no. 173.

176. CAMBRIDGE 1.27. By the Nikosthenes Painter (p. 124 no. 3). Foot AY. For the shape, Bloesch 38, Antimachos Class, no. 7.

177. VILLA GIULIA (part ex Florence), frr. By or near the Nikosthenes Painter (p. 127).

178 (ηηη). AMSTERDAM inv. 888, from Vulci. A–B, *CV*. Scheurleer b pl. 1 (Pays Bas pl. 31), 4–6. I, youth astride a wineskin. A–B, between palmettes and eyes. A, warrior lying in wait; B, the like. Foot AY.

179. VILLA GIULIA 50448. By the Bowdoin-Eye Painter (p. 167 no. 7). Foot AY.

180. LOUVRE G 39. By the Bowdoin-Eye Painter (p. 167 no. 8).

181. LOUVRE C 10468. By the Bowdoin-Eye Painter (p. 167 no. 9).

182. WÜRZBURG 469. By the Bowdoin-Eye Painter (p. 167 no. 10). Foot B. For the shape, Bloesch 65, Pamphaios no. 25.

183. NAPLES, Astarita, 568. By the Bowdoin-Eye Painter (p. 167 no. 11).

184. SWISS PRIVATE, fr. By the Bowdoin-Eye Painter (p. 167 no. 12).

185. ATHENS Acr. 42, fr., from Athens. Near the Bowdoin-Eye Painter (p. 168 no. 1).

186. LOUVRE G 73. Near the Bowdoin-Eye Painter and the Scheurleer Painter (p. 170). Foot AY.

187. LOUVRE G 70. By the Scheurleer Painter (p. 169 no. 6). Foot AY. For the shape, Bloesch 36, Antimachos Class, no. 2.

188. MUNICH 2586. Near the Scheurleer Painter (p. 169 no. 1). Foot AY. For the shape, Bloesch 12 note 27, and 38 no. 4 ('related to the Antimachos Class').

189. VATICAN 500. Near the Scheurleer Painter (p. 170 no. 2). Foot AY. Many-petalled palmettes. For the shape, Bloesch 37, Antimachos Class no. 5.

190. NAPLES, Astarita, 584. I, acontist. A–B, between palmettes and eyes. A, satyr carrying wineskin; B, satyr leading the way. On I, [A]NT[I]-MA[+OS . . . . Near Vatican 500 (no. 189), especially the many-petalled palmettes.

191. HEIDELBERG 32 and DRESDEN. Related to the Scheurleer Painter (p. 170 no. 2).

192 (ζζζ). NEW YORK 56.171.61 (ex Hearst). B, Torr *Gk Music* 26; *Cat. Sotheby July 2 1929* pl. 4. I, youth seated, holding fruits. A–B, between palmettes and eyes. Symposion: A, naked woman reclining, drinking out of a phallus-footed vase; B, naked woman reclining, drinking out of a pointed amphora (or rather, peering into it, Bothmer). Foot AY.

193. WINCHESTER 42. By the Winchester Painter (p. 170 no. 1). Foot AY.

194. DRESDEN ZV. 1395. By the Winchester Painter (p. 170 no. 2). Foot AY.

195. FLORENCE 3930. By the Winchester Painter (p. 170 no. 3). Foot AY.

196. LOUVRE C 10469, frr. By the Winchester Painter (p. 171 no. 4).

197. BREMEN, Schröder. By the Schröder Painter (p. 171 no. 1).

198. LUCERNE MARKET (A.A.). *Ars Ant. Auktion I* pl. 53, 112. I, komast lifting wineskin. A–B, between palmettes and eyes. A, jumper; B, discus-thrower. Foot AY. See p. 153, top.

199. VILLA GIULIA (part ex Florence). By the Thalia Painter (p. 113 no. 2). Foot AY.

200 (δδδ, +). VILLA GIULIA (part ex Florence), and NAPLES, Astarita, 300, frr. A–B, between palmettes and eyes. A, athlete bending to right, with haltēres (the legs and hands remain); B, athlete to right (the legs remain). The Astarita fragment gives the legs on A, except the right heel and the front of the left thigh, which are given by two of the Villa Giulia fragments. Brown inner markings. The palmette-hearts are like those on the cup by the Thalia Painter (p. 112 no. 1) in the Cabinet des Médailles.

201. RENNES 1932.725 (1909.375). I, warrior running. A–B, between palmettes and eyes. A, komast (naked youth kneeling, holding out a cup); B, similar. Foot B. Manner of the Epeleios Painter. For the eyes compare his cup Toronto 351 (p. 146 no. 1). See p. 1628, foot.

A lost eye-cup is abnormal in shape, if the old drawing is to be trusted, and there is no reason why it should not be: a 'Chalcicup' (Bloesch *FAS*. 28–29, 'cups with Ionic foot'; *ABV*. 204–5); the inside is not decorated.

202. Lost. Potter-signature of Pamphaios (p. 128 no. 16).

THE LATE-ARCHAIC CLASS OF EYE-CUPS

The eye-cup was revived (or revivified) for a while in the late archaic period. The old type is modified. The big palmettes flanking the handles give place to a single small palmette, upright, with tendrils, under each handle (e.g. Pottier pl. 98, G 81), and the picture inside is bordered with maeander. The foot, when preserved, is of type B. An old-fashioned feature is the white ring in the eyes.

203. Once BRUSSELS, Somzée. Near the Bonn Painter (p. 352 no. 1).

204. LOUVRE G 81. By the Colmar Painter (p. 356 no. 56). Foot B.

205. ITALIAN MARKET. By the Colmar Painter (p. 356 no. 56 *bis*). Foot B.

206. FERRARA, T 30 D VP, fr. By the Colmar Painter (p. 356 no. 56 *ter*).

207. ATHENS Acr. 244, fr. By the Colmar Painter (p. 356 no. 57).

208. LOUVRE G 288, fr. Manner of Onesimos (p. 331 no. 16).

209. LOUVRE C 10896. By the Antiphon Painter (p. 337 no. 30). Foot B.

210. FERRARA, T. 41 D VP. By the Antiphon Painter (p. 337 no. 30 *bis*). Foot B.

211. LOUVRE G 316. By the Antiphon Painter (p. 339 no. 61).

212. LOUVRE G 289. By the Antiphon Painter (p. 340 no. 74).

213. LOUVRE C 11266, fr. A, between eyes, male reclining (to left: the shoulder remains, with part of the cushion and the back of the couch).

214. LOUVRE C 11267, fr. A, between eyes, komast (the top of a skyphos remains).

215. LOUVRE C 11268, fr. I, (a hand). Outside, the palmette under one handle remains, and part of the left-hand eye on one half. The palmette is almost the same as in no. 210.

216. LOUVRE C 11269, fr. I, (maeander). Outside, the palmette under one handle remains: it is just the same as in no. 210.

217. LOUVRE C 11270, fr. I, (maeander). Outside, part of one eye remains.

218. FLORENCE, fr. I, (maeander). Outside, part of one eye remains.

OTHER BILINGUAL CUPS

To complete the list of *bilingual* cups given above (pp. 40–45) we add four that are not eye-cups:

(i)

(inside, black-figure; outside, red-figure)

LOUVRE F 128. By Oltos (p. 58 no. 50).

(ii)

(inside red-figure; outside, black-figure on a coral-red ground)

LOUVRE F 129. By Skythes (p. 84 no. 20).

PALERMO V 651. By Skythes (p. 85 no. 21).

HEIDELBERG 52, fr. Manner of Onesimos, early (p. 330 no. 1).

To these we may append a cup which is neither Attic nor Etruscan and which is attributed by H. R. W. Smith to an unknown Italic fabric:

BERKELEY, from Barletta. I and A, *AJA*. 1945, 474, 2, and 472, 2. I, rf., symposion (youth reclining, playing kottabos). A–B, silhouette: between eyes, A, youth, B, woman. Foot B.

Lastly, there is a bilingual *stemless* of a peculiar kind:

STEMLESS CUP

BERLIN 1958.7. *Berl. Mus.* 9, 1–2. I, bf., komos (two youths and two men). This belongs to the Segment Class (*ABV*. 212–15 and 689–90) and, within that class, to the Group of London B 460 (ibid. 212), which recalls Painter N (see p. 122). In the upper segment, chequers; in the lower segment, (which is marked off from the chief area by a band of bf. ivy-pattern, rf., a pair of eyes. See p. 1622.

CHAPTER 4

OLTOS

OLTOS

VA. 7–12. Langlotz *Z.* 10. *Att. V.* 10–17 and 461. *BSR.* 11, 156. *Art. Bull.* 19, 537–60 (Johnson). *ARV.*[1] 34–44 and 949. Bruhn *Oltos. Fra Nat.* 1954, 27–36 (Breitenstein). *CB.* iii, text.

Oltos, whose name is known from nos. 64 and 66, is chiefly a cup-painter, but many of his best vases are pots.

The arrangement of the cups is roughly chronological: but the many eye-cups are kept together at the beginning of the cup-list; and the cups that are decorated inside only, at the end. Most of the eye-cups are early, but not all.

Oltos collaborated with many potters:

Nikosthenes (no. 8; see also nos. 10 and 11);
Kachrylion (nos. 51, 54–57, and 60; see also nos. 19 and 39);
Tleson (no. 127);
Pamphaios (nos. 1, 2, and 5; see also no. 17);
Chelis (no. 43; see also no. 78, and p. 67 no. 8);
Euxitheos (nos. 4, 64, and 66).

Bloesch adds Hischylos on stylistic grounds (see nos. 13–16).

Nos. 65 and 139 also bore the signature of a potter, but the name is missing.
In no. 43 part of the decoration is by Oltos, part by the Chelis Painter.
No. 38 also shows collaboration; see also p. 67 no. 8.

NECK-AMPHORAE

(of Nicosthenic type—variant)

1 (3). LOUVRE G 3. Pottier pl. 88, whence Perrot 10, 388–9, Hoppin ii, 303, (A) Swindler fig. 276; B, Pfuhl fig. 363; Jacobsthal O. pl. 44, b–c and pl. 45, b; *CV.* pl. 27, 1–7; A, Ghali-Kahil *H.* pl. 49, 2. A, Menelaos and Helen. B, Chiron with the infant Achilles. On the neck, A, Nereid, B, Nereid. On each handle, helmeted runner. On A, ΦΑΙΦΑΙΟϹ-ΕΠΟΙΕϹΕΝ.

2 (4). LOUVRE G 2. Pottier pl. 88, whence Hoppin ii, 301 and (A) Perrot 10, 390; A, Pfuhl fig. 362; Jacobsthal O. pl. 44, a and pl. 45, a; *CV.* pl. 26, 1 and 3–7; phs. Gir. 25820, 27630, and 27632, whence (A) Buschor 149, (A) Richter and Milne fig. 34, (A) Schnitzler pl. 32, 46; A, ph. Al. 23713, whence Licht ii, 101, Buschor *G. Vasen* 135, Lane pl. 64, Bruhn fig. 54, *Fra Nat.* 1954, 36 fig. 34; *R.I.* xxi. 16. A, satyr and maenad; B, the like. On the neck, A, naked woman doing up her sandal, B, the

like. On each handle, victor. On A, ΦΑΝΦΑΙ ΟϟΕΓΟΙΕΙ. The upper part of the right-hand victor is restored. See p. 1622.

AMPHORAE

(no. 3, type A)

3 (1). VIENNA, Univ., 631a, from Orvieto. A, Albizzati *Due nuovi acquisti* 10; *Jh.* 28, 41–46; *CV.* pll. 7–8. A, Herakles and Apollo: the struggle for the deer. B, (Ares and Aphrodite). The masterpiece of the painter's fully developed style.

(no. 4, type C)

4 (2). LONDON E 258, from Vulci. Gerhard pl. 187; *VA.* 9, whence Hoppin i, 449; *CV.* pl. 5, 1; detail of B, *E.A.A.* ii, 175. A, Achilles; B, Briseis. On one handle, ΕΥ+ϟΙΘΕΟϟ, on the other, ΕΓΟΙΕϟΕΝ retr. See p. 1622.

STAMNOS

5 (5). LONDON E 437, from Cervetri. Panofka *Panph.* pl. 5; Gerhard pl. 115; *WV.* D pl. 6; Hoppin ii, 293; A, Pfuhl fig. 361 (= Pfuhl *Mast.* fig. 36), whence Swindler fig. 279; side, Jacobsthal O. pl. 91; A, Langlotz *F.B.* pl. 14, 1; *CV.* pl. 19, 1, whence (A) Rumpf *MZ.* pl. 16, 5; A, Lane pl. 62; A, *Hist. rel.* 53, below; A, Stella 821; A, *E.A.A.* i, 15. A, Herakles and Acheloos. B, satyr and maenad. On A, ΦΑΝΦ[ΑΙΟϟ]ΕΓΟΙΕΙ.

FRAGMENT OF A POT

6 (7). BOSTON 10.219, fr. *VA.* 7 (mispoised); *CB.* iii pl. 69, 117. (Eros). Still early. See *CB.* iii, text.

PSYKTER

7 (6). NEW YORK 10.210.18 (one fr. ex Villa Giulia, see *CF.* 33 no. 3), from Campagnano. Details, *VA.* 8, Richter *Craft* 53, Alexander *Gk Athl.* 10, 15, 1, and 31, 2, Richter *Sc.* 127 fig. 471, Richter and Milne fig. 87, (whence LS. fig. 50); Richter and Hall pl. 4 and pl. 173, 3, whence (part) *Arch. class.* 2 pl. 8, 1; details, Richter *ARVS.* fig. 35, p. 38 fig. 3, p. 44 fig. 14; part, Richter *H.* 205, c; part, with a new fragment added by Bothmer, *AJA.* 1955 pl. 47 figs. 3–4; the fr. ex Villa Giulia, *ML.* 23, 286, whence Hoppin *Euth. F.* 134. Athletes. On the shape, *CB.* ii, 7, A. 12. I take the inscriptions ΓΟΜΕ and retr. +ΑϟΚΟ to be πῶ με ('drink me', cf. *Cl. Rev.* 57, 102–3) and χάσκω, 'I open my mouth wide'.

KYATHOS

8 (a11). FLORENCE 2 B 11, frr. Part, *CV.* pl. 2, B 11. Satyrs and maenad. [ΝΙΚΟϟΘ]ΕΝΕϟ [ΕΓΟ]ΙΕϟΕΝ. Early.

CUPS

(nos. 9–49, eye-cups)
(nos. 9–29, bilingual eye-cups; nos. 9–24 are early, nos. 25–27 are not)

9 (11). LOUVRE F 127 *ter.* A, Pottier pl. 73; *CV.* b pl. 1, 1–4. I is lost. A–B, between eyes. A, Minotaur. B, laver. Restored. See p. 41 no. 29.

10. VILLA GIULIA 5959, from Corchiano. *CV*. H e pl. 45, 2 and pl. 46, 4–5. I, bf., lion and bull. A–B, between eyes. A, horse; B, horse. Special Nicosthenic foot (see p. 39). As Louvre C 10464 (no. 30). See p. 41 no. 30.

11 (16). MUNICH 2581 (J. 1170), from Vulci. A, Lullies and Hirmer pl. 8, below. I, bf., Dionysos. A–B, between eyes. A, flute-case. B, nose. Restored. For the shape, Bloesch 9, Nikosthenes no. 9. See p. 41 no. 31, and p. 68.

12 (19). FLORENCE 3 B 3 (part ex Villa Giulia), frr. Part, *CV*. pl. 3, B 3. I, bf., citharode (Apollo?). A–B, between eyes. A, altar and palm-tree. See p. 41 no. 32.

13 (12). LOUVRE F 126, from Etruria. I and B, Pottier pll. 72–73; *CV*. b pl. 1, 5–8 and pl. 2, 1; B.Ap. xxi. 40. I, bf., archer. A–B, between eyes. A, discus-thrower; B, acontist. Restored. For the shape, Bloesch 31, Hischylos no. 5. See p. 43 no. 72.

14 (13). LOUVRE F 127, from Vulci. A, Pottier pl. 73; A, Weicker *Seelenvogel* 164 fig. 83; *CV*. b pl. 1, 9 and pl. 2, 2–5. I, bf., warrior. A–B, between eyes. A, siren; B, siren. Restored. For the shape, Bloesch 33, Hischylos no. 11. See p. 43 no. 73.

15 (17). VATICAN 498, from Vulci. *Mus. Greg.* 2 pl. 69, 3, whence (A–B) Klein *Euphr.* 297 and 299; Albizzati pl. 69; Bruhn figs. 13–15; I and B, *Fra Nat.* 1954, 33; A, ph. Al. 35782. I, bf., Dionysos. A–B, between eyes. A, trumpeter; B, warrior lifting his shield. For the shape, Bloesch 33, Hischylos no. 12. See p. 43 no. 74.

16 (23). LEIPSIC T 3371, from Cervetri. I and A, Bruhn figs. 9 and 11. I, bf., archer. A–B, between eyes. A, woman dancing; B, the like. For the shape, Bloesch 33, Hischylos no. 15a. See p. 43 no. 75.

17 (24). ALTENBURG 224. I and A, Bruhn figs. 12 and 10; *CV*. pl. 65 and pl. 67, 3. I, bf., Poseidon. A–B, between eyes. A, victor. B, nose. Restored. For the shape, Bloesch 64, Pamphaios no. 8. See p. 44 no. 76.

18 (25). CASTLE ASHBY, Northampton, 63, from Vulci. *BSR.* 11 pl. 5; A, B.Ap. xxi. 104. 1. I, bf., Hermes. A–B, between eyes. A, Nereid; B, Nereid. See p. 44 no. 77.

19. NAPLES, Astarita, 46. I, bf., trumpeter. A–B, between eyes. A, athlete picking up discus; B, the like. The foot is of type B. Potter-work by Kachrylion. See p. 44 no. 78, and p. 1623.

20. LUCERNE MARKET (A.A.). *Ars Ant. Auktion I* pl. 52. I, bf., komast. A–B, between eyes. A, komast; B, komast. See p. 44 no. 79.

21. RIEHEN, Gsell. I, bf., Minotaur. A–B, between eyes. A, woman with krotala (moving to right, looking round); B, the like. See p. 44 no. 80.

22. NAPLES, Astarita, 492. I, bf., centaur. A–B, between eyes. A, acontist; B, flower? (the lower end of the stalk remaining). [Bothmer]. See p. 44 no. 81.

23 (28). HEIDELBERG 2, and BOSTON. I, Kraiker pl. 1; A, Vorberg *Gloss.* 482. I, bf., Poseidon. A, between eyes, phallus. B is lost. See p. 43 no. 55.

24. BASLE, Cahn, 50, fr. I, bf., male (in long chiton and himation, moving to right; one leg remains). A, between eyes, warrior (running to left, looking round, in helmet, pelt, greaves; spear in right hand, left arm extended holding out the pelt). [Cahn]. See p. 44 no. 82.

25 (29). LONDON 1896.6–21.3. I and A, *JHS.* 41, 118–19. I, bf., slinger. A–B, between eyes. A, donkey. B, leaf. On I, ΚΑ[ΛΟ]Ϟ ΜΕΜ[Ν]ΟΝ. See p. 44 no. 83.

26 (30). MUNICH 2604 (J. 1021), from Vulci. I, bf., satyr. A–B, between eyes. A, donkey. B, trefoil. On I, ΜΜΕΜΕΜΝΟΝ Κ[ΑΛ]ΟϞ. See p. 44 no. 84.

27 (31). OXFORD 515, from Vulci. *JHS.* 24, 303; *CV.* pl. 1, 1 and pl. 5, 1–2. I, bf., warrior. A–B, between eyes. A, discus-thrower; B, athlete. On I, ΚΑΛΟϞΜΕΜΝΟΝ. For the shape, Bloesch 36, Antimachos Class, no. 1. Restored. See p. 44 no. 85.

(nos. 28–29, fragments of eye-cups: bf. interiors)

28 (20). FLORENCE (part ex Villa Giulia), fr. I, bf., youth with flute (to right: head, shoulders, and left hand remain). See p. 42 no. 52.

29. OXFORD G 141.3, fr., from Naucratis. I, bf., youth (head and shoulders remain: Paris, declining to judge?). See p. 42 no. 53.

(nos. 30–37, fragments from the outsides of eye-cups) (all early)

30. LOUVRE C 10464. *CV.* b pl. 18, 8 and pl. 19, 2–3. I is lost. A–B, between eyes. A, horse. See p. 46 no. 117 *bis*, and p. 68.

31 (15). BONN 464, 24, fr., from Cervetri. *AM.* 55 Beil. 53, 3; *CV.* pl. 1, 1. A, between eyes, youth with horse (the winning jockey? see *Dev.* 117 note 28). See p. 46 no. 130.

32 (27). ADRIA B 503, fr., from Adria. *CV.* pl. 1, 1. A, between eyes, warrior. See p. 46 no. 130 *bis*.

33 (26). VILLA GIULIA, frr. A–B, between eyes. A, warrior; B, warrior. On A, moving to right; on B, moving to left. The legs of both remain, with parts of the shields, and, on B, of spear and wrap. See p. 46 no. 131.

34. NAPLES, Astarita, 632, fr. A, between eyes, light-armed warrior (to right, leaning back, with pelta). See p. 46 no. 132.

35. OXFORD, Beazley, fr. A, between eyes, youth (moving to right, looking round; the greater parts of head and of one arm remain, with a trace of the brow of the oculus on the left). [Marie Beazley]. See p. 46 no. 133.

36 (22). LOUVRE S 1393, fr. *CV.* b pl. 2, 7. A, between eyes, woman with flower. See p. 46 no. 134.

37 (21). LOUVRE S 1396, fr. *CV*. b pl. 2, 8. A, between eyes, woman with flower. See p. 46 no. 135.

(*nos. 38–49: red-figured eye-cups*)
(*nos. 38–41: rf. eye-cups of the original type, see p. 39, II*)
(*early middle period, no. 43 somewhat later*)

38 (a). PALERMO V 652, from Chiusi. Inghirami *Chius.* pl. 165; *CV.* pl. 5, 4 and pl. 6. I, warrior. A–B, between eyes. A, discus-thrower; B, athlete bending. Restored. I is by Oltos, but A–B by another hand. See p. 47 no. 151.

39. NAPLES, Astarita, 47. I, Bothmer *Am.* pl. 72, 4. I, Amazon trumpeter. A–B, between eyes. A, bull; B, bull. On I, [+A]+PVL[ION]E[Γ]-OIEϚ[EN]. Potter-work by Kachrylion. See p. 47 no. 152.

40 (32). BOSTON 13.83 and FLORENCE, from Vulci. I and parts of A–B, Bruhn figs. 16–18; the shape, Caskey *G.* 177. I, warrior; A–B, between eyes: A, archer; B, warrior (dancing the pyrrhic?). On I, [M]EMMNO[N]-KALOϚ retr. The Florence fr. adds what was missing on A—the left hand with arrow-head and part of the bow, and part of the oculus. See p. 47 no. 153.

41 (37). LOUVRE G 19. Incompletely, *CV.* b pl. 2, 6 and pl. 3, 1–2. I, naked youth (athlete? the middle is missing and the motive uncertain). A–B, between eyes. A, horseman (jockey); B, the like. On I, MEMNON retr., KALOϚ retr. Other Louvre frr. join, adding a palmette, more of the eyes, and both handles. See p. 47 no. 154.

(*nos. 42–43, red-figured eye-cups, eyes on one half only*)

42. ARLESHEIM, Schweizer. I, hunter returning home (naked youth carrying dead fox over his shoulder and holding a club). A, (without eyes) archer and two horses. B, between eyes, warrior (naked youth, wearing greaves, standing to right, holding a spear). The palmettes on B are closed, on A open. Still early. Restored, B much. See p. 48 no. 166.

43 (33). NAPLES 2615, from Etruria. Hoppin i, 186–7; part, *PP.* pll. 6–7. I, satyr; A, (without eyes) maenad and donkeys; B, between eyes, satyr. I and A are by Oltos, but B (eyes and satyr) are by the Chelis Painter (p. 112 no. 2), and so are the handle-palmettes. On I, [+]ELIϚEΓOIEϚEN, on A, MEMMNON KALOϚ. For the shape, Bloesch 35, Chelis no. 2. See *PP.* 27–28; and here, p. 48 no. 167.

(*nos. 44–49, palmette-eye cups, see p. 39, III*)
(*nos. 44–47 still early, nos. 48–49 early middle*)

44 (35). PROVIDENCE 25.076. A–B, *JHS.* 47, 64; A, *Bull. Rhode* 16, 44 fig. 8; *AJA.* 1928, 435–8; *CV.* pl. 13. I, warrior with horse. A–B, between palmettes and eyes. A, athlete pouring oil into his hand. B, attendant at a sacrifice (youth carrying a leg of meat). For the subject of B see *JHS.* 53, 311, left. See p. 49 no. 169.

45 (14, +). LOUVRE C 11217 and ERLANGEN 459, fr. The Erlangen fr., Bruhn fig. 8 (mispoised); the same, *Jb.* 71, 104 fig. 8 (righted). I, warrior (the forehead and part of the helmet remain). A, between palmettes and eyes, Hyakinthos. The Louvre fragment (composed of three) joins the Erlangen on the left. On the subject of A see *RG.* 88–89 and *EVP.* 49–50. See p. 49 no. 170, and, below, nos. 46 and 62.

46. LOUVRE C 11218, fr. I, (uncertain remains). A, (eye). Not known to be an palmette-eye cup, but placed here because it seemed to belong to C 11217 (no. 45), although I do not see how the remains of I fit the subject. See p. 49 no. 171.

47 (36). FLORENCE I B 32 (part ex Villa Giulia), frr. Part, *CV.* pl. I, B 32; part of B, *CF.* pl. Y, 3. A–B, between palmettes and eyes. A, Herakles and one of the horses of Diomedes; B, Diomedes. See p. 49 no. 172.

48 (38, +). VILLA GIULIA (part ex Florence), and NAPLES, Astarita, 301. Part, *CV.* Fl. pl. I, B 23. I, woman cup-bearer. A–B, between palmettes and eyes. A, one (Dionysos?) reclining; B, maenad. On I, ME[MNON] retr., [KA]LOS retr. The Astarita fragment, unpublished, gives the lower end of couch and table on A, with the tips of two palmette-petals. See p. 49 no. 173.

49 (34). ROMAN MARKET (Basseggio?). B.Ap. xxi. 33. I, satyr (running to right, looking round, drinking-horn in left hand). A–B, between palmettes and eyes. A, warrior with horse; B, the like. See p. 49 no. 174.

(nos. 50–114, without eyes)
(no. 50, bilingual)

50 (39). LOUVRE F 128. A–B, Pottier pl. 73; *CV.* b pl. 3, 3–6 and pl. 4, 1. I, bf., Poseidon. A, Herakles and the lion. B, satyrs and donkey. Restored. Middle period.

(nos. 51–63, early and early middle)

51 (40). LONDON E 41, from Vulci. *WV.* D pl. 7, 1, whence Hoppin i, 156, (I and A) Perrot 10, 383 fig. 228 and p. 384, (I) *Mus. It.* 3,276, (A) Murray 9; I, Murray no. 26; A, Bothmer *Am.* pl. 68, 4. I, Theseus and one of the rescued maidens (the victory dance, cf. the François vase, FR. pl. 13). A, Theseus and Antiope. B, man (or youth) and woman, between two boys on horseback. On B, +A+VLION retr. The verb may have been on one of the missing parts. Parts of the handle-florals are restored. For the shape, Bloesch 45, Kachrylion no. 4. Early. See p. 1622.

52 (41). CAB. MÉD. L 240 (part of de Ridder 525), fr. A, (horse). Cf. the last. Early.

53 (46). MADRID 11267 (L. 151), from Vulci. Klein *L.* 81–82, whence (B) *Jb.* 31, 145; A–B, Ossorio pl. 32; B, Leroux pl. 15, whence Perrot 10, 375 and Pfuhl fig. 319 (= Pfuhl *Mast.* fig. 29); *CV.* pl. 1, 3, pl. 2, 2, pl. 4, 1, and pl. 5, 1; part of B, Simon *G.A.* 21. I, palmettes. A, Theseus pur-

suing the bull. B, symposion (two naked women). On A, ΔΙΟ+ϟΙΓ-ΟϟΚΑLΟϟ. Early.

54 (42). LONDON E 40, from Vulci. *WV*. D pl. 7, 2, whence Hoppin i, 154 and *Fra Nat*. 1954, 35; I, Murray no. 25. I, Amazon. A, Dionysos with satyr and maenad. B, komos. On I, +Α+PVLΙΟΝ ΕΓΟΙΕϟΕΝ retr. Parts of the handle-florals are restored. For the shape, Bloesch 45, Kachrylion no. 1. Early. See p. 1622.

55 (44). FLORENCE 1 B 21 (part ex Villa Giulia), HEIDELBERG 5, BRUNSWICK 537, BALTIMORE (Baltimore Society of the Archaeological Institute of America), and BOWDOIN. *CV*. Fl. pl. 1 B 21; *CF*. pl. X, whence *Fra Nat*. 1954, 34; the Heidelberg fr., Kraiker pl. 3; the Baltimore, *AJA*. 1917, 166 above and 167, and *CV*. Robinson ii pl. 1, 1; the Brunswick, *CV*. pl. 12, 2. I, Pegasos. A, satyrs and maenad. B, komos. On I, [+Α+]-P[VLΙ]ΟΝΕΓΟΙΕΙ. Early.

56 (43). ROME, Torlonia, from Vulci. Noël Des Vergers pl. 37, whence Hoppin i, 171 and (I) Klein *Euphr*. 300. I, warrior. A–B, athletes. On I, +Α+PVL[ΙΟ]Ν [ΕΓΟΙ]ΕϟΕΝ. On A, ΜΕΜΝΟΝ ΚΑLΟϟ. Early.

57. COPENHAGEN, from Italy. *Vente xi Bâle* pl. 19 and pl. 20, 333; *Fra Nat*. 1954, 27–32; Breitenstein *G.V*. 21 and pll. 27–29. I, Poseidon. A, Centauromachy (Kaineus). B, satyrs and maenad. On I, +Α+PVLΙΟΝ-ΕΓΟΙΕ. There may or may not have been an iota after the last epsilon. Restored. Still early. See p. 1622.

58 (47, +). FLORENCE 1 B 20 (part ex Villa Giulia), and CHICAGO, University. Part, *CV*. Fl. pl. 1 B 20; the Chicago fr., *Art Bull*. 19, 539 fig. 1. I, flute-girl. A, heroes quarrelling. B, komos. On A, ΜΕΜΝΟΝΚ[Α]LΟϟ. The inscription on B is ΕVΑΛΟΡΑ retr., complete (see *AJA*. 1950, 317, right). Two new frr. in Florence belong: on one, part of the right arm of the right-hand youth on A, with part of the handle-floral and the final sigma of the kalos-inscription; on the other, more of the handle-floral. Still early. See the next.

59. FLORENCE, fr. Outside, (the letters ΛΑ and, on the right, part of a handle-palmette). Seemed as if it might belong to Florence 1 B 20 (no. 58).

60 (45, +). VILLA GIULIA (part ex Florence), and NAPLES, Astarita, 298. Part, *CV*. Fl. pl. 1 B 51. I, archer. A, fight (with horseman). B, satyr and maenad with donkey. On I, +Α+PVL[Ι]ΟΝ and retr. [ΕΓΟΙ]ΕϟΕΝ. The Astarita fr. joins on the right of A, adding the right shank and foot of the right-hand warrior, part of the floral, and the inscription ... Αϟ with [ΚΑ]LΟϟ below it. Early middle.

61. FLORENCE, fr. (two joining). Outside, (thighs of one in a long chiton moving to right).

62. NAPLES, Astarita, 262, fr. A, (upper part of a boy, wrapt in his himation, to right). Cannot say this was not from an eye-cup. It is early, and indeed recalls the Hyakinthos cup (no. 45).

63 (51, 52, +). ATHENS Acr. 44 and 52, frr., from Athens. Part, Langlotz
pl. 3. I, warrior and youth. A, Adrastos mounting his chariot. On A
(or B), [M]EMM[NON .... A fragment added by Mrs. Karouzou completes the head of the youth on I (*BCH*. 1952, 203, a). For the subject of
A, *AJA*. 1950, 315. Still early. See p. 1622.

(nos. 64–114, developed style, middle and late; most of them are rather rough)

64 (48). BERLIN 2264, from Vulci. Inghirami *Gall.* 2 pll. 254–6; *WV*. D
pl. 2, 1–2, whence Hoppin ii, 249 and (A–B) *Jb*. 17, 55–56; A–B, Lücken
pll. 8–9, whence Licht ii, 168–9; I, Langlotz *G.V*. pl. 3, 6, whence Bruhn
fig. 5; I, Schaal *Rf*. fig. 5; B, Johansen *Il*. fig. 37; A–B, Bruhn figs. 6–7;
A, *Op. Ath*. 2, 63; part of A, *E.A.A*. i, 417. I, trumpeter. A, uncertain
subject (Achilles and Antilochos setting out?). B, fight for the body of
Patroklos. On I, E[V]+SIOEOS EΓOIESE[N], OLTOSEΛ[PAΦ]SEN.
Restored. For the subject of B, Johansen *Iliaden* 108–12, and Sjövall in
Op. Ath. 2, 47–60; for the shape, Bloesch 44, Euxitheos no. 4.

65 (49, +). LONDON E 1, FLORENCE, VILLA GIULIA, and NAPLES, Astarita,
299. Part, *CV*. Fl. pl. 3, B 4. I, trumpeter. A, lion and lioness attacking
bull; B, lion and lioness (or two lions) attacking fawn. On I, ... E]ΓOIE-
S[EN]. The London fragments were attributed to Oltos by Hartwig. The
Astarita fragment joins A, adding the missing part of the lion's tail, and, to
left of it, a bud with tendril, being the missing part of the right-hand half
of the handle-floral.

66 (50). TARQUINIA RC 6848, from Tarquinia. *Mon*. 10 pl. 23–24, whence
Perrot 10, 469–71, Hoppin ii, 251, (I and A) Pfuhl figs. 359–60 (whence,
detail of A, redrawn, Richter *ARVS*. 40 fig. 8), (I and A) Seltman pl.
11, (A) Rumpf *Rel*. fig. 50, (I) Bruhn fig. 4, (I) LS. fig. 49; *WV*. D pl.
1 and pl. 2, 3; A–B, *ML*. 36, 290; A, Romanelli *T*. 140; phs. Mo. 8658–9
and 5857, 2, whence (A–B) Bruhn fig. 3; A, ph. Al. 26045, whence
Bruhn fig. 1 and *Hist. rel*. 192; *CV*. pll. 2–3; A, ph. And. 41005, whence
Stella 39; the Etruscan graffito, *St. etr*. 5 pl. 15, 1. I, warrior. A, deities
in Olympus. B, Dionysos mounting chariot, with satyrs and maenads.
On I, EV+SIOEOS EΓOIESEN retr.; on A, OLTOS EΛPAΦSEN.
Very large. For the shape, Bloesch 44, Euxitheos no. 3. Lücken pl. 7,
Licht ii, 181 and 185, and Bruhn fig. 2 are taken from one of the modern
copies. See p. 1622.

67 (53; 55, 2; 65). COPENHAGEN, Thorvaldsen Museum, 100, VILLA GIULIA,
and FLORENCE 1 B 24. The Thorvaldsen cup: B, Johansen *Il*. fig. 35; B,
Art Bull. 19, 548 fig. 8; Bruhn figs. 37 and 42–43; R.I. x. 37. The Florence
fragment: *CV*. pl. 1, B 24. I, archer. A, Achilles and Ajax playing; B,
fight, Diomed and Aeneas. Restored. The Villa Giulia fragment
(assigned to Oltos in *ARV*.[1] 39, but thought to be from the same cup as
Florence 4 B 38) gives the missing part of Achilles on A, and the hoof of
the horse behind him. The Florence fragment 1 B 24 gives head and

right shoulder of Athena on A, with the missing alpha of the inscription HOΓΑΙS. For the subject of A, CB. iii, text; of B, Johansen *Il.* 105–6, and CB. ii, 19.

68 (54). LOUVRE G 18. A–B, Jahn *Telephos* pl. 2; A–B, *Mon.* 10 pl. 22, 2; *CV.* b. pl. 4, 2–7. I, woman dancing. A, fight: death of Troilos (Troilos as a warrior, Achilles slaying him, Aeneas to the rescue). B, chariot. On I, [M]EMNON ΚΑΛΟS. Restored, I much: the greater part of I is modern; the middle of it, with the foot of the cup, is from a later vase; the upper half of Achilles on A is modern. The inscription ΑVΤΟΒΟV-ΛΟS, retr., on B may be the name of the charioteer—the artist perhaps thinking of Automedon—or may go with the retr. ΚΑΛΟS as a kalos-inscription. The third word is the name ΚΙΝΕΑ (complete, retr.).

69. FLORENCE, frr. A, chariot (to left). B, satyrs and maenads. On A, ΜΙΛΕ-SΙ[ΟS]? But not certain that there were no letters in the break between the Λ and the E. On B, ...ΟΝ... and ...SΚΑΛΟS. Very bad condition. Compare Louvre G 18 (no. 68).

70 (55, part). FLORENCE 4 B 38, fr. *CV.* pl. 4, B 38. A, (warrior, horses). One of the horses may have been ridden, the other led. The Villa Giulia fragment mentioned in *ARV.*[1] is not from this cup, but from Thorvaldsen 100 (no. 67).

71 (56). HEIDELBERG 6, fr. Kraiker pl. 3. A, (mounted warrior).

72 (57). FLORENCE 3923. *CV.* pl. 73 and pl. 116, 1. I, horseman (jockey?). A, heroes quarrelling. B, man or youth mounting chariot. On I, MEM-NO[N] ΚΑΛΟS. On A, [ME]MNONΚΑΛΟS ΑΜΟΡΟ+Ο, on B, ME[MNONΚΑ]ΛΟS. I do not understand the second inscription on A.

73 (58). BERLIN 4221, from Orvieto. I, *Jh.* 1, 43; I, Licht ii, 145; I, Blümel *Sport und Spiel* pl. 24; I, Blümel *S.H.* 67; I, *Arch. class.* 2 pl. 10, 1; A–B, Bruhn figs. 38–39. I, victor. A, fight (heroes parted). B, symposion.

74 (59). MUNICH 2618 (J. 404), from Vulci. Inghirami *Gall. omer.* 2 pll. 238–9; FR. pl. 83, whence (part of A) Jacobsthal *Gött. V.* 43 fig. 66; A, Johansen *Il.* fig. 19; A and foot, Bloesch *FAS.* pl. 14, 1; I and A, Bruhn figs. 36 and 33; Lullies and Hirmer pl. 9, below, and pl. 11. I, youth seated (holding a sprig: the motive not clear to me). A–B, ransom of Hector. On I, ME[M]NON and retr. ΚΑΛΟS. For the shape, Bloesch 50, above, no. 4. See p. 1622.

75 (60). LONDON E 16, from Vulci. I, Murray no. 12; A–B, *Art Bull.* 19, 540; B and foot, Bloesch *FAS.* pl. 14, 2; A–B, Bruhn figs. 40–41. I, boy lifting hydria. A, Ajax leaving home (with chariot). B, Dionysos with maenads and satyrs. On I, MEMNONΚΑΛΟS. On A, MEMNON-ΚΑΛΟS. For the shape, Bloesch 50, middle, no. 2.

76 (61). BERLIN 4220. A, *Dragma* 182; Bruhn figs. 23–25. I, boy fetching cushion. A, Achilles brought to Chiron. B, satyrs and maenad. On I, MEM[NON]ΚΑΛΟS. Furtwängler saw that this was by the same hand

as Berlin 2263 (no. 85). According to Bloesch (*FAS.* 49 no. 2) by the same potter as London E 17 (no. 80).

77 (62). OXFORD 1927.4065. *CV.* pl. 51, 4 and pl. 53, 3–4; A–B, Bothmer *Am.* pl. 68, 6; A–B, Dugas and Flacelière pll. 6–7. I, woman cup-bearer. A–B, Theseus and Antiope. For the shape, Bloesch 54 no. 2.

78. LOUVRE C 11219, fr. (six joining). I, (forearm and hand, holding something, with the letters ... LO ...) A, fight? (the lower halves of the two left-hand figures remain, both male, naked, one running to left, the other sword in hand, rushing to right: inscription .. LIS ([Che]lis??). From the same cup as Louvre C 11220 (no. 79)?

79. LOUVRE C 11220, fr. (four joining). I, satyr (shanks, feet, tail-tip, one hand remain: running to right). Outside, (part of handle-floral). On I, [ME]MNON K[ALOS]. [Bothmer]. From the same cup as Louvre C 11219 (no. 78)?

80 (63). LONDON E 17, from Vulci. I, Murray no. 13; the palmettes, Jacobsthal O. pl. 72, c; part of B (reversed), *The Listener*, 16 April 1959, 665. I, cup-bearer. A–B, fight. On I, KALOS MEMNON. On A, SIMIAΔΕSKAL[O]S. On B, KALOSMEMNON. According to Bloesch (*FAS.* 49, middle, no. 1), by the same potter as Berlin 4220 (no. 76).

81 (64). ATHENS Acr. 45, two frr., from Athens. Langlotz pl. 3. Outside, (woman; woman). Perhaps from a battle-scene, compare the right-hand woman on London E 8 (no. 88). A new Athens fr., with part of one in a himation to left, might be by Oltos, and might be from this cup.

82. ATHENS Acr. 132, fr., from Athens. A, (middle of a woman in chiton, with kolpos, and himation, running to right).

83 (66). LOUVRE G 17. *WV.* 1890–1 pl. 10, whence Perrot 10, 369–71 and (I and A) Bruhn figs. 46–47; *CV.* b pll. 5–6; A, ph. Gir. 25536, whence (part) Grimal 102; phs. Arch. phot. S. 4240.001, AE I, BE I, and CE I. I, youth running with lyre. A, Herakles and Eurystheus. B, Odysseus in chariot, with Hermes. On I, MEMNOON .... On B, MEM[NOO]N-KA[LOS]. Now cleaned. For the subject of B, Robert *Held.* 1188.

84 (67). Once Noël Des Vergers, 137, from Vulci. Noël Des Vergers pl. 38, whence (I and A) Klein *Euphr.* 306 and 81, whence (I) Norman Gardiner *G.A.S.* 307, (I) Norman Gardiner *Athl.* fig. 101. I, jumper. A, Herakles and Geryon. B, Achilles setting out, with chariot. See p. 1622.

85 (68). BERLIN 2263, from Vulci. Bruhn figs. 34 and 31–32; B.Ap. xxii. 108, whence (A) Brommer *Her.* pl. 24, a. I, youth putting on his greaves. A, Herakles and the Amazons; B, chariot of Herakles. On I, MEM-MNON KALOS. See p. 1622.

86 (69). LONDON E 18, from Vulci. Jahn *Dichter* pl. 3; I, Murray no. 14; detail of B, *Jh.* 3, 89; B, *ML.* 19, 96 fig. 11, whence Robert *Herm.* 82 fig.

71; B, Schefold *Bildnisse* 51, 1; A, Bothmer *Am.* pl. 69, 2. I, naked woman tying her sandal. A, Herakles and the Amazons. B, komos (Anacreon and his friends). On I, MEMNON ΚΑΛΟϚ. Bothmer (*Am.* 135) restores the fragmentary Amazon-name on A as [Ky]doi[me]. For the subject of B see CB. ii, 60–61. For the shape, Bloesch 48 no. 2.

87 (70). COPENHAGEN inv. 3877, from Vulci. B, Poulsen *Etr.* pl. 4, 9; *CV.* pl. 137, 2 and pl. 138; Bruhn figs. 26–28. I, naked woman with laver (about to wash). A, Herakles and Kyknos. B, Theseus and Minotaur. On each side of A, and of B, a horseman with a void horse. On I, MEMNONΚΑΛΟϚ. The word ✝ΙΟΝ on A has been thought to apply to the opponent of Herakles, but it should perhaps be taken with the ΚΑΛΟϚ to right of it as a kalos-inscription: the name ✝ΙΟΝ occurs on a cup-fragment in Amsterdam (no. 100); see also p. 1573.

88 (71). LONDON E 8. A–B, Gerhard pl. 84–85; I, Murray no. 5, whence Perrot 10, 372; A–B, *Art Bull.* 19, 547; A–B, Bruhn figs. 44–45; I, Richter *Ancient Italy* fig. 24; B. Ap. xxii. 15. I, boy running with lyre and meat. A, Herakles and Kyknos. B, Dionysos and Giant. On each side of B, warrior with horse, turned towards the handle, and probably to be thought of as pertaining to A.

89 (72). FLORENCE 1 B 37, fr. *CV.* pl. 1, B 37. A, fight (probably Herakles and Kyknos, cf. London E 8, no. 88). [? Λ]ΝΑΘΘΝ .... For this name in Athens about this time see a bf. fragment in Athens, Ceramicus Museum (*Jb.* 61–62 pl. 17, 59).

90 (73). NEW YORK 21.88.174. I, youth with hare (probably about to start it for coursing, compare London E 46, p. 315 no. 1). A, Herakles and the lion. B, warrior, mounted youth, and youth. On I, ME[M]-MNON ΚΑΛΟϚ, on B, ΚΑΛΟϚ, ϚΜΙΚΡΟϚ, ΛΕΚΕϚ, ... Ιϛ✝ ...

91 (74). VILLA GIULIA (part ex Florence). Part, *CV.* pl. 1, B 36. I, naked man running. A, Herakles and Nessos. B, satyr and maenad with donkey.

92 (75). OXFORD 516, from Vulci. *JHS.* 24, 304; *CV.* pl. 1, 2 and pl. 5, 3–4; I, Bruhn fig. 19. I, komast; A–B, symposion: A, youth reclining, and cup-bearer; B, three youths approaching him. On I, MEMNOMOϚ-ΚΑΛΟϚ. Now cleaned.

93 (76). COPENHAGEN, Ny Carlsberg, inv. 2700, from Orvieto. *Nordisk Tidskrift* 1, 353–5; Poulsen *Etr.* pl. 4 fig. 6 and pl. 5; Bruhn figs. 20–22; A–B, Breitenstein *G.V.* pll. 30–31. I, naked woman dancing. A–B, symposion: A, man (Hermes?) reclining, with goats; B, woman reclining, with rams. See p. 1622.

94 (77). FLORENCE 3 B 11, fr. A, *CV.* pl. 3, B 11. I, palmettes. A, komos.

95 (78). LONDON E 19, from Vulci. Jahn *Dichter* pl. 6, whence (I) Klein *Euphr.* 303 and (A–B) Schefold *Bildnisse* 53, 1–2; I, Murray no. 15. I, archer. A–B, komos. On I, MEMNONΚΑΛΟϚ. On A, [ΚΑ]ΛΟϚ

retr., MOLΓIS, OALINOS, +SANΘOS. On B, KALOS retr., NIKON, +ILON, SOLON, KALOS. The kaloses are but loosely attached to the names of the revellers. For the shape, Bloesch 50 no. 5.

96 (79). FLORENCE 81601, from Saturnia. *ML.* 30 pl. 2; *CV.* pl. 74 and pl. 116, 2. I, youth (fragmentary and the motive uncertain). A, komos. B, maenad and satyr with donkey. On A, +IL[ON] retr., AVTOMENES, KALOS, KÁLOS. On B, KALOS +ILOS (sigma written, nu probably intended). For the shape, Bloesch 48 no. 6.

97 (80). FLORENCE (V.), from Chiusi. I, Bruhn fig. 35. I, naked youth (victor?). A, youth attacked by horses. B, (satyr). On I, MEMNO[N] KALOS. For the shape, Bloesch 48 no. 1.

98 (82). HEIDELBERG 3, fr. I, Kraiker pl. 2. I, jumper. All that remains of A–B is a piece of the ground-line. On I, MEMON KALOS. For the shape, Bloesch 50 no. 6. Compare no. 100.

99. NEW YORK 06.1021.300, fr., from Orvieto. Part, *Studies Robinson* ii pl. 50, d; with new fragments, *AJA.* 1955 pl. 47 fig. 1. I, fawn. Outside, a piece of the ground-line remains. On I, MEMMNON[KA]LOS. [Bothmer].

100 (81). AMSTERDAM inv. 2229, fr. *CV.* Scheurleer pl. 6, 5; *Gids* pl. 67, 1. A, athletes. Compare Heidelberg 3 (no. 98).

101 (83). OXFORD G 138.19, fr., from Naucratis. *CV.* pl. 14, 15. A, (satyrs with donkey).

102 (84). MUNICH 2606 (J. 1087), from Vulci. I, Sudhoff i, 27; A, *Art Bull.* 19, 548 fig. 9; I and A, Bruhn figs. 29–30. I, naked woman cleaning her sandals. A, Dionysos seated, with a donkey, and a satyr on a donkey. B, riding lesson? (two youths on horseback, and a man). On I, MEM-[NON] [KAL]OS. On B, KAIKAS SEMONI. Now cleaned. For the shape, Bloesch 50, above, no. 3. For the subject of I compare Naples Stg. 5 (p. 32 no. 4) and the remark of Stratonikos in Athenaeus 351a.

103 (85). ORVIETO 1049, from Orvieto. A, *Mem. Am. Ac.* 6 pl. 17, 3; A, ph. Al. 25985, whence Tarchi pl. 123, 2; A, Vorberg *Gloss.* 266; *CV.* pll. 1–2; A–B, phs. Armoni. I, warrior. A, Dionysos seated, with satyrs and maenads; B, Dionysos on donkey with satyrs and maenads. On I, MEM[N]ON KA[L]OS.

104 (86, +). BRUSSELS R 253, and NAPLES, Astarita, 306. *CV.* pl. 2, 2; I and A, Verhoogen *C.G.* pl. 12, b. I, maenad; A, maenad and satyr with donkey; B, satyrs and maenad. On I, MEMNO[N] KALOS. For the shape, Bloesch 48 no. 11. The Astarita fragment, unpublished, joins on the right of A and gives, with part of the palmette, the last two letters of the inscription KALE.

105 (87). COMPIÈGNE 1093, from Vulci. *CV.* pl. 14, 1–2 and 5. I, cupbearer. A, maenad and satyr with donkey; B, maenads. Restored.

106 (88). VILLA GIULIA (part ex Florence) and HEIDELBERG 4, frr. *CV*. Fl. pl. 1, B 52; the Heidelberg fr., Kraiker pl. 3. A, (satyr, maenad); B, (satyrs).

107. BASLE, Cahn, 51, three frr. A, satyrs with fawn.

108 (89). NAPLES 2617, from Vulci. I, komast. A, satyrs with fawn; B, the like. On I, MILONKΛ complete. On A, KALOϚ retr., ϚTVϚIΓOϚ retr., KALON. On B, ... KIϚ retr., ΦLEBIΓOϚ retr., ΔI[ON?]. For the shape, Bloesch 48 no. 4.

109 (90). LEIPSIC, fr. A, (upper part of a boy, in a chiton ornamented with groups of four dots, to left).

110 (91). VILLA GIULIA, fr. A, (half shank, with foot, of one running to right; on the left, part of a handle-palmette).

111 (92). PALERMO V 791, fr., from Chiusi. *CV*. pl. 7, 5 (misprinted 4 in the text). A, (man—Dionysos?).

112. ATHENS, Agora, P 15964, two frr., from Athens. Outside, (male, spear; man).

113 (93). BOLOGNA 361, from Bologna. *Atti Romagna* 3rd ser., 10 pl. 1; *CV*. pl. 1, 3, pl. 3, and pl. 4, 4–5; I and A, Bruhn figs. 51 and 53; B, *RM*. 63 pl. 43, 2. I, youth running with lyre and meat. A, Herakles and the lion. B, between pegasi, which face the handles, Peleus and Atalanta. [Langlotz]. Late and coarse. For the shape, Bloesch 55 no. 18. See the next.

114 (94). VILLA GIULIA 50388, from Cervetri. R.I. 1867, 20. I, priest. A, Herakles and the Hydra. B, between pegasi (both turned to left), Dionysos and Giant. Restored. Late. As Bologna 361 (no. 113).

114 *bis*. FLORENCE V ix and x, frr., from Chiusi? Outside, komos. Late, coarse; as nos. 113 and 114.

(nos. 115–125; fragments of cups; what remains is the picture inside or part of it; not known if decorated outside or not. Nos. 115 and 116 are early; the rest, middle or late)

115 (95). ROMAN MARKET, fr., from Vulci. I, mounted Amazon (to right: the kidaris is red, the horse's mane white).

116 (96). MUNICH, fr. I, victor (youth bending to left, sprigs in his hands, wreath round his shoulders; on the right a pair of acontia). [Langlotz].

117. ATHENS Acr., two frr. (one composed of two) from Athens. I, woman to right (middle and left arm, and lower part of skirt).

118 (97). GREIFSWALD 278, fr. Peters pl. 22. I, Nereid. [M]EMNO[N ...

118 *bis*. OXFORD, Beazley, fr. I, woman (running to right, looking round: head and shoulders remain, with the greater part of the right arm). Might be a Nereid. On the left, what may be a part of an initial M: inverted, from a retrograde inscription—name of Memnon?

119. NAPLES, Astarita, 248, fr. I, (head of a youth to left). [H. R. W. Smith].

120. NAPLES, Astarita, 142, fr. Bothmer *Am.* pl. 72, 5. I, Amazon. [ME-MN]ON [ΚΑL]OS. [Bothmer].

121 (98). Lost, from Vulci. B.Ap. xxi. 57, whence Vorberg *Ars erot.* pl. 22 and Vorberg *Gloss.* 334. I, naked flute-girl raping a pointed amphora.

122. LOUVRE C 11221, fr. I, satyr (moving to right, a vessel—horn?—in his left hand; the head missing except the end of the beard). ΚΑL . . .

123 (99). MUNICH, fr. I, youth loosing his sandal. MEMNO[N] ΚΑL[O]S.

124 (100). OXFORD G 138. 2, fr., from Naucratis. *BSA.* 5 pl. 8, 10; *CV.* pl. 14, 3. I, youth. ME[MNON] [ΚΑLO]S.

125 (101). BERLIN MARKET (Graupe: ex Prinz Albrecht, *V.D.K.* no. 915), fr. I, Minotaur. ΚΑLOS, ΚΑLOS.

(nos. 126–33: full-size cups, decorated inside only; nos. 126–7 are still early, the rest are not)

126 (102). VATICAN 502. Albizzati pl. 69; Bruhn fig. 50; Buschor *Bilder-welt* 28. I, Herakles. For the shape, Bloesch 37, Antimachos Group no. 7.

127 (103). NAPLES 2627. *RM.* 4, 164, whence Hoppin ii, 455. I, komast. TLESONNVNΛΛ EOEΓOIESEN. For the shape, Bloesch 39.

128 (104). FERRARA, Museo Schifanoia, 269. *Boll. d'Arte* 5, 344; Bruhn fig. 52. I, athlete pouring oil into his hand. MEMON ΚΑLOS. Restored. For the shape, Bloesch 37, Antimachos Group no. 11.

129 (105). PALERMO, from Chiusi. Inghirami *Chius.* pl. 177. I, woman dancing. Apparently mislaid: it was in the Palermo Museum thirty or forty years ago.

130. BASLE MARKET (M.M.). *Vente x Bâle* pl. 20, 413. I, woman dancing. [Hecht].

131 (106). PARMA. Bruhn fig. 48. I, woman.

132 (107). MUNICH 2624 (J. 1092), from Vulci. I, Minotaur.

133 (108). LOUVRE G 94 *bis.* Part, *CV.* b pl. 7, 1; Bothmer *Am.* pl. 72, 6. I, mounted Amazon. Late.

SKYPHOI

134 (109, +). ATHENS Acr. 450, frr., from Athens. Part, Langlotz pl. 38. A, Athena mounting chariot. B, Herakles and the Hydra. A fragment presented by Martin Robertson adds the right hand of Athena on A, with part of her spear, of the reins, of the chariot-car. A new Athens fragment adds the right leg of Athena, with the end of her spear, and on the left the end of an inscription, . . . ES ([Ar]es?).

135 (110). ATHENS Acr. 449, and MUNICH, frr. Part, Langlotz pl. 39 and p. 41. A, Herakles and Apollo: the struggle for the tripod. B, Triptolemos. The Munich fr. gives part of the lower border.

136 (111). ATHENS Acr. AP 430, fr., from Athens. *Hesp.* 4, 284, 153. Herakles and Apollo: the struggle for the tripod. [Pease].

PLATE OR STEMLESS CUP?

137 (10). ODESSA, fr., from Kerch. *Zap. Od.* 22 pl. 3, 1, whence Blavatski 263 and (redrawn) Ebert *S.* 203, whence Ghali-Kahil *H.* pl. 82, 2. Menelaos and Helen.

PLATE

138 (8). ELEUSIS, fr., from Eleusis. *Delt.* 9, 4. Peleus and Thetis.

(STEMMED?) PLATE
(of special type)

139 (9). BERLIN 2313. Gerhard *TG.* pl. 13, 1–2, whence *WV.* 6 pl. 3, 2; *WV.* 7 pl. 4, 3; *AZ.* 1875, 88; Bruhn fig. 49. Athena. . . . ΕΓΟΙΕΙ. Much restored. See p. 68 no. 13 and p. 69. Early.

NEAR OLTOS

ARV.[1] 43–44.

CUPS

(nos. 1–9, eye-cups)

1 (2). VILLA GIULIA 18587, from Falerii. *CV.* H e pl. 45, 1 and 4–5. I, bf., archer. A–B, between eyes. A, nose; B, nose. See p. 41 no. 33.

2 (1). Once MUNICH, Preyss, from Chiusi or Chianciano. I, bf., satyr. A–B, between eyes. A, nose; B, nose. See p. 41 no. 34.

3 (4). FLORENCE 2 B 30 (part ex Villa Giulia). Part, *CV.* pl. 2, B 30. I, bf., Dionysos. A–B, between eyes. A, pear-drop; B, the like. For the shape, Bloesch 62, Pamphaios no. 4. See p. 41 no. 35.

4 (3). HEIDELBERG 1, fr., from near Florence. Kraiker pl. 1. I, bf., archer. [Kraiker]. See p. 43 no. 56.

5 (5). VILLA GIULIA 8343, from Nepi. *CV.* H e pl. 46, 1–3. I, bf., Dionysos. A–B, between eyes. A, maenad; B, maenad. [Kraiker]. See p. 44 no. 86.

6 (l 18). VILLA GIULIA (part ex Florence), frr. Part, *CV.* Fl. pl. 1, B 34. I, bf., doves. A–B, between eyes. A, male (in himation); B, the like. See p. 44 no. 87.

7. LOUVRE C 10460. Incompletely, *CV.* b pl. 18, 1–3. I, bf., satyr. A–B, between eyes. A, donkey. B, trefoil. Other Louvre fragments belong, including one handle. [Villard]. See p. 44 no. 88.

8. CAB. MÉD. 335, from Vulci. The outside pictures are by the Thalia Painter (p. 112 no. 1), but the inside picture may be by Oltos: compare Louvre C 10460 (no. 7), as Villard has done. See p. 44 no. 89.

9 (6). FLORENCE 3 B 10, frr. Part, *CV.* pl. 3, B 10. A–B, between eyes. A, male seated. B, plant. The oculi are not those of Oltos. For the plant compare Cab. Méd. 335 (no. 8). See p. 46 no. 137.

(*nos. 10–13, without eyes*)

10. LONDON E 812.1 and CAMBRIDGE N 142, fr., from Naucratis. See *JHS*. 51, 53 no. 4. The London part, *BSA*. 5, 64; the Cambridge, *CV*. ii pl. 27, 3. I, satyr and maenad. . . . ΕΓ]ΟΙΕϚ[ΕΝ].

11 (8). FLORENCE 1 B 22, fr. *CV*. pl. 1 B 22. A (snake, arm of satyr or maenad).

12. FLORENCE, fr. A (toes to right, then shank and foot of a maenad rushing to right).

STEMMED PLATE
(*of special type*)

13 (9). Once Joly de Bammeville (ex Canino), from Vulci. *RM*. 3 pl. 1, whence Pfuhl fig. 358 and Hoppin ii, 409. Artemis. ϚΙΚΑΝΟϚΕΓΟΙ-ΕϚΕΝ. Bothmer points out that the Canino plate is no. 55 in the Joly de Bammeville sale, *Cat. Sotheby 13 May 1854*. Early. Compared by Rossbach (*RM*. 3, 68) with Berlin 2313 (p. 67 no. 139). See p. 69.

Considering that the kalos-name Memnon is almost confined to Oltos, we may ask whether a lost Memnon vase may not be his:

CUP

Once Noël Des Vergers, 102, from Vulci. I, bf., Poseidon. A–B, between eyes. A, woman dancing; B, the like. ΚΑΛΟϚ ΜΕΜΝ[ΟΝ]. See p. 42 no. 54.

A cup-fragment might be by Oltos:

HEIDELBERG 9, and NAPLES, Astarita, 563. The Heidelberg part: *Anz*. 1916, 174; and Kraiker pl. 1. I, floral. The Astarita fragment joins.

A cup-fragment recalls early Oltos:

LOUVRE C 11265, fr. A, between eyes, horse (standing to left: parts of all four legs and of the red tail remain, with the tear-gland of the right-hand eye). So far as the preservation goes, might belong to Louvre C 10461 (p. 41 no. 36). Compare Louvre C 10464 (p. 56 no. 30) and Villa Giulia 5959 (p. 55 no. 10). See p. 46 no. 129.

In a small fragment of another eye-cup the nose is drawn as in eye-cups by Oltos (Munich 2581, p. 55 no. 11) and near him (Villa Giulia 18587, p. 67 no. 1); Preyss, p. 67 no. 2):

MUNICH, fr. A, between eyes, nose. See p. 46 no. 136.

Close imitation of Oltos, apparently by a beginner:

TWO-HANDLED MASTOID
(rf. version of the common bf. type Richter and Milne fig. 171)

LOUVRE C 10783. Athletes (A, three youths; B, two: several of them characterized as acontists). On A, [ICAL]O$ retr., MEMNON retr., ICALO$, on B, MEMNON retr., ICALO$, ICALO$.

Small fragments are connected by the rare border with two contemporary works, the lost plate signed Sikanos (p. 68 no. 13) and that by Oltos in Berlin (p. 67 no. 139); the remains of the inscription might possibly be from another signature of Sikanos:

OXFORD, Beazley, three frr., from Orvieto. Horse (or horseman) (parts of the hind-legs and of the tail remain. On one fr., ... AN ... (or AN ...); on another, ... OI ... I had thought of these as perhaps part of a lid (of a psykter? or a lidded pelike?), decorated inside; Bothmer suggests that they might be from a stemmed plate not of the same shape as the Sikanos plate, but something like it.

CHAPTER 5

EPIKTETOS

EPIKTETOS

Klein *Euphr.* 14–52. Furtwängler in FR. ii, 82–84. *VA.* 14–18. Langlotz *Z.* 32–34 and 110–14. *Att.V.* 24–29 and 467. *BSR.* 11, 16–17. *Jb.* 44, 141–97 (Kraiker). *JHS.* 51, 41–44. *ARV.*[1] 44–53 and 949.

The name is known from forty signed vases.

Epiktetos collaborated with the potters Hischylos (nos. 1–4 and 7, and p. 79 no. 1), Nikosthenes (nos. 8 and 87), Andokides (no. 90), Pamphaios (nos. 14 and 15), Python (no. 16), and Pistoxenos (no. 205). The plate no. 102 bears the double signature of Epiktetos as potter and Epiktetos as painter. In no. 13 part of the decoration is by Epiktetos, part by the Euergides Painter. Part of no. 29 is by Epiktetos, part in the manner of the Euergides Painter.

The late cups are unsigned. Many of them bear the single word ἐποίεσεν, but the practice is not confined to Epiktetos. No. 31 has a bare ἐγ[ραφσεν] as well as ἐποίεσεν, no. 78 has ἐγραφσεν only.

The cups are arranged here on the same principle as with Oltos (p. 53).

CUPS

(nos. 1–14, eye-cups)
(nos. 1–13, eye-cups of the original type; nos. 1–9 are early)

1 (1). ORVIETO, Faina, 97, from Orvieto? I, A, and, on the left, part of B, Hoppin i, 323; A, *Jb.* 44, 153 fig. 3; I and A, phs. R.I. 1935, 880–1. I, bf., stag. A–B, between eyes. A, runner. B, nose. On I, HIꟻ+VᒪOꟻ ΕΓΟ[ΙΕꟻΕ]Ν. On A, ΕΓΙΚΤΕΤΟꟻ ΕΛΡΑꟻꟼΕΝ. For the shape, Bloesch 32, Hischylos no. 6. See p. 45 no. 100.

2 (2). VILLA GIULIA (part ex Florence) and HEIDELBERG 18. Part, *CV*. Fl. pl. 3, B 1; part, *CF.* pl. Z, 8; the Heidelberg fr., Kraiker pl. 5. I, bf., warrior. A–B, between eyes. A, woman? (one foot and the edge of a long skirt remain). B, horse. On I, H[Iꟻ]+VᒪOꟻ. On B, between the left-hand brow and eye, ΕΓΙκΤΕΤΟꟻ. The verbs were no doubt in the missing parts. The Heidelberg fr. was assigned to Epiktetos by Kraiker. See p. 45 no. 101.

3 (3). LONDON E 3. Palmette, *Jb.* 7, 106 fig. 3 (see Kraiker in *Jb.* 44, 152); I, *JHS.* 29 pl. 12, whence Swindler fig. 277 and Rumpf *MZ.* pl. 17, 1; Hoppin i, 308, whence (parts of A–B) Buschor *Satyrtänze* figs. 49–50; I, *Journ. Walt.* 1, 31; I and B, Schnitzler pl. 31. I, bf., horseman. A–B, between eyes. Satyrs going into battle: A, with drinking-horn; B, with jug, trumpeting. On I, HIꟻ+VᒪOꟻ ΕΓΟΙΕꟻΕΝ. On A, ΕΓΙκΤΕΤΟꟻ.

On B, EΛPAS⊕EN. For the shape, Bloesch 33, Hischylos no. 8. See p. 45 no. 102, and p. 1623.

4 (4). LENINGRAD 645. *Jb.* 44, 154–7. I, bf., komast. A–B. between eyes. A, donkey-man; B, donkey. On I, HIS+V[LO]SEΓOIESEN. On B, EΓIKTETOS EΛPAS⊕EN. See p. 45 no. 103, ibid. no. 99, and p. 1623.

5 (5). ATHENS, fr., from the Argive Heraion. Waldstein *Arg. Her.* ii pl. 62, 29. A, donkey. Probably an eye-cup.

6 (9–11, +). LOUVRE G 8 and TÜBINGEN E 7. (Minus the Tübingen fr.), *CV.* Louvre b pl. 8, 6–7 and pl. 9, 1 and 4; the Tübingen fr., Watzinger pl. 17. I, (lost). A–B, between eyes. A, athlete picking up discus. B, komast. On B, EΓIKTE[TOS]. On A, [EΛP]AS⊕[EN]. See p. 46 no. 120.

7 (6). BERLIN 2100, fr., from Etruria. *Jb.* 1 pl. 12; *JHS.* 29 pl. 9, whence Hoppin *Bf.* 137; Pfuhl fig. 275; Schaal *Sf.* fig. 57; Neugebauer pl. 37, 2. I, bf., komast. [HI]S+V[L]OSEΓOIE[SEN]. [Kraiker]. For the shape, Bloesch 31, Hischylos no. 3. See p. 43 no. 59 and p. 1623.

8 (7). WÜRZBURG 468, from Vulci. Part of A, *AZ.* 1885 pl. 16, 3, whence Hoppin i, 336; Hoppin *Bf.* 462; Langlotz pl. 137, whence (part of A) Rumpf *MZ.* pl. 17, 2. I, bf., komast. A–B, between eyes. A, satyr squatting frontal. B, horse. On A, EΓIKTETOS EΛPAS⊕EN. On B, NIKOSΘENES EΓOIESEN. For the shape, Bloesch 9, Nikosthenes, B, no. 6. See p. 45 no. 105.

9 (8). VILLA GIULIA, fr. A, between eyes, (the lower part of a male squatting frontal). [Giglioli]. See p. 46 no. 139.

10. LOUVRE C 10458, part, frr. *CV.* b pl. 8, 2–3. I, bf., fawn. EΓIKTE-[TOSEΛPAS]⊕EN. May belong to the next, but uncertain. See p. 46 no. 121.

11. LOUVRE C 10458, part, frr. *CV.* b pl. 8, 4–5. I is lost. A–B, between eyes. A, komast (or cup-bearer) at krater. B, nose. See the last, and p. 43 no. 60.

12 (12). FLORENCE 2 B 4. *CV.* pl. 2 B 4; I, *Boll. d'Arte* 29, 266 fig. 15. I, bf., warrior. A, between eyes, jumper. On I, EΓOIE[S]E (rather than EΓOIE[SE]N) and no more. See p. 45 no. 106.

13 (27, +). LOUVRE G 16. One fr., Pottier pl. 90; *CV.* b pl. 11, 2–3 and 6. I, Sisyphos. A–B, between eyes. A, pear-drop; B, the like. On I, HIΓΓAP+OSKALO[S]. I (*CV.* b pl. 11, 2 and 6) is by Epiktetos, but A–B is by the Euergides Painter (p. 44 no. 94): for this collaboration compare Naples 2609 (no. 29). See p. 47 no. 155.

(no. 14, palmette-eye-cup)

14 (13). LOUVRE G 5, from Vulci. A, *BCH.* 1897, 239; Pottier pl. 89, whence Perrot 10, 361–2, Hoppin i, 326–7, and (I) Pfuhl fig. 326; I, (without the restoration), *Jb.* 44, 172; I, Vorberg *Gloss.* 382, 1; *CV.* b pl. 9, 2–3 and pl. 10, 1. I, komast οὐρῶν. A–B, between palmettes and eyes. A, warrior;

B, archer. On I, ΓΑΜΑΦΙΟ$ ΕΓΟΙΕ$ΕΝ. On A, ΕΓΙΚΤΕΤΟ$. On B, ΕΛΡΑΦ$ΕΝ. I is restored. For the shape, Bloesch 64, Pamphaios, iii, no. 10. See p. 49 no. 175.

(*nos. 15–83, without eyes*)
(*nos. 15–43, decorated outside as well as in*)

15 (14). BERLIN 2262, from Vulci. Gerhard pl. 272, 1–4; I, Winter *K.B.*[1] pl. 88, 4; Hoppin i, 305; A–B, Pfuhl fig. 322; B, Swindler fig. 292; I and A, *Jb.* 44, 166–7; A, Schröder *Sport* pl. 55, 1; A, Neugebauer pl. 46; A, Blümel *Sport und Spiel* pl. 17, above; A, Blümel *S.H.* 26–27. I, satyr. A, athletes. B, youth with horses. On I, ΓΑΜΑΦ[Ι]Ο$, ΓΑΜΑ-ΦΙΟ$. On A, ΕΓΙΚΤΕΤΟ$. On B, ΕΛΡΑΦ$ΕΝ ΚΑΛΟ$. Now cleaned. For the shape, Bloesch 64, Pamphaios, iii, no. 11. See p. 1623.

16 (15). LONDON E 38, from Vulci. A, Micali *Storia* pl. 90, 1; I, Murray no. 23; FR. pl. 73, 2, whence Hoppin i, 313, Seltman pl. 12, (I) Buschor 157, (I and B) Swindler figs. 287 and 293; palmettes, Jacobsthal O. pl. 71, a; A and foot, Bloesch *FAS.* pl. 7, 4; I and A, Lane pl. 71; I, Nairn 63; A, *E.A.A.* ii, 226 fig. 340; A–B, ph. Ma. 3172. I, komos (girl dancing and youth playing the flute). A, Herakles and Busiris. B, symposion. On A, ΓΥΟΟΝΕΓΟΙΕ$ΕΝ. On B, ΕΓΙΚΤΕΤΟ$ ΕΛΡΑΦ$Ε[Ν]. Chalcicup (Bloesch 28 no. 13). See p. 1623.

17 (16). LONDON E 37, from Vulci. I, Murray no. 22; Hoppin i, 310–11; Pfuhl figs. 323–4; palmettes, Jacobsthal O. pl. 72, d; B, *Jb.* 44, 177–8; B, Bloesch *FAS.* pl. 17, 3; A–B, Lane pl. C; A–B, ph. Ma. 3171. I, symposion (man reclining, singing). A, Theseus and Minotaur. B, komos. On I, ΗΙΓΓΑΡ[+]Ο ΚΑΛ (not certain that the last letters of the words were ever written). On B, ΕΓΙΚΤΕΤΟ$ ΕΛΡΑ[Φ$]ΕΝ. On A, ΕΛΡΑΦ$ΕΝ. For the shape, Bloesch 64, Pamphaios, iv, no. 14.

18. GREIFSWALD 277, fr. Peters pl. 22. A, komos. [Langlotz].

19 (17). REGGIO C 1143, two frr., from Reggio. *Ausonia* 7, 173. A, Gigantomachy. B, (maenads). [Langlotz].

20 (18). ROME, Antiquarium Forense, fr., from Rome. *Nuova Antologia* 1900, 16, 1; *NSc.* 1900, 177 fig. 26; Ryberg pl. 15, 80a; *Bull. Arch. Com.* 76 pl. 14, 190. A, fight. See p. 1623.

21 (19). LOUVRE G 6, from Vulci. Hoppin i, 328–9; cleaned, *CV.* b pl. 10, 2–9 and pl. 11, 1; A–B, ph. Gir. 25775. I, youth seated playing the cithara. A, fight. B, maenads. On I, ΗΙΓΓΑΡ+Ο[$] ΚΑΛ[Ο]$. On A, [ΕΓ]ΙΚΤΕΤΟ$. On B, ΕΛΡΑΦ$[ΕΝ].

22 (20). FLORENCE 1 B 39, fr. *CV.* pl. 1 B 39. A, (maenad).

23. LOUVRE C 10472, fr. *CV.* b pl. 11, 5. A, (maenad). E . . .

24 (21). VILLA GIULIA 57912, from Cervetri. *Arti fig.* 2 pll. 1–8; phs. R.I. 57.684–6; detail of A, *E.A.A.* i, 280; A, Simon *G.A.* 75. I, naked woman riding a phallus-bird. A, Achilles and Memnon, with Psychostasia.

B, Herakles and Busiris. On I, HIΓΓAP+OϞ. On A, EΓIkTETOϞ. On B, EΛRAΦϞEN. See Ciotti in *Arti fig.* 2, 8–21; and, for the subject of A, CB. ii, 18, and iii, text.

25 (22). ATHENS Acr. 62, frr., from Athens. Langlotz pl. 4 and p. 6. I, maenad. A, (feet). Coral-red used. On I, [H]IΓΓAP+[O]Ϟ k[AL]O[Ϟ]. See the next.

26 (23). ATHENS Acr. 65, frr., from Athens. Langlotz pl. 4. A, Herakles and the lion. Coral-red used. On A, E[ΓIkTE]TOϞ . . . May belong to the last, as Kraiker suggests.

27 (24). VATICAN 506, from Vulci. *Mus. Greg.* 2 pl. 84, 2; A–B, phs. Al. 35827–8, whence (A) *AM.* 41 pl. 34, (B) *Jb.* 44, 189; I, Albizzati pl. 70. I, pyrrhic (pyrrhichist and flute-player). A, harnessing of chariot for Athena and Herakles. B, komos. On I, EΓOIEϞEN. On A, EΓOE[I]-EϞEN. On B, EΓOIEϞEN. Restored. For the shape, Bloesch 57 no. 2.

28 (25). ABERDEEN 744 and FLORENCE 1 B 29, from Vulci. Gerhard pl. 195–6; *Jb.* 44, 187 and 184–5; part of A, *JHS.* 51, 43; I, *Riv. Ist.* 7, 217; the Florence fr., *CV.* pl. 1, B 29, and *JHS.* 51, 41 fig. 2. I, satyr and fawn. A, Achilles and Ajax playing. B, komos. On I, EΓOIEϞEN. On A, HIΓΓAP+OϞ. On B, kALO[Ϟ]. Restored. See *JHS.* 51, 41–42 no. 8.

29 (26). NAPLES 2609. *PP.* pl. 8. I, warrior. A–B, symposion. On I, HIΓΓAP+OϞ kALOϞ. I is by Epiktetos; A–B are not by him, but in the manner of the Euergides Painter (p. 97 no. 2, where also the inscriptions): see *PP.* 28. For this collaboration compare Louvre G 16 (no. 13). Restored. For the shape, Bloesch 66 note 110.

30 (28). PALERMO V 653, from Chiusi. Part, *JHS.* 12 pl. 19 and p. 340; A–B, *CV.* pl. 5, 1–3; part, R.I. xxiii. 39; part, ph. R.I. 7319. I, warrior. A, Herakles and Eurytos. B, fight. On A, EΓOIEϞEN. On B, [EΓOI]-EϞEN. For the subjects, Hartwig in *JHS.* 12, 334–40. See p. 1623.

31 (29). FLORENCE 1 B 35 (part ex Villa Giulia) and BERLIN 2277. Part, *CV.* pl. 1, B 35; the Berlin fragment, *Jb.* 44, 190; I, *Boll. d'Arte* 29, 266 fig. 16. I, hoplite and archer. A, sacrifice. B, women (maenads?) celebrating. On I, EΓOIEϞ[EN]. On B, EΛ[PAΦϞEN].

32. OXFORD, Beazley, fr., from Italy. A, women celebrating (arm to right, upper part of woman to right, looking round; both hold the same objects—not krotala—as two of the women on B of Florence 1 B 35, no. 31). The interior, so far as preserved, is striped horizontally, recalling East Greek cups. [Marie Beazley].

33 (30). FLORENCE, fr. A, fight (middle of a fallen warrior, to left—right arm, part of corslet and of chitoniskos, scabbard).

34 (31). PROVIDENCE 25.077. *AJA.* 1928, 442–4; A–B, *CV.* pl. 14. I, satyr and maenad; A–B, Dionysos with satyrs and maenads.

35 (32). LONDON 1929.11–11.1, from Spina. *BMQ.* 4 no. 4, wrapper, and pl. 55; A, Bloesch *FAS*. pl. 36, 1. I, youth with spear (hunter?). A, Herakles and the Centaurs. B, fight. On I, ЕГΟΙЕЅЕ. On B, ЕГΟΙ-ЕЅΕΝ. For the shape, Bloesch 134 no. 1.

36 (33). LEIPSIC, frr., from Cervetri. *Anz.* 1952, 234. A–B, Herakles and Pholos. A small fragment in Boston, from Cervetri, probably belongs (fore-hooves, to right).

37 (34). Once MUNICH, Preyss, from Chiusi. I, cup-bearer at krater. A, fight. B, satyrs. On I, ΗΙГГΑΡ+ΟЅΚΑLΟЅ.

38 (36). LONDON E 35, from Vulci. I, Murray no. 20; I and part of A–B, *Jb.* 44, 182–3, 150, and 197 fig. 41. I, warrior with horse. A, between pegasi, fight. B, satyrs.

39 (35). PRINCETON 33.41. B, H. R. W. Smith *New Aspects* 55. I, satyr and maenad. A, komos (with naked women). B, fight. Now cleaned.

40 (37). MUNICH 2619. I, two warriors; A–B, fight. On I, Е[ГΟΙ]ЕЅΕΝ. Outside, on one of the shields, ΗΙГГ . . .

41 (38). PALERMO V 654, from Chiusi. Inghirami *Chius.* pll. 85–87; cleaned, *CV*. pl. 7, 1–4 and pl. 16, 1. I, two warriors. A, boxers. B, fight. On I, ЕГΟ[ΙЕЅΕΝ].

42 (39). Once AGRIGENTO, Politi, from Agrigento. Politi *Tazza dell' Amicizia* pll. 1–2, whence Inghirami pll. 259–61, (B) *El.* 1 pl. 47a, (B) *Jb.* 52, 207. I, maenad. A, Herakles in battle (at Troy?). B, return of Hephaistos.

43. GREIFSWALD 280. Peters pl. 25. I, satyr; A, Dionysos and satyrs. B, fight. On I, [Е]ГΙΚ[ΤΕΤΟ]Ѕ.

(nos. 44–53, fragments of interiors; not known if decorated outside; nos. 46, 47, 48, 51, were probably not)

44. NAPLES, Astarita, 572, two frr. I, komast or satyr (neck to waist, with left arm and right elbow). . . . Г . . .

45 (40). ATHENS, Agora NS, AP 1800 a and AP 1920 b, two frr., from Athens. *Hesp.* 9, 240, 261 a–b. I, archer.

46 (41). BOSTON 10.212, fr. *VA.* 15 fig. 9; CB. i pl. 3, 6, whence (redrawn) Richter *ARVS.* 43 fig. 12; Chase *Guide* 63. I, satyr kneeling, drinking.

47 (42). HEIDELBERG 16, fr. Kraiker pl. 3. I, naked woman squatting.

48 (43). ATHENS Acr. 63, fr., from Athens. Langlotz pl. 4. I, symposion (youth reclining). On I, . . . ЕΛΡΑ]ΟЅΕΝ.

49 (44). CAB. MÉD. 596, two frr. One, ph. Gir. 26420, left. I, symposion (man reclining). The other fr. has part of the mattress.

50 (45). ADRIA B 62, fr., from Adria. *CV*. pl. 1, 2. I, symposion (youth reclining). Does not Adria Bc 1 (*CV*. pl. 1, 4) join B 62?

51. AEGINA, fr., from Aegina. Furtwängler *Aegina* pl. 130, i; ph. R.I. 33.244. I, Athena.

52 (46). ATHENS Acr. 70, fr., from Athens. Langlotz pl. 4. I, maenad.

53. ATHENS Acr., fr., from Athens. I, (feet of one standing to left, with part of the line-border).

(nos. 54–83, decorated inside only)

54 (47). Once PARIS, Pourtalès, from Vulci. Panofka *Pourt.* pl. 41, below, whence Hoppin i, 338. I, komast. ΕΓΙΚΤΕΤΟⳞ ΕΛΡΑⳞΦΕΝ. Restored.

55 (48). FERRARA, Museo Schifanoia, 270. *Boll. d'Arte* 5, 342, whence *AJA.* 1912, 271, Hoppin i, 307, *Anz.* 1923–4, 169. I, komast. ΕΓΙΚΤΕΤΟⳞ ΕΛΡΑΦⳞΕΝ. For the shape, Bloesch 64, Pamphaios, iii, no. 9. Restored.

56 (49). BALTIMORE, from Chiusi? *Jb.* 6 pl. 5, 1, whence HM. pl. 9, 1 and Buschor *Satyrtänze* fig. 42; *VA.* 15 fig. 7, whence Hoppin i, 301; *CV.* Robinson ii pl. 1, 3 and pl. 2, 3; *Journ. Walt.* 1, 29 fig. 6. I, satyr reclining, drinking from a pointed amphora. ΕΓΙΚΤΕΤΟⳞ ΕΛΡΑΦⳞ[Ε]Ν. Slightly restored.

57 (50). LONDON E 24, from Nola? Cecil Smith pl. 6, 1, whence Perrot 10, 360; *VA.* 15 fig. 8; Hoppin i, 309, whence LS. fig. 47; Pfuhl fig. 327. I, satyr kneeling, with wine-skin. ΕΓΙΚΤΕΤΟⳞΕΛΡΑΦⳞΕΝ. For the shape, Bloesch 120 no. 9.

58 (51). ROME, Torlonia, from Vulci. *Jb.* 6 pl. 5, 2, whence Hoppin i, 333. I, komast (balancing a skyphos on his thigh). ΕΓ[ΙΚ]ΤΕΤΟⳞ ΕΛΡΑΦⳞΕΝ.

59 (52). COPENHAGEN 119, from Greece. *Ber. Sächs.* 1867 pl. 5, 1; *VA.* 17; Langlotz *GV.* pl. 3, 5, whence Frel *Ř.V.* fig. 152; *CV.* pl. 139, 2, whence Blümel *Gr. Bildhauer an der Arbeit*, ftisp., 1; Cloché *Classes* pl. 27, 1; *Antik-Cab. 1851* 163; Breitenstein *G.V.* pl. 26. I, hermoglyph. ΗΙΓΑΡ+ΟⳞΚΑᏞΟⳞ. [Klein]. See p. 1623.

60 (53). LENINGRAD inv. 14611, from Berezan. Vorberg *Ars erot.* pl. 21; *Jb.* 44, 173; Vorberg *Gloss.* 411. I, μιλησιάζουσα: naked woman using olisboi. ΗΙΓΑΡ+ΟⳞΚΑ[ᏞΟⳞ].

61 (54). ADRIA Bc 54 and B 272, fr., from Adria. Schöne pl. 7, 1; part, *CV.* pl. 1, 3; part, *Riv. Ist.* N.S. 5–6, 31 fig. 1. I, Hermes. +ΑΙΡΙΓΟⳞ Κ[ΑᏞΟⳞ].

62 (55). ATHENS Acr. 68, from Athens. Benndorf pl. 12, 2, whence *WV.* 3 pl. 2, 4; Langlotz pl. 4. I, Minotaur. ΕΓꞋΟΕΙ, but doubtful if the second letter is a pi, more like a nu.

63 (57). CAB. MÉD. 517 *bis*, 516, and another, fr. Ph. Gir. 26420, right. I, youth and naked boy (trainer and athlete?).

64 (58). BOSTON 95. 34, from Italy. Klein *L.* 62; *Jb.* 44, 179; CB. i pl. 3, 5. I, satyr bestriding a wineskin. ΗΙΓΓΑΡ+ΟⳞΚΑᏞΟⳞ. On the skin, ΗΙΓΓᏞΟ+ΟⳞ.

65 (59). TARQUINIA RC 1091, from Tarquinia. *RM.* 5, 340, whence HM. pl. 9, 2; *CV.* pl. 10, 3. I, satyr with wineskin. EΓOIEϟENO+ On the skin, EΓOIEϟ complete.

66. NAPLES, Astarita, 514, fr. I, satyr (left shoulder, part of head and of tail; running to right, looking round). [EΓO]IEϟEN. [Astarita].

67. GENEVA, private. *Auktion xxii Basel* pl. 48, 156. I, satyr (squatting frontal, head to right, horn in right hand). EΓOIEϟEN. [Bothmer].

68 (60). FLORENCE 5 B 4, frr. Part, *CV.* pl. 5, B 4. I, naked youth sitting (balancing himself) on a pointed amphora. [EΓO]IEϟEN. For the subject, CB. ii, 26.

69 (61). NEW YORK 41.162.112. *CV.* Gallatin pl. 47, 4 and pl. 61, 7; Richter *ARVS.* 42. I, warrior. EΓOIEϟEN. [Gallatin].

70 (62). OXFORD, Beazley (ex Arndt), from Orvieto. *Jb.* 44, 191. I, man playing with naked woman. [E]ΓOI[E]ϟEN.

71 (63). Once MUNICH, Preyss. *Jb.* 44, 193. I, komast.

72 (63 *bis*). WASHINGTON 136.380. I, komast. HIΓΓAP+Oϟ[κ]ALO[ϟ].

73 (64). TARQUINIA RC 191, from Tarquinia. *Jb.* 44, 195. I, warrior.

74 (65). BOSTON 01.8074, from Locris. *Jb.* 44, 196; CB. i pl. 3, a and p. 7 fig. 6; the shape, Caskey G. 183 no. 138. I, archer. For the shape, Bloesch 124 no. 18.

75 (66). BALTIMORE, fr., from Chiusi. *JHS.* 12, 347, whence *Mon. Piot* 20, 144; *CV.* Robinson pl. 1, 2. I, komast. EΓOIEϟEN.

76 (67). VILLA GIULIA and HEIDELBERG 17. The Heidelberg fr., Kraiker pl. 4. I, youth grooming horse. EΓOIEϟE[N]. The Villa Giulia fr. gives the greater part of horse and youth.

77 (68). VILLA GIULIA (ex Canino, *Mus. etr.* 1824) from Vulci. I, μιλησι-άζουσα: naked woman using an olisbos. EΓOIEϟEN.

78 (69). BERLIN inv. 4514. *Jb.* 44, 197 fig. 40; A, Bloesch *FAS.* pl. 34, 4. I, satyr. ELPAΦϟEN complete. For the shape, Bloesch 124 no. 19.

79. LOUVRE C 10473. *CV.* b pl. 12, 1. I, komast (or hunter?).

80. ATHENS, Agora, P 24131, from Athens. *Hesp.* 24 pl. 28, d, and p. 65 fig. 3. I, naked woman about to wash (holding a pair of boots). HIΓAP-+Oϟ κALOϟ. [Talcott].

81. ATHENS, Agora, P 24114, from Athens. I, satyr on donkey. EΓOIEϟEN. [Talcott, Philippaki].

82. ATHENS, Agora, P 24110, from Athens. I, boxers. EΓOIEϟEN. [Talcott, Philippaki].

83 (56). Once CANINO (*Mus. etr.* 793), from Vulci. B.Ap. xvi. 10. 3. I, athlete (running with acontia). EΓOIEϟEN.

CUP-SKYPHOI

84 (70). OXFORD 520. A, Panofka *Pourt.* pl. 34, 2; *JHS.* 24, 306; *CV.* pl.

41, 9–10; A, Richter and Milne 7; A. Sparkes, Talcott, and Frantz fig. 17. A, cup-bearers at the krater. B, boy with horses. Restored. Latish.

85 (71). NAPLES, Racc. Porn. 1 (Heydemann p. 620), from Anzi. B, Licht iii, 213; B, Vorberg *Gloss.* 599. A, satyrs and maenad; B, maenad and donkey. Now cleaned. Latish.

SKYPHOS
(shape B, but both handles upright)

86 (72). LONDON E 139, from Capua. Hoppin i, 319; *CV.* pl. 28, 1. A, Dionysos and satyr with donkey; B, satyr with donkeys. On A, [E]ΓΙ-ΚΤΕΤΟ$ ΕΛΡΑΦ$ΕΝ. On B, ΓΙ$[Τ]Ο$+ΕΝΟ$ ΕΓΟ[Ι]Ε$Ε[Ν]. Now cleaned.

KANTHAROI
(no. 87, the exact shape uncertain: perhaps like the Nikosthenes kantharoi Boston 00.334, p. 126, no. 27, and London E 154, p. 127, no. 28)

87 (73). ODESSA, fr., from Leuke. *Zap. Od.* 16 pl. 2, 3, whence *WV.* 1890–1 pl. 7, 3, whence Hoppin i, 321. Komos. [Ν]ΙΚΟ$ΘΕΝΕ[$] ΕΓΟΙ-Ε$[ΕΝ], ΕΓΙΚΤΕΤ[Ο$ . . . . Early.

(no. 88, type A)

88 (74). ATHENS Acr. 553, frr., from Athens. Langlotz p. 50. (Feet). . . . I . . ., . . . ΕΓΟΙΕ . . ., ΕΓ[ΙΚ]ΤΕ[ΤΟ$ . . .

OINOCHOE
(shape 8 A, mug)

89 (85). ORVIETO, Faina, 148, from Orvieto. Satyrs reclining. See p. 152.

CALYX-KRATER

90 (86). VILLA GIULIA, from Cervetri. *ML.* 42, 889–90. A, komos. B, Dionysos and maenads. On A, incised, ΕΓΙΚΤΕ[ΤΟ$Ε]ΛΡΑ$ΦΕΝ. Incised on the foot, [ΑΝΔΟ]ΚΙΔΕ$ΕΓΟΕ complete aft. Early. Ricci (*ML.* 42, 891) rejects the signature of Epiktetos and is reminded of Psiax: I think the drawing is by Epiktetos, although there are certainly resemblances to Psiax; compare also the Brachas vase (p. 9).

PLATES
(nos. 91–101 are early)

91 (75). CAB. MÉD. 509, from Vulci. Hoppin i, 324; Langlotz *GV.* pl. 5, 10; phs. Gir. 8056, 2 and 19298, 1, whence Buschor G. *Vasen* 139. Satyr. ΕΓΙΚΤΕΤΟ$ ΕΛΡΑΦ$ΕΝ.

92 (76). CASTLE ASHBY, Northampton, 79, from Vulci. *Burl. 1888* pl. 19; *Burl. 1903* pl. 96, I 79; Hoppin i, 306; *BSR.* 11 pl. 4, 4, whence Richter *ARVS.* fig. 37. Boy riding cock. ΕΓΙΚΤΕΤΟ$ ΕΛΡΑ$ΦΕΝ. A little boy rides a cock on an oinochoe (shape 3, chous) in Istanbul, inv. 2493.

93 (77). LONDON E 135, from Vulci. Walters *H.A.P.* 1 pl. 37, 2; Hoppin i, 314; Herford pl. 3, c; *Jb.* 44, 165; Lane pl. 70, a; ph. Ma. 3209, middle. Archer. ΕΓΙΚΤΕΤΟϟ ΕΛΡΑϟΦΕΝ. See p. 1623.

94 (78). LONDON E 136, from Vulci. *VA.* 18; Hoppin i, 315; Pfuhl fig. 328 (= Pfuhl *Mast.* fig. 31); Seltman pl. 13, a; *Journ. Walt.* 1, 29 fig. 7; Richter *H.G.A.* 326 fig. 439; ph. Ma. 3209, right. Warrior with horse. ΕΓΙΚΤΕΤΟϟ ΕΛΡΑϟΦΕΝ.

95 (79). LONDON E 137, from Vulci. Cecil Smith pl. 6, 2; Hoppin i, 317, whence LS. fig. 48; *Burl. Mag.* 1921, 231, b; Langlotz *G.V.* pl. 2, 4; Pfuhl fig. 329; Seltman pl. 13, b; *Jb.* 44, 169; Schoenebeck and Kraiker pl. 82, 1; ph. Ma. 3209, left. Two komasts. ΕΓΙΚΤΕΤΟϟ ΕΛΡΑϟΦΕΝ.

96 (80). CAB. MÉD. 510, from Vulci. Hoppin i, 325, whence LS. fig. 46; Pfuhl fig. 325 (= Pfuhl *Mast.* fig. 30); ph. Gir. 8056, 1 and 19298, 2; ph. Arch. phot. BAA 194. Komast. ΕΓΙΚΤΕΤΟϟ ΕΛΡΑϟΦΕΝ.

97 (81). LOUVRE G 7, from Vulci. Pottier pl. 89, whence Perrot 10, 363; Hoppin i, 330; Langlotz *G.V.* pl. 2, 3; Schaal *Rf.* fig. 6; ph. Al. 23733, 1, whence *Arch. class.* 2 pl. 9, 2; *CV.* b pl. 12, 2-6; Villard *GV.* pl. 19, 2. Victor and trainer. ΕΓΙΚΤΕΤΟϟ ΕΛΡΑϟΦΕΝ. See p. 1623.

98 (82). Once ROME, Braun (ex Civitavecchia, Bucci). *Jb.* 44, 159. Dionysos and satyr. ΕΓΙΚΤΕΤΟϟ ΕΛΡΑϟΦΕΝ.

99 (83). VILLA GIULIA, fr. *AJA.* 1935, 480 fig. 5. (Hand—of one dancing?). [ΕΓ]ΙΚΤ[ΕΤΟϟ ...

100. ATHENS Acr., fr., from Athens. (On the left, rear foot of one draped, moving to right, on a ground-line).

101. OXFORD 1929.165. fr. *CV.* pl. 57, 3. Satyr reclining.

102 (84). ATHENS Acr. 6, frr., from Athens. Langlotz pl. 2. Athena. [Ε]ΓΙΚΤΕΤΟϟΕΓΟ[ΙΕϟΕΝ], [ΕΓΙΚΤΕΤΟϟΕΛΡ]ΑΦϟΕΝ.

A cup seemed, through the glass, to be by Epiktetos:

ROME, Torlonia, 158, from Vulci. I, bf., stag. A–B, between eyes. A, jumper (athlete bending with haltēres). B, nose. On I, [ΗΙϟ+Ѵ]ᄂΟϟ ΕΓΟΙΕϟΕ[Ν]. See p. 45 no. 104.

Two scraps of cups are in the manner of Epiktetos and probably from his hand:

CHICAGO, Univ., fr. *AJA.* 1938, 348 fig. 4. A, komos or love-making (parts of a naked woman and of a lampstand are preserved). . . . ΕΛ]ΡΑΦ[ϟΕΝ].

LENINGRAD, fr., from Berezan. A, (head and shoulders of an archer to left).

Another scrap of a cup is contemporary with early Epiktetos, and the letters might be part of his signature:

LEIPSIC T 3770, fr. A, (fingers holding a drinking-horn?) ... TE ...

VASES SIGNED BY EPIKTETOS, UNPUBLISHED AND LOST

CUP

1. Once Magnoncourt 34 (ex Canino *Mus. etr.* no. 1115), from Vulci. I, μιλησιάζουσα (woman using olisboi). A, Herakles and the Centaurs. B, Dionysos reclining, with satyrs. On I, ΕΠΙΚΤΕΤΟΣ ΕΛΡΑΣΦΕΝ. On A, ΗΙΣ+VLΟΣ ΕΠΟΙΕΣΕΝ. No doubt early.

PLATE

2. Once LONDON, Rogers 446 (ex Campanari: bought by David Falcke). χέζων?, assisted by a woman. ΕΠΙΚΤΕΤΟΣ ΕΛΡΑΣΦΕΝ.

MANNER OF EPIKTETOS

CUPS

(nos. 1–7, decorated outside as well as in)

1 (i 2). LENINGRAD inv. 103 n, from South Russia, fr. A, komos (youth to right, bending, holding a drinking-horn, then a hand to left). Early.

2 (i 1). FLORENCE 4 B 4, fr. *CV.* pl. 4, B 4. A, (male with horse). ΕΠΟ ... Early.

3 (iii 4). VILLA GIULIA (part ex Florence). Part, *CV.* Fl. pl. 4, B 1. I is lost. A, between pegasi, maenads. B, between pegasi, fight. On B, [ΕΠΟΙ-Ε]ΣΕ[Ν]. Late.

4 (iii 3). VILLA GIULIA, from Falerii. I, komast (moving to right, looking round, with wineskin). A, Dionysos reclining, with satyrs. B, four warriors. On I, ΕΠΟΙΕΣΕΝ. Late.

5. LOUVRE C 10471, fr. *CV.* b pl. 11, 4. A, boxers. Late.

6 (iii 10). NAPLES 2614, from Etruria. *Mus. Borb.* 14 pl. 29; I, Vorberg *Gloss.* 417. I, man courting boy. A, between sphinxes, Herakles and the lion. B, between sphinxes, fight. On I, ΕΠΟΙΕΣΕΝ. Restored. For the subject of I, *Cypr.* 29, α 49; for the shape, Bloesch 57 no. 1. Late.

7 (iii 11). ATHENS Acr. 170, fr., from Athens. A, Herakles and the lion? (what remains is head and left arm of Athena holding spear and helmet: compare Naples 2614, no. 6). Late.

(nos. 8–10, not known whether decorated outside)

8 (iii 2). FLORENCE, fr. I, warrior. What remains is, on the left, part of the shield (device a satyr's head in outline, as on Tarquinia RC 191, p. 76 no. 73) and of the spear, with the letter ... Α ...

9 (iii 1). Villa Giulia, fr. I, warrior. What remains is, on the left, part of the shield, device as in the last, and the letter . . . E . . .

10 (iii 6). Athens Acr. 71, fr., from Athens. Langlotz pl. 4. I, woman dancing. Late.

(*nos. 11–14, decorated inside only*)

11 (ii 1). Rhodes 13352, from Camiros. *Cl.Rh.* 4, 291; *CV.* pl. 6, 2 and 5. I, athlete using pick. HIΓΓAP+O$. Close to the slighter cups of the painter himself. See p. 1624.

12 (iii 16). Athens 17303, from Greece. *CV.* pl. 11, 1–2. I, naked man assaulting a naked woman. Compare the Princeton cup (p. 74 no. 39).

13 (iii 13). Villa Giulia 47233, from Cervetri. I, woman lifting something (a hydria?). EΓOIE$EN, EΛP[AⵔSE]N.

14 (iii 14). Villa Giulia. I, woman (maenad?) running (to right, looking round: chiton, pelt, saccos). [HOΓ]AI[$] KΛVO$.

The following bear some resemblance to Epiktetos:

CUPS

(*nos. 1–2, decorated inside as well as out*)

1 (iii 12). Athens Acr. 75, frr., from Athens. Part, Langlotz pl. 5. I, owl. A, Achilles and Ajax playing?; B, warriors setting off. For the satyr-head shield-device compare especially Tarquinia RC 191 (p. 76 no. 73).

2 (iii 9). Louvre G 94 *bis*. I, jumper. A–B, Dionysos seated, with maenads and satyrs. The outside is near Epiktetos, the inside not, but they are by the same hand. Coarse. See p. 1624.

(*no. 3, decorated inside only*)

3 (iii 15). Villa Giulia 30284, from Leprignano. I, warrior (naked, helmeted, running to left with spear and shield).

THE GROUP OF LONDON E 33

These coarse imitations of late Epiktetos may be by one hand. They recall the Aktorione Painter (p. 137). See p. 1624.

CUPS

1 (iii 5). London E 33, from Vulci. I, Murray no. 19; I and one figure from B, *Jb.* 44, 192; A and foot, Bloesch *FAS.* pl. 17, 4. I, archer. A, fight. B, komos. On I, EΓOIE$EN. On A, EΓOIE$EN. On B, [EΓOI]-E$EN. For the shape, Bloesch 65, Pamphaios iv, no. 22.

2 (iii 8). Naples 2630. I, youth in vat. A–B, komos. For the shape, Bloesch 56 no. 3.

3 (iii 7). LOUVRE G 40. I, Pottier pl. 91. I, symposion (youth reclining). A, fight? (three males, one striding to right, the second fallen to left, the third striding to left). B, (on the left, two feet remain). On I, ΕΠΟΙΕϟΕΝ. For the shape, Bloesch 43.

Near these the

CUP

ATHENS 1568 (CC. 1165). I, satyr (with pelta and thyrsus). A, satyrs and maenads. B, fight.

THE THALIARCHOS PAINTER

BSR. 11, 17; *ARV.*¹ 53–54.

Four little boxes related to Epiktetos.

PYXIDES
(*shape D*)

1 (1). PARIS, Petit Palais, 382, from Athens. Klein *L.* 88 = Fröhner *Brant.* pl. 5, whence Perrot 10, 682; *CV.* pl. 21, 1–2. Helmet-maker. ⊙ΑLΙ-ΑΡ+Οϟ ΚΑLΟϟ.

2 (2). ATHENS Acr. 574, fr., from Athens. Langlotz pl. 44. Satyr. ⊙ΑLΙ-Α[Ρ+Οϟ ΚΑLΟϟ].

3 (3). ATHENS 1710 (CC. 1600), from Megara. Heydemann pl. 4, 2, whence Klein *Euphr.* 313. Komast. LVϟΙΚLΕϟΚΑLΟϟ.

4 (4). NEW YORK 20.253, from Greece. Richter and Milne fig. 143; Richter and Hall pl. 9, 4 and pl. 178, 4. Squatting satyr. LΙϟΙΚLΕϟΚΑLΟϟ.

The following may perhaps be compared:

PYXIDES
(*type D*)

BOSTON 10.216, fr., from Athens. *Strena Helb.* 92, whence Pfuhl fig. 387, *Dedalo* 7, 406, and *E.A.A.* ii, 342. Dwarf squatting (χέζων?).

BONN, Langlotz. Head of Athena.

CHAPTER 6

SKYTHES

SKYTHES

Mon. Piot 9, 135–78, and 10, 49–54 (Pottier). Pottier *Cat. des vases du Louvre* 3, 891–5. FR. ii, 182–5 (Furtwängler). *Mon. Piot* 20, 101–53 (Rizzo). *Anz.* 1914, 87–90 (Rodenwaldt). *Jb.* 30, 36–40 (Buschor). *VA.* 21–22. Langlotz *Z.* 115–16. *Att. V.* 39–43 and 468. *ARV.*¹ 73–76. *Bull. Ont.* June 1957, 14–16 (Graham); CB. iii, text.

Four cups bear the signature of the painter Skythes: Villa Giulia (no. 1); Louvre S 1335 (no. 4); Villa Giulia 20760 (no. 14); Louvre G 124 (no. 17). Fragments of a fifth are signed, but the name is now missing: Berlin 4041.1 (no. 10). The artist's favourite kalos-name is Epilykos; and Louvre G 10 (no. 3), which is certainly by Skythes, has the misleading inscription ΕΠΙΛѴΚΟ[ЅΕΛΡΑΦ]ЅΕΝΚΑLΟЅ. Another cup by Skythes, in Villa Giulia and Toronto (no. 8) is similarly inscribed— . . . ЅΚΑLΟЅ ΕΛ[ΡΑΦ]ЅΕΝ.

Doubtful if the Skythes whose signature appears on two black-figure plaques is ours; or even if the two plaques are by the same hand: see *ABV.* 352.

Pottier put Louvre G 10, Berlin 4041.1, and Louvre G 10 *bis* together as signed works of 'Epilykos'; added Louvre CA 1527, Cambridge 70, and part of Louvre G 12 as 'from the same workshop' and Boston 10.198 and 10.201 as 'affiliated'.

Furtwängler saw that Louvre CA 1527, Louvre F 129, Palermo V 651, part of Louvre G 12, and the two Boston cups were by the same hand as Louvre G 10, Berlin 4041.1, Louvre G 10 *bis*.

When Villa Giulia 20760 was found, Rizzo attributed Louvre CA 1527, Boston 10.198, Louvre F 129, Cambridge 70 to Skythes.

Rodenwaldt saw that the fragmentary signature on Berlin 4041.1 was probably that of Skythes.

Buschor saw that Louvre G 10 *bis* was signed by Skythes; and denied the existence of a painter 'Epilykos'.

The order of the list that follows is chronological as far as possible.

CUPS

1 (1). VILLA GIULIA, from Cervetri. I, warrior. A, Herakles and Eurystheus. B, athletes. On B, [ЅΚѴ]ΟΕЅΜ[Ε]ΛΡΑΦЅ[ΕΝ]. Very early.

2 (2). MUNICH inv. 8709 (ex Curtius), fr. *Anz.* 1957, 378; ph. R.I. 1935. 2046. I, cup-bearer or komast (balancing a vessel on his foot). Cup-foot of type C.

3 (3). LOUVRE G 10. I, Pottier pl. 89, whence Perrot 10, 367; I, *Mon. Piot* 9, 155; I (cleaned), *Jb.* 30, 38; I, Hoppin i, 343; (cleaned), *CV.* b pl. 13, 1–2 and pl. 14, 1. I, Hermes. A, Herakles and Acheloos. B is lost. On I, ΕΠΙLVΚΟ[ϟΕΛΡΑΦ]ϟΕΝΚΑLΟϟ.

4 (4, 12, +). LOUVRE S 1335. I and A, *CV.* b pl. 13, 3–4. I, komast; A, komos. B, (satyr? and maenad?) On I, ϟΚVΦ[ΕϟΕ]ΛΡΑΦ[ϟΕΝ]. On A, ΕΠ[ΙLVΚΟ]ϟΚΑ[LΟϟ]. The man on A is not a satyr, but the woman is a maenad. Three loose frr. of B. remain: one has the middle of a maenad running to left (and looking round), then the butt of a pine-branch held by the next person; the second has the middle of a naked male to left; the third, part of a handle-palmette.

5. LOUVRE, fr. Outside, (buttocks and arm of a naked male to left, with the small of his back). Belongs to the last, to the male on B?

6. LOUVRE C 10474, fr. *CV.* b pl. 16, 4. I, komast.

7 (5). ATHENS Acr. 249, fr., from Athens. Langlotz pl. 13. I, discus-thrower.

8 (6, +). VILLA GIULIA, and TORONTO 923.13.11. *Bull. Ont.* June 1957 pl. 6, a–c. I, komast. The Toronto fragment attributed to Skythes by Graham. ... ϟΚΑLΟϟ ΕΛ[ΡΑΦ]ϟΕΝ.

9 (7). LOUVRE CA 2997, from Tanagra? *CV.* b pl. 13, 5 and pl. 14, 2. I, youth with cup and wineskin. ΕΠΙLVΚΟϟΚΑLΟϟ. [Plaoutine]. Decorated inside only.

10 (8). BERLIN 4041.1, frr., from Vulci. *AZ.* 1884 pl. 17, 1, whence Hoppin ii, 411 and (part) FR. ii, 182; *Anz.* 1914, 87–90. A, athletes and youths. B, komos. On A, ... ϟΕΝ, ΕΠ[Ι]LV[ΚΟϟ]. On B, ... ΕΛΡΑ]ΦϟΕΝ. [Pottier; Rodenwaldt].

11 (9). BERLIN 4041.2, frr., from Vulci. *AZ.* 1884 pl. 17, 2. A, (satyr). B, (discus-thrower).

12 (10). LOUVRE CA 1527, from Tanagra. *Mon. Piot* 10, 50; *Mon. Piot* 20 pl. 7, 2, whence Pfuhl fig. 335 (= Pfuhl *Mast.* fig. 34), Langlotz *G.V.* pl. 5, 9, Seltman pl. 13, c, Rumpf *MZ.* pl. 21, 3; *CV.* b pl. 13, 6 and pl. 14, 3; ph. Arch. Phot. MNLA 692. I, warrior running. ΕΠΙLVΚΟϟΚ[ΑLΟϟ]. [Pottier; Furtwängler; Rizzo]. Decorated inside only.

13 (11). ATHENS 16269. I, warrior (moving to right, with spear and shield). Decorated inside only.

14 (13). VILLA GIULIA 20760, from Cervetri. *Mon. Piot* 20 pl. 6, pl. 7, 1, and pp. 103–4, whence Perrot 10, 580–1, Hoppin ii, 412–13, (part) Pfuhl figs. 333–4 (fig. 334 and part of 333 = Pfuhl *Mast.* figs. 32–33) (whence, A, Frel *Ř.V.* fig. 156), Swindler figs. 285 and 281, (I) Buschor 156, (part of I, redrawn) Richter *ARVS.* 39 fig. 6; I, *Dedalo* 3, 74; *CV.* pl. 23, pl. 25, 1, pl. 26, 1, and pl. 27; *St. etr.* 1 pl. 35, b; I, Buschor *G.Vasen* 138; I, *ML.* 42, 252; I, Vighi 96; phs. R.I. 57.675–7. I, komast. A, Theseus and the sow; B, Theseus attacking a youth. On I, ϟΚVΦΕϟ ΕΛΡΑΦϟΕΝ. On

A, ΕΠΙLVΚΟ$ ΚΑLΟ$. On B, ΚΑLΟ$. For the shape, Bloesch 120 no. 10.

15 (14). ATHENS, Agora, P 7823, frr., from Athens. A, komos. On A, [ΕΠΙLV]ΚΟ$ ΚΑLΟ$.

16 (23, 24, 25, +). LOUVRE G 76. One fr. of B (G 76), Pottier pl. 97, whence *Jb.* 31, 159 fig. 29; incompletely, *CV.* b pl. 16, 1–3 and 5. I, satyr. A, hoplitodromoi. B, komos (filling the cups). On I, ΚΑ[LΟ$] [Ε]ΠΙLV-ΚΟ$. On A, ... ΚΑLΟ$. On B, a kappa remains. Of the unpublished sherds, one joins A, adding the left shank and foot of the leading youth, the other (S 1340, no. 24 in *ARV.*[1]) does not join, but gives head and chest of the left-hand reveller on B, a bald man looking round to right and holding a cup in his raised right hand.

17 (15, 16, +). LOUVRE G 12. One fr. of B (G 10 *bis*), FR. ii, 183, whence Perrot 10, 583 and Hoppin i, 344, also *Mon. Piot* 20, 123; *CV.* b pl. 14, 4–5 and 7 and pl. 15, 1 and 3–4. I, youth putting on his greaves. A–B, komos: A, Anacreon and his companions; B, filling the cups. On I, ΕΠΙLVΚΟ$ ΚΑLΟ$. On A, ... Ε$. On B, ΕΠΙLVΚΟ$ ΚΑLΟ$, $ΚVΦΕ$ [ΕΛ]RAΦ[$ΕΝ]. The persons in the fragmentary picture B, who wear long chitons, are probably 'Anacreon and his companions' rather than women (see CB. ii, 55–61).

18 (17). ATHENS Acr. 82, two frr., from Athens. One fr., Langlotz pl. 7. A, komos.

18 *bis.* NEW YORK, Love, fr. I, komast? (head, to left, of youth, with his right shoulder and extended upper arm, and his left shoulder with a wrap over it). ΙΚΑ ... retr. [Bothmer].

18 *ter.* SYDNEY, Cambitoglou, fr. *Hesp. Art Bull.* 12, 8. I, man (satyr?) frontal, with frontal face, in or behind a large vessel, on which his right hand is laid. Foot type C.

19 (18). BOSTON 10.198, from Cervetri. Part, *Mon. Piot* 9, 161–2; I, *Mon. Piot* 20 pl. 8, 1; I, *MFA. Bull.* 9, 52; augmented by frr. ex Leipsic (identified by Langlotz) and Oxford, CB. iii pl. 69, 119. I, sphinx. A, Dionysos and satyr. B, komos. At each handle, pegasi. On I, Ε[Π]ΙLVΚ[Ο$] ΚΑLΟ$. [Furtwängler; Rizzo]. See CB. iii, text.

20 (19). LOUVRE F 129. I, Pottier pl. 73; I, *Mon. Piot* 9, 157 = *Mon. Piot* 20, 124 and Perrot 10, 279; A–B, *Mon. Piot* 9, 158, whence (A) Perrot 10, 278 and Pfuhl fig. 271; I, *Mon. Piot* 20, 125; I, *BSA.* 46 pl. 16, b; *CV.* b pl. 14, 6 and 8 and pl. 15, 2 and 5–7. I, komast balancing a pointed amphora on his foot. A–B, coral-red; in bf. on a coral-red background, A, Herakles, B, Kyknos. The meander below is on a reserved ground. The inside is also coral-red except the tondo. On I, [Ε]ΠΙLVΚΟ$ ΚΑLΟ$. [Furtwängler; Rizzo]. Great part of B is modern. For the shape, Bloesch 59 no. 3. As Palermo V 651 (no. 21).

21 (20). PALERMO V 651, from Chiusi. I and A, *Mon. Piot* 9, 159, whence (I) Vorberg *Gloss.* 322; *CV.* pl. 4 (misprinted 3), 1–3. I, satyr violating a pointed amphora. A–B, coral-red; in bf. on a coral ground, A, Nike, B, the like. The key-pattern below is on a reserved ground. The inside is also coral-red except the tondo. On I, [ΕΓΙLV]ΚΟ$ ΚΑLΟ$. [Furtwängler; Buschor]. For the shape, Bloesch 60 no. 2. As Louvre F 129 (no. 20).

22 (21). BOSTON 10.201, frr., from Italy. *Mon. Piot* 9, 167; CB. iii pl. 69, 120. I, satyr and maenad. ΕΓΙLVΚΟ[$]. [Furtwängler; Buschor]. See CB. iii, text.

23 (22). CAMBRIDGE 70, fr., from Vulci. Hartwig 97; E. Gardner pl. 26; *Mon. Piot* 20, 135; *CV.* pl. 25, 1. I, youth running with helmet and shield. ΚΡΑΤΕ$ ΚΑLΟ$. Only the tondo is ancient. [Pottier; Rizzo].

STANDLETS OF SOSIAN TYPE

24 (26). VILLA GIULIA, from Cervetri. Symposion (youth reclining). ΕΓΙLVΚΟ$ΚΑLΟ$.

25. BASLE, Cahn, 25. Woman dancing. ΕΓΙLVΚΟ$ΚΑLΟ$. [Hecht].

The Villa Giulia standlet (no. 24) is of the usual model, but there is only one other standlet of the same model as no. 25, and it has the same border of esses; the very little that remains of the picture is compatible with an ascription to Skythes, and it would be a signed piece:

ATHENS Acr. AP 281, fr., from Athens. *Hesp.* 4, 287, 159. Woman holding a sprig, . . . EN.

THE PEDIEUS PAINTER

ARV.[1] 76–77 and 950.

Called after the kalos-name on nos. 2, 4, and 5.

These cups, especially no. 1, are close to Skythes, and are perhaps late works of his. Louvre CA 581 and Berlin inv. 4855 were attributed to Skythes by Rizzo, Leipsic T 3363 by Langlotz.

1 (1). LOUVRE G 14. Part, *Mon. Piot* 9, 163–5, whence (details of A–B) Pfuhl figs. 336–7, and (detail of A) *Mon. Piot* 20, 139 fig. 15, below; B, Sudhoff i, 56; *CV.* b pl. 17, 1–4 and 7. I, warrior. A–B, naked women: A, sporting with a phallus or phallus-bird; B, washing. On I, ΕΓΙ[LV-ΚΟ$] ΚΑLΟ$. On A, ΕΓΙLVΚΟ$ ΚΑ[LΟ$]. On B, ΚΑ[LΟ]$, ΚΑLΟ$, and on the laver ΚΑLΟ$.

2 (2). LOUVRE CA 581, from Thebes. *Mon. Piot* 9, 175; *Mon. Piot* 20, 136; *CV.* b pl. 17, 5–6. I, woman dancing (or dancing along). ΓΕΔΙFV$ ΚΑLΟ$. Decorated inside only.

3 (3). LEIPSIC T 3363, fr., from Cervetri. I, boy picking up a pointed amphora. A, athletes; B, (foot, heel).

4 (4). TARQUINIA RC 5292, from Tarquinia. I, and detail of A, *Mon. Piot* 20, 138 and 139, 1; I, *RA.* 1918, ii, 51; *Annuario* 4–5, 121–3; I and A, *CV.* pl. 22, 3–4; I and A, phs. Mo. 8304 (8657) and 8661; I and A, phs. R.I. 34. 1880–2. I, horseman; A–B, horse-race. On I, ΓΕΔΙΕΝΣ ΚΑΛΟΣ. On A, ΓΕΔΙΕΝΣ ΚΑΛΟΣ ΚΑΛΟΣ. On B, the like.

5 (5). BERLIN inv. 4855, from Athens. Langlotz *G.V.* pl. 19, 28, whence *Mem. Am. Ac.* 6 pl. 12 a, d; A and foot, Bloesch *F.A.S.* pl. 16, 3. I, maenad. ΓΕΔΙΕΝΣ ΚΑΛΟΣ. For the shape, Bloesch 60 no. 3. Decorated inside only.

In another cup the inside picture must surely be by the Pedieus Painter; I have hesitated over the outside pictures, but they too should be his:

(α). LOUVRE G 13. I, *Mon. Piot* 9, 166; I, *Mon. Piot* 20, 129; I, FR. ii, 184; I, Pfuhl fig. 338; A, Vorberg *Ars erot.* pl. 15; Vorberg *Gloss.* 34, 189–90, and 640; I, ph. Gir. 17545. I, komos (youth and woman); A–B, love-making. On I, ΕΓΙΛΝΚΟΣ ΚΑΛΟΣ. On A, ΕΓΙΛΝ[ΚΟΣΚΑΛΟΣ]. On B, [ΕΓΙ]ΛΝΚΟΣΚΑΛΟΣ. For the drawing of the frontal face on I cf. p. 84 no. 18 ter.

Connected with Skythes and the Pedieus Painter, the

CUP

(β). LONDON E 26, from Camiros. I, komast. For the shape, Bloesch 60 no. 6. Hair and wreath are just as in Skythes and the Pedieus Painter (see below, on the Mannheim cup).

According to Bloesch (*FAS.* 59, foot, no. 1, and p. 60) the following cup is by the same *potter* as the Skythes in Palermo (p. 85 no. 21). The drawing is not by Skythes, nor like him—except in two small points: the contour of the hair, and the wreaths, are thoroughly in his manner. One might con-jecture that these final details—together with the inscriptions—were added by Skythes to the work of another.

CUP

MANNHEIM 13, from Orvieto. *Anz.* 1890, 153, 6; *CV.* pl. 21, 1 and 5, pl. 22, 1–2, pl. 32, 1, and p. 35. I, satyr. A–B, athletes. On I, ΕΓΙΛΝΚΟΣ ΚΑΛΟΣ and on the wineskin ΚΑΛΟΣ. On A, [Ε]ΓΙΛΝΚΟΣ ΚΑΛΟΣ. On B, [Ε]ΓΙΛΝΚΟΣ ΚΑΛΟΣ.

CHAPTER 7

THE EUERGIDES PAINTER

EUERGIDES, POTTER

Bloesch *FAS.* 51–53.

The name of Euergides is preserved, more or less fully, on twelve cups at east. Where the verb remains it is a part of *ποιεῖν*.

London 1920.6–13.1 (p. 88 no. 1).
Leipsic T 3372 (p. 89 no. 23).
Toledo (Ohio) (p. 90 no. 36).
Louvre C 61, frr. (p. 91 no. 45).
Athens Acr. 166, fr. (p. 92 no. 64).
Louvre C 11227, fr. (p. 95 no. 114).
Heidelberg 19, Goettingen, and Dresden (p. 95 no. 116).
Athens Acr. 187, fr. (p. 95 no. 120).
Athens 1430 (p. 95 no. 122).
Athens Acr. 172 and 107, fr. (p. 96).

The first nine of these cups were decorated by one artist, whom we call 'the Euergides Painter'; and the tenth, a small fragment, is probably by the same hand.

For the eleventh and twelfth cups with the signature see p. 1625.

(According to Hauser (*Mon. Piot* 20, 144 note 1) the following cup bore the signature of Euergides:

Once Munich, fr. Hoppin *Bf.* 464. I, satyr attacking maenad.

The fragment is mislaid and I have not seen it: on the photograph I make out, above, ... ϟEL, and, below, EVE ... (or rather ELE ...). I do not think this is a signature of Euergides. The style is not that of the Euergides Painter, it is akin to the late work of the Nicosthenic circle in the wider sense).

THE EUERGIDES PAINTER

JHS. 33, 347–55. *VA.* 19. *Att. V.* 30–37 and 467. *BSR.* 11, 17–19. *ARV.*[1] 59–71 and 950.

Nine of the cups bear the signature of the potter Euergides (see above), and the fragment of a tenth with the same signature is in all probability by the same painter. One cup bear the signature of the potter Chelis (no. 51: see p. 91). Three others were signed (nos. 2, 19, 121); but the name is now missing.

Part of no. 94 is by the Euergides Painter, part by Epiktetos; see also p. 97 no. 2.

CUPS

1 (1). LONDON 1920.6–13.1, from Capua. *Annali* 1849 pl. B, whence *Mon. Piot* 20, 142 and Hoppin i, 367; A–B, *Cat. Sotheby 23 Feb. 1920* pl. 2; Hoppin *Bf.* 463; I, *Burl. Mag.* 39, 231, a; *JHS.* 41 pl. 2; palmettes, Jacobsthal *O.* pl. 71, c; A, Bloesch *FAS.* pl. 15, 1. I, woman dancing. A, acontist and trainers. B, youth with horses. At each handle, sphinxes. On I, EVEPΛIΔEϟEΓOI complete. For the shape, Bloesch 51, Euergides no. 1. See p. 1625.

2 (2). TARQUINIA 699, from Tarquinia. I, warrior. A, Peleus and Thetis. B, Herakles and the Centaurs. At each handle, sphinxes. On I, . . . E]ΓOIE complete aft.

3 (3). MUNICH 2612 (J. 1104), from Vulci. I, and B, *JHS.* 33, 352; I, Reichhold *Skiz.* pl. 55, 1; B, Bloesch pl. 15, 4. I, woman (maenad?). A, man or youth mounting chariot. B, satyrs and maenad. At each handle, sphinxes. Restored. For the shape, Bloesch 53, Euergides.

4 (4). BERLIN 2265. A, *Jb.* 6, 253 fig. 2; I, *JHS.* 33, 351; I, Licht i, 28. I, komast; A–B, symposion (A, youth reclining, drinking; B, youth reclining, with wineskin). At each handle, sphinxes. On I, ΦILOΚOMOϟ. On A, HOΓA[Iϟκ]ALO[ϟ]. On B, κAPT[A]NAI+[I]. For the shape, Bloesch 51, Euergides no. 2. See p. 1625.

5 (5). LEIPSIC T 538 c, fr. A, (handle-sphinx).

6 (6). ATHENS Acr. 143, two frr., from Athens. One, Langlotz pl. 7. A, (handle-sphinx). See the next three.

7 (6 *bis*). ATHENS Acr. 174, fr., from Athens. A, (male, handle-sphinx). [Langlotz]. Might belong to Acr. 143 (no. 6).

8. ATHENS Acr., fr., from Athens. Outside, (handle-sphinx: the upper half of the head remains, to left, with the raised paw and part of the dotted wing). Belongs to Acr. 143 (no. 6)? See also the next.

9. ATHENS Acr., fr., from Athens. Outside, (hair and neck of a handle-sphinx to left, with part of the dotted wing).

10 (7). BOULOGNE 561, from Vulci. *Le Musée* 2, 281, whence (B) *JHS.* 27, 34, (B) Norman Gardiner *G.A.S.* 335, (B) Norman Gardiner *Athl.* 167; B. Ap. xvi. 18. 3; B, ph. Arch. phot. BAA 140. I, cock. A, satyrs and maenad. B, athletes. At each handle, griffins. On I, ΓPOϟAΛOP[EVO]. On A, ΓPOϟAΛ, on B, [O]P[EVO]. See p. 100 no. 19. For the shape, Bloesch 52, Euergides no. 12.

11 (8). MUNICH 2605 (J. 1238), from Vulci. A, *Mon.* 1 pl. 27, 39; palmettes, Jacobsthal *O.* pl. 70, b; A, Bloesch *FAS.* pl. 15, 2. I, jumper. A, naked youth running; B, the like. At each handle, palmettes and griffins. For the shape, Bloesch 51, Euergides no. 4.

12 (9). LEIPSIC T 538 a–b, two frr. A, between pegasi (part of the left-hand one remains), (the shoulder of the left-hand figure remains, with part of the head—a youth to right). The second fragment has part of a right-hand pegasus, whether from A or from B.

13 (10). LONDON E 9, from Vulci. Gerhard pl. 178–9, above; palmettes, Jacobsthal O. pl. 71, d. I is missing (Gerhard pl. 178–9, below, Murray no. 6, as Langlotz noticed, does not belong: see p. 170 no. 4). A–B, Peleus and Thetis. The picture on each half is between two sea-horses. See p. 1625.

14 (11). LONDON, Victoria and Albert Museum, 4807.1901, from Vulci. Gerhard pl. 180–1; de la Beche and Peeks 38; B and part of A, Chittenden and Seltman pl. 17. I, youth in bell-krater (treading grapes). A–B, Peleus and Thetis.

15 (48, 97, +). LOUVRE C 10869. One fr. of B, JHS. 33, 350. I, youth at laver. A, Peleus and Thetis. B, athletes.

16 (12, +). LOUVRE G 87, two frr. (one consisting of five). A, Peleus and Thetis (with Chiron present). On the inscription [ΦΙLΟΚ]ΟΜ[Ο]Ϟ see Eph. 1953–4, 203.

17 (13). ATHENS Acr. 184, fr., from Athens. Langlotz pl. 9. A, (arm with dolphin in the hand—probably from a picture of Peleus and Thetis). Inside, above, black ivy.

18 (14). ATHENS Acr. 183, frr., from Athens. Langlotz pl. 9. Outside, (legs of women running; feet).

19 (15). ATHENS Acr. 147, fr., from Athens. Langlotz pl. 6. I, Triptolemos. A, Herakles and Triton. On I, . . . ΕΓΟΙ]ΕϞΕΝ.

20 (57, 58, +). LOUVRE C 11224. I, Nereid (ΚΑLVΚΕ). A, the Theban Sphinx. B, komos. On B, ΦΙLΟΚΟΜΟ[Ϟ]ΦΙLΕΤΑΙ (Φιλόκωμος φιλεῖται). See Eph. 1953–4, 202–3. At an early stage in the recomposition of this cup, Jacques Bousquet made an important contribution by recognizing that many fragments which I had attributed to the Euergides Painter were from a single cup. He also added one handle. See also no. 83; and p. 1606.

21 (16, +). LOUVRE G 71. Incompletely, Rev. art ancien 1901, 9. I, jumper. A, Herakles and the lion; Theseus and Minotaur; Theseus and Procrustes. B, komos. Now cleaned, and a Louvre fr. added, giving, inside, the forehead-hair, with the H of the inscription, and, outside, the missing part of Herakles and the lion.

22. HEIDELBERG 40, fr. Kraiker pl. 7. A, Herakles and the lion.

23 (21). LEIPSIC T 3372, from Cervetri. I, athlete picking up discus. A, Herakles and the lion. B, satyr and maenads. On I, ΕVΕΡΛΙΔ[ΕϞ-ΕΓΟΙΕ]Ι (or [ΕϞΕΓΟΙΕϞΕ]Ν). For the shape, Bloesch 52, Euergides no. 9.

24 (22). ATHENS Acr. 164, fr., from Athens. Langlotz pl. 6. A, (Herakles, chariot).

25 (23). ATHENS Acr. 91 and 153, fr., from Athens. Part, Langlotz pl. 4. A, (centaur). 153 joins 91 on the left, adding part of the centaur and of a handle-palmette.

26 (17). ATHENS Acr. 149, two frr. from Athens. Langlotz pl. 7. A, Theseus and Minotaur.

27 (18). ATHENS Acr. 152, fr., from Athens. *JHS* 14 pl. 3, 1; Langlotz pl. 7. A, Theseus and Minotaur.

28 (19). LEIPSIC T 496, fr. A, Theseus and Minotaur.

29 (20). OXFORD 1929. 465. *CV*. pl. 51, 3 and pl. 53, 1–2. I, youth in bell-krater. A, Theseus and the bull. B, komos. For the shape, Bloesch 48 no. 8.

30 (24, +). ATHENS Acr. 163, frr., from Athens. Incompletely, Langlotz pl. 6. A, war-chariot. Not certain whether the fr. with Eros (or an Eros-like figure) belongs to A or to B. An Athens fr. joined to it by Mrs. Karouzou almost completes this figure.

31 (25). ATHENS Acr., fr., from Athens (part of 'A 146' which is Acr. 163, but not given by Langlotz under Acr. 163, and hardly belonging to it). A, (muzzle of a horse to right, club).

32 (26). ATHENS Acr. 51, frr., from Athens. Langlotz pl. 3. A, warrior mounting chariot.

33 (27). LONDON E 10, from Vulci. Gerhard pl. 186; I, Murray no. 7. I, sphinx. A–B, Achilles and Ajax playing. Gerhard's draughtsman has suppressed the gaming-table under one handle and substituted the city-gate of Troy which is really under the other. For the subject see CB. iii, text; for the shape, Bloesch 52, Euergides no. 10.

34. ATHENS Acr., two frr., from Athens. A, Achilles and Ajax playing? On one fr., feet and right shank of one squatting to right; on the other, shanks and feet of one squatting to left? Below, border of circumscribed rf. palmettes.

35 (28). LONDON E 20, from Vulci. I, Murray no. 16. I, komast. A, fight at Troy. B, youth with horses. [Cecil Smith].

36. TOLEDO (Ohio). I, cock. A, Herakles and Kyknos. B, fight. On I, EV[E]P[ΛΙ]ΔΕϨΕΓΟΙΕϨΕΝ. See p. 1625.

37 (29). VILLA GIULIA 26039, from Vignanello. A–B, *NSc*. 1916, 45; *CV*. pl. 28. I, youth (holding a garment?). A–B, fight. See p. 1625.

38 (30, +). LOUVRE C 10870 (including S 1363). I, jumper. A, warriors running, B, (what remains is the heel of the last figure but one on the right, and the feet of the last figure, both moving to left).

39 (31). MUNICH, fr., from Athens. A, (shield, muzzle of horse to left).

40 (32). ATHENS Acr. 161, fr., from Athens. Langlotz pl. 7. A, (warrior). From a picture of heroes quarrelling?

41 (33). ATHENS Acr. 151, fr., from Athens. Langlotz pl. 7. A, (helmeted youth).

42 (34). ATHENS Acr. 162, fr., from Athens. Langlotz pl. 7. A, (warrior).

43 (35). ATHENS Acr. 165, fr., from Athens. Langlotz pl. 7. A, arming.

44 (36). BOWDOIN, fr. *JHS*. 33, 355. A, (warrior).

45 (37, +). LOUVRE C 61, frr. I, (sleeve?). A, warrior leading horses. On I, [EVEPΛI]ΔE[ẞ . . . . On A, [HO]ΓAIẞҚΑLO[ẞ]. A Louvre fr. (two joining) with the top of an under-handle palmette and part of the palmette to left of it probably belongs.

46 (38). HEIDELBERG 21, fr. Kraiker pl. 4. A, (horse). . . . E . . .

47 (39). FLORENCE 4 B 39, fr. *CV*. pl. 4, B 39. A, (on the left, horse).

48 (40). ATHENS Acr. 126, fr., from Athens. A, (elbow, horse).

49 (41). LONDON E 21, from Vulci. I, Murray no. 17; A, *Mü. arch. St*. 371; palmettes, Jacobsthal O. pl. 70, c–d; B.Ap. xvi. 14. I, naked youth running. A, youth with horses; B, the like. Now cleaned.

50 (42). CASTLE ASHBY, Northampton. *BSR*. 11 pl. 4, 3 and p. 18. I, youth at bell-krater. A, youths and horse. B, fight.

51 (43). LOUVRE G 15, from Vulci. Pottier pll. 89–90, whence Hoppin i, 190–1 and (I and A) Perrot 10, 366; B, *Mon. Piot* 35, 58; B (augmented by a fr. ex Cab. Méd.), ibid. 59. I, jumper. A, athletes. B, youths with horses. Under each handle a dolphin. On I, +[EL]Iẞ EΓΓOIEẞEN. Restored. For the shape, Bloesch 50.

52 (44). NEW YORK 09.221.47, from Southern Etruria. A–B, *Bull. Metr*. 5, 142 fig. 1; Richter and Hall pl. 3 and pl. 179, 5; detail of A, Alexander *Gk Athl*. 14, 2. I, naked youth with flowers. A–B, athletes.

53 (45). FLORENCE B B 6 (part ex Villa Giulia), frr. Part, *CV*. Fl. pl. B, B6. I is lost. A, athletes. B, komos.

54 (46). CAMBRIDGE 37.15 and VILLA GIULIA, from Vulci. A–B, *Coll. M.E.* pl. 11, 248; I, *VA*. 19; *CV*. ii RS. pl. 8, 4, pl. 9, 1, and pl. 5, 2. I, youth in bell-krater. A, athletes. B, komos. The Villa Giulia fr., unpublished, gives the missing parts of arm and palmettes on A, with the final sigma. For the shape, Bloesch 48 no. 5.

55 (47). DRESDEN xvii. 10. 4, fr. A, athletes (upper part of jumper to right, hand of acontist, inscription . . . ẞA . . .).

56 (49, +). LOUVRE S 1388, frr. Outside, athletes (athlete running, jumper; foot of an athlete, flute-player, discus-thrower).

57 (50). ATHENS Acr. 158, fr., from Athens. Langlotz pl. 7. A, athletes.

58 (51). ATHENS Acr. 160, fr., from Athens. Langlotz pl. 6. A, athletes.

59 (52). ATHENS Acr. 159, two frr., from Athens. One fr., Langlotz pl. 7. A, (athletes).

60 (53, 54, +). ORVIETO, Faina, 171, OXFORD 1927.4075, 1953.1, and 1953.642; and Italian market. The Faina part, I and A, phs. Al. 32472 and 32475; some of the Oxford frr., *CV*. pl. 57, 5 and 21–25. I, komast; A–B, komos. The Faina cup is very much restored: the Oxford frr., some acquired in 1927, others in 1953, give good part of what is missing. Oxford 1953.1 is two of the three fragments formerly in the Italian market and mentioned in *ARV*.[1] under no. 54. The third fragment in the market, now missing, has, outside, the upper part of a youth's head to right, with what is probably a piece of his arm, and the letter H . . . A fragment with part of a leg and the end of a cloak was seen by Bothmer to be by the Euergides Painter; it joins the fragment *CV*. Oxford pl. 57, 25 and has been given by him to Oxford (1953.642).

61 (55). LEIPSIC T 3373, from Cervetri. I, youth in bell-krater. A, komasts at krater; B, the like. For the shape, Bloesch 49, foot, no. 2.

62 (56). LEIPSIC T 495 and FREIBURG, fr. A, komos (youths at krater). The Freiburg fr. gives the right foot of the youth to right of the krater, and the shanks of the youth to right of him.

63 (59). ATHENS Acr. 156, fr., from Athens. A, komos.

64 (60). ATHENS Acr. 166, frr., from Athens. Detail, *Jb*. 14, 154, whence Walter *H.A.P.* i, 227, Perrot 9, 339, Richter *Craft* 73 fig. 68; Langlotz pl. 6, whence *PP*. pl. 1, 2–3. Outside, (vase-painter, with Athena; metal-worker and forge; youths or men with horse). On the subjects see *PP*. 8–10. The horse might be a statue. For the wreath round its neck compare the Bonn cup by Oltos (p. 56 no. 31). The fragment Athens Acr. 345 might belong: inside, EV . . .; outside, part of the maeander below the pictures (see *AJA*. 1950, 317).

65 (61). WÜRZBURG 473, from Vulci. Langlotz pl. 142. I, komast. A, panther attacking fawn, and youth. B, komos (youths at bell-krater). For the shape, Bloesch 51, Euergides no. 3.

66 (62). NEW YORK 41.162.129, from Vulci. *CV*. Gallatin pl. 47, 1, pl. 48, 1, and pl. 61, 4. I, komast. A, panther attacking fawn, and youth. B, athletes.

67 (63). Once ROME, Spagna. B.Ap. xxi. 95. I, naked youth bending. A, panther attacking fawn, and youth; B, two youths hunting a fawn. On the inscriptions, *AJA*. 1927, 347.

68 (64). LOUVRE G 21, from Vulci. I, komast. A, panther attacking fawn, and youth. B, youth with horses. Now cleaned.

69 (65). ATHENS Acr. 150, fr., from Athens. Langlotz pl. 7. A, komos?

70 (66). ATHENS Acr. 123 b, fr., from Athens. A, (male legs).

71 (67). ATHENS Acr. 154, fr., from Athens. A, (middle of a naked male to right).

72 (68). ATHENS, Agora, NS. AP 140, fr., from Athens. *Hesp*. 4, 281, 137. A, (youth). [Pease].

73 (69). ATHENS Acr. 92, fr., from Athens. Langlotz, pl. 4. A, (man lifting the leg of another; or satyr and maenad?)

74 (70). ATHENS, Agora, NS. AP 23, fr., from Athens. *Hesp.* 4, 281, 139. A, (male bending). ... MO ... [Pease]. For the inscription, [Φιλόκω]μο[s]?, *Eph.* 1953–4, 203.

75 (71). MUNICH, fr., from Athens. A, (male armpit). Cf. Agora NS. AP 23 (no. 74) and Athens Acr. 151 (no. 41).

76 (72). MUNICH, fr., from Athens. A, (back of male head to left, with ... Os).

77 (73). ATHENS Acr. 121, fr., from Athens. A, (woman).

78 (74). LEIPSIC T 564, fr. A, (head of youth to left).

79 (75). LEIPSIC T 538 a(?), fr. A, (head of youth to right, with HOΓ [AIs ...).

80 (76). LEIPSIC T 3677(?), fr. A, (forehead to right, with ... ΓAI ...).

81 (77). LEIPSIC T 3653, fr. A, (flute-player and youth, with ... ? ...). The flute is in red.

82 (78). LEIPSIC T 3622, fr. A, (cloak and stick of male, buttocks of another).

83. LOUVRE C 11225, fr. A, (buttocks of a male moving to left, and a thumb). Might belong to Louvre C 11224 (no. 20)?

84. LOUVRE C 11226, fr. A, (head and left shoulder of a naked youth to right).

85 (79). DRESDEN, fr. A, (palmette, then part of one in a cloak).

86 (80). LIVERPOOL, Univ., fr. A, (youths, with ... ΓA ...).

87. ATHENS Acr., fr., from Athens. A, (lower part of a male in a himation leaning to left). Compare the right-hand figure on A of London 1920. 6–13.1 (no. 1). I noted the old number of this fragment as A 190: I do not know if it can be Langlotz's 120, the old number of which he gives as B 190.

88 (81). FLORENCE 5 B 23, fr. *CV.* pl. 5, B 23. A, (youth—komast, or athlete falling?).

89. LOUVRE C 218, fr. A, (a man and a man or youth seizing a woman). Satyrs and maenad?

90 (82). TOURS. B.Ap. xxii. 92. I, naked youth running. A, Dionysos seated, and two satyrs. B, komos.

91 (83). LEIPSIC T 540 (part), T 3599 (part), T 3677, TÜBINGEN E 38, HEIDELBERG 22, fr., from Cervetri. The Tübingen piece, Watzinger pl. 20; the Heidelberg, Kraiker pl. 6. A, (satyr, maenad, and fawn).

92 (84). MUNICH (ex Antiquarium), two frr., joining or nearly. A, (satyr and maenad with donkey).

93 (85). OXFORD G 141.15, fr., from Naucratis. *CV.* pl. 14, 21. A, (satyr).

(no. 94, eye-cup)

94. LOUVRE G 16. *CV*. b pl. 11, 2–3 and 6. I, Sisyphos. A–B, between eyes. A, pear-drop; B, the like. Between the brows, another. On I, HIΓΓAP-+OϞKALO[Ϟ]. The inside is by Epiktetos (p. 71 no. 13), the outside (*CV*. b pl. 11, 3) by the Euergides Painter: for this collaboration compare Naples 2609 (p. 97 no. 2). See p. 47 no. 155.

(nos. 95–121, fragments of cup-interiors: not known whether decorated outside)

95 (86). LOUVRE G 20, fr. Pottier pl. 90. I, komast. To left of the buttocks, the letter I; below the legs, sigma, a pair of interpoints, a fragmentary letter, then room for a letter, then NON and a nondescript letter, unless it be a blot.

96 (88). LENINGRAD 648, fr. I, komast (youth running with wineskin).

97 (aiii 10). ATHENS, Agora, P 287, fr., from Athens. I, komast.

98 (110). LEIPSIC T 3616, fr., from Cervetri. I, komast? (running to left, three-quarter back-view, arm extended in cloak). Leipsic T 3646 probably belongs.

99. ATHENS Acr., fr., from Athens. I, naked youth (back of head, ear, left breast and shoulder, left upper arm, left flank; facing left).

100 (89). ADRIA B 313, fr., from Adria. *CV*. pl. 1, 6. I, youth at bell-krater.

101 (90). BRUNSWICK 500. *CV*. pl. 15, 1. I, youth in bell-krater.

102 (91). FLORENCE PD 441, fr. I, youth (leaning to right).

103 (92). BOSTON 10.214, fr., from Tarquinia. *Bull. MFA.* 9, 54, 2; Sudhoff ii, 37; CB. i pl. 3, 12. I, youth at laver.

104 (93). TÜBINGEN E 41, fr. Watzinger pl. 21. I, youth kneeling on wineskin (ἀσκωλιασμός?).

105 (94). ATHENS Acr. 157, fr., from Athens. Langlotz pl. 7. I, symposion (youth reclining).

106 (a iii 11). ATHENS Acr. 171, fr., from Athens. Langlotz pl. 7. I, athlete. [Langlotz].

107 (95, +). LOUVRE G 96. Incompletely, Pottier pl. 99. I, youth lifting or moving a big stone. A Louvre fr. joins and completes the picture.

108 (96). ATHENS Acr. 144, fr., from Athens. Langlotz pl. 7. I, discus-thrower.

109 (98). ATHENS Acr. 145, fr., from Athens. I, (head and shoulder of a youth to right).

110. LOUVRE C 11226 *bis*, fr. I, (buttocks and right leg of a naked male moving to left).

111 (99). AMSTERDAM inv. 2232, fr. *CV*. Scheurleer pl. 8, 3. I, warrior.

112 (aiii 12). ATHENS, Agora, P 13622, fr., from Athens. I, warrior?

113 (100). LIMENAS, fr., from Thasos. Ghali-Kahil *C.G.* pl. 44, 9. I, warrior (moving to right, in three-quarter back-view, looking round, with spear and shield). On the right, ΗΟΓΑΙϚ. Doubtless decorated inside only.

114. LOUVRE C 11227, fr. I, warrior (shank and foot, running to right). [EVEP]ΛΙ[ΔEϚ . . .

115 (101). LEIPSIC T 3608, two frr., from Cervetri. I, warrior (moving to right, looking round) . . . E . E . . . This might be from a signature of Euergides, whether from the name or from the verb.

116 (102). HEIDELBERG 19, GOETTINGEN, and DRESDEN. The Heidelberg part: *JHS.* 33, 347, whence Hoppin i, 364; Kraiker pl. 5. I, woman running. The Goettingen fr. gives the face, neck, shoulders; the Dresden, the right foot. EV[EPΛ]ΙΔEϚEΓO[IEϚEN].

117 (103). ATHENS Acr. 148, fr., from Athens. I, woman running, a wreath in her hand.

118 (104). ATHENS Acr. 169, fr., from Athens. I, woman running (to right: one foot and part of the skirt remain).

119 (106). LOUVRE S 1383, fr. I, woman running (the upper part remains, head to right, probably looking round).

120 (107). ATHENS Acr. 187, fr., from Athens. Langlotz pl. 9. I, Nereid? (hand holding a fish). [EVEPΛ]ΙΔ[EϚ . . .

121 (108). ATHENS Acr. 103, fr., from Athens. Langlotz pl. 4. I, cock. . . . EΓOIE]ϚEN.

(nos. 122–36, decorated inside only)

122 (109). ATHENS 1430 (CC. 1160), from Corinth. *Eph.* 1885 pl. 3, 2, whence *JHS.* 12, 348, *Mon. Piot* 20, 143, Hoppin i, 362; *CV.* pl. 2, 2, 4, and 6; A, Bloesch *FAS.* pl. 16, 5; ph. Marb. 134755. I, komast. EVEPΛΙΔEϚE complete. For the shape, Bloesch 52, Euergides no. 11.

123. LAON 37.1060. *Coll. M.E.* pl. 6, 150; *CV.* pl. 47, 2 and 4. I, symposion (youth reclining, playing the flute). His right foot modern.

124 (87. +). LOUVRE S 1401, fr. I, komast. A fragment added by Bousquet gives the left leg and part of the cloak.

125 (111). MUNICH 2597 (J. 1157), from Vulci. A and foot, Bloesch *FAS.* pl. 33, 5. I, komast? (youth running). For the shape, Bloesch 121 no. 27.

126 (112). BOULOGNE 183. *Le Musée* 2, 280 fig. 28. I, youth in bell-krater. For the shape, Bloesch 121 no. 29.

127 (113). ATHENS 18709 (ex Empedokles). I, naked youth at bell-krater.

128. LOUVRE C 11228, fr. I, warrior squatting.

129. LOUVRE C 10868. I, hunter (returning with his take, a fox and a hare).

130 (114). ADRIA Bc 56, fr., from Adria. *CV.* pl. 1, 5; *Riv. Ist.* N.S. 5–6, 31 fig. 2; *Mostra* pl. 118, 1. I, jumper.

131. NAPLES, Astarita, 5. I, jumper. ΓΑ[ΙΔΙ]Ι⊂Ο$. This may be the Canino cup with this subject and the word Paidikos: if so, from Vulci.

132. ATHENS Acr. 53, fr., from Athens. I, Athena.

133 (116). LEIPSIC T 499. I, woman running, a wreath in her hand. For the shape, Bloesch 123 no. 37.

134 (117). Lost, from Marion. *Cypr.* pl. 5, 1. I, woman running.

135 (118). LEIPSIC T 501. I, Pegasus. For the shape, Bloesch 121 no. 33. See the next.

136. OXFORD, Beazley. I, hound (bitch rubbing her ear with one hind-leg). Same shape of cup as the last. See p. 172, foot, no. 2, and p. 1625.

A small fragment is most probably by the Euergides Painter:

CUP

ATHENS Acr. 172 and 107, fr., from Athens. *AJA.* 1935, 480 fig. 6. I, one dancing (a hand with crotala remains). ... ΕΓΟ[ΙΕ$ΕΝ], and, outside the line border, ΕVΕΡ[ΛΙΔΕ$ ... See *AJA.* 1935, 480 no. 8.

Two cups must be very early, careful work by the Euergides Painter:

*ARV.*¹ 65, i.

CUPS

1 (ai 1). FLORENCE 1 B 3 (part ex Villa Giulia) and HEIDELBERG 11, frr. Part, *CV.* Fl. pl. 1, B 3; the Heidelberg fr., Kraiker pl. 3, 11. A–B, symposion: A, youth reclining; B, the like.

2 (ai 2). KOENIGSBERG 63, fr., from Athens. Lullies *K.* pl. 9, 63. I, symposion (youth reclining). Already connected with the Euergides Painter by Lullies.

Close to these the cup:

(a). MUNICH 2594 (J. 564), from Vulci. Shape, Lau pl. 18, 5. I, discus-thrower. For the shape, Bloesch 131 no. 5, and 133.

Compare also the cup:

(a). Lost. B.Ap. xxi. 12. I, komast (naked youth running with flower). A, komos (youth with flower and youth with drinking-horn); B, symposion (naked youth reclining).

MANNER OF THE EUERGIDES PAINTER

(i)

ARV.[1] 65–66, ii–iii, and 950.

CUPS

(*nos. 1–3, decorated outside as well as in*)

1 (ii 1). DRESDEN ZV. 1655, from Italy. I, komast. A, satyr and maenad. B, youth with horse. On I, ΓPO[ϟΑΛ]OPEVO. On A, Γ[ΑΙΔΙκO]ϟ. On B, ΓΑΙΔ[ΙκO]ϟ. May be by the painter himself.

2 (ii 2). NAPLES 2609. *PP.* pl. 8. I, warrior. A–B, symposion: A, youth reclining, and boy cup-bearer; B, the like. On I, HIΓΓΑP+Oϟ κΑレOϟ. On A, ΓPOϟΑΛOPEVO. On B, ΓΑΙΔΙκOϟ. Restored. The outside is in the manner of the Euergides Painter, coarse, but very close to him; the inside is by Epiktetos (p. 73 no. 29). For this collaboration compare Louvre G 16 (p. 94 no. 94) and see *PP.* 28. For the shape, Bloesch 66 note 110.

3 (a). MUNICH 2609 (J. 1020), from Vulci. I, warrior. A, one (Aphrodite?) mounting chariot. B, fight. Compare, for B, the cup in Toledo, Ohio (p. 90 no. 36); for A, Munich 2612 (p. 88 no. 3) and Athens Acr. 51 (p. 90 no. 32). For the shape, Bloesch 52, Euergides no. 8.

4 (iii 16). VILLA GIULIA, two frr. A, komos (the upper parts of the two left-hand youths remain, and of the two right-hand). B, (warrior in loin-cloth and helmet to right—the left-hand figure). Coarse.

(*nos. 5–9, not known whether decorated outside*)

5 (a). DRESDEN, fr. I, (hand holding flower). . . . ϟE . . . (perhaps part of a signature). May be by the painter himself.

6. GOETTINGEN H 69, fr. I, discus-thrower.

7 (iii 8). FLORENCE (ex Villa Giulia), fr. I, (hair of one to right, and the letter Δ). May be by the painter himself.

8 (iii 9). FREIBURG, fr. I, (hair of one to left).

9 (iii 5). FREIBURG, fr. I, (buttocks and leg of a naked male running to right).

(*nos. 10–20, decorated inside only*)

10 (ii 3). BRUSSELS R 260. Vorberg *Ars erot.* pl. 19; Vorberg *Gloss.* 341. I, παῖς δεφόμενος at a bell-krater. ΓPOϟΑΛOPEVO, the last three letters retr.

11 (iii 4). VILLA GIULIA. I, youth running (to right, looking round, wrap over both shoulders). . . . V . . . Foot type C. May be by the painter himself.

12 (iii 7). LEIPSIC (T 3361?), from Cervetri. I, komast (youth running to right with wineskin). ΓΑΙϟκΑレOϟ.

13 (iii 13). LONDON E 28, from Marion. I, youth running. ΓΡΟSΑΛΟ-
PEVO.

14 (iii 14). LONDON E 27. *Jb.* 6, 253, above. I, symposion (youth reclining,
or sitting on the ground, holding a pointed amphora).

15 (iii 2). ATHENS 1656 (CC. 1164), from Eretria. I, youth with wineskin.

16 (iii 1). NEW YORK 41. 162.76. *CV.* Gallatin pl. 9, 2. I, komast. Now
cleaned. See p. 101 no. 29 and p. 106.

17 (iii 15). LOUVRE G 98. Pottier pl. 99. I, boy cup-bearer filling a cup at
the krater. See p. 106.

18 (iii 6). LOUVRE G 82, from Campania. *El.* 2 pl. 37. I, komos (two
youths). ΓΡΟSΑΛΟPEVO. Restored.

19. FLORENCE, fr. I, male kneeling, holding a laver (the lower part remains;
to right).

20. FLORENCE, fr. I, (back, buttocks, foot, of a naked male, kneeling or
nearly, to right). Small cup.

(ii)

THE GROUP OF THE PAIDIKOS ALABASTRA

Att. V. 35–36 and 467–8. *BSR.* 11, 19. Angermeier *Das Alabastron* 17–24. Haspels
ABL. 101–4. *ARV.*[1] 68–70 and 950.

ALABASTRA

(α)

Two by the Pasiades Painter; close to the Euergides Painter.

ALABASTRA

(*white ground*)

1 (19). LONDON B 668, from Marion. *JHS.* 8 pl. 82, whence Perrot 10 pl.
19, Hoppin ii, 331, *Mon. Piot* 26, 86, Richter *Sc.* fig. 280, Rumpf *MZ.* pl.
22, 4; Murray *WAV.* pl. 18, a, whence Pfuhl fig. 355 (= Pfuhl *Mast.* fig.
35) and Swindler pl. 13, a; part, Lane pl. 89, c; part, *E.A.A.* ii, 497.Woman
with phiale, woman (maenad?) running with sprigs. On the bottom, rf.
palmette. On the band above the picture, ΓΑSΙΑΔΕS : EΓΟΙΕSΕΝ.
On the topside of the mouth, HOΓΑΙSΚΑΛΟS : See p. 1626.

2 (20). ATHENS 15002, from Delphi. *BCH.* 1921, 519; *Mon. Piot* 26 pl. 3
and pp. 68–77; Hoppin *Bf.* 472; Papaspyridi *Guide* 237; La Coste-
Messelière *Delphes* 32. A, maenad. B, Amazon. On the bottom, rf.
palmette. On the band above the picture, Γ[Α]SΙΑΔ[ΕS :] EΓΟ[Ι-
ΕSΕΝ]. See p. 1626.

(β)

ALABASTRA

(white ground)

Four with floral decoration, by one hand. The palmette on the bottom connects nos. 3 and 4 (Louvre CA 1920 and Athens 2207) with the two alabastra in (α).

3 (25). LOUVRE CA 1920. *Mon. Piot* 26, 87–88. Palmettes; on the bottom, rf. palmette. On the topside of the mouth, ΓΑSΙΑΔΕSΕΓΟΙΕSΕΝ :

4 (28). ATHENS 2207. *Mon. Piot* 26, 89. Palmettes; on the bottom, rf. palmette. On the topside of the mouth, ΗΟΓΑΙSΚΑΛΟSΝΑΙ :

5 (27). NEW YORK 21.80. McClees 65 fig. 81; Richter and Milne fig. 109; Lane pl. 89, a; Richter *H.* 217, h. Palmettes; on the bottom, black palmette on reserved ground. On the topside of the mouth, ΗΙΓΓΑΡ+ΟS= ΚΑΛΟSΝΑΙ : [Haspels].

6 (26). NEW YORK 06.1021.92. Sambon *Canessa* 61, 225; Richter *Hdbk Class. Coll.* 85, 5. Palmettes; on the bottom, black palmette on white ground. On the topside of the mouth, ΗΑΟSΚΑSΕL˙ : [Haspels].

(γ)

The mass of the Group. Some are earlier, some later, but they are all closely interconnected, and may be by one hand: manner of the Euergides Painter.

ALABASTRA

(nos. 7–27, red-figure)

7 (1). LONDON 1902.12–18. 2, from Attica. *JHS.* 41 pl. 8, i, 5. A, woman (mistress); B, woman (maid). On the bottom, rf. palmette. On A, ΓΡΟSΑΛΟΡΕVΟ. On B, ΕΓΟΙΕSΕΝ. On the topside of the mouth, [ΗΟΓ]ΑΙSΚ[ΑLΟS]. Small. Early. Near the Pasiades Painter and the Euergides Painter.

8 (15). ATHENS Acr. 865, fr., from Athens. Langlotz pl. 75. Male and woman at altar.

9 (2). LOUVRE CA 487, from Eretria. *REG.* 1893, 41–44, whence Brueckner *Lebensregeln* 10 and Hoppin ii, 273. A, youth and woman; B, the like. On the bottom, rf. palmette. On A, [ΓΡΟS]Α[ΛΟΡΕVΟ]. On B, ΓΡΟSΑΛΟΡΕVΟ. On the topside of the mouth, ΓΑΙΔΙΚΟSΕΓΟΙ-ΕSΕΝ :

10 (3). LONDON E 717, from Greece. Youth and women. On the topside of the mouth, ... ΚΟSL ... with remains of a letter (not iota) before the kappa. (Most of the alabastra in the lists that follow, pp. 99–100, have inscriptions on the topside of the mouth, but usually meaningless ones.)

11 (4). Once TARPORLEY, Brooks. Youth and women. On the bottom, in silhouette, hunter? (youth kneeling, left arm extended with cloak).

12. BRAURON, fr., from Brauron. On the bottom, in silhouette, hunter.

13 (5). ESSEN (ex Hagen). Phs. Marb. 618689 and 617651. A, woman; B, youth. On the bottom, black palmette. This is probably the alabastron formerly in the van Branteghem collection, 58, from Athens.

14 (6). COPENHAGEN, Ny Carlsberg, inv. 2661. Poulsen VG. figs. 29–30. Youth seated, and woman dancing. On the bottom, black palmette.

15 (7). CAMBRIDGE 37.39, from Greece. CV. ii S. and R. pl. 16, 3. Youth and women. On the bottom, black palmette.

16 (8). OXFORD 1921.1214, from Greece. CV. pl. 41, 1–2. Woman seated and two women. On the bottom, quatrefoil.

17. PRINCETON 31.5. Two women at altar.

18 (10). TÜBINGEN E 49. Watzinger pl. 22. Woman seated, and woman, at altar.

19 (11). NEW YORK 41.162.80. CV. Gallatin pl. 9, 1 and 3. A, woman at altar; B, woman. On A, ΓPOSΛΛ, on B, OPEVO. For the division of the word compare the cup by the Euergides Painter in Boulogne (p. 88 no. 10).

20 (14). NEW YORK 41.162.82. CV. Gallatin pl. 9, 4 and 6. Youth and boy.

21. ATHENS, fr. (Upper half of a woman to right, in spotted chiton, himation, saccos, holding a mirror).

22 (9). COPENHAGEN inv. 3881, from Athens. Poulsen VG. figs. 33–34; CV. pl. 144, 3. Two women. On the bottom, black wheel.

23 (12). OXFORD 1916.6, from Boeotia. Aukt. Helbing 27–28 Juni 1910 pl. 4, 122; CV. pl. 41, 3–4. Youth and woman. On the bottom, quatrefoil. Late. As Würzburg 544 (no. 24).

24 (13). WÜRZBURG 544, from Boeotia. Langlotz pl. 207. Youth and woman. On the bottom, black wheel. Late. As Oxford 1916.6 (no. 23).

25 (16). ARMONK, Pinney. Part, CV. Matsch pl. 8, 3. Two youths. On the bottom, black palmette. Late.

26 (17). ATHENS 12278 (N. 1057), from Atalanti. Two youths. On the bottom, black wheel. Late.

27. ATHENS Acr., fr., from Athens. The lower part remains, with a band of maeander, another of upright strokes (tongues), and on the bottom a black palmette.

(nos. 28–30, white ground)

28 (21). TÜBINGEN E 48. Watzinger pl. 21. A, dancing girl; B, youth. On the bottom, rf. palmette. On A, [HOΓ]A[I]SKΛΛO[S]. On B, ΓPOSΛΛOPEVO. On the topside of the mouth, Γ[P]OS[ΛΛ]O-PEVO. [Watzinger].

29 (22). NEW YORK 41.162.81, from near Bologna. *CV.* Gallatin pl. 27, 6 and 8. Two naked women. On the bottom, in silhouette on a reserved ground, satyr dancing. ΓΡΟ[Ϟ]ΑΛΟΡΕVΟ. On the band above the picture, ΓΡΟϞΑΛΟΡΕVΟ. On the topside of the mouth, ΓΛΙϞ-ΙCΑΛΟϞ. Compare the cup New York 41.162.76 (p. 98 no. 16).

30 (23). BOSTON 00.358. C. Smith *Forman* pl. 12, 366; *Mon. Piot* 26, 85. Woman dancing and two women. On the bottom, in black on a reserved ground, komast? ΓΡΟϞΑΛΟΡΕVΟ. On the topside of the mouth, ΓΛΙϟΚΑLΟϞ :

Other alabastra go with the Paidikos Group in shape and patterns; as to the figure-work, nos. 1 and 2 go together, and are still connected with the Paidikos Group; nos. 3 and 4 are interrelated and more remote:

ALABASTRA

(nos. 1–3, red-figure)

1. ATHENS Acr. 866, from Athens. Langlotz pl. 75. Discus-thrower and flute-player. [Langlotz]. See the next.

2. BARCELONA. *Ampurias* 17–18, 248. Courting: A, youth and boy; B, boy embracing man. On the bottom, rf. palmette. On A, ΓΛΙϟ ΚΑLΟ[Ϟ]. On B, ΓΡΟϞΑΛΟΡΕVΟ. [Trias de Arribas]. Compare the last. Compare also the seated woman on Oxford 1921.1214 (p. 100 no. 16).

3. ATHENS 1239 (CC. 1204), from Athens. CC. pl. 42; Brueckner *Lebensregeln* pl. 1 and pp. 4–7, whence Robert *Herm.* 126–7; *CV.* pl. 1, 3–5. Youth, and servant-boy with food, woman spinning. On the topside of the mouth, ΓΡΟϞΑΡΕVΟ :

(no. 4, white ground)

4. BERLIN inv. 31390, from Athens. *Vereinigung der Freunde: Bericht 1932–4*, 15. Youths, and boy with cat. On the bottom, in silhouette on white ground, archer. Compare the last.

I have not seen the following: from the description it should belong to the Group of the Paidikos Alabastra:

ALABASTRON

(red-figure)

Once BRUSSELS, van Branteghem, 60, from Athens. Woman with phiale at altar. On the bottom, wheel. ΗΟΓΑΙϟΚΑLΙΟϞ.

PASIADES

Hesp. 4, 291–2 (Pease). *ARV.*[1] 70.

WHITE LEKYTHOS

1. ATHENS, Agora, NS AP 422, frr., from Athens. *Hesp.* 4, 291. (Youth, seated woman). There must have been another woman, turned to right, probably seated, on the left of the picture. On the shoulder, incised, ΓΑϚΙΑΔ[ΕϚ]ΕΛΡΑΦ[ϚΕΝ].

The name recurs, but with ἐποίησεν, on three white alabastra. Two of them were decorated by an artist whom we have named 'the Pasiades Painter'; the lekythos in Athens, just described, is not by him. The third alabastron belongs to the same class as the two: it is decorated with palmettes, and one cannot say that it is either by the Pasiades Painter or by the artist of the lekythos in Athens.

2. LONDON B 668, from Marion. See p. 98, Pasiades Painter no. 1.
3. ATHENS 15002, from Delphi. See p. 98, Pasiades Painter no. 2.
4. LOUVRE CA 1921. See p. 99 no. 3.

See also below.

PAIDIKOS, POTTER

The name occurs, followed by ἐποίησεν, on an alabastron:

1. LOUVRE CA 487, from Eretria. See p. 99, Group of the Paidikos Alabastra, no. 9.

It also occurs, but without a verb, on the following:

CUPS

2. NAPLES, Astarita, 5. See p. 96, Euergides Painter no. 131.
3. DRESDEN ZV 1655. See p. 97, manner of the Euergides Painter, no. 1, perhaps by the painter himself.
4. NAPLES 2609. See p. 97, manner of the Euergides Painter, no. 2, and close to him.

All these go together: decorated by the Euergides Painter or in his manner. The alabastron, in point of shape and type, can hardly be separated from those that bear the signature of the potter Pasiades; and it must be considered whether Pasiades and Paidikos are not the same man: 'Paidikos', being a nickname accepted, with satisfaction, by Pasiades. See also Haspels *ABL.* 102.

The word Paidikos occurs on two other cups, but they are lost and nothing is known about the style:

1. Once CANINO, from Vulci. I, warrior. Παιδικος.
2. Once CANINO, from Vulci. I, male with vessels. Παιδικος.

This may also be the name on a cup connected with the Group of Acropolis 96:

FLORENCE D B 8 (part ex Villa Giulia). See p. 105, below, no. 2.

Louvre CA 487, the alabastron with the full signature of Paidikos, has another inscription, προσαγορεύω. This recurs on a good many vases, most of which belong to the same stylistic group as Louvre CA 487:

CUPS

1. BOULOGNE 561. See p. 88, Euergides Painter, no. 10.
2. DRESDEN ZV. 1655. See p. 97, manner of the Euergides Painter, no. 1, perhaps by the painter himself.
3. NAPLES 2609. See p. 97, manner of the Euergides Painter, no. 2, and close to him.
4. BRUSSELS R 260. See p. 97, manner of the Euergides Painter, no. 10.
5. LONDON E 28. See p. 98, manner of the Euergides Painter, no. 13.
6. LOUVRE G 82. See p. 98, manner of the Euergides Painter, no. 18.
7. BOLOGNA 433. See p. 106, Painter of Bologna 433, no. 2.
8. FLORENCE PD 57, from Populonia. NSc. 1926, 370. I, jumper. ΓPOϞ-ΛΛOPEVO. Damaged. Cannot be said to be connected with the Euergides Painter.
9. ROMAN MARKET. Panofka Bilder ant. Lebens pl. 1, 9; Gerhard pl. 272, 5–6. I, naked youth at laver. ΓPOϞΛΛ on the laver. Not connected with the Euergides Painter.
10. AMSTERDAM, Six. I, Dionysos. ΓPOϞΛΛOPEVO. Not connected with the Euergides Painter.
11. PARIS MARKET (ex Canino), from Vulci. I, male kneeling with two amphorae on a pole over his shoulders. προσαγορεvo. Bothmer points out that this is Vente 22 avril 1845 no. 104.

ALABASTRA
(nos. 12–16, red-figure)

12. LONDON 1902.12–18.2. See p. 99, Group of the Paidikos Alabastra, no. 7.
13. LOUVRE CA 487. See p. 99, Group of the Paidikos Alabastra, no. 9.
14. NEW YORK 41.162.80. See p. 100, Group of the Paidikos Alabastra, no. 19.
15. BARCELONA. See p. 101 no. 2.
16. ATHENS 1239. See p. 101 no. 3.

(nos. 17–19, white ground)

17. TÜBINGEN E 48. See p. 100, Group of the Paidikos Alabastra, no. 28.

18. NEW YORK 41.162.81. See p. 101, Group of the Paidikos Alabastra, no. 29.

19. BOSTON 00.358. See p. 101, Group of the Paidikos Alabastra, no. 30.

Add that the alabastron London 1902.12–28.2 (no. 12) has a second inscription, the word ΕΠΟΙΕΣΕΝ sole: cf. p. 70.

CUPS MINGLING EPELEIAN ELEMENTS (p. 146)
AND EUERGIDEAN

ARV.[1] *67. See p. 1626.*

CUPS
(nos. 2–5 go together)

1 (1). FLORENCE A B 4, frr. Part, *CV*. pl. A, B 4. A, athletes.

2 (2). LONDON E 22, from Vulci. I, Murray no. 18; A, *JHS*. 23, 288. I, hoplitodromos; A, hoplitodromoi arming. B, warriors. For the shape, Bloesch 51, Euergides no. 5.

3 (3). MUNICH 2608 (J. 1309), from Vulci. Part of A–B, Jacobsthal *O.* pl. 72, b; B, Bloesch *FAS*. pl. 15, 3. I, satyr; A, satyrs and maenad. B, komos? (two youths stopping a third). Restored. For the shape, Bloesch 51, Euergides no. 7.

4 (4). MUNICH 2607 (J. 1168), from Vulci. I, cup-bearer at krater. A, youths seated, one of them with writing-tablets. B, komos. Restored. For the shape, Bloesch 51, Euergides no. 6. Compare the last.

5. ARLESHEIM, Schweizer. I, jumper. A–B, vintage (satyrs). Restored.

6 (6–8, +). LOUVRE C 11258. I, warrior. A, youths with horses. B, athletes. Below A–B, maeander. This includes the fragments S 1389, S 1392, S 1385, which in *ARV.*[1] were said to be in one style. Many other Louvre fragments join them, and the cup is not far from complete. Two of the fragments composing it had been inserted by Campana's restorer into the cup Louvre G 23 (I, youth at well. A–B, fight: coarse work on the fringe of the Epeleios Group): one of them is the foot of our cup, with the middle of the warrior inside; the other has the head and shoulders of the third figure on B. Louvre G 23 has now been cleaned, the alien foot removed, and several Louvre fragments added, including part of the palmettes, and (S 1364) the head of the right-hand warrior on one half, with parts of his spear and shield.

THE GROUP OF ACROPOLIS 96

ARV.[1] *67, v–vi. Hesp. 15, 279–80 (Vanderpool).*

In *ARV.*[1] 67 I put four small cups together as by 'the Painter of Agora P 1275', and three others as near them and by 'the Painter of Acropolis 96'.

I now run the two groups together, and omit Agora P 1275, which as Vander-pool has pointed out (*Hesp.* 15, 279) is rather different in style and shape from Agora P 1272, P 1273, P 1274.

The eight cups are probably all by one hand, nos. 1–4 being earlier, nos. 5–8 later and nearer to the Euergides Painter.

CUPS

1 (vi 1). ATHENS Acr. 96, from Athens. Langlotz pl. 7, whence *E.A.A.* i, 53 fig. 78. I, komast. For the shape, Bloesch 121 no. 26.

2 (v 2). ATHENS, Agora, P 1272, from Athens. Incomplete, *Hesp.* 15 pl. 30, 33. I, jumper.

3 (v 3). ATHENS, Agora, P. 1274, from Athens. Incomplete, *Hesp.* 15 pl. 30, 35. I, symposion (youth reclining).

4 (v 4). ATHENS, Agora, P 1273, from Athens. *Hesp.* 15 pl. 30, 34. I, sym-posion (youth reclining).

5 (vi 2). ADRIA s.n. 1, fr., from Adria. *CV.* pl. 1, 7; *Riv. Ist.* N.S. 5–6, 32 fig. 3. I, naked youth lifting a vessel.

6 (vi 3). TÜBINGEN E 34. Watzinger pl. 19. I, komast. Already attributed by Watzinger to 'the following of the Euergides Painter'.

7. GELA, from Gela. *NSc.* 1956, 378. I, fish-boy.

8. OXFORD 1947.260 (ex Richmond, Cook). I, komast. Said in *ARV.*[1] 66, iii no. 3, to be in the manner of the Euergides Painter, which is quite true. For the shape, Bloesch 123 no. 39.

Compare with these the small

CUPS

1. ATHENS, Agora, P 1264, fr., from Athens. *Hesp.* 15 pl. 29, 31. I, youth.
2. FLORENCE DB 8 (part ex Villa Giulia). Part, *CV.* pl. D, B 8. I, symposion (youth reclining). . . . IKOϚ (that is, perhaps, [Παιδ]ικος).

Also related, the small

CUP

ATHENS, Agora, P 1275, from Athens. Incomplete, *Hesp.* 15 pl. 30, 36. I, wine-boy: boy carrying two pointed amphorae (empties) on a stick over his shoulder.

Vanderpool noted that a black cup found near Agora P 1272–P 1275 was of the same size, shape, and fabric:
ATHENS, Agora, P 1267, from Athens. *Hesp.* 15 pl. 63, 226.

THE PAINTER OF BOLOGNA 433

Miss Talcott saw that Agora P 24103 was by the same hand as Bologna 433. Related to cups in the manner of Euergides Painter: compare New York 41.162.76 and Louvre G 98 (p. 98 nos. 16 and 17).

CUPS

1. ATHENS, Agora, P 24103, from Athens. I, boxer. [Talcott].
2. BOLOGNA 433, from Bologna. Zannoni pl. 107, 4 and 15; *CV*. pl. 1, 1. I, boxers. [ΓΡΟΣΑ]ΛΟΡΕVΟ. [Talcott].

Compare the fragments of

CUPS

1. ATHENS Acr. 175, fr., from Athens. I, (back of head, ear, shoulder, of a youth to left).
2. ADRIA Bc 92, fr., from Adria. I, acontist.

A small group may perhaps find place at the end of the Euergidean chapter:

THE GROUP OF MONTAUBAN 11

The two may be by one hand.

CUPS

1. MONTAUBAN 11, fr. I, naked youth running.
2. BARCELONA, from Ampurias. García y Bellido pl. 98, 98. I, cup-bearer.

CHAPTER 8

KACHRYLION AND OTHERS, POTTERS

The painters in this chapter are but loosely connected with one another. Many of the vases in it were painted for the potters Kachrylion, Hermaios, Chelis; and it begins with lists of the vases that bear the signatures of these potters.

KACHRYLION, POTTER

Bloesch *FAS.* 45–47 and 161.

The signature occurs on twenty-nine cups and a plate. Many painters are seen to have collaborated with Kachrylion, from Euphronios downwards.

CUPS
(nos. 1–7, by the Hermaios Painter)

1. BOSTON 95.33, fr. P. 110 no. 3.
2. LOUVRE MNC 736. P. 110 no. 5.
3. ADRIA B 485, fr. P. 110 no. 11.
4. LOUVRE G 35. P. 111 no. 13.
5. CAMBRIDGE 71. P. 111 no. 14.
6. BUCAREST, Severeano. P. 111 no. 15.
7. BERLIN 2267. P. 111 no. 16.

(no. 8, perhaps by the Hermaios Painter)

8. VILLA GIULIA, fr. P. 111.

(nos. 9–15, by Oltos)

9. NAPLES, Astarita, 47. P. 57 no. 39.
10. LONDON E 41. P. 58 no. 51.
11. LONDON E 40. P. 59 no. 54.
12. ROME, Torlonia. P. 59 no. 56.
13. FLORENCE (part ex Villa Giulia), HEIDELBERG 5, BRUNSWICK 537, BALTIMORE, and BOWDOIN. P. 59 no. 55.
14. COPENHAGEN. P. 59 no. 57.
15. VILLA GIULIA, and NAPLES, Astarita, 298. P. 59 no. 60.

(nos. 16–17, by Euphronios)

16. MUNICH 2620. P. 16 no. 17.
17. LOUVRE C 11981, fr. P. 17 no. 21.

(the next comes from a large cup like Munich 2620):

18. MARZABOTTO, fr. (part of the foot), from Marzabotto. On the foot (as in Munich 2620) [+A+]PVLIONEΓOIEϚ[EN]. See Bloesch 46, Kachrylion no. 14.

(nos. 19–20, by the Thalia Painter)

19. PALERMO V 655. P. 113 no. 3.
20. LOUVRE G 37. P. 113 no. 5.

(nos. 21–22, by the Painter of Louvre G 36)

21. LOUVRE G 36. P. 114 no. 1.
22. LOUVRE G 38. P. 114 no. 2.

(nos. 23–30, by various painters)

23. LOUVRE C 11229 *bis*, fr. I, (toes to right). A, (foot to right). On I, [+A+]PYLI[ON .... The very little that remains recalls the Thalia Painter.

24. SYRACUSE 21198, from Gela. *ML.* 17, 458, whence Hoppin i, 172, Pfuhl fig. 352, Swindler fig. 302. I, boy grooming horse. Coral-red used. +A+PVLION EΓOIEϚEN. Recalls Louvre G 38 (no. 22).

25. LENINGRAD inv. NB 6484 (ex Russian Archaeological Society), fr. *Zapiski* 7 pl. 1, 1 and pp. 78–80. I, youth with horse. Coral-red used. +A+[PVLIO]N and retr. [EΓOIEϚE]N.

26. LONDON 97.10–28.2, frr., from Orvieto. Part, *JHS.* 41, 121; part, Hoppin i, 158. I, archer. A, sacrifice. B, athletes. Coral-red used. On I, [+A+P]VLI[O]N [EΓOIEϚ]EN. For the style see p. 115.

27. FLORENCE 91456, from Orvieto. *Mus. It.* 3 pl. 2, whence HM. pl. 10, Hoppin i, 153, and Pfuhl fig. 351; I, Jacobsthal O., plates, title-page; I, Greifenhagen *Eroten* 21 fig. 14; A–B, Dugas and Flacelière pll. 4–5; *CV.* pll. 78–80 and pl. 116, 5. I, Eros flying over the sea. A–B, deeds of Theseus: A, Sinis, Minotaur, Procrustes; B, Skiron, Kerkyon, bull. Coral-red used. On A, +A+PV[LION] EΓOIEϚENEΓOEϚE complete aft. On B, +A+PVLION [EΓO]IEϚEN, ΚALOϚ, NAI+I. For the shape, Bloesch 45 Kachrylion no. 6. See below, p. 109.

28. LENINGRAD (ex Botkin). I, male running (to right: parts of the legs remain, of the right arm, and of the hair). A, Dionysos with maenads and satyrs; B, satyrs attacking maenads. On I, [+A+P]VLION and retr. EΓOIEϚEN. Restored, I much. For the subject of B, CB. ii, 96 no. 5. Miserable style.

29. ROMAN MARKET (Basseggio: ex Canino, *Mus. etr.* 1186: now lost), FLORENCE 4 B 19 (part ex Villa Giulia), and CAB. MÉD. (ex Fröhner), from Vulci. The Basseggio part, B.Ap. xxii. 103, whence *WV.* F pl. 1 (whence Hartwig 28–31, whence Hoppin i, 174), and (I) Klein *Euphr.* 314; the Florence part, *CV.* pl. 4, B 19 and *CF.* pl. Y, 13. I, satyr. A, death of

Aigisthos. B, fight. On I, +A+PVLION EΓOIESEN. On A, LEA-
ΛPOS[KA]LOS. On B, [LEAΛ]POÇKALOÇ retr. See *CF*. 10 on *CV*.
Fl. pl. 4 B 19. The Basseggio part of the exterior was very much restored,
and so in the reproductions. To the fragments described in *CF*. add one
in Cab. Méd. (ex Fröhner) which gives the legs of the fifth figure on B
and the upper part of the sixth; and one in Villa Giulia which seems to
give the hand and forearm of Klytaimestra with the elbow of Orestes.
Abominable style.

PLATE

30. ATHENS Acr. 3, fr., from Athens. Langlotz pl. 2. One carrying baskets
on a pole. [+A]+PVLI[ON .... Decent style.

Two cups have some kinship with the Kachrylion cup in Florence (p. 108
no. 27):

LEIPSIC T 497. I, satyr. A, athletes. B, komos. Coral red used.

LONDON E 13, from Vulci. A, *Archaeologia* 32 pl. 10; I, Murray no. 10. I,
Eros. A, Ajax and Odysseus quarrelling. B, Achilles and Troilos. For
the shape, Bloesch 45, Kachrylion no. 12. See p. 1626.

HERMAIOS, POTTER

CUPS

1. BOSTON 03.844, fr. By the Hermaios Painter (p. 110 no. 1).
2. LENINGRAD 647. By the Hermaios Painter (p. 110 no. 2).
3. LONDON E 34. By the Hermaios Painter (p. 110 no. 8).
4. LONDON 96.10–22.1. Probably by the Hermaios Painter (p. 111).

CHELIS, POTTER

Bloesch *FAS*. 35–36, 50, and 161.

CUPS

1. MUNICH 2589. By the Chelis Painter (p. 112 no. 1).
2. NAPLES 2615. Part by Oltos (p. 57 no. 43), part by the Chelis Painter
(p. 112 no. 2).
3. CAB. MÉD. 335. The outside by the Thalia Painter, early (p. 112 no. 1);
the inside perhaps by Oltos.
4. LOUVRE G 15. By the Euergides Painter (p. 91 no. 51).

For the fifth signature of Chelis, on a fragment of a cup, doubtless black-
figure, in the Cabinet des Médailles(Benndorf pl. 29, 20), see *ABV*. 235.

See also p. 62 no. 78.

THE HERMAIOS PAINTER

VA. 14. *Att. V.* 48–49 and 468. *Anz.* 1923–4, 165–72 (Kraiker). *ARV.*[1] 77–79 and 950.

In *ARV.*[1] 78–79 the cups of what I called the Severeano Group were said to be related to the Hermaios Painter, and perhaps to be later work of his, influenced by Oltos, with a new system of proportions. I now take them to be in fact by the Hermaios Painter, later work. In the list that follows, 'S' in the serial number between brackets stands for 'Severeano'.

CUPS

1 (1). BOSTON 03.844, fr. Hoppin ii, 15; CB. i pl. 3, 10. I, horseman. Coral-red used. HE[P]MA[IOSEΓOIESE]N.

2 (2). LENINGRAD 647, from Marion. *Burl. 1888* pl. 3, 5 = Fröhner *Brant.* pl. 3, 3, whence Hoppin ii, 18. I, Dionysos. HEPMAIOS EΓOIESEN.

3 (3). BOSTON 95.33, from Marion. *Burl. 1888* pl. 3, 7 = Hartwig 32 = Fröhner *Brant.* pl. 3, 1; Hoppin i, 150; CB. i pl. 3, 11, and i, 9; the shape, Caskey G. 194 no. 148. I, maenad. +A+PVLION EΓOIESEN. For the shape, Bloesch 119 no. 1.

4. PHILADELPHIA MARKET, fr. Bothmer *Am.* pl. 72, 3. I, Amazon. [Enrico Paribeni]. See Bothmer *Am.* 155.

5. LOUVRE MNC 736, from Velanideza. *Mél. d'arch.* 9, 22, whence Perrot 10, 385, *Zapiski* 7, 83, and Hoppin i, 169. I, warrior. +A+PVL[I]ON-E[ΓOI]ESEN. For the shape, Bloesch 119 no. 2.

6 (5). OXFORD 1919.26, fr. *CV.* pl. 1, 4. I, fish-boy. . . . ISTOS and the tip of the first letter of another word.

7. ATHENS, Agora, P 26228, fr., from Athens. *Hesp.* 28 pl. 22, b. I, Ixion.

8 (6). LONDON E 34, from Marion. *Burl. 1888* pl. 3, 6 = Fröhner *Brant.* pl. 3, 2; *BSA.* 14, 294, a; Sudhoff i, 24; Hoppin ii, 16; A, Bloesch pl. 33, 3. I, naked woman with laver. HEPMAIOSEΓOIESEN. For the shape, Bloesch 119 no. 5. See p. 1626.

9 (a). ATHENS, Agora, P 9356, fr., from Athens. I, symposion (man or youth reclining). . . . NOON, . . . ILOSOΛ. The second inscription may be φ]ίλος ὤν. The first might be the end of a name, [Ξυν]νοῶν, or the end of a verse (compare for example the skolion Diehl 18 (καθαρὸν θεμένη νόον).

10. LONDON 1900.2–14.10, fr., from Naucratis. *BSA.* 5 pl. 8, 12. I, Amazon putting on her greaves.

11 (a). ADRIA B 485, fr., from Adria. Micali *Mon. ined.* pl. 45, 3; Schöne pl. 2, 4, whence Klein *Euphr.* 113, *Jb.* 26, 180, and Hoppin i, 147; part, *CV.* pl. 3, 3; part, *Riv. Ist.* N.S. 5–6, 32 fig. 4. I, symposion (man reclining, playing kottabos). [+A+]PV[LIONEΓ]OIE[SE]N. See p. 1626.

12 (a). HEIDELBERG 36, fr., from Athens. *Anz.* 1923–4, 167; Kraiker pl. 5. I, komast. . . . ΕΓΟΙ]ΕϟΕΝ. [Kraiker].

13 (S1). LOUVRE G 35, fr., from Vulci. Hartwig pl. 2, 2, whence Hoppin i, 161; ph. Al. 23733, right, whence Langlotz *GV.* pl. 9, 14 and Bothmer *Am.* pl. 72, 1; *Enc. phot.* iii, 3, b. I, Amazon. +Λ+PVLION ΕΓΟΙ-ΕϟΕΝ.

14 (S2). CAMBRIDGE 71, from Vulci. E. Gardner pl. 27; Hartwig pl. 2, 3, whence Hoppin i, 151; *CV.* pl. 25, 2. I, komast. +Λ+PVLION ΕΓΟΙ-ΕϟΕΝ. For the shape, Bloesch 45, Kachrylion no. 2. See p. 1626.

15 (S3). BUCAREST, Hist. Mus., from Chiusi. *Demareteion* 1, 5. I, warrior. +Λ+PVLION ΕΓΟΙΕϟ[Ε]Ν.

16 (S4). BERLIN 2267, from Etruria. Hartwig pl. 2, 1, whence Hoppin i, 149; Neugebauer pl. 48, 1 = Diepolder *G.V.* 40. I, satyr balancing a kantharos on his back. +Λ+PVLIONEΓΟΙΕϟΕΝ. For the shape, Bloesch 45, Kachrylion no. 3. Restored. See p. 1626.

17 (a). HEIDELBERG 27, fr. Kraiker pl. 4. A, athletes.

Another cup is probably by the Hermaios Painter:

(a). LONDON 96.10–22.1, from Vulci. *El.* 3 pl. 73; *BSA.* 14, 294, b; Hoppin ii, 17; *Anz.* 1923–4, 171. I. Hermes. ΗΕΡΜΑΙΟϟ [ΕΓΟΙΕϟ]ΕΝ. For the subject compare the Corinthian skyphos Louvre L 173 (Payne *NC.* pl. 31, 10 and p. 129). Burrows and Ure (*BSA.* 14, 295) argue that the cup, now fragmentary, was complete when published in *El.* 3 pl. 73, where the top of the caduceus is given, and the ΕΓΟΙΕϟΕΝ entire. For the shape, Bloesch 120 no. 6.

The following cup is near the Hermaios Painter, and may be his:

BERLIN 2271. R.I. App. Braun xii. 6, b. I, Herakles with the apples of the Hesperides. Restored (the left foot modern). For the shape, Bloesch 120 no. 12.

A cup-fragment recalls the Hermaios Painter:

ATHENS, Agora, P 23172, fr., from Athens. *Hesp.* 23 pl. 15, b. I, hoplito-dromos (at the start: on the attitude see *BSA.* 46, 10–11). [?ΗΙ]ΓΟ-ΜΕ[ΔΟΝ?

A cup-fragment of good style might also be by the Hermaios Painter, but little is preserved:

VILLA GIULIA, fr. I, hunter (part of the head and shoulder of a man in cloak and Robin Hood petasos to right, carrying a fox on a pole over his shoulder). [+Λ+]PVLION . . .

THE CHELIS PAINTER

CF. 7 on pl. 1 B 17. *ARV.*[1] 79–80 and 950.

CUPS

1. (3). MUNICH 2589 (J. 736), from Vulci. FR. pl. 43 and i, 231, whence Hoppin i, 185; palmettes, Jacobsthal O. pl. 75, a; I, Licht iii, 225; I, Vorberg *Gloss.* 735. I, satyr; A, Dionysos with satyr and maenad; B, satyr and maenads. On I, ⊢ΕⱢΙϞ ΕΓΟΙΕΙ. For the shape, Bloesch 35, Chelis no. 3. See p. 1626.

2 (2). NAPLES 2615, from Etruria. Hoppin i, 186–7; part, *PP.* pll. 6–7. I, satyr; A, maenad and donkeys; B, between eyes, satyr. I and A are by Oltos (p. 57 no. 43) (with the inscriptions [⊢]ΕⱢΙϞΕΓΟΙΕϞΕΝ on I, MEMMNON ΚΑⱢΟϞ on A), B (and the handle-palmettes) by the Chelis Painter. See *PP.* 27–28. For the shape, Bloesch 35, Chelis no. 2. See also p. 48 no. 167.

Probably also the small cup-fragment

OXFORD, Beazley, fr. A, (forearm, hand, and tail of a satyr to left, holding a flute; then part of a palmette).

———————

THE THALIA PAINTER

The cup Cab. Méd. 335, which was no. 1 in my earlier list of vases by the Chelis Painter, is not, I now think, by the same hand as the other two; it goes closely with six cups which I then classed as 'the Chelis Group' and spoke of as continuing the Chelis Painter's style and as perhaps being later work by him. I now prefer to make a new heading, 'the Thalia Painter' (named after one of the characters on the Berlin cup inv. 3251, below, no. 7), and to include Cabinet des Médailles 335.

The work of the Thalia Painter varies greatly in quality. The Berlin cup (no. 7) is fine, so is the Acropolis fragment (no. 6); the rest are hasty, and the inside of Louvre G 37 (no. 5), painted for Kachrylion, is particularly poor.

In the bracketed serial numbers, 'C' refers to the 'Chelis Painter' list in *ARV.*[1], 'CG' to the 'Chelis Group' list there.

CUPS

1 (C1). CAB. MÉD. 335, from Vulci. Hoppin i, 188–9; B, Jacobsthal O. pl. 63, a; *CV.* pl. 95, 6–9, and pl. 96, 1–3; part of A, *E.A.A.* ii, 542; phs. Gir. 8051–3 and 26089. I, bf., satyr. A–B, between eyes. A, acontist. B, plant. On I, [⊢]ΕⱢΙϞΕΓΟ[Ι]ΕϞΝ. The inside picture may be by Oltos, see p. 67 no. 8. For the shape, Bloesch 35, Chelis no. 1. See p. 44 no. 89. I is restored.

2 (CGI). VILLA GIULIA (part ex Florence). Part, *CV*. Fl. pl. 1, B 17. I, acontist (running to left); A–B, between palmettes and eyes: A, acontist (running to left); B, jumper (to right). I is restored. See p. 50 no. 199.

3 (CG2). PALERMO V 655, from Chiusi. Inghirami *Chius*. pll. 209–11; Hartwig pl. 1, whence *Zapiski* 7, 84 and Hoppin i, 160; palmettes, Jacobsthal O. pl. 73, a; *CV*. pl. 8, 2 and pl. 9. I, warrior picking up his shield. A–B, komos. On I, +A[+PVL]ION KAL[O]ϟ. Καλός is substituted for ἐποίησεν, whether inadvertently or not: compare Louvre G 10 by Skythes (p. 83 no. 3). For the shape, Bloesch 45, Kachrylion no. 9.

4 (CG3). WARSAW 198514 (ex Pollak). I, *Jh*. 1, 44 fig. 28; A, Michalowski *Sztuka* 31; phs. R.I. 2949–51. I, victor. A–B, komos. Cf. Palermo V 655 (no. 3). (See also p. 114, above, nos. 2 and 3).

5 (CG 4, +). LOUVRE G 37. I, Pottier pl. 91, whence Hoppin i, 164 and Pfuhl fig. 353. I, acontist. A, fight. B, unexplained: what remains is, on the left, a cloven hoof, and above it, a large human foot, both to left. On I, +A+PVLIO[N] EΓOIEϟEN. Several Louvre fragments join the old and have been added: A is not far from complete. A loose fragment should be from the floral to right of B. See below.

6. ATHENS Acr., fr., from Athens. A, (face and front-hair of a youth or woman to left). Coral-red used. Offset lip. Compare Berlin inv. 3251 (no. 7).

7 (CG5). BERLIN inv. 3251 and Florence 1 B 49 (part ex Villa Giulia), from Vulci. Lücken pl. 82, 1 and pll. 80–81; I, Vorberg *Geschl*. pl. 9; part, *CV*. Fl. pl. 1, B 49; I and parts of A–B, Vorberg *Gloss*. 128, 536, and 538. All these without the Florence frr.; the Florence frr., *CF*. pl. Z, 9–15. I, love-making; A–B, love-making. On I, LEAΛPOϟKAL[Oϟ]. Two of the women outside are ⊙ALIA and (retr.) KOPONE. One of the women inside is ϟMIKA, only the last letter remaining, but the rest given in *Réserve etrusque* no. 26. One of the persons outside is E[VNI]kOϟ. For the shape, Bloesch 45, Kachrylion no. 11. See p. 1626.

Near these the cup

(CG6, +). LOUVRE G 68. I, Pottier pl. 96; incompletely, phs. Gir. 28541–2 and 28543, 1. I, satyr and maenad; A–B, Dionysos with maenads and satyrs. Several Louvre frr. join and have been added. With the new frr., phs. Arch. phot. S.4240.004. AE. 1 and BE. 1; one of the new frr., Vorberg *Gloss*. 335, above, left. See p. 115, foot.

A cup-fragment may be compared with Louvre G 37 (above, no. 5):
ATHENS Acr. 196, fr., from Athens. Langlotz pl. 9. I, warrior.

RELATED TO THE THALIA PAINTER

(i)

CUPS

1 (a1). CAMBRIDGE (Massachusetts), Dewing (ex Seltman). I, discus-thrower. ΚΑLΟ$ preceded by an illegible name, the second letter of which is E. Compare the early cups Cab. Méd. 335 and Villa Giulia (pp. 112–13 nos. 1 and 2).

2. LUCERNE MARKET (A.A.). *Ars Ant. Aukt. II* pll. 60–61, 150. I, hunter (youth running with club and cloak). A, komos (youth and man, kneeling facing each other). B, herdsman and bull. Restored. Compare Warsaw 198514 and Palermo V 655 (p. 113 nos. 4 and 3).

3 (a9). Lost. R.I. ix. 35. I, komast (youth moving to left, looking round, drinking-horn in left hand). A, youths leading horses. B, fight. Coral-red used. Compare Warsaw 198514 (p. 113 no. 4).

The cup Naples Stg. 5, no. 7 in the old list of the Chelis Group, is akin to Louvre G 68, but is in a larger style: I said that it seemed to show the influence of Euthymides or of the Kleophrades Painter in his earliest phase, and was to be grouped with an amphora in Leyden and a hydria in Munich. It now appears to me to be by the same hand as they: and I place the three vases, with a fourth recently discovered, under the heading of 'Pezzino Painter' and in a different chapter (p. 32).

THE PAINTER OF LOUVRE G 36

ARV.[1] 82.

These two Kachrylions are akin to Louvre G 37 (p. 113 no. 5), but worse.

CUPS

1 (1). LOUVRE G 36. Pottier pl. 91, whence Perrot 10, 382 and 383 fig. 227, Hoppin i, 163, (rough sketch of I) Norman Gardiner *Athl.* fig. 211; detail of A, Sudhoff i, 34. I, ball-player; A, athletes at laver; B, victor. On I, +A+[PVLI]ON ΕΓ[ΟΙΕ$]E complete aft. Restored. For the shape, Bloesch 47, Kachrylion no. 16.

2 (2, +). LOUVRE G 38. Incompletely, Hartwig 24–27, whence Hoppin i, 166. I, athlete rubbing his arm. A, concert (citharode or flute-player); B, a similar scene: the person in the middle may be singing. On I, +A+PVLION ΕΓΟΙΕ$E complete. Two Louvre fragments join the old and have been added. One gives what was missing of figure and inscription on I; the other, the upper part of the seated man on A. For the shape, Bloesch 47, Kachrylion no. 17.

The Kachrylion cup London 97.10–28.2 (p. 108 no. 26).

ARV.[1] 82–83.

The following are not far from it, but I do not venture to speak of a group:

CUPS

1 (6). CAB. MÉD. 519, fr. A, athletes (athlete moving to right, flute-player standing to left; acontia in the field). Lipped cup.

2 (5). ATHENS, Agora, P 1265, frr., from Athens. *Hesp.* 15 pl. 29, 32, and p. 279. A, athletes (boxers?). Coral-red used.

3 (7). LONDON E 36, from Vulci. I, Murray no. 21; A–B, Cecil Smith pl. 2. I, komast. A–B, deeds of Theseus: A, Procrustes, Kerkyon, Minotaur; B, bull, sow. See p. 1626.

4. ATHENS Acr. 194, fr., from Athens. Langlotz pl. 9. I, Hermes. ΙϹL . . . retr.

PEITHINOS

Att. V. 49–50; *ARV.*[1] 81–82.

There are two signed vases:

CUPS

1. BASLE, Cahn, 52, fr. I, satyr at volute-krater (to left, holding oinochoe and wineskin). All that remains of the outside pictures is the lower edge of a handle-palmette and to left of it an uncertain vestige. On I, ΓΕΙ◊Ι-Ν[ΟϚ] (retr.), followed by [Ε]ΛΡΑΦΕ (not retr.). There may have been a nu at the end of the verb, but there need not have been.

2. BERLIN 2279, from Vulci. Gerhard *Tr.* pl. 9, 1 and pl. 14–15, whence (I) HM. pl. 23; Hartwig pl. 24, 1 and pl. 25, whence Hoppin ii, 335, Licht ii, 93 and 149, (I and B) Perrot 10, 515–17, (detail of A–B) FR. iii, 20, (I) Robert *Herm.* 149 fig. 119, (I) *Hist. rel.* 169; I and part of A, Pfuhl fig. 417 (= Pfuhl *Mast.* fig. 50); I, Langlotz *G.V.* pl. 11, 17; I, Schaal *Rf.* fig. 8; I, Neugebauer pl. 49, 1 = Diepolder *GV.* 41 (whence LS. fig. 51); B, Hofkes-Brukker pl. 9, 20; I, Stella 427, above. I, Peleus and Thetis. A, youths and boys; B, youths and women. On I, ΓΕΙΘΙΝΟϚΕΛΡΑΦϚΕΝ-ΑΘΕΝΟΔΟΤΟϚΚΑLΟϚ. Slightly restored (the fractures repainted). For the subject of A, *Cypr.* 28–9, α 48 (dated too early); for the shape, Bloesch 54. See p. 1626.

But for the signature, no one would have thought of connecting the new fragment (no. 1) with the Berlin Peithinos cup, which is, of course, much later —contemporary with the other cups that bear the same kalos-name—and an exceptional piece, among the most elaborate of all cups (and among the most affected).

The satyr on the new fragment resembles those on the Louvre cup G 68 (p. 113), and might perhaps be early work by the same hand.

A cup-fragment may perhaps be compared with the Berlin Peithinos: ATHENS Acr. 248, fr., from Athens. Langlotz pl. 14; the shape, Bloesch pl. 40. I, youth or man, and boy. ... k]ALOϚ:ϟ[... and, between the two persons, ... IⲪEPO ... (i.e. σο]ὶ φέρω Langlotz). For the shape (Acrocup), Bloesch 141 no. 1, and 143. Mrs. Karouzou conjectures that a new Acropolis fr. may belong: on the left of I, part of a himation and of the line-border, with the inscription ... EΛ]PAⲪϟ[...

CHAPTER 9

APOLLODOROS

THE Epidromos Painter is so close to Apollodoros that it must be considered whether they are not the same: the Epidromos Painter would be early Apollodoros. The works of the Kleomelos Painter and the Elpinikos Painter are very close to each other, and to the Epidromos Painter and Apollodoros: to be considered whether these two groups also are not merely phases of Apollodoros.

i. THE EPIDROMOS PAINTER

Hartwig (*Meist.* 44 and *Jb.* 8, 169) put together six of the cups with the kalos-name Epidromos (nos. 1, 2, 5, 7, 8, 13), but attributed them to 'Kachrylion'.

Att. V. 51–52 and 468; *ARV.*¹ 84–85, 922, and 950. See above.

CUPS

1 (1). BRUSSELS A 1378, from Chiusi. I, Inghirami *Chius.* pl. 35, whence *El.* 3 pl. 87; I, *Jb.* 8, 169; I, Furtwängler *Somzée* pl. 37, iii, 4 = *Vente Somzée* pl. 1, 41; *CV.* pl. 23, 3. I, Hermes carrying a ram. A–B, symposion. On I, ΕΠΙΔΡΟΜ[ΟΣ] ΚΑΛΟΣ.

2 (2). BERLIN inv. 3232. I and B, *Jb.* 8 pl. 2, 1, whence (I) Buschor *Satyrtänze* fig. 64; B, Vorberg *Gloss.* 50; I, ph. Marb. LA 1075.13. I, Herakles sacrificing, assisted by a satyr. A, satyr attacking a sleeping maenad. B, Herakles and Cerberus. On I, ΕΠΙΔΟΡΟΜΟΣ ΚΑΛΟΣ. On A, ΕΠΙΔΟΡΟΜΟΣΚΑΛΟΣ. On B, ΕΠΙΔΟΜΟΣΚΑΛΟΣ. For the subject of A, CB. ii, 96, no. 4; for the shape, Bloesch 94, Hieron no. 25.

3 (3). FLORENCE PD 341, fr., from Populonia. I, (uncertain remains of drapery). A, (feet: symposion?). On I, [ΕΠΙΔ]ΡΟΜ[ΟΣ.

4 (4). LENINGRAD 664, from Vulci. *Izv. M.K.* 1 pl. 15. I, man with hare and dog. ΕΠΙΔΡΟΜΟΣ ΚΑΛΟΣ.

5 (5). Once CANINO, from Vulci. Gerhard pl. 276, 5–6, whence *Izv. M.K.* 1 pl. 16. I, man with dog. ΕΠΙΔΡΟΜΟΣΚΑΛΟΣ.

6. DUBLIN (New Hampshire), Ray W. Smith. *Auktion xviii Basel* pl. 32, 111. I, boxer sitting on the ground, binding his hand. ΕΠΙΔΡΟΜΟΣ ΚΑΛΟΣ. [Cahn].

7 (6, +). LOUVRE G 112. Hartwig pl. 3, 2, whence Rumpf *Rel.* fig. 165; Pottier pl. 105; ph. Gir. 37791. I, sacrifice of a pig. ΕΠΙΔΡΟΜΟΣ-ΚΑΛΟΣ, and on the exergue ΚΑΛΟΣ. Two Louvre frr. have been added since the publications: one completes the picture by giving the rest of

the man's left hand and of the kalos-inscription; the other adds the second handle. With the new frr., ph. Arch. phot. S.4240.005 AE. 1.

8 (7). VIENNA 3691 (ex Oest. Mus. 321), from Cervetri. Masner 41 (= *Jb.* 6, 258), whence HM. pl. 33, 1; *CV.* pl. 2, 4–6 and p. 9. I, Hermes leading a dog disguised as a pig to sacrifice. ΕΓ[Ι]ΔΡΟΜ[ΟΣ]ΚΑ[ΛΟΣ]. The inscription detected by Eichler. For the shape, Bloesch 127, Apollodoros Class, no. 7. See p. 1627.

9 (8). VILLA GIULIA 20775, from Cervetri. I, youth (in himation, leaning on his stick).

10 (9). ADRIA B 1002, fr., from Adria. Schöne pl. 9, 2; *CV.* pl. 2, 2. I, (unexplained subject; two males, one in a long chiton, the other, naked, kneeling).

11 (10). BOLOGNA 436, from Bologna. Pellegrini 207; *CV.* pl. 1, 6. I, symposion (two youths reclining). [Ε]ΓΙΔΡΟΜΟΣ[Κ]ΑΛΟΣ. For the inscription, *JHS.* 49, 288; for the shape, Bloesch 126, Apollodoros Class, no. 6.

12 (11). VILLA GIULIA 20764, from Cervetri. I, Dionysos seated. [ΕΓ]Ι-ΔΡΟΜΟΣΚΑΛΟΣ.

13 (12). LONDON E 43. Hartwig pl. 3, 3 = Klein *L.* 85 = Fröhner *Brant.* pl. 4. I, fight. ΕΓΙΔΡΟΜΟΣΚΑΛΟΣ. Now cleaned. For the shape, Bloesch 121 no. 35. See p. 1627.

14. LUCERNE MARKET (A.A.). I, youth embracing girl; beside them, a water-bird. ΕΓΙΔΡΟΜΟΣΚΑΛΟΣ.

ROUND ARYBALLOS

15 (13). CORINTH C 31.77, fr., from Corinth. Athletes.

---

ii. THE KLEOMELOS PAINTER

Att. V. 52, middle. *BSA.* 29, 205. *ARV.*[1] 85–86 and 950. See p. 117.

Called after the kalos-name on nos. 1 and 2. These surely look like choice work by the Epidromos Painter.

CUP

1 (1). LOUVRE G 111. Girard *L'éd. ath.* 203 fig. 23; Perrot 10 pl. 11, 1; Pottier pl. 105, whence Schröder *Sport* pl. 60, 3; *Dedalo* 4, 732; ph. Gir. 33397. I, discus-thrower. ΚΛΕΟΜΕΛΟΣΚΑΛΟΣ.

OINOCHOE
(shape 3, chous)

2 (2). ATHENS Acr. 703, from Athens. Langlotz pl. 55. Herakles and Apollo: the struggle for the tripod. [ΚΛΕΟ]ΜΕΛΟΣ . . .

ROUND ARYBALLOS

3 (3). NAPLES RC 177, from Cumae. *ML.* 22 pl. 81, 2, whence FR. iii, 247, (part) Schröder *Sport* 161, (part) *Jh.* 31, 1; part, *E.A.A.* iv, 369. Athletes scraping. On the shoulder, A, lion, B, bull.

Near these, the cup-fragment

4. ADRIA B 616, fr., from Adria. Schöne pl. 10, 4. I, (man).

---

iii. THE ELPINIKOS PAINTER

CB. i, 6. *ARV.*[1] 86.

Called after the kalos-name. See p. 117.

CUPS

1 (2). BONN 63, from Orvieto. *AZ.* 1885 pl. 12, 1; *CV.* pl. 3, 5 and pl. 4, 5. I, the Moon. ELΓIN[I]kOϟKALOϟ. For the subject, *JHS.* 59, 150 and *EVP.* 12. For the shape, Bloesch 127, Apollodoros Class, no. 2.

2 (1). MANCHESTER, School of Art, A a 24, from Vulci. *Mem. Manch.* 78 pl. 1, 1; Webster *Gk Interpretations* pl. 4, 1. I, symposion (youth reclining with lyre, playing kottabos). ELΓINIkOϟ KALOϟ. Compare the Florence cup from Orvieto (p. 1) and the cups by Apollodoros in the Paris market (p. 120 no. 12) and in the Louvre (p. 120 no. 1).

3 (3). BOSTON 13. 190, from Cervetri. Incompletely, CB. i pl. 3, 7. I, Menelaos and Helen. ELΓI[NIk]OϟKALOϟ. Now augmented by a fr. ex Leipsic, identified by Kirsten, which gives the right elbow of Menelaos.

Near the Elpinikos Painter, the cup-fragment
LEIPSIC T 609, fr. I, (youth bending).

Related to the Elpinikos Painter, the

CUP

FLORENCE 4221, fr. *CV.* pl. 86, 4. I, symposion (youth reclining, playing kottabos). ELΓIN[IkOϟ . . .

---

iv. APOLLODOROS

Hartwig 628–40. *Att. V.* 52–53 and 468. *JHS.* 53, 69–70. *ARV.*[1] 86–88 and 950.

These cups continue, in the late archaic period, those of the Epidromos Painter; in a mannered, precious form. See p. 117.

CUPS

1 (1, +). LOUVRE G 139–140. Part, Hartwig pl. 69, 2; part, Hoppin i, 47; part, Pottier pl. 115; I, *E.A.A.* i, 475. I, symposion (youth reclining, playing kottabos); A–B, symposion. On I, EVRVΓTOLEMOSKALOS. On A, AΓOLLOA[OROS . . . . On B, EVRVΓTOLEM[OS . . . . A new Louvre fr. joins and adds the right hand of the reveller on the left of B, with the first letter of the inscription; another gives part of the over-handle.

2 (2). TÜBINGEN E 8, fr. Watzinger pl. 17. A, symposion.

3. INNSBRUCK ii. 12. 38, fr. I, (lyre). A, symposion.

4 (3). VILLA GIULIA, and CASTLE ASHBY, Northampton, frr. The Castle Ashby fr., Hartwig pl. 69, 1, whence Hoppin i, 45; all, *JHS.* 53 pl. 6. I, warrior; A, fight; B, warriors advancing (βοηθοί). On I, [EVRVΓTOL]EM[OS . . . . On B, [AΓOLL]OΔOROSEΛRAⴲSEN. See *JHS.* 53, 69–70.

5 (4). FLORENCE 73131 (augmented by frr. ex Florence and Villa Giulia). Part, *CV.* pl. B, B2; *CV.* pl. 88. I, warrior putting on his greaves. A–B, deer-hunt. On I, [EV]PIΓTLEMOS KALOS. For the shape, Bloesch 127, Apollodoros Class, no. 5. [Hartwig, the Florence kernel].

6 (5). ADRIA B 571, fr., from Adria. *CV.* pl. 2, 3. I, (boy, rather than girl).

7 (6). OXFORD 303, from Chiusi. Gardner 29; *CV.* pl. 1, 7. I, Theseus and Minotaur. Restored. For the shape, Bloesch 127, Apollodoros Class, no. 10.

8 (7). TARQUINIA RC 1123, from Tarquinia. *RM.* 5, 343; *CV.* pl. 10, 1. I, warrior attacking a snake.

9 (8). LONDON E 57, from Vulci. Keller *Thiere* 155. I, man with panther-cub. For the shape, Bloesch 127, Apollodoros Class, no. 3. See p. 1627.

10 (9). NEW YORK 18.145.28. Richter and Hall pl. 36, 38. I, youth at altar. Influenced by the early middle—the 'bare'—period of Douris (see p. 425).

11. PRINCETON 33.38. I, komast (youth playing lyre).

12. PARIS MARKET (Koutoulakis). I, symposion (youth reclining, playing kottabos). ΓAMMA+OS KALOS. Slightly restored. Very close to the cup by the Elpinikos Painter in Manchester (p. 119 no. 2).

13 (10). CAB. MÉD., fr. I, (shank, with ankle, of male in cloak moving to right).

14 (11). CAB. MÉD. 682, fr. I, (shank of male in cloak moving to right, with part of the sandalled foot).

15 (12). CAB. MÉD. 624, fr. I, (male in himation standing to left, pouring from an oinochoe; on the right, part of an altar).

16 (13). CAB. MÉD., fr. I, athlete (from navel to ankle, standing with left leg frontal; on the right, his himation on a seat).

17 (a3). ADRIA B 106, fr., from Adria. *CV.* pl. 2, 4. I, warrior approaching altar.

18 (14). CAB. MÉD., fr. I, warrior (greaved, moving to right, spear in right hand, cloak on left arm).

19. ATHENS Acr. (part ex North Slope AP 1255), fr., from Athens. The North Slope part, *Hesp.* 9, 240, 262. I, warrior putting on his greaves. The Acropolis fr. joins the other below, giving more of the shield, and the kappa of the ΚΑΛΟϚ on it.

20 (15). ATHENS Acr. 241, fr., from Athens. Langlotz pl. 10. I, woman (Athena?).

21 (16). VATICAN, from Vulci. *Mus. Greg.* 2 pl. 69, 2, whence Klein *Euphr.* 289; *JHS.* 53, 70; ph. And. 42117, 2. I, trumpeter. For the shape, Bloesch 127, Apollodoros Class, no. 8. Restored. See Bothmer *Am.* 159 (perhaps an Amazon).

22 (17). FLORENCE 4211. *CV.* pl. 86, 2. I, satyr. [Hartwig].

23 (18). Once Alibrandi, from Cervetri. B.Ap. xxii. 94. 3, whence Hartwig 637, whence (redrawn) Buschor *Satyrtänze* fig. 53. I, armed satyr (wearing the drawers of the satyr drama).

24. LEIPSIC T 521, fr., from Orvieto. Hartwig pl. 18, 3, whence *Jb.* 71, 104 fig. 7. I, Hyakinthos.

25 (19). MISSISSIPPI (ex Robinson). *Münzh. Basel 1 Okt. 1935* frontispiece; *CV.* Robinson ii pl. 4; *Jb.* 71, 100. I, Hyakinthos. Restored. See p. 1627.

The name Apollodoros recurs on a tiny cup-fragment in Leipsic. Here it may have been a kalos-name and not a signature (see p. 1565): but what remains of the picture—three triangular ends—can be explained as part of a peculiar shield-apron like those on the Villa Giulia–Castle Ashby cup (p. 120 no. 4); and if so the name is probably from a signature:

LEIPSIC T 3593, fr., from Cervetri. I, (warrior?). ΑΠΟΛΟΔΟ[ROϚ ....

NEAR APOLLODOROS

ARV.[1] 88.

CUPS

1 (2). FLORENCE PD 248, from Orvieto. *NSc.* 1939 pl. 4, 2; *CV.* pl. 86, 3. I, symposion (youth reclining, playing kottabos).

2 (1). OXFORD 1911.621, from Cervetri. Part, *CV.* pl. 2, 2; (augmented by frr. ex Leipsic) *CV.* pl. 51, 6. I, naked man folding his cloak.

Compare also the cup-fragment:

(a). OXFORD, Beazley, fr., from Populonia. I, (sponge and aryballos suspended, ... ΚΑ]ΛΟϚ).

CHAPTER 10

THE COARSER WING, i: THE NIKOSTHENES PAINTER AND HIS CIRCLE

NIKOSTHENES, POTTER

On the black-figured vases, black vases, vase in Six's technique, with the signature of Nikosthenes see *ABV*. 216–35 and 690.[1]

---

[1] The two neck-amphorae by Painter N in the Sligo Collection, nos. 4 and 7 in *ABV*. 225, are the same as the Hodgson vases nos. 5 and 6: I had suspected this, but was informed otherwise. The descriptions should read:

1. BASLE MARKET (M.M.: ex Sligo), from Cervetri. *Auktion xviii Basel* pl. 29, 92. A, horsemen and youths. B, fight. Lower, komos (youths, men, and women dancing), with courting (man and youth: man and boy). Restored.

2. LONDON MARKET (Spink: ex Sligo), from Cervetri. A, Herakles and the lion; B, the like. Lower, komos (youths, man, and women, dancing). Restored.

Add three signed neck-amphorae of Nicosthenic type, by Painter N:

3. PHILADELPHIA MARKET. A, Dionysos with maenads and satyr; B, the like; at each handle, vine. On each handle, warrior. Overlap Group.

4. SWISS PRIVATE. On the shoulder, A, sphinx between lions, B, the like. Lower, satyrs and maenads. On the neck, A, komos: two naked youths at a krater, B, two naked youths.

5. LUCERNE MARKET (A.A.). On the shoulder: A, two sphinxes, between two lions turned toward the handles; B, the like. Lower, floral. On the neck, A, Dionysos with maenad and satyr, B, the like.

6. LUCERNE MARKET (A.A.). On the shoulder, A, between eyes, satyr and maenad, B, the like. On the neck, A, boxers, B, the like (compare Torlonia 1879. 32, *ABV*. 217 no. 8).

7. HANOVER. The body black, except for the base-rays, and three patches on the shoulder. On A, on the patch, a naked youth seated on the ground holding a drinking-horn; on B, a patch to right of one handle and another to left of the other; on each patch a horizontal palmette. On the neck, A, an eye, B, the like. On the topside of the mouth, dolphins. On the left handle, a tripod; on the right handle, floral. Restored. See p. 1627.

To the bf. cups, by various painters, with the signature of Nikosthenes (*ABV*. 232 and 690) add RICHMONZ (Va.). I, gorgoneion. The whole space outside the border of the gorgoneion is striped. A, nose between eyes; B, the like. At each handle, elaborate floral, extending over the space below the eyes, which is reserved. Cup type A: nearest in shape, Berlin 1805 and 1806 (*ABV*. 223–4 nos. 65 and 66). For the handle-florals compare the flowers held by persons on the Nikosthenes pyxis in Florence (76931: *ABV*. 229, vii). See p. 1627.

The cup *ABV*. 231 no. 10 now belongs to a Munich collector; see p. 1627.

The bilingual and red-figured vases with the signature of Nikosthenes are the following:

Group of Louvre F 125:

1. LOUVRE F 125. Cup, bilingual. See p. 161 no. 1.
2. ARLESHEIM, Schweizer. Cup, bilingual. See p. 161 no. 3.

By Oltos:

3. FLORENCE 2 B 11, fr. Kyathos. See p. 54 no. 8.

By Epiktetos:

4. WÜRZBURG 468. Cup, bilingual. See p. 71 no. 8 and p. 45 no. 105.
5. ODESSA, fr. Kantharos. See p. 77 no. 87.

By the Nikosthenes Painter:

6. BERLIN 2324. Skyphoid. See p. 126 no. 26.
7. BOSTON 00.334. Kantharos. See p. 126 no. 27.
8. VILLA GIULIA 20749. Pyxis. See p. 127 no. 30.

By another:

9. BOSTON 95.61. Kantharos. See p. 132.

A small fragment of a bilingual cup may bear the signature of Nikosthenes:

LOUVRE C 10463, fr. CV. b pl. 18, 7. I, bf. All that remains is a little of the figure, and the inscription . . . ΚΟ . . . The cup might go with those in the Group of Louvre F 125 (see above, nos. 1–2; see also p. 42 no. 51).

––––––––––––

THE NIKOSTHENES PAINTER

VA. 23–24 ('Painter of Sleep and Death'). Att. V. 42–45 and 468. BSR. 11, 16–18. ARV.[1] 98–101 and 951. CB. iii, text.

We give this name to the artist who painted nos. 6–8 in the list of red-figured vases that bear the signature of Nikosthenes. He is also one of the painters who worked for Pamphaios (pp. 124–7, nos. 7, 8, 11, 13, 14, 15, 17, 20, 23, 24, 31). His earliest cups are mostly eye-cups, neatly painted. In this phase he must have sat side by side with the Bowdoin-Eye Painter (p. 166) and the Scheurleer Painter (p. 168). His later work is often rough.

We shall give, first, a list of vases by the Nikosthenes Painter; then (corresponding to the list, already given, of vases that bear the signature of the potter Nikosthenes), a list of all the red-figured vases that bear the signature of the potter Pamphaios. These are by various hands (which will be distinguished as far as possible), but some of them are by the Nikosthenes Painter, others are probably so, and others are not far from him. The chapter concludes with a list of coarse cups that may be said to belong to 'the wider circle of the

Nikosthenes Painter'. This arrangement sounds rather complicated, but proved to be the most suitable.

The connexion between the *potters* Nikosthenes and Pamphaios is clear from black-figure as well as red: Pamphaios may have been the younger partner of Nikosthenes.

THE NIKOSTHENES PAINTER

CUPS

1 (1). VILLA GIULIA, frr. A–B, between eyes. A, komast (naked youth to right, bending, lifting a calyx-krater). B, (shanks and feet, to right, and finger-tips, of a male to right, bending). See p. 47 no. 143.

2. MONTAUBAN 1. I, warrior. A–B, between eyes. A, boxer sitting on the ground, binding his hands. B, nose. See p. 48 no. 157, and p. 1627.

3 (2). CAMBRIDGE 1.27. *Cat. Sotheby June 21 1926* pl. 2; *CV.* pl. 25, 3 and pl. 26, 1; A, Norman Gardiner *Athl.* fig. 145; A and foot, Bloesch *FAS.* pl. 11, 1. I, symposion (man reclining, drinking). A–B, between palmettes and eyes. A, acontist; B, athlete bending to pick up haltēres. For the shape, Bloesch 38 no. 7. See p. 49 no. 176.

4 (3). CAMBRIDGE N 141, fr., from Naucratis. *CV.* ii pl. 27, 7. I, athlete bending to pick up haltēres.

5 (4). VILLA GIULIA, fr. I, man lifting calyx-krater. The style and subject are just as in no. 1: I thought that it could not belong, but should like to see it again.

6 (5). VILLA GIULIA. I, komast (naked youth running to right, looking round, holding a wineskin with both hands).

7 (6). CASTLE ASHBY, Northampton, from Vulci. Panofka *Panph.* pl. 2, whence Hoppin ii, 285 and (A–B) Swindler fig. 296; *Burl. 1903* pl. 96, I 65; *BSR.* 11 pl. 7, 4, pl. 6, and p. 17; B.Ap. xxi. 41. I, satyr. A–B, arming. At each handle, pegasi. On I, ΓΑ[N]ΦΑ[ΙΟ]ϚΕΓΟΙΕϚΕΝ. See, for the pattern below the exterior, no. 13.

8 (11). VILLA GIULIA 27250, from Todi. *ML.* 24, 874–5 and pll. 3–4, whence Hoppin ii, 305 and (I) Pfuhl fig. 346; I, *Dedalo* 3, 75; *CV.* pl. 24, pl. 25, 2–3, and pl. 26, 2. I, Odysseus under the ram. A, Herakles and Apollo: the struggle for the tripod. B, chariot of Dionysos. On the foot, ΓΑΝΟΑΙΟϚΕΓΟΙΕϚΕΝ.

9 (12). ITALIAN MARKET, fr. A, (upper part of Dionysos, seated to right, looking round, with kantharos and branch; to left of him, crotala; to right of him, an arm extended to left). Cf. Villa Giulia 27250 (no. 8).

10. OXFORD, Beazley, two frr. I, satyr (to left, looking round, with crotala: one hand and the upper half of the head remain). A, chariot and warriors (youth driving to right, beyond the chariot a warrior running to left; in front of the chariot, spear and calf of one running to right). The smaller fr. of the exterior has a warrior to left. Cf. Villa Giulia 27250 (no. 8).

11 (13). Los Angeles A 5933.50.21 (ex Brooks). *JHS*. 43, 134–5 and pll. 3–4, whence (A) *AJA*. 1924, 184. I, boy preparing a couch. A, Herakles and the Centaurs. B, harnessing chariot for Athena and Herakles. On the foot, ΓΑΝΦΑΙΟΣΕΓΟΙ<ΕΣΕΝ.

12 (14). Washington 136385. I, warrior. A, harnessing the chariot of Athena; B, chariot of Dionysos.

13 (7). Leningrad inv. 3385 (ex Stieglitz), from Vulci. I, youth astride a wineskin. A–B, komos. On the foot, ΓΑΝΦΑΙΟΣΕΓΟΙΕΣΕΝ. Restored (repainted nearly all over). The border below the exterior has the same diamond-pattern as in the Castle Ashby cup (no. 7); the only other examples of it are on cup-fragments in Berlin University (on A, a foot remains and part of the handle-floral) and in Athens, Acr. 89.

14 (8). Leningrad 646 (St. 828). I, komos (man and youth). A–B, fight. On the foot, ΓΑΝΦΑΝΟΣΕΓΟΙΕΣΕΝ.

15 (15). London E 815, from Vulci. A–B and part of I, Hoppin ii, 294–5, (whence (part of I) Pfuhl fig. 348; I, Licht iii, 201; I, Vorberg *Geschl.* pl. 10; I, B, and foot, Bloesch *FAS.* pl. 19, 2; I, Vorberg *Gloss.* 68. I, μλη-σιάζουσα (naked woman using olisboi). A, Hermes playing the lyre, and cattle. B, satyrs and maenads. On I, ΓΑΝΘΑΙΟΣ ΕΓΟΙΕΣΕΝ. For the subject of A, Yalouris in *Eph.* 1953–4, ii, 175–6; for the shape, Bloesch 68, Pamphaios, iv, no. 38.

16 (9). Louvre G 4 *bis*. Hoppin ii, 116–17. I, komast. A, warriors and horsemen; B, youths with horses. The inscriptions are meaningless.

17 (10). Louvre G 4. A–B, Pottier pl. 88, whence Hoppin ii, 115; A–B, ph. Al. 23720. I, naked woman preparing a couch. A, fight; B, warriors, and archers with horses. On the foot, [ΓΑΝΦΑΙ]ΟϟΕΓΟΙΕΣΕΝ. Now cleaned. For the shape, Bloesch 65, Pamphaios, iv, no. 30.

18. Louvre C 10875 (including S 1362, S 1392, and many other frr.). I, satyr (with oinochoe, approaching an altar). A, fight, with chariot wheeling round. B, satyrs with deer, and maenad riding donkey.

19. Louvre C 11253, fr. A, (part of a horse?, and middle of a warrior in corslet and chitoniskos).

20. Melbourne 1730.4, from Vulci. *Qu. Bull. Victoria*, xi, 3, 5–7; Trendall *Felton Vases* pl. 8, a and pl. 7. I, satyr. A, Herakles and Alkyoneus. B, Dionysos with two maenads and two bulls. On the foot, ΓΑΝϘΑΙ-ΟϟΕΓΟΙΕϟΕΝ. [Trendall].

21 (16). London E 14, from Vulci. I, Murray no. 11. I, maenad. A, between sirens, Dionysos and satyrs; B, between sirens, satyr and maenad. Now cleaned, and the foot and one handle, which were alien, removed. Very hasty, but I think by the painter himself.

22 (a). Athens Acr. 113, frr., from Athens. Langlotz pl. 5. I, (one kneeling or nearly; basket hanging). A, (chariot).

23 (a). TARQUINIA RC 2066, from Tarquinia. *Mon.* 11 pl. 24, whence Pfuhl figs. 349–50; *WV.* D pl. 5, whence Hoppin ii, 287; A, Romanelli *T.* 125; *CV.* pl. 6 and pl. 7, 1; A, Greifenhagen *Eroten* 35; I, *Antike und Abendland* 8, pl. at p. 130; A–B, ph. Mo. 8252; A, ph. And. 41004. I, satyr and maenad. A, Herakles and Kyknos. B, athletes. On the foot, ΓΑΝ-ΘΑΙΟϚΕΓΟΙΕϚΕΝ. See p. 1627.

24 (a). LONDON E 12, from Vulci. *Archaeologia* 29, 139 and pl. 16, whence (A–B) Panofka *Panph.* pl. 4; Gerhard pl. 221–2; *WV.* D pl. 3, 1, whence (A) Murray 7, whence Perrot 10, 535; I, Murray no. 9; Hoppin ii, 291; A, Pfuhl fig. 345 (= Pfuhl *Mast.* fig. 37); FR. pl. 156; part of A, *AJA.* 1938, 242 fig. 7; A and foot, Bloesch *FAS.* pl. 19, 1; detail of A, Lane pl. 70, b; detail of A, Stella 303; Trendall *Felton Vases* pl. 8, b and pl. 9; A–B, ph. Ma. I, satyr. A, Hypnos and Thanatos with the body of Sarpedon. A, Amazons arming. On the foot, ΓΑΝΘΑΙΟϚΕΓΟΙΕϚΕΝ. For the shape, Bloesch 68, Pamphaios, 6, no. 37. I think that this splendid cup cannot be denied to the Nikosthenes Painter, in spite of its being on altogether a different level from even the better pieces in the list of his works. The artist would for once be doing his very best; perhaps copying work by another, although to affirm this would not be fair. For the interior, his inspiration, or his model, failed him.

SKYPHOS
(of Corinthian type)

25 (18, +). LOUVRE G 66. Part, Pottier pl. 96; part, phs. Gir. 28508–9. Gigantomachy? (A, Athena in battle; B, Herakles in battle). Louvre S 1399 and many other unpublished fragments join, and the pictures are not far from complete. The subject is doubtful, see Vian *Guerre des géants* 54–55.

SKYPHOID
(of special type)

26 (19). BERLIN 2324, from Vulci. *WV.* 1890–1 pl. 7, 1, whence Hoppin ii, 225 and (part) Perrot 10, 260; general view, Pfuhl fig. 321. A, hunt. B, chariot. On the spout, gorgoneion. On the upper surface, to each side of the spout, a seated youth. On the foot, ΝΙΚΟϚΘΕΝΕϚΕΓΟ[ΙΕ]ϚΕΝ. Much restored.

KANTHAROI
(nos. 27–28, type C)

27 (20). BOSTON 00.334, from Tarquinia. *RM.* 5 pl. 12 and p. 324 = *WV.* 1890–1 pl. 7, 2, whence Perrot 10, 268, Pfuhl fig. 320, Hoppin ii, 227, (the chief picture on A) Buschor *Satyrtänze* fig. 41; the same, Himmelmann-Wildschütz *Eig.* p. 30; CB. iii pl. 68; the shape, Caskey G. 160 = CB. i, 17 fig. 17. A, Dionysos and maenads at altar; B, Dionysos reclining, with satyrs. On the lower part of the vase: A, Herakles and the bull; B, Herakles and the lion. On the foot, ΝΙΚΟϚΘΕΝΕϚΕΓΟΙΕϚΕΝ. See CB. iii, text.

28 (21). LONDON E 154, from Vulci. Genick pl. 26, 1; *CV*. pl. 33, 1. A, war-chariot; B, the like. See CB. iii, text.

(no. 29, type A)

29 (22). LENINGRAD inv. 3386 (ex Stieglitz). A, G.P. 39. A, Herakles and the lion. B, komos. See CB. iii, text.

PYXIS
(of Nicosthenic shape)

30 (23). VILLA GIULIA 20749, from Cervetri. *St. etr.* 1 pl. 35, a; *ML*. 42, 247–50; part, Vighi 95; phs. R.I. 57.662–6; the shape, Hoppin ii, 231. Athletes. On the lid, chariots at the gallop and warriors running. On the foot, NIKOΣOENEΣEΓOIEΣEN.

LARGE VASES (AMPHORAE?)

31 (24). ATHENS Acr. 606, frr., from Athens. Langlotz pl. 46. Unexplained subjects (warriors; woman; others). Among the fragmentary inscriptions, ... ANΦ ... (i.e. [Π]ανφ[αιος ...?).

32 (25). ATHENS Acr. 607, frr., from Athens. Langlotz pl. 46. Unexplained subjects (male leading woman; and other figures). An Athens fragment with forehead and nose of a youthful person to right, and, low down, the letter A . . ., should belong to either this or the last or the next.

33 (26). ATHENS Acr. 605, two frr., from Athens. Langlotz pl. 45. (Feet).

Small fragments of a cup are very like nos. 1–3 in the list (p. 124):

VILLA GIULIA (part ex Florence), frr. A, between palmettes and eyes, warrior bending (to left: shanks, feet, and one hand remain). See p. 49 no. 177.

Another small cup-fragment may be by the painter:

AMSTERDAM inv. 2779, fr. A, (heads of chariot-horses).

For other vases more or less closely related to the Nikosthenes Painter see below, pp. 130–5.

PAMPHAIOS, POTTER

For the black-figured vases with this signature see *ABV*. 235–6 and 324. A list of the red-figured (and bilingual) follows. It will be noticed that Oltos spells the name Phanphaios; Epiktetos, Pamaphios (just as he writes *egrasphen* in his earlier period, and *Pistoschenos*); while all the other cups have Panphaios (or Panthaios), the same form as on the black-figured vases.

(nos. 1–3, by Oltos)

1. LOUVRE G 3. Neck-amphora of Nicosthenic type. P. 53 no. 1.
2. LOUVRE G 2. Neck-amphora of Nicosthenic type. P. 53 no. 2.
3. LONDON E 437. Stamnos. P. 54 no. 5.

(nos. 4–5, by Epiktetos)

4. LOUVRE G 5. Cup. P. 71 no. 14 and p. 49 no. 175.

5. BERLIN 2262. Cup. P. 72 no. 15.

(nos. 6–15, by the Nikosthenes Painter)

6. CASTLE ASHBY, Northampton. Cup. P. 124 no. 7.

7. VILLA GIULIA 27250. Cup. P. 124 no. 8.

8. LOS ANGELES A 5933.50.21. Cup. P. 125 no. 11.

9. LENINGRAD inv. 3385. Cup. P. 125 no. 13.

10. LENINGRAD 646. Cup. P. 125 no. 14.

11. LONDON E 815. Cup. P. 125 no. 15.

12. LOUVRE G 4. Cup. P. 125 no. 17.

13. MELBOURNE 1729.4. Cup. P. 125 no. 20.

14. TARQUINIA RC 2066. Cup. P. 126 no. 23.

15. LONDON E 12. Cup. P. 126 no. 24.

As to the remaining vases with the signature, a list of them will be given first, and after that an attempt made to divide them into stylistic groups.

CUPS

(no. 16, eye-cup of unique type, Chalcicup)

16 (α). Lost. R.I. ix. 124. Inside, nothing. A–B, between eyes. A, goat. B, shield. On the foot, ΓΑΝΘΑΙΟΣΕΓΟΙΕΣΕΝ. The sixth letter looks more like a sigma in the reproduction. See *CF.* 7; and above, p. 51. Early.

(nos. 17–18, eye-cups)

17 (β). BONN 390. *Bonner St.* 198–202, whence Hoppin ii, 281; Hoppin *Bf.* 469; *CV.* pl. 1, 2–4; A and foot, Bloesch *FAS.* pl. 17, 1. I, bf., warrior squatting. A–B, between eyes. A, komast; B, komast. On I, ΓΑΝΘΑΙΟΣΕΓΟ[ΙΕ]ΣΕ[Ν]. For the shape, Bloesch 62, Pamphaios, i, no. 3. See p. 41 no. 28, and p. 131. Early.

18 (γ). FLORENCE 1 B 1, frr. Part, *Boll. d'Arte* 1928, 224 fig. 13, 1; part, *CV.* pl. 1, B 1. A, between eyes, woman? (one arm remains). Below the eyebrows, ΓΑΝΘΑΙΟΣ ΕΓ[ΟΙΕΣΕΝ]. Later and better than the last. See p. 46 no. 138, and p. 131.

(nos. 19–23, no eyes; decorated outside as well as in)

19 (αα). BOSTON 95.32, from Cervetri. Hoppin ii, 282–3; I, *Harv. St.* 52 pl. 2; the shape, Caskey G. 191 fig. 146. I, satyr. A, fight; B, arming. On I, [ΓΑΝΘΑΙΟ]Σ ΕΓΟΙΕΣΕΝ. On A, ΓΑΝΘΑΙΟΝ. On B, ΕΓΟΙ-ΕΣΕΝ. For the shape, Bloesch 66, Pamphaios, iv, no. 31. See p. 131, and p. 133 no. 19.

20 (ββ). Würzburg 471, from Vulci. Langlotz pl. 140; A and foot, Bloesch *FAS*. pl. 18, 1. I, satyr; A–B, satyrs. On the foot, [ΓΑΝ]Φ[ΑΙ]-Ο5ΕΓΟΙΕ5ΕΝ. For the shape, Bloesch 65, Pamphaios, iv, no. 24. See p. 131.

21 (γγ). London 1907. 10–20. 1. Hoppin ii, 296–7; I, Pfuhl fig. 347; A, Swindler fig. 273; A and foot, Bloesch *FAS*. pl. 18, 4. I, warrior running; A–B, warriors running. On the foot, ΓΑΝΟΑΙΟ5ΕΓΟΙΕ5ΕΝ. For the shape, Bloesch 66, Pamphaios, iv, no. 44. See p. 131.

22 (l17). London E 11, from Vulci. Panofka *Panph*. pl. 1, 3 and pl. 3; *WV*. D pl. 4; I, Murray no. 8; Hoppin ii, 289, whence (detail of B) *Arch. class.* 2 pl. 49, 4. I, warrior. A, between pegasi, Dionysos and satyrs; B, between pegasi, satyrs and maenad. On the foot, ΓΑΝΘΑΙΟ5ΕΓΟΙ-Ε5ΕΝ. For the shape, Bloesch 67, Pamphaios, v, no. 34. See p. 130.

23 (δδ). Munich 2620 a (J. 439). Hoppin *Bf.* 470–71; B, Bloesch *FAS*. pl. 18, 2. I, warrior. A, Herakles and the lion. B, komos. On the foot, ΓΑΝΦΑΙΟ5ΕΓΟΙΕ5ΕΝ. For the shape, Bloesch 67, Pamphaios, v, no. 35. See p. 130.

(nos. 24–27, not known if decorated outside; the first probably was)

24 (εε). Louvre C 10877, fr. I, cup-bearer (naked youth filling cup at krater). On the foot, ΓΑΝΘΑΙΟ5ΕΓΟΙΕ5ΕΝ. See p. 131.

25. Louvre C 11254, fr. Half the foot remains, on it ΓΑΝΦΑΙΟ . . .

26. Gela, fr., from Monte Saraceno. I, (rear foot of one moving to left, with the lower edge of the long chiton). [ΓΑ]ΝΦ[ΑΙΟ5 . . .

27. Populonia 1087, fr., from Populonia. *NSc.* 1957, 50, c. Part of the foot remains, on it [ΓΑΝ]ΟΑΙΟ?ΕΓΟ[ΙΕ?ΕΝ].

27 *bis*. Florence 82894, fr., from Orvieto. The foot remains. On it, . . . ΓΓ . ΕΙΕΝ (our dot between Γ and E representing a missing letter; the letter before Γ probably fragmentary); to left of this, reading from right to left, space for one letter, then amorphous traces of three letters. The foot is a Pamphaios foot. At present it is attached to the cup Florence V 47 (I, naked male—satyr?—running with a basket; A–B, horse-race), and Bloesch took it to belong (*F.A.S.* 67 no. 36): but there is no junction; and since the foot is labelled as from Orvieto, while the cup is ex Vagnonville and probably from Chiusi, there appears to be no reason for supposing that the two have anything to do with each other.

(nos. 28–34, decorated inside only)

28 (ζζ). Boston 24.453, from Vulci. *Eph.* 1890, 11, whence Hoppin ii, 284; B.Ap. xvi. 21. 4. I, man treading grapes. On the vat, ΓΑΝΘΛΙΟ5Ε-ΓΟΙ . . . Ν, with uncertain traces of the missing letters. See p. 131.

29. Once Canino, from Vulci. I, 'naked man sitting on rock, with horn' (*Mus. étr.* no. 1513); 'un chasseur tenant en main un cor' (*Rés. etr.* 107 fig. 5). Πανφαιοϲεποιεϲεν.

30 (ηη). LOUVRE CA 2526, from Greece? I, jumper. ΠΑΝΘΑΙΟΣΕΣΕΝ. See p. 131.

31 (θθ). ATHENS 1409 (CC. 1156), from Akraiphia. *Eph.* 1890 pl. 2, whence Hoppin ii, 278; *CV.* pl. 3, 2 and 4. I, naked youth with laver. ΠΑΝΘΑΙΟΣΕΠΟΙΕΣΕΝ. For the shape, Bloesch 64, Pamphaios, iv, no. 13. See pp. 132–3.

32 (υ). FLORENCE PD 249, from Orvieto. *NSc.* 1939 pl. 3, 2; *CV.* pl. 86, 1. I, Pegasus. ΠΑΝΘΑΙ[ΟΣΕΠΟ]ΙΕΣΕΝ. See p. 131.

33 (κκ). BERLIN 2266, from Etruria. Panofka *Panph.* pl. 1, 1, whence Hoppin ii, 279; A and foot, Bloesch *FAS.* pl. 17, 2. I, horse. ΠΑΝΦΑΟΣ ΕΠΟΙΕΣΕΝ. Much restored. For the shape, Bloesch 64, Pamphaios iv, no. 12.

34 (λλ). Once CHIUSI, Casuccini, from Chiusi. Inghirami *Chius.* pl. 133; Panofka *Panph.* pl. 1, 2. I, cup-bearer. Π[ΑΝ]ΘΑΙΟΣΕΠΟΙΕΣΕΝ. Very much restored.

I have not seen the following fragments and I know them from descriptions only. Not known whether the vases were red-figure or black-figure.

35. REGGIO 7560, fr., from Locri. Vase-foot inscribed ΠΑΝΦΑΙΟΣΕΠΟΙΕΣΕΝ. Described by Orsi in *Boll. d'Arte* 1909, 474. See p. 1627.

36. ORVIETO, Faina, 114, fr. Cup-foot inscribed ΠΑΝΟΑΙΣΕΠΟΙΕΣΕΝ. The inscription is said to be incised. Described by Gustav Körte in *Annali* 1877, 131 no. 18 and by Cardella *Museo etrusco Faina* 48.

The following may possibly have borne the signature of Pamphaios:

LARGE VASE (AMPHORA?)

ATHENS Acr. 606, frr. See p. 127, Nikosthenes Painter no. 31.

For the cup-fragments Athens Acr. 221 and Leipsic T 3637, mentioned in *ARV.*[1] 103 as possibly signed Pamphaios, see pp. 1604 and 1605.

———

We now return to the certain signatures.

No. 22 (London E 11) is very like the roughest cups of the Nikosthenes Painter, such as London E 14 (p. 125 no. 21), but I have decided not to put it in the list. The inside picture is especially feeble. The same litter of letters as in London E 14 and E 815 (p. 125 no. 15).

No. 23 (Munich 2620 a), ill preserved, is connected with the later works of the Nikosthenes Painter.

No. 21 (London 1907.10–20.1) is akin to the cups of the Nikosthenes Painter. Miss Talcott has pointed to another vase by the same hand:

LEKYTHOS

ATHENS, Agora, P 24061, from Athens. Part, *Hesp.* 24 pl. 28, c. Three warriors running forth, and a trumpeter. As they run all round the vase, Miss Talcott has proposed to name the artist the Roundabout Painter.

Not enough remains of no. 24 (Louvre C 10877) to associate it for certain with the Nikosthenes Painter. The style is fairly careful.

No. 20 (Würzburg 471), of earlier style, is connected with the Nikosthenes Painter by the net-border below the pictures outside, but in other respects the connexion is slight. Compare the cups

FLORENCE 4 B 46 and 6 B 10, fr. (the two joining). A, *CV*. pl. 4, B 46 and pl. 6, B 10. I, (heel). A, (on the left, satyrs). Here, too, the pattern under the outside pictures connects the cup with our group.

LEIPSIC T 488. I, satyr riding a wineskin. For the shape, Bloesch 67 note 114.

No. 19 (Boston 95.32) is not quite so early as it might seem; it is a singularly artless piece, perhaps by a beginner. It bears some resemblance to the kantharos Boston 95.61 (p. 132).

The three eye-cups, nos. 16–18, differ among themselves, and there is nothing to connect them with the Nikosthenes Painter.

This brings us to the cups decorated inside only. The horse on no. 32 (Florence) looks rather like a dwarfed version of those on Tarquinia RC 2066. No. 28 (Boston 24.453) is a helpless little work: again by a beginner? More can be said about no. 30 (Louvre CA 2526) and no. 31 (Athens 1409). Bothmer has seen that there is another cup by the same hand as Louvre CA 2526:

PARIS MARKET (Segredakis). I, acontist (running to right, about to throw, the acontion in the raised right hand; on the ground between his legs a pick).

Compare also the cup

LEIPSIC, Kunstgewerbemuseum. I, satyr with pelta. A–B, athletes. For the shape, Bloesch 126 no. 1.

I do not know the exact shape of the Segredakis cup; but Louvre CA 2526 is of the same rare model as Athens 1409. A third cup of the same model as these two must also have been fashioned by Pamphaios:

LOUVRE CA 1585, from Greece. I, symposion (youth reclining, playing kottabos). The inscription, ΓΝΑΟЅΕ ΗΑΙΙΟЅΕ is meaningless, but bears a remote resemblance to a signature of Pamphaios.

For drawing, a cup-fragment may be compared with Athens 1409:

ATHENS Acr. 225, fr., from Athens. Langlotz pl. 12. I, naked man (the action not clear).

———————

Returning to the Nikosthenes Painter: some small cup-fragments go with those Pamphaios cups that are near the Nikosthenes Painter:

1. HEIDELBERG 13, fr. Kraiker pl. 3. A, (satyr; and part of a flanking siren or the like).
2. MARSEILLES 9938, fr., from Marseilles. Villard C.G.M. pl. 15, 4; ph. Arch. phot. 920.191528. Outside, (the foot of the right-hand figure on A, and the heel of the left-hand figure on B: satyrs; between them, under the handle, a leaf; below, the same palmette-border as in London E 12, &c.). Placed similarly by Villard.
3. MUNICH, fr. A (part of a sphinx to left, and of the same border as in the last).

Lastly, the second kantharos with the signature of Nikosthenes, a poor work (p. 123 no. 9). The general style is akin to Epeleian (pp. 146–53), although one or two particulars smack of the Nikosthenes Painter. There is some likeness to the Boston cup 95.32 (p. 128 no. 19).

KANTHAROS
(type A)

BOSTON 95.61, from Vulci. A, Licht iii, 199; A, Vorberg Geschl. pl. 5; Vorberg Er. 81 and 84; Vorberg Gloss. 1 and 108; the shape, Caskey G. 161; the shape, CB. i, 15 fig. 12. A, love-making; B, the like. On the foot, ΝΙΚΟΣΟΕΝΕΣΕΠΟΙΕΣΕΝ. Litter of letters in the fields of the pictures.

———————

THE WIDER CIRCLE OF THE NIKOSTHENES PAINTER
ARV.¹ 104–6 and 951.

Many cups, by different hands, might be grouped under this heading: careless, coarse, but sometimes vigorous work.

CUPS

1 (3). HEIDELBERG 33 and VILLA GIULIA. The Heidelberg fragment, Kraiker pl. 6. I, satyr. See JHS. 51, 45 no. 15, and CF. 33 no. 8. Compare Cambridge 37.17 (no. 4). See p. 134.
2 (12). HEIDELBERG 31, frr. Kraiker pl. 5. I, satyr; A, (satyr and donkeys). B, fight. See p. 134.
3 (13). ATHENS Acr., fr. from Athens. (Head, to left, and shoulder, of satyr). As Heidelberg 31 (no. 2).

4 (4). CAMBRIDGE 37.17. Cecil Smith *Forman* pl. 9, whence (A) Pfuhl fig. 343 and (A and part of B) Buschor *Satyrtänze* figs. 44–45; A–B, *Burl. 1903* pl. 96, I 75; cleaned, *CV.* ii RS. pl. 8, 5, pl. 6, below (2, misprinted 1), and pl. 9, 8. Satyr sports: I, satyr lifting a vessel; A, chariot-race (satyr driving a pair of satyrs, satyr driving a pair of maenads); B, 'horse-race' (satyrs riding wineskins). On I, ΕΓΟΙΕϚΕΝ. On B, ΕΓΟΙΕϚΕΝ. For the shape, Bloesch 65, Pamphaios no. 20.

5 (5). TARQUINIA (RC), from Tarquinia. I, male at bell-krater. A, satyrs and maenad; B, satyrs and donkey. Cf. Cambridge 37.17 (no. 4).

6 (6). HEIDELBERG 14, fr. Kraiker pl. 3. A, (satyr and another). Compare the last.

7 (7). GENEVA 239. I and A, phs. Gir. 4962–3. I, satyr; A–B, satyrs and maenads with donkeys.

8 (8). TÜBINGEN E 11, fr. A, Watzinger pl. 17. I, (foot). A, (satyrs and maenad).

9. ATHENS, Agora, P 9281, fr., from Athens. A, (satyr with pelta riding wineskin).

10 (9, +). FLORENCE 4 B 28 and LOUVRE C 11255, frr. Part of the Florence part, *CV.* Fl. pl. 4, B 28. I, satyr; A–B, satyrs with peltae (πυρριχίζοντες?), and flute-player.

11. FLORENCE 4 B 48 and LOUVRE C 11256, fr. The Florence part, *CV.* pl. 4, B 48. A, (satyr with pelta).

12. LOUVRE C 11257, fr. A, (satyr squatting, satyr holding a pointed amphora or the like).

13 (10). VILLA GIULIA 43650, frr., from Vignanello. A–B, *NSc.* 1924, 234; *CV.* pl. 31, 4–5. I, satyr; A, Dionysos(?) with satyrs and donkey. B, fight.

14. AMSTERDAM inv. 2228, fr. A, (satyr, donkey).

15 (11). NEW YORK 22.139.28, from Vulci. I, satyr and maenad; A, satyrs and donkeys. B, fight.

16 (15). ORVIETO, fr., from Orvieto. *NSc.* 1925, 152 fig. 19. A, Herakles and the Hydra.

17 (16). ORVIETO, frr., from Orvieto. *NSc.* 1925, 155. Outside, satyrs.

18 (17). BOULOGNE 556. Ph. Arch. phot. BAA 139. I, satyr (to right). A–B, fight.

19 (19). BRUSSELS A 201. *CV.* pl. 10, 1. I, satyr; A, satyrs. B, fight. Restored. For the shape, Bloesch 65 Pamphaios no. 29; for the palmette border, compare Boston 95.32 (p. 128, no. 19).

20. MYKONOS 14, fr., from Rheneia (originally from Delos). Dugas *Délos xxi* pl. 45, 14. I, satyr and donkey.

21. LOUVRE G 69. Incompletely: *Jb.* 7, 162, whence (A, redrawn) Daremberg and Saglio s.v. maenades fig. 4769; A, Philippart *Bacch.* pl. 13, a. I,

satyr. A, maenads with the limbs of Pentheus. B, fight. Now cleaned.
Four Louvre frr. join and have been added: see CB. ii, 2. Quaint style.

Nos. 1 (Heidelberg 33 and Villa Giulia) and 2 (Heidelberg 31) are connected with a cup which is better than they and which recalls the Group of
London E 33 (p. 80), whereas they do not:

VILLA GIULIA (part ex Florence) and HEIDELBERG 46 and 47. Part, CV. Fl. pl.
5, B 24; the Heidelberg frr., Kraiker pl. 7. I, Sisyphos. A, fish-porters.
B, athletes. To be augmented by a new Villa Giulia fragment which gives
the head of the hindmost porter, a man.

Somewhat more developed than the cups in the previous list, but in the
same tradition, are such cups, with big, rough figures, by various hands, as
the following:

ARV.¹ 105–6 and 951.

1. MUNICH 2622 (J. 139), from Vulci. I, satyr riding wineskin. For the
shape, Bloesch 67 note 114.

2 (1). BRUSSELS A 1377, from Cervetri. A–B, Furtwängler Somzée pl. 37,
iv, 2 = Vente Somzée pl. 1, 38; CV. pl. 10, 2. I, satyr. A, fight. B,
athletes. Cf. Louvre G 92 (no. 3).

3 (2). LOUVRE G 92. A, Brommer Satyrspiele¹ 53 fig. 54 = ²59 fig. 57. I,
athletes. A–B, satyr regatta (satyrs riding on wineskins over the sea). Cf.
Brussels A 1377 and Leipsic T 953 (nos. 2 and 4).

4 (3). LEIPSIC T 953. A and foot, Bloesch FAS. pl. 35, 2. I, boxer squatting,
binding his hands. For the shape, Bloesch 131 no. 12. Cf. Louvre G 92
and Brussels A 1377 (nos. 3 and 2).

5 (4). CAMBRIDGE 29.24. CV. pl. 25, 4 and pl. 26, 2. I, jumper and trainer;
A, athletes; warrior and youth with horse; B, warriors.

6 (5, +). LOUVRE G 94. I, athlete using pick; A, athletes. B, komos.
Many Louvre frr. join this and have been added. For the subject of B,
CB. ii, 61, middle.

7 (6). VILLA GIULIA 50385, from Cervetri. JHS. 4, 255 and pl. at p. 252,
whence (A–B) HM. pl. 29, 1 and 3. I, naked woman running with basket
and alabastron. A, escape from Polyphemos. B, Dionysos mounting
chariot, with satyrs. For the shape, Bloesch 66, Pamphaios no. 32.

8. LOUVRE, frr. A–B, fight. The inside picture pared away.

9. BASLE MARKET (M.M.). I, symposion (man reclining, playing kottabos).
A–B, fight. From the root of one handle a large leaf.

10 (10). PHILADELPHIA 3499, from Orvieto. Trans. Penn. 2, 134 and pll. 33–
34, whence (A) Mon. Piot 20, 131. I, warrior; A–B, fight.

11 (9, +). BERKELEY 8.4, and BRUNSWICK 502, from Cervetri. The Berkeley part: A–B, Furtwängler *Somzée* pl. 37, iv, 5 = *Vente Somzée* pl. 1, 42 (misprint for 39); *CV*. pl. 32, 2. The Brunswick fragment, *CV*. pl. 12, 3. I, woman dancing. A, chariot. B, fight. The Brunswick fragment must give the youth mounting the chariot on A, and the extended arm of the person to right of him.

12. NAPLES, Astarita, 267, fr. A, fight (shield, head of warrior to left, elbow of warrior with spear to right). Compare the last.

13 (11). CAMBRIDGE 37.19. I, *Burl. 1903* pl. 96, I 82; *CV*. ii RS. pl. 8, 6, pl. 7, 2, and pl. 9, 5. I, komast. A, symposion. B, fight. In general character the battle-scenes on nos. 2 and 8–13 resemble those of the Bonn Painter (p. 351).

It is here that we may place the rude and vigorous cup

(a). BOSTON 08.30a (one fr. ex Louvre S 1378), from Vulci. I, Licht iii, 182; I, Vorberg *Geschl.* pl. 3, 2; I, Vorberg *Gloss.* 43; B (without the head of Iris, given by the Louvre fragment), Brommer *Satyrspiele*[1] 22; A, *AJA.* 1954 pl. 61 fig. 23. I, love-making (satyr and woman). A, Iliupersis (Ajax and Cassandra; Aithra; on each side, a warrior attacking a woman). B, Iris assaulted by satyrs. On the subject of B see *Kl.* 270, Haspels *ABL.* 20. The palmette-border inside is a red-figure translation of a black-figure pattern that is a favourite in the circle of the Nikosthenes Painter.

With the Boston cup compare the cup-fragment

(a). WÜRZBURG 494, fr. A, Langlotz pl. 217. I, warrior; A, Achilles and Ajax playing.

See also p. 1628.

CHAPTER 11

THE COARSER WING, ii

THE POSEIDON PAINTER

JHS. 59, 152. *ARV*.¹ 111–12 and 951.

So called after the subject of the Berkeley cup, no. 6.

CUPS

1 (3). LONDON E 15, from Vulci. A, *El.* 1 pl. 63. I, komast. A, birth of Athena. B, Peleus and Thetis. For the shape, Bloesch 45, Kachrylion no. 10. Very large.

2 (1). BOSTON 95.35, from Italy. Shape, Hambidge 119 fig. 7; shape, Caskey G. 185, 140. I, athlete. A, Dionysos on donkey, with satyrs and maenads; B, satyrs and maenads.

3 (2). MUNICH 2613 (J. 803), from Vulci. A, *Jb.* 10, 196, whence *JHS*. 23, 284, Norman Gardiner *G.A.S.* 292, and Norman Gardiner *Athl.* fig. 98; one figure on B, Jüthner 41, a; I, Licht iii, 54; A, Blümel *S.H.* 29; I, Vorberg *Gloss.* 734. I, satyr; A–B, athletes. Restored. See p. 1628.

4 (4). MUNICH 2625, fr. I, komast.

5 (5). NEW YORK 23.160.91. I, maenad.

6 (6). BERKELEY 8.3. Furtwängler *Somzée* pl. 37, iii, 5 = *Vente Somzée* pl. 1, 37; *CV*. pl. 32, 1. I, Poseidon.

7 (7). LEIPSIC, fr., from Taormina. I, warrior or hoplitodromos (head and shoulder of helmeted youth to left, looking round to right, with shield).

8 (8). MUNICH 2621. Licht iii, 152. I, satyr playing the flute. For the shape, Bloesch 55 no. 5.

9 (9). VILLA GIULIA, fr. I, athlete (running to right, between his feet a discus charged with an owl and letters; hanging, a sponge, and an aryballos charged with an owl).

10. LUCERNE MARKET (A.A.). I, pyrrhic (youth standing to right playing the flute, boy with spear and pelta; device a skyphos and a naked youth reclining). Restored.

Compare also the cup

LOUVRE C 10873. I, runner? (naked youth running to left, looking round).

THE AKTORIONE PAINTER

ARV.[1] 112 and 951.

Named after one of the subjects on no. 1.

Influenced, it seems, by late Epiktetos: compare the Group of London E 33 (p. 80).

CUPS

1 (2). ALTENBURG 233, from Vulci. *Jb.* 8, 163; *CV.* pl. 66 and pl. 67, 1–2 and 4. I, satyr at altar. A, Herakles and Cerberus. B, Herakles struggling with two youths (Aktorione, as Hartwig?). For the shape, Bloesch 56 no. 2.

2 (3). BOSTON 13.82. Shape, Caskey G. 197. I, satyr in vat. A, two satyrs quarrelling. B, komos (two youths). For the shape, Bloesch 64, Pamphaios, iv no. 16.

3 (4). LEIPSIC T 489, from Chiusi. I, satyr in vat. A–B, (legs remain). For the shape, Bloesch 65, Pamphaios, iv no. 21. [Kirsten].

4. VIENNA 1930, fr. *CV.* pl. 2, 3. I, satyr in vat.

Not far from these, but less monstrously crude, a cup which Langlotz attributed to the same hand as the Altenburg:

WÜRZBURG 472. A, *Jb.* 8, 162; I, Jacobsthal *Gött. V.* 43 fig. 67; Langlotz pl. 141; B, Schaal *Rf.* fig. 3; A, Brommer *Her.* pl. 27, a. I, symposion (man reclining, playing lyre). A, Herakles and Cerberus. B, youth with horses. Restored. For the shape, Bloesch 56 no. 1.

THE HARVARD PAINTER

ARV.[1] 53.

Close to the Aktorione Painter, and again the last word in crudity. One thinks of small late Epictetan cups.

CUPS

(small, with foot of type C)

1 (1). HARVARD 1925.30.132, from Greece. *CV.* Hoppin pl. 8, 3 and 5. I, naked youth.

2 (2). HARVARD 1925.30.29, from Greece. *CV.* Hoppin pl. 8, 2 and 4. I, naked youth.

3 (3). BERKELEY 8.3309. *CV.* pl. 31, 4. I, komast.

THE CHAROPS PAINTER

ARV.[1] 113.

CUPS

1 (1). COPENHAGEN 127, from Vulci. B, *Mon.* 1 pl. 27, 41; *CV.* pl. 137, 1 and pl. 136; B, *E.A.A.* ii, 538 fig. 740. I, archer. A, Herakles and the lion. B, two maenads. On B, ΚΑLΟ$ +ΑΡΟΦ$. Chalcicup (Bloesch 28, no. 12).

2 (2). ATHENS Acr. 232, fr., from Athens. Langlotz pl. 12. I, youth (workman?). [ΗΙΓ]ΓΑΡ+[Ο$ . . .

THE PAINTER OF THE ACROPOLIS PLATES

ARV.[1] 112–13.

PLATES

1 (1). ATHENS Acr. 22, fr., from Athens. Langlotz pl. 2. Jumper and fluteplayer.

2 (2). ATHENS Acr. 4, fr., from Athens. Langlotz pl. 2, whence *E.A.A.* i, 52 fig. 76. Jumper.

3 (3). ATHENS Acr. 18, fr., from Athens. (Shanks of one dressed in a long chiton, and a chalice standing on the ground).

THE PAINTER OF FLORENCE 1 B 45

Villainous style.

CUPS

1. BARCELONA 1904. García y Bellido pl. 96, 96 and pl. 98, 99. I, satyr. A–B, komos. Very much restored. The head of the fourth figure on A seems alien.

2. FLORENCE 1 B 45, fr. *CV.* pl. 1 B 45. A, (on the right, woman).

The Barcelona cup was published as having been found at Ampurias. This seemed to me improbable, as the restoration looks like Italian work; and Mrs. Trias de Arribas tells me that in fact there is no record of provenience.

Compare the cup

LOUVRE C 11259, frr. A–B, youths leading horses.

THE PITHOS PAINTER

CF. 27 on pl. 20 B 19. *JHS*. 59, 2–4. *ARV*.[1] 116–18 and 952.

So named from the pithoi represented on nos. 1–3 and 8. Exceedingly coarse work.

CUPS

(of type C, coarsely made)

1 (1). LOUVRE G 91. Pottier pl. 98. I, satyr kneeling at pithos.

2 (2). NEW YORK 07.296.32. I, satyr kneeling at pithos. Recalls the Chaire Painter as well (p. 144).

3 (3). PARIS, Villard (ex Mikas). I, satyr kneeling at pithos.

4 (4). LOUVRE G 90. Pottier pl. 98. I, satyr kneeling, with pointed amphora.

5 (5). VIENNA 3215. *CV*. pl. 3, 2 and pl. 13, 8. I, satyr kneeling, with wine-skin.

6. BONN, Perpeet. *Ars Ant. Auktion I* pl. 53, 113. I, satyr with drinking-horn and wineskin. See p. 142.

7 (6). ATHENS, Agora, P 1382 *bis*, from Athens. *Hesp*. 15 pl. 31, 39. I, man kneeling, holding a garment.

8 (7). LONDON E 29, from Camiros. I, youth kneeling at pithos.

9 (8). LONDON E 30, from Camiros. I, athlete kneeling with discus.

(nos. 10–16: I, warrior or hoplitodromos kneeling, to left)

10. ATHENS, Agora, P 23125, from Athens. *Hesp*. 23 pl. 15, g.

11 (9). LOUVRE AM 1065, from Rhodes.

12. LOUVRE C 10883.

13. LOUVRE C 10884.

14 (10). TÜBINGEN E 40, fr. Watzinger pl. 21.

15. GELA, from Gela. *NSc*. 1956, 276.

16 (11). SYRACUSE 19820 a, from Gela.

17. ATHENS, Agora, P 16821 b, fr., from Athens. I, warrior (kneeling to right, looking round).

18 (9). ATHENS, Agora, P 2579, from Athens. *Hesp*. 15 pl. 34, 4, 5. I, warrior (light-armed, kneeling to left).

19. SANTA BARBARA C 18 WL 55. I, archer.

20. AARHUS, Univ., 492, from Athens. *KUML* 1952, 100. I, archer. [Riis].

21 (12). OXFORD, Beazley, fr. I, archer (naked, kidaris, kneeling to left, drawing bow).

22. BRYN MAWR P 934, fr. I, (upper part of male to right, wearing kidaris).

(nos. 23–63: I, symposion: a youth reclining, naked, kidaris on head, seen from behind, to left, looking round to right; usually with a horn, in black, below)

23 (13). RHODES 13386, from Camiros. *Cl. Rh*. 4, 202; *CV*. pl. 5, 2.

24. NICOSIA C 672, from Marion. See *Cypr.* 39.

25. READING, Museum and Art Gallery (found in the Thames). *JHS.* 74, 178. [A. D. Ure].

26 (22). RHODES 14115, from Camiros. *Cl. Rh.* 6–7, 181.

27. RHODES.

28 (19). SALONICA, from Vrastina Kalyvia. *Delt.* 9, suppl., 38 fig. 6 b.

29 (15). THEBES, from Rhitsona. *BSA.* 14 pl. 13, b.

30. ITALIAN MARKET.

31. GELA (Giacomo Pozzo no. 6), from Gela.

32. GELA (INA casa 1954), fr., from Gela.

33. GELA (ex Tedeschi), fr., from Gela.

34. GELA (Acr. amb. 10 no. 4), fr., from Gela.

35 (16). FLORENCE 20 B 19. *CV.* pl. 20, B 19.

36 (17). ATHENS 12268, from Corinth.

37 (23). ATHENS, Agora, P 2800, from Athens. *Hesp.* 15 pl. 37, 60.

38. WASHINGTON 197. 245 (lent by Mrs. E. A. H. Magruder), from Italy. [Bothmer].

39. ST. OMER 6941. [Bothmer].

40 (13 *bis*). BERKELEY, Palestine Institute, fr., from Tell-en-Naṣbeh. *Bull. Am. Or.* 83, 28, 4; McCown *Tell-en-Naṣbeh* 1 pl. 59, 4. [Bothmer].

41. LONDON MARKET (Spink). [Bothmer].

42 (28 *bis*). OXFORD 1954. 239, fr., from Al Mina. *JHS.* 59, 3, 6.

43 (29). Where?, fr., from Al Mina. *JHS.* 59, 3, 7.

44 (30). OXFORD 1954. 240, fr., from Al Mina. *JHS.* 59, 3, 8.

45 (31). Where?, fr., from Al Mina. *JHS.* 59, 3, 9.

46 (32). Where?, fr., from Al Mina. *JHS.* 59, 3, 10.

47 (33). Where?, fr., from Al Mina. *JHS.* 59, 3, 11.

48 (34). Where?, fr., from Al Mina. *JHS.* 59, 3, 12.

49 (35). OXFORD 1954. 242, fr., from Al Mina. *JHS.* 59, 3, 13.

50. ETON, fr., from Al Mina.

51. ETON, fr., from Al Mina.

52. ATHENS Acr., fr., from Athens.

53. ATHENS, Agora, P 16781, fr., from Athens. *Hesp.* 15 pl. 36, 55.

54. (18). ATHENS, Agora, P 6636, fr., from Athens.

55 (20). JERUSALEM (Jordan), Palestine Museum, P 1605, fr., from Tel Jemmeh. *Q. Pal.* 2 pl. 7, 3.

56 (21). SALONICA inv. 458 (R. 199), fr., from Olynthos. Robinson *Olynthus* 5 pl. 107, 199.

57. MYKONOS 15, fr., from Rheneia (originally from Delos).   Dugas *Délos xxi* pl. 45, 15.

58 (24). ATHENS, Agora, P 5293, fr., from Athens.

59 (25). LEIPSIC T 3792, fr.

60. LOUVRE C 11260, fr.

61. ADRIA, fr., from Adria.

62. ADRIA B 1160, fr., from Adria.

63. ADRIA s.n. 9, fr., from Adria.

(nos. 64–67: I, symposion: a youth reclining, or sitting up, to left, left arm raised)

64 (27). LOUVRE G 97.

65. JERUSALEM (Jordan), Palestine Museum, from Tell Abu Hawām. Q. *Pal.* 4 pl. 12, 23.

66 (26). READING, Univ. Formerly in the London market (Spink), where it was shattered by enemy action. Good part of it is in Reading.

67 (28). SALONICA, from Vrastina Kalyvia. *Delt.* 9, suppl., 38 fig. 6a.

(nos. 68–70: I, naked youth kneeling to right)

68 (36). ATHENS, Agora, P 2765, from Athens. *Hesp.* 15 pl. 36, 56.

69. ATHENS, fr., from Perachora. [Corbett].

70. CHIOS, fr., from Kofiná in Chios. *BSA.* 49 pl. 6, 59. Compared by Boardman with Agora P 2765 (no. 68).

71 (37). PARIS MARKET (Mikas). I, hunter? (youth kneeling to left, his left arm extended in his cloak).

DISHIES

72 (38). LONDON MARKET (Sotheby). I, symposion (youth reclining).

73. NEWCASTLE UPON TYNE, Shefton. I, symposion (youth reclining). [Shefton].

NEAR THE PITHOS PAINTER

ARV.[1] 117.

CUPS

1 (1). ATHENS E. I, Sisyphos.

2 (3). LOUVRE S 1352, fr. I, symposion (youth, wearing kidaris, reclining).

3 (2). FLORENCE D B 4. *CV.* pl. D, 4. I, symposion (youth, wearing kidaris, reclining). By the Bonn Painter (p. 352 no. 12).

And a better cup:

LENINGRAD, fr., from Olbia. *Otchët* 1904, 33 fig. 39. I, satyr.

Many other coarse cups, decorated inside only, are more or less closely related to those of the Pithos Painter, and some of them were probably made in the same workshop as they. Among these coarse cups are the Group of Adria 300 and those by the Painter of Agora P 2578, the Heraion Painter, the Chaire Painter.

THE GROUP OF ADRIA B 300

ARV.[1] 117, nos. 4–8.

CUPS

(of type C)

1 (4). ADRIA B 300, fr., from Adria. Schöne pl. 2, 3; part, *CV*. pl. 3, 5. I, symposion (youth reclining).

2 (5). VILLA GIULIA 47259, from Cervetri. I, symposion (archer reclining).

3. ATHENS Acr. 116, fr., from Athens. I, symposion (male reclining).

4 (6). BOSTON Res. 08.31 h, fr. I, symposion (satyr reclining).

5. (7). CASSEL T 504, from Gela. Hartwig 181; Furtwängler *Somzée* pl. 37, iii, 3 = *Vente Somzée* pl. 1, 43. I, naked youth squatting beside a pointed amphora.

6 (8). REGGIO, from Medma. I, naked youth at laver.

7. ATHENS, Agora, P 23178, fr., from Athens. *Hesp.* 23 pl. 15, h. I, naked youth bending.

THE PAINTER OF AGORA P 2578

ARV.[1] 118.

Very close to the Pithos Painter: compare especially the cup p. 139 no. 6.

CUPS

1 (1). ATHENS, Agora, P 2578, from Athens. *Hesp.* 15 pl. 33, 44. I, armed satyr.

2 (2). ATHENS, Agora, P 2576, from Athens. *Hesp.* 15 pl. 33, 42. I, satyr reclining beside a pointed amphora.

3 (3). ATHENS, Agora, P 2577, from Athens. *Hesp.* 15 pl. 33, 43. I, satyr reclining beside a pointed amphora.

THE HERAION PAINTER

JHS. 59, 2. *ARV.*[1] 118–19 and 952.

Named after Delos 658 (no. 19) found in the Heraion of Delos.

Langlotz noted that no. 1 (Würzburg 478) was by the same hand as no. 19 (Delos 658).

CUPS

1 (1). WÜRZBURG 478. Langlotz pl. 217; A and foot, Bloesch *FAS* pl. 33, 7 and pl. 34, 1. I, youth kneeling with flute-case. For the shape, Bloesch 124, North-slope cup no. 4.

2. GELA (Acr. amb. 5 no. 1), fr., from Gela. I, youth kneeling with stick.

3 (2). ATHENS, Agora, P 7258, fr., from Athens. I, youth kneeling.

4 (3). BERLIN, Univ., D 245, fr. I, youth kneeling.

5 (4). ATHENS, Agora, P 11036, fr., from Athens. I, youth kneeling with flute-case.

6 (5). ATHENS, Agora, P 2736, fr., from Athens. *Hesp.* 15 pl. 36, 54. I, youth kneeling.

7. ATHENS, Agora, P 26233, frr., from Athens. I, youth kneeling with flute-case.

8 (6). ATHENS, Agora, P 14942, fr., from Athens. I, youth kneeling.

9. ATHENS, Agora, P 25867, fr., from Athens. I, youth kneeling.

10. ATHENS Acr., fr. (two joining) from Athens. I, male kneeling. The lower part of the painter's usual figure is preserved, with a stretch of net-border.

11. ATHENS, Agora, P 26169, fr., from Athens. I, youth kneeling or reclining.

12. ATHENS Acr., fr., from Athens. I, male (satyr?) kneeling. The middle remains, from navel nearly to mid-thigh, with part of the left hand and of the net-border.

13. ATHENS Acr. 245, fr., from Athens. I, satyr.

14. PARIS MARKET (Mikas). I, satyr kneeling with flute-case (to right, the right foot frontal, flute-case in left hand; egg-border in brown).

15 (5). ATHENS Acr. 131, fr., from Athens. *JHS.* 59, 3, right. I, satyr kneeling.

16 (4). OXFORD 1954. 238, fr., from Al Mina. *JHS.* 59, 3, 5. I, satyr kneeling with flute-case.

17. ATHENS, Agora, P 20389, fr., from Athens. I, satyr kneeling. Kallixenos ostrakon.

CUP OR STEMLESS CUP (RATHER THAN PLATE)

18. ATHENS Acr., fr., from Athens. I, (frontal foot of a male in a himation; egg-pattern border).

PLATES

19 (7). DELOS 658, from Delos. Dugas *Délos x* pl. 54, 658. Youth kneeling.

20 (8). ATHENS Acr. (A 210), frr., from Athens. Youth (kneeling or seated to right, stick in right hand).

21. ATHENS, Agora, P 2786, fr., from Athens. *Hesp.* 15 pl. 36, 57 and pl. 64, 57. (Cloak and elbow remain—of a kneeling youth).

LID

22. ATHENS Acr. 540, from Athens. Langlotz pl. 42. Inside, athlete.

PYXIS
(type D, box)

23. BOWDOIN 15.14, from Athens. Archer kneeling.

NEAR THE HERAION PAINTER

CUPS

1 (2). CAMBRIDGE N 140, fr., from Naucratis. *CV*. ii pl. 27, 4. I, male kneeling, holding (horn?).

2 (1). ADRIA B c 1 *bis*, fr., from Adria. *NSc.* 1879 pl. 3, 7; part, *CV*. pl. 2, 10; part, *Riv. Ist.* N.S. 5–6, 33 fig. 6. I, (youth with hare).

3. NEW YORK 20.206. *Le Musée* 3, 55; *Coll. Arthur Sambon* pl. 19, 101. I, satyr (kneeling: playing boules according to Sambon). Might well be a rather better work by the painter himself.

PLATES

4 (3). ATHENS, Agora (AP), fr., from Athens. *Hesp.* 5, 270, 30. I, symposion? (youth reclining?).

5. ATHENS, Agora, P 8784, fr., from Athens. Male (seated?—stick and feet remain).

THE CHAIRE PAINTER

ARV.[1] 119.

So named from the inscription on nos. 1–2 and 5–7.

New York 07.286. 32, by the Pithos Painter (p. 139 no. 2), recalls the Chaire Painter's cups.

CUPS

1 (1). HEIDELBERG 61. Kraiker pl. 8. I, komast at krater.

2. TORONTO, Wallace, fr. I, komast at krater.

3 (2). ATHENS, Agora, P 5015, fr., from Athens. I, youth at laver.

4 (3). CHIUSI 1842, from Chiusi. Inghirami *Chius.* pl. 164; *E.A.A.* ii, 530. I, naked woman at krater.

5 (4). INDIANAPOLIS 47.37. *Coll. Arthur Sambon* pl. 19, 100; *Bull. Ind.* 34, 19, 1. I, naked woman kneeling at pithos.

6 (5). CERVETRI, from Cervetri. I, youth lifting pointed amphora (naked, to right, bending).

7 (6). READING, Univ., 39. viii. 3, fr. I, male with pointed amphora.

7 *bis*. NAPLES, Astarita, 754, frr. I, komast with with lyre.

8. FERRARA (erratico in 1959), from Spina. I, youth (moving to left, cloak on outstretched left arm).

9 (7). LEIPSIC T 3578, from Cervetri. I, symposion (youth reclining).

Probably also the cup-fragment

OXFORD, Beazley, fr. I, (bare legs of male kneeling to right).

Compare also the cups:

1. ALTENBURG 235, from Vulci. *CV*. pl. 68, 3-4. I, athlete kneeling with discus.

2. YALE 162. Baur 110 fig. 38, left. I, jumper.

3. LOUVRE C 11261, fr. I, one at column-krater (the feet and one shank remain, with part of the krater).

A vase of another shape is more elaborate than any known work of the painter, but like him:

PYXIS

(*type B*)

PARIS MARKET. Symposion (two naked men and two naked women reclining, and a boy cup-bearer filling a skyphos at a column-krater). On the lid, palmettes, with a small wheel in the middle.

CHAPTER 12

THE COARSER WING, iii

THE EPELEIOS PAINTER

VA. 12. *Att. V.* 47–48 and 468. *BCH.* 1936, 12–14 (Dugas). *ARV.*¹ 107–11 and 951.

So called from the kalos-name on nos. 2, 5, 18, and 37. The name is no doubt Ἐπιλέως, but I keep the artist's version of it.

CUPS

1. TORONTO 351. Robinson and Harcum pl. 54. I, naked youth. A–B, between eyes. A, komast; B, komast. Restored (the upper part of the komast on B, and the thing held in the left hand, are modern). The foot of the cup is of type B. See p. 48 no. 164.

2 (1). MUNICH 2619 A (J. 331), from Vulci. FR. pl. 155; I, Licht iii, 147. I, satyr filling krater. A, Peleus and Thetis. B, komos. On I, IϹΑLΟϞ retr., and ΕΓΕLΕΙΟϞ. On B, [Δ]Ο[Ρ]ΟϴΕΟϞ [ΚΑ]LΟϞ ΝΑΙ+Ι, ΙϞΡΑ+ΟϞ (= Ἴσαρχος) ΚΑLΟϞ, ΕΓΕLΙΟϞ and retr. ΚΑLΟϞ, ϴΕΟΔΟΡΟϞ ΚΑLΟϞ. For the shape, Bloesch 50, foot. See p. 1628.

3 (2). FLORENCE 5 B 2 (part ex Villa Giulia), HEIDELBERG 12 and 35, and NAPLES, Astarita, 249. Part, *CV.* Fl. pl. 5, B 2; the Heidelberg frr., Kraiker pll. 3 and 5; I, *Boll. d'Arte* 29, 266 fig. 17. I, symposion (youth reclining). A, sacrifice. B, komos. The Astarita fragment joins, adding the waist and legs of the third youth on B and the right leg of the fourth.

3 *bis* (a 113). FLORENCE V 45, from Chiusi. I is lost. A, bull led to sacrifice. B, satyrs attacking maenads; naked youth attacking a woman.

4. VILLA GIULIA, fr. A, komos (waist and buttocks of a male moving to left, and of another moving to right; between them, the cloak of one).

5 (3). NEW YORK 09.221.48. A–B, *Bull. Metr.* 5, 142 fig. 2; Richter and Hall pl. 7 and pl. 179, 8. I, komast; A–B, komos. On A, ΗΟΓΑΙϞΚΑLΟϞ ΕΓΕLΕΙΟϞ.

6 (4). TARQUINIA RC 5293, from Tarquinia. R.I. xii. 3. I, cup-bearer; A–B, komos.

7 (5). BRUSSELS A 3047, from Vulci. *CV.* pl. 22, 1. I, komast; A–B, komos.

8 (6, 7). FLORENCE B B 5 (part ex Villa Giulia) and AMSTERDAM inv. 2768, fr. Part, *CV.* Fl. pl. B, B5. I, (part of the line-border remains). A–B, komos. The Amsterdam fr. joins on the right of B. See the next.

9 (8). HEIDELBERG 24, fr. Kraiker pl. 2. Outside, komos. This may join the last, on the left of the Amsterdam fragment.

10 (10). LEIPSIC T 562, fr. A, komos (arm, youth playing flute to right).

11 (11). AMSTERDAM inv. 2206, fr. A, komos (youths dancing).

12 (12, +). LYONS, Univ. (including a fr. ex Montpellier, recognized by Dugas), and LOUVRE C 11246. The Lyons part, *BCH*. 1936 pl. 22, 3 and pl. 23. I, naked youth bending. A–B, komos. See p. 1628.

13 (9). HEIDELBERG 25, fr. Kraiker pl. 3. A, komos. Might belong to the last?

14 (13). NEW YORK 96.18.71 (GR 581). I, komast; A–B, komos.

15 (14). ROME, Torlonia, 144. I, komast; A–B, komos.

16. ARLESHEIM, Schweizer. I, komast (naked man capering to left); A–B, komos. On A, two groups, each of four youths: in the right-hand group, a youth, spewing wine, sits on a wineskin, which is in a hand-cart, and his companions seem to be shaking him off.

17 (16). MUNICH 2616 (J. 1234), from Vulci. A and foot, Bloesch *FAS*. pl. 14, 3. I, komast; A, symposion; B, komos. Restored. For the shape, Bloesch 55 no. 15.

18 (17). BRYN MAWR P 96, from Vulci. Gsell pll. 13–16, whence *AJA*. 1916, 324; I, *AJA*. 1916, 323. I, youth leaning on his stick; A, man and youths; B, youths. On I, ΕΓΕΛΕΙΟϟ and retr. ΚΑΛΟϟΝΑΙ+Ι. On A, ΘΕΟ-ΔΟΡΟϟ ΝΑΙ+Ι ΗΟΓΑΙϟ, ΚΑΛΟϟ retr., ΕΓΕΛΕΙΟϟ ΚΑΛΟϟ ΝΑΙ+Ι ΗΟΓΑ[Ιϟ], retr. ΚΑΛΟϟ. On B, ΙϟΡΑ+Ο[ϟ]ΚΑΛ[Οϟ], Ε[ΓΕΛ]ΕΙΟϟ retr., ΚΑΛΟϟ, ΝΑΙ+Ι retr., ΚΑΛΟϟ. Bothmer's readings.

19 (18). WÜRZBURG 475, from Vulci. Gerhard pl. 293–4, 1–4; Langlotz pl. 144. I, naked youth at herm. A, youths and horse; man, boy (the jockey), and youth; B, youths and horse; youths and boy (the jockey?) Restored. For the shape, Bloesch 55 no. 11.

20 (19). FLORENCE 91455. *CV*. pl. 77. I, athlete using pick (the same subject as in Brussels R347, see p. 334). A–B, youths with horses.

21 (20). MUNICH, two frr. Outside, (youth, horses). On one fr., head, to left, breast, right arm of a youth holding a lead, with . . . Ιϟ . . .; on the other, on the right of the picture, part of a horse tied to a column, with . . . ΚΑ]ΛΟϟ.

22 (21). HEIDELBERG 26, fr. Kraiker pl. 3. A, (horse, youth).

23 (22). ORVIETO, Faina, 63, from Orvieto? I, ph. R.I. 1935.862. I, komast. A–B, warriors and horses. For the shape, Bloesch 54, ii no. 1.

24 (23). FLORENCE 4 B 31, two frr. *CV*. pl. 4, B 31. Outside, warriors with horses.

25 (24). VILLA GIULIA 50393. I, warrior; A–B, fight. Restored. For the shape, Bloesch 48 no. 12.

26 (25). CAB. MÉD. 512. De Ridder pl. 21 and pp. 386 and 388. I, warrior; A–B, fight.

27 (26). TORONTO (ex Curtius), fr. Ph. R.I. 1935.234. A, athletes (youth standing to left, acontist moving to right).

28 (27). GOETTINGEN, fr. I, boxer (to right, left hand at head); A (males— athletes?).

29 (28, +). LOUVRE C 10881 (including S 1404, S 1400, and S 1326). I, acontist; A–B, athletes.

30. AMSTERDAM inv. 2203, fr. A, (trainer).

31 (29). AMSTERDAM inv. 2790, fr. A, (youth leaning on his stick).

32. AMSTERDAM inv. 2792, fr. A, (youth).

33. LOUVRE C 11247, fr. A, (males: one moving to right, then a campstool, then one moving to left, a cloak on his right arm, then a youth moving to left, looking round, and another youth in a himation leaning on his stick to left).

34. GREIFSWALD 273, fr. Peters pl. 22. A, (youth seated). [Peters]. See p. 1628.

35 (30). CUXHAVEN, fr. I, cup-bearer (boy to left at krater). Restored.

36 (31). FLORENCE 5 B 9, fr. CV. pl. 5, B 9. I, komast.

37 (32). MUNICH 2595 (J. 469), from Vulci. FR. iii, 243; A and foot, Bloesch FAS. pl. 33, 6. I, maenad. ΕΓΕLΕΙΟ⸱ retr. and ΚΑLΟ⸱. For the shape, Bloesch 123 no. 36.

MANNER OF THE EPELEIOS PAINTER

ARV.[1] 109–11 and 951.

Most of these are very close to the painter and may be from his hand.

CUPS

1 (a 2). NEW YORK 06.1021.168, from Vulci. A–B, Coll. M.E. pl. 11, 247; A–B, Sambon Canessa pl. 5, 77. I, warrior. A, Herakles and the lion; B, Theseus and the bull.

2 (31). ROME, Marchese Giorgio Guglielmi, from Vulci. I, naked youth at laver. A, Herakles and the lion. B, Theseus and the bull.

3 (20). LEIPSIC T 3625, T 3598, part of T 3628, and T 3629 (including a fr. ex Heidelberg 7, recognized by Kirsten), from Cervetri. I and part of A–B, Kirsten LV. no. 2; the Heidelberg fr., Kraiker pl. 3. I, horseman (jockey?). A–B, Theseus and the bull; youths and horses.

4. CHICAGO 89.11. Bull. Art Inst. 23, 130–1 and 140. I, satyr. A, Theseus and the bull; on the left, fight; on the right, fight; B, fight. Restored.

5 (1). MUNICH 2615. I, warrior; A–B, fight. Much restored. For the shape, Bloesch 55 no. 9.

6 (2). PALERMO, fr., from Selinus. A, fight (head, to right, and breast, of bearded warrior with shield).

7 (3). PALERMO, fr., from Selinus. A, fight (shield, head of horse to right).

8. AMSTERDAM inv. 3361, from Vulci. *CV.* Scheurleer b pl. 2; A, *Gids* pl.
68. I, woman dancing. A–B, warriors setting out (A, warrior mounting
chariot, and warrior; B, horsemen and warrior).

9 (4). WÜRZBURG 470, from Vulci. A, *Anz.* 1928, 99 fig. 4; Langlotz pl.
139. I, hoplitodromos. A–B, fight. For the shape, Bloesch 50, middle,
no. 3. For the battle-scene on A compare no. 19.

10 (5). CAB. MÉD. 511. I, A, and part of B, de Ridder pl. 21 and pp. 384–5.
I, jumper. A–B, fight. For the shape, Bloesch 48 no. 9.

11 (6 *bis*). PALERMO V 657, from Chiusi. Inghirami *Chius.* pll. 154 and 171–
2, whence (A) *El.* 1 pl. 4; cleaned, *CV.* pl. 3 (misprinted 4). I, athlete.
A, Gigantomachy. B, fight. For the shape, Bloesch 48 no. 10.

12 (6). FLORENCE 3951 (now augmented by numerous frr. ex Campana added
by Neri and myself: *CV.* pl. 4, B 36–37; pl. 12, B 58 plus pl. 6, B 30; pl.
6, B 33; and others). *CV.* pl. 81 and pl. 116, 6. I, warrior; A–B, fight.

13 (7). MAYENCE, Univ., 101 (ex Preyss); and FLORENCE 6 B 17 (three frr.,
one ex Villa Giulia). Part, *CV.* pl. 6, B 17. I, (lost). A–B, fight. The fr.
ex Villa Giulia, not mentioned in *CF.*, gives part of the leg of the right-
hand horseman on A and part of his horse's flank. See p. 1628.

14 (8). FLORENCE 3965 (augmented by a fragment, part ex Villa Giulia, *CV.*
11 B 47, added by Neri). *CV.* pl. 82 and pl. 116, 7. I, warrior; A–B,
fight. For the shape, Bloesch 55 no. 16. As Laon 37.1054 (no. 23).

15. MUNICH, Bareiss. *Vente xi Bâle* pl. 20, 335. I, komast. A, fight; B,
warriors with horses. Restored.

16 (11). LONDON E 7, from Vulci. I, Murray no. 4. I, warrior; A–B, fight.
On A, HΙΓΓONΚΑLOΣ: on a shield. See no. 59.

17 (12). LEIPSIC T 627, fr. A, fight (upper part of a warrior attacking to left,
inscription . . . A . . .).

18 (13). LEIPSIC T 494, fr. A, fight (leg of warrior to right, legs of wounded
warrior to right).

19 (a 4). CARLSRUHE 244. I and B, Welter pl. 16, 35; *CV.* pl. 25, 1–3. I,
warrior; A, fight. B, youths with horses. For the shape, Bloesch 48
no. 7. See no. 9.

20 (15). COPENHAGEN, Thorvaldsen Museum, 107. Gerhard pl. 293–4, 5–8,
whence (I and B) *JHS.* 24, 191, (B) *JHS.* 27, 26, 15. I, jumper. A, warriors making ready (warriors, youth with horse, youth holding greaves,
warrior with horse). B, athletes. Restored.

21 (16). NAPLES 2616, from Vulci. *Mus. Borb.* 14 pl. 56; ph. So. 11006, iii,
3. I, jumper. A–B, warriors making ready (A, warrior, youth holding
greaves, warriors with horses; B, warriors with horses, youth with
horse). Cf. Thorvaldsen 107 (no. 20).

22. MONTAUBAN 2, from Vulci. *Revue du Louvre* 11, 52–53. I, horseman
(light-armed warrior); A–B, warriors leading horses. See p. 1628.

23 (10). LAON 37.1054 (ex Delessert 28), from Vulci. I, hoplitodromos. A, satyrs and maenad with donkeys. B, fight. Restored. See p. 1628.

24 (17). LEIPSIC T 3630. I, komast. A–B, horses.

25. NAPLES, Astarita, 37, and FLORENCE. I, discus-thrower. A, warrior with horses; B, youth with horses. The Florence fragment gives the flower under one handle. Compare also the fragment Florence 11 B 32 (no. 54: part, CV. pl. 11, B 32).

26. ITALIAN MARKET, four frr. Outside: on one fragment, (on the left, naked youth moving to left blowing a trumpet, then the forepart of a horse, led, to left); on the second, (hindquarters of a horse and lower part of a warrior running, both to left; may be the same horse as before); on the third, (forehead of a warrior to left, with the front of his helmet: may be the same warrior). ΚΕLΑΑΙ. retr., ΕV [. . .] Εϟ.

27 (18). NEW YORK, Scaravaglione, fr. (ex Rome, American Academy). Mem. Am. Ac. 10 pl. 28, 2. A, (youths and horses).

28 (19). DRESDEN, fr. A, (face of horse to right, and the letter ϟ).

29. GREIFSWALD 301, two frr. Peters pl. 29. Outside, (males and horses).

30 (21). LEIPSIC T 3628, part, fr. A, (head, to right, and collarbones, of youth).

31 (33). TÜBINGEN E 30, fr. Watzinger pl. 20 (misprinted E 31). A, youth.

32. LOUVRE C 11248, fr. A, (youth—athlete?—to right: head and upper arms remain, with the letter . . . L . . .).

33 (22, +). LOUVRE C 10879 (including S 1382). I, youth squatting behind a large vessel. A–B, komos.

34 (23). BOULOGNE 52. I, komast; A–B, komos.

35 (24). TURIN 3032. Phs. R.I. 1930.269 and 271–2. I, warrior. A–B, komos. See p. 1628.

36. FLORENCE V.xl and lix, two frr., from Chiusi. Outside, komos.

37 (a 1). MUNICH 2611 (J. 187), from Vulci. I, Licht iii, 126; A and foot, Bloesch FAS. pl. 14, 4; I, Vorberg Gloss. 736. I, satyr. A–B, komos. Restored. For the shape, Bloesch 57 no. 5.

38. GREIFSWALD 274, fr. Peters pl. 22. A, komos. [Peters].

39 (25). VATICAN 504, from Vulci. Mus. Greg. 2 pl. 70, 2; Albizzati pl. 70. I, jumper; A–B, athletes. For the shape, Bloesch 48 no. 3. See p. 1629.

40 (26). VATICAN, from Vulci. Mus. Greg. 2 pl. 70, 1. I, komast. A–B, athletes. Much restored.

41 (27). MONTPELLIER, S.A., 55. I, discus-thrower; A–B, athletes. Restored.

42. LOUVRE C 183, fr. A, athletes (handle, discus-thrower, acontist, runner). Many Louvre frr. join the original C 183.

43. LOUVRE C 11249, three frr. Outside, athletes: on one fr., leg to right,

pair of boxers, legs to right, leg to right; on the second, on the left, sponge hanging, athlete—discus-thrower—to right; on the third, on the right, sponge hanging.

44 (29). HEIDELBERG 23 and (part ex Villa Giulia) FLORENCE 5 B 11. Part, CV. Fl. pl. 5, B 11; the Heidelberg fr., Kraiker pll. 4 and 7. I, athlete with pick; A–B, athletes: A, wrestlers; B, boxers (or pancration).

45 (28). BRUNSWICK 503, 529, 530, 531, and AMSTERDAM inv. 2210 and 2211, frr. CV. Brunswick pl. 14, 2–6. Outside, athletes. A fr. in Bryn Mawr (AJA. 1916, 340, 6) might belong. See p. 1628.

46 (32). PALERMO, fr., from Selinus. A, (middle of male in himation, leaning to left, back-view, right arm akimbo). Compare the last. Also recalls the Painter of Berlin 2268.

47 (30). NEW YORK 41. 162.133, from Vulci. A–B, Cat. Sotheby March 14 1929 pl. 4; CV. Gallatin pl. 47, 3, pl. 49, 1, and pl. 61, 6. I, discus-thrower; A–B, athletes.

48. PALERMO V 658, from Chiusi. Inghirami Chius. pll. 194–6; cleaned, CV. pl. 8, 1 and 3–4. I, acontist; A–B, athletes.

49 (a 6). DRESDEN, fr. A, athletes (jumper, acontist, arm of one in a himation).

50. LOUVRE C 11251, fr. A, athletes at laver.

51. BALTIMORE, Walters Art Gallery, 48.89. I, D. K. Hill Intr., cover. I, naked youth in bell-krater. A, athletes at laver, and athlete; B, the like.

52. LOUVRE G 22. I, discus-thrower. A, youths hunting deer; B, the like. For the shape, Bloesch 48 no. 13.

53. MAYENCE, Univ., 12.2, fr. A, (middle of male—seated?).

54. FLORENCE 11 B 32, fr. CV. pl. 11, B 32. I, athlete. Outside, part of the line-border remains.

55 (34). ATHENS Acr. 167, fr., from Athens. Langlotz pl. 7. I, komast.

56. INNSBRUCK ii.12.20, fr. I, youth (head and left shoulder and arm remain). Compare Louvre C 10881 (p. 148 no. 29).

57 (36). GOETTINGEN (J. 28), fr. Jacobsthal Gött.V. pl. 7, 26. I, seated youth. For the shape, Bloesch 55 no. 8.

58. GOETTINGEN (J. 29), fr. Jacobsthal Gött.V. pl. 8, 28. I, satyr at krater (as cup-bearer).

59. FAYETTEVILLE, Univ. of Arkansas. Hesp. Art. Bull. 5, 6 no. 62. I, warrior running. As London E 7 (no. 16).

60. ATHENS, Agora, P 24101, from Athens. I, warrior picking up his helmet.

61. BOULOGNE 185. Le Musée 2, 280 fig. 29. I, jumper.

62 (37). MUNICH 2623 (J. 1174), from Vulci. Jb. 10, 186 no. 5. I, athlete. For the shape, Bloesch 55 no. 14. See p. 1628, foot.

The following are related to the Epeleios Painter:

(*ARV.*¹ 111)

CUPS

1. LOUVRE C 10878. *Museum* 3, 177 fig. 40. I is lost. A–B, symposion.
2. LOUVRE C 10871. I, athlete (bending). A–B, youths with horses.
3. LOUVRE, fr. I, (maeander). A, (youth leaning on his stick to left).
4 (5). NEW YORK 41.162.128, from Vulci. *CV*. Gallatin pl. 47, 2, pl. 48, 2, and pl. 61, 5. I, discus-thrower; A–B, athletes. For the attitudes on B compare Louvre G 36 (p. 114, below, no. 1). See p. 1629.
5. LOUVRE G 95, fr. Pottier pl. 99. I, man with pointed amphora. The inscription is HOΓ[ΑΙϚ] retr. and ΚΑLΟϚ (not as in Pottier).
6. BASLE MARKET (M.M.). I, naked youth at pithos (to right, bending, his arms in it). Cup type C, North-slope-cup.
7. ITALIAN MARKET. I, warrior (naked, helmeted, running to left, shield-device two dolphins).
8. GRAZ 22, from Capua. *Festschrift des Institutes für Leibeserziehung der Univ. Graz* pl. 1. I, jumper.

OINOCHOE

(*shape 8A: mug*)

9 (7). CRACOW 1259. *CV*. pl. 10, 1. Komos. Restored.

See also p. 158.

———————

For cups mingling Epeleian elements with Euergidean see p. 104.

———————

Two oinochoai have the same shape as the many by the Painter of Berlin 2268 and near him (pp. 156–7 nos. 51–84 and p. 158 nos. 1–3), except for the underside of the foot, which is the same as in the Faina oinochoe by Epiktetos (p. 77 no. 89); the drawing connects them with the Epeleios Painter:

OINOCHOAI

(*shape 8A; mugs*)

1. PALERMO, from Selinus. White ground. Komos (a man and two youths).
2. ATHENS, Agora, P 15918, from Athens. Symposion? (youths reclining or almost, at a krater).

A small fragment has the same underside:

ATHENS, Agora, P 5009, fr., from Athens. (Male sitting on the ground).

See also p. 983.

———————

With New York 41.162.128 (p. 152 no. 4) compare the

CUP

NORTHAMPTON (Massachusetts), Smith College. *Smith College Bull.* 37 (1957), 1–7. I, discus-thrower. A, satyr sitting on the ground, and satyr. B, komos (youths at the krater). Cup type A. Early, See p. 1629.

Compare with these an eye-cup in the Lucerne market (p. 50 no. 198).

———

The following cup is in the manner of the Epeleios Painter (*ARV.*[1] 109 no. 9):

TARQUINIA RC 1130, from Tarquinia. *CV.* pl. 20; I, ph. Mo. 5856, 2. I, naked youth with pole or spear; A, fight; warrior with horse; B, arming (youth with spear and shield, youth holding the shield ready for him); warrior with horse, youth with horse. The youth on I is to be interpreted by comparison with the youth on the right of B.

This cup was never attributed by me to the Colmar Painter—the statement in *CV.* is a muddled version of an illegitimate guess by Philippart (*It. ii,* 121 no. 14). The cup I attributed to the Colmar Painter is Tarquinia RC 1912 (*Att. V.* 229 no. 37; *ARV.*[1] 229 no. 49: below, p. 357, no. 71).

Parts of another cup resemble Tarquinia RC 1130:

ATHENS, Agora, P 24068, from Athens. I, jumper. A, fight; B, arming.

———

THE PAINTER OF BERLIN 2268

Att. V. 46–47 and 468. *V.Pol.* 15. *ARV.*[1] 113–16 and 951.

CUPS

1 (1). NEW YORK 06.1021.166, from Orvieto. *Vente 11 mai 1903,* 41; Sambon *Canessa* 22 and pl. 5, 78; Richter and Hall pl. 6 and pl. 179, 7; I, *AJA.* 1946, 21 fig. 16. I, maenad. A–B, athletes.

2 (2). BERLIN 2268, from Tarquinia. Krause pl. 9b figs. 25 b–d; Lücken pl. 79, 1 and pll. 77–78, whence (I) *E.A.A.* ii, 63 fig. 104; I, Licht ii, 140 = Blümel *Sport und Spiel* pl. 11, above = Zadoks-Jitta 91, 10. I, jumper; A–B, athletes. A–B restored. For the shape, Bloesch 57 no. 6.

3 (3). NAPLES 2636, from Ruvo. A–B, ph. So. 11006, i, 2. I, youth running with hare. A–B, athletes. Restored.

3 *bis.* BASLE MARKET (M.M.). I, man leaning on his stick at laver; A–B, athletes.

3 *ter.* BASLE MARKET (M.M.). I, boxer; A–B, athletes.

4 (4). VILLA GIULIA 20781, from Cervetri. I, youth leaning on his stick; A, jumper and two youths, one of whom is seated; B, male leaning on his stick, between a youth and a man, both seated.

5. MARSEILLES I 6.62, fr., from Marseilles. Villard *C.G.M.* pl. 15, 3. A, athletes (discus-thrower and youth). [Villard].

6 (5). LEIPSIC T 567, fr. A, (discus-thrower).

7. GENEVA I 529. I, satyr running with baskets (fish-baskets?) on a pole. A–B, athletes; on B a herm. For the shape, Bloesch 57 no. 16.

8. LOUVRE C 11232, fr. (two joining). I, (end of a staff or spear). A, athletes? (middles and legs of three naked males to left).

9. LOUVRE C 11233, fr. I, horseman? (legs of a male to left in boots and a long thick cloak). A, (male shank and foot, bare, and lower part of a male in a himation leaning on his stick, both to left).

10. LOUVRE C 11234, fr. A, (youth leaning on his stick).

11. LOUVRE C 11235, fr. I, komast? (male legs to right, with part of the cloak); A, komos? (lower part of a naked male, and leg of a second, moving to right).

12 (6). VILLA GIULIA 20771, from Cervetri. A–B, *ML.* 42, 263–4. I, komast; A–B, komos.

13 (7). AMSTERDAM inv. 52. I, Scheurleer *Cat.* pl. 40, 1; *CV.* Scheurleer b pl. 8, 1–2 and 4. I, warrior. A–B, komos.

14 (8). THE HAGUE, Gemeente Museum, 1712. *CV.* Scheurleer b pl. 7. I, youth at laver. A–B, komos.

15 (9). BERLIN, Univ., D 721. I, komast; A–B, komos.

16 (10). HEIDELBERG 34, fr. Kraiker pl. 12. I, youth leaning on his stick. A–B, komos. For the shape, Bloesch 57 no. 9.

17. LOUVRE C 10887. I, cup-bearer at the krater; A–B, komos.

18 (11, +). LOUVRE C 11236 (including S 1384). I, komast (man); A–B, komos. See nos. 19–20.

19. LOUVRE C 11237, fr. A, komos (upper half of a youth, head to right). Might belong to Louvre C 11236 (no. 18)?

20. LOUVRE C 11238, fr. A, (forehead of a male to right, raising his arm). Might belong to Louvre C 11236 (no. 18)?

21. LOUVRE C 174, fr. A, komos (upper part of a youth to right).

22. LOUVRE C 11239, fr. A, (face, to left, and extended right arm of a youth, inscription [HOΓΑ]Iϟ . . .

23. LOUVRE C 11240, fr. A, (head and breast of a man looking down to right).

24. STRASBURG, Univ., 849, fr. A, (head and right shoulder of man).

25. LOUVRE G 270. A, Pottier pl. 133. I, man holding helmet and shield; A–B, fight. Restored.

26. FLORENCE 4 B 35, frr.   Part, *CV*. pl. 4, B 35.   I, warrior; A–B, fight.

27. NEW YORK 17.194.1900, fr.   I, youth leaning on his stick.   A–B, fight.

28 (12). FLORENCE 3947. *CV*. pl. 83 and pl. 116, 8.   I, youth (cup-bearer) at krater.   A–B, fight.   A Florence fragment joins and adds the ankle of a warrior.   For the shape, Bloesch 131 no. 9.

29 (13). VILLA GIULIA, two frr.   I, (foot to right, hook-pattern border).   A, fight?

30. GELA ILA4, part, two frr., from Gela.   I, warrior putting on his greaves; A–B, fight.

31. VILLA GIULIA 20765–6, from Cervetri.   See p. 1629.

32 (24,+). LOUVRE C 10885.   I, warrior; A–B, fight.

33. LOUVRE C 11241, fr. (two joining).   I, warrior (part of the helmet remains); A, fight (young warrior attacking to right, device three rings, then a warrior fallen, to left).

34. LOUVRE C 10886.   I, fight; A–B, fight.

35. LOUVRE C 11242.   I, male leaning on his stick holding a hare; net-border.   A–B, arming.

36. LOUVRE C 11243, two frr.   Outside, on one, the upper part of a young warrior to left; on the other, a shield charged with a winged dolphin.   Might belong to Louvre C 11242 (no. 35)?

37 (14). CAMBRIDGE 37.16, from Vulci.   I, Cecil Smith *Forman* pl. 10 no. 334; *CV*. ii R.S. pl. 8, 7, pl. 9, 6, and pl. 6, 1.   I, man; leaning on his stick, with helmet and flower; A–B, warriors and youths.   For the shape, Bloesch 57 no. 15.

38 (15). NEW YORK 06.1021.170.   I, Sambon *Canessa* pl. 5, 82; A, *N.Y. Shapes* 18, 3 = Richter and Milne fig. 163, whence LS. fig. 6; Richter and Hall pl. 5 and pl. 179, 6; I, Richter *H*. 215, b.   I, youth with horse; A–B, youths and horses.

39. LOUVRE C 11244, fr.   A, (part of the left-hand figure remains, the head of a horse to left).

40. LOUVRE C 11245, frr.   I, horseman; A (horse's hoof, foot of a youth or man).

41. LOUVRE C 10876.   I, youth holding helmet and shield.   A–B, youths grooming horses.

42 (16). PALERMO, fr., from Selinus.   I, *ML*. 32 pl. 95, 3.   (I, youth).   A, (horse).

43 (18). ORVIETO, Faina, 46, from Orvieto?   I, ph. Al. 32467, whence Tarchi pl. 125, 1; A–B, phs. R.I. 1935.852–3.   I, maenad; A–B, satyrs and maenads.

44 (19). ROMAN MARKET (Depoletti), from Vulci.   B.Ap. xxii. 93.   I, satyr running with phallus-stick and pelta; A, two satyrs (one similarly armed), a maenad, and a donkey; B, satyrs, maenad, and donkeys.

45 (20). ROMAN MARKET (Depoletti), from Vulci. B.Ap. xvi. 36. I, satyr (running to left, looking round); A–B, satyrs and maenads. Alien signature of Hieron, see p. 482 no. 40.

46 (21). LOUVRE C 10888. I, satyr; A–B, satyrs and maenads.

47 (22). PHILADELPHIA 5695. *AJA.* 1934 pl. 35. I, maenad; A–B, satyrs and maenads.

48 (23). CAB. MÉD. 518, fr. I, two athletes (jumper and acontist).

49 (25). CRACOW 1463a. *CV.* pl. 10, 4. I, komast.

50 (26). FLORENCE 11 B 3, fr. *CV.* pl. 11, B 3. I, komast.

OINOCHOAI

(*shape 8A: mugs*)

(*nos. 51–63, warriors*)

51 (27). BOLOGNA 566 *bis*, from Bologna. *Mél. d' arch.* 27, 344.

52 (28). LOUVRE G 102.

53 (30). NEW YORK 06.1021.98, from Capua. *Vente 11 mai 1903,* 32, left, whence *Mü. St.* 494 fig. 26.

54. ITALY, private. (Two light-armed, kneeling, with kidareis and peltae (devices an eye, a dolphin); between, altar and palm).

55 (31). NEW YORK 06.1021.100, from Capua. *Vente 11 mai 1903,* 32, right.

56 (32). NEW YORK x. 21.28 (GR 584).

57 (33). NAPLES RC 130, from Cumae.

58. GIESSEN.

59 (34). CATANIA inv. 4234.

60 (35). CATANIA.

61 (36). READING, frr. The remains of a vase (ex Hearst) which was destroyed by enemy action when in the London market (Spink).

62 (a). WARSAW 142349 (ex Czartoryski 60). *CV.* pl. 23, 3.

63. GELA, from Bubbonia. Fight.

(*nos. 64–71, komos*)

64 (37). NEW YORK 06.1021.172. Sambon *Canessa* pl. 17, 230; *Bull. Metr.* 1, 78 fig. 4; *N.Y. Shapes* 21, 4 = Richter and Milne fig. 186.

65 (38). ATHENS 10460, from the Cabeirion of Thebes. Wolters and Bruns i, 58, left and pl. 40, 2–3.

66 (39). VILLA GIULIA. (Youths kneeling, one to right, with wineskin, the other to left, with cloak; leaf below the handle).

67 (40). TARANTO, fr., from Taranto. (Head and left arm of a youth, and arm, in cloak, of another).

68. RIEHEN, Kuhn. *Vente x Bâle* pl. 20, 414; part, *B. K. Hirsch* pl. 12, 20.

68 *bis.* VIENNA 3448. *CV.* pl. 100, 1–2. [Eichler].

69. SAN SIMEON, Hearst Corporation, 9881.

70. PARIS MARKET (Segredakis). (Two naked youths to right, bending, one of them holding a large wineskin with both hands). [Bothmer].

71. LONDON E 568, from Camiros.

(nos. 72–76, symposion: youths reclining)

72 (42). VILLA GIULIA.

73 (43). TARQUINIA RC 3245, from Tarquinia.

74 (44). TARQUINIA 710, from Tarquinia.

75. NAPLES (ex Spinelli), from Suessula.

76 (45). ATHENS, Agora, P 2230, fr., from Athens.

(nos. 77–80, athletes)

77 (46). CAPUA, from Capua. *CV.* pl. 18, 1–4.

78 (47). BERLIN 2319, from Tarquinia. Blümel *S.H.* 35. *CV.* pl. 144, 1–3 and 7.

79. ATHENS Acr., fr., from Athens. (Arms to left, with a haltēr in one of the hands).

79 *bis.* PADULA, from Padula. Athlete with discus, athlete with haltēres, trainer.

80 (48). OXFORD 1928.25, from Naucratis. *CV.* pl. 62, 4–5.

81. ATHENS, Agora, P 18259, fr., from Athens. (Arm).

82. ATHENS, Agora, P 17620, fr., from Athens. *Hesp.* 17 pl. 66, 1. (Youth leaning on his stick).

83. TEL AVIV. Two satyrs. [Bothmer].

84 (49). BERLIN 2320. Licht iii, 79; *CV.* pl. 144, 4–6 and 8–9. B.Ap. xxi. 92. 2. Horse and phallus-horse at laver.

(special shape)

85 (51). VILLA GIULIA 47235, from Cervetri. *ML.* 42, 967, 1. Satyr on the ground.

ALABASTRA

86 (52). ATHENS, Vlasto, from Koropi. A, a youth courting a boy (the youth leans on his stick, with a hare in his right hand; the naked boy grasps the youth's wrist). B, woman dancing, with crotala.

87 (53). CHICAGO, Univ., from Greece. *AJA.* 1938, 346 fig. 1. Peltasts. On the bottom, black palmette.

88 (54). PROVIDENCE 25.073, from Greece. *AJA.* 1931, 299; *CV.* pl. 17, 3. Satyr with pelta and wineskin.

ASKOS
(type 2)

89 (55). LOUVRE G 609. Symposion (A, youth reclining; B, the like). restored.

A cup-fragment is probably by the painter:

ERLANGEN, fr. A, fight (head and shoulders of a warrior to left, spear in red).

Small fragments of oinochoai (shape 8) may also be his:

ATHENS Acr., fr., from Athens. (Part of a wineskin, with a rough kappa on it, retr.).

ATHENS Acr., fr., from Athens. (Middle of a naked male to left).

A cup may be his, although it is more careful than any of his other works: compare Louvre G 270 and Florence 4 B 35 (pp. 154–5 nos. 25–26).

VILLA GIULIA 50318. *Boll. d'Arte* 7 (1927), 317 figs. 14–15. I, warrior; A–B, fight.

A fragment recalls the painter, and might be from another unusually careful work of his:

OINOCHOE
(shape 8A: mug)

(l 50). ATHENS, Agora, P 447, fr., from Athens. *Hesp.* 17 pl. 66, 2. Man leaning on his stick.

THE GROUP OF MUNICH 2562

Three oinochoai of shape 8A, by one hand, much resemble the many by the Painter of Berlin 2268 (nos. 51–84); the potter-work, too, is just the same: but they also recall the Epeleios Painter, and are therefore placed here in a list by themselves:

OINOCHOAI
(shape 8A: mugs)

1 (a). WARSAW 142459 (ex Czartoryski 58). *CV.* pl. 23, 2. Warriors.

2. MUNICH 2562. *CV.* pl. 96, 1–3. Warriors. Associated with the Painter of Berlin 2268 by Lullies.

3 (l 29). CAPUA 453, from Capua. *CV.* pl. 18, 5–7. Fight.

Two cups with warriors are not far from these, and recall the Epeleios Painter (not the Painter of Berlin 2268):

1. LOUVRE S 1353. I, warrior.

2. LOUVRE C 10872. I, warrior (squatting; device a lionskin).

CHAPTER 13

OTHER EARLY RED-FIGURE CUP-PAINTERS

HARDLY necessary to say that the vases in this chapter do not form a group. They are smaller batches, some early, some later; some by good painters, some not; some connected more or less closely with artists described in previous chapters, others not seen to be so.

THE PAINTER OF THE VATICAN HORSEMAN

JHS. 51, 268 note 20. *CF.* 20 on pl. B 100. *ARV.*[1] 33.

Two very early eye-cups of abnormal type (see p. 37, ii).

CUPS

1 (1). VATICAN, frr. A–B, between eyes. A, horseman (jockey); B, the like.
2 (2). VILLA GIULIA (part ex Florence), CAB. MÉD. (ex Fröhner), and NAPLES, Astarita, 247, frr. Part, *CV.* pl. 12, B 100. A–B, between eyes. A, Dionysos seated; B, the like. The Paris fragment gives the upper part of one Dionysos, the Astarita fragment the lower part, and one of the Villa Giulia fragments the rest of the kantharos.

Near these, two other unique pieces:

CUPS

(special shape and technique: the exterior is reserved, with the figures in outline technique and the floral black)

1. ADOLPHSECK, Landgraf Philipp of Hesse, 29. *CV.* pl. 22, 5, pl. 23, and pl. 24, 1. I, gorgoneion. A, Dionysos seated, and maenad. B, horseman, holding an ivy-branch, and woman. The palmettes recall the bf. cups of the Amasis Painter (*JHS.* 51, 269–73; *ABV.* 157 nos. 87–89). On the shape, Bloesch 23 note 48.

(lip-cup of bf. type, see JHS. 52, 203–4)

2. LONDON E 134. 2, fr., from Naucratis. *JHS.* 52, 202. Outside, what remains is reserved. Inside the lip, (youth reclining).

Yet another unique piece may find place somewhere here:

CUP

(type A)

MAPLEWOOD, Noble, frr. I, bf., hippalektryon and warrior. A–B, rf., between eyes. A, Dionysos seated (or rather reclining) and satyr; B, similar (what remains is head and shoulders of the satyr, and part of the god's branch). On I, hippalektryon to right, and as if standing on its back, a warrior in position of attack to right, looking round. On I, on the left, ... IE final ([επο]ιε?), on the right ... OϚ final. See pp. 1617 and 1621.

THE AMA GROUP

JHS. 51, 275. *CF.* 7 on pl. 1 B 6, and 29 on pl. A, B 1. *ARV.*[1] 33.

Very early.

CUP

FLORENCE 1 B 6, frr. *CV.* pl. 1, B 6. I, satyr. AMΛ ... and E ... (perhaps Aμα[σις] ε[ποιεσεν], see *JHS.* 51, 275, *CF.* 7, *ABV.* 158).

Near this the

CUP

FLORENCE A B 1. Part, *CV.* pl. A, B 1. I, bf., satyr. A–B, between eyes. A, mask of Dionysos; B, satyr dancing. Somewhat recalls the hydria Berlin 2174 (p. 12 no. 8) and the Goluchow Painter (p. 10). See p. 37, iii.

THE PAINTER OF THE BOULOGNE HORSE

ARV.[1] 91, λ–ν.

CUPS

1. BOULOGNE 562 and FLORENCE 6 B 25. A, Hartwig 109, whence Löwy *Nature* fig. 37; the Florence fr., *CV.* pl. 6, B 25. I, bf., warrior (youth in chitoniskos, cloak, kidaris, boots, running to right, looking round, spears in right hand). A–B, between eyes. A, horse. B, nose. The Florence fr. gives part of the left-hand brow on A, and the peg to which the horse is tethered. For the shape, Bloesch 10, Nikosthenes no. 14. See p. 42 no. 42.
2. FLORENCE 1 B 19 (part ex Villa Giulia). Part, *CV.* pl. 1, B 19. I, bf., centaur. A–B, between eyes. A, discus-thrower. B, nose. See p. 42 no. 43.
3. FLORENCE, fr. A, between eyes (the greater part of the left-hand palmette remains and part of the left-hand eye).

See also p. 1629.

The palmettes in these cups have a peculiarity: the heart, red, is bordered above by a pair of relief-lines and the petals *pass through* this border: the same passing-through, but heart and petals different, in the eye-cup fragment Brunswick 539 (*CV.* pl. 12, 1) and another in Freiburg (p. 47 no. 142), in the eye-cup Castle Ashby 6 (p. 42 no. 48), and in the early Phintias cup Munich 2590 (p. 24 no. 12).

THE GROUP OF LOUVRE F 125

AJA. 1957, 11.

These are probably by one hand.

CUPS

(eye-cups)

1. LOUVRE F 125, from Vulci. Pottier pl. 72, whence Perrot 10, 273 and Hoppin ii, 229; cleaned, *CV*. b pl. 7, 2–6 and pl. 8, 1; phs. Gir. 16993, 1, and 16994–5. I, bf., komast. A–B, between eyes. A, naked youth running. B, ram. On I, ΚΟΣΘΕΝΕΣΕΠΟΙ complete aft, and probably fore: there is just room for the first two letters of the name in the missing patch above the right ham, but they would be strangely placed. For the shape, Bloesch 9, Nikosthenes no. 11. See p. 41 no. 26.

2. COMPIÈGNE 1105, from Vulci. *CV*. pl. 13, 1, 3, and 11. I, bf., naked youth running. A–B, between eyes. A, warrior squatting; B, the like. The foot is of the special Nicosthenic type, for which see Bloesch 23 and pl. 6,1, and *ABV*. 231–2. See p. 41 no. 24.

3. ARLESHEIM, Schweizer. I, bf., Dionysos seated. A–B, between eyes. A, warrior squatting; B, the like. On I, ΝΙΚΟΣΘΕΝΕΣΕΠΟΙΕC. Restored. See p. 41 no. 25.

4. FREIBURG, fr. A, between eyes, warrior squatting. See p. 46 no. 127.

5. FREIBURG, fr., from Orvieto. Outside, between eyes, hoplitodromos (bending, to left: the lower half remains). Belongs to the last? See p. 46 no. 128.

6. ADOLPHSECK, Landgraf Philipp of Hesse, 30. A, Bloesch *FAS*. pl. 3, 3; I and B, *CV*. pl. 22, 6, and pl. 24, 2. I, bf., komast. A–B, between eyes. A, hoplitodromos; B, the like. For the shape, Bloesch 9, Nikosthenes no. 7. See p. 41 no. 27.

HISCHYLOS, POTTER

Bloesch *FAS*. 31–35 and 161.

The name of the potter Hischylos appears on sixteen cups. For the three black-figure cups see *ABV*. 166–7, 172, and 688. A list of the thirteen bilingual or red-figure cups follows. (Note that nos. 3 and 4 in Hoppin's Hischylos list (ii, 114–17) do not bear his signature and have nothing to do with him).

1. CAMBRIDGE 37.14. *JHS*. 29 pl. 8 and p. 111, whence Hoppin ii, 113 and *Mus. J.* 23, 25; *CV*. ii RS. pl. 5, 1, pl. 8, 3, and pl. 9, 2. I, bf., warrior and snake. A–B, between eyes. A, nose; B, the like. Under one handle, incised, ΗΙΣ+ΥΛΟΣ: ΕΠΟΙΕΣΕΝ. See the next; and p. 41 no. 40.

2. NAPLES, Astarita, 297, fr. *AJA*. 1957, pl. 6, 4. What remains is, outside, part of the ground-line, a small piece of tendril from a handle-palmette,

and to right of it, under the handle, incised, HI$+VLO$EΓ[OIE$EN].
Cf. Cambridge 37. 14 (no. 1).

(no. 3, by the Hischylos Painter)

3. MUNICH 2588. Below, no. 2.

(nos. 4–9, by Epikletos)

4. ORVIETO, Faina, 97. P. 70 no. 1.
5. VILLA GIULIA, and HEIDELBERG 18. P. 70 no. 2.
6. LONDON E 3. P. 70 no. 3.
7. LENINGRAD 645. P. 71 no. 4.
8. BERLIN 2100. P. 71 no. 7.
9. Once Magnoncourt 34. P. 79 no. 1.

(no. 10, probably by Epiktetos)

10. ROME, Torlonia, 158. P. 78.

(nos. 11–13, by Pheidippos)

11. WÜRZBURG 467. P. 165 no. 2.
12. VILLA GIULIA and HEIDELBERG 8. P. 165 no. 7.
13. LONDON E 6. P. 166 no. 11.

Rumpf told me long ago of a cup with the signature of Hischylos which he had seen for a moment:

14. ROME, private. I, bf., warrior? A–B, between eyes. A, nose? See p. 1630, top.

THE HISCHYLOS PAINTER

ARV.[1] 57 and 950.

CUPS

1 (4). NEW YORK 22.139.81, fr. Richter *ARVS.* fig. 42. A, between eyes, boxer. See p. 46 no. 125.

2 (1). MUNICH 2588 (J. 1160), from Vulci. Hoppin *Bf.* 465; FR. iii, 240–1; I, Schröder *Sport* pl. 52; palmettes, Jacobsthal *O.* pl. 71, b; I, A, and foot, Bloesch *FAS.* pl. 9, 3; I, *Olympia in der Antike* pl. 50; I, *E.A.A.* iv, 42. I, athlete using pick. A, arming. B, youth leading horse. On I, HI$+VLO$ EΓOIE$EN. For the shape, Bloesch 34, Hischylos no. 19.

3 (2). ATHENS Acr. 76, fr., from Athens. Langlotz pl. 4. A, (warrior).

4 (3). ATHENS Acr. 78, fr., from Athens. Langlotz pl. 5. I, warrior.

BELL-KRATER

5 (5). VILLA GIULIA 50590, fr. Ph. R.I. 32. 667. (Dionysos, maenad, and another).

PASEAS (THE CERBERUS PAINTER)

VA. 13–14. Pfuhl 433 ('Io Painter'). *Att. V.* 29–30. *AJA.* 1939, 467–73 (Roebuck). *ARV.*¹ 32, 55–57, and 950. *ABV.* 399–400. *JHS.* 75, 154–5 (Boardman).

For the name see below, p. 164.   His nearest kin is Psiax.   See p. 1630.

PLATES

1 (1). Boston 03.785, from Chiusi. CB. i pl. 1, 2 and p. 3 fig. 3. Discus-thrower and athlete (+ϟENOΦON and ΔOPOΘEOϟ).

2 (2). London E 138, fr. *VA.* 14. (Acontist).

3 (3). Yale 170, from Chiusi. Baur pl. 15. Dionysos and satyr.

4 (4). Yale 169. *VA.* 13, whence Davreux fig. 45; Baur pl. 15. Ajax and Cassandra.

5 (5). Once Blaydes, from Chiusi. *AZ.* 1847 pl. 2, whence Overbeck *KM.* pl. 7, 18, and (wrongly as bf.) *El.* 3 pl. 98. Death of Argos.

6 (6). Boston 01.8025, from Chiusi. *Jb.* 8, 160; Pfuhl fig. 356; CB. i pl. 1, and p. i, 1; Fairbanks and Chase 58; Chase *Guide* 61; *AJA.* 1957 pl. 28, 7; *E.A.A.* ii, 507. Herakles and Cerberus. In the exergue, floral.

7 (7). Louvre G 67. Pottier pl. 96; Pfuhl fig. 357; ph. Gir.. Theseus and Minotaur. Now cleaned.

8 (8). Oxford 310, from Chiusi. *Jb.* 6, 239; Klein *L.* 87; Gardner pl. 13, 1; *CV.* pl. 1, 5, whence Rumpf *MZ.* pl. 16, 8; *JHS.* 71, 213 fig. 1. Mounted archer. MILTIAΔEϟKALOϟ. See Wade-Gery in *JHS.* 71, 210–21.

9 (9). Amsterdam inv. 2474, fr. Athlete and trainer. On the underside, (male running). [EΓIΔ]POMOϟ retr.

CUPS

10 (10). Villa Giulia (part ex Florence) and Heidelberg 20. Part, *CV.* Fl. pl. 1 B 8; I, *CF.* pl. Y, 1; the Heidelberg fr., Kraiker pl. 4. I, naked woman with phallus-bird. A, Herakles and Geryon. B, (unexplained) (males, Artemis). For the shape (Chalcicup), Bloesch 56 no. 11. See *CF.* 7.

11 (11). Florence PD 147, fr., from Populonia. *NSc.* 1923, 133 fig. 6 (misprinted 25); Minto *Pop.* pl. 53, 1. I, seated youth.

KANTHAROID VASE

12 (12). Athens Acr. 551, frr., from Athens. Langlotz pl. 41 and p. 49. An adventure of Herakles. Below, (youth).

ALABASTRON

13 (13). Athens 1740 (CC. 1205), from Athens. Lücken pl. 41; Poulsen *VG.* figs 31–32; *CV.* pl. 1, 1–2 and 6–8. A, woman dancing; B, woman. On the bottom, black palmettes. See p. 1630.

STANDLET OF SOSIAN TYPE

14 (14). LONDON E 809, from Vulci. Woman dancing.

For the black-figured plaques of the Cerberus Painter see *ARV.*[1] 56 and 950; Roebuck in *AJA*. 1939, 467–73; *ABV*. 399–400; and Boardman in *JHS*. 75, 154–5. Boardman shows that three other bf. plaques from the Acropolis, in technique and in style of drawing, go with the five assigned to the Cerberus Painter or associated with him in *ARV.*[1] 56 and 950 and in *ABV*. 399–400: the three are

1. ATHENS Acr. 2588, fr., from Athens. Langlotz pl. 109. White ground. Athena and giant.

2. ATHENS Acr. 2589, fr., from Athens. *JHS*. 75, 154, c. White ground. Athena.

3. ATHENS Acr. 2583, two frr., from Athens. Benndorf pl. 5, 5 and 8; *JHS*. 75, 154, a–b. White ground. Athena and worshipper. [TO]NΓΑSEO: ΛRΑΜΑΤΟΝ retr. See p. 1630.

Boardman is ready to attribute all eight plaques to one hand. Previously I had assigned Acr. 2584 and North Slope R. 253 to the Cerberus Painter, and said that Acr. 2585, Acr. 2587, Acr. 2591 recalled him, and that the first two might be his. I should now follow Boardman and give all eight to the Cerberus Painter. Boardman has thus found the painter's name, Paseas. I also accept Boardman's explanation of the signature in preference to that adopted in *ABV*. 352–3.

NEAR PASEAS

ARV.[1] 57.

PLATE

LOUVRE CA 2181, from Chiusi. Hoppin ii, 420. Man with horse. The incised inscription SOKLEESEΓOIESEN may be genuine but is not certainly so. If it is genuine, the Soklees may or may not be the same as the Soklees whose signature appears on four black-figure cups (see *ABV*. 172–3).

PHEIDIPPOS

Langlotz Z. 34. *Att. V*. 23 and 467. Kraiker in *AM*. 55, 167–80. *ARV.*[1] 54–55 and 950. *Eph*. 1953–4, 200.

The name is known from nos. 11 and 12.

Companion of the young Epiktetos. Collaborated with the potter Hischylos.

CUPS

(eye-cups except the last)

(1). MUNICH 2582 (J. 111), from Vulci. *AM.* 55 Beil. 52, 2, Beil. 53, 1, and p. 167. I, bf., horseman. A–B, between eyes. A, athlete (answering his name). B, nose. On A, M[E]NIϟ KA[LOϟ]. For the shape, Bloesch 31, Hischylos no. 4. [Langlotz]. See p. 44 no. 91.

2 (2). WÜRZBURG 467, from Vulci. I, *JHS.* 29, 113, whence Hoppin ii, 118; A, Jüthner 32 fig. 27b, whence *JHS.* 27, 11, Norman Gardiner *G.A.S.* 320 fig. 74, b, and (debased) Norman Gardiner *Athl.* fig. 115; Hoppin *Bf.* 466; A–B, *AM.* 55 Beil. 59; Langlotz pll. 136 and 164, whence (part of A) Rumpf *MZ.* pl. 17, 5; A–B, Blümel *S.H.* 64–65, below. I, bf., youth (komast?). A–B, between eyes. A, discus-thrower picking up his marker; B, hoplitodromos picking up his shield. On I, HIϟ+VLOϟ and retr. EΓOIEϟEИ. For the shape, Bloesch 33, Hischylos no. 13. [Langlotz]. See p. 44 no. 92.

3 (3). MUNICH 2583 (J. 1232), from Vulci. *AM.* 55 Beil. 57, 1 and Beil. 56; B, Buschor *G. Vasen* 134. I, bf., Minotaur. A–B, between eyes. A, warrior. B, boxer. For the shape, Bloesch 33, Hischylos no. 14. [Langlotz]. See p. 44 no. 93.

4 (4). MUNICH 2584 (J. 1023), from Vulci. *AM.* 55 Beil. 57, 2, Beil. 54, 4, and Beil. 55; B, Bloesch *FAS.* pl. 9, 1. I, bf., komast. A–B, between eyes. A, old man squatting. B, stag. For the shape, Bloesch 33, Hischylos no. 15. [Langlotz]. See p. 44 no. 94.

5 (5). LEIPSIC T 486, from Vulci. A, *Jb.* 10, 192; *AM.* 55 Beil. 52, 1, Beil. 54, 1, and Beil. 53, 2. I, bf., man running. A–B, between eyes. A, hoplitodromos at the tape; B, athlete holding sprig. For the subject of A, *BSA.* 46, 11, no. 1; for the shape, Bloesch 33, Hischylos no. 9. [Langlotz]. See p. 44 no. 95.

6 (6). NEW YORK 41.162.8. *AM.* 55 pl. 9, 2 and Beil. 54, 2–3; *CV.* Gallatin pl. 46, whence (I) LS. fig. 53; parts of A–B, Richter *ARVS.* figs. 39–40; A, Richter *H.* 205, b. I, bf., Dionysos. A–B, between eyes. A, hoplitodromos at the tape; B, runner. For the subject of A, *BSA.* 46, 11 no. 2. See p. 44 no. 96.

7 (7). VILLA GIULIA (part ex Florence) and HEIDELBERG 8. Part, *CV.* Fl. pl. 4, B 29; part of A, *CF.* pl. Z, 4; the Heidelberg fr., Kraiker pl. 3. I, bf., satyr with pointed amphora. A–B, between eyes. A, hoplitodromos. B, nose. On I, HIϟ+VLOϟ [EΓ]OIEϟEN. See p. 44 no. 97.

8 (8). VILLA GIULIA (part ex Florence), frr. I, bf., naked youth running with (wineskin?) (to right, looking round). A–B, between eyes. A, (lost). B, petal. For the petal cf. London E 4 (p. 44 no. 90). See p. 44 no. 98, and the next.

9 (9). HEIDELBERG 15, fr. *AM.* 55 pl. 11; Kraiker pl. 2. A, between eyes, runner at the start. [Langlotz]. For the subject see *BSA.* 46, 9 no. 3. Belongs to the last? See p. 46 no. 140.

10. OXFORD, Beazley, fr. (ex Signorelli 224). A, between eyes, warrior going into ambush. See p. 46 no. 122.

11 (10). LONDON E 6, from Vulci. I, Murray no. 3, whence Hoppin ii, 351; A–B, C. Smith pl. 1, whence Hoppin ii, 351, (A–B) Perrot 10, 368, (A) *JHS.* 23, 273, (A) *JHS.* 27, 13, (A) Norman Gardiner *G.A.S.* 323, (A) Norman Gardiner *Athl.* fig. 21, (B) Swindler fig. 291; *AM.* 55 pl. 9, 1, pl. 10, Beil. 58, and p. 167, below; palmettes, Jacobsthal O. pl. 72, a; A, Bloesch *FAS.* pl. 9, 2. I, archer. A, athletes; B, between eyes, hoplito-dromos. On I, ΗΙϚ+ѴᒪΟϚΕΓΟΙΕϚΕΝ (the first four letters retr.). On A, ΦΕΙΔΙΓΟϚ ΕΛΡΑΦΕ complete. For the left-hand youth on A, *BSA.* 46, 9 no. 4; for the shape, Bloesch 33, Hischylos no. 17. See p. 49 no. 168.

12 (11). LOUVRE C 11223, fr. *Eph.* 1953–4, 201, i, fig. 1. I, komast. [ΦΕ]ΙΔΙ-ΓΟϚ. There may have been a verb. A small cup, probably plain out-side. A Louvre fr. with a foot might perhaps belong (ibid. fig. 2). The potter-work recalls cups decorated by Skythes. See *Eph.* 1953–4, i, 200.

A small fragment may be by Pheidippos:

CUP

DRESDEN, fr. A, (head of a youth, helmeted, to left, with part of his shield).

THE BOWDOIN-EYE PAINTER

VA. 12–13. *Att. V.* 21–22 and 467. *ARV.*[1] 32, 95–96, and 951.

Named after the eye-cup in Bowdoin College (no. 5).

Companion of the Scheurleer Painter (p. 168), and of the Nikosthenes Painter in his earliest phase (p. 123).

CUPS

1 (1). LEIPSIC T 3626, from Cervetri. I, bf., komast. A–B, between eyes. A, male (shanks and feet remain, to left). B, nose. [Rumpf]. See p. 45 no. 107.

2 (3). COPENHAGEN, Thorvaldsen Museum, 92. Part of A, Breitenstein *G.V.* 23. I, bf., komast. A–B, between eyes. A, athlete with acontia; B, hoplitodromos. [Langlotz]. For the attitude of B, *BSA.* 46, 10 no. 5. See p. 45 no. 108.

3. ARLESHEIM, Schweizer. I, bf., satyr. A–B, between eyes. A, naked youth, bestriding a wineskin (bending to right), B, naked youth, his right hand raised, in his left a sprig. I is restored. See p. 45 no. 109.

4 (2). ROME, Torlonia, 151. I, bf., naked youth running. A–B, between eyes. A, boxer; B, athlete. See p. 45 no. 110.

5 (4). BOWDOIN, from Cervetri. I, hoplitodromos (running, with shield, and in his right hand helmet). A–B, between eyes. A, jumper (athlete with haltēres); B, jumper (athlete with haltēres, bending). For the shape, Bloesch 36, Antimachos Class no. 3. See p. 48 no. 160.

6. BASLE 1960.28. Schefold *M*. 167, 156. I, komast with lyre. A–B, between eyes. A, satyr squatting. B, komast or cup-bearer (youth bending at a column-krater). See p. 48 no. 160 *bis*.

7 (5). VILLA GIULIA 50448, from Cervetri. B, *E.A.A*. ii, 158 fig. 235; A–B, phs. G.F. 7156–7. I, komast (youth with wineskin and jug). A–B, between palmettes and eyes. A, jumper (athlete with haltēres, bending); B, athlete using pick. The head shown in the photograph of A belongs to another cup (see p. 48 no. 163) and has now been removed. For the shape, Bloesch 37, Antimachos Class, no. 4. See p. 49 no. 179.

8 (7, 9, 10, +). LOUVRE G 39 (including G 75, C 57, and other frr.). Part of I, Pottier pl. 191, whence Hoppin i, 168; incompletely, *CV*. b pl. 20, 6–8 and pl. 21, 1. I, symposion (youth reclining). A–B, between palmettes and eyes. A, discus-thrower; B, the like. Unpublished frr. add the feet on I, the second handle, and more of oculi and palmettes. The letters on I are not part of a Kachrylion signature: what remains is +, the beginning of a name written retr. (+[ΑΡΟⲰϚ]?, cf. Würzburg 469, no. 10), and Ϙ, the beginning of Ϙ[ΑⳐΟϚ]. See p. 49 no. 180.

9 (8, +). LOUVRE C 10468 (including C 189, C 10470, S 1386, and other frr.). Incompletely, *CV*. b pl. 20, 1–3 and 5 (5, which was S 1386 not S 1368, joins 1). I is lost. A–B, between palmettes and eyes. A, naked youth or man squatting frontal; B, athlete bending, picking up his acontion. Unpublished frr. add parts of the arms on B and of oculi and palmettes. See p. 49 no. 181.

10 (6). WÜRZBURG 469, from Vulci. A, Jüthner 42, whence Norman Gardiner *G.A.S*. 340 = Norman Gardiner *Athl*. fig. 136; Langlotz pl. 138, whence (part of A) Rumpf *MZ*. pl. 17, 4; A, Schaal *Rf*. fig. 7; B. Ap. I, hoplitodromos. A–B, between palmettes and eyes. A, acontist bending; B, the like. On I, [+]Α[ΡΟ]ⲰϚ ϘΑ[Ⳑ]ΟϚ (see *AJA*. 1957, 6). For the attitude on I, *BSA*. 46, 10, no. 4; for the shape, Bloesch 65, Pamphaios no. 25, and p. 67 note 113. Now cleaned. See p. 49 no. 182.

11. NAPLES, Astarita, 568, frr. A–B, between palmettes and eyes. A, naked youth lifting a pointed amphora. B, warrior bending. See p. 49 no. 183.

12. SWISS PRIVATE, fr. A, between palmettes [and eyes], naked youth bending, taking his shield out of its wrapper. See p. 49 no. 184.

13 (11). FRANKFORT, Mus. V.F., from Capua. Hartwig pl. 19, 1 (with false kalos-inscription, since removed); Schaal *F*. pl. 28 and pl. 27, a; Schaal *Rf*. fig. 4. I, komast. For the shape, Bloesch 34, Hischylos no. 18.

14 (12). ALTENBURG 234, from Vulci. *CV*. pl. 68, 1–2. I, youth taking his shield out of its wrapper. For the shape, Bloesch 38 no. 6.

15 (13). BERLIN inv. 3217, from Vulci. Gerhard pl. 50–51, 5–6. I, satyr trumpeting. For the shape, Bloesch 37, Antimachos Class, no. 8.

16 (14). COMPIÈGNE 1101. *CV*. pl. 14, 3 and 6. I, youth putting his sword on.

NEAR THE BOWDOIN–EYE PAINTER

CUPS

1. ATHENS Acr. 42, fr., from Athens. Langlotz pl. 3. A, between palmettes (and no doubt eyes), warrior (or hoplitodromos). See p. 49 no. 185.

2. LOUVRE C 11252, fr. A, komast? (legs of a youth, with cloak, moving to right).

3. LENINGRAD, fr., from Olbia. I, boy running with wineskin and oinochoe.

Compare also
CUP
BOWDOIN 13.17, two frr., from Cervetri. Outside, maenads.

A large vase recalls the Bowdoin-Eye Painter:

AMPHORA
(type A)

LONDON E 256, from Vulci. A, Cecil Smith pl. 10; B, Hoppin *Euth*. pl. 7, whence *Jb*. 31, 142; B, *JHS*. 27 pl. 19, whence Norman Gardiner *G.A.S.* 348 and Swindler fig. 298; detail of B, Herford pl. 3, d; Hoppin *Euth. F.* pl. 9, and pl. 11, above; *CV*. pl. 3, 2; A, *Hesp*. 5, 64; A, Stella 195. A, Apollo with Artemis and Leto. B, athletes. One of the athletes is Phayllos, see CB. ii, 4–5.

THE SCHEURLEER PAINTER
Att. V. 22. *ARV*.[1] 96–98 and 951.

Named after the former owner of no. 1.
Companion of the Bowdoin-Eye Painter.

CUPS

1 (1). AMSTERDAM inv. 997. *Bull. Vereen*. 1, 9; I and A, *CV*. Scheurleer a pl. 1 (Pays Bas pl. 31), 1–3. I, bf., athlete with acontia and pick. A–B, between eyes. A, jumper (athlete with haltēres, bending); B, the like. See the next; and p. 45 no. 112.

2 (2). FLORENCE 4 B 61, fr. *CV*. pl. 4, B 61. Outside, athlete bending. Might belong to B of Amsterdam inv. 997 (no. 1).

3 (3). ROME, Torlonia, 146. I, bf., komast (running to right, looking round). A–B, between eyes. A, jumper. B, warrior (or hoplitodromos) picking up his helmet. See p. 45 no. 113.

4 (4). VATICAN 499, from Vulci. *Mus. Greg.* 2 pl. 69, 4, whence (B) Klein *Euphr.* 291; Albizzati pl. 69. I, bf., hunter (rather than komast). A–B, between eyes. A, acontist bending; B, acontist. (The foot, with the signature of Pamphaios, is of course alien: see Bloesch 63 no. 5, and *ABV.* 236 no. 5). See p. 45 no. 114.

5 (5). FLORENCE and VILLA GIULIA, fr. I, bf., komast (youth running to right, looking round, with wineskin); H[OΓAIϚ] retr. and ҟAL[O]ϟ. Outside, part of the line border remains. See p. 43 no. 62.

6 (6). LOUVRE G 70, from Vulci. Pottier pll. 96–97; *CV*. b pl. 22. I, hunter. A–B, between palmettes and eyes. A, komast astride a wineskin. B, trumpeter. For the shape, Bloesch 36, Antimachos Class, no. 2. See p. 50 no. 187.

7 (7). BRUSSELS R 259, fr. *CV*. pl. 20, 4; Vorberg *Gloss.* 379. I, youth χέζων. Restored.

8 (8). MUNICH SL. 479, part, fr. Sieveking *BTV*. pl. 52, 3. I, youth (reclining?).

9 (9). PAVIA, Stenico (ex Albizzati), fr. *Acme* 10 pl. 1, 1. I, naked youth (running to right, looking round).

A lost vase may be by the Scheurleer Painter:

CUP

ROMAN MARKET (Basseggio). B.Ap. xxi. 27. I, komast (naked youth moving to right, bending, wineskin in right hand, the left raised; HO-ΓAIϚҟALOϟ).

NEAR THE SCHEURLEER PAINTER

CUP

1 (1). MUNICH 2586 (J. 1245), from Vulci. I, Langlotz *GV*. pl. 4, 8; A, Reichhold *Skiz.* 33; A, Bloesch *FAS*. pl. 10, 4. I, athlete with acontia. A–B, between palmettes and eyes. A–B, komos: A, man sitting on the ground; B, youth running with wineskin and drinking-horn. On I, ΔOPOΘEOϟҟALOϟ. On A, ҟALOϟ. On B, ΔOPOΘO[EOϟ]. For the shape, Bloesch 38 no. 4. See p. 50 no. 188.

2 (2). VATICAN 500. Albizzati pl. 69. I, warrior. A–B, between palmettes and eyes. A, discus-thrower; B, jumper. On I, ANTI[M]A+OϞ-ΚΑLOϞ. For the shape, Bloesch 37, Antimachos Class, no. 5. See p. 50 no. 189, and ibid. no. 190.

3. LOUVRE G 89, fr. Pottier pl. 98, whence Buschor *Satyrtänze* fig. 52. I, satyr with pelta.

4 (3). LONDON, part of E 9, fr., from Vulci. Gerhard pl. 178–9, 4; Murray no. 6. I, komast. ΚΑLOϞΦΕΙΔΟΝ. Now separated from E 9, to which it did not belong, see p. 89 no. 13.

The following are also related to the Scheurleer Painter:

CUPS

1 (1). MUNICH 2591. A, Bloesch *FAS.* pl. 10, 2. I, satyr (looking into a pointed amphora). ANTIMA+OϞΚΑLOϞ. Restored. For the shape, Bloesch 37, Antimachos Class no. 10.

2 (2). HEIDELBERG 32 and DRESDEN. The Heidelberg part, Kraiker pl. 6. I, satyr (with horn and wineskin). A, between palmettes and eyes, warrior (or hoplitodromos; hastening to right: the feet, with the greaved shanks, remain). On I, ANTIMA+OϞΚΑ[LOϞ]. See p. 50 no. 191.

A cup is near both the Scheurleer Painter and the Bowdoin-Eye:

LOUVRE G 73, from Vulci. Pottier pl. 97, whence (I) Buschor *Satyrtänze* fig. 51; B, Vorberg *Gloss.* 160; *CV.* b pl. 21, 2–6. I, satyr trumpeting. A–B, between palmettes and eyes. A, discus-thrower (marking his throw). B, komast (balancing a skyphos on his belly). Restored, especially I. See p. 49 no. 186.

THE WINCHESTER PAINTER

CV. Oxford 105 on pl. 51, 1. *ARV.*[1] 106–7.

CUPS

1 (1). WINCHESTER 42. Cecil Smith *Forman* pl. 10, 332. I, satyr. A–B, between palmettes and eyes. A, jumper (bending, with haltēres); B, jumper (with haltēres). Restored. See p. 50 no. 193 and p. 1630.

2 (2). DRESDEN ZV. 1395. A, Schröder *Sport* 113. I, athlete picking up discus. A–B, between palmettes and eyes. A, jumper (bending, with haltēres); B, the like. See p. 50 no. 194.

3 (3). FLORENCE 3930. *CV.* pl. 76 and pl. 116, 4. I, splanchnopt. A–B, between palmettes and eyes. A, athlete picking up haltēres; B, athlete bending (to lift a pick?). See p. 50 no. 195.

4. LOUVRE C 10469, frr. Part, *CV*. b pl. 20, 4. I, acontist (running to left, about to throw). A–B, between palmettes and eyes. A, (legs of a naked male standing to right). B, (one foot of a male moving to left, with half of the shank). See p. 50 no. 196.

Near the Winchester Painter, the cup

1 (1). LONDON E 5, from Vulci. I, Murray no. 2. I, athlete bending, with haltēres. A–B, between eyes. A, athlete bending; B, nose. For the shape, Bloesch 38 no. 5; for the eyes, Louvre G 88 (p. 48 no. 162). See p. 48 no. 161.

Compare also the cup

2 (2). OXFORD 1929.751, from Greece. *CV*. pl. 51, 1. I, naked boy picking up a pointed amphora.

THE SCHRÖDER PAINTER

ARV.[1] 107.

CUPS

1 (1). BREMEN, Schröder, from Vulci. I and A, Schaal *Brem.* pl. 11. I, discus-thrower. A–B, between palmettes and eyes. A, jumper (bending, with haltēres); B, the like. I restored. See p. 50 no. 197.

2 (2). HEIDELBERG 10, fr. Kraiker pl. 2. I, jumper.

3 (3). BRUNSWICK 265, fr. *CV*. pl. 15, 2 and pl. 19, 10. I, komast.

THE MARIO PAINTER

CUPS

1. SWISS PRIVATE (ex Curtius). Ph. R.I. 34.2287. I, symposion (youth reclining to left, right arm extended; hanging, a basket).

2. NAPLES, Astarita, 329. I, symposion (youth reclining to left, his left leg extended with the foot as if pressing against the line-border, about to drink out of a large skyphos held in both hands).

Near these, and probably by the same painter, the cup-fragment

MUNICH, fr. I, symposion (male reclining to left, himation, right arm extended, a cup in the left hand).

HERMOKRATES

ARV.[1] 57.

PLATE

ATHENS Acr. 5, fr. from Athens. *Eph.* 1890 pl. 2, 2, whence Hoppin ii, 19; Langlotz pl. 1. Youth playing the flute. ΗΕΡΜΟΚΡΑΤΕΣ ΕΛΡΑΘΣΕΝ retr. To left of the head, part of a letter (gamma, mu, or nu), the beginning of another inscription, retr.

THE DELOS PAINTER

BSR. 11, 14–15. *ARV.*[1] 58.

The character of the drawing is near early Euergides Painter. See p. 1631.

CUPS

1 (1). CASTLE ASHBY, Northampton, 193. *BSR.* 11 pl. 3, 3–4 and 6. I, bf., horseman. A–B, between eyes. A, Dionysos; B, satyr. See p. 42 no. 47. See p. 1630.

2 (2). LEIPSIC T 500, and VILLA GIULIA. The Leipsic part, *BSR.* 11, 15; one Villa Giulia fr., *CF.* pl. Z, 6; three others give bits of the palmettes. I, woman running with flowers. A, Dionysos seated, and satyr. B, fight. See *CF.* 33 no. 1 *ter.*

3 (3). DELOS 652, from Delos. Dugas *Délos x* pl. 53. I is lost. A, satyr and maenad. B, fight

4. SWISS PRIVATE. I, satyr. A, Herakles and the bull. B, fight (hoplite and archer). The archer, as on the amphora London E 253 (p. 35 no. 2) is named ΣΕΡΑΛVΕ. Compare Delos 652 (no. 3), and, for the floral, Munich 2609 (p. 97 no. 3). See p. 1631.

Probably also:

CUPS

1. ATHENS, Agora, NS R 260, frr., from Athens. *Hesp.* 9, 240, 260. Outside, (Athena, warrior).

2. SANTA BARBARA C17WL55. I, warrior on one knee. Said to have been found with a cup which is by the Euergides Painter (p. 96 no. 136). Both cups appear to be by the same *potter* as Leipsic T 501 (p. 96, Euergides Painter no. 135). See p. 1631.

Cup-fragments are near the Delos Painter:

1. ATHENS, Agora, NS AP 911, fr., from Athens. *Hesp.* 7, 172. A, satyr and maenad.

2. ATHENS, Agora, P 4998, fr., from Athens. I, maenad.

THE AMBROSIOS PAINTER

VA. 19–20; *Att. V.* 28–29 and 468 ; *ARV.*[1] 71–73 and 950.

So called from the inscription on no. 17.

CUPS

(nos. 1–19, decorated inside and out)

1 (1). OXFORD 1911.616, from Cervetri. Incompletely, *CV.* pl. 1, 6, pl. 5, 5–6, and (I, augmented by a fr. ex Leipsic) pl. 51, 2; three frr. of the exterior, ex Leipsic, are unpublished. I, youth with horse. A–B, komos. On I, +SAN[O]ES : KALOS. For the inscriptions (besides *CV.* 2–3 and 105), CB. iii, text.

2 (9). MUNICH 2614 (J. 1096), from Vulci. A, Jahn *Dichter* pl. 4, 1–2, whence Schefold *Bildnisse* 53, 3; A (cleaned) and foot, Bloesch *FAS.* pl. 18, 3; B.Ap. xxi. 30. I, Hermes. A–B, komos. The inscriptions are now seen to be: on I, [HE]PMES; on A, MANTIOEOS, KVΔIAS, ETEOKLES, KALLIAS; on B, between 1 and 2, [.]Λ..., between 2 and 3, EV-AP+OS, between 3 and 4, ... ΦON, and ΓEQES. A Euarchos appears on the stamnos by Smikros in Brussels (p. 20 no. 1). For the shape, Bloesch 65, Pamphaios iv no. 28.

3 (10). BERLIN inv. 3256, from Cervetri. B, Licht iii, 87. I, Amazon. A, komos. B, satyrs.

4 (7). FLORENCE 73127, from Orvieto. *CV.* pl. 75 and pl. 116, 3. I, archer. A–B, symposion: A, Hermes and Herakles reclining; B, Poseidon and Apollo reclining. For the shape, Bloesch 65, Pamphaios iv no. 18.

5 (8). VILLA GIULIA, from Cervetri. Klein *L.* 68–69; phs. G.F. 7163–4 and others. I, komast; A–B, symposion. On I, AN[TIMA+OSKA?]LOS (one of the revellers on A is called ANTIMA+OS). Restored. For the inscriptions, CB. iii, text; for the shape, Bloesch 65, Pamphaios iv no. 19.

6 (18, +). LOUVRE C 11229 *ter* (including S 1398). I, maenad (running to right, looking round, with thyrsus and snake); A–B, symposion: A, maenad and and satyr reclining, and satyr running up to serve; B, two satyrs reclining.

7 (14). AMSTERDAM inv. 2181, fr. A, (satyr and maenad). [Langlotz].

8 (15). ATHENS Acr. 60, fr., from Athens. Langlotz pl. 3. A, (satyr and maenad).

9 (5). BOSTON 01.8024, from Orvieto. Hartwig pl. 5; I, Picard *Vie privée* pl. 6, 2; I, Cloché *Classes* pl. 17, 7; I, Anita Klein pl. 20, f; I, *E.A.A.* i, 317 fig. 455. I, boy fishing (and potting). A–B, satyrs.

10 (6, +). WÜRZBURG 474, from Vulci. Klein *L.*[1] 38, whence *AJA.* 1954 pl. 30; detail of B, Flickinger *Theater* 32 fig. 11; Langlotz pl. 143; parts of A–B (including a fragment ex Louvre S 1366), *AJA.* 1954 pl. 31 fig. 4; A, Himmelmann-Wildschütz *Eig.* pl. 31; A–B, B.Ap. xxii. 55. I, warrior.

A, sacrifice. B, Dionysos on donkey, with satyrs and maenad. For the inscriptions, *AJA.* 1954, 189–90.

11 (3, +). LOUVRE G 72, two frr. Part of A (part of one fr.), Pottier pl. 97. I, warrior. A, Herakles and the lion.

12 (17). ERLANGEN 459 b, fr. A, (Chiron or Pholos).

13 (13). LONDON E 134.1, fr., from Naucratis. A, (Hermes).

14 (16). ATHENS Acr. 57, fr., from Athens. A, (Hermes).

15 (11). VILLA GIULIA 50535, from Cervetri. Phs. G.F. 7160–2. I, youth leaning on his stick with a hare in his hand. A, athletes (boxers, wrestlers). B, deer-hunt. A new fr. gives one of the wrestler's heads on A. For the shape, Bloesch 94, Hieron no. 26.

16 (12). ATHENS Acr. 58, fr., from Athens. I, Langlotz pl. 3. I, (man—Dionysos?). A, (warriors). On A, [ΑΝΤΙ]ΜΑ+ΟϞ.

17 (4). ORVIETO, Faina, 62, from Orvieto? I, Philippart *It.* ii pl. 11, 1; phs. R.I. 1935.885–6. I, komast. A, warriors. B, athletes. On I, ΑΝΒΡΟ-ϞΙΟϞ. For the shape, Bloesch 65, Pamphaios iv no. 27.

18 (12). VATICAN 507, from Vulci. *Mus. Greg.* 2 pl. 74, 2; I, Albizzati pl. 70. I, archer; A–B, fight. For the shape, Bloesch 65, Pamphaios iv no. 26.

18 bis. OXFORD, Beazley, fr. A, (head, to left, and shoulder, of youth).

19. OXFORD, Beazley, fr. A, (head of youth to left; to left of it ... MO).

(nos. 20–28, fragments of interiors; not known if decorated outside as well)

20 (19). LONDON E 42, fr. Hancarville 4 pl. 31, whence Inghirami pl. 119; *VA.* 20; *Mél. Boisacq* pl. 8 fig. 8; *E.A.A.* i, 317, 456. I, Nessos and Deianeira.

21 (20). OXFORD 1917.55, fr. *VA.* 21 fig. 12 *ter*; *CV.* pl. 1, 3. I, Dionysos.

22 (21). BOSTON Res. 08.31 b, fr., from Orvieto. Hartwig 347; Vorberg *Gloss.* 382, 2. I, man ἀποψώμενος.

23 (27). ATHENS Acr. 59, fr., from Athens. Langlotz pl. 3. I, (man).

24 (26). BRUSSELS R 349, fr. *Gaz. arch.* 1887, 111; *CV.* pl. 4, 2. I, naked youth squatting with a laver on his knees. TLEϞON : ΚΑΛΟϞ.

25 (24). LOUVRE G 83, fr. Pottier pl. 98. I, youth running with flute.

26 (22). ADRIA B 99, fr., from Adria. *CV.* pl. 2, 1. I, komast.

27 (23). ATHENS Acr. 56, fr., from Athens. I, komast.

28 (25). LONDON 1900.2–14.11, fr., from Naucratis. I, komast.

(nos. 29–32, decorated inside only)

29. ATHENS, Agora, P 20736, fr., from Athens. I, Dionysos.

30 (28). VATICAN, from Vulci. *Mus. Greg.* 2 pl. 69, 1, whence Klein *Euphr.* 304. I, Amazon. Early. For the shape, Bloesch 123 no. 38.

31 (29). BERLIN 2273, from Vulci. Gerhard pl. 57, 1–2, whence *El.* 1 pl. 38 and Cook *Zeus* i, 216; *Jb.* 27, 257. I, Hephaistos in winged car.

ΚΕΦΙ·ΤΟͶΚΑ[Ⴑ]ΟͶ. The first letter is a poor kappa, and might be a poorer H; if so, ΗΕΦΙ[Ͷ]ΤΟͶΚΑ[Ⴑ]ΟͶ?

32 (30). LONDON E 817, from Vulci. *VA.* 21 fig. 12 *bis.* I, satyr squatting with a laver on his knees.

33 (31). VILLA GIULIA, frr. I, youth carrying a pointed amphora (to right; the vase wreathed with ivy).

34 (32). BOLOGNA 434, from Bologna. Pellegrini 206; *CV.* pl. 109, 1. I, two komasts. Late.

PLATE

35 (33). ATHENS Acr. 17, fr., from Athens. Langlotz pl. 1. Man, embracing woman. [Langlotz].

Probably also the cup-fragment.

HAMBURG, Schauenburg, fr. I, Hermes (seated, with phiale and caduceus).

NEAR THE AMBROSIOS PAINTER

CUPS

1. LOUVRE C 11230, fr. A, (middle of a male with shield rushing to right).
2. WINCHESTER 35, fr. I, komast (upper part of a man with a drinking-horn).

THE HEGESIBOULOS PAINTER

ARV.[1] 77. Akin to Skythes (Furtwängler in FR. ii, 182–5).

CUP

NEW YORK 07.286.47. FR. pl. 93, 2 and ii, 179 and 185, whence Hoppin ii, 11, (A) Jacobsthal *Gött. V.* 44, (I and A) Pfuhl figs. 340–1; I, *Mon. Piot* 29, 113; Richter and Hall pl. 9, 10, and pl. 179, 10; I, *AJA.* 1946, 29 fig. 28; I, Richter *ARVS.* fig. 38; I, Richter *H.* 205, e; *AJA.* 1958 pl. 37. I, old man taking a walk. A, symposion; B, komos. On I, ΕΛΕͶΙΒΟⴑΟͶ retr. and ΕΓΟΙΕͶΕΝ. Coral-red used: see Bothmer in *AJA.* 1958, 173.

Langlotz (*Acr.* p. 48) is probably right in connecting the following with this painter:

SMALL OPEN VASE

ATHENS Acr. 538, fr., from Athens. Langlotz pl. 41. Symposion.

THE CHAIRIAS PAINTER

ARV.[1] 88–89. Nos. 1 and 2, and the Berlin cup 4040, were put together by Hartwig (*Meist.* 177–9), but attributed to Phintias.

CUPS

1 (1). LOUVRE MNB 2040, from Corinth. Hartwig 178 fig. 22; *E.A.A.* ii,
532 fig. 732. I, symposion (youth reclining, playing lyre). +ΑΙΡΙΑϟ
ΙΚΑLΟϟ.

2 (2). ADRIA Bc 45, from Adria. Schöne pl. 7, 2, whence Klein *Euphr.* 308;
part, *CV.* pl. 3, 4; part, *Riv. Ist.* N.S. 5–6, 33 fig. 5. I, symposion (youth
reclining, playing lyre). +ΑΙΡΙΑϟ ΙΚΑLΟϟ. See p. 1631.

Near these:

CUPS

1. AMSTERDAM inv. 323, from Tanagra. Scheurleer *Cat.* pl. 41, 2. I, symposion (youth reclining, with amis).

2. BERLIN 4040, from Corinth. Furtwängler *Sab.* 1 pl. 53, 2; Winter *K.B.*[1]
pl. 89, 1; *CV.* pl. 62, 1. I, komast. +ΑΙΡΙΑ ΙΚΑLΟϟ. For the shape,
Bloesch 126 no. 3.

THE PAINTER OF THE AGORA CHAIRIAS CUPS

Hesp. 24, 72–75 (Talcott).

CUPS

1. ATHENS, Agora, P 24102, from Athens. *Hesp.* 24 pl. 32, b and p. 73, b.
I, naked woman kneeling at an altar, holding a wreath. +ΑΙΡΑϟ. [Tal-
cott, Philippaki].

2. ATHENS, Agora, P 23165, fr., from Athens. *Archaeology* 6, 144; *Hesp.* 23
pl. 15, e; *Hesp.* 24 pl. 32, a. I, naked woman kneeling at a vessel. [Talcott,
Philippaki].

3. ATHENS, Agora, P 24115, from Athens. *Hesp.* 24 pl. 33, d, and p. 73, d.
I, komast. +ΑΙ[ΡΙ]Αϟ ΙΚΑLΟϟ. [Talcott, Philippaki].

4. ATHENS, Agora, P 24315, fr., from Athens. *Hesp.* 24 pl. 33, e, and p. 73,
e. I, komast? The shoulder and part of the back remain; replica, so far
as it goes, of Agora P 24115 (no. 3). +ΑΙΡ . . . [Talcott, Philippaki].

5. NEW YORK MARKET (Morley). I, maenad (in chiton, 'Ionic' himation,
saccos, running to right, looking round, something in right hand, thyrsus
in left). Restored.

6. ATHENS, Agora, P 24116, from Athens. *Hesp.* 24 pl. 33, c, and p. 73, c.
I, maenad. +ΑΙΡΙΑϟ ΙΚΑLΟ[ϟ]. [Talcott, Philippaki].

7. ATHENS, Agora, P 23146, from Athens. *Hesp.* 23 pl. 15, f. I, female head.

Probably also

CUPS

1. AMSTERDAM inv. 591, from Megara. *Coll. M.E.* pl. 10, 223; Scheurleer *Cat.* pl. 42, 1; *CV.* Scheurleer pl. 6, 2 and 4. I, wounded warrior retreating.
2. CORINTH C 34.1077, fr., from Corinth. *Hesp.* 6, 272, 21. I, female head.

Near, the cup-fragments

1. BRYN MAWR, fr. *AJA.* 1916, 340 no. 2. I, youth tuning lyre.
2. MUNICH, fr. I, komast (upper part of a youth to right, cloak over left shoulder, holding a skyphos in his right hand). Very like the Bryn Mawr fragment, but more careful.

Compare also the cup-fragments

1. ATHENS, Agora, P 251, fr., from Athens. I, naked woman.
2. BERLIN 2275, fr. Licht iii, 200; Deubner pl. 3, 2. I, naked woman holding a vessel full of phalli.

With Agora P 24116 (p. 176 no. 6) Miss Talcott and Miss Philippaki compared the cup-fragment

ATHENS Acr. 230, fr., from Athens. Langlotz pl. 12. I, Athena seated.

With that compare the cup-fragment

ATHENS Acr. 233 a, fr., from Athens. Langlotz pl. 13. A, (donkey, satyr?, maenad).

See also p. 1631.

═══════════

THE KISS PAINTER

AV. 22. *Att. V.* 54. *ARV.*[1] 90 and 950.

So named from the subject of nos. 1 and 2.

CUPS

1 (1). BERLIN 2269, from Chiusi. I, Licht ii, 12; I, Greifenhagen *A.K.* pl. 53; *CV.* pl. 62, 2 and 4. I, youth and girl embracing. A–B, komos.
2 (2). NEW YORK 07.286.50, fr., from Arezzo. Richter and Hall pl. 8, 9, whence *E.A.A.* i, 958; part of I, Richter *ARVS.* 38 fig. 4. I, girl kissing youth. A–B, komos? (rather than fight).
3 (3). BALTIMORE, from Chiusi. I, *AZ.* 1885 pl. 19, 2; Hartwig 40–41; *CV.* Robinson ii pll. 5–6; I, *Hesp.* 8, 162, whence *Annuario* N.S. 3–4, 132; B.Ap. xxii. 60. I, boy athlete and man. A–B, komos. On I, ᄂEΛ-ΛΡΟϞ and retr. [κ]ΛᄂΟϞ. On A, E[ΠΙΔΡΟΜΟϞ] ᖇΛᄂΟϞ. On B, [EΠ]ΙΔΡΟΜΟϞ [κ]ΛᄂΟϞ. Restored.

4 (4). FLORENCE, VILLA GIULIA, and HEIDELBERG 38, frr. Part, *CV*. Fl. pl. 12, B 56; part, *CF*. pl. Y, 12 and pl. Z, 7; the Heidelberg fr., Kraiker pl. 7. I, (uncertain remains). A, komos.

5 (5). VILLA GIULIA, fr. I, naked youth (running to left, head bent, right hand raised). Small cup.

THE SALTING PAINTER

Att. V. 50–51. *ARV.*[1] 89, 941, and 950.

Named after the former owner of no. 3.
Akin to the Carpenter Painter (p. 179).

CUPS

1 (1). LEIPSIC T 67. I, youth lifting shield. EΓ[I]Δ[P]OMO[ʃ]ΚΑLOʃ.

2 (2). OXFORD G 138.15, fr., from Naucratis. *CV*. pl. 49, 12. I, naked youth bending.

3 (3). LONDON, Victoria and Albert Museum, C 2496.1910 (ex Salting), from Atalanti. *Greece and Rome* 9 pl. 8, a; Rumpf *MZ*. pl. 20, 9. I, discus-thrower. For the shape, Bloesch 120 no. 19.

4 (4). BRUNSWICK 526, fr. *CV*. pl. 15, 3. I, jumper.

5 (5). Once LONDON, Mitchell, from Greece. *JHS*. 16 pl. 13. I, komast. ΑΚΕʃΤΟR ΚΑLOʃ.

6 (6, +). LOUVRE S 1372. I, athlete scraping. Louvre fragments join the old fragment S 1372, and great part of the figure is preserved.

Two cups go together, are close to those in the foregoing list (especially Louvre S 1372), and are probably later work by the Salting Painter himself:

1 (1). BERLIN 4039, from Corinth. Furtwängler *Sab*. pl. 53, 3; Blümel *S.H*. 66. I, hoplitodromos. For the shape, Bloesch 61, potter Phintias no. 4.

2 (2). WÜRZBURG 476. Langlotz pl. 153; Blümel *S.H*. 100. I, youth lifting lumps of clay. [Langlotz]. For the shape, Bloesch 61, potter Phintias no. 3.

Near these, the cup
WÜRZBURG 477. Langlotz pl. 153. I, boy with grapes. For the shape, Bloesch 61, potter Phintias no. 2.

Also near the Salting Painter, the cup
ROME, Antiquarium Forense, fr., from Rome. Boni *Aedes Vestae* (from *Nuova Antologia* 1 Aug. 1900) 16, 7, whence *Anz*. 1937, 74 fig. 2; *Jh*. 42, 16; with a fragment added by Enrico Paribeni, *Bull. Arch. Com*. 76 pl. 14, 187. I, Ixion. See p. 1631.

A cup recalls the Salting Painter:

LOUVRE G 85. *RA.* 1912, ii, 67, 13. I, jumper.

There is a curious resemblance, in details, between the following cup and those of the Salting Painter: early work by him, with a different system of proportions (cf. p. 110, above)?

CUP

COPENHAGEN inv. 3789, from Etruria. *Mél. d'arch.* 9 pl. 1; *CV.* pl. 139, 1. I, warrior. ϚΤΕϚΑΛΟΡΑ ΚΑLΟϚ, and in the exergue ΚΑL[ΟϚ]. Restored.

THE CARPENTER PAINTER

ARV.[1] 90–91 and 950.

Akin to the Salting Painter (p. 178).

CUPS

1 (1). LONDON E 23, from Chiusi. *El.* 1 pl. 37, whence Blümner ii, 340; Richter *F.* fig. 345; Cloché *Classes* pl. 27, 4. I, carpenter. For the shape, Bloesch 60 no. 5.

2 (2). ORVIETO, Faina, 101, from Orvieto. I, Philippart *It.* ii pl. 11, 3. I, satyr reclining, with cup and lyre. A–B, komos.

HYDRIA

(with picture on the shoulder, framed)

3 (3). VATICAN, from Vulci. *Mus. Greg.* 2 pl. 12, 1; ph. Al. 35841, whence *E.A.A.* ii, 359. Youth attacking boar. Restored.

NEAR THE CARPENTER PAINTER

CUPS

1 (1). BOSTON 00.337, from Corinth or near. I, komast; A–B, komos.

2. LOUVRE C 11230 *bis*, fr. I, komast. Compare Boston 00.337.

3. OXFORD, Beazley, fr. I, komast (running to right, stick in right hand). Compare Louvre C 11230.

HYDRIA

(with picture on the shoulder, framed)

(2). ROUEN 24, from Vulci. Herakles and the lion.

The following, though quite likely made in the same workshop as the cups decorated by Skythes (p. 82), is in a different style from them, and near the Carpenter Painter:

CUP

LOUVRE G 11, fr., from Cervetri. *Mon. Piot* 9 pl. 15, 1 and 3 (not the middle picture, 2, for which see p. 377 no. 98), whence *Mon. Piot* 20, 128, (A) Pfuhl fig. 342, (A) Buschor *Satyrtänze* fig. 55; B, *Mon. Piot* 20, 137, whence Pfuhl fig. 339. A, Herakles resting, with boy cup-bearers, satyr and maenad; B, (satyr, maenads). On A, ΕΠΙLVΚΟϽ ΚΑLΟ[Ͻ]. Under the handle, ΚΑLΟϽ. On B, ΚΑLΟϽ. Restored.

It seems to me that the following cup-fragment may come from the same cup as Louvre G 11:

LOUVRE C 11231, fr. I, (head, to left, right shoulder and upper arm of a youth, wearing a wrap; inscription Κ . . .). Outside, (foot of one moving to left, foot of one in a long chiton moving to left): this would be from B.

The following cup is earlier than all these, but near the Carpenter Painter:

BOSTON 00.336. C. Smith *Forman* pl. 11, 337; CB. i pl. 3, 8 and p. 7; the shape, Caskey G. 181 no. 135. I, archer. For the shape, Bloesch 120 no. 8.

THE GROUP OF LOUVRE G 99

These may be by one hand.

CUPS

1. LOUVRE G 99, fr. Part, Pottier pl. 99. I, youth and girl embracing. A Louvre fragment joins.
2. LECCE 575, from Egnatia. *CV.* pl. 6, 3. I, jumper. For the shape, Bloesch 60 no. 7. See p. 1631.

BOOK III

LATE ARCHAIC POT-PAINTERS

CHAPTER 14

THE KLEOPHRADES PAINTER (EPIKTETOS II)

THE KLEOPHRADES PAINTER (EPIKTETOS II)

Hartwig 400–20 ('Amasis II'). Furtwängler in FR. i, 262–7. Hauser in FR. ii, 228. *JHS*. 30, 38–68. *JHS*. 36, 123–8. *VA*. 40–44. *Att. V*. 69–76 and 469. *Der Kleophrades-Maler* [*Kl*.]. Richter in *AJA*. 1936, 100–15. Den Tex in *AM*. 62, 38–40. *ARV*.¹ 120–31, 949, and 952. Peters *Pan*. 65–67. *AJA*. 1943, 445. Karouzou in *Eph*. 1948–9, 24. *Dev*. 94, 117, and 119. *ABV*. 404–6 and 696. Schnitzler in *Op. Ath*. 2, 47–60. Lullies *Die Spitzamphora des Kleophrades-Malers*. *Antike Kunst* 1, 6–8.

The greatest pot-painter of the late archaic period. He was the pupil of Euthymides, and his earliest vases much resemble his master's. The conventional name by which we continue to call him is taken from the great cup in the Cabinet des Médailles (no. 103) which bears the signature of the potter Kleophrades: his actual name is given by a very late work of little significance, a pelike in Berlin (no. 28): Epiktetos (the second).

Very early work, nos. 1–3, 31–33, 65–67, 79, and 80.

AMPHORAE

(type A)

(nos. 1–4, with framed pictures)

1 (1). WÜRZBURG 507, from Vulci. Gerhard pl. 267; FR. pl. 103 and ii, 226, whence Hoppin *Euth. F*. pl. 12, (B) Pfuhl fig. 377, (A) Rumpf *Rel*. fig. 167, (A) Swindler fig. 305; the woman on B, *Archiv f. Gesch. der Medizin* 3 fig. 5; Langlotz pl. 175, whence (A) *Hist. rel*. 253; B, Wegner *Mus*. pl. 11. A, warrior leaving home (extispicy). B, komos. [Hartwig]. The lid Würzburg 297 must belong (Gerhard pl. 267; part, FR. pl. 103, whence Hoppin *Euth. F*. pl. 12; Langlotz pl. 85: bf., chariot-race: restored: see *Kl*. 23). For the shape, Bloesch in *JHS*. 71, 32, Eukleo Class, D. Very early.

2. LEIPSIC T 666, fr. (Head of youth, and, on the left, part of another figure —of hair-incision and wreath). Very early.

3 (2). VATICAN, from Vulci. *Mus. Greg.* 2 pl. 54, 2; A, ph. Mo., whence *JHS.* 30 pl. 4; Hoppin *Euth. F.* pll. 39–40; A, Herford pl. 3, a; phs. Al. 35822 and 35780, whence (B) Pfuhl fig. 376 and (part of A) *AJA.* 1936, 107 fig. 11; details (the restorations partly removed), *Kl.* pl. 1, whence (detail of B) *AJA.* 1936, 110 fig. 14; phs. And. 42032 and 43034; A, ph. Marb. O. 29168. A, Herakles and Athena. B, komos. [Hartwig]. Restored. For the shape, Bloesch in *JHS.* 71, 32, Eukleo Class, D. Very early.

4 (3). MUNICH 2305 (J. 411), from Vulci. A, *Mon.* 1 pl. 26, 3; details, Hartwig pl. 37, 4 and pp. 409–10; B, Jüthner 69; FR. pl. 52 and i, 262 and 265–6 and ii, 171 fig. 56, whence Hoppin *Euth. F.* pl. 41 and p. 157, Pfuhl figs. 372–3, and (B) Swindler fig. 299; A, Langlotz *GV.* pl. 17, 26; A, Schaal *Rf.* fig. 12; *Kl.* pl. 7; A, mouth, and foot, *JHS.* 71 pl. 17, d, and p. 32 fig. 6; A, Bielefeld *ZV.* pl. 4, 5; Lullies and Hirmer pll. 48–55, whence (B and lid) LS. figs. 69–70; detail of B, *Op. Ath.* 2 pl. 3 fig. 9; *CV.* pll. 173–7, pl. 188, 7, and p. 18. A, warrior leaving home. B, boxers and trainer. On the mouth, *bf.*: A, chariot, horsemen, and youths; B, deer-hunt on horseback. On the lid, *bf.*, chariot-race. [Hartwig]. For the shape, Bloesch in *JHS.* 71, 32, Eukleo Class, D. Early. See p. 1631.

(*no. 5, the pictures not framed*)

5 (4). WÜRZBURG 508, from Vulci. *Mon.* 1 pll. 35–36; FR. pl. 104, whence (restorations omitted) *Kl.* pl. 28, 2; Langlotz pl. 176; B, Buschor *G. Vasen* 168. Warriors parted: A, Ajax and Phoinix; B, Hector and Priam. [Hartwig]. *Ambo truces, ambo abscessere minantes* (Val. Flacc. 7, 653). That the old man on B is Priam is suggested by the inscription on a stamnos by the Triptolemos Painter (p. 361 no. 7). Later.

POINTED AMPHORA

6 (5). MUNICH 2344 (J. 408), from Vulci. FR. pll. 44–45 and i, 234–5, whence (rearranged) *Kl.* pl. 4 (whence, A, LS. fig. 71), (detail) Pfuhl fig. 379, (detail) Swindler fig. 316, (neck A), *JHS.* 27, 265 (= Norman Gardiner *G.A.S.* 353), (neck) Stow pl. 14, (detail of B) Kraiker *M.G.* pl. 28; *Mem. Am. Ac.* 6 pl. 20, 3 and pl. 21, 4; B, Ahrem 86; various details, Buschor 166, Pfuhl fig. 380 (= Pfuhl *Mast.* figs. 44–45), Schaal *Rf.* fig. 10, *Mem. Am. Ac.* 6 pl. 12a, c; *Kl.* pll. 3 and 5–6, whence (A, detail of B) Lane pl. 66, a and pl. 67, (detail of B) Frel *Ř.V.* fig. 162; B, Richter and Milne fig. 28; A and detail of B, Buschor *G. Vasen* 170 fig. 189, and p. 169; part, Vorberg *Er.* 85–87; part, Vorberg *Gloss.* 638–40; Lullies and Hirmer pll. 36–47; *CV.* pll. 199–204 and p. 27; A, Stella 354; Lullies *Die Spitzamphora des Kleophrades-Malers* pll. 1–8 and cover; A and detail of B, *E.A.A.* i, 898–9; detail of A, Richter *H.G.A.* 333; A, Robertson *G.P.* 100–2; B, R.M. Cook pl. 42. Dionysos with maenads and satyrs. On the neck, athletes. Early. See p. 1632.

PANATHENAIC AMPHORAE

7 (6). LEYDEN PC 80 (18 h 35), from Vulci. *JHS.* 30 pl. 6; A, Langlotz *GV.* pl. 25, 38. A, satyr with lyre. B, youth with hare. Still earlyish.

8. MEGGEN, Käppeli. Schefold *M.* 195. Warrior leaving home: A, young warrior drinking from a cup; B, woman with oinochoe and flower. [Cahn]. Perhaps Achilles and Briseis. Later.

9 (7). BOSTON 10.178. Gerhard pl. 275; *JHS.* 36, 130–1; *VA.* 42; *CB.* i pl. 5, whence (A) *Arch. class.* 2 pl. 7, 2; detail of A, *Kl.* pl. 18, 4, whence Chamoux *L'Aurige* pl. 33, 2; Chase *Guide* 64; part of B, Buschor *Bilderwelt* 36; the shape, Hambidge 130; the shape, Caskey *G.* 79. A, victor; B, youth. Later. See p. 1632.

10 (8). BERLIN 2164 and FLORENCE, from Etruria. Gerhard *TG.* pl. 21, whence (B) Overbeck *KM.* pl. 12, 5; details, *Kl.* pl. 30, 1 and 7. A, Herakles shooting. B, Poseidon. Much restored, especially A. The foot of the vase can hardly belong. The unpublished fragment in Florence gives the knuckles of Poseidon's left hand, with part of the trident-head (see *CF.* 33 no. 10). Later.

NECK-AMPHORAE

(nos. 11–18, with twisted handles)

11 (9). HARROW 55. A, *Burl. 1903* pl. 95, H 54; *JHS.* 30 pl. 7; *JHS.* 36, 123–4 and pl. 6, whence Chittenden and Seltman pl. 16, 80; B, *VA.* 43; *Kl.* pl. 29, 1–2, whence (detail of A) *Op. Ath.* 2 pl. 1 fig. 1. A, satyr holding helmet and greaves; B, satyr holding spear and shield. Later.

12 (10). MUNICH 2316 (J. 55), from Vulci. Lützow pl. 29; *JHS.* 30 pl. 8; Lullies and Hirmer pll. 84–87; detail of B, *E.A.A.* ii, 471; *CV.* pl. 209, 3–4 and pl. 211, 4–5. A, Herakles; B, centaur. Later.

13 (11). NEW YORK 13.233. *Bull. Metr.* 9, 233; *JHS.* 36, 125; B, *N.Y. Shapes* 7, 1 = Richter and Milne fig. 20; *Kl.* pl. 29, 3–4; B, *AJA.* 1936, 107 fig. 12; Richter and Hall pll. 14–15, and pl. 169, 13, whence (A) *Arch. class.* 2 pl. 49, 3 and (B) Rumpf *MZ.* pl. 23, 1; B, Richter *H.* 213, e. The struggle for the tripod: A, Apollo; B, Herakles. Later.

14 (12). ROMAN MARKET. Gerhard pl. 268; B.Ap. xxi. 44. A, warrior; B, warrior.

15 (13). LONDON E 270, from Vulci. *Mon.* 5 pl. 10; *CV.* pl. 8, 2, whence (part of B) Wegner *Mus.* pl. 10, b; A, Wade-Gery *The Poet of the Iliad* 30 fig. 2; ph. Ma. A, rhapsode. B, flute-player. Later. See p. 1632.

16 (19, +). LOUVRE G 198 *bis.* A, acontist; B, jumper. Many fragments have been added, mostly by Villard, to that described in *ARV.*[1] 122 no. 19, and the vase is nearly complete. Late.

17 (14). LENINGRAD 613. *JHS.* 36, 126–7. A, discus-thrower; B, trainer. Late.

18 (15). VILLA GIULIA 47836, from Cervetri. B, *ML.* 42, 1015. A, youth; B, boy. The youth on A was meant, as the incised sketch shows, to be offering the boy a hare, which was omitted in the final drawing. Late.

(no. 19, with triple handles)

19 (16). LENINGRAD 609. *Kl.* pl. 21, whence (part of B) *AJA.* 1936, 104, fig. 8, (part of A) *Op. Ath.* 2 pl. 2 fig. 7. A, two acontists. B, two satyrs. Earlyish.

(no. 20, Nolan amphora, with triple handles)

20 (17). OXFORD 273, from Gela. B (with restorations, since removed), Gardner 24 fig. 27 and title-page; cleaned, *CV.* pl. 17, 1 and pl. 18, 4. A, discus-thrower and trainer. B, Artemis. Later.

NECK-AMPHORA?

21 (18). Once CANINO, from Vulci. B.Ap. xvi. 17.1, whence (A) Panofka *Griechinnen* pl. 1, 9. A, youth with writing-tablets (in himation, leaning on his stick to right); B, youth (in himation, standing frontal, head frontal). Late.

LOUTROPHOROS

22 (20). LOUVRE CA 453, from Attica. *Mon. Piot* 1 pll. 5–7, whence *CV.* pl. 57, and (part) Perrot 10, 667, 677, and 679; *CV.* pl. 56; part, *Enc. phot.* iii, 6–7, whence Schnitzler pl. 40. Prothesis. Below, bf., valediction (horsemen). On the neck, A, mourning women, B, the like. Much restored. Later. See p. 1632.

PELIKAI

(nos. 23–27, with framed pictures)

23 (21, +). ATHENS Acr. 612, frr., from Athens. Part of A, *AM.* 15, 29; A, Langlotz pl. 47 and p. 56. A, youth and boy; B, the like. A new Athens fragment joins A on the lower left, adding parts of the borders. Later.

24 (22). VILLA GIULIA, fr. A, (male: what remains is the upper part of the head, to left, the himation covering the back of the head; then the top of a stick; hair-contour incised; above, part of the key-pattern border).

25 (23). LOUVRE G 235. *CV.* pl. 48, 7–9 and pl. 49, 1 and 3. A, youth and boy. B, victor and trainer (the announcement of the victory). Restored. Latish.

26. SWISS PRIVATE. Komos: A, man ('Anacreontic') and flute-girl; B, youth vomiting, and flute-girl. On A, girl to right, playing the flute, man in long chiton, himation, saccos, boots, dancing along to right, looking round; on B, youth leaning on his stick to right, girl standing to left, flute in her left hand at her side. Late.

27 (24). COPENHAGEN 149. *CV.* pl. 133; *AJA.* 1936, 114; *Antik-Cab. 1851* 157. A, youth seated, and woman. B, two athletes. Late.

(*nos. 28–30, the pictures not framed*)

28 (25). BERLIN 2170, from Cervetri. Gerhard pl. 299, whence Hoppin i, 303, whence (B) *AJA*. 1936, 113. A, goddess; B, goddess. On A, ΕΠΙΚΤΕΤΟS ΕΛΡΑΘSΕΝ. On B, ΕΠΙΚΤΕΤΟΣ ΕΛΡΑΘSΕΝ. Restored. Late. See p. 1632.

29 (26). MYKONOS, from Rheneia (originally from Delos). Dugas *Délos xxi* pl. 2, 3. A, satyr. B, youth. Late.

30 (27). AGRIGENTO 34, from Agrigento. A, *Jb*. 8, 183; A, Cloché *Classes* pl. 34, 1. A, oil-seller; B, youth. Late.

CALYX-KRATERS

31 (28). HARVARD 1960.236 (ex Watkins). Part, *AJA*. 1936, 101–3; A, *A.A.A.* pl. 81. Return of Hephaistos. [Richter]. Restored. Very early.

32 (29). COPENHAGEN inv. 13365 (ex Curtius), frr. Part, Breitenstein *G.V.* pll. 32–33; phs. R.I. 36.284; 36.291 A; 35.2052; 36.337. A, symposion; B, komos (Anacreon and his boon-companions). [Curtius]. For B and its inscriptions, CB. ii, 57. On A, . . . ΕΝΙΕS retr. (i.e. [ν]ενιες, or rather [Κλ]ενιες, Ionic?), . . . ΒΕVΕ, and on a cup ΑΙΡΕ . . . Very early.

33 (30). LOUVRE G 48. Pottier pll. 93–94, whence Hoppin *Euth. F.* pl. 43; *CV*. pl. 1, 7, pl. 3, 3, pl. 6, 2, and pl. 7, 1. A, heroes quarrelling. B, arming. Only small parts are antique (see *Kl.* 24–25). Very early.

34. CORINTH T 1332, fr., from Corinth. Athletes and trainer (shanks of athlete standing to right, shanks and feet of trainer in himation standing to left, foot of athlete standing to left). Early.

35 (31). TARQUINIA RC 4196, from Tarquinia. Hartwig 416–17, whence Hoppin *Euth. F.* pl. 42 and (part of A) Norman Gardiner *G.A.S.* 324 fig. 78; A, ph. Mo. 8644, whence Pfuhl fig. 375 (cut down), *Kl.* pl. 16, Buschor *G. Vasen* 173; B and details of A, *Kl.* pl. 17 and pl. 18, 1–3, whence (detail of A) Frel *Ř.V.* fig. 166, (small detail) Chamoux *L'Aurige* pl. 33, 1; *CV*. pl. 15; R.I. Athletes: A, discus-thrower and trainer; B, acontist and trainer. [Hartwig]. Early. See p. 1632.

36 (32). NEW YORK 08.258.58, from Cervetri. A, *Bull. Metr.* 5, 144 fig. 9; part of A, *VA*. 41; A, *Kl.* pl. 19; Richter and Hall pll. 12–13 and pl. 170, 12; detail of A, Richter *ARVS*. fig. 47; A, Richter *H*. 213, d. Arming: A, two warriors; B, two warriors. Early.

37 (33). CAB. MÉD., part of 420, fr. *Kl.* pl. 20, 4. Arming. See *Kl.* 25.

38. ATHENS, Agora, P 20244, two frr., from Athens. On one fragment, (head and staff of Phoinix). On the other, (right arm and flank of a male in chitoniskos and chlamys). [Corbett, Edwards].

39. ATHENS, Agora, P 19582 and P 18278, frr., from Athens. A, Achilles mourning. B, fight. [Corbett, Edwards; the fragment P 6103 added by Shefton].

40 (34). SYRACUSE, two small frr., from Gela. (Upper part of female head to right; above, upright palmettes).

41. ATHENS, Agora, P 17211, fr., from Athens. *Hesp.* 16 pl. 47, 2. (Man).

42 (35). ATHENS Acr. 730, fr., from Athens. *JHS.* 30 pl. 5, 4; Langlotz pl. 58, whence Buschor *Satyrtänze* fig. 59. (Satyr, disguised as Herakles, playing the flute).

43 (36). ATHENS Acr. 883, fr., from Athens. Langlotz pl. 77. (Satyr). Acr. G 17, with part of an amphora on it, seems to belong.

44 (37). ATHENS Acr. L 5–6, fr., from Athens. *Hesp.* 4, 289, 161. (Males). [Pease].

45 (38). ATHENS, Ceramicus Museum, frr., from Athens. *Anz.* 1937, 185, and 1938, 612. Ransom of Hector. [Gebauer, Johannes]. A fragment which according to Gebauer may be from the same vase is mentioned in *Anz.* 1940, 328, middle. Later.

46 (39). ATHENS, Agora, P 10509, fr., from Athens. (Trumpeter: according to Bothmer an Amazon).

47 (40). LOUVRE G 162, from Vulci? *Mon.* suppl. pl. 24; detail, Herford pl. 7, a; *CV.* pl. 12, 8, pl. 13, 2, 5, and 8, pl. 14, 1 and 6, and pl. 16, 1–3; details, *Kl.* pl. 26, whence (detail) Buschor *Bilderwelt* 40; detail, Villard *VG.* pl. 20, 1; detail, *Ant. Kunst* 1 pl. 5, 9. Return of Hephaistos. See *Kl.* 25 no. 34. Now cleaned. Later.

48 (41). BASLE MARKET (ex Giudice), from Favara. Ph. Lo Cascio pl. 90. A, rescue of Theano and Antenor. B, Poseidon and Aithra. On A, a man leads an aged woman; they are preceded by a woman holding an alabastron and a 'plemochoe' and followed by a woman holding a tied fillet; behind her, an aged man grasping his head. See *Kl.* 25–26. Now cleaned. Later.

49 (42). CAB. MÉD. 419, fr. De Ridder 311, whence *Le Musée* 3, 325 fig. 14; *Kl.* pl. 30, 4, whence Frel *Ř.V.* fig. 165. Herakles shooting. [Hauser]. Later.

VOLUTE-KRATERS

50 (43, 80). CAB. MÉD. 385 and BONN 143 b, frr., from Tarquinia. *Mon.* 2 pl. 10, b, whence Overbeck *Gall.* pl. 22, 9, whence Roscher s.v. Thetis, 795; *Kl.* pl. 2 and pl. 30, 6; one fr., B.Ap. xxii. 1, 2, 3. These without the Bonn fragment. The Bonn fragment: *Kl.* pl. 20, 2; *CV.* pl. 17, 4. A, Psychostasia. [Hartwig]. A small fragment with the left hand of Hermes is now missing. Luynes mentions a fragmentary reverse (*Annali* 1834, 296), which has disappeared: he thought of Achilles and Hector: perhaps Achilles and Memnon? See *Kl.* 12 and 26, CB. ii, 18, and CB. iii, text. Early.

51 (44). LOUVRE, part of G 166, frr. The pasticcio in which the fragments were formerly embedded (see *JHS.* 42, 94 note 51, and here p. 206) has now been demolished and the genuine portions taken out. (The pasticcio:

ph. Gir., whence *Mon. Piot* 9, 39; *CV.* pl. 17 and pl. 18, 1–2; ph. Al. 23689). On the neck: on the upper zone, A, Amazonomachy; B, Amazon reinforcements; on the lower zone, B, (Nereids running to Nereus— probably from a representation of Peleus and Thetis). Bothmer, who has seen the fragments since the demolition, reports that the small sherd with Herakles cannot belong to the Amazonomachy as it is not thick enough for the upper zone: it must be either from the lower zone or from another vase. (I have since checked this; the fragment with the upper part of a youth in chiton and himation is also thin and must be from a lower zone).

52 (45). FLORENCE PD 507, fr. On the upper zone of the neck, arming (head and right shoulder of a youthful warrior to right). Bothmer has shown me that the subject is 'arming' rather than 'fight', and that the warrior may be an Amazon. Early.

53 (46). CAB. MÉD. 863, fr. On the neck, arming (Amazons according to Bothmer).

54 (47). ATHENS Acr. 759, fr., from Athens. Langlotz pl. 64. On the upper zone of the neck: A, warriors setting out, with chariot; B, arming.

STAMNOI

55 (82, +). LOUVRE C 10748. Gigantomachy: A, Apollo and Giant, Ares and Giant; B, Dionysos and Giants. Most of the fragments were put together by Villard. Early.

56 (48). TÜBINGEN E 14, three frr. Watzinger pl. 18. A, satyrs. B, komos. [Watzinger].

57 (49). LONDON E 441, from Vulci. *JHS.* 30, 58 and pll. 1–2, whence (B) Pfuhl fig. 374, (B) Seltman pl. 22, a, (A) *Kl.* pl. 28, 1, whence (detail) *Op. Ath.* 2 pl. 1 fig. 3; *CV.* pl. 20, 2 and pl. 21, 1. A, Theseus and Minotaur; B, Theseus and Procrustes. Later. The alien lid has been removed.

58 (50). LOUVRE G 55, from Tarquinia. B, Pottier pl. 95; *CV.* pl. 6, 3 and 5 and pl. 7, 3; B, Langlotz *F.B.* pl. 14, 4; B, Saxl *Mithras* fig. 26; *Kl.* pll. 24–25 and pl. 23, 3; phs. Gir. 19552–3. Centauromachy: A, Kaineus and Centaurs; B, Lapith and Centaurs. Later. See p. 1632.

59 (51). TARQUINIA 711, from Tarquinia. A, ph. Mo. 8658, whence *JHS.* 30 pl. 9, 2; *Kl.* pl. 22 and pl. 23, 1–2; *CV.* pl. 13, 1–2. A, Herakles and Pholos; B, Centaurs coming up. Later. See p. 1632.

60 (52). FLORENCE V 15, from Chiusi. A, athletes and trainer. B, youths and boy. Now cleaned. Later. See p. 1632.

61 (53). ATHENS Acr. 768, frr., from Athens. Part, *JHS.* 30 pl. 5, 2–3; Langlotz pl. 67. A, athletes; B, (athletes and) trainer. Later.

62 (55). PHILADELPHIA L 64.185, from Vulci? A, *Bull. Pennsylvania Mus.* Oct. 1906, 55 fig. 6, whence *AJA.* 1907, 119; *AJA.* 1935, 452; A, *Univ. Mus. Bull.* 5 pl. 5; B, *Die Antike* 17, 218; A, *Proc. Am. Philos. Soc.* 1943

(Dinsmoor *Early American Studies of Mediterranean Archaeology*) 91 fig. 12. A, Herakles and the lion. B, Theseus and the bull. Later. See p. 1632.

63 (56). VILLA GIULIA 26040, from Vignanello. *NSc.* 1916, 47–49, whence (A) *Anz.* 1921, 95, (A) Johansen *Iliaden* fig. 32, (B) Pfuhl fig. 332; *CV.* pl. 6, and pl. 7, 2–3. A, Patroklos taking leave of Achilles; B, warrior leaving home. Late.

STAMNOS?

64 (54). CHIUSI 1847, frr., from Chiusi. Detail of B, *Kl.* pl. 30, 2, whence *Op. Ath.* 2 pl. 3 fig. 10. Now cleaned, and the modern picture (ph. Mo. 10587, whence Giometti 60) removed. On one fragment, (Herakles, Hermes); on the other, (Apollo). Bothmer, who has seen the fragments since the cleaning, tells me that the fragment with Apollo need not be from the same side as that with Herakles and Hermes, and that the shape of the vase is doubtful: not certainly a stamnos, or at least an ordinary stamnos; possibly a long-necked like Louvre G 192 (p. 208 no. 160). The vase is not glazed inside (but neither is, for example, the Oxford stamnos 522, p. 1028 no. 3).

PSYKTERS

65 (57). LOUVRE G 57. Pottier pl. 95; *CV.* pl. 58, 2, 5, and 8, and pl. 59, 2–3; one figure, *AJA.* 1936, 104 fig. 4. Dionysos with satyrs and maenads. Much restored. Very early.

66 (58). COMPIÈGNE 1068, from Vulci. Gerhard pl. 59–60; *CV.* pl. 13, 7–8, pl. 15, 4, and pl. 16, whence (part) Buschor *Satyrtänze* fig. 58; two figures, *AJA.* 1936, 104 fig. 5, and 107 fig. 10; B.Ap. xxii. 21. Dionysos and Herakles, with satyrs. [Richter]. Very early.

HYDRIAI

(no. 67, of bf. shape; the pictures framed)

67 (60). SALERNO inv. 1371, from Fratte. Youths and boys. On the shoulder, satyrs robbing Herakles. Very early: compare Würzburg 507 (no. 1). See p. 33.

(nos. 68–73, kalpides, the picture on the shoulder, framed)

68 (61). ROUEN 25, from Vulci. Licht iii, 95; detail, *AJA.* 1936, 104 fig. 7; Vorberg *Gloss.* 37. Satyrs attacking a sleeping maenad. Very early.

69 (62). VILLA GIULIA 50398. R.I.; Phs. G.F. 7165 and 18275. Herakles and the lion. Early. See p. 1632.

70 (63). LOUVRE G 50, from Vulci. Pottier pl. 94; *CV.* pl. 52, and 4–5; ph. Arch. phot. S.4240.086.AE.I. Herakles attacking men at altar. For the subject compare the cup by Onesimos in New York (pp. 319–20 no. 6). Later.

71 (64). LEYDEN PC 83 (xviii h 20), from Vulci. Roulez pl. 11, 1; Byvanck-Quarles van Ufford *P.* 34. Centauromachy. Later.

72 (65). MUNICH 2427 (J. 347), from Vulci. *JHS.* 30 pl. 9, 1; the maid, Reichhold *Skiz.* 86, 2; *Ant. Kunst* 1 pl. 6 and p. 7. Seated youth, and woman; maid; man and seated woman. Later. See p. 1632.

73. BASLE, Wilhelm, from Vulci. *Ant. Kunst* 1 pll. 2–4, pl. 5, 7–8, and p. 8 (the reproduction of the graffito omits the down-stroke mentioned in the text). Dionysos with maenads and satyr. Later. See ibid. 6–8.

(*no. 74, as before, but the picture running right round the vase*)

74 (66). NAPLES 2422, from Nola. Millin *PVA.* 1 pll. 25–26; Tischbein *Homer* 9 pll. 5–6, whence Kraiker *M.G.* pl. 33; Angelini pl. 5; *Mus. Borb.* 14 pll. 41–43; Gargiulo *Recueil* 2 pl. 31; FR. pl. 34, whence Perrot 10, 627 and pl. 16, *AJA.* 1918, 147, Pfuhl fig. 378, *Die Antike* 5 pl. 22, *Kl.* pl. 27, *R.E.G.* 1936 pl. 8 fig. 7, (detail) Seltman pl. 21, a, LS. fig. 68; ph. Al. 11300, whence *R.E.G.* 1936 pl. 8 fig. 8, (part) *Hist. rel.* 283, (part) *AJA.* 1954 pl. 63, 31; part, Stella 757; detail, Richter *H.G.A.* 332 fig. 447; phs. So. 11075–7; ph. And. 25936; phs. R.I. 57.837–42. Iliupersis (death of Priam; Ajax and Cassandra; Trojan woman attacking a Greek; Aeneas and Anchises; rescue of Aithra). [Hauser]. See *Kl.* 27 (where, right-hand column, line 7, for ἦν read εἰ). Later. See p. 1632.

(*nos. 75–77, kalpides, the picture on the body, not framed*)

75 (67). VILLA GIULIA 50384, from Cervetri. Ph. G.F. 7166. Youth and boy. Later. See p. 1632.

76 (68). MUNICH 2426 (J. 291), from Vulci. Gerhard pl. 83. Iris carrying the infant Hermes. Late. See p. 1632.

77 (69). LONDON E 201, from Vulci. Sudhoff i, 35; *JHS.* 30 pl. 3 and p. 56; Ahrem 70; *CV.* pl. 88, 1. Two naked women washing. Late.

LEKYTHOS

(*standard shape*)

78 (70). MUNICH inv. 7517. *Op. Ath.* 2 pl. 4 figs. 13–14. Herakles with the tripod. Earlyish (and so I described it in *ARV.*[1] 126, not as 'very early' which Schnitzler makes me say in *Op. Ath.* 2, 57 note 116).

FRAGMENTS OF POTS

79 (59). ATHENS, Agora, P 7241, fr., from Athens. (Herakles resting). [Talcott]. Very early. Formerly said to be from a psykter, but Mrs. Ashmead has pointed out that it is not.

80 (71). BRUNSWICK 540, fr. *CV.* pl. 21, 1. (Komast). From an amphora? Very early.

81 (74). ATHENS Acr. 611, fr., from Athens. *JHS.* 30 pl. 5, 5; Langlotz pl. 47; *Kl.* pl. 30, 3. (Satyr). From an amphora?

82 (81, +). FLORENCE 8 B 6, and NAPLES, Astarita, 123, frr. Part, *CV.* pl. 8, B 6. Arming: A, two warriors; B, the like. Probably from a neck-amphora with two figures on each side. See *CF.* 15–16 on pl. 8, B 6,

where an unpublished fragment in Florence is also mentioned. Another unpublished fragment in Florence joins pl. 8 B 11 on the left, adding the rest of the helmet, and part of the shield below it. Of the three Astarita fragments, the first joins, on the left, Florence 8 B 8, adding the greater part of the warrior's arms, part of his corslet, and the point of the spear held by his companion. The second Astarita fragment has one arm, extended, and hand of the left-hand warrior, as it should be, on B, with part of his scabbard, which he seems to be slinging round him. The third Astarita fragment has a foot, and the end of a spear or staff, with a stretch of the net-pattern below the picture; the foot should belong to the left-hand warrior on B.

83. TARANTO, fr., from Locri. (Bare shanks and feet of a male, the left leg frontal, the right leg crossed behind it; below, net pattern).

84 (83). ATHENS Acr. 610, five frr., from Athens. Four of them, Langlotz pl. 47. From a neck-amphora with two figures on each side? Fragments c and d would belong to the left-hand figure on A, a male standing in back-view; fragment b to the left-hand figure on B, a youth (leaning on his stick?) to right; fragment a (a male leaning on his stick to left) would be from the right-hand figure on either A or B. The unpublished fragment has part of the maeander below. Early.

85. ATHENS Acr., fr., from Athens. (Feet of a male in a himation standing to right).

86. FLORENCE, fr. (Part of the buttocks and chitoniskos of one to left, leaning back or falling—a falling warrior?).

87 (85, 86). ATHENS Acr. 898, two frr., from Athens. Langlotz pl. 77, whence Vian R. pl. 38, 385. Gigantomachy.

88 (87). ATHENS Acr. 925, fr., from Athens. Langlotz pl. 76. Centauromachy. Athens Acr. 920 (shield and rump of a wounded warrior) perhaps belongs.

89 (89). ERLANGEN 459 c, fr. Eros. From a hydria?

90 (84). ELEUSIS 597 and 598, two frr., from Eleusis. Delt. 9, 24, pl. 1 at p. 24, 1, and p. 25, fig. 24; the satyr, Kl. pl. 20, 3. Perhaps from an amphora with one figure on each side: (A), Dionysos; (B), satyr.

91. TARANTO, fr., from Locri. Fight (face, left arm, and shield of young warrior to right, and part of another figure). [Enrico Paribeni]. Early.

92. ATHENS Acr. 609, fr., from Athens. JHS. 30 pl. 5, 1; Langlotz pl. 47; Kl. pl. 20, 1. Citharode. From an amphora with one figure on each side?

93 (73). ATHENS Acr. 893, fr., from Athens. Langlotz pl. 77. Citharode. From an amphora with one figure on each side? From the same vase as the last?

94. TARANTO, fr., from Locri. (Satyr: from beard to waist, a horn in the right hand). May be from an amphora.

95 (75–78). ATHENS Acr. 891, 892, 895, and 896, four frr., from Athens. The three first, Langlotz pl. 77. (Maenads).

96 (79). ATHENS Acr. 613, frr., from Athens. Part, Langlotz pl. 47. (Legs; the booted foot might be of Dionysos).

97. ATHENS Acr., from Athens. (A small piece of the himation of one figure; and a piece of the himation of another figure, turned to right).

98. ATHENS Acr., fr., from Athens. (Part of the himation of a figure, probably turned to left). Compare the last.

99. ATHENS, Agora, P 19455, fr., from Athens. (Half shanks, bare, and feet, of a male standing frontal). Might be from a stamnos.

100. LOUVRE C 10838, two frr. On one, (youth and boy); on the other, (boy, male: the boy might be the same as in the first fragment). From a stamnos?

101 (88). GOETTINGEN H 43, fr. (Youth). Probably from a stamnos. [Martin Robertson].

SKYPHOS

(type A)

102 (90). FLORENCE 4218. *JHS.* 1 pl. 3 (incompletely), whence *Die Antike* 5,269; parts, *Kl.* pl. 31, and pl. 23, 4, whence (part) Schnitzler pl. 37, 52, (part) Frel *Ř.V.* figs. 167–8; *CV.* pl. 69; part, Stella 105; part, *E.A.A.* i, pl. p. 900. Iris attacked by Centaurs. Later.

CUPS

103 (91). CAB. MÉD. 535, 699, and other frr., from Tarquinia. Part of A, Luynes pl. 44, whence Hoppin *Euth. F.* pl. 38, Hoppin *Rf.* ii, 139, Pfuhl fig. 371, *Jb.* 44, 125; I and A–B, all in part, Hartwig pl. 37, 1–2, whence Hoppin *Euth. F.* 149 and Hoppin *Rf.* ii, 137; I and A–B, *Kl.* pl. 8, pl. 10, 1, pl. 11–12, pl. 15, 1–6, and pl. 30, 5; the foot of the cup, Bloesch pl. 16, 6. I, warrior putting on his greaves. A–B, Herakles and the Amazons. On the foot, ΚLΕΟΦRΑΔΕΣ ꞉ ΕΓΟΙΕΣΕΝ ꞉ ΑΜΑΣ-
. . . . Σ ꞉ [Hartwig]. Early. See *Kl.* 9–10, 17–18, and 28 no. 77, and, for the shape, Bloesch 58.

104 (92). CAB. MÉD. 536 (part), 647, part of 535, and other frr., from Tarquinia. *JHS.* 10 pl. 2 (incomplete, with alien frr., and restored), whence Hoppin *Euth. F.* pl. 44 and Roscher s.v. Theseus fig. 731; detail of I, Hartwig pl. 37, 3, whence Hoppin *Euth. F.* 163; detail of I, FR. i, 264; detail of I, *C.A.H.*, plates, ii, 32, b; *Kl.* pl. 9, pl. 10, 2, pll. 13–14, and pl. 15, 8–12, whence (detail of I) *Op. Ath.* 2 pl. 2 fig. 6, (detail of I) Kraiker *M.G.* pl. 32, 1, (details of I and of B) Frel *Ř.V.* figs. 163–4; part, ph. Gir. 32792. I, Theseus and Kerkyon; A–B, deeds of Theseus: A, Minotaur, bull; B, Sinis, Skiron, Procrustes. [Hartwig]. Early. See *Kl.* 10, 19–22, and 28 no. 78. A cup-fragment in Cab. Méd. (*JHS.* 10 pl. 2, b; *Kl.* pl. 15, 7) belongs either to this cup or to the last (see *Kl.* 18).

105 (93). ATHENS Acr. 336, from Athens. Langlotz pl. 25, 1, and pl. 24; B, *Kl.* pl. 32, 2. I, uncertain subject: two warriors fighting at an altar. A–B, warriors making ready (A, chariot; B, chariot, arming). See *Kl.* 28–29 no. 79. The warriors on I might be Eteokles and Polyneikes, the subject of A–B the Seven against Thebes (see *Kl.* 28–29 no. 79; also Simon in *Ant. Kunst* 1960, 15). Later.

106 (94). LONDON E 73, from Camiros. *J. Phil.* 7 pll. A–B, whence (B) Robert *Scenen der Ilias* 10 fig. 15, Bulas fig. 19, Johansen *Iliaden* fig. 36; part of A, *Kl.* pl. 32, 1; the palmettes, Jacobsthal *O.* pl. 86, a. I, Peleus and Thetis; in a zone round this, Nereids fleeing to Nereus and Triton. A, Herakles and Kyknos. B, fight (Diomed and Aeneas). Later.

107 (95). BOLOGNA PU 270, probably from Chiusi or near. *Mus. It.* 3, 260–2; *CV.* pll. 111–12 and pl. 113, 1. Deeds of Theseus: I, Theseus and Minotaur; A, Kerkyon, Procrustes; B, bull, Skiron. Restored. Late. See p. 1632.

The Kleophrades Painter has an important *black-figure* side. For his *black-figure* vases see *ABV.* 404–6, 696, and 715. No. 2 of the list there (Louvre F 279) is now cleaned. No. 6 (New York 07.286.79): detail of A, *Op. Ath.* 2 pl. 4 fig. 12; A (after *Dev.*) Frel *Ř.V.* fig. 225. No. 9 (Leyden PC 6): A, *Gids G.V.* fig. 8. No. 19 (once Robinson): *AJA* 1956 pl. 12 and pl. 13, 59–60: now St. Louis, Mylonas. Of the panathenaics in the manner of the Kleophrades Painter, the obverse of Louvre F 276 (*ABV.* 405, foot, no. 3), as Bothmer tells me, is now partly cleaned, and the greater part of Athena's head seen to be alien—from another panathenaic; the obverse, as was said in *ABV.*, is very close to the painter, while the reverse is not at all like him.

Add to his prize Panathenaics

SWISS PRIVATE. A, Athena; B, chariot. Device, as usual in the Kleophrades Painter's panathenaics, Pegasos.

The fragment of a prize Panathenaic, Heidelberg 241, connected in *ABV.* 406 no. 8 with the Cleophradean Panathenaics, is published in *CV.* pl. 38, 3.

See also pp. 1632–3.

To consider, whether the vases by the Boot Painter, chiefly cups (p. 820), which are close to the late work of the Kleophrades Painter, may not be late work by the Kleophrades Painter himself.

Small fragments of a fine piece or fine pieces may be by the Kleophrades Painter. They may be from one vase, but this was not clear to me at the time.

SKYPHOS (OR SKYPHOI)

LEIPSIC T 3840, fr. Wedding of Peleus. This must be the subject: what remains is ear, shoulders, back of head (with the himation covering it) of a woman to left, inscribed ΘΕΤΙϟ, then the top of a quiver, which must belong to Apollo or Artemis.

LEIPSIC, two frr. On one, (feet—the right frontal, the left to right—of one standing, with the lower edge of the chiton), on the other, (part of a chair-leg, and feet of one standing to left, with the lower edge of the chiton).

LEIPSIC, fr. (Ankles of one standing to left, with the lower edge of the chiton).

NEAR THE KLEOPHRADES PAINTER
(i)

In his earliest period.

PSYKTER

1 (5). ATHENS, Agora, P 7240, frr., from Athens. Athletes. [Talcott].

CUP

2 (a). NEW YORK 56.171.62 (ex Torr and Hearst). *Cat. Sotheby July 2 1929* pl. 5, 1; *AJA.* 1945, 474, 1; *Bull. Metr.* summer 1962, 7, 7. I, symposion (man reclining, playing kottabos).

Perhaps also

NECK-AMPHORA
(with convex handles)

VIENNA 3723 (ex Oest. Mus. inv. 1091). *AEM.* 5 pl. 4, whence Hoppin i, 335, *AJA.* 1936, 110 fig. 13, (A) Pfuhl fig. 331; Lücken pll. 83–84, whence (B) Licht ii, 154; detail of A, *AJA.* 1936, 110 fig. 15; A and detail of B, *AM.* 62 pll. 23–24; *CV.* pl. 53. A, boxer; B, athlete scraping. [Richter]. The inscriptions, which are faint, were formerly read as signatures of Epiktetos, but are probably meaningless; see den Tex in *AM.* 62, 38–40, and Miss Richter in *AM.* 1936, 109–12.

I omit the hydria (kalpis, with picture on the body) Munich 2424 (J. 788), from Agrigento (Buschor *G. Vasen* 146 fig. 165), no. 4 in my previous list.

(ii)

Two vases by one hand, near the late style of the Kleophrades Painter. *ARV.*[1] 130, iii.

OINOCHOAI
(shape 5A)

(1). LOUVRE G 242. Two athletes.

(2). NAPLES 3105, from Ruvo. Ph. So. 11069, iv. 1. Two youths.

(iii)

A rough vase recalls the late style of the Kleophrades Painter, and his follower the Boot Painter. Imitation.

HYDRIA

(with picture on the shoulder, framed)

(a). LOUVRE G 177. Pottier pl. 126; *CV.* pl. 54, 1 and 3. Herakles and the lion. Now cleaned.

(iv)

The following recall the bf. neck-amphorae by the Kleophrades Painter (*ABV.* 405 nos. 17–20 and p. 715):

BF. NECK-AMPHORAE

(α)

1. LONDON MARKET (Spink: ex Burg). A, Herakles and the bull; B, Herakles, Athena, and Hermes.
2. ATHENS, Agora P 19879, fr., from Athens. A, Triptolemos.

(β)

Four that go together:

1. LUCERNE MARKET (A.A.). A, Dionysos and two maenads; behind him a goat; B, maenad and two satyrs, all running; behind her a goat.
2. LUCERNE MARKET (A.A.). A, Herakles and Amazons; B, Herakles and Centaurs. Described by Bothmer *Am.* 225 no. 133 *bis.* See the next.
3. LOUVRE F 271, from Vulci. *CV.* pl. 56, 9–10 and pl. 55, 7. A, Herakles in battle. B, Theseus and the bull. Attributed by Bothmer (*Am.* 225) to the same hand as the last.
4. MONTAUBAN, from Vulci. A, *Gaz. B.-A.* 1934, 148. A, Centauromachy (Kaineus); B, two Centaurs.

Bloesch (*FAS.* 117 and *JHS.* 71, 32) has assigned the following vase to the same *potter* as three amphorae by the Kleophrades Painter (pp. 181–2 nos. 1, 3, and 4) and a bf. amphora of the Leagros Group, Munich 1416 (*ABV.* 367 no. 90):

AMPHORA

(type A)

FERRARA, T. 125, from Spina. Aurigemma[1] 57, middle = [2]59 middle. Black. At each handle a rf. palmette with a billet-band above it.

A neck-amphora, in shape and in type of decoration, goes with those by the Kleophrades Painter (pp. 183-4 nos. 11-18), but the figure-work is not in the least like his. The style is mannered; but the vase does not belong to the Mannerist Group.

NECK-AMPHORA
(*with twisted handles*)

PALERMO V 744. *CV*. pl. 26, 1 and 4-5. Komos (A, youth playing the flute; B, youth). Late.

Another vase, as was noted in *JHS*. 36, 124, is linked with Cleophradean neck-amphorae by shape and ornament, although the drawing has no connexion with the Kleophrades Painter:

NECK-AMPHORA
(*with twisted handles*)

WÜRZBURG 502, from Vulci. Gerhard pl. 11, 1-2, whence *El.* 3 pl. 8 and (A) Overbeck *KM*. pl. 12, 1; Langlotz pl. 169; *Delt.* 1930-1, 76-77. A, Poseidon. B, man.

CHAPTER 15

THE BERLIN PAINTER

THE BERLIN PAINTER

JHS. 31, 276–95. *Burl. Mag.* 28, 137–8. *VA.* 35–40 and 953. *JHS.* 42, 70–98. *Att. V.* 76–88 and 469. *BSR.* 11, 20–21. *Der Berliner Maler. Mon. Piot* 35, 49–72 (Merlin and Beazley). *ARV.*¹ 131–46 and 952. Peters *Pan.* 71–75. *AJA.* 1943, 448–50. *JHS.* 70, 23–34 (Martin Robertson). *Dev.* 94–95 and 117–18. *ABV.* 407–9 and 847. *AJA.* 1958, 55–66 (Martin Robertson). *Ant. Kunst* 4, 49–67.

The Berlin Painter (Painter of the Berlin Amphora 2160) issues from the group of Euthymides and Phintias; and the Providence Painter, Hermonax, the Achilles Painter were his pupils.

The earlier vases are the best, and among them are many of the masterpieces of vase-painting. In what I call the middle period the drawing grows conventional, and in the late period mechanical. In the late period it is not always easy to tell the artist's own work from imitations; and over each of the vases marked 'late' in the list this question arises.

Martin Robertson has shown that the two vases attributed in *ARV.*¹ 27–28 to a 'Vienna Painter', whom I had thought of as a forerunner of the Berlin Painter, are really very early works by the Berlin Painter himself. Miss Talcott and Martin Robertson have shown that the cup with the signature of the potter Gorgos (no. 242) is a still earlier work by the Berlin Painter.

AMPHORAE

(nos. 1–2, type A)

(the pictures not framed)

1 (1). BERLIN 2160, from Vulci. Gerhard *EKV.* pll. 8–9; *Jh.* 3 pll. 3–4, pl. 5, 1 and p. 121; *JHS.* 31 pll. 15–16 and p. 276, whence (A) Perrot 10 pl. 17 and (incompletely) Buschor *Satyrtänze* fig. 70; FR. pl. 159, 2 and iii, 255, whence (A) Pfuhl fig. 473, (A) *Berl.* pl. 2, (A) Seltman pl. 23, (A) *G.V. Celle* 21, (A) LS. fig. 72; Lücken pll. 52–53, whence (detail of A, redrawn) Richter *ARVS.* 63 fig. 22; *Berl.* pll. 1 and 3–5 and pl. 22, 2, whence (B) LS. fig. 73; B, Neugebauer pl. 43, whence Diepolder *G.V.* frontispiece; A, Buschor *G. Vasen* 166–7; B, Bielefeld *ZV.* pl. 12; A, Stella 94; A, Pretzell 32; part of A, *E.A.A.* ii, 59. A, satyr and Hermes; B, satyr. See *Berl.* 7, and, for the subject, *Dev.* 114 note 15; also Buschor *Satyrtänze* 99–100, and Martin Robertson in *JHS.* 70, 25 note 9. Early. See p. 1633.

2 (2). LOUVRE CA 2981, from Vulci. *Mon. Piot* 35 pl. 4 and pp. 67–68; there completed by a fragment ex Florence (*CV.* Florence pl. 14, 325; *Mon. Piot* 35, 68: see ibid. 66–67). A, Dionysos; B, satyr. Early. See p. 1633.

(*no. 3, type C*)

3 (3). NEW YORK 56.171.38 (ex Hearst), from Nola. *Cat. Sotheby May 22 1919* pl. 11; *JHS.* 42, 72–73 and pl. 2; *Berl.* pl. 21, whence (A) Buschor *Bilderwelt* 39, (A) Kraiker *M.G.* pl. 30; *Bull. Metr.* March 1957, 176 and cover. A, citharode; B, judge. See *JHS.* 42, 70–74; and below, p. 1633. Early.

PANATHENAIC AMPHORA, OR AMPHORA

4. NAPLES, Astarita, 140, fr. Athlete (discus-thrower?). The head of a youth remains, to left, with his raised forefinger.

PANATHENAIC AMPHORAE

(*no. 5, with framed pictures*)

5 (13). VATICAN, from Vulci. *Mus. Greg.* 2 pl. 58, 2; phs. Al. 35775–6, whence *Berl.* pl. 11, Stella 133 and pl. 2, (A) *E.A.A.* i, 764. A, Athena; B, Hermes. See *Berl.* 9, and, for the subject of A, CB. ii, 42–43. Early.

(*nos. 6–19, the pictures not framed*)

6 (5). MUNICH 2310 (J. 1), from Vulci. A, *VA.* 35; A, *JHS.* 42 pl. 4, 1; A, *Berl.* pl. 7, 2; *CV.* pl. 192 and pl. 198, 1–2. A, discus-thrower; B, jumper. Very early. See p. 1633.

7 (6). CAB. MÉD. 386, plus, four frr. Three of them, de Ridder 280; B, *Berl.* pl. 13, 1. A, Nike. B, woman with oinochoe and phiale. The unpublished fragment gives the front of a left foot, to right. Early.

8 (7). WÜRZBURG 500, from Vulci. Overbeck *KM.* pl. 24, 6 (reversed); FR. pl. 134, 2, whence Perrot 10, 632–3, *Berl.* pl. 9, 2, Pfeiff pl. 13, Schuchhardt and Technau 201 fig. 167, Stella pl. 5; B, Langlotz *G.V.* pl. 14; B, Pfuhl fig. 472, whence Frel *Ř.V.* fig. 170; B, Schaal fig. 17; B, *Berl.* pl. 8, 2; Langlotz pll. 165–6 and 183; A, Buschor *G. Vasen* 170 fig. 190; details, Pfeiff, Beil. 2 at p. 40, 3; A, *Hist. rel.* 113; B, Lane pl. 79; B, Schuchhardt and Technau 200; detail of A, Buschor *Bilderwelt* 35; A, *E.A.A.* ii, 60 fig. 97. The struggle for the tripod: A, Apollo; B, Herakles. See *Berl.* 8. Early. See p. 1633.

9 (8). MUNICH 2311 (J. 52), from Vulci. A, *JHS.* 31, 278; A, *VA.* 36; *JHS.* 42 pl. 5; A, Langlotz *G.V.* pl. 25, 37; *Berl.* pl. 6, whence (A) R. M. Cook pl. 41; Lullies and Hirmer pll. 59–61, whence (part of A) LS. fig. 74; B, Buschor *Bilderwelt*, cover; *CV.* pl. 193 and pl. 195, 1–2; part of A, *E.A.A.* ii, 57. A, satyr; B, satyr. See *Berl.* 7–8; and below, p. 1633. Early.

10 (9). MONTPELLIER 130, from Vulci. *El.* 2 pl. 16, whence *JHS.* 42, 75; *R.E.A.* 1937 pl. 1 and p. 187; detail of A, Wegner *Mus.* pl. 31, a; *Recueil Dugas* pl. 8. 1. A, citharode; B, man. Restored. Early.

11 (10). MUNICH 2312 (J. 54), from Vulci. Micali *Mon. ined.* pl. 44, 3; FR. pl. 134, 1 and iii, 77, whence *Berl.* pl. 9, 1; A, Langlotz *G.V.* pl. 31, 47; Lullies and Hirmer pll. 56–58, whence LS. fig. 78; *CV.* pl. 194 and pl. 195, 2–4; *AJA.* 1958 pl. 8. A, Perseus; B, Gorgon. Early. See p. 1633.

12 (11). MUNICH 2313 (J. 9), from Vulci. A, Kietz fig. 6; A, FR. i, 155 fig. 5; A, *JHS*. 31 pl. 8, 2; *JHS*. 42 pl. 4, 2 and p. 83; A, *Berl*. pl. 7, 3, whence LS. fig. 77; detail of B, Hussong 22; *CV*. pl. 196, pl. 198, 3–4, and p. 25; B.Ap. xvi. 62. A, discus-thrower; B, youth. On A, ⊰OⱤPATE⊰ⱤALO⊰ retr. Early.

13 (12). VATICAN, from Vulci. *Mus. Greg.* 2 pl. 58, 1; A, ph. Mo., whence *JHS*. 31 pl. 8, 1 and Schröder *Sport* pl. 57, 1; phs. Al. 35773–4, whence *JHS*. 42 pl. 3, and (A) *Berl*. pl. 7, 1, whence LS. fig. 76; B.Ap. xxi. 98.1; A, ph. Marb. O. 29173. A, discus-thrower; B, man. Early. See p. 1633.

14 (14). FLORENCE 3989. Parts, Poulsen *Etr.* pl. 8; part, *CV*. pl. 25, 2, pl. 27, and pl. 28, 1; (with the two new fragments added by Neri) Bothmer *Am.* pl. 73, 1. A, Amazon; B, Amazon. Early.

15 (15). PHILADELPHIA 31.16.11, from Vulci. *Mus. J.* 23, 27–30; A, *Univ. Mus. Bull.* 3, 40. A, Nike. B, youth. [Dohan]. Early.

16 (16). BRYN MAWR P 188, fr. *AJA.* 1916, 334; *JHS*. 31 pl. 10, 1; *Berl*. pl. 12, 5, whence *Jh*. 37, 47. A, Athena. Early.

17 (17). ATHENS Acr. 614 a, fr., from Athens. *JHS*. 42, 79; Langlotz pl. 48. B, youth. Early.

18 (18). NAPLES RC 63, from Cumae. *ML*. 22 pl. 82, whence (B) *JHS*. 42, 77, (A) Bethe *Gr. Dichtung* 128, (A) *Berl*. pl. 10 (whence Rumpf *MZ*. pl. 23, 4), (A) Greifenhagen *Eroten* 16; detail of A, *Berl*. pl. 12, 4. A, Eros; B, youth. Early.

19 (19). LEYDEN PC 87 (xviii h 34), from Vulci. *JHS*. 31 pl. 13. A, hoplito-dromos; B, hoplitodromos. Early.

NECK-AMPHORAE

(nos. 20–30, large, with twisted handles)

20 (20). OXFORD 1930.169. *Cat. Sotheby June 18 1930* pl. 5. A, Amazon; B, Amazon. Now cleaned. Early.

21 (21). LONDON E 266, from Vulci. *JHS*. 31 pll. 11–12 and p. 281; *CV*. pl. 8, 3; *Berl*. pl. 14. Komos (A, man; B, youth). Still early. See p. 1633.

22 (22). MUNICH 2319 (J. 8), from Vulci. A, Langlotz *G.V.* pl. 31, 48; A, Pfuhl fig. 764. A, citharode; B, youth. Middle. See p. 1633.

23 (23). LENINGRAD 612 (St. 1638). A, *CR.* 1875, 66. A, citharode; B, man. Middle.

24 (24). LONDON E 268, from Vulci. *El.* 1 pl. 76; *CV*. pl. 9, 2 and pl. 10, 2. A, Athena; B, Hermes. Middle. On B, to right of the knee, there is a 'ghost': the lower edge of a chiton.

25 (25). LEYDEN PC 74 (xviii h 33), from Vulci. *El.* 1 pl. 76 a, whence *Gaz. B.–A.* 1931, 81–82 figs. 11–12; part of A, *Gids G.V.* cover. A, Athena; B, Nike. Middle.

26 (26). BERLIN 2339, from Vulci. B.Ap. xviii. 61, and xxi. 9. A, citharode; B, man. Middle. See p. 1633.

27 (27). LONDON E 269, from Nola. *CV.* pl. 9, 3 and pl. 10, 3. Warrior leaving home: A, young warrior; B, woman. Restored. Middle.

28 (28). LONDON E 267, from Vulci. *Archaeologia* 31 pl. 4, whence Jahn *Dichter* pl. 4, 3–4; *CV.* pl. 9, 1 and pl. 10, 1; *Berl.* pl. 8, 1 and pl. 17, 2. Komos (A, man; B, youth). Middle.

29 (29). VATICAN, from Vulci. *Mus. Greg.* 2 pl. 59, 3. Warrior leaving home (A, warrior; B, old man). Much restored: the lower halves of figures and of vase are modern. Middle.

30 (30). MUNICH 2318 (J. 5), from Vulci. Thiersch *Hell. V.* pl. 5, 2; B, Lau pl. 25, 1; cleaned, *CV.* pl. 210, 1–2 and pl. 211, 6–7. The struggle for the tripod: A, Apollo; B, Herakles. Middle.

(no. 31, large, with ridged handles)

31 (31). LOUVRE G 198, from Vulci. A, Pottier pl. 128; *CV.* pl. 34, 6 and 4 and 7 and pl. 36, 3. A, Nike; B, youth. Now cleaned. Middle.

(nos. 32–44, large, the handles missing)

32. LOUVRE C 10841. A, flute-player; B, man. On A, youth, standing to right, in long sleeveless garment; B, in himation, standing to left. On A, [?AN]TIO+[OS. Many of the fragments were put together by Villard. Early.

33. NAPLES, Astarita, 118, fr. A, Athena (legs, moving to right, with spear). Early.

34 (32). CAMBRIDGE 4.1930. Langlotz *Heyl* pll. 22–23; cleaned, *CV.* pl. 25, 1 and pl. 28, 4–5. A, Amazon; B, Amazon. Early.

35 (33). LOUVRE G 199, part, fr. A, Pottier pl. 128; *CV.* pl. 34, 3 and pl. 36, 1. A, Nike. Much restored. Mouth, neck, handles, foot, of the vase are modern. The ancient part of the reverse is by the Berlin Painter, but does not certainly belong: see the next. Early.

36. LOUVRE G 199, part, fr. *CV.* pl. 34, 8. Male. What is ancient is the feet with a little of the lower edge of the himation, and good part of the pattern-band. The fragment need not be from the same vase as the Nike: it may belong to Louvre C 10842 (no. 37). This portion has been cleaned.

37. LOUVRE C 10842, fr. B, youth (to left, in himation: the greater part of the head remains, with the left shoulder and arm). A Louvre fragment with right hand and half the forearm may belong. See the last. Middle.

38. LOUVRE, fr. (three joining). (Toes of one moving quickly to right, and the same pattern-band as in Louvre G 199 (no. 36)). Might be from the same vase as the next.

39 (187). LOUVRE C 261 *bis*, fr. Male in chlamys moving to right, spears in right hand: the middle remains. See the last.

40 (186, +). LOUVRE C 10843, fr. Hermes (moving to right, looking round). Middle.

41. NAPLES, Astarita, 600, frr. Warrior leaving home: A, young warrior with phiale (shield-device a horse); B, woman with oinochoe. The figures are nearly complete.

42 (a, β). VIENNA, Univ., 631e, and FLORENCE 14 B 4, fr., from Orvieto? *JHS*. 51, 51 fig. 7, whence *CV*. Vienna Univ. 25; the Florence part, *CV*. Florence pl. 14, B 4; the Vienna, *CV*. Vienna Univ. pl. 13, 1. A, warrior. A fragment in Vienna University may belong: it has part of a maeander-band (stopt maeander, addorsed).

43 (34). BONN 464. 25–27, two frr. (from Cervetri according to Greifenhagen, but from Orvieto according to Hartwig). *CV*. pl. 12, 1. A, warrior; B, warrior. Middle.

44 (35). VILLA GIULIA (part ex Florence), four frr. One fr., *CV*. Florence pl. 13, B 62. A, Zeus pursuing, B, Ganymede. See *CF*. 21, right. Middle.

(no. 45, small, fat, with triple handles)

45 (42). OXFORD 1924.3. A, *Spink G.R.A.* 28 no. 55; *CV*. pl. 15, 3–4. A, Zeus and Nike. B, two athletes. Early. For the shape see *ARV*. 517.

(nos. 46–52, small, with double handles: doubleens)

46 (36). MADRID 11114 (L. 184). Gerhard *AB*. pl. 68, 1–2, whence Schreiber 5; A, Norman Gardiner *Athl*. fig. 129; A, *Berl*. pl. 15, 1; *CV*. pl. 22, 2. A, discus-thrower; B, youth. Early.

47. BALTIMORE, Walters Art Gallery, 48. 57. *Journ. Walt*. 15–16, 24–26; detail of A, *Archaeology* Summer 1953, 66, above, and cover; B, museum postcard. A, discus-thrower; B, youth. Early.

48 (37). BOULOGNE 656. A, *El*. 4 pl. 49; *Berl*. pl. 16. A, Eros; B, youth. Early.

49 (38). HARVARD 1227.150 (old 1643.95). A, *VA*. 39; A, Hambidge 45 and frontispiece; A, *Berl*. pl. 17, 1; *CV*. pl. 16, 3. A, Triton; B, Nereid. Early.

50 (39). MADRID 11118 (L. 185), from Nola. *Berl*. pl. 18; *CV*. pl. 22, 1 and pl. 26, 2. A, Ajax quarrelling with, B, Odysseus. Still early.

51 (40). BERLIN MARKET (Graupe: ex Prinz Albrecht 911). *VDK*. pl. 82. Komos: A, youth dancing; B, man dancing. Much restored. Still early.

52 (41). CAPUA 217, from Capua. *CV*. pl. 4, 1, 3–4, and 8. A, man; B, youth. Still early.

(nos. 53–61, small: Nolan amphorae, or doubleens: the handles lost)

53. LOUVRE C 10859, fr. Komast (head and breast of a man moving to right, looking round). C 10860–C 10863 may be from the same vase and C 10864 might possibly belong. Early.

54. LOUVRE C 10860, fr. Komast (head, breast, and right upper arm of a youth moving to right). See the last. Early.

55. LOUVRE C 10861, fr. (End of a cloak). See Louvre C 10859. Early.

56. LOUVRE C 10862, fr. (Middle of a komast with stick and cloak to right). See Louvre C 10859. Early.

57. LOUVRE C 10863, fr. (Male foot to right, with ivy-border below). See Louvre C 10859. Early.

58. LOUVRE C 10865, fr. (Right breast, and waist, with extended right arm, of a male in a himation standing to left). See the next. Early.

59. LOUVRE C 10866, fr. (Middle of a male in a himation to right). Might possibly belong to Louvre C 10865. Early.

60. BERLIN, Goethert, fr. *Anz.* 1958, 11, a. A, Eros (flying to right). The upper part remains. [Peters]. Still early.

61 (47). MUNICH inv. 8541, plus, frr. One fr., *CV.* pl. 102, 5. A, horseman; B, youth (in himation, standing to left). Unpublished fragments in Munich give the tail of the horse and part of its forelegs, and the greater part of the figure on B. Still early.

(nos. 62–99, Nolan amphorae, with triple handles)

62 (48). NAPLES 3137, from Nola. A, ph. So. 11069, iii, 1. Warrior leaving home (A, young warrior; B, woman). Early.

63 (49). LOUVRE G 201, from Nola. B, Pottier pl. 129; *CV.* pl. 36, 7–9 and 12. Symposion: A, Dionysos and satyr reclining; B, satyr drawing wine; under each handle a large ivy-leaf. Early.

64 (50). MANNHEIM 11, from Capua. *CV.* pl. 24, 1, pl. 25, 1–2, and p. 37. A, man offering lyre to youth; B, youth. Early.

65 (51). MANCHESTER III. I. 40 (ex Marshall Brooks). Part of A, *Mem. Manch.* 89 pl. 1; part of A, *AJA.* 1958 pl. 7 fig. 6; detail of A, R. M. Cook pl. 37, a. A, Herakles and Centaur; B, Centaur. Early.

66 (52). NAPLES 3192, from Nola. B, ph. So. x, i, 5. A, athlete with acontion. B, youth. Restored, B much. Early.

67 (53). VIENNA 654. *Berl.* pl. 19; *CV.* pl. 54, 1–2 and p. 10. A, warrior; B, naked youth with spear. Early.

68 (54). NAPLES 3087, from Nola. A, ph. So. 11072, iii, 6. A, citharode; B, man. Early.

69 (55). DRESDEN 289. A, Walter Müller 135, 3. A, Triptolemos; B, Demeter. The neck-palmettes are modern. Early.

70 (56). NEW YORK 07.286.69, from Capua. A, *VA.* 37; B, *N.Y. Shapes* 6, 4 = Richter and Milne fig. 18; A, *Berl.* pl. 15, 2; Richter and Hall pl. 18 and pl. 169, 16. A, satyr; B, satyr. Early.

71 (57). YALE 133. Baur pl. 8, whence (A) Poulsen *Etr.* pl. 10, 17; shape, Hambidge 57. A, Athena; B, Hermes. Middle.

72 (58). NAPLES 3150, from Nola. A, ph. So. 11069, ii, 7. Warrior leaving home (A, young warrior; B, old man). Middle.

73 (59). CARLSRUHE 203 (B 95), from Nola. Welter pl. 14, 30; *CV*. pl. 15, 1 and 3 and (ghost) p. 25. A, Zeus and Athena; B, Nike. Late.

74 (60). ROME, Museo Barracco, 231. A, Nike with cithara; B, citharode. If this is the Castellani vase described in *Bull*. 1868, 219, then from Capua. Late.

75 (61). LOS ANGELES A 5933.50.33 (ex Marshall Brooks). Tischbein 3 pl. 7, whence *El.* 1 pl. 99; A, Tillyard pl. 9, 92; detail of A, *Hesp*. 24 pl. 7, c. A, Nike with cithara; B, youth. Late.

76 (62). LENINGRAD 697 (St. 1628). A, Athena running; B, woman running. Late.

77. SWISS PRIVATE. A, Athena running; B, woman running. On A, to right, holding spear and helmet. B, in chiton, to right, looking round, arms extended to left and right. Restored. Late.

78 (63). TARTU 104, from Capua. Malmberg and Felsberg pl. 3, 3–4. A, Zeus pursuing, B, a woman. Late.

79 (64). ZURICH, Roš (ex Giesecke). A, Nike (standing to right, with torches). B, youth. Late.

80 (65). NEW YORK 41.162.17. *CV*. Gallatin pl. 51, 2. A, Poseidon; B, youth (perhaps Theseus?). Late.

81 (66). LOUVRE G 218, from Capua. *CV*. pl. 41, 7–9. Komos (A, man; B, youth with lyre). Late.

82 (67). FRANKFORT, Mus. V.F., from Agrigento. Schaal *F*. pl. 46; B, *Die Weltkunst* 27, v, 10, above, right. Komos (A, youth with lyre; B, old man). Late.

83 (68). GELA, Salvatore Nocera, from Gela. Komos (A, man with stick; B, youth with stick and skyphos). Graffito ΑΙ. Late.

84 (69). LONDON E 310, from Gela. *CV*. pl. 56, 1. A, young warrior pursuing a woman; B, old man. Late.

85 (70). ZURICH 418, from Nola. A and part of B, *RM*. 58, 187 and 185. A, Apollo pursuing, B, a woman. Restored. Late.

86. ROME, Romagnoli, from Gela. Phs. R.I.42.319 and 321 and 350, whence *RM*. 58 pl. 13, pl. 14, 1, and p. 179. A, Herakles and Apollo: the struggle for the tripod; B, woman (Artemis?). [Tullia Romagnoli]. Late.

87 (71). LONDON E 313, from Nola. Cook *Zeus* ii pl. 1; *CV*. pl. 57, 1. A, Zeus pursuing, B, a woman. Late.

88 (72). NAPLES inv. 126053, from Capua. Ghali-Kahil *H*. pl. 59. A, Menelaos pursuing, B, Helen. Restored. Late.

89 (73). OXFORD 1930.36. A, Nike with hydria; B, youth running. Late.

90 (74). LOUVRE G 204, from Vulci. Dubois *Descr. Pourt*. 27; *Cat. Pourtalès-Gorgier* 29; Cook *Zeus* ii, 745; Pottier pl. 129; *CV*. pl. 37, 8–9 and pl. 38, 1–2; A, *Mon. Piot* 35, 89; A, *Mnemosyne* 4th ser., 3 pl. 2, 4. A, Zeus and, B, Giant. Late.

91. SCARSDALE (N.Y.), private. *Auktion xviii Basel* pl. 38, 118. A, Dionysos; B, maenad. Late.

92 (75). OXFORD 275. *JHS.* 13, 137; *CV.* pl. 17, 7 and pl. 18, 3. A, Eos. B, old man. Late.

93 (76). NAPLES 3214. A, citharode; B, man. Late.

94 (77). BRUSSELS R 307. *CV.* pl. 15, 2. Warrior leaving home (A, warrior and woman; B, old man). Late.

95 (79). VILLA GIULIA 50736, from Cervetri. R.I. xvii. 40. A, acontist running; B, athlete with acontion. Late.

96 (80). LOUVRE G 214, from Nola. *Bull. Nap.* N.S. 6 pl. 7, whence *Jb.* 2, 100, 1–2, *JHS.* 23, 270 fig. 1, Norman Gardiner *G.A.S.* 274, Norman Gardiner *Athl.* fig. 87; *CV.* pl. 40, 3–4 and 7 and 10. A, hoplitodromos; B, man. For the attitude on A, *BSA.* 46, 11 no. 10. Late.

97 (81). MISSISSIPPI (ex Robinson), from Gela. *CV.* Robinson ii pl. 27. A, Triptolemos; B, Demeter. Very late.

98 (82). BASLE 1906.297, from Capua. B, *Hist. Schätze Basels* fig. 3; Schefold *Basler Ant.* ii pl. 22. A, Zeus pursuing, B, a woman. Very late. School-piece?

99 (83). RHODES 13128, from Camiros. A, *Cl. Rh.* 4, 120, 5, and p. 123; A, *CV*, pl. 8, 1. Youth setting out (A, youth; B, old man). Very late. School-piece?

(no. 100, small: with twisted handles, a special model)

100 (45). OXFORD 274, from Gela. Gardner pl. 11; *CV.* pl. 15, 1–2. A, Nike with cithara; B, citharode. Late. School-piece?

(nos. 101–3, small, with twisted handles)

101 (43). VIENNA 741. A, Millin *Mon. ant.* 2 pl. 29; La Borde 2 pl. 34 and pl. 32, 1, whence *Annali* 1849 pl. D; detail of A, Bieber *G.K.* pl. 17, 3; A, Ghali-Kahil *H.* pl. 57, 1; *CV.* pl. 55, 1–2 and pl. 56. A, Menelaos pursuing Helen; B, woman fleeing. Restored. Late.

102 (44). HAVANA, Lagunillas (ex Wilfred Hall). A, Nike (moving to right, looking round, with torches); B, youth (standing to right, right arm extended). Late.

103 (46). COLOGNY, Bodmer (ex Passavant-Gontard 35 and Lederer). A, *Sg Passavant-Gontard* pl. 6, 35; *Aukt. Fischer 21 Mai 1941* pl. 6, 66; Schefold *M.* 205, 219. A, Apollo and Artemis; B, Nike. Same model as the Lagunillas vase (no. 102). Late.

(nos. 104–5. small, with ridged handles)

104. ST. LOUIS 57.55. Passeri pl. 101. A, Nike with cithara; B, citharode. Late. School-piece?

105. VILLA GIULIA, from Cervetri. Youth leaving home (A, youth and man; B, youth). Late.

(nos. 106–7, small, the handles lost)

106. NAPLES, Astarita, 106, fr. A, Dionysos and maenad (maenad standing to right with thyrsus, Dionysos standing to left with kantharos and thyrsus; between them a dog). Late. Probably from a vase like nos. 102–5.

107. CAPESTHORNE, Bromley-Davenport. *JHS*. 78 pl. 12, a–b. A, Eros. B, male. Late. Fragments inserted, as Bothmer tells me, into a black Campanian neck-amphora of the Owl-pillar Class. Now partly cleaned.

LOUTROPHOROS

108 (4). ERLANGEN 526, frr., from Athens. Buschor *Krok.* (= *Mü. Jb.* 1919) pl. 3, whence *AJA.* 1935 pl. 9. Fight (warriors and negroes). On the subject, Buschor *Krok.* 38–39, who compares the bf. amphora by Exekias in Philadelphia (3442: *Mus. J.* 6, 91–92, whence *Dev.* pl. 30; *AJA.* 1935 pl. 8; Technau pl. 23; *ABV.* 145 no. 14): the scene is doubtless laid at Troy, and the negroes are the followers of Memnon. Below, in silhouette, (part of a horseman: from the cavalcade at the funeral; with the gesture of valediction). Still early.

PELIKAI

(nos. 109–11, ordinary, with framed pictures)

109. VIENNA 3725 (ex Oest. Mus. 333), from Cervetri. *Mon.* 8 pl. 15, 1, whence *WV.* 1 pl. 1, 2 and Robert *Herm.* 104–5; FR. pl. 72 and ii, 80, whence Hoppin *Euth. F.* pl. 22, Pfuhl fig. 370 (= Pfuhl *Mast.* fig. 43), *Dedalo* 9, 452–3, Stella 677; A, Lücken pl. 85; *CV.* pll. 68–69 and p. 17. Death of Aigisthos (A, Orestes, Aigisthos, Chrysothemis; B, Klytaimestra, Talthybios). [Martin Robertson]. For the 'ghost' (FR. pl. 72, above, right; *CV.* pl. 69, 4) see *CV.* ii, 17. Very early. See the next.

110. FLORENCE 3985 (part ex Scheurleer). Part, *Mus. It.* 3 pl. 4, whence FR. ii, 81 and Hoppin *Euth. F.* pl. 23; part of A, ph. Al. 17072, 4; *CV.* pl. 31, 2 and pl. 32. A, Theseus and Minotaur; B, Theseus and Skiron. The publication in *CV.* includes the fragment ex Scheurleer added in *Att. V.* 65 (*CV.* Scheurleer pl. 3, 1) and the two Florence fragments added in *CF.* 20, right (*CV.* Florence pl. 13, B5 and pl. 19, B5): two more fragments in Florence join: one adding part of Theseus' left leg on B, with the left heel of Skiron; the other, part of the right-hand side-border on B with the tip of the last sigma. [Martin Robertson]. As Vienna 3725 (no. 109). Very early.

111 (85). VILLA GIULIA 50755. A, ph. G.F. E 18274; R.I. 1867.22. A, Herakles and Apollo: the struggle for the tripod. B, youth, man, and boy. Now cleaned. Early.

(nos. 112–13, ordinary, the pictures not framed)

112 (86). MADRID 11200. Komos (A, youth with lyre; B, man with skyphos). Early.

113 (87). VIENNA 3726 (ex Oest. Mus. 334), from Cervetri. A, Masner pl. 6; *CV.* pl. 71. A, Triptolemos; B, Demeter. Middle.

(*nos. 114–114 bis, neck-pelikai of special shape*)

114 (84). FERRARA, T. 867, from Spina. Aurigemma[1] 87, 2; 89; and ix = [2]93, 2; 95; ix and xiii; part, Arias and Alfieri pl. 12; B, Aurigemma and Alfieri pl. 12, b; Alfieri and Arias *S.* pll. 1–3. On the neck: A, lion; B, lioness. Early. See p. 1633.

114 *bis.* FERRARA, T. 41 D VP, from Spina. Early. Replica of the last.

CALYX-KRATERS

115 (88). CORINTH, fr., from Corinth. *AJA.* 1930, 336; *JHS.* 70, 27 fig. 4 and pl. 9, b. Fight. Very early.

116 (91). CORINTH, fr., from Corinth. (Foot to right, foot to left; on the cul, egg-pattern).

117 (89). ATHENS Acr. 742 and LONDON E 459, from Athens. Langlotz pll. 59–60; one of the London frr., *Berl.* pl. 32; detail of B, with a new fr. identified by Miss Pease, *Hesp.* 5, 260; another new fr. identified by her, *Hesp.* 4, 239, 26. A, Athena mounting chariot, with Zeus and Hermes. B, Apollo with Leto, Artemis, and Dionysos. Two new Athens fragments belong: one joins, adding part of the wheel and car on A; the other gives the top of one of the handle-florals. Early.

118 (90). WINCHESTER 44.4, fr. Herford 72; *Berl.* pl. 13, 4. (Nike). Early.

119 (92). ATHENS Acr. 732, frr., from Athens. Langlotz pl. 58; detail, *Epit. Tsounta* 498 pl. 2, 1. Uncertain subject. There are probably two figures on each side: (1) shanks and feet (of a woman?) to right; (2) upper part of a youth frontal, looking round to left, staff or the like, and something red, in the left hand; (3) goddess with torches; (4) Hermes. 1 and 2 may be from the same side, 3 and 4 from the other. I had thought of Triptolemos: A, Demeter and Triptolemos; B, Persephone and Hermes. But 2 and 1 might also be a bridegroom leading a bride (Peleus and Thetis). A new fragment in Athens joins, adding the elbow of Hermes and the end of his caduceus; another belongs, with part of the mouth of the vase. Early.

120. ATHENS Acr., fr., from Athens. (Part of a wing and of a staff or the like).

121 (93). SYRACUSE 15205, from Terravecchia near Grammichele. *Mon. Piot* 35, 72; A, *CV.* pl. 9, 2. A, Dionysos and satyr; B, maenad. Early.

122 (94). OXFORD 291, from Gela. *CV.* pl. 21, 3 and pl. 12, 6. A, Nike with tripod. B, youth. Middle.

BELL-KRATERS

(*with lugs*)

123 (95, +). LOUVRE G 174 and FLORENCE 12 B 105. *CV.* pl. 6, 8, pl. 7, 4, and

pl. 12, 2 (minus the Florence fr.); part of the Florence fr., *CV*. Florence pl. 12, B 105. A, Herakles resting, waited on by, B, a satyr. Now cleaned. The Florence fragment (two joining) gives the rest of the quiver and cord on A. Early.

124 (96). LOUVRE G 175. *Annali* 1876 pl. C, 2; *JHS*. 31, 284; *CV*. pl. 12, 5 and 7, and pl. 14, 3–4; A, *Berl*. pl. 20, whence LS. fig. 79, and Frel *Ř.V.* fig. 169; *Enc. phot*. iii, 12; *Ant. Kunst* 2 pl. 6, 1–2; A, Robertson *G.P*. 98; A, ph. Gir. 19013. A, Ganymede; B, Zeus. Restored. Early. See p. 1633.

125 (97). ROMAN MARKET (Depoletti), from Cervetri. B.Ap. xxii. 83, 2. A, Ganymede. B, youth. Much restored.

126 (98). TARQUINIA RC 7456, from Tarquinia. A, ph. Mo. 8336, whence *JHS*. 31 pl. 10, 2; A, ph. And. 41014, 1, whence Romanelli *Tarqu*. 123, 1; A, ph. R.I. 1934.1883. A, Europa; B, woman running. Early. See p. 1633.

VOLUTE-KRATERS

127 (99). CAMBRIDGE 5.1952. *JHS*. 70 pll. 6–8, pl. 9, a, and p. 24. A, komast (man with kantharos and lyre). B, youth. On the neck: A, fight; B, fight. See Martin Robertson in *JHS*. 70, 23–34. Early.

128 (100). LEIPSIC T 762, fr. *JHS*. 70, 26. On the neck, athletes. Early.

129 (184). LOUVRE C 10799, fr. A, warrior (rushing to right). Early. See the next.

130 (101). LOUVRE, part of G 166, fr. (eleven joining). *CV*. pl. 19, 1 and pl. 18, 3. The pasticcio in which the fragment was formerly embedded (see p. 186 no. 51) has now been demolished and the genuine portion taken out. On the upper member of the neck, floral; on the lower member, (men, youth, boys). Early. Perhaps from the same vase as the last? Bothmer, who has examined the fragments since they were detached, reports that the floral ones join the others, and that parts of the handles are also preserved.

131. VILLA GIULIA, from Cervetri. A, Vighi 99. A, warrior; B, warrior (running to left). On the neck: A, Herakles and Kyknos; B, athletes. Early.

132 (102). LONDON E 468, from Cervetri. Gerhard pl. 204, whence Robert *Scenen der Ilias* 9 figs. 11–12; *JHS*. 31 pl. 14 and p. 283; detail, *BM. G.R. Life*[3] 94; *Berl*. pll. 29–31, whence (parts) Schoenebeck and Kraiker pl. 14, (A) Schnitzler pl. 45, (A) Stella 728, (B) Frel *Ř.V.* figs. 172–5; B, Lane pl. 78; A, Richter *H.G.A.* 334 fig. 449; ph. Ma. 3141. On the neck: A, Achilles and Memnon; B, Achilles and Hector. Early. See p. 1633.

COLUMN-KRATERS

133 (103). BRUNSWICK 544, fr. *CV*. pl. 22, 1. Part of the lip of the vase remains: on the topside, (lion). Early.

(the pictures not framed)

134 (104). LENINGRAD 635 (St. 1528). A, *CR.* 1873, 22; B, *JHS.* 42, 81 fig. 7. A, Nike. B, youth. On A, ΚΑL[ΟϚ] ϚΟΚΡΑΤΕϚ. Restored. Early.

135 (105). VILLA GIULIA 50510. R.I. xvii. 39. A, Nike. B, youth. Restored. Early.

136. MEGGEN, Käppeli. *Auction xvi Basle* pl. 28, 123, and pl. 29; Schefold *M.* 197. A, flute-player; B, youth. Restored. Early. See p. 1633.

STAMNOI

137 (106). MUNICH 2406 (J. 421), from Vulci. Gerhard pl. 201, whence (A) Robert *Scenen* 8 fig. 8, (A) Furtwängler *Aegina* i, 244; A and part of B, FR. pl. 106, 2 and ii, 234–5, whence (part of A) *Jh.* 37, 45; A, Pfuhl fig. 775; one figure on B, *Berl.* pl. 28, 1; A, Lullies and Hirmer pll. 62–63. A, fight (Athena present: Achilles and Hector?—compare the Providence Painter's stamnos in Barcelona, p. 639 no. 55); B, arming. Early. The ghost of another vase by the same painter, FR. ii, 236. See p. 1633.

138 (107, +). LOUVRE G 56. A, Pottier pl. 95; *CV.* pl. 6, 6–7 and pl. 12, 1 and 4; A, Langlotz *FGB.* pl. 14, 3; phs. Gir. 19559 and another. A, Athena mounting chariot. B, warriors and old man. Now cleaned, and the alien foot removed. Four Louvre fragments belong and have been added. Early.

139 (108). PALERMO V 762, from Chiusi. Inghirami *Chius.* pll. 46–47; Inghirami pll. 77–78 and pl. 381, whence (A) Overbeck *Gall.* pl. 8, 6, whence Baur *Centaurs* 108; *CV.* pll. 29–30. A, Peleus and Thetis approaching Chiron; B, women running to old man (Nereids and Nereus). On A, ΝΙΚΟϚΤΡΑΤΟϚΚΑLΟϚ. Early.

140 (109). LOUVRE G 186, from Chiusi. A, Fröhner *Coll. Barre* pl. 5, whence (redrawn) *JHS.* 1, 139; the Chiron, Morin-Jean 108; part of B, *JHS.* 42, 81 fig. 6; *CV.* pl. 20, 1 and 4; phs. Gir. 19020–1, whence (A) Radermacher *Mythos*² fig. 6, (A) Grimal 153. A, Peleus bringing Achilles to Chiron. B, man and two youths. Restored. Early. See p. 1633.

141 (110). CASTLE ASHBY, Northampton, 25. *BSR.* 11 pl. 8, pl. 9, 1, and p. 21; part of B, *Burl. Mag.* 28, 138, g; *Berl.* pl. 24, 2, pl. 27, 1–3, and pl. 28, 2. A, Athena with Zeus and Hera. B, warrior leaving home. See *BSR.* 11, 20–21. Early.

142 (111, +). LOUVRE G 185. *Mon.* 6–7 pl. 67; heads of the animals, Morin-Jean 186; *CV.* pl. 20, 2 and 5; phs. Gir. 19554–5. A, Dionysos riding a goat; B, Hermes riding a ram. Now cleaned, and the false mouth and the alien handles and foot removed. A good many Louvre fragments belong and have been added. Early.

143. LAUSANNE, Zafiropoulo. *Auktion xviii Basel* pl. 35, 113 and pl. 37, 113; Schefold *M.* 201, 213. A, youth and boy, and man; B, the like. Early. See p. 1633.

144 (112). OXFORD 1912.1165, from Cervetri. A, *Ashm. Report* 1912, 74; *JHS*. 31 pl. 17; the lion, *Burl. Mag*. 28, 137, c; *CV*. pl. 25, 1–2, pl. 20, 10–12, and pl. 30, 5–6; details, *Berl*. pl. 12, 3 and pl. 27, 4, whence (the lion) *Arte antica e moderna* 1, i pl. 6, c. Death of Pentheus. Now augmented by a fragment ex Heidelberg, see *CV*. ii p. vii. Early.

145 (113). CASTLE ASHBY, Northampton, 2. *BSR*. 11 pl. 9, 2, pl. 7, 5, and p. 22; detail, *Berl*. pl. 17, 3 (whence, incomplete, Bethe *Buch und Bild* 43 fig. 20) = *Mon. Piot* 35, 69; detail (= *BSR*. 11 pl. 9, 2), ibid. 70. Dionysos with satyrs and maenads. Much restored. See *BSR*. 11, 21. Early.

146 (114). BERLIN 2187, fr. *Mon. Piot* 35, 71. A, Dionysos and satyrs. Early.

147 (115). LEIPSIC T 652, fr. Warrior leaving home (old man, shield). Middle.

148 (116). VATICAN, from Vulci. *Mus. Greg*. 2 pl. 21, 1, whence (B) Panofka *Pos. u. Dion*. pl. 1, 5; B.Ap. xxii. 64. A, Zeus and Hera with Nike and Athena; B, Poseidon and Hermes; god and goddess. Restored. Middle to late.

149 (117). LONDON E 444, from Vulci. *CV*. pl. 21, 4. Apollo entering Olympus. Middle to late.

150 (118). BERLIN 2186, from Chiusi. *Annali* 1860 pl. L–M, whence (A) Roscher s.v. Boreas, 810. Boreas and Oreithyia. Restored. Late.

151 (122). BOSTON 91.227. A, Edward Robinson *Cat*. 152, whence *Jb*. 29, 30. A, death of Aigisthos. B, man with sceptre, and women. Late.

152 (121). BOSTON 91.226. Dionysos with maenads and satyrs. Late.

153 (124). CAB. MÉD. F 8422, fr. Ph. Gir. 33710, 1. (Women running). Late.

154 (119). NORTHWICK, Spencer-Churchill (part ex Leipsic T 662), frr. Ghali-Kahil *H*. pl. 60. Menelaos and Helen. Late. See the next.

155 (120). HEIDELBERG 182, fr. Kraiker pl. 30. (Woman). Might belong to the last? Late.

156. BASLE, Cahn, 3, fr. Zeus pursuing a woman. Late.

157 (a τ, +). LOUVRE C 10828. Theseus and Minotaur. The vase is now nearly complete. Late.

158 (123). LOUVRE G 371. Strube pl. 1, whence Overbeck *KM*. pl. 15, 20; *CV*. d pl. 10, 3, 5, 7, and 10, and pl. 11, 3; A, *Mél. d'arch*. 62 pl. 2, 4. Triptolemos. Late. See p. 1633.

159. LOUVRE C 10798. Triptolemos. Late.

(nos. 160–1, stamnoi of special shape, long-necked)

160 (125). LOUVRE G 192, from Vulci. *Gaz. arch*. 1875 pll. 14–15; A, Pottier pl. 27; detail of A, Richter *F*. fig. 164; *CV*. pl. 55; A, Villard *GV*. pl. 22;

A, ph. Gir. 17013. A, infant Herakles and the snakes; B, Zeus sending forth Hermes and Iris. Middle. See p. 1633.

161. MUNICH inv. 8738. Peleus and Thetis. [Cahn]. See p. 1633.

HYDRIAI

(nos. 162–8, of bf. shape)

162 (126). BOSTON 03.838, fr. JHS. 70, 33; CB. iii, suppl. pl. 18, 2. Herakles and Cerberus. On the shoulder, floral. See CB. iii, text. Early.

163. HAVANA, Lagunillas, from Vulci? Mon. Piot 20 pl. 5 and p. 72; R.I. ix. 116. Herakles and Apollo: the struggle for the tripod. Early. Now cleaned. See p. 1633.

164 (127). ABERDEEN 695. JHS. 70, 29 and 31. Peleus and Thetis. Early.

165 (128). LONDON E 162, from Vulci. CV. pl. 70, 3; JHS. 70, 27 fig. 5. Herakles and Nereus. Early. See p. 1633.

166 (129). VATICAN, from Vulci. Mus. Greg. 2 pl. 15, 1; Mon. 1 pl. 46; Micali Storia pl. 94; phs. Al. 35778–9, whence Int. Studio Feb. 1927, 23, Berl. pl. 26 (whence LS. fig. 75), Pfeiff pl. 10, (part) Buschor G. Vasen 171; Berl. pl. 25, whence Frel Ř.V. fig. 171; part, Pfeiff pl. 11; ph. Mo. 8575; phs. And. 42071–2, whence Stella 177. Apollo seated on a winged tripod, travelling over the sea. For the subject see ABV. 685; for the shape, only, compare a bf. hydria in Frankfort, Städel Institut (Schaal F. pl. 12; the shoulder-picture, Bothmer Am. pl. 58, 1). Early. See p. 1634.

167 (130). MADRID 11117 (L. 160). Alvarez-Ossorio pl. 35, 3; detail, Burl. Mag. 28, 137, b; the chief picture, BSA. 36 pl. 23; CV. pl. 13, 1; the shoulder, Greifenhagen Eroten 13; R.I. ix. 116. Woman and girl at fountain. On the shoulder, Eros, between florals. Both pictures restored. The shoulder-picture is not free from restoration as Greifenhagen was informed from Madrid: repainting in the middle of the body, in the left forearm, in the feet, and in the right wing. Early.

168 (131). CAB. MÉD. 439, from Vulci. Ph. Gir. 8075, whence Cook Zeus ii, 26. Zeus pursuing a woman. On the shoulder, chariot. Middle to late.

(nos. 169–83, kalpides, the picture on the shoulder, not framed)

169 (132). NEW YORK 10.210.19, from Falerii. Bull. Metr. 6, 34 fig. 14; JHS. 31 pl. 9 and p. 285; Hdbk Cl. Coll. 122; Int. Studio Feb. 1927, 22; Berl. pl. 22, 1; Richter and Hall pl. 16 and pl. 172, 14, whence E.A.A. ii, 60 fig. 98; details, Richter ARVS. 40 fig. 7; p. 60; and p. 64 fig. 26; Richter Gk Ptg 9, 2; Richter H. 213, g; Bothmer Am. pl. 71, 1. Achilles and Penthesilea. Very early.

170 (133). BALTIMORE, Walters Art Gallery, 48.79. Bothmer Am. pl. 73, 2. Greek and Amazon. Much restored. [Robinson]. Early. For the subject, Bothmer Am. 157, top.

171 (134). Once FLORENCE, Guarducci. Inghirami pl. 63. Herakles and the lion. Early.

172 (135). OXFORD 1927.4502. *CV.* pl. 61, 4; *Berl.* pl. 23, 2. Europa. Early.

173 (137). VIENNA 3739 (ex Oest. Mus. 331), from Cervetri. Masner pl. 7 and p. 49. Apollo and Artemis. Early.

174 (138). LENINGRAD 628 (St. 1588), from Vulci. *Burl. Mag.* 28, 137, a and p. 138, d–f; *Berl.* pl. 24, 1, whence Thompson *Tholos* 105; G.P. 62. Polyxene and Achilles at the fountain. Slightly restored. Early.

175 (139). BOULOGNE 449, from Vulci. Dionysos and maenad. Early.

176 (140). ATHENS Acr. 934, fr., from Athens. *Berl.* pl. 13, 5; Langlotz pl. 77. (Flute-player). Early.

177 (141). ATHENS Acr. 933, fr., from Athens. Langlotz pl. 77. Komos (woman with skyphos). Early.

178 (142). ELEUSIS, fr., from Eleusis. Komos (upper part of a man moving to right, his left arm extended holding a cup, his head thrown back). Early.

179 (143, +). FLORENCE 8 B 7, and NAPLES, Astarita, 105, fr. Part of the Florence part, *CV.* pl. 8, B 7. Seated god (or goddess), and woman, at altar. The unpublished fragment in Florence (already added in *CF.* 16) joins above on the right, giving the left shoulder and arm of the woman; one of the two Astarita fragments joins on the right, below, giving more of her chiton and himation; the other Astarita fragment joins on the left, below, giving the lower part of the seated deity. Early.

180. LOUVRE C 10800, frr. Triptolemos. Early.

181 (144). COPENHAGEN, Ny Carlsberg, inv. 2696, from Orvieto. *Nordisk Tidskrift* 1, 356–7; Poulsen *Etr.* pll. 6–7, whence *Mél. d'arch.* 1950 pl. 1, 2; Breitenstein *G.V.* pll. 34–35. Triptolemos. Early to middle. See p. 1634.

182 (145). BOSTON 03.843, fr. CB. iii, suppl. pl. 20, 5. (Old man seated). See CB. iii, text. Early to middle.

183 (146). CAB. MÉD. 441. De Ridder 333. Apollo and Artemis. Restored. Late.

OINOCHOAI
(nos. 184–5, shape 1)

184 (176). LONDON E 513. *El.* 1 pl. 93, whence Roscher s.v. Nike, 329 fig. 6; ph. Ma. Nike. Early.

185 (177). LONDON E 514, from Vulci. *El.* 2 pl. 12. Apollo and Artemis. Late.
(nos. 186–7, shape 3, choes)

186 (179). NEW YORK 22.139.32, from Vulci. *Cat. 7 juin 1922* pl. 4, 56; *AJA* 1926, 37; detail, Richter *Sc.* fig. 484; Richter and Milne fig. 119; Richter and Hall pl. 17, 15 and pl. 177, 15; Bieber *H.T.* 2 fig. 4; detail, Richter *ARVS.* fig. 48; Richter *H.* 213, h. Komos (youth with lyre, and boy). The patterns are by another hand. Early to middle. See p. 1634.

187 (180). MUNICH 2453 (J. 789), from Sicily. *CV.* pl. 87, 1, pl. 86, 11–12, and pl. 92, 10; van Hoorn *Choes* fig. 319. Athlete and youth. Middle.

LEKYTHOI

(standard shape)

188 (147). PALERMO V 669, from Gela. *CV*. pl. 19, 3 and 5. Nike. Early.

189 (148). HARVARD 4.08. *CV*. pl. 17, 4. Nike. Early.

190 (149). ATHENS 1274 (CC. 1363). Pottier *Peint. industr.* fig. 34. Horseman. Early.

191 (150). CORINTH, fr., from Corinth. *AJA*. 1930, 335, a–b. Athena. [Payne]. Early.

192 (151). ATHENS 12394 (N. 1028), from Eretria. *Eph.* 1907, 234; *Epit. Tsounta* 498 fig. 3. Komast. Early.

193 (152). PALERMO V 666, from Gela. *CV*. pl. 19, 1 and 4. Komast (man with lyre). Early.

194 (153). PALERMO V 667, from Gela. *CV*. pl. 20, 1. Warrior. Early.

195 (154). PALERMO V 670, from Selinus. *CV*. pl. 19, 2. Nike. Early.

196 (155). COPENHAGEN, Ny Carlsberg, inv. 2701, from Orvieto. *Nordisk Tidskrift* 1, 358; Poulsen *Etr.* pl. 9; Breitenstein *G.V.* pl. 36. Woman playing lyre. Early.

197 (156). NEW HAVEN, Watkins. *A.A.A.* pl. 80, 272. Dionysos (standing to right, kantharos in right hand, knotty staff and sprig of ivy in left; below, ivy border). Early.

198 (157). SYRACUSE 20534, from Gela. *ML.* 17 pl. 19, whence Bethe *Gr. Dichtung* 172. Triptolemos. Early.

199 (158). MUNICH 2475. *Berl.* pl. 12, 1. On the shoulder, lion. Early.

200 (159). ADRIA B 180 and B 404, two frr., from Adria. One fr., *Berl.* pl. 12, 2; both, *CV*. pl. 5, 8–9. On the shoulder, lioness between flowers. The second fr. added by Miss Riccioni. Early.

201 (160). PHILADELPHIA 5706 (ex Giudice). *Mus. J.* 19, 74. Maenad. Early.

202 (161). MUNICH inv. 7515. Demeter. Middle.

203 (162). NEW YORK 21.88.163. *RM.* 58 pl. 14, 2. Woman running with torch and phiale. Late.

204 (163). TARANTO 4535, from Taranto. Maenad. Late.

205 (165). CAMBRIDGE 37.28 (ex Giudice). *CV*. ii RS. pl. 13, 2. Woman fleeing. Late.

206 (166). AGRIGENTO 28, from Agrigento. Woman running with torch. Restored. Late.

207 (167). TARANTO, from Metapontum. Woman spinning (to right, at wool-basket). Late.

207 *bis*. GELA, from Gela. Youth attacking with spear; on the shoulder, Centaur (fleeing). Late. See p. 1634.

208 (168). PARIS MARKET, from Sicily. *Coll. Lambros* pl. 7, 55. Nike. Late.

209 (169). PARIS MARKET, from Sicily. *Coll. Lambros* pl. 7, 54. Nike (running with torches). On the shoulder, griffin between flowers. Restored. Late.

209 *bis*. PADULA, from Padula. Poseidon. On the shoulder, griffin between flowers. Late.

210 (171). SYRACUSE 21884, from Gela. *ML.* 17 pl. 15, 2. Poseidon. On the shoulder, Pegasos, between flowers. Late.

211 (170). PALERMO V 671, from Gela. *CV.* pl. 20, 5. Poseidon. On the shoulder, Pegasos, between flowers. Late.

212 (172). BERLIN 2208, from Nola. Genick pl. 39, 3 (reversed); Lücken pl. 48, 1 (reversed), whence Licht i, 90. Dionysos. Restored. Late.

213 (173). COMPIÈGNE 1036, from Vulci. *CV.* pl. 14, 7. Woman running with torches. Late.

LEKYTHOS?

214 (175). Once AGRIGENTO, Granet, from Agrigento? R.I. xii. 18. Nike (to right, with oinochoe and phiale, at thurible). Early.

LEKANIS

215 (181, +). TARANTO and REGGIO, from Locri. Poseidon pursuing a woman. Middle to late. Compare Munich inv. 8738 (no. 161). See p. 1634.

FRAGMENTS OF POTS

216 (191). FLORENCE 6 B 48, fr. *CV.* pl. 6, B 48. (Male). Early.

217 (190). FLORENCE 6 B 53, fr. *CV.* pl. 6, B 53. Horseman. See the next two. Early.

218. NAPLES, Astarita, 154, fr. (Hind-legs of an animal to right). May belong to Florence 6 B 53 (no. 217). Early.

219 (193). FLORENCE (ex Villa Giulia), fr. (Tip of a himation, with part of the border below—stopt key and saltire-square). May belong to Florence 6 B 53 (no. 217)—from the other side. Early.

220. INNSBRUCK ii. 12. 21, fr. *Jh.* 37, 44. Athena. [Sitte]. Early.

221 (194). BRUSSELS A 2492–5, four frr. Komos. A 2496 may also belong. Early.

222 (202). AMSTERDAM inv. 2275, fr. *Berl.* pl. 13, 2. (Staff or the like, woman with oinochoe and phiale). Early.

223. ATHENS Acr., fr., from Athens. (Thighs of a male in a cloak moving to left). Early.

224 (199). BERLIN, Univ., fr. (Feet, with edge of chiton). Early.

225 (196). LEIPSIC T 690, two frr. (Warrior; chiton). Early.

226 (201). FRANKFORT, Liebieghaus, 128, fr. (Arm with shield to right, cloak and raised arm of another person). Early.

227 (200). CAB. MÉD., fr. (Buttocks and thigh of warrior in chitoniskos to right, with part of the scabbard at his side). Early.

228 (185). VILLA GIULIA, fr. (Head of woman, in spotted saccos, to left, with part of one shoulder: the face missing except the eye). Early.

229 (189). FLORENCE 19 B 25, fr. *CV.* pl. 19, B 25. Warrior. Early.

230 (198). LEIPSIC, fr. (Belly and penis of naked male moving to left, with part of the thighs). Early.

231 (197). LEIPSIC, fr. (Part of a chitoniskos with crosses on it and engrailed lower edge). Early.

232 (203). AMSTERDAM inv. 2870, fr. (Male foot, frontal, with the end of a staff, acontion, or the like; below it, the left corner of the stopt-key border). Early.

233. BERLIN, Goethert, fr. *Anz.*1958, 11, b. Eros (the forearms and hands remain, holding a hare). [Peters]. From an oinochoe? Early.

234 (192). FLORENCE, fr. (ex Villa Giulia). (Head and breast of youth in himation to left, right arm extended). Early.

235 (206). FLORENCE 6 B 51, fr. *CV.* pl. 6, B 51. Zeus and Ganymede. From a small vase—Nolan amphora or the like. See the next. Early.

236 (205). FLORENCE 6 B 52, fr. *CV.* pl. 6, B 52. Male. From a small vase. May be from the same as the last—from the other side. Early.

237 (204). FLORENCE 7 B 14, fr. *CV.* pl. 7, B 14. Dionysos and satyr. From a small vase. Might be from an oinochoe of shape 3. Early.

238 (195). ATHENS Acr. 702, frr., from Athens. *Berl.* pl. 13, 3; Langlotz pl. 54; part, Vorberg *Gloss.* 496, 2. Unexplained subject: man with a phallus-staff, and phalli sprouting from his nose and forehead: see *Berl.* 21, also Herter *Vom dionysischen Tanz zum komischen Spiel* 16, 17, and 20; and here p. 346 no. 78. From a hydria or an oinochoe shape 3? Still early.

239 (207). CORINTH, fr., from Corinth. Satyr as boxer. From a Nolan amphora?

240 (208). HEIDELBERG 114, two frr. Kraiker pl. 20. Amazon. Late. From a small panathenaic?

SKYPHOS

241. ATHENS Acr. 454, fr., from Athens. Langlotz pl. 38. (God and goddess seated side by side). Very early. Langlotz compared this with the two very early pelikai in Vienna and Florence (nos. 109 and 110).

CUPS

242. ATHENS, Agora, P 24113, from Athens. I and B, *The Times* 13 Sept. 1954, 12; *Hesp.* 24 pl. 30; A, *Anz.* 1954, 715; A, *BCH.* 1955, 214 fig. 3; A, *Arch. Reports 1954*, 4; *AJA.* 1958 pl. 6 and pl. 7 figs. 3–5. I, youth with hare. A, fight: Achilles and Memnon. B, Dionysos with maenad and satyrs. On I, ΛΟRΛΟΣΕΠΟΙΕΣΕΝ. On A, ΚRΑΤΕΣ, on B, ΚΑΛΟΣ. [Talcott.] Miss Talcott saw that this cup was curiously close, in many respects, to the Berlin Painter, and she suggested that it might be from his hand, his earliest extant work. This view has been persuasively argued

by Martin Robertson (*AJA*. 1958, 55–56) and should, I think, be accepted. There are differences which made me hesitate, but the resemblances are so great as to outweigh them. See p. 1634.

243. ATHENS, Agora, P 26245, fr., from Athens. *Hesp.* 28 pl. 22, c and a. I, (maeander). A, (athlete). The maeander is not the least like the Berlin Painter's patterns.

PLATES

244 (182). ATHENS Acr. 427, frr., from Athens. Part, *Eph.* 1886 pl. 8, 5; Langlotz pl. 32. White ground. Athena. Early.

245 (183). ATHENS Acr. 23, two frr., from Athens. Part, Langlotz pl. 1. Herakles. An unpublished fragment joins 23a and adds his foot. Early.

I omit from the list the Madrid hydria 11125 (L. 161), no. 136 in *ARV*.[1] 140 (*Berl.* pl. 23, 1, whence LS. fig. 80; *CV.* pl. 11, 2 and pl. 14, 1).

A small fragment of a fine vase really ought to be by the Berlin Painter:

CALYX-KRATER

AEGINA 1966, fr., from Aegina. What remains of the picture is the upper part of a helmet to left, and to left of it NE . . . retrograde—$Ne[o-\pi\tau o\lambda\epsilon\mu os]$?, so Death of Priam?

For the *black-figured* Panathenaic amphorae by the Berlin Painter or from his workshop see *ABV.* 407–9, 482, 517, 685, and 715; and add his prize Panathenaics:

FERRARA, T. 11 C VP, from Spina. A, Athena; B, chariot.

HANOVER (New Hampshire), Dartmouth College. *Dartmouth Alumni Magazine* June 1959, 24–25. A, Athena; B, wrestlers. [Bothmer].

A fragment of a bf. Panathenaic is probably also his:

TARANTO 16599, fr., from Taranto. A, Athena (the right arm remains, with part of the aegis).

MANNER OF THE BERLIN PAINTER

ARV[1]. 144–6 and 952. See also above, p. 196.

(i) Various

PANATHENAIC AMPHORA

1 (α). LONDON E 287, from Nola. *CV.* pl. 47, 2. A, Nike; B, youth. Small. Late.

NECK-AMPHORAE

(small)

(nos. 2–6, Nolan amphorae, with triple handles)

2 (γ). Louvre G 219. *CV.* pl. 42, 1–2. A, youth with phiale; B, youth. Miserable. Late.

3 (δ). Capua 214, from Capua. *CV.* pl. 3, 1–2 and pl. 5, 7–8. A, discus-thrower; B, trainer. Late.

4 (ε). Mykonos, from Rheneia (originally from Delos). Dugas *Délos xxi* pl. 17, 46 and pl. 45, 46. A, Dionysos and maenad; B, satyr.

5 (l 78). Naples 3116, from Nola. A, ph. So. 11072, ii, 5. A, Dionysos and maenad; B, maenad. Late.

6 (ζ). Palermo V 746. *CV.* pl. 27, 1–2 and pl. 26, 3. A, horseman; B, youth. Coarse. Late.

(no. 7, with twisted handles)

7. Angers 12, from Basilicata. *RA.* 1923, i, 55–56; *La nature* 3133 (1 avril 1947), 112 fig. 4; A, Henry de Morant *Guide* 15; Henry de Morant pll. 9–10 and pl. 37, b. Warrior leaving home (A, warrior and woman; B, man). Restored. Late.

LOUTROPHOROI

8. Tübingen E 101, fr. Watzinger pl. 29. On the neck, warriors. Slight, but may be from a scamped part of a vase by the painter himself.

9. Athens, Acropolis Museum, fr., from Athens. (Head, to left, and left shoulder, of Hermes). Very late.

CALYX-KRATER

10 (ν). Cincinnati, Univ. A, Apollo and Nike; B, Zeus and Hermes. Middle to late.

STAMNOI

11 (ι). Philadelphia 4872, from Orvieto. *Mus. J.* 4, 157. Athletes. Middle.

12 (κ). Roman market (Basseggio). Lost at sea. Gerhard pl. 156. Death of Orpheus. Late.

HYDRIA

(kalpis, with picture on the shoulder)

13 (ο). Athens Acr. 1009, fr., from Athens. Langlotz pl. 79. Old priestess at altar. On the inscription see Peek in Langlotz, 131. May be by the painter himself. Not late.

LEKYTHOI

(standard shape)

14. Gela 21, from Gela. *NSc.* 1956, 328 fig. 16. Nike. [Orlandini]. Still early.

15. Naples, Astarita, 494. Eros (flying to left with phiale, looking round). [Astarita].

16. ONGAR, Capel Cure, from Nola. Eros (flying to right, with right leg frontal, looking round, lyre in left hand). For the shoulder palmettes compare Palermo V 670 (p. 211 no. 195).

17 (ρ). OXFORD 323, from Gela. *CV.* pl. 35, 3-4. Arming: youth holding greaves and woman holding spear and shield. Very like the Berlin Painter, except the heads, which recall the Briseis Painter. Middle.

18. GELA 24, from Gela. *Arch. class.* 5 pl. 13; *NSc.* 1956, 329 fig. 19 and p. 330. Eos and Kephalos. Middle.

19 (σ). LONDON E 574, from Sicily. Ph. Ma. 3195, middle, whence Walters *H.A.P.* pl. 36, 2. Nike. Bad. Late.

20 (1 164). GELA (ex Navarra-Jacona), from Gela. Benndorf pl. 49, 2. Woman running with oinochoe and phiale.

FRAGMENT OF A POT

21. FLORENCE 15 B 43, fr. *CV.* pl. 15, B 43. Satyr. From a small neck-amphora? Very late. Recalls Hermonax.

(ii)
THE GROUP OF LONDON E 311
ARV.[1] 323, ii.

A very late group. The three vases must be by one painter. In all three the reverse has a more old-fashioned look than the obverse, yet the hand must be the same. The obverses recall a pupil of the Berlin Painter—Hermonax.

NECK-AMPHORAE
(*small*)

(*no. 1, Nolan amphora, with triple handles*)

1 (1). LONDON E 311, from Nola. *El.* 1 pl. 39; *CV* pl. 56, 2. A, a man pursuing, B, a woman.

(*no. 2, the exact shape uncertain: Nolan?*)

2 (2). PARIS MARKET. *El.* 1 pl. 82. A, Zeus; B, Athena.

PANATHENAIC AMPHORA

3 (4). CAB. MÉD. 378. Luynes pl. 40. A, youth with stone and spear, attacking; B, woman fleeing. Small.

Near these, a larger work from the late following of the Berlin Painter:

STAMNOS

(5). OXFORD 521, from Vulci. *Annali* 1865 pl. P–Q, whence *JHS.* 24, 307; details, *JHS.* 24, 308; A, Pickard-Cambridge *Dith.* fig. 49; *CV.* pl. 26 and pl. 31, 5. Herakles and Busiris.

(iii)

THE GROUP OF LONDON E 445

These also are very late. The coarse stamnoi in London and Trieste are by one hand, and the Indianapolis vase is at least very close to them. All three are of the same shape as Oxford 521. Here again there is a flavour of Hermonax.

STAMNOI

1 (λ). LONDON E 445, from Vulci. Gerhard pl. 174–5, whence (B) Panofka *Pos. u. Dion.* pl. 1, 4, (A) *AJA*. 1937, 603 fig. 2; *CV*. pl. 21, 5. A, judgement of Paris. B, Poseidon, Nike, and Dionysos.

2 (μ). TRIESTE S 424, from Vulci. Gerhard pl. 146–7 (the first ten figures; for the others see p. 498 no. 3); phs. Al. 40212–14, whence (B) Pickard-Cambridge *D.F.A.* fig. 201; A, Stella 836; part of A, *Gymnasium* 66 pl. 2. Herakles entering Olympus.

3. INDIANAPOLIS 31.299 (ex Canino), from Vulci. A, *Bull. Ind.* 19, 1; A, *Bull. Ind.* 23, 4; part, *Studies Robinson* ii pl. 51, a–b; (reversed) B.Ap. xxii. 24. Return of Hephaistos. See p. 1636.

Two other vases from the late school of the Berlin Painter may be placed near these:

NECK-AMPHORA

(small, with ridged handles)

1 (θ). CAB. MÉD. 374. Caylus 2 pl. 35, 2; Millin *PVA*. 2 pl. 34. A, Eos and Kephalos; B, companion fleeing.

LEKYTHOS

(standard shape)

2. TARANTO 52220, from Taranto. Nike (flying, with torch). Associated with the Berlin Painter by Campi.

Three hydriai must be, each in its way, imitations of the Berlin Painter:

HYDRIAI

(kalpides, with picture on the shoulder, not framed)

1. LOUVRE C 11056. Amazonomachy (young Greek and Amazon). See Bothmer *Am.* 143 no. 23 and p. 144. Early.

2. FLORENCE, and NAPLES, Astarita, 112, two frr. Women fleeing to man. On the Florence fragment (two joining) the middle of a woman running to right, her left arm raised, and the legs of a seated man in chiton and himation to left, with part of his sceptre; on the Astarita fragment, breast to mid-shanks, with left hand, of a woman running to left. Later.

3. LOUVRE G 178, from Vulci. *CV*. pl. 54, 2, 5, and 7. Peleus and Thetis. Some details recall the Harrow Painter. Later.

Martin Robertson has noted (*AJA*. 1958, 64–66) a distinct resemblance between the gorgoneion on the following vase and those of the Berlin Painter:

HYDRIA
(*kalpis, with picture on the shoulder, not framed*)

LONDON E 180, from Tarquinia. Panofka *Blacas* pl. 10; *CV*. pl. 71, 4; *AJA*. 1958 pl. 9; ph. Ma. 3155. Gorgoneion. See *Antike Kunst* 4, 59.

THE GROUP OF THE FLORAL NOLANS

H. R. W. Smith, and Luce, in *CV* Providence, 25. *JHS*. 53, 311.

H. R. W. Smith proposed to attribute Providence 24.509 (no. 1) to the Berlin Painter, by comparison with vases in Yale (p. 201 no. 71) and London (p. 206 no. 132). Luce observed that New York 06.1153 (no. 5) had 'the same design' as the Providence vase. The vases in Providence and New York belong to a group of Nolans, decorated with bands of patterns only (floral and other), which are more or less closely connected with the Berlin Painter. Four lekythoi belong to the same group, and two oinochoai.

NECK-AMPHORAE
(*Nolan amphorae, with triple handles*)

1. PROVIDENCE 24.509. *CV*. pl. 15, 3.
2. VIENNA 848. *CV*. pl. 57, 3–4.
3. SAN SIMEON, State Monument, 9487 (ex Sotheby, *Cat. 22–23 May 1919* no. 272, and Revelstoke).
4. Once NAPLES, Hamilton. Hancarville 2 pll. 46–47. (The handles are not given as triple).
5. NEW YORK 06.1153.
6. PARIS MARKET (Segredakis).
7. VIENNA 847. *CV*. pl. 57, 1–2.
8. VILLA GIULIA (ex Castellani).
9. GELA, from Gela. A, *NSc*. 1956, 324, b.
10. BIRMINGHAM 1616.85.

LEKYTHOI
(*standard shape*)

11. GELA, from Gela. *NSc*. 1956, 324, c.
12. GENEVA MARKET (Hirsch, 153), from Gela.

13. SYRACUSE. Poulsen *Aus einer alten Etruskerstadt* pl. 11 fig. 20.

14. COPENHAGEN, Ny Carlsberg, from Orvieto. Poulsen *Aus einer alten Etruskerstadt* pl. 11 fig. 19. See p. 1636.

OINOCHOAI
(shape 2)
(the model is not the same: no. 15 is squatter than no. 16, and the foot and handle are different)

15. VILLA GIULIA (ex Castellani).

16. MUNICH 2450, from South Italy. Lau pl. 22, 2; Pfuhl fig. 786; *CV*. pl. 89, 1–2 and pl. 91, 11–12.

The Nolans nos. 1–8, the lekythoi nos. 11–12, and the two oinochoai nos. 15–16 go together. Nos. 2 and 3 are particularly close to no. 1. Nos. 9 and 10 go together. Of the lekythoi, no. 12 goes with no. 11, and no. 14 with no. 13. Nos. 13 and 14 are not so near the Berlin Painter: for the maeander band, however, on no. 14 compare no. 8, and for the floral band on no. 13 compare that on the oinochoe New York 22.139.32, the figure-work of which is by the Berlin Painter (p. 210 no. 186). See also p. 1636.

For the drawing of the floral bands on nos. 1–9, 11–12, and 16 compare vases from the Berlin Painter's middle period: the oinochoe in Munich (p. 210 no. 187), the Nolan in Yale (p. 201 no. 71), the lekanis in Taranto (p. 212 no. 215).

The drawing of the floral on no. 15 is the same except in one detail, the mid-petal of the flower, which is the same as in earlier vases by the Berlin Painter: the calyx-krater Acropolis 742 and London E 459 (p. 205 no. 117), the volute-krater London E 468 (p. 206 no. 132).

There is a complication in an oinochoe by the Dutuit Painter, London E 510 (p. 307 no. 8): the floral is indistinguishable from that on our nos. 1–9, 11–12, and 16, or indeed on the vases by the Berlin Painter which we have compared with them. Bothmer is inclined to attribute the New York Nolan (no. 5) to the Dutuit Painter.

The Villa Giulia oinochoe (no. 15) is linked with the Dutuit Painter by two small particulars: the drawing of the palmette at the lower end of the handle (compare p. 307 nos. 10, 12, 13); and the horizontal bud in the middle of the floral, to left and right of the loops (compare the London oinochoe E 510, p. 307 no. 8).

CHAPTER 16

THE NIKOXENOS PAINTER AND THE EUCHARIDES PAINTER

THE NIKOXENOS PAINTER

BSA. 19, 229–47. *VA.* 25–26. *Att. V.* 91–93 and 469. *ABS.* 24 and 48. *ARV.*[1] 147–50 and 952–3.

So called from the inscription on no. 6. For his black-figure vases (neck-amphorae, an amphora, pelikai, hydriai), which may be counted as belonging to the Leagros Group, see *ABV.* 392–3 and 696. They are really better than his red-figure, which belong to the coarser wing of archaic red-figure vase-painting.

His work, in both techniques, is continued by his pupil the Eucharides Painter (p. 226).

AMPHORAE

(with framed pictures)
(nos. 1–3, type A)

1 (1). MUNICH 2304 (J. 405), from Vulci. A, Gerhard pl. 7; A, *RA.* 1912, ii, 56; *BSA.* 19 pl. 18; A, FR. pl. 158; detail of A, Richter *F.* fig. 33; *CV.* pll. 178–81 and pl. 188, 8. A, deities in Olympus (Zeus and Hera with Iris; Poseidon with Athena and Hermes). B, Apollo, with Dionysos and a maenad and Hermes and a goddess. For the subject of A, Simon *O.G.* 63.

2. PAESTUM, from Paestum. B, Sestieri *Mus. di Paestum* 35; *Riv. Ist.* N.S. 2, 6–14; B, *Anz.* 1956, 438. A, Herakles and Cerberus. B, Amazons arming. [Enrico Paribeni, Sestieri].

3 (2). LOUVRE G 46. Pottier pl. 93; *CV.* pl. 31, 2–3 and 5 and 8 and pl. 29, 7. A, warrior leaving home (extispicy). B, Dionysos with satyrs and maenads. Restored.

(no. 4, type B)

4 (3). NEW YORK 06.1021.99. Sambon *Canessa* pl. 16, 227 and p. 62, whence (B) *BSA.* 19, 236; Richter and Hall pl. 19 and pl. 169, 17; *AJA.* 1954 pl. 60 fig. 21. A, death of Priam; B, the like.

PANATHENAIC AMPHORAE

(nos. 5–8 bis, the pictures framed)

5 (4). BOSTON 95.19. *Harv. St.* 17, 143; *BSA.* 19 pl. 16; shape, Caskey *G.* 77. A, Athena; B, Athena. On A, ΓΙΦΟΝΚΑLΕ on the shield; on B, ΝΙΚΕ-ΚΑLΕ on the shield.

6 (5). MISSISSIPPI (ex Stroganoff and Robinson), from Capua. Klein *L.* 121, whence *BSA.* 19, 233; Pollak and Muñoz pl. 34; *CV.* ii pl. 24, 1 and pl. 25, whence (A) Rumpf *MZ.* pl. 21, 5. A, Athena; B, Athena. On A, NIKO+SENOS on the shield, and in the field IIALOII.

7 (6). BERLIN 2161, from Nola. A, *BSA.* 19 pl. 17, 1. A, Athena with cithara; B, citharode.

8 (7). MUNICH inv. 8728. 1–8, frr. A, *CV.* pl. 190, 1 and p. 23. A, Athena; B, jumper and flute-player. On A, NIKE retr. and KALO[S], also . . . PE (perhaps [χαι]ρε).

8 *bis.* ZURICH, private. A, Hermes (with phiale, at altar between two columns, each surmounted by a cock); B, the like. See p. 1636.

(nos. 9–10, the pictures not framed)

9 (8). LOUVRE G 60. Pottier pl. 95; *CV.* pl. 31, 7 and 4 and pl. 32, 1 and 6; A, ph. Gir. 25509, 2. A, Athena; B, priest.

10 (9). LOUVRE G 61. *BSA.* 19, 230–1; *CV.* pl. 31, 9 and 6, and pl. 32, 4–5; R.I. xxi. 7; A, ph. Gir. 25509, 1. A, Athena; B, priestess.

PELIKAI

(with framed pictures)

11. LOUVRE C 10782. A, satyr and maenad. B, man approaching altar.

12 (10). AMSTERDAM inv. 1313. *Bull. Vereen.* 1, 10 fig. 4; *CV.* Scheurleer pl. 3, 3–4. A, satyr and maenad; B, the like.

VOLUTE-KRATERS

13. TARANTO, from Turi. On the neck: A, boys playing (with astragaloi one would say, although the astragaloi are not represented); B, horse-race.

14 (11). MUNICH 2381 (J. 542). from South Italy. *Philologus* 1868 pl. 4, whence (A) Buschor *Satyrtänze* fig. 47; Brommer *Satyrspiele*[1] 54–57 =260–61. On the neck: A, satyrs as athletes; B, athletes. Much restored.

15 (12). OXFORD G 136.36 and G 138.40, two frr., from Naucratis. *CV.* pl. 50, 12–13. On the neck, komos.

16 (13). AMSTERDAM inv. 2269, fr. On the neck, fight.

CALYX-KRATERS

17 (14, +). ATHENS Acr. 727, from Athens. Part, Langlotz pll. 56–57. A, fight. B, youths leading horses. On the cul: A, satyr dancing; B, symposion (youth reclining). 'A fragment in Freiburg, Baumgarten collection' (Langlotz); Martin Robertson found another on the Acropolis and gave it to the Museum; Miss Pease added three others from recent excavation (*Hesp.* 5, 258–9); a new Athens fragment has part of the mouth of the vase; a fragment in Munich seems to give the middle of the seated youth on B.

18 (15). SYRACUSE, fr., from Gela. Komos (upper part of youth, to right, facing left).

HYDRIAI

(no. 19, of bf. shape, with framed pictures)

19 (16). LONDON E 160, from Vulci. *BSA.* 19 pl. 19, pl. 17, 2, and p. 234; *CV.* pl. 70, 2 and pl. 72, 2; ph. Ma. 3148. Achilles and Ajax playing. On the shoulder, chariot. For the shape, Bloesch in *JHS.* 71, 37.

(nos. 20–27, kalpides, the picture on the shoulder, framed)

20 (17). LENINGRAD. B.Ap. xxii. 19. 1. Dionysos and satyr.

21 (17 *bis*). FLORENCE. Satyr and maenad.

22 (18). LENINGRAD 623, from Cervetri. B.Ap. xxii. 9; one figure, *BSA.* 19, 237. Herakles resting, and satyr.

23 (19). LENINGRAD 626. One figure, *BSA.* 19, 238, whence Pfuhl fig. 390. Athletes.

24 (20). ABINGDON, Robertson, fr., from Greece. *AJA.* 1962 pl. 83. Athletes (jumper, and youth kneeling).

25 (21). WÜRZBURG 531, from Vulci. Langlotz pll. 196 and 210. Athletes.

26 (22). FLORENCE 8 B 18. *Boll. d'Arte* 1928, 187; *CV.* pl. 8, B 18. Warriors leaving home.

27 (23). CORINTH C 30.53, fr., from Corinth. (Male seated with lyre, male).

FRAGMENTS OF POTS

28 (24). ATHENS Acr. 907a, fr., from Athens. *BSA.* 19, 239; Langlotz pl. 76. (Jumper).

29 (25). ATHENS Acr. 907b, fr., from Athens. Langlotz pl. 76. (Boxer).

PLAQUE

30 (26). ATHENS Acr. 1043, fr., from Athens. Langlotz pl. 81. (Chariot). [Langlotz].

For the *black-figure* work of the Nikoxenos Painter see *ABV.* 392–3 and 696. The bf. neck-amphora ibid. 392 no. 12 (already *ARV.*[1] 952 no. 36 *bis*) is now in Achimota, University of Ghana. Add the

BF. NECK-AMPHORA

MAYENCE, Univ., 73, from Vulci. Hampe and Simon *G.L.* pll. 14–15; *CV.* pl. 34 and p. 36. A, Dionysos, and two satyrs lifting maenads. B, warrior leaving home. [Bothmer].

MANNER OF THE NIKOXENOS PAINTER

*ARV.*¹ 150.

HYDRIA
(kalpis, with picture on the body)

1 (1). CERVETRI, from Cervetri. Man with horse, and youth.

VOLUTE-KRATER

2 (3). VILLA GIULIA, from Veii. On the neck: A, warriors lying in wait; B, symposion.

A black-figured vase is near the Nikoxenos Painter and the Eucharides Painter:

BF. HYDRIA
(kalpis, with picture on the body)

MONTREAL 39C b 1, from Vulci. Dionysos, and two satyrs playing citharae. [Bothmer].

For the vases by the black-figure associates of the Nikoxenos Painter—the Painter of Munich 1519 and others—see *ABV.* 393-5 and 696.

AKIN TO THE NIKOXENOS PAINTER

*ARV.*¹ 150-1 and 953.

VOLUTE-KRATERS

1 (β). NEW YORK, Bothmer, fr. Ph. R.I. 37.190. On the neck, (satyrs).

2. TORONTO 959.17.187 (ex Curtius), fr. Ph. R.I. 37.451. On the neck, mission to Achilles (on the left, shield and helmet, then part of Phoinix seated, [ΦΟ]ΙΝΙ+Ϟ retr.).

3 (δ). AMSTERDAM inv. 2770, fr. On the neck, fight.

4 (γ). RHODES, fr., from Camiros. *Cl. Rh.* 6-7, 175. On the neck, fight.

HYDRIA
(kalpis, with picture on the body)

5 (2). Once CANINO, from Vulci. Gerhard pl. 28, whence *El.* 2 pl. 36a. Apollo with Artemis and Leto. Restored. For the subject, Simon *O.G.* 16, 24, and 99.

PELIKAI
(with framed pictures)

6 (ε). ATHENS 1425 (CC. 1080), from Aegina. *CV.* pl. 8, 2 and 4; B, Licht iii, 141. A, warrior (in forest-fighting). B, naked woman washing at fountain.

7 (*v*). TARQUINIA, from Tarquinia. Vorberg *Gloss.* 41 and 111; *CV.* pl. 12, 2–3; phs. Mo. 8648 and 8268; A, ph. R.I. 1934.2215. Love-making (A, inspection; B, penetration).

CUP

8 (m4). FLORENCE 3924, from Chiusi. *CV.* pl. 91, 2 and pl. 116, 13. I, komast.

Perhaps also the

CUP

9. Once CANINO, from Vulci. A, *El.* 3 pl. 2. I, 'hunter'. A, Poseidon (or Nereus) on a sea-horse; B, the like.

THE KARKINOS PAINTER

So named from a peculiar shield-device on no. 1—a crab grasping what looks like a double-flute: see p. 1636.

No. 2 was described in *ARV.*[1] 150, α, as akin to the Nikoxenos Painter, which was right so far as it went.

VOLUTE-KRATERS

1. NEW YORK 59. 11. 20. On the neck, Theseus and Antiope (on B, five mounted Amazons).
2. NEW YORK 21.88.74. *AJA.* 1923, 268, and 269 fig. 5; McClees 103 and 73; Richter and Hall pl. 20 and pl. 171, 18. On the neck: A, five mounted warriors (Amazons?); B, symposion.
3. REGGIO, fr., from Locri. On the neck, (warrior leading a horse, warrior mounting his chariot: Amazons according to Bothmer). On the upper section of the neck, the same palmettes as in nos. 1 and 2. See Bothmer *Am.* 151 no. 56 and p. 156.

Compare with these the fragment of a

VOLUTE-KRATER

ATHENS, Agora, P 368, fr., from Athens. On the neck, (head of a horse— from a chariot-team?—then a woman running).

THE PAINTER OF LONDON E 2

Six cups were put together in *ARV.*[1] 151 as akin to the work of the Nikoxenos Painter, which they are, but they were not described as a group. In *ABV.* 390 they became 'the Group of London E 2' and were said to be probably by one painter—a black-figure artist. They are in fact so. The list that follows is repeated, exceptionally, from *ABV.*, but with additions and a correction.

CUPS

1 (ζ). LONDON E 2, from Vulci. I, ph. Ma., whence Walters *H.A.P.* pl. 37, 1; detail of I, *JHS.* 77, 315 fig. 4. I, komast (youth lifting a pointed amphora). Round this, bf., ships. A–B, komos (A, two youths dancing, with a pointed amphora between); B, the like.

2 (η). AMSTERDAM inv. 2182, fr. *CV.* Scheurleer a pl. 6 (Pays Bas pl. 30), 8–9. Scheurleer saw that this was from just such a cup as the last. I, (the tondo lost). Round it, bf., ships. A, (one hand of the figure on the left remains).

3 (λ). DIJON 1223, from Vulci. I, Micali *Storia* pl. 97, 2, whence Milani *Filottete* pl. 1, 6. I, splanchnopt. A–B, komos. The statement in *ABV.* 390 no. 6 that the exterior is largely modern is untrue.

4 (θ). LOUVRE G 93, from Poggio Sommavilla. Pottier pl. 99; A–B, *Mem. Am. Ac.* 6 pl. 14, 3–4; I, *AJA.* 1935 pl. 10, a; I, ph. Arch. phot. MNLA 1307A. I, negro warrior (henchman of Memnon). A, Dionysos and maenads; B, maenads. Restored. By the same potter as London E 2 (no. 1). For the provenience, *Bull.* 1837, 73.

5 (κ). MADRID 11266 (L. 153). A–B, Alvarez-Ossorio pl. 8, 2; *CV.* pl. 1, 2, pl. 2, 3, and pl. 3; R.I. M 38, 55, and 12, b, whence (A–B) Buschor *Satyrtänze* 93. I, komast. A, symposion (Herakles and a man—Iolaos?—, waited on by a satyr); B, the like.

6 (ι). BONN 315, from Chiusi. *CV.* pl. 2, 5 and pl. 3, 1; A and foot, Bloesch *FAS.* pl. 13, 2. I, symposion (youth reclining, playing kottabos). For the shape, Bloesch 47, Kachrylion no. 15.

7. LUCERNE MARKET (A.A.). I, symposion (youth reclining, right hand raised with the fingers turned down). Compare the last. See p. 1636.

It was noted in *ABV.* 390 that the bf. ships on nos. 1 and 2 were in the same style as those on the black-figured cup Cab. Méd. 322 (de Ridder 219–23; *CV.* pl. 52, 3–6, pl. 53, and pl. 54, 1–2; phs. Gir. 8048–50: restored), which belongs to the Leagros Group, and within it to the Antiope Group I (*ABV.* 380 no. 296). See also Williams in *JHS.* 77, 316; and below, p. 1636.

THE PAINTER OF MUNICH 2306

Att. V. 93. *ARV.*[1] 152.

Akin to the Nikoxenos Painter. Doubtless a black-figure artist.

AMPHORAE

(*no. 1, type A; with framed pictures*)

1 (1). MUNICH 2306 (J. 406), from Vulci. Palmettes, Lau pl. 13, 4 and pl. 12, 3; *CV.* pll. 182–5 and pl. 188, 9. A, Herakles and Cerberus. B, Apollo in chariot.

(no. 2, type C; the pictures not framed)

2 (2). LENINGRAD 602 (St. 1639). *CR.* 1868, 58 and 5, whence Overbeck *KM.* pl. 24, 5. Struggle for the tripod (A, Apollo; B, Herakles).

=====

THE EUCHARIDES PAINTER

BSA. 18, 217–33. *BSA.* 19, 245. *VA.* 45–47. *Att. V.* 93–97 and 470. *V.Pol.* 16 and 79. *ARV.*[1] 153–8 and 953. *AJA.* 1943, 446–7. *ABV.* 395–8 and 696. *Scritti Libertini* 91–95.

Called after the kalos-name on no. 35.
Pupil of the Nikoxenos Painter. He too has his black-figure side: see *ABV.* and what is there quoted; and below, p. 232. His latest works, poor in quality, already belong to the early classic period. See also p. 1637.
It is falsely stated in *Delt.* 9, 35 that I attributed the fragment ibid. fig. 36 to the Eucharides Painter.

NECK-AMPHORAE
(nos. 1–2, large, with ridged handles; the pictures framed)

1 (1). LONDON E 279. Inghirami pll. 347–8; *BSA.* 18 pll. 11–12 and p. 220, whence (B) Rumpf *MZ.* pl. 24, 1; *CV.* pl. 15, 2; neck A, Jacobsthal *O.* pl. 88, b. A, Dionysos; B, Ariadne.

2 (2). LONDON E 278, from Vulci. *Mon.* 1 pl. 23, whence *El.* 2 pl. 55 and Inghirami pl. 45; *BSA.* 18 pll. 13–14 and p. 221, whence *Jb. Berl. Mus.* N.S. 1, 22, (A) *VA.* 45, (B) Pfuhl fig. 389; *CV.* pl. 15, 1; neck B, Jacobsthal *O.* pl. 88, a. Death of Tityos: A, Apollo; B, Tityos and Leto.

(no. 3, large, with twisted handles)

3 (3). MUNICH 2317 (J. 2), from Vulci. Lützow pl. 18 and p. 30. A, woman with lyre; B, man with lyre. See p. 1637.

(no. 4, small, with ridged handles)

4 (4). LOUVRE G 202. *BSA.* 18, 222; Pottier pl. 129; *CV.* pl. 36, 10–11 and pl. 37, 1–3; side, Jacobsthal *O.* pl. 54, c, whence Richter *H.G.A.* 377. A, satyr; B, maenad.

(nos. 5–6, small, with double handles)

5 (5). BRUSSELS A 721. FR. pl. 162, 2, and iii, 268; side, Jacobsthal *O.* pl. 74, a; *CV.* pl. 14; B and side, Schnitzler pl. 44. A, acontist; B, the like.

6 (6). NAPLES Stg. 249. B, ph. So. 11096. A, Dionysos; B, satyr.

PANATHENAIC AMPHORAE

7 (7). PARIS MARKET (Mikas), from Vulci. Votaries (A, man in himation to right, holding a stick and sprigs with a pinax tied to one of them; B, man in himation, frontal, looking round to right, with stick, sprigs, and pinax as before).

8 (8). LOUVRE G 221. *CV*. pl. 41, 10–11. A, man holding a sucking-pig; B, man. Much restored.

AMPHORAE

(the pictures not framed)
(no. 9 is of type B)

9 (9). NEW YORK 07.286.78, from Agrigento. Part of B, *VA*. 46; B, Richter and Milne fig. 5; Richter and Hall pl. 21, pl. 22, 19, and pl. 169, 19; A, Richter *H*. 213, c. A, Apollo and Artemis. B, athlete and trainer.

10. LOUVRE C 10839, four frr. A, male and woman. B, male and youth at laver. On A, middle and left hand of one in a himation standing to right, middle of a woman in a chiton standing to left, oinochoe in right hand; on B, left hand of a male in a himation leaning on his stick to right, laver with ΚΑΛΟ$ on it, head and shoulders of a youth standing to left, with part of his himation.

CALYX-KRATERS

11 (10, +). LOUVRE G 47. Pottier pll. 93–94; *CV*. pl. 1, 1, 4, and 9, pl. 3, 1–2 and 4–5, and pl. 14, 2. A, arming; B, warriors setting out. Much restored. A Louvre fragment belongs: it gives part of the spear of the foremost warrior on B and part of a palmette. Early.

12 (11, +). LOUVRE G 163, from Cervetri. *Mon*. 6–7 pl. 21 and *Annali* 1858 pl. P; Pottier pl. 124, whence (B) Friis Johansen *Iliaden* fig. 28; *CV*. pll. 8–9; *Enc. phot*. iii, 16–17, whence (A) Stella 282; phs. Gir. 32504–6, whence Béquignon *Il*. 148 and 138; detail of A, Bille-de Mot 110. A, Hypnos and Thanatos with the body of Sarpedon; B, the mission to Achilles. On the cul: A, satyrs; B, komos. Now cleaned. Five Louvre fragments belong, all from A and all with pieces of wings. One of them has, besides a piece of Thanatos' wing, a small raised forearm with hand, and the elbow of the other arm: these must be part of an eidolon of Sarpedon, fluttering over the body and making lament. Another of the fragments has, with part of wing, small remains not yet explained.

13 (12). NAPLES, part of 2201, frr., from Apulia. *Mus. Borb*. 15 pl. 15. What is ancient is, in A, a foot, some clothing, parts of the komos on the cul, and small parts of B. Fragments of a later bell-krater have been combined with this. Most of the vase is modern.

14 (13). ATHENS Acr. 745, fr., from Athens. Langlotz pl. 62. (Seated god).

15 (14). ATHENS Acr. 738, fr., from Athens. Langlotz pl. 62 (misprinted 758), whence *AJA*. 1934, 433, below, and *Jb*. 52, 7 fig. 4. (Winged goddess).

16 (15). ATHENS, Agora, P 13367, fr., from Athens. Triptolemos.

17. ATHENS, Agora, P 19291, fr., from Athens. *Hesp*. 18 pl. 45, 5. (On the right, boy athlete). [Corbett].

18. BIRMINGHAM, Univ., fr., from Patara. (Head of a youth to left: symposion?).

19 (15 *bis*). Syracuse 49295, from Monte Casale. A, *CV*. pl. 9, 3. Komos: A, man and woman; B, youth. Very late.

VOLUTE-KRATERS

20 (16, +). Athens Acr. 755, plus, and Munich, seven frr., from Athens. Three of the Athens frr., Langlotz pl. 62; a fourth, added by Miss Pease, *Hesp.* 5, 262 fig. 10, 11. On the neck, symposion. A new Athens fragment has the head of a youth playing the flute to left. The two remaining fragments are in Munich.

20 *bis*. Pompeii 225. 4, fr., from Pompeii. On the neck, symposion. [Bothmer].

21 (17). Eleusis, fr., from Eleusis. *Delt.* 9, 23 fig. 20. On the neck, (woman running).

COLUMN-KRATERS
(*nos. 22–24, the pictures framed*)

22 (18). Florence 3990 and Goettingen '89'. The old Florence part, *CV*. pl. 38, 1 and pl. 40, 1–2; the new Florence fragment, *CV*. pl. 8, B2. A, warrior leaving home. B, satyrs and maenad. The Goettingen sherd was attributed to the painter by Martin Robertson.

23 (19). Palermo (1484), from Chiusi. A, Inghirami *Chius*. pl. 80. A, Herakles and Pholos. Largely modern. B is lost.

24 (21). Ferrara, T. 694, from Spina. A, *Mouseion* 16 pl. 8, 3–4. A, symposion. B, youths and boy. Late.

(*nos. 25–29, the pictures not framed*)

25 (22). Eleusis, from Eleusis. *Eph.* 1931, 52–60. A, warrior leading horse. B, satyr leading donkey. [Mylonas].

26 (20). Oxford, Beazley, fr. B, komast (youth running to left, looking round, with stick and cup).

27 (23). Ferrara, T. 539, from Spina. *Jb.* 71, 114–15. A, Zephyros pursuing, B, Hyakinthos. Late.

28 (24). Ferrara, T. 931, from Spina. A, man and youth; B, youth. Late.

29 (25). Ferrara, T. 245, from Spina. A, man and boy; B, youth with torch. Late.

STAMNOI

30. (26). Leningrad 642 (St. 1357), from Cervetri. *Mon.* 1856 pl. 8, whence Overbeck *KM*. pl. 6, 4; part of A, *VA*. 47. A, Danae and Perseus. B, Amazons. Restored. See p. 1637.

31 (28). Paris, Ganay (ex Bourguignon). *Coll. 18 mars 1901* pl. 3, 30 and 30A, and p. 10. A, Peleus and Thetis. B, Nereus mounting chariot.

32 (40, +). Louvre C 10754. One fr., *Mon. Piot* 29 pl. 7, 4; *Scritti Libertini* pll. 1–2. A, satyrs using mallets; B, preparations for the sacrifice of a bull. On the subject see ibid. 91–95. Many of the fragments were put together by Villard.

33. LOUVRE C 10827, frr. A, warriors with horses; B, the like.

34 (42, +). LOUVRE C 10797, frr. Athletes.

35 (27). COPENHAGEN 124. A, *BSA.* 18 pl. 10; *CV.* pl. 134; A, *Antik-Cab. 1851*, 135; detail of A, *Studies Robinson* I pl. 47, a. A, youth and women; B, the like; over each handle, Eros. On A, EV+APIΔEϟ retr. and KΛLOϟ, on B, KΛLOϟ.

36 (29). WÜRZBURG 516, from Vulci. *BSA.* 18 pl. 15; Langlotz pll. 185 and 210. Warriors leaving home. Restored.

37. OXFORD, Beazley, frr. Komos (on A, 1, youth to right, lifting the skirt of, 2, girl to left, playing the flute; 3, youth with stick to left, looking round; on B, 1, youth with cup to right, 2, youth to left, 3, youth to right with lyre; 4, (head to left).

HYDRIAI
(no. 38, the picture on the shoulder, framed)

38 (30). VATICAN, from Vulci. *Mus. Greg.* 2 pl. 12, 2; Gerhard pl. 202, 1–2, whence Robert *Scenen der Ilias* 9 fig. 13; ph. Mo. 8602; ph. Al. 35841A, whence Friis Johansen *Iliaden* fig. 41 and *Enc. It.* s.v. Ettore. Achilles and Hector.
(no. 39, the picture on the shoulder, not framed)

39 (31). LONDON E 174, from Vulci. *El.* 3 pl. 19; *CV.* pl. 78, 2 and pl. 79, 3. Poseidon and Aithra. Later.

(nos. 40–45, the picture on the body)

40 (32). ATHENS 1482 (CC. 1246), from Attica. Heydemann pl. 7, 1. Pholos.

41 (33). LENINGRAD, from South Russia. Nike flying with tripod.

42. LOUVRE C 10786. Apollo and Artemis at altar.

43 (34). WÜRZBURG 533, from Vulci. Langlotz pll. 184 and 197. Dionysos and Ariadne.

44 (35). ATHENS Acr. 688, fr., from Athens. Langlotz pl. 53. Warrior leaving home (warrior and woman). Later.

45 (36). VIENNA 582. Komos. Late.

OINOCHOE
(shape 3, chous)

46 (36 *bis*). ATHENS, Agora, P 15010, from Athens. Van Hoorn *Choes* fig. 74. Nike at altar.

LEKYTHOI
(standard shape)

47 (37). OXFORD 315, from Gela. Gardner pl. 24, 3; *CV.* pl. 33, 1. Triptolemos.

48 (38). AGRIGENTO, fr., from Agrigento. Hesperid.

FRAGMENTS OF POTS

49 (39). LOUVAIN, fr., from Athens. Fight (Greeks and Oriental). From a loutrophoros?

50. ATHENS, Agora, P 25957, seven frr., from Athens. One, *Hesp.* 27 pl. 42, n. (Fight—chariot—back of a head, and a boy behind it). From a volute-krater according to Miss Talcott.

51 (44). FLORENCE 13 B 27, fr. *CV.* pl. 13, B 27. (One in long chiton with staff or spear at altar).

52. NAPLES, Astarita, 107, fr. Sacrifice (1, boy in chitoniskos standing to right, holding meat on a spit over the altar, 2, man or youth standing to right, probably holding a vessel in his right hand, the left arm raised; altar with the figure of a lion in the pediment). May be from an amphora.

53. NAPLES, Astarita, 122, two frr. Apollo and Artemis: Apollo's left hand remains, with part of his cithara, of his himation, of the phiale in his right hand; middle of Artemis, and her right hand, holding an oinochoe.

54 (45). HEIDELBERG 116, fr. Kraiker pl. 20. (Man—Hermes?).

55 (47). ATHENS Acr. 909, fr., from Athens. Langlotz pl. 76 and p. 84. (Youth, and hand of one holding a helmet).

56 (49). ATHENS Acr. 910, fr., from Athens. (Foot of one in a long chiton; below, running maeander, rightward).

57. ATHENS Acr., fr. (two joining), from Athens. (Left foot, turned to right, of one standing, with the lower part of the long chiton; diagonally across the shanks, part of a staff or the like).

58. ATHENS Acr., fr., from Athens. (Front middle of a male leaning on his stick to right, then a little of another draped figure).

59 (48). ATHENS Acr. 908, frr., from Athens. Langlotz pl. 76. Amazons making ready. See Bothmer *Am.* 152 no. 65 and p. 157.

60 (41). ATHENS, Agora, P 3299, fr., from Athens. Fight.

60 bis. ELEUSIS 599, fr. from Eleusis. Komos (head of youth playing the flute).

61 (50). ELEUSIS 608, fr., from Eleusis. *Delt.* 9, 33. Komos.

62 (51). ELEUSIS, fr., from Eleusis. *Delt.* 9, 12, δ and (joining) p. 34, δ. Komos.

63 (52). ELEUSIS, fr., from Eleusis. Komos (legs of male in cloak moving to left, flute-case).

64 (53). ELEUSIS, fr., from Eleusis. *Delt.* 9, 34, β. Komos.

65 (54). ELEUSIS, fr., from Eleusis. *Delt.* 9, 34, γ. (Male).

66 (55). ELEUSIS, fr., from Eleusis. (Himation of one to right).

67 (56). ELEUSIS 581, frr., from Eleusis. *Delt.* 9, 12, ε. (Woman).

68 (57). ELEUSIS, fr., from Eleusis. *Delt.* 9, 31 fig. 32, 1. (Satyr).

69 (58). ELEUSIS, fr., from Eleusis. *Delt.* 9, 27 fig. 26, α. (Satyr).

70 (59). ELEUSIS, fr., from Eleusis. (Feet of one standing to right; below, left-ward maeander, pattern-square, rightward maeander).

71 (46). HEIDELBERG 127, fr. Symposion (part of couch, of table, of hi-mation). From a stamnos or a column-krater?

72 (a). ADRIA B 82, fr., from Adria. *CV.* pl. 5, 7. (Naked male).

73. INNSBRUCK ii 12. 33, fr. (The Theban Sphinx carrying off a youth). Bothmer thinks this may be from a hydria.

SKYPHOI
(no. 74, type A)

74 (60). LEIPSIC T 681, fr. Arming.

(no. 75, of Corinthian type)

75. MAYENCE, Univ., 113. Hampe and Simon *G.L.* pl. 24. A, man seated playing the lyre; B, youth seated, with lyre.

CUPS

76 (61). CAMBRIDGE 37.18. *CV.* ii RS. pl. 7, 1, pl. 8, 8, and pl. 9, 7. I, satyr. A–B, warriors (A, attackers; B, defenders in ambush). For the subject, CB. ii, 22.

(nos. 77–87, decorated inside only)

77 (61 *bis*). ATHENS, Agora, P 12072, fr., from Athens. I, (woman).

78 (62). LOUVRE G 136, from Vulci. Emmanuel 262; *BSA.* 18, 227; Pottier pl. 113; ph. Gir. I, pyrrhic. ΑΡΙϚΤΕΙΔΕϚ ΕΙϚVΚΛ complete.

79 (63). FERRARA, T. 503, from Spina. *Riv. Pop. d'It.* Nov. 1928, 42, middle; Aurigemma[1] 69 and 67, 4 = [2]73 and 71, 4; Arias and Alfieri pl. 10; Stella 497; *E.A.A.* iii, 1. I, Danae, Perseus, and Akrisios. See p. 1637.

80 (64). NEW YORK 19.182.32, from Cervetri. I, love-making (male and woman).

81. ITALIAN MARKET. I, athlete (bending, with a marker in his right hand). ΚΑLΟϚ retr.

82. (65). PHILADELPHIA 4842, from Orvieto. *Mus. J.* 4, 156. I, boy seated writing.

83. NAPLES, Astarita, 656. I, youth seated, holding a book.

84. LUCERNE MARKET (A.A.). I, youth with lyre (in himation, to left, bending, stick in left hand, with right hand laying a lyre on a seat, or picking it up).

85 (66). MUNICH 2679. I, woman pouring warm water into a laver.

86 (67). VILLA GIULIA (ex Castellani). I, priest (in robe, standing frontal, head to left, holding something over a basin; on the right, altar).

87 (67 *bis*). SYDNEY 46.40, from Vulci. Gerhard pl. 302–3, 3–4; *Burl. 1903* pl. 89, G 13; Trendall *Hdbk Nich.*[2] 295; *JHS.* 71 pl. 40, a. I, woman spinning.

For the *black-figure* work of the Eucharides Painter (panathenaics prize and other; pelikai; amphorae; hydriai) see *ABV*. 395–8 and 696, and add

BF. PELIKE

1. SAMOTHRACE 57.565, from Samothrace. A, *BCH*. 1958, 773; A, *Archaeology* 12, 164 fig. 2, left. A, Hermes seated playing the flute, goat dancing, and satyr. B, citharode and man.

BF. HYDRIAI
(kalpides, with picture on the body)

2. LENINGRAD (1517). Hermes and three nymphs. [Bothmer].

3. CAPESTHORNE, Bromley-Davenport. *JHS*. 78 pl. 9. Herakles and Cerberus. [Bothmer]. Now cleaned.

The bf. prize panathenaic formerly in the Hearst collection at San Simeon (*ABV*. 395, foot, no. 3) is now New York 56.171.3. The bf. prize panathenaic Munich inv. 8746, said in *ABV*. 397, middle, to be either by the Eucharides Painter or near him, is in fact his. The panathenaic in Leningrad (*ABV*. 396 no. 10): A, Blavatski 262, left. The pelike in Leningrad (*ABV*. 396 no. 24): A, ibid., right.

As to the bf. vases said in *ABV*. 397 to be near the Eucharides Painter, A of no. 1 (Hamburg 1906.380) is reproduced in *Gymnasium* 67 pl. 8, 1; A of no. 4 (Naples 2481) ibid. pl. 12, 1; ibid. p. 397 no. 34 (Bronxville, Bastis) in Bothmer *A.N.Y.* pl. 76, 208 and pl. 78, 208.

See also p. 223.

CHAPTER 17

MYSON AND OTHER PAINTERS OF COLUMN-KRATERS

THE GROUP OF ACROPOLIS 787

No. 1 was said in *ARV.*[1], 151, μ, to be akin to the work of the Nikoxenos Painter.

COLUMN-KRATERS

1. ATHENS Acr. 787, frr., from Athens. Langlotz pl. 70. A, maenad mounting chariot, with satyrs. B, (horses, warrior).

2. ATHENS, Agora, P 17462, two frr., from Athens. On one fragment, (chariot: forearms of the driver with reins and goad, forearm of the passenger holding the rail); on the other, (lyre, maenad, vine-branch held by Dionysos).

THE PAINTER OF NAPLES RC 132

Att. V. 45. ARV.[1] 101 and 159.

Recalls the rough cups from the circle of the Nikosthenes Painter (p. 132).

COLUMN-KRATER
(with framed pictures)

1 (1). NAPLES RC 132, from Cumae. A, gigantomachy (Athena and Giant). B, satyr attacking maenad. See p. 236.

LOUTROPHOROS

2 (2). ATHENS 1452 (CC. 1168). A, CC. pl. 42. A, prothesis; B, valediction; on the neck, A, mourning women, B, the like.

Near these, the

LOUTROPHOROS

(a). ATHENS, Vlasto, fr., from Koropi. A, prothesis.

THE GOETTINGEN PAINTER

ARV.[1] 158-9.

COLUMN-KRATERS
(nos. 1-14, with framed pictures)

1 (2). GOETTINGEN H 36 and H 37. A, Dionysos and satyrs. B, komos (two youths).

2 (a2). VILLA GIULIA 47232, from Cervetri. *ML.* 42, 971–2. A, satyrs and maenad; B, two satyrs.

3 (3). PALERMO, fr., from Selinus. *ML.* 32 pl. 95, 4. (Satyr).

4 (8). Once AGRIGENTO, Giuffrida. A, satyrs and maenad (satyr dancing to right, maenad running to right, looking round, with a fawn in her left hand, satyr running to left, holding a drinking-horn). B, (?).

5 (11). TARANTO 20319, from Taranto. A, Peleus and Thetis. B, Herakles and a youth (supporting each other), Dionysos, and a satyr.

6 (1). VILLA GIULIA 1342, from Falerii. *CV.* pl. 16, 4–5; A, ph. R.I. 1929.326. A, horseman (ἀκοντίζων ἀφ᾽ ἵππου). B, two satyrs. See p. 1638.

7 (9). CORINTH, from Corinth. B, *AJA.* 1939, 593 fig. 6. A, (horse and male). B, komos (two youths).

8. LOUVRE C 10777. A, Herakles and Kyknos. B, (satyr, fingers).

9 (4). NAPLES RC 131, from Cumae. *ML.* 22, 518–19. A, fight. B, komos.

10 (5, +). NEW YORK 06.1021.97 (part ex Greifswald 341). B, Sambon *Canessa* pl. 8, 88; the Greifswald fr., Peters pl. 37. A, fight (Greeks and Oriental). B, komos. Bothmer observed that the Greifswald fragment joined the New York vase.

11 (10). HARVARD 1925.30.126. *CV.* Hoppin pl. 7. A, warriors lying in wait; B, the like. On the neck, A, in silhouette, centaurs fleeing: see p. 235. Restored. See *Antike Kunst* 4, 64.

12. GOETTINGEN, fr. *Auction xvi Basle* pl. 28, 122. A, komos.

13 (6). ATHENS, Agora, P 4674, fr., from Athens. Komos.

14 (7). ATHENS, Agora, P 4694, fr., from Athens. (Youth). Belongs to the last?

(no. 15, the pictures not framed)

15 (12). LENINGRAD 634 (St. 1713). A, *CR.* 1869, 161; A, Licht i, 279. A, naked woman juggling with phialai; B, komast.

MANNER OF THE GOETTINGEN PAINTER

ARV.[1] 159.

Nos. 1–4 and 6, at least, may well be by the painter himself.

COLUMN-KRATERS
(with framed pictures)

1 (1). NEW YORK 91.1.462. A, Richter and Milne fig. 46. A, Herakles and (Kyknos?). B, komos (two youths). On the neck, A, in silhouette on white ground, hunters and hounds: see p. 235.

2. ERLANGEN P 114. A, Bothmer *Am.* pl. 70, 3. A, Herakles and the Amazons. B, satyr with donkey. Restored as a stamnos. See Bothmer *Am.* 141.

3. GREIFSWALD 342, three frr. One, Peters pl. 37. A, (warriors).

4. GREIFSWALD 351, fr. Peters pl. 37. Komos (two youths at column-krater).

5. GREIFSWALD 345, fr. Peters pl. 37. (Youth—komast?).

6. GELA (Acr. amb. 10 no. 5), fr., from Gela. (Komos?—fingers, upper part of a youth's head to left).

7 (3). NEW YORK 41.162.73, from Cumae. *Coll. B. et C.* pl. 19, 158; B, *Cat. 7 juin 1922* pl. 3, 58; *AJA.* 1924, 278-9; *CV.* Gallatin pl. 9, 5 and 7-8. A, Theseus and the bull. B, fight.

8. PORTLAND (Oregon) 26.305. A, woman with bull. B, boxers. [Amyx]. B much restored.

9 (4). PARIS MARKET (Segredakis). A, *Coll. Woodyat* pl. 3, 45. A, youths at laver. B, fight.

10. ATHENS, Agora, P 17751, fr., from Athens. B, (youth).

The following recalls the Goettingen Painter:

COLUMN-KRATER

ATHENS, Agora, P 19579, frr., from Athens. (Males, horse?).

The small figures in silhouette, with mock inscriptions, on the neck of Harvard 1925.30.126 (p. 234 no. 11) and New York 91.1.462 (p. 234 no. 1) link those vases with two black-figured column-kraters of the Leagros Group: Brussels R 324 (*CV.* H e pl. 16, 2: *ABV.* 376 no. 225) and Bologna 52 (*CV.* H e pl. 28, 1-2: *ABV.* 376 no. 231). Another bf. column-krater of the Leagros Group, Bologna 51 (*ABV.* 376 no. 234) has a similar band on the neck, but I have not noted whether the style of the silhouette figures is the same as in the four—particularly as in Harvard 1925.30.126, where the subject is the same, four centaurs fleeing to right. A fragment of a column-krater, Hildesheim 1630, is from a neck-picture in the same style as the four (a naked man sitting on the ground, with goats): one cannot say whether the main pictures were black-figure or red-figure. A red-figured column-krater by the Chairippos Painter, in the Lucerne market (p. 236 no. 7) has a similar band on the neck, but there are no inscriptions and the style is rather different.

Other coarse early column-kraters are akin to those of the Goettingen Painter, but cannot be said to be in his manner:

ARV.[1] 160 and 954.

(*with framed pictures*)

1 (α). PORT SUNLIGHT 2139. A, Tillyard pl. 20, 123. A, Dionysos reclining, and satyr. B, komos.

2 (β). LONDON MARKET (ex Lamb). Destroyed by enemy action: fragments are in Reading. A, Dionysos reclining, and satyr. B, fight.

3 (γ). LENINGRAD (St. 1629). A, komos. B, Herakles and Acheloos.

4 (δ). BARI 4979, from Rutigliano. *RM.* 19, 80–83; phs. R.I. 1529–32b. A, naked women washing. B, komos (two youths). See p. 1638.

Also akin, the column-krater Naples RC 132 (p. 233, middle, no. 1) and those of the Chairippos Painter.

THE CHAIRIPPOS PAINTER

Att. V. 106. *ARV.*[1] 160–1.

Named after the kalos name on no. 8.
Allied to the Goettingen Painter, but less old-fashioned.

COLUMN-KRATERS
(nos. 1–5, with framed pictures)

1 (9). FLORENCE 3991. *CV.* pl. 38, 3 and pl. 41, 1–2. A, fight. B, komos (two youths).

2 (5). OXFORD 1954.236, five frr., from Al Mina. *JHS.* 59, 2, 3. A, Theseus and the bull. See no. 6.

3 (7). ATHENS Acr. 795 and 792, frr., from Athens. Langlotz pl. 71. A, Centauromachy.

3 *bis.* ELEUSIS 634, fragmentary, from Eleusis. A, chariot of Dionysos (satyr with one foot in the car, maenad); B, three satyrs.

4 (10). TARQUINIA RC 2398, from Tarquinia. A, *CV.* pl. 9, 1. A, komos; B, komos.

5. LOUVRE C 10771. A, athletes. B, komos.

(no. 6, not known if the pictures framed)

6 (6). OXFORD 1954.237, four frr., from Al Mina. *JHS.* 59, 2, 4. B, komast. Would seem to belong to no. 2. If a fifth fragment, with a hand raised holding a stick, is from the same vase as 1954.237, the picture was unframed: this would be an objection to its belonging to 1954.236, but not a fatal one as is shown by the Lucerne vase (no. 7).

(no. 7, on A the picture framed, on B not)

7. LUCERNE MARKET (A.A.). *Ars Ant. Aukt. II* pl. 61, 151. A, maenad, satyr, and donkey; B, satyr. On the neck, A, in silhouette, athletes (boxers, jumpers, wrestlers).

(nos. 8–12, the pictures not framed)

8 (1). SYRACUSE 21138, from Gela. A, *ML.* 17, 402 and pl. 22, whence Robert *Herm.* 230 fig. 182a. A, komos (man and youth). B, satyr. On A, +ΛΙΡΙΓΓΟϚΚΛLΟϚ.

9 (2). COPENHAGEN inv. 3759. *CV.* pl. 126, 1. A, boxer. B, komast.

10 (3). FLORENCE 3980. *CV.* pl. 38, 4 and pl. 41, 3–4; A, *E.A.A.* ii, 532 fig. 733. A, athletes (discus-thrower and acontist). B, satyr. On A, ΑΦΡΟΔΙϟ[Ι]Α ΚΑΛΕ.

11. LUCERNE MARKET (A.A.). A, Dionysos on donkey; B, satyr. On A, to right, looking round, with kantharos and vine; on B, to left, looking round, with wineskin.

12. BESANÇON. A, *Bull. mus. France* Sept. 1947, 10. A, satyr and maenad; B, satyr. [Loye].

13 (4). ATHENS Acr. 793, fr., from Athens. Langlotz 75. Satyr.

FRAGMENTS
(may all be from column-kraters)

14 (11). ELEUSIS 585, fr., from Eleusis. *Delt.* 9, 21 fig. 18. Naked male felling another (probably boxers or pancratiasts).

15 (12). ELEUSIS 583, fr., from Eleusis. (Upper parts of male to left and of naked youth to right).

16. ELEUSIS 587, fr., from Eleusis. (Youth). Belongs to the last?

17 (13). ELEUSIS 613, fr., from Eleusis. *Delt.* 9, 12, foot, left. (Youth). See the next.

18 (13). ELEUSIS, fr., from Eleusis. *Delt.* 9, 12, foot, right. (Komast). Belongs to the last?

19 (14). ATHENS Acr. 928, fr., from Athens. A, (jumper and acontist). See the next.

20 (15). ATHENS Acr. 918, fr., from Athens. (Middle of a naked male moving to right). Belongs to the last?

Compare also the fragment (of a column-krater?)

(1). MUNICH, fr., from Athens. (Middle and right arm of naked male moving to left).

MYSON

VA. 48–52. *Att. V.* 97–99 and 470. *V.Pol.* 16 and 79. *ARV.*[1] 169–73 and 954.

The name is given by a small vase (no. 42) which he signs both as painter and as potter.

His earlier vases recall Phintias, and Phintias may have been his master. Compare Athens 636 and 766 (p. 25 nos. 1–2).

Most of his works are very ordinary column-kraters, but five excellent vases show him at his best: the amphora in the Louvre (no. 1), the calyx-krater in London (no. 16), the panathenaic in Florence (no. 2), the Astarita psykter (no. 77), and the Florence cup (no. 83). No. 16 was compared with no 1 by de Witte (*Coll. Durand* 152 no. 411).

Myson was the father of the Mannerists (p. 562). The Pig Painter (p. 562) is especially close to him, continues his style in fact; and it is not easy to say where Myson ends and Pig Painter begins.

AMPHORA
(type A; the pictures not framed)

1 (47). LOUVRE G 197, from Vulci. *Mon.* 1 pll. 54–55, whence Inghirami pll. 319–20 and *JHS*. 18, 268; *FR*. pl. 113 and ii, 277 and 282 fig. 99, whence (B) Radermacher[2] *Mythos* fig. 20; Pottier pl. 128; *CV*. pl. 35 and pl. 94, 5; *Mon. Piot* 29, 178–9; *Enc. phot.* iii, 10–11, whence (A) Frel *Ř.V.* fig. 161; *Bull. Vereen.* 29, 18–19; B, Dugas and Flacelière pl. 8; A, *E.A.A.* ii, 927 fig. 1189; phs. Gir. 17826–7; B, phs. Arch. phot. MNLA 1344. A, Croesus on the pyre. B, Theseus and Antiope. See p. 1638.

PANATHENAIC AMPHORA

2 (48, +). FLORENCE 3982 and LOUVRE. Incompletely, *CV*. Florence pl. 25, 1 and pl. 26. The struggle for the tripod: A, Apollo; B, Herakles. A fragment in the Louvre, and three in Florence, belong. The Louvre fragment gives the right thigh of Herakles and part of the tripod; one of the Florence fragments, the middle foot of the tripod; the second, the left upper-arm of Apollo and part of his cloak; the third (two joining) his left hand, holding arrows, and part of the cloak at that point.

PELIKAI
(nos. 3–14, with framed pictures)

3 (36). SYRACUSE 15709, from Gela. *CV*. pl. 1; B, ph. R.I. 5421.299. A, boy victor with youth and trainer. B, komos.

4 (37). NAPLES 3051, from Nola. A, ph. So. 11009, v, 1. A, komos. B, two two satyrs.

5 (39). SYRACUSE 20065, from Gela. A, *Anz.* 1936, 342 fig. 5; *CV*. pl. 7, 1–2. A, naked woman with olisboi; B, naked woman.

6 (38). SYRACUSE 20066, from Gela. A, komast; B, komast.

7 (40). MISSISSIPPI (ex Robinson), from Athens? *CV*. ii pl. 24, 2 and pl. 26; A, *A.A.A.* pl. 80, 271. A, komast. B, satyr. Restored.

8 (41). FLORENCE 8 B 17. Part, *CV*. pl. 8, B 17. A, komast; B, naked woman cup-bearer (ladling from a psykter).

9. LOUVRE C 11100, fr. (six joining). Woman at laver. On this and the next five see also p. 242, foot.

10. LOUVRE C 11097, fr. (ten joining). A, armed acrobat.

11. LOUVRE C 11101, fr. (five joining). One lifting a vessel (or setting it down).

12. LOUVRE C 309 *bis*, fr. (four joining). Naked male bending. Belongs to the last?

13. LOUVRE C 11098, fr. (two joining). Komast? (legs of male moving to right).

14. LOUVRE C 281, fr. Youth (chin, breast, parts of arms). Belongs to the last?

(no. 15, the pictures not framed)

15 (42). PALERMO (1495), from Chiusi. A, komos (two youths). B, man (or Zeus?) pursuing a woman.

CALYX-KRATERS

16 (46). LONDON E 458. *Mon.* 2 pll. 25–26; A, *VA.* 49, whence *Mon. Piot* 29, 181; B, Herford pl. 7, d; B, Stella 154, above; B, ph. Ma. 3138. A, rescue of Aithra. B, Herakles and Apollo: the struggle for the tripod.

17 (a). BERLIN inv. 3257, from Falerii. *Anz.* 1893, 88; Lücken pll. 39–40; Licht ii, 132. A, fight; B, warriors setting out. On A, NIKON, and on shields KALOS and HIΠON. See p. 1602.

COLUMN-KRATERS
(nos. 18–29, with framed pictures)

18 (1). NAPLES 2410, from Ruvo. A, Stella 377, above; B, ph. So. 11071, iii, 1. A, chariot of Dionysos (Ariadne mounting chariot, and Dionysos). B, Centauromachy (Kaineus).

19 (2). WÜRZBURG 526, from Vulci. Langlotz pl. 193, pl. 135, and pl. 211; B.Ap. xxi. 26. A, Dionysos and satyrs. B, komos.

20. LOUVRE C 10759, frr. A, Dionysos and satyrs. B, komos.

21 (3). VILLA GIULIA 984, from Falerii. A, *Boll. d'Arte* 10, 341; A, *Dedalo* 3, 78; *CV.* pl. 15; A, ph. Al. 41215; A, ph. G.F. 9177, left. A, Herakles and the lion. B, athletes.

22 (4). NEW YORK 56.171.45 (ex Hearst). *AJA.* 1945, 475, 1; A, *Bull. Metr.* March 1957, 175, 3. A, fight. B, komos.

23 (5). VILLA GIULIA 1044, from Falerii. *CV.* pl. 16, 1–2; A, ph. Al. 41191. A, athletes. B, komos.

24. NICOSIA MK 50, from Mines near Kazaphani. A, symposion (male running to left, male reclining to left; the left-hand part of the picture lost); B, komos.

25 (7). Once CATANIA, Ricupero. A, Benndorf pl. 41, 2. A, symposion (youth reclining and youth with lyre). B, athletes.

26 (6). ATHENS Acr. 804, fr., from Athens. Langlotz pl. 70. A, symposion? (man—reclining?)

27 (8). ATHENS, Agora, P 7249, fr., from Athens. Komos. [Talcott].

28. LOUVRE C 11211, fr. Komos? (head and shoulder of youth).

29 (9). ATHENS, Agora, P 6890, fr., from Athens. (Man).

(nos. 30–39, not known whether the pictures framed)

30. NEW YORK, Mirsky, fr. A, (Dionysos: his head remains, to left, with part of his vine-branch). [Bothmer].

31. ATHENS, Agora, P 7244e and f, two frr., from Athens. I, symposion. As the next.

32. ATHENS, Agora, P 7244, part, from Athens. I, symposion.

33. LOUVRE C 11212, fr. A, symposion.

34 (10). ATHENS Acr. 800, fr., from Athens. Langlotz pl. 70. A, symposion? (man—reclining?).

35 (30). AMSTERDAM inv. 2893, fr. B, komast (youth with pointed amphora).

36. ATHENS, Agora, P 5557, fr., from Athens. (Komast—arm with oinochoe in the hand, stick).

37 (31). ELEUSIS, fr., from Eleusis. Komos? (head and breast of youth to right, a drinking-horn in his left hand).

38. ATHENS, Agora, P 14711, part, fr., from Athens. (Raised hand, naked youth).

39 (34). ATHENS Acr. 801, fr., from Athens. Langlotz pl. 70. (Youth—komast?) Under this number Langlotz mentions two other fragments, which I have not seen.

(nos. 40–76, the pictures not framed)

40. LOUVRE C 10757, fr. A, Herakles and Apollo: the struggle for the tripod. B, komast.

41 (11). FLORENCE 3981. *CV*. pl. 38, 2 and pl. 40, 3–4. A, Herakles with the tripod. B, acontist.

42 (12). ATHENS Acr. 806, from Athens. *Mon. Piot* 29 pl. 7, 5–6; Langlotz pl. 72. A, Athena and male at altar; B, Athena seated, and youth. On the neck, ΜΥΣΟΝΕΛΡΑΦΣΕΝΚΑΓΟΙ ΕΣΕΝ. Small.

43 (13). LENINGRAD 632 (St. 1602). A, Bothmer *Am.* pl. 73, 6. A, mounted warrior. B, komast. According to Bothmer the warrior is probably an Amazon (*Am.* 159).

44 (14). LOUVRE CA 1947, from Orvieto. *CV*. pl. 24, whence *Die Antike* 6, 8; *Mon. Piot* 29 pl. 6. A, satyrs demolishing a tomb. B, athletes (acontist, jumper, and flute-player).

45 (15). NEW YORK 07.286.73. A, *VA*. 48; A, Richter and Milne 26; Richter and Hall pl. 23, 20 and pl. 170, 20, whence (A) Rumpf *MZ*. pl. 23, 3; part of A, Richter *ARVS*. fig. 49; A, Richter *H*. 213, f. A, Dionysos. B, komast.

46 (16). BOLOGNA 265, fr., from Bologna. Pellegrini 108. A, Dionysos.

47 (17). FLORENCE 13 B 47, frr. Part, *CV*. pl. 13, B 47. A, male (Dionysos or Hephaistos) riding a donkey. B, komast.

48 (18). COPENHAGEN 3836, from Orvieto. *CV*. pl. 126, 2. A, satyr. B, komast.

49. LUCERNE MARKET (A.A.). A, satyr (in panther-skin, moving to right, looking round, an aulos in each hand). B, komast (naked youth moving to right, looking round, skyphos in right hand, the left raised).

50. LOUVRE C 10755. A, satyr (moving to right, looking round, with wine-skin and skyphos). B, male (moving to right).

51 (a9). FERRARA, T. 223, from Spina. *NSc.* 1927, 147, whence *Anz.* 1928, 130. A, maenad; B, satyr. Late. Recalls the Pig Painter.

52 (10). OXFORD 561. *JHS.* 28 pl. 31; A, *VA.* 50; *CV*. pl. 23, 1 and pl. 22, 5; A, Norman Gardiner *Athl.* fig. 130. A, discus-thrower. B, komast. B restored.

53 (a3). ATHENS, Agora, P 11025 a–b, two frr., from Athens. A, discus-thrower.

54 (20). Once AGRIGENTO, Giudice, 593, from Gela. Ph. Lo Cascio pl. 6. A, acontist; B, athlete.

55 (21). VIENNA 2157, fr., from Orvieto. *CV*. pl. 86, 4. Athlete.

55 *bis.* NAPLES, Museo di Capodimonte, 987. A, athlete with pick; B, trainer. [Bothmer].

55 *ter.* RIEHEN, Hoek. A, warrior (standing to right, looking round, device a lion). B, naked youth (running to left, looking round). [Hecht].

56. BASLE, Cahn, 4 frr. Naked youth with shield (the upper half remains). [Hecht].

57 (22). VILLA GIULIA 25004, fr. *ML.* 14, 299; *CV*. pl. 16, 3. A, symposion (youth reclining).

58 (32). ATHENS, Agora, P 7244 a–b, two frr., from Athens. Komast. [Talcott].

59. ATHENS, Agora, P 7244 d, fr., from Athens. Komast (a hand holding a skyphos remains). [Talcott].

60. ATHENS, Agora, P 7244 c, fr., from Athens. Komast. [Talcott].

61. ATHENS, Agora, P 7244 h, fr., from Athens. Komast. [Talcott].

62 (24). PHILADELPHIA 5688, from Chiusi. *Mus. J.* 23, 32–33; R.I. ix. 97. Komos: A, naked woman cup-bearer; B, youth with pointed amphora.

63 (25). PALERMO (1494). Komos: A, naked woman cup-bearer (with ladle and skyphos, at a pointed amphora); B, komast. Much restored.

64. GELA, from Gela. *NSc.* 1960, 138–9. A, komast; B, komast.

65 (26). NAPLES RC 153, from Cumae. A, komast; B, komast.

66 (27). MUNICH inv. 7528. Komos: A, youth; B, naked woman.

67 (28). ALTENBURG 279. *CV*. pl. 54. A, komast; B, komast.

68 (29, +). LOUVRE C 10778 (including S 1315), frr. A, komast; B, komast. Many Louvre fragments belong to S 1315.

69 (a5). ATHENS, Agora, P 7250, fr., from Athens. Komast.

70 (a4). ATHENS, Agora, P 10578, from Athens. A, komast (playing the flute). B, discus-thrower.

71. LUCERNE MARKET (A.A.). Komos: A, youth with stick and pointed amphora; B, youth with wineskin and skyphos.

72 (a6). CRACOW inv. 1321, fr. *V.Pol.* pl. 7, 1; *CV.* pl. 10, 3. Komast.

73 (a7). NEW YORK 21.88.82. A, *Bull. Metr.* 18, 255 fig. 7; A, *V.Pol.* pl. 7, 2; A, Richter and Milne 5; Richter and Hall pl. 23, 21 and pl. 170, 21. A, komast; B, komast.

74 (a8). FLORENCE, from Orvieto. *NSc.* 1939, 32–33. A, komast; B, komast.

75 (33). ATHENS Acr. 803, fr., from Athens. Langlotz pl. 70. Youth—komast?

76 (35). ATHENS Acr. 802, fr., from Athens. Langlotz pl. 70. Naked woman with olisbos.

PSYKTER

77. NAPLES, Astarita, 428. Theseus and Antiope. [Bothmer]. See Bothmer *Am.* 129–30.

OINOCHOAI
(nos. 78–79, shape 3, choes)

78. SALONICA 799. Dionysos and satyr (Dionysos seated to right, satyr to left, bending, taking grapes out of a basket).

79. ATHENS, Agora, P 25965, fr., from Athens. *Hesp.* 27 pl. 45, d; *JHS.* 78, Reports, 4, b; *Anz.* 1957, 59; *BCH.* 1958, 666 fig. 16; Sparkes, Talcott, and Frantz fig. 16; *Fasti arch.* 12 pl. 7, 18. Komos (two youths). See p. 1638.

(no. 80, shape 1)

80 (43). BOSTON 03.786, from Vulci. Youth with sword pursuing a woman.

FRAGMENTS OF POTS

81 (44). ADRIA B 515 and B 1412, fr., from Adria. Part, Schöne pl. 10, 8; *CV.* pl. 5, 4; *Riv. Ist.* N.S. 5–6, 34 fig. 8. A, return of Hephaistos. From a column-krater or a volute-krater?

82 (45). LENINGRAD, fr. (Head and shoulders of youth facing right).

CUP

83 (a). FLORENCE 3 B 15. Part, *Boll. d'Arte* 1928, 183 and 185; *CV.* pl. 3, B 15. I, satyr and maenad. A, warriors. On I, ᒪEΛΛP[Oϟ . . .

MANNER OF MYSON

(i)

These small fragments go with the Louvre pelike-fragments p. 238 nos. 9–14; may be from the same vases, and, whether or not, are Mysonian.

PELIKAI

1. LOUVRE C 11110, fr. (On the right, above, something that recalls the saccos of the woman in Louvre C 11100 (p. 238 no. 9).
2. LOUVRE C 11104, fr. (Basket hanging).
3. LOUVRE C 11105, fr. (Bottom of a basket).
4. LOUVRE C 11096, fr. (four joining). (Wineskin hanging).

(ii)

various

PELIKAI

(nos. 1-2, ordinary)

1. LOUVRE C 11119, fr. Komos (hand with skyphos, middle of naked male moving to right).
2 (13). ERLANGEN 292, from Nola. A, jumper and trainer. B, man and youth. Framed pictures.

(no. 3, neck-pelike)

3 (14). CATANIA 714. A, Libertini pl. 81. A, maenad; B, satyr.

COLUMN-KRATERS

(with framed pictures)

4 (1). BERLIN inv. 31404, from near Taranto. *Vereinigung der Freunde antiker Kunst, Bericht 1934*, frontispiece and p. 18; *Staatliche Museen, Erwerbungen 1933-5*, 7-8. A, youth with panther-cub, and youths. B, groom currying horse, and youth. [Zahn, Langlotz]. All rather coarse Mysonian, except the naked bodies from collar-bone to waist, which are in the manner of the Eucharides Painter. Restored.

5 (10). MITTELSCHREIBERHAU, Guthmann. Neugebauer *ADP*. pl. 69. A, komos; B, komos. Odd the youth on B who plays the part of Sisyphos. Restored.

FRAGMENTS OF POTS

6 (16). BRYN MAWR P 975, fr. (Upper part of a satyr to right, looking round).
7. ATHENS Acr., fr., from Athens. (Cup-bearer: what remains is right hand, holding a ladle, and left arm, with a cup in the hand, of one to right). Might be from a column-krater or a pelike. May be by Myson himself.
8. FLORENCE PD 352, fr. (Middle of a naked male to right, turning round).
9. ATHENS Acr. 810, frr., from Athens. One, Langlotz pl. 71. A, symposion. From a column-krater?
10 (17). ATHENS Acr. 947, fr., from Athens. Langlotz pl. 79. (Woman).
11 (18). ATHENS Acr. 929, fr., from Athens. Langlotz pl. 77. (Youth). From the same vase (pelike?) as the last?

12 (19). ATHENS Acr. 930, fr., from Athens. Langlotz pl. 77. (Youth). [Langlotz].

13. MUNICH inv. 8740, fr. Naked woman running with wineskin. From the reverse of a column-krater?

14 (20). HEIDELBERG 117, two frr., from Cervetri. Kraiker pl. 19. On one fr., (Apollo and Artemis), on the other, (woman). From a psykter? Mannered.

CHAPTER 18

THE SYLEUS SEQUENCE

THE SYLEUS SEQUENCE

The Painter of the Munich Amphora—the Gallatin Painter—the Diogenes Painter—the Syleus Painter: these form a stylistic sequence. In the lists that follow I still keep the groups apart: but it is very likely that the Diogenes Painter is an earlier phase of the Syleus, the Gallatin a still earlier; and even the Painter of the Munich Amphora might be the nonage of the Syleus.

THE PAINTER OF THE MUNICH AMPHORA

Att. V. 108–9 and 470. *ARV.*[1] 161–3.

AMPHORAE

(no. 1, type A; with framed pictures)

1 (1). MUNICH 2303 (J. 749), from Agrigento. A, Richter *F.* fig. 163; cleaned, *CV.* pll. 186–7, pl. 188, 10, and p. 21; A, *E.A.A.* i, 392. A, unexplained subject: a man reclining, a woman offering him a wreath, a hunter approaching: see *ABV.* 700. B, Dionysos with satyr and maenad.

(nos. 2–3, type C)
(no. 2, the pictures framed)

2 (2). LOUVRE G 62. *CV.* pl. 32, 2–3. A, satyr and maenad; B, two satyrs.

(no. 3, the pictures not framed)

3 (3). LENINGRAD (St. 1637). *CR.* 1866 pl. 5, 1–3, whence Overbeck *KM.* pl. 6, 9, Cook *Zeus* i, 531, (A) Jahn *Entf. der Europa* pl. 5, 6; A, R.I. xxi. 11. A, Europa; B, Zeus.

PELIKAI

(with framed pictures)

4 (4). BERLIN inv. 3154. *Anz.* 1889, 92, left; B.Ap. xxii. 10, whence (A) *Jb.* 59–60, 77. A, Herakles and a king. B, naked youth (Theseus?) attacking a man.

5 (5). BONN 75. *CV.* pl. 13, 1–4; B.Ap. xxii. 29. A, Apollo and Artemis. B, komos (two youths). A restored.

COLUMN-KRATERS

(no. 6, the pictures framed)

6 (6). SALERNO 1130, from Fratte. A, Theseus and Procrustes; Theseus and Minotaur. B, komos.

(no. 7, the pictures not framed)

7 (7). TARQUINIA RC 992, from Tarquinia. A, girl dancing and woman seated playing the lyre. B, komos.

STAMNOI
(no. 8, the pictures framed)

8 (8). LOUVRE G 54 *bis*, from Nola. Millingen *Coghill* pl. 23; *CV*. pl. 6, 1 and 4. A, Dionysos and satyr. B, warrior leaving home (warrior and woman). On A, ΜΕΝΑΔΡΟ϶ and ΚΑΛΟϚΗΕΟ (= καλῶς χέω, see *AJA*. 1941, 599), both retr. On B, ΗΟΓΑΙΚΑΛΟϚ retr. Now cleaned.

(no. 9, the pictures not framed)

9 (9). TARQUINIA RC 2460, from Tarquinia. A, Ghali-Kahil *H*. pl. 42, 2. A, Menelaos and Helen. B, komos.

HYDRIAI
(of bf. shape; with framed pictures)

10 (10). COMPIÈGNE 1054, from Vulci. *CV*. pl. 13, 6 and pl. 15, 2–3. Herakles and Athena, both seated, with Hermes; on the shoulder, Herakles and the lion.

11 (11). BERLIN 2175, from Etruria. Genick pl. 29, whence Ghali-Kahil *H*. pl. 102, 2; Lücken pl. 42; phs. Marb. LA 1079. 6–7 and 1081.36. Theseus carrying off Helen. On the shoulder, death of Priam. See p. 247.

FRAGMENTS OF A POT
(with framed picture)

12 (12). ATHENS Acr. 813, frr., from Athens. Langlotz pl. 73. Woman and youth, both seated.

A lost vase, as Brommer has seen, may be by the Painter of the Munich Amphora:

AMPHORA
(with framed pictures)

ROMAN MARKET (Campanari). B.Ap. xxii. 22, whence *Jb*. 52, 208–9 and (B) Buschor *Satyrtänze* fig. 66. A, return of Hephaistos; B, satyr and (man?). Restored. See Brommer in *Jb*. 52, 210–11.

Near the Painter of the Munich Amphora, and possibly a late work of his:

PELIKE
(the pictures not framed)

BERLIN inv. 4560. A, *Coll. M.E.* pl. 10, 226; A, Schröder *Sport* pl. 100, 1; A, Licht i, 105; A, Blümel *S.H.* 85. A, athlete at laver; B, youth. See p. 1639.

The following is by the same *potter* as the Berlin hydria 2175 (above, no. 11); the pattern on the mouth, and the small handle-palmettes, are also the same as there:

HYDRIA
(of bf. shape)

WÜRZBURG 322. Langlotz pl. 98. Black.

THE GALLATIN PAINTER

ARV.[1] 163. CB. ii, 11–13. See p. 245.

Named after the former owner of no. 3.

HYDRIAI
(no. 1, of bf. shape; with framed pictures)

1 (1). BOSTON 13. 200, from Gela? (or rather Suessula?) *MFA. Bull.* 12, 6; *VA.* 51, whence *Bull. Vereen.* 17, 5 fig. 10; *Historia* 4, 208; Cloché *Les Classes* pl. 26; Casson *Technique* fig. 82; Cook *Zeus* iii pl. 38; the chief picture, Blümel *Griechische Bildhauer an der Arbeit* 35; Fairbanks and Chase 47 fig. 45; CB. ii pl. 34; the shape, Caskey G. 107. Danae. On the shoulder, Theseus and the bull. See CB. ii, 11–13.

(no. 2, kalpis, the picture on the shoulder, framed)

2 (2). VATICAN, from Cervetri. *Mus. Greg.* 2 pl. 12, 3; Pareti *Tomba Regolini-Galassi* pl. 51, 393; the shoulder, ph. And. 42068. Herakles and the lion. See p. 1639.

AMPHORA
(type B; with framed pictures)

3 (3). NEW YORK 41.162.101. *CV.* Gallatin pl. 51, 1; A, *Bull. Metr.* 37, 55; A, *AJA.* 1944, 38; part of A, Richter *ARVS.* fig. 51; A, Richter *H.* 214, a. A, Theseus and Skiron; B, Theseus and Minotaur.

A fragment is near both the Gallatin Painter and the Diogenes:

HYDRIA
(of bf. shape, with framed picture)

MYKONOS, fr., from Rheneia (originally from Delos). Dugas *Délos xxi* pl. 4, 11. Achilles and Polyxene at the fountain. Troilos was doubtless represented as well.

THE DIOGENES PAINTER

VA. 52. *Att. V.* 111–12 and 470. *ARV.*[1] 163–4 and 954. See p. 245.

Named after one of the inscriptions on no. 2.

COLUMN-KRATER
(the pictures not framed)

1 (1). LENINGRAD, from Kerch. *Otchët 1899*, 27 fig. 39; *VA*. 53. A, Zeus and Athena. B is lost.

AMPHORAE
(type B; the pictures framed)

2 (2). LONDON E 261, from Vulci. Gerhard pl. 273; *Gaz. arch.* 1875 pll. 3–4; detail of A, *VA*. 52; *CV*. pl. 4, 2; B, ph. Ma. 3120. A, youths and B, Dionysos and satyrs. On A, ΛΝΤΙΜΕΝΟΝ, ΟΡΛ∫VΚLΕΙΔΕ∫, ΔΙΟΛΕΝΕ∫, all retr., and ΚΛLΟ∫. Diogenes seems to be the boy, and the *kalos* may go with the *Diogenes*.

3 (3). VATICAN, from Vulci. *Mus. Greg.* 2 pl. 56, 1; A, Overbeck *KM*. pl. 12, 25, whence Vian *R*. pl. 39, 364; A, ph. Al. 35754, whence Cook *Zeus* iii pl. 2 and Stella 394; A, ph. Mo. 8572. A, Poseidon and Giant. B, warriors leaving home. See p. 1639.

LOUTROPHOROS

4 (4). AMSTERDAM inv. 301, frr., from Athens. *CV*. Scheurleer b pl. 5 (Pays Bas pl. 76). Prothesis; valediction (horsemen); on the neck, mourning women.

FRAGMENTS OF STANDS OR STANDED VASES

5 (5). TÜBINGEN E 15 and E 13, OXFORD 1921. 866 and 1937. 891 frr., from Athens. The Tübingen frr., Watzinger pl. 18; one of the two Oxford, *CV*. pl. 50, 5. (Dionysos, Apollo (?), Hermes, and other deities). See *CV*. 44 on pl. 50, 5. The unpublished fragment in Oxford gives the left shoulder, breast, arm of Hermes and the sleeve of a person to right of him.

6 (6). ELEUSIS 601, fr., from Eleusis. *Delt*. 9, 8 fig. 6, 1. (Dionysos, maenad). See the next.

7 (7). ELEUSIS 586, fr., from Eleusis. *Delt*. 9, 12, α. (Man—Hermes?). Belongs to the last?

Perhaps also:

VOLUTE-KRATER

1 (a). SOFIA, fr., from Apollonia Pontica. Ghali-Kahil *H*. pl. 104, 3. On the neck, Theseus carrying off Helen.

CALYX-KRATER?

2 (a). ATHENS, Agora, P 9191, fr., from Athens. (On the right, man).

HYDRIA
(kalpis, with picture on the shoulder, not framed)

3. SAN SIMEON, Hearst State Monument, 9966 (ex Holford 156). Citharode, and two seated listeners. Now partly cleaned.

THE SYLEUS PAINTER

VA. 66–67. *Att. V.* 160–2 and 473. *ARV.*[1] 164–8 and 954.

Called after the subject of no. 36.

AMPHORAE

(no. 1, type A; with framed pictures)

1 (1). KANSAS CITY 30.13, from Paestum. A, unexplained subject: Athena, two warriors, and an old man. B, Dionysos and satyrs. On A, Athena holds a phiale, and each of the two warriors holds a leaf; one of them dips it in the phiale. The subject should be the same as in the volute-krater Ferrara T. 579, by the Painter of Bologna 279 (p. 612 no. 1): purification, Argonauts? (see Aurigemma[1] 216 = [2]254).

(no. 2, type A or B)

2 (2). REGGIO 4380, fr., from Locri. (Parts of two female heads, with a thyrsus between).

(nos. 3–4, type B)
(no. 3, with framed pictures)

3 (3). TOURS, Brunet. A, *Vente Ready* 47 no. 317. A, Dionysos and satyr; B, satyr and maenad. Early. See p. 1639.

(no. 4, the pictures not framed)

4. ATHENS 18543, from Markopoulo. A, Theseus and, B, the bull.

(no. 5, type C, with framed pictures)

5 (4). WÜRZBURG 509. Langlotz pll. 177–8; B, Richter and Milne fig. 11; A, Wegner *Mus.* pl. 18. A, citharode and man. B, jumper and trainer.

POINTED AMPHORA

6 (5). BRUSSELS R 303, from Vulci. Noël Des Vergers pll. 32–36; *CV.* pll. 8–9, whence (A) *Bull. Vereen.* 24–26, 24; side, Jacobsthal O. pl. 74, b; A, *AM.* 50 pl. 1; A, Messerschmidt *Vulci* 101; part of the lower zone, Byvanck-Quarles van Ufford P. 36. Above: A, Gigantomachy; B, Theseus and the bull. Below, Centauromachy. Restored.

PANATHENAIC AMPHORAE

7 (6). WÜRZBURG 501, from Vulci. Gerhard pl. 18; Langlotz pll. 167–8. A, Athena; B, Hermes. Early.

8 (7). ROME, Conservatori, 27. A, ph. R.I. 57.450. A, Athena. B, youth. Early. Restored.

9 (8). NEW YORK 20.244, from Vulci. *AJA.* 1923, 269 fig. 6 and pp. 270–1; A, Richter and Milne fig. 25; Richter and Hall pll. 25–26 and pl. 169, 25. Procession: A, youth with skaphe and sprigs; B, youth with sprigs.

10 (9). ABINGDON, Robertson, fr., from Greece. B, man (the head remains, to right). [Robertson].

NECK-AMPHORA

(with triple handles)

11. LOUVRE C 10788. A, man and boy. B, satyr.

LOUTROPHOROS

12 (10). OXFORD 1923.269, fr., from Greece. *CV.* pl. 49, 1–3. Prothesis; valediction.

PELIKAI

(nos. 13–17, with framed pictures)

13 (11). CAB. MÉD. 390, from Vulci. De Ridder pl. 14 and pp. 284–6. A, citharode. B, Dionysos and satyrs. Early. Restored. See p. 254.

14 (12, +). LOUVRE G 228. B, *Mém. Ac. Inscr.* 34 (1895) pl. 3; B, Pottier pl. 131; *CV.* pl. 45, 2–3 and 8, and pl. 44, 1, whence (A) Vian *R.* pl. 38, 339. A, Gigantomachy (Athena, Herakles, and Giant). B, the Theban Sphinx. Now cleaned. Three Louvre fragments belong and have been added. Early. See p. 254.

15 (13). LOUVRE G 226. *Mon.* suppl. pl. 25; *CV.* pl. 44, 4–7 and 9. A, wedding of Peleus. B, Dionysos and satyrs. Much restored. A Louvre fragment with the lower part of a handle-palmette may belong. Early. See p. 254.

16 (14). LOUVRE G 223. A, Pottier pl. 130; *CV.* pl. 43, 1–2 and 8, and pl. 42, 8, and 10. A, Zeus seated and Nike. B, satyr and maenad. Now cleaned. Early. See p. 254.

17 (15). LENINGRAD (St. 1591). A, naked women at laver. B, youth and seated woman.

(nos. 18–26, the pictures not framed)

18. PARIS, Niarchos. *Auktion xviii Basel* pl. 36. A, Apollo; B, goddess. Early.

19 (22). VILLA GIULIA 50505. A, Dionysos and maenads. B, men and youth. Much restored.

20. LOUVRE C 10792. A, three men; B, two men. See p. 255.

21 (16). ERLANGEN 486. A, *AM.* 65 pl. 2, 2, whence Rumpf *MZ.* pl. 23, 6; A, Grünhagen *Ant. Or.* pl. 16. A, man chopping meat, with a boy. B, man and boy. See p. 1639.

22 (19, +). LOUVRE G 225. *CV.* pl. 43, 6–7. A, man with sceptre seated, and youth (Zeus and Ganymede?) B, man and boy. Now cleaned. Two Louvre fragments belong and have been added.

23 (20). VATICAN, from Cervetri. *Mus. Greg.* 2 pl. 62, 1; A, Pareti *Tomba Regolini-Galassi* pl. 51, 395; A, ph. And. 42083. A, Theseus and Minotaur. B, man and boy.

24 (21). LOUVRE G 232, from Chiusi? Heydemann, Hilfstafel 1; *VA.* 66; Pottier pl. 131; *CV.* pl. 47, 1–5. A, Eos with the body of Memnon. B, woman with hydria, and man. Restored.

25 (17). ORVIETO, Faina. A, ph. Al. 32491, whence Zadoks-Jitta 87, 11 and Tarchi pl. 121, 4; A, ph. R.I. 38. 262, whence *Ant. Kunst* 2 pl. 8, 5. A, youth pursuing boy; B, boy fleeing. Restored.

26 (18). LOUVRE G 233. *CV*. pl. 47, 6–9. A, Athena. B, old man. Restored.

VOLUTE-KRATERS

27 (23). REGGIO 4379, two frr., from Locri. *NSc.* 1917, 147. Birth of Athena.

28 (24, +). ANTIOCH, frr., from Al Mina. *JHS.* 59 pl. 1 and pp. 4–6, 15 (minus the fragment with the head of Zeus on B, recognized by Clairmont and now published in *Berytus* 11 pl. 26, 1). A, Zeus seated, with Eros and Nike. B, Zeus pursuing Ganymede. On the neck: (A?), men and boys; (B?), lions attacking bull. It occurs to me that Hera may have been present, on the right, in the scene on A: but I did not think of this at the time.

STAMNOI

29 (25, +). LOUVRE G 182 *bis*, from Nola. B, Pottier pl. 127; *CV*. pl. 15, 6 and 3. A, citharode. B, athletes and trainer. Now cleaned. The Louvre fragment C 300 belongs, adding lower parts of the two right-hand figures on A; another Louvre fragment has part of the citharode's robe. A Louvre fragment with shoulder-tongues may belong. Miss Philippaki suggests that the handles formerly attached to Louvre G 185 may belong to Louvre G 182 *bis*. Early.

30. TOLEDO (Ohio). A, Poseidon and Amphitrite, both seated, and Nike. B, boxers and trainer. Restored. Early. See p. 1639.

31 (26). FLORENCE PD 538, and CHICAGO, Univ. The Chicago part, *AJA.* 1938, 346 fig. 3. A, Herakles and the lion. B, three satyrs dancing. Early.

(nos. 32–38, the pictures not framed)

32 (27). BERLIN 2182, from Tarquinia. *AZ.* 1883 pl. 15; A, *Jb.* 31, 203. A, judgement of Paris. B, Dionysos and maenads.

33. ROME?, Besozzi, from Vulci. *Arch. class.* 8 pll. 4–5. Peleus and Thetis. [Enrico Paribeni].

34 (28). PALERMO V 763, from Chiusi. Gerhard pl. 148, whence Radermacher *Mythos²* fig. 5; *CV*. 31; A, *Hist. rel.* 235, below. A, Herakles and the Hydra. B, Athena, Hermes, and Nereus, running.

35. SWISS PRIVATE. A, Amazonomachy (Achilles and Penthesilea). B, Agamemnon seated, a woman serving him with wine, and a man.

36 (29). COPENHAGEN inv. 3293, from Orvieto. *Mon.* 11 pl. 50; *CV*. pl. 135, whence *Jb.* 59–60, 70–71; side, Jacobsthal *O.* pl. 102, b. A, Herakles and Syleus. B, Dionysos and maenads.

37. LOUVRE C 11073. A, *RA.* 28 (1947), 6–7. Gigantomachy: A, Dionysos and Giant; B, Poseidon and Giant. Five Louvre fragments belong and have been added.

38 (30). Louvre G 181, from Nola. *CV*. pl. 13, 1, 4, and 7. A, Zeus with Hera and Nike. B, komos. Restored. See p. 1639.

HYDRIAI

(no. 39, of bf. shape, the pictures framed)

39 (31). Once Rome, de Ferrari, fr. *Rend. Pont. Acc.* 10, 205. (On the right, man leaning on his stick). On the shoulder, lion and lioness attacking fawn.

(nos. 40–42, kalpides, the picture on the shoulder, not framed)

40 (32). New York 21.88.1. *Singleton Abbey* pl. at p. 49, no. 709; Richter and Hall pl. 24, 27. Herakles and the lion. Early.

41 (33). Leningrad 629 (St. 1624). B.Ap. xxii. 97. Dionysos seated, with satyr and maenad.

42 (34). Athens Acr. 707, fr., from Athens. Langlotz pl. 54. Komos.

(nos. 43–52, kalpides, the picture on the body, not framed)

43. Bronxville, Bastis. Bothmer *A.N.Y.* pl. 82, 231 and pl. 87, 231. Poseidon and Giant (Poseidon in chitoniskos and cloak to right with trident and island, young giant down on one knee to right, looking round, with spear and shield, device the hindquarters of a horse).

44 (36). Florence 8 B 16, fr. *CV*. pl. 8, B 16. Youth and boy.

45 (37). New York 11.212.7, from Bolsena. *AJA*. 1923, 272 fig. 9; Richter and Hall pl. 27 and pl. 172, 26; side, Richter *Craft* 52; Richter *H*. 213, i. Youth and boy.

46 (38). Athens 12882 (N. 1043). Demeter and Persephone.

47 (39). Vatican, from Vulci. *Mus. Greg.* 2 pl. 14, 1; Gerhard pl. 12, whence *El*. 3 pl. 5 and Overbeck *KM*. pl. 13, 2; ph. Al. 35724, whence Stella 398, above, and *E.A.A.* i, 179; *Arch. class.* 8 pl. 6. Poseidon and Aithra.

48 (40). Leipsic, from Cervetri. Youth pursuing woman.

49 (41). Leipsic, fr., from Cervetri. Eos and Kephalos.

50 (42). Florence 8 B 15, fr. *CV*. 8 B 15. (Young hero—Theseus?).

51 (43). Cab. Méd. 440. Luynes pl. 28; *Mon. nouv. ann.* 1837 pl. 9, whence Inghirami pl. 384, Overbeck *KM*. pl. 1, 19, *Jb*. 6, 47, Cook *Zeus* i, 708. Zeus entrusting the infant Dionysos to the Nymphs.

52 (44). Berlin 2179, from Vulci. Gerhard *EKV*. pll. 6–7, whence *WV*. 3 pl. 6, 1 and *ML*. 14, 55; Neugebauer pl. 45. Theseus leaving Ariadne.

FRAGMENTS OF POTS

53 (a2). Eleusis, two frr., from Eleusis. *Delt.* 9, 7, αβ. On one fr., (woman?); on the other, (sleeve, hand). From the neck of a loutrophoros (as Papaspyridi)? The two fragments ibid. γδ might belong.

54. LOUVRE C 10823, nine frr. From a large vase with two rows of figures. In the upper row (fragment ε), hooves of horses—probably a chariot-team—to right. What follows is from the lower zone. Fragment α (composed of six) gives the shield of a warrior (Aeneas) to left, the middle of a woman to left holding a dove (Aphrodite), a chariot to left, and on the off side of the chariot the shield of another warrior. The subject of the zone, therefore, or one of the subjects, was the combat between Dio-med and Aeneas. Fragment β (C 293) has part of the shield, chitoniskos, scabbard, spear of a warrior moving to left, then part of another warrior. Fragment γ has part of a warrior moving to right, then part of a fallen warrior and part of the garment of a woman (?) to left: I do not know if these can be the Aeneas and Aphrodite of fragment α, with the Diomed of the group; or not rather Memnon, Eos, Achilles from another scene. Fragment δ (two joining) has the middle of a warrior moving to left, then the middle of a charioteer in a chariot-car to right. Fragment ε has (besides the vestige of the upper picture already described) the forepart of a chariot-team in action to right, then parts of two oxen—the hindquarters of one animal to right, and the head, to left, of another. Fragment ζ must come from the same scene as ε: tail and rump of an ox to left, then parts of two chariot-horses to left. Fragment η has the shoulder-piece of a warrior's corslet, θ and ι have unexplained remains and ι the first two let-ters of the graffito *su*[*thina*].

55 (46). ATHENS Acr. 964, fr., from Athens. Theseus and Minotaur.

56 (47). ATHENS Acr. 965, fr., from Athens. Langlotz pl. 78. Male and boy chopping meat.

57 (45). ATHENS Acr. 772, fr., from Athens. Langlotz pl. 67. (Youth—athlete?).

58 (48). ATHENS Acr. 627, frr., from Athens. Langlotz pl. 49. (Youth; woman). From an amphora?

59 (49). ATHENS Acr. 778, fr., from Athens. Langlotz pl. 68. Man or youth, and man, with panther-cub.

60 (50). ATHENS Acr. 811, fr., from Athens. Komos (youth and male at krater). A fragment in Munich, with the upper left-hand part of a krater. might belong.

61 (51). MUNICH, fr., from Athens. (Youth—chin, to left, and breast, re-main). May be from the same vase as the Munich fragment just described and as another Munich fragment with knee and thighs of a naked male moving to left.

62. ATHENS Acr., fr., from Athens. (Forepart of a foot moving to right: below it a red band).

NEAR THE SYLEUS PAINTER

FRAGMENT OF A POT

(1). ATHENS Acr. 691, fr., from Athens. Langlotz pl. 53. (Man). Probably from a hydria. Early.

PELIKE

(with framed pictures)

ATHENS Acr. 620, fr., from Athens. Langlotz pl. 48. (Head).

Perhaps also the fragment of a

CALYX-KRATER

TARANTO, fr., from Locri. (Upper half of a satyr with a drinking-horn moving to right, then a branch). See now p. 1639.

THE CLASS OF CABINET DES MÉDAILLES 390

The three very large pelikai nos. 13–15 in the list on p. 250 have the same shape, patterns, and handle-palmettes. Other pelikai go with them: shape and handle-palmettes the same as there, patterns sometimes the same.

PELIKAI

(with framed pictures)

1. CAB. MÉD. 390. Syleus Painter no. 13.

2. LOUVRE G 228. Syleus Painter no. 14.

3. LOUVRE G 226. Syleus Painter no. 15.

4. LOUVRE G 229. Siren Painter (p. 289 no. 3). Very large.

5. ITALIAN MARKET. A, the Theban Sphinx (on a column, sejant; between two seated youths). B, two satyrs. Recalls the Syleus Painter, especially Louvre G 228 (p. 250 no. 14).

6. LOUVRE G 223. Syleus Painter (p. 250 no. 16).

7. GENEVA 498. Vian R. pl. 38, 340. Gigantomachy: A, Hermes and Giants; B, Ares and Giants. Much restored. Recalls the Argos Painter (p. 288).

With the Geneva pelike compare

HYDRIA

(kalpis, with picture on the body)

1. SALERNO 1128, from Fratte. Herakles and Amazon. Bothmer points out (*Am.* 141) that this is the subject, and not Herakles and Kyknos.

COLUMN-KRATER

(the pictures not framed)

2. VIENNA 688. A, La Borde 1 pl. 41; Millingen *AUM.* pll. 7-8, whence (A) *El.* 1 pl. 5, (A) Overbeck *KM.* pl. 13, 1, whence Vian *R.* pl. 40, 366; *CV.* pl. 86, 1-3 and p. 25. Gigantomachy: A, Poseidon and Giant (Ephialtes); B, Giant.

With the Bastis hydria (p. 252 no. 43) compare the hydria (with picture on the body):

ROMAN MARKET (Castellani). Overbeck *KM.* pl. 12, 27. Poseidon and Giants. Much restored.

THE PAINTER OF BRUSSELS A 2482

ARV.[1] 168.

Near the early work of the Syleus Painter; compare especially the Louvre pelike C 10792 (p. 250 no. 20).

PELIKAI

1 (1). BRUSSELS A 2482. A, youths and woman; B, man pursuing a youth.
2 (2). LENINGRAD 618 (St. 1681). A, men and woman; B, man pursuing a woman.

CHAPTER 19

THE SYRISKOS GROUP

THE SYRISKOS GROUP

It consists of two artists, 'brothers', the Copenhagen Painter and the Syriskos Painter, who are sometimes hard to tell apart.

In *ARV*.[1] I said that the Kephalos Painter continued the style of the Syriskos Painter: I now take the two artists to be the same: 'the Kephalos Painter' being the later, the early classic, phase of the Syriskos. In this phase the likeness to the Copenhagen Painter has disappeared.

THE COPENHAGEN PAINTER

VA. 63 note 1. *Att. V.* 156–7. *V.Pol.* 21, 35, and 80. *ARV*.[1] 192–5.

An academic artist, akin to the later phase of Douris.
Named after no. 1.

AMPHORA

(type B)

1 (1). COPENHAGEN 125, from Vulci. Ussing *To graeske Vaser* pl. 1 and p. 7; *CV*. pl. 130; A, Cloché *Classes* pl. 2, 3; A, *Antik-Cab. 1851*, 131; A, Breitenstein *G.V.* pl. 37. A, old man with negro slave-boy. B, youth buying an amphora.

POINTED AMPHORA

2 (2). LONDON E 350, from Vulci. Cecil Smith pl. 13 and pl. 18, 1; side, Jacobsthal *O.* pl. 106, a; *CV*. pl. 18; ph. Ma. 3146. A, Dionysos and Nymphaia; B, two nymphs. On B, ΚΑΡΤΟΝΚΑΛΟΣ retr.

PANATHENAIC AMPHORA

3 (3). ATHENS, Agora, P 7257, frr., from Athens. A, victor with tripod; B, Nike.

VOLUTE-KRATER

4 (4). ATHENS Acr. 761, frr., from Athens. Langlotz pl. 66, whence (B) *AJA*. 1934, 436, 4. A, Herakles and Apollo: the struggle for the tripod; B, Leto and Artemis.

STAMNOI

5 (5). WÜRZBURG 515. *AZ*. 1883 pl. 12 and pp. 215 and 218, whence (A) Farmakovski i, 219 and (A) *AJA*. 1918, 151; *Klio* 20 pll. 1–4; A, Langlotz *F.G.B.* pl. 14, 5; Langlotz pll. 182–3 and 210, whence (A) Schnitzler pl. 47; detail of A, *E.A.A.* ii, 803. Death of Hipparchos. Restored.

6 (7). BERLIN 2184, from Vulci. Gerhard *EKV*. pl. 24, whence (A) *Annali* 1853 pl. H, (A) *WV*. 1 pl. 1, 1, (A) FR. ii, 77, (A) *Jb*. 29, 31, (A) Pfuhl fig. 478, (A) Bieber *Entw*. 31, Herbig *Terrakottagruppe* fig. 27, (detail) *Jb*. 11, 27, 9 = *Jb*. 26, 175; part of A, *Hist. rel.* 284. A, death of Aigisthos. B, athlete with man and youth. On B, N[I]KOϚTRATOϚ. Restored.

7. LOUVRE C 11139. A, death of Aigisthos; B, woman running to right, man moving to right, looking round, woman (?) standing to left.

8 (8). MUNICH 2408 (J. 343), from Vulci. Gerhard pl. 157, 3–4. A, Pelias and his daughters. B, Pelias seated, and his daughters. See p. 1640.

9 (9). LONDON E 442, from Vulci. *CV*. pl. 21, 2. A, Theseus and Procrustes; B, Theseus and the bull.

10 (a3). FREIBURG S 68, fr. (Legs of a figure like the London Procrustes, with rocky ground below).

11. SWISS PRIVATE. A, Theseus and Minotaur (on the left, Ariadne; on the right, Minos). B, unexplained: three women and three young boys; two of the women show concern: mothers at Athens, in fear of the tribute? See p. 1640.

12 (13). ELEUSIS, six frr., from Eleusis. Three of them, *Delt.* 9, 39 and 43. The fragments reproduced are doubtless from the front of the vase (A). The youth or man ibid. 39 is the left-hand figure. An unpublished fragment gives the upper half of his head, with part of the neck of the vase. The hand, holding a phiale, in the fragments ibid. 43 may belong to this figure, but uncertain. The woman there no doubt held an oinochoe. The two other fragments, unpublished, must come from B. One of them has the hand of a man or youth to right, holding a stick, with the inscription HOΓAIϚ KALOϚ; the other, the feet of a woman in chiton and himation standing to left, with part of the maeander below.

13 (14). VATICAN. Gerhard pl. 145, whence (A) *JHS*. 71, 131 fig. 3; without the Douris fragment which had been used in antiquity to mend it, *JHS*. 71, 130. A, Herakles and Nereus. B, youth and boy. Restored.

14 (10, +). LOUVRE G 114. A, Daremberg and Saglio s.v. stamnos, fig. 6565; A, Pottier pl. 107; *CV*. pl. 6, 9, pl. 7, 2 and pl. 12, 6 and 3. A, symposion: Dionysos and Herakles; B, three maenads. On A, TOITENΔE retr., and LVKOI. Much restored. A Louvre fragment belongs, adding part of the vine and pelt on the right of A, and a small piece of the back of Dionysos' head.

15 (a2). WARSAW 142330 (ex Czartoryski 50), from Cervetri. Part of A, and B, *V.Pol.* pl. 12, 2 and pl. 11, 3; *CV*. pl. 19; R.I. xvii. 46. A, Herakles and Antaios. B, arming. Late.

16 (12). ATHENS Acr., fr., from Athens. (Upper part of a female head to left wearing a stephane ornamented with esses; on the left, what may be the tips of two fingers of her raised hand).

17 (6). Once PARIS, de Witte (ex Campanari), from Vulci. Gerhard pl. 301,

whence (A) Bieber *G.K.* 9 fig. 12; B.Ap. xvi. 29. A, women folding clothes. B, youth, woman, and man.

18 (15). CHICAGO 16.140. *AJA.* 1930, 158–60. A, woman spinning, and women. B, male and two women. Much restored, especially B.

19. (11). LOUVRE G 190, from Nola. *CV.* pl. 20, 7 and pl. 21, 5. Men and youths. Now cleaned.

20. LUCERNE MARKET (A.A.) *Ars Ant. Auktion I* pl. 54. Komos: A, three youths and a man; B, two men and a youth.

21 (a1). NORTHWICK, Spencer-Churchill. Symposion. Late. See p. 1640.

22. BROOKLYN 03.8. B, *Brooklyn Mus. Quarterly* 21 (April 1934), 45, 2 and p. 69. Symposion. Now cleaned. Late. See p. 1640.

23 (a4). PARIS, Delepierre, from Vulci. A, *Tabl. I.P.* pl. 9, 34. Hoplito-dromoi. Late.

CALYX-KRATERS

24 (16). BOSTON 03.871, fr., from Athens. (Head of woman).

25 (a). BONN 71, from Attica. *CV.* pl. 17, 1–2 and pl. 21, 1, whence (part) Vian *R.* pl. 39, 352. A, Zeus; B, Giant.

HYDRIAI

(no. 26, of bf. shape; the picture not framed)

26 (17). LONDON E 163, from Vulci. Cook *Zeus* ii pl. 14; *CV.* pl. 70, 4; B.Ap. xxii. 45. 1; ph. Ma. 3149. Medea rejuvenating Jason. See p. 1640.

(no. 27, kalpis, with picture on the shoulder, not framed)

27 (18). ATHENS Acr. 694, fr., from Athens. Langlotz pl. 53. (Woman and another).

FRAGMENTS OF POTS

28 (19). ATHENS Acr. 780, fr., from Athens. Langlotz pl. 69. Dead Mino-taur.

29 (20). ATHENS Acr. 779, frr., from Athens. A, Langlotz pl. 68. A, uncer-tain subject (woman: sacrifice?). B, (male).

30 (21). ATHENS Acr. 975, fr., from Athens. Langlotz pl. 83. (Woman?)

31. NEW YORK, Bothmer, fr. (Upper half of a boy in a himation standing to left, and arm, with stick, of a man or youth).

A small fragment (of a stamnos?) is to be compared with the Munich stamnos 2408 (p. 257 no. 8) and the London hydria E 163 (p. 258 no. 26): ATHENS Acr. 983, fr., from Athens. Langlotz pl. 78. Daughters of Pelias.

The difficulty, already mentioned (p. 256), of distinguishing the Copenhagen Painter from the Syriskos comes to a head in the case of a New York
vase: in *ARV.*[1] (196 no. 8) it was given to the Syriskos Painter, and it seems
perfectly in place among his works; but on the other hand I do not know
how to separate it from the Copenhagen Painter:

STAMNOS

New York 56.171.50 (ex Torr and Hearst). A, *Cat. Sotheby July 2 1929* pl. 6,
   1. A, men with sceptres, and women; B, men and youths.

Two other vases of just the same shape as the New York are close to both
artists. In *ARV.*[1] the Munich vase was assigned to the Syriskos Painter (196
no. 7). The Rouen was said there to be in his manner (199 no. 1): perhaps I
should have named the Copenhagen Painter rather than the Syriskos: my
notes are imperfect.

STAMNOI

1. Munich 2409 (J. 356), from Vulci. A, *Mon.* 1 pl. 27, 28. Men. See
   p. 1640.
2. Rouen 18, from Vulci. A, Zeus pursuing a woman. B, Nike, woman,
   and youth, running.

A rough vase recalls the Copenhagen Painter:

PELIKE
(the pictures not framed)

Athens 1685 (CC. 1187). A, woman with perfume-vase; B, youth.

THE SYRISKOS PAINTER

VA. 63–65. *Att. V.* 148–60 and 473. *V.Pol.* 17–18, 21, 35, and 75. *ARV.*[1] 195–200
and 954.

'Brother' of the Copenhagen Painter, and sometimes hard to distinguish
from him.

He painted two skyphoi for the potter Pistoxenos (nos. 86 and 87), and an
astragalos for Syriskos (no. 67).

In *ARV.*[1] 195 I said that his style was continued by the Kephalos Painter.
I now consider that the vases ascribed to 'the Kephalos Painter' in *Att. V.*
307–8 and 476 and *ARV.*[1] 350–1 are the late, the early classic, work of the
Syriskos. The late vases are marked so in the list; and 'K' before the serial
number in brackets refers to the Kephalos list in *ARV.*[1]

CALYX-KRATERS

1 (1). Athens Acr. 735, from Athens. *Eph.* 1885 pll. 11–12, whence *AM.*
   16, 200–1, Harrison and Verrall cxxv–cxxvi, Robert *Herm.* 142 and 143
   fig. 112; Langlotz pl. 61. A, Theseus and Minotaur. B, Orneus, Pallas,

Nisos, and Lykos. A fragment in Athens joins, adding the rest of Lykos' feet, with the lower edge of his himation.

2 (2). CAB. MÉD. 418, from Agrigento. *Mon.* 1 pll. 52–53, whence (A) Overbeck *Gall.* pl. 13, 10, (A) *JHS.* 18, 278, (A) Jacobsthal *Thes.* pl. 1, 2, detail of A, Richter *H.G.A.* 360 fig. 480; Luynes pll. 21–22; phs. Gir. 8058 and 8060, whence (A) *Hist. rel.* 261, above. A, Poseidon and Theseus; B, Nereids. Later.

BELL-KRATER
(with lugs)

3 (3). FRANKFORT, Liebieghaus, L 116, fr. (a lug). On the lug, satyr (kneeling to left, looking round).

VOLUTE-KRATERS

4 (4). ATHENS Acr. 758, frr., from Athens. Langlotz pl. 63. On the neck, athletes and men.

5 (5). SYRACUSE 15076, fr., from Gela. On the neck, symposion.

6. AGRIGENTO, fr., from Agrigento. On the neck, boys dancing (the two left-hand figures on one side remain, to right, in ungirt chitoniskoi). Later.

7 (a2). LOUVRE G 194, fr. *Jb.* 7, 209, whence (part) Schröder *Sport* 127 fig. 33; Pottier pl. 128; *CV.* pl. 22, 4. Part of one handle remains; on it: above, Theseus and Skiron; below, Theseus and Kerkyon.

8 (K1). BOLOGNA PU 283, from Orvieto. A, Pellegrini *VPU.* 45; A, *E.A.A.* iv, 339. A, Eos and Kephalos; B, youth fleeing to man. Late.

COLUMN-KRATERS
(with framed pictures)

9 (K2). ATHENS Acr. 814, frr., from Athens. Langlotz pl. 74. A, Boreas and Oreithyia. B, (on the left, woman). Late.

10 (K3). PALERMO V 794. *CV.* pl. 47. A, Dionysos reclining, and maenad; B, satyr pursuing maenad. Late. See p. 1640.

11 (K4). FERRARA, T. 445, from Spina. A, Aurigemma[1] 95 = [2]101. A, satyrs and maenad. B, three youths. Late. See p. 1640.

12 (K5). TARQUINIA RC 8261, from Tarquinia. Schnabel *Kordax* pll. 1–2, whence (A) *Zap. Od.* 30 pl. 1, (A) Bieber *Th.* 176, (A) Licht i, 174, (A) Bieber *H.T.* 84; phs. Mo. 8264 and 5854, 3; ph. And. 41008. Grotesque dancers; on A, two of them are masked. Late.

13 (K7). BARI 3798. A, komos. B, youth and boy. Late.   ·

14 (K6). ORVIETO, Faina. A, (hoplitodromos, trainer). B, men and youth. Largely modern. Late.

15. NEW YORK, private. A, Simon *O.G.* pl. 4, 2; *Ars Ant. Auktion I* pl. 56, 119. A, Zeus and Hera seated, with Nike (or rather Iris) and

Hermes. B, youths and woman. Attributed to the Kephalos Painter by Miss Simon. Late. For the subject, Simon loc. cit. 58–63.

16 (Ka1). REGGIO, frr., from Locri. A, old king seated, with three women. Late. See p. 1640.

STAMNOI

(no. 17, the pictures not framed)

17 (6). WÜRZBURG 527, from Tarquinia. Gerhard pll. 285–6; Langlotz pl. 212. A, men and boys; B, men. Now cleaned, and the alien mouth and foot removed.

(no. 18, with framed pictures)

18. NAPLES, Astarita, 627, three frr. Three women preparing a couch. Later. See p. 1640.

NUPTIAL LEBES

19 (9). MYKONOS, from Rheneia (originally from Delos). Dugas *Délos xxi* pl. 5, 12, pl. 6, pl. 7, 12, and pl. 57. Apollo, and Muses (or Delian women) dancing. Later.

NECK-AMPHORAE

(nos. 20–23, small, with triple handles)

20 (10). ORVIETO 1040, from Orvieto. *CV.* pl. 4, 1–2; phs. Armoni. A, Dionysos and maenad; B, two maenads.

21 (11). ORVIETO 1045, from Orvieto. *CV.* pl. 4, 3–4; phs. Armoni. A, man and boy; B, man and boy.

22 (12). BOSTON 13.90. A, man and boy; B, man and boy. Restored.

23 (13). VATICAN. A, youth (in himation, phiale in right hand); B, youth (in himation).

(no. 24, Nolan amphora, with ridged handles)

24 (15). OXFORD 1920.105. *CV.* pl. 17, 9 and pl. 18, 11. A, Poseidon; B, woman running. Later. See p. 1641.

(no. 25, exact shape unknown)

25 (K11). Lost, from Agrigento. Politi *Ercole ed Apollo*, whence *El.* 2 pl. 58 and FR. iii, 280. A, Apollo and Orion; B, Artemis. Late.

(no. 26, squat, with convex handles)

26 (14). NAPLES. A, Dionysos and maenad; B, maenad.

LOUTROPHOROS

27. ARLESHEIM, Schweizer. Wedding; on the neck, A, Nike with torches, B, woman with torches. Later.

PANATHENAIC AMPHORA

28 (49, +). NAPLES, Astarita, 115, and FLORENCE 7 B 42, two frr. The Florence fr., *CV.* pl. 7, B 42. Procession: A, man with branch; B, youth. One

of the Astarita fragments joins the Florence below, continuing the figure down to the waist; the other Astarita fragment has the head, to right, of the youth on B.

AMPHORA

(type C)

29. BASLE, Staechelin. *Auction xvi Basle* pl. 31, 125. A, victor; B, man.

PELIKAI

(nos. 30–33, with framed pictures)

30 (17). BERLIN inv. 4496. *Vente 11–14 mai 1903* pl. 5; parts of A and B, *G.V. Celle* 18 and cover. A, women at their toilet, and a little maid. B, man and boy.

31. OXFORD, Beazley, frr. (six, composed of fourteen), from Vulci. A, male and woman at laver. B, man and boy. On A, male leaning on his stick to right, woman standing frontal holding an alabastron by its thong. On B, man to right, leaning, boy standing to left.

32 (19). CRACOW 1320, fr. *V.Pol.* pl. 7, 4 (reversed); *CV.* pl. 10, 2. Youth and boy.

33 (K10). NAPLES 3048, from Nola. A, ph. So. 11009, v, 4. A, Dionysos and maenad. B, youth and boy. Late.

(nos. 34–40, the pictures not framed)

34 (18). NAPLES 2891. A, ph. So. 11009, vi, 4. A, man with sceptre seated, and woman (Zeus and Hebe?). B, two women. On A, ΚΑLΟS and retr. +ΑΙΡΙΑS.

35. GREIFSWALD 344. Peters pl. 38. A, flute-player; B, boy. Restored.

36 (19 *bis*). HEIDELBERG 125. Kraiker pll. 21–22. A, satyr; B, satyr.

37. GENOA 1150, from Veii. *Le Arti* 3 pl. 67, whence *Anz.* 1941, 386 figs. 21–22; *CV.* pll. 1–2. A, satyr seated; B, satyr (in himation). Restored.

38 (K8). LECCE 573, from Rugge. *CV.* pl. 1, 1–2 and pl. 2, 1. Komos: A, two men; B, man and youth. Late.

39 (K9). LONDON E 365, from Camiros. Komos (A, youth; B, youth). Late.

40. GENOA, Castello d'Albertis. *CV.* pl. 1 (Italia 938), 6–7. A, satyr pursuing maenad; B, the like. Late.

HYDRIAI

(no. 41, of bf. shape; with framed pictures)

41 (20). LONDON E 161, from Vulci. The chief picture, *VA.* 64; *CV.* pl. 71, 1 and pl. 72, 3; ph. Ma., whence (the chief picture) *Hist. rel.* 282, above; the chief picture, Ghali-Kahil *H.* pl. 50. Menelaos and Helen. On the shoulder, symposion.

(no. 42, of bf. shape; the picture not framed)

42. ATHENS 16351, fr., from Greece. *Epit. Tsounta* 498 pl. 1 and pl. 2, 2. Hermes leading a man (Sisyphos?).

(nos. 43–50, kalpides, with picture on the shoulder, not framed)

43 (28). LONDON E 168, from Vulci. *CV.* pl. 73, 3 and pl. 74, 2. Herakles and the lion.

44 (21). ATHENS Acr. 689, fr., from Athens. Langlotz pl. 53. (Male and boy).

45 (22). TRIESTE S 423. Gerhard pl. 278–9, 5–6; ph. Al. 40211; B.Ap. xvi. 11. 2. Men and seated youth.

46 (23). FLORENCE 6 B 56 (part ex Villa Giulia), frr. Part, *CV.* pl. 6, B 56. Seated male, man, and old man (mission to Achilles?—Achilles, Odysseus, Phoinix?).

47 (24). FLORENCE 6 B 49, frr. Part, *CV.* pl. 6, B 49. (Youth; man).

48 (25). FLORENCE 6 B 55, fr. *CV.* pl. 6, B 55. (Woman seated, and woman).

49 (26). ROMAN MARKET (Depoletti). B.Ap. xxi. 91. Men and woman (man leaning on his stick to right, with purse, woman standing to right, with mirror, man leaning on his stick to left).

50 (27). SALERNO 1132, from Fratte. Youth seated with lyre, and boy with lyre.

(no. 51, kalpis, with picture on the body)

51. OXFORD, Beazley, two frr., composed of seven, from Vulci. Three maenads (1, dancing to right, wing-sleeves; 2, moving to right, looking round, with thyrsus; 3, moving to right, no doubt looking round). Late.

PSYKTER

52 (a). BALTIMORE, Walters Art Gallery, 48.77, from Tarquinia. Hartwig 265–6 (A is reversed); *Journ. Walt.* 2, 112; B, *Bull. Walt.* 6 no. 7 (April 1954), 3; phs. Mo. A, athlete tying up his penis, and servant-boy. B, youth and boy. The lid, and the greater part of the boy on A, with the dog, are now missing.

OINOCHOE
(shape 8A, mug)

53 (29). TARANTO 4550 (69), from Taranto. Man (in himation, moving to left, looking round, stick in right hand).

WHITE LEKYTHOS
(standard shape, but an unusual model)

54 (30). BERLIN 2252, from Athens. *AZ.* 1880 pl. 11; Riezler pl. 1 and p. 89; *Die Antike* 1 pll. 30–31 and p. 280, whence Rumpf *MZ.* pl. 24, 6; Neugebauer pl. 55, 1; the shoulder, Greifenhagen *Eroten* 85. Woman seated, and man; on the shoulder, Eros. HOΓΑΙϟΚΑΛΟϟ retr., ΙΚΑΛΟϟ, retr. OLVNΓΙ+ΟϟΚΑΛΟϟ. See p. 1641.

SQUAT LEKYTHOI

55 (31). NAPLES 3135, from Locri. Arditi *Ill.*; Dubois-Maisonneuve pl. 77, 6; Inghirami *Mon. etr.* pl. 30; *Mus. Borb.* 3 pl. 12, 3–4; ph. So. 11069, iv, 8. Woman seated with lyre. The mouth of the vase is alien.

56 (32). BOWDOIN 20.4. Man and boy.

ROUND ARYBALLOS

57 (33). TARANTO 4553 (3799), from Taranto. Klein *L.* 102–3; Riezler 54– 56; *Die Antike* 1, 282–3. White ground. A, men and boy. B, man leading horse. On the bottom, wheel. On A, ΛIOΛENEϟKAΛOϟ retr., KAΛOϟ retr. On B, ΛIOΛENEϟKAΛOϟ. On a band above the pictures, HI[ΓΓ]OΛO+OϟKAΛOϟ :

ALABASTRA

(*nos. 58–65, white ground*)

58 (34). ATHENS, Vlasto, from Athens. Woman with flute and flower at altar.

59. SWISS PRIVATE. Woman with alabastron and mirror at altar.

60 (35). BRUSSELS R 397. *CV.* Jb pl. 1, 4. Woman with alabastron.

61. ATHENS (ex Stathatou), from Attica. *Acta arch.* 18, 189 and 191; Amandry *Coll. Stathatos* 10 fig. 10. Woman. [Holmberg].

62 (36). BARCELONA (ex Gerona), from Ampurias. Botet y Sisó pl. 3, 2; *Anuari* 1908, 224 fig. 43, whence *Anz.* 1912, 447; *R.A.* 1917, i, 121 fig. 22; Bosch Gimpera *L'art grec a Catalunya* fig. 41; García y Bellido *Hallazgos* pl. 83, 1; García y Bellido pl. 93; Almagro and García y Bellido *Ars Hisp.* 192 fig. 203. Woman.

63. DUNEDIN F 54. 78. Anderson *H.G.V.* pl. 12, 84. Woman with torches approaching altar.

64 (37). ATHENS, Acropolis Museum, fr., from Athens. *Delt.* 1, suppl., 40 fig. 15. (Woman).

65 (38). AMSTERDAM inv. 2193, fr. Archer.

(*no. 66, red-figure*)

66 (K12). KOENIGSBERG 78, from Greece. Lullies *K.* 13. Man and boy. APIϟTON KAΛOW (the inscription genuine according to Lullies). Late.

ASTRAGALOS

67 (39). VILLA GIULIA 866, from Falerii. *Boll. d'Arte* 10, 345–6; Hoppin ii, 442–3; phs. And. 6294–5, whence (B) Della Seta *Mus. V.G.* pl. 27, 1; *Mü. Jb.* 1919 (Buschor *Krok.*) 18 fig. 27; *Dedalo* 3, 82; *CV.* pl. 1 and pl. 2, 1–2; part, Greifenhagen *Eroten* 25; phs. Al. 23257–8, and 41162 left. Nike. Eros. Lion. ϟVPIϟKOϟEΓOIEϟEN TIMAP+OϟKAΛ[Oϟ].

FRAGMENTS OF POTS

68 (47). ATHENS Acr. 626, frr., from Athens. Langlotz pl. 49. A, male and seated youth; B, the like.

69 (50). OXFORD 1912.39.2, fr., from Naucratis. *CV.* pl. 50, 7. (Youth).

70. (48). GOETTINGEN H 44, fr. (Dionysos). From a hydria?

71. ATHENS Acr. 706, fr., from Athens. Langlotz pl. 54. (Man). From a hydria?

72. NAPLES, Astarita, 631, fr. (Head of a youth). From a panathenaic or an amphora type C?

73. *Vacat.*

74. OXFORD, Beazley, fr. (Upper part of a woman's head to right, with the back of the neck). Late: as no. 51. Might be from a neck-amphora.

RHYTON

(ram's head)

75 (40). LONDON E 795, from Capua. *CV.* pl. 41, 1 and pl. 42, 2; Lane pl. 92, c; part, *Ant. Kunst* 4 pl. 12, 2. Symposion.

RHYTA OR KANTHAROI

76. VILLA GIULIA, fr., from Veii. (Youth and boy: the boy stands to right, the youth leans on his stick to left; between them a pillar inscribed ΚΑΛΟΣ). A fragment (mislaid?) of a cat-head rhyton may belong: of the picture, the feet of a male figure in a himation, to right, remained.

77 (41). BRYN MAWR P 247, fr. (Hand holding cup).

HEAD-KANTHAROI

(no. 78, woman's head)

78 (42). BOSTON 98.928, from Tanagra. *JHS.* 49 pl. 5, 2 and p. 48; B, *AJA.* 1935 pl. 11, b. White ground. A, woman with mirror. B, negro. For the plastic part, p. 1534 no. 16. See also p. 267.

(no. 79, janiform, women's heads)

79 (43). NAPLES Stg. 60, from Capua. A, *Mü. Jb.* 1919 (Buschor *Krok.*) 14 fig. 21; ph. So. 11029. A, woman seated, and two women; B, youths and woman. [Buschor]. For the plastic part, p. 1537 no. 2.

(nos. 80–81, janiform: Herakles' head and woman's head)

80 (a ii 1). CAB. MÉD. 866. Phs. Gir. 8122, a, and 8119, a, whence Farma-kovski i, 214–15; A, de Ridder 509. A, man (Zeus?) seated, with Nike, and youth. B, youths and boy. For the plastic part, p. 1538 no. 1. The drawing in this and the five that follow is very poor, but I cannot separate them from nos. 78–79; see also p. 1538 no. 3.

81 (a ii 2). NEW YORK 96.18.77 (GR 599). A, ph. Mo. 11106, whence *Mü. Jb.* 1919 (Buschor *Krok.*), 14 fig. 22; cleaned, *JHS.* 49, 59 fig. 12. A,

Athena and two women (goddesses?), all seated. B, symposion (youth reclining and seated woman). For the plastic part, p. 1538, below, no. 2.

(nos. 82–84, janiform: satyr's head and woman's head)

82 (a ii 3). BOSTON 95.37 (R. 463 a), from Capua or Nola. Fröhner *Coll. Hoffmann* pl. 21; Edward Robinson 168. Symposion: A, youth reclining; B, the like. For the plastic part, p. 1539, above, no. 6.

83 (a ii 4). BOSTON 98.880. *JHS*. 49, 67. A, youths and seated woman. B, symposion (youth reclining). For the plastic part, p. 1545 no. 1.

84. ARLESHEIM, Schweizer. Symposion: A, satyr and maenad reclining; B, Dionysos reclining. For the plastic part, p. 1539, above, no. 7. See p. 1641.

(no. 85, janiform: head of satyr and head of Dionysos)

85. FERRARA, T. 256 B VP, from Spina. A, man cutting up a carcass, assisted by a boy. B, symposion: Dionysos reclining. Might also be a school-piece. For the plastic part, p. 1537 no. 5.

SKYPHOI

(nos. 86–89, type A)

86 (45). BRUSSELS A 11. Furtwängler *Somzée* pl. 39, i, 5 = *Vente Somzée* pl. 5, 46; Hoppin *Bf*. 473; *CV*. pl. 18, 2; bottom, H. R. W. Smith *Lewismaler* pl. 30, d. A, men and boys; B, women. Under one handle, ΓΙΣΤΟ-+[ΣΕΝΟΣ ΕΓΟΙΕΣΕ]Ν.

87. LOUVRE C 10818. A, warrior leaving home; B, arming. Under one handle, [ΓΙ]ΣΤΟ+ΣΕΝΟϟ [Ε]ΓΟΙΕϟΕΝ. On A, 1, boy standing to right holding helmet and spear, 2, man in himation with sceptre standing to right, 3, bearded warrior standing to left with spear and shield, 4, woman standing to left holding spear; B, 1, youth putting on his greaves, to right, 2, woman standing to left holding spear and shield, 3, man in himation standing to left, 4, youth in himation standing to left. A loose fragment with part of a spear and of a shield resting with its edge on the ground must be under one of the handles. Very poor, but I think by the painter himself.

88. TARANTO, two frr., from Locri. On one fr., upper half of a man in chiton and himation moving to right. On the other, upper parts of a woman running to right, looking round, and of a man in a himation moving to left, holding out a scabbard in his left hand; inscription ...EYϟ retr. ([Ter]eus?).

89 (46). PALERMO, fr. (two joining), from Selinus. (Upper half of woman facing to left, right arm extended).

(no. 90, with offset lip)

90 (44). ATHENS Acr. 482, frr., from Athens. Langlotz pl. 39. Komos.

NEAR THE SYRISKOS PAINTER

All these may be by the painter himself.

PELIKE
(the pictures framed)

1. LOUVRE C 11112, frr. A, two women at an altar. B, one in a himation, and a woman with a phiale.

FRAGMENTS OF POTS

2 (4). ATHENS Acr. 963, fr., from Athens. Langlotz 88. Males at laver.

3 (5). ATHENS Acr., part of 820 (G 202a), fr., from Athens. (Males: one leaning on his stick to left, with purse, the second standing to right, the third leaning on his stick to left).

4. ATHENS Acr., fr., from Athens. BCH. 1940-1 pl. 10, 3. (Man).

5. LENINGRAD, fr. (Head and shoulders of a youth in a himation standing to left). From a stamnos?

6. NAPLES, Astarita, 212, fr. (Hand, with sceptre, of one standing to right, waist and raised arm of a woman approaching, to left).

The following is a poor imitation:

PELIKE
(the pictures not framed)

(3). PARIS, Musée Rodin, 949. CV. pl. 21, 1-2. A, woman running. B, man.

THE GROUP OF THE NEGRO ALABASTRA

Winnefeld in AM. 14, 41-50. Bethe in AM. 15, 243-5. Buschor Krok. 37. Beardsley The Negro 48-54. JHS. 49, 51. Fraser in AJA 1935, 41-44. Angermeier Das Alabastron 26-29. Haspels ABL. 103-4 and 167 note 1. ARV.^{1} 200-1 and 955. Webster in Mem. Manch. 89, 6-10. Bothmer Am. 158.

These depend upon the Syriskos Painter: compare his white alabastra (p. 264 nos. 58-65) and his head-kantharos Boston 98.928 (p. 265 no. 78); and many of the negroes are indistinguishable in style from that on the head-kantharos (JHS. 49, 48).

ALABASTRA
(white ground)

All but the two last have a figure of a negro; no. 32 has two negroes.

1 (1). LONDON B 674, from Tanagra. AJA. 1935 pl. 10, b; Lane pl. 89, b.

2 (2). AMSTERDAM inv. 1900. AZ. 1872, 36, c; CV. J pl. 1, 3.

3 (3). TÜBINGEN E 51. Watzinger 40.

4 (4). COPENHAGEN inv. 1946, from Greece. CV. pl. 174, 3.

5 (5). RHODES 13270, from Camiros. *Cl. Rh.* 4, 134; *CV.* a pl. 2, 3 and 5.

6 (6). WILNO, Society of Friends. *CV.* pl. 1 (Pologne pl. 124), 3.

7 (7). COMPIÈGNE 1078, from Nola. Fröhner *Deux* 16, whence Perrot 10, 693; *CV.* pl. 13, 4–5.

8 (8). LENINGRAD, from South Russia? See p. 1641.

9 (9). ATHENS 422 (CC. 1088), from Thebes.

10 (10). ATHENS 423 (CC. 1089), from Thebes.

11 (11). ATHENS 481 (CC. 1090), from Athens.

12 (12). BERLIN 2260. *AZ.* 1872, 36, d.

13 (13). DRESDEN 102 (ZV. 649), from Crete.

14. PRAGUE, Nat. Mus., 1684, from Greece. *Sborník* 1959 pl. 7, 47. [Frel]. Restored.

15. CINCINNATI, Boulter. *Auction xvi Basle* pl. 27, 114.

16 (14). COPENHAGEN inv. 8224, from Rhodes. *CV.* pl. 174, 2.

17 (15). BOSTON 98.927. *AJA.* 1935 pl. 11, a.

18 (16). DELPHI, fr., from Delphi. *Mon. Piot* 26, 97, h; *R.A.* 1962, 108, 2.

19 (17). BRUSSELS A 1391. *CV.* Jb pl. 1, 3.

20 (18). Once DARDANELLES, Calvert. Ph. A.I. 143, 2.

21 (19). PALERMO 2270.

22 (20). NEW YORK MARKET (Joseph Brummer). A, *Coll. Lambros* pl. 8, 39; B, *Amer. Art Galleries 6–8 Jan. 1927* no. 5.

23 (21). SYRACUSE, from Gela.

24 (22). LOUVRE MNC 673. *AJA.* 1935 pl. 10, c, 2.

25 (23). LOUVRE MNC 476. *AJA.* 1935 pl. 10, c, 1; *Enc. phot.* iii, 43.

26 (25). DUNEDIN 48.362 (ex A. B. Cook).

27. MANCHESTER, Univ., III. 1. 42. *Mem. Manch.* 89 pl. 4.

28 (27). MUNICH 2290. *Coll. M.E.* pl. 9, 147.

29 (28). AMSTERDAM, fr.

30 (29). ATHENS 412 (CC. 1091), from Tanagra. *AM.* 14, 43.

31 (30). ATHENS 13887.

32 (32). Where?, from Megara. *AM.* 14, 45 and 41. Unusual.

33 (35). LONDON B 673, from Camiros. Fröhner *Deux* pl. 2, whence Perrot 10, 692; Bothmer *Am.* pl. 73, 3. Amazon. See p. 270.

PLATES
(white ground)

34 (40). TARANTO inv. 61, from Taranto. *AM.* 15, 243; *E.A.A.* i, 972, 1224. Negro.

35 (41). TÜBINGEN E 47, fr. Watzinger pl. 16. Negro.

There are some white alabastra in my former Negro list on which my notes are too brief for me to be sure that they belong to the Group of the Negro Alabastra:

(24). LENINGRAD. Half-size; side border.

(26). PARIS, Rothschild.

(31). RHODES.

(32 *bis*). GOETTINGEN, fr.

(33). LEIPSIC T 2406, fr.

(36). ATHENS Acr. 870, fr., from Athens. (Archer).

―――――――

THE PAINTER OF NEW YORK 21.131

Bothmer *Am.* 158–9.

Bothmer points out that two alabastra in Reggio and Palermo which I had placed in my Negro list as nos. 37 and 38 are not in the same style as the rest, but go with some others. The style is earlier than in the Group of the Negro Alabastra and somewhat recalls the Group of the Paidikos Alabastra (pp. 98–101). There is a close connexion, however, with the Negro Group.

ALABASTRA

(white ground)

1. NEW YORK 21.131. Bothmer *Am.* pl. 73, 4. Amazon. Youth leaning on his stick. [Bothmer].
2. MEGGEN, Käppeli. Schefold *M.* 187, 202a. The like; with a heron.
3. NEW YORK MARKET (Ernest Brummer). Bothmer *Am.* pl. 73, 5. Amazon. [Bothmer].
4. PALERMO, from Selinus. *ML.* 32, 330 fig. 140. Amazon. [Bothmer].
5. REGGIO 5347, from Locri. *NSc.* 1917, 138. Amazon. [Bothmer].

Near these:

(i)

ALABASTRON

(white ground)

BERLIN inv. 3382. Amazon; negro.

PLATE

(white ground)

ATHENS Acr. 425, from Athens. Langlotz pl. 32. Amazon. [Bothmer]. See Bothmer *Am.* 158–9.

(ii)
THE GROUP OF THE CRACOW ALABASTRON

These can hardly be separated from the Painter of New York 21.131; the chief difference is the use of 'second white' on nos. 1 and 2.

ALABASTRA
(*white ground*)

1. CRACOW inv. 1292. *V.Pol.* pl. 32, 3; *CV.* pl. 13, 7. Amazon.
2. LOUVRE C 10712, frr. Amazon. See Bothmer *Am.* 152 no. 73 *bis* and p. 158.

PLASTIC KANTHAROS
(*white ground*)

3. OXFORD, Beazley, fr. (two joining). Amazon (fallen, or sitting on the ground). See Bothmer *Am.* 152 no. 77 *bis*.

I have left the white alabastron London B 673, with some hesitation, in the group of the Negro Alabastra (p. 268 no. 33). It is close to the Painter of New York 21.131, and especially to the Group of the Cracow Alabastron.

CHAPTER 20

OTHER PAINTERS OF LARGE VASES

THE PAINTER OF FLORENCE 3984

ARV.[1] 174.

HYDRIAI

(*kalpides, with the picture on the shoulder, framed*)

1 (2). MILAN, Scala. *Coll. B. et C.* pl. 21, 155; *Cat. Jules Sambon* pl. 1, 10. Athletes (runner practising starts, jumper, trainer, hoplitodromos). For the left-hand figure see *BSA.* 46, 9 no. 7.

2 (1). FLORENCE 3984. *CV.* pl. 57, 1 and pl. 58, 1. Herakles and the lion.

Probably also the

HYDRIA

(*of the same type*)

(3). BERLIN 2176, from Castelluccio in Basilicata. *Annali* 1849 pl. I; Johansen *Iliaden* fig. 29; B.Ap. xii. 28. Mission to Achilles.

━━━━━━━

THE PAINTER OF GOLUCHOW 37

JHS. 52, 142. *JHS.* 56, 89. *ARV.*[1] 158.

Somewhat recalls the Eucharides Painter.

CALYX-KRATER

1 (1). FERRARA, T. 323, from Spina. A, Aurigemma[1] 81 = [2]87; A, Aurigemma and Alfieri pl. 9, b; A, Alfieri and Arias *S.* pll. 4–5; A, *Mostra* pl. 68, 2. A, satyr and maenad. B, athlete and trainer. See p. 164[1].

STAMNOS

2 (2). ATHENS Acr. 775, fr., from Athens. Langlotz pl. 68. Maenads.

HYDRIA

(*with picture on the body*)

3 (3). WARSAW 142285 (ex Czartoryski 37), from Cervetri. *CV.* pl. 20, 1. Nike (or Iris).

Probably also

COLUMN-KRATER

(with framed pictures)

(a). REGGIO 10557, fr., from Locri. Komos (upper part of a youth to right; black palmette side-border).

THE HARROW PAINTER

JHS. 36, 128 and 132–3. *VA*. 56. *Att. V*. 118–21 and 471. *ARV*.[1] 177–82 and 954.

Named after no. 76.

NECK-AMPHORAE

(nos. 1–9, with twisted handles)

1 (1). VILLA GIULIA 50471, from Cervetri. A, ph. G.F. 7168. A, Dionysos pursuing a woman; B, woman fleeing.

2 (2). MISSISSIPPI (ex Robinson). A, *Cat. Sotheby Dec. 16 1926* pl. 3, 71; *CV*. ii pl. 29, 2. A, Dionysos pursuing a woman; B, woman fleeing. The provenience 'Vari' given in *CV*. cannot be correct.

3 (4). TARQUINIA RC 7455, from Tarquinia. A, youth and woman; B, youth.

4 (5). VATICAN. A, man leaning on his stick, and boy; B, youth.

5 (6). VATICAN. A, man leaning on his stick, and boy seated holding a lyre; B, man.

6 (9). VILLA GIULIA 47799, from Cervetri. A, *ML*. 42, 1011; phs. R.I. 57. 673–4. A, youth and boy; B, youth.

7 (7). LOUVRE G 222. A, Pottier pl. 130; *CV*. pl. 42, 5–7. A, man on platform, and man; B, youth. Restored.

8 (10). ARLESHEIM, Schweizer (ex Jandolo). A, Fallani *Racc. Signorelli* pl. 8, 226, and cover. A, man attacking with sword (Aristogeiton, as Bothmer?). B, youth. A is restored.

9 (8). SARASOTA (ex Parrish). A, Nike (running to right, a torch in each hand). B, youth (standing to right).

(nos. 10–18, with triple handles)

10 (11). LENINGRAD 607 (St. 1532). A, *CR*. 1873, 42. A, Zeus and Ganymede. B, youth.

11 (12). LENINGRAD 606 (St. 1642). A, Zeus pursuing a woman. B, man. Much restored.

12 (13). LENINGRAD 605 (St. 1640). A, youth and woman; B, woman.

13 (14, +). LOUVRE G 215. *CV*. pl. 40, 11–12. A, acontist and flute-player. B, man. A Louvre fragment (composed of three) joins, adding part of the flute-player's robe. Restored.

14 (15, +). LOUVRE G 208. *CV.* pl. 38, 7–8. A, Dionysos and maenad; B, satyr and maenad. Now cleaned. A Louvre fragment joins, adding the foot of the maenad's oinochoe on A and the middle of the god's himation.

15 (16, +). LOUVRE G 207 *bis. CV.* pl. 38, 9 and 13. A, Dionysos and satyr; B, maenad. Restored.

16 (17). NAPLES inv. 126062. A, Zeus. B, youth.

17 (18). ALTENBURG 288, from Nola. *CV.* pl. 44, 2, pl. 45, 3, and pl. 47, 3; R.I. ix. 89. A, man (leaning on his stick). B, youth.

18 (19). MUNICH 2326 (J. 253), from Vulci. B, FR. i, 148; *CV.* pl. 55, 1, pl. 56, 5, and pl. 57, 3; B.Ap. xvi. 18. 1. A, komast ('Anacreontic'). B, youth. See CB. ii, 58 no. 5.

(nos. 19–20, with ridged handles)

19 (20). SCHWERIN 1293. A, satyr petting fawn; B, satyr.

20 (21). NAPLES, from Nola. A, ph. So. 11072, i, 3. A, Dionysos (standing to right, holding out a drinking-horn). B, youth.

(nos. 21–24, the handles missing)

21 (22). LEIPSIC, from Cervetri. A, woman with hydria on her head, and youth holding out a circlet. B, man and boy.

22 (23). BALTIMORE, from Taranto? *CV.* Robinson ii, pl. 29, 1 and pl. 30 (with alien lid); A, *Anz.* 1941, 46; A, *A.A.A.* pl. 83, 278. A, Silenos led captive; B, man (Midas?). Restored; the upper part of Silenos, for example, is modern.

23 (24). LOUVRE G 207. *CV.* pl. 38, 4–5. A, Dionysos and satyr. B, man. Restored.

24. LOUVRE C 11049, two frr. On one (five joining), (male standing to right, the left-hand figure on one side, or the sole). On the other, (part of a woman standing to right, the left-hand figure, or the sole, on the other side).

PANATHENAIC AMPHORA

25 (25). BERLIN 2162, from Vulci. A, Eros. B, Athena. Small. Cleaned.

AMPHORA

26 (26). FLORENCE 8 B 21, two frr. *CV.* pl. 8, B 21. (Satyr; satyr).

PELIKAI
(nos. 27–30, the pictures framed)

27 (27). TARQUINIA RC 973, from Tarquinia. A, man and seated youth; B, man seated, and man.

28 (28). SYRACUSE 36257, from Gela. A, komos (youth, and woman playing the flute). B, youth and boy.

29 (29). AGRIGENTO, from Agrigento. A, two males at laver; B, two males.

30 (30). ATHENS Acr. 625, frr., from Athens. Part, Langlotz pl. 48. A, cockfight. B, (males).

(no. 31, not known if the picture framed)

31 (31). ERLANGEN 840, fr. (Upper arm of man with stick to left).

(nos. 32–34, the pictures not framed)

32. LOUVRE C 10789. A, man and boy (with dog); B, male and boy.

33. LOUVRE C 10867, fr. A, youth and boy. B, (part of the ess-border remains, and of a stick?).

34. PHILADELPHIA MARKET, frr. A, girl. B, athlete. On A, in transparent chiton, standing frontal, head to left, mirror in right hand.

STAMNOI

35 (32). MUNICH 2407 (J. 415), from Vulci. *Mon.* 6–7 pll. 27 a–b. A, Herakles and the lion. B, Hermes, Poseidon, and another. See p. 1641.

36 (33). Once AGRIGENTO, Giudice. A, Dionysos and maenads. B, (youths?). Much restored.

37 (34). FRANKFORT, Städel Institut. Schaal *F.* pll. 43–44. A, maenads; B, maenads.

38. LOUVRE C 10821, frr. A, (male, man, old man); B, male and boy, two males.

COLUMN-KRATERS

(nos. 39–58, with framed pictures)

39 (35). HARVARD 60.339 (ex Robinson), from Ruvo. A, *RM.* 9 pl. 8, whence *JHS.* 18, 279 and Jacobsthal *Thes.* pl. 3 fig. 5; A, *Cat. Am. Art Ass. March 6 1936*, 11, 38; *CV.* Robinson ii pll. 31–33. A, Poseidon and Theseus. B, citharode.

40 (36). ATHENS Acr. 817 and MUNICH, frr., from Athens. One fr. of B, Langlotz pl. 74. A, uncertain subject: Hermes, or a herald, and woman; old man, youth, and another. B, man and males. The Munich fragment gives the lower parts of four figures on A.

41 (37). ROME, Conservatori, 23. A, Bothmer *Am.* pl. 70, 2; phs. R.I. 57.507 and 503. A, Herakles and the Amazons. B, three youths. Restored.

42 (38). LONDON MARKET (Sotheby, *Cat. July 11 1927* no. 161: ex Holford), from Poggio Sommavilla. A, R.I. ix. 68, whence Jüthner 9. A, athletes. B, man and youths.

43. PHILADELPHIA MARKET. *Hesp. Art. Bull.* 2 no. 68. A, athletes (jumpers and trainer). B, man and boy.

44 (39). FERRARA, T. 475, from Spina. A, Aurigemma[1] 59, above = [2]61, above = Aurigemma and Alfieri pl. 7, above. A, athletes. B, three youths. For the right-hand figure on A see *BSA.* 46, 9 no. 8. See p. 1641.

45 (40). AGRIGENTO (ex Giudice 208), from Agrigento. A, ph. Lo Cascio pl. 5; A, ph. R.I. 4933. A, arming. B, men and youths.

46 (41). BOLOGNA 189, from Bologna. A, Pellegrini 71; *CV*. pl. 24, 4–5. A, warriors leaving home. B, youths and boy.

47 (42). FLORENCE 3999. *CV*. pl. 39, 2 and pl. 42, 2–4. A, symposion. B, man and youths.

48. MONTAUBAN 3. A, symposion (man reclining, and man playing the flute). B, male and boy.

49 (43). FLORENCE PD 373. A, symposion (man reclining, and man with lyre). B, two youths.

50 (44). VILLA GIULIA 1054, from Falerii. A, *Boll. d'Arte* 10, 342; A, ph. Al. 41213, whence Greifenhagen *Eroten* 41. A, youth and woman, with Erotes. B, komos.

51. LOUVRE C 10753. A, youth and boy; man and boy; B, youths and boy.

52 (45). AGRIGENTO 18, from Agrigento. A, youth with lyre, youth, and man; B, youths. Much restored.

53 (46). HARVARD, from Poggio Sommavilla. *CV*. Hoppin pl. 12, 1–2. A, youth seated with lyre, man, and youth; B, man and youth.

54 (47). MUNICH 2373 (J. 413). A, men and boy; B, youths and boy. Restored.

55 (48). VATICAN. A, woman seated, with youth and man; B, two youths.

56 (49). ATHENS Acr. 818, fr., from Athens. (Man).

57 (50). ATHENS Acr. 816, fr., from Athens. Langlotz pl. 74. B, two men.

58 (a). PALERMO V 792, from Agrigento. A, Politi *Cinque vasi di premio* pl. 1; A, *Dioniso* 3, 162; *CV*. pl. 46, 1–2 and pl. 45, 3 (*not* pl. 46, 3). A, man, seated woman, and youth. B, youths and boy. Late.

(nos. 59–68, the pictures not framed)

59 (51). BERLIN inv. 3163, from Etruria. A, *Anz*. 1890, 89, below. A, winged goddess and seated youth (Thetis and Achilles?). B, youth.

60 (52). NAPLES 3152, from Telese. A, ph. R.I. 56.495, whence *Ant. Kunst* 2 pl. 10, 3; A, ph. So. 11071, i, 2. A, Zeus and Ganymede. B, youth.

61 (53). VIENNA 3737 (ex Oest. Mus. 340), from Cervetri. A, Masner pl. 6, 340; *CV*. pl. 87, 1–2. A, Poseidon. B, youth.

62 (54). AGRIGENTO (ex Giudice 168), from Gela. Ph. Lo Cascio pl. 2. A, youth driving calf. B, man.

63 (55). FLORENCE 4024. A, Passeri pl. 150; *CV*. pl. 39, 1 and pl. 42, 1. A, symposion (man reclining). B, youth.

64 (56). VILLA GIULIA, from Falerii. A, symposion (youth with lyre reclining). B, youth.

65 (57). NAPLES inv. 86304, from Cumae. A, youth at herm. B, youth.

66 (58). ATHENS Acr. 815, fr., from Athens. Langlotz pl. 74. A, komast.

67 (59). VILLA GIULIA 50520. A, man and youth; B, youth.

68 (60). ATHENS Acr. 805, fr., from Athens. Langlotz pl. 70. Youth (komast?).

CALYX-KRATER

69 (61). ATHENS Acr. 734, fr., from Athens. Langlotz pl. 58. (One offering a lyre to a boy).

HYDRIAI

(no. 70, of bf. shape; with framed pictures)

70. MAPLEWOOD, Noble, from Vulci. Woman seated, boy, man, and youth. On the shoulder, fight.

(nos. 71–72, kalpides, the picture on the shoulder, framed)

71 (62). ROMAN MARKET, from Sicily. Man and youths (1, youth standing to right, holding a hare; then a dog; 2, man with stick, seated to right; then a dog; 3, youth bending to left).

72 (63). ROMAN MARKET, from Sicily. Youths and man (man to right with stick, youth seated to right, youth leaning on his stick to left).

(nos. 73–75, kalpides, the picture on the shoulder, not framed)

73 (64). ATHENS Acr. 690, fr., from Athens. Langlotz pl. 53. (Nike).

74 (65). ATHENS Acr. 693, fr., from Athens. Langlotz pl. 53. Mistress and maid.

75 (66). LONDON MARKET (Spink: ex Norfolk). Destroyed by enemy action except for fragments which are in Reading. Dionysos and maenads (maenad to right with thyrsus, Dionysos to right with grapes and ivy, maenad to left with oinochoe and fruit).

OINOCHOAI

(nos. 76–78, shape 1)

76 (67). HARROW 56. *Burl. 1903* pl. 95, H 53; *JHS.* 36 pl. 7, 2 and p. 133, whence Chittenden and Seltman pl. 18, 81; *VA.* 56. Boy with hoop.

77 (68). CAMBRIDGE 164. Ernest Gardner pl. 33; *CV.* pl. 35, 4 and pl. 40, 4; B.Ap. xxi. 64. Woman with oinochoe and phiale.

78 (69). COPENHAGEN, Thorvaldsen Museum, 97. B.Ap. xxii (the second number missing). Athena. Slightly restored.

(no. 79, shape 5)

79 (70). BASLE 1921.363. Schefold *Basler Ant.* ii pl. 24, a. Symposion (man reclining).

(no. 80, shape 6)

80 (71). NEW YORK 12.229.13, from Athens. Stackelberg pl. 24, 5; *JHS.* 36 pl. 7, 1; Richter and Hall pl. 33, 24, whence *Bull. Vereen.* 17, 11 fig. 26. Satyr athlete.

FRAGMENTS OF POTS

81 (74). LEIPSIC T 664, fr. (Lower parts of two persons in long chiton and himation, one at least of them male). From a neck-amphora or a pelike?

82. LOUVRE C 11008, two frr. On one, (middle of a male standing to right, with stick); on the other, a small piece of drapery. From a neck-amphora or a pelike?

83 (73). LENINGRAD, fr., from Kerch. (Upper part of a man leaning on his stick to right). From a pelike?

84 (75). ATHENS Acr. 987, two frr., from Athens. On one, (athlete). On the other, (part of a himation, then bare legs).

85 (76). ATHENS Acr. 988, fr., from Athens. Langlotz pl. 79. (Man). From a hydria or a pelike?

86. NAPLES, Astarita, 141, fr. Part of the right-hand figure remains, the legs of a woman standing to left, then net-dot side-border. From a hydria (with picture on the shoulder) or a pelike?

PLATE

87 (72). ATHENS Acr. 27, frr., from Athens. Part, Langlotz pl. 1. Woman.

The following is probably by the Harrow Painter:

COLUMN-KRATER
(*the pictures not framed*)

VIENNA 1103. A, Millin *PVA.* 2 pl. 24; *AZ.* 1854 pl. 66, 1, whence Robert *Herm.* 213; A, Lücken pl. 86; cleaned, *CV.* pl. 87, 3–4. A, Klytaimestra and Talthybios (extract from a 'Death of Aigisthos'). B, komast.

A fragment might be by the Harrow Painter:

COLUMN-KRATER
(*the picture not framed*)

LOUVRE C 10819, fr. A, symposion (one reclining).

Compare also the
COLUMN-KRATER
(*framed pictures*)

(2). BOLOGNA 232, from Bologna. Zannoni pl. 68, 3 and 6–7; A, Pellegrini 92. A, symposion. B, youth, boy, and man.
This recalls the Walters Painter as well (p. 278).

In the following the reverses appear to be by the Harrow Painter himself. The obverse of no. 2 may be his (late work); the other obverse is not well known to me.

COLUMN-KRATERS

(*with framed pictures*)

1. MARKET. A, Dionysos with satyr and maenad. B, youths and boy. On A, maenad moving to right, thyrsus in right hand, snake in the muffled left, Dionysos moving to right, with kantharos and thyrsus, satyr to left, right arm extended, thyrsus in left hand.

2. PHILADELPHIA 2464. A, symposion. B, youths and boy.

THE PAINTER OF FERRARA T. 756

Near the Harrow Painter.

COLUMN-KRATERS

(*small; the pictures framed*)

1. FERRARA, T. 756, from Spina. Symposion: A, man reclining; B, youth reclining.

2. FERRARA, T. 274, from Spina. Symposion: A, man and youth reclining; B, two men reclining.

THE WALTERS PAINTER

ARV.[1] 182.

Near the Harrow Painter, but weaker. See also p. 277.

COLUMN-KRATERS

(*with framed pictures*)

1 (1). BALTIMORE, Walters Art Gallery, 48.70. *Bull. Walt.* 6, 6 (April 1954), 2, below; detail of A, *Bull. Walt.* 11, 7 (April 1959), 3, above. A, man, woman, and youth; B, man, youth, and man. On the neck, A, in silhouette, lions and bull.

2 (2). VILLA GIULIA 857. A, man and boy; man and youth; B, two males and a woman.

3. BROOKLYN 03.9, from Capua. A, warrior and man; male and man. B, three satyrs.

4. LOUVRE C 10746. A, symposion. B, males.

5. LOUVRE G 191. *CV.* pl. 22, 1–2. A, athletes. B, man seated and woman. Was restored as a stamnos: now cleaned, and a Louvre fragment (two joining) added, which gives the upper part of the right-hand athlete on A.

6. NAPLES inv. 86306, from Cumae. A, Dionysos with satyrs and maenad. B, man and youth. B restored.

PELIKE
(with framed pictures)

7. NAPLES inv. 146679, from Naples. A, *NSc.* 1935, 259. A. two satyrs. B, two youths.

_____

Probably also:

COLUMN-KRATERS
(with framed pictures)

1. VILLA GIULIA 50760. A, symposion. B, hoplitodromoi and trainer.
2. BOULOGNE. A, two youths, two males; B, two males and a woman, who moves away, holding a mirror.

Compare also the

COLUMN-KRATER

LOUVRE G347, from Agrigento. Millingen *Coghill* pl. 24; *CV.* d pl. 24, 4–5. A, satyrs. B, man and youth. Much restored.

_____

THE FLYING-ANGEL PAINTER

VA. 57–59. *Att. V.* 106–7 and 470. *ARV.*[1] 182–5 and 954. CB. iii, text.

So called from the subject of no. 7.

AMPHORAE
(type C)

1 (1). LENINGRAD 603 (St. 1593). A, athlete with acontion; B, man.
2 (2). PARIS, Petit Palais, 307, from Capua. *CV.* pl. 12, 1–3 and 6. A, naked woman holding a phallus-bird and uncovering a basket full of phalloi; B, naked woman holding a phallus.
3. VILLA GIULIA, from Cervetri. A, a youth throwing a stone at a hawk which has lifted a hare into the air. B, youth (leaning on his stick, the right arm akimbo).
4. VILLA GIULIA, from Cervetri. A, man attacking with sword (Robin Hood petasos, left arm extended in chlamys). B, satyr attacking with fir-branch.
5 (3). LOUVRE G 212. *CV.* pl. 39, 10–11 and pl. 40, 5. A, man with spear; B, man. Restored.
6 (4). LENINGRAD 604 (St. 1601). A, *VA.* 59. A, satyr with pantheress-cub; B, satyr.
7 (5). BOSTON 98.882, from Capua. *VA.* 58; A, Richter and Milne fig. 10; A, *E.A.A.* i, 393, 536; CB. iii pl. 82, 124; the shape, Caskey G. 80. A, satyr holding his son flying-angel; B, satyr brandishing a phallus. See CB. iii, text.

8. MUNICH 8726. *CV*. pl. 189, pl. 190, 2-3, and p. 22. A, warrior; B, warrior.

9 (6). VIENNA 3724 (ex Oest. Mus. 332), from Cervetri. A, Masner pl. 6, 332, and p. vii; *CV*. pl. 52, 1-2 and p. 9. A, warrior; B, man.

10 (7). BRUSSELS A 2483-5, frr. B, *CV*. pl. 23, 2. A, warrior lifting a dead body; B, warrior.

11 (8). LOUVRE G 220. Pottier pl. 130, whence *BCH*. 1942-3, 251; *CV*. pl. 42, 3-4; *Revue des Arts* 8, 202 and 207-8 (A cleaned). A, komast; B, komast. Both 'Anacreontic', see CB. ii, 58 no. 4. Restored.

PANATHENAIC AMPHORA
(small; with framed pictures)

12 (9). LONDON E 259. *CV*. pl. 5, 2. A, komast; B, komast.

NECK-AMPHORAE
(no. 13, with twisted handles)

13. VILLA GIULIA 47214, from Cervetri. A, *ML*. 42, 671; phs. R.I. 56.1551-2. A, Eros pursuing a boy; B, man. Eros holds a whip; the boy, plectrum and lyre: for the subject compare two vases by the Oionokles Painter, London E 297 (p. 647 no. 13) and Charlecote (p. 648 no. 32), and the aryballos by Douris in Athens (p. 447 no. 274).

(no. 14, small; of special shape; the handles lost)

14 (10). TARANTO 4546, from Taranto. A, satyr. B, youth (komast?).

PELIKAI
(nos. 15-18, with framed pictures)

15 (11). LENINGRAD 619 (St. 1208). A, warrior leaving home; B, the like.

16 (13). VILLA GIULIA (ex Mus. Art. Ind.). A, *RM*. 38-39, 88; A, ph. R.I. 4407. A, jumpers. B, komast.

17 (15). FLORENCE 76895, from Chiusi. *CV*. pl. 31, 3 and pl. 33, 3-4. Komos: A, youth and flute-girl; B, youth.

18 (21). MYKONOS, from Rheneia (originally from Delos). Dugas *Délos xxi* pl. 3, 7. A, man embracing boy. B, komos (two men). A is by the Triptolemos Painter (p. 362 no. 21). Late.

(nos. 19-26, the pictures not framed)

19 (12). BRUSSELS A 2487-9, frr. A, two males; B, youth and woman.

20 (14). NAPLES 3213. A, youth and woman. B, komos (man and youth).

21 (18). DRESDEN 292 (ZV. 737). A, citharode; B, man (judge).

22 (17). HEIDELBERG 120, fr. Kraiker pl. 30. B, youth.

23 (19). LONDON E 364, from Camiros. A, Herakles; B, Syleus.

24 (20). TÜBINGEN E 54, from (the Rhodian?) Chalki. A, Watzinger pl. 25. A, satyr; B, satyr.

25. LOUVRE C 10791. A, warrior (or hoplitodromos). B, komast.

26 (16). MYKONOS, from Rheneia (originally from Delos). Dugas *Délos xxi* pl. 3, 5–6. A, (male). B, komast (youth dancing).

COLUMN-KRATERS
(*nos. 27–35, with framed pictures*)

27 (22). PHILADELPHIA 2465. A, boxers and trainer. B, two youths.

28 (23). OXFORD 1917.56. Tischbein 4 pll. 37 and 44, whence Inghirami pll. 272 and 82; Tillyard pl. 20, 124; *CV.* pl. 23, 2 and pl. 22, 4. A, Dionysos reclining, and satyrs. B, two athletes.

29 (24, +). FLORENCE 8 B 1 and HEIDELBERG 121. The Heidelberg fr., Kraiker pl. 17; part, *CV.* Florence pl. 8, B 1. A, satyr and maenad. B, komos (two youths). A new Florence fragment joins the Heidelberg above, completing the skyphos in the reveller's hand.

30 (25). ATHENS, Agora, P 7251, frr., from Athens. A, satyrs treading wine. B, komos. [Talcott.]

31. FERRARA, T. 344, from Spina. A, youth leading horse, and man with sceptre. B, two athletes.

32 (26). FERRARA, T. 482, from Spina. A, symposion. B, three athletes.

33 (27). CHIUSI 1849, from Chiusi. B, ph. Al. 37492, whence Levi *Mus. Civ. Chiusi* 114; *Boll. d'Arte* 35 (1950), 333 figs. 5–6. A, symposion (Dionysos and Herakles reclining). B, komos. Late.

34 (28). FLORENCE V 5, from Chiusi. B, *Jh.* 8, 145, and p. 10, 118; B, *St. e mat.* 1, 64–65, whence Buschor *Feldmäuse* 8; B, Milani *Mus. Top.* 69; *Mon. Piot* 29 pl. 5, whence (B) *Bull. Vereen.* 17, 6 fig. 14, (B) Buschor *Satyrtänze* fig. 73, (part of B) *Hist. rel.* 175. A, athletes. B, satyrs demolishing a tomb. Late.

34 *bis.* MILAN 74. 1957. *CV.* pl. 7 and pl. 5, 2–4. A, athletes and trainer. B, two naked youths dancing. Restored.

35 (29). LOUVRE G 354. *CV.* d pl. 25, 5 and 7. A, komos; B, komos (youths dancing). Late.

(*nos. 36–39 bis, the pictures not framed*)

36 (30). HEIDELBERG 122, fr. A, youth with shield.

36 *bis.* SYDNEY 51.46, fr. B, naked youth.

37 (31). LENINGRAD (St. 2186), from near Kerch. A, *ABC.* 160 (131), 1. A, komast. B, jumper.

38 (32). PALERMO. A, warrior (bearded, frontal, head to right, holding helmet and spear). B, jumper. Restored.

39. LUCERNE MARKET (A.A.). *Ars Ant. Auktion I* pl. 55, 115. A, citharode. B, komast.

39 *bis.* ITALIAN MARKET. A, satyr (moving to the attack, to right, with phallus-staff and panther-skin). B, komast (youth, wrap over arms, running to right, looking round, right arm extended to left).

LEKYTHOI

(secondary shape: Class ATL, p. 709, but in a neat version; see also pp. 282–3)

40 (33). LONDON E 583, from Gela. Schlesinger pl. 9. Satyr with flute.
See below.

41 (34). PALERMO V 690, from Gela. *CV*. pl. 24, 5–6. Athlete using pick.
See below.

FRAGMENTS OF POTS

42 (35). ATHENS Acr. 830, frr., from Athens. Langlotz pl. 74. Maenads.
From a column-krater or a stamnos?

43 (36). ATHENS Acr. 828, fr., from Athens. (Satyr).

44 (37). ATHENS Acr. 945 and 942, two frr., from Athens. Langlotz pl. 78
and pl. 77. (Youth; boy). From an amphora?

45. LENINGRAD Б 6472, fr., from South Russia. (Youth—Kephalos?).

The following looks like a coarse imitation of the painter's late work:

COLUMN-KRATER
(with framed pictures)

LONDON E 487, from Capua. A, athletes. B, satyrs as porters stacking bags,
and a man looking on: for the subject compare the Arkesilas cup (FR. pl.
151). For the style compare Louvre G 354 (p. 281 no. 35).

The following is near the painter:

FRAGMENT OF A POT

BRYN MAWR P 184, fr. *AJA*. 1916, 343, 25. (Youth).

In shape and ornament a lekythos goes with the two by the Flying-angel
Painter (above, nos. 40–41); the style of the figure, though looser, is not far
off:

LEKYTHOS
(secondary shape)

NEW YORK 22.139.74. Satyr with lion-cub.

In shape and pattern-work this lekythos and Palermo V 690 (above, no.
41) go with a group of four white lekythoi; the style of the figures, too, is
at least similar. The maeander of London E 583 (above, no. 40), and the shape
so far as it is preserved, are the same as in all these. The white lekythoi are
placed under the heading 'Painter of Munich 2774', but he is very probably
the same as the Flying-angel Painter.

THE PAINTER OF MUNICH 2774

The shape is a neater version of 'ATL' (see p. 709).

LEKYTHOI (WHITE)
(secondary shape)

1. LONDON 1914.5–12.1. Youth and woman.
2. MUNICH 2774 (J. 199). Fairbanks i, 92; *AM.* 52 Beil. 28, 4. Youth and boy.
3. GELA, from Gela. *Boll. d'Arte* 39 (1954), 78–79; *NSc.* 1956, 296, 5, p. 297 fig. 12, and p. 298. Satyr and maenad.
4. COPENHAGEN inv. 6328, from Gela. *CV* pl. 170, 1; Breitenstein *G.V.* pl. 25. Achilles brought to Chiron.

THE PAINTER OF LOUVRE G 238

Near the Flying-angel Painter; and linked by the maeander with the Geras and Argos Painters (pp. 285 and 288).

PELIKAI
(with framed pictures)

1. LOUVRE G 238. One head, *CV.* pl. 50, 1 (pl. 50, 2 is modern). A, man and two women; B, man, man or youth, and woman. Now cleaned, and new Louvre fragments added.
2. LOUVRE G 227. A, *Annali* 1862 pl. C, whence Frickenhaus *Len.* pl. 2, 12; *CV.* pl. 45, 1 and 4. A, satyrs at idol of Dionysos. B, man, man or youth, and boy. Now cleaned. Two Louvre fragments belong: one has part of the maeander, the other joins B and gives the subject: 1, a man leaning on his stick to right, holding out a head-fillet, 2, a boy to left with a cock in his hand, 3, a man or youth to left.
3. LENINGRAD 617. A, two men and a boy; B, the like. Very much restored.
4. ROME, Conservatori. Phs. R.I. 57.493–4. A, komos (man—'Anacreontic' —playing the lyre, and two women with krotala). B, man, boy, and male. Much restored.
5. LONDON MARKET (Spink: ex Samuel Rogers 382). Destroyed by enemy action: a few fragments are in Reading. A, mission to Achilles. B, youth leaving home (or returning) (1, woman to right, a flower in her left hand, shaking hands with, 2, a youth in a chitoniskos, holding a spear, to left; 3, an old man). Described by Panofka in *Annali* 1849, 255.

THE MATSCH PAINTER

Bull. Vereen. 24–26, 20.

Named after the former owner of no. 2. Akin to the Flying-angel Painter.

PELIKAI

(*no. 2, the pictures not framed*)

1. VILLA GIULIA 48238, from Cervetri. *Studies Robinson* ii pl. 36 and pl. 37, c; *ML.* 42, 1021-2; A, Vighi 100; phs. R.I. 57.682–3, whence (A) *Jb. Mainz* 5 pl. 23. A, Herakles and Geras. B, Dionysos and maenad.

(*no. 2, the pictures framed*)

2. EASTON (Pennsylvania), Williams (ex Matsch). *CV.* Matsch pl. 7. A, man, and woman with basket on her head. B, youth and girl. Now cleaned.

NECK-AMPHORAE

(*with twisted handles*)

3. VILLA GIULIA 50462. A, ph. GF. 7167. A, a man offering a hare to a boy; B, man.

4. NEW YORK 56.171.39 (ex Hearst). A, *Vend. Sarti* pl. 20, 290; A, *Coll. B. et C.* pl. 20, 170; A, *Bull. Metr.* March 1957, 177, 4. A, warrior leaving home (warrior and old man); B, man. Wrongly ascribed to the Harrow Painter in *ARV.*[1] 178 no. 3.

COLUMN-KRATER

(*with framed pictures*)

5. STOCKHOLM, Medelhavsmuseum. *Ars Ant. Aukt.* IV pl. 46, 135. A, youth with spears (Theseus?) pursuing a woman; B, two women fleeing to a king. To left of the pair on A, a youth moving to left, looking round, and an old man moving to right, right arm extended.

Near the painter:

NECK-AMPHORA

(*with twisted handles*)

VILLA GIULIA 14213. A, ph. Al. 41172; phs. R.I. 1935.1627–8. A, woman with hydria on her head. B, youth. The vase is of a different model from nos. 3 and 4.

Compare also:

COLUMN-KRATER

(*the picture not framed*)

PADULA, fr., from Padula. (Man to right, with phiale).

THE GROUP OF VIENNA 895

Eichler is probably right in assigning these to one hand (*CV.* Vienna ii, 19). The shape, also, is the same in both.

PELIKAI
(with framed pictures)

1. ADOLPHSECK, Landgraf Philipp of Hesse, 42. A, Brommer *A.K.F.* fig. 15; *CV.* pl. 32, 1–2, and p. 22, above. A, sale of oil (man seated, and woman). B, youth and woman. [Eichler].

2. VIENNA 895. *CV.* pl. 72, 3–4, and p. 19, above. A, sale of oil (man seated, and girl). B, two youths. [Eichler].

THE GERAS PAINTER

VA. 56–57. *Att. V.* 109–10 and 470. *ARV.*[1] 174–6 and 954.

So called from the subject of no. 16.
Close to the Argos Painter (p. 288), who may be said to continue his style.

PELIKAI
(nos. 1–2, the pictures framed)

1 (1). LOUVRE G 224, from Vulci. Pottier pl. 130; A, Jacobsthal *Akt.* 6; *CV.* pl. 43, 3–5, pl. 42, 9, and pl. 44, 3, 8, and 10; A, R.I. xxi. 14 b. A, death of Actaeon. B, Zeus and Ganymede. Now cleaned.

2. BASLE MARKET (M.M.). A, Dionysos and satyr; B, satyr. The satyr on A wears a himation, let down from the waist, and a petasos, holds an oinochoe and a bunch of grapes; the satyr on B wears the drawers of the satyr-play, and dances, sword in one hand and scabbard in the other.

(nos. 3–22, the pictures not framed)

3 (2). ATHENS 1413 (CC. 1176), from Atalanti. *CV.* pl. 9, 2–4. A, man offering hare to boy; B, man.

4. LOUVRE C 11013, fr. A, warrior between palmettes.

5 (3). BERLIN 2171. Gargiulo *Recueil* (1845) ii pl. 66, whence (A) *El.* 3 pl. 47; B, Licht ii, 147; B.Ap. xviii. 2. A, Triptolemos and Demeter. B, man offering hare to boy. Restored.

6 (3 *bis*). BASLE 1906.301. A, van Hoorn *Choes* fig. 109; Schefold *Basler Ant.* ii pl. 23. A, komos (man and youth). B, youth and boy. See p. 1642.

7 (4). HARVARD 1925.30.34. *CV.* Hoppin pl. 12, 3–4, whence (incomplete) Buschor *Satyrtänze* fig. 65. A, Herakles carrying a pair of pointed amphorae; B, satyr at well.

8 (5). CAB. MÉD. 397, from Capua? De Ridder 292 (misprinted 291) and pl. 14, whence (A) Buschor *Satyrtänze* fig. 63. A, uncertain subject: Herakles

and a man. B, youth at herm. Herakles seems to be putting on his lion-skin rather than taking it off. The other person on A is not characterized as a satyr: Rumpf thinks of Antaios. De Ridder had already thought of a hero, and compared, for the attitude, that of boxers at the punch-ball.

9 (6). Leipsic T 643. A, *Jh.* 11, 191, 35. A, Dionysos chastising a satyr, who holds a flute. B, male at herm.

10. Berkeley 8.4583. *AJA.* 1945, 509. A, satyrs cooking; B, satyr running with situla and pointed amphora. [Amyx]. For the subject, Amyx in *AJA.* 1945, 508–18.

11 (7). Vienna 728, from Nola. A, La Borde 1 pl. 83, whence *El.* 1 pl. 55; *CV.* pl. 73, 1–2. A, birth of Athena. B, youth and boy. Restored.

12 (8). Vienna 905, from Nola. La Borde 2 pl. 29, left; *CV.* pl. 73, 3–5. A, Nike and victor; B, discus-thrower.

13. Agrigento, Soprintendenza, from Monte Saraceno? A, *Fasti arch.* 10, 119. A, Europa. B, boar.

14 (9). Louvre G 536, from Nola. *Annali* 1862 pl. H; A, Pottier pl. 155; *CV.* pl. 45, 5, 7, and 11. A, peasant riding a ram; B, peasant riding a goat. Both youths play the flute.

15 (10). Cab. Méd. 391, from Vulci. Fröhner *Mus. de France* pl. 8; A, ph. Gir. 8077. A, Dionysos arming, with satyr; B, Dionysos and maenad.

16 (11). Louvre G 234, from Capua? A, *Philologus* 50 (1891) pl. 1, whence Roscher s.v. Personifikationen 2083 fig. 2 and Pfuhl fig. 493; A, Pottier pl. 131; *CV.* pl. 48, 1–6; A, ph. Gir. 17297, whence Richardson *Old Age* fig. 1, *Anz.* 1952, 62, and (parts) *Studies Robinson* ii pl. 37, d–e. A, Herakles and Geras. B, Poseidon. See p. 1642.

17 (12). Once Magnoncourt 55, from Nola. Gerhard *AB.* pl. 117, 2–3. A, Theseus and Minotaur. B, Nike (or Iris).

18 (13). Berlin 2173, from Vulci. A, Licht iii, 78; Buschor *Satyrtänze* fig. 78; B.Ap. xxi. 65. A, satyr running to fountain; B, woman at fountain. Restored.

19 (14). New York 01.8.8 (GR 578), from South Italy. A, Richter and Milne fig. 36, whence LS. fig. 3; Richter and Hall pl. 22, 22 and pl. 173, 22; B, Richter *ARVS.* 61 fig. 19, and fig. 50; A, Richter *H.* 214, c. A, Dionysos; B, satyr.

20 (15). Leningrad 724. A, Dionysos; B, satyr. Restored.

21 (16). Oxford 283, from Sirignano. *CV.* pl. 19, 2–3. A, man holding helmet. B, satyr (in himation and petasos).

22 (17). Villa Giulia (ex Castellani). A, man holding helmet. B, youth.

NECK-AMPHORAE
(*small, with triple handles*)

23 (18). Munich 2327 (J. 251), from Vulci. *Annali* 1839 pl. Q; *CV.* pl. 55, 2, pl. 56, 6, and pl. 57, 4–5. A, Herakles; B, Acheloos.

24 (19). COPENHAGEN, Thorvaldsen Museum, 99, from Vulci. A, Micali *Storia* pl. 100, 1; A, *El.* 2 pl. 99; Jacobsthal *Akt.* 4–5; B, *Die Antike* 6 pl. 20; B.Ap. xxii. 76. A, death of Actaeon. B, satyrs playing ephedrismos.

25. NAPLES (ex Spinelli), from Suessula. A, Dionysos and maenad; B, maenad pursuing a satyr.

STAMNOS

26 (20). LONDON 1929.5–13.2. Zahn *Sg Schiller* pl. 30; *BMQ.* 4 pl. 16. A, Herakles and the Hydra; B, Herakles and the lion.

VOLUTE-KRATERS

27 (21). MUNICH 2382 (J. 783), from Sicily. A, Zancani Montuoro and Zanotti-Bianco *Heraion* ii, 195 fig. 46. A, Herakles and the Kerkopes. B, Artemis. On the neck, A: Dionysos reclining, with maenad and satyr.

28 (22). ATHENS Acr. 733, fr., from Athens. Langlotz pl. 58. On the neck, (Ganymede).

COLUMN-KRATERS
(the pictures not framed)

29 (23). CAB. MÉD. 415, from Vulci. De Ridder 306. A, Herakles and Athena. B (de Ridder 307, whence Weege *Tanz* 104) is modern.

30. BRNO 2624. *Epit. Haken* pl. 3. A, man at stele; B, man.

HYDRIA
(with picture on the body, framed)

31 (24). ATHENS 1176 (CC. 1172), from Pikrodafni. *CV.* pl. 8, 3 and pl. 9, 1. Man offering lyre to boy.

OINOCHOE
(shape 5A)

32 (25). NAPLES inv. 126056. Brommer *Satyroi* 63, whence Herbig *Pan* pl. 7, 1; *Marb. Jb.* 15, 21. Pan.

FRAGMENT OF POTS

33 (26). VILLA GIULIA, fr. (Head of woman to left). From a neck-amphora?

34 (27). FLORENCE 6 B 40, fr. *CV.* pl. 6, B 40. (Girl).

A fragment recalls both the Geras Painter and the Argos Painter: FLORENCE 19 B 14, fr. *CV.* pl. 19, B 14. Woman. Might belong to Florence 6 B 40?

With the volute-kraters by the Geras Painter (above, nos. 27–28) compare the

VOLUTE-KRATER

CARLSRUHE 207, from Agrigento. Wagner and Eyth pll. 42 and 60; *CV.* pl. 18. A, goddess. B, komast.

THE ARGOS PAINTER

Att. V. 110–11. *ARV.*[1] 176–7 and 954.

So called from the subject of no. 1. Very like the Geras Painter, but less old-fashioned.

STAMNOI

1 (1). VIENNA 3729 (ex Oest. Mus. 338), from Cervetri. A, *Annali* 1865 pl. I–K, whence Overbeck *KM.* pl. 7, 10, *WV.* 1890–1 pl. 11, 1, Cook *Zeus* iii pl. 49, 2; A, Wolff *Heldensagen* pl. at p. 272; part of A, *Zalmoxis* 1 pl. at p. 12; A, *E.A.A.* i, 627; *CV.* pl. 66 and p. 15. A, death of Argos. B, youth, boy, and man. On A, ΚΑLΟϚ ΛΑΜΑϚ. See Pfeiffer *Ein neues Inachos-Fragment des Sophokles* 23. See also p. 1642.

2 (2). VILLA GIULIA 868, from Falerii. *CV.* pl. 5 and pl. 7, 1; A, ph. Al. 41162, 2. Herakles and Pholos.

3 (3). OXFORD 1911.625, fr., from Cervetri. Part, *CV.* pl. 25, 3. A, (man— god?—with phiale, and woman with phiale). ΑΠΟLLΟ[ΔΟΡΟϚ? Now augmented by a new fragment ex Leipsic, see *CV.* Oxford ii, 7.

4 (4). OXFORD, fr., from Cervetri. *CV.* pl. 66, 4. (One seated on a throne). Might be from the same vase as the last.

PELIKAI

(nos. 5–11, with framed pictures)

5 (5). BERLIN 2166, fr., from Cervetri. *AZ.* 1875 pl. 10, above. A, Zeus and Poseidon with Nike.

6 (6). BERLIN 2167, frr., from Cervetri. A, *AZ.* 1875 pl. 10, below. A, Zeus and Poseidon with Nike. B, (on the right, hand, woman with oinochoe).

7 (7). ROMAN MARKET, from Veii. Campanari *Isola Farnese* pl. 4; *El.* 3 pl. 61, whence Overbeck *KM.* pl. 15, 17. A, Triptolemos and Demeter. B, man with sceptre, boy with hoop, and youth.

8. LOUVRE C 11166, fr. A, Dionysos and maenads. B, (citharode and man). Another Louvre fragment may belong, giving part of the citharode's robe.

9. LOUVRE C 11167, fr. A, (Dionysos: part of his vine-branch remains). B, (hair?). The mouth and neck of the vase remain. See the next.

10. LOUVRE C 11168, fr. (On the left, middle of a male leaning on his stick to right). May belong to Louvre C 11167.

11 (8). LENINGRAD 614 (St. 1603). *CR.* 1875 pl. 5, 1–3; A, Waldhauer *A.R.V.* fig. 18; A, *Bonner Jahrbücher* 155–6 pl. 3 fig. 1; A, R.I. xxi. 13. A, negro leading a camel. B, citharode, judges, and listener. Late.

(nos. 12–15, the pictures not framed)

12 (9). LOUVRE G 236. *CV.* pl. 49, 2 and 4–6; A, Villard *VG.* pl. 25; A, ph. Arch. phot. S.4240.007. AE 1. A, man with phiale and woman with oinochoe at altar. B, jumper.

13 (10). VIENNA 1090. La Borde 2 pl. 30, 2 and pl. 31, 2; *CV*. pl. 70. A, Dionysos; B, satyr.

14 (11). NEW YORK 96.18.29 (GR 580). Richter and Hall pl. 24, 23 and pl. 173, 23; the shape, Hambidge 93. A, woman with mirror; B, woman. Now cleaned.

15 (12). LENINGRAD (St. 1606). B.Ap. xxiii. 35. 1. A, woman holding thurible; B, old man. Late.

A fragment may be compared:

ZAGREB, fr. (Hand of a male holding a stick, to right, mouth to knees of a woman to left holding out a mirror).

THE SIREN PAINTER

Hauser in FR. iii, 26. *Att. V.* 117 and 471. *ARV.*[1] 177.

STAMNOI
(with framed pictures)

1 (1). LONDON E 440, from Vulci. *Mon.* 1 pl. 8, whence HM. pl. 30; FR. pl. 124, whence (A) Perrot 10, 637, (A) Pfuhl fig. 479; *CV*. pl. 20, 1; A, *Hist. rel.* 286; part of A, Grimal 184; B, Greifenhagen *Eroten* 32; phs. Ma. 3223-4. A, Odysseus and the Sirens. B, three Erotes flying over the sea; the leader is named Himeros. [Hauser]. See p. 1642.

2 (2). LOUVRE G 180, from Vulci. Pottier pll. 127-8; *CV*. pl. 12, 9, pl. 13, 3, 6, and 9, and pl. 14, 5. A, Herakles and Apollo: the struggle for the tripod. B, Perseus pursued by a Gorgon, with Athena. See p. 1642.

PELIKE
(with framed pictures)

3 (3). LOUVRE G 229, from Vulci. B, *Mon.* 2 pl. 59, 5; B, Panofka *Argos* pl. 3, whence Overbeck *KM.* pl. 7, 12; Gerhard pl. 116; B, *El.* 3 pl. 100; Pottier pl. 131; *CV*. pl. 45, 5-7 and pl. 46, 2; part of A, ph. Gir. 25512. A, Herakles with Deianeira, Hyllos, and Oineus. B, death of Argos. [Hauser]. Now cleaned. See p. 254 no. 4, and p. 1642.

THE TYSZKIEWICZ PAINTER

AJA. 1916, 144-52. *VA.* 54-55. *Att. V.* 113-17 and 470. *ARV.*[1] 185-90 and 954. CB. ii, 13-21.

Named after no. 1, which was formerly in the Tyszkiewicz collection. The late works belong to the early classic period; some of them were grouped under the heading 'Iliupersis Painter' in *Att. V.* 116-17, but later I saw that they were really by the Tyszkiewicz (*ARV.*[1] 185).

CALYX-KRATERS

1 (1). BOSTON 97.368, from Vulci. Robert *Scenen der Ilias* pll. 1–2, and p. 3; Fröhner *Coll. Tyszk.* pll. 17–18, whence Furtwängler *Aegina* 345, (B) *VA.* 54, below, (B) Bulas *Il.* fig. 18; *AJA.* 1916, 145–6; A, *VA.* 54, above; B and side, Jacobsthal O. pl. 62; A, Fairbanks *Philostratus* 29 fig. 3; B, Richter and Milne fig. 56, whence LS. fig. 9; B, Fairbanks and Chase 66 fig. 71; CB. ii pll. 35–36 and suppl. pl. 13, 1. A, fight: Achilles and Memnon. B, fight: Diomed and Aeneas. On A, on the rim of a shield, ᛚΛᛏΕΛϟ : ΚΛᛚΟϟ. See CB. ii, 13–21.

2 (2). BERLIN, Univ., fr. (Middle of male in chitoniskos and cloak moving to right).

VOLUTE-KRATERS

3 (3). SYRACUSE 9318, from Syracuse. B, *NSc.* 1891, 412. On the neck: A, Herakles and the lion; B, Theseus and the bull.

3 bis. PADULA, fr., from Padula. On the neck, part of the right-hand figure on one side remains, the head of a youth to left.

COLUMN-KRATERS
(nos. 4–11, with framed pictures)

4 (4). MUNICH 2370 (J. 746), from Magna Graecia. Stackelberg pl. 41. A, Herakles and Pholos. B, satyrs and maenad.

5 (5). VILLA GIULIA 8346, from Nepi. A, ph. G.F. 18278. A, Herakles and Dionysos with Hermes and satyr. B, komos.

6 (6). SALERNO 1656 (or 1156?), from Fratte. A, Peleus and Thetis; B, Nereids fleeing to Nereus.

6 bis. LUCERNE MARKET (A.A.). A, Zeus pursuing a woman. B, satyr pursuing a maenad. See p. 1642.

7 (7). TARQUINIA 683, from Tarquinia. A, return of Hephaistos. B, komos.

8 (8). LENINGRAD inv. 14119, from Kerch. A, *Otchët 1903*, 159 fig. 318. A, Dionysos and maenads; B, satyrs and maenad. Late.

9 (9). VILLA GIULIA 3578, from Falerii. *St. e mat.* 3, 160–1; *Dedalo* 3, 77; *CV.* pl. 18, whence (A) *Ant. cl.* 6 pl. 4, 12; A, *AJA.* 1954 pl. 63 fig. 32. Iliupersis: A, death of Priam; B, Trojan woman attacking a Greek. Late.

10 (10). FERRARA, T. 154, from Spina. A, arming (youth putting on his greaves, woman holding his spear and shield, woman with sceptre). B, komos. Late.

11 (a1). FERRARA, T. 153, from Spina. A, symposion; B, komos. Late.

(nos. 12–13, the pictures not framed)

12 (11). SYRACUSE 19841. A, Poseidon pursuing a woman. B, (?). Late.

13 (12). PALERMO V 791, from Selinus. A, *Bull. Comm. Sic.* 1872 pl. 5 fig. 1; *CV.* pl. 44. A, youth with phiale and woman with oinochoe; B, youth. Late.

STAMNOI

(nos. 14–24, the pictures framed)

14 (13). OXFORD 1911.620, from Cervetri. Part of A, *AJA*. 1916, 144; part of A, *CV*. pl. 50, 8; augmented by frr. ex Leipsic, *CV*. pl. 65, 31–32. A, Hephaistos and Thetis. B, athletes.

15 (14). GOETTINGEN 574 h, fr. Komos.

16. OXFORD, Beazley, three frr., from Orvieto. A, (unexplained vestiges of of the right-hand figure). B, (part of the right-hand figure: a foot to right, and part of an object—wineskin?) These frr. may be from the same vase as Goettingen 574 h (no. 15), and if so the foot belongs to the komast whose upper part is preserved in Goettingen.

17 (15). FLORENCE 7 B 16, frr. (two of them ex Villa Giulia). Part, *CV*. pl. 7, B 16. Herakles and Athena. It was said in *CF*. 14 that the Florence fragment *CV*. pl. 13 B 64 might come from the other side of the same vase. As this does not seem to have occurred to me when I last saw the fragment it has been given a number of its own (no. 81). See p. 295.

18. BASLE MARKET (M.M.). *Auction xvi Basle* pl. 30, 124. A, Herakles and Linos. B, komos (two youths).

19. PHILADELPHIA MARKET, fr. A, death of Aigisthos.

20. NAPLES, Astarita, 530, fr. Death of Aigisthos. This is probably the subject: on the left, male in corslet, with sword (right arm to knees preserved), attacking one wearing long chiton and himation, who falls back (one shank and foot preserved).

21 (16). BRUSSELS A 3092. *Coll. Bougard* pl. 2, 97; A, cleaned, *Bull. Mus. Roy.* 1936, 53 fig. 5b; cleaned, *CV*. pl. 23, 1. A, Amazons arming; B, the like. See Bothmer *Am*. 153 no. 80 and p. 159.

22 (17). CAMBRIDGE, Trinity College. A, arming; B, the like.

23. PARIS MARKET (Segredakis). A, Dionysos and maenad; B, satyr and maenad. On A, maenad with oinochoe and krotala, Dionysos with kantharos and vine-branch; on B, satyr in panther-skin pursuing a maenad.

24 (19). ATHENS, Vlasto, from Koropi. A, Dionysos, maenad, and Giant; B, satyr driving a satyr-biga. See CB. ii, 71.

(nos. 25–30, the pictures not framed)

25 (20). Once ROME, Cippico. Komos ('Anacreontics', and women, or a woman). See CB. ii, 58 no. 7. If this is the vase described in *Bull*. 1843, 90 (see ibid. 60 no. 28), then from Chiusi.

26. WORCESTER (Massachusetts) 1953.92, from Taranto. A, *Bull. Worc*. 19 (April 1954), 27–28; A, *Art Quarterly* 1954, 181, 2. Peleus and Thetis.

27 (21). LENINGRAD 643 (St. 1531). Part, *AJA*. 1916, 149–50. Peleus and Thetis. Restored.

28 (22). DETROIT 24.13. A, *Art in America* 15 fig. 11; B, *Bull. Detroit* 6, 12

fig. 3b; Clairmont *P.* pll. 31–32. Judgement of Paris: A, Hermes with a goddess (Athena?) and Aphrodite; B, Aphrodite and the Horai.

29 (23). LONDON E 443, from Vulci. Gerhard pl. 64; *AJA.* 1916, 147–8; B, *VA.* 55; *CV.* pl. 21, 3, whence Vian *R.* pl. 34, 344; B, Pickard-Cambridge *D.F.A.* fig. 198. Gigantomachy: A, Apollo and Giant; B, Dionysos and Giant. See p. 1642.

30 (24). ROMAN MARKET. Gerhard pl. 162, 1–2. A, Theseus and the bull. B, men.

AMPHORAE
(type C)
(nos. 31–32, with framed pictures)

31 (26). ORVIETO, Faina, 33. A, ph. Al. 32490, whence Tarchi pl. 121, 3; A, *Ant. Kunst* 2 pl. 6, 3; B, ph. Al. 32753. A, Zeus and Ganymede. B, youth and boy. Restored.

32 (25). THE HAGUE, Gemeente Museum, 2026 (ex McCormick). Gerhard pl. 276, 1–2; B, *Burl. 1903* pl. 99 no. 83. A, man at herm. B, man and youth. Restored.

(no. 33, the pictures not framed)

33 (27). MILAN, Scala, 416. *Vend. Sarti* pl. 19, 289; *Coll. B. et C.* pl. 20, 169; *Coll. Jules Sambon* pl. 1, 9. A, trumpeter; B, warrior.

PANATHENAIC AMPHORAE
(with framed pictures)

34 (28). FERRARA, T. 603, from Spina. A, Aurigemma[1] 83–85 = [2]89–91; part of A, Arias and Alfieri pl. 11; part of A, Stella 418, below; A, Aurigemma and Alfieri pl. 11, a; Alfieri and Arias *S.* pll. 6–7. A, Herakles and Nereus; B, Nereid fleeing to Doris. See p. 1642.

35. BIRMINGHAM (Alabama). A, Zeus pursuing a woman. B, man and woman at altar. [Bothmer].

NECK-AMPHORAE
(nos. 36–37, with triple handles)

36 (29). LENINGRAD (St. 1530). A, warrior; B, trumpeter. Very much restored.

37. BALTIMORE, Walters Art Gallery, 48.58. A, man leaning on his stick; B, woman.

(no. 38, Nolan amphora, with triple handles)

38 (30). LONDON MARKET (Christie: ex Basseggio 62 and Jekyll). A, Zeus and Nikai; B, Hera with Nike and a goddess holding torches.

PELIKAI
(nos. 39–57, with framed pictures)

39 (32). VATICAN, from Vulci. *Mus. Greg.* 2 pl. 62, 2; Gerhard pl. 161. A. Theseus and Minotaur. B, man with youth and woman.

40 (38). VILLA GIULIA (ex Castellani). A, Apollo and Tityos. B, three clothed figures.

41 (39). VILLA GIULIA 50441, from Cervetri. Phs. GF. 7169–70; R.I. xvii. 38. A, Hephaistos and Thetis; B, mission to Achilles (Achilles and Odysseus).

42. LOUVRE C 10794, frr. A, (on the right, feet of a woman standing to left). B, Achilles and Odysseus. Compare Villa Giulia 50441. The subject of A, too, might be the same as there.

43. LOUVRE C 11007, two frr. On one, from A, (Zeus in pursuit). On the other, from B or A, (on the left, legs of a woman standing to right).

44 (49). BOLOGNA 161, from Bologna. A, Pellegrini 54. A, Zeus and Hera with Nike. B, youth, woman, and man.

45 (41). FLORENCE 13 B 8, fr. CV. pl. 13, B 8. (Hand holding helmet.) See the next.

46 (42). FLORENCE (ex Villa Giulia), fr. (Hair, in krobylos, of the left-hand figure on one side, with parts of the net-borders above the picture and at the side). May belong to Florence 13 B 8 (no. 45). A third fragment that may belong is Florence 13 B 6 (CV. pl. 13, B 6; on the left, youthful figure).

47 (34). BOULOGNE 134. Panckoucke Héracléide fig. 45; Le Musée 2, 279; ph. Arch. phot. BAA 120. A, youth giving cock to boy; B, man holding hare, and boy.

48 (35). Once MUNICH, Preyss. A, man giving cock to boy. B, komos.

49 (31). VILLA GIULIA 1129, from Falerii. A, youth and seated woman; B, man and woman.

50 (33). COPENHAGEN, Ny Carlsberg, inv. 2659. Poulsen VG. figs. 35–36. A, man and woman; B, man and youth.

51 (36). COPENHAGEN inv. 3634. A, AJA. 1916, 151; CV. pl. 132. A, man and youth; B, man and youth.

52 (37). LOUVRE G 237. CV. pl. 50, 3–5. A, seated youth, and woman; B, seated woman, and youth.

53 (40). FLORENCE 14 B 2, frr. Part, CV. pl. 14, B 2. (On the right, woman).

54 (43). CAMBRIDGE 6.1952, from Chiusi. A, youth and boy; B, man and boy.

55 (44). LEIPSIC T 3805, from Cervetri. A, boy with hoop, and male. B, komos.

56 (45). Once Vescovali. B.Ap. xxi. 16, a. A, discus-thrower and trainer; B, jumper and trainer.

57 (50). SYRACUSE 20967, from Gela. A, ML. 17, 178; A, CV. pl. 7, 3. A, man and woman; B, youth and woman. Late.

(nos. 58–59, the pictures not framed)

58 (46). ROMAN MARKET. Gerhard pl. 159, whence Robert *Herm.* 260–1. A, Theseus and Procrustes; B, Theseus attacking a man.

59 (48). DRESDEN 293. A, Dionysos; B, maenad (running with oinochoe).

PSYKTER

60 (52). VILLA GIULIA 49796, from Cervetri. *ML.* 42, 827–8. Theseus and Minotaur.

HYDRIAI

(nos. 61–62, with picture on the shoulder, framed)

61 (53). UTRECHT. *Mnemosyne* 3rd ser., 10 pl. 1; *Nederlands Jaarboek* 1955, 23. Women washing. Restored.

62 (54). LONDON E 165, from Vulci. *El.* 1 pl. 3; *CV.* pl. 71, 3 and pl. 72, 4; Cook *Zeus* iii pl. 10; B.Ap. xxii. 36; ph. Ma. 3150, left. Gigantomachy (Zeus and Giant, Athena and Giant).

(no. 63, with picture on the body?)

63. Once Pembroke. *Gaz. arch.* 1877 pl. 6, whence *Jb.* 26, 158. Deities with Nike. The head of the seated figure on the left must be restored, and the subject may be Zeus and Hera with Nike (or Iris).

(nos. 64–66, with picture on the body, framed)

64 (55). LOUVRE G 53, from Vulci. Pottier pl. 94; *CV.* pl. 53, 3 and 6. Peleus and Thetis. Now cleaned.

65 (56). MUNICH 2425 (J. 283). *Mon.* 1 pl. 27, 26; Gerhard pl. 169, 1–2; Ghali-Kahil *H.* pl. 87, 3; ph. Marb. 115622. Menelaos and Helen.

66 (58). VILLA GIULIA. Two women dancing (1, to right, 2, to right, looking round, with krotala). Late.

FRAGMENTS OF POTS

67 (60). ATHENS Acr. 812, fr., from Athens. Langlotz pl. 73. Ajax and Cassandra.

68 (61). ATHENS Acr. 784, frr., from Athens. Part, Langlotz pl. 71. Centauromachy.

69 (62). ATHENS Acr. (G 334), fr., from Athens. (Male to left, hand). ('G 354' in *Att. V.* is a misprint, hence the error in Langlotz p. 88 no. 957 pl. 83).

70 (63). ATHENS Acr. 959, fr., from Athens. Langlotz pl. 79. (Woman holding shield and spear, hand: Thetis and Achilles, as Langlotz?).

71 (64). ATHENS Acr. 623, fr., from Athens. Langlotz pl. 48. (Man).

72 (65). ATHENS Acr. 956, fr., from Athens. Langlotz pl. 79. (Youth).

73 (66). ATHENS Acr. 958, fr., from Athens. (Middle of a clothed figure, arm).

74 (67). ATHENS Acr. 901, fr., from Athens. Langlotz pl. 77. (Dionysos and satyr). Athens Acr. 986 (Langlotz pl. 78) might perhaps belong.

75 (68). ATHENS Acr. 1004, fr., from Athens. Langlotz pl. 79. (Woman).

76 (47). BONN 144, fr., from Greece. CV. pl. 13, 5. Citharode. From a pelike or an amphora.

77 (69). TARANTO, fr., from Taranto. (Feet to right; below, key-pattern border).

78 (70). FLORENCE 7 B 5, fr. CV. pl. 7, B 5. (Boxer). A fragment Naples, Astarita, 222, with the legs of a naked male—athlete—to left, falling back, might perhaps belong.

79. FLORENCE 13 B 31, fr. CV. pl. 13, B 31. (Acontist).

80. FLORENCE 13 B 35, two frr. Part, CV. pl. 13, B 35. The fragment 13 B 58 has part of the right-hand figure on one side, a male in a himation standing to left; a Florence fragment joins on the right and adds the lower right-hand corner of the maeander. The fragment 13 B 75 has one heel of the left-hand figure on one side, standing to right on a platform.

81. FLORENCE 13 B 64, fr. CV. pl. 13, B 64. (Male and woman). See no. 17.

82. FLORENCE, three frr. On one, the lower part of the himation of the right-hand figure on one side, standing to left, with part of the net side-border to right of it; on the second, a small part of the himation of one to right; on the third, part of the net side-border. Inside, broad bands, darker and lighter. From a pelike?

83 (18). AMSTERDAM inv. 407, fr., from Athens. (Warrior). From a stamnos?

84. VILLA GIULIA, fr., from Cervetri. NSc. 1955, 103 fig. 69. (On the left, youth). From a stamnos?

85 (72). ATHENS, Agora, P 5094, fr., from Athens. (Head). From a stamnos?

86. NAPLES, Astarita, 198, fr. (Athena—parts of her aegis and right arm remain). Probably belongs to no. 17.

87. PRAGUE, Univ., part of E 128, fr., from Greece. Sborník 1959 pl. 12, 79. Peleus and Thetis? (male running to right—part of chiton and of thigh remains—, leg of woman running to right). From a column-krater according to Frel.

88 (a 6). OXFORD, Beazley (d.d. Spranger), fr. (Head, to left, and shoulder, of youth). Late. From a stamnos or a column-krater.

The following are probably by the Tyszkiewicz Painter:

FRAGMENTS OF POTS

1 (4). ATHENS Acr. 991, fr., from Athens. Langlotz pl. 79. Procession.

2 (2). PALERMO, fr. (Head of youth to right). From a stamnos?

A complete vase is close to the painter in many respects, but has an unusual look:

PELIKE

(a). Würzburg 510. *Kunstbesitz eines nordd. Sammlers* pl. 21, 816; side, Jacobsthal O. pl. 47, c; Langlotz pl. 179. A, mistress and maids; B, youths and woman. See p. 1643.

THE TROILOS PAINTER

JHS. 32, 171–3. *VA.* 61. *Att. V.* 122–3 and 471. *ARV.*[1] 190–1 and 954.

Named after no. 15. See p. 1643.

AMPHORAE
(type A; with framed pictures)

1 (1). Vatican, from Cervetri. *Mus. Greg.* 2 pl. 54, 1; Gerhard pl. 126, whence (A) *Die Antike* 15, 286; A, ph. Mo. 8577. A, Herakles and Apollo: the struggle for the tripod. B, komos.

2 (2). Louvre G 196. *CV.* pl. 34, 9–10. A, Athena mounting chariot. B, Dionysos and satyr. Much restored.

NECK-AMPHORA
(not certain that neck and triple handles belong)

3 (3). Orvieto, Faina. A, Herakles and Athena. B, Dionysos. Restored. This seems to be the vase described in *Bull.* 1859, 105; if so, from Chiusi.

PELIKE
(with framed pictures)

4 (4). Philadelphia 3443, from Orvieto. A, Dionysos and satyr; B, the like.

STAMNOI

5 (5, +). Louvre G 182. B, Pottier pl. 127; *CV.* pl. 15, 1 and 4, and pl. 16, 4–5; phs. Gir. 25988 and 25751. A, Zeus with Poseidon and Hera. B, victor (boxer) with flute-player and trainer. Restored. A Louvre fragment adds part of the flute-player's garment.

6 (6). Louvre G 184, from Nola. *CV.* pl. 15, 7–8. A, Dionysos, Poseidon, Hermes, and goddess. B, warrior leaving home. Restored.

7. Louvre C 10747. A, Herakles and Apollo: the struggle for the tripod. B, komos.

8 (7). Mannheim 60, from Orvieto. *CV.* pl. 29, 1–3 and 5. A, Zeus with Nike and Athena. B, youths and boy.

9 (8). Florence 3986, from Orvieto. *CV.* pl. 47, 1, pl. 49, 1, and pl. 50, 1–2. A, boxers. B, naked women about to wash.

10 (9). Villa Giulia (ex Castellani). A, Theseus and Sinis. B, komos (two youths).

CALYX-KRATER

11 (10). COPENHAGEN 126. B, *Annali* 1846 pl. M, whence *JHS*. 24, 185 fig. 7 and Norman Gardiner *G.A.S.* 303; B, Lange *Darstellung* 100; *VA*. 60; A, *Mon. Piot* 29, 171; *CV*. pll. 127–9; side, Jacobsthal *O.* pl. 52; A, *Antik-Cab. 1851*, 159. A, Athena mounting chariot, with Herakles. B, athletes.

HYDRIAI
(nos. 12–13, with picture on the shoulder, framed)

12 (11). OXFORD 1914.731. *CV*. pl. 31, 1–2. Uncertain subject: youth with sword attacking another who also has a sword; naked youth, unarmed, attacking another. Doubtful if the attacker is Theseus.

13 (12). MUNICH 2428 (J. 342), from Vulci. Micali *Storia* pl. 90, 2; FR. pl. 73, 1; *Riv. Ist.* 6, 213. Herakles and Busiris. See p. 1643.

(no. 14, with picture mainly on the shoulder, not framed)

14 (13). NEW YORK 56.171.53 (ex Torr and Hearst), from Vulci. *Cat. Sotheby July 2 1929* pl. 6, below, and pl. 7; *AJA*. 1945, 471, 2; *Bull. Metr.* March 1957, 175, 1; *Bull. Metr.* Oct. 1957, 54. Triptolemos.

(nos. 15–17, with picture on the body, not framed)

15 (14). LONDON 99.7–21.4, from Vulci. Fölzer pl. 10, 23; *JHS*. 32 pl. 2; *CV*. pl. 78, 4; ph. Ma. 3131, left. Troilos and Polyxene.

16 (15). MUNICH Z3, fr. (Upper parts of two heads). The upper part of the vase remains.

17 (16). LONDON E 175. *JHS*. 32 pl. 3; *CV*. pl. 78, 3. Youth and boy.

LEKYTHOS
(standard shape)

18 (17). STOCKHOLM G. 1700. *Nationalmusei Årsbok* 4, 127, right, and 139; Kjellberg fig. 1. Death of Orpheus. Restored.

For the *black-figured* neck-amphora by the Troilos Painter see *ABV*. 400.

THE HEPHAISTEION PAINTER
ARV.[1] 192 and 954.

So called from no. 4. Some kinship with such members of the Brygan circle as the Dokimasia Painter (p. 412).

STAMNOI

1 (1). BERLIN 2188, from Vulci. The Medea, Helbig *Hom. Epos*[2] 357; side, Jacobsthal *O.* pl. 96, a; A, Neugebauer pl. 57; A, Brendel *Schafzucht* pl.

60, 2; graffito, Kirchner pl. 11, 22; A, *Gymnasium* 61 pl. 5, 1. A, Medea and a daughter of Pelias, with the ram. B, youths and boy. On A, KALOΣ. On B, KAL[O]Σ, NIKO[ΣTPATOΣ] . . ., KALOΣ retr. [Talcott]. Restored.

2 (a). LEYDEN PC 88 (xviii g 32), from Vulci. Side, Jacobsthal *O.* pl. 94, a. A, youth seated, youth, woman holding helmet (Achilles, Antilochos, and Thetis?). B, Dionysos with maenad and satyr. See p. 1643.

3. GREAT NECK (Long Island), Pomerance. A, *Man in the Ancient World* 169. A, Poseidon pursuing, B, Aithra. On A, in long chiton and cloak, running to right with trident and dolphin; on B, running to right, looking round, in her left hand a wool-basket. See p. 1643.

CALYX-KRATER

4 (2). ATHENS, Agora, P 9462, from Athens. Dinsmoor *Heph.* 133, 60. A, Dionysos; B, maenad. [Talcott].

BELL-KRATER

5 (3). ATHENS, Agora, P 8776, frr., from Athens. Youth leaving home? (male in chitoniskos and chlamys, with spears; one in chiton and himation; male).

COLUMN-KRATER
(the pictures not framed)

6 (4). FERRARA, T. 745, from Spina. A, maenad; B, maenad.

In shape and in type of decoration another stamnos goes with the Pomerance (no. 3); the general character of the drawing, too, is not unlike:

STAMNOS

LONDON E 439, from Vulci. Cecil Smith pl. 15, whence (A) Jane Harrison *Prol.* 451; *CV.* pl. 19, 3; A, ph. Ma. 3222. A, Dionysos (μαινόμενος); B, satyr playing the flute. For the motive of A, the cup by the Briseis Painter, London E 75, might be compared (p. 406 no. 2). See p. 1643.

THE PAINTER OF PALERMO 1108

Att. V. 224. *ARV.*[1] 191–2.

Follower of Makron.

CALYX-KRATER

1 (1). PALERMO V 771 (1108). *CV.* pl. 33. Komos: A, man and flute-girl; B, man with lyre.

PANATHENAIC AMPHORA

2 (2). MUNICH 2315 (J. 51), from Vulci. Benndorf pl. 9, whence *Jh.* 8, 41; *CV.* pl. 191 and pl. 190, 4–5. A, youth with plaque and sprigs; B, youth carrying a panathenaic amphora.

HYDRIA

(with picture on the body)

3 (3). MUNICH 2431 (J. 358), from Vulci. Gerhard pl. 300. Goddess (Aphrodite?) and two women (the Horai?) See p. 1643.

CUP

4 (4). ZURICH, private (ex Preyss). *Auktion xxii Basel* pl. 49, 167 and pl. 54, 167. I, youth with flower, and boy seated; A, boy running with lyre, man, and youth; B, boy, man, and youth. Already recalls the cups by Hermonax.

CHAPTER 21

PAINTERS OF SMALL VASES

THE DIOSPHOS WORKSHOP

(Workshop of the Diosphos Painter and the Sappho Painter)

Haspels *ABL*. 94–130, 225–41, and 368–9. See also under the several painters.

THE DIOSPHOS PAINTER

So named by Rumpf from the inscription on the black-figured neck-amphora Cabinet des Médailles 219 (see Haspels *ABL*. 96–97 and 238 no. 120).

Longpérier in *RA*. 1868, i, 351–2. Luce in *AJA*. 1916, 439–59. Hoeber in *Monats-hefte für Kunstwissenschaft* 11 (1918), 42–52. *V.Pol*. 6–7 and 79. Haspels, *ABL*. 94–130, 225–41, and 368. *ARV*.¹ 203, 928, and 940. *ABV*. 346, 482, 507, 508–11, 668, 702–3, 716.

The list of black-figure vases by the Diosphos Painter could be considerably increased, but I make only one addition, and that for the sake of the kalos-inscription:

BF. LEKYTHOS

(*of Little-Lion type, see p. 301*) (*the body white-ground*)

ATHENS, from Vari. Horseman and two warriors. On the shoulder, hound and hare. In large rough letters, $\text{SONAVTIOSKA}\Lambda\text{OS}$. For the name compare Σωναύτης, Σώφορτος, and see *Hesp*. 12, 88.

THE SAPPHO PAINTER

So named from the inscription on his hydria (of Six's technique) in Warsaw (142333: ex Czartoryski 32: *CV*. pl. 16, 3).

Haspels *ABL*. 94–130, 225–9, and 369. *ARV*.¹ 203–4, 928, and 940. Haspels in *Bull. Vereen*. 29, 29. *ABV*. 507–8, 675, 677, and 702. Boardman in *BSA*. 50, 62–63 (on no. 39 see *AJA*. 1957, 5–6).

The two painters, as Miss Haspels showed, worked side by side, and count as 'brothers'. The great majority of their many vases are black-figured; but they also used Six's technique, and, occasionally, 'semi-outline' on a white ground (Haspels *ABL*. 111). Miss Haspels also showed (111–12) that the semi-outline lekythoi stood at the head of a series of white lekythoi decorated with outline figures flanked by large black palmettes ('side-palmette lekythoi'), in some of which the drawing is more or less closely connected with the Diosphos Painter and the Sappho.

The *potter-work* of the vases, black-figure or other, decorated by the Sappho and Diosphos Painters is characteristic; and the semi-outline lekythoi mentioned above were fashioned by the Diosphos *Potter*. Many other side-palmette lekythoi were fashioned by him. We give a list of side-palmette lekythoi, in two sections. The first section consists of vases fashioned by the Diosphos Potter, the second of side-palmette lekythoi not fashioned by him.

SIDE-PALMETTE LEKYTHOI

I. Fashioned by the Diosphos *Potter*

Nearly all these are of the Diosphos Potter's principal type, which we call DL; one is of another, smaller type, the 'Little Lion' (LL), to which many of the black-figured lekythoi from the Diosphos Workshop belong, as well as many black ones and many in Six's technique (Haspels *ABL*. 98–100, 107, 109–10, 116–20, 227, 235–6; *ABV*. 512–16 and 703).

The pattern-work in these vases is the same as in the black-figured lekythoi from the Diosphos Workshop.

WHITE LEKYTHOI

(no. 1, of Little-Lion shape—Class LL)

1. LOUVRE MNB 911, from Athens. Haspels *ABL*. pl. 40, 1. Achilles and Ajax playing. Near the Diosphos Painter. [Haspels]. See p. 303, foot.

(nos. 2–21, of the Diosphos Potter's principal shape—Class DL)

2. BOSTON 99.528, from Sicily. Politi *Esposizione di sette vasi* pl. 2, 2 (reversed); Fairbanks i pl. 1, 3; side, Jacobsthal *O*. pl. 53, a; the shape, Caskey *G*. 212. Semi-outline. Warrior with horse. By the Diosphos Painter. See p. 1643.

3. NEW YORK 06.1070. *Bull. Metr*. 2, 82–83; Fairbanks i pl. 4; *Hdbk Cl. Coll.*⁵ 129 fig. 85; Jacobsthal *O*. pl. 53, b–c; Richter *ARVS*. fig. 71; Richter *H*. 216, e. Semi-outline. Perseus and Medusa. By the Diosphos Painter.

4. LOUVRE MNB 909, from Attica? Perrot 10, 691 fig. 78; Fairbanks i pl. 3, 1; Haspels *ABL*. pl. 39, 1, whence (part) Rumpf *MZ*. pl. 21, 1. Semi-outline. Herakles and the lion. By the Diosphos Painter [Haspels].

5. STUTTGART MARKET. *Auktion Kricheldorf 28–29 Mai 1956* pl. 26, 1273. Achilles in retirement (seated to left, brooding; hanging, sword and shield). Restored. See p. 304, and for the subject compare the aryballos Berlin 2326 (p. 813 no. 97).

6. LOUVRE MNC 650, from Attica? Part, Fairbanks i pl. 2, 2; Riezler 4 fig. 3, 2; Villard *VG*., cover, 4. Nike. See p. 304.

7. NEW YORK 51.163, from Greece. Centaur. See p. 304.

8. SYRACUSE 43052, from Vittoria. Komast? (man in himation moving to right, stick in hand). Restored. See p. 304.

9. ATHENS 12769 (N. 981), from Eretria. *CV.*Jb pl. 1, 4. Warrior. By the Painter of Würzburg 517 (p. 305 no. 6).

10. THEBES R. 46.84, from Rhitsona. *JHS.* 29 pl. 24. Woman. By the Painter of Würzburg 517 (p. 306 no. 7).

11. ATHENS 12471. Maenad. May be by the Painter of Würzburg 517 (p. 306).

12. MUNICH 2773 (J. 245). The side-palmettes, Lau pl. 23, 2a, below; Fairbanks i, 69. Maenad. Now cleaned. See p. 304.

13. NAPLES 2763, from Locri. Fairbanks i, 71; ph. So. 11070, iv, 1. Satyr (in himation) with goat. See p. 304.

14. WARSAW 142470 (ex Czartoryski 92), from Locri? *CV.* pl. 42, 5. Youth with dog. By the Painter of Copenhagen 3830 (p. 724 no. 9). Restored.

15. ZURICH, Schuh. Youth leaning on his stick. By the Painter of Copenhagen 3830 (p. 724 no. 10).

16. PALERMO. *AM.* 52, Beil. 28, 1. Youth leaning on his stick. Compare Warsaw 142470 and Schuh (nos. 14 & 15). See also p. 724.

17. TEL AVIV, from Greece. Youth and boy (youth to right, with stick, boy to left; both in himatia; above, leftward key). Mock inscriptions in the manner of the Diosphos Painter.

18. AGRIGENTO, from Agrigento. Maenad (moving to left, looking round, with wing-sleeves).

(nos. 19–21 have black palmettes on the shoulder instead of lotus-buds)

19. WARSAW (ex Breslau). *Sg Vogell* pl. 3, 13; Michalowski *Sztuka* 32. Woman with mirror. I take the neck and mouth of the vase to be restored.

20. ATHENS MARKET. *Bonner Jahrbücher* 122 pl. 5, 1. Nike (flying, head frontal, with thurible).

21. HARVARD 1925.30.51. *CV.* Hoppin pl. 19, 5. Hunter returning.

The exact shape of the following side-palmette lekythoi is not known to me, nor are the patterns of the Barre and Raimondi vases:

WHITE LEKYTHOI

1. Once Barre, from Attica. *Coll. A. B*[*arre*] 45, 353. Herakles (leaning on his club to right, at altar, holding kantharos and fruit). The side-palmettes unusual. For the figure of Herakles compare the Nolan amphora by the Dutuit Painter, Louvre G 203 (p. 306 no. 1). See pp. 304 and 1643.

2. Once Raimondi. Politi *Esposizione di sette vasi* pl. 2, 7 (reversed). Woman seated playing ball.

3. PALERMO, from Randazzo. *AM.* 52, Beil. 28, 2. Youth. Palmettes on shoulder. Restored. See p. 1643.

II. Not by the Diosphos *Potter*

WHITE LEKYTHOI

(nos. 1–7: Class PL—see p. 675— or near it)

1. PARIS, Petit Palais, 336. *CV.* pl. 33, 3–4. Komast ('Anacreontic'). By the Painter of Petit Palais 336 (p. 305 no. 1).
2. PARIS, Petit Palais, 335. *CV.* pl. 33, 1–2. Woman with mirror. By the Painter of Petit Palais 336 (p. 305 no. 2).
3. WARSAW 142304 (ex Czartoryski 90). *CV.* pl. 42, 6. Dancing-girl. Restored.
4. NEW YORK 41.162.95. *CV.* Gallatin pl. 27, 2. Wounded warrior.
5. MARKET, from Taranto or near. Youth (standing frontal, head to left, in chitoniskos and black chlamys, right arm akimbo, spears in left hand).
6. OXFORD 1922.18. Woman with perfume-vase. By the Vlasto Painter (p. 696 no. 5).
7. MARKET. Maenad (in chiton, fawnskin, saccos, striding to right, thyrsus in right hand, left arm extended in wing-sleeve). Mouth and neck of the vase modern.

(nos. 8–9 may be of Class PL or near it, but my notes are insufficient)

8. TARANTO. Woman with lyre (moving to right, looking round, in chiton, wrap, saccos, black boots, with lyre).
9. ATHENS 1858 (CC. 1014). Dumont and Chaplain i pl. 11, 2. Warrior.

(nos. 10–13 are of other shapes; they belong to the early classic period)

10. ATHENS 2023 (CC. 1018), from Attica. Benndorf pl. 19, 3. Nike. Recalls the Providence Painter and, a little, the school of Douris.
11. CAMBRIDGE 138. By the Carlsruhe Painter (see p. 735 no. 98).
12. DRESDEN ZV 2963. Woman seated. Full size. Much restored.
13. CAMBRIDGE 3.17. Full size. Late straggler. By the Painter of Cambridge 3.17 (see p. 1241 no. 1).

─────────

We now return to

THE DIOSPHOS PAINTER

By him the three white lekythoi in semi-outline, nos. 2–4 in the list of side-palmette lekythoi (p. 301), namely:

1. BOSTON 99.528.
2. NEW YORK 06.1070.
3. LOUVRE MNB 909. [Haspels].

Near the Diosphos Painter, a lekythos of a different type, Louvre MNB 911: see p. 301 no. 1. Shape and pattern-work of another lekythos are the same as in Louvre MNB 911, except that there are no side-palmettes; and what little remains of the picture may be in the manner of the Diosphos Painter. Black-figure, save the column on the left, which is in the outline technique.

WHITE LEKYTHOS
(of Little-Lion shape)

SYRACUSE, from Megara Hyblaea. Chariot.

It may be added here that there are also semi-outline white lekythoi by the Bowdoin Painter (see p. 689: the shape is of course different); and that many white lekythoi have so many black areas in the drawing as to be almost 'semi-outline': but we do not use the term unless the flesh is black.

Most of the side-palmette lekythoi in List I—the list of those by the Diosphos *Potter* (pp. 301-2)—though by several hands, have a certain general kinship, in style of drawing, with the vases of the Diosphos Painter. Nos. 6 and 8–11 were associated with him by Miss Haspels; and we may add nos. 5, 7, 12, 13, also the Barre lekythos (p. 302 no. 1), and nos. 1 and 2 in list II on p. 203—the list of those not by the Diosphos Potter. Some of these can be assigned to their painters.

We return to

THE SAPPHO PAINTER

Miss Haspels saw that the following was near him:

WHITE LEKYTHOS

LENINGRAD 671. Haspels *ABL*. pl. 39, 3. Hoplite and two archers. See Haspels *ABL*. 113.

THE PAINTER OF WÜRZBURG 557

Haspels *ABL*. 112–13. *ARV*.¹ 204.

Not far from the Sappho Painter.

WHITE ALABASTRA

1 (1). WÜRZBURG 557, from Eretria. Langlotz pl. 207. Two women washing. [Haspels].

2 (2). PALERMO, from Selinus. *ML*. 32, 330 fig. 141. Two women dressing. [Haspels].

Near these, as Langlotz and Miss Haspels saw, the

WHITE LEKYTHOS

(with glaze outlines)

TÜBINGEN E 56. Watzinger pl. 22. Theseus and the bull.

━━━━━━━━

THE PAINTER OF PETIT PALAIS 336

Akin to the Sappho and Diosphos Painters.

WHITE LEKYTHOI

(of Class PL, so called after these, see pp. 675–6; see also p. 303 nos. 1–2)

1. PARIS, Petit Palais, 336. *CV*. pl. 33, 3–4. Komast (Anacreontic). For the subject, CB. ii, 58 no. 8.
2. PARIS, Petit Palais, 335. *CV*. pl. 33, 1–2. Woman with mirror.

━━━━━━━━

THE PAINTER OF WÜRZBURG 517

ARV.[1] 204: 'Group of Würzburg 517' there, but I am now able to substitute 'Painter' for 'Group'. Although most of his vases are large, he is not at home in large vases, and he is placed here because his connexions are with the circle of the Diosphos and Sappho Painters.

STAMNOI

1 (1). MUNICH 2405 (J. 352), from Vulci. A, the Sphinx of Thebes (the Sphinx and two youths); B, the like. See p. 1644.
2 (2). WÜRZBURG 517. Langlotz pll. 186 and 184. A, warrior leaving home; B, the like.
3 (3). NAPLES 3172, from Nola? A, ph. So. x, iv, 1. A, three maenads; B, satyr and maenads.

PELIKAI

(with framed pictures)

4. VILLA GIULIA, from Cervetri. A, maenad (with thyrsus and snake); B, satyr (carrying a pointed amphora).
5. VILLA GIULIA, from Cervetri. A, Athena; B, warrior at altar.

WHITE LEKYTHOI

(side-palmette lekythoi of Class DL, see p. 302 nos. 9–10)

6. ATHENS 12769 (N. 981), from Eretria. *CV*. Jb pl. 1, 4. Warrior.

7. THEBES R. 46.84, from Rhitsona. *JHS.* 29 pl. 24. Woman with mirror and pomegranate.

Another white lekythos of the same type may also be his: ATHENS 12471. Maenad. See p. 302 no. 11.

Compare also the

ALABASTRON

LONDON E 718. A, woman; B, maid. On A, ΑΦΡΟΔΙSΙΑΚΑΙΕ, ΤΟS-ΔΟΚΕΙ ΕV+ΙΡΟΙ. On B, ΗΟΓΑΙSΚΑΙΟS, ΕΡΟSΑΝΘΕΟΚΑΙΕ. On the topside of mouth, ΑΦΡΟΔΙSΙΑΚΑΙΕ. The last inscription but one is probably Ἡροσάνθη, ὦ καλή.

=====

THE DUTUIT PAINTER

JHS. 33, 106–10. *VA.* 69. *Att. V.* 127–8 and 471. *ARV.*[1] 205–6 and 955. *CB.* ii, 36–37.

So called from a former owner of no. 11. Connected with the circle of the Diosphos Painter.

NECK-AMPHORAE

(*small*)

(*nos. 1–4, Nolan amphorae, with triple handles*)

1 (1). LOUVRE G 203, from Nola. A, Hancarville 3 pl. 49; A, Winckelmann *Mon. ant. inediti* (Rome, 1767) fig. 159, whence Greifenhagen *Griechische Vasen auf Bildnissen der Zeit Winckelmanns und des Klassizismus* (from *Nachrichten der Göttinger Gesellschaft* N.S. 3, no. 7) 206; parts in Pompeo Batoni's portrait of Karl Wilhelm Ferdinand, Duke of Brunswick and Lüneburg (in Brunswick; replica in Schloss Blankenburg, Harz: reproduced in Greifenhagen op. cit. pl. 1, pl. 2, 1, and pl. 3, 1); Millin *PVA.* 2 pl. 41, whence Inghirami *Mon. etr.* 5 pl. 37 and Welcker *A.D.* 3 pl. 4; *CV.* pl. 37, 4–7; phs. Gir. 36248, whence Greifenhagen op. cit. pl. 4 and pl. 3, 2; palmettes, Jacobsthal *O.* pl. 51, b. A, Herakles and Athena; B, Hermes. For the figure of Herakles compare a white lekythos formerly in the Barre collection (p. 302 no. 1); and see below, p. 308.

2 (2). BOSTON 13.188, from Suessula. *RM.* 2, 241–2; *JHS.* 33 pl. 11 and p. 110, whence (A) Curtius *Astragal* pl. 2, 3; part of A, Richter *ARVS.* fig. 53; A, Fairbanks and Chase 70 fig. 75; *CB.* ii pl. 44, above, and p. 36; the shape, Hambidge 60 and Caskey *G.* 67. A, Hephaistos and Thetis. B, Nike. See *CB.* ii, 36–37.

3 (3). ATHENS, Iolas (ex Segredakis). A, satyr and maenad; B, satyr. On A, the satyr embraces the maenad, climbing round her; on B the satyr runs to right with arms extended to right and left.

3 *bis.* LISBON, Gilbert. A, Dionysos; B, satyr. See p. 1644.

4 (4). BERLIN 2330, from Nola. A, Dionysos; B, maenad.

(*nos. 5-6, with double handles: doubleens*)

5 (5). NAPLES 3155. A, ph. So. 11072, iii, 5. A, citharode; B, man. On A, AP+INO[Ϛ]KALOϚ.

6 (6). LOUVRE G 137. Pottier pl. 115; *CV.* pl. 33, 8–10 and pl. 34, 1–2, whence (neck A) Rumpf *MZ.* pl. 24, 4. On the neck: A, Nike; B, Nike. On A, AP+INOϚ KALOϚ. On B, AP+INOϚ retr. and KALOϚ.

HYDRIA
(*with picture mainly on the shoulder, not framed*)

7 (7). LONDON E 179, from Nola. *JHS.* 33 pl. 12; *CV.* pl. 81, 4. Nike.

OINOCHOAI
(*nos. 8–11, shape 1*)

8 (8). LONDON E 510, from Vulci. *JHS.* 33 pl. 9; part, *E.A.A.* iii, 198; ph. Ma. 3199, left. Satyr and maenad.

9 (9). LONDON E 511, from Vulci. *JHS.* 33, 107 and pl. 8; back, Jacobsthal O. pl. 51, a, whence Buschor G. *Vasen* 172 fig. 193; ph. Ma. 3199, right. Dionysos and satyr.

10 (10). LOUVRE G 240, from Vulci. *JHS.* 33 pl. 10; back, Jacobsthal O. pl. 51, c. Dionysos and maenad.

11 (11). PARIS, Petit Palais, 315, from Nola. Fröhner *Nap.* pl. 1 = Fröhner *Musées de France* pl. 4; Lenormant *Dutuit* pl. 14, 1; *JHS.* 33, 106, whence Herford 104; *CV.* pl. 19, 1–6 and pl. 20, 2. Winged Artemis petting fawn.

(*nos. 12–15, shape 5B*)

12 (12). MUNICH 2445 (J. 300), from Vulci. Lau pl. 24, 3; Genick pl. 33, 2; Pfuhl fig. 782; *CV.* pl. 85, 4–6, pl. 86, 8, and pl. 91, 10. On the neck, Eros.

13. WORCESTER (Massachusetts) 1953.93, from Vulci. *Bull. Worc.* 19, 29. Woman with mirror and flower.

14 (13). LOUVRE G 239. Jacquemart 242 (reversed); *Enc. phot.* iii, 30, a. On the neck, maenad.

15. VILLA GIULIA, from Cervetri. On the neck, youth and Maltese dog.

LEKYTHOI
(*nos. 16–20, standard shape*)

16 (14). MUNICH inv. 7516. Nike.

17 (15). NEW YORK 13.227.16. *Bull. Metr.* 9, 234; Richter and Hall pl. 28 and pl. 175, 28; part, Richter *ARVS.* fig. 52 and p. 65 fig. 29; Richter *H.* 214, f. Nike.

18. PADULA, from Padula. Apollo and a goddess.

19 (16). SYRACUSE 20536, from Gela. *ML.* 17, 394. Woman with thurible and phiale.

20 (17). SYRACUSE 23611, from Camarina. Winged Artemis petting fawn.

         (*no. 21, secondary shape, Class PL, p. 676 no. 1*)

21 (18). NEW YORK 41.162.27. *CV.* Gallatin pl. 18, 1; Richter *H.* 216, c. Woman at thurible.

The following, though very poor, seems to be by the same hand:

NECK-AMPHORA
(*small, with double handles*)

(a). BERLIN inv. 3309, from Greece. A, Dionysos with satyr and maenad. B, horseman and youth.

Heydemann (*Bull.* 1869, 146 no. 6) describes 'a very small amphora' [neck-amphora] with Herakles and Athena, then in the Torrusio collection, from Nola, as 'so like [our no. 1] that it might almost seem to be the same vase'. See also p. 219.

THE TERPAULOS PAINTER

AJA. 1957, 6, xii.

OINOCHOAI
(*shape 2*)

1. VILLA GIULIA, from Cervetri. Satyr playing the flute. He is named ΤΕΡΓΓΑVLΟ$.

2. VILLA GIULIA, from Cervetri. Victor.

3. VILLA GIULIA, from Cervetri. *ML.* 42, 834; ph. R.I. 57.661. Warrior retreating. LVEAKALΟ$, ΝΑΙ+Ι ΔΟΚΕΙΤΟΙ, and retr. ΚΑLΟ$. On the band serving as ground-line, LVEAKALΟ$. For the other inscriptions, *AJA.* 1957, 6, xii.

Probably also:

OINOCHOE
(*shape 1*)

4. ST. LOUIS, Washington University, 3283. Jacobsthal *O.* pl. 118, a, and p. 80; *AJA.* 1940, 209–10. Maenad.

LEKYTHOS

5. AGRIGENTO 23, from Agrigento. Politi *Un leckitos* pl. 1; Gàbrici *Vasi ined.* pl. 1 and fig. 6; Haspels *ABL.* pl. 21. Arming. See Haspels *ABL.* 70–74. She finds a connexion with the Sappho and Diosphos Painters.

THE TITHONOS PAINTER

VA. 69–70. *Att. V.* 128–9 and 471. *ARV.*¹ 206–7. CB. ii, 37–38.

So called after the subject of no. 1. Related to the Berlin Painter.

NECK-AMPHORAE

(Nolan amphorae, with triple handles)

1 (1, +). BOSTON 03.816, and NAPLES, from Suessula. CB. ii pl. 44, below; the shape, Caskey G. 63. A, Eos and Tithonos; B, boy (Priam?) fleeing. The publication does not give the two Naples sherds, which add the left foot of Eos, the missing part of Tithonos' right foot and of the border below (trios of maeander alternating with trios of stopt key), and part of his himation.

2 (2). LOUVRE G 205, from Vulci. *El.* 3 pl. 23; *CV.* pl. 37, 12–13 and pl. 38, 3. A, Poseidon and Amphitrite; B, woman.

3 (3). BERLIN 2328, from Nola. A, boy offering lyre. B, youth fleeing.

4 (4). LOUVRE G 213. *CV.* pl. 40, 1–2, and 6 and 8. A, Antilochos; B, Nestor.

5 (5). NAPLES 3182, from Ruvo. A, Schröder *Sport* pl. 55, 2; A, ph. So. x, i, 4. A, acontist; B, trainer.

6 (6). LONDON E 296, from Nola. Raoul-Rochette pl. 44, 1; *El.* 4 pl. 48; *CV.* pl. 50, 3; A, Greifenhagen *Eroten* 14. A, Eros; B, youth. On A, ΔΙΟΚLΕΕϟΚΑLΟϟ. Slightly restored.

7 (7). BUDAPEST. Procession: A, boy with thurible; B, boy with oinochoe.

8 (8). FLORENCE 4011. *CV.* pl. 25, 3 and pl. 28, 2–3. A, Dionysos; B, maenad.

9 (9). HAMBURG 1893.100. A, Ballheimer 41; *Kunst u. Künstler* 18, 128; B, *Anz.* 1928, 491 = Mercklin *GR.* pl. 13. A, komast; B, komast.

LEKYTHOI

(standard shape)

10 (10). BOSTON 00.340, from Syracuse. *VA.* 68; CB. ii, suppl. pl. 10. Woman with mirror.

11 (11). ABERDEEN 706. Woman with alabastron and perfume-vase.

12 (13). NEW YORK 25.78.2, from Gela. Side, Richter and Milne fig. 96, whence LS. fig. 22; Richter and Hall pl. 29, 30 and pl. 175, 30; part, Richter *ARVS.* fig. 55 and p. 65 fig. 30. Hermes.

13 (12). GELA (ex Navarra-Jacona), from Gela. Benndorf pl. 47, 2. Nike.

14 (15). OXFORD 1917.58. Millingen *Coghill* pl. 22, 2, whence Inghirami *Mon. etr.* 5 pl. 66 and *El.* 1 pl. 92; Tillyard pl. 13, 106; *CV.* pl. 34, 2. Nike.

15 (14). NEW YORK 27.122.6. *Bull. Metr.* 23, 109 fig. 5; *Gaz. B.-A.* 1931, 81 fig. 10; Richter and Hall pl. 29, 29 and pl. 175, 29; Richter *H.* 216, b. Athena.

16. GELA 29 and 41, frr., from Gela. Athlete with strigil and acontion.

17 (16). SYRACUSE 21197, from Gela. *ML.* 17 pl. 33, 2. Warrior adjusting his greave.

18 (17). HILLSBOROUGH (California), Hearst (ex Torr), from Athens. Torr *Gk Music* 3; *Cat. Sotheby July 2 1929* pl. 8, 33. Boy seated with lyre.

19 (18). ATHENS 1644 (CC. 1393) from Eretria. Warrior.

STAMNOS

20 (19). MUNICH SL. 480, frr. Sieveking *BTV.* pl. 53, 1; *CV.* pl. 245, 3–6. A, Zeus and Hera with Nike (or Iris). B, (male).

Probably also

LEKYTHOS
(standard shape)

(1). CHANIA 2, from Kydonia. Citharode. See p. 1644.

FRAGMENT OF POT (LEKYTHOS?)

(2). ADRIA B 622, fr., from Adria. Schöne pl. 4, 3. Youth playing lyre, with Eros.

THE PAINTER OF PALERMO 4

V.Pol. 9. *ARV.*[1] 208 and 955.

LEKYTHOI
(nos. 1–10, standard shape)

1 (1). PALERMO V 680 (4), from Gela. *CV.* pl. 25, 2 and 5. Nike with greave and spear.

2 (2). NEW YORK 41.162.88, from Sicily? *CV.* Gallatin pl. 58, 2. Nike.

3. ATHENS, private. Nike (running with phialai).

4. GELA, Hornbostel, from Gela. Nike (moving to right, hands raised).

5 (3). Once AGRIGENTO, Giudice. Woman running with mirror (to left, looking round).

6 (4). SYRACUS E 19865, from Gela. Woman running with mirror.

7 (5). ROME, Museo Barracco. Woman seated with mirror.

8 (6). LONDON E 643, from Camiros. *AM.* 5 pl. 14, 1. Nike.

9. ROME, Romagnoli. Ph. R.I. 42.317. Nike (standing to right, phiale in right hand, left hand raised). [Bothmer].

10 (a2). NEW YORK 06.1021.146. *Vente 11 mai 1903* pl. 2, 9; Sambon *Canessa* 31. Woman.

(*no. 11, secondary shape*)

11 (7). CRACOW, Univ., 1087. Bieńkowski O *lec.* 14; *CV*. pl. 8, 11. Athena.

OINOCHOE
(*shape 1*)

12 (8). LONDON E 515, from Nola. Athena. Restored.

NEAR THE PAINTER OF PALERMO 4

LEKYTHOI
(*nos. 1–2, standard shape*)

1 (1). ATHENS 1193 (CC. 1476). Eros.

2. LONDON E 642, from Gela. Woman dancing. Also recalls the manner of the Bowdoin Painter.

(*nos. 3–4, secondary shape, near Class PL*)

3 (3). DUNEDIN E 30.202 (ex Seltman). Anderson *H.G.V.* pl. 12, 86. Athena seated. Restored. Also recalls early vases by the Sabouroff Painter (see p. 856, xii).

4. CATANIA. Athena.

THE ASTUTO GROUP

These go together, and are not far from the Vlasto Painter (p. 696).

LEKYTHOI
(*secondary shape: near Class PL*)

1. PALERMO V 694 (ex Astuto). *CV*. pl. 22, 3. Woman spinning.
2. PALERMO V 688 (ex Astuto). *CV*. pl. 22, 1. Man leaning on his stick.

THE PAINTER OF THE LENINGRAD HERM-MUG

OINOCHOAI
(*no. 1, shape 5B*)

1. LONDON MARKET (Spink: ex Wilfred Hall). On the neck, Poseidon (standing with both legs frontal, head to left, dolphin in right hand, trident in left; naked, wrap round both shoulders).

(*no. 2, shape 8C, mug*)

2. LENINGRAD inv. 1898.42. Man at herm (palm-tree, rock-seat, man in himation, to right, holding cup, then altar, and herm to left).

THE CLASS OF VIENNA 3717

Eichler noticed that in shape these went together.

PYXIDES

(type D)

1. OXFORD 1922.67. *CV.* pl. 4, 4 and pl. 47, 13. Satyr eating grapes.
2. VIENNA 3717 (ex Oest. Mus. 383). *CV.* pl. 48, 1 and 4. Cock.

THE PAINTER OF ACROPOLIS 573

PYXIDES

(type D)

1. ATHENS Acr. 575, from Athens. Langlotz pl. 44. Siren.
2. ATHENS Acr. 573, from Athens. Benndorf pl. 12, 4; Langlotz pl. 44; Vorberg *Gloss.* 501, below. Phallus-bird.

BOOK IV

LATE ARCHAIC CUP-PAINTERS

CHAPTER 22

ONESIMOS

ONESIMOS

'The style of Onesimos so directly continues that of the Panaitios Painter that late Panaitios Painter is almost indistinguishable from early Onesimos; and Furtwängler's conjecture (FR. iii, 134) that the two are the same may be correct' (*ARV.*[1] 209). Furtwängler afterwards abandoned his conjecture, but I have always laid stress upon it (*VA.* 88; *ARV.*[1] 209 and 218–19; CB. ii, 32); and I now venture to identify the two artists: I take the vases which I assigned to the Panaitios Painter to be by Onesimos, his earlier works; his later works—the vases of my old Onesimos lists—continue the grand and forcible style of his earlier period in a graceful and often exquisite form.

The name of Onesimos is known from a single cup, Louvre G 105 (p. 324 no. 60), on which the potter-signature of Euphronios is accompanied, for once, by the painter-signature of Onesimos. Of the cups that bear the signature of the potter Euphronios without naming the painter, seven were decorated by Onesimos, and so were fragments of an eighth cup that was probably signed Euphronios. The seven are Louvre G 104 (p. 318 no. 1), London E 44 (p. 318 no. 2), Cab. Méd. 526 plus (p. 319 no. 5), New York 12.231.2 (p. 319 no. 6), Amsterdam (p. 322 no. 27), Boston 95.27 (p. 325 no. 79), and Perugia (p. 320 no. 8). The fragments of the eighth cup are Louvre C 11335 (p. 330 no. 4), to which Louvre C 11336 may belong. Fragments of a ninth cup with the potter-signature of Euphronios, Acropolis 434, are at least near Onesimos (p. 330 no. 5). Other possible remains of the signature are on the cup-fragments Louvre C 11346 *bis*, which is at least in the manner of Onesimos (p. 330 no. 6), and Acropolis 441, which is not remote from him (p. 333).

(Later than all these, and not connected with Onesimos, are three cups decorated by the Pistoxenos Painter: Berlin 2282, Acropolis 439, Taranto: see pp. 858-9 nos. 1-3. The Berlin cup bears the signature of the potter Euphronios. The other two were also signed: the name is now missing, but it was probably Euphronios).

Cups with the *potter*-signature of Euphronios were formerly assumed to have been decorated by Euphronios, whose work as a *painter* is known from several signed vases (p. 13). It was Furtwängler who first separated 'the Panaitios Painter' from Euphronios (FR. ii, 110-12: see above, p. 13).

Several of the cups in the lists that follow were attributed by Klein, Hartwig, and others, to their composite 'Euphronios': these attributions were based on just observation, on comparison with the cups signed Εὐφρόνιος ἐποίησεν, and are therefore acknowledged below, where they are marked 'Klein E.', 'Hartwig E.', &c.

Under the heading of 'the Proto-Panaetian Group' I have collected, as before, a number of fine cups which I began by thinking of as the earliest work by the Panaitios Painter. Their exact relation to him is not clear: they are close to him and lead on to him. Some of them are quite probably from his hand: but which? They differ a good deal among themselves, and it is hard to arrange them, as one might have expected to do, in a chronological sequence. If they are all his, he oscillated considerably before settling down. This is conceivable in an adventurous young man; but one cannot assume it. The question remains difficult, and the expression 'the Proto-Panaetian Group' had better be retained.

Before describing the Proto-Panaetian Group, we deal with a few vases by a painter who is connected with it and might almost be said to form part of it:

THE ELEUSIS PAINTER

CF. 23; *ARV.*[1] 209-10 and 955; CB. ii, 21-23.

CUPS

1 (2). VIENNA, Univ., 53 c 23-25 and 20, five frr., from Orvieto. One fr., and part of another, *A.E.M.* 16, 115-16, whence Davreux fig. 64; *CV.* pl. 10, 1-4 and 7, whence (two frr. and part of a third) *AJA.* 1954 pl. 61 fig. 26. I, (woman?) running. Outside, Iliupersis. I took *CV.* pl. 10, 3 and 5 to be from this cup. (The obverse of pl. 10, 2 and the reverse of pl. 10, 7 are not figured in *CV.*). Outside, LEA[ΛΡΟ$], also ΚΑLΟΝ retr., and ΚΑLΟ[$] (whether either pertains to the Leagros or not). Early.

2 (1). BERLIN inv. 3239 and VILLA GIULIA, from Vulci. Part, Hartwig pl. 4, whence (I) *Riv. Ist.* 6, 210; the Villa Giulia fr., *CF.* pl. Y, 10. I, Egyptian; A-B, Herakles and Busiris. On I, LEAΛPO[$] EIΚALO$. On A, LEA-ΛP[O$. . .], ΚΑ[LO$]. And traces of other inscriptions.

3 (3). ELEUSIS 618, frr., from Eleusis. *Delt.* 9 pl. at p. 24, 2, whence Philippart *C.A.B.* pl. 13, a; Kourouniotes 116; Robertson *G.P.* 97. I, white ground, Triton . . . . Ο$ and ⊕ . . .

4 (5). ELEUSIS 619, fr., from Eleusis. *Delt.* 9, 16, whence Philippart *C.A.B.* pl. 13, b; Kourouniotes 117; the shape, Bloesch *F.A.S.* pl. 37, 1. I, white ground, Athena and Giant. L[EAΛPOS] retr. and KA[LOS].

5 (4). MANILA, Zobel de Ayala (ex Curtius), fr. *Cat. Hecht Gr. u. röm. Münzen* (1954) i, 1; *Archaeology* Summer 1956, cover, back, inside; ibid. Autumn 1956, 223; ph. R.I. 37.192. A, komos (man with lyre, hand with drinking-horn). As no. 7.

6 (6). BOSTON 10.196, from Cumae. Hartwig pl. 10; CB. ii suppl. pl. 5, 1 and suppl. pl. 6. I, warrior and archer; A, fight; B, cavalrymen with horses. On I, retr., KALO? and [LEAΛR]OS. On B, [L]EAΛROS. See CB. ii, 21–23.

SKYPHOS

7 (7). BONN, Langlotz, fr., from Taranto. Komos (lyre-player and youth side by side). As no. 5.

Close to these, and very likely by the same hand, but rather weaker, the cup-fragments

ATHENS, Agora, P 9052, two frr., from Athens. A, (women fleeing; on the smaller fr., elbow and sleeve of a raised arm).

Near the Eleusis Painter, the cups

1. BASLE, Cahn, 101, fr. I, fight (youth with sword and youth with pelta). A, boxers, B, (on the right, heel). Early.

2. LONDON E 816, from Vulci. Vorberg *Ars erot.* pl. 16. I, love-making (elderly man, and woman). LEAΛROS KALOS.

THE PROTO-PANAETIAN GROUP

ARV.[1] 210–12 and 955. See above, p. 314.

The Group is here divided into two sections: in the first, the cups that seem specially akin to early Onesimos ('Panaitios Painter'); in the second, various cups that seem somewhat less near him: but the division is perhaps rather arbitrary.

(i)

1 (1). LONDON E 46 and LEIPSIC, from Cervetri. Fröhner *Brant.* pll. 15–16 (= Hartwig pl. 8 = Klein *L.* 74–75), whence (I) HM. pl. 16, 1, *Int. Studio* Feb. 1927, 24, 1, and 25, 2, (I) Perrot 10, 387, (I) Buschor 162, (I) Swindler fig. 284; I (augmented by two frr. found by Nachod and Rumpf in Leipsic), *Disj.M.* 2, whence Pfuhl fig. 413; I, Botsford and C. A. Robinson[3] pl. 25; I, *Mitt.* 5 pl. 4, 4; I, Rumpf *MZ.* pl. 25, 1; A and the foot, Bloesch *F.A.S.* pl. 21, 1. I, youth starting a hare (for the subject cf. the kyathos p. 333 no. 2). A–B, komos. On I, retr., LEAΛROS

ΚΑΛΟϚ, and, not retr., ΗΟΓΑΙϚ ΚΑΛΟϚ. On A, [L]ΕΑΛR[Ο]Ϛ
ΚΑ[L]ΟϚ. [Hartwig E.]. The cup has now been cleaned, and the two
Leipsic frr. have been joined to it. A third fr., still in Leipsic, gives the
missing part of the middle figure on B, a youth playing the flute to left.
The forerunners of these komasts are those on the neck of the volute-
krater by Euphronios in Arezzo (p. 15 no. 6). For the shape, Bloesch
75, Euphronios no. 24.

2 (2, +). Louvre G 77, fr. Part, Pottier pl. 97. A, komos. A Louvre fr.
joins on the right, giving the rest of the skyphos, and the upper half of
another youth, playing the flute, to right.

3 (3). Once Rome, de Ferrari. I, *Burl. Mag.* 41, 123, 1, whence Philippart
C.A.B. pl. 11, a; *Cat. Sotheby June 8 1925* pl. 1; phs. R.I. 7618–20. I, lovers
(woman lying on couch and man taking off his sandals); A–B, symposion
(youths and naked women). On I, ΑΟ[ΕΝ]Ο[ΔΟΤΟϚ] retr., and
ΚΑ[LΟ]Ϛ. Much restored. See *Burl. Mag.* 41, 121–2. Compare Cab.
Méd. 523 (no. 4). See p. 1645.

4 (4). Cab. Méd. 523, from Vulci. Hartwig pl. 16 and pl. 15, 2, whence
JHS. 23, 278, Norman Gardiner *G.A.S.* 385 and 286, (I) Swindler fig. 307;
phs. Gir., whence (I) Norman Gardiner *Athl.* fig. 157. Athletes: I, wrestlers; A, wrestlers, boxers; B, hoplitodromoi. Very much restored (repainted). The inscriptions, now largely obliterated by repainting, *Mus.*
étr. pl. 36, 1645 and 1645 *bis*, whence Hartwig 135. [Hartwig E.]. On B,
ΚΕΦΙϚΟΦΟΝ ΚΑΛΟϚ. ΔΟΡΟΘΕΟϚ retr. and ΚΑΛΟϚ. ΚΑΛΟϚ
ΟLΥΝΓΙΟΔΟΡΟϚ. Dorotheos and Olympiodoros are 'early' names,
and among the other names of athletes are the 'early' Ambrosios, Euagoras,
Antias, Antimachos. Compare especially the de Ferrari cup (no. 3). For
the shape, Bloesch 70, Euphronios no. 1. See p. 1645.

5 (12). Louvre G 25, from Chiusi. Fröhner *Brant.* pll. 17–18 = Hartwig pl.
9 and Klein *L.* 77–78; phs. Gir. 28594–5. I, komast (man vomiting).
A–B, warriors in ambush. On I, LΕΑΛΡΟϚ. On A, LΕΑΛΡΟϚ ΚΑΛΟϚ.
On B, LΕΑ[Λ]ΡΟϚ ΚΑΛΟϚ. [Hartwig E.]. Restored.

6 (6). Louvre C 91, fr. A, *Hesp.* 8th suppl., pl. 1, 1. I, (part of a cloak remains on the left). A, (on the right, Dionysos? reclining, and satyr).
Cf. the Baltimore cup no. 7.

7 (7). Baltimore, from Chiusi. Inghirami *Chius.* pl. 48, whence Klein *Euphr.*
278; Hartwig pl. 44, 1; *CV.* Robinson ii pl. 7. I, satyr balancing himself on
a wineskin. ΓΑΝΑΙΤΙΟϚΚΑΛΟϚ. [Hartwig E.]. Restored. Cf. Louvre
C 91 (no. 6).

8 (13). London E 45, from Vulci. I, Murray no. 28; Hartwig pl. 13; I,
Beazley and Ashmole fig. 58, whence *Bull. Vereen.* June 1941, 27; I and A,
Lane pl. 73; A and foot, Bloesch *F.A.S.* pl. 21, 4; A–B, Bothmer *Am.* pl.
69, 4. I, two Amazons running; A–B, Herakles and the Amazons.
[Hartwig E.]. For the shape, Bloesch 78, Euphronios no. 38. See p. 1645.

9 (14). BOSTON 01.8018, from Orvieto. Hartwig pl. 14, 2, whence Klein *L.* 84, Perrot 10, 386, FR. iii, 22; Langlotz *GV.* pl. 6; cleaned, CB. ii pl. 38, above, and p. 24; the shape, Caskey G. 207 no. 160. I, symposion: youth vomiting and man playing the flute. ΕΠΙΔΡΟΜΟΣ ΚΑLΟΣ. [Hartwig, E.]. This may really be an early work by 'the Panaitios Painter'. See CB. ii, 24–25; and below, p. 1645.

(ii)

10 (9). BOSTON 98.876. I, *Handbook B.M.F.A.* (1914), 86; I, Stow pl. 11, 1; CB. ii pl. 37 and p. 23; I, Villard *VG.* pl. 20, 2; I, *Olympia in der Antike* pl. 51; the shape, Caskey G. 205 no. 159. I, athlete running with haltēres; A–B, athletes. On I, ΑΘΕΝΟΔΟΤΟΣ ΚΑLΟΣ. See CB. ii, 23–24.

11 (11). FLORENCE 4 B 60 and VILLA GIULIA, two frr. The Florence fr., *CV.* Fl. pl. 4, B 60. Outside, on one fr., head, to right, and extended arm, of a youth, with the inscription . . . ΟΣ; on the other fr., man with stick to left.

12. LEIPSIC T 558 and GREIFSWALD 275, fr. The Greifswald part, Peters pl. 22. The Greifswald fr. joins the Leipsic on the right. A, athletes (head of a youth to right, upper part of a youth rushing to right, looking back and down, holding an acontion, as it must be—the top remains—in his right hand).

13. LOUVRE G 26 and G 26 *bis*, two frr. A of part of one fr., Pottier pl. 90. I, warrior or hoplitodromos. A, cavalrymen with horses; B, (one with a horse). On I, [LE]ΑΛROΣΚ[ΑLΟ]Σ. On A, LEΑΛROΣ ΚΑLΟΣ. On B, LEΑΛ[ROΣ . . .]. Villard has joined to G 26 a fragment giving more of the right-hand horse.

14. LEIPSIC, fr., from Orvieto. I, archer (forehead, eye, and hand holding up an arrow, to right, with ΚΑLΟΣ. A, athletes (foot to right, hand with haltēr to left).

15 (10). BRUSSELS A 723. Hartwig pl. 7; *CV.* pl. 11, 1. I, satyr astride a wineskin; A, procession of satyrs: the chief of them rides a phallus-bird, accompanied by a satyr playing the flute and three others turning somersaults. B, komos. On I, ΚRΑΤΕΣΚΑLΟΣ and on the wineskin ΚRΑΤΕΣ ΚΑLΟΣ. On A, ΚRΑΤΕΣ ΚΑLΟΣ ΚΑLΟΣ. On B, ΚRΑΤΕΣ ΚΑLΟΣ ΚRΑΤΕΣ on one pointed amphora, ΚRΑΤΕΣ; on the other, ΚΑLΟΣ. [Hartwig, E.]. Much restored. This is a difficult piece to place exactly: the inside is very Panaetian; the outside is less so, and it combines old-fashioned traits with more modern ones.

Another cup not easily placed is nearest, perhaps, to Cab. Méd. 523 (p. 316 no. 4):

16 (5). MUNICH 2636 (J. 272), from Vulci. *Philologus* 26 pl. 3, 1–2; Hartwig 129 and pl. 15, 1; I, Licht iii, 122. Symposion: I, naked woman reclining. playing kottabos; A, man and another, reclining; B, two youths reclining,

[Hartwig E.]. Now cleaned. The woman inside calls TOITEN[ΔE] (retr.), the youth on B who holds the μυρρίνη, K[ALO]SEI (retr.); the inscription to left of the man's head on A is EΛEI ... (retr.), perhaps the beginning of a poem, ἔγει[ρε], cf. Pindar O. 9, 47. For the shape, Bloesch 76 no. 30, Euphronios.

A small cup is related to the Proto-Panaetian Group:

OXFORD 302, from Gela. Eckstein fig. 8a; CV. pl. 1, 9. I, komast. ΠΑΝΑΙ-ΤΙΟΣ ΚΑLΟΣ.

====

ONESIMOS (INCLUDING 'THE PANAITIOS PAINTER')

See p. 313.

Hartwig 95–153 and 444–502 ('Euphronios'), and 503–62. Furtwängler in FR. ii, 110–12 and 134. VA. 82–89 and 194. Langlotz in Gnomon 4, 326–8. Att. V. 165–75 and 473. V.Pol. 21–23 and 80. ARV.¹ 208–24 and 955. CB. ii, 23–26 and 102.

The cups are grouped according to subject. Those marked 'early' belong to the 'Panaetian' period of the painter. 'P', in the serial numbers between brackets refers to the Panaitios list in ARV.¹, 'O' to the Onesimos list, 'Pi' to the 'early Panaitios Painter' list in ARV.¹ 212–13, 'PO' to the lists 'between Panaitios Painter and Onesimos' ibid. 218–19, 'PP' to the Proto-Panaetian Group ibid. 210–12.

1 (P 10). LOUVRE G 104 and FLORENCE PD 321, from Cervetri. Mon. gr. 1872 pll. 1–2, whence WV. 5 pl. 1, Klein Euphr. 182 and 194–5, (I) HM. pl. 14, Perrot 10 pl. 10 and pp. 422–3, (I) JHS. 18 pl. 14, (A–B) Hoppin i, 399, below; A–B, JHS. 35 pl. 4; FR. pll. 5 and 141, whence (I) Jacobsthal Thes. pl. 1, 1, (I) Buschor 165, (I) Langlotz GV. pl. 15, (I) Hoppin i, 399, above, (I and B) Swindler pl. 9 and fig. 300, (A–B) Schnitzler pl. 41, 56, (A) Radermacher Mythos fig. 15, (A–B) Stella pl. 13; I, Perrot 10 pl. 9; Pottier pll. 102–4; I, ph. Al. 23725, whence Pfuhl fig. 398 (= Pfuhl Mast. fig. 48), Bieber Entw. pl. 12, Buschor G.Vasen 151, Die Antike 17, 222, Radermacher Mythos fig. 18, Stella 396; I, Enc. phot. iii, 9, whence LS. fig. 57 and Frel Ř.V. fig. 157; I, Dugas and Flacelière pl. 9; Richter H.G.A. 329; A–B, ph. Gir. The Florence fr., Hesp. 8th suppl., pl. 1, 2. I, Theseus and Amphitrite, with Athena; A–B, deeds of Theseus: A, Skiron, Procrustes; B, Kerkyon, bull. On I, EVΘRO[NIOSE]ΠΟΙΕSEN. The drawing of A–B in FR. is restored: see the drawing in Mon. gr. For the shape, Bloesch 71, Euphronios no. 5. Early. See p. 164⁵.

2 (P 11). LONDON E 44, from Vulci. WV. 5 pl. 7, whence Klein Euphr. 98 and 88–89, HM pl. 12 and pl. 13, 2, (A) Murray 10; I, Murray no. 27, whence Perrot 10, 425; FR. pl. 23, whence Hoppin i, 389, (A–B) Perrot 10, 426–7, (A–B) Pfuhl figs. 401–2; I, Pfuhl fig. 405 (= Pfuhl Mast. fig.

49); I, Langlotz *GV.* pl. 18; I, Schaal *Rf.* fig. 18; I, Licht ii, 46; I, Schoene-beck and Kraiker pl. 83, 2; detail of A, Lane pl. 72, b; the foot, Bloesch *F.A.S.* pl. 20, 2. I, lovers (woman and old man). A, Herakles and Eurystheus. B, chariot (young driver, warrior who has just alighted, Hermes at the horses' heads). On I, ΓΑΝΑΙΤΙΟ꒱ ΚΑ⅃Ο꒱. Incised on one handle, ΕVꝺꝶΟΝΙΟ꒱ ΕΓΟΙΕ꒱ΕΝ. For the subject of B, Robert *Held.* 1188: he shows that it may be the same as in the Louvre cup G 17 by Oltos (p. 62 no. 83): if so, the chariot of Odysseus. For the shape, Bloesch 70, Euphronios no. 4. Early.

3 (P 2). LONDON E 47, from Orvieto. I, god and giant; A–B, Gigantomachy. On I, ΑΘΕΝΟΔ[ΟΤΟ꒱] and on the ground-line ΚΑ[⅃Ο꒱]. [Hartwig E.]. Early. See p. 1645.

4. LOUVRE C 11335, two frr. I, (warrior: part of a shield remains, the device a bull; and what seems to be part of a cloak). Outside, deeds of Theseus?: on one fr., the feet of a giant figure, to right, lying on its back (Mino-taur?), and the legs of a female figure rushing to left; then the head of an animal, fallen; on the other fr., the legs of a youth or man standing to right, with a stick, and part of a bull lying on its back. On I, . . . ΕΓΟΙ]Ε꒱ΕΝ. To be considered, whether another Louvre fragment, C 11336, worn like the others, may not be from the same cup; outside, what may be the edge of a draped figure to left, with the inscription . . . ΝΙ . . . ([*Εὐφρο*]*νι*-[*οϲεποιεϲεν*]?). Early.

4 *bis.* OXFORD, Beazley, fr. A, Theseus and Antiope; what remains is the hindquarters of a chariot-team speeding to left, with the hands and forearms of the driver; and, beyond the chariot, part of a warrior rushing to left. Inscription, retr., [ΑΝΤΙΟ]ΓΕΙΑ.

5 (P 27). CAB. MÉD. 526 (part), 743, 553, L 41, plus, frr., from Tarquinia. Part, *Mon.* 2 pl. 10, a, whence *WV.* 5 pl. 5, 1, Klein *Euphr.* 152 and 137 (without the paper restorations), Hoppin i, 395 (with restorations), (A) Panofka *Namen* pl. 4, 6, (part, without restorations) Bulas *Il.* fig. 22; two further frr., *AZ.* 1882, 47, whence (one fr.) Klein *Euphr.* 155; a new fr., *Hesp.* 8th suppl., pl. 1, 4; for other new frr. see *JHS.* 54, 85. I, warrior (holding out his helmet; a small fr. gives two toes of his right foot, frontal). A, Dolon. B, uncertain subject (legs of male in himation, frontal foot, sandalled and stockinged, of a male rushing to right, foot of an animal; Agamemnon seated to left). On I, [Ε]VꝺꝶΟΝ[ΙΟ꒱ΕΓΟΙΕ꒱Ε]Ν. Outside, under one handle, [ΕVꝺꝶ]ΟΝΙΟ꒱ and below it [ΕΓΟΙ]Ε꒱ΕΝ. Early.

6 (P 28). NEW YORK 12.231.2, from Cervetri. I, *Bull. Metr.* 8, 153; *AJA.* 1916 pll. 2–6 and p. 126, whence Hoppin i, 393 and (I) Pfuhl fig. 400: I, *Hdbk Cl. Coll.* 115; augmented by frr. found by Rumpf in Leipsic and by me in Dresden, Richter and Hall pll. 37–39 and pl. 179, 39; detail of I, Richter *ARVS.* fig. 59; I, Richter *H.* 214, d. I, Herakles and a little boy (Philoktetes?) carrying his luggage; A, Herakles and the sons of Eurytos;

B, unexplained subject; Herakles attacking a man or youth at an altar (cf. p. 188 no. 70). On I, ΕVΦΡΟΝΙΟSΕΓΟΙ[ΕSΕΝ]. For the shape, Bloesch 70, Euphronios no. 8. Early.

7 (P 29). CAB. MÉD. 601, 714, 567, 731, part of 521 (L 282), 759, plus, frr. I, uncertain subject (symposion?: an old man reclining, and a woman standing in front of him). Outside, unexplained subject: symposion, with two men or youths seizing a youth. The style of the inside picture is a little unusual. Early.

8 (O 56). PERUGIA 89, from Vulci. Gerhard pll. 224–6, whence *WV.* 5 pl. 6, Klein *Euphr.* 220 and 214–15, HM. pll. 17–17a; Hartwig pl. 59, 1 and pl. 58, whence Hoppin i, 403 (details) *Mon. Piot* 16, 131–2, (I) Pfuhl fig. 399. I, Achilles slaying Troilos; A, Achilles dragging Troilos to the altar; B, arming. On A, ԼVԿΟՏ. On B, ΕVΦΡΟΝΙΟSΕΓΟΙΕSΕΝ. [Hartwig]. Restored. For the shape, Bloesch 71, Euphronios no. 12.

9 (Oa 3). CERVETRI 374, fr., from Cervetri. *Hesp.*, 8th suppl., pl. 2, 3. A, capture of Silenos? See ibid. 4–5.

10 (P 12). BALTIMORE, from Cervetri. Hartwig pl. 45, whence (part of A) *VA.* 85; *CV.* Robinson ii pll. 8–9. I, satyr; A, satyrs attacking a sleeping maenad; B, the like. On I, ΓΑΝΑΙΤ[ΙΟSԿΑԼ]ΟS. [Hartwig E.]. Early.

11 (P 14, +). LOUVRE S 1339, S 1328, and two other frr. One fr., A, *Hesp.*, 8th suppl., pl. 1, 3. I, satyr; A, satyrs attacking a sleeping maenad; B, similar. The fr. S 1328 was attributed to the Panaitios Painter in *Att. V.* (167 no. 22) but by an oversight omitted in *ARV.*[1]: it gives, inside, toes of the satyr and one hand, holding a bunch of grapes; outside, one leg of the left-hand figure on B, a satyr moving to right. The third fragment has the knee of the same satyr, and his elbow; and one arm, with crotala in the hand, of a maenad lying on the ground, to right. The fourth fragment has the legs of this maenad, and those of another satyr, moving to left. Early.

12 (P 13). FLORENCE 3917. Part, Hartwig pl. 44, 2 and p. 453. Now augmented by new frr., see *JHS.* 51, 47 no. 25 and *CF.* on pl. 6 B 42. The new frr., A–B, *CV.* pl. 6, B 42 and 45, *CF.* pl. Y, 4 and pl. Z, 3 and 26. All, *CV.* pl. 87. I, komast. A, satyrs attacking a sleeping maenad; B, the like. On I, ΓΑ[ΝΑΙ]ΤΙΟSԿΑԼΟ[S]. [Hartwig E.]. Early.

12 *bis.* OXFORD, Beazley, fr. A, (flank and thigh of a naked male—satyr?—wearing a goatskin). Early. Compare No. 93 *bis*? See p. 1645.

13. LOUVRE C 10892. I, satyr; outside, one figure on each half: A, satyr; B, satyr. On I, ԼVԿΟS ԿΑԼΟ[S]. Early.

14 (2). BOSTON 01.8021, from Orvieto. Hartwig pl. 12, whence (I) Pfuhl fig. 407; I, Licht i, 96; A, *Jb.* 53, 109; cleaned, CB. ii pl. 39, 75; the shape, Caskey G. 205 no. 158. I, boxer. A–B, fight. On I, ΑΘΕΝΟΔΟΤΟS

and retr. ΚΑΛΟΣ; also ΚΑΛΟΣ and retr. ΚΑΛΟΣ. See CB. ii, 26–28, and, for the shape, Bloesch 77, Euphronios no. 34. Early.

15 (O 22). CAB. MÉD. 604 and L 155, frr. I, archer: round the tondo, a white zone; A–B, fight.

16 (O 23). GOETTINGEN, part of 566, frr. I, warrior; A–B, fight.

17 (Pi 3). TÜBINGEN E 18, fr., from Taranto. Watzinger pl. 19. I, athlete? A, arming. Early.

18 (O 24). LEIPSIC T 552, fr., from Orvieto. I, archer (legs, moving to left); A, arming (archer with his bow between his legs, male leg to right, toes to left).

19 (Pi 4). CAB. MÉD. 524, fr. De Ridder 394. I, komast. A, athletes (wrestlers, or pancration). [Hartwig E.]. Early.

20 (Pi 5). BOSTON 98.877, fr. CB. ii, suppl. pl. 7, 2–3. I, athlete; A, athletes. On I, ΑΘ[ΕΝΟΔΟΤΟΣ] and retr. Κ[ΑΛΟΣ]. See CB. ii, 28–29. Early.

21 (Pi 6). BOSTON 10.207, from Orvieto. Hartwig pl. 14, 1 and p. 120 fig. 17; CB. ii pl. 39, 76 and suppl. pl. 7, 1. I, two archers. A–B, athletes. On I, ΑΘΕΝ[ΟΔΟΤΟΣ] ΚΑΛΟΣ. [Hartwig E.]. See CB. ii, 27–28. Early.

22 (P 5). BOSTON 01.8020, from Orvieto. AZ. 1884 pl. 16, 2, whence Klein Euphr. 285–6, Norman Gardiner G.A.S. 326 fig. 80 and p. 305, (A and one figure from B) Jüthner 15 fig. 14 and p. 26, (I, A, and one figure from B) JHS. 24, 183 fig. 3, and 27, 20; A–B, VA. 83; A, Langlotz G.V. pl. 7; A, Int. Studio Feb. 1927, 24, 2; A, Schröder Sport pl. 54, below; I and A, Alexander Gk Athl. 15 and 11; I and A, Norman Gardiner Athl. figs. 114 and 105; I, Buschor G. Vasen 153 fig. 171; cleaned, CB. ii pl. 40 and p. 29; Olympia in der Antike pll. 46–48; the shape, Caskey G. 189 no. 143. I, discus-thrower; A–B, athletes: A, jumpers; B, discus-thrower and jumper. On I, ΠΑΝΑΙΤΙΟΣΚΑΛΟΣ. [Meier E.]. See CB. ii, 29–31, and, for the shape, Bloesch 76, Euphronios no. 29. Early.

23 (P 7). BERLIN inv. 3139, from Italy. I, Klein L. 109; Hartwig pl. 46, whence (I) Festschr. Benndorf 21, (I) Pfuhl fig. 408, (I) Swindler fig. 304; I, Langlotz G.V. pl. 12; I, Zschietzschmann H.R. pl. 151, 1. I, trainer with tablets; A–B, athletes. On I, ΠΑΝΙΤΙΟΣ ΚΑΛΟΣ. On A, ΠΑΝΙΤ-[ΙΟΣ . . .]. [Klein E.]. Early.

24 (P 6). LOUVRE G 287. I, VA. 84. I, discus-thrower and trainer; A–B, athletes. Early.

25 (P 22). HEIDELBERG 53, fr. Kraiker pl. 8. A, (athlete).

26 (23). VILLA GIULIA, fr. (two joining). I, athletes (one moving to right, the other kneeling to left: feet and parts of the legs remain); A, athletes (foot of jumper, legs of athlete bending with haltēres, both to right). Another fr. in Villa Giulia may belong: inside, on the left, a bare arm and shoulder; outside, legs of an athlete to left, for example a boxer, then the head of one to right.

27 (28). AMSTERDAM inv. 1820. I, acontist and jumper (athlete with halteres); A–B, athletes. On I, EVⲪRONIOϚ EΓ[OIEϚ]EN ΚΑ[Ⳑ]OϚ. Ruined.

28 (PO i 1). MUNICH 2637 (J. 795), from Vulci. *AZ.* 1878 pl. 11, whence Klein *Euphr.* 284, Norman Gardiner *G.A.S.* 105, *Mnem.* 4th ser., 3, 198; I, Blümel *S.H.* 62; I, A, and foot, Bloesch *F.A.S.* pl. 20, 1; I, Neutsch *Sport* fig. 20; parts of A–B, *RM.* 63 pl. 41, 1–2. I, discus-thrower and acontist; A–B, athletes. On I, ΓΑΝΑΙΤΙΟϚ ΚΑⳐΟϚ. For the shape, Bloesch 71, Euphronios no. 7.

29 (O 25). FLORENCE PD 265, from Chiusi. *CV.* pl. 92. I, naked boy running with tray (of food?). Round the tondo, white zone. A–B, athletes. On I, [HO]Γ[ΑI]ϟ ΚΑⳐΟϚ, and on the white zone EPOⲾEMIϟ.

30 (O 26). DRESDEN and FREIBURG, fr. I, athlete stringing his acontion; A, athletes. See *CF.* 34 no. 17.

31 (O 27). FREIBURG, fr. I, acontist (shank with foot, to left, and hand with acontion; two-line border); A, athlete (legs to right, and acontion).

32 (O 28). FREIBURG, fr. A, athlete (arm with haltēr in the hand, to right). Might belong to the last.

33 (O 29). FREIBURG, fr. I, (two-line border). A, (part of male in himation).

34 (O 30, O 34, +). LOUVRE C 10893. I, warrior. A–B, acontists. Many Louvre frr. join those previously mentioned, and the cup is not far from complete.

35 (O 32, +). LOUVRE G 297, G 297 *bis*, plus. One fr. of A, Pottier pl. 134. I, athlete at laver; A–B, athletes scraping themselves. Many Louvre frr. join, and the cup is not far from complete.

36 (O 31, 33, 51, +). LOUVRE G 291. Part, Hartwig 258–9; part of I, Sudhoff i, 17; part of I and one fr. of B, Pottier pl. 134. I, athlete; A, athletes at well; B, athletes at laver. Many Louvre frr., including G 298 and S 1368, join G 291, and the cup is not far from complete; the alien foot has been removed and the proper one substituted.

37. SWISS PRIVATE. I, youth with hare (bending to right, head frontal). A–B, athletes: A, pancration; B, boxers. On A, ΓΑΝΑΙΤΙΟϚΚΑⳐΟϚ. On B, ⳐVΚΟϟ and on a discus-bag ΙΚΑⳐΟϚ. Cup type C. Slightly restored. [Astarita].

38 (O 36). PARIS, Petit Palais, 325, from Tarquinia. *CV.* pl. 20, 1, 4, 6, and 9; B.Ap. xvi. 10. 2. I, athlete with acontion; A–B, athletes. Restored.

39 (O 37). ROME, Torlonia, 241, from Vulci. *R.I.* ix, 61, whence (I and A) Jüthner 41, c and p. 31 fig. 26. I, athlete with acontion; A–B, athletes.

40 (O 38). FRANKFORT, Liebieghaus, L 108 (inv. 554), fr. I, discus-thrower; A–B, athletes?

41 (O 42). CAB. MÉD. 667 and L 301, two frr. I, discus-thrower (right leg frontal, discus in left hand); A, athletes.

42 (O 41). CAB. MÉD. 666, two frr. I, athlete bending with haltēres; A–B, acontists.

43 (O 40). CAB. MÉD. 799, fr. I, (on the left, male arm); A, athletes.

44 (O 39). CAB. MÉD. 785, 659, plus, two frr. I, athlete (bending, to right); A–B, athletes.

45 (O 44). CAB. MÉD. (part of 658?), fr. A, (trainer: the upper part remains moving to left, looking round; bearded).

46 (O 46). CAB. MÉD., fr. A, (athlete: armpit and arm extended to right, horizontal acontion or wand).

47 (O 45). CAB. MÉD. 520 (L 124), fr. I, (stopt maeander). A, (part of the right-hand figure remains, a naked boy to left, looking round, a bag over his shoulder). This may be from an athlete cup; there is a similar figure on the cup in Amsterdam (no. 27).

48 (O. 47). LEIPSIC T 3374. I, athlete holding a pick; outside, one figure on each half: A, athlete (jumper?); B, athlete with acontia.

49 (O 48). FLORENCE PD 382, fr. I, athlete (haltēr in one hand); A, boxers; B, athletes.

50 (O 49). FLORENCE PD 396, fr. I, (maeander). A, (athlete bending to right: (victor?—cf. Louvre G 296, p. 331 no. 15).

51. LOUVRE C 11336 bis, fr. A, (athlete: frontal, looking round to left with face in three-quarter view; thongs, suspended).

51 bis. OXFORD 1953.5, fr. A, (athlete: upper half, frontal, looking round to right, strigil in right hand).

52 (O 50). MISSISSIPPI (ex Robinson), fr. CV. Robinson ii pl. 21, 2. I, symposion (youth reclining; and one playing the flute?). A, athletes (wrestlers?). [Robinson].

53 (Oa 2). VILLA GIULIA, fr. I, athlete holding acontion (his head remains, to right; key border); A, athletes (toes and hand, holding haltēr, of an athlete bending to right; then an acontion, and the heel of one to right).

54. VILLA GIULIA, fr. A, (part of an upright acontion, thonged, and legs of an athlete moving to right).

55. NEW HAVEN, Watkins, from Greece. I, hoplitodromos; A–B, hoplito-dromoi. See BSA. 46, 10–11.

56. ARLESHEIM, Schweizer. Schefold M. 189, 203. I, hoplitodromos (bearded athlete with his helmet in his left hand; two-line border); A–B, hoplito-dromoi. On I, ΓΑΝΑΙΤΙΟ§ΚΑLΟ§ and on the shield ΗΟΓΑΙ§. Re-stored.

57 (O 43). CAB. MÉD., fr. I, (maeander). A, hoplitodromoi (leg to left, leg to left with shield, leg to left).

58. INNSBRUCK ii, 12.27, fr. I, (on the left, youth in chitoniskos, petasos at nape). A, (horse's hoof).

59 (P 26). LEIPSIC, fr. A, (cavalryman: what remains is the breast of one wearing chitoniskos, Thracian cloak, alopeke; then the tail of a horse to right).

60 (O 1). LOUVRE G 105, from Vulci. *Mon. gr.* 1885–8, 7 and 10–11, whence
(I) HM. pl. 16, 2, (A–B) Perrot 10, 448–9; Hartwig pl. 53, whence Hoppin i, 401, (I) Perrot 10, 447, (I) *Mon. Piot* 16, 135, (I) Pfuhl fig. 404; I and
B, Pottier pl. 104; (I) Cloché *Classes* pl. 2, 2; I and A, phs. Gir. 28507 and
28543, 2. I, horseman; A–B, horsemen. On I, EV[Φ]RONIOϚ EΓOI-
EϚEN, ΚΑLOϚ]E]ROⲐEMIϚ, and, on the exergue, L[V]ΚOϚ (the
letter after this is modern). On A, ΚΑLOϚ EROⲐEMIϚ, and on the
echinus LVΚOϚ. On B, ONEϚIMOϚEΛRAⲐϚ[EN]. The first four
letters of Ὀνήσιμος are now missing, but the name was complete in 1829
and was recorded as late as 1845 (see p. 1645). Restored. For the shape,
Bloesch 73, Euphronios no. 17.

61 (O 2). MUNICH 2639 (J. 515), from Vulci. *AZ.* 1885 pl. 11, whence Klein
Euphr. 287 and Norman Gardiner *G.A.S.* 474; I, Langlotz *G.V.* pl. 13;
part of B, Schröder *Sport* pl. 83, above; B, Norman Gardiner *Athl.* fig.
58. I, youth with spear and panther-skin (light-armed? hunter?). A–B,
youths with horses. Restored.

62 (O 3, +). LOUVRE G 113, two frr. I, (male: the legs, to left). A, youths
and horse; B, (horse). On A, LVΚOϚ.

63 (O 4). BONN 1227, from Falerii. I, *CV.* pl. 7, 1. I, man at the altar of
Hermes. A–B, males and horses. On I, LVΚOϚΚ[A]LOϚ.

64 (O 5). VIENNA, Univ., 501, from Orvieto. *CV.* pl. 11, 2 and 4, and pl. 12,
3–4. I, athlete. A–B, a single group on each half: A, boy leading horse:
B, the like.

65 (O 6). BOSTON 95.29, from Chiusi. I and part of B, *RM.* 46 pl. 21, 2 and
pl. 19, 2; CB. ii pl. 43, 81, whence (detail of I) *Hesp.* 27 pl. 47, b; I,
Sparkes, Talcott, and Frantz, fig. 27. I, komast. A–B, youths and horses.
See CB. ii, 34–36; and below, p. 1645.

66 (O 7). HEIDELBERG 63, frr., from Orvieto. A–B, Kraiker pl. 9. I, (uncertain remains). Outside, (horse-race; mounted boy; male and horse).

67. OXFORD 1927.4608, fr., from Orvieto. A, *CV.* pl. 14, 42. I, (uncertain
remains). Outside, (youth holding a horse, behind it a boy; on the right
the heel of a male in a himation to right, leaning).

68 (O 8). HEIDELBERG 64, fr. Kraiker pl. 9. A, (youth, horse).

69 (O 9). HEIDELBERG 62. I, Kraiker pl. 8; I, *RM.* 46 pl. 20, 1. I, athlete.
A–B, youths and horses.

70 (O 10). BERLIN, Univ., fr. A, (youth, horse).

71 (O 11). BRYN MAWR, P 935 and P 931, two frr. Part of the outside, *AJA.*
1916, 343, 20–21. I, male and dog. Outside, males and horses. A Bryn
Mawr fr. joins 20, adding the middle of the male. [Swindler].

72. BRYN MAWR P 246 and P 984, two frr. Outside, (raised head of horse to
right; hindquarters of a horse to left and outstretched right arm of a male
to left who holds a cord in his right hand and in his left a pair of javelins.

The two frr. are probably from the same cup. That with the horse's head, P 246, is mentioned by Miss Swindler in *AJA*. 343, 342 as in the manner of Onesimos: she implied that it came from the same cup as no. 71, but this did not seem certain to me.

73 (O 12). SCHWERIN 1307. I, Pretzell 72 fig. 58, 4. I, youth. A, youth leading horses; B, boys and horses. On I, ARIΣTAR+OΣ KALOΣ. On A, ARIΣTAR+OΣ. On B, retr., KALOΣ NAI+I.

73 *bis*. BASLE, Cahn, 56. I, discus-thrower (bending to right, discus in left hand). A, hunting boar; B, hunting deer.

74 (P 1). CRACOW 31, from Vulci. Hartwig pl. 11, whence (I) Robert *Herm*. 229; *V.Pol*. pl. 8, 1 and pl. 9, 1–4; *CV*. pl. 8, 1. I, komast; A–B, komos. On I, KALOΣ AΘENOΔOT[O]Σ. On A, AΘENOΔOTOΣ. On B, KAL[OΣ]. [Hartwig E.]. Restored. Early.

75 (PP 8, O 18, +). LOUVRE G 28. I, komast (youth moving to right, stick in left hand); A–B, komos (A, two youths and a woman; B, three youths). Many Louvre frr. (including G 161 *bis*) join the original fr. G 28, and the cup is preserved in great part.

76 (P 31). BOSTON 95.27, from near Viterbo. *Burl*. *1888* pll. 4–6 = Fröhner *Brant*. pll. 10–14; Hartwig pl. 48, 1 and pl. 47, whence Perrot 10, 769–71, Hoppin i, 387, and Pfuhl figs. 409–11 (whence, B, *Mnem*. 4th ser., 3, 199); I, Eckstein fig. 12; I, Chase *Guide* 65; I, *Harv*. *St*. 52 pl. 4; CB. ii pll. 41–42. I, komos; A–B, komos. On I, EVΦRONIOΣEΓOΓIEΣEN. On A, retr., ΓANAITIOΣ KALOΣ. On B, ΓANAITIOΣ KALOΣ. See CB. ii, 31–33, and, for the shape, Bloesch 71, Euphronios no. 6. Still early.

77 (P 32). LENINGRAD 651, from Capua. Hartwig pl. 48, 2 and pl. 49, whence Perrot 10, 773–5 and (A) Pfuhl fig. 406; I and A, *Anz*. 1913, 93; A, Peredolskaya *K probleme* 166. I, komos: man vomiting, helped by a boy; A–B, komos. [Hartwig E.]. Restored. Still early.

78 (Pa 13). CAB. MÉD. 591, 563, plus, frr. Part of I, de Ridder 441. I, komos (male and flute-girl); A–B, komos.

79 (Pa 5). FLORENCE 4 B 6, fr. *CV*. pl. 4, B 6. A, komos (bald man playing the lyre and singing). Florence *CV*. pl. 4, B 7 is not in the same style (as was stated in *CF*.).

80 (O 13). ERLANGEN Pr 20 (ex Preyss). I, ph. R.I. 2853. I, komast (youth vomiting); A–B, komos. On I, ΓANAITIOϞ and on the basin KALOϞ.

81 (O 14). FLORENCE V., from Chiusi. I, komast (bearded, bending); A–B, komos (on each half, naked woman between youth and man).

82 (O 15). BOSTON 10.211, VILLA GIULIA, and FLORENCE. I, incomplete, *VA*. 88; part of the Florence part, *CV*. pl. 6 B 35; all, CB. ii pl. 43, 80, suppl. pl. 8, 1, and suppl. pl. 9. I, komast; A–B, komos. See CB. ii, 33–34.

83 (O 17). FLORENCE PD 383, fr. I, love-making? (on the right, part of a youthful head, probably a girl's, remains); A, komos.

84 (O 19). FLORENCE 11 B 68, fr. *CV*. pl. 11, B 68. A, komos? (neck, chest, left arm, of a youth with a stick).

85 (O 20). ERLANGEN 459 d, fr. A, komos (fair-haired youth dancing, hand on head).

86 (O 21). DRESDEN, fr. A, komos, or love-making? (upper part of a youth, seen from behind, head to left, then a jug and a stick).

86 *bis*. LUCERNE MARKET (A.A.). I, komast (elderly man kneeling). A–B, love-making. Still early.

87. LOUVRE C 11337, two frr. I, komast (the end of his stick remains, and suspended, a flute-case); A–B, love-making. A much-worn fragment in the Louvre might belong (outside, beard and arm to right, chin, back, arm of one—a woman?—to left).

88. LOUVRE C 11338. I, symposion (youth reclining, tying a long sash round his head); A–B, symposion: A, two males reclining; B, a male and a naked woman reclining. Early. See the next.

89. LOUVRE C 11339, fr. A, symposion (what remains is head and right shoulder of a naked woman to left; on the left, part of a cup held high— by her?; on the right, fingers—hers?). May belong to Louvre C 11338 (no. 88). Early.

90. LOUVRE C 11340, fr. I, (maeander). A, symposion (on the right, head and breast of a naked woman to left). Early. A Louvre fragment, C 11341, might perhaps belong: I, (maeander); outside, half a handle, and to left of it, hair wreathed with ivy.

90 *bis*. REGGIO C 1140, fr., from Reggio. I, komast (part of the head remains, and one hand with a skyphos); A, symposion.

91 (P 16). FLORENCE 10 B 106 and HEIDELBERG 55, frr. The Florence part, *CV*. pl. 6, B 43 and pl. 10, 106, and *CF*. pl. Y, 15; the Heidelberg fr., Kraiker pl. 9. I, komos (a drunk man led by a naked girl); A–B, symposion (naked women reclining). Early. See p. 1645.

92 (P 30). VILLA GIULIA 18558, from Falerii. I, *Hesp*., 8th suppl., pl. 2, 2. I, komast (man vomiting); A–B, symposion. Still early.

93 (O 55). OXFORD G 138. 3, 5, and 11, frr., from Naucratis. One fr., *BSA*. 5, 65, whence Walters *H.A.P.* ii, 264; part, *JHS*. 25 pl. 7, 4–5 and pl. 6, 5, whence (one fr.) FR. iii, 90 = Birt *Buchrolle* 148 fig. 80 = *Bonner Jahrbücher* 123, 279; *CV*. pl. 14, 27–31. I, man and seated youth: the man is no doubt dictating; A–B, school. For the writing on the roll see *AJA*. 1948, 337–8.

93 *bis*. OXFORD, Beazley, fr. I, (part of the border remains, with a morsel of the picture). A, (lower part of a naked male, fattish, squatting frontal). Early. Compare no. 12 *bis*? See p. 1645.

94 (P 17). BONN 349, fr. *CV*. pl. 3, 3. A, (woman, man seated playing the lyre and singing). ΓΑΝΑΙ[ΤΙΟ$ ... Still early.

95. NAPLES, Astarita, 312, fr. I, athlete? (chest to mid-thighs of a naked male to right). A, athletes? (foot of one running to left, foot of one running to right). Early.

96. FLORENCE, fr. A, komos? (penis to near mid-thighs of a male to left, cloak over both arms). Worn. Early.

97. LOUVRE C 11342, fr. A, (shoulder to mid-thigh of a man or youth leaning on his stick to right). Still early.

98 (Pa 4). FLORENCE 4 B 9, fr. *CV*. pl. 4, B 9. A, (flute-player: may be from an athletic scene, but need not be). Still early.

99 (PO ii 3). VILLA GIULIA, fr. (two joining). I, (no doubt an athlete, since part of a pickaxe remains). A, (pair of feet to right, end of stick).

100 (PO ii 4). MUNICH, fr. A, (waist to mid-thighs of a naked male moving to right).

101 (O 54). TÜBINGEN E 37, two frr. Watzinger pl. 20. Outside, on one fr., part of the right-hand figure, a male with a stick; on the other, a male with a stick.

102 (O 16). FLORENCE, fr. (Triangular fr., with, outside, part of the breast, middle, and extended right arm of a naked male to left).

103. BERLIN, Goethert, fr. A, *Anz*. 1958,14. Inside, white ground, or at least a white zone. A, (head, extended right arm, waist, of a youth leaning on his stick to left). [Peters].

(nos. 104–9, not known if decorated outside)

104. OXFORD, Beazley, fr. I, naked male (running to left, spits? in left hand). Early. See p. 1645.

105 (P 19). ELEUSIS 584, fr., from Eleusis. *Delt*. 9, 20. I, male leaning on his stick. Early.

105 *bis*. OXFORD, Beazley, fr. I, man seated, head bent, stick in left hand. Early. See p. 1645.

106. OXFORD, Beazley, fr. I, two workmen at a furnace, one poking, the other squatting and plying the bellows. Early. See p. 1645.

107 (P 15). FLORENCE PD 316, fr. *Hesp*., 8th suppl., pl. 2, 1. I, two archers. Early.

108 (PO ii 2). Once ROME, Curtius, fr. Ph. R.I. 37.444. I, archer.

109 (O 53). FLORENCE, fr., from Orvieto. I, (middle of naked male, moving to right, inscr. . . . . ΑΙ . . .).

(nos. 110–32; decorated inside only)

110 (Pi 1). BOSTON 10.179, from Orvieto. *AZ*. 1885 pl. 10; detail, Buschor 163; *VA*. 82; Langlotz *G.V*. pl. 8; Pfuhl fig. 414; Buschor *G. Vasen* 148; Schoenebeck and Kraiker pl. 83, 1; Lane pl. 72, a; CB. ii pl. 38, below, and and p. 25; the shape, Caskey *G*. 181 no. 136. I, satyr sitting on a pointed

amphora. LEΛΛROSΚΑLΟЅ retr., ΑΘΕΝΟΔΟΤΟЅ ΚΑLΟЅ, and on
the amphora ΚΑLΟЅ. See CB. ii, 25–26, and, for the shape, Bloesch 76,
Euphronios no. 25. Very early. [Meier E.].

111 (P 4, +). LOUVRE G 130, fr. Part, Pottier pl. 112; part, *Anz.* 1923–4,
170. I, komast. [ΓΑ]ΝΑΙΤΙΟЅ. A Louvre fr. joins the published one
on the left, adding the toes of the left foot and more of the stick. Early.

112 (P 3). SYRACUSE 22479, fr., from Gela. *Sumbolae de Petra* 81; *RM.* 46,
191. I, archer. ΑΘΕΝΟΔΟΤΟЅ ΚΑLΟЅ. Coral-red used outside.
Early.

113 (P 8). BRUSSELS R 348, from Cervetri. *Gaz. arch.* 1887, 112, whence
Perrot 10, 373; *CV.* pl. 1, 1; Verhoogen *C.G.* pl. 16, a. I, athlete with
pick. [ΓΑ]Ν[Α]ΙΤΙΟЅ ΚΑLΟЅ. [Hartwig E.]. Early.

114 (P 9). BOWDOIN 30.1, from Cervetri. Incompletely, *VA.* 86, whence
(redrawn) Richter *ARVS.* 62 fig. 21; incompletely, *JHS.* 39 pl. 2, 1 and
p. 83; R. M. Cook pl. 40. I, naked girl at krater. [ΓΑΝΑΙΤ]ΙΟЅΚΑ-
LΟ[Ѕ], and on the skyphos ΔΟΡΙЅ. Two new frr. found by Rumpf in
Leipsic and now added give the shanks of the girl (close together) and
the bottom of the krater. Early.

115 (P 18). ELEUSIS 607, fr., from Eleusis. *Delt.* 9, 19. I, youth seated with lyre.
... ΟVΚΟLΟИ retr., need not be complete aft. This should be [*B*]ουκολος,
presumably as a kalos-name. The right spelling would be ΒΟΚΟLΟЅ, but
ΟV is occasionally written for the impure diphthong, for instance in *Αυτο-
βουλος* (p. 68 no. 68) or in *Περιθους* on the amphora by Euthymides in
Munich (p. 27 no. 4); see also Raubitschek *Dedications* 281 and 383. Early.

116 (P 20). HEIDELBERG 54, fr. Kraiker pl. 9. I, male and dog. Still early.

117 (P 21). ATHENS, Agora, P 13600, fr., from Athens. I, (woman). Still
early.

118 (P 24). VILLA GIULIA, fr. I, (on the right, legs of two males—athletes?
—moving to left, side by side or nearly, and ΚΑLΟЅ retr.; two-line
border).

119. LOUVRE C 11343, fr. (two joining). I, komast (youth bending, his left
leg raised over a skyphos which stands on the ground; line-border).

120 (PO iii 1). FERRARA, T. 196, from Spina. Aurigemma[1] 63 = [2]65; Aurigemma and Alfieri pl. 8, a. I, satyr putting bunches of grapes into a
basket.

121 (PO 2). BARI, from Vulci. I, symposion (youth reclining, face frontal,
holding a sash). LVΚΟЅΚ[ΑLΟ]Ѕ.

122. SWISS PRIVATE. I, youth with hare (in himation, leaning to right, right
foot frontal, holding the hare by ears and hind-legs). LVΙΚΟЅ and retr.
ΚΑLΟ⸰. [Astarita]. Conefoot cup.

123. (Oa 14). VILLA GIULIA, fr. I, youth with ladle (in himation, right leg
frontal, leaning to right, ladle in right hand; four-line border).

124 (PO 5). PHILADELPHIA L 64.261, fr. I, komast (man to right, playing the flute).

125. LOUVRE C 11344, fr. I, (shanks and shod feet of a male standing to right, with the lower edge of his himation).

125 bis. KINGS POINT (N.Y.), Schimmel. Ars Ant. Aukt. II pl. 60, 153. I, stable–boy grooming a horse. LVΙCOˀ ΙCΑLOˀ.

126 (O 57). LOUVRE S 1324, fr. I, naked girl. The fragment Louvre C 11345 is Onesiman and probably belongs: on the left, right arm holding jug, and the inscription . . . ΙϞ retr.

127. LOUVRE C 11350, fr. I, (arm and foot of one running to right).

128 (O 58). VIENNA 1848. VA. 89; Lücken pl. 75, above; Langlotz G.V. pl. 19, 29; Licht ii, 122; RM. 46 pl. 20, 2; Eichler 11; JHS. 59, 114; CV. pl. 5, 1 and pl. 3, 7. I, youth with stick (in—entering—the palaestra).

129 (O 59). ROME, Mus. Art. Ind., from Tarquinia. Ber. Sächs. 1878 pl. 5, whence Benndorf Gjölb. 112 fig. 115; ph. R.I. 4400, whence RM. 38–39 pl. 2, 1 and p. 84 fig. 9 and RM. 46 pl. 21, 1; Schröder Sport pl. 100, below; Sparkes, Talcott, and Frantz fig. 26; R.I. 1866.33. I, athlete drawing water from well.

130 (O 60). BRUSSELS A 889, from Chiusi. Fröhner Brant. pl. 28, whence Perrot 10, 647, Sudhoff i, 49, and Jb. 30, 91; Bull. Mus. Roy. 1908, 83; Langlotz G.V. pl. 20, 30, whence Rumpf MZ. pl. 25, 3 and Frel Ř.V. fig. 158; CV. pl. 1, 3; RA. 1933, i, 156; Verhoogen CG. pl. 16, b; Robertson G.P. 105. I, naked girl about to wash. See p. 1645.

131 (Oa 9). COPENHAGEN, Thorvaldsen Museum, 105, from Vulci. Micali Storia pl. 97, 3; Panofka Bilder ant. Leb. pl. 15, 5; Langlotz G.V. pl. 20, 31; Cloché pl. 36, 1; B.Ap. xvi. 25. 2. I, fish-boy. [Langlotz]. Conefoot cup.

132 (Oa 10). ORVIETO, Faina, 65, from Orvieto. Jb. 3 pl. 4; ph. R.I. 1935. 858. I, mounted archer. ΚΑ[LOϞ] LVΚΟϞ ΝΑΙ+[Ι]. Unexplained the further inscription ΤΟRΙ (with room for a letter in a gap after the iota).

STEMLESS CUP

133 (Oa 16). ATHENS Acr. 205, fr., from Athens. Langlotz pl. 9. I, two males and a dog.

KYATHOI

134 (P 33). BERLIN 2322, from Vulci. Micali Storia pl. 103, 1, whence Klein Euphr. 283; Bonner Jahrbücher 123, 279 fig. 6; Neugebauer pl. 55, 2; Hof kes-Brukker pl. 11, 23; Zschietzschmann H.R. pl. 152. Youth reading and youths listening. ΓΑΝΑΙΤΙΟˀ ΚΑLΟ[ˀ] retr., and ΚΑLΟϞ. Restored. Early. For the inscriptions, +ΙΡΟΝΕΙΑ on the roll, and ΚΑLΕ on the box, see AJA. 1948, 337.

135 (P 35). CAB. MÉD. 848. De Ridder pl. 24 and p. 499. Satyrs and maenad. [Langlotz]. Restored. Early.

136 (P 34). ATHENS Acr. 463, fr., from Athens. Langlotz pl. 38. (Male, dog).

PLATE

137 (Pa 17). ATHENS Acr. 15, fr., from Athens. Langlotz pl. 1. Archer. Early.

Two small cup-fragments may be by Onesimos, but not enough remains for certainty:

(Oa). FLORENCE PD 115, frr., from Populonia. *St. etr.* 12 pl. 62, 3–4. I, symposion? EP[OOEMIᛋ] KAᒐOᛋ. The two frr. seem to be from the same cup.

_____

MANNER OF ONESIMOS

(i)

CUPS

1 (Pa 1). HEIDELBERG 52, fr. I, Kraiker pl. 9. I, satyr. A, in bf. on a coral-red ground, (bit of cloak). [Kraiker]. Early.

2 (Pa 2). CAB. MÉD. 534, 527, and 538 *bis*, fr. Part, de Ridder 401 fig. 99, and p. 397. I, Centaur and Lapith; A, Centauromachy. Early.

3 (Pa 3). CAB. MÉD., part of 577, fr. I, warrior pursuing a woman. A, unexplained subject (quarrel of Ajax and Odysseus?); inscription [?AᑎᒐA-ME]MNON retr. The outside of the fr. is described by de Ridder under no. 577 (p. 436, top), but coupled (p. 435, foot) with an interior which has no connexion with it. Cf. pp. 319–20 nos. 5 and 9. The exterior is extremely like the painter, the interior seems less so.

4 (Pa 9). BERLIN inv. 3376, fr. *Theoria* 64–67; *CV.* pl. 51, 5–7. I, white ground, (Eros). A, komos. Early. May be by the painter himself.

5 (Pa 11). ATHENS Acr. 434 (and a lost piece), frr., from Athens. A–B, Benndorf pl. 29, 1 (incomplete, but with the lost piece); A–B, *JHS.* 14, 383; Langlotz pll. 35 and 33, whence (I) Philippart *C.A.B.* pl. 15. I, white ground, Athena. A–B, one figure on each half: A, man with phiale and spear invoking Zeus; B, male pouring libation. On I, in the zone outside the picture, [EVⵁPO]NI[O]ᛋEⵁOIEᛋEN. On A, ᛍEVᛋOTEP retr., and, on the left, ICVI with the first letter of another word below it. On B, ᛋⵁENᐱOTOIᐱAIMONITOIᐱᐱAⵔ[OI]. The outside is near the painter, the inside not definitely so. Early. See p. 1646.

6. LOUVRE C 11346, fr. A, (part of a horse's mane and ear to left, with the inscription . . . IME . . .). [Ἀντ]ιμέ[νων] suggests itself, but many other names are possible. The fragment Louvre C 11346 *bis* might possibly belong: outside, on the right, part of a horse's tail—or a satyr's tail—to left, with the inscription . . . ᛋE . . . ([Εὐφρονιο]σε[ποιεσεν]?). Early.

7. LOUVRE C 11347, fr. I, (a sword in its sheath, hanging or held, not worn). Outside: on the left of A, a horse's leg to right; on the right of B, what

may be the heel of a sandalled foot moving to left; under the handle [κ]ΑLΟ*ΓΑ[ΝΑΙΤΙΟ*]. Cf. Cab. Méd. 526 (p. 319 no. 5). See the next.

8. LOUVRE C 11348, fr. I, (the lower end of a spear? and a toe?). Outside, (legs of a horse to left). May belong to the last.

9. LOUVRE C 11349, fr. I, (maeander). Outside, (a horse's leg to right, and and one leg of another horse).

10. FLORENCE 6 B 50 (part ex Villa Giulia), fr. Part of A–B, *CV.* pl. 6, B 50. I, komast; A–B, symposion.

11 (Pa 14). BOSTON 10.205, frr., from Capua. Hartwig pl. 36, 4–5; CB. ii, suppl. pl. 8, 2–3. I, seated woman; A, (woman spinning, and youth). See CB. ii, 33; and the next. Still early.

12 (Pa 15). HEIDELBERG 56, fr. Kraiker pl. 8; CB. ii, suppl. pl. 8, 4. A, (youth). Still early. Cf. the last.

13 (a). HEIDELBERG 65, fr. A, Kraiker pl. 9. I, (foot). A, (athlete). Seems Onesiman rather than Antiphontic.

14 (l O 52). LEIPSIC T 593, fr. I, youth leaning on his stick. A, athletes? (hand to right, then bare shin and foot of one moving to left). Also recalls the Antiphon Painter.

15 (Oa 5, +). LOUVRE G 296, fr. I, Pottier pl. 134, whence *Arch. class.* 2 pl. 10, 3; I, ph. Gir. 31352, whence *RM.* 46, 195. I, victor; A, boy wrestlers; B, similar. A fr. added by Marie Beazley gives one arm of the left-hand wrestler on B. The interior also recalls the Antiphon Painter, but the exterior does not.

16 (Oa 4). LOUVRE G 288, fr. I, youth (the hair remains). A, between eyes, athlete with haltēres. Two Louvre frr. join this, giving more of the right-hand eye; a third may belong. Also recalls the Antiphon Painter. See p. 51 no. 208.

17 (Oa 1). LENINGRAD 656 (St. 888). A, G.P. 49. I, athlete (a cord in the right hand is indicated in the incised sketch); A, wrestlers; B, athletes. Seemed to me an imitation rather than by Onesimos himself.

18. AMSTERDAM inv. 2815, fr. A, (youth).

19 (Oa). VILLA GIULIA, fr. I, (hair?, [H]ΟΓΑΙ*, and line-border). A, komos (youth with stick dancing to right, male dancing to left). Seemed Onesiman rather than Antiphontic, but I am not sure.

(nos. 20–33, decorated inside only)

20. HARVARD (ex Boas), from Greece. Klein *L.* 108; Hartwig pl. 44, 3, whence *Jh.* 12, 86. I, ἀφευομένη: naked woman filling lamp to singe herself. ΓΑΝΑΙΤΙΟ* ΚΑLΟΝ. Restored. Early.

21 (Pa 8). LENINGRAD 660, fr. Herford pl. 7, b. I, satyr. The head recalls the Eleusis Painter.

22. OXFORD, Beazley, fr. *AJA.* 1957 pl. 5, 1. I, warrior putting on his

greaves. ΓΑΝΑΙΤΙΟⳞ ΚΑΛΟⳞ. Early. May be by the painter himself.

23. LOUVRE C 11351, fr. I, male squatting, holding a sacrificial basket, his right arm extended (probably putting something—incense—on an altar).

24 (Pa 7). ATHENS Acr. AP 286, fr., from Athens. *Hesp.* 4, 284, 143. I, Herakles. ⊙ . . . Still early.

25 (PO iii, 2). ROMAN MARKET (Basseggio). B.Ap. xxi. 24. I, old man seated with lyre, singing.

26 (PO ii, 1). LEIPSIC T 3605, fr. I, symposion (male reclining). For the shape, Bloesch 128, Conefoot Class no. 13.

27 (Pa 12). ATHENS Acr. 432, frr., from Athens. Benndorf pl. 11, 3; Langlotz pl. 33, whence Philippart *C.A.B.* pl. 17. I, white ground, Herakles and Apollo: the struggle for the tripod (see *Gnomon* 13, 290-1). Still early.

28. ADRIA B c 17, fr., from Adria. Schöne pl. 12, 7; *CV*. pl. 26, 9. I, male with (weapon?).

29 (Oa 7). BERLIN, part of inv. 30894. Phs. R.I. 1930, 623-5, whence *RM.* 46 pll. 17-18 and pl. 19, 1. I, archer. [Technau].

30 (Oa 11). DRESDEN 301, from Italy. *Anz.* 1898, 136. I, horse-race (jockey). ΛV[Κ]Ο[Ⳟ] ΚΑΛΟⳞ ΝΑΙ+Ι. May be by Onesimos himself. Cf. Faina 65 (p. 329 no. 132). For the shape, Bloesch 128, Conefoot Class no. 7.

31 (Oa 12). ROME, Conservatori. *RM.* 63 pl. 42, 3; ph. R.I. 57.501. I, acontist. Conefoot cup.

32 (Oa 8). LEIPSIC T 492, fr., from Capua. *St. etr.* 2 pl. 44, 4-5. I, satyr riding donkey. For the Etruscan graffito, Rumpf in *St. etr.* 2, 404-5 and Danielsson in *St. etr.* 4, 259-60.

33 (Oa 13). TÜBINGEN E 16, frr., from Orvieto. Watzinger pl. 19. I, komast. ΛVΚΟⳞ . . .

STEMLESS CUP

34 (Oa 15). TÜBINGEN E 22, fr. Watzinger pl. 20. I, woman cup-bearer.

PYXIS
(type A)

35 (Pa 18). ATHENS Acr. 559, fr., from Athens. Langlotz pl. 42. (Seated youth).

(ii)

THE OINOPHILE PAINTER

ARV.[1] 217-18 and 955.

LEKYTHOS

1 (3). LONDON 1922.10-18.1, from Sicily. Haspels *ABL.* pl. 22, 4. Komos (youth and old woman). The γραῦς is ΟΙΝΟΦΙLΕ (retr.); a second inscrip-

tion is ill written and hard to read, ·POSHIΛΛMAS. The first letter is
smudged; and the fourth from the end might be omikron. On the wineskin ICA[L]OS, on the skyphos standing on the ground, ICALOS.
Miss Haspels points out that the shape of the lekythos links it with the
black-figured lekythoi of the Marathon Painter and that it is probably from
the same workshop.

KYATHOI

2 (1). BRUSSELS A 2323. *CV.* pl. 20, 1. Hare-coursing. kAL[OS] retr.,
kALOS retr., ΓANΛITIOS. Restored.

3 (2). BERLIN 2321, from Vulci. Gerhard pl. 50-51, 3-4, whence Klein
Euphr. 282 and Vian *R.* pl. 41, 373. Dionysos and Giants. ΓANAI-
TIO[S] kALOS. Restored.

Compare with these the cup-fragment

(a). OXFORD G 138.13, fr., from Naucratis. *CV.* pl. 14, 18. A, (youth).

Also the kyathos

LONDON E 808, from Vulci. FR. pl. 74, 2, and ii, 87; *CV.* pl. 34, 4 and pl. 35,
4. Fight. Restored.

(iii)

In the list of cups in the manner of Onesimos there were several fragments
that were said to recall the Antiphon Painter more or less vividly. A cup of
unusual style may be described as in the manner of Onesimos, but with
strong Antiphontic influence:

LOUVRE C 10891. I, youth (in himation, moving to left, looking round, with
stick); A-B, youths and boys. C 10891, put together from many fragments, includes G 317, C 212, and C 247.

Compare the cup-fragment

LOUVRE C 199, fr. Outside, (youth). I do not know that this might not belong to C 10891.

A cup-fragment may find place at the end of this chapter:

(a). ATHENS Acr. 441, fr., from Athens. A, *JHS.* 14, 382; A, Langlotz pl.
37. A, white ground, (Dionysos). The interior, so far as preserved, is also
white, with an inscription, of which ... PO ... remains, in the outer zone.
This might be [Ευφ]ρο[νιος εποιεσεν], cf. Athens Acr. 434 (p. 330 no. 5),
or might be [E]ρο[θεμις], cf. Florence PD 265 (p. 322 no. 29). The style
of what little remains is not remote from Onesimos.

The following cup-fragment was not attributed by me to the Panaitios Painter as is stated in *RM*. 63, 90 owing to a confusion with Brussels R 348 (p. 328 no. 113), which was misnumbered R 347 in *Att. V*. 168 no. 36 but not in *ARV.*¹ 213 no. 8:

BRUSSELS R 347, fr. *Gaz. arch.* 1887, 113, whence Perrot 10, 374 fig. 221; *CV.* pl. 4, 1; Norman Gardiner *Athl.* fig. 56; part, *RM.* 63 pl. 42, 1. I, athlete using a pick.

CHAPTER 23

THE ANTIPHON PAINTER

THE ANTIPHON PAINTER

VA. 111–12 ('Lysis-Laches-Lykos Group'). *Att. V.* 230–5 and 475. *V.Pol.* 26.
*ARV.*¹ 230–9 and 955–6.

Called after the kalos-name on no. 1.

His style derives from the earlier ('Panaetian') style of Onesimos, and runs parallel to the later style of the master. The two artists are sometimes rather close to one another, but the Antiphon Painter's figures are more massive.

It is not always easy to tell the Antiphon Painter from his imitators, especially in fragments; and a good deal of what is here classed, for safety, under the heading of 'manner' may be by the painter himself.

The cups are grouped according to the subjects of the exteriors.

SLENDER STAND

(1). BERLIN 2325, from Pomarico. Gerhard *AB.* pl. 67, 1–2; Genick pl. 14–15, 3; Langlotz *G.V.* pll. 23–24, whence (one figure) Rumpf *MZ.* pl. 25, 2; *Dedalo* 4, 738–9; FR. pl. 162, 1, and iii, 264; part, Neugebauer pl. 54, 2; Blümel *Sport u. Spiel* pl. 17, below; Blümel *S.H.* 82–83, whence (part) Neutsch *Sport* fig. 18; part, Diepolder *G.V.* 31; part, *E.A.A.* i, 438. Athletes. ΑΝΤΙΦΟΝ ΚΑΛΟΣ, ΑΝΤΙΦΟΝΚΑΛΟΣ.

CUPS
(nos. 2–26, decorated inside only)

2 (2). FLORENCE 11 B 5 (part ex Villa Giulia, see *JHS.* 51, 50 no. 36). Part, *Boll. d'Arte* 1928, 214; *JHS.* 51, 51 fig. 6; part, *CV.* pl. 11, B 5; *Boll. d'Arte* 29, 267 fig. 18. I, komast.

3 (3). ORVIETO, Faina, from Orvieto. I, komast. ΛV[ΣΙ]ΣΚΑΛΟΣ.

4 (4). BRUSSELS R 265 and VILLA GIULIA (see *CF.* 34 no. 18). Minus the Villa Giulia fragment, *CV.* pl. 4, 3; also Verhoogen *C.G.*, cover, back. I, komast.

5 (5). CHICAGO, Univ. *AJA.* 1938, 346 fig. 2. I, komast.

6 (6). VILLA GIULIA 12.2.1880, from Falerii. I, komast (moving to right, looking back, with stick and cup; billet-maeander).

7 (7). LOUVRE S 1426, fr. I, komast.

8 (8). VIENNA 212. Hartwig pl. 70, 1; *CV.* pl. 7, 1. I, komast. ΛVΣΙΣ.

9 (9). FLORENCE 10 B 180. Incompletely, *CV.* pl. 10, B 180, whence Bielefeld *Von gr. Mal.* fig. 9. I, komast (man dancing), and boy.

9 *bis*. BASLE MARKET (M.M.). I, symposion (youth reclining, right arm extended with flute, skyphos in left hand). ΗΟΓΛΙϚ ΙϹΛLΟϚ retr. He says ΔΟϚ (retr.). See p. 1646.

10 (10). BERLIN 2303, from Vulci. Hartwig pl. 70, 2, whence Richter *F*. 209; A and foot, Bloesch *F.A.S.* pl. 21, 5; I, ph. Marb. 1075.12. I, symposion (man reclining). LVϚIϚIϹΛLΟϚ. For the shape, Bloesch 79, Euphronios no. 52.

11 (11). COMPIÈGNE 1103. *CV*. pl. 14, 4 and 8. I, jumper. Early.

12 (14). CHIUSI 1841, from Chiusi. I, jumper. Very much restored (modern above the navel).

13 (12). MADRID 11269 (L. 152). Alvarez-Ossorio pl. 34, 1; Leroux pl. 16; *CV*. pl. 1, 5 and pl. 5, 2. I, athlete with strigil. LVΚΟϚ and retr. ΚΛLΟϚ.

14 (13). BERLIN 2314 and VILLA GIULIA (see *CF*. 34 no. 19), from Vulci. The Berlin part: Gerhard *TG*. pl. 13, 5–6; also Blümel *Sport u. Spiel* pl. 4, above. I, athlete pouring oil into his hand. L . . . (the beginning of a kalos-name). On the athlete's thigh, as if he were a statue, LΛ+ΕϚΚΛLΟϚ. On the pillar, ΗΟΓΛΙϚ, ΝΛΙ+I, ΚΛLΟϚ, each word in a separate line. The Berlin part much restored. For the shape, Bloesch 79, Euphronios no. 48. See p. 1646.

14 *bis*. WINTERTHUR, Bloesch. I, youth leaning on his stick, and boy athlete with his right hand raised and haltēres in his left.

15 (15). LEIPSIC T 516, from Orvieto. Hartwig pl. 62, 1. I, hoplitodromos. [ΗΟ]ΓΛΙϚ ΙϹΛL[ΟϚ] and on the shield LVΙϹΟ[Ϛ].

16. BALTIMORE, Walters. *Antike Kunst* 2, i, advertisement pages, 6; *Hesp. Art. Bull.* 8, 4 no. 4. I, hunter (youth and boar). ΛΡΙϚΤΛΡ+ΟϚ ΙϹΛLΟϚ. [Hecht]. See p. 1646.

17 (16). ABERDEEN 743. Gerhard pl. 162, 3–4. I, hunter (youth and boar).

18 (17). BOSTON 01.8030, from Orvieto. Hartwig pl. 62, 2; without the restorations, CB. iii pl. 81, 145; the shape, Caskey G. 196. I, youth with spear (light-armed; perhaps a περίπολος, as Hartwig). LVΙϹΟϚ [ΙϹΛ]LΟϚ. See CB. iii, text, and, for the shape, Bloesch 80, Euphronios no. 61.

19 (18). VILLA GIULIA. I, warrior (standing frontal, head to left, with phiale and upright spear; billets).

20 (19). VIENNA 2008. *Kunst u. Kunsthandwerk* 14, 259; *CV*. pl. 7, 4–5; ph. R.I. 1935. 1632, 1. I, warrior lifting his shield.

21 (20). LEIPSIC T 505, from Capua. I, warrior running.

22 (22). OXFORD 518, from Orvieto. *Vente 18 mars 1901*, 17; *JHS*. 24, 305, 518; FR. iii, 81, whence Richter *F*. fig. 102; (without the restorations) *CV*. pl. 2, 8; (redrawn, and the restorations reinserted) Cloché pl. 23, 5, whence (further degraded, and reversed) Béquignon *Il*. 156, 1. I, helmet-maker. Much restored. See p. 1646.

23 (23). GOETTINGEN H 70, fr., from Orvieto. I, youth (or girl?) lifting laver.

24 (24). PHILADELPHIA 2448, from Chiusi. *Trans. Penn.* 2 pl. 36, whence *AJA.* 1909, 210; *Mus. J.* 4, 162. I, acolyte (boy with sucking-pig and sacrificial basket).

25 (25). WÜRZBURG 485. Langlotz pll. 153 and 164; Bieber *G.K.* pl. 39, 2; A and foot, Bloesch *F.A.S.* pl. 21, 6. I, youth leaning on his stick. For the shape, Bloesch 80, Euphronios no. 57.

26 (26). BOSTON 10.199, from Orvieto. Hartwig pl. 63, 1, whence Perrot 10, 665 and Ebert xi pl. 54; *MFA. Bull.* 9, 53; Cloché pl. 37, 1; Stow pl. 1, below; CB. iii pl. 81, 144. I, she-ass. NIKOSTRATOSICA[L]OS and in the exergue LA+ESICALOS. See CB. iii, text.

(no. 27, not known if decorated outside)

27. NAPLES, Astarita, 260, fr. I, komast? (middle of a male with a cloak moving to right). [Bothmer].

(nos. 28–89, decorated outside as well as in)

28 (27, +). VILLA GIULIA, FLORENCE 6B2 and another fr., and NAPLES, Astarita, 266. One of the Florence frr., *CV.* pl. 6, B2. I, youth with stick (in himation, standing, back-view, head to right). A, a youth leading a horse towards a seated youth; B, two youths and a horse; one of the youths holds a stick, the other a brush. Two fragments in Villa Giulia join the cup. One gives, inside, part of the right arm and the S K of the inscriptions [H]OΓAIS KALOS, and, outside, in the left-hand youth on B, the toes of the left foot, with the lower edge of the himation and one of the horse's hind hooves; the other gives the right hand and buttocks of the youth leading the horse on A, with part of his chlamys. The first Astarita fragment gives the back of the horse on A and branches of the tree behind it. The second Astarita fragment gives part of one handle-area. A fragment in Florence gives the shoulders of the horse on A. Bothmer saw that another fragment in Florence (*CV.* pl. 6, B2) came from the same cup as the two Astarita fragments: it gives the back of the horse on B.

29 (28). OXFORD 1927.4603, frr., from Orvieto. *CV.* pl. 14, 6–7 and 32–38. I, komast. Outside, (youths, boy, and horses).

30. LOUVRE C 10896. I, horseman (with Thracian hat, cloak, boots, and two spears). A–B, between eyes. A, horse. See p. 51 no. 207. Two worn fragments in the Louvre, C 11352 and C 11353, each with part of a horse outside, recall this splendid cup.

30 *bis.* FERRARA, T. 41 D VP, from Spina. A, athlete. A–B, between eyes. A, horse (tied to a column); B, youth leaning on his stick. See p. 51 no. 210.

31 (29). ATHENS Acr. 281, fr., from Athens. Langlotz pl. 15. I, naked girl with skyphos; A, komos.

32 (30). ATHENS Acr. 282, fr., from Athens. A, Langlotz pl. 15. I, komast; A, komos.

33 (31). ATHENS Acr. 286, fr., from Athens. Langlotz 23. A, komos.

34. LOUVRE C 11354, fr. I, komast (moving to left, with skyphos); A–B, komos: on A, 1, male rushing to left, with skyphos, 2, naked woman squatting to right, playing the flute, 3, youth to left with stick; on B the right-hand figure is a naked woman bending to left.

35. FLORENCE, fr. A, komos (part of the head, and fingers, of one—a woman rather than a youth?—playing the flute to right, evidently seated on the ground; inscription . . . |ϟκ[ΑLΟϟ].

36 (32). TARQUINIA, from Tarquinia. I, komast (moving to right, with mug and stick); A–B, komos.

37. LOUVRE C 10901 (including S 1429). I, komast (moving to left, with stick and wineskin): A–B, komos. On A, 1, youth squatting to left, looking round, with stick, 2, youth sitting on the ground to left, playing the flute, 3, youth leaning on his stick to left, holding out a flute-case; on B, 1, youth squatting to right with skyphos, 2, youth squatting to right, looking round, 3, hand to left.

38 (a 20). Once PARIS, Morin-Jean, fr. R.E.G. 1919, 404. A, komos.

39 (33). HEIDELBERG 103 and 106 (joining), fr. I of 103, Kraiker pl. 16; A of 106, Kraiker pl. 20. I, youth. A, komos. On I, [LV]ϟΙϟ ΚΑLΟϟ. [Kraiker].

40 (34). HEIDELBERG 99, frr. A–B, Kraiker pl. 15. I, (male: bit of himation and foot). A–B, komos.

41 (35). HEIDELBERG 100, fr. Kraiker pl. 15. A, komos.

42 (36). AMSTERDAM inv. 2247 and OXFORD 1929.114 (joining), fr., from Greece. I of the Amsterdam part, CV. Scheurleer pl. 10, 1, also Langlotz G.V. pl. 30, 45; the Oxford part, CV. pl. 57, 1 and 4. I, komast; A, komos. On I, LVϟ[Iϟ . . . .

43 (37). DRESDEN, two frr. I, komast (knee with part of shank and toes, to right, with the end of the cloak); outside, komos (foot to left, stick, skyphos on the ground; rump, flute-case, hand).

44 (38). CAB. MÉD., fr. A, komos (belly, thighs, knees, cloak of a komast moving to right, leaning back, and toes of a komast dancing to left).

45 (40). CAB. MÉD. 636 and 708 (joining), fr. I, warrior. A, komos (male squatting to right, male rushing to left, male with stick rushing to right).

46 (41). NEW YORK 16.174.42. Richter and Hall pl. 65 and pl. 181, 62. I, komast; A–B, komos.

47 (42, +). FLORENCE 10 B 151, VILLA GIULIA, and NAPLES, Astarita, 261. I, incompletely, Boll. d'Arte 1928, 213, also CV. pl. 10, 151. I, komast; A–B, komos. The Astarita fragment, which had been assigned to the Antiphon Painter by Bothmer, gives, inside, the feet with the missing

part of the border below them, and, outside, the lower part of a komast running to left, with the hand and shin of another.

48 (43). ORVIETO 1048, from Orvieto. Incompletely, *CV.* pl. 5, 3–4; also (I) ph. Armoni. I, trainer. A–B, komos. On I, ⅃A+ES⅃KA⅃OS. Becatti (*CV.* p. 9) is mistaken in saying that the cup is uninscribed: the inscription can even be seen in Armoni's photograph. An unattached fragment gives the last three letters and the top of the wand.

49 (a 18). ERLANGEN 454. Hartwig 256–7, whence *Festgabe Erlangen* 36; I, *Festgabe Erlangen* pl. at p. 34; I, Grünhagen *Ant. Or.* pl. 22. I, komast; A–B, komos. [V. Wade-Gery]. For the chief inscription, Wilamowitz in *Hermes* 61, 282.

50 (44, +). ATHENS Acr. 261, frr., from Athens. Part, Langlotz pl. 14. I, youth at laver. A–B, komos. A fragment given by Ashmole joins 261 b, inside, below.

51 (46). ORVIETO 585 (452), from Orvieto. A, Vorberg *Gloss.* 109, 1; *CV.* pl. 6; phs. Armoni. I, komast; A, love-making; B, komos (naked girl sitting on the ground, drinking out of a pointed amphora, and two youths).

52 (45). VIENNA 107 b, fr., from Adria. Hartwig 643; *CV.* pl. 7, 2–3. I, symposion (youth reclining); A, love-making. On I, ⅃VSI[S . . .

53. LOUVRE C 11355, frr. I, (head, shoulder, one foot, of a bald man remain). A, love-making; B, the like.

54 (47). FLORENCE, from Chiusi. I, komast; A, love-making; B, the like.

55 (48). Once MUNICH, Arndt. Vorberg *Ars erot.* pll. 10–12; A, Licht iii, 192. I, symposion (youth reclining); A, love-making; B, the like.

56 (51 *bis*). DUNEDIN 39.108. I, youth. A, symposion; B, komos. A very informal symposion though. Restored.

57 (49). MUNICH 2635 (J. 705), from Vulci. I, jumper. A–B, symposion (A, two men; B, two youths). Restored. For the shape, Bloesch 80, Euphronios no. 59.

58 (50). ATHENS Acr. 287, frr., from Athens. Part of A, Langlotz pl. 15. I, symposion? (male right shoulder and extended right arm). A–B, symposion. On I, ⅃VS[IS . . .

59 (51). FLORENCE 4 B 55, frr. Part of A, *CV.* pl. 4, B 55. I, (maeander). A–B, symposion.

60 (53). AMSTERDAM inv. 2804, fr. I, (bare forearm). A–B, symposion. On I, ⅃VSI[S . . .

61 (54, a67, +). LOUVRE G 316. I, male leaning on his stick. A–B, between eyes: symposion: A, youth reclining, singing; B, male reclining. Many Louvre frr. join G 316 (among them S 133 and S 1435) and the cup is preserved in good part. See p. 51 no. 211. The youth on A sings HOΓAIS, retr.

62 (55). VILLA GIULIA 50430. *Dedalo* 4, 734–7, whence (A) Norman Gardiner *Athl.* fig. 46 and (B, redrawn) fig. 119; phs. G.F. 7174–6. I, man. A–B, athletes. I is restored.

63 (56). DRESDEN 304. *Anz.* 1892, 164; parts of A–B, Blümel *S.H.* 126–7. I, komast. A–B, athletes. For the shape, Bloesch 79, Euphronios no. 53.

64 (57). LENINGRAD 655 (St. 859). Hartwig pl. 61, whence *Trans. Penn.* 2, 143. I, boxer; A–B, athletes. On I, ⌐VⱯOϟ ⱯAⱢOϟ. Restored.

65 (58). BALTIMORE, from Cervetri. Hartwig pl. 64, whence (detail of A) Perrot 10, 629, (A) Norman Gardiner *G.A.S.* 437, (A) Norman Gardiner *Athl.* fig. 189; *CV.* Robinson pll. 17–18, whence (I) Buschor *G. Vasen* 153 fig. 172. I, boy; A–B, athletes (A, pancration; B, wrestlers or pancratiasts).

66 (59). NEW YORK 96.18.67 (GR 567). I, youth (in himation, with stick); A–B, athletes. Now cleaned.

67 (60). VILLA GIULIA, fr. I, (crown of a head). A, athletes (legs and one hand, holding a haltēr, of an athlete to left, then part of the himation of a male leaning on his stick to left).

68 (62). CAB. MÉD. 663, fr. I, male (the feet remain, one of them seen from behind). A, athletes (on the right, leg to right, legs to left with haltēr).

69 (63). CAB. MÉD. 665, 517, and 693, frr. I, athlete (moving to right, looking round, with haltēr); A, athletes (on the right, foot moving to left, and acontion, then the legs of an athlete moving to left, behind him an acontion).

70 (64). BRUNSWICK 558, fr., from Orvieto. *CV.* pl. 12, 5–6. I, athlete; A, athletes.

71. NAPLES, Astarita, 658. I, athlete; A–B, athletes . On I, youth in scrumcap standing to left, looking down, holding an acontion. See p. 1646.

72 (65). MUNICH. I, youth sitting on a rock. A–B, athletes.

73 (66). OXFORD 1914.729 and FLORENCE 9 B 38, from Vulci. *Mém. Ac. Brux.* 16 pll. 1–3; Gerhard pl. 271, whence Jüthner 40 fig. 35 and Norman Gardiner *G.A.S.* 473; *CV.* Oxford pl. 2, 5 and pl. 6, 1–2; Norman Gardiner *Athl.* fig. 52; detail of B, Gow *Theocritus* pl. 4, b; the Florence fragment, *CV.* Florence pl. 9, B 38. I, boy acontist and trainer; A–B, athletes. On I, ⱯIOⱯENEϟ ⱰAⱢOϟ. For the shape, Bloesch 71, Euphronios no. 10; the foot alien.

74 (a80, +). LOUVRE G 289. I, komast (moving to right, looking round, with skyphos and stick). A–B, between eyes. A, jumper; B, jumper. Many Louvre frr. join G 289, and good part of the cup is preserved. See p. 51 no. 212.

75. LOUVRE C 10897. I, discus-thrower (moving to left); A–B, hoplitodromoi.

76 (a 56, +). LOUVRE C 10905 (including G 320, S 1418, and many other frr.). I, hoplitodromos putting on his greaves; A–B, hoplitodromoi.

77 (67). BERLIN 2307, from Tarquinia. Gerhard pl. 261, whence *Jb.* 2, 105, Norman Gardiner *G.A.S.* 288 and *Athl.* fig. 96; I, Blümel *Sport u. Spiel* pl. 21; Blümel *S.H.* 63, 64, above, and 65, above; I, Stow pl. 8, 1; I, Schuchhardt and Technau 149. I, hoplitodromos; A–B, hoplitodromoi. Restored. For the shape, Bloesch 80, Euphronios no. 56.

78 (68). ATHENS Acr. 264, fr., from Athens. A, Langlotz pl. 14. I, (maeander). A, (hoplitodromos).

79 (69). AMSTERDAM inv. 2246, fr. I, (male). A–B, hoplitodromoi.

80 (70). FLORENCE PD 362, from Populonia. *CV.* pl. 97. I, youth leaning on his stick. A–B, hoplitodromoi. On A, ᒥ[Vᔓ]ᒍᔓᛕ[ᐱᒪOᔓᎏ].

81 (71). LEIPSIC T 3614, frr. I, warrior running; A–B, warrior running.

82 (72). NEW YORK 96.9.36 (GR 575), from Tarquinia. Richter and Hall pl. 62 and pl. 181, 61. I, youth with flute adjusting his phorbeia. A, youths and boy; B, youths and boy.

83 (73). CAB. MÉD. 555 (not 549), fr. I, youth (in himation). A, (male in himation leaning to right, toes of another person to left).

84 (39). CAB. MÉD. 701, fr. I, komast. A, (foot).

85. LOUVRE C 11356, fr. A, (youth leaning on his stick to left).

86. LOUVRE C 250 (plus), frr. I, (the end of a garment). A, satyrs and donkey. There are two frr., one consisting of three.

87 (74). ADRIA Bc 20 and B 69, from Adria. A, Micali *Mon. ined.* pl. 46, 3; A, Schöne pl. 6, 1; *CV.* pl. 6, 7–8; *Riv. Ist.* N.S. 5–6, 37. I, hunter? A, Herakles and the bull. B, Herakles and Antaios?

88 (75, +). FLORENCE 3920. I and A, *Mus. It.* 3, 253–6; *CV.* pl. 96 and pl. 116, 17. I, komast. A, Theseus and the bull; B, the like. A Florence fragment joins, giving the missing part of the bull's hindquarters on A, and part of the cloak to right of them.

89 (a69). LOUVRE G 263. Phs. Gir. 19312 and 17296, whence Grimal 104–5 and (A) Brommer *Her.* pl. 17. I, komast. A, Herakles and the deer; B, Herakles and the bull. On I, . . . ᑎᐱᒪᐱᐞᔓ. Now partly cleaned.

FRAGMENT
(of an oinochoe shape 8, mug?)

90 (a82). BOWDOIN 30.34, fr., from Athens. Eros.

MANNER OF THE ANTIPHON PAINTER

*ARV.*¹ 234–7 and 956.

CUPS

(*nos. 1–25, decorated inside only*)

1 (1). COMPIÈGNE 1102, from Vulci. *CV.* pl. 17, 2 and 5; part, Sparkes, Talcott, and Frantz fig. 19. I, cup-bearer. ᒪVᔓᒥᔓᛕᐱᒪOᔓ.

2. GREIFSWALD 316, two frr. Peters pl. 30. I, cup-bearer? (one with ladle at psykter).

3 (2). VILLA GIULIA, fr. I, komast (legs, dancing, with stick; line-border). Worn.

4 (3). VILLA GIULIA. I, komast (walking to left, looking round, skyphos in right hand, cloak on left arm.) Very close to the painter, but rather dwarfish proportions.

5. LOUVRE C 11357. I, komast (youth dancing, with crotala).

6. STUTTGART MARKET. *Auktion VI Kricheldorf* pl. 16, 42. I, komast.

7. LOUVRE G 314. I, komast. Perhaps recalls the Cage Painter (p. 348). Restored.

8. STUTTGART MARKET. *Auction xiv Basle* pl. 19, 75; *Auktion Kricheldorf 28–29 Mai 1956* pl. 27, 1274. I, komast. [Bothmer]. See no. 37.

9 (10). ERLANGEN 531. Ph. R.I. 1935.1628. I, youth seated playing the flute.

10 (4). VILLA GIULIA and BOSTON 03.840 (see *CF.* 34 no. 20). The Boston fr., *CF.* pl. Z, 2. I, symposion (youth reclining).

11 (5). PERUGIA 11. I, athlete. ᒐVᛕOᛑ and retr. ᛕAᒐOᛑ. Dwarfish figure.

12 (6). VILLA GIULIA, fr. I, (male foot to right, and shield on the ground).

13. LOUVRE C 11358. I, warrior running. ᛕAᒐOᛑ [ᒐ]Vᛑᛁᛑ. May be by the painter himself.

14 (7). ORVIETO, Faina, 110, from Orvieto. Ph. R.I. 35.902. I, warrior running. ᒐVᛑᛁᛑ, ᕼOᒑAᛁᛑ.

15. VIENNA 3702, frr. *CV.* pl. 5, 5–6. I, hoplitodromos or warrior.

16. LOUVRE C 11359, fr. I, youth (back-view) picking up his crest.

17 (8). DRESDEN ZV 1398, from Chiusi. I, trumpeter. ᒐVᛕOᛑ ᛕA[ᒐO[ᛑ. [Kraiker].

18 (9). VIENNA 2149. *F. Benndorf* 66; Lücken pl. 91; *CV.* pl. 7, 6–7. I, archer. Coarse forms.

19 (l 21). BOSTON 01.8073, fr. *Jb.* 14 pl. 4, whence Perrot 9, 338, Perrot 10, title-page, Richter *Craft* 72; Cloché pl. 20; *Technical Studies* 10, 8; *AJA.* 1960 pl. 85 fig. 3; CB. iii pl. 81, 146. I, vase-painter. May be by the painter himself. See *PP.* 10–11 and CB. iii, text.

20. LOUVRE C 11360, fr. I, youth lifting laver.

21 (11). FLORENCE, fr. I, male (frontal knee, stick or the like, and end of cloak). Should be by the painter himself.

22 (12). FLORENCE 9 B 24, fr. *CV.* pl. 9, B 24. I, (head and shoulder of youth). See p. 1646.

23. LOUVRE C 10910, fr. I, youth with stick (to right). ᕼOᒑAᛁ[ᛑ] ᛕA]ᒐOᛑ.

24 (13). ADRIA B 1036 (or B 1130), fr., from Adria. I, (feet and left shank of male in himation to left; billets).

25. LOUVRE C 10903, frr. I, naked woman.

(nos. 26–31, not known if decorated outside)

26 (72). VILLA GIULIA, fr. I, komast (middle, moving to left, stick in right hand, cloak).

27. LOUVRE C 11385, fr. I, warrior. May be by the painter himself.

28 (73). BRYN MAWR P 194, fr. I, warrior or hoplitodromos. May be by the painter himself.

29. LEIPSIC T 607, fr. I, warrior or hoplitodromos. Same attitudes as in the last.

30. (74). VILLA GIULIA, fr. I, boy moving to right, short garment tied round his waist, holding a dinos; on the left, a lampstand? Close to the painter.

31 (21). VILLA GIULIA, fr. I, komast (waist and thighs, running to left, with cloak).

(nos. 32–114, decorated outside as well as in)

32. LOUVRE C 10904. I, symposion (youth reclining, with drinking-horn and skyphos); A–B, komos.

33. NEW YORK, Bothmer. I, symposion (two youths reclining); A–B, komos. [Bothmer]. Bothmer notes that the foot of the cup is of Python's type. Recalls the Cage Painter (p. 349).

34. LOUVRE C 11365, fr. I, komast (booted; one shank and foot remain, with the toes of the other foot); A, komos.

35. LOUVRE C 11366, frr. I, archer? (part of one leg?, and, in the field, arrow and quiver suspended). A–B, komos. An elderly man vomits. Recalls the Cage Painter (p. 348).

36 (14). CAB. MÉD. 765, 809, 710 (which seems to consist of two frr. now labelled 710 and 750), frr. I, komast (bearded, with skyphos); A–B, komos.

37 (15). ROMAN MARKET (Feoli? or Depoletti?). B.Ap. xxi. 31. I, komast (bearded, moving to right, with stick and skyphos); A–B, komos. Restored. Late. Compare, perhaps, the cup in the Stuttgart market (no. 8).

38 (16). FLORENCE, fr. I, komast (on the right, cloak); A, komos (on the right, foot of one rushing to right, and toes of his other foot). Burnt.

39 (17). FLORENCE 9 B 55, fr. CV. pl. 9, B 55. A, komos. Burnt.

40 (19, +). LOUVRE S 1321, fr. I, (couch?). A, komos (male reclining, or almost, holding a calyx-krater). A Louvre fr. joins above, giving the upper part of the krater.

41 (22). GOETTINGEN, part of 566, frr. A–B, komos.

42 (23). MUNICH, part of S.L. 513, fr. A, komos (arm extended to right, legs of male rushing to left).

43. Louvre C 11367, three frr. I, (male in himation leaning, to left). A–B, (males: komos?). Damaged.

44 (24). Athens Acr. 304, fr., from Athens. Langlotz pl. 19. A, komos?

45. Louvre C 11368, fr. A, komos? (upper part of youth rushing to right, looking round).

46. Louvre C 11369, fr. A, komos? (head of youth to left, with crotala?)

47 (l 52). Goettingen J. 32. Jacobsthal *Gött. V.* pl. 9. I, youth with basket (of sand, in the palaestra). A–B, symposion.

48 (29). Roman market (Hartwig), two frr. I, warrior (right leg frontal, shield on ground—device a tripod—, spear). Outside, symposion.

49 (30). Siena (ex Chigi), fr. A, symposion (head of youth, frontal, drinking, head of youth to left, and his right arm, raised to his forehead).

49 *bis*. London market (Christie, *Cat. 14 July 1959* no. 64; ex Nathan). I, symposion (youth reclining, playing kottabos); A–B, symposion (A, two reclining, with a boy cup-bearer between; B, three reclining). [Corbett].

50 (31). Leipsic T 571, two frr. Outside, symposion. Leipsic T 3632, with part of a cup-bearer, might belong.

51 (32). Leipsic T 3579, fr., from Cervetri. I, (male in himation standing to left). A, symposion. On A, ΛVΣΙ[Σ . . . .

52 (33). Heidelberg 104, fr. Kraiker pll. 16 and 18. I, youth starting hare (coursing). A, symposion.

53. Louvre C 11370, fr. I, (maeander). A–B, symposion.

54 (26). Munich, fr. I, (stick, foot). A, symposion? Burnt. May be by the painter himself.

55 (27). Munich, fr. A, symposion? (head of youth to right). Burnt.

56 (28, +). Louvre G 315, frr. I, (foot). A–B, symposion. Several Louvre fragments belong and some join. Outskirts of the group.

57. Louvre C 10898. I, komast. A, wrestlers; B, the like.

58 (34). Munich, fr. A, wrestlers (the head of the right-hand one remains). Burnt. Another Munich fr. (I, cloak, stick; A, leg to left) might possibly belong.

59. Louvre C 10908. I, komast. A–B, athletes. On I, ΛVΣΙΣ ΚΑΛΟΣ. Close to the painter; the figures rather short.

60. Louvre C 11371, fr. I, athlete; A, athletes (end of cloak, acontia, pillar, wand, foot to left). May be by the painter himself.

61 (l 61, +). Louvre C 10900 (including S 1430). I, jumper; A–B, athletes. Many Louvre frr. join S 1430, and the cup is preserved in great part.

62. Louvre C 11372, fr. I, discus-thrower; A–B, athletes.

63. Louvre C 11373, fr. I, youth with shield; A, athletes.

64 (36). Philadelphia 2444, from Cortona. *Trans. Penn.* 2, 140 and pl. 35, whence (A) Norman Gardiner *G.A.S.* 392. I, athlete; A–B, athletes. On I, ΚΑ[ΛΟΣ] retr. and ΛVΚΟΣ.

65 (37). New York 06.1133, Florence 9 B 11, and Villa Giulia. The New York frr.: Hartwig pl. 70, 3; A, McClees 95; A, Alexander *Gk Athl.* 11, 2; Richter and Hall pl. 66, 63; the Florence, (I) *CV.* pl. 9, B 11; the Florence and Villa Giulia, *CF.* pl. Y, 21–22. I, komast. A, wrestlers; B, athletes. On I, ᒷᐯᏕᛁᏕ. Very close to the painter, but the figures dwarfish.

66 (38, +). Louvre G 132, fr. Hartwig pl. 63, 2, whence (detail of A) *JHS.* 27, fig. 17 = Norman Gardiner *G.A.S.* 331. I, komast. A, athletes. On I, ᒷᐱᛕᎬᏕ ᛕᐱᒷᎾᏕ. A Louvre fragment joins, adding the right hand of the discus-thrower and half of the handle. Cf. the last.

67 (39). Cracow 1463 and Villa Giulia (see *CF.* 34 no. 21). The Cracow part, Hartwig 572–3, also *CV.* pl. 9, 1. I, komast. A–B, athletes. On I, ᒷᐱᛕᎬᏕᛁᏟᐱᒷᎾᏕ retr. On A, ᒷᐱᛕᎬᏕ . . .. Miserable style, dwarfish figures. Restored.

68. Louvre C 11374, two frr. Outside, athletes: on one fr., chin to buttocks of an athlete to left, and hand of another, with . . . ᑎᐱᛁᏞ+ᛁ; on the other, arms? of one, and extended arm of another. May be by the painter himself.

69 (40). Heidelberg 105 and (ex Villa Giulia) Florence, frr. (see *JHS.* 51, 50 no. 37). The Heidelberg fr., Kraiker pl. 17. I, (maeander). Outside, runners.

70 (41). Florence, fr. A, athletes (on the left, acontia, then a male arm and flank to right).

71 (42). Louvre G 292. Pottier pl. 134. I, discus-thrower; A–B, athletes. Weak. Restored.

72 (43). Leipsic T 3364, from Cervetri. I, boxer; A–B, runners. Late. For the shape, Bloesch 79, Euphronios no. 46.

73 (44). New York 07.286.48, from Chiusi. R.I., whence (detail of A) Jüthner 32 fig. 27, a, whence Norman Gardiner *G.A.S.* 320, a. I, discus-thrower; A–B, athletes. The New York cup must be that formerly in the Ciaj collection at Chiusi reproduced in the R.I. drawing; some fragments may have been lost. A different picture was originally planned inside, see *AJA.* 1953, 40, left. See p. 1647.

74 (45). Dresden, two frr. I, (frontal foot). Outside, athletes: on one fr., hand and shank of an athlete rushing to right, hand of another, bending to left with haltēr; on the other, face and upper arms of an athlete bending to left). Near the painter, late.

75 (46). Cab. Méd. 568, fr. I, youth leaning on his stick; A–B, athletes. Late; gross forms.

76 (47). Cab. Méd. 569 and 695 (joining), fr. I, trainer; A–B, athletes.

77 (48). Leipsic T 3580, frr., from Cervetri. I, athlete; A–B, athletes. Close to the painter.

78 (49, +). Louvre C 11375 (including C 192 and S 1420). I, barbarian: a figure like those on the cup by the Pistoxenos Painter in the Faina

collection (p. 860 no. 14), compare also the frr. by the Berlin Painter in Athens (Acr. 702: p. 213 no. 238): he stands to right, dressed in shoes and a long fringed or furry garment, and holding a phallus-staff. A, boxers or rather pancratiasts; B, hoplitodromoi. Should be by the painter himself.

79 (50, +). LOUVRE S 1419, fr. I, (hair of male). A, athletes. Three Louvre frr. join S 1419.

80. LOUVRE C 11376, fr. A, (athlete: middle, to left).

81. LOUVRE C 11377, fr. A, (athlete, neck to thighs, bending to left).

82. LOUVRE C 11378, fr. A, (athlete: his breast, right arm, back of head).

83 (51). VIENNA 2151. CV. pl. 8, 1–4. I, jumper; A–B, athletes. For the attitude of the right-hand athlete on B see BSA. 46, 9 no. 9.

84 (52). PARIS, Musée Guimet. I, man with hare. A–B, athletes. On I, LVSIS KALOS. Much restored.

85. LOUVRE C 10909. I, komast. A–B, athletes. Recalls the Cage Painter.

86 (54). FLORENCE, fr. A, hoplitodromoi (shield, arm of runner, KA]LO[S). May be by the painter himself.

87 (55). CAB. MÉD. 639, fr. A, hoplitodromoi (helmet, hand).

88. LOUVRE C 11379, fr. I, symposion (youth reclining to right). A–B, hoplitodromoi. May be by the painter himself.

89 (57, +). LOUVRE S 1428. I, hoplitodromos; A–B, hoplitodromoi. Several Louvre frr. join S 1428.

90. LOUVRE C 11380, two frr. Outside, hoplitodromoi or warriors (on one fr., on the right of A, shield of one moving to left, device a bird; on the other, shield and middle of one running to left, device a leaf).

91 (58). LEIPSIC T 3592, from Cervetri. I and detail of A, Kirsten L.V. no. 3. I, youth; A–B, youths. On I, LVSIS   KALOS.

92 (59). HEIDELBERG 102, fr. Kraiker pl. 16. I, man leaning on his stick; A, males.

93 (61). ERLANGEN, fr. A, (himation of male to left, youth with stick to left, ...ΠAIS...). By the painter himself or close to him.

94 (62). FLORENCE 15 B 11, fr. Part of A, CV. pl. 15, B 11. I, (outline of arm?; sponge and aryballos hanging). A, (on the right, stick, male with stick to left); B, (on the left, male leaning, to right).

95. GENEVA, Robert Boehringer. I, man (in himation, left foot frontal, head to left, stick in right hand); A, man, boy, and youth; B, youths and boy.

96 (63). FREIBURG S 128, S 148, S 149, and other frr. I, man seated, and woman; palmette border). Outside, males; maeander below.

97 (64). CAB. MÉD. 671, frr. I, youth with stick; outside, males; one is a boy.

98 (65). MUNICH 2619. Put together by Hauser from a Munich fragment and another ex Berlin 2297 (Hartwig pl. 35, 3 and p. 325). Jb. 10, 162–3. I, komos (elderly drunk assisted by a boy). A–B, men and youths. Late; gross, dwarfish figures.

99 (66). STRASBURG 838, and lost. Hartwig pl. 71. I, youth with armour. A, Nike and youths; B, youths and boy. What is in Strasburg is one handle, with part of the left-hand youth on A, the flower under the handle, and the basket on the right of B.

100. LOUVRE C 11381, two frr. I, (hand of a male and part of his cloak). A (on the left, bare leg and stick of one to left; on the right, feet of one leaning to left). B, (on the left, foot of one to left; on the right, legs of one to left). May be by the painter himself.

101. LOUVRE C 11382, fr. I, (feet of one leaning, to right). A, (youth and boy); B, (on the right, pillar).

102. LOUVRE C 11383, fr. I, male leaning on his stick; A, (male and boy).

103 (35). VILLA GIULIA, fr. I, athlete (mid-breast to mid-thigh, to left, acontion in left hand, . . . Α . . .). A, (foot to right). May be by the painter himself.

104. LOUVRE C 11384, fr. A, (head of youth to left).

105 (68). LOUVRE G 155, fr. A, *Annali* 1878 pl. E; A, Pottier pl. 123. I, komast. A, Herakles in the house of Nereus. By the painter himself?

106 (70). VATICAN, from Vulci. *Mus. Greg.* 2 pl. 85, 1; I, ph. Al. 35837. I, man leaning on his stick. A–B, Centauromachy. On I, ΛΑ+ΕΣ ΚΑΛΟΣ. Restored.

107 (53). CAB. MÉD. 772, fr. I, (uncertain remains). A, (on the right, shank and foot of a male rushing to left).

108 (71). FREIBURG, fr. I, (sponge, aryballos, and strigil, hanging). A, (foot of one moving to left, feet of one moving to right).

109 (77). VILLA GIULIA, fr. (three joining). I, komast (arm with wrap). A, (bare shank and foot moving to left).

110 (78). VILLA GIULIA, fr. I, (forehead and forehead-hair to right). A, legs, the left one frontal, of a male in a cloak leaning to left). May be by the painter himself.

111 (75). VILLA GIULIA, fr. I, (maeander). A, (knee and shank of a male moving to right).

112 (76). VILLA GIULIA, fr. I, (foot of one to right: billet-maeander). A, (legs of male moving to right).

113 (79). FLORENCE 11 B 64, fr. *CV.* pl. 11, B 64. A, (male leg, fingers).

114. HEIDELBERG 107, fr. Kraiker pl. 15. A, (athlete?). [Kraiker].

SKYPHOS

115 (81). ATHENS, Agora, P 2787, fr., from Athens. *Hesp.* 15 pl. 34, 58. (Trainer). May be by the painter himself.

RELATED TO THE ANTIPHON GROUP

I

THE CAGE PAINTER

ARV.[1] 237–8.

So called after the subject of the tondo in no. 2.

CUPS

1. LOUVRE G 295. I, horse-race (jockey); A–B, horse-race. Many Louvre frr. join the old, and the cup is almost complete. For the lebetes on pillars compare the limestone dedications in Samos (*A.M.* 55 Beil. 10–12).

2 (1). LONDON 1901.5–14.1, from Orvieto. *Vente 18 mars 1901*, 18; I, *Le Musée* 3, 78; I, *JHS.* 41, 126, whence *Die Antike* 6 pl. 18, d. I, boy seated opening a bird-cage; A, youths and seated boy; B, the like. Now cleaned. See p. 1647.

3 (2). LOUVRE G 318. A, Girard *L'éduc. ath.* 205 fig. 25; A, Pottier pl. 135; one figure on B, D.S. s.v. reticulum fig. 5935. I, komast. A, seated man, and youths; B, seated youth, and youths.

4 (4). TARQUINIA 701, from Tarquinia. Hartwig 343. I, seated man with boy on his lap; A, seated boy, with man and youth; B, seated boy, with youth (or man) and youth.

5 (5). FLORENCE V 53, from Chiusi. I, athlete (moving to left, haltēr in hand, bending). A, youth and males; B, three males. Now cleaned.

6 (6, +). LOUVRE G 134. I, Pottier pl. 113. I, komast. A, youths and boy; B, similar. On I, ⌐VƧIƧΚΛLOƧ. Many Louvre frr. join the old, and the cup is not far from complete.

7 (3). LOUVRE G 133. Pottier pl. 113; one figure on A, D.-S. s.v. scyphus fig. 6252; part of A, Villard *VG.* pl. 1, 1; phs. Gir. 31994–5, whence (I) *Hist. rel.* 170. I, boy cup-bearer; A–B, symposion. On I, [L]VƧIƧΚΛLOƧ. Restored.

By the Cage Painter or very near him, the

PYXIS

(*type A*)

LIVERPOOL 49.50.7. Woman at laver; youth with a table in front of him.

Compare also the cups, all in the manner of the Antiphon Painter:

1. LOUVRE G 391. Pottier pl. 140. I, youth seated, holding a bag (phormiskos). The handles have been added by Marie Beazley.

2. BONN. *Auktion xviii Basel* pl. 34, 115. I, youth seated, looking round. See the next.

3. PERUGIA, from Perugia. *St. etr.* 26, 260. I, Symposion (youth reclining, playing kottabos). As the last. Attributed to the Antiphon Painter by Bizzarri.

4. BASLE MARKET (M.M.) *Auktion xviii Basel* pl. 37, 116. I, youth seated.

Bothmer's cup (p. 343 no. 33) recalls the Cage Painter, and so do Louvre G 314 (p. 342 no. 7) and Louvre C 11366 (p. 343 no. 35).

II

THE ADRIA PAINTER

ARV.[1] 238.

CUPS

1 (1). ADRIA B 326, fr., from Adria. *CV.* pl. 7, 6; *Riv. Ist.* N.S. 5–6, 39 fig. 17. I, komast.

2 (2). ADRIA B 293, fr., from Adria. *CV.* pl. 7, 4. I, komast.

3 (3). ADRIA B 310, fr., from Adria. *CV.* pl. 7, 2. I, komast.

4 (4). ADRIA Bc 32, fr., from Adria. *CV.* pl. 7, 3; *Riv. Ist.* N.S. 5–6, 38 fig. 16. I, komast.

The following are connected with the Adria Painter, but they are no longer Antiphontic and they recall the Ancona Painter (p. 874).

CUPS

1. FERRARA, T. 45 C VP, from Spina. I, male seated with lyre; A–B, school (youths seated: on A, one holds stylus and tablets, the two others volumes; on B, one holds stylus and tablets, the second a lyre, the third a volume).

2. ADRIA B 471, from Adria. Schöne pl. 2, 1; *CV.* pl. 7, 5; *Riv. Ist.* N.S. 5–6, 38 fig. 15; *E.A.A.* i, 74, 114. I, naked youth trick-drinking. See p. 1674.

Compare with these the

CUP

NAPLES inv. 126058. I, satyr (moving to right, looking round, with stick and pelt). Restored.

III

THE GROUP OF BOLOGNA 440

I substitute this for 'the Group of Bologna 441' (*ARV.*[1] 238, foot). Bologna 441 bears a superficial resemblance to the three cups in the list that follows, but is in the manner of the Tarquinia Painter (p. 872 no. 18). Amsterdam inv. 2262 (*CV.* Scheurleer pl. 10, 4) should probably be separated too.

CUPS

1. BOLOGNA 440, from Bologna. Zannoni pl. 42, 4 and 7; *CV*. pl. 109, 2. I, youth.
2. BOLOGNA 450, from Bologna. *CV*. pl. 109, 3. I, youth.
3. VILLA GIULIA 8347, from Nepi. I, youth; A, seated youth, and youths; B, seated youth, and youths.

IV

ARV.[1] 239, IV.

These two fragments are close to one another:

CUPS

1 (1). OXFORD 1927.4076 a, fr. *CV*. pl. 57, 28. A, (jumper and youth).
2 (2). LEIPSIC T 561, fr. A, (youth leaning to left, holding up a flower).

CHAPTER 24

THE COLMAR PAINTER

THE BONN PAINTER

Att. V. 45. ARV.[1] *225–6.*

Called after no. 1.

These coarse cups are connected (1) with fight-cups from the later phase of of the wider circle of the Nikosthenes Painter (see p. 135 no. 13), (2) with the Pithos Painter, (3) with the earliest works of the Colmar Painter. The third connexion is so close that we must consider whether the Bonn Painter may not be the very earliest phase of the Colmar Painter himself.

CUPS

1 (1). BONN 1644. A–B, *CV.* pl. 2, 1–2. I, archer. A–B, Centauromachy.

2 (2). TARANTO, fr., from Taranto. *Dedalo* 2, 624. A–B, Centauromachy.

3. RIEHEN, Gsell, fr., from Vulci. A–B, *Vente xi Bâle* pl. 20, 334. I, satyr. A–B, Centauromachy.

4 (3). VATICAN 505, from Vulci. *Mus. Greg.* 2 pl. 82, 2; *Scritti Nogara* pii. 26–28; Albizzati pl. 70; A, *E.A.A.* ii, 135; I, ph. Al., whence Stella 557; I, ph. And. 42110; I, ph. Marb. 29176. I, centaur. A, Theseus and the bull. B, fight. For the shape, Bloesch 57 no. 8; for the partridge on the pelta the Philadelphia cup p. 134 no. 10.

5 (4). BOLOGNA 363, from Bologna. Zannoni pl. 105, 3–4; Pellegrini 178–81; *CV.* pl. 1, 1, pl. 2, and pl. 4, 3. I, fight; A–B, fight. For the shape, Bloesch 57 no. 3.

6. LUCERNE MARKET (A.A.). Part of A–B, *Revista I.N.C.* 1, iii–iv, 8–9; *Ars Ant. Aukt. IV* pl. 45. I, archer; A–B, fight.

7 (5). FLORENCE 4 B 33, frr. Part, *CV.* pl. 4, B 33. Outside, fight.

8. ARLESHEIM, Schweizer, from Vulci. *Cat. Sotheby July 5 1928* pl. 2, 2 and pl. 1; Schefold *M.* 169. I, woman with crotala. A, deer-hunt. B, athletes (discus-throwers, acontist, and jumper, with trainer and flute-player).

9 (7). AMSTERDAM inv. 2773, fr. I, (head and shoulders of youth to left).

10 (8). VIENNA 1862, from Chiusi? *CV.* pl. 5, 2 and pl. 3, 6. I, warrior.

11 (9). FERRARA, T. 475, from Spina. Aurigemma[1] 61, and 59, below = [2]63, and 61, below = Arias and Alfieri pl. 7, below = Aurigemma and Alfieri pl. 7, below. I, archer. IΠΠAP+OϚ. See p. 1647.

12 (12). FLORENCE D B4. *CV*. pl. D, B4. I, symposion (youth reclining). Manner of the symposion-cups by the Pithos Painter (pp. 139–41 nos. 23–63).

_____

Cup-fragments are close to the Bonn Painter and may be from his hand: ORVIETO, frr., from Orvieto. *NSc*. 1925, 153–4 (I take the three fragments to be from one cup). A–B, fight.

_____

NEAR THE BONN PAINTER

CUPS

1 (l 6). Once BRUSSELS, Somzée, 40. I, Furtwängler *Somzée* pl. 37, iii, 1 = *Vente Somzée* pl. 1, 40. I, warrior. A–B, between eyes. A, warrior crouching. B, nose? See p. 51 no. 203.

2. MADRID, private. I, satyr reclining (to left, looking back and down, right hand grasping head; in the exergue a drinking-horn. Manner of symposion-cups by the Pithos Painter (pp. 139–41 nos. 23–63), but better, better also than Florence D B 4 (above, no. 12).

3 (a). LEIPSIC T 502, from Italy. *Jb*. 11, 184. I, komast. Doubtful whether the inscription ΓΡΟⳞΕLΟΟΟⳞ was meant, as Hartwig thought, for προσ-αγορεύω.

4 (l 10). FLORENCE PD 356. *CV*. pl. 88, 5. I, warrior running.

5 (l 11). VILLA GIULIA. I, warrior running (to right, looking round, naked, helmeted; head and middle missing).

See also p. 135 no. 13.

_____

THE COLMAR PAINTER

VA. 81–82. *Att. V*. 227–30. *ARV*.[1] 226–9 *and* 955.

Named after no. 9.

His earliest works are very close to those of the Bonn Painter: see p. 351. His developed style was formed under the influence of Onesimos (in both stages of that artist's career) and the Antiphon Painter. He probably sat side by side with them in the workshop of Euphronios.

The cups are arranged according to the subjects of the exteriors.

CUPS

1 (2). ORVIETO, Faina, 48, from Orvieto. I, ph. Al. 32468, whence Philippart *It*. ii pl. 12, 1; phs. R.I. 1935. 887–9, whence (I) *E.A.A*. ii, 744. I, archer. A, boxers; B, boxers. Very early. See p. 357, foot.

2 (3). TARQUINIA (696?), from Tarquinia. I, athlete with acontia and athlete with haltēres; A, wrestlers; B, wrestlers. Very early.

3. LOUVRE G 27. One fr. of B, Pottier pl. 90. I, symposion (one reclining). A, wrestlers; B, similar. On B, LEΛΛRO[ϛ]. Several Louvre frr. join the published one: the lower parts of all four figures on A are preserved; and the left-hand figure on B. Very early.

4 (34). FLORENCE 3944. CV. pl. 85 and pl. 116, 10. I, warrior putting on his greaves. A, wrestlers; B, wrestlers. For the shape, Bloesch 78, Euphronios no. 37.

5. LOUVRE C 11306, fr. I, youth at altar. A, wrestlers.

6. LOUVRE C 11307, fr. I, (head of youth to right). A, (athlete?—bare leg to left).

7 (42). VILLA GIULIA (part ex Florence), frr. I, symposion (youth reclining to left). A–B, athletes: on one fr., the lower part of the left-hand figure on one half, a naked male striding to right, then a stick; on another fr., the feet of two figures; on a third, one foot of one moving to left, the legs of male in a himation moving to left, and part of a pillar on a base.

8 (7). FLORENCE C B 1. I, Boll. d'Arte 1928, 216; CV. pl. 10, 156 and pl. C. I, warrior. A, boxers; B, wrestlers.

9 (17). COLMAR 48 (ex Campana). I and A, Anz. 1904, 53; details of B, RM. 63 pl. 42, 4. I, symposion (man reclining). A–B, athletes. Restored.

10 (20). VILLA GIULIA (part ex Florence), fr. Part, CV. Fl. 11, B2. I, cup-bearer (boy with ladle and cup to left). A, athletes (three, running to right). Compare Munich 2667 (no. 11).

11 (21). MUNICH 2667 (J. 562), from Vulci. A, Jüthner 47 fig. 41, whence JHS. 27, 262 = Norman Gardiner C.A.S. 349 and Norman Gardiner Athl. fig. 142; A–B, RM. 63 pl. 41, 3–4; the foot, Bloesch F.A.S. pl. 21, 2. I, cup-bearer. A–B, athletes. Restored. For the shape, Bloesch 77, Euphronios no. 31.

12 (22). CAB. MÉD., part of 521 (L 27 only), plus, frr. I, jumper and acontist; A–B, runners.

13 (35). LEIPSIC T 577, fr. A, (athlete to right, looking round; on the left a pair of acontia).

14. ATHENS, Agora, P 20074, fr., from Athens. A, (athlete?).

15 (28). Once BRUSSELS, van Branteghem, 82 (later, market, Lambros), from Italy. I, Cat. 15 juin 1881 pl. 9 no. 213. I, youth running with hare. A–B, hoplitodromoi.

16 (29). VILLA GIULIA and FLORENCE. Part, CV. Fl. pl. 9, B 1. I, hoplito-dromos; A–B, hoplitodromoi. On I, LV[ϛI]ϛ kΛLOϛ.

17 (30). LEIPSIC T 3700, frr. Outside, hoplitodromoi. See the next two.

18 (31). LEIPSIC T 587, fr. Outside, (hoplitodromos). Belongs to Leipsic T 3700?

19 (33). LEIPSIC T 3622(?), fr. Outside, (middle of hoplitodromos or warrior, running). Belongs to Leipsic T 3700?

20 (a). LOUVRE G 24. Part, Hartwig 91–92. I, satyr reclining. A–B, fight. On I, LEΛΛPOϟ retr. Several Louvre frr. join the old. Early.

21. LOUVRE C 11308, frr. I, warrior (youth, helmet, wrap, running to right, looking round, with spear and shield, device a horse); A–B, fight.

22 (19). LEIPSIC T 3594, from Cervetri. I, athlete running with haltēres and acontia. A–B, fight.

23 (8). NEW YORK 14.105.9. I, *Bull. Metr.* 10, 124; Richter and Hall pl. 36, 37. I, athlete. A–B, warriors (pyrrhic). On I, ΓΑΝΙΤΙΟϟ retr. and ICΛLOϟ. The first letter of the name is more like √.

24 (9). LONDON 97.10–28.1, from Falerii. *JHS.* 41 pl. 3, ii, 1. I, warrior; A–B, warriors (pyrrhic). On I, ΑΘΕΝΟΔΟΤΟϟ. On A, LEΛΛR[Οϟ] KΛLOϟ and on a shield LEΛΛPΟϟ retr. On B, KΛLOϟ retr. and on a shield KΛLOϟ. For the shape, Bloesch 76, Euphronios no. 26.

25 (5 *bis*). WASHINGTON 136375, from Orvieto. I, cup-bearer; A–B, symposion. On I, L[EΛΛPO]ϟ and retr. KΛ√[O]ϟ. On A, [L]EΛKPOϟ [KΛLO]ϟ. On B, [ϟΑΝΤ]ΙΛϟ. Very early.

26 (1, +). FLORENCE 11 B 22, HEIDELBERG 96, LEIPSIC T 522, TÜBINGEN E 12, DRESDEN 305, BRUNSWICK 538, AMSTERDAM inv. 2215, and STRASBURG 848, frr. Part, *CV.* Fl. pl. 11, B 22; the Heidelberg fr., Kraiker pl. 13; the Tübingen, Watzinger pl. 18; the Brunswick and Dresden frr., and part of the Florence, *CV.* Brunswick pl. 12, 7. I, warrior. A–B, symposion. On I, ΑΝΤΙ[Α]ϟ retr., KΛLOϟ, KΛLOϟ. Early. See p. 1647.

27 (4). ORVIETO, Faina, 175, from Orvieto. I, ph. R.I. 1935. 898. I, warrior. A–B, symposion. Early.

28 (12, +). HEIDELBERG 95, FLORENCE, and VILLA GIULIA, frr. The Heidelberg fr., Kraiker pll. 17 and 14; the Villa Giulia fr., *CF.* pl. Y, 19. I, fight. A–B, symposion. Two frr. in Florence belong; one of them joins the Heidelberg and adds the foot of the falling warrior.

29. LONDON 1953.12–2.6, fr. A, (head and shoulders of a youth playing the flute to left: I take this to be from a symposion).

30. BARCELONA 467, fr., from Ampurias. I, García y Bellido pl. 98, 100. I, komast; A, symposion.

31 (10). VILLA GIULIA 16337. *ML.* 24 (Cultrera) pl. 7; *CV.* pl. 29; ph. G.F. 9160, left. I, jumper. A–B, symposion.

31 *bis.* NAPLES, Astarita, 688, eleven frr. I, cup-bearer; A–B, symposion.

32. LOUVRE C 246, fr. I, one at a column-krater; A–B, symposion (the left-hand youth on A, and the right-hand youth on B, remain).

33. LOUVRE C 11309, fr. I, komast? (shank, foot, cloak-ends of a male to right). A, symposion (youth to left, playing the flute, male to left, holding an empty cup by one handle).

34 (39). PHILADELPHIA 4871, fr., from Orvieto. I, *JHS.* 39 pl. 2, 2. I, cup-bearer; A, symposion.

35 (40). NEW YORK 16.174.41. Richter and Hall pl. 35 and pl. 179, 36; I, Richter H. 215, a. I, acontist. A–B, symposion.

36. BARCELONA 4296, fr., from Ampurias. I, warrior (parts of helmet and crest remain). A, symposion. [Trias de Arribas].

37 (41). ANCONA, from Belmonte Piceno. A–B, Dall'Osso 133, 4. I, satyr filling oinochoe at krater. A–B, symposion.

38 (44). VILLA GIULIA 50492, from Cervetri. I, youth with hare. A–B, symposion.

39 (6). FLORENCE 73749, from Orvieto. CV. pl. 84 and pl. 116, 9. I, Dionysos reclining, with satyr; A–B, symposion: A, satyr and naked maenad, reclining; B, the like. On I, LΕΑΛΡΟϟ retr. and ΚΑLΟϟ. On A, LΕΑΛΡΟϟ. On B, LΕΑΛΡΟϟ.

40 (11, +). LOUVRE G 78. One fr. of A, Pottier pl. 97. I, satyr; A–B, symposion: A, satyr and naked maenad reclining; B, the like. Great part of the cup is preserved.

41 (15, +). LEIPSIC T 490, VILLA GIULIA, and STRASBURG 850. I, satyr and maenad; A–B, satyrs and maenads. See CF. 34 no. 16. One of the Strasburg frr., with the upper part of a satyr, facing left, joins the Leipsic portion; the other Strasburg fr. has the middle of a satyr to left, holding a horn. See the next.

42 (16). LEIPSIC T 559, fr. Outside, (maenad). Probably belongs to the last.

43 (14). FLORENCE V., from Chiusi. I, satyr (running with kantharos and wineskin); A–B, satyrs and maenads. For the shape, Bloesch 70. Euphronios no. 45.

44 (18). VIENNA 1919. I, JHS. 39 pl. 2, 3; I, Licht ii, 134; Lücken pl. 79, 2 and pl. 97; CV. pl. 6, 1–3 and pl. 8, 5. I, symposion (youth reclining). A, satyrs and maenad; B, satyrs and donkeys. For the shape, Bloesch 76, Euphronios no. 27.

45 (25). LOUVRE G 135, from Vulci. I, Pottier pl. 113; I, ph. Al. 23731, whence Ahrem 75 fig. 73. I, symposion (man reclining and woman playing the flute). A–B, return of Hephaistos. On I, on a cup, LVϟIϟΚΑLΟϟ. Now cleaned. For the shape, Bloesch 73, Euphronios no. 16.

46 (24). FLORENCE V., from Chiusi. I, komast. A, Herakles and Antaios. B, Theseus and Skiron. For the shape, Bloesch 78, Euphronios no. 36.

47 (13). ATHENS Acr. 243, frr., from Athens. Langlotz pl. 13. I, fight. A–B, komos.

48 (26). VATICAN, from Vulci. Mus. Greg. 2 pl. 71, 4. I, hoplitodromos. A–B, komos. On I, on the shield-rim, L[V]ϟIϟ. For the shape, Bloesch 79, Euphronios no. 44. Restored.

49 (37). FLORENCE 7 B 9, fr. CV. pl. 7, B 9. A, (lyre, komast).

50. ATHENS, Agora, P 17531, fr., from Athens. Hesp. 17 pl. 68, 2. A, (birdcage, boy).

51. HANOVER. *Auktion xviii Basel* pl. 34, 112 and pl. 35, 112. I, youth leaning on his stick at a pillar; A, youths and boy; B, the like.

52. NAPLES, Astarita, 509, fr. A, (upper part of a youth leaning on his stick to right).

53 (27). HARROW 53, from Chiusi. I, cup-bearer. A–B, youths. On A, on a pillar, ᒷᐯᔑIᔑᐱᗅᒷ○ᔑ.

54 (a). HEIDELBERG 98, fr. Kraiker pl. 15. A, (back of a youth's head). Cf. Florence C B 1 (no. 8).

55 (23). CAB. MÉD. 607, 2, fr. I, (white zone). A, (youth with stick running). Cab. Méd. 605 may belong: I, (leg of one in a chiton); outside, (leg of male in chlamys). Cab. Méd. 607,1 may also belong: outside, (legs of an animal).

56 (42 *bis*). LOUVRE G 81, from Vulci. I and A, Pottier pl. 98; phs. Gir. 31990–1. I, symposion (two youths reclining). A–B, between eyes. A, boy with hoop and hare; B, youth. For the shape, Bloesch 70, Euphronios no. 3. See p. 51 no. 204.

56 *bis*. ITALIAN MARKET. I, symposion (youth reclining to left, looking round, holding a cup by a finger passed through one handle). A–B, between eyes. A, youth running with oinochoe and cushion. See p. 51 no. 205.

56 *ter*. FERRARA, T. 30 D VP, fr., from Spina. I, symposion. Outside, between eyes. A, komast (youth running). See p. 51 no. 206.

57. ATHENS Acr. 244, frr., from Athens. Part of I, Langlotz pl. 13. I, symposion (male reclining). A, between eyes, (foot and uncertain remains). Under the handle, floral of the same kind as in Louvre G 81 (no. 56). A new Athens fragment joins 244a on the right. See p. 51 no. 207.

(nos. 58–60, not known if decorated outside)

58 (45). FLORENCE 3 B 19, fr. *CV.* pl. 3, B 19. I, warrior.

59. VILLA GIULIA, fr., from Veii. I, warrior (running to left, looking round, with spear and shield, device a cup). Foot type C.

60 (36). VILLA GIULIA, fr. I, komast? (boy moving to right, looking round, in cloak: preserved from ear almost to knees, with a little of the left calf).

(nos. 61–73, decorated inside only)

61 (a). BALTIMORE, Walters Art Gallery, 48.1920. Furtwängler *Somzée* pl. 37, iii, 2 = *Vente Somzée* pl. 1, 36; *Coll. B. et C.* pl. 21, 146; D. K. Hill *Soldiers* 1; *AJA.* 1945, 505; *Bull. Walt.* 11, 7 (April 1959), 3, below. I, warrior. Very early.

62. LOUVRE C 11310, fr. I, archer. Very early.

63. NAPLES 2633. Ph. So. 11006, vi, right. I, naked boy running. For the shape, Bloesch 45, Kachrylion no. 8. Very early.

64 (5, +). LOUVRE S 1402. I, symposion (youth reclining). A Louvre fr., joining, adds the right-hand part of the figure.

65. LOUVRE C 11311, fr. I, komast (male moving to right with cup, lyre, and stick).

65 *bis.* LONDON, Embiricos. I, komast (youth moving to right with stick and skyphos). LVSIS KALOS. See p. 1647.

66. NAPLES, Astarita, 6, fr. I, two acontists. The border is a pair of lines.

67 (46). FLORENCE D B 5, frr. Part, *CV.* pl. D, B 5. I, symposion (youth reclining). LVSI[S] KAL[OS]. The fr. with the right arm is misplaced in *CV.*

68 (52). HARVARD 1925.30.128. *CV.* Hoppin pl. 13, 1–2. I, maenad.

69 (47). OXFORD 300, from Chiusi. Gardner pl. 22, 1; *VA.* 81; *CV.* pl. 1, 8; Norman Gardiner *Athl.* fig. 55; *Ashm. Guide* pl. 36, a. I, boy running with hoop and food. For the shape, Bloesch 76, Euphronios no. 28.

70 (48). VILLA GIULIA 48352, from Cervetri. I, satyr (with horn, moving towards a krater).

71 (49). TARQUINIA RC 1912, from Tarquinia. *CV.* pl. 10, 2. I, youth leaning on his stick at a pillar.

72 (50). ADRIA B 809, fr., from Adria. *CV.* pl. 6, 4. I, komast (running with lyre).

73 (51). FLORENCE D B 7. *CV.* pl. D, B 7; *Arch. class.* 2 pl. 10, 2. I, victor with hare.

RHYTON

(*donkey-head*)

74 (53). PARIS, Petit Palais, 367, from Capua. *CV.* pl. 28; Hoffmann *A.R.R.* pl. 1, 3–4. Komos (old man and youth).

The following recall the Colmar Painter:

CUPS

1. LUCERNE MARKET (A.A.). I, warrior (to left, naked, helmeted, with spear and shield, device four circles with the centres marked, attitude as in p. 354 nos. 23 and 24).

2. HEIDELBERG 72, fr. Kraiker pl. 15. I, youth (komast?).

The following cup is close to the earliest athletic cups by the Colmar Painter, especially Faina 48 (p. 352, foot, no. 1):

BOLOGNA 362, from Bologna. Zannoni pl. 97, 3–5; I and A, Pellegrini 177, whence (A) Pfuhl fig. 354; *CV.* pl. 5 and pl. 4, 1–2. I, athlete at laver; A, wrestlers; B, the like.

See also p. 1647.

THE PAINTER OF NEW YORK GR 576
ARV.[1] 229.

Recalls the Colmar Painter and Onesimos. See also p. 1648.

CUP

1 (1). NEW YORK 96.9.23 (GR 576). I, youth and naked boy (athlete?).
2 (2). CHICAGO, Univ., fr. *AJA.* 1938, 348 fig. 6. I, (youth). A, (stick).

THE PAINTER OF THE LOUVRE KOMOI

Rough work, somewhat akin to that of the Colmar Painter but on a much lower level.

CUPS

1. LOUVRE C 11315. I, komast; A–B, komos. On I, a youth plunging an oinochoe in a column-krater.
2. LOUVRE C 11316, fr. I, warrior (moving to left, with spear). A, komos. B, (youth). On A, the left-hand figure remains, a youth with a cup rushing to right, then the foot of another to right, with a pointed amphora. On B, the right-hand figure remains, a youth in a himation leaning on his stick to left.
3. LOUVRE C 11317, fr. I, (arm). A, komos; the legs of the left-hand figure remains, rushing to right; on the left, below the handle, a column-krater.
4. LOUVRE C 11318, fr. I, (maeander). A, komos (youth running to right, looking round, youth with skyphos running to left). See the next.
5. LOUVRE C 11319, fr. A, komos (shoulder, cup). Might belong to Louvre C 11318 (no. 4).
6. LOUVRE C 11320, fr. I, (maeander). A, komos (middle of male rushing to right).
7. LOUVRE C 11321, two frr. I, komast (running to right, looking round, krotala in right hand; between his legs a cup; ess-border); A–B, komos (A, two males and a woman; B, the like). See the next.
8. LOUVRE C 11322, two frr. Outside, komos. On one fr., head and right arm of a youth rushing to right, holding a pointed amphora; on the other, upper parts of a woman running to right, looking round, and of a youth to left. May belong to Louvre C 11321 (no. 7).
9. LOUVRE C 11323, fr. I, komast (part of a cup remains: ess-border); A, komos (lower part of a male rushing to right).
10. LOUVRE C 11324, fr. I, (foot to left). A, komos (two youths rushing to right, the second looking round and holding a stick).
11. LOUVRE C 252 and C 253, two frr. I, (the end of a couch?; maeander with billets). A–B, komos.

12. Louvre C 11325, fr. I, (foot to left). A, komos (on the left, youth rushing to right).

13. Louvre C 11326, fr. A, komos. On A, the right arm of the left-hand figure remains, a male with a skyphos rushing to right; on B, one hand, holding krotala, of the middle figure, and the upper half of the right-hand one, a youth with a skyphos bending to left.

14. Louvre C 11327, fr. A, komos (head, to left, and right arm of a youth holding krotala).

15. Louvre C 11328, fr. A, komos (middle of a male rushing to right, in three-quarter back-view).

16. Louvre C 11329, fr. I, komast (parts of shank and stick remain); A, komos? (leg of male squatting to right).

17. Louvre C 11330, fr. A, (one shank of the left-hand figure remains, with part of the other shank and of the rump).

18. Louvre C 11331, fr. A, komos? (on the left, wineskin).

19. Orvieto 589, from Orvieto. CV. pl. 7. I, symposion (male reclining to left, playing lyre); A–B, komos.

20. Louvre C 11332, fr. A, (upper half of the bent head of a youth to left).

21. Louvre C 11333, fr. I, komast (hand holding skyphos); A–B, symposion.

22. New York 06.1021.169. Sambon Canessa pl. 5, 79; AJA. 1917, 161. I, maenad; A, satyrs and maenad; B, satyrs.

23. Louvre S 1380, plus, fr. A, satyrs and maenad (satyr to right, one arm extended, maenad to right, looking round, with krotala, satyr to left, looking round). A Louvre fr. joins S 1380 on the left. See the next.

24. Louvre C 11334, fr. A, (head, to left, and shoulder, of satyr). May belong to Louvre S 1380 (no. 23).

25. Florence 11 B 11, fr. Part, CV. pl. 11, B 11. I, cup-bearer.

26. Basle market (M.M.). I, komast (youth scuttling to right, looking round, with oinochoe and skyphos).

27. Basle market (M.M.). I, woman cup-bearer (to right, moving towards krater, with oinochoe and cup).

The following cup-fragments may be by the Painter of the Louvre Komoi:

1. Villa Giulia, fr. I, (part of arm and cloak). A, (male foot, with part of a cloak, to right).

2. Florence, fr. I, komast? (a little of the hair remains, and of the fillet round the head; leftward maeander). A, komos? (waist, and part of the legs, of a male rushing to left). Damaged.

3. Florence PD 298, fr. A, komos? (forearm, hand, cloak, of one moving to right).

CHAPTER 25

THE TRIPTOLEMOS PAINTER

THE TRIPTOLEMOS PAINTER

VA. 98–99 note 1. *Att. V.* 151–5 and 473. *ARV.*¹ 239–44 and 956. *BSA.* 46, 7–15. *Charites Langlotz* 136–9.

Named after the stamnos no. 2.

Moiseëv, publishing the pelike-fragments in Leningrad (no. 20), saw that they were by the same hand as the Berlin cup 2286 (no. 59). Buschor (*Jb.* 31, 74–76) added the stamnos Louvre G 187 (no. 2) and the Nolan amphora Brussels R 308 (no. 16), and attributed the group to Douris on the strength of the signature on Berlin 2286. In *VA.* 98–99 note 1 I increased the group to eighteen, but rejected the evidence of the signature, being unable to reconcile the style of the Berlin cup with what is known of Douris. Buschor told me later that he had come round to my view.

It may be asked whether there are other links between the Triptolemos Painter and Douris besides the inscription on Berlin 2286. There are three: (1) on several of his early cups (Leipsic T 504, Leipsic T 513, Cab. Méd. 657, Adria Bc 62 *bis*, Lucerne market: nos. 35, 43, 36, 40, 41) the Triptolemos painter uses the same rare border as Douris on some of his earliest cups (pseudo-maeander with uprights); (2) on some of the later cups (Vatican, Berlin 2988, Heidelberg 81, Berlin 2286: nos. 49, 52, 33, 59) the cross-square is especially like Douris' (although the maeander element is quite different); (3) according to Bloesch (*FAS.* 97 and 99) the potter-work of Berlin 2286 and Louvre G 138 (nos. 59 and 61) is by Python the chief collaborator of Douris. In the figure-work I can see no connexion.

On the inscription of the Berlin cup 2286 see *PP.* 41–42.

Chiefly a cup-painter, the Triptolemos Painter has an important pot side, and some of his finest work is on pots. His early vases are all cups.

In *ARV.*¹ 243–4 I placed a number of cups under the heading 'Manner of the Triptolemos Painter', but I added that they must all, I thought, be early works of the painter himself. They are in fact so, and are included in the list that follows, where they have the letter e before the old serial number.

CALYX-KRATER

1 (1). LENINGRAD 637 (St. 1723), from Cervetri. Gerhard *Danae* pl. 1, whence Overbeck *KM.* pl. 6, 2–3 (whence *HM.* pl. 34) and Cook *Zeus* iii, 457. Danae: A, the golden rain; B, the chest. See p. 1648.

STAMNOI

2 (2). LOUVRE G 187, from Vulci. Inghirami pll. 36–37; *El.* 3 pll. 59–60, whence *Jb.* 31, 82–83; *CV.* pl. 20, 3 and 6; part of A, *Enc. Phot.* iii, 21, whence *Mél. d'arch.* 1950 pl. 1, 4, Stella 486; A, *Recueil Dugas* pl. 28, 2; phs. Gir. 19018–19 and four others. A, Triptolemos with Demeter and Persephone; B, Plouton (rather than Keleos) with Demeter and Persephone. For the subject of B, Simon *O.G.* 74–76. See p. 1648.

3 (3, 4, +). LOUVRE C 10834 and FLORENCE 19 B 41. Part of the Florence frr., *CV.* pl. 19, B 41; A, *Charites Langlotz* pl. 18. A, Marpessa. B, men and youths. See *Charites Langlotz* 136–9.

4 (5). HEIDELBERG 124, fr. Kraiker pl. 17. (Dionysos, Ares).

5. LOUVRE C 10835, frr. (Men and women). There are five frr., each composed of several. On fr. (α), a hand holding out a wreath, and a king seated to right. On fr. (β) (two joining), shanks and feet of one in chiton and himation seated to right, probably the king in fr. (α). On fr. (γ) the upper part of a woman to left, the right arm extended. On fr. (δ) (several joining), the lower part of the right-hand figure on one side, in chiton and himation, standing to left: this may be the woman of fr. (γ); also toes, turned to left, of the left-hand figure on the other side of the vase, with part of his stick. On fr. (ε) (seven joining), the lower part of the right-hand figure on this side of the vase, a male in a himation standing with right foot frontal, stick in left hand. In fact: A, king seated, and two women. B, three males.

6. LOUVRE C 10826, frr. A, (women). B, men. On A, a hand holding a mirror, and the arms and middle of a woman to left. On B, parts of three men. Reddish and damaged.

7. SWISS PRIVATE. A, fight: Ajax and Hector. B, mission to Achilles. On A, ΦΟΙΝΙ+Ϩ, ΗΕΚΤΟΡ, ΓΡΙΑΜΟϨ. On B, ΝΙΚΟϨ[Τ]ΡΑΤΟϨ ΚΑLΟϨ, and ΔΙΟΜΕΔΕϨ, ΟLVΤΤΕVϨ, Α+ΙLLΕVϨ, ΦΟΙΝΙ+Ϩ.

8 (6). LENINGRAD 641 (St. 1712). A, Zeus, Hera, and Nike; B, Nike and two men.

COLUMN-KRATERS

(nos. 9–11, with framed pictures)

9. LUND, from Cervetri. A, Triptolemos. B, jumper and trainer. On A, Persephone with flower, Triptolemos with phiale and ears of corn, Demeter with phiale. Restored.

10 (7). OXFORD 1937.1005, from Sicily. A, athletes; B, komos.

11 (8). VILLA GIULIA 50532. A, ph. G.F. 7173. A, komos (two men and a naked woman); B, komos (youths dancing).

(nos. 12–13, the pictures not framed)

12 (9). VILLA GIULIA, fr. A, Centauromachy (heads of a Lapith and of a centaur).

13 (10). ROME, Ruspoli, from Cervetri. A, maenad; B, satyr.

PANATHENAIC AMPHORA

14 (11). MUNICH 2314 (J. 1185), from Vulci. A, *Mon.* 1 pl. 26, 6; Gerhard pl. 244; A, Poland, Reisinger, and Wagner 198; *CV.* pl. 197 and pl. 198, 5–6. A, Athena with stylus and tablets; B, acontist.

NECK-AMPHORAE
(small)
(no. 15, doubleen)

15 (12). CAMBRIDGE 37.24. Millingen *Coghill* pl. 22, 1; *CV.* ii RS. pl. 11, 2 and pl. 17, 7 and 11. A, woman spinning; B, youth. See p. 1648.

(nos. 16–17, Nolan amphorae, with triple handles)

16 (13). BRUSSELS R 308, from Orvieto. *Jb.* 31, 78–79; *CV.* pl. 15, 3; R.I. 23, 20. Warrior leaving home: A, warrior and woman; B, youth. Restored.

17 (14). NAPLES 3097, from Nola. A, ph. So. 11069, iii, 2. A, warrior arming; B, youth.

AMPHORA
(type B)

18 (15). FERRARA, Museo Schifanoia, 265. A, Dionysos; B, satyr. Very much restored: little of B is ancient, and less of A.

PELIKAI
(nos. 19–21, with framed pictures)

19 (16). COPENHAGEN, Ny Carlsberg, 2695, from Orvieto. Poulsen *Etr.* pll. 12–13 and pl. 14 fig. 25. A, Triptolemos. B, Theseus and Poseidon.

20 (17). LENINGRAD inv. NB 3425 (ex Russian Archaeological Society, 33. 160–1 and 144 and 146), frr., from South Russia. *Zapiski* 7 pl. 2, whence *Jb.* 31, 76–77 and (A) Poulsen *Etr.* pl. 14 fig. 26. Uncertain subjects. A, god with goddess (Nike?) and one seated. B, (young hero and woman). The head of the youth on B is now lost.

21 (18). MYKONOS, from Rheneia (originally from Delos). Dugas *Délos* xxi pl. 3, 7. A, man courting boy. B, komos. A (pl. 3, 7 a) is by the Triptolemos Painter; B (pl. 3, 7 b) is not by him but by the Flying-angel Painter (p. 280 no. 18). For the subject of A see *Cypr.* 30–31, γ 18.

(no. 22, the pictures not framed)

22. VILLA GIULIA 48339, from Cervetri. A, man; B, youth. Wretched.

HYDRIAI
(with picture on the shoulder, not framed)

23 (19). OXFORD 1914.734. *CV.* pl. 31, 3–4. Music-lesson (teacher and youth, both seated, with lyres).

24 (20). BERLIN 2178, from Vulci. One figure, *Jh.* 6, 20; Blümel *S.H.* 84; Greifenhagen *A.K.* pl. 42, 1; B.Ap. xviii. 58. 1. Athlete and youth.

OINOCHOAI
(no. 25, shape 5B)

25 (21). VIENNA, Liechtenstein, K 135. Man with lyre.

(no. 27, shape 7)

26. GENEVA, Robert Boehringer. *Ars Ant. Auktion I* pl. 55, 116; Schefold *M.* 201, 214. Boy with lyre, and man.

(no. 27, shape 6)

27 (22). BERLIN 2189, from Chiusi. Inghirami *Chius.* pl. 68, whence *El.* 4 pl. 28; *F. Benndorf* 188; *AJA.* 1907, 424; Pfuhl fig. 792. Women in sacrificial procession.

(no. 28, shape 8C, mug)

28. TARANTO, fr., from Locri. Youth playing the flute (head and shoulders remain).

ALABASTRA

29 (23). LOUVRE CA 2575. White ground. A, woman with alabastron; B, woman with box.

29 *bis.* PROVIDENCE 25.087, from Greece. *AJA.* 1931, 4; *CV.* pl. 20, 2. Woman and youth. Not attributed by me to the Carlsruhe Painter as alleged in *AJA.* 1931, 4.

FRAGMENTS OF POTS

30. LOUVRE C 10837, fr. (Hand). Might be from a stamnos.

31 (25). VILLA GIULIA, fr. (Head of a woman in a saccos to left; above, egg-pattern).

32 (26). AMSTERDAM inv. 2278, fr. (Head and shoulders of youth). Perhaps from a Nolan amphora.

CUPS

33 (e 1, +). LOUVRE S 1423, S 1410, plus, two frr. I, discus-throwers; A, athlete with acontion, and jumper; B, two athletes (the legs of the left-hand one remain, and one foot of the other). Early.

34 (e 2). LOUVRE S 1413, S 1415, and S 1411, two frr. I, athlete scraping his leg; A–B, athletes: on A, athlete with acontion, jumper, trainer; on B, the feet of the right-hand athlete remain. Early. A fragment with a handle might belong.

35 (e 3). LEIPSIC T 504. I, hoplitodromos; A, hoplitodromos and trainer; B, jumper and trainer. Early. For the shape, Bloesch 78, Euphronios no. 43.

36 (e 4). CAB. MÉD. 657, 800, 669, 761, 642, and 635, frr. I, trainer; A–B, athletes (victors). Early.

37 (37). OXFORD, Beazley, two frr. (one composed of four). I, athlete; A, boxers.

38 (38). FLORENCE PD 301, fr. I, (bare shank and foot); A, athletes (toes, foot, acontion).

39 (36). TORONTO (ex Curtius), fr. Part, ph. R.I. 1936.332. A, (trainer). A fr. joining on the left gives his right foot and part of a pillar.

40 (41). ADRIA B c 62 *bis*, fr., from Adria. *Jh.* 31, 18; *CV.* pl. 17, 5. A, (acontists).

41. LUCERNE MARKET (A.A.). I, youth at altar. A–B, hoplitodromoi. On I youth in himation standing to right, holding a kantharos over an altar; A–B, three on each half, running. Restored. Earlyish.

42 (35). OXFORD 1947.262 (ex Richmond, Cook). I, *Burl. 1903* pl. 92, G 17; I, *Ashm. Report* 1947 pl. 3, a; *BSA.* 46, pl. 5, pl. 7, a, and p. 7, whence (I) *BCH.* 1957, 155 fig. 13; I, *Ashm. Guide* pl. 35, b. I, trainer; A–B, hoplitodromoi. See *BSA.* 46, 7–15.

43 (e 5). LEIPSIC T 513, from Orvieto. Hartwig 526–7. I, youth trying his sword in the scabbard; A–B, fight. For the shape, Bloesch 78, Euphronios no. 42. Early.

44 (e 11). LEIPSIC T 534, fr., from Orvieto. A, fight; B, (warriors, horse). Early.

45 (e 12). BERLIN 2295, from Orvieto. Hartwig pl. 56, 2 and pl. 57; I, Lücken pl. 82, 2; *CV.* pl. 64, 3–4. I, hoplite and archer; A–B, fight. Still early. For the shape, Bloesch 73, Euphronios no. 14.

46 (e 13). EDINBURGH 1887.213, from Italy. Hartwig pl. 56, 1 and pl. 55; Cecil Smith *Cat. Ed.* pl. 3, 1 and pl. 2. Fights: I, Greek and Persian; A–B, Greeks and Persians. Still early.

47. STRASBURG 851, fr. A, fight (upper part of a young warrior attacking to right).

48 (e 14). VILLA GIULIA, fr. A, fight (leg of a warrior moving to right, legs of an archer to left).

49 (28). VATICAN, from Cervetri. *Mus. Greg.* 2 pl. 86, 2; *Annali* 1875 pll. F–G; phs. Al. 35791–3; I, ph. And. 42074. Warriors leaving home: I, warrior and seated man; A–B, warriors and men. For the shape, Bloesch 85, Brygos no. 21.

50 (e 7). VIENNA 3692 (ex Oest. 322), from Cervetri. A–B, *Annali* 1878 pl. D; *CV.* pl. 3, 4 and pl. 4. I, youth with helmet and shield. A, Herakles and Antaios. B, Theseus and the bull. Early. For the shape, Bloesch 78, Euphronios no. 41.

51 (e 8). LEIPSIC, Kunstgewerbemuseum, inv. 781.03.G. A, Jacobsthal *Gött. V.* 45, whence *Jb.* 31, 146. I, komast; A–B, symposion. Early. For the shape, Bloesch 78, Euphronios no. 39.

52 (29). BERLIN 2298, from Vulci. *CV.* pl. 64, 1–2; R.I. M 34. I, porter carrying a sack past a herm. A–B, symposion.

53. BRUNSWICK 534, fr. *CV.* pl. 12, 4. A, symposion.

54 (e 10). Louvre G 311. I, Emmanuel 225; I, Pottier pl. 134. I, boy dancing and youth playing the flute; A–B, komos. Now cleaned. Early.

55 (31). Adria B 481, fr., from Adria. *CV*. pl. 17, 4; I, *Riv. Ist.* n.s. 5–6, 45 fig. 30. I, komast; A–B, komos.

56 (32). Florence PD 478, fr. I, man (head and shoulders, to right). A, komos? (legs of two males). [Spranger].

57 (33). Heidelberg 81, fr. Kraiker pll. 11 and 13. I, (male). A, komos?

58 (30). Louvre G 250. Pottier pl. 132; B.Ap. xxii. 100. I, satyr and maenad; A–B, Dionysos and maenads. Now cleaned.

59 (27). Berlin 2286, from Cervetri. *AZ*. 1883 pl. 4, whence Hoppin i, 217 and (A) Pfuhl fig. 465; I, *Jb*. 31 pl. 2; I, Pfuhl fig. 465. I, symposion (man and woman reclining). A, man, and man or youth, and woman; youth and woman; B, men and woman; man or youth, and woman. On I, ΛΟΡΙ5ΕΛΡΑΦ5ΕΝ. For the shape, Bloesch 97, Python no. 12 (the foot is missing); for the question raised by the signature, *PP*. 41.

60 (e 6). Tarquinia, from Tarquinia. I, komast (youth playing the flute). A, boy between two youths; one youth offers the boy a hare; B, boy between youth and man. Early.

61 (e 9). Louvre G 138. Hartwig pll. 65–66, whence (part) Perrot 10, 787–9, (I) Licht ii, 183; Pottier pll. 114 and 116; I, ph. Al. 23727. I, Dionysos and a boy (Oinopion). In a zone round this, procession of youths and men: A, procession of youths and men; B, marshal and spectators (a man and youths). Now cleaned. For the shape, Bloesch 99, Python no. 24 (the foot seems alien). Early.

62 (45). Freiburg, four frr. I, one seated and a male standing (1, toes to right, 2, legs of a male in a himation, standing with left leg frontal). A, (bare legs). B, males as if in procession, (two of them holding lyres). See the next.

63. Bryn Mawr P 210, fr. I, (on the left, a youth seated to right). A, (bare legs). Belongs to the Freiburg frr. (no. 62)?

64 (49). Naples 2645. *Mus. Borb.* 4 pl. 51; A, ph. So. 11006, iv, 3. I, youth; A–B, youths. Restored.

65. Louvre C 11312, fr. I, (maeander). A, (legs of two males in himatia, standing to right, with stick, the other standing frontal).

66. Louvre, fr. I, (maeander with Douris cross-square). A, (thighs of one in himation to left).

67 (34). Leipsic T 565, fr. A, (head of a flute-player to right).

68 (39). Adria B 113 *bis*, fr., from Adria. *CV*. pl. 13, 2. I, (columns). A, (on the left, male).

69 (40). Adria B 576 and B c 67, fr., from Adria. Schöne pl. 10, 1; *CV*. pl. 17, 6. A, (naked youth, youth seated).

70 (43). ADRIA B 1319, fr., from Adria. *CV.* pl. 15, 4. A, (male). Misnumbered B 761 in *ARV.*[1]

71 (45). ADRIA B 692, fr., from Adria. A, (middle of a naked male bending to right).

72 (48). FREIBURG (ex Technau), fr., from Orvieto. A, (head and shoulders of the left-hand figure, a youth wrapped in his himation to right).

73 (46). BRUNSWICK 536, fr. *CV.* pl. 17, 5. A, (youth).

74. CAIRO, fr. A, (head and shoulders of a boy in a himation standing to left). Lipped cup.

75. ATHENS, Agora, P 19574, fr., from Athens. A, (youth). Lipped cup.

76 (47). ATHENS, Agora, P 4688, fr., from Athens. I, (arm of one standing to right, head of youth in himation seated to left).

77. LENINGRAD inv. 6469, fr., from Berezan. *Zapiski* 7 pl. 1, 2, p. 98, and p. 99 fig. 20. I, seated youth. [Peredolskaya].

78 (e 15). TÜBINGEN E 42. Watzinger pl. 21; Schröder *Sport* pl. 60, 1; Blümel *S.H.* 36. I, discus-thrower. Early.

79 (52). LEIPSIC, from Cortona. I, athlete pouring oil into his hand.

80. LOUVRE C 10913. I, athlete and youth (youth in himation with stick, and athlete squatting on the ground).

81 (59). NEW YORK 14.105.7, fr. I, athlete tying his penis up.

82 (57). MUNICH, fr. I, youth (in himation, standing frontal, head to left, wand upright in his right hand).

83 (e 16). BOSTON 13.81. CB. i pl. 3, 13 and p. 10; the shape, Caskey G. 195 no. 149. I, komast. Early.

84 (56). FLORENCE 11 B 9. *Boll. d'Arte* 1928, 212; *CV.* pl. 11, B 9. I, komast (youth playing the flute).

85 (61). TARQUINIA RC 1916, from Tarquinia. I, youth (in himation, standing frontal, head to right, with stick; on the right a laver).

86 (50, +). LOUVRE G 245. I, komast (youth with lyre; in front of him a column-krater, behind him a herm). Two Louvre fragments join and have been added: they give the feet and parts of the maeander, and one of them reaches the rim.

87 (51). ATHENS Acr. 256, fr., from Athens. I, male at herm. For the graffito see Peek in Langlotz ii, 130.

88 (53). TARQUINIA RC 1918, from Tarquinia. I, man with cup praying at altar.

89. NAPLES, Astarita, 574. I, acolyte (youth standing at a block with the severed head of a bull lying on it; the right hand may have held a chopper).

90 (54). MUNICH 2672. I, youth taking his shield down.

91. BASLE MARKET (M.M.). I, youth (in himation, standing to left, stick in right hand; on the left, seat; on the right, suspended, aryballos and strigil).

92 (60). Once MUNICH, fr. Ph. Mus. I, satyr (running to left, looking round, with a pelta, to which a panther-skin is attached by way of apron).

93 (e 17). TARQUINIA, from Tarquinia. FR. iii, 252 fig. 119, whence Vorberg *Ars erot.* pl. 18, 1; ph. Mo. 8269, 1, whence Vorberg *Ars erot.* pl. 17, 1; *CV.* pl. 11, 2; ph. R.I. 1934.2218. I, love-making (man and woman). Early.

94 (55). TARQUINIA, from Tarquinia. Vorberg *Gloss.* 44; *CV.* pl. 11, 1; ph. R.I. 1934.2217. I, love-making (baldhead and woman).

95 (58). NORWICH, fr. I, (head of youth to left).

96. LOUVRE C 11313, fr. I, (foot).

SKYPHOI
(no. 97, type A)

97 (62). CAB. MÉD. 839, from Nola. A, Raoul-Rochette *Lettres arch.* pl. 1, whence *El.* 3 pl. 80 and Gerhard *Ak. Abh.* pl. 63, 4. A, herm; B, youth at altar.

(nos. 98–101, type A or B)

98 (63). ADRIA B 454 and B 63, fr., from Adria. *CV.* pl. 8, 4. Herm.

99 (64). ADRIA B 556, fr., from Adria. *CV.* pl. 8, 3; *Riv. Ist.* N.S. 5–6, 47 fig. 33. Youth.

100 (65). ADRIA B 495, fr., from Adria. *CV.* pl. 33, 4. Male.

101 (66). ELEUSIS 593, fr., from Eleusis. *Delt.* 9, 32 fig. 34, 1. Herm.

(nos. 102–5, type B, glaukes)

102. MAPLEWOOD, Noble, from Vulci. Cecil Smith *Forman* pl. 11, 358; A, *Burl. 1903* pl. 96, I 80; *BSA.* 46 pl. 6, c–d, whence (A) *BCH.* 1957, 151; A, *Cat. Christie July 14 1959* pl. 6, 3. A, athlete using the pick; B, athlete seated on the ground watching him. See *BSA.* 46, 15. Was not in the Melchett collection as stated in *ARV.*[1] 956, top. See p. 1648.

103 (67). SALERNO 1131, from Fratte. A, *St. etr.* 3 pl. 11, below, left. A, athlete; B, youth.

104 (68). BERLIN 2594, from Nola. *CV.* pl. 141, 1 and 3. A, herm; B, herm.

105 (69). MUNICH 2551 (J. 763), from Sicily. *CV.* pl. 95, 3–4. A, satyr threatening, B, satyr.

The following recall the Triptolemos Painter:

CUP
LOUVRE C 11314, fr. I, male (bare legs and the end of a cloak). Early.

LEKYTHOS
(standard shape)
PALERMO V 693. *CV.* pl. 22, 4–5. Woman spinning.

CHAPTER 26

THE BRYGOS PAINTER AND HIS CIRCLE

THERE are fourteen signatures of Brygos, all on cups. The verb where preserved is always ἐποίησεν. One of the cups is lost and nothing is known about the style (p. 398 no. 10). Of three others a handle is all that remains (p. 398 nos. 11–13). The five finest of the rest were decorated by a single artist, whom we call 'the Brygos Painter' (p. 398 nos. 2–6). The tenth cup (p. 398 no. 7), weak, is in the manner of the master, and resembles the work of the Castelgiorgio Painter, an imitator of his. The eleventh is by a follower of the Brygos Painter, the Briseis Painter (p. 398 no. 8), and was evidently painted under the master's influence and indeed from his designs. The twelfth (p. 398 no. 9) is by a fourth artist, who bears no special relation to the Brygos Painter. The thirteenth (p. 398 no. 1), very fragmentary, stands apart from all the rest: it is far earlier, and is not connected with them. For more about the potter Brygos see pp. 398–9, and there for the fourteenth cup.

THE BRYGOS PAINTER

Hartwig 307–74. *VA.* 89–93. Langlotz *Z.*, *passim.* Langlotz *GV.* 11–15. Pfuhl 459–66. *Att. V.* 175–86 and 473. *V.Pol.* 23–25, 28, and 80. *BSR.* 11, 19–20. Caskey in *CB.* i, 13–26. *ARV.*[1] 245–261 and 956. *Studies Robinson* ii, 74–83.

The earlier work of the Brygos Painter runs parallel with the work of Onesimos in that artist's later—post-Panaetian—phase (p. 313), and has a good deal in common with it, but the temperament is different.

Most of the smaller cups, of those decorated inside only (nos. 88–170), are late, and many of them weak, but I cannot be sure that any in the list are school-pieces. In later life the fire burned down: and the 'weak Brygan' vases seem to be the late work of the Brygos Painter himself. Besides cups, a good many lekythoi belong to this phase, also a squat lekythos and a Nolan amphora.

It must be admitted, however, that the 'weak Brygan' cups lead on to those which I count as school-pieces and attribute to the Painter of Munich 2676 (p. 391). There is the same problem here as with the latest phases of other artists, the Berlin Painter for example (p. 196), or Douris (p. 426).

A very large and famous piece, the Alkaios vase in Munich, was attributed to the Brygos Painter by Furtwängler. I counted it as a school-piece, but am now disposed to accept it as a very late work of the painter himself (p. 385 no. 228); grouping with it two skyphoi in the Louvre (p. 381 nos. 174 and 175).

CUPS

1 (1). LOUVRE G 152, from Vulci. Heydemann *Iliupersis* pl. 1, whence Davreux fig. 23; *WV*. 8 pl. 4; FR. pl. 25, whence Perrot 10, 569–71, Hoppin i, 118, (A–B) Buschor 168–9, (A) Robert *Herm.* 135, (A–B) Pfuhl figs. 419–20 (fig. 419 = Pfuhl *Mast.* fig. 52), (A) Swindler fig. 311, (detail of A) Seltman pl. 21, b, (I) LS. fig. 81; Pottier pl. 121; A–B, Perrot 10 pll. 12–13; I, ph. Al. 23726, whence Pfuhl fig. 428 and Schaal *Rf.* fig. 22; *REG.* 1936 pll. 4 and 7; *Enc. phot.* iii, 18–19, whence (part) Frel *R.V.* figs. 177–9; A–B, phs. Gir. 17459–62, whence (A) Buschor *G.Vasen* 154, (B) Davreux fig. 23 b, (A and part of B) *AJA.* 1954 pl. 60 fig. 22, (part of B) Grimal 178–9, (detail of A) *E.A.A.* ii, 200 fig. 298; detail of A, *E.A.A.* i, 751; I, ph. Arch. Phot. MNLA 768A. I, Phoinix served with wine by Briseis; A–B, Iliupersis. On one handle, BPVΛOϟEΓOIEϟEN. For the shape, Bloesch 82, Brygos no. 3. See p. 1649.

2 (2). LONDON E 69, from Vulci. *Archaeologia* 32 pll. 8–9 and 11; *WV*. 6 pl. 2; I, Murray no. 47, whence Perrot 10, 635; the armour under one handle, Hartwig 359; B, Méautis *Âme* fig. 25; A–B, Hofkes-Brukker pl. 10; A, Scheurleer pl. 28, 79; I, Ghali-Kahil *H.* pl. 86, 1; I, Stella 643. I, uncertain subject: a hero leading a woman. A–B, the armour of Achilles: A, the quarrel; B, the vote. [Klein]. For the shape, Bloesch 82, Brygos no. 10. The persons on I may be Agamemnon and Briseis; but the petasos is perhaps against this; and Donald Robertson suggests that they may be Odysseus and Chryseis (*Il.* i, 439–45).

3 (3, +). LOUVRE G 154. *Mon. Piot* 16 pll. 15–17, whence Pottier pl. 221, (A–B) Roscher s.v. Troilos 1226 and (detail) *Hesp.* 8, 301. I, warrior and old man. A–B, Achilles pursuing Troilos. A Louvre fragment joins, giving the middle of the woman on the right of A. For the subject of I compare, perhaps, Athens Acr. 355 by the Stieglitz Painter (p. 827 no. 29).

4 (4). TARQUINIA RC 6846, from Tarquinia. *Mon.* 11 pl. 33; *WV*. D pl. 8, 2 = *WV*. 1890–1 pl. 8, 2, whence (A) F. Benndorf 67 and (B) Robert *Scenen der Ilias* 4 fig. 1; I, ph. Mo. 8362, whence Ahrem 99 fig. 103; I, ph. Al. 26053, whence Philippart *It.* ii pl. 13, 1, *Corolla Curtius* pl. 48, and Grimal 149; A–B, phs. R.I. 1934, 1890–5a and 2277–84, whence *Corolla Curtius* pll. 48–50; B and part of A, *ML.* 36 pl. 8, 1–2; I, Romanelli *Tarqu.* 126; *CV.* pll. 4–5; I, Stella 694; I and A, phs. And. 40999 and 41003. I, Phoinix served with wine by Briseis; A, Paris returning to his father's house after the judgement; B, fight: Achilles and Memnon. [Duemmler]. On the subjects see Hampe in *Corolla Curtius* 142–7; and here, p. 406. For the shape, Bloesch 132 no. 16.

5 (5). ATHENS Acr. 293, from Athens. Langlotz pll. 17–18, and p. 25, above. I, Odysseus and Circe; A–B, Circe. On one handle, B[PVΛOϟEΓOIEϟEN].

6 (6). VATICAN, from Vulci. *Mus. Greg.* 2 pl. 83, 1, whence (A–B) *El.* 3 pl. 86 and *AZ.* 1844 pl. 20; detail of A, van Hoorn *De vita* 9; detail of A,

Bull. Vereen. 24–26, 7; phs. Al. 35783–5, whence (A) Stella 306; A–B, *Eph.* 1953–4, ii, 177–8. I, symposion (man and youth reclining). A–B, Hermes and the cattle of Apollo. [Duemmler]. Restored. For the shape, Bloesch 85, Brygos no. 23.

7 (7, +). ATHENS Acr. 288, frr., from Athens. Part, *Jb.* 2, 230–1, 1–4 and 6–7; Langlotz pl. 16. I, Herakles and Eurytos (Eurytos reclining, Herakles arriving breezily); A–B, Herakles in the house of Eurytos. [Furtwängler]. A new fragment, added by Mrs. Karouzou, joins, giving, inside, the left arm of Eurytos with part of his middle, and, outside, one foot of the left-hand person on B.

8 (8). CAB. MÉD. L 243, L 46, L 78 (these probably part of de Ridder's '583'), 600, and another fr. One fr. of I, Hartwig pl. 35, 4a; all, *Studies Robinson* ii pll. 27–28; I (except one fr.) and part of A–B, parts of phs. Gir. 28876, 28877, and 28879. I, symposion (man reclining, and cup-bearer). A, Herakles in the house of Eurytos. B, symposion. See *Studies Robinson* ii, ii, 77–82.

9 (9). LEIPSIC T 582, two frr. Outside, unexplained subject (on one fr., youth running, with an arrow? in his hand; bow and quiver hanging; on the other, cloak—hanging?—, tree).

10 (10). BERLIN 2293, from Vulci. Gerhard *Trinkschalen* pl. 8, 2 and pll. 10–11, whence (I) *El.* 2 pl. 117, (A–B) Overbeck *KM.* pl. 4, 12, Vian *R.* pl. 35; I, Winter *KB.*¹ pl. 89, 3; FR. pl. 160, whence (I) Swindler fig. 289 and (I and B) Schnitzler pl. 43, 59 and 59a; A, Neugebauer pl. 50; A and foot, Bloesch pl. 22, 3; A, Diepolder *G.V.* 36–37; A, Schnitzler pl. 43, 59 b; I and part of A–B, Stella 325 and 751; I and B, Greifenhagen *A.K.* pl. 58, 2 and pll. 59–60; *CV.* pll. 67–68. I, Selene. A–B, Gigantomachy. [Furtwängler]. For the shape, Bloesch 82, Brygos no. 8.

11 (11, +). Once Paravey 76; and NAPLES, Astarita, 130. B.Ap. xxi. 107 (minus the Astarita fragment). I, woman spinning. A, Eos mounting chariot; B, similar, but the deity is not winged: Selene? The upper half of the figure (except the head) is given by the Astarita fragment, which also supplies the first two letters of the inscription HOΓΑΙ*K[A]*LOΣ.

12 (12). HEIDELBERG 69, fr. Kraiker pl. 11. Outside, (winged goddess—Iris?).

13 (13). LONDON E 65, from Capua. *Mon.* 9 pl. 46; *WV.* 8 pl. 6, whence HM. pll. 27–28; I, Murray no. 43, whence FR. i, 239, Perrot 10, 564, Hoppin i, 110, and Pfuhl fig. 429; A–B, FR. pl. 47, 1, whence Hoppin i, 110, (A–B) Perrot 10, 563, (A–B) Seltman pl. 25, (A) Pfuhl fig. 424, (A–B) Bieber *H.T.* 20 fig. 25, (A–B), Buschor *Satyrtänze* figs. 76–77; A, mouth, and foot, Bloesch pl. 36, 2, whence (A) *AJA.* 1945, 158; I, Richter and Milne 29; I, *AJA.* 1945 pl. 7; I, Lane pl. 74; A–B, Stella 207 below and 106; A, *E.A.A.* ii, 199. I, Chrysippos served with wine by Zeuxo. A–B, Hera and Iris attacked by satyrs. On the foot, BRVΛOΣEΓOIEΣEN. For the shape, Bloesch 134 no. 4; for the co-finds, *AJA.* 1945, 156–8.

14 (15). CAB. MÉD. 576. Hartwig pl. 33, 1 and pl. 32, whence Pfuhl figs. 426–7 and 430 (fig. 426 = Pfuhl *Mast.* fig. 57), (I) HM. pl. 38, (I) Farnell *Gk Cults* 5 pl. 44; phs. Gir. 8064, 18943, and 28871, whence (I) Langlotz *G.V.* pl. 16, 23, (I) Schefold *Bildnisse* ftisp., (part of I) Wegner *Mus.* pl. 15, a, (I) Richter *A.G.A.* fig. 216, (I) Buschor *Bilderwelt* 38, (part of B) *Hist. rel.* 227, (I) *E.A.A.* ii, 202 fig. 302, (I) Richter *H.G.A.* 330; B and foot, Bloesch *F.A.S.* pl. 22, 1. I, Dionysos and satyrs; A–B, Dionysos with satyrs and maenads. [Hartwig]. For the shape, Bloesch 81, Brygos no. 1.

15 (14). MUNICH 2645 (J. 332), from Vulci. F. Thiersch *Ueber die hellenischen bemalten Vasen* pl. 4, whence (I) HM. pl. 15, 2; FR. pl. 49 and i, 250, right, whence (I) Perrot 10, 713, (I) LS. fig. 82; I, Reichhold, *Skiz.* 125; I, Langlotz *G.V.* pl. 22, 34, whence Frel *Ř.V.* 176; I, Schaal *Rf.* fig. 26; I, Philippart *C.A.B.* pl. 3; A and foot, Bloesch *F.A.S.* pl. 23, 1; I, Buschor *G.Vasen* 156, whence Rumpf *MZ.* pl. 25, 4; I, Lane pl. 89, d; Lullies and Hirmer pll. 64–69, whence (A and part of B) LS. figs. 83–84; I, Robertson *G.P.* 107. I, white ground, maenad; A–B, Dionysos with maenads and satyrs. [Furtwängler]. For the shape, Bloesch 84, Brygos no. 16. See p. 1649.

16 (16). CASTLE ASHBY, Northampton, fr. Hartwig pl. 33, 2; BSR. 11 pl. 10, 3–4. A, Dionysos with satyrs and maenads. [Furtwängler].

17 (17). FLORENCE, two frr., from Populonia. One, *ML.* 34, 402, also Minto *Populonia* pl. 53, 5a. Outside, Dionysos with satyrs and maenads. The unpublished fragment has the upper part of a satyr to left, and of another satyr dancing to right: this is not the fragment figured by Minto pl. 53, 5b, for which see p. 444 no. 240.

18. INNSBRUCK ii. 12.36 and 50, fr. I, satyr and maenad (one foot of each remains); A, (maenad, satyr). [Bothmer].

19. INNSBRUCK ii. 12.52, fr. Outside, (satyr, maenad).

20 (18). LEIPSIC T 528, fr., from Orvieto. Hartwig 318. A, (satyr and maenad). [Hartwig].

21 (a 7). TÜBINGEN E 24, fr. Watzinger pl. 20. A, (satyr). [Watzinger].

22 (19). FRANKFORT, Liebieghaus, 109, fr. A, (satyr and maenad—elbow of maenad with thyrsus, upper part of satyr rushing, with head, to right, thrown back, crotala in right hand).

23. MUNICH, Bareiss, fr. A, (satyr throwing the discus, then Dionysos or a maenad). [Cambitoglou].

24 (21). LONDON E 68, from Vulci. Jahn *Dichter* pl. 7; I, Murray no. 46; Hartwig pl. 35, 1 and pl. 34, whence (I) HM. pl. 37, (A–B) Farmakovski i, 226, (A) Perrot 10, 619, (detail of B) Richter *F.* fig. 173; detail of A, *VA.* 93 fig. 61; I, Pfuhl fig. 432; I, Licht ii, 51; A, Hofkes-Brukker pl. 12, below; A and foot, Bloesch pl. 23, 4; A, Lane pl. 75, b. I, symposion (youth reclining and girl dancing); A–B, symposion. On A, ΔΙΓΙLΟ𝟓 ΚΑLΟ𝟓, ΝΙΚΟΓΙLΕ ΚΑLΕ. On B, ΓΙLΟΝ ΚΑLΟ𝟓. [Duemmler]. For the shape, Bloesch 85, Brygos no. 22; for π instead of φ in the inscriptions, Hartwig 320–1. See p. 1649.

25. OXFORD, Beazley, fr. A, symposion (arm of male with crotala, part of man reclining to left). [Bothmer].

26 (23). CAB. MÉD., part of 583 (L 337), part of 588 (L 217), part of 546 (L 127), plus, frr. One fr., Hartwig pl. 35, 4b; all, *Studies Robinson* ii pl. 25, α–β; phs. Gir. 27790 (part) and 28879 (part). Outside, symposion. See *Studies Robinson* ii, 74–76.

27. *Vacat.*

28 (24). CAB. MÉD. 585, 717, and part of 583 (L 242 and part of L 243), frr. (Minus a small fragment of I) *Studies Robinson* ii pl. 25, γ–ε and pl. 26; one fr. of I, ph. Gir. 28876, part (marked 592 in pencil). I, symposion (man or youth, and man, reclining); A–B, symposion. See *Studies Robinson* ii, 76–77.

29 (25). LONDON E 71, from Vulci? *AZ.* 1870 pl. 39; I, Murray no. 49; B.Ap. (xxi. 11?). I, komast; A–B, symposion. [Hartwig].

30. LOUVRE C 11458, fr. I, (maeander). A, symposion, with love-making.

31 (26). FLORENCE 3921 (including a fr. ex Trieste, recognized by Studniczka). I, Hoppin ii, 495; I, Pfuhl fig. 431; I, Langlotz *G.V.* pl. 30, 44; A–B, Vorberg *Ars erot.* pll. 13–14; A and foot, Bloesch pl. 23, 2; A–B, Vorberg *Gloss.* 187–8. I, komos (man and flute-girl); A–B, love-making. On one handle, BRVΛOϟEΓOIEϟEN. For the shape, Bloesch 84, Brygos no. 19.

32 (27). WÜRZBURG 479, from Vulci. Urlichs *Brygos* plate; *WV.* 8 pl. 5, whence HM. pl. 26, 2 and pl. 25; FR. pl. 50 and i, 250, left, whence Perrot 10, 565–7, Hoppin i, 121, (I) Buschor 171, (A–B) Pfuhl figs. 422 a and 423 a, (I and part of A) Seltman pl. 26, (A) Philippart *It.* i pl. 4, a (= Philippart ~~C.A.B. pl. 4, a~~), (A) ~~Mitt. 1952 pl. 11, 1~~; Pfuhl figs. 421–3 (figs. 421–2 =Pfuhl *Mast.* figs. 54 and 53), whence (I) LS. fig. 85; I, Langlotz *G.V.* pl. 26, whence Frel *Ř.V.* fig. 184; A–B, incompletely, Schaal *Rf.* figs. 19 and 24–25; Langlotz pll. 145–9 and 164; signature, Zadoks-Jitta pl. 77, 10; A and foot, Bloesch pl. 22, 2; I and B, Buschor *G.Vasen* 157–8; Schoenebeck and Kraiker pll. 84–85; I, *Marb. Jb.* 14, 15 fig. 18; B, Lane pl. 75, a; B, Wegner *Mus.* pl. 14; I and detail of B, *E.A.A.* ii, 201 and 200 fig. 299; I, Robertson *G.P.* 104; B, R. M. Cook pl. 43. I, komos (youth vomiting, assisted by a girl); A–B, komos. On one handle, BPVΛOϟEΓOIEϟEN. For the shape, Bloesch 82, Brygos no. 4. See p. 1649.

33 (28). ORVIETO, Faina, 37, from Orvieto. Hartwig pl. 36, 1–3; I. ph. Al. 32476; A–B, phs. R.I. 1935. 890–1. I, komos (drunk man dancing, and boy playing the flute); A–B, komos. [Hartwig].

34 (33). CAB. MÉD. 594 and 744, two frr. I, komos (one dancing—a hand remains—and a youth playing the flute); A–B, komos. See the next.

35 (34). CAB. MÉD. 687, fr. A, (on the right, youth to left). May belong to the last.

36 (29). COPENHAGEN inv. 3880, from Italy. Fröhner *Brant*. pll. 24–27 = Hartwig 332–3; *CV*. pll. 141–2, whence (I) Rumpf *MZ*. pl. 25, 5; Breitenstein *G.V*. pll. 38–42; I, Sparkes, Talcott, and Frantz fig. 21. I, symposion (man reclining, vomiting, assisted by a boy); A–B, komos. [Hartwig]. For the shape, Bloesch 82, Brygos no. 5. Restored. Close to the Brygos Painter, but might be by the Dokimasia Painter (p. 412) rather than the master himself. See p. 1649.

37 (30). ATHENS Acr. 265, four frr., from Athens. I, symposion (man reclining); outside, komos. See the next.

38 (31). ATHENS Acr. 291, fr., from Athens. Langlotz pl. 15. A, komos. May belong to the last.

39 (32). ATHENS Acr. 292, fr., from Athens. I, Langlotz pl. 15. I, komast; A, komos.

40 (35). MUNICH 2642, fr. I, komast (youth holding flute-case); A–B, komos.

41 (39). VILLA GIULIA, fr. A, komos (upper part of a man with a wrap over his shoulders moving to left, bending).

42. STRASBURG, Univ., 858, fr. A, komos (youth rushing to right, looking round).

43 (40, +). BOSTON 10.200, fr. I, *VA*. 91; CB. i pl. 9, 23 and p. 23. I, komast (man vomiting); A–B, komos. An unpublished fragment joins and has been presented to the museum: it gives, inside, the feet, and, outside, part of B—the legs of a male dancing, then a cloak and a stick. See p. 1649.

44 (36). ATHENS Acr. 289, two frr., from Athens. One, *Jb*. 2, 231, 5; both, Langlotz pl. 16. Outside, komos.

45 (38). VILLA GIULIA 50433. I and A, phs. G.F. 7158–9. I, man leaning on his stick; A–B, komos. For the shape, Bloesch 132 no. 22. See no. 120.

46 (37). BERLIN 2309, from Capua. Detail of A, *Jb*. 31, 158 = Weege *Etr. Mal*. 120; Lücken pl. 90, 1 and pll. 88–89; I and A, Licht ii, 152 and 117; A, Neugebauer pl. 47; A, foot, and mouth, Bloesch pl. 39, 1; A, Greifenhagen *A.K*. pl. 58, 1. I, komos (man vomiting, assisted by a boy); A–B, komos. [Furtwängler]. For the shape, Bloesch 142, Acrocup no. 2.

47. LOUVRE C 11459, five frr. I, man or youth in himation at altar. A–B, girls dancing and youths watching.

48 (41). VATICAN, from Vulci. *Mus. Greg*. 2 pl. 81, 2; Gerhard pll. 269–70, whence (I) Benndorf *Gjölb*. 211; phs. Al. 35809–11, whence (A) *Mnem*. 4th ser., 3 pl. 1, 1; I and A, phs. And. 42118 and 42105; B.Ap. xxi. 43. I, arming (youth putting his greaves on, and old man); A–B, arming. [Duemmler]. For the shape, Bloesch 82, Brygos no. 7. See p. 1649.

49 (42). ATHENS Acr. 266, three frr., from Athens. A–B, Langlotz pl. 12. I, two warriors (arming). A, horse-race. B, arming. See the next.

50 (43, +). ATHENS Acr. 269, three frr., from Athens. One fr., Langlotz pl. 14. A, horse-race. The two unpublished fragments were added by Mrs.

Karouzou (*BCH.* 1952, 204). Probably belongs to Athens Acr. 266 (no. 49).

51. ATHENS Acr., fr. from Athens. Outside, part of the left-hand figure on one half remains, the helmeted head of a youth. Lip-cup. I do not know whether this could belong to Athens Acr. 266 (no. 49).

52 (44). ATHENS Acr. 295, four frr., from Athens. Three of them, Langlotz pl. 15 (for *c* and *e* read *b* and *c*). I, (maeander). Outside, arming. *c* on Langlotz's plate is not given completely.

53 (45). ATHENS Acr. 296, fr., from Athens. A, Langlotz pl. 15. I, (maeander). A, (unexplained subject: male legs). Might belong to the last?

54 (46). ELEUSIS, frr., from Eleusis. *Delt.* 9, 37–38. I, archer and dog. A, fight; B, (archer with horse, warrior).

55 (47). FLORENCE 15 B 21, fr. Part, *CV.* pl. 15, B 21; I, *CF.* pl. Y, 17. I, (male, shield). A, youths with horse.

56. LOUVRE C 11460, three frr. Outside, youths and horses. On one fr., part of the left-hand figure on one half, a youth in a himation standing to right, then tail and hind-legs of a horse to right; on the second, part of a youth in chitoniskos, Thracian cloak, and boots, moving to right, leading a horse; on the third, part of a similar figure. Cf. Florence 15 B 21 (no. 55).

57 (48). ATHENS Acr. 258, fr., from Athens. Langlotz pl. 14. I, (seated male). A, (male running, male doing up his sandal).

58 (50, +). FLORENCE 14 B 29, LEIPSIC T 539 and T 533, and STRASBURG, Univ., 833, frr. Part, *JHS.* 51, 49; part, *CV.* Florence pl. 14, B 29. I, (male seated, male standing). A, boxers; B, (seated man, males). The unpublished fragment in Strasburg joins: it adds, inside, the elbow of the right-figure and part of an arrow which he must be holding; outside, the rest of the right-hand boxer's right foot, the legs of the person leaning on his stick to right of him, and, under the handle, a dog to right.

59 (50 *bis*). LEIPSIC T 589, fr. A, (athlete tying his penis, man or youth to right).

60 (61). NEW YORK 22.139.80, fr., from Chiusi. Richter and Hall pl. 41, 45. A, (man leaning on his stick).

61 (49, +). COPENHAGEN, Thorvaldsen Museum, 112, and GREIFSWALD 308. Gerhard pl. 281, whence (A–B) Norman Gardiner *G.A.S.* 475; A–B, Norman Gardiner *Athl.* fig. 45; A, *RM.* 63 pl. 43, 1; these minus the Greifswald fragment; the Greifswald fr., Peters pl. 30. I, male seated, holding cup, male leaning on his stick; A–B, athletes and men. [Hartwig]. Now cleaned. The Greifswald fragment gives, on B (the half with the seated youth), the capital of the column, the upper ends of the acontia to left of it, and the knot of the discus-bag. See p. 1649.

62 (51). ROMAN MARKET (Basseggio), VILLA GIULIA, and FLORENCE 12 B 16, from Vulci. (Minus the Villa Giulia and Florence frr.), Gerhard pl. 278–

9, 1–4; the Florence fr., *CV*. pl. 12, B 16; the Florence fragment, and two of the three Villa Giulia, *CF*. pl. Y, 25 and 20. I man and boy; A–B, men, youth, and boys. The lost Basseggio part was assigned to the Brygos Painter by Milani: for the Villa Giulia and Florence frr. see *CF*. 19 on pl. 12 B 16.

63. NAPLES, Astarita, 3. I, youth or man, and boy; A–B, men and boys. On I, male leaning on his stick to right, boy standing to left: both in himatia. HOΓAI[Ϛ] [ΚALO]Ϛ. Outside, two of the men hold hares, and there is a Maltese dog.

64 (52). VILLA GIULIA, three frr. Outside, (youths and male in the palaestra). All wear himatia: on one fr., elbow of a male, aryballos and strigil hanging, then head, to left, and shoulder, of a youth, with (Κ]AL[OϚ]; on the second, aryballos and strigil hanging, then nose, upper lip, and arm of a youth leaning on his stick to left, with ΚA[LOϚ]; on the third, aryballos-thong and top of strigil, then arm of a male leaning on his stick to right, with ... NO ...

65 (53). VILLA GIULIA, fr. A, (part of the middle of a male in a himation to left, then part of a tree; pairs of dots on the himation).

66 (59). ROMAN MARKET (Hartwig), fr., from Chiusi. I, (maeander, a little drapery, and [ΚA]LOϚ). A–B, males (in himatia: on the left of A, male standing to right, dog to left, stick; on the right of B, male leaning on his stick to left, tree, male standing to left, dog to left).

67 (60, +). FLORENCE, and NAPLES, Astarita, 274, two frr. On the Florence fr.: inside, maeander; outside, knee of one to right, holding out a hare, then a dog seated to right, and the stick of one leaning on it to left, with the edge of his thigh. On the Astarita fragment: inside, maeander, and, on the left, sponge hanging, and arm of the left-hand figure; outside, dog seated to left, legs of male in himation and shoes leaning on his stick to left. Both fragments worn.

68 (57). VATICAN, from Vulci. *Mus. Greg.* 2 pl. 80, 3; A–B, phs. Al. 35834–5, whence (A) Philippart *It.* i pl. 4, b (= Philippart *C.A.B.* pl. 4, b) and (A) Hofkes-Brukker pl. 9, 19. I, plain white. A–B, men, youths, and boys. For the shape, Bloesch 82, Brygos no. 6.

69 (58). BRYN MAWR P 190, fr. *AJA*. 1916, 343, 16. A, (youth and boy). [Swindler].

70 (56). PHILADELPHIA MARKET (ex Curtius), fr. Phs. R.I. 1935.2069–70. I, symposion? (naked man lying on the ground, and a male in front of him, who might be playing the flute). A, (toes). School-piece?

71 (62). ATHENS Acr. 255, frr., from Athens. I, Langlotz pl. 13. I, athlete rubbing his shank, and man or youth. Outside, (males). See the next.

72 (63). ATHENS Acr. 263, fr., from Athens. Langlotz pl. 14. A, (naked youth). May belong to Athens Acr. 255 (no. 71).

73 (64). CAB. MÉD. 547, fr. A, (man).

74 (65). CAB. MÉD. L 232, fr. A, (upper part of a boy in a himation looking round to right).

75 (a v3). ROME, Antiquarium Forense, fr., from Rome. I, *Bull. Arch. Com.* 76 pl. 17, 211. I, komast. Outside, part of the two-line border remains.

(nos. 76–87, not known if decorated outside)

76 (20). VILLA GIULIA, fr. I, (satyr:—face, looking up to right, beard, and part of the panther-skin).

77 (54). VILLA GIULIA, fr. I, (belly to mid-calf of a hairy man standing to left, spotted himation over his right arm).

78 (55). VILLA GIULIA, fr. I, (waist, with left hand and forearm, of a man or youth in a spotted himation leaning to right: below, a great chip).

79 (66). VILLA GIULIA, fr. I, (fingers of one playing the flute to right, then the middle of a small boy, naked, standing to right—singing?).

80. NAPLES, Astarita, 281, fr. I, (aryballos and strigil hanging, then the upper half of a boy's head to left, with [ʞ]ΑⱢ[ΟϚ]).

81 (67). ROME, Van Buren, fr., from Orvieto. *JHS.* 39, 79–80. I, komast. [E. D. Van Buren].

82 (68). BOSTON 10.202, fr. CB. i pl. 9, 24. I, komast playing the flute.

83 (69). TORONTO 959.17.78 (ex Curtius), fr. Ph. R.I. 1935.2059. I, cup-bearer (naked boy with ladle and cup).

84 (70). FLORENCE PD 425, fr. I, woman seated (cooking?).

85. OXFORD, Beazley, fr., from Populonia. I, woman seated holding a distaff, man or youth leaning on his stick and taking hold of her arm.

86 (71). CAB. MÉD., fr. I, komast (armpit to mid-thigh of a youth or man in a himation to right, his right arm extended to left).

87 (96). ~~ERLANGEN 459 k, fr. I, Nike.~~

(nos. 88–170, decorated inside only)

88. LOUVRE C 11461, fr. I, (on the left, youth in a himation standing to right, head bent).

89 (72). FLORENCE 9 B 32, fr. *CV.* pl. 9, B 32. I, boy singing and one playing the flute.

90 (74). FLORENCE 3949. Hartwig pl. 35, 2; *CV.* pl. 91, 1 and pl. 116, 12. I, symposion (youth reclining, singing). [Hartwig]. For the shape, Bloesch 128, Conefoot cup no. 5.

91 (75). NEW YORK 16.174.43, from Chiusi. *AJA.* 1923, 273 and 272 fig. 10; Richter and Hall pl. 44, 44 and pl. 180, 44. I, komast. [Albizzati].

92 (76). CAB. MÉD. 552, 787, 707, and another, fr. (composed of four). Two of the four, ph. Gir. 28879 (part). I, komast (youth to right, bending, stick in left hand).

93 (77). BOSTON 01.8038. *AJA.* 1915 pl. 9; CB. i pl. 10, 28; the shape, Caskey G. 203 no. 157. I, athlete.

94 (81). ATHENS Acr. 257, fr., from Athens. Langlotz pl. 14. I, archer.

95 (80). FLORENCE B B 3. *CV.* pl. B, B3; *Boll. d'Arte* 29, 267 fig. 19. I, archer.

96 (78). BERKELEY 8.921, from the territory of Falerii, probably Narce. *CV.* pl. 33, 1. I, youth and dog.

97. FLORENCE fr. I, (a stretch of the same border as in Berkeley 8.921 and other cups by the Brygos Painter; hardly anything of the picture remains).

98 (79). LOUVRE S 1336. *Mon. Piot* 9 pl. 15, middle (Furtwängler pointed out that it did not belong to the cup with which Pottier published it, see p. 180). I, maenad. Restored.

99 (82). BRUSSELS R 350. *CV.* pl. 4, 4. I, boy with dog.

100 (83). ERLANGEN 459 g, fr. I, youth playing the flute.

101 (84). LEIPSIC T 526, fr., from Orvieto. Vorberg *Gloss.* 552. I, love-making (man or youth, and woman). [Rumpf].

102 (85). LEIPSIC T 530, from Orvieto. Incompletely, *Jb.* 26, 114; incompletely, *R.A.* 1933, i, 160. I, woman at well. [Hartwig]. The second reproduction gives a fragment not in the first, but both omit a fragment with the raised right arm.

103 (86). CAB. MÉD. 652, fr. I, ph. Gir. 28878. I, woman (washing clothes?— or preparing food, as Bothmer suggests?).

104 (87). CAB. MÉD. 632 (L. 48), fr. I, woman seated at wool-basket. A small fragment with the corner of a hanging basket probably belongs.

105 (88). YALE 164, from Vulci. Baur pl. 14. I, komast (youth playing the flute at altar). Recalls the Foundry Painter, see p. 405.

106 (89). LOUVRE G 313, from Vulci. Pottier pl. 135. I, komast.

107 (90). MUNICH. I, komast (youth standing to right, stick in left hand; on the right, a skyphos on the ground, and, hanging, a flute-case). Damaged. Cone-foot cup.

108 (91). CAB. MÉD. (587 and 677?), two frr. I, komast (man to right, mouth open, a thick fillet round his head).

109 (92). VIENNA, Univ., 502, from Orvieto. Benndorf *Gjölb.* 113 fig. 117; *R.A.* 1933, i, 158; *CV.* pl. 11, 1 and 3. I, woman at well.

110 (93). LOUVRE C 92, fr. I, Dionysos.

111 (94, +). LOUVRE C 223, two frr. I, Nike.

112 (95). ATHENS Acr. 360, fr., from Athens. Langlotz pl. 23. I, Nike.

113 (97). FLORENCE 80528, from Saturnia. *M.L.* 30, 686. I, Hermes spinning a top.

114 (98). CAB. MÉD. 581, from Vulci. De Ridder pl. 21; ph. Gir. 28872. I, woman with lyre at altar. [De Ridder].

115 (99). BRUSSELS R 263. *CV.* pl. 1, 4; *R.A.* 1933, i, 159; Richter *A.G.A.* fig. 215. I, girl cup-bearer. For the shape, Bloesch 128, Conefoot cup no. 8.

116. LOUVRE C 11462, fr. I, youth at herm.

117. LOUVRE C 11463, fr. I, youth with oinochoe.

118. LOUVRE C 11464, fr. I, komast.

119 (100). LEIPSIC T 598, fr. I, komast.

120. OXFORD, Beazley. I, komast (youth in himation moving to right, sky-phos in left hand; on the left, stick and basket; on the right, table). Compare Villa Giulia 50433 (no. 45). Very small.

121 (101). BOWDOIN 13.20, fr. I, woman dancing.

122 (102). WAIBLINGEN, Oppenländer (ex Preyss). Part, Bieber G.K. pl. 8, 1. I, naked woman folding her chiton. Restored.

123 (103). PALERMO V 660, from Chiusi. Inghirami Chius. pl. 134; cleaned, CV. pl. 11, 1. I, woman dressing.

124. LOUVRE C 11465, fr. I, woman running (the legs remain; in front of her a chest, behind her a door: one thinks of Althaia).

125. LOUVRE C 11466, fr. I, woman at (altar?).

126. LOUVRE C 11467, two frr. I, woman running or dancing.

127. LOUVRE (ex Troyes 27), fr. I, woman (the upper part remains). A Louvre fragment with part of the same border might belong.

128. ADRIA Bc 84, fr., from Adria. CV. pl. 8, 6. I, woman. [Riccioni].

129 (104). BERLIN 2301, from Tarquinia. AZ. 1854 pl. 66, 2; Bloesch pl. 24, 3. I, Klytaimestra. [Hartwig]. Running to help Aigisthos, as in the Vienna pelike (p. 204 no. 109) and elsewhere (Robert Held. 1310). For the shape, Bloesch 86, Brygos no. 27.

130 (105). TARQUINIA RC 5590, from Tarquinia. CV. pl. 17, 1. I, komast (youth with crotala). Restored. Conefoot cup.

131 (106). SYDNEY 40. I, youth seated playing the flute. Restored.

132. GODALMING, Charterhouse. I, youth seated playing the flute. Replica of Sydney 40.

133. FLORENCE V 67, from Chiusi. I, man seated at a table.

134. Vacat.

135. ARLESHEIM, Schweizer. Schefold M. 189, 204. I, maenad. Conefoot cup. Restored.

136 (106 bis). BOWDOIN 13.21, fr. I, woman (might be a cup-bearer).

137. OXFORD, Beazley (ex Durand 666, Roger, and Pourtalès 396), from Vulci. I, man courting boy. See Cypr. 29, α 51. Conefoot cup.

138. NEW YORK 58.11.4. A.A.A. pl. 80, 276. I, trainer. [Clairmont]. Compare the last.

139. LOUVRE C 11468, fr. I, woman.

140 (107). OXFORD 1925.73, from Capua. CV. pl. 2, 6. I, woman with mirror and circlet. For the shape, Bloesch 89 no. 1.

141. BUDAPEST 50.89. Szilágyi and Castiglione *Führer*, cover; *Arch. Ért.* 1961, 166–7. I, Nike (or Iris) at altar. [Also Szilágyi].

142 (108). FLORENCE 76103, from Chiusi. *R.A.* 1935, 201; *CV.* pl. 102, 3 and pl. 116, 19. I, woman at well. For the shape, Bloesch 90 no. 11. Late.

143 (109). BRYN MAWR P 186, fr. *AJA.* 1916, 340, 15. I, girl cup-bearer.

144 (109 *bis*). FLORENCE 4 B 47, fr. Part, *CV.* pl. 4, B 47. I, woman at fountain.

145 (110). MILAN 266. Brizio *Marz.* pl. 9, 19, whence J. Hülsen *Nymphaeum* (*Milet* i, 5) 82; *R.A.* 1933, i, 155; *CV.* pl. 1; part, *Cisalpina* 1 (Belloni) pl. 2, 3. I, woman at well. Late and especially poor.

146. LONDON 1950.1–4.10. *BMQ.* 16 pl. 9. I, warrior advancing. [Martin Robertson]. Conefoot cup. Late.

147 (111). BOSTON 10.197. CB. i pl. 10, 26. A, Apollo. Late.

148. NEW YORK MARKET. I, man leaning on his stick, holding out a sash (in himation, to right, right leg frontal; on the left a seat, and, hanging, aryballos and strigil). Conefoot cup. Late.

149 (112). MANCHESTER, School of Art, Aa 37, from Italy. *Mem. Manch.* 78 pl. 1, 2; Webster *Gk Interpretations* pl. 4, 2. I, komast. Restored. Late.

150 (113). NEW YORK 21.88.150. A, Richter and Milne fig. 164; Richter and Hall pl. 44, 50 and pl. 180, 50. I, komast. For the shape, Bloesch 128, Conefoot cup no. 12. Late.

151 (114). MUNICH 2675 (J. 271), from Vulci. I, woman running to altar. For the shape, Bloesch 90 no. 9. Restored. Late.

152 (116). ADRIA Bc 31, from Adria. Part, Micali *Mon. ined.* pl. 46, 8; Schöne pl. 3, 1; part, *CV.* pl. 8, 7; part, *Riv. Ist.* N.S. 5–6, 41. I, maenad. Late.

153. ADRIA B 120, fr., from Adria. *CV.* pl. 8, 5. I, maenad. Late.

154. ADRIA s.n. 53, fr., from Adria. I, maenad (legs, running to right). Late.

155. ADRIA Bc 90, fr., from Adria. *CV.* pl. 22, 5. I, (youthful head). Late. Or school-piece? Recalls the Painter of Munich 2676.

156 (117). NEW YORK 96.9.37 (GR 577). Richter and Hall pl. 47, 49 and pl. 180, 49; lithograph in R.I. I, Thracian woman (extract from a 'Death of Orpheus'). For the shape, Bloesch 128, Conefoot cup no. 10. Late.

157 (118). FLORENCE 10 B 154 (part ex Villa Giulia). Part, *CV.* pl. 10, B 154; *Boll. d'Arte* 29, 267 fig. 21. I, youth with cup. Late.

158 (119). OXFORD 1929.464. *CV.* pl. 51, 7. I, woman at wool-basket. For the shape, Bloesch 90 no. 10. Late.

159. OXFORD, Beazley, fr. I, (on the right, tips of three fingers holding one aulos of a flute); border as in Florence 10 B 54 and Oxford 1929.464 (nos. 157 and 158).

160 (120). ROME, Torlonia. I, woman spinning. Late.

161 (121). VILLA GIULIA (part ex Florence). I, woman with phiale at altar. Late.

162. LOUVRE C 11469, two frr. I, youth (in chlamys, right arm raised holding something). Late.

163. LOUVRE C 11470. I, seated youth (in himation). Late.

164 (115). Once CHIUSI, Mazzetti. Lithograph in R.I. I, woman fleeing to altar (to left, looking round, arms extended to right). Late.

165 (122). FLORENCE V, from Chiusi. I, archer (to right, drawing bow). For the shape, Bloesch 128, Conefoot cup no. 6. Late.

166 (123). FLORENCE 72724, from Pacchierello. I, male with (go-cart? or roller?). Late.

167 (124). TARQUINIA RC 5589, from Tarquinia. I, youth seated with lyre, singing. Forms a group with Berlin 2302 and Brussels R 332 (nos. 168–9). Late.

168 (125). BERLIN 2302, from Vulci. B.Ap. xviii. 59, 2. I, woman fleeing. Restored. For the shape, Bloesch 128, Conefoot cup no. 9. Late. See no. 167.

169 (126). BRUSSELS R 332. CV. pl. 1, 2. I, komast ('Anacreontic'). Conefoot cup. Late. See no. 167; and, for the subject, CB. ii, 59 no. 11.

170 (127). LOUVRE G 285, from Vulci. El. 4 pl. 93; Pottier pl. 134. I, komast ('Anacreontic'). Late. For the subject see CB. ii, 59 no. 12.

SKYPHOI

(nos. 171–5, type A)

171 (129). VIENNA inv. 3710 (ex Oest. Mus. 328), from Cervetri. Mon. 8 pl. 27, whence Robert Herm. 170 and (B) FR. ii, 122; A, WV. 1 pl. 3, 1; FR. pl. 84, whence (A) Wade-Gery The Poet of the Iliad 81 fig. 3; A, Buschor 172; details of A, Löwy Altgr. Graphik 4–5; handle and bottom, H. R. W. Smith Lewismaler pl. 30, a–b; A, Buschor G. Vasen 161; CV. pll. 35–37; A, E.A.A. i, 29; A, Recueil Dugas pl. 43, 1. A, ransom of Hector; B, Greek heroes. [Duemmler].

172 (130, +). LOUVRE G 156, from Nola. Langlotz G.V. pl. 27; Pottier pl. 123; A, ph. Al. 23693, whence Ahrem 85 fig. 84, Int. Studio Feb. 1927, 26, 1, (part) Kraiker M.G. pl. 29; phs. Gir., whence (A) Hofkes-Brukker pl. 11 below; B, Enc. phot. iii, 20, 1, whence Frel Ř.V. fig. 181; detail, E.A.A. ii, 202 fig. 301. Komos. [Hartwig]. Restored. Three unpublished Louvre fragments join, giving (1) the booted feet, with part of the skirt, of the woman to left of the boy holding cup and lamp, (2) the right foot, with part of the skirt, of the woman to left of the lyre-player, (3) the upper part of the girl playing the flute under one handle, with a piece of the tree. See p. 1649.

173 (131). BOSTON 10.176, from Greece. *AJA*. 1915, 130-4 and pll. 7-8, whence (A) Norman Gardiner *Athl*. fig. 102; detail, *VA*. 90 fig. 58; A, Pfuhl fig. 425 (= Pfuhl *Mast*. fig. 56); CB. i pl. 7, whence Chase *Guide* 69 and (A) Stow pl. 9; Schröder *Sport* pl. 53; B, Buschor *Bilderwelt* 37; A, Villard *GV*. pl. 20, 3; the shape, Hambidge 111 fig. 15 and Caskey *G*. 157 no. 115. Athletes. [Caskey].

174. LOUVRE G 195 (plus), two frr. Part of one fr., Pottier pl. 128. A, adventures of Theseus; B, Theseus received by Aigeus. The smaller fragment gives the foot of one (fallen) to left, then shank and foot of a male moving to right, then the shanks and feet of Theseus dragging the sow to left. The larger fragment gives good part of B; on the right of A, one seated to left (perhaps Phaia?), and under the handle, Theseus and Kerkyon. Very late. See p. 368, foot.

175. LOUVRE C 10813, two frr. Komos. On A, feet of a male, and the greater part of a woman playing the flute, both moving to right; on B, an old man ('anacreontic') moving to right, with a lyre, and a woman moving to left, looking round. As the last. Very late. See p. 368, foot.

(nos. 176-7, hybrid, between type A and type B: type A, but with the handles of type B)

176 (132). NEW YORK 29.131.4. *Bull. Metr*. 25, 137 figs. 7-8; B, Richter and Milne fig. 175; Richter and Hall pl. 42 and pl. 178, 42, whence (A) Buschor *Bilderwelt* 41; A, Bieber *H.T*. 10 fig. 13; B, Richter *Gk Ptg* 11, 2. A, maenad dancing; B, maenad playing the flute.

177 (133). THEBES, from Rhitsona. *BSA*. 14 pl. 14; Vorberg *Gloss*. 490. A, armed satyr. B, warrior (light-armed).

(nos. 178-9, type B, glaux)

178 (134). CAMBRIDGE 12.1955 (ex Lamb). *JHS*. 38 pl. 4; Tillyard pl. 28, 184. A, satyr; B, satyr.

179 (135). MUNICH 2550 (J. 775), from Sicily. *CV*. pl. 95, 1-2. A, youth dancing; B, woman playing the flute.

FRAGMENTS (OF KANTHAROI?)

180. LENINGRAD Ol. 3622, fr., from Olbia. *Soobshcheniya* 9, 47, left. Symposion or komos? (man playing the flute). [Peredolskaya].

181. ATHENS Acr., two frr., from Athens. One, *BCH*. 1952, 203, b. Diosysos leading Ariadne away. [Karouzou].

181 *bis*. ATHENS Acr., fr., from Athens. (Nose, beard, outstretched left arm, with a wrap over it, of a man moving to right; tree, ΚΑΛ . . ..).

181 *ter*. MUNICH, fr., from Athens. (Lower part of the cloak, patterned with small circles, of one moving to right).

KANTHAROI
(no. 182, type A)

182 (136). BOSTON 95.36, from Thebes. Tarbell *Canth*. (*Chicago Dec. Publ*.

6) pll. 2–3 and p. 3, whence (B) Pfuhl fig. 433 (= Pfuhl *Mast.* fig. 55); Tonks *Brygos* pll. 1–2; A, *VA.* 90 fig. 57; A, Hambidge pl. at p. 68; A, *N.Y. Shapes* 20, 2 = Richter and Milne fig. 167, whence LS. fig. 5; B, Richter *Craft* 23 fig. 30; B, *Int. Studio* Feb. 1927, 25, 1; CB. i pl. 6; B, Lane pl. 76, a; the shape, Hambidge 68 and Caskey G. 162. A, Zeus pursuing Ganymede; B, Zeus pursuing a woman (Aigina?). [John Marshall].

(nos. 183–4, plastic: janiform, women's heads)

183 (137). NEW YORK 12.234.5, from Capua. Pollak and Muñoz pll. 35–36; *Bull. Metr.* 8, 158; A, *VA.* 92; A, *JHS.* 49, 57; B, *N.Y. Shapes* 23, 2; A, Richter *Sc.* fig. 483; Richter and Hall pl. 43 and pl. 178, 43, whence (A) Simon *G.A.* 65; detail of A, Richter *ARVS.* 61 fig. 18; B, Richter *A.G.A.* fig. 217; A, Richter *H.* 214, h. Symposion: A, satyr reclining; B, the like. On the plastic part see p. 1538.

184 (138). LONDON E 784, from Capua. *CV.* pl. 36, 1 and pl. 38, 1; A, *E.A.A.* ii, 499, 1; ph. Ma. 3217 middle. Symposion: A, youth reclining. [Cecil Smith]. On the plastic part see p. 1533 no. 8.

RHYTA

(nos. 185–6, ram's head, with stand)

185 (139). Once GOLUCHOW, Czartoryski, 119. De Witte pll. 31–32; *V.Pol.* pl. 10 and pl. 11, 2; *CV.* pl. 23, 4. Satyrs attacking sleeping maenads; behind, below, Dionysos and satyr. [Gallatin]. See p. 1649.

186 (140). GENOA 1158, from Veii. Campanari *Isola Farnese* pl. 5; part, *Anz.* 1938, 644 fig. 9; *Le Arti* 3 pl. 67; *CV.* pl. 3 and pl. 4, 1–3. Symposion.

(nos. 187–8, hound's head; two-handled)

187 (141). VILLA GIULIA 867, from Falerii. *Boll. d'Arte* 10, 343, whence *AJA.* 1917, 457; *Dedalo* 3, 81; *CV.* pl. 2, 3–5; Richter *Animals* fig. 159; ph. Al.; phs. R.I. 1935.1684–5. Symposion: A, man and youth reclining; B, man reclining. See p. 1649.

188 (142). LENINGRAD 679 (St. 360). *CR.* 1865, 159 and 186, whence Roscher s.v. Pygmaien 3295 figs. 8–9 and (part) *Ausonia* 2, 151; part, *G.P.* 54. Pygmies and cranes. See p. 1649.

(nos. 189–95, donkey's head)

189 (143). BOSTON 03.787. Hirth *Formenschatz* 1908, 85; Buschor 155; Buschor *Krok.* (= *Mü. Jb.* 1919) 15; CB. i pl. 9, 22; part, Richter and Milne fig. 178, whence LS. fig. 21; part, Chase *Guide* 70; part, Hoffmann *A.R.R.* pl. 3, 1. Satyrs and maenad. [Tonks].

190 (144). ORVIETO 1051, from Orvieto. *CV.* pl. 3, 1–3; ph. Armoni. Komos.

191 (145). LENINGRAD 680 (St. 407). *CR.* 1881, 5, 49, 60, and title-page; Waldhauer *K.O.* pl. 11 fig. 11. Komos. As Leningrad 679 (no. 188).

192 (146). Lost. Noël Des Vergers pl. 11. Komos. Very much restored.

193. LOUVRE C 11741, fr. Komos. To left of one ear, youth (reclining?) to left, playing the flute; to right of the ear, youth or man to left, leaning back.

194. LOUVRE C 11472, four frr. (Old man seated, man or youth leaning on his stick).

195 (147). NAPLES 2961, from Ruvo. *Mus. Borb.* 5 pl. 20, 1; Inghirami pl. 118, 1; Panofka *Trinkhörner* pl. 2, 1-2. Eros and boys. See p. 1649.

KYATHOI

196 (148). ATHENS Acr. 545, frr., from Athens. Langlotz pl. 41. Zeus and Ganymede.

197 (149). ATHENS Acr. 546, fr., from Athens. Langlotz pl. 41. (Youth seated, singing and playing the lyre).

NECK-AMPHORAE

(Nolan amphorae, with triple handles)

198 (150). VIENNA 695. *CV.* pl. 54, 3-4 and pl. 55, 3-4. A, Dionysos; B, satyr. Restored.

199 (151). BOSTON 26.61, from Gela. *MFA. Bull.* 24, 39-40; CB. i pl. 8 and suppl. pl. 1, 19, whence (A) Buschor G. *Vasen* 172 fig. 192 and (B) *N. Jb.* 10 pl. 2, 3. A, citharode; B, youth listening. [Caskey].

200. HAMM inv. 3690, from Nola. *AJA.* 1947 pl. 63; *Anz.* 1948-9, 133-6. A, warrior; B, warrior. Ex Torrusio, see Heydemann in *Bull.* 1869, 191 no. 15. See no. 217.

201 (152). NEW YORK 25.189.3, from Gela. A, Eos and Tithonos; B, boy fleeing. Late.

LEKYTHOI

(of standard shape)

202 (153). BERLIN 2205, from Armento. Millingen *AUM.* 1 pl. 32; Lücken pl. 48, 2; Neugebauer pl. 54, 1; Ghali-Kahil *H.* pl. 85, 2. Wedding of Menelaos and Helen. Late. For the subject see CB. ii, 44; for the suggestion that it is not exactly the wedding, but Menelaos leading Helen away after the award, compare Pindar *P.* 9, 121-3.

203 (154). BERLIN 2206. Gerhard *A.B.* pl. 9, whence *El.* 2 pl. 10. Apollo and Artemis. Restored. Late.

203 bis. SWISS PRIVATE. Apollo pursuing a woman. He holds a sceptre in his right hand.

203 ter. REGGIO, fr., from Locri. Woman holding armour (standing to left, right arm extended with helmet, left hand supporting shield; on the right, upright spear, and helmet-bag).

204 (155). NEW YORK 09.221.43. *Bull. Metr.* 5, 142 fig. 4; Richter and Hall pl. 41, 41 and pl. 175, 41; Richter *H.* 214, i; Himmelmann-Wildschütz *Eig.* 21. Athena.

205 (156). NEW YORK 28.57.12. Richter and Hall pl. 40 and pl. 175, 40. Hera. [Richter]. Bothmer has found the last letter of the inscription [HEP]Λ.

206 (157 *bis*). PROVIDENCE 35.707. *Cl. Studies Capps* 244 fig. 3. Hera and Nike.

207 (157 *ter*). Once NAPLES, Hamilton. Tischbein 4 pl. 16, whence *El.* 1 pl. 32. Hera and Nike.

208 (157). PROVIDENCE 25.078, from Gela. *Bull. Rhode* 16, 46; *AJA.* 1928, 53–54; *CV.* pl. 19, 1. Hera.

209. NEW YORK, private. *Charites Langlotz* pl. 19. Hera. Extract from a judgement of Paris; the sheep, part of Paris' flock, makes friends with the visitor. Late. Compare especially New York 25.189.1 (no. 211).

210 (158). LONDON 99.2–17.3, from Eretria. *JHS.* 19, 203. Woman running out. ALKMEON KALOS.

211 (160). NEW YORK 25.189.1, from Gela. *Bull. Metr.* 22, 19 fig. 4; Richter and Hall pl. 46, 48 and pl. 175, 48; *Trans. Int. Num. Congress 1936*, 25; part, Richter *ARVS.* fig. 60 and p. 63 fig. 23; Richter *H.* 214, g. Athena with aphlaston. Late.

212. PAESTUM, from Paestum. *AJA.* 1954 pl. 68 fig. 5, 4; *Anz.* 1954, 98, 4 and p. 100; *Fasti arch.* 8, 127. Woman with parasol and girl with sprigs. Late.

213. OXFORD, Beazley, fr., from Italy. *Charites Langlotz* pl. 20, 3. Woman. Late.

214 (161). BOSTON 13.189, from Gela. CB. i pl. 10, 29 and p. 25; the shape, Caskey G. 217 no. 171. Woman working with wool. Late.

~~215 (162). OXFORD 318, from Gela. Gardner pl. 24, 1; cleaned, *CV.* pl. 38,~~ 11. Nike. Late.

216 (159). NEW YORK 24.97.28, from Gela. Richter and Hall pl. 46, 47 and pl. 175, 47. Woman playing the flute. [Richter]. Late.

217. SWISS PRIVATE. Warrior (bearded, standing to left, looking round, spear upright in right hand, shield on left arm, device a crescent within four rings). Compare especially Hamm 3690 (no. 200).

218 (163). BOSTON 10.180. CB. i pl. 9, 21 and title-page, whence *Jb.* 56, 41; Greifenhagen *Eroten* 11. Eros.

219 (164). GELA (ex Navarra-Jacona), from Gela. Benndorf pl. 48, 2, whence Roscher s.v. Eros 1354; Greifenhagen *Eroten* 17. Eros. A lekythos-fragment in Reggio, from Locri, may be compared: Eros: preserved, the left wing, and, to right of it, the upper part of the lyre.

220 (165). PALERMO V 668, from Selinus. *CV.* pl. 20, 2–3. Eros.

221 (166). GLASGOW, from Lipari. Woman playing the flute.

222 (167). LOUVRE G 381, from Italy. Millingen *AUM.* 1 pl. 6, whence *El.*

2 pl. 108a and Roscher s.v. Eos, 1258; ph. Gir. 25515, whence Stella 289. Nike with hydriai. Now cleaned. On the subject see *V.Pol.* 20. Late.

(*no. 223, white-ground*)

223. GELA (ex Navarra-Jacona), from Gela. Benndorf pl. 46, 1. Aeneas and Anchises.

SQUAT LEKYTHOS

224 (168). VATICAN. Albizzati *Due acquisti,* 16, 18–19, and 21–22. Death of Orpheus. Late.

OINOCHOAI

(*no. 225, shape 6*)

225 (169). ORVIETO 490, from Orvieto. *NSc.* 1887 pl. 13 fig. 68; ph. Al. 25984, 1, whence Philippart *It.* ii pl. 12, 4; *CV.* pl. 3, 4–6; ph. Armoni; phs. R.I. 56.110–12. Komos.

(*nos. 226–7, shape 8, mugs*)

(*no. 226, shape 8B*)

226 (170). BOSTON 00.339, from Locri. Cecil Smith *Forman* pl. 12 no. 361; CB. i pl. 8, 20; Schröder *Sport* pl. 42, 2; shape, Caskey G. 147 no. 100. Komos (youth dancing and girl playing the flute). [Cecil Smith].

(*no. 227, shape 8A*)

227 (171). ADOLPHSECK, Landgraf Philipp of Hesse, 62, from Taranto? *CV.* pl. 41, 5–6. Athlete.

KALATHOID VASE WITH SPOUT

228 (a 27). MUNICH 2416 (J. 753), from Agrigento. Millingen *AUM.* 1 pll. 33–34, whence Dubois-Maisonneuve pl. 81; Lau pl. 30, 1; FR. pl. 64, and ii, 22, whence (A) Perrot 10 pl. 15; A, Christ *Gr. Lit.*5 fig. 6; A, Pfuhl fig. 772; Licht ii, 33; Schaal *Rf.* figs. 28–29; A, *Die Antike* 7, 91; A, Richter and Milne fig. 90; A, Schefold *Bildnisse* 55; A, Wegner *Mus.* pl. 15, b; Lullies and Hirmer pll. 94–96, whence (part of A), *E.A.A.* i, 198; A, *E.A.A.* ii, 500. A, Alcaeus and Sappho. B, Dionysos and maenad. On A, ΔΑΜΑΚΑΛΟϚ. [Furtwängler]. Very late: as the Louvre skyphoi G 195 and C 10813 (nos. 174–5). See p. 1649.

PLATE

229 (128). ATHENS Acr. 20, frr., from Athens. Ross *Arch. Aufsätze* i pl. 10, whence Klein *Euphr.* 52; Langlotz pl. 1, whence *AJA.* 1934, 418. (Komast.) [Duemmler].

MANNER OF THE BRYGOS PAINTER

I

THE CASTELGIORGIO PAINTER

Att. V. 184–5, iii and 473. *ARV.*[1] 257–8 and 956.

CUPS

1 (1). FLORENCE 82894, from Castelgiorgio near Orvieto. Now augmented by a fragment ex Tübingen, see *CF*. 33 no. 12. Minus the Tübingen fragment, *Atene e Roma* 20, 191 and 193; the Tübingen, Watzinger pl. 20, E 23; A–B, all, Ghali-Kahil *H.* pl. 104, 1–2; detail of A, *E.A.A.* ii, 408; *CV.* pll. 100–1. I, symposion. A–B, Theseus carrying off Helen.

2 (2). VIENNA, Univ., 53 c 17, fr., from Orvieto. *CV.* pl. 10, 13. Outside, (chariot, man).

3 (3). LONDON E 67, from Vulci. Gerhard *TG.* pl. D, whence (B) Cook *Zeus* iii, 1051 fig. 845; I, Murray no. 45. I, seated man served with wine by woman (Zeus and Hebe?). A, fight: Achilles and Memnon; B, Zeus and Hera in Olympus, with Ares. Now cleaned. For the shape, Bloesch 132 no. 15, and, for the subject of B, Simon *O.G.* 66, 9. See p. 1649.

4 (4). PALERMO V 661, from Chiusi. *CV.* pl. 11, 2–3 and pl. 12. I, youth and boy (or woman?); A–B, youths and women. For the shape, Bloesch 84, Brygos no. 15.

5 (5, +). ATHENS Acr. 297, frr., from Athens. Part, Langlotz pl. 15; part, with new frr. identified by Mrs. Karouzou, *BCH.* 1947–8, 425 and pl. 64. I, (feet of a male in a himation). A–B, death of Orpheus.

6 (6). ATHENS Acr. 300, frr., from Athens. Langlotz pl. 18 and p. 26. I, satyr and maenad; A–B, chariot of Dionysos, with maenads.

7 (7). ATHENS Acr. 298, frr., from Athens. Outside, unexplained subject (women).

8 (8). ATHENS Acr. 299, fr., from Athens. A, Langlotz pl. 15. I, (maeander). A, (women).

Close to these is the weak cup with the signature of Brygos in Frankfort, which Cecil Smith had already compared with London E 67:

FRANKFORT, Städel Institut, from Vulci. *Annali* 1850 pl. G; Gerhard *TG.* pl. A–B; *WV.* 8 pl. 2, whence Hoppin i, 109; Schaal *F.* pl. 30, a, and pl. 31, whence (A) *Mél. d'arch.* 1950 pl. 2, 2. I, Poseidon pursuing a woman (Aithra?). A, Triptolemos. B, Herse and Aglauros. On one handle, ΒRVΛΟϟΕΓΟΙΕϟΕΝ. For the shape, Bloesch 84, Brygos no. 20.

The following cup is in the manner of the Brygos Painter and is connected with the Castelgiorgio Painter:

(a). CAB. MÉD. 571, plus, frr. Part, Luynes pl. 42; another fr., de Ridder

427; phs. Gir. 27789 (part), 27790 (part), 27791 (part), 32792, and 32826, whence (one fr.) Davreux fig. 107, (one fr.) Ghali-Kahil *H.* pl. 47, 3; A–B, *AJA.* 1954 pl. 61, 24. I, arrival of a youth? A–B, Iliupersis. The person who greets the youth on I may be either male or female: perhaps Aigeus and Theseus, compare the Louvre skyphos G 195 (p. 381 no. 174)?

Fragments of a somewhat later-looking cup are also connected with the Castelgiorgio Painter:

(a). ATHENS Acr. 334, frr., from Athens. One fr., Langlotz pl. 23. Outside, Peleus and Thetis.

II

THE SCHIFANOIA GROUP

These are probably by one hand. They may be said to look back towards the Castelgiorgio Painter, and forward to the later work of the Painter of Munich 2676 (p. 391). Coarse, lively style. No. 1 was associated with the Brygos Painter by Negrioli, no. 2 with the workshop of Brygos by Pottier.

CUP

1. FERRARA, Museo Schifanoia, 277, from Vulci. A–B, *Boll. d'Arte* 5, 344 figs. 3–4; B.Ap. xxii. 59. I, a king served with wine by a woman (Zeus and Hebe?). A–B, maenads and satyrs. Restored. For the shape, Bloesch 81, Brygos no. 2.

KANTHAROS

(type D, Sotadean kantharos)

2. LOUVRE G 248. *Ant. Kunst* 2 pl. 10, 1–2. A, Zeus pursuing Ganymede; B, a man pursuing a boy. Restored.

III

Manner of the Brygos Painter: sundry.

ARV.[1] 259–60 and 956.

CUPS

1. VIENNA, Univ., 53 c 19 and part of 20, two frr., from Orvieto. *CV.* pl. 10, 5–6 (only). Outside, uncertain subject (woman and girl fleeing; old man). Early-looking: compare, perhaps, the Frankfort cup (p. 386, foot) and those of the Castelgiorgio Painter.

2. LOUVRE C 11475, two frr. A–B, komos. See the next, and p. 1650.

2 *bis.* NAPLES, Astarita, 689, seven frr. I, (on the left, part of a table?, and of a stick). A–B, komos. Very like the last. See p. 1650.

3. ATHENS, Agora, P 8119 and (joining) P 10865, fr., from Athens. I, symposion (male reclining); A, komos. [Talcott].

4 (2). ADRIA B 429, fr., from Adria. *CV.* pl. 24, 2. A, komos. May belong to the 'Mild Brygan Group' (p. 400). For the flute-case compare Naples Stg. 273 (p. 413 no. 13).

5. ADRIA B 573 and (joining) B 869, fr., from Adria. *CV.* pl. 13, 5 and pl. 15, 6. A, (woman).

6. GREIFSWALD 306, fr. Peters pl. 30. I, athlete and trainer; A, wrestlers. [Langlotz].

7. GREIFSWALD 310, fr. Peters pl. 30. A, komos? (thighs of a male in a cloak). [Langlotz].

8. GREIFSWALD 307, fr. A, komos? (male rushing to right). [Peters].

9. GREIFSWALD 304, fr. I, komast; A–B, komos.

10. GREIFSWALD 311, fr. A, komos. [Peters].

11 (6). FRANKFORT, Liebieghaus, fr. A, komos (upper part of youth moving to right, looking round, cloak over shoulders).

12 (4). ATHENS Acr. 290, fr., from Athens. Langlotz pl. 15 and p. 24. A, komos. [Langlotz].

13 (5). PARMA, fr. A, (upper half of fair-haired boy to right, looking round, in himation).

14 (8). CAB. MÉD. 723, fr. I, male (part of himation and stick remain, with the foot of the cup). Cab. Méd. 622 may belong: I, (foot of male); A, (one seated on rock).

15. BRYN MAWR P 200, fr. I, (woman running). A, Herakles pursuing one in a long chiton and himation—Nereus?

16. FLORENCE 16 B 9, fr. *CV.* pl. 16, B 9. A, (male, woman).

17. HEIDELBERG 70, fr. Kraiker pl. 11. A, (Dionysos, and maenad or satyr). [Kraiker]. See the next.

18. VILLA GIULIA, fr. A, (Dionysos, maenad). (Sleeve, then the upper part of Dionysos to right, krobylos, kantharos in right hand, the face missing). Cf. Heidelberg 70 (no. 17).

19. TODI 464, from Todi. I, Becatti *Tuder-Carsulae* pl. 19, 6; *CV.* pl. 1, 2 and pl. 4, 2. I, youth with spears; A, youth or man leaving home. B, males at laver. Near 'weak Brygan'.

20. ADRIA B 253 and B 577, two frr., from Adria. *CV.* pl. 9, 3–4. I, (maeander). Outside: on one fr., (woman fleeing); on the other, (warrior running).

(nos. 21–23, not known if decorated outside)

21. REGGIO, fr., from Locri. The foot of the cup remains, with a small part of the inside picture—the upper middle of a male in a spotted himation to right. May be by the painter himself.

21 *bis*. ADRIA B c 70, fr., from Adria. Schöne pl. 12, 9; *CV*. pl. 15, 8. I, woman at laver. May be by the painter himself.

22. OXFORD, Beazley, fr., from Vulci. I, (legs of a woman—or at least one in a chiton with kolpos—running to right). Compare, for example, Ferrara T. 499 (p. 415 no. 2), Berlin 2301 (p. 378 no. 129), Boston 03.787 (p. 382 no. 189).

23. MAYENCE, Brommer, fr. I, male running (to right: the middle remains; in chitoniskos and chlamys. [Brommer].

(nos. 24–44, decorated inside only)

24 (l 73). CHIUSI, from Chiusi. Levi *Mus. Chius.* 115. I, symposion (man reclining and woman playing the flute). [Levi]. Seems more or less Brygan, but hard to place. Restored.

25. VILLA GIULIA 48426, from Cervetri. *ML*. 42, 1006 (misnumbered 48427). I, komos (man and flute-girl). [Ricci].

26 (11). ATHENS Acr. 285, fr., from Athens. I, komast.

27 (12). ORVIETO, Faina, 111, from Orvieto. Ph. R.I. 1935.872. I, komast, Cf. Athens Acr. 28 (no. 46).

28 (13). MUNICH 2678 (J. 516), from Vulci. A and foot, Bloesch pl. 34, 7. I, komast. Much restored. For the shape, Bloesch 128, Conefoot cup no. 14.

29 (21). VILLA GIULIA. I, youth (in himation, leaning on his stick to right, holding a cup; on the left, couch-head with wine-skin on it; on the right, table with cup on it).

30 (22). VILLA GIULIA. I, youth (in himation which covers the back of his head, leaning on his stick, to right, at laver).

30 *bis*. FLORENCE V viii, from Chiusi. I, man or youth; beyond, a couch. Compare Villa Giulia 50523 (p. 416, top, no. 8).

31 (23). FLORENCE 3911. *CV*. pl. 102, 4 and pl. 116, 20. I, youth seated, holding out lyre. Near the Painter of Munich 2676 (p. 391). For the shape, Bloesch 134 no. 12.

32. BASLE, Cahn, 57, fr. I, Nike (the head remains, with part of the wings). Recalls the Painter of Munich 2676 (p. 391).

33 (18). CAB. MÉD. 793, plus, fr. I, Herakles (on the left, his arm holding the club, and part of the tail of the lion-skin).

34. LOUVRE C 11476, fr. I, male seated and male (both in himatia).

35. LOUVRE C 11477, fr. I, male sitting on the ground (athlete?) and male.

36. LOUVRE C 11478, two frr. I, two warriors.

37 (20). VILLA GIULIA, fr. I, (satyr: the upper part of the right-hand figure remains, moving to left, three-quarter back-view, panther-skin on left arm).

38 (16). CAB. MÉD. 616, fr. I, maenad.

39 (15). AMSTERDAM inv. 2829, from Orvieto. I, maenad.

40. LOUVRE C 11479. I, maenad (with frontal face). Small Conefoot cup.

41 (17). CAB. MÉD. 670, fr. I, woman running (part of the skirt, and the toes of one foot, remain).

42. GREIFSWALD 325, fr. Peters pl. 31, 25. I, woman.

43 (19). PERUGIA 84. I, woman with flute. Much restored. For the shape, Bloesch 89 no. 7.

44 (14). BERLIN inv. 3218. *Anz.* 1893, 90 no. 36; Licht ii, 89; Diepolder *G.V.* 42. I, naked woman laying her clothes down. [Furtwängler]. For the shape, Bloesch 128, Conefoot cup no. 1. Recalls the Foundry Painter.

ALABASTRON

45 (26). ATHENS Acr. 864, fr., from Athens. Langlotz pl. 75. Youth; boy.

PLATE

46 (25). ATHENS Acr. 28, fr., from Athens. Male and another. Cf. Faina 111 (no. 27).

NECK-PELIKE

47. NAPLES 3178, from Ruvo. B, ph. So. 11009, vi or vii, 1. A, man and boy; B, man and boy. Imitation, somewhat recalling the Painter of Munich 2676.

A small fragment recalls the Brygos Painter:

SKYPHOS

AEGINA 1963, fr., from Aegina. *Jb. Mainz* 8 pl. 36, 2. A, (on the left, Hephaistos: one arm and side remain, with part of the back-hair, and the axe).

So does a small vase, damaged:

PYXIS

(type D, box)

BASLE, Cahn, 14. On the lid, discus-thrower.

IV

THE PAINTER OF LONDON D 15

ARV.[1] 261, vi.

ALABASTRA

(white ground)

1 (1). LONDON D 15, from Greece. Klein *L.* 151; ph. Ma. 3117, right. Youth with dog; acontist. +AIPIΓΓOS KALOS, +AIPIΓΓOSKALOS.

2 (2). ATHENS 18570 (ex Empedokles). Two naked youths and a cock. ΦΑΝΟΣΚΑΛΟΣ. On the inscriptions, *AJA*. 1957, 7, xvi.

Probably also the Brygan

RHYTON

(in the shape of a bird)

(a). LENINGRAD 682, from Capua. *CR*. 1872 pl. 4, 1–2. A, Eos carrying off Kephalos. B, satyr and maenad.

V

THE PAINTER OF MUNICH 2676

I collect under this heading the vases that in *ARV*.[1] formed three separate groups:

   (i) the Painter of Acropolis 564 (*ARV*.[1] 259);

  (ii) the Group of Munich 2676 (*ARV*.[1] 261);

 (iii) the Group of Cambridge 74 (*ARV*.[1] 555).

(i) and (ii) are coarse imitations of the late Brygan style; (iii), the Group of Cambridge 74, is still coarser, and no longer Brygan; but I cannot separate it from (i) and (ii). So far as I can make out, all three groups are by one man, who began as an imitator of the Brygos Painter, but in his later, early classic period had lost touch with Brygan style.

The cups are the direct continuation of the 'weak Brygan' cups (p. 368), and the earlier ones are not always easy to keep apart from those.

Another early classic artist, the Painter of the Yale cup, is very close, in style and quality, to the late phase of the Painter of Munich 2676, and is therefore dealt with in this chapter (although he has nothing to do with the Brygos Painter) rather than among the other early classic cup-painters as in *ARV*.[1]

In the following list, 'A' in the serial number within brackets refers to the vases placed under 'the Painter of Acropolis 564' in *ARV*.[1]; 'M' to 'the Group of Munich 2676' there; 'C' to 'the Group of Cambridge 74'.

CUPS

(nos. 1–39, decorated inside only)

1 (M 2). ADRIA s.n. 2, fr., from Adria. *CV* pl. 10, 4. I, komast. Early. Formerly numbered B 469, but another fr. has that number (p. 392 no. 23)

2 (M 3). ADRIA B 511, fr., from Adria. *CV*. pl. 10, 5. I, komast? (head of youth). As the last. Early.

3 (M 5). VILLA GIULIA (part ex Florence), five frr. I, komast (youth in himation to right, skyphos in left hand, stick held across his shoulder with the right). Early. As no. 6.

4 (C 10). VILLA GIULIA 5239. I, komast (moving to left, looking round).

5. OXFORD, Beazley. I, komast (man in himation and shoes to right, with cup and stick; on the left a couch, on the right a table). As Florence D B 1 (no. 13) and Adria B 469 (no. 23).

6 (M 4, +). FLORENCE (part ex Villa Giulia), and NAPLES, Astarita, 314. I, youth running to altar (in himation, to left, a little round thing in his right hand, a sceptre in his left). The Astarita fragment gives the middle of the picture, which is now nearly complete. Conefoot cup. Early. As no. 3.

7. LOUVRE C 11473, two frr. I, youth (moving to left); the upper half of the head remains, and one heel with a piece of the himation). As the last. Early.

8. LOUVRE C 11474, fr. I, male (moving to left; the feet remain, with the lower part of the himation). Early.

9 (M 6). FREIBURG, fr. I, (foot of male to right, with the lower edge of the himation). Early. See no. 11.

10 (M 7). FREIBURG, fr. I, (on the right, forearm of male in himation to right, holding a stick). Early. See no. 11, and p. 1650.

11. MAYENCE, Univ., 2, fr., from Orvieto. I, male (leg, moving to right, in himation, with stick). Early. Joins the Freiburg fragments, nos. 9 and 10?

12. LUCERNE MARKET (A.A.). I, youth (in himation, to right, stick in left hand).

13 (C 7). FLORENCE D B 1 (part ex Villa Giulia). Part, CV. pl. D, B 1. I, youth leaning on his stick. See no. 46.

14. ADRIA B 540, fr., from Adria. CV. pl. 23, 3. I, youth.

15. ADRIA B 566, fr., from Adria. CV. pl. 23, 4. I, youth.

16 (M 10). VILLA GIULIA (part ex Florence) and HEIDELBERG 71. CV. Florence pl. 7, B 44; the Heidelberg fr., Kraiker pl. 16. I, man and boy. Early.

17. BASLE, Cahn, 86, fr. I, (head of youth—rather than woman?).

18. LOUVRE C 11785, fr. I, (on the left, part of a rock and of a himation).

19. ADRIA s.n. 55, fr., from Adria. I, one running (to right: one foot remains).

20 (A 1). DRESDEN, fr. I, woman (goddess?) at altar. The upper half of the picture remains: frontal, head to left, right arm extended, with phiale, over altar, sceptre in left hand. Small cup. Early.

21 (C 8). ADRIA B 470, from Adria. Schöne pl. 6, 2; CV. pl. 39, 5; Mostra pl. 118, 3. I, woman with sceptre (goddess?) at altar. See no. 32.

22. LOUVRE C 11782, fr. I, (on the right, hand holding sceptre).

23 (C 9). ADRIA B 469, from Adria. CV. pl. 39, 6. I, woman with sceptre approaching altar.

24. LOUVRE C 10938. I, woman running to altar.

25. LOUVRE C 11783, frr. I, woman at altar.

26. ADRIA B 757, fr., from Adria. *CV.* pl. 24, 4. I, woman. As Louvre C 11783 (no. 25).

27 (M 1). MUNICH 2676 (J. 676), from Vulci. I, woman playing ball. For the shape, Bloesch 89, v, no. 4.

28. BASLE, Cahn, 83, fr. I, woman (head and left shoulder, to right).

29. LOUVRE C 11784, fr. I, woman running (the shanks and feet remain). Compare the Faina cup (no. 34).

30. ADRIA B 250, fr., from Adria. *CV.* pl. 39, 3. I, woman singing.

31 (C 5). ADRIA B 250 (*bis?*), fr., from Adria. I, woman (standing to right, at wool-basket).

32. ADRIA B 748, fr., from Adria. *CV.* pl. 15, 3. I, woman. Compare Adria B 470 (no. 21).

33 (C 3). ROME, Conservatori, 9. Ph. R.I. 57.502. I, Nike.

34 (C 4). ORVIETO, Faina, from Orvieto? Ph. R.I. 1935.871. I, Nike. As the last.

35. BASLE, Cahn, 82, fr. I, Nike (to right: wing and shoulder remain). As nos. 33 and 34.

36 (C 6). COPENHAGEN, Thorvaldsen Museum, 116. I, symposion (woman reclining). As Conservatori 9 (no. 33).

37 (C 1). OXFORD 307, from Nola. *CV.* pl. 2, 7. I, satyr and maenad.

38. LOUVRE C 11779, fr. I, maenad (the left hand, holding a thyrsus, remains).

39 (C 2). CAMBRIDGE 74, from Bari. *CV.* pl. 25, 6, whence *E.A.A.* ii, 284. I, maenad.

(nos. 40–45, decorated outside as well as in)

40 (A 2). ADRIA B 58, fr., from Adria. *CV.* pl. 9, 6. A, (man). Small cup. Early.

41 (A 3). NEW YORK, Bothmer (ex Curtius), fr. A, (upper part of woman with head to right, left forearm extended). Early.

42. LOUVRE C 11780, frr. I, Nike (flying with torches to altar). A, youth and males; B, women.

43. LOUVRE C 11781, fr. Outside, part of a palmette remains. Would have been expected to belong to the last, but does not seem to find place.

44. ADRIA B 926, fr., from Adria. I, woman; A, (male leaning on his stick).

45. NAPLES, Astarita, 38, frr. I, maenad (moving to right towards an altar, thyrsus in right hand, left arm extended). A–B, women.

STEMLESS CUP

46 (C 11). SYRACUSE 24611. I, maenad. As Florence D B 1 (no. 13).

ALABASTRA
(nos. 47–50, rf.)

47 (C 12). BONN 84 a, from Boeotia. *CV.* pl. 25, 2–4. Two women.

48. PARIS MARKET (Mikas). Man and woman (man in himation, frontal, head to right, leaning on his stick, right arm akimbo, flower in left hand; chair; woman frontal, holding wool, at wool-basket).

49. ATHENS MARKET. Two women (one standing with right leg frontal, head to right, holding a lump of something, the other standing to left, holding a basket; between, a chair; on the right a stone seat, and, hanging above it, a saccos).

50. ATHENS 16456. *CV*. pl. 11, 3–5. A, maenad; B, maenad.

(no. 51, white ground)

51. ARLESHEIM, Schweizer. Woman seated (to right); woman with distaff at wool-basket (standing frontal). Restored.

FRAGMENT (OF A PYXIS ?)

52 (A 4). ATHENS Acr. 564, fr., from Athens. Langlotz pl. 42. (Woman). Early.

NEAR THE PAINTER OF MUNICH 2676

(i)

CUPS

1 (M 8). CAB. MÉD. 690, fr. I, male and seated woman (the feet of the woman remain, to right, with the edge of her chiton; and one foot of the male, to left, with a little of his himation). Early.

2 (M 9). CAB. MÉD. 562, plus, two frr. Incompletely, ph. Gir. 28878, part. I, seated woman, and man. Giraudon's photograph omits a joining fragment which gives the man's right foot and the toes of the left. Early. Better.

3. ADRIA B 327, fr., from Adria. *CV*. pl. 14, 2. I, woman spinning and seated boy. Early.

4. LOUVRE, fr. I, (foot of male in himation standing to left). Early.

5. LOUVRE C 10992. I, male (in himation, standing to left, looking round; on the left, door; on the right, rock-seat). Much worn.

6. LOUVRE C 11777, fr. I, woman (standing to left: the feet remain, and part of the chiton). Compare the last.

7. HOUSTON 34.135, from Rhodes. I, maenad (running to right, with thyrsus and snake). Acrocup. Should be by the painter himself.

8. ADRIA B 511 *bis*, fr., from Adria. I, woman running (the lower part of the chiton remains).

9. LOUVRE G 473. I, old man seated, holding something (a cake?).

10. OXFORD 1946.49 (ex Seltman and Marshall Brooks), from Greece. I, youth at altar. Acrocup.

11. NAPLES Stg. 266. I, woman with mirror at wool-basket. Cup type C.

ALABASTRON

12. CARLSRUHE B 3056, from Haliki. *CV.* pl. 29, 1 and p. 34. Zeus and Hera (rather than a Hora).

See also p. 1650.

(ii)

These recall the Painter of the Yale Cup as well:

CUPS

1. FLORENCE PD 452 and PD 453, two frr. I, one at altar.
2. FLORENCE D B 6. *CV.* pl. D, B 6. I, youth at altar. See the next.
3. LOUVRE C 11775, fr. I, male at altar. Replica of the last, in the same style.
4. LOUVRE C 11776, fr. I, woman. As Athens Acr. 30 (no. 5).

STEMLESS CUP

5. ATHENS Acr. 30, fr., from Athens. I, one in himation (standing to right). As Louvre C 11776 (no. 4).

THE PAINTER OF THE YALE CUP

VA. 96–97. *Att. V.* 271–2 and 476. *ARV.*[1] 553–4 and 962. Nos. 20, 22, and 24 had been put together by Collignon and Couve.

See p. 391.

CUPS

(nos. 1–15, decorated outside as well as in)

1 (1). DRESDEN 358. I and A, Bloesch pl. 38, 1. I, woman running: A–B, youths. For the shape, Bloesch 139, Vicup no. 2.
2 (2). PFORZHEIM, private. I, woman (standing with right leg frontal, head to left, her right hand extended over a wool-basket; on the right, indication of a house); A, youths and woman; B, youths. Vicup.
3. LOUVRE C 10940. I, woman spinning; A–B, youths. Vicup.
4 (3). ATHENS 18723 (ex Empedokles). I, woman with ball; A–B, youths. Vicup.
5 (4). LONDON. I, youth leaning on his stick; A–B, youths. Vicup.
6 (5). PARIS MARKET (Segredakis). I, youth; A–B, youths. Vicup.
7 (6). COPENHAGEN 205a, from Nola. *CV.* pl. 161, 2. I, seated youth; A–B, youths. Acrocup. Restored.
8 (7). COPENHAGEN 205b, from Nola. *CV.* pl. 161, 1. I, youth at altar; A–B, youths. Acrocup. Restored.
9 (8). ISTANBUL, from Lindos. Blinkenberg *Lindos* i pl. 129, 2707. I, youth; A–B, youths.

10. LOUVRE C 11774. I, male at laver; A–B, males.

11 (8 *bis*). LONDON MARKET, from Greece: destroyed by enemy action. I, symposion (youth reclining to left, looking round). A–B, youths. Vicup.

12 (18). FRANKFORT, Museum V.F., 102 (ex Haeberlin). I, phot. Heidelberg. I, woman at laver; A–B, youths and women. For the shape, Bloesch 139, Vicup no. 5.

13 (9). FLORENCE PD 456, fr. A, (youth).

14 (10). OXFORD G 701, fr., from Naucratis. *CV.* pl. 57, 18. A, (youths).

15 (21 *bis*). OXFORD, fr., from Naucratis. A, (males).

(nos. 16–47, decorated inside only)

16. LOUVRE G 332. I, woman in doorway, holding out a saccos.

17 (11). YALE 165, from Bari. Baur 109; the shape, Hambidge 117 fig. 3. I, woman. Cup type C.

18 (12). ATHENS, Talcott. *Hesp.* 5, 338. I, woman. Vicup.

19 (13). FERRARA, T. 605, from Spina. I, woman with mirror.

20 (14). ATHENS 1574 (CC. 1212). CC. pl. 43. I, woman with mirror. Cup type C.

21 (15). PARIS MARKET (Mikas). I, woman (standing with right leg frontal, head to left, left arm extended; on the left a chair, on the right a wool-basket. Vicup.

22 (16). ATHENS 1575 (CC. 1213). I, woman at altar. Cup type C.

22 *bis*. FERRARA, T. 366 A VP, from Spina. I, woman at (tall laver or the like).

23 (17). LONDON E 91, from Camiros. I, woman seated. Cup type C.

24 (19). ATHENS 1576 (CC. 1214). I, woman running. Cup type C.

~~25 (20). LONDON E 134. 8, fr., from Naucratis. Petrie *Naukratis* i pl. 13, 15.~~ I, woman.

26 (21). OXFORD G 138.9, fr., from Naucratis. *CV.* pl. 14, 9. I, woman.

27 (22). HEIDELBERG 139, from Greece. Kraiker pl. 27. I, youth. Vicup.

28. BARCELONA 618, from Ampurias. I, youth (standing to right).

29 (23). FLORENCE (V, ex Servadio). I, youth at altar.

29 *bis*. LENINGRAD Б 4516. *Soobshcheniya* 15, 42–43. I, youth at altar. [Skudnova].

30 (24). LONDON E 92, from Camiros. I, youth at altar. Vicup.

30 *bis*. EASTON (Pennsylvania), Williams, from Argolis. I, youth at altar (frontal, looking round to left; on the left a laver). Vicup. [Williams].

31. FERRARA, T. 212 B VP, from Spina. I, youth at altar.

32 (25). BERNE 12302. I, youth at altar.

32 *bis*. MILAN 264. *CV.* pl. 4; part, *Cisalpina* i (Belloni) pl. 3, 6. I, youth. [Belloni].

33. FERRARA, T. 983, from Spina. I, youth.

34. BARCELONA 425, fr., from Ampurias. I, male at altar.

35 (26). ANCONA 3324, from Numana. I, youth running to altar. Vicup.

36 (27). VIENNA 216, from Sicily. A, Bloesch pl. 38, 2; CV. pl. 16, 6–7. I, youth leaning on his stick. For the shape, Bloesch 140, Vicup no. 10.

37. LAON 37.1063. CV. pl. 45, 2 and 4. I, youth leaning on his stick. Cup type C.

38 (33). LENINGRAD, fr., from Olbia. Otchët 1905, 33 fig. 58. I, youth.

39 (28). BOLOGNA 445, from Bologna. I, male at laver.

40 (29). BOLOGNA 452, from Bologna. Zannoni pl. 107, 5 and 14. I, youth.

41 (30). BOLOGNA 449, from Bologna. Zannoni pl. 30, 6; CV. pl. 110, 1. I, youth running with phiale.

42 (31). LONDON 1910.3–7. 8, fr. I, youth.

43. ADRIA B 89, fr., from Adria. I, (feet of male in himation).

44 (32). CYRENE, fr., from Cyrene. Afr. It. 4, 212, 2. I, (youth?). See the next.

45. CYRENE, fr., from Cyrene. Afr. It. 4, 211, 5 (upside down). I, male. Belongs to the last?

46 (34). OXFORD, fr., from Naucratis. I, (middle of one in himation).

47 (35). DRESDEN 359. I, satyr at pithos. For the shape, Bloesch 139, Vicup no. 7.

STEMLESS CUP
(with ring-foot—saucer-foot)

48 (36). LONDON E 123, from Camiros. I, komast.

SKYPHOS
(type A)

49 (37). HEIDELBERG 138, from Athens. A, Kraiker pl. 23. A, maenad; B, maenad.

LEKYTHOI
(of secondary shape: Munich 7689 and Moore are of type CL, p. 677 nos. 5–6, and so probably is Athens E 1445)

50 (38). ATHENS E 1445. Nike running with mirror.

51 (39). MUNICH inv. 7689. Nike.

52 (40). EUGENE (Oregon), Moore, from Greece. Eros flying to altar.

The following are in the manner of the painter and may be from his hand:

CUP OR STEMLESS CUP

1 (1). ARLES (ex Mazel), from the lake of Vaccarès. Mém. Inst. Hist. Provence 5 (1928), 88; Benoit Arles 21; Préh. 2, 54. I, youth at altar.

STEMLESS CUP

(*with ring-foot—saucer-foot*)

2. ATHENS, Agora, P 23826, fr., from Athens. I, satyr. Compare Dresden 359 (no. 47).

Perhaps also the

LEKYTHOS

(*of secondary type*)

MUNICH inv. 7692. Youth running (in chlamys, to right, looking round). Restored.

BRYGOS, POTTER

Bloesch *FAS.* 81–90 and 161. *ARV.*[1] 245, 261–3, and 956.

The signature appears on fourteen cups:

1. CAB. MÉD. 570 plus. See p. 399.

(*nos. 2–6, by the Brygos Painter*)

2. LOUVRE G 152 (p. 369 no. 1).
3. ATHENS Acr. 293 (p. 369 no. 5).
4. LONDON E 65 (p. 370 no. 13).
5. FLORENCE 3921 (p. 372 no. 31).
6. WÜRZBURG 479 (p. 372 no. 32).

(*no. 7, manner of the Brygos Painter, near the Castelgiorgio Painter*)

7. FRANKFORT, Städel Institut (p. 386).

(*no. 8, manner of the Brygos Painter, by the Briseis Painter*)

8. LOUVRE G 151 (p. 406 no. 8).

(*no. 9, by the Painter of the Oxford Brygos*)

9. OXFORD 1911.615 (p. 399).

(*nos. 10–13, the style of the drawing unknown: a lost cup, and three handles*)

10. Lost (Gerhard i, 217). I, 'Amazons'. A, Triptolemos. B, Menelaos and Helen. On one handle, Βρυγοσεποιεσεν.
11. BOSTON 95.57, fr., from Athens. Fröhner *Brant.* no. 74 = Hartwig 372; *CB.* i pl. 9, 25. Handle with BRVΛOϚ : EΓOIEϚEN.
12. ATHENS Acr. 294, fr., from Athens. Langlotz 25, below. Part of handle with BRVKOϚ . . .
13. ATHENS, Acropolis Museum (Apotheke), inv. 5791, from Athens. *Delt.* i, suppl., 40 fig. 13, left. Part of handle with [B]RVΛOϚΓOIEϚEN.

The fourteenth cup with the signature of Brygos is known to me from a brief description only:

GENEVA MARKET. I, ransom of Hector; A–B, the like. On I, Priam, bending, approaches Achilles; on A–B, the treatment is similar to that on the Vienna skyphos (p. 380 no. 171). My informants thought that the drawing was by the Brygos Painter. See p. 1650.

The cup with the signature of Brygos in the Cabinet des Médailles:

CAB. MÉD. 570, 578, 580, and perhaps 722: frr.; from Tarquinia. Part, *WV.* C pl. 7, 2, whence Hoppin i, 115. I, seated deity, and Nike. A–B, obscure subjects: deities, among them Poseidon and a goddess—Amphitrite?; Nike; Aphrodite (?) and Eros. On the foot, which no doubt belongs, BRV[ΛOS... On the handle (if it belongs?), B with a bit of the rho after it.

This cup is much earlier than the other cups with the signature of Brygos, and has no connexion with them in drawing.

A small cup-fragment is connected by its patterns with the Cabinet des Médailles Brygos; and what little remains of the pictures is not unlike in style:

FREIBURG S 212, fr. I, (obscure remains). A, white ground, (foot, chitons).

In general character (and no more) the cup in the Cabinet des Médailles is akin to such others, by different hands, as Cabinet des Médailles 543 (p. 448) and Athens Acr. 208, from Athens (Langlotz pl. 11): elaborate cups with something senile about them: the end of a mode, the last of the 'Parade Cups' (Haspels in *BCH.* 1930, 444–51).

THE PAINTER OF THE OXFORD BRYGOS

This cup was not decorated by the Brygos Painter, and the style is not like his:

OXFORD 1911.615, from Cervetri. Part, *JHS.* 34 pl. 9 (whence Hoppin i, 113 and Pfuhl fig. 434) and p. 108; augmented by two frr. found by Nachod and Rumpf in Leipsic (*Disj. Membra* no. 4) and by two found by me in Frankfort (*CV.* Oxford 3–4 and 113–14), *CV.* pl. 2, 1, pl. 6, 3–4, and pl. 61, 1–3. I, uncertain subject: two warriors (Odysseus and Diomed? see *CV.* Oxford, 3). A, fight (Greeks and Persians); B, arming. On one handle, BRVΛOSΕΓΕSΕΝ.

A lost cup seems to be by the same hand.

ROMAN MARKET (Basseggio). B.Ap. xxi. 35; R.I. M 35. I, old man seated, and little girl. A–B, arming.

The following cup is related:

CAB. MÉD. 559 and part (L 247) of 544, frr. I, de Ridder 418; part of A, Hartwig 219. I, arming; A–B, arming.

Compare also the cup-fragments

MARSEILLES, fr., from Marseilles. *C.R.A.I.* 1910, 431; Vasseur pl. 13, 8–10; ph. Arch. phot. 920.191528. A, uncertain subject: the Seven against Thebes (Amphiaraos, Polyneikes). This is somewhat nearer to the Brygos Painter than the others are.

ATHENS, Vlasto, fr., from Glyphada. I, (foot of a male in a himation to right). A, music (1, youth leaning on his stick to right, holding a flute-case; 2, man seated to right with lyre; 3, male leaning on his stick to left, playing the flute).

––––––––––

After these digressions we return to the neighbourhood of the Brygos Painter and examine six artists who (together with the vases already described as in his manner) may be said to form his circle:

(1) The Foundry Painter.

(2–5) The Briseis Painter; the Dokimasia Painter; the Painter of Agora P 42; the Painter of Louvre G 265.

(6) The Painter of the Paris Gigantomachy.

The Foundry Painter is an excellent artist: with his forcible, sometimes even brutal, style he often equals the Brygos Painter. The Briseis Painter and three whom we have grouped with him have less fire than the Brygos Painter, and their style might be described as a 'mild Brygan':[1] three of the four are good, the Painter of Louvre G 265 is inferior. The Painter of the Paris Gigantomachy has vigour, but no subtlety, and most of his work is mechanical and repetitive. He stands nearer to the Foundry Painter than to the Brygos Painter himself.

THE FOUNDRY PAINTER

Nos 1–3 were put together by Hartwig (381–9).

VA. 93–94. *Att. V.* 183–9 and 474. Caskey in *CB.* i, 26–30. Dohan in *Mus. J.* 23, 23–44. Van Ingen in *Harv. St.* 46, 155–66. *ARV.*[1] 263–6 and 956.

CUPS

1 (1). BERLIN 2294, from Vulci. Gerhard *Trinkschalen* pl. 9, 2 and pll. 12–13; FR. pl. 135, whence Perrot 10, 653–7, (I) Johansen *Il.* fig. 31, (A) *Jb.* 44, 9 fig. 2, (detail of B) *Metr. St.* 4, 200, (details of A–B) Lippold *A.G.* pl. 20, 110, (I) Stella 212; (A) Buschor 178; A, Schaal *Rf.* fig. 30; A, Neugebauer pl. 53; A–B, Casson *Technique* figs. 52–53; A–B and part of I, Cloché *Classes* pl. 24, pl. 25, 1, and pl. 23, 6; B and foot, Bloesch pl. 20,

––––––––––

[1] Not to be confused with 'weak Brygan', for which see p. 368.

3; I, Béquignon *Il.* 155; A, *E.A.A.* ii, 184; A, cleaned, Greifenhagen *A.K.* pl. 64. I, Hephaistos and Thetis; A–B, foundry (sculptors). On A, ΔΙΟΛΕΝΕ϶ ΚΑLΟ϶ ΝΑΙ+Ι. [Hartwig]. I was slightly restored, now cleaned. For the shape, Bloesch 73, Euphronios no. 19. See p. 1651.

2 (2). MUNICH 2650 (J. 400), from Vulci. Gerhard pl. 229–30, whence (A) Overbeck *Gall.* pl. 25, 3; A, *Jb.* 44, 25; B and foot, Bloesch pl. 20, 4; I and A, Stella 744 and 746; B, Carpenter *Esthetic Basis* pl. at p. 48. I, two men. A, sculptor making a marble horse. B, men and youths. [Hartwig]. Restored. For the shape, Bloesch 74, Euphronios no. 22. The costume of the two elders on A is perhaps in favour of the old interpretation as Epeios making the model for the Trojan horse.

3 (3). LONDON E 78, from Vulci. I, Murray no. 55, whence Norman Gardiner *G.A.S.* 406; detail of A, Hartwig 392, whence *Jh.* 31, 3; detail of B, *JHS.* 23, 285, 13; A–B, *JHS.* 26 pl. 13, whence Norman Gardiner *G.A.S.* 436 and *Athl.* 213 fig. 188; I, Norman Gardiner *Athl.* fig. 174; part of A, Hilker fig. 13, whence Neutsch *Sport* fig. 31. I, boy boxer and trainer; A–B, athletes: A, pancration, boxers; B, boxers, hoplitodromos. [Hartwig]. For the shape, Bloesch 73, Euphronios no. 20.

4 (4, +). HEIDELBERG 73 and 74, and NAPLES, Astarita, 275, frr. The Heidelberg part, Kraiker pl. 10. Outside, athletes. The Astarita fragment joins Heidelberg 74 on the right, adding the athlete's left arm and shoulder, and the finger-tips of another person on the left. See the next.

5 (5). NEW YORK 07.156.8, fr. Richter *ARVS.* fig. 97. A, (on the right, trainer). May be from the same cup as the last.

6 (6, part). FLORENCE 6 B 47, fr. *CV.* pl. 6, B 47. A, (boxer). See the next. Compare the last two.

7 (6), part). FLORENCE 9 B 44, fr. *CV.* pl. 9, B 44. A, (trainer). May be from the same cup as the last.

8 (7, +). LOUVRE S 1417, plus, two frr. I, boxer (legs and bit of thong); outside, athletes (on one fr., boxers; on the other, on the left, athlete with acontia, hand of trainer with wand).

8 *bis.* BASLE, Cahn, 102. I, man and boy. A, boxers; B athletes.

9 (8, +). LOUVRE G 290. I, ph. Gir. 31998. I, acontists; A–B, athletes. Several Louvre frr. join, among them C 190. For the shape, Bloesch 137, Eleusis Class, no. 3.

10 (9). COPENHAGEN, Thorvaldsen Museum, 111. I, boy acontist and trainer; A, hoplitodromoi; B, acontist, boxer, trainers. Restored.

10 *bis.* LUCERNE MARKET (A.A.). I, symposion (man reclining, right arm extended holding a cup, another cup in the left hand). A–B, athletes (A, jumper and youth, athlete picking up discus; B, discus-thrower and two youths). Restored. See p. 1651.

11 (11). BOSTON 01.8034. Detail of A, *VA.* 93 fig. 62; CB. i pl. 12 and p. 28;

shape, Caskey G. 189 no. 144. I, symposion (man and youth reclining); A–B, symposion.

12 (12). CAMBRIDGE, Corpus Christi College. Fröhner *Coll. Lecuyer* 2 pl. E5 = *Cat. Lecuyer* 63; *JHS*. 41, 224 and pll. 15–16, whence (part) Chittenden and Seltman pl. 19. I, symposion (man reclining, playing the flute, and boy dancing); A–B, symposion. For the shape, Bloesch 73, Euphronios no. 18. See p. 1651.

13 (13). BERLIN inv. 3198. *Anz.* 1892, 101; I, Licht ii, 205; B.Ap. xxi. 90. I, komast οὐρῶν; A–B, komos.

14 (14). BASLE, Kambli. I and A, *Coll. M.E.* pl. 10, 225. I, komast; A–B, komos.

15 (15). BOSTON 10.195, from Orvieto. CB. i pl. 11 and p. 27; I (with the restoration), *AJA*. 1935, 45. I, warrior; A–B, arming.

16 (16). HARVARD 1917.149 (1642.95). *Harv. St.* 46, 156–7; *CV*. pl. 13; *Archaeology* 1954, 132. I, warrior; A, arming; B, fight.

17 (17). BRUSSELS R 322. I, *Bull. Mus. Roy.* 1908, 82; *CV*. pl. 3, 1. I, warrior; A–B, arming.

18 (18). AREZZO 1421, two frr. Outside, arming? On one fr., (man, spear, arrow), on the other, (man with face in three-quarter view).

19. RIEHEN, Gsell. I, komast playing the flute. A–B, fight (on A, 1, attacking to right, 2, falling to left, 3, to left, striking with sword; on B, 1, running to left, 2, retreating to left, looking round, 3, attacking to left with sword). Restored, I much.

20 (21). PHILADELPHIA 31.19.2, from Italy. *Mus. J.* 23, 34–38 and 42–43 figs. 16 and 18. I, cup-bearer. A, Centauromachy. B, fight.

21 (22). MUNICH 2641, from Cervetri. FR. ii, 133–5; A–B, *Mus. J.* 23, 40–41. I, youth arming, and boy; A–B, Centauromachy. For the shape, Bloesch 79, Euphronios no. 51.

22 (20). MUNICH 2640 (J. 368), from Vulci. Benndorf *Gjölb.* 183 and 186; Hartwig pl. 59, 2 and pl. 60, whence (I) HM. pl. 39; FR. pl. 86 and ii, 132, whence (I) Buschor 167, (I) Pfuhl fig. 403, (I and A) Byvanck-Quarles van Ufford P. 31–32, (I) LS. fig. 92; I, Buschor G. *Vasen* 160, whence Frel *Ř.V.* fig. 185; Lullies and Hirmer pl. 80, above, and pll. 81–83. I, Lapith and Centaur; A–B, Centauromachy. Restored. For the shape, Bloesch 71, Euphronios no. 13. See p. 1651.

23 (a). BOSTON 98.933, from Cervetri. Gerhard pl. 203, whence (A–B) Benndorf *Gjölb.* 155; cleaned, Pollak *Zwei* 22 and pl. 8, whence (A–B) Bulas *Il.* fig. 20, (A–B) Fairbanks and Chase 71; CB. i pl. 14; A–B, *Bull. Vereen.* June 1940, 28; B.Ap. xxii. 77. I, Phanas and Empedion. A–B, Achilles pursuing Hector.

24 (23). VILLA GIULIA 50407. Hartwig pl. 54. I, horseman; A, hoplite and cavalry; B, cavalryman with horses. Restored. For the shape, Bloesch 84, Brygos no. 17. See p. 1651.

25 (24). LENINGRAD 663. I, youth and boy. A, boys on horseback and, youth. B, man in mule-cart, with man and youths.

26 (26). BOSTON 13.204, from Cervetri. CB. i pl. 13, 33. I, maenad; A–B, satyrs and maenads.

27 (25, +). ADRIA B 600 and B 551, fr., from Adria. Part, Micali *Mon. ined.* pl. 46, 6; *CV.* pl. 12, 2; *Riv. Ist.* N.S. 5–6, 42 fig. 24. A, (on the left, boy holding hare, and man or youth). Miss Riccioni has seen that B 551 (wrongly attributed to the Triptolemos Painter in *ARV.*[1] 242, no. 44) joins B 600 below.

28 (a). FLORENCE 9 B 36, fr. *CV.* pl. 9, B 36. A, (boy).

29. NAPLES, Astarita, 128 and 129, two frr. Outside, on 128, (on the left, bent head, minus the chin, of a fair-haired boy to right, then the extended right arm of a man or youth holding a stick; behind the arm an aryballos hanging); on 129, (strigil and aryballos hanging from a thong).

30 (19). LEIPSIC T 542, fr., from Orvieto. I, warrior (wiping his helmet?). A, (feet).

(nos. 31–36, decorated inside only)

31 (27). TÜBINGEN E 27. Watzinger pl. 20. I, athlete.

32 (28). BOWDOIN 13.26, from Cervetri. I, two athletes (one of them seated on the ground, holding an acontion).

33 (29). ADRIA B 498, fr., from Adria. *CV.* pl. 20, 2. I, athlete seated on the ground, and trainer.

34. CHRISTCHURCH (N.Z.), Canterbury University College, 17. I, symposion (man reclining). A fragment in my possession had the man's left arm, part of his chest and middle, part of the couch: I have given it to Canterbury University College.

35. TODI 463, from Todi. *CV.* pl. 1, 1. I, youth seated, playing the flute.

36 (a). BOSTON 13.95, from Cervetri. CB. i pl. 10, 27. I, satyr. Now augmented by a fragment ex Leipsic, see *CF.* 33 no. 12 *bis.*

SKYPHOS

(hybrid: body of type A, handles of type B: cf. p. 381 nos. 176–7, and p. 899 no. 143)

37 (30). ATHENS 14705. *Eph.* 1920, 94 and 96. A, boy running with hoop, and loaves on a platter; B, youth.

OINOCHOE

(shape 2 rather than 1)

38 (a 8). LONDON D 13, from Locri?. Newton and Thompson *Cast.* pl. 13; *Guide G.R. Life*[3] 133 fig. 147, whence Wiegand *Spinnerin* 6 and Bieber *G.K.* 2 fig. 4; Bieber *Entw.* pl. 1, 2; Cloché pl. 28, 3; ph. Ma. 3197, 3. White ground. Woman spinning. See below, p. 405.

The following cup is probably by the Foundry Painter rather than the Brygos Painter, to whom it was attributed in *ARV.*[1] 247 no. 22 and in *Studies Robinson*:

CAB. MÉD. L 114 (?), 766, and 593, frr. I, *Studies Robinson* ii pl. 29, a; I, symposion (man reclining and youth playing the flute); A–B, symposion. See ibid. 82–83.

MANNER OF THE FOUNDRY PAINTER

ARV.[1] 265–6.

CUPS

1 (a). CAB. MÉD. 557 and (joining) 676, fr. I, *Studies Robinson* ii pl. 29, b; phs. Gir. 28876 (part), 28877 (part), 28879 (part). I, naked boy playing the flute, and male seated holding a flute. A, (males).

2 (1). ROMAN MARKET (Basseggio), from Vulci. B.Ap. xxii. 101. I, maenad dancing and satyr seated playing the flute; A, satyrs carrying off a maenad; B, maenads and satyr. [Rumpf].

3 (l 10). ROMAN MARKET (Depoletti), from Tarquinia. B.Ap. xxi. 94. 1. I, trainer (leaning on his stick to right); A–B, athletes: A, boxers and youth; B, discus-thrower, trainer, and acontist.

4. VILLA GIULIA, fr. I, boxer (head to right, and extended left arm, holding a thong with both hands); A, pancration.

5. FLORENCE 11 B 42, fr. *CV.* pl. 11, B 42. A, (boxer).

6 (2). TÜBINGEN E 29, fr. Watzinger pl. 20. A, (youth).

7 (3). CAB. MÉD., part of 713, fr. A, (front-hair, and hand with stick, of male).

8. OXFORD, Beazley, fr. I, (on the right, head of boy or girl in himation to left).

9 (5). ORVIETO, Faina, 56, from Orvieto. Ph. R.I. 35.879. I, acontist (youth standing to right, upright acontion in his left hand). See p. 405.

10 (6). FLORENCE B B 4. *CV.* pl. B, B 4; *Boll. d'Arte* 29, 267 fig. 20. I, komast.

11 (7). BERLIN inv. 3757, from Orvieto. Licht ii, 72; Vorberg *Gloss.* 378; *CV.* pl. 74, 2; ph. Marb. 1075.14. I, naked woman οὐροῦσα.

The following cup is connected with the Foundry Painter:

LINCOLN. *AJA.* 1959 pl. 38 figs. 19–21. I, warrior; A–B, warriors.

A cup-fragment resembles the Perugia cup by Onesimos (p. 320 no. 8), but the crest recalls the Foundry Painter:

(a). HEIDELBERG 67, fr., from Athens. Kraiker pl. 9. A, (youth holding helmet).

See also p. 1651.

With the white oinochoe in London, D 13 (p. 403 no. 38), compare the

WHITE ALABASTRON

BERLIN 2258, from Tanagra. *Die Antike* I pll. 28–29; B, Neugebauer pl. 55, 3; B, Blümel *S.H.* 76; Greifenhagen *A.K.* pl. 72. Nike; athlete.

————————

Two fine cups go together (*ARV*.¹ 256–7, 1): they are close to the Brygos Painter at his height, but hardly from his hand. They might be by the Foundry Painter at the point in his career when he was nearest to the Brygos Painter.

1. TARQUINIA RC 5291, from Tarquinia. *Mon.* 11 pl. 20, whence (A) Buschor 173; *WV.* D pl. 8, 1, whence (A) HM. pl. 35; I and B, Ghali-Kahil *H.* pl. 86, 2 and pl. 56, 2; *CV.* pl. 18; 1, phs. Mo. 9038 and 5854, 6; I, ph. Brogi 18467; A, phs. R.I. 34.1887 and another. I, hero leading a woman (Agamemnon and Briseis?). A, Theseus leaving Ariadne. B, Menelaos and Helen.
2. LONDON 95.5–13.1. Hartwig 350–1; I, Licht ii, 131; I, Nairn 52; B.Ap. I, komos (youth playing the flute, and man seated listening); A–B, komos.

Other cups are nearer to the Foundry Painter than to the Brygos: compare London 95.5–13.1:

MANNHEIM 183, from Italy. Hofmann pl. 2; *CV.* pl. 21, 2 pl. 23, 1–2, and pl. 32, 3. I, komast; A–B, komos. Close to the Foundry Painter; compare the Kambli cup (p. 402 no. 14).

BASLE, Cahn, 58, fr. A, arming? (head and shoulders of a youth in a chitoniskos bending to right, as if putting on his greaves, then a greave, frontal, probably hanging, then what seems to be part of another person's arm and hair).

BERLIN inv. 3240, from Cervetri. Hartwig 373–4; I, Licht i, 27; I, Philippart *C.A.B.* pl. 5; *CV.* pl. 71, 1–7. I, youth and boy; round the tondo a white zone. A, woman spinning, and youths; B, woman and males. Restored. For the shape, Bloesch 91, Hieron no. 8.

Faina 56 might perhaps be placed here (p. 404 no. 9); compare also Yale 164 (p. 377 no. 105).

————————

THE 'MILD BRYGAN' GROUP

See p. 400. It consists of the Briseis Painter, the Dokimasia Painter, the Painter of Agora P 42, and the Painter of Louvre G 265. The first three, closely interconnected, are good, the fourth inferior.

THE BRISEIS PAINTER

VA. 109–11. *Att. V.* 194–6 and 474. *ARV.*[1] 266–70 and 956–7.

Named after the subject of no. 1. Mild–Brygan Group.

CUPS

1 (1). LONDON E 76, from Vulci. Gerhard *TG.* pll. E–F; I, Murray no. 53; Hartwig pl. 42, 1 and pl. 41, whence Farmakovski ii, 274 and 272, (A) Perrot 10, 793, (A) Bulas *Il.* fig. 1, (A) Johansen *Iliaden* fig. 25. I, old man seated, and man; A, Briseis led away from Achilles; B, Briseis brought to Agamemnon. The men on I are probably Greek heroes like two of the persons on A and three on B: the old man perhaps Phoinix. For the shape, Bloesch 88, below, no. 2.

2 (2). LONDON E 75, from Vulci. I, Murray no. 52; Hartwig pl. 42, 2 and pl. 43, whence (I) Farmakovski ii, 273 and (A) Farnell *Greek Cults* 5 pl. 45; B and foot, Bloesch pl. 24, 4; I, *E.A.A.* ii, 176. I, old man at door, and guard (Priam at the tent of Achilles?). A–B, Dionysos with maenads and satyrs. For the shape, Bloesch 88, below, no. 3.

3 (4). OXFORD 1944.87, from Greece. Phs. A.I. varia 695–7. I, satyr and maenad; A–B, Dionysos with maenads and satyrs.

4. NEW YORK MARKET. I, satyr and maenad; A–B, satyrs and maenads. On I, maenad dancing to right, wing-sleeves, and satyr to left, playing the flute, then a fancy rock; on A, two groups of a satyr attacking a maenad; on B, two groups of a maenad rounding on a satyr. Cup type C.

5 (5). ADRIA Bc 21, fr., from Adria. I, Schöne pl. 2, 2; *CV.* pl. 12, 1; I, *Riv. Ist.* N.S. 5–6, 42 fig. 23. I, love-making (on the right, naked woman, wineskin). A, (maenad); B, (maenad).

6 (7). FLORENCE PD 386–8, frr. Outside, unexplained subjects: on one fr., toes of one fallen, lower part of woman running to left, chitoniskos of male to right; on the second, hand, to right, of a woman; on the third, bow and quiver hanging, and part of a sleeve: the subject, or one of the subjects, may have been an adventure of Herakles.

7. NEW YORK 53.11.4. *Bull. Metr.* Oct. 1954, 62–63; B, Richter *ARVS.*[2] fig. 62. I, Theseus and Amphitrite; A, Theseus, Triton, Poseidon, and Nereids; B, Theseus returning to Athens.

8 (22). LOUVRE G 151, from Cervetri. *Mon.* 1856 pl. 14, whence (B) Robert *Bild und Lied* 91, (B and part of A) Davreux fig. 22; *WV.* 8 pl. 3, whence (I) HM. pl. 26, 1, and Hoppin i, 116; part, Perrot 10, 559–61; Pottier pl. 120; A, ph. Gir. 34080, whence (detail) *Ant. class.* 6 pl. 1, 4; B, ph. Al., whence *Corolla Curtius* pl. 51, 2–3; A, *Recueil Dugas* pl. 12, 2. I, Apollo and Artemis; A, judgement of Paris; B, Paris returning to his father's house after the judgement. On one handle, BPVΛOϞE[ΓOIEϞEN]. For the subject of B compare Tarquinia RC 6846 (p. 369 no. 4) and see Hampe

in *Corolla Curtius* 144; for the shape see Bloesch 85, Brygos no. 26. Now cleaned. See p. 398 no. 8.

9 (6). ADRIA B 275, fr., from Adria. *CV.* pl. 24, 1. A, (youth attacking with sword).

10 (23). OXFORD 1927.4604 and (ex Leipsic T 541) 1932.1, fr. Part, *CV.* pl. 14, 10 and 23. I, woman with kithariskos. A, arming? (youth running, woman holding shield, male).

11 (8). HAMBURG 1900.518. Ballheimer 31–32, 35, and 39; I, Schröder *Sport* pl. 109; I, Blümel *S.H.* 101; A–B, *Anz.* 1935, 154. I, youth with pick and acontia; A–B, wrestlers. See p. 1651.

12. BOWDOIN 13.19, fr. A, victor.

13 (13). LEIPSIC T 510, from Orvieto. I and parts of A–B, *Jb.* 11, 187. Youth (peripolos). A, boy folding his himation, and youths; B, the like. For the shape, Bloesch 128, Conefoot cup no. 3.

14. FERRARA, T. 173 C VP, from Spina. *Arte Antica e Moderna* 1 pl. 8, pl. 9, a, and pl. 10. I, man. A, man and horses; B, youth and horses.

15. BARCELONA 478, fr., from Ampurias. I, youth (head and shoulders, standing to right). A, (frontal foot of male in himation, three hooves).

16 (9). LOUVRE G 278 and FLORENCE Z B 27, from Vulci. See *CF.* 16 on pl. 9, B 37. I, *RA.* 1851–2, ii pl. 168; I, Pottier pl. 133; I, Vorberg *Gloss.* 453; the Florence fr., *CF.* pl. Z, 27. I, man embracing boy. A, Nike and youths; B, similar. Restored. For the shape, Bloesch 88, below, no. 1; for the subject of I, *Cypr.* 28, α 47. The fragment Florence 9 B 37 does not belong (see no. 28).

17 (3). BRYN MAWR P 267, fr. I, *AJA.* 1916 pl. 13. I, old man seated, and man or youth. A–B, males seated and standing. For I, compare London E 76 (no. 1).

18 (10). NEW YORK 27.74. Pollak and Muñoz pll. 39–41; *Bull. Metr.* 23, 108 fig. 1, and 110; A, Richter and Milne fig. 156; Richter and Hall pl. 47, 51, pl. 48, and pl. 180, 51; *AJA.* 1941, 534 and pl. 14; detail of A, Richter *ARVS.*[1] fig. 62. I, boy, at a wooden erection of uncertain purpose; A, boys singing to the flute; B, the like. On the subjects see Miss Bieber in *AJA.* 1941, 529–36. For A–B she thinks of a tragic chorus in training: rather, χορὸς παίδων training for a dithyrambic contest.

19 (11). BERLIN inv. 3359. *CV.* pl. 74, 1 and 3–4. I, countryman. A, boy seated playing the flute, and youths; B, youth offering a boy a lyre, and youth.

20 (12). TARQUINIA, from Tarquinia. I, (bit of chair). A, youth singing, youth playing the flute, and youth listening; B, the like.

21 (16). NORTHWICK, Spencer-Churchill. A–B, *Coll. B. et C.* pl. 21, 180. I, man; A, youths and boy; B, youth, man, and boy.

22 (17). BOWDOIN 20.2 (bought at Sirolo). I, youth; A–B, youths and boys.

23. BARCELONA 511, fr., from Ampurias. A, (youth, boy; in a building). Cup type C. [Shefton].

24 (18). MARZABOTTO, fr., from Marzabotto. A, (upper part of a youth in a himation to left; on the left, sponge and strigil). Another fragment in Marzabotto may belong: outside, tree, altar, goat's horns.

25. OXFORD, Beazley, three frr., from Vulci. I, (on the right, a small piece of the person's garment, and, hanging, bag and strigil). Outside: on one fragment the upper half of a youth in a himation leaning on his stick to right, the right arm akimbo: probably the left-hand figure on one half; on the second, waist almost to ankle of a male in a himation seated to right; on the third, heel, with himation, of the right-hand figure on one half, a male standing to left, then a column, and a rock-seat under the handle.

26. NAPLES, Astarita, 271, fr. A, (nose and upper front of a boy in a himation standing to right, then, hanging, a writing-case; then the nose of another, to left). [Bothmer].

27. WASHINGTON (neg. 37625 D), fr., from Orvieto. A, (upper front part of a boy in a himation standing to right, and forearm with hand of a male holding an upright stick).

28 (20). FLORENCE 9 B 37, fr. *CV*. pl. 9, B 37. A, (youth leaning on his stick).

29 (21). FLORENCE 20 B 39, fr. *CV*. pl. 20, B 39. A, (boy).

30. STRASBURG, Univ., 844, fr. A, (middles of two males in himation to left, the second one leaning on his stick).

31 (19). ADRIA B 792, fr., from Adria. A, (face of a youth to left).

32 (15). TARQUINIA 703, from Tarquinia. *CV*. pl. 8. I, youth standing and youth seated; A, youth and woman; man and woman; B, men and women.

33 (14). RUVO, Jatta, 1539, from Ruvo. I, *Annali* 1877 pl. Q; Philippart *C.A.B.* pl. 8; I and A, *Japigia* 3, 18; I, *E.A.A.* ii pl. p. 174. I, white ground, satyr. A, women and youth; B, women. Restored. (The inscription Αλκιβιαδες καλος is modern: doubtful if over ancient traces). For the shape, Bloesch 89, above, no. 4.

34. BASLE, Cahn, 59, fr. A, (head and shoulders of a naked woman bending to right, with part of a tree: probably from a bathing scene, cf. London 96. 6–21. I, no. 42).

35 (a2). ATHENS, Vlasto, fr., from Athens. I, (head, breast, right upper arm, of an old man to left; on the left, a crest?).

36 (27). TARQUINIA, from Tarquinia. FR. iii, 252 fig. 120; ph. Mo. 8269, 2, whence Vorberg *Ars erot*. pl. 18, 2 and Vorberg *Gloss*. 110, 1; Vorberg *Ars erot*. pl. 17, 2; ph. R.I. 1934.2216, whence *AM.* 57 Beil. 2, 1; *CV*. pl. 12, 1. I, love-making (man and woman).

37 (26). OXFORD, Beazley, from Cervetri. Vorberg *Gloss*. 109, 2; ph. R.I. 1931.243. I, love-making (man and woman).

38 (28). ADRIA Bc 76; and once ADRIA, Bocchi: fr., from Adria. Part (Bc 76), *CV*. pl. 20, 7. I, love-making (man or youth, and woman). The small fragment Bc 76 is all that remains; but a rough sketch by Bocchi shows that about half the picture was found in the year 1803.

39 (30). LOUVRE G 312. Ph. Gir. 31999. I, komos (youth and flute-girl).

40 (35). FREIBURG, fr. I, (on the right, lower part of one in a himation, standing, with upright stick).

41 (31). GOETTINGEN H 91 and VILLA GIULIA. See *CF*. 34 no. 22. I, seated youth, and girl.

42 (25). LONDON 96.6–21.1, from Vulci. Sudhoff i, 33; *JHS*. 41, 125. I, naked woman at laver.

43 (32). BERLIN 2300, from Chiusi. *Annali* 1847 pl. M; Gerhard *TG*. pl. 9, 5–6, whence HM pl. 33, 3; Richter *F*. fig. 224. I, king (Thoas?) in chest.

44 (33). ADRIA B 496, from Adria. Schöne pl. 3, 2; *CV*. pl. 17, 3. I, death of Orpheus.

45 (34). ADRIA B 323, frr., from Adria. Schöne pl. 7, 3; *CV*. pl. 9, 1–2. I, Europa. Compare the cup-fragments Adria B 558 (*CV*. pl. 28, 10) and Adria B 701 (*CV*. pl. 28, 11).

46 (29). ADRIA B 548, fr., from Adria. *CV*. pl. 14, 4; *Riv. Ist.* N.S. 5–6, 43 fig. 26. I, satyr.

PANATHENAIC AMPHORA

47 (37). BERLIN 2163, from Locri. Gargiulo *Recueil* (1845) 2 pl. 67; B, Genick pl. 2. A, Zeus; B, Iris.

NECK-AMPHORAE

(nos. 48–50, small, with ridged handles: see CB. ii, 39–40)

48 (38). LONDON 1928.1–17.56, from Nola. *BCH*. 1899, 158 and 160, whence *Mü. St.* 341; *Burlington 1903* pl. 89, G 11; A, *BMQ*. 2 pl. 55, b; *CV*. pl. 59, 2. The sons of Boreas: A, Zetes and umpire; B, Kalais. For the subject, Miss Hutton in *BCH*. 1899, 157–64.

49 (39). BOSTON 01.8028, from Capua. A, *VA*. 110; CB. ii pl. 45, 86 and p. 40; shape, Caskey G. 72. A, maenad and satyr; B, satyr. See CB. ii, 39–40.

50 (40). LONDON E 319, from Nola. *CV*. pl. 59, 1. A, satyr and maenad; B, satyr.

(nos. 51–58, Nolan amphorae, with triple handles)

51 (41). CAMBRIDGE 37.23. A, *Burl. 1903* pl. 92, G 22; A, *VA*. 109; *CV*. ii RS. pl. 11, 1 and pl. 17, 3, 6, and 8. A, Zeus and Ganymede; B, old man.

52 (42). PARIS, Peyrefitte. A, woman with torches (moving to right); B, king (standing to left).

53 (43). NAPLES 3198. A, ph. So. 11072, i, 7. A, woman with oinochoe and phiale; B, old man.

54. LENTINI, from Leontinoi. A, *Boll. d'Arte* 1957, 72. A, Nike; B, man.

55 (44). MAYENCE, Univ., 111, (ex Preyss), from Sicily. A, *Coll. Lambros* pl. 10, 59; A, Hampe and Simon *G.L.* pl. 26. A, Nike; B, woman with phiale. Small.

56. LONDON MARKET (Spink: ex Sligo). A, Nike (or Iris); B, woman. On A, to right, with phiale and caduceus; on B, to left, with oinochoe. Small. Especially close to the last.

57 (45). SYRACUSE 17250, from Gela. A, *CV.* pl. 8, 1. A, Zeus and Nike; B, woman.

58 (46). SYRACUSE 19860, from Gela. A, seated man with spears. B, woman carrying couch.

COLUMN-KRATER
(the pictures not framed)

59 (47). NAPLES RC 146, from Cumae. Fiorelli pl. 15, whence *Bull. Nap.* N.S. 5 pl. 10, 19. A, Eos and Tithonos; B, woman.

OINOCHOE
(shape 1)

60 (a 1). LEYDEN PC 84 (xviii e 24), from Vulci. Roulez pl. 8, 1, whence Overbeck *KM.* pl. 24, 9; *Rijksmuseum, Gids* 35, 1. Herakles and Apollo: the struggle for the tripod.

LEKYTHOI
(standard shape)

61. GELA INA casa 1954, from Gela. *NSc.* 1960, 164. Zeus and Ganymede.

61 *bis* (a 4). LONDON E 646, from Gela. Woman holding sword and shield.

62 (48). Once AGRIGENTO, Giudice, 401 (59), from Gela. Ph. Lo Cascio pl. 99, b. Woman seated and man with purse. Restored.

ALABASTRON

62 *bis.* ATHENS 16277. A, woman with mirror; B, woman with thurible.

PYXIDES
(no. 63, type A)

63 (49). LONDON E 769, from Athens. Part, Richter *F.* fig. 195. Women.

(no. 64, type D, box)

64 (50). OXFORD 1929.4, from Greece. *CV.* pl. 52, 7 and pl. 65, 7. Boy.

STEMMED DISHES

65 (24). LOUVRE C 108, fr. I, man and boy.

66. LOUVRE C 10912. I, woman (standing to right, holding a basket).

PLATE

67 (36). NAPLES RC 138, from Cumae. *ML.* 22 pl. 83, 1. Woman seated, with mirror.

MANNER OF THE BRISEIS PAINTER

ARV.[1] 270 and 956-7.

(i)

For some of the fragments, especially the smaller ones, other members of the Mild-Brygan Group (p. 400) cannot be excluded—the Painter of Agora P 42 (p. 415) and the Dokimasia Painter (p. 412):

CUPS

1. ADRIA B 673 and B 259, fr., from Adria. *CV.* pl. 22, 3 and pl. 13, 1; part (B 259), *Riv. Ist.* N.S. 5-6, 44 fig. 27. A, (boy singing, and youth—probably seated and playing the flute). B 673 joins B 259 on the left. B 259 was attributed to the Briseis Painter by Miss Riccioni, who compared New York 27. 74 (p. 407 no. 18); compare also Bowdoin 20. 2 (p. 407 no. 22).

2. ADRIA B 294, fr., from Adria. *CV.* pl. 13, 8. A, (male).

3. ADRIA B 105, fr., from Adria. *CV.* pl. 24, 3. A, (male). [Riccioni].

4. ADRIA B 765, fr., from Adria. *CV.* pl. 13, 7. A, (male). [Riccioni].

5. THE HAGUE, Museum Meermanno–Westreenianum, 629. I, Byvanck *Gids* pl. 32. I, youth putting on his greaves; A–B, arming. [Rumpf].

6. OXFORD G 138. 27, fr., from Naucratis. *CV.* pl. 14, 22. A, (arming).

7. TÜBINGEN E 26, fr. A, Watzinger pl. 20. I, (so far as preserved, white ground). A, (youth, man: perhaps from a procession).

8. OXFORD 1929.167, fr. *CV.* pl. 57, 4 and 13. I, (hand with writing-case). A, (one in long chiton and himation, seated); B, (foot of woman running). Recalls the Painter of Agora P 42.

9. ADRIA B 839, fr., from Adria. *CV.* pl. 24, 5. I, (boy).

(ii)

No. 1 is really very like the Briseis Painter; the others resemble it, but seem farther from him:

CUPS

1 (3). ADRIA B 254 and B 483, fr., from Adria. A, Micali *Mon. ined.* pl. 47, 1-2; *CV.* pl. 11; I, A–B, *Riv. Ist.* N.S. 5-6, 40. I, male and boy. A, (on the right, boy with lyre, seated man); B, (on the left, boy, male).

2 (4). ADRIA B 543, fr., from Adria. Micali *Mon. ined.* pl. 47, 3; *CV.* pl. 13, 3; *Riv. Ist.* N.S. 5-6, 44 fig. 28. Outside, (youth).

3. ADRIA B 590, fr., from Adria. *CV.* pl. 17, 2. A, (hunter attacking boar).

4. ADRIA B 611, fr., from Adria. *CV.* pl. 6, 3. Outside, (youth—hunter?). Compare the last.

5 (5). ADRIA B 587, fr., from Adria. *CV.* pl. 29, 5. A, (man).

Compare also the cup-fragment

(6). ADRIA B 545, fr., from Adria. Schöne pl. 10, 5; *CV*. pl. 10, 1. A, komos.

THE DOKIMASIA PAINTER

Att. V. 193. *ARV.*[1] 271-2 and 957.

Named from the subject of no. 1. Mild-Brygan Group.

CUPS

1 (1). BERLIN 2296, from Orvieto. *AZ*. 1880 pl. 15, whence Helbig *Hippeis* 74; Lücken pl. 90, 2 and pll. 45-46; I, Schaal *Rf*. fig. 14; A and foot, Bloesch pl. 22, 4; *CV*. pl. 75. I, archer with horse. A–B, youths with horses (inspection, see Gustav Körte in *AZ*. 1880, 177-81, and Helbig *Hippeis* 78-79). For the shape, Bloesch 83, Brygos no. 13.

2 (2). LEIPSIC, fr., from Cervetri. I, (youth in himation: head and shoulders, to right, remain). A, youth leading horse (from a scene like that on Berlin 2296, no. 1).

3 (3, 4). ADRIA B 553 and B 88, two frr., from Adria. One fr., *CV*. pl. 10, 3; I of one fr., *Riv. Ist.* N.S. 5-6, 39 fig. 18. I, (man); A, youth leading horse; B, youth leading horse. The scene outside may have been of the same nature as in Berlin 2296 (no. 1). Inside there may have been a second man, seated, and the pair would correspond to the officials beside the tree.

4 (5). ADRIA B 97, fr., from Adria. A, (on the left, man leaning on his stick, then a horse's tail).

5. ADRIA B 98 and B 98 *bis*, two frr., from Adria. *CV*. pl. 27, 12-13. I, (feet). Outside, (youth, horses). [Riccioni].

6 (8). FLORENCE PD 56, from Populonia. *NSc*. 1926 pl. 11; I, Minto *Populonia* pl. 45, 1. I, komast (youth playing the flute at a krater). A, boy with horse, and man; B, (man, horse).

7. FLORENCE V xxxix, fr., from Chiusi. I, athlete (on the left, a pillar). A, (forelegs of horse to left, stick and shod foot of a male to left).

8 (6). ADRIA B 425, fr., from Adria. *CV*. pl. 16, 1; A, *Riv. Ist.* N.S. 5-6, 45 fig. 29. I, (male in himation, seated). A, youth and donkeys.

9 (7). BOLOGNA 366, from Bologna. Zannoni pl. 53, 6 and 13-14; *CV*. pl. 7; A, Cloché pl. 13, 5. I, boy holding a piece of meat. A, copulation of donkeys. B, bull-calves and heifer coming home from grazing.

10 (9). LONDON E 818, from Vulci. B, *JHS*. 23, 285, whence Norman Gardiner *G.A.S.* 289; I, Vorberg *Gloss*. 119 and 544. I, love-making (man and woman). A, wrestlers; B, hoplitodromoi.

11 (10). FERRARA, T. 931, from Spina. I, man and dog. A, athlete and youths; B, man and boy and youth. See p. 1651.

12. PARIS MARKET (Segredakis). I, komast (man running to left, looking round, playing the flute); A–B, komos (on A, youth with stick and krotala, youth making water, youth with skyphos leaning on his stick to left; on B, old man leaning on his stick to left, two youths dancing). I is restored.

13 (11). NAPLES Stg. 273. I, komast; A–B, komos. See p. 388 no. 4.

14. LEIPSIC T 527, from Tarquinia. A, Hartwig 335; A, Bielefeld *Z.V.* pl. 10 fig. 12. I, komast; A–B, komos.

15. NEW YORK 06.1021.188. *Vente 11 mai 1903*, 44–45; Sambon *Canessa* 24 no. 80, and 23; cleaned, Richter and Hall pl. 45 and pl. 180, 46. I, komast; A–B, komos.

16 (14). COPENHAGEN inv. 6327, from Capua. *CV.* pl. 143. I, youth at herm. A, boar-hunt; B, deer-hunt.

17 (15). LONDON 1952.12–2.12, fr. A, (man attacking with sword—hunter?).

18 (18). ADRIA B 532, fr., from Adria. *CV.* pl. 15, 2. A, (youth in chlamys—hunter?).

19 (20). LENINGRAD 657 (St. 848). I, warrior at altar; A–B, fight.

20 (19). ORVIETO 588, from Orvieto. *CV.* pl. 8, 4–6. I, warrior; A–B, warriors.

21 (22). CAB. MÉD. 685 (L 134), fr. Ph. Gir. 28876 (part) and 28877 (part). I, (on the left, neck to middle of a youth in a himation to right). A, (foot of one moving to left). Another fragment in the Cabinet des Médailles is in the same style and should belong: I, (feet of a male in a himation to right), but I have no note of the outside.

22 (23). DELOS, frr., from Delos. Dugas *Délos x* pl. 54, 655–6. Outside, (youths and boys).

23 (12). LENINGRAD 653 (St. 879). R.I. xii, 10 a–b, whence *Annali* 1875 pl. Q, 1–2 and pl. R, 1. I, warrior. A, Dolon; B, the like.

24 (13). FLORENCE V 58, from Chiusi. I, youth running with spear. A, Herakles and the lion, with satyrs; B, Theseus and the bull, with satyrs. Restored.

25 (a). FLORENCE 70800, from Tarquinia. *Mus. It.* 3 pl. 3, whence Pottier *Pourquoi Thésée* (from *Revue de l'art ancien et moderne*), 3, 5, and 7, and (B) *Jh.* 1, 193; *CV.* pll. 98–99 and pl. 116, 18. Deeds of Theseus: I, Theseus and Minotaur; A, Sinis, Skiron, Procrustes; B, bull. For the shape, Bloesch 83, Brygos no. 14. See p. 1651.

26 (24, +). LOUVRE G 159. I and part of B, Pottier pl. 124. I, maenad; A–B, Dionysos with satyrs and maenads. Four Louvre fragments join the old, adding the hand and left arm of the satyr on the left of A, and his middle, the face and left upper arm of the left-hand satyr on B, with the rest of the maenad's thyrsus.

27. OXFORD 1911.622 and 623, frr., from Cervetri. *CV*. pl. 14, 39–41. A–B, satyrs. Now augmented by a splinter ex Leipsic, see *CV*. ii p. vi.

28 (25). ADRIA B 487, fr., from Adria. Micali *Mon. ined.* pl. 45, 4; Schöne pl. 3, 4; *CV*. pl. 14, 5; *Riv. Ist.* N.S. 5–6, 43 fig. 25. I, satyr and maenad.

29 (26). Once TARQUINIA, Avvolta, from Vulci. B.Ap. xxii. 17. I. I, two satyrs, one holding oinochoe and kantharos, the other squatting and eating grapes.

30. BASLE, Cahn, 60. I, komast ('Anacreontic'): Anacreon himself?—man in long chiton, cloak, saccos, ear-ring, moving to right with lyre, head thrown back, singing, beside him his dog).

31 (16, +). VILLA GIULIA, FLORENCE, and NAPLES, Astarita, 318. I, hunter or light-armed warrior (youth in chitoniskos and pilos running to left, spear in right hand, left arm extended with a goat-skin over it). The Astarita fragment has the middle of the figure and completes the picture.

32 (21). BERLIN inv. 3233. I, warrior putting on his corslet. For the shape, Bloesch 89 no. 6.

SKYPHOS

33 (17). ADRIA B 71, B 609, and B 93, frr., from Adria. Schöne pl. 11, 1–2; *CV*. pl. 33, 1–2. Boar-hunt.

STAMNOS

34 (27). NORTHWICK, Spencer-Churchill. Gerhard pl. 290; side-view, Jacobsthal O. pl. 94, b; graffito, *AJA*. 1927, 349. A, youth leading horse, with man and youth. B, youth with hare, man, and dog. Restored.

FRAGMENT OF A POT

35. TURIN, fr. (head, to left, and shoulders, of a maenad dancing).

NEAR THE DOKIMASIA PAINTER

ARV.[1] 272.

CUPS

1. BOSTON 01.8075. CB. i pl. 13, 34 and pp. 30–31; I, *Olympia in der Antike* pl. 42. I, athlete folding his himation; A–B, athletes.

2. LONDON 1952.12–2.10, two frr., from Vulci. A, komos (what remains is, on one fragment, the upper part of a naked girl, moving to left, looking round, and, on the other fragment, the thighs of a naked girl, doubtless the same, to left, with part of her right hand). May be by the painter himself.

Compare also

CUPS

1. VILLA GIULIA, fr. I, archer (middle, standing to right, chitoniskos, corslet, helmet, greaves, quiver, bow in left hand, big battle-axe in right).

2. FERRARA, T. 499, from Spina. I, Aurigemma[1] 73 = [2]77; *Riv. Ist.* 6, 208–11; I, Arias and Alfieri pl. 9; I, Stella 409; I, Aurigemma and Alfieri pl. 8, b; I, *E.A.A.* ii, 226 fig. 339. I, Egyptian fleeing; A–B, Herakles and Busiris.

PANATHENAIC AMPHORA

3. VATICAN, from Vulci. *Mus. Greg.* 2 pl. 59, 1. A, warrior; B, woman holding spear and shield. Restored.

STAMNOS

4. LEIPSIC, frr., from Cervetri. Arming. On A, 1, male in himation to right, 2, warrior to left, with shield, 3, woman to left holding spear and shield; on B, 1, male holding spear and shield, 2, warrior to right, 3, woman to left holding shield. See p. 1652.

─────

III

THE PAINTER OF AGORA P 42

ARV.[1] 273 and 957.

Mild-Brygan Group. Near the Dokimasia Painter.

CUPS

1 (1). ATHENS, Agora, P 42, from Athens. *Hesp.* 2, 216–23; B and foot, Bloesch *F.A.S.* pl. 29, 1. I, warrior at altar; A–B, warriors about to leave home: A, two warriors, and a woman holding a shield; B, king and woman, old man seated, woman (?) with lyre. For the subjects, Talcott in *Hesp.* 217–24; for the shape, Bloesch 103, Three-edge Class, no. 1.

2 (2). Once ROME, Stroganoff, from Capua? Pollak and Muñoz pll. 37–38. I, king at altar; A, king seated, with a woman and a winged goddess; B, king and two women. For the subjects, Simon *O.G.* 73–77 and 121: she takes the king in all three pictures to be Plouton; on A, with Persephone and Iris; on B, with Demeter and Persephone. This is very attractive. Slightly restored.

3 (3). ADRIA B 583, fr., from Adria. *CV.* pl. 20, 1. A, (on the right, woman).

4 (4). ADRIA B 608, fr., from Adria. *CV.* pl. 14, 1; I, *Riv. Ist.* N.S. 5–6, 42 fig. 22. I, old man; A, (two in long chiton and himation, one seated, the other standing).

5. ADRIA s.n. 14, fr., from Adria. *CV.* pl. 15, 7. I, (woman); A, (woman). Already compared with Adria B 608 (no. 4) by Miss Riccioni.

6 (5). PALERMO, two frr. Outside, arming: on one fragment, (one holding sword, youth standing frontal, head to left); on the other, (arm of male with spear to left).

7 (6). BOLOGNA 365, from Bologna. Zannoni pl. 119, 7 and 14–15; I, Pellegrini 182; I, Sudhoff ii, 38; *CV.* pl. 9; I, *E.A.A.* i, 143. I, uncertain subject: naked boy with oinochoe at pot. A, woman at laver, woman, and young boy; B, youths and boy. For the shape, Bloesch 129, Conefoot cup no. 15.

8 (7). VILLA GIULIA 50523. I, woman with mirror (standing to right; beyond, a couch). Much restored.

IV

THE PAINTER OF LOUVRE G 265

CV. Oxford 4–5. *ARV.*[1] 273.

Mild-Brygan Group; weak. See p. 405.

CUPS

1 (1). LOUVRE G 265, FLORENCE, and VILLA GIULIA, from Vulci. See *CF*. 34 no. 14. I, Pottier pl. 133. I, youth leading a woman away (wedding of Menelaos and Helen?). A–B, deeds of Theseus: A, bull (with satyr), Procrustes; B, sow, Sinis.

2. LAUSANNE, private. Death of Orpheus: I, two Thracian women; A, Orpheus and four Thracian women; B, five Thracian women.

3 (2). OXFORD 305. Gardner 29 fig. 35, and pl. 19; *CV*. pl. 2, 3 and pl. 7, 1–2, whence (A) Wegner *Mus*. pl. 27, b; I, *E.A.A.* iv, 699 fig. 847. I, woman running. A, man playing the flute, and boys, at herm; B, man seated, boy, and youth. For the shape, Bloesch 89 no. 3.

4 (3). PROVIDENCE 25.066. *CV*. pl. 21, 1. I, youth; A–B, komos.

5 (4). Once VIENNA, Univ. (perhaps only for restoration). I, winged woman pursuing a boy (Eos and Tithonos, one would have said, but she holds a caduceus: Iris?). A is fragmentary (women: pursuit?); B, women fleeing to an old man.

6 (5). ORVIETO 590, from Orvieto. *CV*. pl. 8, 1–3. I, youth with spear; A–B, fight.

7 (s 3). LEYDEN PC 75 (xviii a 6), from Vulci. Roulez pl. 2. I, voting on the arms of Achilles; A–B, the like. Restored.

8. LUCERNE, Kofler. I, youth and boy. A–B, athletes. Cup type C. On I the youth takes the boy by chin and right forearm.

9 (a 1). VIENNA, Univ., 53a. A–B, *WV*. C pl. 7, 1; *CV*. pl. 11, 5 and pl. 12, 1–2. I, male at altar. A, Dionysos, and a satyr-boy leading a donkey; B, satyr watering donkey.

10 (a 2). LEIPSIC T 622, fr. I, discus-thrower. A, (foot, and male leaning on his stick).

Near these:

CUPS

1. VIENNA, Univ., 53 c 10 and part of 53 c 11, frr., from Orvieto. A–B, *CV*. pl. 18, 10–12 and 15–18. I, (maeander). A–B, athletes.

2. BOULOGNE 12. I, youth with spears; A–B, arming.

3. TÜBINGEN, fr. I, (boy). A, (legs of a male in himation and shoes leaning on his stick to left).

Compare also the

HYDRIA

(the picture on the shoulder, not framed)

NAPLES 3103, from Nola. Dionysos and maenads. Much restored.

THE PAINTER OF THE PARIS GIGANTOMACHY

VA. 94–96. *Att. V.* 189–93 and 474. *V.Pol.* 25–26. CB. i, 26. *ARV.*[1] 274–8 and 957.

Called after no. 1. See p. 400.

CUPS

1 (1). CAB. MÉD. 573, from Vulci. Luynes pll. 19–20, whence Gerhard *Trinkschalen* pll. A–B (whence Vian *R.* pl. 36, 335) and Overbeck *KM.* pl. 5, 1; Cook *Zeus* 3 pl. 3; A and foot, Bloesch pl. 24, 2; phs. Gir. 8070–2 and 33383–4. Gigantomachy: I, Poseidon and Giant; A, Poseidon and Giant, Hephaistos and Giant, Apollo and Giant; B, Dionysos and Giant, Apollo and Giant, Ares and Giant. Restored. For the shape, Bloesch 85, Brygos no. 25. According to Vian (*Guerre des Géants* 118) the right arm of Hephaistos is 'only half drawn': it is so in Gerhard's copy, but in the original it is complete. See p. 1652.

2 (2). ORVIETO, Faina, 44, from Orvieto. Hartwig 550–1, whence (A) Byvanck-Quarles van Ufford *P.* 38; I, ph. Al. 32466, whence Tarchi pl. 125, 2; A–B, phs. R.I. 1935.892–4. I, fight. A–B, Centauromachy. For the shape, Bloesch 84, Brygos no. 18.

3 (3). VATICAN, from Vulci. *Mus. Greg.* 2 pl. 72, 1; phs. Al. 35794–6, whence (I) Byvanck-Quarles van Ufford *P.* 33. I, Lapith and Centaur; A–B, Herakles and Centaurs.

4 (4). ROMAN MARKET (Basseggio), from Vulci. Gerhard pl. 166, whence (I and B) Schachermeyr pl. 24, 1. I, Greek and Persian; A–B, Greeks and Persians.

5 (6). VILLA GIULIA 3586, from Falerii. *CV.* pl. 32; ph. G.F. 9155, right. I, youth leaning on his stick. A–B, fight.

6 (7). DRESDEN ZV 1610. I, youth leaning on his stick. A–B, fight.

7 (8, 14, +). VILLA GIULIA, FLORENCE 6 B 21, LEIPSIC T 514, AMSTERDAM inv. 2250, and NAPLES, Astarita, 264. Some of the Florence frr., *CV.* Florence pl. 6, B 21. I, warrior; A–B, fight. The Astarita fragment gives shield and spear-point of the left-hand warrior on A, and the upper part of the middle warrior.

8 (9). VILLA GIULIA, fr. I, komast or satyr (moving quickly to right, holding

a wine-skin: shank and foot remain). A, fight (shield and leg of a warrior, down, to right, legs of a warrior striding to left, frontal toes of a third, rushing to right).

9 (10). FLORENCE, fr. A, fight (knee of a warrior, down, to right, with part of his shield and shield-apron).

10 (11). VILLA GIULIA, fr. A, (part of a warrior to left).

11 (12). BASLE MARKET (M.M.). I, warrior (naked youth standing with right leg frontal, head to left, helmet in right hand, shield on left arm); A–B, fight.

12 (13). MUNICH, frr. I, warrior; A–B, fight.

13 (16 bis). ATHENS, Agora, P 14040, fr., from Athens. A, fight. Our old no. 16 was the same as this.

14 (15, +). LOUVRE S 1347, plus, frr. I, woman running. A–B, fight.

15 (5). CAB. MÉD. 572 bis, 590 (one fr.), 769, 770, 721, plus, frr. Part of A–B, de Ridder 428. I, Peleus and Thetis; A–B, Peleus and Thetis.

16 (17). BASLE. I, two maenads dancing; A, Dionysos with satyrs and maenads. For the shape, Bloesch 88.

17. BASLE, Cahn, 61, frr. A–B, satyrs and maenads.

18 (18). CAB. MÉD. 577, 720, and parts of 558, frr. I, satyr and maenad; A–B, satyrs and maenads.

19 (22). AMSTERDAM inv. 2251, fr. A, (satyr).

20 (23). ADRIA B 516, fr., from Adria. CV. pl. 16, 2. A, (satyr).

21 (24). FLORENCE 9 B 60, fr. Part, CV. pl. 9, B 60. A, (satyr).

22 (19). LENINGRAD 650 (St. 892). I, symposion (two youths reclining and a woman playing the flute). A–B, satyrs and maenads.

23 (20). LOUVRE G 252, from Italy. Millin 2 pl. 63; phs. Gir. 18315–16. I, symposion (youth reclining). A–B, satyrs. See p. 1652.

24 (21). LEIPSIC T 491, fr. I, satyr with wine-skin; A, (satyrs).

25 (26). MUNICH 2649 (J. 279), from Vulci. A–B, Schröder Sport pl. 89; A–B, Jh. 31, 14. I, komos (man and flute-girl). A–B, boxers. Early. For the shape, Bloesch 88, iii, no. 1.

26. PARIS MARKET (Segredakis). I, acontist, trainer, and boy boxer; A–B, athletes (A, boxers; acontist; B, acontists, discus-thrower). Early.

27 (27). BONN 143 c, fr., from Tarquinia. CV. pl. 5, 5. A, athletes.

28 (29). ROMAN MARKET? B.Ap. xxi. 82, whence (I and A) Jb. 10, 190, whence JHS. 23, 278, 8 (= Norman Gardiner G.A.S. 287) and (parts of B) Jüthner 41 fig. 36, b, and p. 48 fig. 43. I, hoplitodromoi; A, hoplitodromoi; B, acontists. See p. 1652.

29 (28). TARQUINIA RC 2067, from Tarquinia. I, youth and boy. A, boxers; B, athletes.

30 (51). CAB. MÉD. 617, fr. A, (boxer).

31 (52, +). FLORENCE 11 B 15, fr. Part, *CV*. pl. 11, B 15. I, athlete; A, boxers. Four frr. (three of them ex Villa Giulia) join the original one, and we have arm and leg of the right-hand boxer, and the lower half of a trainer leaning on his stick to left, together with his left elbow.

32 (31). COPENHAGEN, Thorvaldsen Museum, 110. A–B, *AJA*. 1928, 49. I, youth with stick; A–B, boxers. Much restored.

33 (33). BRUSSELS R 337. *CV*. pl. 3, 2; A–B, *AJA*. 1928, 48. I, youth leaning on his stick; A–B, boxers.

34 (34). TORONTO 357, from Orvieto. *AJA*. 1928, 42–47; Robinson and Harcum pl. 60 and p. 167. I, symposion (youth reclining). A–B, boxers.

35 (32, +). AMSTERDAM inv. 2253, fr. (two joining), from Orvieto. I, (on the left, hand holding stick); A, (boxers).

36. WASHINGTON 136390, fr., from Orvieto. A, boxers.

37. LOUVRE C 11480, two frr. Outside, boxers. The two frr. need not be from the same half of the cup.

38 (41). LEIPSIC T 539, fr. I, (feet). A, boxers.

39 (36). ADRIA B 103 and B 538 (joining), fr., from Adria. *CV*. pl. 18, 1; *Riv. Ist.* N.S. 5–6, 46 fig. 31. A, boxers.

40 (39). ADRIA B 1011, fr., from Adria. *CV*. pl. 26, 6. I, (maeander). A, boxers.

41 (40). ADRIA B 1072, fr., from Adria. A, boxers.

42 (37). ADRIA B 431, fr., from Adria. *CV*. pl. 26, 2. I, warrior at altar. A, athletes.

43 (38). ADRIA B 1037, fr., from Adria. *CV*. pl. 26, 1. I, (pillar). A, athletes.

44. ADRIA B 722, fr., from Adria. *CV*. pl. 26, 4. I, (pair of shod feet). A, (jumper, trainer).

45 (35). PARIS MARKET, from Orvieto. I, *Vente 11 mai 1903*, 42, above. I, symposion (youth reclining). A–B, athletes. Restored.

46 (43). BOLOGNA 364, from Bologna. Zannoni pl. 77, 1–2 and 5, whence (A) Norman Gardiner *G.A.S.* 304 and (A) Norman Gardiner *Athl.* fig. 103; A, Jüthner 17 fig. 16, whence *JHS*. 24, 186; *CV*. pl. 6. I, komast. A–B, athletes. See p. 1652.

47 (44). FLORENCE 75590, from Falerii. I, Milani *Mus. Top.* 82. I, symposion (youth reclining). A–B, athletes.

48. LOUVRE C 11481, fr. I, youth. A, athletes.

49. LOUVRE C 11482, fr. A, (athlete).

50 (46). BRAUNSBERG, fr. A, *Anz*. 1933, 426. I, (maeander). A, athletes. [Greifenhagen].

51. LOUVRE C 11483, fr. A, athletes. See the next.

52. LOUVRE C 11484, fr. I, (on the right, the top of a pillar). Outside, (legs

of the left-hand figure, a male in a himation, leaning, to right). May belong to the last.

53 (47). Leipsic T 535, fr. I (maeander). A, athletes (a trainer remains).

54 (47 bis). Lost. B.Ap. xxiii, last, left, below. A, (head and shoulders of athlete bending to right, then aryballos and strigil hanging).

55 (48). Amsterdam inv. 2805, fr. A, (athlete).

56 (30). Cracow inv. 1211. I, V.Pol. pl. 8, 2; CV. pl. 9, 2. I, youth, at laver; A–B, athletes.

57 (45). Naples 2611, from Nola. Mus. Borb. 3 pl. 13; A–B, ph. So. 11006, i, 7. I, youth leaning on his stick; A–B, athletes. For the shape, Bloesch 134 no. 6.

58 (49). Geneva 14985. I, youth leaning on his stick; A–B, athletes. For the shape, Bloesch 134 no. 8.

59 (92). Ancona, from Numana. I, youth leaning on his stick; A–B, athletes (each, trainer between two jumpers). Late.

60 (60). Philadelphia 2445, from Vulci. AJA. 1913, 480–3. I, komast; A–B, komos. Early.

61. Innsbruck ii.27.2. I, komast; A–B, komos. According to Bothmer the small fragment Innsbruck ii. 12. 55 may belong.

62. Seattle 20.35. I and B, Art Qu. 1960, 183, 6–7. I, symposion (two youths reclining, each playing kottabos, with a cup in his raised right hand, and a skyphos in his left); A–B, komos (A, man, and four dancing youths, two of them naked; B, five youths).

63 (57). Cab. Méd. 556 and 808, frr. I, VA. 95. I, komos (two youths); A–B, komos.

64 (58). Cab. Méd. 683, 684, 756, 746, and 790, frr. Part (nos. 683 and 756), phs. Gir. 27789 (part) and 27790 (part). I, male and boy; A–B, komos.

65 (59). Cab. Méd. 740, fr. I, (head of youth to left). A, (lost). Might belong to one of the two last.

66 (61). Louvre G 161, fr. Pottier pl. 125. A, komos.

67 (62). Tübingen E 25 a, fr. A, komos.

68 (63). Florence 12 B 51, fr. CV. pl. 12, B 51. A, komos.

69 (64). Florence 9 B 5, fr. CV. pl. 9, B 5. A, komos.

70 (65). Florence 9 B 4, fr. CV. pl. 9, B 4. A, komos.

71 (66). Villa Giulia, two frr. I, (leftward maeander). Outside, komos (on one fragment, legs of two naked males, running or dancing, one to right, the other to left; on the other fragment, legs of a naked male running or dancing to right, booted).

72 (67). Villa Giulia, fr. A, komos (male dancing to right, booted, and naked male to right).

73 (68). VILLA GIULIA, fr. A, komos (face and shoulder of youth looking up to left).

74 (69). CAB. MÉD. 608, frr., from Tarquinia. I, white ground, maenad. A, (shoe). 606 probably belongs.

75 (70). SÈVRES 2617.1–2, frr. CV. pl. 18, 1–2. I, (a white band). Outside, komos. Probably belongs to the last, see JHS. 51, 54 no. 9 and JHS. 56, 252.

76. VILLA GIULIA, fr., from Cervetri. I, ML. 42, 891. I, komast; A–B, komos? [Ricci].

77. BASLE, Cahn, 63, fr. A, symposion (youth reclining to left, with crotala). Lipped cup.

78 (71). LONDON E 70, from Vulci. I, Murray no. 48; I, VA. 96. I, symposion (two youths reclining, and boy cup-bearer); A–B, symposion.

79 (72). ORVIETO, Faina, 39, from Orvieto. Phs. R.I. 1935.906 and 899. I, youth leaning on his stick. A–B, symposion.

80 (73). FLORENCE A B 5, frr. Part of I, CV. pl. A, B 5. I, symposion (youth reclining); A–B, symposion.

81 (74). MUNICH 2664 (J. 801), from Vulci. I, youth and woman; A–B, youths and women. For the shape, Bloesch 88, iii no. 2.

82. OXFORD, Beazley, fr. (five joining). A, (males and woman: middle of male leaning on his stick to right, right arm akimbo, purse in left hand, woman moving to left, right hand raised, male leaning on his stick to left).

83 (75). HILLSBOROUGH (California), Hearst (ex Oppenheimer). Gerhard pl. 283–4, 1–3; Burl. 1903 pll. 95 and 96, I 70; I and A, Cat. Christie July 22 1936 pl. 6. I, youth and boy; A–B, youths and boys.

84 (76). OXFORD 1947.263 (ex Richmond, Cook). Burl. 1903 pl. 95, H 51. I, youth and boy; A–B, youths and boys. For the shape, Bloesch 82, Brygos no. 11.

85 (77). BRUSSELS A 3048. CV. pl. 22, 2. I, symposion (two youths reclining). A–B, youths and boys.

86 (78). FLORENCE V. 55, from Chiusi. I, warrior. A–B, youths and boys.

87 (79). FLORENCE 11 B 14, fr. I, CV. pl. 11, B 14. I, youth leaning on his stick; A, (males).

88. LOUVRE C 11486, fr. I, youth leaning on his stick; A, youths and boy; B, (male). Another Louvre fragment may belong, giving the right shoulder and upper arm of the left-hand person on B.

89. LOUVRE C 11485, fr. I, (maeander). A, (male and boy).

90 (88). AREZZO 1225. I, youth, at laver; A–B, youths and boys. Late. Restored.

91. LOUVRE C 11487, two frr. I, (maeander). A–B, youths and boys. Late. See the next.

92. LOUVRE C 11488, fr. A, (youth leaning on his stick). Late. Might belong to the last.

93 (89). FLORENCE 18 B 49, fr. A, *CV*. pl. 18, B 49. I, male. A, youths and boy. Late.

94 (90). Once MUNICH, Preyss. I, youth, at laver; A–B, youths and boys. Late.

95 (91). ROME, Torlonia, 160. I, satyr (moving to left, bending). A, youths and boy; B, the like. Late.

96. FERRARA (erratico Dosso B, 31.5.1958), from Spina. I, archer. A, youths and boy; B, the like. Late.

97 (50). CAB. MÉD. 638, frr. A, ph. Gir. 27790 (part). I, warrior (or hoplito-dromos) holding helmet. A, (male leaning on his stick).

98 (81). ADRIA B 723, fr., from Adria. I, *CV*. pl. 16, 4. I, symposion (youth reclining). A, (heel).

99 (83). MUNICH, fr. I, symposion (male reclining, right arm raised). A, (foot; two-line border).

100. BASLE, Cahn, 62, fr. I, symposion (two youths reclining). Outside, (two-line border).

101. LOUVRE C 11489, fr. I, symposion. A, (legs of male in himation to left). See the next.

102. LOUVRE C 11490, fr. I, (maeander). A, (legs of male in himation, lean-ing, to left). May belong to the last.

103. BARCELONA 4293, fr., from Ampurias. I, (on the right, forehead of male to left. A, (legs of male in himation leaning on his stick to left). [Shefton].

103 *bis*. FREIBURG S 159, fr. I, (feet of one moving to left). A, (male legs, bare). Under one handle a stone seat.

104 (80). LONDON XY 2, fr. A, (legs and belly of naked male).

105 (84). FREIBURG, fr. I, (leftward maeander). A, (shod feet of male to left).

106 (85). CAB. MÉD. 807, fr. A, (back of youth's head to left).

107 (42). LEIPSIC T 723, fr. A, (head and breast of youth to left).

108 (53). VILLA GIULIA, fr. A, (middle of the right-hand figure, a male in a himation, leaning, to left).

109 (54). FLORENCE, fr. A, (arm of the right-hand figure, a male in a hima-tion, leaning, to left).

110 (55). FLORENCE P D 303, fr. I, (rightward maeander). A, (feet of a male in a himation, leaning, to left).

111 (56). FLORENCE P D 351, fr. A, (middle of the right-hand figure, a male in a himation, leaning, to left). [Anna Magi].

112. STRASBURG, Univ., 834, fr. I, (on the right, one in a himation,

probably a boy: compare the boy on the San Simeon cup, no. 83). Outside, floral under the handle.

113 (25). TORONTO 959.17.160 (ex Curtius), fr. Phs. R.I. 1935.229–30. I, satyr and maenad. A, (foot of the left-hand figure).

(no. 114, not known if decorated outside)

114 (82). HEIDELBERG 101 (ex Dresden), fr. Kraiker pl. 15. I, symposion.

(no. 115, probably decorated inside only)

115 (85 *bis*). Once CHIUSI, Casuccini, from Chiusi. Inghirami *Chius.* pl. 175. I, youth leaning on his stick at altar. Neither Inghirami, nor Brunn in *Bull.* 1859, 107, mentions outside pictures.

(nos. 116–18, decorated inside only)

116. OXFORD, Beazley, fr. I, (on the right, Centaur—rather than satyr: the upper part of the figure remains).

117 (87). TARQUINIA 698, from Tarquinia. I, boy acontist and youth.

118 (86). VILLA GIULIA (ex Castellani). I, youth in himation leaning on his stick at an altar, holding a purse.

NECK-AMPHORA
(Nolan amphora, with triple handles)

119 (93). LONDON E 288, from Nola. *CV.* pl. 47, 3; A. ph. Ma. A, discus-thrower and trainer; B, flute-player.

LEKYTHOI
(standard shape)

120 (94). FRANKFORT, Museum für Kunsthandwerk. Schaal *F.* pll. 32–33. Eos and Tithonos.

121 (102). PALERMO V 678. *CV.* pl. 25, 1. Nike.

122 (96). PALERMO V 679, from Selinus. *CV.* pl. 25, 3–4. Nike.

123 (97). BOSTON 24.450. CB. i pl. 10, 30. Maenad.

124 (103). VIENNA 608. Woman fleeing.

125 (95). BERLIN 2211. Millingen *AUM.* i pl. 29, whence *El.* 1 pl. 96. Nike holding an aphlaston.

126 (100). GELA (ex Navarra-Jacona), from Gela. Nike (flying, holding a head-band).

127 (99). LONDON 99.2–18.71. Nike.

128 (101). GELA (ex Navarra-Jacona), from Gela. Benndorf pl. 47, 1. Nike.

129. AARHUS, Univ., 142 (on loan from Copenhagen, inv. 11480), fr., from Agrigento. *Acta arch.* 16, 145, 70. (Woman). [Breitenstein].

130. MAPLEWOOD, Noble. *Auction xiv Basle* pl. 19, 77. Woman holding oinochoe and phiale; on the shoulder, mirror, crotala, and saccos.

131 (104). ATHENS 1627 (CC. 1458), from Tanagra. Woman with phiale.

132 (98). OXFORD 319, from Gela. Gardner pl. 24, 2; cleaned, *CV*. pl. 38, 12. Warrior.

OINOCHOAI

(*no. 133, shape 1*)

133 (105). VATICAN. Ph. Al. 35728; ph. And. 42080, 1. Athena.

(*no. 134, shape 6*)

134 (106). VIENNA 3771 (ex Oest. Mus. 330), from Cervetri. Masner 48. Komos.

A cup-fragment recalls Cab. Méd. 608 (no. 74):

(a). VILLA GIULIA, fr. I, white ground, (maenad: her elbow; holding a snake). A, (toes of the left-hand figure, to left; and part of the floral under the handle).

CHAPTER 27

DOURIS

DOURIS

Hartwig 200–30, 582–627, and ('Master with the Sprig') 657–80. Furtwängler in FR. i, 246–8 and 262–75, and ii, 85–86. Frucht *Die signierten Gefässe des Duris*. Buschor in *Jb*. 81, 74–95. *VA*. 97–100. *JHS*. 39, 84–87. Pfuhl 475–85. *Att. V*. 199–210 and 474. Papaspyridi-Karouzou and Kyparissis in *Delt*. 1927–8, 91–110. *ARV*.[1] 279–94, 918, 957, and 968. CB. iii, text.

The signature of Douris occurs on 39 vases: 35 cups, a kantharos, a psykter, an aryballos, and a lost fragment which was said not to be from a cup. Douris nearly always signs as painter: on the kantharos he signs as potter also; on the aryballos as potter only. One of the cups is not by Douris: see p. 360.

The long career of Douris may be divided into four periods: (1) very early, and early; (2) early middle; (3) middle; (4) late. In periods 1 and 2 Chairestratos is the favourite kalos-name; in period 3, Hippodamas; in period 4, kalos-names are rare, but there are Polyphrasmon and Hiketes. Period 3 slips gradually into period 4; there is more of a break between periods 2 and 3; period 1 is experimental.

In the lists that follow, the cups that are decorated outside as well as in are kept apart, as usual, from those that are decorated inside only. Within these categories the order is in the main chronological (with fragments it is sometimes difficult, of course, to be precise).

Early in period 1 are the signed cups Vienna 3694 and Boston 00.338 (nos. 3 and 4). Limber figures, stretching out. Nos. 1–25 belong to this period, and, among the cups decorated inside only, nos. 211–15. The Vlasto kantharos (no. 255) is also very early.

With period 2, the early middle period, the style of Douris settles down. The cup with the Arms of Achilles in Vienna, 3695 (no. 26), is already early middle. Characteristic of period 2 is the *bare* type of decoration (as opposed to the richer type adopted in period 3): figures only, no palmettes at the handles, and the simplest of borders—a line round the tondo (the elaborate Vienna cup is exceptional in its borders): London E 39 (no. 29) is a typical 'bare' cup. The figures are more compact than before. Nos 26–45 are of period 2, also nos. 216–24, the Brussels kantharos (no. 256), the white lekythos in Palermo (no. 266), the lekythos Boston 95.41 (no. 270).

With period 3, the middle period, the period of Hippodamas, Douris changes to a richer type of cup-decoration: round the tondo, a border of maeander and cross-square; at the handles, a large design of palmettes: palmettes and border both of characteristic design. Typical examples on the

Theseus cup London E 48 (no. 47) and the Berlin cup 2285 (no. 48). Nos. 47–116 belong to this period; among the cups decorated inside only, nos. 226–9; also the Rosenberg stemless (no. 252), the London psykter (no. 262), the aryballos in Athens (no. 274). Before the end of period 3, the signatures cease.

The transition to the late period, period 4, as was said above, is gradual. Late in the third period the border is sometimes modified slightly: the maeander-unit is a pair instead of single: so, for example, in Berlin 2289 (no. 95) and London E 54 (no. 96). In period 4 this becomes usual. Towards the end of the fourth period the typical Hippodamas border is at last abandoned, giving place to a commonplace type. Nos. 128–58 belong to period 4; also nos. 234–51 among the cups decorated inside only; the cup-skyphos in Bologna (no. 253), the Adria skyphos (no. 254), the rhyta (nos. 257–61), the oinochoe (no. 265), the lekythoi in Vienna University and in Boston, 13. 194 (nos. 272–3).

A number of late cups by Douris were put together by Hartwig, but attributed to a 'Painter with the Sprig' whom he took to be a pupil. These are marked 'Hartwig R' in our list ('R' for 'Ranke').

The list of cups decorated outside as well as in concludes with fragments (nos. 189–206) in which all that remains is part of the characteristic handle-palmettes. These fragments belong either to the third period or to the fourth. It should be said, however, that in the cups of the Oedipus Painter, a close follower of Douris (p. 451), the handle-palmettes are indistinguishable from those of Douris himself.

Imitations of Douris began at least as early as period 2. In period 4 they became numerous: there was a 'school of Douris', and some of the late vases in the list may be school-pieces rather than from the painter's own hand: I have done my best to distinguish, but it is not always easy; nor am I even quite certain at what point in the chronological development of the Douris *sequence* Douris himself stops and the succession of Douris begins. In early classic times the school of Douris flourished. Many pupils and followers can be specified, and the influence of Douris extended even beyond his immediate circle: one might almost say that the whole academic wing of early classic vase-painting was more or less closely akin to the art of Douris. The school-pieces that are nearest to the painter's own late work are described in this chapter; later vases by pupils and followers are reserved for a subsequent one (pp. 781–806); but the line dividing the two batches is rather artificial: the 'later' continue the 'earlier' without a real break.

The association between the painter Douris and the potter Python began very early: Vienna 3694 (no. 3) bears the signature of Python as potter as well as of Douris as painter. Two other cups have the same pair of signatures (nos. 26 and 78). An early cup bears the signature of the potter Kleophrades (no. 21); and a cup from the middle period (no. 74) that of the potter Kalliades, otherwise unknown. Bloesch has shown that some of the early cups, though unsigned, were fashioned by the potter Euphronios. But the vast majority of Douris' cups, early, middle, late, are seen to have been fashioned by Python.

Douris himself was potter on occasion as well as painter. The kantharos in Brussels (no. 256) is signed not only by Douris as painter but by Douris as potter; and although he painted the round aryballos in Athens (no. 274) he signs it as potter only.

CUPS

(nos. 1–206, decorated outside as well as in)

(The list is in the main chronological: for the periods to which the several cups belong see above, pp. 425–6; but I repeat here that nos. 1–25 are very early—period 1).

1 (1). LOUVRE G 127. Hartwig pl. 19, 2 and pl. 20; I, Pottier pl. 112. I, komast; A–B, komos. On I, +AIPE𐤔TATO𐤔KALO𐤔. On A, +[A]I-[P]E𐤔.... On B, hard to read, +A[I]PE, then room for several letters, then TO, then room for several letters, then TO𐤔. [Hartwig]. Now cleaned. For the shape, Bloesch 70, Euphronios no. 2.

2 (a i 1). VATICAN, from Vulci. *Mus. Greg.* 2 pl. 81, 1; I, ph. Mo. 8596, whence Wolters *Faden und Knoten als Amulett* (suppl. to *ARW.* 8), 6 (what appears, however, at the left ankle of the man is not an ankle-band but the border of his himation, and as a matter of fact is modern) and Ahrem 75, fig. 74; I and A–B, phs. Al. 35825–6, whence Licht i, 181, 177, and 179, Zadoks-Jitta pl. 87, 8, (A) Sparkes, Talcott, and Frantz fig. 5, (I and part of A) Zschietzschmann *H.R.* pl. 264, 2 and pl. 261. I, symposion (man vomiting, helped by a woman); A–B, symposion. Much restored. For the shape, Bloesch 71, Euphronios no. 9. As Agora P 10271 (no. 213).

3 (6). VIENNA 3694 (ex Oest. Mus. 324), from Cervetri. *WV.* 7 pl. 1; FR. pl. 53 and i, 275, 2, whence Hoppin i, 266–7, (A) Perrot 10, 547, (I) Pfuhl fig. 456; A, Pfuhl fig. 455; A–B, Lücken pll. 100–1; A and foot, Bloesch *F.A.S.* pl. 27, 2; *CV.* pll. 9–10. I, warrior leaving home (warrior and woman): A–B, arming. On I, ΔORI𐤔EΛRAΦ𐤔EN. On A, HOΓAI𐤔-KALO𐤔. On B, [+]AI[RE𐤔TRA]TO𐤔 KALO𐤔. On the edge of the foot, ΓVOON retr. For the shape, Bloesch 96, Python no. 5.

4 (8). BOSTON 00.338, from Tarquinia. *RM.* 5, 332–3; Hartwig pl. 21, whence Hoppin i, 229, Pfuhl figs. 451–2, (I) Perrot 10, 528; I, Langlotz *G.V.* pl. 9, 15; I, *Dedalo* 4, 741; I, *Harv. St.* 52 pl. 6; Chase *Guide* 68; CB. iii pl. 70; the shape, Caskey G. 187 fig. 142. I, discus-thrower. A–B, fight. On I, ΔORI𐤔EΛRAΦ𐤔EN. On A, [+AI]RE𐤔TRATO𐤔KALO𐤔. On B, +[AIR]E𐤔TRATO[𐤔]KALO𐤔. For the shape, Bloesch 100, Python no. 34. See CB. iii, text.

5 (4). ATHENS Acr. 303 (B 4, and, joining on the left, B 54), fr. Part, Langlotz

pl. 19. A, (woman running towards a man; his fingers remain, with the head of his stick). . . . ΟΣΚΑΛ[ΟΣ]. [Langlotz].

6 (10). TÜBINGEN E 20, fr., from Taranto? Watzinger pl. 19. A, (youth with writing-case). [+ΑΙRΕΣ]ΤR[ΑΤΟΣ . . .

7. FLORENCE V. xxxvii–xxxviii, two frr., from Chiusi. I, komast or satyr. A–B, komos. On I, [+ΑΙRΕ]ΣΤ[RΑΤΟΣ . . .

8 (5, part). ATHENS, North Slope, AP¸2267, fr., from Athens. I, (maeander, of Douris' earliest type). A, (on the left, legs of a male in a himation to left).

9 (5, part). ATHENS, North Slope, AP 2262, fr., from Athens. *Hesp.* 9, 240, 270. Outside, (woman). Belongs to the last?

10 (11). LOUVRE G 122. Hoppin i, 258; Pottier pl. 111, whence (B) Pfuhl fig. 454. I, woman playing the lyre. A–B, one figure on each half: A, seated youth; B, youth. On I, ΔΟ[R]Ι[Σ]Ε . . .. On B, +ΑΙ[R]ΕΣ[ΤRΑ-ΤΟΣ . . . Now cleaned.

11 (12). LOUVRE G 276. I and A, Pottier pl. 133; I, ph. Gir. 19014, whence Philippart *C.A.B.* pl. 1. I, youth and boy; round the tondo a white zone. A–B, two figures on each half: A, youth pursuing boy; B, youth or man, and seated woman (she spinning, he holding out a kalathos). Now cleaned. The inscription on I is [ΗΟ]ΓΑ[Ι]ΣΚ[Α]ΛΟ[Σ], on A, [ΗΟ-Γ]ΑΙΣΚΑ[ΛΟΣ].

12 (13). BERLIN inv. 3255. Lücken pll. 14–15 (B is reversed). I, flute-girl; A–B, komos: one figure on each half: A, youth; B, flute-girl. For the shape, Bloesch 100, Python no. 35.

13 (14). BERLIN inv. 3168, from Etruria. *Anz.* 1891, 117–18; Hartwig pl. 27, whence (part of A) *Delt.* 1927–8, 95 and (A) *Die Antike* 6 pl. 15, a. I, boy in winged chariot (Hyakinthos?). A, Eros pursuing a boy; B, athletes. For the shape, Bloesch 77, Euphronios no. 33.

14 (7). CAB. MÉD. 675, 600, 597, 727 (part), 774, L 224, and parts of 586, frr. I, youth seated, and male with tablets; A–B, men and youths.

15 (9). FREIBURG, fr. A, (athlete?: head, shoulders, upper arms of a naked youth bending to right).

16 (15). CAB. MÉD. 538. *Mon.* 2 pl. 11, 1–2; I, Bothmer *Am.* pl. 71, 3. I, Greek and Amazon. A, unexplained subject (Achilles in Skyros has been suggested). B, fight. The drawing in *Mon.* gives one fragment which I cannot find—left flank, with shield, of the left-hand warrior on B; but it omits the left leg of the right-hand figure on A. See Bothmer *Am.* 143 no. 26 and pp. 145–6.

17 (16). CAB. MÉD., part of 526, fr. A, (corslet, shield, spear, of warrior to right).

18. CAB. MÉD., part of 574, fr. A, Gigantomachy? (head of Athena attacking to right).

19 (17). CAB. MÉD. 537 and 598, frr., from Tarquinia? I, *Mon.* 2 pl. 11, 3; part of I, B.Ap. xxii. 1, 2, part. I, Ajax with the body of Achilles. A, unexplained subject: on one fragment, male with bow and arrows, woman, male, all rushing to right, then foot of one to left; on the other fragment, upper part of a woman moving to right.

20 (18). LONDON D 1, frr., from Naucratis. Part, Hartwig pl. 50; another fr., *JHS.* 25 pl. 6, 4; I, Philippart *C.A.B.* pl. 2. White ground. I, Europa. A, Herakles and Apollo: the struggle for the tripod. B, fight. For the shape, Bloesch 137, Potter of the Eleusis Group, no. 2. See p. 1652.

21 (19). BERLIN 2283, and NAPLES, Astarita, 134, from Vulci. *AZ.* 1883 pll. 1–2, above, whence Hoppin i, 211, above, and 213, above; I, Lücken pl. 43; detail of A, Pfuhl fig. 450; detail of B, Schröder *Sport* pl. 94, 2. I, Nike and warrior. In a zone round the tondo, chariot-race. A–B, athletes. On I, ΚΑΛ . . . and, in the zone, [ΗΟ]ΓΑΙ< ΚΑΛΟ<, ΓΑΝΑΙΤΙΟ-[<ΚΑΛΟ]<. On A, . . . ΚΑΛ[Ο<] retr. On B, ΓΑΝΑΙΤΙΟ<[κ]Α-ΛΟ[<] retr. The foot (Bloesch *FAS.* pl. 16, 7) with the inscription on the edge (now, according to Bloesch, almost illegible), ΚΛΕ[Ο]ΦΡΑ-[ΔΕ<ΕΓΟ]ΙΕ<Ε[Ν], belongs either to this cup or to the next. The unpublished fragment in the Astarita collection was seen by the owner to belong, and to join *AZ.* 1883 pl. 1 on the left above, giving, inside, the arms of the charioteer and the rest of the reins and kentron, with the ΓΑΙ< of the inscription, and, outside, the middle of the last athlete but one on A. For the shape, Bloesch 58, Kleophrades no. 2. See also p. 1566.

22 (20). BERLIN 2284, frr., from Vulci. *AZ.* 1883 pll. 1–2, below, whence Hoppin i, 211, below, and 213, below; A, Schröder *Sport* pl. 90, 2; A, Blümel *Sport und Spiel* pl. 11, below; A, Blümel *S.H.* 30. Replica, so far as it goes, of the last. I, in the zone, chariot-race. A–B, athletes. On I, in the zone, +ΑΙΡΕ<Τ[ΡΑΤΟ< . . .. On A, ΔΟΡΙ<ΕΛΡΑ[Φ<ΕΝ].

23 (21). PALERMO, fr., from Selinus. *ML.* 32 pl. 95, 6; *AJA.* 1935, 481. A, Achilles and Memnon (part of the Thetis remains).

24 (22). VILLA GIULIA, fr. I, (foot to left, with maeander). A, (end of stick, foot—thin—of one moving to right).

25 (24). Once Joly de Bammeville. *AZ.* 1861 pl. 150, 1–2 and pl. 149, whence (I) *Jb.* 11, 28 and (A–B) *Jb.* 59, 74; B.Ap. xxii. 56. I, cup-bearer (woman with oinochoe and phiale). A, Herakles and Antaios; B, Herakles and Syleus.

26 (28). VIENNA 3695 (ex Oest. Mus. 325), from Cervetri. *Mon.* 8 pl. 41, whence *WV.* 6 pl. 1, whence (B) Robert *Herm.* 133 fig. 101; FR. pl. 54 and i, 275, 1, and 269, whence Perrot 10, 540–1, Hoppin i, 268, Stella 735, (A) Swindler fig. 312, (A) Scheurleer pl. 28, 78, (B) Seltman pl. 27, a; I, Langlotz *G.V.* pl. 21; Pfuhl figs. 463 and 459–60 (= Pfuhl *Mast.* figs. 61–63); I and B, Lücken pll. 102–3; I, Licht ii, 170; B and foot, Bloesch *FAS.* pl. 27, 3; I, Buschor *G. Vasen* 152; *CV.* pll. 11–12 and pl. 13, 1–2; A–B, *E.A.A.* i, 169; I, *E.A.A.* ii, 822. The armour of Achilles: I, Odysseus

and Neoptolemos; A, Ajax and Odysseus quarrelling; B, the vote. On I,
ΛΟRΙ≤ΕΛRΑⵕ≤ΕΝ. On A, ΗΟΓΑΙ≤ΚΑͰΟ≤. On B, +ΑΙRΕ≤ΤRΑ-
ΤΟ≤ΚΑͰΟ≤. On the side of the foot, ΓVΘΟΝ. For the shape,
Bloesch 97, Python no. 8.

27 (26). Cab. Méd. 575 and 648, frr. Part, de Ridder 433. I, Amazonomachy; A–B, Herakles and the Amazons. See Bothmer *Am.* 132 no. 1
and p. 140.

28 (27). Cab. Méd., fr. A, (middle of warrior to right). Belongs to the
last?

29 (29). London E 39, from Vulci. *WV.* 8 pl. 1, whence Hoppin i, 237; I,
Murray no. 24; *JHS.* 26 pl. 12, whence Norman Gardiner *G.A.S.* 404;
A and foot, Bloesch *F.A.S.* pl. 27, 1. I, boxer at altar; A–B, boxers. On
I, +ΑΙRΕ≤ΤRΑΤΟ≤ΚΑͰΟ≤. On A, ΔΟRΙ≤[ΕΛ]RΑⵕ≤ΕΝ. On B,
ΚΑͰΟ≤. For the shape, Bloesch 96, Python no. 1.

30 (30). Palermo V 663, from Chiusi. Inghirami *Chius.* pll. 109–11;
cleaned, *CV.* pl. 16, 3 and pl. 15. I, man (trainer) seated; A–B, athletes.
On I, ΔΟRΙ≤ΕΛRΑⵕ≤ΕΝ. On A, ΗΟ+ΑΙRΕ≤ΤR[ΑΤΟ≤]ΚΑͰΟ≤.
On B, ΗΟ+ΑΙRΕ≤[Τ]RΑΤΟ≤ Κ[Α]ͰΟ≤. For the shape, Bloesch 96,
Python no. 2 (the underfoot has the usual offset).

31. Basle market (M.M.). Schefold *M.* 193. I, trainer; A–B, athletes (A,
acontists; B, jumpers). On I, ΛΟRΙ≤ΕΛRΑⵕ≤ΕΝ.+ΑΙRΕ≤ΤRΑΤΟ≤-
ΚΑͰΟ≤.

32 (31). Florence 73750, from Orvieto. Hoppin ii, 496. I, man with hare;
A–B, athletes and men. On I, Δ[ΟRΙ]≤ΕΛRΑⵕ≤Ε. Not certain that
there was a final nu.

33 (32). Dresden, Kunstgewerbemuseum. Hoppin *Bf.* 461. I, man with
purse; A–B, men and youths (one a boy victor). On I, ΛΟRΙ≤ΕΛΡΑⵕ-
≤ΕΝ and +ΑΙRΕ≤ΤRΑΤΟ≤ΚΑͰΟ≤. On the shape, Bloesch 96, Python
no. 4.

34 (33). Leningrad (ex Orloff Davydoff). *R.A.* 1913, i, 33–37, whence
Hoppin i, 262–3. I, trainer; A–B, athletes (A, men; B, youths). On I,
[ΛΟR]Ι≤ΕΛRΑⵕ≤ΕΝ.

35 (34). Louvre G 118. *WV.* 6 pl. 9, whence Hoppin i, 250; I and part of A,
Pottier pl. 107; part of A, Perrot 10, 549; I, *Enc. phot.* iii, 13, c; phs. Gir.
17823–5. I, trainer; A–B, athletes. On I, ΛΟRΙ≤ΕΛRΑⵕ≤ΕΝ.+ΑΙRΕ≤Τ-
RΕ≤ΤRΑΤΟ≤ΚΑͰΟ≤. Restored.

36. Louvre C 10907. I, symposion (man reclining, and boy cup-bearer).
A, Herakles and the lion; B, Herakles and the bull. On I, +ΑΙRΕ≤[Τ]-
Ρ[Α]ΤΟ≤ΚΑ[ͰΟ≤] and in the exergue ΚΑͰΙΜΑ+[Ο≤] with ΚΑͰΟ[≤]
below it. For the inscriptions, *Eph.* 1953–4, 201 and *AJA.* 1954, 190.

37 (35, 36, +). Louvre G 119. I, incompletely, *WV.* 7 pl. 4, 2, whence Hoppin i, 252. I, trainer; A–B, boxers. On I, ΛΟRΙ≤[Ε]ΛRΑⵕ≤[ΕΝ].
Louvre S 1349 and several other Louvre fragments belong.

38 (37). LEIPSIC T 3366, fr. I, seated male; A, athletes (athlete to left, victor between two men or youths in himatia leaning on their sticks). [Rumpf].

39 (38). BONN 1931, fr. CV. pl. 5, 3–4. I, one seated; A, (athlete and males). On I, Λ[ORIꓢEΛRΑⵔꓢEN].

40 (39). HEIDELBERG 75 and FLORENCE 16 B 5, fr. The Heidelberg part, Kraiker pl. 10; the Florence, CV. pl. 16, B 5. A, (on the right, youth, and man or youth, boy).

41 (40). BRUNSWICK 528, fr. CV. pl. 17, 3. A, (on the left, man or youth, and boy).

42 (41). VILLA GIULIA, fr. I, (on the right, right middle of the right-hand figure, a male in himation with knotty stick; line-border). A, (the legs of the right-hand figure remain, a male in a short himation leaning on his stick to left). B, (shank and heel of the left-hand figure remain, a small boy to right).

43. NAPLES, Astarita, 131, five frr. I, Hermes at altar. A, gods and goddesses in Olympus (Zeus and Hera, with Ganymede; Poseidon and Amphitrite; Dionysos; there were others). B, fight: Achilles and Hector. I have given my part (AJA. 1955, 71, left) to Astarita. As Louvre G 116 (no. 44).

44 (42). LOUVRE G 116. WV. 7 pl. 2, whence Hoppin i, 246; A, Perrot 10, 539; I, Pottier pl. 109; B, ph. Al. 23732, whence Stella 420; A–B, cleaned, ph. Gir. 33535. I, Poseidon and goddess. A–B, Peleus and Thetis. On I, ΛOR[Iꓢ]EΛRΑⵔSEN.

45 (43). BOSTON 98.930. Hoppin i, 226–7; I, Langlotz G.V. pl. 22, 33, whence Mem. Am. Ac. 6 pl. 12 b, a; I, Pfuhl fig. 457; CB. iii pl. 72. I, komast; A–B, komos. On I, ΛORIꓢEΛRΑⵔꓢEN. See CB. iii, text.

46 (45). ADRIA B 812, fr., from Adria. I, (breast and waist of youth). A, (foot?).

47 (46). LONDON E 48, from Vulci. Gerhard pl. 234, whence (A–B) Perrot 10, 537; WV. 6 pl. 3, 1, whence (A–B) Hoppin i, 238; I, Murray no. 29, whence Perrot 10, 538 and Hoppin i, 238; Walters H.A.P. pl. 1; detail of A (Theseus and Kerkyon), Norman Gardiner Athl. fig. 166; A–B, ph. Ma.; B.Ap. xxii. 57. Deeds of Theseus: I, Minotaur; A, Skiron, Kerkyon; B, sow, Sinis. On I, ΛORIꓢEΛRΑⵔꓢEN. For the shape, Bloesch 98, Python no 13.

48 (47). BERLIN 2285, from Cervetri. Mon. 9 pl. 54, whence WV. 6 pl. 6, (A) Perrot 10, 551, (I) FR. iii, 87, whence Hoppin i, 214; AZ. 1873 pl. 1; A–B, FR. pl. 136, 1, whence Hoppin i, 215 and Bieber H.T. 3; A, Pfuhl fig. 468 (= Pfuhl Mast. fig. 65); A, Neugebauer pl. 52; B, Buschor 176; details of A, Birt Buchrolle 138, Schubart Buch² 153 and 156, and Kirchner pl. 11, 21; A–B, Zadoks-Jitta 93, 7 and 9; A, Buschor G. Vasen 159; B, Wegner Mus. pl. 12; A, Schefold Bildnisse 15; A, Mnem. 4th ser., 3 pl. 1, 3; detail of A, Das Altertum 1, frontispiece; A, Greifenhagen A.K. pl. 61; I, ph. Gir. 30084. I, athlete taking his sandals off. A–B,

school. On I, ΛΟΡΙΣΕΛΡΑΦΣΕΝ. On A, ΗΙΓΟΛΑΜΑSΚΑLΟS. On B, ΗΙΓΟΛΑΜΑS[ΚΑ]LΟS. For the shape, Bloesch 98, Python no. 14; for the writing on the roll, *AJA.* 1948, 337–8 no. 2. See p. 1653.

49. FLORENCE (ex Villa Giulia), fr. A, (knees of one in a himation seated to right, middle of one in a himation standing to left). Compare Berlin 2285 (no. 48): this too may be from a school-scene. It might belong to the next.

50 (48). VILLA GIULIA, fr. I, concert: a boy, probably singing, and a youth or man, probably playing the flute, standing on a platform, between two listeners, one of whom sits, the other stands; A, school? (what remains corresponds to feet and stool of the youth with tablets on B of Berlin 2285, to the feet of his pupil, to the back stool-leg of the man on the right). See the last.

51 (49). FLORENCE 7 B 29, HEIDELBERG 76 and 77, and VILLA GIULIA, frr. The Florence frr. (part), *CV.* pl. 7, B 29; the Heidelberg, Kraiker pl. 10; the Villa Giulia, *CF.* pl. Y, 18. Outside, music-lesson.

52 (50). LONDON E 49 and VILLA GIULIA, from Vulci. *WV.* 6 pl. 10, whence Hoppin i, 241; I, Murray no. 30; part of A, Schaal fig. 35; detail of A, Richter *H.G.A.* 362 fig. 481; A–B, ph. Ma. 3171: these without the Villa Giulia fragment, which is *CF.* pl. Z, 25. I, komast; A–B, symposion. On I, ΛΟΡΙΣΕΛΡΑΦΣΝ retr. For the shape, Bloesch 98, Python no. 15.

53 (51). VATICAN, fr. Hartwig pl. 67, 3, whence Hoppin i, 261, (A) Perrot 10, 530, (A) Brueckner *Leb.* 15, (A) Pfuhl fig. 469, I, *JHS.* 71, 131 fig. 6; *JHS.* 71, 131 figs. 4–5; A, ph. And. 42101, 1. I, symposion? (part of a woman's head remains: cf. no. 97); A, symposion. On I, [ΛΟR]ΙS-ΕΛΡΑΦ[ΣΕΝ]. See p. 1653.

54 (52). ~~FREIBURG, fr. A, symposion (part of a~~ man reclining to left, cup in his left hand, with his right stroking his beard).

55 (54). FLORENCE 3922, from Chiusi. I and A, Jacobsthal *Gött.* 58, whence (A) Pfuhl fig. 464; *CV.* pl. 90 and pl. 116, 11. I, symposion (man reclining); A–B, symposion. [Hartwig]. For the shape, Bloesch 97, Python no. 10.

56 (55). VILLA GIULIA, fr. A, symposion (hair of one to right, and the lower part of a cup hanging).

57 (56, +). LOUVRE G 126 *bis* (including S 1327 and another fr.), fr. I, symposion (youth, and a youth or man, reclining); A–B, symposion. One fr. was attributed to Douris by Pottier.

58 (57). FLORENCE V 48, from Chiusi. I, symposion (man reclining): A–B, symposion. For the shape, Bloesch 97, Python no. 9.

59 (58). LONDON E 52, from Vulci. I, Murray no. 32. I, man; A, youth and boy victor; men and boy; B, youths and boys. [Hartwig]. For the shape, Bloesch 97, Python no. 6.

60 (59, 95, +). LOUVRE S 1350. I, woman looking in her mirror (face and

right leg frontal, mirror in left hand, alabastron in right; on the left a laver, on the right, a wool-basket on a chair). A–B, men (or men and youths) and boys.

61 (53). FREIBURG, two frr. I, (unexplained remains, with Hippodamian maeander). Outside, on one fr., unexplained remains; on the other, part of the handle-floral—of the middle palmettes.

62 (60). LOUVRE G 117. *WV.* 7 pl. 3, whence Hoppin i, 249; I, Pottier pl. 109; I, R.I.; ph. Gir. 32353. I, fight: Greek and Persian. A–B, fight. On I, Λ[Ο]ΡΙ ΣΕΛ[Ρ]ΑΦΣΕΝ. Now cleaned.

63 (61). NAPLES, Astarita, 48 (ex Basseggio), VILLA GIULIA, and FLORENCE 12 B 38. See *JHS.* 51, 48 no. 28 and *CF.* 20 on pl. 12 B 38. *WV.* 6 pl. 5, whence Hoppin i, 275 and (A) Robert *Scenen der Ilias* 5; the Florence fr., *CV.* pl. 12, B 38; the Villa Giulia, *CF.* pl. Z, 5. I, warrior; A–B, fight. On I, ΛΟΡΙ ΣΕΛΡΑΦΣΕΝ.

64 (62). FLORENCE, fr. (now detached from the Makron cup in which the restorer had inserted it, see p. 460 no. 15). Hartwig pl. 28, above, right, whence Hoppin ii, 57, above, right. A, fight.

65 (63). LEIPSIC T 724, fr. I, (maeander). A, fight (end of a quiver, middle of a warrior).

66 (64). LEIPSIC T 626, fr. A, fight (on the right, warrior to left, striking with sword).

67 (65). VILLA GIULIA, fr. A, (small pieces of crest and shield, with ΗΙΓ- [ΓΟΛΛΑΜΑΣ . . .]. Rim-fragment. A small rim-fragment in Florence, with part of a crest, recalls this.

68 (67). BERLIN 2287, from Cervetri. *AZ.* 1883 pl. 3, whence Robert *Scenen der Ilias* 6 and Hoppin i, 219; I, Greifenhagen *A.K.* pl. 62; phs. Marb. LA 1075. 15–17. I, fight; A–B, fight. On I, in the exergue, ΛΟΡΙ ΣΕΛΡΑΦ- ΣΕΝ. Now augmented by Leipsic fragments identified by Rumpf; see also the next two numbers. See p. 1653.

69 (68). LEIPSIC, fr. Outside, fight (east palmette, then helmet and shield of a falling warrior). Almost certainly belongs to Berlin 2287, see *CF.* 32 no. 11 *bis.*

70 (69). TÜBINGEN E 21, fr. Watzinger pl. 19. Outside, fight. Probably belongs to Berlin 2287, see *CF.* 32 no. 11 *bis.*

71. NAPLES, Astarita, 133, six frr. I, (there remain: on one fr., on the right, the foot of one running to left; on another fr., a sceptre-head; the subject might be, for example, Zeus pursuing Aigina). A–B, warriors: the voting on the arms of Achilles. [Astarita]. The fragment Astarita 135, with part of a palmette in the style of Douris, may belong. See p. 1653.

72. NAPLES, Astarita, 132, two frr. I, warrior seated, and another. The warrior wears a himation over his armour; in the exergue, palmettes. A, the voting on the arms of Achilles (counting the votes); B, (on the right,

a warrior). [Astarita]. The two fragments Astarita 136 and 139, with parts of palmettes in the style of Douris, may belong. See p. 1653.

73. *vacat*.

74 (70). LOUVRE G 115, from Capua. Fröhner *Nap.* pll. 2–4 = Fröhner *Mus. de France* pll. 10–12, whence *WV.* 6 pl. 7, (A–B) Robert *Scenen der Ilias* 12 and 7, (I) H.M. pl. 18, (A–B) Robert *Herm.* 205–6; Pottier pll. 107–8, whence (A–B) Perrot 10, 532–3, Hoppin i, 245; I, Perrot 10 pl. 11, 2; I, Langlotz *G.V.* pl. 28; I, Pfuhl fig. 466 (= Pfuhl *Mast.* fig. 64), whence LS. fig. 87; phs. Al. 23723–4, whence (I) *ML.* 28, 279 and (A–B) Jacobsthal *O.* pl. 77, a; I, Cloché pl. 22, 2; I, Zadoks-Jitta 77, 7; A–B, Johansen *Iliaden* figs. 39–40; *Enc. phot.* iii, 14–15, whence Frel *Ř.V.* fig. 186; phs. Gir. 17458 and 17471, whence (A–B) Béquignon *Il.* 131 and 135; I, Stella 298. I, Eos with the body of Memnon; A–B, fights: A, Menelaos and Paris; B, Ajax and Hector. On I, ΛΟΡΙ$ ΕΛΡΑΘ$ΕΝ, ΚΛΛΙΑΛΕ$ ΕΓΟΙΕ$ΕΝ, ΗΕΡΜΟΛΕΝΕ$ ΚΛΛΟ$. For the shape, Bloesch 134 no. 3; for the mysterious inscription on I, *AJA.* 1960, 219.

75 (71). BONN 76 and FLORENCE 11 B 39. *WV.* 7 pl. 5, whence Hoppin i, 222; *Festschrift Clemen* (Winter *Schale des Duris*) 122–4; *CV.* Bonn pl. 4, 1–2 and pl. 5, 1–2; these without the Florence fragment, which is *CV.* Florence pl. 11, B 39. I, warrior; A–B, arming. On I, ΛΟΡΙ$ΕΛΡΑΘ$Ε retr.

76 (72). AMSTERDAM inv. 4623, fr. Outside, (upper part of man to left, arms extended).

77 (73). VILLA GIULIA, fr. Outside, (head and shoulders of a man in a himation, wreathed, seated on a chair to right, arms extended).

78 (74, +). LOUVRE G 121. *WV.* 6 pll. 8 a and 8 b, whence Hoppin i, 255 and 257; Pottier pl. 110, whence (part of I) Perrot 10, 550; phs. Al. 23728–9. I, youth with hare, seated; in a zone round this, men and youths; A–B, men and youths. On I, ΛΟΡΙ$ΕΛΡΑΘ$ΕΝ retr. and ΗΟΓΑΙ$ ΚΛΛΟ$. On A, ΚΛΛΟ$, ΚΛΛΟ$, [ΗΙΓΓ]ΟΛΛΜ[Α$]. On B, [Κ]ΛΛΟ$, ΚΛΛΟ$, ΗΙΓΓΟΛΜΑ[$]. On the side of the foot, ΓVΘΟΝ. Now cleaned, and one or two fragments added. For the shape, Bloesch 99, Python no. 22.

79 (75, +). LOUVRE C 11386, four frr. Replica of the last. Several other fragments in the Louvre belong to either this or the last.

80. LOUVRE C 11387, fr. (three joining). A, (one seated to right: the hair remains, then the upper part of a stick, and, hanging, a shield; on the left, . . . Ο$).

81. LOUVRE C 201, two frr. I, (maeander). Outside, (on one fr., the middle of the left-hand figure on one half, a male leaning on his stick to right; on the other fr., parts of the middles of three persons in himation).

82. LOUVRE C 11388, four frr. Outside, (on one fragment, man in himation seated to left; on the second, part of a similar man; on the third, the

middle of a man in a himation seated to right; on the fourth, which consists of three, a shield hanging, and to right of it a palmette).

83. LOUVRE C 11389, fr. Outside, (middle of one in a himation leaning to left, then a small part of another to right).

84. LOUVRE C 11390, fr. I, (shanks of a male in a himation leaning to right; on the left. . . . O . . .). A, (feet to right). Worn.

85. LOUVRE C 11391, fr. A, komos? (shoulders to buttocks of a naked male moving to left, with a stick).

86. STRASBURG, Univ., 776, fr. I, (maeander and HO . . .). A, komos? (legs of males moving to right).

87 (76). LONDON E 53, from Vulci. I, Murray no. 33. I, man seated at altar. A–B, komos. [Hartwig.] For the shape, Bloesch 99, Python no. 29.

88 (77). LEIPSIC T 524, fr., from Tarquinia. Hartwig 610, whence Hoppin i, 265. I, warrior. A, satyrs. On I, [ΛO]RISEΛRAⵙSE[N]. Unusual border for Douris.

89 (78). BOSTON 00.499, from Orvieto. *AJA.* 1900 pl. 1 and pp. 185, 188, 189, whence Hoppin i, 230, (A–B) *Mem. Am. Ac.* 6 pl. 16, 2, and (I) Yavis *Gk Altars* 166; I, Richter *F.* fig. 117; I, *Harv. St.* 52 pl. 7; CB. iii pl. 73. I, Dionysos at altar; A–B, satyrs and maenads. On I, ΛORISEΛRAⵙSEN. On A, HIΓΓOΛΛΑΜΑSΚΑⵏOS. Restored. See CB. iii, text.

90 (79). ERLANGEN 459 e, fr. A, (head and breast of man to left, with wand or stick).

91 (80). TARQUINIA, from Tarquinia. *RM.* 5, 338–9, whence *Festschrift Clemen* (Winter *Schale des Duris*) 127. I, warrior; A–B, men. [Reisch].

92 (81). LOUVRE G 125, fr. A, Pottier pl. 111. I, warrior at altar; A, warriors leaving home. [Pottier].

93 (82). CAB. MÉD. 540. De Ridder pl. 21 and pp. 408–10. I, komast. A–B, warriors leaving home. [De Ridder].

94 (83, +). LOUVRE G 123. Hartwig pl. 68; I, Pottier pl. 111, whence Perrot 10, 601; I, Beazley and Ashmole fig. 57, whence *Hundertes Winck.* 46. I, Zeus carrying off Ganymede. A–B, men and youths. [Hartwig]. Now cleaned, and the alien fragment removed (p. 460 no. 15). A Louvre fragment joins, adding the middle of the two left-hand figures on A. The figure in the arms of Zeus is male (Kunze *Hundertes Winck.* 39; *EVP.* 297, foot; CB. ii, 52).

95 (84). BERLIN 2289, FLORENCE 7 B 28, and VILLA GIULIA, from Vulci. See *CF.* 15 on pl. 7 B 28. Gerhard *TG.* pl. 14, 1–4; I, *Jh.* 12 pl. 1, whence Perrot 10, 659, Ahrem 99 fig. 104, Bieber *G.K.* 1, Cloché pl. 28, 1; I, Pfuhl fig. 461; I, Neugebauer pl. 49, 2; I, Brendel *Schafzucht* pl. 66, 2; A–B, Lücken pll. 11–12; A, Greifenhagen *A.K.* pl. 63; the Florence part, *CV.* pl. 7, B 28 (and pl. 24, B 9); the Villa Giulia, *CF.* pl. Y, 16. I, women preparing wool. A–B, komos. [Furtwängler]. For the shape, Bloesch 99,

Python no. 23; for the subject of I compare the cup by the Stieglitz Painter in Florence (3918: p. 826 no. 7).

96 (85). LONDON E 54, from Vulci. I, Murray no. 34, whence Pfuhl fig. 458. I, komos (two men); A–B, komos. [Hartwig]. For the shape, Bloesch 100, Python no. 30.

97 (86). PARIS, Ganay (ex Kopf), fr., from near Tarquinia. I, *Festschrift für Benndorf* 86, whence *JHS*. 66, 123 fig. 2; I, Pollak *Kopf* pl. 5, 98; *JHS* 69, 73. I, symposion (man reclining and woman binding her head). A–B, men and woman. [Hartwig].

98 (85). Once LONDON, J. C. Robinson, from Vulci. I, *JHS*. 66, 123 fig. 1. I, symposion (man reclining and woman sleeping). A–B, komos. [Martin Robertson].

99 (87, +). LOUVRE S 1351, fr. (five joining). I, (maeander). A, (two men, column, man or youth raising his hand to his head).

100. LOUVRE C 11392, fr. Outside, (hair of one to left, forehead-hair and hand, holding stick, of a male to left). Might belong to the last.

101. LOUVRE C 11393, fr. Outside, (thong of an aryballos).

102. LOUVRE C 222, fr. Outside, (part of two males in himatia). Might belong to Louvre S 1351 (no. 99).

103. LOUVRE C 11394, fr. (two joining). A, (the upper part of the right-hand figure remains, a man leaning to left, then part of the NW. handle palmette).

104. LOUVRE C 11395, fr. A, (thigh and penis of a naked male moving to right, legs of a male in a himation seated, or rather reclining on the ground, to left).

105. LOUVRE C 11396, fr. A, (sandals hanging, arm of male leaning to right).

106. LOUVRE C 11397, fr. Outside, (part of E. palmette, arm of male leaning to right).

107. LOUVRE C 11398, fr. I, (maeander). A, (buttocks of two males in himatia).

108 (88). VILLA GIULIA, fr. A, (part of the E. palmette, then head, to right, shoulders, left hand resting on stick, of the left-hand figure, a man in a himation).

109 (89). VILLA GIULIA, fr. Outside, (S. palmette, then shanks and feet of the left-hand figure on one half, a male in a himation leaning to right).

110 (90, +). LOUVRE G 124. I, Pottier pl. 111. I, man or youth, and woman. A–B, warriors leaving home. Four Louvre frr. belong, including the handles, and have been added.

111. CLEVELAND 508.15. *AJA*. 1954 pll. 41–42. I, Dionysos and satyr; A–B, satyrs and maenads.

112 (91). HARVARD 1925.30.129, from Capua. Details of I and A, *JHS*. 44, 242 fig. 14, 1–2; *CV*. Hoppin pll. 9–10; the shape, Caskey G. 203 no. 156.

I, satyr and maenad; A–B, Dionysos with satyrs and maenads. [Hoppin]. Compare the last.

113 (92). LOUVRE S 1319, fr. A, (youth and another). Compare Harvard 1925.30.129 (no. 112).

114. NEW YORK 52.11.4. *Bull. Metr.* Nov. 1952, 100–1. I, man and seated youth; A–B, men and youths. [Langlotz, Bothmer].

115. SWISS PRIVATE. I, man and woman; A–B, men and youths. On I the man leans on his stick, the woman holds up a distaff. [Astarita].

116 (93). VATICAN, from Cervetri. *Mon.* 2 pl. 35; *Mus. Greg.* 2 pl. 86, 1; detail of A, Hartwig 669; I, ph. Mo., whence *Rend. Lincei* 29, 53 and Ahrem 95 fig. 97; I and A, phs. Al. 35830 and 35829, whence (I) Pfuhl fig. 467, (I) Seltman pl. 27, b, (I) *Hist. rel.* 271, (I) Radermacher *Mythos*² fig. 10; I, ph. And. 42056, whence Stella 579; I, ph. Marb. O 29171. I, Jason disgorged by the dragon; and Athena. A–B, men and youths. [Hartwig R.]. Restored. For the shape, Bloesch 99, Python no. 25. See p. 1653.

117 (94). WÜRZBURG 484, fr. A, Langlotz pl. 152. I, (maeander). A, men and boys. Cf. the Vatican cup no. 116.

118 (94 *bis*). MUNICH SL 513, part. A, (the upper part of the right-hand figure remains, a man in a himation to left, then part of the W. palmette).

119 (96). CAB. MÉD. L 133, fr. A, (part of the left-hand figure remains, a youth in a himation standing to right; on the left, part of the E. palmette).

120 (97). ADRIA B 500, fr., from Adria. *CV.* pl. 21, 6; I, *Riv. Ist.* N.S. 5–6, 47 fig. 34. I, man seated with lyre, and boy standing in front of him, perhaps singing. A, (males).

121 (98). Once William W. Hope, 76 (ex Pembroke). I, *El.* 4 pl. 98. I, warrior and woman; A–B, warriors.

122 (99). BOSTON 10.208, fr. Hartwig 620; CB. iii pl. 20, 3–4. I, man and youth; A, (males and boy). [Hartwig].

123 (105). BRYN MAWR P 182, fr. *AJA.* 1916, 340, 9. A, (youth).

124. LONDON 1952.12–2.1, fr. A, symposion.

125 (106). OXFORD 1927.4605, fr., from Orvieto. *CV.* pl. 14, 13 and 26. I, (woman). A, (males).

126 (104). BRYN MAWR P 245, fr. *AJA.* 1916, 340, 14. A, komos.

127 (102). HEIDELBERG 88, fr. A, Kraiker pl. 12. I, on the right, woman; A, (women; or gods and goddesses).

128 (108). MUNICH 2646 (J. 371), from Vulci. A, *Ber. Sächs.* 1853 pl. 10; FR. pl. 105, and ii, 230, whence (I) *Mem. Am. Ac.* 6 pl. 12 c, b; I, Langlotz *G.V.* pl. 29, 43; palmettes, Jacobsthal *O.* pl. 78, a; Lullies and Hirmer pll. 92–93; I, *E.A.A.* ii, 863. I, symposion (man reclining, singing, and youth playing the flute). A, Herakles and Linos. A, men and youths. [Hartwig]. For the shape, Bloesch 100, Python no. 32. See p. 1653.

129 (109). LOUVRE G 126. I, *Gaz. arch.* 1883, 481; I and A, Pottier pl. 112; R.I. I, Theseus and Skiron. A–B, Peleus and Thetis. [Hartwig]. Now cleaned.

130 (110). BERLIN 2288, from Vulci. Panofka *Skiron* pll. 1–2; *Jb.* 31 pl. 4 and pp. 86–87; I, Radermacher *Mythos*² fig. 14; I, Stella 534. I, Theseus and Skiron. A, fight. B, men and youths. [Furtwängler]. For the shape, Bloesch 98, Python no. 20.

131 (111). BRYN MAWR P 936, fr. I, (on the right, male in himation standing to left, dog). A, fight.

132 (112). MUNICH 2647 (J. 793), from Vulci. *Jb.* 31 pl. 3 and pp. 84–85; A, *Delt.* 1927–8, 103; A–B, Vorberg *Erotik* 77; B.Ap. xxii. 99. I, komos (two men). A–B, Dionysos with satyrs and maenads. On A, ΓΟLVΦPAϟ-ϟM[ON]. On B, ΓΟLVΦPAϟϟMON]ΚALO[ϟ]. For the shape, Bloesch 99, Python no. 28; for the scene inside, CB. ii, 59 no. 10. See p. 1653.

133 (113). CAB. MÉD. 542, from Vulci. *Mon.* 5 pl. 35, whence (I) *St. e mat.* 3, 214 and Roscher s.v. Prometheus, 3086; phs. Gir. 35674 and another, whence (I) *Hist. rel.* 180. I, Prometheus and Hera. A, return of Hephaistos. B, komos. [Hartwig R.]. For the shape, Bloesch 99, Python no. 27; for the subjects, Simon O.G. 90. See p. 1653.

134 (114). CAB. MÉD. 539, from Vulci. Luynes pll. 33–34, whence (A–B) *El.* 1 pll. 44–45 and (A)*WV.* 1 pl. 9, 1; phs. Gir. 8066–7. I, Peleus and Thetis. A, return of Hephaistos; B, satyrs attacking maenads. [Hartwig].

135 (114 *bis*). VILLA GIULIA, fr. I, (tail of satyr to right). A, (the heel of the left-hand figure remains, moving to right; to left of it, part of the S. palmette).

136 (100). VILLA GIULIA, fr. (three joining). I (maeander, Dourian pairs). Outside, (the left-hand part of the N. palmette remains, with parts of the tendrils to left of it).

137 (101). VILLA GIULIA, fr. Outside, (the upper part of the N. palmette remains, with parts of the tendrils to right of it).

138 (115). CHRISTCHURCH (N.Z.), Canterbury Museum, AR 430, from Orvieto. I, Panofka *Eigennamen* pl. 1, 10, whence Klein *Euphr.* 100; I, Klein *Liebl.* 94, whence Perrot 10, 387; *JHS.* 71 pl. 40, b–d; B.Ap. xvi. 33. 1. I, girl embracing youth. A–B, symposion. On I, HIΚET[Eϟ]ΚALOϟ.

139 (116). LEIPSIC T 550, frr. Hartwig 661–2. I, symposion. A, women. B, (youths). [Hartwig R.].

140 (117). HARVARD 1959.124 (ex Robinson), from Capua. *AJA.* 1921 pll. 1–3; *CV.* Robinson ii pll. 13–14. I, symposion (man and woman reclining); A–B, symposion.

141 (118). BOSTON 00.343, from Tarquinia. Hartwig pll. 74–75, whence (I) Pfuhl fig. 470; I, Vorberg *Erotik* 83; CB. iii pl. 74, 132 and pl. 75. I, satyrs and maenad. A–B, warriors leaving home. [Hartwig R.]. See CB. iii, text.

142 (119). MUNICH, fr. I, (middle of a woman, moving to right—pursued?). A, (foot moving to left, foot to right, foot to left).

143 (120). ADRIA B 112, fr., from Adria. I, (ram—Phrixos?) A, komos? (feet of males).

144 (121). OXFORD 1929.166, fr. *CV*. pl. 57, 2 and 11. I, male pursuing woman. A, (Herakles and Linos?).

145 (122). HEIDELBERG 79, fr. Kraiker pl. 10. I, (male and woman). A, (foot, shank and foot—Herakles and Linos?). On I, Ƨ with what may be the lower arm of an epsilon before it: [HIKET]EƧ?

146 (123). BRYN MAWR P 236, fr. I, (on the right, a woman). A, (on the right, males moving to right); B, (on the left, foot of one running to left).

147 (124). BRYN MAWR P 940, fr. I, (cloak). A, (on the right, shank and cloak of male running to right).

148. BRYN MAWR, fr. I (maeander, Dourian pairs). A, (middles of males in himatia).

149. BRYN MAWR P 939, fr. I, (unexplained remains). A, (on the right, part of a woman and of the handle-floral).

150. BRYN MAWR P 941, fr. I, (maeander). Outside, (parts of the N. and S. palmettes).

151 (125). VILLA GIULIA, fr. I, symposion (bit of table, and of a himation above it). A, (toes to left).

152 (126, 127, +). FLORENCE 7 B 25 (part ex Villa Giulia) and BOWDOIN, frr. Part, *CV*. pl. 7, B 25. A–B, warriors leaving home. The Bowdoin fragment joins. Another Florence fragment joins, adding one handle and part of the N. palmette. See also nos. 153–7.

153 (145). FLORENCE, fr. A, (right upper arm, and upper part of himation, of male to right). Probably belongs to Florence 7 B 25 (no. 152).

154 (128). VILLA GIULIA, fr. A, (upper half of warrior's head to right, with the top of his shield, seen from inside). Probably belongs to the last.

155 (129). VILLA GIULIA, fr. Outside, (right corner of the E. palmette, then left shoulder, and back of head, of a man in chiton and himation to right holding a sceptre). May belong to Florence 7 B 25 (no. 152).

156. VILLA GIULIA, fr. Outside, (edge of the E. palmette, then shoulder to near waist of one in a himation to right). May belong to Florence 7 B 25 (no. 152).

157 (161). FLORENCE (ex Villa Giulia), fr. Outside, (upper part of an upper palmette). May belong to Florence 7 B 25 (no. 152).

158 (130). VILLA GIULIA, fr. I, (scrap of himation, and end of a wand or perhaps a crest). A, (edge of shield? on the ground, then two feet to left).

159 (131). BONN 464.34, VILLA GIULIA, and FLORENCE, frr. The Bonn fr. (assigned to Douris by Greifenhagen), *CV*. pl. 6, 4. I, two men at a herm. A–B, (males). On I, [H]IK[ETEƧ . . . . The five frr. (making three) in

Italy give inside, forehead, eye, nose, right hand of the man on the left, with the lower part of his himation and of his stick and of the herm; front-hair of the man on the right, with part of his right leg and his right hand, on his hip; outside, legs in himatia.

160. NAPLES, Astarita, 265, fr. A, (arm of male holding stick, bent head of man to left and his hand holding a stick).

161. *Vacat.*

162 (132 *bis*). VILLA GIULIA, fr. I, (Dionysos: leg, in chiton and himation, to left, and beside it part of his thyrsus). A, komos? (shank and foot moving to left, shank and foot moving to right, heel to right).

163 (132). VILLA GIULIA, fr. I, (shank of one in chiton and himation). A, (shank of male moving to left, stick, ends of cloak).

164 (133). VILLA GIULIA, fr. A, (forearm with part of garment).

165 (134). VILLA GIULIA, fr. A, (shank of male in himation to right).

166 (135). VILLA GIULIA, fr. A, (middle of male in himation with stick transverse).

167 (136). VILLA GIULIA, fr. A, (piece of stick and of himation).

168 (137). VILLA GIULIA, fr. I, (elbow of one in himation to left). A, (ground-line and tip of S. palmette).

169 (138). VILLA GIULIA, fr. A, komos (hand holding cup by handle, knotty stick). ... |LL[O$?] retr. with part of a letter before the iota.

170 (139). FLORENCE 7 B 47 and VILLA GIULIA, frr. Part, *CV*. Florence pl. 7, B 47. Outside, komos. See no. 173.

171 (140). VILLA GIULIA, fr. A, (on the right, edge of a male shoulder and cloak, then the W. palmette). Might belong to the last.

172 (141). FLORENCE, fr. A, (on the left, waist and buttocks of a naked male to right; to left of this, the lower part of the E. palmette).

173 (139). FLORENCE 7 B 39, fr. *CV*. pl. 7, B 39. A, komos. Belongs to Florence 7 B 47 (no. 170)?

174 (144). VILLA GIULIA, fr. A, (raised hand).

175. FLORENCE, fr. (ex Villa Giulia). A, komos? (belly of male in cloak to right, right arm of male in cloak to right).

176 (157). LEIPSIC, fr. I, (maeander, Dourian pairs). Outside, (upper part of N. palmette).

177 (156). AMSTERDAM inv. 2803, fr. A, (on the left, a small piece of a clothed figure; to left of it, the E. palmette).

178 (147, +). LOUVRE G 319, fr. I, woman seated and youth. A, youth standing, between a man (or a youth) and a man, both seated. Two Louvre fragments join, giving, inside, the top of the head of the seated person, and outside, the right-hand figure on A.

179 (146). TARQUINIA 692, from Tarquinia. I, man seated and youth; A–B, men and youths.

180 (107). LONDON E 56, from Vulci. *WV*. C pl. 3, 1–2; I, Murray no. 36. I, Achilles and Odysseus; A–B, warriors leaving home. For the shape, Bloesch 99, Python no. 21.

181 (148). AREZZO 1414. Philippart *It. ii* pl. 9. I, symposion. A–B, men and youths. For the shape, Bloesch 97, Python no. 7.

182. BRYN MAWR P 942, fr. I, (bit of himation, and bud). A, (legs of the two left-hand figures remain: one in chiton and himation standing to right, woman running to left: perhaps a Nereid fleeing to Nereus, compare Munich 2648 (no. 185)?

183 (149). ATHENS Acr. 305, frr., from Athens. Part, Langlotz pl. 19. I, (floral in the field). A–B, (males).

184 (150, +). FLORENCE 3960. *CV*. pl. 93 and pl. 116, 15. I, woman greeting youth. A–B, warriors leaving home. For the shape, Bloesch 100, Python no. 31. School-piece? See p. 1653.

185 (151). MUNICH 2648 (J. 369), from Vulci. *WV*. A pl. 1; FR. pl. 24; palmettes, Jacobsthal O. pl. 78, b; I, Richter and Milne 19; I, *JHS*. 59, 109; A and foot, Bloesch *FAS*. pl. 27, 4; Lullies and Hirmer pl. 80, below, and pll. 88–91, whence Stella pl. 17, p. 421, and p. 427, below, and (I) LS. figs. 88–89. I, Herakles and Athena. A–B, Peleus and Thetis. For the shape, Bloesch 98, Python no. 17. Compare the next. School-piece?

186 (152). NEW YORK 23.160.54. I, *Bull. Metr.* 20, 129; *AJA*. 1926, 32–34; B, *RM*. 47 pl. 2; Richter and Hall pl. 61, pll. 63–64, and pl. 181, 59; I, Richter *Gk Painting* 12; detail of I, Richter *ARVS*. fig. 65; I, Schnitzler pl. 42; I, Richter *H*. 228, d; part of I, Buschor *Bilderwelt* 42. I, two naked women laying their clothes down. A, boy with lyre, and women; B, women and youths. [John Marshall]. School-piece? See p. 1653.

187 (153). ROUEN inv. 450, from Vulci. Vesly *Notes arch.* 1914, 3–5, whence *Ant. cl.* 1, 245; *Musée des antiquités, Guide* 43–44. I, satyrs dancing. A, athletes; B, men and youths. [Pottier R.]. Much restored. School-piece?

188 (154). NEW YORK 22.139.82, fr. Richter and Hall pl. 66, 60. I, (satyr). A, komos. School-piece?

189. LOUVRE C 11399, fr. Outside, (W. palmette).

190. LOUVRE C 11400, fr. Outside, (W. palmette).

191. LOUVRE C 11401, fr. Outside, (W. palmette).

192. LOUVRE C 11402, fr. Outside, (W. palmette).

193. LOUVRE C 11403, fr. Outside, (N. and E. palmettes).

194. LOUVRE C 11404, fr. Outside, (E. palmette).

195. LOUVRE C 11405, fr. Outside, (E. or W. palmette).

196. LOUVRE C 11406, fr. Outside, (W. palmette).

197 (155). CAB. MÉD., fr. Outside, (corner of E. or W. palmette).

198. FLORENCE, fr. Outside, (lower right-hand part of W. palmette).

199 (162). VILLA GIULIA, fr. Outside, (right upper quarter of E. or W. palmette).

200 (142). VILLA GIULIA, fr. Outside, (left upper part of E. or W. palmette).

201 (143). VILLA GIULIA, fr. Outside, (right upper corner of E. or W. palmette).

202 (158). VILLA GIULIA, fr. Outside, (left upper quarter of E. or W. palmette).

203 (159). VILLA GIULIA, fr. Outside, (left upper corner of E. or W. palmette).

204 (160). VILLA GIULIA, fr. (two joining). Outside, (left part of E. or W. palmette).

205 (163). VILLA GIULIA, fr. Outside, (right part of W. palmette).

206. FLORENCE, fr. Outside, (upper left-hand piece of E. or W. palmette).

(nos. 207–10, not known if decorated outside)

207 (44). VILLA GIULIA, fr. I, (shanks of a male in a himation standing to left).

208. LOUVRE C 11407, fr. I, (stick, himation). On the left, the letter .. O and the upright of another letter.

209 (66). VILLA GIULIA, fr. I, (greaved shank of a warrior running to right).

210 (103). FLORENCE PD 335, fr. I, symposion (two youths reclining).

(nos. 211–51, decorated inside only)

(The order is again, so far as possible, chronological: see pp. 425–6; nos. 211–15 are very early).

211 (2). LOUVRE G 128, fr. Part (the border omitted), Pottier pl. 112. I, komast (youth with lyre, singing). [+ΛIRE϶T]RΛTO϶K[ΑLO϶]. Very early.

212 (3). TÜBINGEN E 19, from Taranto. Watzinger pl. 19. I, komast (youth with lyre, singing). [+ΛIRE]϶TRΛT[O϶ ... Very early.

213 (a). ATHENS, Agora, P 10271, from Athens. Foot and mouth, Bloesch *FAS.* pl. 24, 1. I, komos (man singing and woman playing the flute). There is no border, and the part of the interior outside the tondo, and the greater parts of the exterior, are reserved: the original intention was probably to cover them with coral-red. Same style as the Vatican cup no. 2. Very early. For the shape, Bloesch 83, potter Brygos, no. 12.

214. Once ROME, Giglioli, fr. *Arch. class.* 2, 86. I, (youth with lyre). ...϶K .... Early.

215 (164). BALTIMORE, from Chiusi. Hartwig pl. 22, 2; *CV.* Robinson ii pl. 11. I, two warriors running. According to Bothmer not Amazons. +ΛIRE϶TRΛTO϶ KΑLO϶. [Hartwig]. Early.

216 (165). LEIPSIC T 509 (?), from Orvieto. Hartwig pl. 17, 2, whence Hoppin

Euth.F. 108 and Hoppin ii, 364. I, youth seated, playing the lyre and singing. [ΔOPIϟE]ΛPΑⵔⵔEN ⵙ +ΑIP[EϟTPATOϟⱢΑⵔOϟ]. [Langlotz].

217. READING 39. viii. 5, fr., from Etruria. *CV*. pl. 24, 4. I, male seated with lyre. ... ΑⵔⵔEN. [A. D. Ure].

218 (166). ATHENS Acr. 178, fr., from Athens. Langlotz pl. 8. I, (youth, sprig). [+ΑIPEϟ]TP[ΑTOϟ ...

219 (167). MUNICH inv. 8710 (ex Curtius), fr. *Anz.* 1957, 379; Ph. R.I. 1935.2056. I, youth seated, chin on hand; hanging in front of him, a fox.

220 (169). FLORENCE, fr., from Orvieto. *NSc.* 1939, 15. I, youth or man seated writing.

221 (170). ROMAN MARKET (Basseggio). R.I. ix. 72. I, youth (in himation, leaning on his stick to left, holding a wreath with both hands; on the left, hanging, sponge, aryballos, and strigil; on the right, a seat). HO-ΓΑIϟⱢΑⵔOϟ.

222 (186). ADRIA Bc 44, fr., from Adria. Schöne pl. 4, 5. I, youth seated. +ΑIREϟTRAT[OϟⱢΑⵔOϟ]. [Hartwig].

223 (171, +). LOUVRE G 120. Part, Hoppin i, 253; part, Pottier pl. 107. I, naked youth with phiale. ΛORIϟEΛRAⵔⵔEN ⵙ +Α[IREϟTRATOϟ-ⱢΑⵔOϟ]. Two Louvre frr. have been added, one by Bousquet, both reaching the rim.

224 (175 *bis*). MUNICH 2631. Vorberg *Gloss.* 461. I, man embracing boy. For the subject see *Cypr.* 30, γ 17.

224 *bis.* BASLE, Cahn, 64. I, athlete (moving to right, looking round, discus-bag in left hand). [HOΓ]ΑIϟⱢΑⵔO[ϟ].

225 (172). BOSTON 95.31, from Tarquinia. Fröhner *Brant.* pl. 19 = Hartwig pl. 22, 1, whence Perrot 10, 553 and Hoppin i, 225; CB. iii pl. 71, 127; R.I. M 38. I, Zephyros and Hyakinthos. ΔORIϟEΛRAⵔ[ϟ]EN ⵙ +ΑIRE-[ϟTRATOϟⱢΑⵔOϟ]. See CB. iii, text.

226 (173). BOSTON 01.8029, from Orvieto. Hartwig pl. 67, 1, whence Perrot 10, 599; *Int. Studio* 1927, 27, 1; CB. iii pl. 74, 128; the shape, Caskey G. 187 no. 141. I, naked youth at laver. HIΓOΛΑΜΑϟⱢΑⵔOϟ. [Hartwig]. For the shape, Bloesch 100, Python no. 36. See CB. iii, text.

227 (174). LONDON E 50, from Falerii. Hartwig pl. 67, 4. I, symposion (youth reclining). ⱢΑⵔOϟ HIΓOΛΑΜΑϟ. [Hartwig]. For the shape, Bloesch 100, Python no. 37. See p. 1653.

228 (176). ATHENS Acr. 306, fr., from Athens. I, (foot of one in chiton standing to right).

229 (178, +). LOUVRE G 286. I, komast ('Anacreontic'). Several Louvre frr. have been added by Marie Beazley. On the subject, CB. ii, 108 no. 9.

230 (177). FLORENCE V 497, from Chiusi. I, boxer kneeling. For the shape, Bloesch 96, Python no. 3.

230 *bis*. STOCKHOLM, Medelhavsmuseum. *Ars Ant. Aukt. II* pl. 60, 152. I, boy (fleeing? wrapped in his himation, hastening to left, looking round; on the left, suspended, a flute-case). HOΓAIϟ KALOϟ.

231 (179). HEIDELBERG 78, frr. Part, Kraiker pl. 13. I, warrior (light-armed, in Thracian costume).

232. PRINCETON 33.34. I, woman with crotala (dancing?) at altar. Probably by Douris himself.

233 (181). FLORENCE PD 194, fr. I, (arm, kantharos).

234 (182). CAB. MÉD. 515 (plus frr. of the border), frr. I, warrior putting on his greaves. . . . K]ALOϟ.

235 (183). VILLA GIULIA, fr. (five joining). I, Herakles?—man moving to left, club (?) in right hand, baldrick, left arm extended. HOΓAIϟKALOϟ.

236. LOUVRE C 11408, fr. I, (on the left, a wing).

237. LOUVRE C 11409, fr. I, (maeander, Dourian pairs).

238. FREIBURG, fr. I, (maeander, Dourian pairs).

239 (186). WÜRZBURG 482, from Vulci. Hartwig pl. 72, 3, whence Licht ii, 150; Langlotz pll. 152 and 164; the foot, Bloesch *FAS.* pl. 28, 3. I, man and boy. [Hartwig R.]. For the shape, Bloesch 100, Python no. 38.

240 (187). FLORENCE P D 106, fr., from Populonia. *NSc.* 1921, 323; Minto *Pop.* pl. 53, 5 b. I, (satyr).

241. LUCERNE MARKET (A.A.). I, love-making (man and woman). HEΓAIϟ-KALE, and, said by the man, HE+EHEϟY+Oϟ (ἔχε ἥσυχος, 'keep still', the earliest evidence for the expression). School-piece? For ἔχε compare the bf. fragment Athens Acr. 2644 (Graef pl. 112).

242 (188). ORVIETO, Faina, 60, from Orvieto. I, symposion (man and woman reclining).

243 (189). VILLA GIULIA 5294. I, trainer.

244 (190). BOULOGNE 157, fr. I, komast ('Anacreontic': in long chiton and himation, with cup and parasol). Restored.

245. VERDUN. I, symposion (man reclining and woman cup-bearer). [Bothmer]. As the next. School-piece?

246 (184, +). WÜRZBURG 483 and LOUVRE C 11410, from Vulci. The Würzburg part, Langlotz pl. 152. I, symposion (man reclining, and woman cup-bearer). The four Louvre fragments (one composed of two) join the Würzburg, completing the picture and one of them reaching to the rim. As the last. School-piece?

247. LOUVRE C 11411, fr. I, symposion (part of the couch, of the table, of the boots below the table).

248 (191). BOSTON 97.369, from Falerii. CB. iii pl. 74, 131. I, woman at laver.

249. NAPLES, Astarita, 760. I, woman perfuming a vessel.

250 (192). TARQUINIA RC 1116, from Tarquinia. *Eranos Vind.* 381; *CV.* pl. 10, 4. I, woman at laver. Cf. New York 23.160.54 (no. 186).

251 (193). BALTIMORE, from Chiusi. Hartwig pl. 72, 2, whence Wolters *Salbgefäss* 89 fig. 7; *CV.* Robinson ii pl. 12, where Zschietzschmann *H.R.* pl. 181, 2. I, Hermes teaching a boy to spin a top. [Hartwig R.].

STEMLESS CUP

252. CAMBRIDGE (Massachusetts), Rosenberg (lent to Harvard, 501.1937), from Greece. *CV.* pl. 19, 2; *Harv. St.* 52 pl. 1; Forbes *Studies in Ancient Technology* iii, 113. I, youth. [Holland, Chase]. On the inscription, TPIKOTVLOꝶ, read by Immerwahr, see his article in *P.A.P.A.* 79, 184–90.

SKYPHOI
(no. 253, cup-skyphos)

253 (194). BOLOGNA 470, fr., from Bologna. Part, Pellegrini 213. A, Dionysos and satyr. [Pellegrini]. Late.

(no. 254, type A)

254 (195). ADRIA B 601, fr., from Adria. Schöne pl. 10, 9; *CV.* pl. 22, 4; *Riv. Ist.* N.S. 5–6, 48 fig. 35. (Man). Late.

KANTHAROI
(no. 255, type A)

255 (196). ATHENS, Vlasto, from Keratea. Komos: A, man moving to right with lyre; B, youth leaning on his stick, holding a cup. Very early. For the shape, CB. iii, text.

(no. 256, type C)

256 (197). BRUSSELS A 718. *Memorie* 2 pl. 11; *WV.* 7 pl. 4, 1; *FR.* pl. 74, 1, whence Perrot 10, 543—5, Hoppin i, 233; A, Pfuhl fig. 453 (= Pfuhl *Mast.* fig. 60); *CV.* pll. 5–6, whence (part of B) Rumpf *MZ.* pl. 25, 7, (A) LS. fig. 91; B, Richter and Milne fig. 168; A, Schnitzler pl. 41, 57; Verhoogen *C.G.* cover and pll. 14–15; Bothmer *Am.* pl. 70, 4. Herakles and the Amazons (A, Herakles; B, Telamon). On A, ΛΟΡΙꝶΕΛΡΑΦꝶΕΝ: ΛΟΡΙꝶΕΓ[ΟΙΕꝶΕΝ]. On B, ⊦ΑΙΡΕꝶΤΡΑΤΟꝶ ΚΑLΟꝶ. For the shape, CB. iii, text. See p. 1653.

RHYTA
(nos. 257–8, lion's head)

257 (198). LOUVRE MNB 1294. B, Villard *VG.* pl. 21, 1; B, Bille-de Mot 107; ph. Arch. phot. MNLA 788. A, komast; B, komast. Late.

258 (199). LONDON E 796, from Capua. Walters *H.A.P.* pl. 46; *CV.* pl. 41, 2. Woman pursuing boy. Late. See p. 1653.

(no. 259, donkey's head)

259 (a ii 33). CHICAGO 05.345, from Nola. *Cat. vente Piot 27–30 mai 1890,* 47. Satyr and maenad. Late. See p. 1653.

(nos. 260–1, eagle's head)

260 (200). BRUSSELS, Bibliothèque Royale, 8, from Capua. *Cat. Cast.* pl. 3; Buschor *Krok.* (*Mü. Jb.* 1919) 16; Feytmans *V.B.R.* pll. 18–20. Floral. ΛΕΟϟϟΟΕΝΕϟΚΑΛΟϟ. The inscription read by Mrs. Callipolitis-Feytmans. Late. See p. 1653.

261 (a). LONDON E 802, from Capua. *CV.* pl. 43, 2; Hoffmann *A.R.R.* pl. 5, 2. What painting there is must be by the same hand as in the last.

PSYKTER

262 (201). LONDON E 768, from Cervetri. *WV.* 6 pl. 4; FR. pl. 48, whence Perrot 10, 529, Buschor 175, Hoppin i, 242, Licht iii, 30, Buschor *G. Vasen* 165, Buschor *Satyrtänze* fig. 71, (detail) Richter *ARVS.* fig. 64, (part) LS. fig. 90; *CV.* pl. 105, whence Buschor *G. Vasen* 164; detail, Bieber *H.T.* 21; part, Brommer *Satyrspiele*[1] 64 = [2]68; part, Lane pl. 77; part, Pickard-Cambridge *D.F.A.* fig. 199; detail, Richter *H.G.A.* 332 fig. 446; ph. Ma. 3211. Satyrs. ΔΟRIϟΕΛRΑΦϟΕΝ. ΑRIϟΤΑΛΟRΑϟ ΚΑΛΟϟ. For the shape, CB. ii, 7, A, A 20. Early middle.

NECK-AMPHORAE
(small; doubleens)

263 (202). LENINGRAD inv. 5576, from Capua. *CR.* 1874 pl. 7, 4–6, whence *Arch. class.* 2 pl. 13, 1; *Anz.* 1930, 29–30. A, Nike; B, victor.

264. LOUVRE S 3853. A, Nike (flying to left, looking round, holding a sash); B, youth (in himation, moving to right, holding a sprig). Restored.

OINOCHOE
(shape 7)

265. OBERLIN 55.11. *Bull. Allen* 13, 4–6; *Bull. Allen* 1959, 165. Satyr. Late.

LEKYTHOI
(standard shape)
(no. 266, white ground)

266 (203). PALERMO, from Selinus. Incompletely, *ML.* 32, 331 and pl. 94, whence *Anz.* 1929, 155; Marconi *Pal.* pl. 57, 1–2. Sacrifice of Iphigeneia. [Gàbrici]. Early middle. Compare especially Vienna 3695 (no. 26).

(nos. 267–73, red-figure)

267 (204). BOLOGNA PU 321, from Etruria. Pellegrini *VPU.* 54 fig. 43 and p. 55, whence (detail) Schröder *Sport* 117; *Arte antica e moderna* i, pl. 6, a–b, and pl. 7. Nike and victor. On the shoulder, lion between palmettes. ΔΙΟΛΕΝΕϟΚΑΛΟ[ϟ], and on the topside of the mouth ΜΕΝΟΝΚΑΛΟϟ. Much restored (notwithstanding the flattering reaction under fluorescent light reported in *Arte antica e moderna* i, i).

268. PAESTUM, from Paestum. Nike (flying to right, with oinochoe and phiale). Badly damaged, but seems to be by the painter himself. [Enrico Paribeni].

269 (205). Syracuse 26830, from Gela. *ML.* 19 pl. at p. 128, fig. 12. Nike. ΓVΘΑΙΟξΚΑLΟξ. Slightly restored.

270 (206). Boston 95.41, from Athens. Buschor G. *Vasen* 172 fig. 194; the shoulder, *AJA.* 1946, 105 fig. 10, b; the shape, Caskey G. 217 no. 172; CB. iii pl. 84, 134. Jumper. +ΑΙ[R]EξTR[ΑΤ]Οξ ΚΑLΟξ. The figure is a replica of one on a cup in the Basle market (no. 31). See CB. iii, text. Early middle.

271 (207). Syracuse 19896, from Gela. Man attacking with sword.

272 (209). Vienna, Univ., 526 a, from Gela. *Festblatt zur Versammlung deutscher Philologen*; Löwy *Altgr. Graphik* (from *Die graphischen Künste* 1923), 1; *CV.* pl. 13, 2–3; Greifenhagen *Eroten* 65. Eros blowing trumpet.

273 (208). Boston 13.194, from Gela. *AJA.* 1918, 119; CB. iii pl. 84, 135. Youth playing lyre. Late. School-piece. See CB. iii, text.

ROUND ARYBALLOS
(one-handled, flat-bottomed)

274 (210). Athens 15375, from Athens. *Anz.* 1928, 571; *Delt.* 1927–8 pll. 4–5, suppl. plate, and pp. 94 and 102, whence Stella 265, (part) Bielefeld *ZV.* pl. 20; part, Richter and Milne fig. 106; Greifenhagen *Eroten* 59. Erotes pursuing boy. ΛΟRΙξ ΕΓΟΙΕξΕΝ, ΑξΟΓΟΛΟRΩΗΕLΕ-ΛVΘΟξ. See *BSA.* 29, 205 no. 8; and below, p. 1653.

PYXIDES
(no. 275, type A)

275 (211). London E 807, fr., from Attica. Hartwig 625. (Woman fleeing). ...E... Δ... [Hartwig].

(no. 276, tripod-pyxis)

276 (212). Mannheim 124, from Athens. *CV.* pl. 26, 1 and 6–7 and pl. 32, 5. Uncertain subject (not Menelaos and Helen): A, warrior running; B, woman running, a small box in her hand; C, woman running up.

A small cup-fragment may be by Douris:

Innsbruck ii. 12. 29, fr. A, warriors (part of one warrior's shield, then beard and helmet-nape of another warrior, with part of his black shield). [Bothmer].

LOST VASES SIGNED BY DOURIS
CUPS

1. Lost. (De Witte in *Rev. phil.* 2, 513; Klein no. 11; Hoppin no. 38). I, male seated with purse. A–B, males and youths. On A, Δοριςεγραφσεν, on B the like.

2. Once William Hope (ex Durand 118 and Magnoncourt 23), from Vulci. (Brunn *KG.* 2, 669 no. 5; Klein no. 8; Hoppin no. 37). I, komos (man and youth); A–B, komos. On I, Δοριϛεγραφϛεν.

SHAPE? (according to Tsountas not a cup)

3. Lost?, from Athens (Acropolis). (*Eph.* 1885, 56; Klein no. 24.) Δοριϛε...

The Braun cup (Brunn *KG.* 2, 670 no. 11; Klein no. 3; Hoppin no. 39) is probably, as Plaoutine suggested, Louvre G 118, our no. 35.

On the cup Berlin 2286 see p. 360 and p. 365 no. 59.

MANNER OF DOURIS

See p. 426.

I

Early (period 1).

CUPS

1. LOUVRE C 11412, fr. (four joining). I, warrior (the feet remain, standing to right, and part of the earliest-Dourian maeander); A, warriors: parts of of the right-hand figures remain, running to right. Probably by Douris himself: very badly preserved.

2. LOUVRE C 11413, fr. I, (maeander, of earliest-Dourian type). A (naked cup-bearer, with a ladle, bending to right). Probably by Douris himself: ill preserved.

3. OXFORD, Beazley, fr. I, (maeander, of earliest-Dourian type). A, symposion (parts of two males reclining; below, a line and the same maeander). May be by Douris himself.

4 (i 2 2). ATHENS, Agora P 6159, fr., from Athens. I, (toes). A, komos.

5 (l 23). VILLA GIULIA, fr. I, (bare shank and foot, to left, on a thick ground-band).

A large cup is akin to the very earliest works of Douris:

CAB. MÉD. 543, part of 536, plus, frr. Part, Hartwig pl. 23; some frr. (wrongly combined with another cup, Cab .Méd. 536, see p. 191 no. 103), *JHS.* 10 pl. 2 (see *Kleophr.* 19); part, phs. Gir. 8062–3 (the photographs include several alien fragments). I, Dionysos seated, and maenad; A–B, satyrs and maenads. Outside, remains of the kalos-name Chairestratos (+ ...,... PΑ ...,... T ...,... OϚ). See also pp. 399 and 1566.

II

Various. Periods 2–4.

CUPS

1. FLORENCE PD 587, fr. A, (middle of male in himation to left). May be by Douris himself.

2 (8). VATICAN, from Vulci. *Mus. Greg.* 2 pl. 74, 1; Gerhard pl. 109 and pl. 202, 3–5, whence (A–B) Robert *Scenen der Ilias* 8 figs. 9–10, (A) Robert *Herm.* 204, (I) *Boll. d'Arte* 30, 40 fig. 3; I, ph. Al. 35831, whence Dölger Ἰχθύς iv pl. 163 and Radermacher *Mythos²* fig. 2; I and A, phs. And. 42106 and another, whence Stella 316 and 720. I, Herakles in the bowl of Helios. A, fight (Achilles and Hector); B, the like. Attributed to Douris by Hartwig. Coarse imitation of the Hippodamas style (period 3). For the shape, Bloesch 99, Python no. 26. Restored.

3 (9). LONDON E 55, from Vulci. I, Murray no. 35; palmettes, Jacobsthal O. pl. 77, b. I, maenad; A–B, Dionysos with satyrs and maenads. Attributed by Hartwig to Douris. Stiff imitation, late middle period: as London E 51 (no. 4). For the shape, Bloesch 98, Python no. 18.

4 (10). LONDON E 51, from Vulci. I, Murray no. 31, whence Pfuhl fig. 462. I, woman smelling a flower; A, youths and women; B, men and women. As London E 55 (no. 3). With these two compare also the Harvard cup (p. 436 no. 112). For the shape, Bloesch 98, Python no. 19. See p. 1653.

5. FLORENCE PD 332, fr. A, (boy, stick).

6 (26). FREIBURG, part of S 144, three frr. I, (male: a hand remains, holding a stick). Outside, (males in himatia: on one fr., part of a left-hand figure, holding a purse; on the second, part of a right-hand figure; on the third, parts of two figures confronted, one of them holding a knotty stick). Late. See p. 1653.

7 (23). LONDON E 60, from Vulci. I, Murray no. 39. I, boy on horseback. A, fight; B, arming. For the shape, Bloesch 100, Python no. 33.

8 (27). AMSTERDAM inv. 2180, fr. A, *Bull. Vereen.* 1, 11, 4; A, *CV.* Scheurleer pl. 9, 1. I, (maeander). A, men and boys. Late. See the next.

9 (28). LONDON, Webster, fr. A, (men and boy). Late. As Amsterdam inv. 2180 (no. 8).

10 (14, +). LOUVRE C 58 and C 59, plus, two frr. I, (maeander and obscure remains). A–B, komos. Two Louvre frr. (one added by Villard) join C 58 on the right, outside; a third joins C 59 in the same place. Late. Near the Oedipus Painter (p. 451).

11 (17). FLORENCE V 59, from Chiusi. I, two satyrs. A–B, boxers. Late. Restored.

12 (17 *bis*). FLORENCE 17 B 19, fr. *CV.* pl. 17, B 19. A, athletes. Late. Compare Florence V 59 (no. 11).

13 (18). CHICAGO, Univ., fr., from Orvieto. *AJA.* 1938, 348 fig. 7. Outside, athletes. Late. See the next.

14 (19). CHICAGO, Univ., fr., from Orvieto. *AJA*. 1938, 348 fig. 9. Outside, athletes. Late. Probably belongs to the last.

15 (21). HEIDELBERG 80, fr. A, Kraiker pl. 10. I, (maeander). A, (naked male). Late. [Kraiker].

16. LOUVRE C 11414, fr. A, (komast or satyr with flute). Late.

17 (24). AMSTERDAM inv. 2245, fr. A, (Nike).

18 (29). BERLIN inv. 3389, fr. *CV*. pl. 99, 3–5. I, Nike and victor. A, pursuit (woman fleeing, foot); B, (woman running). Late imitation.

(no. 19, not known if decorated outside)

19. OXFORD, Beazley, fr., from Vulci. I, (on the left, man or youth in himation leaning on his stick to right). . . . Ϟ . . . Probably late period 3.

(nos. 20–31, decorated inside only)

20 (1). VILLA GIULIA 50327, fr. *Boll. d'Arte* 1927, 318 fig. 18. I, athlete with discus. [+ΑΙΡΕϞΤΡ]ΑΤ[ΟϞΚΑ]ΛΟϞ. Rough imitation of period 2, the bare style (p. 424).

21 (2). CAB. MÉD., fr. I, male leaning on his stick (middle, in himation, to right, right arm akimbo; line border). On the left, retr., . . . ΟVΔ . . . or the like. Period 2.

22 (3). Once PARIS, Pourtalès, 388, from Vulci. B.Ap. xvi. 21. 3, whence Vorberg *Gloss*. 507. I, naked woman squatting, drinking from a phallus-spouted skyphos. Period 2.

23 (l 175). CHICAGO 07.323, from Greece. Fröhner *Brant*. pl. 20 = Klein *L*. 104=Hartwig pl. 67, 2, whence HM. pl. 19 and Perrot 10, 598. I, Artemis. ΗΙΓΓΟΛΑΜΑϞ ΚΑΛΟϞ. Slightly restored. Close to Douris, period 3, but very weak.

23 bis. PHILADELPHIA MARKET, I, komast (man moving to right, head back, wrap over shoulders, with lyre, plectrum, basket).

24. RICHMOND (Virginia). *Auction xvi Basle* pl. 30, 126. I, man and boy. The man says ΑΓΟΔΟϞ.

25. MUNICH, part of S.L. 513, fr. *Anz*. 1938, 452 fig. 34. I, youth and boy. Late. [Lullies].

26. SWISS PRIVATE. I, woman with basket. ΙΚΑΟΛϞ.

27 (11). BONN 1624, fr. *CV*. pl. 7, 2. I, (on the left, naked youth). Imitation.

28. ADOLPHSECK, Landgraf Philipp of Hesse, 34, fr. *CV*. pl. 28, 1. I, satyrs dancing. Late. Near the Oedipus Painter (p. 451).

29 (30). BOSTON 28.476. *Cat. Sotheby July 5 1928* pl. 2, above; CB. iii pl. 71, 133. I, satyr. Late. Compare the Oedipus Painter. See CB. iii, text..

30 (32). ADRIA B 328 and Bc 55, fr., from Adria. *CV*. pl. 22, 1; *Riv. Ist*. N.S. 5–6, 48 fig. 36. I, woman with basket. Late.

31 (31). BERLIN 2305, from Nola. Hartwig pl. 72, 1; Licht ii, 153; *Jb*. 71, 120. I, Zephyros and Hyakinthos. Attributed by Hartwig to 'the Master with the Sprig'.

PYXIS

(*type A*)

32 (34). CAMBRIDGE 1933.1, from Greece. Part, *Friends of the Fitzwilliam, Reports* 26 (1934), 3 fig. 4. Nereids.

PELIKE

33 (35). BOLOGNA PU 278, from Athens. Pellegrini *VPU*. 43–44. I, youth and seated woman; B, man and boy. Period 2.

LEKYTHOI

(*standard shape*)

34. HARVARD 1959.193 (ex Watkins), from Sicily. *Coll. Lambros* pl. 7, 51; *Coll. Hirsch* pl. 3, 169. Woman with alabastron.

35. NEW YORK 25.78.1, from Gela. Nike (flying, with sash).

A small fragment recalls Douris:

CUP

(*decorated inside only*)

FREIBURG S 133, fr. I, (on the right, part of a flute-case, probably suspended, with . . . ΚΑΛΟ϶). Not late.

III

THE OEDIPUS PAINTER

These two cups were put together, as by one hand, in *CV*. Oxford, ii, 107 and *ARV*.[1] nos. 296 nos. 12 and 13. Close to the late work of Douris. The Vatican cup had already been attributed to 'the Master with the Sprig' by Hartwig, and to Douris by Buschor; the Oxford cup had been associated with Douris by Zahn.

1. VATICAN, from Vulci. *Mus. Greg.* 2 pl. 80, 1; Hartwig pl. 73, whence (I) *Mü. Jb.* 1906, 3 fig. 8; I, ph. Mo. 8600; phs. Al. 35800–2, whence (B) Licht i, 34, (I) *Int. Studio* Feb. 1927, 26, 2, (B) *JHS.* 57 pl. 2, 2, (A) Brommer *Satyrspiele* 35; A, *JHS.* 57 pl. 2, 1; I, Zadoks-Jitta 96, 6; I and B, phs. And. 42112 and 42107, whence (I) Stella 637. I, Oedipus and the Sphinx. A–B, satyrs. [Hartwig R.]. Restored. For the shape, Bloesch 97, Python no. 11. The Etruscan cup Paris, Musée Rodin, 980, as Plaoutine saw, copies the outside of the Oedipus cup (*JHS.* 57 pl. 1; *CV*. pll. 28–30; *EVP*. pl. 4, 1–3, with pp. 3 and 25–27; see also *Festschrift Rumpf* 10).

2. OXFORD 1929.752. *CV*. pl. 52, 1 and pl. 54, 1–2. I, symposion: Dionysos and Herakles. A–B, arming.

3. BASLE MARKET (Borowski). I, satyr; A, three women spinning; B, arming. The satyr bends, holding out a box, and should probably be thought of

as attending upon women—such women as those on A. Behind him, on a block, a large pelike.

Another cup, close to late Douris, is probably by the Oedipus Painter: OXFORD, Beazley. I, athlete with haltēres, and man. Trimmed round.

Compare with all these the cup-fragments Louvre C 58–59 (p. 449 no. 10) and Adolphseck 34 (p. 450 no. 28), and the cup Boston 28.476 (p. 450 no. 29). See also p. 426, middle, and p. 1653.

IV

THE CARTELLINO PAINTER

Att. V. 210; *ARV.*[1] 297–8.

No. 1 bears the name ΛΟRΙϚ without verb, on a cartellino, nos. 2–5 have the same on a garment.

LEKYTHOI
(standard shape; Class BL)

1 (1). SYRACUSE 22666, from Gela. *Sumbolae de Petra* 74, whence Perrot 10, 525 and Hoppin i, 273; *E.A.A.* ii, 378. Nike. ΛΟRΙϚ on a cartellino.

2 (2). ATHENS 1305 (CC. 1188), from Eretria. *Eph.* 1886 pl. 4, 1, whence *JHS.* 27, 23 and Hoppin i, 270; *Eph.* 1907, 230 fig. 4, 2; *CV.* pl. 10, 1. Discus-thrower. ΛΟRΙϚ on his garment.

3 (3). BERLIN inv. 4858, from Greece. *Eph.* 1907, 222; Hoppin i, 221. Woman with torches. ΛΟRΙϚ on her himation.

4 (4). ATHENS 1633 (CC. 1189), from Eretria. *Eph.* 1907, 226 and pl. 10, 1, whence Hoppin i, 271; *CV.* pl. 10, 3. Woman with lyre. ΛΟRΙϚ on her himation.

5 (5). ATHENS 12803 (N. 1030), from Eretria. *Eph.* 1907, 225 and pl. 10, 2, whence Perrot 10, 527 and Hoppin i, 272; *CV.* pl. 10, 2; Papaspyridi *Guide* 329 fig. 68. Boy with lyre. ΛΟRΙϚ on his himation.

6 (6). ATHENS 12781 (N. 1027), from Eretria. *Eph.* 1907, 229 fig. 4. Acontist.

The following, as Seyrig saw, is related to Douris; it recalls Athens 12781 (no. 6):

LEKYTHOS
(secondary shape; Class CL, see p. 677 no. 7)

PARIS, Seyrig. *AJA.* 1948 pl. 34. Boy seated, holding an open scroll. For the writing on the scroll see *AJA.* 1948, 336–37, and 1950, 318–19.

The following cup cannot be said to be in the manner of Douris: yet in composition and in the cut of the figures the resemblance to the 'bare cups' of Douris (p. 425) is too distinct to be accidental, although the 'bare cups' have an earlier look:

CUP

FLORENCE PD 269, from Chiusi. *CV*. pl. 94 and pl. 116, 15. I, athlete; A–B, athletes.

CHAPTER 28

THE ASHBY PAINTER AND OTHERS

The painters in this chapter do not form a group.

THE H.P. PAINTER

'H.P.' for 'Herakles and Pholos'. 'Pholos Painter' would have been simpler, but the name of Pholos has been used already for a group of black-figure vases.

CUP

SWISS PRIVATE. I, symposion (youth reclining, with skyphos, woman seated playing the flute). A–B, Herakles and Pholos: A, Herakles and Pholos reclining, and two centaurs coming up; B, Herakles fighting with four centaurs.

Another cup seems to be an early work of the same painter:

STOCKHOLM, Throne-Holst. I, youth seated (to right, himation from waist, a curiously shaped stick in his right hand). A, fight (youth and man with spears and shields, archer). B, komos (man with krotala between youth playing the flute and youth with oinochoe).

===

THE ASHBY PAINTER

Att. V. 54. BSR. 11, 18–19. CF. 13–14. ARV.[1] *299 and 957.*

Named after no. 8. See also p. 1654.

CUPS

1. LOUVRE C 10916, frr. I, komast (οὐρῶν). A–B, athletes. On A, jumper, athlete with acontia, athlete, all running: on B, the right-hand figure is an athlete running to right. Very early.
2. LOUVRE, frr. of at least one other athlete cup in the same style as the last.
3 (2, +). VILLA GIULIA, FLORENCE 7 B 1, HEIDELBERG 37 and 39, and MUNICH S.L. 479, part. Part, *CV*. Florence pl. 7, B 1; the Heidelberg frr., Kraiker pll. 6 and 4; the Munich fragment, Sieveking *BTV*. pl. 52, 6. I, athlete using pick. A, Herakles and the lion. B, Theseus and the bull. A Villa Giulia fragment not mentioned in *CF*. seems to give the missing parts of Herakles' left foot and right leg.
4 (3). FLORENCE 1 B 44, VILLA GIULIA, and HEIDELBERG 41, frr. *CV*. Fl. pl. 1, B, 44; the Heid. frr., Kraiker pl. 8. A, youths mastering a bull; B, the like.

5 (4 part, +). BRYN MAWR P 240, P 181, and P 239, frr. *AJA*. 1916, 340 nos. 3–5. A, Theseus and the bull. B, hunt or the like. See *CF*. 14 on pl. 7 B 1. A fragment in another collection joined P 239 (*AJA*. 1916, 340, 5) on the right, and has now been presented to Bryn Mawr.

6 (4 part). BRYN MAWR P 191, fr. *AJA*. 1916, 340, 1. A, (Athena). Same style as the last: I thought it might belong: Athena present at the taming of the bull by Theseus, and seated, so on a larger scale.

7 (5). ATHENS Acr. 191, fr., from Athens. Langlotz pl. 9, whence *E.A.A.* i, 706. I, (youth).

8 (6). CASTLE ASHBY, Northampton, from Vulci. *AZ*. 1885 pl. 17; *BSR*. 11 pl. 7, 1–3; B.Ap. I, trumpeter. A–B, symposion.

9 (6). LONDON E 64, from Vulci. *Mon*. 3 pl. 12, whence (I) *El*. 2 pl. 22, (I) Overbeck *KM*. pl. 26, 1; I, Murray no. 42. I, Apollo pursuing a woman. A–B, symposion. See p. 1654.

10 (8). CAB. MÉD. 532 and four other frr. I, Luynes pl. 45, whence *AZ*. 1853 pl. 52, 3–4, whence *Arch. class*. 2 pl. 13, 2; A–B, incompletely, de Ridder 400. I, man binding victor with fillet; A–B, athletes. Late. Powerful drawing, vying with Panaetian.

11 (9). CAB. MÉD., part of 525, fr. Hartwig 460. A, (man with stylus and tablets, and two males). Late.

CUP-SKYPHOS

12 (1). ATHENS, Agora, P 7899, frr., from Athens. A, Herakles and the Hydra. (B?), (upper part of a youth).

THE THORVALDSEN GROUP

In *CV*. Gallatin 9. *ARV*.[1] 299.

Near the Magnoncourt Painter and the earliest Douris.

CUPS

1 (1). NEW YORK 41.162.1, from Vulci. *CV*. Gallatin pll. 10–12: I, *Bull*. *Metr*. 37, 49; detail of I, Richter *ARVS*. fig. 58; I, Richter *H*. 214, e. I, warrior with spear, and boy. A–B, athletes. For the inscription on I, *AJA*. 1950, 318.

2 (3). COPENHAGEN, Thorvaldsen Museum, 115, from Vulci. B.Ap. xxi. 83. I, woman at laver. A–B, komos.

3 (2). BERLIN 2270. *CV*. pl. 92, 1–2. I, satyr. A–B, symposion.

Compare the cup

FLORENCE 80565, from Saturnia. *ML*. 30, 670. I, uncertain subject, a man rising from his couch, with a sword (Tereus?).

THE MAGNONCOURT PAINTER

Att. V. 171. *CF.* 17. *ARV.*[1] 300 and 957.

Named after the former owner of no. 2.

CUPS

1 (1). MUNICH 2638, from Cervetri. I, *JHS.* 8, 440–1, whence HM. pl. 13, 1 and Robert *Herm.* 264. I, Aedon and Itys. A–B, satyrs and maenads. On I, ITVϞ, ΑΕΔΟΝΑΙ complete, [ΓΑ]ΝΑ[ΙΤ]ΙΟϞ. On A, [ΓΑ]ΝΑΙ-ΤΙΟϞ and retr. ΚΑLΟϞ. On B, Γ[ΑΝΑΙΤΙΟϞΚΑ]LΟϞ, [Κ]ΑLΟ[Ϟ]. Now cleaned. See p. 1654.

2 (2). NEW YORK 41.162.6 (ex Magnoncourt), from Vulci. I, Panofka *Eigenn.* pl. 4, 7, whence Klein *Euphr.* 280 and Pfuhl fig. 412; cleaned, *CV.* Gallatin pl. 47, 5 and pl. 49, 2. I, satyr and maenad; A, Dionysos mounting chariot; B, Ariadne mounting chariot. On I, ΓΑΝΑΙΤΙΟϞΚΑLΟϞ.

3 (3, +). LOUVRE G 129 (including C 93, C 204a, C 204b, S 1314, S 1337, S 1342, S 1343, and other fragments). One fr., Pottier pl. 112. I, youth pursuing boy. A–B, satyrs and maenads. On I, Γ[ΑΝΑΙ]ΤΙΟϞΚΑ[L]ΟϞ-ΚΑLΟϞ. On A, ΓΑΝΑΙΤΙΟϞΚΑLΟ[Ϟ]. The cup is now nearly complete. See p. 1566.

4 (4, +). LOUVRE C 10917 and FLORENCE 10 B 99. The Florence fr., (I), *CV.* pl. 10, B 99. I, komos (two youths). A–B, satyrs. The inscriptions are hard to read: on A, ΑΡΙϞϞΑΛΤΛΟ ... (for Aristagoras) [Κ]ΑL[ΟϞ]. On B, ΦΑΙΔΡΙ[ΑϞ?. See p. 1566.

The following cup may be compared with New York 41.162.6 (no. 2) for the composition of the tondo, and the drawing bears a certain resemblance to that of the Magnoncourt Painter:

LOUVRE G 34. Hartwig pl. 6, whence (I) HM. pl. 31; I, *Enc. phot.* iii, 3, c. I, satyr and maenad; A, Dionysos and his chariot; B, satyrs and maenads. Much restored.

THE BRYN MAWR PAINTER

ARV.[1] 300.

PLATES

1 (1). BRYN MAWR P 95. *AJA.* 1916, 331. Symposion (man reclining).

2 (2). HARVARD 60.350, from Vari. *CV.* Robinson ii pl. 22 and pl. 23, 1, whence *E.A.A.* ii, 203. Symposion (woman reclining). Slightly restored.

3 (3). HARVARD 60.351, fr., from Vari. *CV*. Robinson ii pl. 23, 2; detail, *R.M.* 63 pl. 42, 2. Athlete. Restored. The attitude recalls the interior of the Florence–Boston Aristagoras cup (pp. 1565–6 no. 3).

Probably also

PLATE

OXFORD, Beazley, fr. I, (on the left, the upper part of a youth in a himation leaning on his stick to right, holding a sprig; there was no doubt another figure on the right).

CHAPTER 29

MAKRON

MAKRON

Hartwig 270–306 ('Hieron'). Furtwängler in FR. ii, 129–31. Leonhard *Ueber einige Vasen aus der Werkstatt Hierons*, and *Hieron* in Pauly-Wissowa. *VA.* 101–6. *AJA.* 1921, 325–36. Langlotz Z. 85–87 and 110. Pfuhl 467–75. *Att. V.* 211–21 474–5. *BSA.* 29, 192. *ARV.* 301–15 and 958. *Bull. Vereen.* 29, 12–15. CB. iii, text.

The vases that bear the signature of the potter Hieron (see pp. 481–2), with three exceptions, were decorated by Makron, whose signature appears, together with that of Hieron, on the Boston skyphos (no. 1), and perhaps appears on a small pyxis in Athens (no. 336). In the list that follows, I have counted attributions to 'Hieron' as attributions to Makron, and acknowledged them as such, although Hartwig and others thought that Makron was not the painter of the 'Hieron cups'. Furtwängler seems to have been the first to insist that he was.

The cups are grouped according to the subjects of the exteriors.

The long association between Hieron and Makron is comparable to that between Python and Douris (p. 426).

For the followers of Makron in the early classic period, who continue the the style of his cups in a mannered form, see p. 807. Another early classic follower is the Syracuse Painter (p. 517), nearly all of whose vases are not cups but pots. Earlier than these artists is the Painter of Palermo 1108 (p. 298).

SKYPHOI

(type A, but nos. 1 and 2 have diagonal handles)

1 (1). BOSTON 13.186, from Suessula. *Gaz. arch.* 1880 pll. 7–8, whence *AZ.* 1882, 3–6 and *WV.* C pl. 1; FR. pl. 85, whence Perrot 10, 474–5, Pfuhl figs. 435–6, Hoppin ii, 53, (A) Seltman pl. 28, b, (detail of A) *AJA.* 1921, 333, (A) Stella 702, (B) L.S. fig. 86; Herford pl. 8, a; A, *International Studio* Feb. 1927, 27, 2; A, *Hist. rel.* 274; Fairbanks and Chase 65 and 74 fig. 80; Chase *Guide* 66; incompletely, Ghali-Kahil *H.* pll. 4 and 48; A, *E.A.A.* i, 119; A, Richter *H.G.A.* 331; CB. iii pll. 76–77; the shape, Hambidge *Dyn. Sym.* 109 fig. 10 and Caskey *G.* 158. A, Paris leading Helen away; B, Menelaos attacking Helen. Incised on one handle, HIEPON-ΕΠΟΙΕΣΕΝ. On A, ΜΑΚΡΟΝ : ΕΛΡΑΦΣΕΝ. See CB. iii, text.

2 (2, +). LOUVRE G 146. *Mon.* 6–7 pl. 19, whence *WV.* C pl. 6, Robert *H.* 178–9, Hoppin ii, 81, *AJA.* 1934 pl. 14, Bulas *Il.* figs. 2 and 5; Perrot 10, 484–5; Pottier pl. 118; A, ph. Al. 23692, whence Johansen *Il.* fig. 26 and

(A) Stella 717; ph. Gir. 33399, whence Béquignon *Il.* 128 and 137 and (A) *Hist. rel.* 278. A, Briseis led away; B, mission to Achilles. An unpublished fragment in the Louvre joins and has been added, giving the left foot of Agamemnon on A, the right foot of Briseis and the toes of her left, with part of her chiton. Incised on one handle, HIEPONEΓOIE-ϟEN. Restored.

3 (3). LONDON E 140, from Capua. *Mon.* 9 pl. 43, whence Overbeck *KM.* pl. 15, 22, Rumpf *Rel.* fig. 51, (A) Perrot 10, 487; *WV.* A pl. 7, whence Hoppin ii, 61; Hambidge *Diagonal* 114–15; FR. pl. 161 and iii, 259, whence Nilsson *G.G.R.* i pl. 43, (B) Pfuhl fig. 437 (whence Seltman pl. 28, a), (part of A) *Mél. d'arch.* 1950 pl. 2, 1; *CV.* pl. 28, 2; detail of A, Schaal *Rf.* fig. 16; A, Bieber *Entw.* pl. 13, 1–2; A, Lane pl. 69; A, ph. Ma., whence *Hist. rel.* 173; B, *E.A.A.* i, 390; A, *Recueil Dugas* pl. 30, 1. Triptolemos. Incised on one handle, HIERONEΓOIEϟEN. For the co-finds see *AJA.* 1945, 156–8. See p. 1654.

3 *bis*. REGGIO 4062, fr., from Locri. (Upper part of a man in chiton and himation, moving to right, right arm extended: may be a pursuer). [Procopio].

CUPS

4 (4). BERLIN 2291, from Vulci. Gerhard *TG.* pl. 11–12, whence (A) Perrot 10, 490, (B) Ghali-Kahil *H.* pl. 3, 3; *WV.* A pl. 5, whence Hoppin ii, 43, (B) *AZ.* 1882, 2, (detail of A) *AJA.* 1921, 332; A, Pfuhl fig. 441; details, Jacobsthal *O.* pl. 76; detail of A, Greifenhagen *Eroten* 67; detail of A, Himmelmann-Wildschütz, *Eig.* 15; A, *Recueil Dugas* pl. 12, 1. I, man and boy (the boy is HIΓΓOΔAMAϟ). A, judgement of Paris; B, Paris leading Helen away. Incised on one handle, HIEPONEΓOIEϟEN. For the shape, Bloesch 92, Hieron no. 11. See p. 1654.

5 (5). ATHENS Acr. 310, frr., from Athens. A, Langlotz pl. 19. A, judge-of Paris. [Studniczka].

6 (6). LEIPSIC T 3656 (?), fr. A, (uncertain subject: herald?—and woman? —judgement of Paris?).

7. INNSBRUCK ii. 12. 34, fr. A, (uncertain subject; woman, and Hermes or a herald: here also one thinks of the judgement of Paris; but doubtful). [Bothmer].

8 (7). ATHENS Acr. 308, fr., from Athens. A, Langlotz pl. 19. I, (a male foot). A, (uncertain subject: Hermes and others).

9 (8). ATHENS Acr. 342, fr., from Athens. A, (parts of two figures, one of them apparently Hermes).

10 (9). ATHENS Acr. 323, fr., from Athens. A, (on the right, Athena and another).

11 (10). ATHENS Acr. 315, frr., from Athens. A, Langlotz pl. 19. A, voting on the armour of Achilles.

12. LOUVRE C 11271, frr. I, (foot of warrior to right, foot of one in long chiton to left). A–B, Ajax and Odysseus quarrelling. The two figures on the right of B doubtless belong to the same scene as A. A loose fragment has the raised hand and forearm of one moving to right, and the same part of another, moving to left.

13 (11). LENINGRAD 649 (St. 830). *Mon.* 6–7 pl. 22; *WV*. A pl. 8, whence (I) HM. pl. 22, 2, Hoppin ii, 83; I, Pfuhl fig. 445; I, Dugas and Flacelière pl. 10. I, Theseus attacking Aithra. A, Diomed and Odysseus quarrelling over the Palladion; B, Greek princes. Incised on one handle, HIEPON EΓOIEϟEN. Restored. See p. 1654.

14 (12, +). LOUVRE G 153. Two frr. of I, Pottier pl. 122; *Bull. Vereen.* 29, 12–15. I, ransom of Hector (Achilles reclining, with the body of Hector below the couch). A–B, sacrifice of Polyxene. On one handle, in red, HIEPON.EΓOIEϟEN. See *Bull. Vereen.* 29, 12–15.

15 (13). FLORENCE 3929. Hartwig pl. 28, whence Hoppin ii, 57; cleaned, *CV.* pl. 95. I, winged goddess (Eos? Nike?). A–B, Achilles and Ajax playing. Now cleaned, and the alien fragment (right upper corner of the reproduction) removed (see p. 433 no. 64). The handle with HIEPON-EΓOIEϟEN in red does not certainly belong. See CB. iii, text.

16 (14). BOSTON 03.856, three frr. CB. iii, suppl. pl. 19, 2. A, Peleus and Thetis? (parts of Nereus and four Nereids remain). See CB. iii, text. Early.

17. LOUVRE C 11272, fr. A, Peleus and Thetis? (part of a Nereid remains, on the right of the picture).

18 (15). FLORENCE PD 278, PD 280, and PD 281, three frr. CB. iii, suppl. pl. 19, 3. Outside, Peleus and Thetis? (parts of three or four Nereids remain).

19 (16). ATHENS Acr. 328, from Athens. Langlotz pl. 22. I, Herakles and Athena. A–B, Achilles brought to Chiron. Late.

20 (17, +). ATHENS Acr. 325, from Athens. Part of A–B, *Jb.* 6 pl. 1, a–c, whence Farmakovski i, 195; part of A, Frickenhaus *Len.* 22, whence Cook *Zeus* i, 707; incompletely, Langlotz pll. 20–22; part of A–B, *Hesp.* 4, 233; a new fr., assigned to Makron by Mrs. Karouzou and to this cup by Miss Pease, ibid. 232, 22; I, Brommer *Her.* pl. 11; I, ph. Marb. 154392. I, Herakles and the Hydra. A–B, Zeus bringing the infant Dionysos to his nurses. A new fr. in Athens belongs, giving, inside, part of the maeander, and, outside, part of chiton, himation, sceptre, of the right-hand figure on B, joining the fragment with foot and sceptre on Langlotz pl. 21. Mrs. Karouzou has added a handle with the incised signature HIERONEΓOIE-ϟEN.

21 (18). ATHENS Acr. 319, frr., from Athens. Langlotz pl. 21. A, (unexplained subject—on the left, hill, two women). For the hill compare Acr. 325 (no. 20).

22 (a β). ATHENS Acr. AP. U.G. 435, fr., from Athens. *Hesp.* 4, 284, 147. A, (Athena: doubtless from a Gigantomachy). Early.

23 (19). ATHENS Acr. 327, frr., from Athens. Langlotz pl. 21. I, Athena and Giant; A–B, Gigantomachy.

24 (20 *bis*). ATHENS, Agora, P 15003, fr., from Athens. A, (Zeus?—in the Gigantomachy?).

25 (20). ATHENS Acr. 313, fr., from Athens. Langlotz pl. 19. A, (unexplained subject: man: recalls Poseidon in the Gigantomachy).

26 (21). CAB. MÉD. 550, 565, 789, 609, 804, 579, part of 536 (see *Kleophr.* 19, 5), part of 558, plus, frr. I, (on the right, king or god). A–B, unexplained subject (pursuit or the like).

27. LOUVRE C 11273, fr. A, (part of the left-hand figure remains, a king or god to right).

28. ATHENS Acr. fr., from Athens. A, (parts of the heads of a god and goddess, side by side, to right).

29 (a). ATHENS Acr. 333, fr., from Athens. Langlotz pl. 23. A, (Nike). Very early.

30 (24). ATHENS Acr. 317, fr., from Athens. A, (shoulder of a male in a cloak to right, with the back of the head, and the petasos at the nape).

31 (25). ATHENS Acr. 309, frr., from Athens. Outside, (uncertain subject: one in long chiton and himation, and goat). Need not be from a judgement of Paris, since a goat appears under the handle in thiasos cups (nos. 45 and 51).

32 (22). LOUVRE G 266, from Vulci. A, Pottier pl. 133 A, *Antike und Abendland* 9 pl. 11, 34. I, warrior cresting his helmet. A–B, the Theban Sphinx. Restored.

33 (23). LOUVRE G 271, from Capua. B, Pottier pl. 133; B, Hamilton *Greece* 69, 1. I, boy running with a dove in his hand. A, departure, with chariot; B, arming.

34. LOUVRE C 11274, fr. I, (foot of one moving to left, with a little of the shank). A, fight (on the left, Greek and Oriental); B, (one foot of the right-hand figure remains, rushing to left).

35. LOUVRE C 11275, fr. I, (maeander). A, fight (shield, scabbard, then part of one fallen to left).

36 (26). BOSTON 01.8072. A–B, Vorberg *Gloss.* 47–48; CB. iii pl. 78, 138. I, komast. A, satyrs attacking a sleeping maenad; B, the like; she wakes. Early. See CB. ii, 96 no. 10, and iii, text.

37 (27). MUNICH 2644 (J. 273), from Vulci. I, Emma von Sichart *Kostümkunde* 62; A–B, *Mem. Am. Ac.* 6 pl. 21, 5 and pl. 19, 5; B and foot, Bloesch *FAS.* pl. 25, 1. I, Amazon. A–B, Dionysos with satyrs and maenads. For the shape, Bloesch 91, Hieron no. 1. Early. Restored.

38 (28). FLORENCE 75589, from Saturnia. I, man with purse. A, satyrs and maenad; B, satyrs. Early.

39 (29). ORVIETO, Faina, 36, from Orvieto. I, ph. Al. 32465; A, phs. R.I. 1935.882–4. I, maenad; A–B, satyrs and maenads.

40 (30). BRYN MAWR P 193, fr. *AJA*. 1916, 343 no. 17. A, (maenad). [Swindler].

41 (31). BRUSSELS R 247, from Vulci. *Gaz. arch. 1887* pl. 14, 2 and pl. 15, 1–2, whence Hoppin ii, 55 and Rumpf *MZ*. pl. 25, 6; I, Langlotz *GV*. pl. 16, 24; B, *Mem. Am. Ac.* 6 pl. 20, 1; *CV*. pl. 11, 2. I, Dionysos and satyr; A–B, satyrs and maenads. On one handle, HIEPONEΓOIEϟEN. For the shape, Bloesch 91, Hieron no. 5.

42 (32). MISSISSIPPI (ex Warren and Robinson), from Capua. *CV*. Robinson iii pll. 4–5. I, maenad; A–B, Dionysos with satyrs and maenads. The HIEPONEΓOIEϟEN incised on one handle has been doubted.

43 (33). LOUVRE G 144. Hoppin ii, 76–77; B, Pottier pl. 117; I, Pfuhl fig. 443; I and A, phs. Gir. 19043 and 19041, 2. I, satyr and maenad; A–B, Dionysos with satyrs and maenads. On one handle, in red, HIEPONEΓOIEϟEN. Restored.

44 (34). PARIS, Rothschild, from Vulci. *Tabl. I.P.* pl. 10, 38. I, Dionysos and satyr; A–B, Dionysos with satyrs and maenads. [Plaoutine].

45 (35). NEW HAVEN, Watkins, from Vulci. I and part of A–B, *A.A.A.* pl. 82, 275. I, satyr and maenad; A–B, satyrs and maenads. Restored. [Richter].

46. LONDON 1952.12–2.9, fr. A, (satyr and maenad). [Martin Robertson].

47 (36). MUNICH 2654 (J. 184), from Vulci. *WV*. A pl. 2; FR. pl. 46, whence Hoppin ii, 63; I, Langlotz *GV*. pl. 29, 42, whence Frel *Ř.V.* fig. 180; I, Pfuhl fig. 442; I and A, Licht iii, 151 and 207; I and part of A, Vorberg *Erotik* 75–76; I and A, Vorberg *Gloss*. 741–2; A and foot, Bloesch *FAS*. pl. 25, 3. I, satyr and maenad; A–B, satyrs and maenads. Incised on one handle, HIEPONEΓOIEϟEN. For the shape, Bloesch 92, Hieron no. 19.

48 (37). BERLIN 2290 and VILLA GIULIA, from Vulci. See *CF*. 34 no. 13. Gerhard *TG*. pll. 4–5, whence (A) Perrot 10, 495, (A–B) Swindler fig. 313; *WV*. A pl. 4, whence HM. pl. 21, Hoppin ii, 41, (A–B) Frickenhaus *Len*. 6–7; B, Buschor 177; B, Pfuhl fig. 438 (= Pfuhl *Mast*. fig. 58); Licht i, 23 and 114, whence (A–B) Frel *Ř.V.* figs. 182–3; B, Schaal *Rf*. fig. 32; B, Richter *Sc*. fig. 287; B, Neugebauer pl. 51; A, Buschor *G. Vasen* 155; A, Diepolder *GV*. 38; part of A, *Hist. rel*. 47; I, A, and part of B (cleaned), Greifenhagen *A.K.* pll. 65–67. All these without the Villa Giulia fragment: the Villa Giulia fragment, *CF*. pl. Z, 1. I, Dionysos and satyr; A–B, maenads dancing at the image of Dionysos. Incised on one handle, HIERONEΓOEϟEN. For the shape, Bloesch 92, Hieron no. 18.

49 (38, +). VILLA GIULIA (part ex Florence), HEIDELBERG 89, BRUNSWICK 498, NAPLES, Astarita, and HALLE, private. Part, *CV*. Fl. pl. 7, B 18; the Heidelberg fr., Kraiker pl. 13; all (except the Astarita and Halle frr.), *CV*. Brunswick pl. 16 and p. 25. I, woman seated, holding a wreath. A–B, satyrs. The Halle fragment (though said to be from the Acropolis of Athens) gives the left hand of the first satyr on A (*CV*. Brunswick pl. 16,

1), and the right arm and hand, breast, hair of the second; Astarita 269 joins the Halle on the right, adding the face and left arm of the second satyr, with part of the third satyr's tail.

50 (40). LOUVRE G 145. Hoppin ii, 78–79; phs. Gir. 19042, 1; 19041, 1; and 19040. I, two maenads dancing; A–B, maenads. Incised on one handle, HIEPONEΓOIEϚEN.

51 (41). BALTIMORE, from Cervetri. Hartwig pl. 30, 3 and pl. 31, whence (I and A) *Mem. Am. Ac.* 6 pl. 19, 1 and pl. 20, 4; *CV.* Robinson ii pll. 15–16. I, maenads; A–B, Dionysos with satyrs and maenads. [Hartwig].

52 (42). NEW YORK 06.1152. Pollak *Kopf* pl. 5, 97; A, *Int. Studio* Feb. 1927, 28; Richter and Hall pl. 57, 55, pll. 59–60, and pl. 180, 55; detail of A–B, Richter *ARVS.* fig. 63. I, satyr and maenad; A–B, satyrs and maenads.

53. MEGGEN, Käppeli. B, *Bull. Vereen.* 30, 22–23 = *Fasti arch.* 10, 73; Schefold *M.* 191. I, maenad (moving to right, looking round, thyrsus in left hand); A–B, maenads (four in each half: one playing the flute, the others dancing, one with crotala).

54 (43). FLORENCE 82896, part (PD 15–26), from Castelgiorgio. I, (feet of one in a long chiton to left); outside, satyrs and maenads.

55 (44). CAB. MÉD., part of 558, fr. A, (satyr, thyrsus; to left, handle-palmette).

56 (45). CAB. MÉD. 618 (plus?), four frr., probably all from one cup. Outside, (satyrs and maenads).

57 (128). OXFORD 1953.2, two frr., from Vulci. I, (toe, pillar). Outside, (satyr, maenads).

58 (47). VILLA GIULIA, three frr. I, (maeander). Outside, (satyrs and mae-nads). On one fr., small satyr kneeling, and tail and leg of satyr to right. On the second, skirt to left, tail and leg of satyr with drinking-horn to right. On the third, leg of satyr to right, legs of maenad to left.

59 (48). HEIDELBERG 91, fr. Kraiker pl. 11. A, (satyr).

60 (49). HEIDELBERG 92, fr. Kraiker pl. 11. A, (hand with thyrsus, satyr).

61 (50). FLORENCE 7 B 21, fr. *CV.* pl. 7, B 21. A, (Dionysos).

62 (51). FLORENCE 11 B 53, fr. *CV.* pl. 11, B 53. A, (satyr and maenad).

63 (52). VILLA GIULIA, fr. A, (bent head, and arms, of a fair-haired maenad dancing to right, and elbow of a satyr). See the next.

64 (53). VILLA GIULIA, fr. A, (raised forearm, with hand, of a dancing mae-nad, and the ends of her streaming hair: rim-fragment). May belong to the last.

65 (54). VILLA GIULIA, fr. I, (a little of the border remains). A, (tail and shank of satyr to right).

66 (55). VILLA GIULIA, fr. A, (head of a satyr to left playing the flute).

67 (56). VILLA GIULIA, fr. A, (extended hand of a satyr wearing a panther-skin to right, head, to left, and hand of a maenad striking at him with her thyrsus).

68 (57). BRUNSWICK 542, fr. *CV*. pl. 12, 8. A, (satyr and maenad). Might, for the attitudes, be the same persons as in the last.

69 (58). BRUNSWICK 565, fr. *CV*. pl. 12, 9. A, (maenads).

70. LOUVRE C 11276, two frr. Outside, (satyrs and maenad). On one, upper part of a maenad to right, with wing-sleeves, and shoulder of a satyr to right; on the other, wreath and extended arm of one to right, extended hand of satyr wearing a panther-skin to left.

71 (59). FLORENCE V. xviii, from Chiusi. I, (uncertain remains). A, satyrs and maenads (three figures in each half).

72 (60). VILLA GIULIA 3575, from Falerii. I, man holding a cuttle-fish. A–B, satyrs and maenads. For the shape, Bloesch 94, Hieron no. 34.

73 (61). MUNICH, fr. I, (maeander). A, (satyrs, or komos: bare leg to right, toes of another to left; between, the end of a wine-skin).

74. BASLE, Cahn, 103, fr. I, Dionysos (to right, with kantharos and branch). A, (maenads?—legs of woman to right, leg of woman to left).

75. LONDON 1952.12–2.8, fr. A, komos (upper part of a man with a skyphos moving to right, looking round, right hand raised). Early.

76 (62). TORONTO 356. *AJA*. 1928, 33–40; Robinson and Harcum pl. 59 and pl. 163; *B.R. Ont.* pl. 5, a, and pl. 6. I, komast; A–B, komos. Early. Much restored.

77 (63). BONN 143 d, fr., from Tarquinia. *CV*. pl. 3, 4. A, komos. Early: cf. Toronto 356.

78 (64, +). LOUVRE G 157. I and part of A, Pottier pl. 123. I, woman playing the flute to a man; A–B, komos. Two Louvre frr. join and have been added: the first gives the space above one handle, the second (composed of four) the upper part of the right-hand figure on A, a man carrying a basket slung from his stick. Early.

79 (65). LOUVRE G 277. A, Pottier pl. 134; I, phs. Gir. 19015 and 26290, 3. I, boy victor, and man announcing the victory. A–B, komos. Early. Restored.

80 (66). BRUSSELS R 264 and VILLA GIULIA. The Brussels part, *CV*. pl. 2, 1, also Verhoogen *C.G.* pl. 12, a and pl. 13. I, youth. A–B, komos. One of the fragments in Villa Giulia gives the missing part of the pointed amphora under the handle, the other the calyx-krater on A, with a bit of the woman's chiton, the man's toe, and the end of his stick. Early. Restored.

81 (67). VATICAN, from Vulci. *Mus. Greg.* 2 pl. 78, 2; phs. Al. 35797–9, whence (A) Licht i, 171, (A) *Mnem.*, 4th ser., 3 pl. 1, 2. I, man at altar. A–B, komos. For the shape, Bloesch 92, Hieron no. 14. See p. 1654.

82 (68). VILLA GIULIA 50396, from Cervetri? Hartwig pl. 29 and pl. 30, 2, whence Hoppin ii, 84–85 and (A) Robert *H.* 230 fig. 182. I, Dionysos. A–B, komos. On one handle, HIEPONEΓOIEϽEN. For the shape, Bloesch 92, Hieron no. 12. See p. 1654.

83 (69). TORONTO 959.17.113 (ex Curtius), fr. I, (maeander). A, komos? (the lower half of the circumscribed palmette under the handle, then the bare leg of the left-hand figure, a male rushing to right).

84 (71, +). LOUVRE G 141. Parts of I and A, Hoppin ii, 71, also Pottier pl. 115; detail of A, Villard *VG.* pl. 21, 2; part of B, ph. Gir. 19042, 2. I, man and boy. A–B, komos. Many Louvre frr. join and have been added, and the cup is now almost complete. Incised on one handle, HIEPONEΓOI-EϽEN.

85. TOULOUSE 26.126(370). I, youth and boy. A–B, komos.

86 (72, +). LOUVRE G 150. Part of A, Pottier pl. 119. I, komast (man with oinochoe and skyphos approaching a column-krater); A–B, komos (three males and a flute-girl in each half). Several Louvre frr. have been added by Villard.

87 (73). FLORENCE 7 B 10, fr. A, *CV.* pl. 7, B 10. I, (stick of one and toes of another). A, komos.

88 (74). CAB. MÉD. 679, 735, 736, part of 586, and probably '53', frr. I, male in himation with stick and lyre (standing to left). A–B, komos.

89 (75). CAB. MÉD. 704, fr. I, (stick, male). A, komos? (male feet, female foot). Uncertain if it belongs to the last.

90 (76). CAB. MÉD. 692, fr. I, (shod foot). A, (feet).

91 (77). FLORENCE 20 B 46, fr. A, *CV.* pl. 20, B 46. I, (maeander). A, komos.

92. FLORENCE PD 512, fr., from Populonia. I, youth seated, holding a sprig. A–B, komos. [Anna Magi].

93. FLORENCE PD 517, fr., from Populonia. I, (maeander). A, komos. [Anna Magi].

94. LOUVRE C 10919, frr. I, komast (on the right, raised hand, and skyphos); A–B, komos. Lipped cup.

95. LOUVRE C 11277, fr. A, komos (the upper part of the left-hand figure remains, a youth running to right, looking round, a large sash tied round his head). Lipped cup.

96. LOUVRE C 11278, frr. I, Dionysos (to left). A–B, komos (males and woman; under one handle a krater).

97. LOUVRE C 11279, frr. I, one seated playing the lyre. A–B, komos.

98. LOUVRE C 11280, fr. A, komos (head and shoulder of a woman, facing right, holding up an aulos).

99. LOUVRE C 215 (plus), two fragments. I, (on the right, a cup held high). Outside, komos (under one handle a dog).

100. LOUVRE C 11281, fr. A, komos (on the left, youth playing the flute, male with oinochoe).

101. LOUVRE C 11283, fr. A, komos (youth playing the flute, then what is probably an elbow).

102. LOUVRE C 11282, frr. I, (on the right, part of a hairy man in a himation to left). A–B, komos (men in himatia).

103. OXFORD, Beazley, two frr., from Vulci. Outside, komos. On one fr., the upper half of the left-hand figure on A remains, a youth holding a cup; on the other, face and shoulder of a youth, holding (a lyre?). Burnt grey.

104 (78). NAPLES Stg. 269. I, *AJA*. 1935, 482. I, komast; A–B, komos. For the name ⏀VPMO⟩ on I, *AJA*. 1935, 481–2; for the shape, Bloesch 94, Hieron no. 30.

105. FLORENCE 9 B 61, fr. I, *CV*. pl. 9, B 61. I, komast. A, komos (heel with wineskin).

106 (79). LENINGRAD 652 (St. 850). A, G.P. 51. I, komast; A–B, komos.

107 (80). BERKELEY 8.3222, from Etruria. *CV*. pl. 33, 2. I, boy. A–B, komos. Restored. [H. R. W. Smith].

108. GENEVA, Robert Boehringer. *Vente xi Bâle* pl. 21 and pl. 22, 336; Schefold *M*. 190. I, seated youth. A–B, komos. On I, ⌐OⱢVΔEMO⟩ KAⱢO⟩.

109 (81). BOULOGNE 51. I, male with phiale at altar. A–B, komos.

110. HAVANA, Lagunillas. I, youth leaning on his stick. A–B, komos; on A, three youths hastening; on B, 1, male leaning on his stick to right, 2, male seated to right, 3, youth seated to left, holding out a cup. [Bothmer].

111. BASLE, Cahn, 65 b–c, two frr. Outside, komos. On one fragment, youth running to left, looking round; on the other, youth moving to left, look-round, cup in left hand. [Cahn].

112. BASLE, Cahn, 65 e, fr. Outside, (head of man to left, with his right shoulder). [Cahn]. Belongs to the last?

113. BASLE, Cahn, 74, fr. I, warrior (helmeted head of youth to left, with the top of his shield). A, komos? (legs of male moving to left, foot of another to left).

114. BASLE, Cahn, 72, fr. I, (maeander). A, komos? (lower half of male moving to left, with stick).

115. BARCELONA 26.9.11, fr., from Ampurias. I, (foot to left). A, komos (leg of a woman to right, flute-case, leg of a male in a himation to left).

116 (70). VILLA GIULIA, fr. I, (male shank and end of himation to right). A, komos? (feet to right).

117 (82). WÜRZBURG 481. Langlotz pll. 150–1, and pl. 164. I, youth seated with lyre. A–B, symposion. For the shape, Bloesch 91, Hieron no. 9. Early.

118 (83). New York 20.246, from Vulci. I, *Bull. Metr.* 18, 253; *AJA.* 1923, 274–6; Richter and Hall pl. 50, 53, pll. 53–54, and pl. 180, 53. I, satyr and maenad. A–B, symposion. On I, POΔO[Γ]IS K[A]LE. Incised on one handle, HIEPONEΓOESEN.

119 (84). Gotha 49. I, Hofkes-Brukker pl. 12, above; I and A, Elisabeth Rohde *Kleinkunst* 64–65 figs. 9–10. I, symposion (man reclining and seated woman); A–B, symposion. See CB. iii, text.

120 (85). Florence PD 317, fr. A, symposion (parts of two couches and a table).

121 (86). Villa Giulia, fr. I, (wreathed head). A, symposion (part of a table).

122 (87). Leipsic T 3367. I, symposion (man reclining and youth playing the flute); A–B, symposion.

123. Louvre C 11284, two frr. I, (on the right, close to the border, a youthful head to left). A–B, symposion (males reclining on the ground, and a basket). See nos. 124–5.

124. Louvre C 11285, fr. A–B, symposion. A handle remains, with part of the left-hand figure on A and of the right-hand figure on B, also, under the handle, a column-krater. Belongs to Louvre C 11284 (no. 123)?

125. Louvre C 11286, fr. A, symposion (two reclining to left, the first a man turning round and playing the flute). Belongs to C 11284 (no. 123)?

126 (88). Munich 2643 (J. 596), from Vulci. I, komast; A–B, symposion. For the shape, Bloesch 92, Hieron no. 21.

127 (89). Vienna 3699 (ex Oest. Mus. 320), from Cervetri. A, Masner 40; *CV.* pl. 15, pl. 13, 6, and p. 17. I, symposion (youth reclining); A–B, symposion. For the shape, Bloesch 132 no. 18.

128. Basle, Cahn, 65 a, fr. A, symposion (part of one reclining). [Cahn].

129 (90). Oxford 1911.631 (augmented by frr. ex Leipsic), from Cervetri. *CV.* pl. 49, 10–11, pl. 51, 5, and pl. 58, 4–5. I, komast; A–B, symposion. Leipsic T 570 (outside, hand with cup) might belong: it would be from the right-hand figure on B. For the shape, Bloesch 132 no. 19.

130. Louvre C 10918, frr. I, man cooking; A–B, cooking.

131 (91). Copenhagen inv. 703. *CV.* pl. 140, 2. I, athlete using pick; A–B, athletes. Early. Restored.

132 (92). Rome, Torlonia, 148. R.I. 1879.34, whence (one figure on A) Jüthner 58, whence Norman Gardiner *G.A.S.* 351 = *Athl.* fig. 146. I, boxer; A–B, athletes. Early.

133 (93). London E 58, from Vulci. *Mon.* 4 pl. 33, whence (I) *El.* 3 pl. 89; I, Murray no. 37; I, Stella 93, below. I, Hermes running with lyre. A–B, athletes. For the shape, Bloesch 91, Hieron no. 3. Early.

134. Bryn Mawr, fr. I, (maeander). A, athletes? (bare shank of one rushing to left, leg of male in himation striding to left).

135 (94, +). LOUVRE G 158 (including G 293, S 1414, S 1422, S 1424). Part of A, Pottier pl. 124. Many Louvre frr. join and have been added. I, athlete folding his himation; A, boxers; B, athletes.

136. LOUVRE G 294, two frr. One fr., Pottier pl. 134. I, (maeander). A, athletes answering their names; B, boxers. The new fr. gives the greater part of A.

137. LOUVRE C 11287, frr. I, symposion (youth reclining, head frontal, an aulos in each hand). A, boxers. See the next.

138 (177). LOUVRE S 1377, fr. A, (upper part of a youth in a himation). Placed here because it may belong to C 11287 (no. 137).

139 (95). LONDON E 63, from Orvieto. I and A, Cecil Smith pl. 3, whence detail of A) Norman Gardiner G.A.S. 403 fig. 132. I, boxers and trainer; A, boxers answering their names; B, athletes. [Cecil Smith]. Lately cleaned, and an alien fragment removed (see the next).

140 (96). LONDON, part of E 63, fr., from Orvieto. A, (athlete?—leg of male moving to right).

141 (97). VILLA GIULIA, fr. I, (maeander). A, athletes (male in himation to right, wand, bare legs to right).

142 (98). CAB. MÉD. 661, fr. I, (head of youth). A, athletes? (bare legs).

143 (99). CAB. MÉD. 561, 711, and another fr. (part of 560?), frr. Part, de Ridder 423. I, (woman). A, males and woman. Still early.

144 (100). CAMBRIDGE 12.27, from Poggio Sommavilla. CV. pl. 25, 5 and pl. 28, 1. I, woman embracing a male; A–B, youths and women. Incised on one handle, HIEPONEΓOIEϞEN. For the shape, Bloesch 91, Hieron no. 7. See p. 1654.

145 (101). LONDON E 61, from Vulci. WV. C pl. 5, whence Hoppin ii, 59, (A) Murray 14, (A) Perrot 10, 498; I, Murray no. 40, whence Perrot 10, 499; I, Richter H.G.A. 362 fig. 482. I, girl dancing and woman playing the flute; A, youths and women; B, men and woman. Incised on one handle, HIEPONEΓOIEϞEN. For the shape, Bloesch 92, Hieron no. 22.

146 (102). NEW YORK 12.231.1, from Vulci. AJA. 1917 pll. 1–3, whence Hoppin ii, 68–69 and (A–B) Pfuhl fig. 448; part of A, Richter Sc. 74 fig. 288; I, Hdbk Cl. Coll. 117; B, Richter and Milne fig. 166; Richter and Hall pl. 49, 52, pll. 51–52, and pl. 180, 52; detail, Richter ARVS. 62 fig. 20; I, Richter H. 215, d. I, man and woman; A, man and woman; youths and women; B, youths and women; man and woman. On I, ANTIΦANEϞ ΚΑ··TOϞ (ΚΑLITOϞ de Witte Descr. no. 12, and perhaps the word was complete in his time—καλιτος would be a miswriting for καλιστος= κάλλιστος, cf. NIΚOTPATE on the exterior). On A, N[AV]ΚLEA-ΚΑLE. Bothmer's readings. Incised on one handle, [HI]EPONEΓOIEϞEN. For the shape, Bloesch 92, Hieron no. 16.

147 (103). HEIDELBERG 90, fr., from Orvieto. Kraiker pl. 11. A, (woman embracing man).

148 (104). LOUVRE G 143, from Vulci. Hoppin ii, 74–75; Pottier pl. 117; I, Pfuhl fig. 440. I, man and woman; A, men and women; youth and woman; B, men and women. Incised on one handle, HIERONEΓOEϞEN. For the shape, Bloesch 92, Hieron no. 17.

149 (105). BOSTON 01.8022, from Orvieto. Hartwig 279–80, whence Jacobsthal *Gött. V.* 19; CB iii pl. 78, 141 and pl. 79; the shape, Hambidge 121 fig. 10, and Caskey G. 191 no. 145. I, symposion (man reclining, and woman). A, men and women; youth and woman; B, man and woman; youths and women. [Hartwig]. See CB. iii, text.

150 (106). GOETTINGEN J 30 and H 83, two frr. One fr., Jacobsthal *Gött. V.* 18. I, symposion. A, (woman); B, (male); under each handle a seat. [One fr., Jacobsthal].

151 (107). VILLA GIULIA, fr. Outside, (seat under handle).

152. OXFORD, Beazley, fr. *AJA.* 1957 pl. 6 fig. 6. I, symposion. A, (man or youth; man and woman). On the handle, incised, H[IEPONEΓOIEϞEN]. See *AJA.* 1957, 7, xv.

153. OXFORD, Beazley, fr. Outside, (middle—thighs and right upper arm— of a woman seated to right).

154 (108). VATICAN, from Vulci. *Mus. Greg.* 2 pl. 78, 1; Gerhard pl. 295–6, 1–4; phs. Al. 35806–8, whence (A) Licht ii, 84. I, youth and woman; A–B, men and women. Much restored. For the shape, Bloesch 92, Hieron no. 15. [Studniczka].

155 (109). CAB. MÉD., part of 560; 752; 715; frr. Part, de Ridder 420–1. I, man and woman; A–B, men and women. [Hartwig].

156 (110). CAB. MÉD., part of 588 (L 30), fr. A, (woman, sponge). Probably belongs to the last.

157 (111). CAB. MÉD. 550, fr. A, (back of woman's head).

158 (112). NEW YORK 41.162.130, from Italy. *Cat. Sotheby March 14 1929* pl. 2, 2 and pl. 1; *CV.* Gallatin pl. 47, 6 and pl. 50, 1. I, man (or god) enthroned, with phiale. A, woman dancing to man and youth; B, men and woman. Now cleaned.

159 (113). ADRIA B 318, from Adria. I, Micali *Mon. ined.* pl. 45, 2; *CV.* pl. 19, 5; I, *Riv. Ist.* N.S. 5–6, 46 fig. 32. I, komast. A, male seated between male and another; B, (male, woman).

160 (114). FLORENCE 7 B 20, fr. *CV.* pl. 7, B 20. A, (woman).

161 (115). FLORENCE, fr. A, (right arm and middle of hairy man to right, his stick under his armpit). Put in this place because it might belong to the last.

162 (116). FLORENCE 7 B 23, fr. *CV.* pl. 7, B 23. A, (woman).

163 (117). VILLA GIULIA, fr. A, (head of woman to left). Ruddy.

164 (118). VILLA GIULIA (part ex Florence), fr. A, (middles of male in himation, frontal, and of woman in chiton to right, her right arm bent up).

165 (119). Villa Giulia, two frr. I, (bit of himation). Outside feet of woman in chiton to right, and stick of male; feet of woman to left, legs of male leaning on his stick to right).

166 (120). Villa Giulia, fr. I, (back of male head to right). A, (feet of woman to right and of male to left).

167 (121). Florence, fr. A, (shoulders and arms of woman to right, fingers). Corroded.

168 (122). Florence 7 B 11, fr. A, CV. pl. 7, B 11. I, (maeander). A, (woman).

169 (123). Freiburg, fr. A, (woman seated to right with mirror).

170 (124). Florence 11 B 46, fr. A, CV. pl. 11, B 46. I, (maeander). A, (woman, male).

171 (125). Villa Giulia, fr. A, (hand, raised arm of woman to left).

172 (126). Villa Giulia, fr. A, (flute-case, woman bending to right).

173 (127). Florence, fr. I, (maeander). A, (end of flute-case, lower part of woman in chiton and himation to right). Reddish.

174. Bryn Mawr, fr. I, (maeander). A, (foot of a woman to right, foot to left).

175 (129). Florence, two frr., from Vetulonia. NSc. 1895, 304 fig. 17; Montelius ii pl. 178, 24–25. Outside, (women).

176 (130). Amsterdam inv. 2814, fr. A, (woman).

177 (131). Athens Acr. 318, fr., from Athens. Langlotz pl. 19, A, (woman). See the next.

178. Athens Acr., fr., from Athens. A, (chin, neck, shoulders, breast, of a woman to right). Ought to join the last, but it did not occur to me at the time.

179 (132). Athens Acr. 324, fr., from Athens. Part, Langlotz pl. 21. A, (woman). An Athens fr. joins the published fr. below, adding the lower part of the woman's face, with the neck, left shoulder, breast, and the rest of the flower. On the name KALONI[KE] see Eph. 1953–4, 203–4, 7.

180 (135, +). Louvre G 148. I and part of A, Pottier pll. 118–19. I, man and boy; A, men and boy; youth and boy; B, men and women. Now cleaned, and several Louvre frr. added, including the handles. Early, and crude.

181. Louvre C 11288, fr. A, (middles of two women, one to left, the other to right, with part of a third person, to left).

182. Louvre C 11289, fr. A, (hairy man leaning on his stick to right, and the knees of one seated to left).

183. Louvre C 11290, two frr. A, (on the left, nape, breast, right arm of a hairy man, leaning, to right). The smaller fr. has part of the reserve over one handle.

184. LOUVRE C 11291, fr. A, (part of a male in a himation, leaning, to right, right arm akimbo: right shoulder to right thigh remains).

185. LAUSANNE, private. I, warrior and old man (bearded warrior leaning on his spear to right, old man seated to left). A, men and women; youth and woman; B, men and youths. Incised on one handle, HIEPONEΓOIEϟEN.

186 (133). MUNICH 2656 (J. 603), from Vulci. I, youth with purse; A–B, youths and boys. On I, ΓPA+ϟITELEϟ KALOϟ. On A, APIϟTA-ΛOИϟ KALOϟ, ΓPA+ϟITELEϟKALOϟ. On B, [Γ]PA+ϟITELEϟ: KALOϟ, ΓPA+ϟITELEϟ. [Hartwig]. Early. For the shape, Bloesch 91, Hieron no. 4.

187 (134). CAB. MÉD. 716, 564, 730, plus, frr. I, (male); A–B, (males). Early.

188. LOUVRE C 10923. I, (maeander). A–B, men and youths. Under each handle a palmette with pointed mid-petal. Early.

189. LOUVRE C 10920, fr. A, (hand to right holding sprig, boy standing to right). See the next.

190. LOUVRE C 203 a, fr. A, (elbow of boy, right side of male). Probably belongs to C 10920 (no. 189).

191. LOUVRE C 11292, fr. A, (hand, to right, of one holding out a lyre, face of a boy to left with part of his himation).

192. LOUVRE C 11293, fr. A, (on the left, hand holding a hare by the ears).

193 (136). VIENNA 3698 (ex Oest. Mus. 323), from Cervetri. WV. C pl. 4, whence Hoppin ii, 89; A–B, Lücken pll. 104–5, whence (B) Licht ii, 143; CV. pl. 14, pl. 13, 3–4, and p. 16. I, youth and girl; A–B, men and boys. On one handle, HIEPONEΓOIEϟEN. For the shape, Bloesch 92, Hieron no. 13. See p. 1654.

194 (137). LONDON E 62, from Vulci. I, Murray no. 41. I, man and boy; A, men and youth; B, men. [Hartwig]. For the shape Bloesch 92, Hieron no. 20.

195 (138). BERLIN 2292, from Vulci. WV. A pl. 6, whence Hoppin ii, 45. I, man and girl; A–B, men. Incised on one handle, HIEPONEΓOIEϟEN. Restored.

196 (139). MUNICH 2655 (J. 804), from Vulci. Gerhard pl. 280; WV. A pl. 3, whence Hoppin ii, 65; A, Pfuhl fig. 444; A, From the Coll. 3, 133. I, youth and boy; A, youths and boys; man and boy; B, youths and boys. On I, HIΓΓOΔAMAϟ KALOϟ. On one handle, HIEPONEΓOI-EϟEN. For the shape, Bloesch 91, Hieron no. 10.

197 (140). VILLA GIULIA 916, from Falerii. Hoppin ii, 87; CV. pl. 30 and pl. 31, 1–3; A–B, ph. Al. 41190; A–B, phs. R.I. 3180–2. I, (maeander). A, men and boys; youth and boy; B, men and boys. Incised on one handle, HIEPONEΓOIEϟEN. For the shape, Bloesch 92, Hieron no. 24.

198 (141). LOUVRE G 142, from Chiusi? Detail of A, Mon. gr. 1876, 15; Hoppin ii, 72–73; Pottier pl. 116. I, boy with lyre, and man; A–B, men

and boys. Incised on one handle, HIEPONEΠOIEϟEN. For the shape, Bloesch 92, Hieron no. 23.

199 (142). FRANKFORT, Univ., frr., from Orvieto. *AZ*. 1884 pl. 17, 3, whence Hoppin ii, 91; part, Schaal *F*. pl. 30, b. I, (male); A–B, (men, youth). Incised on one handle, HIEPONEΠOIEϟEN.

200 (143). BOSTON 89.272 (R. 389), from Vulci. Gerhard pl. 282; *AZ*. 1885 pl. 18 and pl. 19, 1; CB. iii pl. 81, 142 and 80, 142; the shape, Caskey *G*. 183 no. 137. I, youth and boy; A–B, men and boys. [Wernicke]. See CB. iii, text.

201. LOUVRE C 11294, frr. I, (maeander). A–B, man, youths, and boys. Under each handle a circumscribed palmette.

202. LOUVRE C 11295, fr. (four joining). A, (male leaning on his stick to right, boy to left, looking round, hands of one holding a wreath). Very like Louvre C 11294 (no. 201).

203. LOUVRE C 11296, fr. (four joining). A, (male to left, with stick, man leaning on his stick, with purse, raised arm to left).

204. LOUVRE C 11297, two frr. I, (maeander). Outside: on one fr., part of the left-hand figure on A, legs from mid-thigh to mid-shank of a male in a cloak to right; on the other fr., part of the himation of the right-hand figure on A, to left, and part of the himation of the left-hand figure on B, to right.

205. LOUVRE C 11298, fr. A, (upper part of a youth in a himation, leaning, to left, stick in left hand, the head missing).

206. LOUVRE C 11299, fr. I, (maeander). A, man and boy; youth and boy; man or youth, and boy.

207 (144). NEW YORK 08.258.57, from Falerii. A, *Bull. Metr*. 5, 142 fig. 5; *AJA*. 1917 pll. 4–6; Hoppin ii, 66–67; Richter and Hall pl. 50, 54 and pll. 55–56. I, man and youth; A, man with lyre, and men; youth playing the flute, and male; man and boy; B, men and youths. Incised on one handle, HIEPONEΠOIEϟEN.

208 (145). FREIBURG S 129, two frr. Outside, (middles of two males, one to left, with stick, the other to right; middles of two males, one to right with stick, the other—a boy?—to left).

209 (146, +). LOUVRE S 1318. I, youth and boy; A–B, men and boys. Many Louvre frr. join S 1318, and the greater part of the cup is preserved. Incised on one handle, HIEPONEΠOESEN.

210 (a 1). PALERMO V 661 a, fr., from Chiusi. I, Inghirami *Chius*. pl. 69; I, Benndorf *Gjölbaschi* 180, whence Rumpf *Rel*. fig. 166; cleaned, *CV*. pl. 14; I, Zschietzschmann *H.R*. pl. 44, 2. I, sacrifice. A, (males, one with lyre); B, (males). Late.

211 (147). LOUVRE G 147. I, *Annali* 1863 pl. C, whence HM. pl. 22, 1; I, Pottier pl. 118; I, *Enc. phot*. iii, 13, d; I, ph. Gir. 25516, whence *Hist. rel*.

172 and Stella 628. I, Procne and Philomela with Itys. A–B, men and youths. [Hartwig]. For the shape, Bloesch 132 no. 17; for the subject of I, Robert *Held*. 155. Restored. See p. 1654.

212 (148). LOUVRE G 149, from Vulci. Pottier pl. 119. I, youth at altar. A, man and boy; youth and boy; B, the like. [Hartwig].

213 (149). MADRID 11268 (L. 154). Hartwig 297–8; I, Alvarez-Ossorio pl. 34, 3; I and A, Leroux pll. 17–18; *CV*. pl. 1, 4 and pl. 42. I, komast. A, youth seated with lyre, and youth; male and boy; B, male seated and males. Much restored. [Hartwig].

214 (150). DRESDEN, fr. I, (crown of male head). A, (males in himatia, one to right with stick, the other—a boy?—to left).

215 (151). FREIBURG, fr. A, (upper part of man with flower to right).

216 (152). FREIBURG, fr. I, (legs of a male, leaning to right, and of a male—boy?—standing to left). A, (himatia, foot to left).

217 (153). CHICAGO, Univ., fr. *AJA*. 1938, 348 fig. 5. A, (male). [Johnson].

218. BASLE, Cahn, 104, fr. A, (middle of male in himation leaning on his stick to right, right arm extended).

219 (154). FLORENCE 7 B 22, fr. I, *CV*. pl. 7, B 22. I, (male). A, (leg of a male, leaning, to right).

220 (155). FLORENCE 20 B 73 (part ex Villa Giulia), two frr. Part, *CV*. pl. 20, B 73. Outside, (males).

221 (156). LEIPSIC T 624, fr. A, (man with purse and stick).

222. ATHENS Acr., fr., from Athens. A, (leg of a male in a himation to right).

223 (157). CAB. MÉD., part of 560; 777; 727; frr. Part of A, de Ridder 422; part of A, part of ph. Gir. 27791. I, (male); A–B, (males, some with lyres). See p. 1654.

224 (158). CAB. MÉD., part of 588 (L. 88), fr. A, (man with purse leaning on his stick to left).

225 (159). CAB. MÉD. 768, fr. I, (folds). A, (foot).

226 (160). CAB. MÉD. (parts of 545 and 595?), frr. Outside, (heads of youths).

227 (161). GOETTINGEN, fr. A, (on the right, youth to left with flower).

228 (162). AMSTERDAM, fr. A, (male left arm with stick).

229 (163). BERLIN, fr. A, (upper part of man in himation leaning forward to left).

230 (164). VILLA GIULIA, two frr. I, (shoulder, and back of head, of woman facing to right; on the left, crotala). A, (stick?, and edge of himation).

231 (165). VILLA GIULIA, fr. I, (a bit of the himation of the left-hand figure). A, (toes to right, toes to left).

232 (166). VILLA GIULIA, fr. I, (maeander). A, (a bit of the himation of a male to left).

233 (167). VILLA GIULIA, fr. I, (legs of the left-hand figure, a male in a himation, leaning, to right). A, (feet to left, feet to right).

234 (168). VILLA GIULIA, fr. A, (beard, chest, arm, of a man to right, holding
a wreath).

235 (169). VILLA GIULIA, fr. A, (hand with flower).

236 (170). VILLA GIULIA, fr. I, (maeander). A, (shank of male in himation,
leaning, to left).

237 (171). VILLA GIULIA, fr. I, (maeander). A, (shanks of male in himation,
leaning, to right).

238 (172). VILLA GIULIA, fr. I, (maeander). A, (foot to right, feet of a male
in a himation to left).

239 (173). ATHENS Acr. 320, fr., from Athens. Langlotz pl. 19. A, (youth).

240 (174). ATHENS Acr. 321, fr., from Athens. *Jb.* 6 pl. 1, d = *Jb.* 11, 259,
2; Langlotz pl. 19. A, (youth with lyre).

241 (175). ADRIA B 572, fr., from Adria. A, (head and shoulders of a boy
to right).

242 (176). AMSTERDAM inv. 2897, fr. A, (youth).

243. LOUVRE C 11300, fr. A, (upper part of youth leaning on his stick to
right).

244. LOUVRE C 11301, fr. A, (ball-bag, then the upper part of a youth leaning on his stick to right).

245. LOUVRE C 11302, fr. A, (male arm raised, with stick, then the arm of
another, extended to left; letter N or M).

246. LOUVRE C 11303, fr. A, (on the right, upper part of a male, leaning, to
left).

247 (178). MUNICH, fr. A, (middle of a male in a himation leaning on his
stick to right).

248 (179). AMSTERDAM inv. 2205, fr. *CV.* Scheurleer pl. 10, 6. A, (youth).

249 (180). BRYN MAWR P 202, two frr. I, symposion (male reclining, and
male standing—fluting?). A, (on the left, male and youth, male).

250 (228). BRYN MAWR P 203, fr. I, symposion (youth reclining, his left arm
extended, holding a cup). A, (persons seated). [Swindler].

251 (181). VILLA GIULIA, fr. I, symposion (part of himation and of cushion).
A, (feet of two males leaning on their sticks, one to left, the other to right).

252. INNSBRUCK ii. 12. 35, fr. I, symposion (part of the table remains). A,
(stick of male leaning to right, legs of male in cloak moving to left).
[Bothmer].

253. CAMBRIDGE, Museum of Classical Archaeology, UP 130, fr. I, symposion. A, (foot).

254 (182). ADRIA B 276, fr., from Adria. *CV.* pl. 20, 4. I, symposion. A
boy between two seated males. See the next.

255. ADRIA B 910, fr., from Adria. A, (middle of male in himation to left). Probably belongs to the last.

256. ADRIA B 654, fr., from Adria. I, (foot of male in himation). A, (foot of male).

257. ADRIA, fr., from Adria. I, (heel to right). A, (toes of male leaning on his stick to right, with the lower edge of his himation).

258 (183). FLORENCE PD 360, fr., from Populonia. A, (on the right, part of a male in a himation, to left, then a stick).

259 (184). BERKELEY 8.2184, from Saturnia. I, *ML.* 30, 683, ii, 2; *CV.* pl. 34, 1. I, girl cup-bearer. A, youths; B, males. [H. R. W. Smith].

260 (185). HILDESHEIM RM 1, from Tarquinia. I, Roeder *Pelizaeus-Museum* 176; *R.I.* 1875.71. I, man seated playing the lyre. A, youth playing the flute, between a seated man and a youth; B, youths seated and youth offering lyre. [Hartwig].

261. PARIS, Bérard. I, satyr dancing (frontal, head to left, arms akimbo; on the left, a kantharos on a table). A, youth seated with lyre, between two youths; B, boy seated, between a youth and a seated youth.

262 (186). AMSTERDAM inv. 2179 (part ex Villa Giulia, see *JHS.* 52, 142 and *CF.* 34 no. 13 *bis*), from Campagnano. Part, *Bull. Vereen.* i, 2, 5; part, *CV.* Scheurleer pl. 10, 2–3 and 5; the Villa Giulia part, *ML.* 23, 283. I, youth; A, youths and boy; B, the like.

263 (187). FREIBURG, fr. I, (maeander). A, (legs of male in himation, leaning, to left).

264 (188). COPENHAGEN, Ny Carlsberg, 34, from Orvieto. Poulsen *Etr.* pll. 15–16. I, komast. A, youths and boy; B, men and boy.

265 (189). BOSTON 08.293. CB. iii pl. 78, 143 and pl. 80, 143. I, boy running home; A, youths pursuing a boy; B, youths and man pursuing a boy. See CB. iii, text.

266 (190). LONDON E 59, from Nola. Gargiulo *Recueil* (1845) ii pll. 72–73, whence (A) Panofka *Bilder ant. Leb.* pl. 4, 4; I, Murray no. 38. I, boy with hare; A, youth seated playing the flute, between youths; B youth seated, between youths. For the shape, Bloesch 95, Hieron no. 40.

267 (191). MUNICH 2657 (J. 507), from Vulci. Gerhard pl. 283–4, 4–7; I, Brommer *Satyrspiele* 13. I, satyr dancing: he wears the drawers of the satyr-play. A, boy between seated man and seated youth; B, youths and boy, seated. Restored.

268 (192). LENINGRAD 659 (St. 1614). Gerhard pl. 283–4, 8–10. I, youth with purse; A, youths seated and man; B, youths seated, and youth.

269 (193). NEW YORK 96.18.70 (GR 573), from Capua. Richter and Hall pl. 58 and pl. 180, 57. I, youth leaning on his stick with flower; A, youth, man, and boy; B, youths and boy.

270 (194). VILLA GIULIA (part ex Florence) and HEIDELBERG 93, frr. Part,

CV. Fl. pl. 18, B 11; the Heidelberg fr., Kraiker pl. 11. I, (maeander). A, youth seated with lyre, between male and youth; B, youth running, between youth and males.

271 (195). BRUNSWICK 532, fr. *CV*. pl. 17, 4. A, (youth).

272 (196). BRUNSWICK 533, fr. *CV*. pl. 17, 7. A, (youth).

273 (197). BRYN MAWR P 206, frr. *AJA*. 1916, 340, 10–11. Outside, (youths). [Swindler].

274 (198). VILLA GIULIA, from Falerii. I, youth leaning on his stick, holding a flower; A–B, males (A, one moving to right with a flute-case, between two others leaning on their sticks; B, one moving to right, between a lost figure and one leaning on his stick).

275 (199). MUNICH 2658 (J. 505), from Vulci. A–B, Poulsen *Etr*. pl. 17; A and foot, Bloesch *FAS*. pl. 26, 4. I, youth; A, youth with hare, running, between men; B, youth running, between youth and man. For the shape, Bloesch 95, Hieron no. 42.

276 (200). ADRIA B 673 *bis*, fr., from Adria. *CV*. pl. 19, 2. A, (youth, stick).

277 (201). VILLA GIULIA, fr. I, (on the left, satyr to right: hair, back, tail remain: no doubt attacking a maenad: inscription . . . INO . . .). A, (feet). See the next.

278 (202). VILLA GIULIA, fr. I, (piece of a maenad to left). Might belong to the last.

279 (203). FLORENCE, fr. I, (foot and half-shank of a maenad to left; to the left, tail and paw of her panther-skin). A, (toes to right, toes to left).

280 (204). CAB. MÉD. 599, fr. I, woman with flute. A, (feet). Still early.

281 (46). ADRIA B 606, fr., from Adria. I, *CV*. pl. 19, 1. I, (satyr). The stopt maeander is very rare in Makron, but does occur on Torlonia 148 (no. 132).

282 (205). VILLA GIULIA, fr. I, (maeander). A, (bit of one in chiton and himation to right).

283. LOUVRE C 11304, fr. I, woman with flower. A, (stick, stick, frontal foot).

284. BASLE, Cahn, 65 d, fr. A, (head and arms of youth to right, holding out a wreath). [Cahn].

285. BASLE, Cahn, 71, fr. I, man holding cock and hen. Outside, (male leg moving to left, seat, legs of male leaning on his stick to right, foot of male moving to right).

286. BASLE, Cahn, 70, fr. I, (feet of male to left). A, (feet of male with stick seated to right, feet of male in himation standing to left).

287. BASLE, Cahn, 73, fr. I, (on the left, head of youth to right). A, (stick, foot of male in himation to left).

288 (207). CAB. MÉD. 566, fr. I, male with lyre and plectrum (moving to right). Outside, all that remains is a piece of the line border.

289 (208). VILLA GIULIA, fr. I, (stick of male to right). Outside, a piece of the line border.

290 (209). VILLA GIULIA, fr. Outside, the greater part of the circumscribed palmette under one handle remains.

(*nos. 291–307, not known if decorated outside*)

291 (210). ATHENS Acr. 358, frr., from Athens. Langlotz pl. 27. I, Herakles and the Hydra.

292 (γ). ATHENS Acr. 322, fr., from Athens. Langlotz pl. 21. I, Hermes and Athena.

293 (211). LONDON E 134. 3, fr. I, satyr attacking maenad. [Cecil Smith].

294 (212). VILLA GIULIA, fr. I, satyr attacking maenad. The fragment includes the stem.

295 (226). NEW YORK 07.286.49, fr., from Arezzo. Richter and Hall pl. 49, 58. I, unexplained subject: two males reclining, and the youth ΛΜVϞΟϞ, naked, lying on the ground.

296. ADRIA B 133, fr., from Adria. *CV.* pl. 18, 3. I, symposion (male reclining).

297 (213). ATHENS, Agora, NS AP 499, fr., from Athens. *Hesp.* 4, 281 no. 148. I, deities? (one with sceptre seated, and one standing).

297 *bis.* ATHENS Acr. 277, fr., from Athens. Langlotz pl. 14. I, youth arriving or leaving home.

298. ATHENS Acr., fr., from Athens. I, (part of the right arm and chest of a male in chitoniskos and chlamys).

299 (216). ATHENS Acr. 251, fr., from Athens. Langlotz pl. 13. I, (small boy holding his master's stick and cloak).

300. ATHENS Acr., fr., from Athens. I, (shoulder and right arm of a man in a himation leaning on his stick to right).

300 *bis.* CAB. MÉD. 724, fr. I, (middle of a woman seated to right, forearms raised).

301. LOUVRE C 205, fr. I, male and woman (she standing frontal, lifting her skirt, and a hand touching her breast).

302 (217). ADRIA B 306, fr., from Adria. *CV.* pl. 21, 2. I, (seated male).

303 (214). ADRIA B 534, fr., from Adria. *CV.* pl. 19, 7. I, male with lyre and dog.

304 (δ). ADRIA B 517, fr., from Adria. *CV.* pl. 10, 2. I, youth playing the flute.

305 (215). VILLA GIULIA, fr. I, woman (standing to right, flute in hand: inscription . . . ΟΔΟ . . ., i.e. [Ρ]ΟΔΟ[ΓΙϞ]?

305 *bis.* ROME, Antiquarium Forense, fr., from Rome. *Bull. Arch. Com.* 76 pl. 16, 205. I, (woman playing the flute). [Enrico Paribeni].

306. BOSTON 08.31 e, fr., from Orvieto. Vorberg *Gloss.* 450. I, man or youth courting boy. See *Cypr.* 29 α 50.

307. BASLE, Cahn, 66, fr. I, Iris (in peplos, moving to left, with caduceus). [Cahn].

(nos. 308–33, decorated inside only)

308 (218). ATHENS Acr. 307, fr., from Athens. Langlotz pl. 19. I, Dionysos.

309 (219). BOSTON 13.67, from Vulci. Gerhard pl. 57, 3–4; Edward Robinson 144; B.Ap. xxi. 97, 2; CB. iii pl. 78, 139. I, Dionysos and satyr. See CB. iii, text.

310. ITALIAN MARKET. I, satyr (moving to right, bending, skyphos in right hand, left hand raised; between his legs a curious horn-like or shell-like object).

311 (220). FLORENCE 3943. *CV.* pl. 91, 3–5 and pl. 116, 14. I, satyr and maenad.

312 (221, +). LOUVRE G 160. Part, Pottier pl. 125, and *Mem. Am. Ac.* 6 pl. 21, 2. I, maenad. Two Louvre frr. join and have been added, giving the head of the fawn and parts of the maeander.

313. BASLE, Cahn, 69, fr. I, Hermes and a male (feet and shanks remain). [Cahn].

314 (222). ATHENS Acr. 311, fr., from Athens. *Jb.* 2, 164; Langlotz pl. 19. I, komast. ΗΙΠΠΟΔΑΜΑΣ ΚΑΛΟΣ. [Studniczka].

315 (223). CAB. MÉD. 696, 747, 734, 798 and a fr. joining it. I, komast (man with stick and skyphos).

316 (224). MUNICH 2673 (J. 669), from Vulci. B and foot, Bloesch *FAS.* pl. 26, 3. I, komast. For the shape, Bloesch 94, Hieron no. 31.

317 (225). OXFORD 301. ~~Gardner pl. 22, 3;~~ *CV.* pl. 2, 4 and pl. 47, 5. I, komast.

318 (227). ATHENS Acr. 312, fr., from Athens. Langlotz pl. 19. I, symposion (one reclining and one standing). [Η]ΙΠΠΟ[ΔΑΜΑΣ . . .

319 (229). NEW YORK 96.9.191 (GR 1120). *VA.* 101; Pfuhl fig. 439; McClees 77 fig. 96; Richter and Hall pl. 57, 56 and pl. 180, 56; *Harv. St.* 52 pl. 5; detail, Richter *ARVS.* 64 fig. 27; Richter *H.* 215, c. I, youth, and girl dancing. Early.

320 (230). WÜRZBURG 480. Langlotz pl. 150. I, a youth offering a hare to a seated boy. For the shape, Bloesch 94, Hieron no. 32.

321 (231). VILLA GIULIA, fr. I, youth (or satyr?) (singing?) and man seated playing the flute.

322 (232). ADRIA B 544, fr., from Adria. *CV.* pl. 22, 2. I, (on the right, man with stick).

323. BASLE, Cahn, 67, fr. I, youth and seated male (head of youth, crown of the other's head and top of his stick). Between, downwards, ΗΙΚΕ[ΤΕΣ . . .

The upright of the epsilon is preserved. The name may have been followed by καλος. See the next.

324. BASLE, Cahn, 68, fr. I, male and seated male (the legs remain). Should belong to the last.

325 (233). Once CANINO, from Vulci. Gerhard pl. 276, 3-4. I, man holding out a hare. Restored.

326 (234). MUNICH 2674 (J. 275), from Vulci. Anita Klein pl. 20, d; A and foot, Bloesch *FAS*. pl. 26, 2. I, boy running with hoop and meat, and a dog. For the shape, Bloesch 94, Hieron no. 29.

327 (235). ADRIA B 509, fr., from Adria. *CV*. pl. 19, 6. I, boy with cock.

328 (236). PHILADELPHIA 2515, from Chiusi. I, jumper.

329 (237). BASLE, Cahn, 107 (ex Curtius), fr. I, (head of a man to right). Line border.

330. GODALMING, Charterhouse. *The Times* 14 Feb. 1946, 6; Chittenden and Seltman pl. 18, 82. I, naked woman laying her boots down.

331. BARCELONA, fr., from Ampurias. I, (head and shoulders of the left-hand figure remain, a man to right). [Shefton]. See the next.

332. BARCELONA, fr., from Ampurias. I, (on the right, the foot of a woman, with the edge of her skirt). Probably belongs to the last. [Shefton].

333. LOUVRE C 11305, three frr. I, (uncertain subject: a foot—of a statue?— to right, on a block, then part of a furnace?; on the second fr., part of a stick; on the third, part of an unexplained object).

STEMLESS CUP

(saucer-like)

334. ATHENS Acr., fr., from Athens. I, symposion (male reclining to left: the right foot remains—encroaching on the maeander—and part of the legs).

PLATE

335 (238). COPENHAGEN inv. 3878. Fröhner *Coll. Brant.* pl. 23 = Hartwig pl. 30, 1; *CV*. pl. 139, 3; Breitenstein *G.V.* pl. 43. Man with lyre and flower. [Klein].

PYXIS

(type A)

336 (239). ATHENS Acr. 560, from Athens. *JHS*. 14 pl. 3, 2; Langlotz pl. 43. Women. Still early. MELITA : KA[LE?], but the KA ... might also be the beginning of another name. In white, on a red sash, KA ... and HIΠΠOΔAMASKALE. The fragmentary inscription MAKP .. may be part of a woman's name, but considering the rarity of women's names derived from μακρ- one must ask whether it may not be part of the artist's signature.

ROUND ARYBALLOS

337 (240). OXFORD 1929.175, from Athens. *CV*. pl. 64, 1–7; *BSA*. 29 pll.
3–4 and pp. 190–1; part, Richter and Milne fig. 105. Boys playing with
toy chariots. On the topside of the mouth, in relief-lines, ΗΙΓΓΟΔΔ-
ΜΑϚ ˙ ΚΑLΟϚ. See *BSA*. 29, 187–93. Möbius has pointed out to me
that a cup from the school of Makron has the same subject (p. 809 no. 20);
so has a hydria in Bloomfield Hills (Michigan), Cranbrook Academy of
Arts (1940.40; *Art News* 3 Feb. 1940, 4).

ASKOI

(no. 338, shape 2)

338 (241). PROVIDENCE 25.074. *AJA*. 1931, 300; *CV*. pl. 17, 4. Symposion:
A, maenad reclining; B, the like. Early.

(no. 339, shape 1)

339 (242). BOWDOIN 23.30. *AJA*. 1921, 325 and 328–30; Greifenhagen
Eroten 21 figs. 15–16 and p. 88. A, Eros; B, Eros.

Miss Anna Magi is probably right in attributing two cup-fragments to
Makron (rather than his school): I know them from sketches only:

1. FLORENCE PD 584, fr. A, (man, and youth with lyre).
2. FLORENCE PD 584 a, fr. A, (on the right, man leaning on his stick to left).

Three cups go together, and I take them to be early work by Makron:

*ARV.*¹ 315, top, and 958.

1 (1). MUNICH 2617 (J. 605), from Vulci. B, Bloesch *FAS*. pl. 26, 1. I,
komast. A, Herakles and Antaios; B, Herakles and Alkyoneus. For the
shape, Bloesch 94, Hieron no. 27.
2 (2). PALERMO V 659, from Chiusi. A–B, *AZ*. 1871 pl. 48; Hartwig 538–9;
CV. pl. 16, 4 and pl. 10. I, warrior; A, death of Troïlos; B, fight. For
the shape, Bloesch 77, Euphronios no. 32.
3 (3). TARQUINIA 689, from Tarquinia. I, youth running with helmet; A–B,
fight.

The following cups are near Makron:

*(ARV.*¹ 315)

1 (α). ATHENS Acr. 216, fr., from Athens. Langlotz pl. 13. A, (hands holding
wreath, and one seated on a throne). Early. For the sleeve compare
Boston 13.67 (p. 478 no. 309).

2. FLORENCE 7 B 15, fr. *CV*. pl. 7, B 15. A, (Dionysos and maenad?:—arm of woman, kantharos).

3. GREIFSWALD 279. Peters pll. 23–24. I, warrior; A–B, fight. Damaged. May be by Makron himself.

4. VILLA GIULIA, fr. A, (head and hand of a youth playing the lyre, to right). The cup is lipped inside.

5. GREIFSWALD 322, fr. Peters pl. 31. I, male with purse, and woman (spinning?). Trimmed round to make a game-piece or peever. Compared by Peters with Athens Acr. 322 (p. 477 no. 292).

6 (ε). VILLA GIULIA, fr. I, (middle, and upper arm, of male to right; above, (chipped). Makron or his school.

7 (ζ). MUNICH, fr. A, (breast and shoulders of youth in himation, leaning, to right). Probably school rather than himself.

8. FLORENCE, fr. I, (maeander). A, (piece of a shin and foot).

HIERON, POTTER

Bloesch *FAS*. 91–96 and 161.

The name occurs on thirty-one vases decorated by Makron:

(*nos. 1–31*)

SKYPHOI

BOSTON 13.186. P. 458 no. 1.

LOUVRE G 146. P. 458 no. 2.

LONDON E 140. P. 459 no. 3.

CUPS

BERLIN 2291. P. 459 no. 4.

LENINGRAD 649. P. 460 no. 13.

LOUVRE G 153. P. 460 no. 14.

FLORENCE 3929 (if the handle belongs). P. 460 no. 15.

ATHENS Acr. 325. P. 460 no. 20.

BRUSSELS R 247. P. 462 no. 41.

MISSISSIPPI. P. 462 no. 42.

LOUVRE G 144. P. 462 no. 43.

MUNICH 2654. P. 462 no. 47.

BERLIN 2290 and VILLA GIULIA. P. 462 no. 48.

LOUVRE G 145. P. 463 no. 50.

VILLA GIULIA 50396. P. 465 no. 82.

LOUVRE G 141. P. 465 no. 84.

NEW YORK 20.246. P. 467 no. 118.

CAMBRIDGE 12.27. P. 468 no. 144.

LONDON E 61. P. 468 no. 145.
NEW YORK 12.231.1. P. 468 no. 146.
LOUVRE G 143. P. 469 no. 148.
OXFORD, Beazley, fr. P. 469 no. 152.
LAUSANNE, private. P. 471 no. 185.
VIENNA 3698. P. 471 no. 193.
BERLIN 2292. P. 471 no. 195.
MUNICH 2655. P. 471 no. 196.
VILLA GIULIA 916. P. 471 no. 197.
LOUVRE G 142. P. 471 no. 198.
FRANKFORT, Univ., frr. P. 472 no. 199.
NEW YORK 08.258.57. P. 472 no. 207.
LOUVRE S 1318. P. 472 no. 209.

(nos. 32–33)

Two cups decorated by the Telephos Painter:

32. BOSTON 95.28, VILLA GIULIA, and FLORENCE (pp. 816–17 no. 1).
33. BOSTON 98.931 (p. 817 no. 2).

(no. 34)

A kantharos decorated by the Amphitrite Painter:

34. BOSTON 98.932 (p. 832 no. 36).

(nos. 35–40)

Besides, on a lost vase, and five cup-handles where the pictures are lost:

35. Lost, from Bomarzo. A, Dionysos and maenads; B, maenads. Signature of Hieron. Uncertain shape ('diota' according to Vittori *Bomarzo* 59: probably a skyphos, as Klein suggested, *Meist.* 172).

CUPS

36. CAB. MÉD., part of 558, fr., from Tarquinia. Ph. Gir. 8062, below, left; Hoppin ii, 70. Handle with HIEPON ᛬ ΕΠΟΙΕϚΕΝ.
37. ATHENS Acr. 326, fr., from Athens. Langlotz 29. Handle with HIEPON᛬ ΕΠΟΙΕϚ[ΕΝ] incised.
38. VILLA GIULIA, fr. Handle with HIEPON . . . incised.
39. MUNICH, part of 2648 (J. 369), fr., from Vulci. FR. pl. 24, below, left. Handle with HIEPONEΠΟEϚEN incised, used in antiquity to mend an alien cup (p. 156 no. 45).
40. ROMAN MARKET (Depoletti), from Vulci, fr. B.Ap. xvi. 36. Foot with HIEPONEΠΟΙΕϚEN attached to an alien cup: see p. 156 no. 45. See Wernicke in *AZ.* 1885, 258.

BOOK V

EARLY CLASSIC PAINTERS OF LARGE POTS

CHAPTER 30

HERMONAX

HERMONAX

VA. 123–7. *Att. V.* 299–304 and 476. Pallottino *Studi sull'arte di Hermonax* (in *Atti della Reale Accademia d'Italia, Memorie,* ser. vii, i, 1). *ARV.*[1] 317–24 and 958. *Classical Studies Oldfather* 73–81 (F. P. Johnson). *AJA.* 1945, 491–502 (F. P. Johnson). *AJA.* 1947, 233–47 (F. P. Johnson).

The name is known from ten signed vases (nos. 1, 5–7, 24–27, 33, and 132). Pupil of the Berlin Painter.

STAMNOI

1 (1). Louvre G 336. Hoppin ii, 25, whence (B) Swindler fig. 280; Pottier pl. 135; *CV.* d pll. 12–13; A, ph. Al. 23701. Komos. HERMONA+[ϟ] EΛRAⱰϟEN. Restored. See p. 1655.

2 (2). Heidelberg 170, fr., from Cervetri. Kraiker pl. 32. Komos.

3 (3). Florence PD 421, frr. Komos.

4. Athens, Agora, P 25357, fr., from Athens. (Head of youth—komos?) [Philippaki].

5 (4). Orvieto, Faina, 66, from Orvieto. *AZ.* 1878 pl. 12, whence Hoppin ii, 23 and Pallottino 37; Pallottino 34–35; *Anz.* 1941, 415–16; *Boll. Restauro* 23–24, 164; phs. R.I. 1935.821–4, and 40.11, 12, 15, and 17–18. Youth pursuing a woman. HERMONA+ϟ EΛRAⱰϟEN.

6 (5). Boston 01.8031, from Orvieto. Detail, *VA.* 123; Hoppin ii, 21. Youth pursuing a woman. [HERMON]E+ϟ [EΛRAⱰϟE]N. Replica of the last. Much restored.

7 (6). FLORENCE 3995. A, *Mem. Acc. Nap.* 1918 pl. at p. 24; *CV.* pl. 52, 1–5 and pl. 48, 2: both incompletely. Eos and Tithonos. ΗΕΡΜΩΝΑ+Ϟ Ε[Λ]ΡΑΦϞΕΝ. The fragment *CV.* pl. 14 B 9 belongs and has been inserted: so has a second fragment, recognized by Neri, with part of Tithonos' lyre; a third Florence fragment adds part of the neck and mouth of the vase. The fragment Florence 14 B 5 does not belong, see the next. See p. 1655.

8. FLORENCE 14 B 5, fr. *CV.* pl. 14, B 5. (Youth).

9 (7). VILLA GIULIA 5241, from Narce. *Dedalo* 3, 84–85; *CV.* pl. 12, and pl. 14, 2–3; details, Pallottino 30 and 32; detail of B, *AJA.* 1947 pl. 57, 1. Peleus and Thetis.

10 (8). LENINGRAD 805. Details, *VA.* 125; A, G.P. 71. Boreas and Oreithyia.

11 (9). LENINGRAD inv. 4121 (ex Stieglitz 84). Parts, *AJA.* 1947 pll. 49–50. Satyrs and maenads.

12. LOUVRE C 11067, frr. The lower part of the vase remains. A, satyr and two maenads; B, (maenad, satyr). See the next.

13. LOUVRE C 11062, fr. (Thyrsus, head and hand of a maenad moving to right, head of a satyr with a lyre to right). I do not know if this could be from the same vase as C 11067.

14. LOUVRE C 11065, four frr. (Middles of a satyr and three maenads).

15 (10). LENINGRAD 803 (St. 1692). *CR.* 1874 pl. 3. Return of a youth (probably Theseus).

16 (11). LENINGRAD 804 (St. 1711). *CR.* 1874 pl. 4; part of A, *AJA.* 1947 pl. 56. Theseus victorious over the Minotaur.

17 (12). LOUVRE G 416, from Nola. *Mon.* 9 pl. 30; *CV.* d pl. 19, 1, 4, and 6–7, and pl. 20, 1–2. Death of Orpheus. [Ducati]. See p. 1655.

18 (13). FULDA, Welz (ex Kalebdjian). *Mon.* 6–7 pl. 58, 1. Zeus and Hera with Nike; Dionysos, two goddesses, god, and Plouton. Very much restored.

19 (14). ROMAN MARKET (Basseggio). B.Ap. xxii. 84. Zeus and Ganymede; Hermes pursuing a boy. See CB. ii, 52.

20 (15). ROMAN MARKET (Campanari). B.Ap. xxii. 33. 2. A, Poseidon and two women. B, man and two women.

21 (16). VATICAN, from Vulci. *Mus. Greg.* 2 pl. 20, 1; phs. Al. 35739–40, whence Pallottino 68–69 and (A) *E.A.A.* i, 175. Zeus pursuing Aigina. Late.

22 (17). LOUVRE G 413, from Cervetri. *Mon.* 6–7 pl. 8, whence (detail) Pfuhl fig. 490; A, Pottier pl. 142; *CV.* d pl. 18, 1–4; A, ph. Gir. 35654, whence Béquignon *Il.* 98, *Hist. rel.* 277, and Bielefeld *ZV.* pl. 7. Philoktetes bitten. Now cleaned: B, which was largely repainted, is preserved with the exception of a few fragments: it continues A. Late. See p. 1655.

BELL-KRATER

23. ARGOS, from Argos. A, *BCH.* 1956, 373 fig. 18; A, *AJA.* 1956 pl. 99 fig. 10; A, *Archaeology* autumn 1956, 174; A, *Arch. Reports* 1955, 10; A, *Fasti arch.* 10, 136. A, Theseus and Minotaur. B, woman with man and man or youth. [Karouzou]. The potter-work of another bell-krater from Argos is the same (see p. 633 no. 1). See p. 1655.

PELIKAI

24 (20). VIENNA 3728 (ex Oest. Mus. 336), from Cervetri. *Mon.* 8 pl. 45, whence *WV.* 1889 pl. 8, 10 (whence Robert *Oidipus* i, 54), Hoppin ii, 29, and Pfuhl fig. 517; Pallottino 52–57; *AJA.* 1947 pl. 48; *CV.* pl. 74 and p. 19, below. The Sphinx of Thebes. On A, HERMONA+ξ EΛRAΦ-ξEN. See p. 1655.

25. VILLA GIULIA, from Cervetri. Perseus and Polydektes. On A, HER-MONA+ξ EΛRAΦξEN.

26. SWISS PRIVATE. Zeus and Ganymede. On B, HERMONA+ξ EΛRAΦ-ξEN.

27 (21). VILLA GIULIA 50459, from Cervetri. Hoppin ii, 27; Pallottino 18–24; *Anz.* 1941, 411–14. Dionysos with maenads and satyrs. On A, HERMONA+ξ EΛRAΦξEN. See p. 1655.

28 (22). LOUVRE G 374. *Mon.* 6–7 pl. 20; *CV.* d pl. 45, 1–4 and 6; ph. Gir., whence (parts) Pallottino 66; during cleaning, *Museum* 3, 178 fig. 44. Mission to Achilles. Now cleaned, and the alien parts removed. Five Louvre fragments belong and have been added. A sixth, with part of a himation held over one arm, is by Hermonax and may belong.

29 (23). CHICAGO, Univ., and HEIDELBERG 171. The Heidelberg frr., Kraiker pl. 33; *Class. Studies Oldfather* pll. 2–6. A, unexplained subject: Hermes and a youth or man welcomed by an old man who holds a sceptre; a woman is present. B, woman seated spinning, and woman; woman seated, and woman. [The two Heidelberg fragments were assigned to Hermonax by Kraiker, the Chicago part by Johnson, who also observed the pertinence].

30 (24). GLASGOW 1883.32 a. A, Power *A Kelvingrove Jubilee* 32, left, below, middle. A, youth leaving home. B, woman with man and youth.

31 (25). LOS ANGELES A 5933.50.41 (ex Marshall Brooks). *AJA.* 1945, 501; *Hesp.* 24 pl. 7, d–f and pl. 8. A, youth leaving home. B, man and two women.

32 (25 *bis*). TÜBINGEN inv. 1583, fr. Part of the left-hand figure remains, a woman standing to right: compare the left-hand figure on A of the last.

33. VILLA GIULIA, from Cervetri. Pallottino pll. 1–2 and pp. 3–14; *Anz.* 1941, 407–10; phs. R.I. 57.678–9. Boreas and Oreithyia. On A, HERMONA+ξ EΛRAΦξEN.

34 (26). ATHENS, Agora, P 8959, frr., from Athens. A, Boreas and Oreithyia; B, one seated, and a woman running towards him (Erechtheus, and
Herse or Aglauros). See p. 1655.

35. LOUVRE C 10765. A, Eos and Kephalos. B, man and two women.

36. LOUVRE C 10766, frr. A, Eos and Kephalos. B, man, woman, and
another. I took the head of Eos, now built into B, to come from A. See
the next.

37. LOUVRE, fr. (Head of a youth in chlamys, shoulder of a male.) Now built
into C 10766 (no. 36), but not clear to me that it belongs.

38. LOUVRE C 11064, frr. A, Peleus and Thetis.

39. LOUVRE C 11060, two frr. (B?), (man).

40 (27). LONDON E 374, from Camiros. AJA. 1945, 498. A, man and boy;
B, man.

41 (28). BRUSSELS A 1579, from Rhodes. CV. d pl. 9, 2. A, Nike; B,Nike.

42 (29). MANCHESTER iii. I. 41 (ex Marshall Brooks). A, AJA. 1945, 497
fig. 12; Mem. Manch. 89 pll. 2–3. A, youth with sword pursuing a
woman (Theseus and Aithra?). B, man and youth.

43 (30). MARSEILLES 7023. A, Dionysos and maenad. B, youth and woman
at altar. See p. 1655.

44 (31). LONDON E 371, from Camiros. AJA. 1945, 496. A, Dionysos;
B, maenad.

45 (32). LENINGRAD 727 (St. 1455), from Nola. B, AJA. 1945, 497 fig. 8.
A, youth and boy. B, maenad.

46 (33). LONDON E 405. Hancarville 1 pl. 112 and 2 pl. 43, whence Inghirami pl. 114 (whence FR. ii, 242), (A) Panofka Bilder ant. Leb. pl. 8, 1, (A)
El. 1 pl. 83. A, arming (youth holding helmet, and woman holding his
spear and shield). B, man at altar. See p. 1655.

47 (34). MARSEILLES 1630. A, athlete and man; B, youth.

48 (35). VIENNA 1095. CV. pl. 75, 1–2. A, man and boy; B, youth.

49 (36). BERNE 26454, from Nola. AJA. 1945, 497 fig. 9. A, man and boy;
B, youth.

50 (37). LOUVRE G 546. CV. d pl. 45, 8–9. A, youth and woman; B,
woman.

51. NAPLES (ex Spinelli 2028), from Suessula. A, maenad and youth; B,
youth with thyrsus.

NECK-AMPHORAE

(nos. 52–54, large, with twisted handles)

52 (38). LENINGRAD 696 (St. 1671). A, CR. 1875, 199; A, Waldhauer K.O.
pl. 10 fig. 9. A, citharode; B, woman.

53 (39). ROMAN MARKET (Depoletti). B.Ap. xxi. 45. 1. A, warrior leaving
home (woman standing to right holding oinochoe and helmet, young

warrior standing frontal, head to left, phiale in right hand, spear in left). Restored. I am not sure that what Gerhard gives as B (man and woman at altar) really belongs to this vase.

54 (40). WARSAW, (ex Potocki). A, *CV*. pl. 1 (Pologne pl. 129), 4. A, arming (youth and woman). B, man and woman. See p. 1655.

(nos. 55-56, large, with triple handles)

55 (41). WÜRZBURG 504, from Vulci. FR. pl. 107, 2; A, *Anz.* 1928, 99 fig. 6; Langlotz pll. 171-2 and 184. Arming (A, youth and woman; B, youth and woman).

56 (42). BOULOGNE 125. A, Panckoucke *Héracléide* no. 10; details, *AJA.* 1945, 494. A, warrior leaving home (warrior and man). B, man and woman.

(no. 57, large, with ridged handles)

57 (43). MADRID 11098 (L. 172). Side, Jacobsthal *O*. pl. 81, a; *CV*. pl. 20, 1; *AJA.* 1945, 492-3. A, warrior leaving home (warrior and woman); B, youth leaving home (youth and man).

(nos. 58-59, small, with double handles; doubleens)

58 (44). NORWICH 36.96. *AJA.* 1947 pl. 52, b. A, god and woman (Zeus and Hebe?); B, man.

59 (45). SAN SIMEON, Hearst Corporation, 12359 (ex Lloyd and Spink). A, *Connoisseur* Dec. 1936, cover, back. A, Eos and Kephalos; B, youth with lyre, fleeing. B is restored. See CB. ii, 38, top.

(nos. 60-61, small, with double handles; another model)

60 (46). NAPLES 3098, from Nola. A, ph. So. 11072, ii, 4. A, youth with spear; B, man.

61 (47). LENINGRAD (St. 1461), from Nola. *AJA.* 1945, 500 figs. 15-16. A, youth with spears (Theseus?) pursuing, B, a woman.

62 (48). ALTENBURG 289, from Nola. *AJA.* 1945, 500 figs. 13-14; *CV*. pl. 45, 1-2 and pl. 47, 4-5. A, maenad; B, satyr.

(nos. 63-64, small, with ridged handles)

63. BASLE MARKET (M.M.). *Auktion xviii Basel* pl. 38, 119. A, Nike; B, king (Zeus?) The mouth of the vase is as in doubleens (e.g. nos. 58-59), the foot is a double ogee and of just the same shape as in the next.

64. CHRISTCHURCH (N.Z.), Canterbury University College. A, king and woman; B, man. Mouth in two degrees (as, for example, in no. 52). As the last.

(nos. 65-79, Nolan amphorae, with triple handles)

65 (49). LONDON E 312, from Nola. *CV*. pl. 56, 3. A, Nike; B, victor.

66 (49 *bis*). OXFORD, Beazley. *AJA.* 1947 pl. 53. Death of Orpheus: A, Thracian woman; B, Orpheus. See CB. ii, 74 no. 15.

67 (50). LENINGRAD 699 (St. 1674). *AJA*. 1947, 236 fig. 2 and pl. 51. A, satyr with donkey; B, Dionysos.

68 (51). LOUVRE G 376, from Vulci. *CV*. d pl. 36, 1 and 5. A, Dionysos; B, maenad.

69 (52). NAPLES 3385, from Nola. A, ph. So. x, i, 3. A, Eos; B, Kephalos.

70 (53). NAPLES. A, Zeus (standing to right, right arm extended, sceptre in left hand); B, woman with torches. B much restored.

71 (54). GOTHA 50. *AJA*. 1947, 240. Komos (A, youth playing the flute; B, man).

72. WIESBADEN. A, woman with lyre. B, man. [Shefton].

73 (55). LENINGRAD 700 (St. 1672). B, *VA*. 126; B, *AJA*. 1947, 239. A, satyr and maenad; B, maenad.

74 (56). MUNICH, Haniel. Langlotz *Sg Heyl* pl. 24. A, satyr and maenad; B, maenad.

75 (57). MOSCOW 601. *AJA*. 1947 pl. 54. A, satyr and maenad; B, satyr. [Peredolskaya].

76 (58). MOSCOW 1072. *Zhizn Muzeya* 1930, 27–28. A, satyr; B, satyr. [Loseva].

77 (59). ST. LOUIS, Washington University, 3271, from Capua. *AJA*. 1940, 208. A, man pursuing a boy; B, boy with lyre fleeing.

78. COLOGNE, Univ. A, youth with sword pursuing, B, a woman. On A, naked, wrap over left arm, to right, sword in right hand, scabbard in left; on B, running to right, looking round. Theseus and Aithra? [Bothmer].

79 (a). BALTIMORE, Walters Art Gallery, 48.55. A, D. K. Hill *Ancient Gk Dress* 16. A, youth pursuing, B, a woman. Now cleaned.

LOUTROPHOROI

80 (60). TÜBINGEN E 99, fr. Watzinger pl. 27. On the neck, mourning women.

81 (61). TÜBINGEN E 90, fr. Watzinger pl. 27; *Mus. J.* 23, 22; *Arte ant. e mod.* 4, 324 fig. 113 d. Fight.

82 (62). ATHENS, Vlasto, two frr. Prothesis; Valediction. [Vlasto].

83. ATHENS, Agora, P 25018, fr., from Athens. On the neck, three women.

84. ATHENS, Acr. Mus., fr., from Athens. (Male—bridegroom—mounting chariot, and women).

85. ATHENS, Acr. Mus., frr., from Athens. Wedding (with door). Below, rf. palmettes.

86. ATHENS, Acr. Mus., frr., from Athens. Wedding. Below, maeander and saltire-squares.

87. ATHENS, Acr. Mus., fr., from Athens. Wedding. Below, wreath.

88. ATHENS, Acr. Mus., fr., from Athens. Wedding (the mother touching the shoulder of the bride).

89. ATHENS, Acr. Mus., fr., from Athens. (Elbow of one in himation, hand and sleeve of woman holding up torch). May belong to the last.

90. ATHENS, Acr. Mus., fr., from Athens. (Woman seated, holding wool, and women).

91. ATHENS, Acr. Mus., fr., from Athens. (Upper part of woman's head to left).

92. ATHENS, Acr. Mus., fr., from Athens. (Middle of one in himation).

93. ATHENS, Acr. Mus., fr., from Athens. (Nike with torch, girl with long hair).

94. ATHENS, Acr. Mus., fr., from Athens. Procession (hymenaios) (two women, and a girl carrying a loutrophoros).

95. ATHENS, Acr. Mus., fr., from Athens. (Leg of a woman standing to right).

96. ATHENS, Acr. Mus., fr., from Athens. (Woman; two Erotes flying towards each other).

97. ATHENS, Acr. Mus., fr., from Athens. On the neck, three women.

98. ATHENS, Acr. Mus., fr., from Athens. On the neck, (woman with flower, woman with sash).

99. ATHENS, Acr. Mus., fr., from Athens. On the neck, (head and shoulders of woman to right).

100. ATHENS, Acr. Mus., fr., from Athens. On the neck, (feet of one standing to left).

HYDRIAI

101 (64). RHODES 12884, from Camiros. *Cl. Rh.* 4, 108–9; *CV.* pl. 5, 1. Woman seated, and two women.

102. BRISTOL H 4631. Two women seated, and a woman. [Shefton].

103 (65). CATANIA 706. Libertini pl. 78. Woman seated, and a woman.

104 (66). LONDON, Victoria and Albert Museum, 4816.58, from Nola. *AJA.* 1947 pl. 52, a; B.Ap. xxiii. 33. 2. Dionysos and maenad.

OINOCHOAI

(nos. 105–12, shape 2)

105 (68). PARIS MARKET (Minerva). Satyr.

106 (69). LOUVRE G 573. Artemis.

107 (70). FERRARA, T. 607, from Spina. Woman with oinochoe.

108. FERRARA (erratico B, 31.5.1958), from Spina. Satyr (with oinochoe, approaching a column-krater).

109 (71). FERRARA, T. 377, from Spina. Maenad.

110 (72). FERRARA, T. 733, from Spina. Man with stick.

111 (73). BOLOGNA 344, from Bologna. Tithonos.

112. FERRARA, T. 216 C VP, from Spina. Tithonos.

(no. 113, shape 5 A)

113 (74). FERRARA, T. 897, from Spina. Komast.

LEKYTHOI
(standard shape)

114 (76). CAB. MÉD. 489. Ph. Gir. 8076, whence Cook *Zeus* ii, 732 and Richer 380 fig. 220; ph. Gir. 29088, whence *Delt.* 1930–1, 79 and *Mnemosyne* 4th ser., 3 pl. 2, 5; *AJA.* 1947, 238; B.Ap. xxii. 81. Zeus; on the shoulder, woman fleeing, between flowers. Restored. See p. 1655.

115 (77). NEW YORK 41.162.19. *AJA.* 1924 pl. 9; *CV.* Gallatin pl. 16, 2, and pl. 17; Swindler pl. 10, a; *Bull. Metr.* 37, 57; detail, Richter *ARVS.* fig. 77; Richter *H.* 225, e and p. 88. Maenad; on the shoulder, satyr eating grapes, between flowers.

116. BARCELONA 581, from Ampurias. Woman running with phiale. On the shoulder, centaur, between flowers.

116 *bis*. LUCERNE MARKET (A.A.). Youth leaving home (youth in chlamys to right, right arm akimbo, spears in left hand, bald man in long chiton and himation to left, stick in left hand). See p. 1655.

117 (78). HEIDELBERG 172, fr. Kraiker pl. 31. Demeter.

118 (79). AGRIGENTO, from Agrigento. Woman spinning.

119 (80). PALERMO V 672, from Gela. *Bull. Comm. Sic.* 1864, ii, plate, whence Overbeck *KM.* pl. 12, 3; *CV.* pl. 20, 4 (misprinted V 674). Poseidon pursuing a woman. See p. 1655.

120 (81). SYRACUSE 24552, from Gela. *ML.* 17 pl. 55, 2. Woman running with helmet, shield, and spear. See *Antike Kunst* 4, 59.

121 (82). HARTFORD (Connecticut) 30.184 (ex Giudice). *AJA.* 1947 pl. 55. Maenad. Restored.

122 (83). NEW YORK 26.60.77. *Bull. Metr.* 23, 109 fig. 4; Richter and Hall pl. 89 and pl. 175, 85. Maenad.

123 (84). PALERMO V 673, from Gela. *CV.* pl. 20, 6; ph. R.I. 7322,whence Stella 352, right, and Zschietzschmann *H.R.* pl. 15, 1. Dionysos.

124 (85). MUNICH 2477 (J. 757), from Sicily. Woman with torches.

LEKANIS

125 (86). FERRARA, T. o, from Spina. *Arte ant. e mod.* 7 pll. 116–20. Gigantomachy. See p. 1655.

FRAGMENTS OF POTS

126 (88). ABINGDON, Robertson, fr., from Greece. (Male pursuing a woman). [Robertson].

127 (89). LENINGRAD inv. NB 6463 (ex Russian Archaeological Society), fr. (Warrior: the head remains, bearded, in a 'Thracian' helmet, to right). From a stamnos?

128. ISTANBUL A 33.2322, from Xanthos. (Satyrs and maenad).

129. LOUVRE C 11068, fr. (Youth with spear running to left, right arm extended).

130. LOUVRE C 11061, fr. (Lower part of a pillar, and legs of one in long chiton and himation standing to right).

131. ATHENS, Agora, P 25357, fr., from Athens. (Male face).

CUPS

132. ATHENS, fr., from Brauron. *Praktika* 1949, 87 fig. 16 a, 2 (above), and fig. 16 b, below, left. I, (white ground), (wing). A, rf., (woman). On I, HERM[O]NA+ϟ. There was doubtless the verb ἔγραψεν.

133 (90). BRYN MAWR P 209, fr. I, *AJA.* 1916, 340 no. 12; I, *VA.* 127. I, woman fleeing to man. A, (woman, foot).

134 (91). ANCONA, fr., from Castelbellino. I, (back of the left-hand figure, to right). A, (on the right, one in long chiton standing to right, one in long chiton and himation standing to right, with sceptre—king?—then two women running to left); B, (on the left, woman running to left, looking round, woman running).

135 (92). ANCONA, three frr., from Castelbellino. I, (on the right, feet of one in a himation seated to left). A, (on the right, man seated, and boys).

136 (93). VIENNA, Univ., 503. 50, fr., from Orvieto. *CV.* pl. 21, 14. A, (youth).

137 (94). ADRIA B 785, fr., from Adria. *CV.* pl. 29, 4. A, (part of a youthful head and hand).

138 (95). ADRIA B 34, fr., from Adria. *CV.* pl. 29, 3. I, boy seated and male with stick.

139. ADRIA B 451 *bis*, B 1069, B 296, and B 296 *bis*, frr., from Adria. *CV.* pl. 29, 1–2. I, male; A–B, males seated. [Riccioni].

140 (96). TÜBINGEN E 43, fr. I, Watzinger pl. 21. I, youth. A, (feet).

141. LOUVRE C 11944, fr. A, komos (man with skyphos, youth playing the flute, youth with flute-case and stick).

142 (97). GOETTINGEN H 74, fr. A, (woman and man).

143 (98). HEIDELBERG 173, fr. Kraiker pl. 25. A, (man seated, hand).

144. INNSBRUCK ii. 12. 66, fr. A, (youth, man).

145. INNSBRUCK ii. 12. 67, fr. A, (arm, then head of male).

146 (99). DRESDEN, fr. A, (on the right, man leaning on his stick to left, then sandals hanging).

147. MAPLEWOOD, Noble. I, boy seated; A, man seated, youth leaning on his stick, youth seated; the man holds a fruit and a stick; B, man seated, youth leaning on his stick, boy standing; the man holds a stick and looks round. See p. 1655, foot.

148. Louvre C 11945, fr. I, youth (leaning on his stick to left, holding out a lyre); A, (on the left, male leaning on his stick to right, then a chair-leg). A Louvre fragment with knees and hand of one seated to right should belong.

149. Louvre C 11946, fr. A, (on the left, male to right).

150. Louvre C 11947, fr. A, (on the right, head of man seated to left).

151. Louvre C 11948, fr. I, (maeander). A, (male leaning on his stick to right, boy moving to right, looking round, holding a lyre which is also held by a third person, whose hand remains).

152. Louvre C 11949, fr. A, (youth standing to right, elbow of one seated to right).

153. Louvre C 11950, fr. A, (sandals hanging, head, bare shoulder, and raised hand, of youth to left).

154. Louvre C 11951, fr. A, (hand with stick, youth, youth seated). See the next two.

155. Louvre C 11952, fr. A, (head and shoulder of man seated to right). Might belong to Louvre C 11951 (no. 154).

156. Louvre C 11953, fr. A, (man seated to right). Might belong to Louvre C 11951 (no. 154).

157. Louvre C 11954, fr. A, (youth leaning, to right).

158 (101). Orvieto, Faina, 43, from Orvieto A, *AJA.* 1947, pl. 57, 2. I, (feet of male). A, men and boy; B, youth, and youth or man, and boy).

159. Louvre C 10955. I, centaur; A–B, centauromachy.

160. Istanbul A 33. 2350, frr., from Xanthos. I, maenad; A–B, satyrs and maenads.

161 (100). Louvre G 268. I, siren; A–B, sirens. Much restored. See p. 1655.

(no. 162, decorated inside only)

162. Oxford, Beazley, fr. I, satyr (to right, playing the flute: head and shoulders remain).

CUP-SKYPHOS OR STEMLESS CUP

163. Barcelona 4233–6, fr., from Ampurias. A, unexplained subject: a woman attacking another at the altar of Hera, who sits behind it. [Shefton].

MANNER OF HERMONAX

(i)

THE PAINTER OF BRUSSELS R 284

ARV.[1] 323, i.

A group of three weaklings by one hand; they seem to lead on to the Loeb Painter (p. 1004).

NECK-AMPHORAE

(*Nolan amphorae, with triple handles*)

1 (1). BRUSSELS R 284. *El.* 3 pl. 22, whence (part of A) Overbeck *KM.* pl. 12, 4; *CV* d pl. 7, 2. A, Poseidon pursuing a woman; B, youth.

2 (2). DRESDEN 309. A, Nike (flying to right with phiale and oinochoe); B, youth.

3 (3). DRESDEN 310. Youth leaving home: A, youth (petasos, wrap, standing frontal, head to right, spears in right hand); B, woman (standing to left).

(ii)

VARIOUS

ARV.[1] 323-4, ii.

The following, in the tradition of the Berlin Painter, is either by Hermonax or near him:

NECK-AMPHORA

(*small, with ridged handles*)

(3). BERLIN MARKET (Graupe: ex Prinz Albrecht). *VDK.* pl. 85, 912. A, Apollo and Artemis. B, youth attacking with sword. Restored. For B compare the Nolan in Cologne (p. 488 no. 78).

Near Hermonax, each in its way:

STAMNOS

1. MANNHEIM 59, from Petrignano near Castiglione del Lago. *CV.* pll. 27-28, pl. 30, 3, and p. 40. Warrior leaving home.

HYDRIA

2 (l 63). BRUSSELS A 3098, from Capua. *Coll. Bougard* pl. 3, 106; *CV.* pl. 15, 1 and pl. 16, 2; detail, White *P.* pl. 4, b. Mistress and maids.

FRAGMENTS

3 (l 87). ATHENS Acr. 692, fr., from Athens. Langlotz pl. 53. (Athena).

4. VIENNA, Univ., 503.21, fr., from Orvieto. *CV.* pl. 21, 12. (Youth).

A fragment is near Hermonax and his follower the Painter of the Birth of Athena:

ATHENS, Agora, P 25105, fr., from Athens. (Athena). [Talcott]. From a hydria?

A vase recalls Hermonax:

LEKYTHOS
(*standard shape*)

(7). ATHENS 1632 (CC. 1194), from Eretria. *CV.* pl. 17, 1 and 3; ph. A.I. NM 3048. Youth setting out.

For other vases described in *ARV.*[1] 323 under 'ii', see pp. 216–17.

For the oinochoe Florence and Buschor, no. 67 in *ARV.*[1] 321, see p. 874 no. 6.

A vase attributed to Hermonax in *ARV.*[1] (p. 321 no. 75) is at best a weak imitation:

OINOCHOE
(*shape 5A*)

ALTENBURG 297, from Nola. *Zeitschrift für Kunst* 1950, 182 fig. 152; Bielefeld *G.E.T.A.* pl. 7, 2; *CV.* pl. 63 and pl. 64, 1–3; R.I. ix. 96. Komos.

===

THE PAINTER OF THE BIRTH OF ATHENA
Att. V. 304–5 and 476. *ARV.*[1] 324 and 958.

Follower of Hermonax. Named from the subject of no. 1.

PELIKAI

1 (1). LONDON E 410, from Vulci. Gerhard pl. 3–4, whence *El.* 1 pll. 64–65 and *WV.* 8 pl. 11, 9; A, A. H. Smith *Parthenon* 7; A, Cook *Zeus* iii pl. 56; part of A, *Jb.* 72, 11; A, ph. Ma. 3206. Birth of Athena.

2 (2). VILLA GIULIA 20846, from Cervetri. *ML.* 42 pl. 5 and pp. 291–2 figs. 47 a–b. A, Poseidon and Amymone. B, Zeus pursuing a woman.

3 (3). VILLA GIULIA 20847, from Cervetri. *St. etr.* 1 pl. 37, a–b; *ML.* 42, 293–4. A, Poseidon and Amymone. B, Zeus pursuing a woman. Replica of the last. The chief figures on B are inscribed Poseidon and Amymone, but by mistake: see CB. ii, 90, top (where the numbers of this and the last are interchanged and the reference to *St. etr.* is given incorrectly).

4. SWISS PRIVATE. *Ars Ant. Aukt. II* pl. 63. Dionysos with satyrs and maenads. One satyr takes hold of Dionysos by the shoulder. Very large.

5. LOUVRE, frr. Satyrs and maenads. One of the figures in chiton and himation may be Dionysos. Very large.

STAMNOI

6 (4). VILLA GIULIA 20844–5, from Cervetri. A, *St. etr.* 1 pl. 37, c; *ML.* 42, 291–2 figs. 46 a–b and pl. 4. A, Zeus pursuing a woman; B, the like.

7 (5). VILLA GIULIA, frr., from Cervetri. (Pursuit). As the last.

8. LUCERNE, Kofler. A, Zeus pursuing a woman; B, three women running (the middle one holding torches).

9 (6). MUNICH, and ERLANGEN 567, frr. Maenads.

10 (7). LENINGRAD (St. 1443 a). A, woman with woman and man; B, women running.

FRAGMENTS OF A POT

11 (8). FLORENCE 13 B 1, frr. Part, *Boll. d'Arte* 1928, 217–18, whence *Anz.* 1929, 74; part, *CV.* pl. 13, B 1. Prothesis of a woman. *CV.* pl. 19 B 28 joins pl. 13 B 4 below. Two fragments, Naples, Astarita, 228 and 226, as Astarita has seen, probably belong.

THE PAINTER OF MUNICH 2413

These two vases have a good deal in common with Hermonax, but there are also differences, and I now follow Pallottino in detaching them from the list of works by Hermonax.

STAMNOI

1. MUNICH 2413 (J. 345), from Vulci. *Mon.* 1 pll. 10–11, whence Inghirami pll. 73–74, *El.* 1 pl. 84, and 3 pl. 11, (A) *Jb.* 26, 167; FR. pl. 137 and iii, 95, whence (Erotes) *Jb.* 30, 190, (A) Cook *Zeus* iii pl. 23, (B) *Jb.* 56, 42, (A) Lippold *A.G.* pl. 3, 14, (A) Stella 144, above; side, Jacobsthal *O.* pl. 100; A, Buschor *G. Vasen* 182; B, Rumpf *MZ.* pl. 30, 5; the Erotes, Greifenhagen *Eroten* 28–31; side, Simon *G.A.* 73. A, birth of Erichthonios. B, Zeus and Nike. At each handle, floral with two Erotes. Neck and mouth of the vase are modern. Slightly restored. For the Erotes compare a loutrophoros in the Acropolis Museum (p. 489 no. 96).

2. HEIDELBERG 169, fr., from near Florence. Kraiker pl. 31. (Woman).

Fragments may perhaps be compared:

OINOCHOE

ATHENS, Agora, P 11810, three frr., from Athens. *Hesp.* 8, 268–9; Pickard-Cambridge *D.F.A.* fig. 25. Actors dressing and boy holding a tragic mask. See Talcott in *Hesp.* 8, 267–73 and Webster *G.T.P.* 38.

CHAPTER 31

OTHER EARLY CLASSIC PAINTERS
OF LARGE POTS

THE OREITHYIA PAINTER

Att. V. 292–3. *V.Pol.* 19–20. *ARV.*[1] 324–6.

Nos. 1, 2, and 5 had already been connected with one another by Jahn (*Beschr.* clxxxiv note 1223).

POINTED AMPHORAE

1 (1). BERLIN 2165, from Vulci. *Nouv. annales* 1839 pl. H; Gerhard *EKV.* pll. 26–29, whence FR. ii, Beil. at p. 186 figs. 66–67; details, ibid. Beil. at p. 187 figs. 68–69. Boreas and Oreithyia. [Jahn].

2 (2). MUNICH 2345 (J. 376), from Vulci. *Mon. nouv. ann.* 1839 pll. 22–23; Lau pl. 24, 1; FR. pll. 94–95 (slightly restored) and ii, 191–2; *CV.* pll. 205–8. Boreas and Oreithyia. [Jahn]. See p. 1656.

STAMNOI

3 (3). EDINBURGH 81.44.24. *Mus. J.* 23, 70–73; B.Ap. xxii. 65. A, a youth pursuing a woman. B, warrior leaving home. See p. 1656.

4 (4). PHILADELPHIA 48.30.3 (ex Hegeman). *Mus. J.* 23, 67–69. A, warrior leaving home. B, king and two women. [Dohan]. Much restored.

BELL-KRATER
(with lugs)

5 (5). PALERMO V 779, from Agrigento. Politi *Cinque vasi di premio* pll. 7–8, whence (A) *El.* 3 pl. 62, (A) Overbeck *KM.* pl. 15, 30, (B) Raoul-Rochette *Pomp.* 5, (A) Cook *Zeus* i pl. 18; *CV.* pll. 35–36 and pl. 37, 1–3. A, Triptolemos. B, Eos and Thetis appealing to Zeus. [Jahn].

BELL-KRATER OR CALYX-KRATER

6. MUNICH inv. 8717, fr. *Mü. Jb.* 1955, 262; *Anz.* 1957, 390. (Thracian woman).

CALYX-KRATER

7. AGRIGENTO, from Agrigento. Politi *Due parole* pl. 1 and frontispiece 2. A, Dionysos; B, satyr.

HYDRIAI
(the picture on the body)

8 (6) WARSAW 142288 (ex Czartoryski 38). De Witte pl. 6; *V.Pol.* pl. 14, 1; *CV.* pl. 20, 2. Nike.

9 (7). MUNICH 2430 (J. 351), from Vulci. Gerhard pl. 82. Nike (or Iris).

10 (8). LONDON E 176, from Vulci. *ML.* 9, 22; *CV.* pl. 73, 4; ph. Ma. 3153, left. Herakles and Nessos.

11 (9). TÜBINGEN E 102, fr. Watzinger pl. 27. (God or king).

LEKYTHOI
(*standard shape*)

12. GELA 26, from Gela. *NSc.* 1956, 332–3. Zeus and Ganymede (with Eros).

13. GELA 25, fr., from Gela. Part, *NSc.* 1956, 331. (Woman: there may have been another figure, for instance a deity whom she is serving with wine).

ALABASTRON

14 (a 2). OXFORD 1934.328, fr., from Attica. (Woman holding a garment).

Probably also
(*ARV.*¹ 325–6.)

FRAGMENT, PROBABLY OF A HYDRIA

1 (1). BOWDOIN 27.18, fr. Zeus and Ganymede.

FRAGMENT OF A POT

2 (3). ERLANGEN 367, fr. (Man in long chiton and himation, and arm of woman).

Near the painter, and perhaps his, the

LEKYTHOS
(*standard shape*)

NEW YORK 20.197. Nereid. See below.

Small fragments might be by the Oreithyia Painter:

CALYX-KRATER

LEIPSIC T 688 and T 689, two frr. (Part of the head of Dionysos).

Rather like the lekythos New York 20.197 (see above), but not by the same hand, the
LEKYTHOS
(*standard shape*)

ATHENS 12891 (N. 1032), from Eretria. Ph. A.I. NM 3035. Woman running with thyrsus and dolphin.

THE CONCA PAINTER

BELL-KRATER

VILLA GIULIA 11688, frr., from Conca. *AJA*. 1953 pll. 45–48 (pl. 47 fig. 5 and pl. 46, γ are upside down). Herakles on the pyre. For the subject, *EVP*. 103–4 and Clairmont in *AJA*. 1953, 85–89.

Fragments may be by the same hand:

CALYX-KRATER

ATHENS Acr. 737, two frr., from Athens. Langlotz pl. 62. (Male running, woman running.)

THE DEEPDENE PAINTER

VA. 194–5. *Att. V*. 293–6 and 476. *V.Pol*. 30–31. *ARV*.[1] 326–8 and 958.

Named after no. 28, which was once in Deepdene.

No. 17 bears the signature of the potter Oreibelos, otherwise unknown.

STAMNOI

1 (1). NEW YORK 17.230.37, from Rome. *AJA*. 1923, 279–81; side, Jacobsthal O. pl. 97, a; Richter and Hall pll. 85–86 and pl. 173, 82, whence Stella 70–71. Danae and Perseus. See CB. ii, 12; and below, p. 1656.

2 (2). NEW YORK 18.74.1, from Capua. A, *Bull. Metr*. 14, 9; A, Richter and Milne fig. 65; Richter and Hall pl. 87 and pl. 173, 83. A, Eos and Kephalos. B, youth with spear, and women. For the provenience, *AJA*. 1945, 157. See p. 1656.

3 (4). WÜRZBURG 519, from Vulci. Gerhard pl. 182; side, Jacobsthal O. pl. 97, b; Langlotz pl. 188; B.Ap. xxii. 34. A, Peleus and Thetis; B, Nereid fleeing to Nereus and Doris. B is repeated in Gerhard pll. 146–7, the last three figures—tacked on by error to a stamnos in Trieste (p. 217 no. 2).

4 (11). LOUVRE G 189. *CV*. pl. 20, 8 and pl. 21, 2. A, youth pursuing a woman (Peleus and Thetis?). B, three women. Much restored.

5 (5). CARLSRUHE 211 (B 1904), from Capua. Welter pl. 13 and pl. 12, 2; *CV*. pl. 21. A, Boreas and Oreithyia. B, Eos and Kephalos. For the provenience see *AJA*. 1945, 157.

6 (14). LOUVRE G 188 *bis*, from Nola. *CV*. pl. 22, 3. A, Zeus and Athena. B, (woman). Now cleaned. The reverse given in *CV*. pl. 22, 5 is alien. Seven Louvre fragments belong to our vase, and one of them has the shoulder of the left-hand figure on B, a woman standing to right.

7 (7). COPENHAGEN inv. 3612. *CV*. pl. 150, 1; side, *Marb. Jb*. 15, 236 fig. 175. A, Triptolemos and Demeter; B, worthies of Eleusis (two men with sceptres, and a woman). See no. 11.

8 (6). BRUSSELS A 131, from Nola. Raoul-Rochette pl. 44 b; *CV.* pl. 7, 3. A, Dionysos and maenad; B, Boreas and Oreithyia.

9 (10). BERLIN 4030. A, Dionysos and maenad. B, three women (maenads?).

10 (15). WARSAW 142351 (ex Czartoryski 44), from Capua. Minervini *Barone* pl. 7; de Witte pll. 15–16, whence Frickenhaus *Len.* pl. 2, 14, *Annuario* 4–5, 133, *A.M.* 53, 81, (A) Rumpf *Rel.* fig. 16; *CV.* pl. 27. Feast of Dionysos (Lenaia): A, maenads at the image; B, maenads.

11 (8). NEW YORK 41.162.20. B, Carroll *Coll. Clarke* pl., no. 627; *CV.* Gallatin pl. 14; A, Richter *H.* 225, h; B, Ghali-Kahil *H.* pl. 69. A, arming (of Achilles?). B, Menelaos and Helen. Bothmer noted that this and no. 7, the Copenhagen stamnos, were called pendants by Fröhner in *Cat. d'une coll. d'antiquités, Vente 23–26 mars 1868* [Jérôme Bonaparte] 33 nos. 62 and 63. Bothmer presumes that the two vases were found together.

12 (3). FLORENCE V., from Chiusi. A, arming (youth putting on his greaves, old man, and woman); B, warrior leaving home (warrior, old man, and woman). See p. 1656.

13. LOUVRE C 11117, fr. (four joining). A, (head of male in Thracian cap standing to right, head of male in Thracian cap, with spears, standing to left, forehead and nose, to right, of male with sceptre).

14 (9). BRUSSELS A 3093, from Capua. *Coll. Bougard* pl. 3, 98; *CV.* d pl. 13, 1 and pl. 14, 5. A, citharode. B, men and woman.

15 (13). VILLA GIULIA 50455. Side, Jacobsthal *O.* pl. 101, c. A, man with phiale, and two women; B, three women (one playing the flute, another with krotala).

16 (12). CAMBRIDGE 2.1935. A, three women; B, three women. See p. 1656.

VOLUTE-KRATER

17 (16). ATHENS Acr. 762, fr., from Athens. Hoppin ii, 267; Langlotz pl. 62 and p. 72. (Athena and another). On the neck, OREIBELOS : EΓOIESEN HIEROSTESAΘE[NAIAS]. Small.

COLUMN-KRATERS

(nos. 18–22, the pictures framed)

18. LOUVRE G 359. *CV.* d pl. 26, 5 and 8. A, warrior leaving home. B, male, boy, and youth. Now cleaned. Two Louvre fragments belong, adding parts of B. In *ARV.*[1] Louvre G 346 was substituted for Louvre G 359 in error: see p. 515 no. 3.

19 (17). LONDON E 474, from Agrigento. Detail of A, Schlesinger *Aulos* pl. 8. A, komos. B, three youths.

20 (20). MADRID inv. 32656. *CV.* pl. 15, 1. A, Dionysos with satyr and maenads. B, three youths.

21 (21). Once NAPLES, Hamilton. Tischbein 4 pl. 30, whence *El.* 4 pl. 20 and Sudhoff i, 55, whence Richter and Milne 21. A, women washing. Tischbein 4 pl. 48 (whence Inghirami pl. 383) may be the reverse of this: youth with old man and man. See p. 1656.

22 (18). LENINGRAD, fr. A, komos (woman moving to right, looking back, naked youth moving to right pursuing a woman moving to right, looking back; there must have been a youth on the left corresponding to the youth preserved).

(no. 22 bis, not known whether the pictures framed)

22 *bis.* REGGIO, fr., from Locri. (Head of youth to left).

(nos. 23–26, the pictures not framed)

23 (22). MUNICH 2380 (J. 752), from Sicily. Komos: A, youth and flute-girl; B, youth.

24 (23). FERRARA, T. 732, from Spina. A, youth seated, and youth. B, komast.

25. FERRARA, T. 71 B VP, from Spina. A, youth and girl; B, youth.

26 (24). VILLA GIULIA 3573, from Falerii. *CV.* pl. 19, 4–5. A, Nike running, holding a helmet. B, komast.

CALYX-KRATER

27. SALONICA inv. 34.277, from Olynthos. Robinson *Olynthus 13* pll. 33–35. A, youth with spears (Theseus?) pursuing a woman. B, Nike and warrior. [Robinson]. Bothmer notes (*A.J.Phil.* 1953, 216–17) that the pieces are put together wrongly, and that the subjects are as above.

AMPHORA
(type A, the pictures not framed)

28 (25). LOS ANGELES A. 5933. 50. 27 (ex Marshall Brooks). Tischbein 2 pll. 22–23; Tillyard pl. 8, 84; *Cat. Sotheby 14 May 1946* pl. 2. A, Herakles and Athena. B, Dionysos and maenad.

NECK-AMPHORAE
(Nolan amphorae, with triple handles)

29 (26). SYRACUSE 21967, from Gela. A, *ML.* 17 pl. 10, 1; *CV.* pl. 8, 2. A, Theseus and Procrustes. B, youth.

30 (27). DRESDEN 317. A, woman with torches. B, youth.

PELIKAI

31 (28). NAPLES 3030, from Capua. A, Sudhoff i, 45; A, ph. So. 11009, v, 5. A, women washing; B, youth and woman.

32 (29). WARSAW 142310 (ex Czartoryski 67), from Nola. *V.Pol.* pl. 19, 1–2; *CV.* pl. 31, 4. A, girl dancing and woman playing the flute; B, the like.

33 (30). NAPLES 3034, from Nola. A, ph. So. 11009, v, 7. A, youth and seated woman. B, man and boy.

34 (32). BRUSSELS R 250. *CV*. pl. 19, 3. A, Dionysos and maenad; B, two maenads.

35 (31). LONDON E 377, from Nola. Panofka *Pourt*. pl. 9, 2. A, satyr putting on greaves, and maenad; B, Dionysos and maenad.

LOUTROPHOROS

36. ATHENS, Acr. Mus. fr., from Athens. On the neck, two women.

HYDRIAI

(with picture on the body)

37 (33). NEW YORK 56.171.54 (ex Oppenheimer and Hearst). *Bull. Metr.* March 1957, 175, 2. Mistress and maid.

38. ASHEVILLE (N.C.), Beecher. Girl dancing and woman playing the flute. Same composition as on A of Warsaw 142310 (no. 32), but the girl wears a chitoniskos. [Bothmer].

ALABASTRON

39 (34). ATHENS, Vlasto, from Spata. Woman with mirror; woman with alabastron.

FRAGMENT OF A POT

40 (35). ATHENS Acr. 1006, fr., from Athens. (Woman). From a small stamnos or neck-amphora?

NEAR THE DEEPDENE PAINTER

ARV.[1] 328.

PYXIS

(type A)

(2). CAMBRIDGE 1.22, from Athens. *CV*. pl. 39, 1; part, ph. A.I. varia 293, 1. Mistresses and maid; two maids.

THE PAINTER OF THE YALE OINOCHOE

VA. 61–62. *Att. V*. 287–8. *V.Pol*. 31. *ARV*.[1] 328–30. Called after no. 25.

STAMNOI

1 (1). OXFORD 292. Gardner pll. 16–17 and p. 27; *CV*. pl. 27, 1–2; detail, Jacobsthal *O*. pl. 98, b. A, Demeter and three women; B, Persephone, two women, and a man. See p. 1656.

2 (5). WARSAW 142353 (ex Czartoryski 51), from Nola. De Witte pll. 18–19; palmettes, *V.Pol*. pl. 28, 4; *CV*. pl. 28. A, king (or god) at altar, with women and Nike. B, youth with spear (Theseus?) pursuing a woman.

3 (6). NAPLES 3095, from Nola. A, ph. So. x, iv, 3. A, women (or goddesses) at altar. B, king and two women. See p. 1656.

4 (2). LONDON E 446, from Capua. CV. pl. 22, 1. A, youth with sword pursuing a woman (Theseus and Aithra?). B, man and women at altar.

5 (3). CREFELD. B, ph. R.I. 40.568. A, youth with spear (Theseus?) pursuing a woman; B, a youth pursuing a woman.

6 (9). BRUSSELS R 311, from Nola. CV. pl. 7, 1. A, warriors setting out. B, young warrior pursuing a woman. Restored.

7 (7). COPENHAGEN 540, from Nola. Welcker AD. 3 pl. 33, 1–2; AZ. 1866 pl. 206, 3–4; cleaned, CV. pl. 150, 2; side, Jacobsthal O. pl. 98, a. A, Phineus and the Boreads? B, Nike with youth and man. [Jacobsthal].

8 (8). FRANKFORT, Museum V.F., 58 (ex Haeberlin), from Capua. A, Anz. 1910, 460. A, citharode. B, youth and women.

COLUMN-KRATER
(with framed pictures)

9 (9). BARI 1396. A, Theseus and the bull. B, komos.

BELL-KRATERS
(nos. 10–11, with lugs)

10 (10). LOUVRE G 368. CV. d pl. 8 figs. 2–3 and pl. 11 fig. 2; A, Mél. d'arch. 1950 pl. 5, 4; A, Recueil Dugas pl. 33, 2; A, ph. Al. 23683. A, Triptolemos and Demeter; B, Demeter and Persephone. Restored.

11 (11). LENINGRAD 777 (St. 1786). A, youth with sword pursuing a woman (Theseus and Aithra?); B, youth with spear (Theseus?) pursuing a woman.

(no. 12, not known if lugs or handles)

12 (a). LEIPSIC T 661 and BRYN MAWR, fr. (see JHS. 51, 56 no. 13). Selene.

CALYX-KRATER

13 (12). FLORENCE 4013, from Chiusi. CV. pl. 36, 3 and pl. 37, 1–2. A, goddess and woman (Hera and Hebe?). B, woman running. Small.

NECK-AMPHORA
(with twisted handles)

14 (13). NEW YORK 41.162.155, from Apulia. A, Canessa Coll. (1919) no. 71; A, AJA. 1924, 281; CV. Gallatin pl. 18, 2 and 4. A, youth with sword pursuing a woman (Theseus and Aithra?). B, youth, and boy with lyre. See p. 1656.

LOUTROPHOROI

15 (14). AMSTERDAM inv. 2310, fr. B, valediction.

16. ATHENS, Acr. Mus., fr., from Athens. On the neck, (women).

17. ATHENS, Acr. Mus., fr., from Athens. On the neck, (two women).

PELIKE

18 (15). MARSEILLES 1631. A, woman seated, and woman; B, woman.

HYDRIAI

(no. 19, the picture on the shoulder)

19 (16). LOUVRE G 428. *Mon.* 1 pl. 6; *CV.* d pl. 51, 1 and 4–6. Peleus and Thetis.

(nos. 20–24, the picture on the body)

20 (17). LONDON E 178. *CV.* pl. 81, 3; ph. Ma. 3154. Judgement of Paris.

21 (18). SAN SIMEON, State Monument, 9936. *Cat. Sotheby 22–23 May 1919* pl. 10, left. Women gathering fruit.

22 (19). HARVARD 60.340 (ex Robinson), from Vari? *CV.* Robinson ii pll. 34 and 34 a. Woman seated, and woman, with herons.

23 (20). LONDON 83.11–24.26. *CV.* pl. 90, 7. Woman seated, with heron, and maid.

24 (21). COPENHAGEN inv. 5, from Capua? *CV.* pl. 154, 1; *Festskrift Poulsen* 86 fig. 11. Woman spinning, and two women seated holding baskets.

OINOCHOE

(shape 5A)

25 (22). YALE 143, from Athens. *VA.* 61; Baur 97 and pl. 10. Poseidon and Theseus.

Probably also

FRAGMENT

(of a stamnos or volute-krater)

TARANTO, fr., from Locri. (Head and breast of a woman running to right, looking round, then the top of a sceptre).

MANNER OF THE PAINTER OF THE YALE OINOCHOE

DISH

(calathoid, but very shallow, compare Athens 1616 by the Painter of London E 489, p. 549 no. 58)

1. ATHENS, Agora, P 18414 and (joining) P 18007, frr., from Athens. Boreas and Oreithyia; Peleus and Thetis.

STAMNOS

2. WARSAW 142359 (ex Czartoryski 49). A, *V.Pol.* pl. 21, 1; *CV.* pl. 29, 1. A, Boreas and Oreithyia. B, arrival of youth. Imitation. The florals exactly as in Oxford 292 (p. 501 no. 1).

THE AEGISTHUS PAINTER

AJA. 1916, 147. *VA*. 193. *Att. V*. 290–2. *V.Pol*. 21 and 80. *ARV*.[1] 330–3 and 958. Peters *Pan*. 80–81. *AJA*. 1943, 450. *ABV*. 407.

His style seems derived from the later style of the Copenhagen Painter (p. 256).

CALYX-KRATERS

1 (1). LOUVRE G 164. *Mon*. 1856 pl. 11, whence (A) Overbeck *KM*. pl. 23, 6; Pottier pl. 125; *CV*. pll. 10–11; A, FR. pl. 164, whence Stella 167; A, ph. Gir. 25510, whence Swindler figs. 328–9 and Pfeiff *Apollon* pl. 15; A, ph. Al. 23679, whence Schaal *Rf*. fig. 40, Buschor G. *Vasen* 181, *Jb. Berl. Mus*. N.S. 1, 26, *E.A.A*. iii, 249. A, Apollo and Tityos. B, old man, and woman, running. Restored. See p. 1657.

2. REGGIO, three frr., from Locri. On one, woman running to left, looking round, holding one end of her himation; columns, with architrave. On the second, head of an old man to left; abacus, architrave. On the third (two joining), part of the floral above the picture. Compare no. 7.

2 *bis*. REGGIO (three frr.) and TARANTO (one), from Locri. On one fragment, a male in a himation (head missing) seated on a block to right, staff in left hand. On a second fragment, pursuit: male arm extended to right, with a cloak over it, then the middle of a woman in a chiton, with kolpos, and a cloak, and the fingers of her right hand. A fragment in Taranto is by the Aegisthus Painter, and I take it to belong to this vase, giving the head, shoulders, breast, of the pursuing youth, with part of the cloak over his left arm. I think that his legs, striding to right, with the lower edge of his cloak, are given by a third fragment in Reggio.

2 *ter*. OXFORD, Beazley, fr. (On the right, head of boy in himation standing to left).

3 (2). LONDON E 509.6, fr., from Camiros. Male, and boy with lyre.

4 (3). ADRIA B 160, fr., from Adria. *CV*. pl. 27, 1. (Feet of male).

5 (4). VIENNA 1102. *AZ*. 1877 pl. 14; Lücken pll. 108–9; Licht ii, 124 and i, 89. A, man and boy; B, youth.

6 (5). BOLOGNA 288, from Bologna. Zannoni pl. 34, 1–3; *CV*. pl. 71, above. A, two youths at altar; B, youth and woman at altar.

CALYX-KRATER?

7. COLUMBIA (Missouri), Univ. of Missouri, fr. (Woman running to left, arms extended, then forearms of a similar figure; Doric columns).

COLUMN-KRATERS

(*nos. 8–9, the pictures framed*)

8 (6). BOLOGNA 230, from Bologna. Zannoni pl. 79, 1–3, whence (A) FR. ii, 78, (A) *Jb*. 29, 32, (B) Vorberg *Gloss*. 38; *Dedalo* 9, 454–60; *CV*. pll. 37–38; detail of A, Stella 676; A, *Mostra* pl. 43. A, death of Aegisthus. B, komos (youths and women).

9 (7, +). ADRIA B 208, B 575, B 297, and B 114, three frr., from Adria. Part of one fr., Micali *Mon. ined.* pl. 46, 10; all, *CV.* pl. 31, 1–4. Komos. B 575 was associated with B 208 in *ARV.*[1] 958. B 297 and B 114 were added by Miss Riccioni: uncertain if from the same side of the vase as the others. The remains on the right of pl. 31, 1 are the shoulder of a komast.

9 *bis.* DURHAM (N.C.), Ruestow, fr. *Hesp. Art Bull.* 12, 7 no. 104. B, komos? (on the left, the upper half of a youth moving to right, looking round).

(*nos. 10–12, not known if the pictures framed*)

10. GELA, fr., from Gibil-Gabib. (Eyebrow to upper lip of a man facing right). A fragment might belong (on the left, foot of one moving to right, toes of one standing to left): if so, the pictures framed.

11. GELA (ILA cassetta 8, part), fr., from Gela. Symposion (middle of a male reclining to left, right arm extended).

12 (29). ETON, six frr., from Al Mina. Warrior leaving home.

(*nos. 12 bis–15, the pictures not framed*)

12 *bis.* FERRARA, T. 42 D VP, from Spina. A, Eos and Tithonos. B, komast.

12 *ter.* REGGIO 10603, fr., from Locri. A, komast (youth with kantharos and lyre). [Procopio]. It occurs to me now that another Reggio fragment might belong (to B?) (komast; head, to left, raised, and shoulders of a man moving to left, wrap, dotted hand-band; the face missing).

13 (8). VIENNA, Univ., 551 a. *CV.* pll. 14–15. A, symposion (man reclining, and naked girl); B, komast.

14 (9). NAPLES, from Cumae. A, *ML.* 22 pl. 84, 4. A, man and youth. B, youth with cup.

15 (10). ADRIA s.n. 3, fr., from Adria. A, *CV.* pl. 31, 9. A, youth and boy. B, (crown of a head).

STAMNOI

16 (11). VATICAN, from Vulci. *Mus. Greg.* 2 pl. 19, 1. A, man reclining, and Nike serving him with wine. B, man and woman; man and youth.

17 (13). VILLA GIULIA (ex Castellani). A, symposion; B, the like.

18 (12). FLORENCE 3994. *CV.* pl. 48, 1 and pl. 49, 3–4. A, Nike and two boys. B, three women. See p. 509 and p. 1657.

19 (14). VIENNA, Univ., 631 c and part of 631 d, frr. Part, *CV.* pl. 16, 1 and 3 and p. 26. (B?), two women fleeing to an old man. The two fragments pl. 16, 3 are wrongly detached from 631 c (pl. 16, 1) and put with fragments of other vases (see p. 620 no. 29). According to my note pl. 16, 3, left, joins pl. 16, 1. Pl. 16, 3, right, belongs, and probably gives part of a woman (1) to the left of the first (2), with a little of 2's heel and skirt. Other fragments, not reproduced, have the toes of a foot to left, parts of the maeander, and the mouth of the vase.

PELIKAI

20 (15). LONDON E 375, from Vulci. *El.* 1 pl. 50; side, Jacobsthal *O.* pl. 102, a. A, Zeus pursuing a woman. B, youth and woman.

20 *bis.* REGGIO, fr., from Locri. A, (knees of one seated to right?; then a youth in a himation standing to left, stick in left hand; above, a little of the floral border).

21 (16). CAMBRIDGE 37.26. *CV.* ii RS. pl. 12, 2. A, man pursuing a boy; B, man and boy.

22. ADRIA B 249, fr., from Adria. *CV.* pl. 30, 2 (the number misprinted B 1171). A, woman; B, girl. [Riccioni].

NECK-AMPHORAE

(no. 23, with double handles)

23 (a ii 2). MYKONOS, from Rheneia (originally from Delos). Dugas *Délos xxi* pl. 21, 56. A, woman running with helmet and shield. B, male.

(no. 24, broad, with convex handles)

24 (17). NAPLES 3033. A, ph. So. x, i, 7. A, youth and boy; B, youth.

PANATHENAIC AMPHORA

25. LONDON MARKET (Spink): destroyed by enemy action; fragments are in Reading. Complete, *AJA.* 1959 pl. 86 figs. 41–42. Procession: four persons in himatia, to right: A, 1, youth playing the flute; 2, man frontal, looking round to left, his right hand raised, a sprig in his left; between the two, on the ground, a panathenaic amphora; B, 3, youth with a long branch, serving as a stick, in his left hand; 4, man holding a sprig in his left hand.

LOUTROPHOROI

26. ATHENS, Acr. Mus., fr., from Athens. Boreas and Oreithyia.

27. ATHENS, Acr. Mus., fr., from Athens. (Upper part of a man in a himation, wearing chaplet and vine-wreath).

HYDRIAI

(no. 28, the picture mainly on the shoulder, framed)

28 (18). ADRIA B 1171, from Adria. Micali *Mon. ined.* pl. 46, 1; *CV.* pl. 30, 1 and 3 (only); *Riv. Ist.* N.S. 5–6, 49; *Mostra* pl. 119. Woman seated, with youth and man.

(nos. 29–33, the picture mainly on the shoulder, not framed)

29 (19). LOUVRE CA 2587. *Ant. 3 juin 1926* pl. 5 no. 64; *Mon. Piot* 30, 27 and pl. 4; *CV.* d pl. 50, 3–6; ph. Arch. phot. MNLA 650. Thracian women at the fountain. Slightly restored.

30 (20). LONDON E 197, from Camiros. *CV.* pl. 80, 2. Komos (youth pursuing a woman).

OINOCHOAI
(no. 31, shape 1)

31 (21). MUNICH 2449 (J. 262), from Vulci. *CV*. pl. 85, 1, pl. 86, 4–5, pl. 91, 9, and pl. 92, 3. Man and boy.

(no. 32, shape 2, thin)

32 (22). FERRARA, T. 732, from Spina. Woman with flute-case.

FRAGMENTS OF POTS

33 (23). LOUVRE CA 2955, fr. Part, *Eph.* 1937, 186; detail, *Enc. phot.* iii, 20, b. Prothesis; valediction. Above, chariot-race. Unique shape? not an ordinary loutrophoros.

34 (24). BERLIN 2378, fr. Athena.

35 (25). MUNICH inv. 8712 (ex Curtius), fr. *Anz.* 1957, 382; *Ant. Kunst* 2 pl. 9, 1; ph. R.I. 1936. 287–8. Zeus and Ganymede.

36 (26). ELEUSIS, fr., from Eleusis. *Delt.* 9, 35 fig. 37. (Woman).

37 (27). ATHENS Acr. 992, fr., from Athens. Langlotz pl. 79. (Woman).

38 (30). ADRIA B 875, fr., from Adria. *CV* pl. 31, 8. (Head).

39. ADRIA, s.n. 5, fr., from Adria. *CV*. pl. 31, 5. (Youth). Might be from a column-krater.

40. BASLE, Cahn, 37, two frr. On one (head and breast of Poseidon); on the other (upper half a woman holding a mirror).

For his black-figured prize Panathenaic, Naples Stg. 693, see *ABV*. 407.

————————

A fragment is either by the Aegisthus Painter or by his follower the Painter of the Florence Stamnoi (p. 508):

LOUTROPHOROS

ATHENS E 23, fr. (Head of a youth to left, head of a youth to right).

————————

The following are in the manner of the Aegisthus Painter and probably from his hand:

ARV.[1] 332–3.

HYDRIA
(the picture mainly on the shoulder, not framed)

1 (i 1). ATHENS 1174 a (CC. 1171), from Athens. Heydemann pl. 2, 1; *CV.* pl. 7, 2–3; *Eph.* 1937, 235; phs. A.I. NM. 3065–7. Poseidon pursuing a woman.

FRAGMENTS OF POTS

2 (ii 6). ATHENS Acr. 628, frr., from Athens. Part, Langlotz pl. 49. Theseus and the bull. From an amphora?

3 (ii 7). ATHENS Acr. 629, fr., from Athens. Langlotz pl. 49. (Youth). From an amphora? Belongs to the last?

4 (ii 8). ATHENS Acr. 954, frr., from Athens. Langlotz pl. 78. (Theseus and Skiron, Theseus and the bull).

Other vases are in the manner of the Aegisthus Painter:

ARV.[1] 332–3.

COLUMN-KRATERS

(*nos. 1–2, with framed pictures*)

1 (ii 1). BOLOGNA 247, from Bologna. A, Pellegrini 99; *CV.* pl. 23. A, symposion; B, komos. B recalls the Painter of Syracuse 23510 (p. 510).

2 (l 28). REGGIO, fr., from Locri. (Head, shoulders, right hand, of a boy in a himation to right, and hand, holding stick, of a male to left; hanging, sandals).

(*no. 3, the pictures not framed*)

3. REGGIO, fr., from Locri. (Upper half of a boy's head, with a circlet round it, to left).

NECK-AMPHORA

(*with triple handles*)

4 (ii 3). MYKONOS, from Rheneia (originally from Delos). Dugas *Délos xxi* pl. 22 and pl. 24, 57. A, komos ('Anacreontic', and woman playing the flute). B, man and woman. See CB. ii, 59 no. 15.

AMPHORA

(*type C*)

5 (ii 4). LOUVRE AM 1064 *bis*, from Rhodes. *CV.* d pl. 37, 8–9. A, woman with lyre. B, youth. Restored.

HYDRIA

(*the picture mainly on the shoulder, not framed*)

6 (ii 5). BOWDOIN 13.32, from Cumae. Woman seated, and two youths. Her name is ΝΙΚΑΡΕΤΕ.

THE PAINTER OF THE FLORENCE STAMNOI

Att. V. 292. *ARV.*[1] 333–4.

Follower of the Aegisthus Painter.

STAMNOI

1 (1). LOUVRE G 188, from Vulci. *CV.* pl. 20, 9 and pl. 21, 1 and 3–4. A, Zeus entrusting the infant Dionysos to the nymphs of Nysa; B, nymphs of Nysa. See p. 1657.

2. NAPLES (ex Spinelli 1949), from Suessula. A, Philippart *It.* ii pl. 6, iv, 6. A, Menelaos and Helen. B, youth and women (1, woman running to left, looking round, 2, youth in himation standing to right, 3, woman running to left, then a Doric column).

3 (2). FLORENCE 3993. *CV.* pl. 51 and pl. 47, 3. A, man with sceptre and phiale, and two women; B, three women, one of them with a sceptre. Three small fragments in Florence belong, adding parts of the handle-florals and of the maeander. See p. 1657.

4 (3). FLORENCE 4008. *CV.* pl. 49, 2, pl. 47, 2, and pl. 50, 3. A, warrior and women. B, youths and man. See p. 1657.

PANATHENAIC AMPHORA

(*with framed pictures*)

5 (4). BOLOGNA 154, from Bologna. Zannoni pl. 83, 1–3; A, Ghali-Kahil *H.* pl. 53, 1. A, youth with sword pursuing a woman; B, woman fleeing to man.

A vase that recalls the Aegisthus Painter may be by his follower, the Painter of the Florence Stamnoi:

NECK-AMPHORA

(*with triple handles*)

(a). LENINGRAD inv. 15495, from Kerch. *Otchët 1906*, 88. A, youth and woman. B, two youths.

In the following stamnos, the floral work at the handles, and the maeander below the pictures, are in the same style, and must be by the same hand, as those parts of the stamnoi by the Painter of the Florence Stamnoi and of one stamnos by the Aegisthus Painter (Florence 3994, p. 505 no. 18); the shape of the vase, too, is similar; the figure-work is nearer to the Painter of the Florence Stamnoi than to the Aegisthus Painter, but can hardly be said to be his:

STAMNOS

BALTIMORE, Walters Art Gallery, 48.2034 (ex Garrett). A, Eos and Titho-nos. B, man, youth, and woman. See p. 1657.

With the Baltimore stamnos compare the

HYDRIA

LONDON Embiricos (ex Sligo). Eos and Tithonos.

THE PAINTER OF SYRACUSE 23510

ARV.[1] 334.

Related to the Aegisthus Painter.

COLUMN-KRATERS

(with framed pictures)

1 (1). SYRACUSE 23510, from Gela. A, *ML.* 17 pl. 42 and p. 502. A, warrior leaving home. B, komos.

2 (2). MADRID 11043 (L. 166). A, Alvarez-Ossorio pl. 29, 1; A, Leroux pl. 21, 1; *CV.* pl. 15, 2. A, komos; B, komos.

3. BALTIMORE, Walters Art Gallery, 48.69. B, D. K. Hill *Dance* 5. A, Hermes pursuing a woman. B, komos.

See also p. 508 no. 1.

———

THE FRÖHNER PAINTER

ARV.[1] 416–17. CB. ii, 68–69.

Recalls the Altamura Painter (p. 589), but not so that he can be counted as belonging to the same group.

VOLUTE-KRATER

1 (1). CAB. MÉD., three frr. (ex Fröhner). The neck-fragment, *Le Musée* 2, 193 fig. 7. (Man or youth attacking with sword; behind him Athena; on the left a woman, probably fleeing.) On the neck, Peleus and Thetis.

VOLUTE-KRATER ?

2. REGGIO, two frr., from Locri. Gigantomachy? On one fragment, thighs and left knee of a woman moving quickly to right, then hand with sword, to left, of her fallen opponent. Besides chiton and himation she wears an ependytes which is ornamented with a row of stars between two rows of animals and is bordered below by a band of spirals. The other fragment has right shank and foot of a woman moving quickly to right; the costume is the same; the animals in the lower row are griffins.

CALYX-KRATER

3 (2). BOSTON 95.23, from Orvieto. Side-view, Jacobsthal O. pl. 61, b; CB. ii suppl. pl. 14 and suppl. pl. 13, 2; A, *E.A.A.* iii, 741 fig. 911; the shape, Caskey G. 124. A, Zeus pursuing Thetis; B, Nereid fleeing to Nereus. See CB. ii, 68–69.

———

THE KAINEUS PAINTER

JHS. 59, 304. *ARV.*[1] 334 and 958.

Recalls the Fröhner Painter. See also p. 663.

COLUMN-KRATERS
(with framed pictures)

1 (1). PALERMO V 786, from Agrigento. Politi *Cinque vasi di premio* pl. 6, whence (A) Pace *Arte e civiltà*[2] i, 49; *CV.* pl. 45, 1–2 and pl. 46, 3 (*not* pl. 45, 3). A, Centauromachy (Kaineus). B, three youths. See p. 1657.

2. NAPLES, Museo di Capodimonte, 958. A, heroes quarrelling: two armed men attacking each other with swords; each is held back by a man; between the armed men, a woman. B, three youths. See p. 1657.

3 (2). AGRIGENTO 15, from Agrigento. A, women dressing. B, three youths.

4. STOCKHOLM G. 1698. A, Kjellberg fig. 4; A, Antonsson 96. A, Dionysos with satyrs and maenad; B, satyrs and maenad.

Compare with these the

COLUMN-KRATER
(framed pictures)

ERLANGEN. A, Dionysos on donkey, with satyrs and maenad; B, three maenads.

THE PAINTER OF BOLOGNA 228

ARV.[1] 335–7. See p. 775.

VOLUTE-KRATERS

1. ANCONA, from Numana. A, Marconi and Serra pl. 51. A, chariot, with hero or deity mounting; B, kings and women. Misattributed to the Boreas Painter in *ARV.*[1] 337 no. 1.

2 (10). FERRARA, T. 436, from Spina. *NSc.* 1927, 187; Alfieri and Arias *S.* pl. 23. A, Nike; B, citharode. Small.

COLUMN-KRATERS
(nos. 3–9, with framed pictures)

3 (1). BOLOGNA 228, from Bologna. *Mon.* 11 pl. 19, whence (A) Roscher s.v. Herakles 2239; *CV.* pll. 41–43, whence (detail of A) *E.A.A.* ii, 128; A, Stella 50; A, ph. Al. 37788. A, Herakles entering Olympus. B, men and women.

4 (2). NEW YORK 29.131.7. *Bull. Metr.* 25, 96–98; Richter and Hall pl. 82, pl. 88, 80, and pl. 170, 80; A, Richter *H.* 225, i. A, war-chariot: the warrior has alighted. B, Dionysos and maenads.

5 (3). FERRARA, T. 308, from Spina. A, Aurigemma[1] 77 and 79 = [2]83 and 85; details of A, Aurigemma and Alfieri pl. 10; Alfieri and Arias *S.* pll. 24–27. A, Artemis in chariot, with Apollo and Hermes. B, satyrs and maenad. See p. 1657.

5 *bis*. REGGIO, two frr. (nearly joining), from Locri. A, woman (Artemis ?) in chariot (to right), with one (Apollo?) standing beyond the horses. Another fragment in Reggio has part of a cithara, with a hand behind the strings, and the neck of a chariot-horse to right, but I could not affirm that it belongs.

6 (4). BOLOGNA 233, from Bologna. A, Mingazzini *Apoteosi* pl. 2, 1. A, chariot of Herakles (Iolaos driving, Herakles has alighted). B, men and woman.

6 *bis*. FERRARA, T. 256 B VP, from Spina. A, Herakles and Centaur. B, women and youth.

6 *ter*. FERRARA, T. 62 B VP, from Spina. A, Dionysos with satyrs and maenad; B, satyrs and maenad.

7 (5). FERRARA, T. 123, from Spina. A, Dionysos and satyr riding donkeys. B, youths and boy.

8 (6). TARANTO, from Pisticci. A, *NSc*. 1902, 316. A, Dionysos on donkey, with satyr and maenad. B, three youths.

9 (7). VILLA GIULIA (ex Castellani), fr. A, warrior leaving home (two in long chiton and himation standing to right; warrior with phiale standing to left, shield-device a snake; male with stick standing to left).

(no. 9 bis, not known whether the pictures framed)

9 *bis* (18). REGGIO 10561 (4377), fr., from Locri. A, (upper part of a man in a chiton to right).

(nos. 10–11, the pictures not framed)

10 (8). MUNICH 2379. A, Pfuhl fig. 776; A, FR. pl. 166, 1 and iii, 286; A, Bothmer *Am*. pl. 83, 1. A, Amazon dismounting. B, man.

11 (9) AGRIGENTO (ex Giudice 184), from Gela. A, ph. Lo Cascio pl. 7, whence Schauenburg *Helios* fig. 9. A, Helios. B, man. Now cleaned.

NUPTIAL LEBES ?
(part of the stand remains)

12. OXFORD, Beazley, fr., from Attica. (Deities: cithara of Apollo, head and right shoulder of a bearded god).

LOUTROPHOROI

13 (11). ATHENS 1170 (CC. 1167), from Pikrodafni. *Mon*. 8 pl. 5, 2; detail, *AM*. 21, 368; detail, *AM*. 53, Beil. 16–17, 96; phs. Al. 24488–9, whence (detail) Buschor 182 and (part, redrawn!) Perrot 10 pl. 18, whence Swindler fig. 322; part of A. Buschor *Grab* 17; *CV*. pll. 21–23, pl. 24, 3–4, pl. 25, and pl. 26, 1. Prothesis; valediction; cavalcade; on the neck, mourning women. See p. 1657.

14 (12). ATHENS E, fr. (Head of woman to left).

15 (13). NEW YORK 07.286.70, fr. Richter and Hall pll. 83–84 and pl. 173, 81. On the neck: A, two warriors; B, warrior and old man.

16. ATHENS, Acr. Mus., fr., from Athens. On the neck, procession (hymenaios).

NECK-AMPHORAE

(with triple handles; the pictures framed)

17 (14). BOLOGNA 156, from Bologna. A, Pellegrini 51. A, Theseus and Minotaur. B, man and boy.

18 (15). BOLOGNA 157, from Bologna. A, Pellegrini 52. A, Zeus and Nike. B, man and youth.

19 (16). BOLOGNA 155, from Bologna. Zannoni pl. 80, 10-12. A, warrior leaving home; B, youth and woman.

20. FERRARA ('T. 224?'), two frr., from Spina. Uncertain subject (hero with sword attacking a man or youth).

FRAGMENTS OF POTS

21 (17). TÜBINGEN E 86 and AMSTERDAM inv. 2307 and 2308, frr. See *JHS*. 51, 55 no. 12. The Tübingen frr., Watzinger pl. 27. (Male in chariot, male with sceptre, woman with torch and staff, man—Hermes?—woman with torch). These are probably all deities.

22. REGGIO, two frr., from Locri. On one fragment, breast to middle of one in chiton and himation standing frontal, left forearm extended to right (the hand missing). On the other fragment, neck nearly to the waist of Nike in chiton and himation, standing frontal, with the right arm to past the elbow. Reserved inside. From a neck-amphora?

23 (19). AMSTERDAM, fr. Komos or symposion? (head and shoulder of a man to right).

────────────

NEAR THE PAINTER OF BOLOGNA 228

(i)

NECK-AMPHORAE

(with double handles)

1. MYKONOS, from Rheneia (originally from Delos). Dugas *Délos xxi* pl. 19, 51. A, komast; B, komast.

2. MYKONOS, from Rheneia (originally from Delos). Dugas *Délos xxi* pl. 20, 52. A, Zeus and Nike. B, maenad and satyr.

(ii)

A small vase might be by the painter:

CUP-SKYPHOS

(lipped, solid, not very shallow)

BRUSSELS, Bibliothèque Royale, 11, from Capua. Fröhner *Nap.* pl. 5 = Fröhner *Mus. France* pl. 6, whence (B) Buschor *Satyrtänze* fig. 54; Feytmans

V.G.B. pll. 25–28. A, Dionysos and Giant; B, satyr driving satyr-biga. For B see CB. ii, 71. There is a general affinity to Sotadean cup-skyphoi (pp. 764 no. 5; 768 nos. 34–37; 769–70).

(iii)

THE GROUP OF NAPLES 3169

Nos. 1 and 2 seem to be by one hand; no. 3 resembles them, but is stiffer and perhaps a little earlier.

NECK-AMPHORA

(with triple handles)

1. NAPLES 3169, from Nola. A, Angelini pl. 6; A, ph. So. 11069, i, 6. A, Eos and Tithonos. B, youth.

STAND

2. AMSTERDAM inv. 2468 and 2469, two frr. On one (two women with torches, and part of a third figure); on the other (middle of a figure in chiton and himation, and buttocks of another).

COLUMN-KRATER

(with framed pictures)

3. VILLA GIULIA 3579, from Falerii. *St. mat.* 1, 160–1; A, *Boll. d'Arte* 10, 340; A, *Dedalo* 3, 79; *CV.* pl. 17. A, Tereus. B, youths and boys.

Probably also the

COLUMN-KRATER

(with framed pictures)

FERRARA, T. 253, from Spina. A, symposion. B, youths and boy.

════════

THE MYKONOS PAINTER

ARV.[1] 354–5 and 958.

NUPTIAL LEBETES

(type 1)

1 (3). MYKONOS, from Rheneia (originally from Delos). Dugas *Délos xxi* pl. 33, 91, pl. 34, pl. 36, 91. Mistress (bride) and maids. The fragments inserted by the restorer into the lower part of the stand must be alien (ibid. pl. 33, 91, below, and pl. 39, 91).

2 (4). COPENHAGEN inv. 9165, from Greece. *Fra Nat.* 1932, 40–42. A, bride seated holding a nuptial lebes, and two women; under each handle, Nike; B, woman with sceptre and woman running with torches. Slightly restored.

COLUMN-KRATERS
(with framed pictures)

3. Louvre G 346, from Nola. *CV.* d pl. 29, 1 and 3. A, Zeus and goddess; Poseidon and Nike. B, komos. Now cleaned. Mouth and neck (*CV.* d pl. 29, 8) were alien. Misattributed in *ARV.*[1] 327 no. 19 owing to a confusion of numbers.

4 (6). Florence 75586, from Falerii. A, Nike and two kings or gods. B, youths and woman.

5 (5). Corinth C 32.93 (6), fr., from Corinth. A, (Dionysos and maenad). B, (youths).

CALYX-KRATERS

6 (7). Catania 697. Hancarville 4 pl. 126; Millin *PVA.* 2 pll. 3–4, whence Inghirami pll. 70–71; Libertini pll. 74–75. Perseus. See p. 1657.

7 (a 1). Los Angeles A 5933.50.34 (ex Marshall Brooks), from Agrigento. A, Hermes pursuing a woman; B, woman fleeing to king. See p. 1657.

8. Harvard 1916.264. *CV.* pl. 19, 1. A, Dionysos and maenad; B, satyr and maenad.

BELL-KRATERS

9. Athens, Agora, P 14322, fr., from Athens. (Youth).

(no. 9 bis, with lugs)

9 *bis.* Ferrara, T. 112 D VP, from Spina. Dionysos with maenads and satyrs.

AMPHORA
(type B)

10. Athens, Agora, P 24141, frr., from Athens. A, (youth, in chlamys—leaving home?). B, (Nike).

LOUTROPHOROI

11 (8). Athens, Vlasto, frr., from Koropi. Prothesis, valediction.

12. Athens, Acr. Mus., fr., from Athens.

NECK-AMPHORA
(Nolan amphora, with triple handles)

13 (9). Ferrara, T. 437, from Spina. A, Zeus; B, Nike.

HYDRIAI

14 (1). Warsaw 142361 (ex Czartoryski 72), from Nola. *CV.* pl. 33, 3. Mistress and maids, and youth.

15 (2). Ferrara, T. 918, from Spina. Eos and Tithonos.

FRAGMENTS OF POTS

16 (10). Athens Acr. 1007, fr., from Athens. Langlotz pl. 79. (Women).

17 (11). ATHENS, Agora, P 9464, fr., from Athens. Dinsmoor *Heph.* 136, 20. (Woman).

CUP

18 (12). BERLIN 2521, from Vulci. *AZ.* 1865 pl. 204, whence Overbeck *KM.* pl. 15, 21 and (I) Cook *Zeus* i, 219; *CV.* pl. 96. I, Triptolemos. A, warriors leaving home. B, young warrior pursuing a woman.

Near the Mykonos Painter, the

COLUMN-KRATER

(with framed pictures)

(a 2). PERUGIA 73. A, *Jb.* 47, 197; A, ph. R.I. 1468. A, infant Herakles and the snakes.

Parts of the following, especially the Nikai, recall the Mykonos Painter:

NUPTIAL LEBES

(type 1)

BONN 1520, from Athens. *CV.* pl. 12, 4 and pl. 14, 4. A, woman seated, with girl and woman; at each handle, Nike; B, three women; on the stand, three women.

THE CLEVELAND PAINTER

Panm. 19. *ARV.*[1] 351.

COLUMN-KRATERS

(with framed pictures)

1 (1). CLEVELAND 30.104, from Paestum. A, *Bull. Clev.* 1930, 142, 1; A, *Report Clev.* 1930, 41, above. A, goddess mounting chariot (Artemis?: with Hera?, Apollo, Leto?). B, komos.

2 (2). RHODES 13301, from Camiros. *Cl. Rh.* 4, 259–61; *CV.* pl. 1, 1 and pl. 2, 2–3. A, Dionysos with satyrs and maenad. B, satyrs and maenad.

3 (3). ABINGDON, Robertson, fr., from Greece. A, (on the left, satyr and maenad).

4 (4). NEW YORK 41.162.10. *CV.* Gallatin pl. 57, 2. A, vintage: satyrs treading wine, and Dionysos; B, satyrs and maenad.

5 (5). HARROW 50, from Vitorchiano. *JHS.* 17 pl. 6 and p. 295, whence (part of A) Chittenden and Seltman pl. 20; A, *Burl. 1903* pl. 97, H 44; *Ant. class.* 4 pl. 28, 3; B.Ap. xxii. 14. A, Centauromachy (Kaineus). B, satyrs and maenad.

6 (6). FERRARA (sequestro Venezia), from Spina. A, centauromachy (Kaineus). B, komos. This is not, as said in *Panm.* 19, the vase figured in *NSc.* 1924, 287, for which see p. 1114, no. 14.

7. ATHENS MARKET. *Hesp. Art Bull.* 2, 7 no. 69. A, Herakles and Busiris. B, satyrs and maenad. See p. 1658.

8 (7). VIENNA 683. Tischbein 5 pll. 34–35; A, Dubois-Maisonneuve pl. 6; *CV.* pl. 88, 4–5. A, komos; B, komos.

9 (8). CHIUSI 1850, from Chiusi. A, ph. Al. 37493, whence *E.A.A.* ii, 717. A, komos. B, three youths.

NECK-AMPHORA
(with convex handles)

10 (9). LOUVRE G 200. *CV.* pl. 36, 1 and 4–6. A, warrior; B, woman. Now cleaned.

OINOCHOE
(shape 1)

11 (10). COPENHAGEN, Ny Carlsberg, inv. 2697, from Orvieto. Poulsen *Etr.* pl. 21, whence (part) *Mél. d'arch.* 1950 pl. 2, 3; part, *Recueil Dugas* pl. 28, 1. Triptolemos and Demeter. By the same *potter* as the Orchard Painter's oinochoe in New York, 21.88.148 (p. 527 no. 74).

THE PAINTER OF BOLOGNA 235

COLUMN-KRATERS
(with framed pictures)

1. FERRARA, T. 30 C VP, from Spina. A, three women at laver. B, komos.

2. FERRARA, T. 368, from Spina. A, symposion; B, komos.

3. FERRARA (scolina del Dosso C, VP), from Spina. A, Nike, boy, male, and man. B, komos.

4. BASLE, Erlenmeyer. A, youths and man leading a bull to sacrifice. B, komos.

5. FERRARA, T. 910, from Spina. A, youth and woman; man and youth. B, komos.

6. BOLOGNA 235, from Bologna. A, Ghali-Kahil *H.* pl. 56, 1. A, Menelaos and Helen. B, komos.

THE SYRACUSE PAINTER

VA. 132. *Att. V.* 313–14. *ARV.*[1] 352–4 and 958. CB. iii, text.

Called after no. 32.

Follower of Makron.

STAMNOS

1 (1). BOSTON 10.177, from Cumae. A, *Jb.* 26, 133; side, Jacobsthal O. pl. 101, a; A, Simon *G.A.* 76; CB. iii pl. 83 and pl. 82, 147. A, Psychostasia; B, old man, man and youth. See CB. iii, text; and below, p. 1657.

COLUMN-KRATERS

(nos. 2–8, with framed pictures)

2 (6). LOS ANGELES A 5933.50.12 (ex Marshall Brooks). A, Tischbein 4 pl. 41, whence *El.* 3 pl. 95; A, *Cat. Christie July 23 1917* pl. 2, 48; A, Tillyard pl. 20, 125. A, Hermes pursuing a woman. B, man and youths.

3 (7). NORTHWICK, Spencer-Churchill, from Bomarzo. Detail of A, Seltman *Athens* 29 fig. 21; B.Ap. xxii. 66. A, arming. B, Herakles and Alkyoneus.

4. LOUVRE C 10774. A, Dionysos and satyrs: vintage; B, satyrs and maenad·

5 (a). COPENHAGEN, Ny Carlsberg, inv. 2754. A, *Coll. Woodyat* pl. 3, 47; *From the Coll.* 2, 126–7. A, Dionysos with satyr and maenad. B, komos.

6 (8). LOUVRE G 349, from Nola. *CV.* d pl. 24, 6 and 3; A, Villard *GV.* pl. 26, 1. A, three maenads. B, man, boy, and youth.

7 (9). FLORENCE V, from Chiusi. A, youth leaving home (youth, man, and woman). B, man, woman, and youth.

8 (a 4). NAPLES 3128, from Telese. A, ph. So. 11071, ii, 3. A, youth leaving home. B, man and youths.

(no. 9, not known if the pictures framed)

9. SALONICA 277 a.1934, fr., from Olynthos. (Shoulder to buttocks of one in a himation standing to left: may be the right-hand figure on one side).

(nos. 10–15, the pictures not framed)

10 (2). NAPLES Stg. 700, from Cumae. A, ph. So. 11028. Arming (A, youth and youth; B, old man).

11 (3). VILLA GIULIA 836, from Falerii. *CV.* pl. 8; A, ph. Al. 41212. A, satyr carrying maenad. B, komast.

12 (3 *bis*). THEBES, two frr., from Halai. *Hesp.* 9, 457, above. A, satyr and maenad. The fragments ibid., below, can hardly belong.

13 (5). TARANTO, from Mesagne. A, two maenads. B, god pursuing a sea-nymph (Zeus and Thetis? See CB. ii, 69 note 1). B is rough, has the look of prentice-work.

14. Where? (seen in Naples at the restorer's). A, man pursuing a boy with a lyre; B, man running.

15 (4). BOLOGNA 251, from Bologna. Zannoni pl. 59, 4–6. A, komast; B, komast.

AMPHORA

(type A; the pictures not framed)

16 (10). NEW YORK 06.1021.151. A, Sambon *Canessa* pl. 4, 95; A, Richter and Milne fig. 8, whence LS. fig. 2; Richter and Hall pl. 93, 91 and pl. 169, 91. A, Dionysos and satyr. B, Poseidon and Nike.

NECK-AMPHORAE

(no. 17, with triple handles)

17 (11). ATHENS 1335 (CC. 1222), from Tanagra. A, Eos and Tithonos. B, man with sceptre, and woman.

(nos. 18–19, Nolan amphorae, with convex handles)

18 (12). SYRACUSE 24649, from Gela. A, *ML.* 17, 347 fig. 253; A, *CV.* pl. 8, 6. A, Dionysos; B, maenad.

19 (13). SYRACUSE 33502, from Gela. A, *ML.* 17, 349 fig. 255; A, *CV.* pl. 8, 7. A, woman running with torches; B, youth running.

(no. 20, Nolan amphora, with ridged handles)

20 (14). SYRACUSE 33503, from Gela. A, *ML.* 17, 350 fig. 256; A, *CV.* pl. 8, 8. A, Nike; B, youth running.

LOUTROPHOROI

21 (15). COPENHAGEN inv. 9195 (ex Seltman). *Festskrift Poulsen* 86 figs. 1–4. A, prothesis; B, valediction. On the neck: A, mourning women; B, men (valediction). Much restored.

22. ATHENS 17420, frr. One fr., *Anz.* 1943, 293. Prothesis, valediction. Below, in black, horsemen (inverted).

23. ATHENS, Acr. Mus., fr., from Athens. (Head and shoulders of woman to right).

24. ATHENS, Acr. Mus., fr., from Athens. (Youth leaning on his stick, woman, and another). On the neck, three women.

25. ATHENS, Acr. Mus., fr., from Athens. (Youth and woman; then, under handles, tree and siren or Nike to right). On the neck, three women.

26. ATHENS, Acr. Mus., fr., from Athens. (Under handle, palm-tree and woman to right).

27. ATHENS, Acr. Mus., fr., from Athens. (Nose to waist of woman facing left).

28. ATHENS, Acr. Mus., fr., from Athens. (Nose to waist of woman to right).

29. ATHENS, Acr. Mus., fr., from Athens. (Head of youth to left).

30. ATHENS, Acr. Mus., fr., from Athens. (Lower part of youth's face to right, with his breast and right arm).

31. ATHENS, Acr. Mus., fr., from Athens. On the neck, A, woman (standing to right). B, woman (moving to right, looking round).

31 *bis*. ATHENS 17456. Women; on the neck, A, a woman; B, the like. Small.

PELIKAI
(*nos. 32–33, the pictures not framed*)

32 (16). SYRACUSE 21834, from Gela. A, *ML*. 17, 370 and pl. 16; A, *CV*. pl. 3, 4. A, Dionysos and satyr; B, satyr and maenad.

33 (17). DRESDEN 294, from Nola. B.Ap. xxiii. 19. 1; B, R.I. xi. 39. A, Poseidon. B, woman running with oinochoe and phiale.

(*no. 34, with framed pictures*)

34. GALAXIDI. *BCH*. 1950 pl. 5. A, man and girl; B, man and boy.

HYDRIAI

35. RIEHEN, Gränacher. *Auction xvi Basle* pl. 33, 129. Apollo and three goddesses at altar.

36 (20). OXFORD 531. *JHS*. 25, 68; *CV*. pl. 32, 9. Woman seated, and two women.

37 (21). LONDON E 211, from Vulci. *CV*. pl. 89, 3. Old man seated, woman seated, and woman.

38 (22). LOUVRE MN 712, from Cyrenaica. *CV*. d pl. 53, 7 and 9. Men and woman.

39 (18). PARIS MARKET. *Coll. Lambros* pl. 10, 71. Three maenads.

40 (19). PARIS MARKET, from Sicily. *Coll. Lambros* pl. 10, 92. Fleeing women.

41. ABINGDON, Robertson, fr., from Greece. Eos and Tithonos (upper part of a boy in a himation moving to left, looking round, and extended arms of a woman to left).

42 (23). MYKONOS, from Rheneia (originally from Delos). Dugas *Délos xxi* pl. 27, 67. Youth and woman.

OINOCHOAI
(*nos. 43–44, shape 1*)

43 (24). NEW YORK 26.60.80. Part, Richter and Milne fig. 125, whence LS. fig. 12; Richter and Hall pl. 93, 92 and pl. 177, 92. Satyrs and maenads.

44 (25). CATANIA 710. Libertini pl. 80. Zeus pursuing a woman.

(*no. 45, shape 5 A*)

45 (26). LONDON E 557, from Camiros. Dionysos.

LEKYTHOI
(*of standard shape*)

46 (27). ATHENS 12120 (N. 1031), from Eretria. *AM*. 32 Beil. 3 fig. 13; Nicole pl. 15, 3. Nike.

47 (28). REGGIO 4105, from Locri. Nereid (running to altar).

48. MANNHEIM 300. *CV.* pl. 32, 6–7. King.

49 (29). AGRIGENTO 26 (715), from Agrigento. Boy running with meat in his hand.

50 (30). PALERMO, fr. (two joining), from Selinus. Man and woman (man to right, right arm extended, woman with head to left: heads and shoulders remain).

51 (31). ATHENS 1310 (CC. 1195), from Eretria. Man and boy.

52 (32). ATHENS 1643 (CC. 1196), from Eretria. Fight.

53. ATHENS 1306 (CC. 1367), from Eretria. Youth riding, and leading a void horse (Troilos?).

FRAGMENTS OF POTS

54. PRAGUE, Univ., I 311, fr., from Greece. Benndorf pl. 55, 6; *Listy fil.* 74 pl. 3, 3; Frel *Ř.V.* fig. 40. (Woman with oinochoe).

55. ATHENS Acr. 832, fr., from Athens. Langlotz pl. 74. Hermes. From a small column-krater?

55 *bis.* REGGIO, fr., from Locri. (Youth in himation standing to right, his right hand raised behind his head; missing, shanks and feet, left hand). From a small vase.

SKYPHOS

56. PALERMO, fr., from Selinus. (Head and shoulders of a man, doubtless leaning on his stick, to right). Misattributed in *ARV.*¹ 447 no. 69.

CUPS

57 (33). FLORENCE V 63, from Chiusi. I, komast. A, youths and boy; B, the like. Restored.

58 (34). MUNICH 2659 (J. 513), from Vulci. I, centaur. A, komos. B, youths.

MANNER OF THE SYRACUSE PAINTER

(i)

Near the Syracuse Painter and perhaps by him:

*ARV.*¹ 354.

COLUMN-KRATERS

(nos. 1–2, with framed pictures)

1 (2). AMSTERDAM inv. 4643, fr. (Head of woman, to left).

2 (3). SYRACUSE, fr., from Gela. (Upper part of maenad dancing to left, looking round).

(no. 3, the pictures not framed)

3 (1). BOLOGNA 250, from Bologna. A, komast; B, komast.

LOUTROPHOROI

4. ATHENS, Acr. Mus., fr., from Athens. (Head of woman to left, then a sash hanging).
5. ATHENS, Acr. Mus., fr., from Athens. (Legs of woman standing to right; on the left, under the handle, siren).
6. ATHENS, Acr. Mus., fr., from Athens. On the neck, (sash hanging, then the upper part of a woman's head to right).

FRAGMENT OF A POT

7. ATHENS Acr., fr., from Athens. *BCH.* 1940–1 pl. 10, 6. (Athena).

(ii)

THE PAINTER OF MUNICH S.L. 477

ARV.[1] 481.

Close to the Syracuse Painter, and put here, rather than among the painters of smaller vases, for that reason.

LEKYTHOI

(standard shape)

1 (1). Once ROME, Curtius. Athena (standing frontal, head to right, bareheaded, upright spear in right hand, left arm akimbo, shield leaning against her left thigh, device a wreath).
2 (2). MUNICH S.L. 477, from Gela. *Coll. B. et C.* pl. 24, 167; Sieveking *BTV.* pl. 51, 4. Woman with alabastron and dish of loaves.
3 (a). AMSTERDAM inv. 698, from Athens. Scheurleer *Cat.* pl. 43; *CV.* d pl. 1, 4. King, and woman with flower. ΛΙ+ΑΣ ΚΑΛΟΣ.

In the manner of the Syracuse Painter, and probably by the same hand as these:

LOUTROPHOROS

ATHENS, Acr. Mus., fr. (two joining), from Athens. On the neck, (woman to right with torch, woman facing left: head, shoulders, arm of the first remain, the head of the second).

THE ORCHARD PAINTER

VA. 133–4. *Att. V.* 311–13. *ARV.*[1] 346–9.

So called after the subject of no. 1.

Related to the Painter of Brussels R 330 (p. 925).

COLUMN-KRATERS
(nos. 1–31 bis, the pictures framed)

1 (1). New York 07.286.74. Part of A, *Bull. Metr.* 12, 245 = *Hdbk Cl. Coll.* title-page; Richter and Hall pl. 91, pl. 90, 87, and pl. 170, 87. A, women in orchard, picking fruit. B, youths and women.

2 (2). New York 06.1021.149. A, Sambon *Canessa* pl. 8, 90; Richter and Hall pl. 92, 89 and pl. 170, 89. A, Poseidon pursuing a woman, Hermes pursuing a woman. B, youth and women.

2 *bis*. Padula, from Padula (T. xxxviii, no. 7). A, a god (Hermes?) pursuing a woman. B, woman (?) with man and male.

3 (3). Ferrara, T. 627, from Spina. A, Hermes pursuing a woman. B, youth, male, and woman.

4. Louvre C 10763. A, fight: Achilles and Memnon. B, youths and woman.

5. Mariemont G 130. A, *Coll. Warocqué* i, 49; *Ant. Mariemont* pl. 42. A, Centauromachy (Kaineus). B, youths and woman.

6 (4). New York 25.78.45. Millingen *Coghill* pll. 12–13; A, *Cat. Sotheby 7–8 July 1924* pl. 2, left. A, warrior leaving home. B, youths and woman.

7 (5). Bologna 240, from Bologna. A, youth with horse leaving home. B, youths and woman.

8. Manchester iii. 1. 39. *Mem. Manch.* 87 pl. 4. A, youth in chariot leaving home. B, youth, woman, and old man.

9 (6). Naples 3369. A, ph. So. 11071, i, 1. A, sacrifice to Hermes (procession of three women and a girl). B, man, youth, and woman.

10. San Simeon, State Monument, 9956, from Sicily. A, man and Nike; woman with phiale and sceptre, and old man. B, maenad (woman with torch and thyrsus), man, and youth.

11 (7). London 1914.5–20.1, from Cyrenaica. A, youth, woman, and man. B, maenad, male, and youth.

12 (8). Villa Giulia 50391. A, men and women; B, men and woman.

12 *bis*. Berlin market (Propyläen-Kunsthandlung). A, old man and woman; man and woman; B, man, woman, and youth. Restored.

13 (9). Bari, from Ceglie. *Japigia* 1, 247. A, man and woman; youth and woman.

14 (10). Lecce 601, from Rugge. *CV.* pl. 10, 3–4. A, man and youths; B, man and youths.

15. Louvre C 10767. A, man, male, and woman; B, man, male, and youth.

16 (11). Tarquinia RC 3217, from Tarquinia. A, youth and boy; man and boy; B, man, youth, and boy.

16 *bis*. Padula, from Padula (Valle Pupina, T. xxxv, no. 3). A, symposion: Dionysos and Herakles reclining; with a maenad. B, men and woman.

17 (13). BOLOGNA 226, from Bologna. Zannoni pl. 30, 2–5. A, symposion. B, youths and woman.

17 *bis*. LOUVRE, fr. (two joining). A, symposion (upper part of a man reclining to left, phiale in left hand; the upper part of the head missing).

18 (14). HEIDELBERG 181, fr. Kraiker pl. 34. A, symposion.

19 (15). FERRARA, T. 364, from Spina. A, symposion. B, youth, man, and woman.

20 (16). BOLOGNA 234, from Bologna. Zannoni pl. 40, 1–3 and 5; A, *Jb*. 38–39, 130; A, Deubner pl. 21, 3. A, komos ('Anacreontic'). B, youths and woman. See CB. ii, 60 no. 24.

21 (12). NAPLES, from Cumae. A, youths pursuing women. B, youths and woman. Restored.

21 *bis*. REGGIO, fr., from Locri. A, a man pursuing a woman. These are the two right-hand figures; preserved, the man's head, to right (petasos at nape) and his right hand, the head of the woman, looking round to left, with her right shoulder; between them a column. See the next.

21 *ter*. REGGIO, fr., from Locri. (On the left, head and shoulders of a woman running to left, looking round to right, arms extended). May belong to the last.

22 (17). LONDON E 479. A, Dionysos with maenads and satyr. B, youths and woman.

23 (18). FERRARA, T. 483, from Spina. A, Dionysos with maenad and satyrs. B, youths and woman.

24 (19). FERRARA, T. 1009, from Spina. A, satyr and maenads. B, old man, and woman.

25 (20). BOLOGNA 241, from Bologna. A, *Mus. It.* 2 pl. 1, 3; *CV*. pl. 28, 1–3. A, vintage: satyrs treading grapes, and maenad. B, men and youth.

26. FERRARA, T. 254 C VP, from Spina. A, vintage. B, youth and boys.

27 (21). BOLOGNA 190, from Bologna. A, Heydemann *Jason* pl. 1, 4; A, Zannoni pl. 122, 4 and d; *CV*. pl. 24, 1–3; A, *AJA*. 1935, 183 fig. 3 and p. 184; detail of A, Bieber *H.T.* 19; A, *E.A.A.* iii, 749. A, satyr as Jason, seizing the fleece; with Dionysos. B, youth pursuing a woman. [Richter].

28 (22). NEW YORK 34.11.7. A, *Bull. Metr.* 30, 87; A, *AJA*. 1935, 182 and 183 fig. 2, whence *R.E.G.* 1936 pl. 3, 2; Richter and Hall pl. 90, 88 and pl. 170, 88, whence (A) Radermacher *Mythos*[2] fig. 9, (A) Stella 576; A, Richter *H.* 225, g. Jason and the fleece. B, youths and woman. [Richter]. The figures of Jason and Athena are in an abominable style, as if the painter had left them to a beginner to line in.

29 (a). TARANTO 7482, from Montescaglioso. A, naked women washing. B, man and boys.

30. SAMOTHRACE, fr., from Samothrace. *Hesp.* 22 pl. 2, d. (Woman).

31 (23). BOSTON 86.605 (F. 360. 3), fr., from Naucratis. Fairbanks pl. 39. (Woman).

31 *bis.* REGGIO, fr., from Locri. (The upper part of the left-hand figure remains, a youth in a himation standing to right).

(nos. 32–39, the pictures not framed)

32 (24). GELA (ex Navarra-Jacona), from Gela. A, maenad running (with torches and thyrsus); B, woman running.

33 (25). LONDON MARKET (Sotheby). A, man and boy; B, man. Graffito NV.

34 (26). Once LONDON, Spetia, from Spina. A, youth and boy; B, youth.

35 (27). FERRARA, T. 717, from Spina. A, man and woman; B, man. On A, man to right, holding a stick; woman moving to right, looking round, holding a sprig of ivy; on B, to left, holding a sprig of ivy.

36 (28). BOSTON 89.274 (R. 421). Shape, Caskey G. 122. A, man and woman; B, youth and woman. On A, the woman holds a torch and a sprig, the man a stick.

37. FERRARA, T. 105 C VP, from Spina. A, woman with torches; B, youth.

37 *bis.* FERRARA, T. 103 B VP, from Spina. A, symposion (man reclining); B, komast.

38 (29). Once MUNICH, Preyss. A, symposion (man reclining). B, youth.

39. FERRARA, T. 790, from Spina. A, woman fleeing. B, youth holding sprig.

NECK-AMPHORAE

(no. 40, with convex handles; framed pictures)

40 (31). VATICAN, from Vulci. *Mus. Greg.* 2 pl. 55, 2. A, woman holding phiale and shield, and two men. B, woman with torches, youth, and man.

(no. 41, with triple handles; framed pictures)

41 (30). DRESDEN 307, from Nola. B.Ap. xxiii. 33. 1. A, Dionysos and maenad; B, two maenads.

(no. 42, small, with double handles; the pictures not framed)

42 (a 1). LONDON E 344, from Camiros. *CV.* pl. 69, 1. A, Dionysos. B, youth.

(no. 43, small, with ridged handles; the pictures not framed)

43 (a 2). LONDON E 345. *CV.* pl. 66, 3. A, komast; B, komast.

(nos. 44–46, special shape, small, squat, with convex or flat handles; framed pictures)

44 (32). BOLOGNA 160, from Bologna. Zannoni pl. 52, 2 and 6–7. A, man doing his need, molested by two satyrs. B, youth and woman.

45 (33). MYKONOS, from Rheneia (originally from Delos). Dugas *Délos xxi* pl. 17, 47. A, two youths; B, male and youth.

46 (34). NAPLES 3170. A, ph. So. 11009, iii, 8. A, youth and woman; B, youth and boy.

PELIKAI
(nos. 47–57, with framed pictures)

47 (36). MARKET. A, Theseus and Minotaur. B, man and woman. On A, Theseus has his sword in his right hand and takes the monster by the horn with his left.

48 (38). SAN SIMEON, Hearst Corporation, 12292 (ex Serrure and Rothschild). A, youth, man, and woman; B, man and boys.

49 (37). LONDON E 358, from Camiros. A, man and woman; B, man and youth.

50 (35). LENINGRAD (St. 2163). A, youth and woman; B, man and woman.

51 (40). NAPLES. A, ph. So. 11009, v, 3. A, youth and woman; B, youth and woman. Above, lotus-buds.

52. ADOLPHSECK, Landgraf Philipp of Hesse, 43. *CV*. pl. 22, 3–4. A, youth and woman; B, youth and boy. [Brommer].

53 (41). DRESDEN 325. A, youth and boy; B, youth and boy.

54 (39). MYKONOS, from Rheneia (originally from Delos). Dugas *Délos xxi* pl. 12, 31. A, two youths; B, youth and woman.

55. NAPLES (ex Spinelli 129), from Suessula. A, two youths; B, the like.

56. PARIS MARKET (Feuardent). A, Tischbein 4 pl. 4, whence *El*. 1 pl. 61; A, Tillyard pl. 13, 99. A, Athena and woman. B, man and woman.

57 (41 *bis*). MYKONOS, fr., from Rheneia (originally from Delos). Dugas *Délos xxi* pl. 9, 30. A, (maenad); B, (man).

(nos. 58–60, the pictures not framed)

58 (42). LENINGRAD 730 (St. 1273 e). A, warrior pursuing woman. B, woman running with helmet, shield, and spear.

59 (43). Where?, fr., from Al Mina. *JHS*. 59, 9, 25. Man and woman.

60 (44). VATICAN. A, Pistolesi 3 pl. 63, 3. A, Eos; B, Tithonos.

LOUTROPHOROI

61. ATHENS, Acr. Mus., fr., from Athens. Wedding (the bride's head is completely covered).

62. ATHENS, Acr. Mus., fr., from Athens. Male pursuing a woman.

63. ATHENS, Acr. Mus., fr., from Athens. On the neck, (youth and woman).

64. ATHENS Acr. 653, fr., from Athens. Langlotz pl. 52. On the neck, (woman).

HYDRIAI
(no. 65, the picture on the body, framed)

65. PARIS MARKET (Geladakis). Woman seated, with man and woman (man leaning on his stick to right, forearm extended; column, wool-basket;

woman seated to right, looking round, in her left hand an alabastron; woman standing to left).

(nos. 66–71, the picture on the body, not framed)

66 (47). PARIS, Rothschild. *Cat. Sotheby July 5 1928* pl. 3, 1. Women and little girl.

67 (48). OXFORD 1962.272, fr., from Greece. Boreas and Oreithyia.

68. CHICAGO 89.95. Eos and Tithonos. Restored.

69 (49). ATHENS 16262. Two women and a seated man.

70. SAN FRANCISCO, Legion of Honor, 1633. *CV.* pl. 15, 1 and pl. 16, 1. Nike.

71. MAPLEWOOD, Noble. Nike (running to right, a torch in each hand). Bothmer saw that this was by the same hand as the last.

(no. 72, the picture on the shoulder, framed)

72. ATHENS, Agora, P 15086, fr., from Athens. (On the left, head of man).

OINOCHOAI
(shape 1, large)
(nos. 73–74, the picture framed)

73 (50). FLORENCE 4025. Inghirami pl. 314; *CV.* pl. 66, 3 and pl. 68, 1–3. Wedding.

74 (51). NEW YORK 21.88.148. *AJA.* 1926, 42; Richter and Hall pl. 92, 90 and pl. 177, 90. Woman seated, with man and youth. By the same *potter* as the Cleveland Painter's oinochoe in Copenhagen, Ny Carlsberg, inv. 2697 (p. 517 no. 10).

(no. 75, the picture not framed)

75 (52). Once St. Audries, 81. Dionysos and maenad (she standing to right, with kantharos and thyrsus, he standing to left, with forked sprig).

FRAGMENTS OF POTS

76 (54). TÜBINGEN E 55, fr. Watzinger pl. 18. (Dionysos and satyr). From a pelike?

77 (46). MUNICH inv. 1742, fr. *CV.* pl. 102, 7. (Man). From a pelike or a hydria. 'W.' in *ARV.*[1] 348 no. 46 is a misprint for 'M.'

78. MYKONOS, fr., from Rheneia (originally from Delos). Dugas *Délos xxi* pl. 46, 118. (Man). [Dugas].

79. ELEUSIS 605, fr., from Eleusis. (Upper part of a man, and a sprig of ivy held by another person—a woman?).

CUP

80. DUNEDIN E 48.232. A, *JHS.* 71, 190 fig. 8. I, Dionysos and satyr; in the zone round this, satyrs attacking maenads; A, satyr and woman, satyr and Nike; the satyrs on A wear himatia; B, the like.

SKYPHOS

(type A)

81 (53). YALE 158. A, Baur 106; the shape, Hambidge 62 fig. 4. A, youth and boy; B, the like.

82. LOUVRE G 560. A, Pottier *Dessin* pl. 14, 57. A, two maenads. B, youth and boy. Restored. In *ARV*.[1] 616 no. 50 this was attributed to the Painter of Brussels R 330, but it can hardly be separated from Yale 158 (no. 81), and I now take it to be by the Orchard Painter. The two artists have points in common.

A ruined vase seems to be by the Orchard Painter:

COLUMN-KRATER

(with framed pictures)

(a). VILLA GIULIA 5951, from Corchiano. A, Dionysos with maenad and satyrs. B, youth, man, and woman.

The following may be his:

COLUMN-KRATERS

(no. 1, not known if the pictures framed)

1. REGGIO, fr., from Locri. (Hand, extended to right; then beard to waist of a man in a himation standing to left, holding a staff).

(the pictures not framed)

2. FERRARA, T. 697, from Spina. Komos (A, man and flute-girl; B, man or youth).

In the manner of the Orchard Painter, the

COLUMN-KRATER

(with framed pictures)

LECCE 599, from Rugge. *CV.* pl. 9, 1–2. A, two old men and two women; B, old man and two women.

The following recalls the Orchard Painter:

COLUMN-KRATER

(with framed pictures)

STRALSUND. A, *Jb.* 69, 132–3. A, Eos and Tithonos. B, youth.

THE ALKIMACHOS PAINTER

VA. 134–8. *Att. V.* 296–9 and 476. *V.Pol.* 29. *ARV.*[1] 356–60, 936, 942, and 958.
CB. iii, text.

So called from the kalos-name on nos. 19 and 20.

At times influenced by the Pan Painter.

NECK-AMPHORAE

(*nos. 1–18, Nolan amphorae, with triple handles*)

1 (1). NEW YORK 41.162.16. A, *AJA.* 1924, 287; *CV.* Gallatin pl. 22. A,
Greek and Amazon. B, youth.

2 (2). NEW YORK MARKET (Ernest Brummer: ex Parrish). A, *Cat. Sotheby
5 July 1928*, pl. 3, 24. Centauromachy (A, Centaur and Lapith; B,
Lapith).

3 (4). LONDON E 306, from Nola. *CV.* pl. 54, 3. A, warrior. B, youth.

4 (5). WARSAW 142335 (ex Czartoryski 53). *V.Pol.* pl. 18; *CV.* pl. 30, 1.
A, warriors setting out. B, youth.

5. BASLE MARKET (M.M.). A, youth and man setting out. B, youth. The
youth on A (chitoniskos, chlamys, petasos at nape) moves to right, looking round, a pair of spears in his left hand; the man (chlamys, woollen hat)
follows him, to right, in his right hand a stick, in his left a bag held over
his shoulder. On B, in himation, standing to right, with stick.

6 (6). OXFORD 1919.23. *CV.* pl. 17, 8 and pl. 18, 8. A, warrior setting out.
B, youth.

7 (3). HARVARD 1927.148 (1641.95). *CV.* pl. 16, 1; A, *Die Antike* 17, 225;
A, Radermacher *Mythos*[2] fig. 16. A, Theseus and Sinis. B, youth.

8 (7). SAINT-GERMAIN 7565, from Italy. Reinach *Cat.* ii, 108. A, Eos and
Kephalos. B, woman.

9 (8). MADRID 11102 (L. 177), from Nola. *CV.* pl. 22, 5; B.Ap. xxiii. 34,
2. A, woman with sceptre; B, woman bringing her a phiale.

10 (9). NEW YORK, Gallatin, from Campania (Capua or Curti). *CV.* pl. 54,
1. A, jumper; B, trainer. See p. 1658.

11. PLOVDIV 2572, from Brezovo. ‖*RA.* 38 (1951), 32–38, whence *BCH.*
1957, 150, 7 and 155 fig. 12. A, athlete; B, trainer.

11 *bis.* LISBON, Gilbert. Rocha Pereira *Notícia* 3 figs. 16–17; Rocha Pereira
G.V.P. pll. 24–25. A, athlete; B, youth.

12 (a i 2). LONDON 1928.1–17.57. A, *Burl. 1903* pl. 89, G 10; A, *BMQ.* 2 pl.
55, c; *CV.* pl. 46, 2 and pl. 51, 3; A, *BSA.* 40 pl. 12, 42. A, Athena and
Hermes. B, youth. Compare Leningrad 611 (no. 26). Unusually plea-
sant for this painter.

13 (10). NAPLES 3050, from Nola. A, ph. So. 11072, ii, 6. A, Dionysos.
B, youth. On A, ΚΑΛΟΣ ΛΙΤΑΣ.

14. PALERMO V 745, from Gela.   A, *AZ*. 1871 pl. 45, 1, whence (detail) *Jb*. 40, 218 fig. 17; *CV*. pl. 28, 1–2 and pl. 27, 2.   A, Nike.   B, youth.

15 (11). PARIS, Rothschild.   A, Nike.   B, youth.   On A, ΛΙ+ΑΣ.

16 (12). NAPLES 3180, from Nola.   A, ph. So. 11072, ii, 3.   A, youth with lyre at altar.   B, youth.

17 (14). Once NAPLES, Pacileo.   B.Ap. xxiii. 32. 1.   A, youth with lyre; B, man.   On A, in himation, standing to right, lyre in left hand, at column. On B, in himation, standing to left.

18 (13). MADRID inv. 32671 (red 181).   *CV*. pl. 24, 2.   A, youth at column; B, youth.

(no. 18 bis, Nolan amphora, with ridged handles)

18 *bis*. FRANKFORT MARKET (Henrich).   B, *Ant. Kunst* 2, i, advertisement pages, 1. A, (?).   B, man (moving to left, with stick).

(nos. 19–22, small, with ridged handles: on the shape see CB. ii, 40)

19 (16). MUNICH 2325 (J. 227), from South Italy (Nola?).   Millingen *PAV*. pl. 9; A, *Jb*. 29, 130; A, Richter *F*. fig. 151; *CV*. pl. 58, 1 and pl. 59, 1 and 3.   A, Theseus and Procrustes.   B, woman.   On A, ΑΛΚΙΜΑ+ΟΣ ΚΑΛΟΣ.

20 (17). LONDON E 318, from Nola.   A, *Mon*. 1 pl. 9, 3; *CV*. pl. 58, 3; A, Stella 839; A, ph. Ma. 3158, 2.   A, Herakles and Apollo: the struggle for the tripod.   B, old man.   On A, in three lines, ΑΛΚΙΜΑ+ΩΣ ΚΑΛΩϹ ΕΓΙ+ΑΡΟΣ.

21 (18). NAPLES 3125, from Nola.   A, Angelini pl. 9; A, ph. So. 11072, iii, 3.   A, Boreas and Oreithyia; B, woman fleeing.   On A, ΚΛΕΝΙΑΣ ΚΑΛΩΣ.

22 (19). LOUVRE G 206, from Capua.   A, *Annali* 1878 pl. I, 1 (= Furtwängler *KS*. i pl. 9, 1), whence HM. pl. 36, 1; *CV*. pl. 37, 10–11 and pl. 38, 6. A, satyr attacking a sleeping maenad.   B, woman running.

(nos. 23–25, small, with double handles)

23 (20). MADRID 11101 (L. 178).   *RM*. 3, 106; A, Alvarez-Ossorio pl. 35, 1; *CV*. pl. 20, 4.   A, Neoptolemos and Astyanax; B, warrior.   Restored.

24 (21). LONDON E 286, from Nola.   *CV*. pl. 47, 1.   A, warrior; B, light-armed man.

25 (22). LONDON E 285.   A, Hancarville 4 pl. 74; *CV*. pl. 46, 3.   A, warrior; B, slinger.

(no. 26, larger, with twisted handles)

26 (a i 1). LENINGRAD 611.   A, Waldhauer *ARV*. fig. 15; B, Waldhauer *KO*. pl. 10 fig. 8.   A, Hermes pursuing a boy (Ganymede); B, Hermes and a boy (Paris?).   Compare London 1928.1–17.57 (no. 12).   For the subjects, CB. ii, 52.

(no. 27, larger, with triple handles)

27 (15). MUNICH 2343 (J. 1181), from Vulci. *CV.* pl. 209, 1–2, pl. 211, 1–3, pl. 216, 5, and p. 7. A, Dionysos and maenad; B, Dionysos and satyr.

(no. 28, fat, with convex handles; framed pictures)

28 (a ii 1). LONDON E 283, from Vulci. *CV.* pl. 17, 2. A, woman and Nike. B, komos (youth with skyphos, and boy).

PELIKAI

(nos. 29–30, with framed pictures)

29 (25). DRESDEN ZV 2535. A, *Anz.* 1925, 121; A, Brommer *Satyrspiele* 61. A, satyr at herm. B, Nike running with torch and thurible.

30 (27). MARSEILLES 1624. A, warrior leaving home (youth and woman). B, two youths.

(nos. 31–34, the pictures not framed)

31 (23). LONDON E 404, from Camiros. A, two women; B, woman and old man.

32 (24). VIENNA 1093. *CV.* pl. 76, 4–5. Komos (A, youth with stick and skyphos, and youth with lyre; B, youth dancing).

33 (26). LENINGRAD 734 (St. 1721). *CR.* 1868, 129 and 168. A, satyr and boy; B, satyr.

34 (28). PARIS, Rothschild (ex Torr), from Rhodes. A, satyr and boy; B, youth. On A, satyr in himation leaning on his stick to right, boy in himation standing to left; on B, in himation, with stick, moving to left.

LOUTROPHOROI

35. ATHENS, Acr. Mus., fr., from Athens. Women (with chaplet, basket, flowers, sash, basket).

36. ATHENS, Acr. Mus., fr., from Athens. (Women with alabastron, girl with basket).

37. ATHENS, Acr. Mus., fr., from Athens. (Woman, woman with torch).

COLUMN-KRATERS

(nos. 38–52, with framed pictures)

38 (29). NEW YORK 56.171.46 (ex Hearst). A, Gerhard *A.B.* pl. 117, 1; A, *Cat. Sotheby July 11 1927* pl. 9, 160. A, Theseus and Minotaur. B, three youths. Now cleaned.

39 (30). SYRACUSE 23511, from Gela. A, *ML.* 17 pl. 45 and p. 511. A, Dionysos with satyrs and maenad. B, three youths.

40 (32). BOLOGNA 244, from Bologna. Zannoni pl. 42, 3 and 8–9; *CV.* pl. 29. A, Dionysos and maenad with donkeys. B, komos.

41 (31). VIENNA 835. *CV.* pl. 90, 1–2. A, maenad with donkey, and satyrs. B, three youths.

42 (33). BOLOGNA 238, from Bologna. A, Pellegrini 95; *CV.* pl. 30, 1–3. A, satyrs and maenads. B, youths and woman.

43 (34). MUNICH 2377 (J. 791), from Sicily. A, satyrs and maenad. B, komos (two youths).

44 (35). BOLOGNA 236, from Bologna. A, *Mus. It.* 2 pl. 1, 1, whence Roscher s.v. Kora, 1378; A, *Ausonia* 9, 72; *CV.* pl. 25; A, Stella 442; A, *E.A.A.* i, 261. A, wedding of Hermes to the daughter of Dryops (*H. H. Pan* 33). This interpretation is Miss Milne's. B, komos.

45 (36). BOLOGNA 237, from Bologna. A, Pellegrini 94. A, Centauromachy. B, komos.

46 (37). LENINGRAD, from Kerch. A, *Otchët 1903*, 157 fig. 314. A, young warrior pursuing a woman. B, komos (youths and woman).

47 (38). SYRACUSE, from Camarina. A, young warrior pursuing a woman. B, youths and woman.

48. FERRARA, T. 377, from Spina. A, Boreas and Oreithyia. B, old man and two youths.

49 (40). MADRID 11042 (L. 168). A, Alvarez-Ossorio pl. 29, 3; A, Leroux pl. 21, 2; *CV.* pl. 16, 1. A, arming. B, three youths.

49 *bis.* FERRARA, T. 67 B VP, from Spina. A, warrior setting out. B, woman, old man, and youth.

50 (41). BOLOGNA 239, from Bologna. Part of A, Pellegrini 96. A, komos ('Anacreon and his companions'). B, old man, woman, and male. For the subject of A, CB. ii, 60 no. 23.

51 (39). RHODES 12063, from Ialysos. A, *Cl. Rh.* 3, 280; A, *CV.* pl. 10, 1–2. A, horse-race. B, athletes and trainer.

52. BERKELEY 8.3838, fr. B, (youth).

(nos. 53–55, the pictures not framed)

53 (42). NAPLES, from Cumae. A, *ML.* 22 pl. 83, 2. A, dadouchos and mystes. B, woman. For the subject of A, *Num. Chr.* 1941, 7.

54 (43). ANCONA, from Numana. A, Marconi and Serra pl. 48, 1. A, woman holding spear and shield and old man holding helmet. B, youth.

55 (44). FERRARA, T. 143, from Spina. A, symposion (man reclining); B, komast (youth).

HYDRIA
(the picture mainly on the shoulder)

56 (45). BASLE 1906.295. Eos and Tithonos.

LEKYTHOI
(standard shape)

57 (46). BERLIN inv. 30035, from near Taranto. *Amtl. Ber.* 9, 219–22; *VA.* 137; *Stephanos* pl. 6; the Herakles, Licht i, 238; Schaal fig. 36; part,

Bieber *G.K.* pl. 35, 2; Diepolder *G.V.* 45; Züchner *Abb.* 8.   Herakles and Perithoos in Hades.   See CB. iii, text.

58 (47).   BOSTON 95.39, from Eretria.   *VA.* 135, whence Philippart *Ic. Bacch.* 18 and Cook *Zeus* iii, 8 fig. 24; Fairbanks and Chase 36; CB. iii pl. 84, 148.   Birth of Dionysos from Zeus.   See CB. iii, text.

59 (48).   SYRACUSE 2411.   Youth advancing with spear and sword.

59 *bis.*   REGGIO 5236, from Locri.   *NSc.* 1917, 129 fig. 35.   Demeter.

OINOCHOE
(*shape 1*)

60 (a i 3).   SCHWERIN 1308.   Apollo and Artemis.

CUPS

61 (49).   FERRARA, T. 308, from Spina.   I, Eos and Kephalos.   A–B, women.

62.   LEYDEN PC 89 (xviii a 4), from Vulci.   I, *Jb.* 2, 99, whence Schröder *Sport* 103 fig. 22; I, Weege *Bronzestatuette eines antiken Waffenläufers* fig. 3; I, *Gids G.V.* fig. 12.   I, hoplitodromos.   A, Dionysos with satyr and maenad; B, satyrs and maenad.   For the subject of I, *BSA.* 46, 11 no. 11.

63.   BARCELONA 4306, and AMPURIAS, fr., from Ampurias.   I, satyr squatting, playing the flute; A, maenad on donkey, and satyrs; B, (donkey, maenad). [Shefton].

64.   AMPURIAS 7.10.1920, fr., from Ampurias.   I, satyr with pointed amphora; A, (Dionysos, satyr, and another).

65.   BARCELONA, fr., from Ampurias.   *Riv. st. lig.* 15, 84, above, right = Almagro *Guía*² 110, above, right.   A, Boreas and Oreithyia.

MANNER OF THE ALKIMACHOS PAINTER
*ARV.*¹ 358–60 and 958.

COLUMN-KRATERS
(*nos. 1–3, with framed pictures*)

1.   BARCELONA 477, fr., from Ampurias.   A, (the upper part of the left-hand figure remains, a naked youth, helmeted, to right).

2 (6).   VILLA GIULIA, from Corchiano.   A, Dionysos and maenads with donkeys.   Ruined.

3 (7).   NAPLES 3115.   A, ph. So. 11071, i, 5.   A, warrior pursuing a woman (Menelaos and Helen).   B, komos.   Compare Milan (p. 534, foot no. 1). Perhaps late work of the painter himself?

(*nos. 4–4 bis, the pictures not framed*)

4 (5).   RUVO, Jatta, 873 *bis,* from Ruvo.   A, Boreas and Oreithyia; B, woman fleeing.

4 *bis*. PALERMO (2120), from Gela. A, *Jb*. 10, 198, 32. A, hoplitodromos and judge; B, old man.

PELIKE

5 (4). KOENIGSBERG 65. A, Lullies *A.K.K.* pl. 9, below; phs. A.I. varia 385–6. A, Eos and Kephalos. B, jumper and trainer. May be by the painter himself. Restored.

NECK-AMPHORAE

(no. 6, small, with convex handles)

6 (a). LONDON E 326, from Nola. A, *JHS*. 27 pl. 17; *CV*. pl. 63, 1. A, youth leaving home (youth and old man). B, woman holding out lyre and flute, and youth. May be by the painter himself—but something has happened to the woman on B—left to a beginner?

(nos. 7–8, small, the handles lost)

7. MYKONOS, from Rheneia (originally from Delos). Dugas *Délos xxi* pl. 18, 49, whence (B) *BCH*. 1957, 153. A, youth settting out (youth, and woman—or Athena?). B, youth. On B, on a pillar, TIMOK[PATEξ-K]ΑΛΟξ.

8 (a). FLORENCE 19 B 46. Part, *CV*. pl. 19, B 46. A, Eos and Kephalos. B, male.

(no. 9, Nolan amphora, with triple handles)

9. CARLSRUHE 204, from Nola. A, Wagner and Eyth pl. 58; Welter pl. 15; *CV*. pl. 15, 2 and 4. A, Pegasus. B, boy running. On A, NIKONΔAξ-KΑΛΟξ.

(no. 10, Nolan amphora, with ridged handles)

10 (2). WINCHESTER, Sharpe, from Vulci. Gerhard pl. 274, 3–5; B.Ap. xvi. 7. 1. A, Eos; B, youth (companion of Tithonos?).

LOUTROPHOROS

11. ATHENS, Acr. Mus., from Athens. Wedding (of Peleus?: the bridegroom mounting a chariot). On the neck, two women and a man.

Related to the Alkimachos Painter, two by one hand:

COLUMN-KRATER

1. MILAN, from Spina. A, warrior pursuing a woman (Menelaos and Helen). B, three youths.

CALYX-KRATER

2. ATHENS, Agora, P 8447, fr., from Athens. A, (woman—probably pursued).

The following recall the Alkimachos Painter:

LEKYTHOI

(*standard shape*)

1 (a 9). ATHENS 1300 (CC. 1369), from Eretria. Ph. A.I. NM 3031. Woman with lyre and phiale (Artemis holding Apollo's lyre?).

2 (2). SYRACUSE 21972, from Gela. *ML.* 17 pl. 11, whence Perrot 10, 649 and Licht ii, 88; Matt 88, right; ph. Al. 33388, 3. Naked woman laying her clothes on a chair.

3 (3). NEW YORK 21.88.72, from Sicily. *Coll. Lambros* pl. 9, 53; *Coll. Hirsch* pl. 3, 172; *Bull. Metr.* 18, 254. Maenad.

NECK-AMPHORA

(*Nolan amphora, with triple handles*)

4 (a 3). BOSTON 95.20. The shape, Caskey G. 69. A, Nike. B, woman with torch. On A, NIKON ΚΑΛΟΣ.

BELL-KRATER

5 (4). LONDON E 507, from Camiros. A, Dionysos and maenads; B, satyr and maenads. Wretched drawing, but akin to the Dionysiac column-kraters of the Alkimachos Painter.

VOTIVE SHIELD

6 (a 10). ATHENS Acr. 1071, fr., from Athens. Langlotz pl. 83. Nike with aphlaston.

THE ARISTOMENES PAINTER

ARV.[1] 360.

Somewhat recalls the Alkimachos Painter.

LEKYTHOI

(*standard shape*)

1 (1). SYRACUSE 21130, from Gela. *ML.* 17 pl. 18, whence *E.A.A.* i, 651. Warrior and old man. ΚΑΛΟΣ ΑΡΙΣΤΟΜΕΝΗΣ.

2 (2). SYRACUSE 21129, from Gela. *ML.* 17 pl. 17. Woman holding a helmet.

CHAPTER 32

THE BOREAS-FLORENCE GROUP

THE BOREAS—FLORENCE GROUP

The Boreas Painter, the Florence Painter, the Painter of London E 489 —these form a group. They are mainly painters of second-rate column-kraters. The Boreas Painter sometimes rises above that; the others, so far as can be told at present, do not.

The Painter of London E 489 is the youngest of the three. The Boreas Painter and the Florence Painter are 'brothers', and one sometimes hesitates between them, especially in the Dionysiac vases. I have shifted three kraters from the old Boreas list to the Florence: Cape Town (no. 45), Syracuse 22758 (no. 54), Baltimore, Walters, 48.66 (no. 37).

In the next generation the tradition is continued by the Naples Painter (p. 1096).

THE BOREAS PAINTER
VA. 133. *Att. V.* 305–7. *ARV.*[1] 337–41 and 958.

I now take the Ancona volute-krater, no. 1 in my previous list, to be by the Painter of Bologna 228 (p. 511 no. 1).

VOLUTE-KRATERS

1 (2). FERRARA, T. 749, from Spina. A, Aurigemma[1] 141–5, p. 1, above, and p. xvii =[2] 181–5, p. 1, above, and p. xvii; detail of A, Arias and Alfieri pl. 30; Alfieri and Arias S. pll. 14–17; detail, *E.A.A.* ii, 140. Youth with spears (Theseus?) pursuing a woman (Helen?). On the neck: A, animals (lion and panther attacking fawn; on the left, lion and boar; on the right, the like). B, symposion. See p. 1658.

2 (3). BOLOGNA 273, from Bologna. Part of A, Pellegrini 116; detail of A, Stella 299; *CV.* pll. 51–52. Boreas and Oreithyia.

3 (4). BOLOGNA 274, from Bologna. A, Pellegrini 117; *CV.* pll. 53–54 and pl. 55, 7. Warrior arming.

4. FERRARA, T. 18 C VP, from Spina. Alfieri and Arias S. pll. 18–21; *Mostra* pl. 77. Neoptolemos leaving Skyros. See p. 1658.

COLUMN-KRATERS
(nos. 5–34, with framed pictures)

5 (5). NEW YORK 96.19.1 (GR 1244). Richter and Hall pl. 94 and pl. 170, 86. A, Zeus and Aigina. B, man and three women.

6 (6). SYRACUSE 2408, from Còmiso. A, Franz Müller 93; A, *NSc*. 1937 pl. 17, 2; A, B.Ap. xxii. 44. 1; A, ph. R.I. 307. A, Penelope and the suitors; B, suitors. Now cleaned.

7 (7). COPENHAGEN, Ny Carlsberg, inv. 2681. A, Pollak *Woodyat* pl. 4, 49; Poulsen *VG*. figs. 37-38. A, Herakles and Nereus. B, youth pursuing a woman.

8 (8). BOLOGNA 196, from Bologna. A, Pellegrini 74; A, *CV*. pl. 30, 4. A, Herakles and Nereus. B, three women.

9 (9). MUNICH 2375 (J. 748), from Sicily. A, Lau pl. 32, 1: A, Winter *J.A.V*. 21. A, Boreas and Oreithyia. B, old king and three women.

10 (10). BOLOGNA 204, from Bologna. A, Pellegrini 79; *CV*. pl. 40, 1-2. A, Eos and Kephalos. B, youths and woman.

11. OXFORD, Beazley, frr. A, uncertain subject: two warriors (one bearded, one young) pursuing a woman; on the left, a youth and a woman (he pursuing her?). B, four males. Good part is preserved.

12 (11). BOLOGNA 206, from Bologna. A, *Mus. Ital*. 2 pl. 1, 2; *CV*. pl. 27, whence (A) *BCH*. 1952, 617. A, old man at herm, woman at herm. B, youths and woman.

13. SAN SIMEON, State Monument, 9855. A, *Coll. Gagliardi* pl. 6, 421. A, Zeus and Hera, with Nike (or Iris) and Hermes. B, youth with spear, and three youths. Slightly restored. Compare Lecce 598 (no. 14), and, for the subject, a column-krater by the Syriskos Painter (p. 260 no. 15).

14 (12). LECCE 598, from Ruvo. *CV*. pl. 5, 3-4 and pl. 6, 2; A, Bernardini pl. 45, 1. A, Zeus and Nike (or Iris); between two youths. B, four youths. Compare the last.

15 (13). GOETTINGEN (Berlin 2370 on loan), from S. Agata de' Goti. A, man with phiale, served with wine by a woman, in presence of a man and two youths, all three sceptred. B, four youths. Restored.

16 (14). LONDON MARKET (Spink: ex Richmond, Cook). A, two horsemen. B, three youths.

17 (15). Once AGRIGENTO, Giudice. A, two horsemen. B, youths.

18. SYRACUSE, from Syracuse. *NSc*. 1938, 262-3. A, two mounted warriors. B, youths and boy.

19 (16). ADOLPHSECK, Landgraf Philipp of Hesse, 75. *CV*. pl. 45, 1-2. A, youth with horse leaving home. B, athlete and youths.

20 (17). NAPLES inv. 127929, from Cumae. A, *ML*. 22 pl. 84, 5. A, racing-chariot and judge. B, three youths.

21. FERRARA, T. 15 C VP, from Spina. A, komos; B, athlete, youths, and man.

22 (18). LONDON E 475, from Gela. A, komos. B, three youths.

23 (19). GELA (ex Navarra-Jacona 286), from Gela. A, komos (three men, and a youth playing the flute). B, man and three youths.

24 (20). BOSTON 86.604 (F. 360.4), fr., from Naucratis. Fairbanks pl. 39. B, komos.

25 (23). WELWYN, Wilshere, from Agrigento. Millingen *Coghill* pll. 16–17. A, satyrs and maenads. B, komos.

26 (22). SYRACUSE, from Camarina. A, satyr and maenads (a satyr grasping a maenad, between two maenads holding torches). B, four youths. As the next.

27 (a 2–3). CATANIA 694 and 695. Libertini pl. 73. A, satyrs and maenads. B, komos. As the last.

28 (26). FLORENCE PD 420, fr. A, satyr and maenads. B, youths and woman.

29 (27). BOLOGNA 208, from Bologna. Zannoni pl. 27, 9–13. A, satyr and maenads; one of them chastises him with a sandal; B, three maenads.

30 (28). BOLOGNA 227, from Bologna. A, three maenads. B, male and two boys.

31 (29). MARZABOTTO, fr., from Marzabotto. Gozzadini pl. 9, 4–5. (Woman—maenad?—with torch).

32. GELA (Acr. amb. 5 no. 2), fr., from Gela. A, (thumb, then head of a woman moving to right, looking round to left).

32 *bis.* REGGIO, fr., from Locri. A, (head of a woman in a saccos to left). Worn.

32 *ter.* REGGIO, fr., from Locri. Youths and woman (upper part of youth in himation to right, head of woman to left, upper part of youth in himation to left).

32⁴. REGGIO, fr., from Locri. (Upper half of a youth's head to left, including the nape).

32⁵. REGGIO, fr., from Locri. (Upper half of a youth's head to left, minus the nape).

33 (30). BOLOGNA, fr., from Bologna (Certosa). (Heads of two youths to left, the second one holding a stick).

34 (31). OXFORD G 712, fr., from Naucratis. *CV.* pl. 66, 12. (Youth).

(nos. 35–37, the pictures not framed)

35 (32). PALERMO V 793. *CV.* pl. 49. A, satyr and maenad; B, maenad.

36 (33). VILLA GIULIA 3574, from Falerii. *CV.* pl. 19, 1–3. A, satyr and maenad; B, satyr.

37 (34). NAPLES, from Cumae. A, Zeus pursuing a woman. B, two youths.

KRATER (BELL-KRATER ?)

38. BASLE, Cahn, fr. (Head of young warrior to left).

PANATHENAIC AMPHORA

39 (35). LONDON E 282, from Vulci. *JHS.* 9 pl. 3 and p. 11; *CV.* pl. 17, 1. A, warrior; B, wife holding child.

LOUTROPHOROS

40. ATHENS 1249 (CC. 1226), from Pirnari. B, Collignon and Couve pl.
43, 1226; A, ph. Al. 24480, 1, whence Herford pl. 3, b; A, *Eph.* 1936, 52
fig. 3; A, Zevi (*Mem. Linc. 6*) 363. Wedding; on the neck, A, woman
with torch, B, the like.

AMPHORA

(type B)

41. ATHENS, Agora, P 21859, from Athens. *Hesp.* 22 pl. 21. A, man pursuing a woman; B, woman fleeing. [Talcott]. See p. 1658.

PELIKE

42 (37). VILLA GIULIA. A, *Coll. Delessert* pl. 3, 30; *Boll. d'Arte* 1927, 176–82.
A, warrior leaving home (warrior and woman). B, man and youth.

HYDRIA

(the picture mainly on the shoulder)

43 (38). ATHENS, Vlasto, from Kitsi. Part, Clairmont *P.* pl. 33, a. Judgement of Paris.

OINOCHOAI

(no. 44, shape 1)

44 (39). ATHENS 14504 (15110), from Attica. Bride, with women and man.
Compare Bologna 206 (no. 12).

(nos. 45–46, shape 5A)

45 (40). LONDON E 559, from Camiros. Man and boy. Rough.

46 (41). LONDON E 558, from Camiros. Komast. Rough.

FRAGMENT OF A POT

47 (43). ATHENS Acr. 1024, fr., from Athens. Langlotz pl. 79 and p. 92.
(Woman). From a calyx-krater?

VOTIVE SHIELD

48 (42). ATHENS Acr. 1072, fr., from Athens. Langlotz pl. 83, whence *Hesp.*
23, 201; *Charites Langlotz* pl. 20, 1. Woman holding aphlasta.

NEAR THE BOREAS PAINTER

COLUMN-KRATERS

(no. 1, the pictures not framed)

1. PADULA, from Padula. A, woman with flute, and man; B, man. May be
by the painter himself.

(no. 2, with framed pictures)

2 (4). BOLOGNA 201, from Bologna. A, Boreas and Oreithyia. B, youths
and woman.

DINOS

3 (1). Bologna 330, from Bologna. Pellegrini 168 (with alien stand). Men.

AMPHORA

(type B)

4 (5). Louvre CA 1852, from Greece. A, *Le Musée* 3, 54; A, *Coll. B. et C.* pl. 24, 185; *CV* d pl. 38, 1–2; A, ph. Gir. 15263. A, man buying an amphora; B, youth with amphora, and man. Restored.

OINOCHOE

(shape 5A)

5 (6). Athens 1415 (CC. 1291), from Phocis. Women.

FRAGMENT OF A POT

6. Athens, Agora, P 20682, fr., from Athens. (Woman, loutrophoros). From a nuptial lebes?

A lost vase, probably a column-krater, may be by the Boreas Painter: Lost. A, Tischbein 5 pl. 4. A, youth pursuing a woman.

A vase is related to the Boreas Painter and the Florence Painter:

COLUMN-KRATER

(with framed pictures)

Los Angeles A 5933.50.37 (ex Cowdray). A, Millingen *Coghill* pl. 41, whence Inghirami pl. 268; A, *Cat. Christie July 23 1917* pl. 2, 62; A, Tillyard pl. 21, 130; A, *Cat. Sotheby Dec. 2 1946* pl. 3. A, Dionysos, satyr with a midget satyr on his shoulders, and satyr with donkey. B, man and youths.

Another vase is akin to the work of the Boreas Painter:

COLUMN-KRATER

(the pictures not framed)

Palermo V 795, from Agrigento. Politi *Vasi di premio* pll. 4–5; *CV*. pl. 48. A, Zeus pursuing a woman. B, woman running with torch.

―――――――

THE FLORENCE PAINTER

Att. V. 308–9 (Painter of the Florence Centauromachy). *ARV.*[1] 341–4.

'Brother' of the Boreas Painter: see p. 536.

··The vases marked 'late' are weaker than the rest, but I take them to be by the painter himself.

COLUMN-KRATERS

(nos. 1–56, with framed pictures)

1 (1). FLORENCE 3997. Heydemann *Ober.* pl. 3, 1; A, ph. Al. 17071, above, right, whence Milani *Mus. Fir.* pl. 42, 3 = Minto *R. Mus. Fir.* pl. 46, above, right; A, Pfuhl fig. 489 (= Pfuhl *Mast.* fig. 74); A, FR. pl. 166, 2, whence Norman Gardiner *Athl.* fig. 181, Byvanck-Quarles van Ufford *P.* 29, Kraiker *M.G.* pl. 37, *Riv. Ist.* N.S. 4, 185; *CV.* pl. 39, 3, pl. 43, 1–3, and pl. 44, 2–3, whence Rumpf *MZ.* pl. 28, 4; A, ph. Al. 45762, whence Buschor *G. Vasen* 186 and Stella 561; A, Dugas and Flacelière pl. 11; A, *E.A.A.* iii, 701. A, Centauromachy at the wedding of Perithoos. B, komos.

2. LOUVRE C 10751. A, judgement of Paris. B, males and youth.

3 (2). FERRARA, T. 577, from Spina. A, Aurigemma[1] 159 = [2]189; A, Ghali-Kahil *H.* pl. 61. A, Menelaos and Helen. B, youths and woman,

4 (3). SYRACUSE 21189, from Gela. Part of A, *ML.* 17, 323. A, a god (Zeus?) pursuing a woman. B, youths and boy.

4 bis. FERRARA (erratico Dosso D, Nov. 1959), fr., from Spina. A, (upper front half of a female head to left). A fragment found in the same quarter may belong (leg of one in long chiton and himation standing to right, foot of a male moving to right).

5 (4). CEFALÙ. A, ph. R.I. 4932 = 5016. A, Eos and Tithonos.

6 (4 bis). Once NEW YORK, Hyde. A, *Cat. Parke-Bernet March 15–16 1940*, 52, 280. A, Eos and Tithonos. B, Nike, man, and youth.

7 (5). FERRARA (sequestro 30.11.28), from Spina. A, death of Orpheus. B, youths and woman. Late.

8 (6). LOUVRE G 360, from Nola. *CV* d pl. 26, 6–7. A, youth returning home. B, males and boy. Restored.

9 (7). BOLOGNA 203, from Bologna. A, Pellegrini 78 fig. 48; *CV.* pl. 47. A, youth returning home. B, youths and boy.

10 (8). BOLOGNA 207, from Bologna. A, youth returning home. B, three youths.

11 (9). FERRARA, T. 376, from Spina. A, youth returning home. B, youths and boy.

12 (10). MUNICH 2374 (J. 779), from Sicily. A, woman offering sword and shield to youth. B, three youths.

13 (15). SANTA BARBARA, Brundage. A, woman offering sword and shield to youth (between two men; device a wolf's head; replica of A on Munich 2374, no. 12). B, youths and boy.

14. FERRARA, T. 24 C VP, from Spina. A, woman offering sword and shield to youth. B, youths and boy. Replica of the last two.

15 (11). COPENHAGEN inv. 8178, from Bomarzo. *CV.* pl. 145, 2. A, woman offering phiale and sword to youth. B, youths and boy.

16 (12). FLORENCE 3998. *CV*. pl. 44, 4 and pl. 39, 4. A, woman offering phiale and sword to youth. B, youths and boy.

17 (13). SALONICA inv. 253 (R. 105 a), from Olynthos. A, Robinson *Olynthus 5* pl. 64, below. A, woman offering phiale to youth. B, (on the left, part of a clothed figure remains).

18 (14). FERRARA (sequestro S. Alberto di Romagna, dic. 1928), from Spina. A, woman offering phiale to youth. B, youths and boy.

19 (16). LENINGRAD 800 (St. 1682). A, warrior leaving home. B, youths and boy.

20 (17). PERUGIA (ex Guardabassi). A, warrior leaving home. B, youths and male. Restored.

20 *bis* (30). ALTENBURG 283, from Apulia. *CV*. pl. 55, 2 and pl. 56, 4. A, youth leaving home. B, youths and woman. Late. Misnumbered and misdescribed in *ARV*.[1] See p. 1658.

21 (18). MUNICH, Lenbachgalerie. A, youth and Nike with male and man. B, youths and male.

22 (19). LOUVRE G 350. *CV*. d pl. 24, 8–9. A, komos. B, youths and boy.

23. FERRARA, T. 611 B VP, from Spina. A, komos. B, youths and woman.

24 (20). FERRARA, T. 702, from Spina. A, komos. B, youths and boy.

25 (21). BOLOGNA 209, from Bologna. Zannoni pl. 93, 2–4. A, komos. B, youths and boy.

26. LOUVRE C 10760. A, komos. B, youths and boy.

27 (22). SYRACUSE (24036?), from Camarina. A, komos (youth with skyphos and stick, woman playing the flute, man with stick, man with stick looking round). B, youths.

27 *bis*. REGGIO, fr., from Locri. (Head of a woman playing the flute, to right; bobbed hair).

28 (23). LONDON E 484. Hancarville 4 pl. 29. A, komos. B, youths.

29 (24). LOUVRE G 352, from Agrigento. *CV*. d pl. 25, 3–4. A, komos. B, youths and boy.

30 (25). TARANTO. A, komos (replica of that on Louvre G 352, no. 29). B, youths and boy.

31 (26). OXFORD, Beazley, fr., from North Italy. Komos (upper part of man with skyphos).

32 (27). FERRARA, T. 746, from Spina. A, komos. B, youths and boy.

33 (28). LONDON MARKET (Spink: ex Richmond, Cook). A, komos. B, youths and woman. As Florence 4023 (no. 34). Late.

34 (29). FLORENCE 4023. Dempster 1 pl. 39; *CV*. pl. 46, 4 and pl. 38, 6. A, komos. B, youths and woman. Late.

35. BOLOGNA PU 284. Drawings, from the collection of Cassiano Dal Pozzo, in Windsor, whence *P.A.P.S.* 102, 206 fig. 21. A, komos. B, youths and woman. Compare Florence 4023 (no. 34). Late.

36 (B 21). BALTIMORE, Walters Art Gallery, 48.66, from Tarquinia. A, ph. Mo. A, symposion; B, komos (old man dancing, and two youths). Now partly cleaned. The style of the reverse is rather unusual.

37 (31). VILLA GIULIA, from Todi. A, *ML*. 24, 870. A, symposion. B, youths and boy. Late.

38. ALBANY (N.Y.), Nelson A. Rockefeller. A, symposion. Compare Villa Giulia and Taranto (nos. 37 and 39). Late.

39 (32). TARANTO 20931, from Conversano. A, symposion. B, youths and woman. Late.

39 *bis*. RENNES 716. A, men and boys; B, youths and boy.

40 (33). NAPLES Stg. 289. A, man and woman, man and youth with lyre. B, youths and woman. Late.

41 (34). BOLOGNA 259, frr., from Bologna. A, man and woman, two males. B, three males.

42 (35). VILLA GIULIA 48240, from Cervetri. A, *ML*. 42, 1023. A, youths and woman; B, the like. Late.

43 (36). NEW YORK 27.122.28, fr. A, Dionysos and satyrs. As Cefalù (no. 44).

44. CEFALÙ, from Lipari. A, Zagami pl. 7, a and pl. 8. A, Dionysos with satyrs and maenad. B, youths and woman. As New York 27.122.28 (no. 43).

45. CAPE TOWN (ex Champernowne). A, *Spink G.R.* 32 no. 63; A, *Cat. Sotheby July 20 1928* pl. 4. A, Dionysos on donkey, with satyr and maenad. B, youths and boy. See p. 1658.

46. FERRARA, T. 208 A VP, from Spina. A, Dionysos and maenads. B, youths and boy.

47 (37). LUCERNE MARKET (A.A.: ex Hirsch 300). *Ars Ant. Aukt. II* pl. 62, 157. A, satyrs and maenads. B, youths and woman.

48. STUTTGART MARKET. *Ant. Trau* ii pl. 5, 80; *Auktion iii Kricheldorf* pl. 9. A, satyrs and maenads. B, youths and boy.

49 (38). RUVO, Jatta, from Ruvo. A, *Japigia* 3, 20. A, satyrs and maenads. B, youths and boy.

50. LOUVRE C 10750. A, satyrs and maenads. B, youths and boy.

51. LOUVRE C 10752. A, satyrs and maenads. B, youths and boy.

51 *bis*. FERRARA, T. 840 B VP, from Spina. A, satyrs and maenads. B, youths and boy.

52 (39). FERRARA, T. 560, from Spina. A, satyrs and maenads. B, youths and woman.

53 (40). FERRARA, T. 1039, from Spina. A, satyrs and maenads. B, youths and woman.

53 *bis*. FERRARA, T. 212 B VP, from Spina. A, satyrs and maenads. B, youths and woman. Late. Manner, not self: see p. 1683.

54. SYRACUSE 22758, from Camarina. A, *ML.* 14 pl. 48. A, satyrs. B, youths and boy.

55. ATHENS, Agora, P 17532, fr., from Athens. (Head of youth to right, hair of head to left).

56. VATICAN, fr. (Head and shoulders of youth in himation to left).

56 *bis.* BOLOGNA, fr., from Bologna. *St. etr.* 23, 373. B, (boy).

(*no. 56 ter, not known whether the pictures framed*)

56 *ter.* REGGIO, fr., from Locri. (Bare legs of a male, right leg, frontal, of a woman in a chiton, both moving to right). The chiton has a kolpos and a pair of vertical stripes. Between the two figures, what may be part of a thyrsus; if so, satyr and maenad.

(*no. 57, the pictures not framed*)

57 (41). BOLOGNA 254, from Bologna. Zannoni pl. 58, 1–3; *CV.* pl. 33. Komos (A, man and flute-girl; B, youth).

STAMNOS

58 (42). NEWCASTLE UPON TYNE (ex Tynemouth, Hall). B, *Museums and Galleries* cover, below, r. A, Zeus pursuing a woman. B, woman offering phiale to youth (between two men). Restored.

NUPTIAL LEBES
(*type 1*)

59 (43). ATHENS 1251 (CC. 1234), from Attica. Bridegroom mounting biga. On the stand, youths and woman.

PELIKAI
(*nos. 60–63, the pictures framed*)

60. LOUVRE C 11019, frr. A, satyr and maenad. B, youth and woman.

61. LOUVRE C 11020, fr. A, satyr and maenad. B, youth and woman.

62 (45). FLORENCE 19 B 42. *CV.* pl. 19, B 42–45 and 47. A, komos (youth and woman). B, youth and boy.

63 (44). LONDON E 353, from Camiros. A, man and boy; B, youth and boy.

(*no. 64, the pictures not framed*)

64 (46). MYKONOS, from Rheneia (originally from Delos). Dugas *Délos xxi* pl. 12, 32. A, youth and boy; B, two boys.

OINOCHOAI
(*no. 65, shape 1*)

65. VILLA GIULIA, from Cervetri. Youth, and young girl seated.

(*nos. 66–67, shape 3, choes*)

66 (47). PARIS MARKET (Mikas). Van Hoorn *Choes* fig. 100. Symposion (man reclining, and youth with lyre). Late.

67 (48). ATHENS, from Athens. Youth and woman.

Fragments are either by the Florence Painter or by the Boreas:

COLUMN-KRATERS

1. ATHENS, Agora, P 19150, fr., from Athens. A, male pursuing a woman.
2. REGGIO, fr., from Locri. A, (lower parts of two horses' heads, to right, then a male moving to right—the tail of his chitoniskos is preserved). White reins. Compare the last.
3. REGGIO, fr., from Locri. (Head—except the part above the eye—to left, right shoulder, and breast, of a man in a himation standing frontal, right arm probably akimbo).

MANNER OF THE FLORENCE PAINTER

COLUMN-KRATERS
(with framed pictures)

1. SALONICA inv. 724 (R. 105), fr., from Olynthos. Robinson *Olynthus 5* pl. 64, above; part, Robinson *Olynthus 13* pl. 128, 8. A, youth, male with horse, and male.
2. FERRARA, T. 607, from Spina. A, satyrs and maenads. B, three youths.
3. REGGIO, fr., from Locri. (Heads of satyr and of Dionysos, both facing left, with an upright thyrsus between them).
4. FERRARA (sequestro), fr. (two joining), from Spina. B, youths and woman (arm with stick, upper part and left side of woman frontal, looking round to left, upper part of youth to left, stick in left hand).
5 (a). SYRACUSE 2409. A, youth with spears (Theseus?) pursuing a woman. B, youths and woman. Late.
6 (a). SYRACUSE 36388, from Syracuse. A, warrior leaving home. B, youths and woman. Late.
7 (1). Once AGRIGENTO, Politi, from Agrigento. A, Politi *Ill. ad un vaso fittile rappresentante Cassandra* pl. 1; A, Raoul-Rochette pl. 2, whence Inghirami pl. 378. A, man pursuing a woman. B, youths and woman.

NUPTIAL LEBES
(type 1)

8 (2). ERLANGEN 434. A, mistress and maid (woman seated, and woman); at each handle, Nike; B, two women. The stand black. Late.

HYDRIA
(rather than oinochoe shape 2)

9 (3). MYKONOS, from Rheneia (originally from Delos). Dugas *Délos xxi* pl. 27, 66. Seated woman, and woman. Small. Late.

The following is near the late work of the Florence Painter:

PELIKE
(with framed pictures)

SAN SIMEON, Hearst State Monument, 10083. A, youth with spears (Theseus?) pursuing a woman. B, man and woman. Restored.

THE PAINTER OF LONDON E 489

Att. V. 310. ARV.[1] 344–6.

Connected with the Boreas Painter and the Florence Painter.

COLUMN-KRATERS
(with framed pictures)

1 (1). NAPLES 2423. A, ph. So. 11071, ii, 5. A, Zeus pursuing a woman. B, komos.

2 (2). VIENNA 642. A, Tischbein 5 pl. 32; *CV.* pl. 88, 1–3. A, youth with spears (Theseus?) pursuing a woman. B, three youths.

3 (3). BOLOGNA 210, from Bologna. A, youth with spears (Theseus?) pursuing a woman. B, three youths.

4 (4). FERRARA, T. 446, from Spina. A, youth with spears (Theseus?) pursuing a woman. B, komos.

5. FERRARA (sequestro Carabinieri di Comacchio 7–8.9.57), from Spina. A, youth with spears (Theseus?) pursuing a woman. B, youths and woman.

6 (6). BOLOGNA 213, from Bologna. A, youth pursuing a woman. B, three youths.

7 (6). SYRACUSE 12359, fr. A, youths with spears pursuing women.

8 (7). VILLA GIULIA 50646. A, men pursuing women. B, komos.

9. PARIS MARKET (Mikas). A, Eos and Kephalos. B, komos. On A, Eos grasping Kephalos, who turns round; he holds spears and club; then a bald man with sceptre standing frontal, head to left. On B, youth, man with stick, youth with skyphos.

10. FERRARA, T. 179 A VP, from Spina. A, Centauromachy. B, three youths.

11 (8). FLORENCE PD 574. A, Amazonomachy. B, youths and a woman.

12 (9). Once SYRACUSE, Gargallo (later in the Italian market), from Syracuse. A, *NSc.* 1907, 745. A, fight (horse and foot). B, youths and woman (one of the youths holds a skyphos).

13. SYRACUSE, from Camarina. A, fight (horse and foot).

14. FERRARA, T. 240 A VP, from Spina. A, fight (horse and foot). B, komos.

15. ITALIAN MARKET. A, fight. B, komos. On A, two men and a youth attacking to right; the foremost man wears a cap and wields a club, the

other has helmet, spear, and shield; facing the three a fully armed warrior (device a bull's head). For the man in the cap compare a fragment in Florence (*CV*. pl. 15, B 2).

16. FERRARA, T. 722, from Spina. A, mounted warriors (and the forepart of a second horse). B, komos? (three males).

17 (12). BOLOGNA 211, from Bologna. Zannoni pl. 56, 1–3. A, two horsemen. B, youths and woman.

18. FERRARA, T. 7 C VP, from Spina. A, two horsemen. B, woman with torch, and youths.

19 (13). VILLA GIULIA 969, from Falerii. A, two horsemen. B, Nike, youth, and man.

20. NEW YORK, Fox, fr. A, horsemen (head of horse, upper part of youth in chlamys, head of youth in petasos, all to right). [Bothmer].

21 (15). FERRARA, T. 212, from Spina. A, horsemen setting out. B, youths.

22 (16). BOLOGNA 202, from Bologna. A, *Atti Romagna* 21 (1903), 268 fig. 3; *CV*. pl. 45. A, Amazons setting out (horse and foot). B, youths.

23 (14). BOLOGNA 212, from Bologna. *CV*. pl. 36, 3–4. A, horseman leaving home. B, youths and boy.

24 (17). COPENHAGEN 147. Millingen *AUM*. pl. 40; *CV*. pl. 148, 2; A (cleaned), *AJA*. 1950, 318. A, Memnon setting out (on horseback). B, three youths. On the inscription see *AJA*. 1950, 319.

25. FERRARA, T. 263 A VP, from Spina. A, horseman, preceded by a woman running (not necessarily pursued). B, three youths.

26 (10). SYRACUSE 34430, from Syracuse. A, racing-chariot (with a woman, and a man holding a wand). B, three youths.

27 (11). BOLOGNA 215, from Bologna. Pellegrini 84; *CV*. pl. 44, 1–2. A, racing-chariot (with Nike, and a man holding a wand). B, man and youths.

28 (18). PARIS MARKET (Feuardent), from Agrigento. Politi *Descr. di due vasi-fittili* pll. I and A. A, youth leaving home. B, komos.

29. FERRARA, T. 5 B VP, from Spina. A, youth leaving home. B, (male).

30 (19). MANCHESTER, Univ., III I 3. *Mus. Disn.* pll. 113–14. A, youth leaving home. B, youth and woman.

31 (20). LONDON E 489, from Nola. A, komos. B, youths and boy.

32 (21). FLORENCE 4009. *CV*. pl. 45, 1–2, pl. 39, 5, and pl. 46, 1. A, komos; B, komos.

33. FERRARA, T. 85 A VP, from Spina. A, komos. B, three youths.

34 (22). BROOKLYN 09.6, from Agrigento. A, Millingen *Coghill* pl. 8, whence Inghirami pl. 356; A, *Cat. de Morgan Jan. 16 1909* pl. 1, 141; *Studies Robinson* ii pl. 51, c–d. A, symposion. B, youths and woman.

35. MILAN, from Spina. A, *Corriere della Sera* 31 July 1957. A, symposion.

36 (23). FERRARA, T. 813, from Spina. A, symposion; B, youths and woman (one of the youths holds a skyphos).

37. FERRARA (erratico VP C), frr., from Spina. A, symposion.

38 (24). FERRARA, T. 912, from Spina. A, youths and women; B, youths and woman.

39. FERRARA, T. 23 C VP, from Spina. A, man and three youths; B, youths and boy.

40 (25). AGRIGENTO 16, from Agrigento. A, satyrs attacking maenads. B, three youths.

41 (26). PALERMO. A, satyrs attacking maenads (two pairs). B, youths and woman.

41 *bis*. FERRARA (sequestro Firenze), from Spina. A, satyrs and maenad (two pairs; the right-hand maenad holds a torch). B, Nike and two youths.

42. MARIEMONT G 132 (85). A, *Coll. Warocqué* 50; A, *Ant. Mariemont* pl. 42, G 132. A, Dionysos with satyrs and maenad. Restored.

NUPTIAL LEBETES
(*no. 43, type 1*)

43 (27). ATHENS 1254 (CC. 1235). Ph. A.I. 3092. A, seated woman (bride) with Eros and two women; at each handle, Nike; B, three women, two of them with torches.

(*no. 44, type 2*)

44 (28). GENEVA H 239. A, woman seated, and two women; at each handle, Nike; B, two women.

NECK-AMPHORA
(*with triple handles; framed pictures*)

45. PADULA, from Padula. A, warrior setting out, with horsemen (the hindquarters of one horse are shown, and the forehand of the other). B, youths and woman.

PELIKE
(*with framed pictures*)

46. PORT SUNLIGHT (on loan in Preston). A, youth and woman; B, youth and boy.

LOUTROPHOROI

47–53. ATHENS, Acropolis Museum, from Athens. Seven fragments, from several vases.

HYDRIAI
(*the picture on the body*)

54 (29). LONDON E 192, from Camiros. *CV*. pl. 87, 1. Woman seated and two women.

55 (30). JENA 355. Woman seated and two women.

56. LOUVRE C 10850. Woman seated and two women.

OINOCHOE

(shape 1)

57. FAENZA 48, from Spina.   Youth with spears pursuing a woman.

DISH

(shallow)

58 (31). ATHENS 1616 (CC. 1599), from Velanideza.   Youth with spears pursuing a woman.

FRAGMENT OF A POT

59. ATHENS, Agora, P 23863, fr., from Athens.   (Head of a woman, hair of another woman.)   From a neck-amphora?

CHAPTER 33

THE PAN PAINTER

THE PAN PAINTER

JHS. 32, 354–69. *VA*. 113–18. *Att. V*. 99–105 and 470. *Der Pan-Maler. JHS*. 55, 67–70 (Martin Robertson). *ARV*.¹ 361–9 and 959. *CB*. ii, 45–55 and 102.

Called after one of the pictures on no. 1.

Pupil of Myson. A mannerist, and connected with the earlier members of the Mannerist Group (p. 562), but far above them: an exquisite artist.

BELL-KRATERS
(with lugs)

1 (1). BOSTON 10.185, from Cumae. FR. pl. 115, whence Pfuhl figs. 475–6, (A) Buschor 184, (A) *VA*. 113, (A) *Zeitschr. fur Bildende Kunst* 55, 98 fig. 6, (A) *C.A.H.* plates ii, 32, 3, (A) Walter Müller 139, 1, (A) *Int. Studio* Dec. 1927, 70, below, (A) Beazley and Ashmole fig. 81, (A) Seltman pl. 24, a, (A) Hoenn *Artemis* 74, (detail of A) *Jb*. 26, 182 fig. 82, (B) Rumpf *Rel*. fig. 29, (B) Herbig *Pan* pl. 35, 1, (A) Stella 183, (A) *E.A.A.* i, 693; A, Hambidge 88; A, Pfuhl fig. 783; A, Jacobsthal *Akt*. 8; part of B, Picard *Vie privée* viii, 1; part of B, Cloché *Classes* pl. 14, 3; *Panm*. pll. 1–4, whence (detail of B) Buschor *Bilderwelt* 44, (B) Stella 385, (A) Frel *Ř.V*. fig. 187; A, Buschor G. *Vasen* 178; A, Schoenebeck and Kraiker pl. 88; A, Lane pll. 82–83; B, *Marb. Jb*. 15, 16; A, Fairbanks and Chase 52 fig. 51; part of B, Richter *ARVS*. fig. 67; CB. ii pl. 47, 94, pll. 48–49, and p. 46; detail of A, Schwabacher *Demareteion* pl. 2, 2; part of A, Robertson G. *P*. 118–19; A, *Mü. Jb*. 9–10 (1958–9), 10; A, R. M. Cook, pl. 44; the shape, Hambidge 88 and Caskey G. 127–7. A, death of Actaeon. B, Pan pursuing a goatherd. See CB. ii, 45–51; and below, p. 1658.

2 (2). PALERMO V 778, from Agrigento. Politi *Cinque vasi di premio* pll. 2–3, whence Hartwig 471; *Panm*. pll. 31–32 and pl. 27, 2; *CV*. pl. 34. A, Dionysos and maenad. B, komos. See *Panm*. 17 and 20; and below, p. 1659.

CALYX-KRATER

3 (3). BASLE MARKET (M.M.: ex Elgin). Detail of A, *Panm*. pl. 25, 2. A, Achilles and Penthesilea. B, Herakles and Syleus. Ruined. See *Panm*. 20 and Bothmer *Am*. 145.

COLUMN-KRATERS
(nos. 4–12, the pictures not framed)

4 (4). BARI 4402, from Binetto. A, Poseidon (with trident and aphlaston). B, komast (youth playing the flute). See *Panm*. 20.

5 (5). BERLIN 4027, from Altamura. *Annali* 1877 pl. W. A, Herakles going to, B, the fountain. See *Panm.* 20–21.

6 (8). NEW YORK 16.72. A, *Bull. Metr.* 11, 256 = *N.Y. Shapes* 9, 3, McClees 31, 5, and Richter and Milne fig. 47, whence LS. fig. 8; *Int. Studio* Dec. 1927, 72–73; the Dionysos, McClees 72; the satyr on A, Richter *Sc.* fig. 482; the same, *Panm.* pl. 25, 3; Richter and Hall pll. 67–68 and pl. 170, 64, whence (A) Stella 363; Richter *H.* 225, a. A, Dionysos and satyr; B, satyr. See *Panm.* 21.

7. LOUVRE C 10761. A, Dionysos and satyr; B, satyr.

8 (6). VATICAN. A, *Panm.* pl. 26, 2. A, two satyrs; B, satyr.

9 (7). MUNICH 2378 (J. 777), from Sicily. Detail, *Hermes* 1903, 268, whence D.S. s.v. nota fig. 5332; A, *Panm.* pl. 26, 1; A, Zschietzschmann *H. R.* pl. 247. A, Thracian woman; B, Thracian woman. Extract from a Death of Orpheus. See *Panm.* 21.

10 (10). BERLIN inv. 3206, from Etruria. Licht iii, 81 and ii, 30; B, Deubner pl. 4, 2. A, youth at herm. B, naked woman carrying a monster phallus. Restored. See *Panm.* 21.

11. NAPLES MARKET. A, love-making (youth and woman). B, no picture. [Bothmer].

12 (9). ATHENS, Ceramicus Museum, fr., from Athens. (Head and shoulders of woman to right).

(nos. 13–19, the pictures framed)

13 (12). LONDON E 473, from Etruria? A, *JHS.* 32, 356; A, *Panm.* pl. 27, 1; part of A, Byvanck-Quarles van Ufford *P.* 37; R.I. Centauromachy: A, Kaineus and Centaurs; B, Centaur and Lapith. See *Panm.* 21.

14 (13). PALERMO V 788, from Chiusi. *CV.* pl. 41. A, Dionysos and satyrs; B, the like. [Marconi Bovio].

15 (14). NAPLES, from Cumae. *ML.* 22 pl. 80 and pl. 81, 1, whence (A) Pfuhl fig. 477, (A) Rumpf *Rel.* fig. 30, (A, with a few corrections) *Panm.* pl. 30, 1, (detail of A) *Jb.* 40, 214 fig. 6. A, sacrifice to Hermes. B, komos. See *Panm.* 21.

16 (15). SYRACUSE 12781, from Sant' Anastasia near Randazzo. A, *Panm.* pl. 30, 2 and pl. 29, 2. A, komos; B, komos. See p. 1659.

17. LOUVRE C 10758, fr. A, komos (women dancing, and male). Two of the women wear the himation only, the third wears chiton as well and dances or shuffles grotesquely; the male leans on his stick; there may have been a fifth figure.

18 (10). BOLOGNA 229, from Bologna. Zannoni pl. 143, 8–10. A, chariot (warrior leaving home). B, men and youths. See *Panm.* 21.

19 (11 *bis*). SYDNEY 42. *The Canon* Aug. 1950 pl. 1; A, *Hdbk Nich.*² pl. 7. A, citharode. B, men and boys.

VOLUTE-KRATERS

20 (16). ATHENS Acr. 760, frr., from Athens. Part of A, *Eph.* 1886 pl. 7, 3; B, Jacobsthal *Akt.* 7; B, *Panm.* pl. 12, 2; Langlotz pl. 65, whence (A) Vian *R.* pl. 41, 375. A, Dionysos and Giant. B, death of Actaeon. Langlotz does not figure a floating fragment of A which gives the end of Dionysos' ivy-branch. A new Athens fragment joins this on the right and adds part of the tongues above the picture, with the spring of the handle. Early. See *Panm.* 15–16.

21 (17). BOSTON 95.58, fr., from Falerii. *VA.* 116 fig. 73; *Panm.* pl. 13, 3; CB. ii, suppl. pl. 11, 4. A, (deities—Dionysos and another). Early. See CB. ii, 45.

STAMNOI

22. LOUVRE C 10822, frr. Ransom of Hector.

23 (19). ROME, Ruspoli, from Cervetri. A, sacrifice. B, flute-player with judges. See *Panm.* 22.

STAMNOS?

(or rather a psykter?)

24 (18). LEIPSIC T 651, frr. *Jb.* 11, 190–1, 34. Herakles and Busiris.

NUPTIAL LEBES

(or the like)

25 (20). ATHENS Acr. 675, frr., from Athens. Langlotz pl. 52; *Panm.* pl. 28, 3. On the stand: (Athena, Poseidon; hand with flute, arm). See *Panm.* 26.

NUPTIAL LEBETES

26 (21). TÜBINGEN E 103, fr. Watzinger pl. 29. (Hermes, woman). See *Panm.* 26.

27 (21 *bis*). PROVIDENCE 28.020. A, *Bull. Rhode* 16, 47; A, *Bull. Rhode* 27, 34; *CV.* pl. 22, 2. A, woman and youths; under each handle, sphinx; B, mistress and maids. On the stand: Poseidon pursuing a woman; youth pursuing a woman. Hasty.

DINOS

28 (22). ATHENS, Vlasto, frr., from Athens. Symposion, with love-making.

AMPHORA

(type B)

29 (22 *bis*). LONDON MARKET, from Greece (destroyed by enemy action). A, Eros (flying to left, face frontal, with hare and lyre). B, man (in himation, standing with right leg frontal, stick in right hand).

PANATHENAIC AMPHORA

30 (23). NEW YORK 20.245, from Vulci? A, *AJA.* 1923, 278; A, *Panm.* pl. 28, 2; Richter and Hall pl. 70, pl. 72, 66, and pl. 169, 66. A, citharode; B, judge.

NECK-AMPHORAE

(no. 31, special shape: pointed amphora ?)

31 (24). ATHENS Acr. 618, fr., from Athens. Langlotz pl. 18. Sacrificial procession. See *Panm.* 22.

(nos. 32–33, with triple handles; framed pictures)

32 (25). NAPLES Stg. 225. A, *Jb.* 76, 68; B, ph. So. 11096. A, flute-duet. B, herald and women. See *Panm.* 22.

33 (26). LAON 37.1023, from Nola? *Cat. Serrure 27 juin 1913* pl. 2 no. 63, whence *JHS.* 55, 69 fig. 2; *CV.* pll. 26–27. A, warrior leaving home (youth and woman). B, youth at two herms.

(nos. 34–43, Nolan amphorae, with triple handles)

34 (27). ZURICH 18, from Capua. *Panm.* pl. 15, 1, pl. 16, 1, and pl. 17, 1, whence *Bull. Vereen.* 24–26, 22; Bloesch *A.K.S.* pll. 30–31, pl. 1, 2, and p. 63. A, Nike. B, youth.

35 (28). TARANTO, from Novoli. A, Nike. B, youth. On A, flying to left with lyre and three phialai. On B, standing to left, in himation.

36 (29). COPENHAGEN inv. 4978, from Sicily. A, *JHS.* 32, 360; *CV.* pl. 131, 1. A, Hermes; B, woman running.

37 (30). SCHWERIN 1295, from South Italy? *Panm.* pl. 19, 1, pl. 20, 1, and pl. 21, 1. A, Poseidon (in Gigantomachy). B, youth.

38 (31). SCHWERIN 1304, from South Italy. *Panm.* pl. 19, 2, pl. 20, 2, and pl. 21, 2, whence (part of A) *G.V. Celle* 26, (A) Herbig *Terrakottagruppe* fig. 26. A, Nereid; B, old man (Nereus?). Extract from a 'Peleus and Thetis' or the like.

39 (32). BOSTON 10.184, from Suessula. A, *RM.* 2, 240 fig. 9; A, FR. pl. 159, 1, whence (corrected by the omission of the upper border added by Reichhold) *Panm.* pl. 18, 1, whence Sichtermann *Ganymed* pl. 2, 2; A, *Int. Studio* Dec. 1927, 71, above, left; CB. ii pl. 50, 95; A, *Ant. Kunst* 2 pl. 8, 4; the shape, Hambidge 78 and Caskey G. 64. A, Zeus and Ganymede; B, boy running with a leg of meat in his hand. See CB. ii, 51–53.

40 (33). BOSTON 01.8109, from Cumae. One figure from A, *VA.* 115; A, *Int. Studio* Dec. 1927, 71, above, right; A, *Panm.* pl. 16, 3; CB. ii pl. 50, 96; the shape, Hambidge 61 and Caskey G. 66. A, boy victor, and trainer. B, youth (attendant at a sacrifice) dragging the skin of an ox. See CB. ii, 53–54.

41 (34). Once DEEPDENE, Hope. Millingen *Coghill* pl. 31, 1; A, Tillyard pl. pl. 9, 90; B, *Panm.* pl. 16, 2. A, Dionysos; B, satyr. See *Panm.* 23.

42 (35). MADRID 11119 (L. 174), from Nola. A, Alvarez-Ossorio pl. 35, 2; *Panm.* pl. 22; *CV.* pl. 20, 2 and pl. 24, 3. A, Artemis. B, youth.

43 (37). BOWDOIN 13.30, from Gela. *Panm.* pl. 11, 2. A, youth playing the flute and youth listening; B, youth.

(no. 44, small, with double handles: doubleen)

44. LONDON, University College. A, youth offering a hare to, B, a boy. [Martin Robertson].

(no. 45, small, with ridged handles)

45. BONN, Langlotz. A, woman playing a small cithara and singing; B, youth dancing. [Langlotz].

LOUTROPHOROI

46–78. ATHENS, Acropolis Museum, from Athens. Thirty-two fragments, or groups of fragments, from many vases.

79 (38). HOUSTON 37.10. Side, *Bull. Houston* 10, 2 (Spring 1948). Wedding procession (boy flute-player, and women holding chaplets, loutro-phoros, torches, basket); on the neck, the like (women holding loutro-phoros, torch, chaplet). Loutrophoros-hydria.

80 (30). AMSTERDAM inv. 2313, fr. Women at tomb.

81 (40). OXFORD, Beazley, fr., from Greece. B, valediction. [Marie Beazley].

PELIKAI

(nos. 28–93, the pictures not framed)

82 (41). ATHENS 9683 (CC. 1175), from Boeotia. A, Dumont and Chaplain pl. 18, whence (detail) *Jb.* 29, 141 fig. 14; A, Collignon and Couve pl. 41; A, Herford pl. 9, d; detail of B, *Delt.* 9, 28; *Panm.* pll. 7–10 and pl. 11, 1, whence (part of A) *Corolla Curtius* pl. 65, 2, (B) Buschor G. *Vasen* 179, (A) Lane pl. 84, (A) Schnitzler pl. 46, (A) Schachermeyr *Indogermanen und Orient* pl. 20, 2, (part of A) Rumpf *MZ.* pl. 24, 7, (detail of A) Buschor *Bilderwelt* 45, (B) LS. fig. 95, (A) Frel *Ř.V.* figs. 188–9; Vorberg *Gloss.* 489, 2; phs. A.I., whence (detail of A) *E.A.A.* i, 974. Herakles and Busiris. See *Panm.* 12–13. Kraiker has shown that the thing held by the left-hand man on B is a case of knives (*Gnomon* 8, 644–5); so also Fuhr-mann in *Jh.* 39, 27–30.

83 (42). FERRARA, from Spina. Aurigemma[1] 91 and 93 = [2]97 and 99; part of A, and B, Stella 341 and 722; A, Aurigemma and Alfieri pl. 11, b; A, Alfieri and Arias *S.* pl. 22. A, Triptolemos. B, youth (Achilles?) receiving his armour.

84. ARLESHEIM, Schweizer. Schefold *M.* 202. A, youth leaving home. B, man and boy. Restored.

85. MUNICH inv. 8725. *Anz.* 1957, 383–6 and 380; *Mü. Jb.* 9–10 (1958–9), 7–8; A, Schauenburg *Perseus* pl. 40, 1. A, Perseus. B, komast playing the flute.

86 (44). MADRID 11201 (L. 157). *CV.* pl. 9, 3. A, woman working (wash-ing clothes?); B, youth. See *Panm.* 22.

87 (43). OXFORD 282, from Gela. Gardner pl. 10, 1 and p. 23, whence (A) Richter *F.* fig. 192, (A) Richter *H.G.A.* 364; *CV.* pl. 19, 1 and 4. A, boy carrying couch and table; B, man. See *CV.* Oxford i, 17 and ii, 6.

(nos. 88–93, small: the first five form a class)

88 (45). VIENNA 3727 (ex Oest. Mus. 335), from Cervetri. *AEM.* 3 pl. 3, whence FR. ii, 293, whence Cloché pl. 38, 2; *Panm.* pl. 23, 1–2; *CV.* pl. 76, 1–3. A, fishers; B, fisher-boy running to town (past a herm). See *Panm.* 13.

89 (46). LOUVRE G 547. A, Sudhoff i, 19; A, *Panm.* pl. 23, 3; *CV.* d pl. 46, 1–3 and 6; phs. Gir. A, woman and girl working (washing clothes?). B, man and girl. See *Panm.* 23; and below, p. 1659.

90 (47, +). LOUVRE G 472. Part of A, Pottier pl. 150; the same part, *Panm.* pl. 23, 4. A, unexplained subject: old man catching a pig by the hind-legs; beside him a phallus-stick. B, boy chasing a fawn. See *Panm.* 13. Several Louvre fragments join the one already known.

91 (48). BERLIN inv. 4283, from Falerii. A, Jacobsthal *Gött.* 9 fig. 10, whence *Jb.* 29, 243 and *Annuario* 8,200. A, bird-headed monster. B, the like. See *Panm.* 23.

92 (49, 50, +). LOUVRE C 10793. Procession to herms: A, three herms; B, girl with sacrificial basket on her head, youth bending, lifting a hydria or rather putting it down.

93. LOUVRE C 11016, fr. (Maenad dancing, to right, with wing-sleeves).

(no. 94, the pictures framed)

94 (51). LONDON E 357. Buck pl. 7. A, two women dancing; B, woman dancing. Small.

HYDRIAI
(nos. 95–99, the picture on the shoulder or mainly so)

95 (52). LENINGRAD 627 (St. 1538), from Vulci. Gerhard pll. 50–51, 1–2, whence *Annali* 1845 pl. B; the Hermes, *VA.* 117; the Hermes, Pickard-Cambridge *D.F.A.* fig. 200; B.Ap. xxii. 26. 4. Unexplained subject (Hermes, two old men, and Dionysos). See *Panm.* 23.

96 (53). LONDON E 181, from Capua. *JHS.* 32 pl. 6 and p. 357, whence Pfuhl fig. 474, *Panm.* pl. 5, 1, *Jh.* 38, 13, *BCH.* 1953, 309 fig. 12, Stella 501; *CV.* pl. 80, 1; ph. Ma. 3131, right. Perseus and Medusa. See *Panm.* 11.

97 (53 *bis*). SAN FRANCISCO, De Young Museum, 707, from Nola. *CV.* pl. 15, 2 and pl. 16, 2. Apollo and Artemis. [H. R. W. Smith]. Gargiulo *Cenni* pl. 7, 19 is perhaps an inaccurate version of this.

98. TARANTO, from Metaponto. *Anz.* 1956, 279. Youths and girl. Restored.

99. LOUVRE C 11053, fr. (Male seated—the top of his stick remains—and youth in himation with stick).

(no. 100, the picture on the body)

100 (54). NAPLES Stg. 192. Gerhard pl. 78, whence *El.* 2 pl. 24; part, *Panm.* pl. 17, 3, whence *Mitt.* 5 pl. 1, 2. Apollo with Artemis and Leto.

PSYKTER

101 (55). MUNICH 2417 (J. 745), from Agrigento. Politi *Esposizione di un vaso* pl. 1, whence Inghirami pll. 282–3 and (the Marpessa) *AM.* 48, 151; *Mon.* 1 pl. 20; F. Thiersch *Über die hellenischen bemalten Vasen* pl. 5, 1; Lau pl. 30, 2; FR. pl. 16 and i, 77 and 79, whence *Panm.* pl. 12, 1 and (part) *Jh.* 16, 105; part, Pfuhl fig. 771; Langlotz *GV.* pl. 32; the Artemis, *Panm.* pl. 13, 1; partly cleaned, Lullies and Hirmer pll. 70–79, whence Stella 168–9; part, *E.A.A.* ii, 497 fig. 688 and iv, 876 fig. 1041; detail, *Mü. Jb.* 9–10 (1958–9), 9 fig. 4, Marpessa. See *Panm.* 15.

LEKYTHOI
(nos. 102–20, rf.)
(nos. 102–19 bis, standard shape)

102 (56). OXFORD 312, from Gela. Gardner pl. 23, 2, whence *Izv. Mat.* 2 pl. 27; *CV.* pl. 33, 2; *Panm.* pl. 14, 2, whence *Jb.* 56, 40. Nike. See *Panm.* 16 and 24.

103 (57). OXFORD 1920.58, fr. Welcker *Alte Denkmäler* 3 pl. 32 (made up with fragments of other vases into a curious olio, see *CV.* i, 44); cleaned, *CV.* pl. 40, 4; *Panm.* pl. 6, 1; Greifenhagen *Eroten* 19. Eros.

104 (58). PROVIDENCE 25.110, from Gela. *CV.* pl. 19, 2; *Class. Studies Capps* 244 fig. 2. Nike.

105. PROVIDENCE 35.708. *Class. Studies Capps* 243 fig. 1. Nike. [Luce].

106. PROVIDENCE 56.062, from Gela. *Bull. Rhode* May 1957, 2. Nike. [Bothmer].

107. PARIS, private, from Agrigento. Hermes (with right leg frontal, head to left, holding a caduceus, and a phiale over an altar).

108 (59). TARANTO, from Novoli. *Ant. Kunst* 2 pl. 8, 3. Zeus and Ganymede. See CB. ii, 51.

109 (59 *bis*). ADOLPHSECK, Landgraf Philipp of Hesse, 53, from Gela. *CV.* pl. 39, 4 and 6–7. Woman (doubtful if Athena) holding shield. [Landgraf Philipp of Hesse]. Restored (see *AJA.* 1957, iii, top).

110 (60). BRUSSELS, Bibliothèque Royale, 10, from Capua? *Gaz. arch.* 4 pl. 25, 1; *Panm.* pl. 15, 2: Feytmans *V.B.R.* pll. 23–24, whence (part) *Bull. Vereen.* 24–26, 23; *Oudh. Meded.* N.S. 37, 5. Woman with mirror and woolbasket.

111 (61). LENINGRAD. *Izv. Mat.* 2 pl. 25, pl. 24, 2, p. 280, and p. 285, 5; *Panm.* pl. 17, 2. Woman with torches (Hecate?). [Trever]. See *Panm.* 24.

112 (62). TARANTO, from Taranto. Citharode (Apollo?: moving to right, looking round, with cithara and phiale).

113 (63). BOSTON 13.198, from Gela. *VA.* 114; *Int. Studio* Dec. 1927, 69; *Panm.* pl. 24, 1 and pl. 13, 2; CB ii pl. 51, 97; Kraiker *M.G.* pl. 31; *Mü. Jb.* 9–10 (1958–9), 9 fig. 5; the shape, Caskey G. 214 no. 169. Hunter (Kephalos?). See CB. ii, 54–55; and below, p. 1659.

114 (67). BOSTON 01.8079, from Gela. *JHS.* 32, 361–2; *Panm.* pl. 6, 3; CB. ii pl. 51, 2; Greifenhagen *Eroten* 20. Eros catching a fawn. See CB. ii, 55.

115 (64). NAPLES 3118, from Nola. Angelini pl. 18; *Panm.* pl. 28, 1. Woman playing lyre. Restored.

116. HAVERFORD COLLEGE. Comfort no. 24. Woman seated, and maid. [Bothmer, Richter]. See Bothmer in *AJA.* 1957, 310; and below, p. 1659.

117 (65). LONDON E 579, from Gela. *JHS.* 32 pl. 7, whence *Panm.* pl. 25, 1, Seltman pl. 24, b, Pfeiff *Apollon* pl. 41, a. Apollo and Artemis.

118 (66). SYRACUSE 15498, from Gela. *Panm.* pl. 24, 3. Hunter.

119 (69). ADOLPHSECK, Landgraf Philipp of Hesse, 51, from Gela. Brommer *A.K.* fig. 17; *CV.* pl. 38; Greifenhagen *Eroten* 6–10; part, *Arch. class.* 10 pl. 87, 2. The body black save for a strip of maeander at the top. On the shoulder, two Erotes. See Greifenhagen 8–12.

119 *bis.* LONDON, Embiricos. Youth seated with lyre, and a naked boy standing facing him. Black palmettes on the shoulder.

(no. 120, secondary shape, small)

120 (68). ATHENS 1602 (CC. 1364), from Athens. *Panm.* pl. 6, 4. Siren.

(nos. 121–2, white ground; standard shape)

121 (70). LENINGRAD 670. *Jh.* 16 pl. 2, whence Rumpf *MZ.* pl. 24, 8 and (detail) Richter *ARVS.* fig. 66; *Izv. Mat.* 2 pl. 26, pl. 24, 1, and p. 281; *Panm.* pl. 14, 1, whence LS. fig. 94 and Frel *R.V.* fig. 203. Artemis and a swan. Second white used. See p. 1659.

122 (71). SYRACUSE 19900, from Gela. *Arch. Ért.* 1907, 5 fig. 14, whence Láng *Onos* 51. Woman with yarn.

ALABASTRA
(no. 123, ordinary shape)

123 (72). BERLIN 2254, from Pikrodafni. *Panm.* pl. 29, 1; *Anz.* 1932, 15–16 fig. 3. Woman spinning, youth and maid. See *Panm.* 24–25.

(no. 124, Columbus alabastron)

124 (73). ATHENS 17207, from Athens. *Anz.* 1932, 15–16 fig. 2. Youth and woman. See *Panm.* 25.

OINOCHOAI
(nos. 125–6, shape 1)

125 (75). LONDON E 512, from Vulci. *JHS.* 32 pl. 8 and p. 363; *VA.* 116 fig. 72 *bis*; *Panm.* pl. 5, 2; ph. Ma. 3200, right. Boreas and Oreithyia. The picture framed. See *Panm.* 11–12.

126 (74). MUNICH 2455. *CV.* pl. 86, 9–10 and pl. 92, 6. Woman at altar.

(no. 127, shape 2)

127 (76). NEW YORK 23.160.55. *AJA.* 1926, 36; *Panm.* pl. 18, 2, whence
Sichtermann *Ganymed* pl. 2, 3; Richter and Hall pl. 69, 65 and pl. 177, 65;
Richter *ARVS.* fig. 68; Richter *H.* 225, b; *E.A.A.* iii, 905. Ganymede.

(no. 128, shape 8A, mug)

128 (77). TARANTO, from Novoli. Flute-player and man (youth in costume
playing the flute to right, the phorbeia lowered and resting round his neck,
man leaning on his stick to left).

FRAGMENTS OF POTS

129. ATHENS Acr., fr., from Athens. *BCH.* 1940–1 pl. 10, 4. (Man, wand).
Might be from a stamnos.

130. LOUVRE C 10833, two frr. Triptolemos.

131 (a 13). ATHENS, Agora, P 6576, fr., from Athens. Uncertain subject
(woman, hand).

132 (96). ATHENS Acr. 771, fr., from Athens. Langlotz pl. 67. Uncertain
subject (old man seated).

133 (97). ATHENS Acr. 769, two frr., from Athens. One fr., including a new
piece added by Miss Pease, *Hesp.* 4, 224. (Males leading an ox).

134 (98). ATHENS Acr. 770, fr. (two joining), from Athens. Langlotz pl. 67.
(Old man; on the left, under one handle, boy).

135. ATHENS Acr., fr., from Athens. (Under one handle—the roots remain
—upper part of a youth's head, wreathed, to right).

136. ATHENS Acr., fr., from Athens. Procession to sacrifice (legs of two
males in long chitons to right, one of them holding an oinochoe).

137 (100). ATHENS Acr. AP 283 and AP 400, two frr., from Athens. *Hesp.*
4, 289, 166. (Boy, male; man). [Marie Beazley].

138. Private, fr. (Head and shoulders of a girl). [Cambitoglou].

139 (99). GOETTINGEN, fr. (Head and shoulders of youth to left). From an
amphora or a hydria?

140 (102). ATHENS, Agora, P 9463, fr., from Athens. Dinsmoor *Heph.* 136,
17. (Maenad?). Should be from a hydria.

141 (a 12). MARBURG 1704, fr., from Greece. (Hand of one holding a chaplet, arm of Nike with part of one wing). Compare Houston 37.10
(no. 79).

KANTHAROS

142 (78). ATHENS 2038, frr., from Menidi. *Jb.* 14, 104. A, sacrificial procession. B, (shield). See *Panm.* 25.

SKYPHOI
(no. 143, type uncertain)

143 (79). ATHENS Acr. 490 and MUNICH, frr., from Athens. Part, Langlotz
pl. 40. Oxen led to sacrifice. The Munich fragment gives pattern and
two hooves. Two new Athens fragments, with parts of palmettes and
rays, belong, and one of them probably joins fragment b on the right.

(no. 144, type A)

144 (80). ATHENS Acr. 469 a, fr., from Athens. Langlotz pl. 38; *Panm.* pl.
24, 2; detail, *Jh.* 31, 16 fig. 10. Eos and Kephalos. I am not sure if the
fragment 469 b (Langlotz pl. 38) belongs.

(nos. 145–6, small; type A or B)

145 (85). ATHENS Acr. 468, fr., from Athens. Langlotz pl. 38. Youth.
See *Panm.* 25.

146 (86). ATHENS Acr. 467, fr., from Athens. Langlotz pl. 38. Male with
lyre and dog.

(nos. 147–50, type B, glaukes; small)

147 (81). AGRIGENTO, fr., from Agrigento. *Atti Soc. M.G.* 1931, 72 fig. 43;
Jh. 33, 26; *JHS.* 68, 27 fig. 2. A, youth attacking with sword (Harmo-
dios?). See *JHS.* 68, 26.

148 (82). WISBECH. *JHS.* 55 pl. 8 and p. 67. A, warrior lying in wait; B,
archer. [D. S. and Martin Robertson]. See Martin Robertson in *JHS.*
55, 67–70.

149 (83). BERLIN 2593, from Nola. A, *JHS.* 32, 368; B, *JHS.* 55, 69 fig. 3;
CV. pl. 141, 4 and 7. A, boy with lyre; B, youth. See *Panm.* 25.

150 (84). NEW YORK X. 22.25 (GR 585). A, *N.Y. Shapes* 22, 3; *Int. Studio*
Dec. 1927, 70, above, and 71 below; Richter and Hall pl. 69, 67 and pl.
178, 67. A, Theseus; B, Minotaur.

CUPS
(nos. 151–3, decorated outside as well as in)

151 (87). LEIPSIC T 3365, frr., from Cervetri. Philippart *C.A.B.* pl. 7. I,
(white ground), (remains of two figures). A–B, infant Herakles and the
snakes. See *Panm.* 25.

152 (88). OXFORD 1911.617, from Cervetri. *JHS.* 32 pl. 9; *CV.* pl. 2, 9 and
pl. 7, 3–4, whence (A) *Hesp.* 19 pl. 11 fig. 31; the shape, Bloesch *FAS.*
pl. 37, 2. I, youth with skaphe and man with writing-case; A–B, sacrifice.
Now augmented by small fragments ex Leipsic. The exact subject uncertain: see *CV.* Oxford, i, 6–7, and ii, 6, also *Panm.* 17 and 25; for the
shape, Bloesch 137, Eleusis-cup no. 5.

153 (90, +). LEIPSIC T 529, and STRASBURG, Univ., 836, frr., from Orvieto.
I, (toes); in a zone round this, symposion; A–B, komos. The Strasburg
fragment joins one of those in Leipsic, adding parts of the symposion and
of the komos, with the other handle. Late.

(no. 54, not known if decorated outside)

154 (89). VIENNA, Univ., inv. 53 c 1, fr., from Orvieto. *CV*. pl. 10, 18. I, (youth carrying a vessel; at a well?). See *Panm.* 25.

(nos. 155-8, decorated inside only)

155 (91). COPENHAGEN 120, from Greece. *CV*. pl. 144, 1; *Antik-Cab. 1851* 164. I, Eros. Now cleaned.

156 (92). VILLA GIULIA 50422. *Philologus* 54 pl. 1, whence *Panm.* pl. 6, 5; Deubner pl. 23, 1; ph. R.I. 1932, 1562-3. I, boy in festal costume holding a branch. See *Panm.* 26.

157 (93). FLORENCE (V.), from Chiusi. I, athlete (jumper) and flute-player. Now cleaned.

158 (94). OXFORD 1927.73. *CV*. pl. 51, 9. I, boy fleeing. For the shape, Bloesch 142, Acrocup no. 5.

STEMLESS CUP

(small; with ring-foot—saucer foot)

159 (95). BERLIN inv. 4951. *Sg Vogell* 18 fig. 8; *Panm.* pl. 6, 2; *Mü. Jb.* 9-10 (1958-9), 12. Medusa. [Zahn]. See *Panm.* 11 and 26.

NEAR THE PAN PAINTER

COLUMN-KRATERS

1. LIMENAS, fr., from Thasos. Ghali-Kahil *C.G.* pl. 46, 30 *bis*. A, (head of Dionysos, to left).

2. LIMENAS, fr., from Thasos. Ghali-Kahil *C.G.* pl. 50, 79. B, (woman, youth, hand of male with stick). Might belong to the last?

HYDRIAI

(the picture on the body)

3 (2). NAPLES 3139. *Mus. Borb.* 5 pl. 35, 2; ph. So. 11068. Boreas and Oreithyia. Restored.

4 (3). NAPLES Stg. 205. Eos and Kephalos. Now cleaned. Also recalls the Alkimachos Painter.

LEKYTHOI

(standard shape)

5 (5). TARANTO, from Taranto. *Jh.* 38, 1-2; *Jh.* 41, 78-81. Theseus and Ariadne. The young boy on the left is not Perithoos as has been held, but something in the nature of the Naxian παῖς ἀμφιθαλής, see Pfeiffer *Callimachus* i, 581. See p. 1659.

6 (6). OXFORD 313. Gardner pl. 23, 3; *CV*. pl. 33, 4. Nike. See the next.

7 (7). OXFORD 314. *CV*. pl. 33, 3. Nike. Replica of the last, by the same hand. See *Panm.* 24.

8 (8). PARIS MARKET, from Gela. *Coll. B. et C.* pl. 20, 161. Nike. Compare the two last.

9 (9). OXFORD 321, from Gela. Gardner pl. 25, 1; *CV.* pl. 38, 5. Man. ΗΙΠΠΟΝ ΚΑΛΟΝ.

SKYPHOI
(no. 10, of Corinthian type)

10. LOUVRE G 563. A, woman with phiale at altar; B, woman with oinochoe.

(no. 11, type A)

11. HILLSBOROUGH (California), Hearst, from Capua. *Jb.* 10, 191, whence Schröder *Sport* 105 and Norman Gardiner *Athl.* fig. 97; A, *Coll. 18 mars 1901* pl. 2, 49 and p. 16; *AJA.* 1945, 475, 2; *BSA.* 46 pl. 6, a–b. A, hoplitodromos at the start; B, trainer. Small. See *BSA.* 46, 13.

FRAGMENTS OF POTS

12. ATHENS Acr. 658, two frr., from Athens. Langlotz pl. 52. On one fragment, two persons at an altar; on the other a woman.

13 (10). SYRACUSE 19840, fr., from Gela. Athena fighting (in Gigantomachy?). Another fragment in Syracuse may belong (right hand and buttocks of male in himation, with sceptre, moving to right).

14. ABINGDON, Martin Robertson, fr., from Greece. (Youth, woman, waterbird, male). Compare the fragment Marburg 1704 (p. 558 no. 141).

15 (l 101). AMSTERDAM inv. 2281 and 2289, two frr. Eos and Tithonos? On one fragment, part of Eos (?) grasping Tithonos (?); on the other, part of youth in a himation moving to right, looking round, with a stick.

Compare also:

NECK-AMPHORA
(with twisted handles)

1 (1). SANTA BARBARA, Brundage, from Chiusi. A, Merlo 15 fig. 5. A, warrior (naked, loin-cloth, helmet, moving to left, looking round, right arm raised with spear). B, youth (leaning on his stick to left).

FRAGMENT OF A POT

2. ADRIA B 68 (2), fr., from Adria. Komos (what remains is the upper part of a man playing the flute).

CHAPTER 34

EARLIER MANNERISTS

THE MANNERIST GROUP

VA. 118–22 and 194. *Att. V.* 239–55, 415–18, 475, and 478. *ARV.*¹ 369–400 and 959. *P.P.* 11–13.

One workshop, specializing in third-rate column-kraters, pelikai, hydriai, can be traced from the archaic period down to the end of the fifth century or near. We have come across it already: it began as the workshop of Myson (pp. 237–8). He was the founder of the style: the early Mannerists were his pupils. On the workshop in general see *PP.* 11–13: we even have a view of it, on a hydria by one of the early Mannerists, the Leningrad Painter (p. 571 no. 73).

In *Att. V.* and *ARV.*¹ the Later Mannerists were dealt with in the same chapter as the Earlier. They are now separated: the Earlier Mannerists treated here, the Later reserved for a subsequent chapter (pp. 1106–25).

THE EARLIER MANNERISTS

In the lists that follow, the letter *u* before the bracketed serial number signifies that in *ARV.*¹ the vase appeared under the heading 'undetermined mannerists'.

EARLIER MANNERISTS. i. THE PIG PAINTER

VA. 118–20 ('Seesaw Painter': but the vase after which I named him is by a brother mannerist, see p. 569 no. 49). *Att. V.* 239–41 and 475. *BSR.* 11, 21–22. *ARV.*¹ 370–3.

Continues the style of Myson (p. 238).

Named after the pigs on the Cambridge pelike (no. 27).

COLUMN-KRATERS
(nos. 1–12, with framed pictures)

1 (1). CASTLE ASHBY, Northampton. A, *BSR.* 11, 23 fig. 17; A, *Ant. cl.* 4 pl. 28, 1. A, chariot of Dionysos (Ariadne mounting chariot, and Dionysos). B, athletes.

2 (2). LENINGRAD (ex Shuvalov). A, chariot of Poseidon (Amphitrite mounting chariot, and Poseidon); B, chariot of Dionysos (Ariadne mounting chariot, and Dionysos).

3 (3). ZURICH B 21. A, Dionysos and two maenads. B, youth with man and woman.

3 bis. ROME, Banca Romana. Phs. R.I. 59.383–5. A, Dionysos, satyr playing the flute, and maenad; B, satyrs and maenad. Restored.

4. NAPLES, Museo di Capodimonte, 960. A, *La donazione Mario de Ciccio* pl. 7 (the number misprinted 860). Vintage: A, satyrs making wine, with Dionysos; B, satyrs making wine. Restored. Placed by Bothmer in the Mannerist Group.

5 (4). BRUSSELS R 305. *CV.* pl. 16, 1 and pl. 17, 1. A, Theseus and Minotaur. B, athletes.

6 (5). FERRARA, T. 503, from Spina. A, *Mouseion* 16 pl. 8, 1–2; A, Aurigemma[1] 65 and 67, 3 = [2]69 and 71, 3; A, Aurigemma and Alfieri pl. 9, a; A, Alfieri and Arias *S.* pl. 8. A, Theseus and Minotaur. B, three youths. See p. 1659.

7. LUCERNE MARKET. A, Centauromachy (Kaineus). B, two men and a boy.

8 (7). HARVARD 60.346, from Agrigento. *CV* Robinson iii pll. 6–7. A, komos (man, youth, and naked women); B, komos (man, youth, and naked woman).

9. CLEVELAND 26.549. A, *Acta arch.* 13, 224. A, komos ('Anacreontic'); B, komos. On the subject of A see CB. ii, 59–60 no. 21.

10 (6). LOUVRE G 355. *CV.* d pl. 25, 8–9 and 11. A, symposion; B, komos. Much restored.

11 (8). TARANTO, from Cavallino. A, woman seated playing the flute, with youth and man. B, youths and boy.

11 bis. REGGIO, fr., from Locri. A, (on the left, woman to right, and youth to right, looking round to left, a phiale in his raised right hand). Lotus-buds on the neck of the vase.

12 (9). PALERMO V 790, from Agrigento. *CV.* pl. 42. A, youth and boy; man and boy. B, youths at herm.

(no. 12 bis, not known whether the pictures framed)

12 bis. REGGIO, fr., from Locri. (Face and fingers of a man playing the flute to left).

(nos. 13–26, the pictures not framed)

13 (10). NEW YORK 56.171.47 (ex Holford and Hearst). A, *Cat. Sotheby July 11 1927* pl. 9, 159. A, Dionysos and satyr; B, satyr.

14. DUNEDIN E 50.198. *JHS.* 73 pll. 6–7 and p. 141. A, Dionysos and satyr; B, satyr. [Corbett].

14 bis. ITALIAN MARKET. A, Dionysos and maenad; B, satyr pursuing maenad. On A, both moving to right, the maenad with crotala, Dionysos with stick and kantharos.

15 (11). NEW YORK 06.1021.152.   A, *Vente 11 mai 1903* pl. 2, 8; A, *Le Musée* i, 209, 13; Sambon *Canessa* 28–29 and pll. 8–9 no. 89; Richter and Hall pl. 72, 69. A, satyr and maenad; B, satyr.

16 (12). ADOLPHSECK, Landgraf Philipp of Hesse, 74. *CV.* pl. 44, 5–6 and p. 31. Komos: A, youth and woman; B, man. On the graffito see *AJA.* 1957, 111, left.

17 (13). PARIS, Musée Rodin, 993. A, *CV.* pl. 22, 1–3. Komos: A, two men; B, youth.

18 (14). CLEVELAND 24.197. *The Canessa Coll.* (1924) no. 62; *Bull. Clev.* 1924, 66 and 49. Komos: A, man and boy; B, youth. Inside the neck, as Bothmer tells me, the ghost of another column-krater (with framed pictures: A, two youths dancing; B, youth leaning on his stick).

19 (15). Where? (seen in Naples at the restorer's). Komos: A, woman with lyre, and youth; B, man.

20 (16). PALERMO V 789. *CV.* pl. 43. Komos: A, man and flute-girl; B, man.

21 (17). LECCE 572, from Rugge. *CV.* pl. 3 and pl. 4, 1; A, Bernardini pl. 36, 1. A, girl dancing, and woman playing the flute; B, youth.

22 (18) BOLOGNA 252, from Bologna. A, Zannoni pl. 142, 1. A, man and woman. B, komast.

23 (19). CAB. MÉD. 414. A, de Ridder pl. 16. A, man and boy victor. B, youth.

23 *bis.* LISBON, Gilbert. Rocha Pereira *Notícia* 3 figs. 12–13; Rocha Pereira *G.V.P.* pll. 26–27. A, victor and man; B, youth.

24 (20). NEW YORK 41.162.86. A, Tischbein 4 pl. 59; A, Tillyard pl. 20, 127; *CV.* Gallatin pl. 57, 1. A, man and boy; B, youth.

25 (*u* 3). ADRIA B 209, fr., from Adria. *CV.* pl. 5, 3; *Riv. Ist.* n. s. 5–6, 35 fig. 9. A, man and another (woman or youth).

26. ZAGREB. A, youth offering a cock to a boy; B, youth. [Bothmer].

PELIKAI

(nos. 27–30, with framed pictures)

27 (21). CAMBRIDGE 9.17. Dubois-Maisonneuve pl. 54, 3; Tillyard pl. 12, 98; *CV.* pl. 33, 2 and pl. 34, 4; A, Cloché *Classes* pl. 14, 2. A, Odysseus and Eumaios? B, man and youth. See p. 1659.

28 (22). RHODES 13129, from Camiros. *Cl. Rh.* 4, 120, left, and 124–5; *CV.* pl. 3. Komos ('Anacreontic'): A, man with lyre, and woman with crotala; B, two men. For the subject, CB. ii, 59 no. 20.

29 (26). ATHENS 1427 (CC. 1182), from Corinth. A, boy with man and youth; B, the like.

30 (a 1). MADRID 11122 (L. 158). A, Alvarez-Ossorio pl. 10, 1; *CV.* pl. 9, 2. A, man with lyre approaching a herm. B, man pursuing a boy who holds a hoop (not necessarily Zeus and Ganymede). Much restored.

(no. 31, not known if the pictures framed)

31 (27). LONDON E 436.2, fr., from Naucratis. (Man).

(nos. 32–33, the pictures not framed)

32. GELA (ex Navarra-Jacona), from Gela. A, Theseus and Minotaur; B, man and boy; youth and boy.

32 *bis* (23). MUNICH 2346 (J. 293), from South Italy. *CV.* pl. 70 and pl. 72, 3–4. A, komos; B, komos.

33 (28). TORONTO 365, from Capua or near? Robinson and Harcum pl. 64; *B.R. Ont.* pl. 9, a. A, youth with lyre, and youth, at altar. B, man and boy. Much restored, especially B.

AMPHORAE
(type B; with framed pictures; small)

34 (29). LONDON E 260, from Camiros. *CV.* pl. 5, 3. A, youth and woman; B, man and woman.

35 (30). VIENNA 634. La Borde 1 pll. 29–30; *CV.* pl. 52, 3–4. A, Theseus and Minotaur. B, komos (man and youth).

NECK-AMPHORAE
(of special shape, with convex handles)

36 (31). CAMBRIDGE 37.22. *CV.* ii RS. pl. 10, 2 and pl. 17, 9–10. A, Theseus and Procrustes. B, winged goddess pursuing a youth (Eos and Tithonos, one might have said, but the goddess holds the lyre and the youth a sprig).

37 (32). NEW YORK 56.171.40 (ex Hearst), from Capua. *Vente 18 mars 1901* pl. 2, 31 and p. 11; A, *Jb.* 10, 199; A, *Bull. Metr.* 1956–7, 177, 1. A, hoplitodromos and trainer. B, komos (woman playing lyre, and youth).

38 (33). MAGDEBURG (ex Kemma). A, man and woman; B, man and woman. On A, he offers her a ball or fruit, and she holds a fruit; on B, she seems to hold a skein; between the two, a mirror.

39 (34). PALERMO. Passeri pll. 30–31. A, naked woman washing, and woman. B, youth and woman. See p. 1659.

HYDRIAI
(the picture on the shoulder, framed)

40. SAN SIMEON, Hearst Corporation, 12274. Women at the fountain, and two men. This is the vase *ARV.*[1] 173, no. 15, said there to be in the manner of Myson, which is not wrong.

41 (35). SCHWERIN 1294. Music-lesson.

42 (36). LONDON E 172, from Camiros. *Annali* 1878 pl. O; *CV.* pl. 75, 4 and pl. 77, 2; detail, Richter *H.G.A.* 362 fig. 484; ph. Ma. 3152, left. Music-lesson.

43 (37). ATHENS 1691 (CC. 1173), from Greece. Heydemann pl. 8, 1; CC. pl. 40, 1173. Theseus and Minotaur.

44 (38). LENINGRAD (St. 2184), from Kerch. ABC. pl. 63 a, 4 and 4 a. Goddess mounting chariot.

FRAGMENTS OF POTS

45. REGGIO, fr., from Locri. (Neck to middle of a woman to left, right arm extended, a round fruit or the like in the left hand). May be from a column-krater.

46 (40). LIMENAS, fr., from Thasos. Ghali-Kahil C.G. pl. 49, 68. (Head of youth playing the flute). From a pelike?

MANNER OF THE PIG PAINTER

ARV.¹ 372–3.

COLUMN-KRATERS

(no. 1, with framed pictured)

1. ATHENS, Agora, P 7243, frr., from Athens. A, Centauromachy (Kaineus); B, (centaur).   *(nos. 2–4, the pictures not framed)*

2. COPENHAGEN inv. 13111. A, satyr and donkey; B, maenad dancing, and donkey. May be by the painter himself; also near Myson.

3. HARVARD 1959.125 (ex Robinson), fr., from Vari? CV. Robinson ii pll. 28 and 28 a. A, komast ('Anacreontic'). For the subject, CB. ii, 59 no. 18.

4. ATHENS, Agora, P 7242, two frr., from Athens. A, komast ('Anacreontic'); B, komast. Compare the last. For the subject, CB. ii, 59 no. 19.

PELIKAI

(nos. 5–7, with framed pictures)

5 (2). NEW YORK 56.171.43 (ex Hearst). *Vente 11 mai 1903* pl. 1, 10 and 8. A, Dionysos and satyr. B, youth and boy.

6 (l 25). ADOLPHSECK, Landgraf Philipp of Hesse, 41. CV. pl. 31. A, man and seated woman; B, man and woman.

7 (3). ATHENS, from Perachora. JHS. 56 pl. 10. A, youth with lyre approaching herm; B, man at herm.

(no. 8, the pictures not framed)

8 (l 24). HARVARD 1959.188 (ex Watkins). A, komos; B, komos.

FRAGMENTS OF POTS

9. NAPLES, Astarita, 114, two frr. A, (foot of woman running, with part of the skirt). B, youth and woman. From a neck-amphora?

10. ADRIA B 1025, fr., from Adria. CV. pl. 5, 6. (Man). [Riccioni].

11 (l 39). ATHENS, Agora, P 9465, fr., from Athens. (Hand with purse, and boy—or woman). May be from a column-krater. Also recalls the Agrigento Painter.

EARLIER MANNERISTS. ii. THE LENINGRAD PAINTER

Att. V. 245–8. *V.Pol.* 40–44 and 80. *ARV.*[1] 373–7 and 959.

Called after the amphora no. 70.

'Brother' of the Pig Painter, but less Mysonian.

COLUMN-KRATERS

(nos. 1–43, with framed pictures)

1 (1). NAPLES 2415, from Ruvo. A, ph. So. 11071, iii, 3. A, symposion; B, symposion.

2 (2). TRIESTE. Phs. Al. 40207 and 40215; A, *E.A.A.* iv, 561 fig. 657. A, symposion. B, man and youths.

3 (3). LOS ANGELES A 5890.48.1 (ex Warren), from Agrigento. A, *Cat. Parke-Bernet April 24 1943*, 9 no. 50; *Los Ang. Bull.* Spring 1949, 15–16. A, symposion; B, komos.

4 (4). MILAN, Torno, from Ruvo. A, *Annali* 1868 pl. C, whence Philippart *It. ii*, 29. A, symposion; B, komos. Restored, B much.

5. ATHENS, Agora, P 19282, fr., from Athens. *Hesp.* 18 pl. 45, 4. A, symposion or komos? (woman playing the flute). [Corbett].

6 (5). NEW YORK 41.162.60. A, *AJA.* 1924, 284; *CV.* Gallatin pl. 23, 3–4. A, komos; B, komos.

7 (6). BOLOGNA 191, from Bologna. Zannoni pl. 116, 8 and 11–12. A, komos; B, komos.

8 (8). NAPLES inv. 116117. A, komos; B, komos.

9. RANCATE, Züst. A, komos; B, komos. On A, youth with stick, youth with column-krater, youth playing the flute, man to left with stick.

10 (9). VIENNA 947. *CV.* pl. 91, 1–2. A, komos. B, youths.

11 (10). VILLA GIULIA 18247, from Falerii. A, komos. B, youths.

12 (11). SYRACUSE, from Syracuse? A, komos; B, komos. On A, youth holding column-krater, youth playing lyre, youth with oinochoe and stick.

13 (12). VILLA GIULIA. A, komos (youth to right with cup, youth to right with lyre and stick, youth to left with oinochoe and stick).

14. BONN, Langlotz, fr. A, komos (head and shoulders of youth to right, holding a pointed amphora).

15. ANCONA. A, komos; B, komos.

16 (13). ESSEN, Krupp, from Capua. *VDK.* pl. 83; A, Neugebauer *ADP.* pl. 70, 163. A, komos; B, komos. Restored.

17 (14). BOLOGNA 181, from Bologna. *CV.* pl. 26, 3–4. A, komos; B, komos.

18 (15). MUNICH 2372 (J. 747), from Sicily. A, Genick pl. 18. A, komos. B, flute-player and two youths.

19 (u 15). AGRIGENTO 7, from Agrigento. A, komos.

20. LOUVRE C 10781, fr. A, komos (on the right, head of male with lyre, head of youth with stick).

21 (16). OXFORD G 711, frr., from Naucratis. *CV*. pl. 66, 10–11. A, komos.

22 (17). BOLOGNA 266, fr., from Bologna. Pellegrini 109. Komos.

23 (18). ATHENS, Agora, P 12511, fr., from Athens. Komos.

24 (19). NAPLES 3084, from Nola. A, ph. So. 11071, ii, 4; B.Ap. xvi. 78. A, athletes; B, athletes.

25 (20). AGRIGENTO (ex Giudice 194), from Gela. Ph. Lo Cascio pl. 13; A, Griffo *Guide* fig. 59. A, arming. B, youths.

26 (21). ROMAN MARKET (Jandolo). A, arming.

27 (22). ETON, fr., from Al Mina. *JHS*. 59, 9, 23. A, arming (woman holding shield).

28 (23). TRIESTE 993. A, warrior leaving home. B, procession (women with torches).

29 (36). LOUVRE G 356. A, Millin *PVA*. 2 pl. 22; A, *AZ*. 1852 pl. 44, 2; A, Pottier pl. 137; *CV*. d pl. 26, 1–4. A, warrior mounting chariot. B, three youths. On the graffito see *AJA*. 1927, 350.

30 (24). LONDON MARKET (Burney). A, two young horsemen. B, three youths (1, running to right, left arm extended, 2, to left, looking round, stick in right hand, 3, running to right, looking round).

31 (25). TÜBINGEN E 96, fr. Watzinger pl. 28. A, (man with cock, and boy).

32 (26). FLORENCE 81268, from Chiusi. *CV*. pl. 44, 1 and pl. 36, 5. A, victorious lyre-player (boy with lyre, and two Nikai). B, youth running and others.

33 (27). FERRARA, T. 3, from Spina. A, youths and boys; B, youths and male.

34 (28). CORINTH C 32. 72, fr., from Corinth. A, (head and shoulder of Dionysos). The fragment C 32.165 may belong (muzzle of donkey, kantharos).

35 (29). FERRARA, T. 306, from Spina. A, return of Hephaistos; B, satyrs and maenad.

36 (30). MADRID 11040 (L. 167). A, Alvarez-Ossorio pl. 9, 2; *CV*. pl. 15, 3. A, Dionysos and satyrs. B, three youths.

37. FERRARA, T. 263 C VP, from Spina. A, Dionysos with maenad and satyrs.

38 (31). Once LECCE 77. A, satyrs and maenad; B, maenads. On A, satyr dancing to right, maenad running to left, looking round, with both hands raised, satyr dancing with head to left.

38 *bis*. REGGIO, fr., from Locri. (Raised arm of one in chiton, satyr moving to left with a pointed amphora in his left hand).

39 (32). LECCE 602, from Rugge. A, *Apulia* 3, 7 fig. 6; *CV*. pl. 5, 1–2 and pl. 6, 1; A, Romanelli and Bernardini 45, left; A, Bernardini pl. 36, 2; B, Bernardini *Vasi a soggetto sportivo* (from *St. Sal.* 9), 9–10. A, vintage: satyrs making wine. B, athletes and trainer.

40. MILAN, Torno, from Ruvo. A, Jatta *Caputi* pl. 6, whence Frickenhaus *Len.* pl. 2, 13 and *AM.* 53, 83. A–B, Lenaia: A, maenads at idol of Dionysos; B, maenads.

41 (34). LENINGRAD 636 (St. 1272). A, *CR.* 1873 pl. 5, 1–2. A, Herakles and Pholos. B, youths.

42 (35). LOUVRE G 364, from Altamura. A, *Annali* 1882 pl. O, whence Roscher s.v. Phineus 2366, 1; A, Pottier pl. 138; *CV.* d pl. 27, 8–11 and pl. 28, 2. A, Phineus (but the exact subject is not clear). B, three youths.

43 (37). DETROIT 24.120. A, *Bull. Detroit* 6, 9; A, *Art in America* 15 fig. 10; A, Schauenburg *Helios* fig. 17. A, Helios in his chariot. B, athletes and youth. B restored.

(nos. 44–51, the pictures not framed)

44 (38). SYRACUSE 24663, fr., from Gela. *ML.* 17, 306. A, komos (youth and man).

45. LUCERNE MARKET (A.A.). Komos: A, man to right, right arm extended, stick in left hand, youth to left playing the flute; B, youth playing the flute, youth dancing to left with head thrown back.

46 (39). Once AGRIGENTO, Giudice, 591, from Gela. Phs. Lo Cascio pl. 8. Komos: A, youth playing the flute, and youth with stick dancing; B, man. Restored.

47 (40). VILLA GIULIA 48334, from Cervetri. A, citharode and youth. B, komos (two youths).

48 (41). NAPLES (one number—not Heydemann's—2626). A, man playing the flute, and boy. B, youth and woman. Much restored. Small.

49 (a 4). BOSTON 10.191, frr. A, *MFA. Bull.* 9, 54, 1 ; A, *VA.* 119, whence *Die Antike* 6 pl. 16, b; A, Anita Klein pl. 23, b; CB. iii pl. 85, 149. A, see-saw. B, male. See CB. iii, text.

50. GELA (ILA cassetta 5), fr., from Gela. A, (head and shoulders of man to right).

51 (42). ADRIA B 212 and B 164, frr., from Adria. *CV.* pl. 35, 3. (Youths).

VOLUTE-KRATER

52 (43). BOLOGNA 276, from Bologna. Zannoni pl. 135, 4–5; *CV.* pl. 57 and pl. 58, 4–6. A, Dionysos with satyrs and maenad; B, satyrs and maenads.

PELIKAI
(nos. 53–66, with framed pictures)

53 (46). BRUNSWICK 269. *CV.* pl. 21, 2–3. Komos (A, youths and flute-girl; B, man with lyre, and youths).

54 (47). PARIS MARKET (Mikas). Komos (A, youth playing the flute and youth with oinochoe; youth with stick and youth with oinochoe).

55. LOUVRE ('juin 1928'). Komos (A, youth playing the flute and youth with cup; B, youth and woman).

56 (49). LONDON E 351, from Solygeia near Corinth. *Annali* 1879 pl. U; B, Schlesinger *Aulos* pl. 5. Komos (A, youth and boy; B, two youths).

57 (50). NAPLES Stg. 238. A, citharode and youths. B, youth and boy.

58 (50 *bis*). MYKONOS, from Rheneia (originally from Delos). Dugas *Délos xxi* pl. 8, 18. A, youths and boy; B, two youths.

59 (51). LENINGRAD, fr. Youth and boy (the upper halves remain: youth leaning on his stick, offering a wreath to a boy).

60 (54). BOLOGNA 163, from Bologna. Zannoni pl. 17, 3–5. A, man and boy; B, youth and boy.

61 (53). Where?, frr., from Al Mina. *JHS.* 59, 9, 24. Fragments β and γ show a boy, and the right hand of a male talking to him; fragment α (male leaning on his stick) is either from the same figure as the hand, or from a corresponding figure on the other side of the vase.

62 (52). Once TREBEN, Leesen. *Kat. von Leesen* pl. 2, 30. A, two youths; B, two youths.

63. TARANTO 52341, from Taranto. A, youth and seated woman; B, youth and woman.

64 (55). BOLOGNA 162, from Bologna. Zannoni pl. 38, 2–3 and 7. A, acontist and flute-player; B, jumper and youth.

65 (57). SYRACUSE 21968, from Gela. A, *ML.* 17 pl. 10, 2; A, *CV.* pl. 2, 1. A, youths and cock. B, youth running.

66 (58). PALERMO V 749, from Gela. *CV.* pl. 28, 3–4. A, satyr and maenad; B, maenad.

(no. 67, not known if the pictures framed)

67 (56). REGGIO, fr., from Locri. (Head and breast of youth to right; above, lotus-bud border).

(nos. 68–69, the pictures not framed)

68 (44). FLORENCE PD 60 a, from Populonia. *St. etr.* 12 pl. 63, 3–4. A, arming; B, arming.

68 *bis*. BEAUNE (Louvre C 10285 on loan). A, *Musées de France* 1949, 4, 5. A, Dionysos with satyrs and maenad; B, satyrs and maenad. Assigned to the Mannerist Group by Devambez.

69. CAMBRIDGE 1.1958. Part, *Arch. Reports 1961–2*, 50, 9. Komos. [Nicholls].

AMPHORAE
(type B; with framed pictures)

70 (59). LENINGRAD, from South Russia. A, G.P. 69. A, citharode, with listeners; B, listeners.

71 (45). ADRIA B 248, frr., from Adria. *CV*. pl. 32; *Riv. Ist.* N.S. 5–6, 51. A, komos ('Anacreontic'); B, komos. Adria B 1220 probably belongs.

NECK-AMPHORA
(with twisted handles)

72 (60). MUNICH 2323 (J. 416), from Vulci. Handle-floral, Lau pl. 25, 3; side, Jacobsthal O. pl. 61, c; *CV*. pl. 213, 3–5 and pl. 217, 2. A, victorious lyre-player (youth with lyre, Nike, and woman). B, three youths.

HYDRIAI
(nos. 73–84, with picture on the shoulder, framed)

73 (61). MILAN, Torno, from Ruvo. *Annali* 1876 pl. D–E, whence HM. 11 fig. 4, FR. ii, 307, Perrot 9, 343, *ML*. 28, 100, Richter *Craft* 71, Cloché *Classes* pl. 21, 1; Singer *Hist. of Technology* ii pl. 16; detail, Richter *H.G.A.* 307; detail, *Archaeology* 12, 243; *AJA*. 1960 pl. 84. Vase-painters. See *PP*. 11–13; and below, p. 1659.

74. CORINTH T 1144, frr., from Corinth. *Hesp.* 24 pl. 85. Scene from a tragedy with Persian subject: see *Hesp.* 24, 305–19.

75 (a 5). BOSTON 03.788. Brommer *Satyroi* 69; Brommer *Satyrspiele* 14, whence *Bull. Vereen.* 17, 11 fig. 24; F. F. Jones *The Theater in Ancient Art* fig. 1; *Hesp.* 24 pl. 86, 2; CB. iii pl. 86, 151. Scene from a satyr-play: satyrs about to set up a couch. See *Hesp.* 24, 310–11, and CB. iii, text.

76 (62). WARSAW 142290 (ex Czartoryski 55). *Gaz. arch.* 1884 pll. 44–46; de Witte pl. 22, whence Cook *Zeus* i, 424 fig. 305 and Rumpf *Rel.* fig. 173; *CV*. pl. 32, 3. Ceremonial cleansing of a youth (nuptial bath according to Rumpf). See *V. Pol.* 40–44.

77 (63). LONDON E 167. Hancarville 4 pl. 50; *AJA*. 1917, 39–40; *CV*. pl. 73, 1 and pl. 79, 1; *Hesp.* 24 pl. 86, a; Bothmer *Am.* pl. 70, 1. Herakles and the Amazons.

77 *bis*. REGGIO, two frr., from Locri. Herakles and Busiris. One of the fragments was already attributed to the painter by Procopio.

78 (64). LONDON MARKET (Spink: ex Richmond, Cook). Youths and men (1, youth seated to right; 2, man to right; 3, man seated in chair to right; 4, youth frontal, looking round; 5, youth seated to left: all wear the chlamys, and 1, 2, 4 have spears).

79 (65). LONDON 1920.3–15.3, from Capua. *Bull. Nap.* 6 pl. 2, 1–2; *CV*. pl. 73, 2 and pl. 79, 2. Centauromachy (Kaineus).

80 (66). BOLOGNA 169, from Bologna. Pellegrini 57. Pygmies and cranes.

81 (u 65). SAN SIMEON, State Monument, 9933, from Capua. *Vente 18 mars 1901*, 12. Woman spinning, women, and youths.

82 (64). RHODES 13261, from Camiros. *Cl. Rh.* 4, 160–1; *CV*. pl. 5, 3. Women working with wool, and youths.

83. ATHENS E 4, fr. (On the left, youth seated to right).

84. TARANTO, fr., from Locri. (Upper part of naked youth to right, bending).

(no. 85, the picture on the shoulder, running right round the vase)

85 (67). ATHENS MARKET. Dionysos with donkey, and satyrs and maenads.

(no. 86, the picture mainly on the shoulder, not framed)

86 (68). MYKONOS, from Rheneia (originally from Delos). Dugas *Délos xxi* pl. 26, 62. Unexplained subject; youth with lyre, woman with torches, and king, at altar.

(nos. 87–88, the picture on the body)

87 (69). VATICAN, from Vulci. *Mus. Greg.* 2 pl. 14, 3; ph. Al. 35738. Apollo mounting chariot, with two goddesses (Leto and Artemis?).

88 (u 82). CHICAGO 11.456. Girl kissing youth, with women and youth. One of the women holds a braiding-frame.

FRAGMENTS OF POTS

89 (70). MUNICH inv. 8542. *CV.* pl. 102, 6. (Citharode—Apollo?).

90 (71). DELPHI, fr., from Delphi. *FD.* v, 170 fig. 714. Komos.

91. ETON, fr., from Al Mina. Komos? (thigh and ham of a male in a cloak moving to left).

92. ADRIA B 217, fr., from Adria. *CV.* pl. 35, 4. (Youth). [Riccioni]. From a column-krater?

––––––––––––

A vase which I know from tiny photographs only is early mannerist and may be by the Leningrad Painter:

COLUMN-KRATER
(with framed pictures)

ADALIA, from Aspendos. A, komos (three youths). B, arming (three naked youths, one holding a greave, another picking up a shield).

––––––––––––

MANNER OF THE LENINGRAD PAINTER
ARV.[1] 377.

COLUMN-KRATERS
(no. 1, with framed pictures)

1 (1). AGRIGENTO (ex Giudice 583), from Gela. Ph. Lo Cascio pl. 3. A, symposion; B, komos. Also recalls the Pig Painter.

(nos. 2–3, not known whether the pictures framed)

2. NEW YORK, Bothmer, fr. Komos? (head, to right, with right shoulder, left shoulder and arm, of a naked youth running to left and looking back). Probably by the painter himself.

3. IKARIA (isle of), fr., from Ikaria. *Prakt.* 1939, 155 fig. 18. (Youth).

PELIKAI
(nos. 4–7, with framed pictures)

4 (l 47 *bis*). PAESTUM, frr., from Paestum. *JHS*. 59, 226 fig. 11; part, *Anz*. 1940, 530. Komos.

5 (u 49). MYKONOS, fr., from Rheneia (originally from Delos). Dugas *Délos xxi* pl. 46, 20. A, komos? (youth playing the flute and one dancing).

6 (u 47). NAPLES 3045, from Nola. B, ph. So. 11009, vi, 3. A, Hermes pursuing a woman; B, old king, and woman running.

7 (u 56). MYKONOS, from Rheneia (originally from Delos). Dugas *Délos xxi*, pl. 8, 19. A, youth and old man (or youth?); B, male and boy. Imitation.

(no. 8, not known whether the pictures framed)

8 (2). MUNICH, two frr. On each, beard and upper part of a man or god in chiton and himation to right; on one, holding a phiale; on the other, with a sceptre across his shoulder.

(nos. 9–10, the pictures not framed)

9 (u 46). LOUVRE G 373, from Bomarzo. Pottier pl. 139; *CV*. d pl. 40, 1–7. Peleus and Thetis.

10 (u 45). PARIS MARKET (Brimo; ex de Domenicis). Gerhard pl. 210; B.Ap. xvi. 13. A, Athena mounting chariot, and warrior; B, men and youths looking on. Restored.

AMPHORA
(type B; with framed pictures)

11 (3). VATICAN, from Vulci. *Mus. Greg.* 2 pl. 57, 2. A, warriors leaving home (a hoplite and two archers, with a woman). B, kings and women. Much restored: the upper part of the vase is modern, with the heads of all the figures. Should be by the painter himself.

HYDRIAI
(with picture on the shoulder, framed)

12. MISSISSIPPI (ex Robinson), fr., from Vulci. *AJA*. 1956 pl. 15 figs. 66–67. Unexplained subject (Zeus, Poseidon, Nike or Iris, youth—Apollo?; there was another figure, on the left). [Enrico Paribeni].

13. FERRARA, T 619 B VP, fr., from Spina. (Woman seated with mirror or distaff, woman running up, male leaning on his stick).

FRAGMENTS OF POTS

14 (6). CORINTH CP 998, fr., from Corinth. Komos ('Anacreontic': hand and shoulders of a man in chiton, cloak, saccos, to right, looking up). Perhaps from a column-krater.

15. ETON, fr., from Al Mina. (Middle of a male to left, arm extended—komos?). Compare the right-hand figure on the front of the Harvard pelike, p. 566 no. 8).

See also pp. 584 no. 11 and 587 nos. 55 and 56.

EARLIER MANNERISTS. iii. THE AGRIGENTO PAINTER

VA. 120–1. *Att. V.* 242–5 and 475. *ARV.*[1] 377–82, 959, and 968.

Called after the calyx-krater no. 55.

Takes off from the Pig Painter.

COLUMN-KRATERS
(nos. 1–50 bis, the pictures framed)

1 (1). NAPLES 2414, from Ruvo. A, ph. So. 11071, iii, 2. A, goddess mounting chariot, and Nike bringing a tripod; B, goddess mounting chariot, and woman with torches.

2 (2). RUVO, Jatta, from Ruvo. A, *Japigia* 3, 19; A, Philippart *It. ii* pl. 1, 1 and pl. 2, 3. A, goddess mounting chariot, and Nike with cithara. A, youths and boy.

3 (3). OXFORD 1927.1, from Valenzano. *CV.* pl. 60, 5–6. A, Zeus pursuing Thetis; B, Nereids fleeing to Nereus. On the subject see CB. ii, 68–69.

4 (4). LENINGRAD inv. 210 (St. 1724). A, Apollo and Muse, with Artemis and Hermes. B, youth with lyre, and youths.

5 (5). NAPLES MARKET (Barone), from Anzi. Minervini *Mon. Barone* pl. 10, whence Overbeck *Gall.* pl. 1, 14, (A) Brunn *K.S.* iii, 22. A, the Theban Sphinx. B, man and youths.

6 (6). NAPLES inv. 146739, from Naples. A, *NSc.* 1935 pl. 15, 3; A, Brommer *Satyrspiele*[1] 49 = [2]55, whence Pickard-Cambridge *DFA.* fig. 33. A, Orpheus with a Thracian and a satyr. B, youths and boy.

7 (7). SYRACUSE, from Leontinoi. Part of A, *Riv. Ist.* 2, 173. A, Amazonomachy. B, youths and boys.

8 (8). CHIUSI, frr., from Chiusi. *NSc.* 1931, 218, 4–6. A, Amazonomachy.

9 (9). NEW YORK 15.27, from near Naples. A, *Bull. Metr.* 10, 123 fig. 3; Richter and Hall pl. 73 and pl. 170, 70; A, Richter *H.* 225, d. A, Herakles and Busiris; B, Egyptians fleeing.

10 (10). BOSTON 10.188, fr. A, Herakles and Busiris.

11 (11). VILLA GIULIA 14217. *ML.* 24 (Cultrera) pl. 10, 23; *CV.* pl. 20, 1–2; A, ph. Al. 41167; A, ph. R.I. 1931.2350, 2. A, Theseus and Minotaur. B, youths and boy.

12 (12). LENINGRAD 801 (St. 1626), from Sicily. A, Theseus and Minotaur. B, youths and boys.

13 (13). NAPLES 3156. A, ph. So. 11071, i, 3. A, Theseus and Minotaur. B, youths and boy.

14 (14). BOLOGNA 183, from Bologna. A, Pellegrini 67; *CV*. pl. 32, 3-4. A, Eos and Kephalos. B, youths and boy.

15. SYRACUSE, from Megara Hyblaea. *NSc*. 1954, 103. A, Nike (or Iris) pursuing a boy who holds a lyre (Eos and Tithonos, one would have said, but the goddess holds a caduceus). B, youths and boy.

16 (15). TORONTO 364, from Tarquinia. Robinson and Harcum pl. 63; A, *B.R. Ont.* pl. 7, b. A, Dionysos with maenad and young satyr; B, satyrs and maenad.

17 (16). VIENNA 3738 (ex Oest. Mus. 341). *CV*. pl. 92, 1-2. A, Dionysos with maenad and satyr. B, satyrs and maenad.

18. FERRARA, T. 26 C VP, from Spina. A, Dionysos with maenad and satyr; B, satyrs and maenad.

19 (17). TURIN 3029. A, Barocelli *Mus. Tor.* pl. 41, 4; A, Philippart *It. ii* pl. 1, 2. A, Dionysos with maenad and satyr; B, satyrs and maenad.

20 (18). VILLA GIULIA 846, from Falerii. A, Dionysos, inebriated, with satyrs and maenads; B, satyrs and (maenad?).

21 (19). BOLOGNA 194, from Bologna. A, Pellegrini 73; *CV*. pl. 31. A, Dionysos on donkey, with boy satyr. B, youths and boy.

22 (20). BOLOGNA 258, from Bologna. A, Pellegrini 103, whence *Mem. Am. Ac.* 6 pl. 18, 1; A, *CV*. pl. 50, 2-3. A, four maenads. B, males.

23 (21). BARI. A, three maenads.

24. BALTIMORE, Walters Art Gallery, 48.71. A, komos; B, komos.

25 (22). PALERMO (955). A, komos (three youths, and a flute-girl). B, youths and boys.

26 (22 *bis*). BARCELONA 607, from Ampurias. *Mem. Mus. Arqu. Prov.* 1940 pl. 8; García y Bellido pl. 97. A, komos; B, komos.

26 *bis*. LONDON MARKET (Sotheby). A, komos. B, youths and woman. On A, 1, youth to right, playing the flute, 2, man to right, looking round, 3, youth to right with lyre, 4, man to left with cup and stick.

27 (24). BOLOGNA 184, from Bologna. Zannoni pl. 59, 1-3. A, komos. B, youths and boy.

28 (25). SYRACUSE, from Camarina. A, *ML*. 14 pl. 53 and p. 858. A, komos; B, komos.

29 (26). BREMEN, Focke Museum. Schaal *Brem.* pll. 14 and 12. A, komos. B, youths and boy. [Schaal].

30 (27). PARIS MARKET (Feuardent). A, komos. B, youths and boy. On A, man with stick and pointed amphora, bending, woman playing the flute, youth running with raised stick.

31. Where? (seen in Naples at the restorer's). A, komos. B, youths and boy. On A, youth with stick, woman playing the flute, youth looking round.

32 (28). Once Burgon (ex Englefield). A, Tischbein 3 pl. 16; A, Moses *Englefield* pl. 24. A, komos. B, three draped persons.

33 (29). VIENNA 770. A, La Borde 1 pl. 38, whence *El.* 4 pl. 91; *CV.* pl. 92, 3–4. A, komos ('Anacreontics', and woman with cithara). B, youths and boy. For the subject of A, CB. ii, 60 no. 22.

34 (31). SYRACUSE 23509, from Gela. A, *ML.* 17, 499 and pl. 41, whence Philippart *It. ii*, 30. A, symposion; B, komos.

35 (32). VATICAN. A, symposion; B, komos.

36 (32 *bis*). CHICAGO, Univ., fr. *AJA.* 1938, 353 fig. 13. A, symposion.

37 (a 1). ANCONA 3264 (999), from Numana. A, Marconi and Serra pl. 48, 2. A, symposion; B, symposion.

38. FERRARA, T. 430 B VP, from Spina. A, young warrior pursuing a a woman. B, youths and boy.

39. FERRARA, T. 5 A VP, from Spina. A, arming. B, youths and boy.

40. FERRARA, T. 31 A VP, from Spina. A, arming. B, youths and boys.

41 (33). BOLOGNA 180, from Bologna. *CV.* pl. 34, 1–2. A, warrior leaving home; B, youths with armour.

42 (34). LENINGRAD 797 (St. 1273). A, youth leaving home. B, youths and boy.

43. BASLE MARKET (M.M.). A, youth seated, man holding helmet, man, and youth. B, youths and boy.

44. BARCELONA 558, fr., from Ampurias. A, (youth and Eros).

45 (35). YALE 1933.175, from near Taranto. A, *Cat. de Morgan* (*16 Jan. 1909*) pl. 4, 139; *Am. Art Gall., Coll. Clarke* no. 373; A, *Bull. Yale* 7, 11. A, man and boy, youth and boy; B, youths and boy.

46 (39). OXFORD, Beazley, fr., from South Russia. *Sborník* 1961 pl. 24, 1. A, (head and shoulders of an old man with a stick in his right hand).

47 (36). MARZABOTTO, fr., from Marzabotto. (Head of man looking up to right.) Worn.

48 (37). PALERMO, fr., from Selinus. B, (one in himation to right, upper part of youth in himation leaning on his stick to right, right hand extended holding strigil).

49 (38). SYRACUSE 21889, fr., from Gela. B, (on the right, head, to right, of boy, upper part of youth leaning on his stick to left).

50 (40). LEIPSIC T 668, fr. (Head of youth to left).

50 *bis*. REGGIO, fr., from Locri. (Head and shoulders of a youth to left, with part of the tongue-pattern above; no relief-contour).

(no. 51, the pictures not framed)

51 (41). NAPLES 3111, from Nola. A, ph. So. 11071, ii, 2. Komos: A, youth and flute-girl; B, youth.

DINOS

52 (42). ATHENS 1489 (CC. 1597). Part, *Bull. MFA.* 46, 48. Boar-hunt.

STAMNOI

53 (43). BOLOGNA 177, from Bologna. A, Theseus and Minotaur. B, man offering lyre to youth, and male. See p. 1659.

54 (44). BOLOGNA 178, from Bologna. A, Eos and Kephalos. B, boy with youth and male. See p. 1659.

CALYX-KRATER

55 (45). AGRIGENTO, from Agrigento. A, Gabrici *Vasi ined.* (from *Atti Pal.* 15) fig. 9. A, Herakles and Nessos. B, youths and boys.

BELL-KRATERS OR CALYX-KRATERS

56 (45 *bis*). MYKONOS, fr., from Rheneia (originally from Delos). Dugas *Délos xxi*, pl. 36, 80. A, (man).

57 (u 33). OXFORD G 138.32, fr., from Naucratis. *CV.* pl. 50, 14. (Maenad?).

58. ATHENS, Agora, P 12051, fr., from Athens. A, (warrior).

59. ATHENS, Agora, P 10846, fr., from Athens. Komos.

BELL-KRATERS
(no. 60, with lugs)

60 (46). LOUVRE G 369. Detail, Emmanuel *Danse* 211 fig. 461; *CV.* d pl. 9, 2–3 and pl. 11, 1 and 5. A, komos; B, komos.

(no. 61, unknown whether lugs or handles)

61 (47). LENINGRAD, fr. Komos (hand with cup, and youth playing the flute to right).

(nos. 62–63, with handles)

62 (48). ROMAN MARKET (Depoletti). B.Ap. xxii. 113. A, youth with sword pursuing a woman; B, woman running to youth.

63 (49). BERLIN 4028. A, komos; B, komos.

AMPHORA
(type A; with framed pictures)

64 (50). ROME, Torlonia, 91. A, Hermes and woman; Poseidon and woman with torch. B, (one with a cithara, woman with oinochoe and phiale, and other figures which I could not see).

PELIKAI
(nos. 65–80, with framed pictures)

65 (51). TARQUINIA 705, from Tarquinia. A, ph. And. 41010, 1; A, *E.A.A.* i, 157. A, Theseus and Minotaur. B, youth, boy, and man.

66. FLORENCE, from Populonia. A, Theseus and Minotaur. B, youth, boy, and man.

67. MUNICH inv. 8737. *Vente xi Bâle* pl. 23, 342; *Anz.* 1957, 391-4. A, unexplained subject: youth stealing up to a woman who is picking flowers or fruit, and a man looking on. B, man, boy, and youth.

68. CHARLECOTE, Fairfax-Lucy. A, youth with sword pursuing a woman (Theseus and Aithra?). B, woman running to youth.

69 (52). Once BROOMHALL, Elgin. Stackelberg pl. 22, whence (A) Weege *Tanz* 35 fig. 41. A, pyrrhic. B, youth and boy.

70. LOUVRE. A, warrior leaving home (warrior standing frontal, woman standing to left with oinochoe and phiale; also a dog). On B, part of the net-border at the side is all that remains.

71. LOUVRE C 10790. A, discus-thrower and acontist; B, jumper and trainer.

72 (53). FERRARA, T. 563, from Spina. A, komos (two youths and a woman with a lyre). B, youths and boy. See p. 1660.

73 (59). LENINGRAD (St. 1529). Komos: A, two youths; B, youth playing the flute, and youth.

74 (54). LENINGRAD. A, youth and boy; B, the like. On A, youth leaning on his stick to right, a lyre in his left hand, boy standing to left, his right hand raised.

75. PARIS, Musée Rodin, 4. *CV.* pl. 21, 3-4. A, youth and boy; B, man and boy. Restored.

76 (55). PARIS MARKET (Geladakis). A, youth and boy; B, youth and boy. On A, boy to right, youth leaning on his stick to left; on B, youth holding (a box?) and boy. Wreath-border above.

77 (56). PARIS MARKET (Segredakis). A, youth and boy; B, the like. The boy stands to right, the youth leans on his stick to left. Key-pattern above.

78 (58). REGGIO 963, fr., from Locri. (Part of a head to right, then the head of a woman in a saccos to left).

79. SALONICA, Univ., from Karabournou. *Epit. Tsounta* 385-6. A, Dionysos and satyr; B, satyr and maenad.

80 (61). ATHENS 1399 (CC. 1276), from Boeotia. A, ph. A.I. 3106. A, satyr squatting on a table, with a kantharos in one hand, and maenad playing the flute. B, youth and boy.

(no. 81, not known whether the pictures framed)

81 (57). ERLANGEN 841, fr. (Head and shoulders of youth to right).

(no. 82, the pictures not framed)

82 (60). ATHENS 12492 (N. 1085). A, Amazonomachy. B, youths and boy. See Bothmer *Am.* 182-3 no. 66.

HYDRIAI

(with picture on the shoulder, framed)

83 (u 69). INDIANAPOLIS 47.34 (ex Perry and Simkhovitch). *AJA.* 1917, 38 and 46; *Cat. Am. Art Ass. March 6–7 1936*, 9, 31; *Bull. Ind.* 34, 21. Return of Hephaistos.

84 (62). BOSTON 08.417, from Capua. *Harv. St.* 12, 335, whence *Jb.* 18, 43 and *RM.* 21, 100; *AJA.* 1917, 41 and 52; Fairbanks and Chase 47 fig. 44; CB. iii pl. 86, 150 and Suppl. pl. 21, 1; the shape, Hambidge 71; the shape, Caskey G. 114. Death of Argos. See CB. iii, text.

85 (64). PIRAEUS. Theseus and Minotaur (with Minos and Nike).

86 (65). CHICAGO, Univ., fr. *AJA.* 1938, 353 fig. 14. Youth with spears (Theseus?) pursuing a woman. [Johnson].

87 (63). LONDON E 171, from Camiros. *Annali* 1878 pl. P; *CV.* pl. 75, 3 and pl. 76, 2, whence Wegner *Mus.* pl. 13; (reversed) *The New Oxford History of Music* pl. 10, b; ph. Ma. 3152, right. Music-lesson.

88 (67). RHODES 12266, from Camiros. *Cl. Rh.* 4, 210, middle, and 211. Youths and boys.

FRAGMENTS OF POTS

89 (68). HEIDELBERG 164, fr., from Orvieto. (Seated youth). From a stamnos?

90. BARCELONA (? mislaid), fr., from Ampurias. Komos (head of a youth to right, playing the flute, then the hand of another person to left— dancing?). [Shefton].

MANNER OF THE AGRIGENTO PAINTER

PELIKE

(with framed pictures)

ATHENS. A, man and girl; B, youth and boy. [Philippaki].

EARLIER MANNERISTS. iv. THE OINANTHE PAINTER

Att. V. 251. *V.Pol.* 44. *ARV.*[1] 383.

So called from the inscription on no. 2.

Near the early phase of the Nausicaa Painter (p. 1106).

AMPHORA

(type B; with framed pictures)

1 (1). LONDON E 264, from Vulci. *WV.* 1890–1 pl. 8, 1; *CV.* pl. 7, 1; A, Stella 710. A, Theseus arriving in Athens. B, youth leaving home (or arriving: youth with Nike and old man).

HYDRIAI

(*with picture on the body*)

2 (2). LONDON E 182, from Vulci. Gerhard pl. 151, whence *El.* 1 pl. 85, Robert *Arch. Märchen* 191, Sauer *Theseion* 60; *CV.* pl. 85, 1; Cook *Zeus* iii pl. 22; detail, *RM.* 47 pl. 1, 3; Simon *G.A.* 16; ph. Ma. 3156. Birth of Erichthonios. OINANOEKALE.

3 (3). LEYDEN PC 73 (xviii d 21), from Vulci. Roulez pl. 1; *Gids* 35, 3. Zeus and Hera with Nike (or Iris) and Hermes. For the subject, Simon *O.G.* 58, 62–64, and 132.

Probably also the

PELIKE

(*the pictures not framed*)

(u 41). VATICAN, from near Norcia. *Mus. Greg.* 2 pl. 63, 1. A, Apollo, with two goddesses, a boy, and Hermes; under each handle, Nike; B, Zeus and Hera, and Nike holding a lyre, at an altar. For the subject, Simon *O.G.* 41 and 65.

Near these, a slighter work:

COLUMN-KRATER

(*with framed pictures*)

(a). PARIS MARKET (Mikas: ex Feuardent). A, Tillyard pl. 21, 129. A, women running to king. B, man and youths. B somewhat recalls Copenhagen inv. 7030 (p. 1109 no. 33).

––––––––

EARLIER MANNERISTS. v. THE PAINTER OF LOUVRE G 231

ARV.[1] 382.

Akin to the Oinanthe Painter.

AMPHORAE

(*type B; with framed pictures*)

1 (1). VATICAN, from Vulci. *Mus. Greg.* 2 pl. 57, 1; Gerhard pl. 160; part of A, *Jb.* 43, 131; A, ph. And. 42039, whence Bille-de Mot 108; A, ph. R.I. 1928.155; A, ph. Marb. O. 29167. A, Theseus and Minotaur. B, youth setting out (with Nike and an old man). Restored.

2 (2). CAMBRIDGE 37.21. *CV.* ii RS. pl. 10, 1 and pl. 17, 1–2 and 4–5. A, Athena greeting a young warrior. B, a youth welcomed by a man.

3 (a). LONDON E 262, from Vulci. Gerhard pl. 76, 1 and pl. 143; *CV.* pl. 6, 1. A, Artemis in chariot, with Apollo. B, Herakles entering Olympus (Herakles, Nike, and Zeus). See also under p. 1030 no. 36.

PELIKE
(the pictures not framed)

4 (3). LOUVRE G 231. A, *Mon.* 10 pl. 22, 1, whence Roscher s.v. Polyxene 2731 fig. 7; *CV.* pl. 46, 5 and 7–8; B, Schauenburg *Perseus* pl. 13, 1. A, Achilles and Troilos. B, Perseus (with Athena and Hermes). Much restored.

EARLIER MANNERISTS. vi. THE PERSEUS PAINTER
Att. V. 241–2. *ARV.*[1] 382–3.

Called after no. 16.

PELIKAI
(the pictures not framed)

1. NOSTELL PRIORY, St. Oswald. A, Poseidon and (?) Nereid; B, Nereid (?). On A, Poseidon seated to right with phiale and trident, Nereid standing frontal, head to left, with phiale and aphlaston; on B, woman running up with oinochoe. Restored.

2 (4). BERKELEY 8.4582, from Cortona. *CV.* pl. 43, 1. A, satyr and maenad. B, mistress and maid? (seated woman, and woman). With A compare a pelike in the Noble collection at Maplewood (*AJA.* 1956 p. 115 figs. 44–45), which is not, however, by the Perseus Painter and does not even belong to the Mannerist Group (see p. 1659).

3. CYRENE, from Cyrenaica. A, man and woman; B, youth and woman. On A, man in long chiton and himation holding a cock by the wings, woman holding a box; between them, a wool-basket. On B, youth to right with stick, woman to left with perfume-vase.

4 (5). BERLIN 2172, from Etruria. Gerhard *Ak. Abh.* pl. 67, 1; B, Licht iii, 80; Vorberg *Gloss.* 491–2. A, herm, bird, and altar; B, acolyte and herm.

5. ATHENS, Agora, P 17001, fr., from Athens. A, Dionysos; B, satyr.

NECK-AMPHORAE
(small, with double handles)

6 (6). CAMBRIDGE 166, from Nola? A, E. Gardner pl. 34; *CV.* pl. 32, 1 and pl. 40, 5. A, Dionysos; B, maenad.

7. Once NEW YORK, Simkhovitch. A, Dionysos (or hierophant, see *Num. Chron.* 1941, 7) moving to left, looking round, a torch in each hand; B, woman (running to right).

LOUTROPHOROI

8 (7). LOUVRE S 1672. Neck, A, Emmanuel *Danse* 273 fig. 552. A, prothesis; B, valediction; on the neck, A, two women mourning, B, the like.

9. ATHENS, Acr. Mus., fr., from Athens. (Heads of youth—Hermes?—, of Nike, of bride and bridegroom—in chariot?).

10. ATHENS, Acr. Mus., fr., from Athens. (Head and shoulders of youth, petasos at nape).

11. ATHENS, Acr. Mus., fr., from Athens. On the neck, (youth playing the flute).

12. ATHENS, Acr. Mus., fr., from Athens. On the neck, (woman carrying a loutrophoros).

COLUMN-KRATER
(with framed pictures)

13. NAPLES (ex Spinelli 1950), from Suessula. A, Philippart *It. ii* pl. 5, v, 3. A, Dionysos on donkey, and maenad. B, youths and boy.

BELL-KRATERS
(no. 14, with lugs)

14 (8). BOLOGNA 311, from Bologna. Zannoni pl. 52, 4 and 14–15. A, satyr and maenad. B, youth and woman.

(no. 15, not known whether lugs or handles)

15. LOUVRE C 11195, fr. Woman running with torch. Small.

HYDRIAI
(with picture on the body)

16 (1). BERLIN 2377, from Vulci. *Annali* 1851 pl. O; Schauenburg *Perseus* pl. 41; B.Ap. xviii. 58. 2. Athena and Perseus.

17 (2). COPENHAGEN, Thorvaldsen Museum, 95. Apollo and goddess. Restored.

18 (3). LONDON E 252.4, fr., from Camiros. (Apollo and Artemis).

19. ADOLPHSECK, Landgraf Philipp of Hesse, 39. *CV.* pl. 29, 4. Two women picking fruit.

FRAGMENT OF A POT

20. ATHENS, Agora, P 17137, fr., from Athens. (Head and hand of a woman). From an amphora or a pelike.

Probably also

NUPTIAL LEBES
(type 1)

1 (u 30). ATHENS 1255 (CC. 1237). B, ph. A.I. 3094. A, male, man, and woman; B, three women; on the stand, man and woman, youth and woman.

OINOCHOE
(small; the pictures not framed)

2. NAPLES inv. 86297, from Cumae. A, Oedipus and the Sphinx; B, the like. Much restored.

EARLIER MANNERISTS. vii. THE PAINTER OF LONDON 95

Charites Langlotz 138.

AMPHORAE

(type B; with framed pictures)

1 (u 61). LONDON 95.10–31.1. Gerhard pl. 46, whence *El.* 3 pll. 57a and 57b, (one figure on A) Overbeck *KM.* pl. 20, 11, (A) Roscher s.v. Idas p. 103; *CV.* pl. 4, 1 and pl. 12, 4. A, Marpessa. B, Triptolemos. On the subject of A see *Panm.* 15 note 30, *CF.* 27, and *Charites Langlotz* 136–8.

2. LUCERNE MARKET (A.A.). A, Herakles and Athena (Hermes to right, woman holding sash, Herakles to right with kantharos and club, Athena to left with oinochoe and spear, altar). B, young warrior (Achilles) receiving his armour (woman to right, holding greaves, youth to right, spear in left hand, receiving a helmet from a woman standing to left, holding a shield, old man with stick, head to left). Restored.

———

EARLIER MANNERISTS. viii. UNDETERMINED

Att. V. 248–51, 418, and 475. *ARV.*[1] 395–400 and 959.

Many of the vases in those lists are now assigned to particular mannerists.

The list in *ARV.*[1] is now divided, and the earlier vases separated from the later. Here the earlier: for the later see pp. 1106–25.

COLUMN-KRATERS

(nos. 1–5, the pictures not framed)

1 (4). TARQUINIA 682, from Tarquinia. A, komast? (the lower half remains: in long chiton, with lyre: 'Anacreontic'?). B, satyr.

2 (5). ATHENS Acr. 808, fr., from Athens. Langlotz pl. 70. Youth—komast?

3 (10). VILLA GIULIA. A, symposion: youth reclining, seen from behind, playing kottabos with a skyphos; B, komast.

4 (14). LUCCA, from Ponte a Moriano. *NSc.* 1893, 405–7. A, Theseus and Minotaur. B, komos (two revellers).

5 (11). BOLOGNA 249, from Bologna. A, warrior and woman; B, Nike. Small.

(no. 6, the picture not framed?)

6 (9). MUNICH, fr., from Athens. (Head and shoulders of naked youth to left, looking round to right).

(nos. 7–7 ter, not known if the picture framed)

7. GELA (ILA 4, part), fr., from Gela. A, return of Hephaistos.

7 *bis.* REGGIO, fr., from Locri. Komos (naked male holding a pointed amphora, a flute-case hanging from his wrist, then one in chiton and

wrap, stick in right hand; both moving to right). Compare a Reggio fragment (legs of a naked male moving to right, then part of a garment).

7 *ter*. REGGIO, fr., from Locri. A, (head and breast of youth moving to right, looking round).

(nos. 8–30, the pictures framed)

8 (6). ATHENS Acr. 789, part, frr., from Athens. One, Langlotz pl. 71. Maenad and donkeys. See the next.

9 (7). ATHENS Acr. 789, part, fr., from Athens. Langlotz pl. 71. Komos (youth, naked woman, and another). Same style as the last: may be from the reverse of the same vase.

10 (8). ATHENS Acr. 798, fr., from Athens. Langlotz pl. 71. (Youth). Compare the last.

11 (21 *bis*). Once NEW YORK, Untermyer, from Capua. A, *Untermyer Coll.* 73, no. 108. A, satyrs and maenad. B, three youths. Looks like the Leningrad Painter in the small reproduction.

12 (17). CHIUSI, fr., from Chiusi. A, satyr and (maenad?) with donkeys.

13. Lost. Dempster 1 pl. 17; Passeri pl. 169. A, Dionysos and satyrs. B, komos.

14 (18). ATHENS, Agora, P 7259, fr., from Athens. A, one mounting chariot.

15 (1). OXFORD G 710, frr., from Naucratis. *CV*. pl. 66, 7–9. A, Herakles and the Amazons.

16 (2). HEIDELBERG 118 (ex Dresden) and DRESDEN, frr. The Heidelberg part, Kraiker pl. 18. Komos. Three fragments remain in Dresden.

17 (16). FLORENCE, fr. Komos (on the right, hands of one playing the flute, middle of male, both to right).

18. LOUVRE, fr. (composed of seven). Komos? (feet and shanks remain).

19. LIMENAS, fr., from Thasos. Ghali-Kahil *C.G.* pl. 46, 31. Komos? (the left-hand top corner of the picture remains, with forehead and eye of a male to right).

19 *bis*. PADULA, from Padula. A, *Apollo* (Salerno) 1, 112, 2. A, Ajax and Odysseus quarrelling. B, warrior leaving home.

19 *ter*. CORINTH CP 2635, fr., from Corinth. (Upper half of a youth in a chlamys moving to right, looking round).

20 (19). VIENNA 723. A, Tischbein 5 pl. 93; A, *Philologus* 27 pl. 4, 3 and p. 22; *CV*. pl. 90, 3–5. A, Dionysos and his chariot. B, athletes and trainer.

21 (20). BONN 72. *CV*. pl. 18; B.Ap. xvii. 39. A, Dionysos and satyrs; B, satyrs and maenad. See p. 1660.

22 (21). MUNICH 2371 (J. 303), from South Italy. A, Dionysos on donkey, with satyrs; B, satyr and maenads. Much restored.

23 (22). BERLIN 2185, fr., from Agrigento. A, symposion.

24 (23). NEW YORK 10.210.14, from Ruvo. A, *RM.* 23, 332 and 338; detail of A, McClees[1] 80 = ²⁸5; Richter and Hall pl. 71, pl. 75, 68, and pl. 170, 68. A, warrior arming; B, youth with Nike and old man.

25 (25). BERLIN inv. 3155. A, B.Ap. xvi. 53. 1. A, Dionysos reclining, with satyr; B, maenads.

26 (26). HAVANA, Lagunillas (ex Hirsch). A, warrior leaving home (woman, youth holding helmet, spear, and shield, device a lion, with KAㄴOƧ, man). B, man and two youths.

27. LONDON MARKET. A, Menelaos pursuing Helen; B, two women fleeing to altar. On A, Aphrodite, Eros in hand, flees as well as Helen. Shield-device a vulture. Compare Athens 1172 (no. 33). See p. 1660.

28 (27). LOUVRE G 366, from Vulci. *Gaz. arch.* 1 pl. 9 and 3 pl. 18; *CV.* d pl. 28, 5-7; phs. Gir. 33688, whence Stella 54 and 14. A, Kronos and Rhea. B, old man, woman, and Nike.

29 (24). CHICAGO 89.16. A, *AJA.* 1899 pl. 4, whence Roscher s.v. Salmoneus. A, Salmoneus. B, woman and Nikai. Compare Louvre G 366 (no. 28).

30. OLYMPIA, frr., from Olympia. A, (horse). B, males.

COLUMN-KRATER?

31. Once NAPLES, Hamilton. A, Tischbein 4 pl. 33, whence Inghirami pl. 198. A, komos. Pig Painter rather than Leningrad Painter?

BELL-KRATER

32. REGGIO, fr., from Locri. A, Apollo with Artemis and Leto (legs of one goddess standing to right and of Apollo standing frontal; beside her a fawn; feet of the other goddess, standing to left). Below, egg-and-dot pattern. Large. Compare the Vatican pelike by the Painter of Louvre G 231 (p. 580 no. 1).

NUPTIAL LEBES
(type 1)

33 (31). ATHENS 1172 (CC. 1229). A, CC. pl. 43; side, *AM.* 32, 96 Beil. 1 fig. 10; part of side, *Jh.* 31, 93; phs. A.I. 3079-83. Wedding (of Peleus?); on the stand, Apollo with Artemis, Leto, and Hermes. Compare no. 27.

PELIKAI
(nos. 34-36, the pictures not framed)

34 (38). LONDON E 362, from Nola. Panofka *Blacas* pll. 13-15, whence Panofka *Bilder ant. Leb.* pl. 13, 3 and Daremberg and Saglio s.v. Dionysos fig. 2420; A, Simon *O.G.* pl. 3. Dionysos with satyrs and maenads. For the subject, Simon *O.G.* 52-54; and below, p. 605 no. 65 *bis.*

35 (40). LEIPSIC T 654, fr., from Gela. *Jb.* 11, 189-90, whence Sauer *Theseion* 61 and (A) *Jb.* 26, 108. A, birth of Erichthonios; B, daughters of Kekrops.

36 (44). LONDON E 363, from Camiros. *Mon.* 11 pl. 8. A, Achilles receiving his armour; B, youth (Achilles?), and women holding armour.

(nos. 37–38, not known if the pictures framed)

37 (42). BRYN MAWR P 197, fr., from Attica. *AJA.* 1916, 337. A, (Dionysos and satyr).

38 (51). REGGIO 4383, fr., from Locri. (Head of woman in saccos).

(nos. 39–53, with framed pictures)

39. MAPLEWOOD, Noble. A, satyr with goat, and maenad; B, the like. [Bothmer].

40 (36). LONDON MARKET (Spink: ex Giudice). A, jumper and trainer. B, komos (two youths).

41 (37). PALERMO (1249). A, man and boy; B, youth and boy.

42. LOUVRE C 11006, fr. A, acontist and trainer.

43. LOUVRE C 11010, fr. A, komos (youth playing the flute, and male). B, (back of the right-hand person's head).

44 (50). AMSTERDAM inv. 2930 and 2941, two frr. On the right of one side, male with stick or spear; on the other fragment, part of a man with a stick.

45. PORTLAND (Oregon) 26.310. A, youth and boy; B, youth and boy. [H. R. W. Smith].

46 (48). MADRID 11038 (L. 156). A, Alvarez-Ossorio pl. 34, 2; *CV.* pl. 9, 1 and pl. 10. A, Peleus and Thetis; B, Nereids fleeing to Nereus.

47 (39). BERLIN inv. 3223. B, *Anz.* 1893, 90, right; A, Weinreich *Epigramm u. Pantomimus* pl. 1; *Hesp.* 24 pl. 87; Greifenhagen *A.K.* pll. 40–41. A, maenad and flute-player; B, the like. For the subject, *Hesp.* 24, 312–13.

48 (52). SYRACUSE, fr., from Camarina. A, (on the left, head of woman to right); B, (on the right, head and shoulders of woman to left).

49. FERRARA (erratico Dosso B 31.5.1958), from Spina. A, male and woman; B, old man and boy.

50 (54). HARROW 51, from Solygeia near Corinth. A, Theseus and Minotaur; B, Theseus and Procrustes. Recalls the Agrigento Painter.

51 (53). FLORENCE 73140, from Orvieto. *St. e mat.* 3, 162–3; *CV.* pl. 31, 4 and pl. 34, 1–2; *AJA.* 1954 pl. 64 fig. 37. A, death of Priam; B, Trojan elders. See p. 1660.

52 (54). ATHENS 1416 (CC. 1178), from Phokis. A, Zeus and Ganymede; B, Zeus and Hera.

53 (55). LONDON E 352, from Camiros. A, two men and a seated woman. B, two youths. The artist's ideal seems to have been the Agrigento Painter.

HYDRIAI

(nos. 54–69, with picture on the shoulder, framed)

54 (63). WÜRZBURG 532. Langlotz pll. 195 and 210. Herakles and the lion.

55 (62). OXFORD, Beazley, fr., from Greece. Unexplained subject: (on the left, 1, youth in chlamys and pilos striding to left, looking round, drawing his sword, 2, woman in a chiton rushing to right). Recalls the Leningrad Painter.

55 *bis.* PADULA, from Padula (Valle Pupina, T. xiv, no. 1). Peleus and Thetis (with Chiron looking on).

56. ALEXANDRIA 23446, fr., from Egypt? *Berytus* 11 pl. 27, 3. Woman, man, youth, all seated, and women. Recalls the Leningrad Painter. Compare the Robinson fragment (p. 573 no. 12).

57 (66). ATHENS MARKET (Minerva). Two women, man, and youth.

58. NAUPLIA, fr., from Argos. (Head, to right, and shoulders, of a woman).

59 (75). MYKONOS, fr., from Rheneia (originally from Delos). Dugas *Délos xxi* pl. 45, 63. (Seated youth).

60 (67). LONDON MARKET (Spink). Women and youths. Graffito Γ retr. standing on a horizontal stroke.

61 (68). NAPLES 2666, fr. Women seated, with youth and women.

62 (70). ATHENS 1262 (CC. 1174), from Attica. Ph. A.I. 3068. Dionysos with satyrs and maenad.

63. ATHENS, Agora, P 8892, fr., from Athens. Pygmies and cranes.

64 (72). Once Higgins. *Burl. 1903* pl. 95, H 55. Death of Aigisthos.

65 (71). LONDON E 173, from Camiros. *CV.* pl. 78, 1. Youth with spear pursuing a woman.

66 (73). ATHENS Acr. 686, fr., from Athens. Langlotz pl. 53. Oedipus and the Sphinx.

67 (74). REGGIO 886, fr., from Locri. (On the right, woman running to right, looking round).

68. CORINTH T 620, two frr., from Corinth. On one, (male and another); on the other, (woman, youth).

69. MYKONOS, from Rheneia (originally from Delos). Dugas *Délos xxi* pl. 26, 64. Poseidon pursuing a woman. With this and a few other trifling hydriai, one hesitates between Earlier and Later Mannerists.

(no. 70, the picture on the shoulder, running right round)

70 (80). RHODES 12145, from Camiros. *Cl. Rh.* 4, 61; *CV.* pl. 7, 2–3. Horse-race. Restored.

(nos. 71–72, with picture on the body)

71 (83). OXFORD 1929.13, frr. *CV.* pl. 67, 27. Judgement of Paris. Recalls the Oinanthe Painter.

72 (83 *ter*). CAB. MÉD. 456, from Cyrenaica. De Ridder 348, whence Cook *Zeus* iii, 849. Thracian woman with the head of Orpheus. Small.

LEKYTHOS
(standard shape)

73 (84). BOSTON 13.199, from Gela. CB. ii pl. 51, 99; the shape, Caskey G. 214, 168. Komast ('Anacreontic'). See CB. ii, 55–61.

FRAGMENTS OF POTS

73 *bis*. REGGIO, fr., from Locri. (Rear foot of one moving to right, with the lower part of the chiton and one corner of the himation).

73 *ter*. REGGIO, fr., from Locri. (Eye to waist of a maenad in chiton and panther-skin moving to left, looking round and down, thyrsus in left hand). Recalls the Pig Painter.

74 (86). ATHENS Acr. 777 and 608, two frr., from Athens. Langlotz pll. 67 and 45. (Woman with flower; youth with lyre).

75 (97). ATHENS Acr. 941, fr., from Athens. Langlotz pl. 77. (Youth, arm with bow). Perhaps from a hydria.

76 (34). ATHENS, Agora, P 9053, fr., from Athens. (Part of chiton).

77. HEIDELBERG P. 13.71, fr. Komos? (on the right, booted shank and foot). From an amphora?

78. OLYMPIA, fr., from Olympia. *Jb.* 56, Olympiabericht iii, 61. (Two men). Seems near the Pig Painter.

79. FLORENCE PD 586, fr., from Vetulonia. (Man in chlamys).

80 (90). CASSEL, Lullies, fr., from Greece. Ph. A.I. 19411, 4. (Male, in chitoniskos and chlamys, leading a woman by the wrist).

81. MUNICH, fr., from Athens. (Forepart of a foot to right; below, maeander).

82 (89). BRYN MAWR P 967, fr. Death of Orpheus?

83 (91). SYRACUSE, fr., from Camarina. (A hand grasping the knee of a male in a chlamys).

84 (92). SYRACUSE 23634, three frr., from Camarina. One, *ML.* 14, 903 fig. 99. Return of Hephaistos.

85 (94). NEW YORK 07.286.57, fr. (Head and hand of a youth wearing a fur hat).

86 (95). ATHENS Acr. 622, fr., from Athens. (Youthful head).

87. ATHENS, Agora, P 13411, two frr., from Athens. (Athena and Hephaistos; woman). From a pelike?

88 (96). ATHENS Acr. 774, fr., from Athens. Langlotz pl. 67. (Woman with torches, youth).

89 (93). LONDON E 252.2, fr., from Mytilene. Death of Orpheus.

CHAPTER 35

THE NIOBID PAINTER AND HIS GROUP

THE GROUP OF THE NIOBID PAINTER

The Group consists of the Altamura Painter, 'elder brother' to the Niobid Painter; the Blenheim Painter who stands between the Altamura Painter and the Niobid; the Niobid Painter himself; and his followers, the chief of whom are the Painter of Bologna 279, the Painter of the Woolly Satyrs, the Geneva Painter, the Painter of London E 470, the Painter of the Berlin Hydria, and the Spreckels Painter.

THE ALTAMURA PAINTER

VA. 143–5. *Att. V.* 333–6 and 477. *ARV.*[1] 412–16 and 960. CB. ii, 69–70.

Called after no. 1.

'Elder brother' of the Niobid Painter.

VOLUTE-KRATERS

1 (1). LONDON E 469, from Altamura. The chief picture, Heydemann *Gigantomachie* pl. 1, whence (details) *Jb.* 29, 133, and (incomplete) Pfuhl fig. 510, whence *Mon. Piot* 35, 75 and Vian *R.* pl. 36, 337; A, Webster *N.* pl. 1; A, ph. Ma. 3142. Gigantomachy. On the neck: A, Triptolemos; B, victorious citharode.

2. ATHENS, Agora, P 14729, four frr., from Athens. Triptolemos. On the neck, (foot of one in long chiton). [Talcott].

3 (2). FERRARA, T. 381, from Spina. Aurigemma[1] 151–5 = [2]171–5; detail of A, Rostovtzeff *Mystic Italy* frontispiece; A, *Jb.* 65–66, 117; A, Stella 362; A, Aurigemma and Alfieri pl. 21; Alfieri and Arias *S.* pl. 9; detail of B, *Mostra* pl. 89, 1. A, Zeus giving the infant Dionysos to his nurses. B, athletes. On the neck: A, victorious citharode; B, men, youths, and boys. See p. 1660.

3 *bis.* REGGIO, two frr. (one composed of three), from Locri. (Athena, Poseidon, goddess). On one fragment, 1, forehead of a goddess to right, holding up a sprig, 2, head and shoulders of Athena to left, 3, hand of Poseidon, with trident, to left; on the other fragment, a flower of the handle-floral, then ear and back-hair of the goddess 1.

3 *ter.* REGGIO, fr., from Locri. Part of the left-hand figure on one side remains, an old man standing to right; to left of him, part of the handle-floral.

3⁴. REGGIO, fr. (three joining), from Locri. A, (the legs of the left-hand figure remain, standing to right: he wears a short chiton, to past the knees, and a fawn-skin—Dionysos?). B, (part of the right-hand figure remains, standing to left, in long chiton and himation, with staff). Handle-floral.

3⁵. REGGIO, fr., from Locri. Part of the right-hand figure on one side remains, the bare shank of a male moving to left. Handle-floral.

3⁶. REGGIO, fr., from Locri. On the neck, Theseus and Minotaur.

3⁷. REGGIO, fr., from Locri. On the neck, (head, and right hand with spear, of a young warrior to left; and part of another warrior?).

4 (3). CAIRO 32378, from Saqqarah. Edgar pl. 11; B, *Jb.* 52, 210. Return of Hephaistos (A, Hephaistos and Dionysos; B, satyr with lyre, Hermes, and Hera).

5 (4). VATICAN. Dempster pl. 15; Passeri pl. 151; B, Pistolesi 3 pl. 70, 2; A, Panofka *Dionysos und die Thyaden* pl. 3, 12. A, Dionysos and Ariadne; B, satyr and maenad.

6 (5) BOLOGNA 277, from Bologna. *CV.* pl. 58, 3 and pl. 59, above. A, Apollo and Leto; B, god and goddess.

7 (6). BOLOGNA 271, from Bologna. Zannoni pl. 85, 5–7; *CV.* pl. 60. A, Herakles and Linos. B, man and youth.

8 (7). BOLOGNA 272, from Bologna. Part of B, Pellegrini 114; *CV.* pl. 61. Unexplained subjects. A, Zeus, Hera?, and a goddess. B, man running, with oinochoe and another object, male running. As the left-hand person on B has a beard, the subject is not Poseidon and Amymone.

8 *bis.* PADULA, from Padula. A, citharode (or Apollo?), with two Nikai. B, (much damaged) two women? [Panebianco].

9 (7 *bis*). FERRARA, T. 124, from Spina. A, citharode (with Nike and judge). B, flute-player. Recalls the Blenheim Painter (p. 597).

10 (7 *ter*). FERRARA, T. 231, from Spina. Alfieri and Arias pll. 12–13. A, Dionysos with maenad and satyr; B, satyr and maenad.

DINOS

10 *bis.* NEWCASTLE UPON TYNE. Fight (with chariot). See p. 1660.

CALYX-KRATERS

11. BOSTON 59.176. *ILN.* Oct. 10 1959, 398–9; CB. iii pll. 92–95 and Suppl. Plates 22–23. Iliupersis: A, Ajax and Cassandra; death of Priam; two warriors fighting; B, Aeneas and Anchises.

12 (8). LOUVRE G 342, from Agrigento. Millingen *PAV.* pll. 49–50, whence *AZ.* 1845 pl. 36, 4 and pl. 35, 3; A, Pottier pl. 137; *CV.* d pl. 4, 2–3 and pl. 5, 1–2; A, ph. Al. 23673, whence Stella 715, (detail) Schaal *Rf.* fig. 23; A, ph. Gir. 25513, whence (detail) *Mus. Helv.* 7, 51; B, ph. Arch. phot. 5.4240.008.AE.1. A, Achilles and Memnon. B, Philoktetes bitten. A restored, B almost entirely modern.

13 (9). BOLOGNA 285, from Bologna. Zannoni pl. 11, 3–4 and pl. 12, 1, whence (A) Robert *Sc. der Il.* 9 fig. 14. A, Achilles and Memnon. B, warriors leaving home.

14. ATHENS, Sisilianos, fr., from Athens. Fight (upper part—from nose to waist—of a young warrior in a metal corslet, moving to right, shield on left arm).

15 (10). LENINGRAD 639 (St. 1207). *CR.* 1862 pl. 2; A, G.P. 72; B.Ap. xxii. 70. A, Triptolemos; B, kings and women (worthies of Eleusis).

16 (11). VILLA GIULIA 24403, frr., from Falerii. Triptolemos.

17 (12). LENINGRAD 638 (St. 1600). *CR.* 1867 pll. 4–5. Dionysos arming.

18 (13). LENINGRAD 768 (St. 1356). A, *CR.* 1875 pl. 5, 4–5. A, victorious citharode. B, two women. Restored.

19 (14). NEW YORK, Aiken (ex Gallatin), from Catania. *CV.* pl. 56, 2. A, Dionysos and maenads. B, two youths.

20 (15). VIENNA 985. La Borde 1 pll. 49–50, whence (A) *El.* 1 pl. 48; B, Studniczka *Ein vermeintlicher Kriegsheld* fig. 3; Lücken pll. 106–7; A, Licht i, 268; A, Eichler *Führer* 13, a; A, *AM.* 59 Beil. 13, 3; A, Brommer *Satyrspiele*[1]25 = [2]28. A, return of Hephaistos; B, satyr and maenad.

21 (16). NAPLES Stg. 701. B, ph. So. 11091. A, return of Hephaistos; B, satyr and maenads.

22. HAMBURG 1960.34. *Auction xvi Basle* pl. 33, 130. A, Apollo and two goddesses (Artemis and Leto). B, Dionysos and maenad. See p. 1660.

23 (17). MUNICH 2383 (J. 299), from South Italy. A, Lau pl. 31, 1; A, Lücken pl. 51. A, Triptolemos. B, king and woman.

24 (18). LYONS. *JHS.* 71, 59, pl. 25, above, and pl. 26; *Recueil Dugas* pl. 35, 1–2 and pl. 36. A, Triptolemos. B, satyr and maenad.

25. BALTIMORE, Walters Art Gallery, 48.262. A, *Am. Art Gall., Coll. Clarke* pl. 1, 625; A, D. K. Hill *Soldiers* 9; A, *Bull. Walt.* 3 no. 5, 3. A, warrior and woman at altar; B, man. [Bothmer].

26 (60). BARCELONA 531, fr., from Ampurias. Bosch Gimpera *L'art grec a Catalunya* fig. 42, 3; García y Bellido pl. 100, 107. (Youth—leaving home?).

26 *bis*. REGGIO, fr., from Locri. (Legs of the right-hand figure, one in long chiton and himation, standing to left; below, stopped maeander, rightward, with cross-squares).

CALYX-KRATERS OR BELL-KRATERS

27 (19). ATHENS, Agora, P 9757, fr., from Athens. (Middle of woman). [Talcott]. See no. 39.

28 (20). SALONICA inv. 8. 54 (R. 108), fr., from Olynthos. Robinson *Olynthus* 5 pl. 65, 108. (Dionysos in Gigantomachy). [H. R. W. Smith].

29 (28, +). CORINTH C 33. 129 and 138, frr., from Corinth. Youth with spears (Theseus?), pursuing a woman; Athena and a man look on. Two of the fragments were added by Clairmont.

30. ATHENS, Agora, P 10748, fr., from Athens. (Hand, head of woman).

31 (21). BOLOGNA, fr., from Bologna. B, (head and breast of a man frontal, head to right). Another fragment, with the middle of a figure, may belong.

31 *bis*. REGGIO, fr., from Locri. (Middle—from the elbow almost to the knees—of Zeus standing to left, thunderbolt in left hand).

31 *ter*. REGGIO, fr., from Locri. (Athena moving to right: the lower part of the aegis remains, with something of the peplos).

31⁴. REGGIO, fr., from Locri. (Warrior moving to right: the left shoulder with part of the arm and of the inside of the shield).

BELL-KRATERS

(nos. 32–36, with lugs)

32 (22). PALERMO V 780, from Gela. *AZ*. 1870 pl. 33, whence (A) Walters *H.A.P.* ii, 107, (A) Jacobsthal *Theseus* pl. 2, 3; *CV*. pll. 38–39 and pl. 37, 4. A, Herakles entering Olympus. B, Zeus pursuing a woman.

33 (23). AMSTERDAM inv. 372, fr., from Athens. Scheurleer *Cat*. pl. 40, 2; *CV*. Scheurleer pl. 3, 2. (Dionysos and maenad). The shape of the mouth of the vase suggests that this was a krater with lugs.

33 *bis*. LONDON 1961.7-10.1. A, warriors leaving home: 1, woman with phiale, 2, young warrior wearing a quiver (Teucer?) (shield-device a scorpion), 3, bearded warrior (Ajax?) (shield-device a serpent, on the shield-apron an eye), 4, man. B, komos (two youths dancing, between them a girl playing the flute). See p. 1660.

34 (24). BOLOGNA 312, from Bologna. A, Pellegrini 155; *CV*. pl. 89, above, and pl. 90, below. A, Dionysos and maenad; B, two maenads.

35 (25). VIENNA 321, from South Italy. Millingen *PAV*. pl. 10. A, Theseus and Procrustes. B, man seated and man.

36 (26). PARIS, Petit Palais. A, *Coll. Lambros* pl. 11; *Mon. Piot* 35 pl. 5 and p. 81; *CV*. pl. 23, 1–5; A, phs. Arch. phot. Gigantomachy (A, Zeus and Giant Porphyrion; B, Poseidon and Giant).

(nos. 37–40, the handles or lugs missing)

37 (27). COPENHAGEN, Thorvaldsen Museum, 96, and ERBACH, frr., from Locri. Tischbein 5 pl. 111 (omits one of the two Erbach frr.); the other Erbach fr., Tischbein *Homer* 7 and 32, whence *El*. 1 pl. 29, 1; both Erbach frr., *Bonner Jahrbücher* 96, 342; the Thorvaldsen fr., Breitenstein *G.V.* pl. 44. (Deities: on the Thorvaldsen fragment, hand, goddess, Poseidon; on one Erbach fr., goddess—Athena?; on the other, part of a bow, so Apollo or Artemis).

38 (29). TÜBINGEN E 94, fr. Watzinger pl. 28 (mispoised). (Oriental).

39 (30). ATHENS, Agora, P 3037, fr., from Athens. (Legs of two clothed figures, one moving to left, the other to right). Might belong to Agora P 9757 (no. 27).

40 (31). ATHENS, Agora, P 5563 a, fr., from Athens. (Phiale, head of man). Two small fragments (c and d) may belong.

(no. 41, with handles)

41 (32). FERRARA, T. 311, from Spina. A, NSc. 1927 pl. 16; A, Anz. 1928, 131; A, Philippart Bacchantes pl. 4, b; A, Riv. Pop. d'It. Nov. 1928, 42, left; A, Aurigemma[1] 149 and 147, 3 = [2]179 and 177, 3, whence (part) Rumpf MZ. pl. 31, 3; A, Jb. 65–66, 116; part of A, Stella 360; detail of A, E.A.A. i, 277; A, Alfieri and Arias S. pll. 10–11; detail of A, Mostra pl. 75, 1. A, Dionysos and Oinopion. B, acontist with flute-player and Nike. For the subject of A, Fuhrmann in Jb. 65–66, 118–21. See p. 1660.

STAMNOI

42 (33). LENINGRAD 807, from Orvieto. R.I. 1875.13, whence R.I. 53.660 and 661, whence (B) Bothmer Am. pl. 70, 5b; A, ibid. pl. 70, 5a. A, Herakles and the Amazons; B, Amazons. See Bothmer Am. 142.

43 (34). BOLOGNA 174, from Bologna. Zannoni pl. 23, whence (detail of A) Jb. 29, 134; CV. pl. 71, 5, pl. 93, and pl. 94, 6–8. A, Herakles and Busiris. B, youth leaving home.

44 (35). MUNICH SL. 471. Sieveking BTV. pl. 47, pl. 51, 3, and p. 60. A, Theseus and Minotaur; B, rescued youths and maidens. See p. 1660.

45 (36). NEW YORK 56.171.51 (ex Hearst). Cat. Sotheby May 22 1919 pl. 13; B, Langlotz F.B. pl. 14, 6; Bull. Metr. March 1957, 177, 2–3. A, Peleus and Thetis; B, Nereids fleeing to Nereus.

46 (37). LYONS. JHS. 71, 61, pl. 25, below, and pl. 27; Recueil Dugas pl. 35, 3–4 and pl. 37. A, victorious citharode. B, four youths with lyres and a man with a flute. See p. 1660.

47 (38). ORVIETO, Faina, 67, from Orvieto. Boll. Restauro 23–24, 157; A, ph. Armoni. A, Athena and Giant. B, warrior leaving home.

48. LOUVRE C 10831. Arming.

49. LOUVRE C 10832, two frr. (Man and males).

NECK-AMPHORAE
(with twisted handles)

50 (39). PHILADELPHIA 5466, from Capua. Le Musée 3, 432 and pl. 63, 1; Mus. J. 8, 20 and 24; part of A, Archaeology 12, 248 fig. 9. A, Apollo and Artemis. B, Dionysos and maenad. See p. 1660.

51 (40). NAPLES Stg. 28, from Nola. Panofka V. di premio pl. 5, whence (A) El. 2 pl. 32. A, Apollo and Artemis. B, king and woman.

PELIKAI

52 (41). LOUVRE G 230. Millingen *Coghill* pll. 14–15; *CV.* pl. 46, 1, 3–4, and 6. A, Eos and Kephalos. B, two athletes. Restored.

53 (42). NEW YORK 56.171.44 (ex Oppenheimer and Hearst). Detail of A, *Ant. class.* 4 pl. 32, 1; *Cat. Christie July 22–23 1936* pl. 9; A, *Bull. Metr.* 1956–7, 175, 4. A, warrior leaving home (warrior and woman); B, warrior and woman.

AMPHORA

(type B, with framed pictures)

54 (a 5). LONDON E 263, from Vulci. A, Gerhard pl. 169, 3–4; *CV.* pl. 62; A, Ghali-Kahil *H.* pl. 62, 1; A, ph. Ma. 3121. A, Menelaos and Helen. B, three maenads. Very poor, but by the painter himself. Compare the reverse of the Aiken calyx-krater (no. 19).

HYDRIAI

(no. 55, of bf. shape)

55. TARANTO, fr., from Locri. Tereus pursuing Prokne (the upper part of Tereus' head remains, with a small bird perched on it; inscription TER-[EVϛ]. The shoulder of the vase is black, except for a tongue-pattern at the top.

(nos. 56–61, kalpides, with picture on body, but, except in London E 177, rather high up)

56 (43). LONDON E 177, from Vulci. *VA.* 141; *CV.* pl. 81, 2. Apollo with two goddesses (Leto and Artemis).

57 (44). NAPLES Stg. 197. *Jb.* 71, 110. Youth in two-horse chariot, with Apollo and goddess. Restored. Uncertain who the youth is; on a bf. column-krater in New York, 07.286.76, the charioteer of Apollo is Lykomedes.

58 (45). ROMAN MARKET (Campanari), from Vulci. Gerhard pl. 27, whence *El.* 2 pl. 33; B.Ap. xxii. 31. Apollo with Artemis and Leto.

59 (46). CAMBRIDGE 28.7. Gerhard pl. 30, whence *El.* 2 pl. 34; *Cat. Sotheby Dec. 19 1927* pl. 6, 195; *CV.* ii pl. 26, 2 and pl. 28, 2. Apollo with Artemis, Leto, and Hermes.

60. FERRARA, T. 55 C VP, from Spina. Triptolemos.

61 (47). VATICAN, from Vulci. Gerhard pl. 152, 1–2, whence *WV.* 2 pl. 9, 2; ph. Al. 35753, whence Stella 301. Boreas and Oreithyia. Restored.

OINOCHOAI

(nos. 62–71, shape 1)

62 (48). BOSTON 97.370, from Sunium. Fairbanks and Chase 26 fig. 16; CB. ii, suppl. pl. 15 and p. 69; shape, Caskey G. 137. Apollo and Artemis. See CB. ii, 69–70.

63 (49). LOUVRE CA 154. Apollo and goddess.

64 (50). VILLA GIULIA, fr. Menelaos and Helen.

65 (51). BOLOGNA 338, from Bologna. Pellegrini 171; CV. pl. 91, 1–2 and pl. 92, 3–4. Dionysos, and maenads bringing him his armour.

66 (52). ANCONA, from Numana. Marconi and Serra pl. 52. Dionysos and Giant.

67 (53). VILLA GIULIA, frr. Victorious citharode (citharode and Nikai).

67 bis. FERRARA, T. 62 B VP, from Spina. Victorious flute-player (flute-player with Nike and judge).

68 (54). HILLSBOROUGH (California), Hearst, from Spina. Cat. Sotheby Dec. 13 1928 pl. 14; AJA. 1945, 475, 3, and 476, 1. Warrior leaving home.

69. FERRARA, T. 15 C VP, from Spina. Warrior leaving home (youth with man and Nike).

70. FERRARA T. 15 C VP, from Spina. Death of Priam.

71. HOBART. Two women at altar; above, half seen, a small herm with youthful head and arm holding a sprig of ivy; the women also hold branches of ivy: probably maenads in the sanctuary of Dionysos. [Bothmer]. Bothmer thinks that the image may show both arms, and may be female.

(no. 72, shape 3)
(with framed picture)

72. LENINGRAD, from South Russia. Webster N. pl. 10, b. Cutler. Ascribed to the Niobid Painter, as early work, in ARV.¹ 423, but I now think by the Altamura.

LEKANIS-LIKE VESSEL (BUT NOT A LEKANIS)

73 (55). CAB. MÉD. (ex Fröhner), frr. of the lid. Iliupersis (death of Priam; warrior seizing woman; and other scenes). Above, (bull).

SHAPE UNKNOWN (NECK-AMPHORA?)

74 (56). Once NAPLES, Hamilton. Tischbein 4 pll. 19–20. A, Greek and Amazon. B, arming.

FRAGMENTS OF POTS

75 (57). OXFORD, Beazley, fr., from Brindisi or near. (Middle of goddess with staff or spear).

76. REGGIO, two frr., from Locri. On one, middle of a woman standing to right, chiton ornamented with crosslets, kolpos, cloak, with her forearm, a staff or the like in the hand. On the other fragment, middle of a woman standing frontal, in a peplos, with the elbow of the raised right arm, the sunk left forearm and part of the left hand; bracelet.

77 (a 2). LEIPSIC T 671 and T 672, two frr. (Head of woman; hand of woman holding an oinochoe, with part of her peplos).

78 (59). LIMENAS, fr., from Thasos. Ghali-Kahil C.G. pl. 46, 32. (On the left, middle of a woman standing to right, then part of a palm-tree).

MANNER OF THE ALTAMURA PAINTER

ARV.[1] 416.

PELIKE

1 (1). BERNE 12227. *RA.* 1910, i, 218–21; Bloesch *AKS.* pll. 36–37 and p. 69; Schefold *M.* 199, 224. Sale of perfume: on A the maid receives an alabastron of perfumed oil from the vendor, on B she delivers it to her mistress: see Bloesch *AKS.* 67–69 and 172–3.

BELL-KRATERS

2. ATHENS, Agora, P 15700, fr., from Athens. [Youth].

3. REGGIO, fr., from Locri. (Head and shoulders of a satyr, a pelt round his shoulders, standing to right).

FRAGMENTS

4. REGGIO, fr., from Locri. Warrior leaving home (hilt of sword held up; head, to left, and left shoulder, of a woman standing frontal; face, shoulder, and right hand with T-topped stick, of an old man standing to left).

5. REGGIO, fr., from Locri. (Foot of one standing to left, with the lower edge of the shield held by her or him; shod feet of a male with a stick, standing to left, and the lower edge of his long fringed chiton; below, rightward maeander with saltire-squares).

6. REGGIO 10559, fr., from Locri. (Upper part of a youth, standing, a pair of spears in his right hand).

7. REGGIO 4051, fr., from Locri. (Artemis, holding oinochoe and sprig, standing at an altar). Seems Altamura Painter rather than Niobid Painter.

8. REGGIO, fr., from Locri. The feet of the right-hand figure remain, standing to left, with the lower edge of the long fringed chiton; below, rightward maeander with saltire-square. Reserved inside.

9 (4). ISTANBUL, fr., from Lindos. Blinkenberg *Lindos* i pl. 129, 2698. (Woman).

10. ATHENS, Agora, P 23214, fr., from Athens. (Head and shoulders of a king or god). [Talcott].

11 (3). HEIDELBERG 178, fr. Kraiker pl. 30. (Woman). Might be from a picture of Menelaos and Helen: compare the oinochoe fragment in Villa Giulia (p. 595 no. 64). May well be by the painter himself.

12. GOETTINGEN '167', fr. (Head of a woman to left).

13. ATHENS, Agora, P 18554, fr., from Athens. (Dionysos).

PHIALE?

14. ATHENS 16442, fr. *JHS.* 71, 101 fig. 6. Seems to be the omphalos of a phiale: on it, head of Apollo. [Karouzou].

The following fragments might be by the Altamura Painter:

CALYX-KRATER

FLORENCE, frr.   What remains is good part of the leftward-slanting palmettes on the mouth of the vase, and the upper edge of the palmette-design at one handle.

The following is an imitation of his work:

NECK-AMPHORA
(with triple handles)

VIENNA 772.   La Borde 1 pll. 81–82, whence *Annali* 1830 pl. M and *El.* 2 pll. 95–96; *CV.* pl. 62.   A, woman (goddess?) with phiale and sceptre, and woman with oinochoe and flower, at altar (Hera and Hebe?); B, youth (Apollo?) with phiale and sceptre, and woman with oinochoe and sprig, at altar.   [Cambitoglou].

A vase without figure-work resembles the neck-amphorae with twisted handles by the Altamura Painter (p. 593 nos. 50–51):

NECK-AMPHORA
(with twisted handles)

BONN, Langlotz.   Black.   On the neck, ivy; on the mouth, maeander and cross-squares.

A weak piece bears a certain resemblance to calyx-kraters by the Altamura Painter:

CALYX-KRATER

MISSISSIPPI (ex Robinson), from Populonia.   *CV.* Robinson ii pl. 38, 1. A, return of Hephaistos (Hephaistos and satyr); B, satyr and maenad. Attributed to the painter by Robinson.

See also below, under 'Blenheim Painter'.

THE BLENHEIM PAINTER
ARV.[1] 417–18.   CB. ii, 70–72.

Named after no. 1.

Between the Altamura Painter and early Niobid Painter.   I have sometimes thought that these vases might be late work by the Altamura Painter himself.

VOLUTE-KRATER

1 (1).   BLENHEIM, Marlborough.   A, Moses *Coll.* pl. 16; Tillyard pl. 17, 115. A, Dionysos and maenads; B, satyr and maenads.

CALYX-KRATERS

2 (2). LENINGRAD 765 (St. 1274), from Agrigento. A, Millin *Gal. myth.* I pl. 88, 236; Inghirami pl. 117; *CR.* 1867 pl. 6; A, Stella 373. A, Dionysos and Giant; B, satyr and maenad. The lower half of B is modern.

3 (3). BOLOGNA 286, from Bologna. A, Pellegrini 131; Webster *N.* pl. 7; *CV.* pll. 75-76. A, Dionysos and Giant. B, Apollo with Artemis and Leto.

STAMNOS

4 (4). BOSTON 00.342, from Athens. B, *VA.* 143; side, Jacobsthal O. pl. 99, a; A, Vian *R.* pl. 41, 382; CB. ii pll. 55-56; the shape, Caskey *G.* 95. A, Dionysos and Giant; B, satyr driving satyr-biga. See CB. ii, 70-72.

OINOCHOE
(shape 1)

5 (5). FLORENCE 4016. Ph. Al. 17072, 6, whence Minto *R. Mus. Fir.* pl. 46, right, 6, and *E.A.A.* ii, 114; *CV.* pl. 66, 2 and pl. 67, 2-4; ph. Brogi 10752, ii, 3. Dionysos and maenads.

A fragment belongs to the *Group* of the Niobid Painter and is especially close to the Blenheim Painter: compare in the above list the right-hand maenad on no. 5 and the left-hand maenad on no 4:

CALYX-KRATER

REGGIO, fr., from Locri. (Legs of a maenad in chiton and fawn-skin hastening to left).

THE NIOBID PAINTER

The volute-kraters Bologna 269, Berlin 2403, Naples 2421 (nos. 8, 9, 13), were put together by Milchhöfer (*Jb.* 9, 74 note 44), Halle 211 (no. 4) added by Robert (*Marathonschlacht* 55), Bologna 268, Palermo G 1283, Louvre G 343 (nos. 1, 2, 17) by Furtwängler (FR. i, 130-4). They do not speak of a painter.

VA. 145-50. *Att. V.* 336-42 and 477. Webster *Der Niobidenmaler.* Dugas in *REA.* 1937, 185-96. *ARV.*[1] 418-26 and 960. CB. ii, 72-82 and 102. Simon *O.G*, 20-22, 47, and 58-59.

Named after no. 22.

'Younger brother' of the Altamura Painter.

VOLUTE-KRATERS

1 (1). BOLOGNA 268, from Bologna. *Mon.* 11 pll. 14-15, whence *REA.* 1937 pl. 3 and (B) Benndorf *Gjölb.* 232 fig. 178; Webster *N.* pl. 6; B, Davreux fig. 54; A, Byvanck-Quarles van Ufford *P.* 44; A, *AJA.* 1954 pl. 63 fig.

33; A, Stella 759; part of A, *Riv. Ist.* N.S. 4, 111 fig. 17; *Recueil Dugas* pl. 9; parts, *Mostra* pl. 40, 2 and pll. 45–46; *CV.* pl. 97, 1–2 and pll. 98–100. Iliupersis (A, death of Priam; B, Aithra, Cassandra). On the neck: A, centauromachy; B, Herakles and Pholos. Early.

2 (2). PALERMO G 1283, from Gela.   Details, FR. i, 125, 128–9, and 132, whence *Jb.* 33, 13–14 and Swindler figs. 356 and 359–60; A, Della Seta *It. ant.*[1] 101, b = [2]111, b; A and side, Marconi *Mus. Pal.* pl. 49; A, Buschor G. *Vasen* 184; A, Byvanck-Quarles van Ufford *P.* 21; A, ph. Al. 33019, whence Bothmer *Am.* pl. 74, 3; part, *AJA.* 1960 pl. 49. Amazonomachy. On the neck: A, centauromachy; B, Herakles and Pholos. Early. For the chief subject, Bothmer *Am.* 161 no. 5 and pp. 166–7.

3 (3). LENINGRAD inv. 6796, fr.. Webster *N.* pl. 9, b (mispoised); Bothmer *Am.* pl. 82, 3. Amazonomachy. Early. [Waldhauer].

4 (4). HALLE inv. 211 (KN 63), frr., from Ruvo. Part, *Jb.* 1 pl. 10, 2; Robert *Mar.* 56; Webster *N.* pl. 12, whence (one fr.) LS. fig. 113; Bielefeld *Halle* 125–6 figs. 1–3; part, Bielefeld *ZV.* pl. 10 fig. 11. Rape of the daughters of Leukippos. Early.

5 (5). REGGIO, fr., from Locri. Part, *NSc.* 1911, suppl., 74. Ajax and Cassandra? An unpublished fragment in Reggio joins the published part, adding the rest of the woman's head, her left shoulder, and of her assailant the right flank and thigh, with part of the right arm.

6 (6). FERRARA, T. 740, from Spina. A, Alfieri and Arias *S.* pl. 40. A, warrior leaving home (warrior, with Nike, and a woman holding his helmet and shield). B, goddess and two women. Middle.

7. IZMIR inv. 3361, frr., from old Smyrna. *BSA.* 53–54 pl. 40 and pl. 41, 118. Warriors making ready, with a horse (probably a chariot). On the neck: A, winged youth pursuing a woman; B, youth or man with spears (Theseus?) pursuing a woman. Late. The winged youth on the neck may be Zephyros rather than Boreas; or Zetes, pursuing Phoibe (compare the Etruscan cup with *Zetun* and *Phuipa* in the Vatican, G. 112, see *R.G.* pl. 32 with pp. 89–90, and *EVP.* pl. 12 and pl. 4, 5, with pp. 4 and 55).

8 (7). BOLOGNA 269, from Bologna. *Mon.* 10 pll. 54 and 54a, whence *REA.* 1937 pl. 2 and (one figure) *Jb.* 11, 24; *Dedalo* 9, 325–32; Webster *N.* pl. 13; A, Byvanck-Quarles van Ufford *P.* 45; A, Ghali-Kahil *H.* pl. 58, 2; *Recueil Dugas* pl. 10; part of A, and B, *Mostra* pll. 32–33; CB. pl. 97, 3–4 and pll. 101–4; A, ph. Al. 10647, middle. A, Iliupersis (Menelaos and Helen; Aithra). B, warriors setting out, with chariot. On the neck: A, youth pursuing a woman; B, women and men at altar. Late.

9 (8). BERLIN 2403, frr. *AZ.* 1883 pl. 17, 1–2, whence Farmakovski ii, 340, FR. ii, 247, and *Mnemosyne* 4th ser., 3, 209; Schrader *Phidias* 170–1; Webster pl. 24, b–c; Schuchhardt and Technau 210. Centauromachy (at the wedding of Perithoos). Late.

10 (9). ERBACH, two frr. What remains of the chief picture is part of a raised

axe-blade (cf. the last). On the neck, (woman running to right, woman fleeing to left, looking round). Late.

11 (10). ATHENS, fr., from the Argive Heraion. Waldstein *Arg. Her.* ii pl. 62, 34. On the neck, (male, woman).

12 (11). BOSTON 33.56, from Italy. *Bull. MFA.* 40, 11–13; CB. ii pll. 58–60. Warriors leaving home. On the neck: A, youth or man (Theseus?) pursuing a woman; B, (women). For the fragmentary neck-picture B compare Bologna 269 (no. 8) and the fragment from the Argive Heraion (no. 11). See CB. ii, 77–82. Late.

13 (12). NAPLES 2421, from Ruvo. Gargiulo *Recueil* (1845) ii pll. 54–56; Schulz *Amazonenvase*; the chief picture, and A of the neck, FR. pll. 26–28 and i, 126 and 137, whence (A) Pfuhl fig. 505, (A) *Jb.* 33, 9, (A) Swindler fig. 358, (details) *Jb.* 29, 131 and *Jb.* 31, 221, (A) Stella 569, below; A, Bothmer *Am.* pl. 74, 4; phs. So. 11049 and 11045; A, ph. Al. 11285, whence Webster *N.* pl. 23; details, *Arte ant. e mod.* 4, 317 fig. 112; Maiuri *Mus. Naz.* 139. Amazonomachy. On the neck: A, Peleus and Thetis; B, youth with spears (Theseus?) pursuing a woman. Late. For the chief subject, Bothmer *Am.* 167.

14. FERRARA, T. 11 C VP, from Spina. Details, *Arte ant. e mod.* 4 figs. 113a–b; A, *Archaeology* 13, 210, 4; parts, *Mostra* pl. 83 and pl. 87, 1. Amazonomachy. On the neck: A, Dionysos with maenads and satyrs; B, winged youth (Zephyros?) pursuing a woman (see no. 7). Late. See p. 1661.

15 (13). HEIDELBERG 176, fr., from Athens. *Jb.* 32, 65; Kraiker pl. 32. On the back of the handle, citharode. Late.

16 (14). SYRACUSE 24127, fr., from Gela. On the neck, symposion. Late.

16 *bis.* REGGIO, fr. (three joining), from Locri. (Parts of two women: one to right, her left hand on her shoulder, the other to left, holding out an open box. On the neck, a youth, with sword, pursuing (a woman: Theseus and Aithra?). Late.

16 *ter.* REGGIO, fr., from Locri. On the neck, (foot of one moving to right, as if pursued, legs of male in himation, with stick, standing to left, a dog beside him). Not clear from my notes whether this belongs to the last or not.

16⁴. REGGIO, fr., from Locri. On the neck, (Greek and Amazon). [Procopio].

17 (15). LOUVRE G 343, from Etruria. Dempster 1 pll. 47–48; the chief pictures, Hancarville 2 pll. 106 and 129; Millingen *AUM.* 1 pll. 20–24, whence Panofka *Vasi di premio* pll. 1–2, Inghirami pll. 8–10 and 163, and (neck A) *El.* 3 pl. 63b; Pottier pl. 137; *CV.* d pl. 5, 3–4, pl. 6, and pl. 7, 2; neck-picture A, and part of the chief picture, *Mél. d'arch.* 1950 pl. 3; the same portions, *Recueil Dugas* pl. 31. A, warriors leaving home, with chariot; B, fight. On the neck: A, Triptolemos; B, deer-hunt. Very late.

CALYX-KRATERS

18 (16). FERRARA, T. 936, from Spina. A, Aurigemma[1] 177 = [2]235; detail
(restored), Spinazzola *Pompei* i, 155 fig. 191; A, *AJA*. 1954 pl. 63 fig. 34;
part of B, Ghali-Kahil *H.* pl. 68, 4; A, Alfieri and Arias *S.* pll. 37–39;
detail of B, *Gymnasium* 67 pl. 17, 1; A, *Mostra* pl. 82. Iliupersis (death of
Priam; Aeneas and Anchises; Menelaos and Helen). Early. See p. 1661.

19 (17). ERLANGEN 842, fr. Pyrrhic. Early or early middle.

20 (18). LONDON E 461, from Vulci. Gerhard pl. 304, whence (A) Farmakovski ii, 283, (A) Licht ii, 29; A, Schaal *Rf.* fig. 41; detail of A, *RM.* 47
pl. 1, 2; A, ph. Ma. 3139. A, Muses; B, Muses. Restored. Middle.

21 (19). LOUVRE G 165. Pottier pl. 126; *CV.* pl. 23; phs. Gir., whence
Webster *N.* pl. 18. A, Athena mounting chariot. B, horseman leaving
home. Restored. Middle.

21 *bis.* REGGIO 4055, fr., from Locri. A, (Herakles: might be from a 'struggle
for the tripod'). [Procopio]. Late.

22 (20). LOUVRE G 341, from Orvieto. *Mon.* 11 pll. 38–40, whence *JHS.*
10, 118, (A) *Mon. gr.* 1895–7, 26, (A) Farmakovski ii, 350, (one figure)
Jb. 11, 45; details, *Mon. gr.* 1895–7, 19–23, whence Farmakovski ii, 338–
9; FR. pl. 108, pl. 165, and ii, 244 and 251, whence *JHS.* 39, 132 and 130,
Swindler figs. 319, 349, and 351–3, Webster *N.* pl. 5 (whence LS. figs.
107 and 112), (A) Buschor 189, *Jb.* 33, 2, (A) Pfuhl fig. 492, (A) Seltman
pl. 33, a, (A) Dugas *Aison* fig. 1, (A) Beazley and Ashmole fig. 82, (A)
Buschor *G. Vasen* 197; part of A, ph. Al. 23684, whence Langlotz *GV.*
pl. 34, Pfuhl *Mast.* fig. 77, Zadoks-Jitta 75, 10, Stella 574; Pottier pl. 136;
CV. d pll. 1–3 and pl. 4, 1, whence Rumpf *MZ.* pl. 28, 1–2; Webster *N.*
pll. 2–4, whence (detail of B) Seltman pl. 33, b–c, LS. figs. 105–6 and 110–
11, (details of A) Frel *Ř.V.* figs. 196–9; *Enc. phot.* iii, 22–23, whence (B)
Frel *Ř.V.* fig. 195; phs. Gir. 31932–3 and 31935–8, whence (A and detail
of B) *Hist. rel.* 154 and 208, (B) Schnitzler pl. 49, (part of A) Schuchhardt
and Technau 208, (part of A) Grimal 123, (B) Lane pl. 87, (B) Stella 152,
Kraiker *M.G.* pll. 38–40; part of A, Dugas and Flacelière pl. 14; detail of
A, Richter *H.G.A.* 335; A, Robertson *G.P.* 124. A, Herakles and the
Argonauts. B, slaughter of the Niobids. Late. See p. 1661.

(nos. 23–24, with two rows of figures)

23 (21). LONDON E 467, from Altamura. *JHS.* 11 pll. 11–12 and p. 280,
whence Cook *Zeus* i pl. 38, *Hesp.* 24 pl. 88, a, (lower part of B) *RM.* 6,
273, (A) Bieber *Th.* 101, (A) *Marb. Jb.* 15, 25 fig. 32; Pickard-Cambridge
Dith. figs. 14–15; A, Bieber *Th.* pl. 51; details, *Metr. St.* 5, 138; Webster
N. pll. 14–15; details of the lower picture on A, *Marb. Jb.* 15, 20; the lower
picture on B, Brommer *Satyrspiele*[1] 37 = [2]41; A, ph. Ma. 3140. Above:
Pandora, with chorus of women. Below: A, chorus of Pans; B, family
of satyrs playing ball. Middle. See *Hesp.* 24, 316–18.

24 (22). FERRARA, T. 313, from Spina. *Riv. Pop. d'It.* Nov. 1928, 34–35; A, *Metr. St.* 5, 129; A, *Webster N.* pl. 16; Aurigemma[1] 167 middle and 169–71 = [2]201 middle and 203–5; the lower picture on A, *Mél. d'arch.* 1950 pl. 4; the upper picture, and the lower picture on A, *Vian R.* pl. 37, 338; *Arch. class.* 6 pll. 92–109; detail, Stella 215; B, Aurigemma and Alfieri pl. 23; Alfieri and Arias *S.* pl. 34–36; the lower picture on A, *Recueil Dugas* pl. 32; A, *Mostra* pl. 81. Above, Gigantomachy. Below: A, Triptolemos; B, Dionysos with maenads and satyr. Late. See p. 1661.

BELL-KRATERS OR CALYX-KRATERS

25. TARANTO, fr., from Locri. Gigantomachy (Dionysos (?) and giant—head and shoulders of the giant remain, and a serpent held out by the deity; then, from another group, the raised right arm of the attacker). Early.

25 *bis.* REGGIO 960, fr., from Locri. (Head and shoulders of a youth leaning to right, a hand under his chin).

25 *ter.* REGGIO, fr., from Locri. (Middle—right hip, navel—of a naked male moving to right, his cloak ornamented with crosslets).

25⁴. REGGIO, fr. (two joining), from Locri. Youth leaving home (middle of a youth in a chlamys standing frontal, spear in left hand, thighs and half the right knee of another male standing frontal, in an ornamented chitoniskos).

25⁵. REGGIO, fr. (two joining), from Locri. (Upper part of a man standing frontal, head to left, right arm raised; he wears an ornamented chitoniskos, with a cloak over the left shoulder, and a petasos at his nape). May be the second person on the last: the preservation, however, is different.

25⁶. REGGIO 4053, fr., from Locri. (Upper part of a man wearing a petasos, to right).

25⁷. REGGIO, fr., from Locri. (Head of a woman to right; above, slanting palmettes).

26 (23). NICOLAEV, fr., from Olbia. Farmakovski *Rozk. Olb. 1926,* 49 fig. 32. (Hermes). Late.

27 (33 *bis*). ISTANBUL, frr., from Samaria, 2159, 2786, and 1834. *Harv. Exc. Sam.* 2 pl. 71, h, 2 and 4–5. Youth pursuing a woman. Late.

BELL-KRATERS
(no. 28, with lugs)

28. LOUVRE C 10846, fr. A, pyrrhic. B, (boy with lyre, and youth).

(nos. 30, 34, 35, 36, 38, 41 with handles; the rest, not known whether with handles or lugs)

29 (24). LONDON E 509.5, fr. A, symposion. Early.

30 (26). BOLOGNA 313, from Bologna. Zannoni pl. 39; A, *Webster N.* pl. 19, b; A, Stella 59. A, Zeus pursuing a woman (Aigina); B, her sisters fleeing to a king (Asopos). Early. For shape and palmettes compare the bell-krater by the Altamura Painter in Ferrara (p. 593 no. 41).

31. ATHENS, Agora, P 16616, fr., from Athens. *Hesp.* 17 pl. 68, 3. A, (Apollo). Early. [Talcott].

32 (25). ATHENS, Agora, P 13083, fr., from Athens. A, (on the right, woman holding small cithara).

33. BENGHAZI M 87, fr., from Euhesperides. A, (on the left, hind-legs of a horse standing to right).

34 (27). PERUGIA, from Orvieto. A, Roscher s.v. Kora, 1370 fig. 17; *St. etr.* 6 pll. 26–27, whence *Mél. d'arch.* 1950 pl. 5, 3; R.I. A, Triptolemos. B, Zeus and Hera with Nike (or Iris) and another goddess. Middle.

35 (28). TÜBINGEN E 104. A, Watzinger pl. 30 and p. 47; A, Webster *N.* pl. 20. A, youth leaving home. B, man and women. Middle. Already connected by Watzinger with Cab. Méd. 425 and the hydriai in Basle and Leningrad (nos. 36, 67, 72).

36 (29). CAB. MÉD. 425. Dubois-Maisonneuve pl. 12, whence *El.* 3 pl. 70; A, de Ridder pl. 17. A, youth leaving home. B, three women. Much restored. Late middle.

37 (30). KOENIGSBERG 67, fr. Ph. A.I. varia 416, 5. (Woman with lyre).

38 (31). KIEV, fr., from the government of Kiev. *Izv. Imp. Arkh. Kom.* 40 (1911), 50 figs. 6–7. (Man, woman, and another).

39. ATHENS, Agora, P 3832, fr., from Athens. (Legs of one in long chiton and himation).

40 (32). REGGIO, fr., from Locri. *NSc.* 1917, 154 fig. 60. A, Triptolemos. Late. See p. 609 no. 13 *bis.*

41 (33). ISTANBUL, from Samaria, 2914. *Harv. Exc. Sam.* 2 pl. 70 and pl. 69, 0; part of A, *Jb.* 40, 220; A, Wright *Bibl. Arch.* 205. A, sacrifice to Apollo. B, youth pursuing a woman. Late.

41 *bis.* REGGIO, fr., from Locri. (Head of a woman to right, playing the flute; with part of the ledge above the picture).

PELIKAI

42. LOUVRE C 11039, frr. A, male with sceptre (Zeus?) pursuing a woman.

43. CYRENE, fr., from Cyrenaica? Eos and Kephalos (the feet of Eos remain, with part of her chiton, and the greater part of Kephalos and of his hound Lailaps).

44 (34). KOENIGSBERG 66, from Piraeus. A, ph. A.I. varia 384, whence Webster *N.* pl. 11, b; A, Lullies *K.* pl. 10. A, Eos and Kephalos. B, man and woman. Early middle.

45 (35). LONDON E 381. Hancarville 1 pl. 122 and 4 pl. 61, whence (A) *El.* 1 pl. 21. A, king and woman at altar. B, Eos and Tithonos. Middle.

46 (36). CAPUA 1391 (204), from Capua. *CV.* pl. 6. A, Nike, and youth with spear, at altar; B, youth with spear, and woman. Restored. Early or middle.

47 (37). WÜRZBURG 511. Side, Jacobsthal *O.* pl. 82, b; Langlotz pl. 180, whence *Mnemosyne* 4th ser., 3 pl. 2, 6; A, Webster *N.* pl. 11, a. A, Boreas and Oreithyia; B, Pandrosos and Aglauros fleeing to Erechtheus. Middle.

48 (38). LOUVRE G 431. *CV.* d pl. 42, 7, 9, 11, and 5. A, warrior leaving home. B, Poseidon and two women. Restored. Middle.

49 (39). CARLSRUHE 205 (B 2402), from Bolsena. A, Welter pll. 9–10; *CV.* pl. 16; A, Simon *O.G.* pl. 4, 1; detail of A, Schnellbach fig. 21. A, Apollo with Artemis and Leto. B, three maenads. Late.

AMPHORAE
(type B)
(no. 50, with framed pictures)

50 (41). LONDON E 257, from Vulci. A, Gerhard pl. 176, 1, whence *AJA.* 1937, 603 fig. 3; *CV.* pl. 7, 2; B.Ap. xxii. 43. A, judgement of Paris. B, Dionysos and maenads. Middle.

(no. 51, the pictures not framed)

51 (40). PARIS, Seillière, from Vulci. *El.* 2 pll. 90–91, whence (A) FR. iii, 284 and (part of A) *Jb.* 11, 35; phs. Gir. 31958 and another, whence (A) Webster *N.* pl. 8, a. A, Artemis and Niobe. B, woman seated, and youth (sale of—oil?). Restored, especially B. Early. See p. 1661.

PANATHENAIC AMPHORA

52 (42). LENINGRAD, from South Russia. A, Webster *N.* pl. 10, a; A, G.P. 77. A, Athena and warrior. B, sacrificial procession (man with sprig and youth with oinochoe and kantharos). Early middle.

NECK-AMPHORAE
(nos. 53–56, with twisted handles)

53 (43). LONDON E 274, from Vulci. Part of A, *VA.* 149; *CV.* pl. 13, 2; part of A, Jacobsthal *O.* pl. 65, c. A, Apollo and Artemis. B, Triptolemos and Demeter. Middle.

54 (44). TARQUINIA RC 2240, from Tarquinia. *CV.* pl. 7, 2–3. A, Dionysos and maenad; B, two maenads. Middle.

55 (45). MUNICH 2324 (J. 326), from Vulci. A, *Mon.* 1 pl. 26, 13; palmettes, Lau pl. 25, 2; side, Jacobsthal *O.* pl. 61, d; Webster *N.* pl. 17; *CV.* pl. 215 and pl. 216, 2–4 and 6–8. A, warrior leaving home (warrior and two women). B, man and two women. Middle.

56 (46). OXFORD 280, from Nola. Millingen *PAV.* pll. 55–56, whence Inghirami pll. 310–11; Gardner pl. 12, p. 22, and p. 25 fig. 29; *CV.* pl. 16, 3–4. A, warrior leaving home; B, youths leaving home. Middle.

(nos. 57–58, with concave handles)

57. BROOKLYN 59.34. A, death of Orpheus. B, sacrifice (man with kantharos pouring wine on the altar, boy acolyte with oinochoe).

58 (47). LEYDEN PC 78 (xviii h 38), from Vulci. Roulez pl. 6. A, Eos and Kephalos; B, youths fleeing to man. Middle.

(no. 59, with triple handles)

59 (48). LEYDEN PC 76 (xviii h 37), from Vulci. Roulez pl. 4. A, Triptolemos and Demeter. B, Zeus and Iris. Middle.

(nos. 60–61, with ridged handles)

60 (49). VATICAN, from Vulci. *Mus. Greg.* 2 pl. 55, 1; A, Webster *N.* pl. 8, b. A, warrior leaving home; B, youth leaving home. Early.

61 (50). NEW YORK 99.13.2 (GR 579), from Capua. B, *Scribner's Magazine* Apr. 1888, 425, 2; A, Richter and Milne fig. 21; Richter and Hall pl. 100 and pl. 169, 97. A, Dionysos and maenads. B, king and women. Middle. For the provenience, *AJA.* 1945, 154.

(no. 61 bis, the handles missing)

61 *bis.* REGGIO, 4058, plus, three frr., from Locri. A, warrior leaving home. B, (on the right, youth in himation). The first fragment has a hand holding an oinochoe, a column, a young warrior with phiale in his right hand, helmet in his left; shield-device, gorgoneion. The second fragment has what remains of B; the third is from neck and shoulder of the vase. [Procopio].

HYDRIAI
(nos. 62–81, with picture on the body)

62 (52). BOSTON 90.156, from Foiano. Edward Robinson *Cat.,* frontispiece, whence *Jb.* 29, 27, Guthrie *Orpheus* pl. 4; back, Jacobsthal *O.* pl. 60, b; CB. ii pl. 57 and pl. 47, 107; the shape, Hambidge 87; the shape, Caskey G. 110. Death of Orpheus. Early. See CB. ii, 72–76.

63. CAMBRIDGE 5.1961. Warriors leaving home: in the middle, warrior taking the hand of a horseman; on the right, warrior taking the hand of a seated woman (the mother); on the left, seated man (the father), with woman, warrior, man. One of the elders is inscribed ΓΡΙΑΜΟξ, so Hector leaving home? [Hecht]. Early. See no. 93.

64 (53). LENINGRAD 755 (St. 1650), from Vulci. *Mon.* 3 pl. 54; cleaned, Webster *N.* pl. 9, a. Amphiaraos leaving home. Early.

65. PRINCETON 33.42, from South Italy. King and two women. Early.

65 *bis.* Private. Dionysos and two maenads. The young Dionysos, μαινό-μενος, dances at his altar, brandishing the torn body of a kid, half in each hand. One maenad holds snake and thyrsus; the other, oinochoe and kantharos. For the subject compare the London pelike E 362 (p. 585 no. 34). Dionysos wears an ependytes as there. I take the chief figure to be Dionysos rather than a maenad: for a youthful Dionysos at this period (wearing an ependytes) see the Salonica fragment 8.54 (p. 591 no. 28).

66. NAPLES, Astarita, 120, fr. (On the right, head and breast of a woman wearing chiton, himation, veil, standing to left, her right hand raised to her shoulder and chin). Early or middle.

67 (55). BASLE 1906.296, from Capua. *Mon.* 9 pl. 17, 2; Schefold *Basler Ant.* ii pl. 21. Boreas and Oreithyia. Middle. For the provenience, *AJA.* 1945, 154.

68 (54). BOWDOIN 08.3. Back, Jacobsthal *O.* pl. 60, a. Boreas and Oreithyia. Middle.

69. LUCERNE MARKET (A.A.). *Ars Ant. Aukt. II* pl. 65. Boreas and Oreithyia. [Also Bothmer]. Middle.

70 (56). SYRACUSE 35182, from Syracuse. Warrior leaving home. Middle.

71 (57). CAB. MÉD. 443, from Nola. Gerhard pl. 29, whence *El.* 2 pl. 36; B.Ap. (xxi. 11?). Apollo seated, with Artemis, Leto, and Hermes. Restored. Middle.

72 (58). LENINGRAD, from Capua. *Mon.* 9 pl. 17, 1; *RM.* 42, 239 and Beil. 34–35; Webster *N.* pl. 21, a. Apollo seated, with Artemis, Leto, and Hermes. Middle. For the provenience, *AJA.* 1945, 154; for the subject, Simon *O.G.* 21–22.

73. OXFORD 1947.312, 314, and 338, three frr. Youth with spears (Theseus?) pursuing a woman.

74 (59). TARANTO, from Ceglie. Youth with sword and spears pursuing a woman. Late middle.

75 (60). ATHENS 1486 (CC. 1253). Eos and Kephalos. Late.

76 (61). ANCONA, frr., from Castelbellino. (?Dionysos and) maenads at altar. Late.

77 (62). FERRARA, T. 325, from Spina. Detail, Alfieri and Arias *S.* pl. 41. Dionysos and maenads at altar. Late.

78 (63). NAPLES Stg. 199, from Sorrento. Dionysos and maenads at altar. Late.

79 (64). LONDON E 198, from Nola. *VA.* 146; *CV.* pl. 87, 4. Youth with spears (Theseus?) pursuing a woman. Late.

80 (65). NEW YORK 41.162.98. *CV.* Gallatin pl. 56, 1; *Bull. Metr.* 37, 58; detail, Richter *ARVS.* fig. 75. Triptolemos. Late.

81 (66). RHODES 12060, from Ialysos. *Cl. Rh.* 3, 249; Webster *N.* pl. 21, b. Apollo with Artemis and Leto. Restored. Late.

(no. 82, with picture on the shoulder)

82. TARANTO, fr. (Eros to left, girl in chitoniskos playing ball to right).

OINOCHOAI
(nos. 83–87, shape 3, choes)
(nos. 83–84, the picture not framed)

83 (69). CAB. MÉD. 460. Luynes pl. 29. Dionysos and Ariadne. Late.

84 (71). Munich 2454 (J. 282), from Vulci. The shield, *Jh.* 5, 170; Webster pl. 22, b; *CV.* pl. 87, 2, pl. 88, 1–3, and pl. 91, 1–4. Arming. Late.

(nos. 85–87, the pictures framed)

85 (70). Florence 4007. Inghirami pl. 146; Webster *N.* pl. 22, a; *CV.* pl. 66, 4 and pl. 68, 4–5. Satyr and maenad. Late.

86 (72). Louvre CA 2993, from Nola. *Bull. nap.* n.s. 6 pl. 5, 1; ph. Gir., whence van Hoorn *Choes* fig. 497. Huntress (Artemis? or Prokris?). Late. For the subject compare the lekythos in Mayence (p. 693 no. 5), and the Italiote volute-krater in Naples, 3249 (FR. pl. 179: see Ines Jucker *Der Gestus des Aposkopein* 98).

87 (73). Louvre L 62, from Athens. Farmakovski ii, 346; Webster *N.* pl. 22, c–d; ph. Gir. 34139, 1. Herakles and Athena. Late. See p. 1661.

(no. 88, shape 1)

88 (67). Athens 14503, from Greece. Return of warrior. Late.

LEKANIS

89 (73). Naples 2638, from Locri. *Mon.* 1 pl. 37; Schweitzer *M.H.* pl. 6, 2. Peleus and Thetis. Restored. Early.

FRAGMENTS OF POTS

90 (75). Villa Giulia, fr. Webster *N.* pl. 24, a. (Woman seated). Early.

91 (76). Oxford, Beazley, fr., from Greece. (Forearm of warrior holding a spear, thigh of warrior). Early.

92 (77). Chicago, Univ., fr., from Athens. *AJA.* 1938, 355, 19. (Warrior). [Johnson]. Perhaps from a lekanis? Early.

93. Florence 19 B 20, and Naples, Astarita, 110, frr. Three of the Florence frr., *CV.* pl. 19, B 23, and pl. 13, B 55. Chariot. The chariot stands to right; on this side of it is a man or a youth leaning on his stick to left, and facing it a man or youth to left (his stick remains, and a small piece of his leg). To left of it (?), the toes of one standing to right, and the lower part of a woman standing to right. A Florence fragment joins 19 B 20 on the right, adding the toes of the woman's left foot; another Florence fragment joins below, giving the lower part of the maeander. A Florence fragment joins 13 B 55 on the right, giving the stick of the person facing the chariot and a small piece of his leg. Two other fragments in Florence have parts of the horses. The four Astarita fragments have parts of wheel and of horses, the legs of the man leaning on his stick this side of them, and the lower part of a door. Early. From a hydria? Compare the hydria in the London market (no. 63). In *ARV.*[1] the fragment Florence 19 B 20 is wrongly ascribed to the Altamura Painter, as no. 58. See the next.

94 (a 25). Florence, fr. (Lower part of head of old man to left, with his shoulder, in a himation, his hand on his mouth). I do not know that this might not belong to the last.

95 (78). FLORENCE 15 B 1, fr. *CV*. pl. 15, B 1. (Woman or youth).

96 (79). ABINGDON, Robertson, fr., from Greece. (Head of woman to left). [Robertson].

97. LOUVRE C 10855, fr. (Head and shoulders of youth to right).

98 (80). NEW YORK 41.86, fr. (ex Richter). (Youth). Middle.

98 *bis*. REGGIO, fr., from Locri. (Feet, and half the shanks, of a woman in a peplos with embattled border standing frontal; below, rightward maeander with saltire-square).

99 (81). CHICAGO, Univ., fr. *AJA*. 1938, 357 fig. 25. (Woman seated— playing the lyre?). From an oinochoe of shape 3? The picture framed. Late.

100 (82). ATHENS, Ceramicus Museum, fr., from Athens. (Herakles and Iolaos). From an amphora? Late.

101. GELA, fr., from Gela. (Raised forearm, then head and shoulder of a king seated to right). Late.

MANNER OF THE NIOBID PAINTER

VOLUTE-KRATERS

1. NEW YORK 24.97.113, fr., from Gela. (Youth leaning on his spear). Early.

2 (1). Once ROME, Izard. Appears in J. S. Copley's portrait of Mr. and Mrs. Ralph Izard in the Museum at Boston (*Museum of Fine Arts, Boston; the Oil Paintings illustrated*). *Nachr. Gött*. 1939 pl. 8; *Proc. Am. Phil. Soc*. 87 (1943), 75 fig. 4. A, Apollo with Artemis and Leto. [Caskey]. May be by the painter himself.

3. FERRARA, T. 113 A VP, from Spina. A, warrior leaving home. B, Poseidon and women.

3 *bis*. REGGIO, fr., from Locri. On the neck, (thyrsus, Doric column, upper part of maenad with torch and thyrsus).

CALYX-KRATERS

4 (2). BOLOGNA 287, from Bologna. Zannoni pl. 141, 7–8; *CV*. pl. 71, middle. A, woman with sceptre, and two youths (perhaps Leda and the Dioskouroi, as Pellegrini). B, old man seated, and two males. Early.

5 (3). BOLOGNA 291, from Bologna. *Eos* 34 pl. 3, 5 and pl. 2, 4. Armour of Achilles. [Bulas].

6 (4). Once ROME, Curtius, two frr. Phs. R.I. 35.235–6. On one, warrior with man and woman; on the other, (hand with wreath, warrior). Near the painter himself.

6 *bis*. REGGIO, two frr., from Locri. Iliupersis. On one fragment, raised arm of a warrior, then the upper part of a girl's head in a saccos, both to right; above, the floral on the mouth of the vase. On the other fragment, more of the floral, and, reaching into it, the head of a sceptre—Priam's.

(no. 7, with two rows of pictures)

7 (5). ATHENS, Agora, P 104, P 110, and P 223, frr., from Athens. Above, fight. Below, (on one fragment, hand, woman; on the other, king). Near the painter himself.

CALYX-KRATERS OR BELL-KRATERS

8 (6). CORINTH C 33.141, fr., from Corinth. (Hand with phiale, woman with oinochoe).

9. ATHENS, Ceramicus Museum, fr., from Athens. (Upper part of an old man in himation standing to left, holding a sceptre or the like).

10. ISTANBUL, fr., from Xanthos, A 33.3060. (Apollo).

11. ATHENS, Agora, P 19175, fr., from Athens. (Youth). Perhaps recalls the Painter of the Berlin Hydria (p. 615).

BELL-KRATERS

(nos. 12, 15, and 19–21 with handles; the rest, not known whether handles or lugs)

12. ATHENS, Agora, P 21352, frr., from Athens. *Hesp.* 22 pl. 23; A, Ghali-Kahil *H.* pl. 63, 1. A, Menelaos and Helen. B, women fleeing to king. [Talcott].

13. CAMBRIDGE, Museum of Classical Archaeology, fr., from Al Mina. (Head of woman, wearing a stephane, to left).

13 *bis*. REGGIO, two frr., from Locri. On one, legs of Demeter in peplos standing frontal, holding corn-ears, then the handle-floral. On the other, handle-floral, then the right foot of a woman standing frontal, with the edge of her right leg. In *ARV.*[1] 421 no. 32 these were taken to belong to the Reggio fragment p. 603 no. 40, but when I saw them again it did not seem quite certain that they did. I could not find a fragment which I had seen before, with handle-floral and then the upper part of a woman holding a pair of torches.

14. LOUVRE C 10848, fr. A, male leaving home (upper part of woman to right with oinochoe and phiale, hand of male with spears). Two Louvre fragments may belong: on the first, the middle of one in a himation to right; on the second, which would come from B, arm and breast of a male in a himation to left.

14 *bis*. REGGIO, fr., from Locri. (Legs of a male in a chlamys to left, holding a pair of spears and leading a horse).

15. LOUVRE C 10845. A, symposion; B, komos (males dancing).

16. LOUVRE, fr. (Part of a woman in a peplos, then the lower part of a male in a himation leaning on his stick to right, then leg of one in long chiton and himation). Fired red outside.

17. LOUVRE C 10847, fr. (Hand holding a box or the like, middle of woman seated to left holding a writing-case).

18 (10.) BONN 306, fr., from Athens. *Jb*. 14, 166; *CV*. pl. 19, 3. (Man). Trial-piece.

19 (7). BOLOGNA 315, from Bologna. A, Pellegrini 156. A, komos. B, three youths.

20 (8). VIENNA 559. A, woman seated and two women; B, three women. Small.

21 (9). CHICAGO 22.2197, from Capua. *AJA*. 1930, 172–3; A, Webster *N*. pl. 19, a. A, warrior at home; B, youth holding armour, and two women. [Rich]. For the subject, Simon *O.G.* 102 note 67.

STAMNOS

22. WASHINGTON 136402, fr., from Orvieto. (On the right, shanks and feet of a male in a himation standing to left, then part of the handle-floral). May be by the painter himself.

PELIKAI

23 (11). COPENHAGEN inv. 596. *CV*. pl. 153, 1. A, woman seated with lyre and woman with flute. B, king and woman at altar.

24 (12). RHODES 13205, from Camiros. *Cl. Rh.* 4, 257–8; *CV*. pl. 4. A, youth leaving home. B, youths and boy. Late.

25 (13). ATHENS MARKET. A, youth leaving home (1, woman standing to right, 2, youth, wearing petasos, standing to left, with spears, 3, king with sceptre standing to left). B, two youths.

26 (14). GELA, Aldisio, from Gela. A, warrior leaving home (1, woman frontal, head to right, oinochoe in right hand, 2, young warrior frontal, head to left, with phiale, 3, woman to left, right hand raised). B, man and women at altar (1, woman to right with oinochoe and sprig, 2, woman frontal, head to left, with phiale, sceptre, and sprig, 3, man to left).

27 (15). SAN FRANCISCO, Legion of Honor, 1813, from Greece. *CV*. pl. 18, 1, pl. 19, 1, and pl. 20, 1. A, warrior leaving home. B, three youths. Late.

28 (17). VILLA GIULIA 50524. A, warrior leaving home. B, boy with lyre, and youths. Restored. Late.

29. PARIS MARKET (Segredakis). A, Apollo with Artemis and Leto. B, three youths. On A, Leto to right, holding a wreath, 2, Apollo seated to right with phiale and laurel-staff, 3, Artemis frontal, head to left, with oinochoe and bow.

30. LOUVRE C 11037, two frr. (one composed of eleven). A, women (on the left, a woman standing frontal; on the right, a woman moving to right); B, (on the left, a woman standing to right).

31. Louvre C 11038, frr.   A, (woman and girl: woman seated to right, girl
—the right-hand figure—standing to left); B, (on the right, youth leaning
on his stick to left).

NECK-AMPHORAE
(no. 32, with concave handles)

32 (18). Würzburg 503.   Part of A, FR. iii, 285; detail of A, Bieber *G.K.*
pl. 4, 4; side, Jacobsthal *O.* pl. 82, a; Langlotz pl. 170, pl. 172, and pl.
184; part of A, Bieber *Entw.* pl. 14, 2; A, Buschor *G. Vasen* 198; A, Pfeiff
Apollon pl. 41, b; A, Dinsmoor *Proc. Am. Phil. Soc.* 87 (1943), 74 fig. 5;
A, *Mitt.* 5 pl. 3; A, Simon *O.G.* pl. 1; A, Himmelmann-Wildschütz *Eig.*
pl. 28.   A, Apollo with Artemis and Leto.   B, Dionysos and maenad.
[Rumpf].   Now cleaned.   Late.   For the subjects, Simon *O.G.* 134.
Close to the painter himself.   See p. 1661.

(nos. 33–34, the handles missing)

33 (l 51). Athens, Vlasto, fr., from Koropi.   (Warrior standing frontal,
head to left, then the hand of another person).   Early.

34 (20). Villa Giulia, two frr.   On one, part of a youth in himation and
kidaris standing to left; on the other, part of a right-hand figure—booted
legs moving to right.

HYDRIAI
(with picture on the body)

35 (21). Mississippi (ex Robinson), from Vari.   *AJA.* 1932 pll. 16–17;
CV. Robinson ii pll. 36–37 and pl. 37a.   Satyrs and maenads.   Restored.
[Robinson].

36 (22). London E 190, from Kimissala in Rhodes.   *CV.* pl. 86, 3.   Woman
seated reading, and woman.   Late.

37. Laon 37.1027.   *CV.* pl. 34, 1 and pl. 35, 1.   Zeus, Hera, and Nike (or Iris).
Late.

38 (23). Athens 1261 (CC. 1244), from Attica.   Youth leaving home.

39 (24). Athens, Agora, P 12954, fr., from Athens.   (Woman).

? OINOCHOE
(shape 3, chous)

40. Athens, Agora, P 18538, fr., from Athens.   *Hesp.* 17 pl. 68, 5.   Odysseus
(in Skyros?).   For the subject, Homer Thompson and Corbett in *Hesp.*
17, 189–90.   May be early, delicate work by the painter himself.

FRAGMENTS OF POTS

40 bis. Rimini, Museo Missionario, fr., from S. Maria di Pesaro.   *St. etr.* 25,
suppl., pl. 18 fig. 6.   Fight?   Attributed by Zuffa to the circle of the Niobid
Painter and more precisely to the Painter of Bologna 279, whom it indeed
recalls, but the style of what remains is pure for that artist, and the
Niobid Painter himself must be considered.   From a volute-krater?   See
p. 1661.

41. ATHENS, Agora, P 19174, fr., from Athens. (Apollo and Artemis: what remains is part of a cithara and the head of a woman holding a sprig). From a volute-krater?

42 (27). DELOS, frr., from Delos. One fr., Plassart *Délos xi*, 51; two, Dugas *Délos xxi* pl. 56, 1a and 1b. Fight. The three unpublished fragments give: greaved calf of a warrior to right with the ends of his shield-apron, and the calf of another warrior to right; part of a warrior's thigh; lower part of a warrior's corslet with part of his chitoniskos and of a spear. May be by the painter himself.

43 (26). KOENIGSBERG 71, fr. Lullies *K.* pl. 14. (Old man, grieved). From a loutrophoros? Should be by the painter himself.

44. ATHENS, Agora, P 6985, fr., from Athens. (Thracian woman?—so from a Death of Orpheus?—what remains is part of one arm, and the ends of the apoptygma).

45. ATHENS, Agora, P 10176, two frr., from Athens. (Youth—Hermes?). [Talcott]. From an amphora? or a pelike? Late.

46. REGGIO, fr., from Locri. (Foot to right; below, rightward maeander with saltire-square).

THE PAINTER OF BOLOGNA 279

JHS. 56, 92. *ARV.*[1] 428.

Follower of the Niobid Painter.

VOLUTE-KRATERS

1 (1). FERRARA, T. 579, from Spina. *Riv. Pop. d'It.* Nov. 1928, 39–40; B of neck, *ML.* 33 pll. 1–3 and p. 6, whence *RM.* 47, 124, *Bull. Vereen.* 17, 7 fig. 15, Brommer *Satyrspiele*[1] 46 (= [2]49), *Hesp.* 24 pl. 88, b; B of neck, in part, Buschor *Feldmäuse* 19 fig. 7; Aurigemma[1] 213 middle, 215–19, and 53 above = [2]255 middle, 257–61, and 52 above, whence (A) Rumpf *MZ.* pl. 28, 6; A of neck, *Riv. Ist.* 6 pl. 1; B, Arias and Alfieri pl. 40; Stella 648 and 588; A, Aurigemma and Alfieri pl. 29; Alfieri and Arias *S.* pll. 42–44; *A, E.A.A.* ii, 129; detail of A, *St. etr.* 25, suppl., pl. 19; A, *Ant. Kunst* 3, i, pl. 5, 2; A, *Mostra* pl. 84; detail of neck B, *E.A.A.* iii, 374. A, Seven against Thebes. B, Argonauts. On the neck: A, Herakles and Busiris; B, rising of a goddess (Persephone?), with satyrs. For the subjects of the chief pictures, Aurigemma[1] 214–16 = [2]256–8; for the subject of neck B, *Hesp.* 24, 311–12. See p. 1662.

2. SWISS PRIVATE. Amazonomachy. On the neck, symposion.

3 (2). BOLOGNA 279, from Bologna. *Atti Romagna* 21 pl. 2 and p. 258, whence (the chief picture) Pfuhl fig. 508 (= Pfuhl *Mast.* fig. 75); *CV.* pll. 62–66; detail, *E.A.A.* iv, 1127. Amazonomachy. On the neck, symposion. For the subject, Bothmer *Am.* 169.

A late imitation of the Niobid Painter (*ARV.*¹ 426 no. 19) may be slight work by the Painter of Bologna 279:

NECK-AMPHORA
(with ridged handles)

NAPLES 3159, from Nola. A, ph. So. 11069, i, 5. A, youth leaving home (or returning). B, three youths.

THE PAINTER OF THE WOOLLY SATYRS

Att. V. 343 and 477. *ARV.*¹ 427–8. *JHS.* 79, 16–18.

Called after no. 6.

Follower of the Niobid Painter.

VOLUTE-KRATERS

1 (1). NEW YORK 07.286.84, from Numana. FR. pll. 116–17, whence (part) *Jb.* 29, 149, (part) *Jb.* 33, 4–5 and 8, (A) Pfuhl fig. 506, (A) Swindler fig. 350, (neck A, incomplete) *Jh.* 35, 88; A, *N.Y. Shapes* 9, 2; B and side, Richter and Milne figs. 51–52, whence (B) L.S. fig. 10; Richter and Hall pll. 97–98 and pl. 171, 98; details, Richter *Gk Ptg* 13, 1 and 3; A, *Hist. rel.* 263; Richter *H.* 227, a; Bothmer *Am.* pl. 75; A, *E.A.A.* i, 307 and 901; detail of the neck-picture on A, Richter *H.G.A.* 334 fig. 450; A, Robertson *G.P.* 123. Amazonomachy. On the neck: A, Centauromachy at the wedding of Perithoos; B, youths and women. For the chief subject, Bothmer *Am.* 167–9. See p. 1662.

2 (a, +). LOUVRE C 10749 (one fr. ex Tübingen E 97). The Tübingen fr., Watzinger pl. 28. A, Centauromachy at the wedding of Perithoos. B, three women (two with sceptres, the third with an oinochoe). Shefton pointed out that the Tübingen fragment, said in *ARV.*¹ 426, no. 28, to be in the manner of the Niobid Painter and to recall the Painter of the Woolly Satyrs, joined Louvre C 10749.

3. LOUVRE CA 3482. A, *Rev. des Arts* 7, 123. A, death of Actaeon. B, women and youths.

CALYX-KRATERS

4 (2). PALERMO. Detail of A, *Jb.* 49, 42. A, uncertain subject (Herakles and the lion; Iolaos before Eurystheus?). B, two women running and a youth.

5 (2 *bis*). BOWDOIN 30.8, fr. A, symposion.

BELL-KRATERS

6 (3). SYRACUSE 23508, from Gela. A, *ML.* 17 pl. 44 and p. 510, whence *AM.* 52, 232, Nilsson *GGR.* i pl. 35, 1, and *Boll. d'Arte* 1950, 197 fig. 6; A, *CV.* pl. 14. A, uncertain subject: Dionysos, Circe?, and satyrs (see Buschor in *AM.* 52, 232). B, youths and woman.

7 (4, +). LOUVRE G 649, frr. Part of one fr., Pottier pl. 160. A, Herakles, Nike, and (Eurystheus?). On one fragment, the legs of Herakles seated on a rock to right, then part of Nike standing frontal; on the other, part of Nike and a man seated on a rock.

8. LOUVRE MNB 2774, fr. A, (satyrs wearing the drawers of the satyr-play: thighs of one to right, a second dancing, a third to right, bending).

PELIKAI

9 (6). COLOGNY, Bodmer. A, *Auktion Fischer 21 Mai 1941* pl. 67; A, Schefold *M.* 233, 283. A, Hera and Nike at altar. B, two youths.

10 (7). ATHENS 1426 (CC. 1274), from Corinth. A, two women; B, two women.

HYDRIA
(but without back-handle; two rows of pictures)

11 (5). VATICAN, from Vulci. *Mus. Greg.* 2 pl. 19, 2; detail, Jacobsthal *Mel.* 194 fig. 71. Above, uncertain subjects: A, warrior at altar, two women with sceptres, and a seated woman; B, seated man, and two women with sceptres. Below, Hermes pursuing a woman.

OINOCHOE
(shape 1)

12 (a). FERRARA, T. 607, from Spina. Amazonomachy. See Bothmer *Am.* 175–6, and *JHS.* 79, 17.

FRAGMENT OF A POT

13. COULOMMIERS, Majurel, fr., from La Monédière. *JHS.* 79 pl. 1, a. Amazonomachy. See *JHS.* 79, 16–18.

Probably also

HYDRIA

1 (a). ODESSA, Univ. Farmakovski pl. 17. Amazon archer.

BELL-KRATER

2 (a). OXFORD 1954.246, four frr., from Al Mina. One, *JHS.* 59, 9, 26. (Hand holding a helmet).

FRAGMENT OF A POT

3. TARANTO 52387, fr., from Taranto. (Breast of a warrior moving to right).

THE GENEVA PAINTER

Att. V. 342. *ARV.*[1] 430.

Niobid Group; near the Painter of the Woolly Satyrs.

CALYX-KRATER
(with two rows of pictures)

1 (1). GENEVA MF 238. FR. ii, 314 fig. 105, whence Swindler fig. 374, (detail) Pfuhl fig. 509 (= Pfuhl *Mast.* fig. 76), (part) Rumpf *MZ.* pl. 28, 3; A, Deonna *Choix* pl. 42; A, *E.A.A.* iii, 898; phs. Gir. 4028–9. Above, Amazonomachy. Below: A, youth with spears (Theseus?) pursuing a woman; B, boy with lyre, and youths. Restored. For the subject, Bothmer *Am.* 169–70.

HYDRIA

2 (2). LOUVRE G 427. Pottier pl. 142; *CV.* d pl. 52, 1–3 and 5. Youth with sword and spears pursuing a woman (Theseus and Aithra?). Restored.

The following vase is connected with the Geneva Painter:

VOLUTE-KRATER

LOUVRE G 482, from Tarquinia. Raoul-Rochette pl. 80; *CV.* d pl. 30, 1–3 and 7; A, *Anthemon* pl. 21, 3; B and sides, Ghali-Kahil *H.* pl. 70; B, Villard *VG.* pl. 26, 4. A, armour of Achilles. B, young warrior pursuing a woman.

THE PAINTER OF LONDON E 470

Corbett perceived that these two vases went together. See Clement in *Los Angeles Bulletin* 9, iii, 5–15.

Niobid Group; near the Geneva Painter and the Painter of the Woolly Satyrs.

VOLUTE-KRATERS

1. LOS ANGELES A 5933.51.108. A, *Cat. Sotheby Jan. 17–18 1951* pl. 3, whence Ghali-Kahil *H.* pl. 62, 2; cleaned, *Los Angeles Bull.* 9, iii p. 10, p. 11 figs. 3–4 and 6, p. 12 figs. 11–13, p. 13 figs. 14 and 16–19, p. 14 figs. 20 and 23–24, and p. 15; detail, *Archaeology* 12, 248 fig. 10. A, Menelaos and Helen. B, symposion.

2. LONDON E 470, from South Italy. Raoul-Rochette pl. 60, whence (B) *AZ.* 1848 pl. 14, 2; B, Jacobsthal *Mel.* 51; B, Davreux fig. 60; B, side, and part of A, *BSA.* 46 pl. 14, c–d; A, ph. Ma. 3143. A, warrior leaving home. B, Ajax and Cassandra.

THE PAINTER OF THE BERLIN HYDRIA

VA. 150–2. *Att. V.* 344–5. *ARV.*[1] 428–9. CB. ii, 82–83.

Named after no. 11.

Follower of the Niobid Painter.

VOLUTE-KRATER

1 (1). BOSTON 00.347, from near Licata. The Apollo, *VA*. 150; A, *AJA*. 1922, 416; A, Miller *Daedalus and Thespis* iii fig. 43, 12; CB. ii pl. 61; the shape, Caskey G. 123. A, Apollo with Artemis and Leto. B, three women at altar (one holding a sceptre: priestess and attendants). See CB. ii, 82–83, and Simon *O.G.* 131.

CALYX-KRATERS

2 (2). LENINGRAD 766 (St. 1271). *CR.* 1874 pll. 5–6; A, *G.P.* 78. A, warrior leaving home in chariot; B, youth leaving home.

3 (3). NEW YORK 07.286.86, from Numana. FR. pll. 118–19 and ii, 325, 3, whence (A) Pfuhl fig. 507, (A) Swindler figs. 325–6; A, Richter *Craft* 24 fig. 32; B, *N.Y. Shapes* 10, 1; Richter and Hall pl. 99 and pl. 170, 99; B, Buschor G. *Vasen* 196; detail, Richter *Gk Ptg* 13, 2; detail, Richter *ARVS*. 91; A, Schuchhardt and Technau 209; Richter *H*. 227, b; Bothmer *Am*. pl. 74, 2. Amazonomachy. For the subject, Bothmer *Am*. 165–6.

BELL-KRATERS

3 *bis*. BASLE, Cahn, 22, frr. A, Theseus and Skiron (with Athena). B, (on the left, youth in chlamys).

4 (3 *bis*). REGGIO 498, frr., from Locri. A, warrior leaving home.

NECK-AMPHORAE
(*nos. 5–7, with twisted handles*)

5 (4). LENINGRAD (ex Stroganoff), from Capua. *CR.* 1874 pl. 7, 1–3. A, youths with spears; B, warrior leaving home (warrior and woman). For the provenience, *AJA*. 1945, 154–5.

6 (5). LONDON E 275, from Vulci. Part of A, *VA*. 151; the same, Herford pl. 9, c; *CV*. pl. 14, 1. A, Nike and warrior; B, goddess and Nike.

7 (6). VATICAN, from Vulci. *Mus. Greg.* 2 pl. 60, 1; Gerhard *TG*. pl. J, 1–2; A, ph. Al. 35712, whence Stella 493; B.Ap. xxii. 48. 1 and xxii. 47. 2. Death of Orpheus (A, Orpheus and Thracian woman; B, Thracian woman and Thracian youth). See p. 1662.

(*no. 8, with triple handles*)

8 (7). COPENHAGEN, Ny Carlsberg, inv. 2698, from Orvieto. Poulsen *Etr*. pll. 18–20; part of A, Breitenstein *G.V*. pl. 45. A, warrior leaving home; B, youth leaving home.

AMPHORAE
(*type A*)

9 (8). VATICAN, from Vulci. *Mus. Greg.* 2 pl. 56, 2. A, warrior leaving home; B, youth leaving home.

10 (9). LONDON MARKET (Christie: ex Jekyll). B.Ap. xxi. 87. A, youth leaving home; B, the like.

HYDRIAI

11 (10). BERLIN 2381, from Nola. Gerhard *AB*. pl. 49, whence *El.* 3 pl. 39;
Jb. 26, 160; B.Ap. xviii. 5. Nike and two seated goddesses.

12 (11). VIENNA 1073. Athena and two women at altar.

13 (a). HARVARD 60.341 (ex Robinson), from Vari. *AJA.* 1932 pll. 14–15;
CV. Robinson ii pl. 35. Mourning women. Restored.

14. FERRARA, T 253 C VP, from Spina. Three women. Weak.

THE SPRECKELS PAINTER

Named after the donor of no. 1.

The pelike reminded me of the krater (*ARV.*[1] 426); H. R. W. Smith saw
(*CV.* San Francisco 40–41) that the two were in fact by one hand, and he
gave the artist the name which I adopt. The pelike imitates the Niobid
Painter; the krater cannot be said to do so.

PELIKE

1. SAN FRANCISCO, Palace of the Legion of Honor, 1814a, from Athens (gift
of Mrs. Alma de Bretteville Spreckels Awl). *CV.* pl. 18, 2 and pl. 19, 2.
A, Apollo seated, with Artemis and Leto. B, youths and boy. Placed
under 'manner of the Niobid Painter' in *ARV.*[1] 425 no. 16.

CALYX-KRATER

2. NEW YORK 07.286.66, from Agrigento. Richter and Hall pl. 126, pl. 129,
127, and pl. 170, 127, whence (A) *Hesp.* 8, 294, (A) Stella 519; part of A,
Richter *Gk Ptg* 14, 2; detail of A, White *P.* pl. 5, d. A, Kadmos.
B, man and two women. On A, EVMLKOϟ KMLOϵ and ΛLONHϟ
KMLOϟ. Peculiar alphas. The first inscription should be Εὔαλκος καλός
(as Richter): the name in the second must be badly misspelt.

CHAPTER 36

THE VILLA GIULIA PAINTER
AND HIS GROUP

THE GROUP OF THE VILLA GIULIA PAINTER

The Group consists of the Villa Giulia Painter; his follower the Chicago Painter; a few imitators; and the Methyse Painter. See also p. 634.

THE VILLA GIULIA PAINTER

RM. 27, 286–97. *RM.* 28, 125. Frickenhaus *Lenäenvasen* 35. *VA.* 153–4. *Att. V.* 349–53 and 477. *V.Pol.* 46–48. *ARV.*[1] 401–7 and 959.

So called after no. 1.

He belongs to the academic wing of early classic vase-painting, and is connected with the followers of Douris. His best work has a quiet nobility.

CALYX-KRATERS

1 (1). VILLA GIULIA 909, from Falerii. FR. pll. 17–18; B, ph. And. 6325, whence Della Seta *Mus. V.G.* pl. 28, 1; detail, *Dedalo* 3, 87; *CV.* pll. 21–22. Women dancing. See p. 1662.

2 (2, +). LOUVRE G 344, fr. Part, *CV.* d pl. 7, 1 and 3. A, woman playing the flute, and women. B, king, and two women running. Several Louvre fragments join the published part.

3 (3). CARLSRUHE 208 (B 3), from Agrigento. Creuzer *Gall.* pl. 2, 3; *RM.* 27 pl. 10, 2 and Beil. p. 286, 1; Welter pl. 11; A, Brommer *Satyrspiele* [1]36 = [2]40; *CV.* pl. 19, whence (A) Rumpf *MZ.* pl. 31, 1; A, Schnellbach fig. 19. A, satyr family. B, king, and two women running.

4 (4). MOSCOW, Hist. Mus., from Nola. A, *Zhizn Muzeya* 1926, frontispiece; A, ibid. 1930, 48 fig. 3; A, Blavatski 205, above; A, *Putevoditel* 61. A, Hermes with the infant Dionysos. B, old king, and two women running.

5 (5). MARZABOTTO, from Marzabotto. A, Dionysos and satyrs. B, athletes and youths.

6 (6). SCHWERIN 1261. A, Apollo and Muses. B, athletes and trainer. Restored.

7. GELA (INA casa 1954), fr., from Gela. (Head, to right, and right shoulder, of a woman wearing a saccos). A Gela fragment with the lower edge of a shield resting on the ground may belong: if so, an arming scene or a departure.

8 (7). DRESDEN 349. A, *Anz.* 1892, 165, 32. A, arming. B, three youths.

9 (8). BERLIN inv. 4497, from Capua. A, *Le Musée* 1, 1; *Vente 11–14 mai 1903*, 31 and pl. 2 figs. 6 and 10; Lücken pll. 54–55. A, Troilos and Polyxene. B, satyrs and maenad.

10 (9). TÜBINGEN E 32, fr. Watzinger pl. 20. (Satyr).

11 (10). TARANTO, fr., from Taranto. B, athletes (leg of athlete moving to left, legs of athlete moving to right, of male in himation to left with stick).

11 *bis*. REGGIO, two frr., from Locri. White ground. On one fragment, part of the left-hand figure on one side remains, Athena (AΘEN[AIA):—the top of the hair, with a little of the spear. On the other fragment, head, shoulders, breast, right forearm, of a woman standing frontal, head to left, right hand covering her mouth, with a child asleep on her left shoulder. This is the same figure as on the Providence alabastron (no. 88), and as on the Boston skyphos by the Euaichme Painter (p. 784 no. 2) where the woman is named Astyoche. Second white used.

12 (11). LAUSANNE 3700, fr., from Tarsus. White ground. (Upper part of woman, led, to right). Second white used. Restored.

(no. 13, with two rows of pictures)

13 (12). PALERMO (1817), fr. Above, horse-race. Below, (top of head).

BELL-KRATERS

14 (13). CORINTH, frr., from Corinth. A, Theseus leaving home. B, athlete and youths.

14 *bis*. REGGIO 4070, fr., from Locri. A, (part of the left-hand figure remains, AIΘPA, so the subject was doubtless Theseus leaving home).

15 (14). CARLSRUHE 209 (B 40), from Locri. *RM.* 27 pl. 10, 1; A, Welter pl. 12, 1; *CV.* pl. 20; A, Schnellbach fig. 20. A, Polydeukes and Castor. B, old king, and women running.

16 (15). LONDON E 492, from Nola. A, Millin *PVA.* 2 pl. 13, whence Inghirami pl. 65; Panofka *Pourt.* pl. 27; part of A, *VA.* 153, whence Scheurleer pl. 34, 95; detail of A, Richter *ARVS.* fig. 84; A, Stella 98, above; A, ph. Ma. 3135. A, Hermes with the infant Dionysos. B, athlete and trainers. Restored.

17 (16). NEW YORK 24.97.96. *The Canessa Coll.* (*Jan. 25–26 1924*) no. 63; *Bull. Metr.* 20, 265 figs. 4–5; B, Richter and Milne fig. 60, whence LS. fig. 7; Richter and Hall pl. 101 and pl. 171, 100; A, *Mitt.* 5 pl. 2, 1; A, Richter *H.* 228, a. A, Apollo with Artemis and Leto. B, old king, and two women.

17 *bis*. REGGIO, fr., from Locri. A, (Apollo: the head remains, to right, bent, with part of the egg-pattern on the ledge above the picture).

18 (17). LONDON E 493, from Camiros. *RM.* 27 pl. 11. A, Perseus and Medusa. B, (athlete and trainer). See p. 1662.

19 (18). MADRID 11010 (L. 169). *Museo español* 1 pl. 20, whence (part of

A) Studniczka *Perseus* fig. 2; A, Alvarez-Ossorio pl. 31, 1; A, Leroux pl. 22, 1; *CV.* pl. 17, 1 and pl. 18. A, Perseus and Medusa. B, old king, and two women running.

20 (19). AMSTERDAM inv. 307, fr., from Athens. (Perseus: the back of his head remains).

21 (20). REGGIO 960, fr., from Locri. (Upper half of a woman, probably a maenad, to right).

22. BASLE MARKET (M.M.). A, maenad and satyrs. B, three youths. On A, satyr moving to left, looking back, maenad moving to right, head thrown back, with thyrsus, satyr moving to right, playing the flute. Very slight.

22 *bis.* REGGIO, fr., from Locri. (Satyr and maenad?—arm outstretched to right, shoulder of a woman in a sleeveless chiton to right).

23 (21). LONDON E 496, from Vulci. A, *RM.* 27, Beil. at p. 286, 2. A, Triptolemos. B, athletes.

24. TARANTO 52932, from Rugge. A, mounted youth, and man with sceptre. B, youth and males. Restored.

25 (22). TÜBINGEN inv. 1567, fr. (Upright spear, and upper half of youth in himation to left).

26 (23). FLORENCE PD 572, fr. A, (athlete).

VOLUTE-KRATER

27 (24). HALLE 92, frr. Part, *Jb.* 52, 211. Return of Hephaistos.

COLUMN-KRATER
(*with framed pictures*)

28 (25). FERRARA, T. 350, from Spina. A, warrior and women. B, three youths.

STAMNOI

29 (26). VIENNA, Univ., 551 b and part of 631 d, from Orvieto? *CV.* pl. 17, and pl. 16, 4, left. A, young warrior pursuing a woman. B, male, and two women running. In *CV.* the fragment of the reverse (*CV.* pl. 16, 4, left) is wrongly detached from 551 b and put with fragments of other vases.

30 (27). OXFORD 524. *JHS.* 24, 312-13, whence (A) Farnell 4 pl. 20; *CV.* pl. 28, 3-4, pl. 30, 9, and pl. 12, 4; palmettes, Jacobsthal O. pl. 101, d. A, Apollo and Muses; B, Muses. The provenience Gela given by Gardner is false: the vase is *Coll. Castellani* (1884) no. 81. See p. 1662.

31 (28). NEW YORK 06.1021.176, from Capua. A, Sambon *Coll. Canessa* pl. 8, 97; B, Richter and Milne fig. 66, whence LS. fig. 11; Richter and Hall pl. 102 and pl. 173, 101; the shape, Hambidge 102. A, arming; B, king, woman with oinochoe and phiale, and two youths. Bothmer has found the lid.

32 (29). LENINGRAD 806 (St. 1714). A, G.P. 80. A, maenads; B, maenads.

33 (30). VILLA GIULIA 983, from Falerii. Frickenhaus *Len.* 8–9 no. 19; A, *Dedalo* 3, 83; *CV.* pl. 13 (reversed) and pl. 14, 1; detail of A, *Annuario* 4–5, 137; A, ph. Al. 41192, whence Pickard-Cambridge *D.F.A.* fig. 11, a. Lenaia: A, maenads at idol of Dionysos; B, maenads.

34 (31). BOSTON 90.155 (R. 418). Frickenhaus *Len.* pl. 3, 16; the shape, Caskey G. 93. Lenaia: A, maenads at idol of Dionysos; B, maenads.

35 (32). LONDON E 451, from Vulci. Panofka *Dionysos und die Thyaden* pl. 2, 1; B.Ap. xxii. 42, whence Frickenhaus *Len.* 8–9 no. 18; *CV.* pl. 23, 2; A, *Hist. rel.* 69. Lenaia: A, maenads at idol of Dionysos; B, maenads.

36 (33). WÜRZBURG 520, from Vulci. Langlotz pl. 189. Lenaia: A, maenads at idol of Dionysos; B, maenads. Was completely painted over, now cleaned.

37 (35). FLORENCE 4005. *CV.* pl. 53, 3–4 and pl. 48, 3. Lenaia: A, maenads at idol of Dionysos; B, maenads.

38 (35 *bis*). FLORENCE 14 B 6, fr. *CV.* pl. 14, B 6. Lenaia: A, women at idol of Dionysos (a small part of the idol remains).

39 (34). LOUVRE G 408, from Vulci. *Mon.* 6–7 pl. 65, whence Frickenhaus *Len.* pl. 3, 17 and Nilsson *G.G.R.* 1 pl. 37, 1; A, Pottier pl. 142; *CV.* d pl. 15, 2 and 7, and pl. 16, 2; B.Ap. xxii. 27. 1. Lenaia: women at idol of Dionysos; maenads. Now cleaned. See p. 1662.

40 (35 *ter*, +). LOUVRE C 10762. Lenaia: maenads at idol of Dionysos; maenads. Many fragments join that originally described, and the vase is not far from complete.

41 (36). OXFORD 523, from Gela. *JHS.* 24 pl. 9 and p. 310, whence Frickenhaus *Len.* 10, (A) Pfuhl fig. 516, (A) Pickard-Cambridge *D.F.A.* fig. 12; *CV.* pl. 28, 1–2 and pl. 12, 5; palmettes, Jacobsthal *O.* pl. 104, a; B, Pickard-Cambridge *D.F.A.* fig. 11, b. Lenaia: the same scene as in nos. 33–40, but the idol not indicated. The palmettes are as in the stamnos by the Danae Painter Louvre G 411 (p. 1075 no. 2), and may be by the same hand; the maeanders are also like. See p. 1662.

42 (37). SAN SIMEON, Hearst Corporation, 12211 (ex Forman 352), from Capua. B, *Amer. Art Ass. March* 6–7 1936, 9, 2. Lenaia: maenads.

43. LOUVRE, fr. (Right foot of a woman moving quickly to right, with parts of her shanks, and, below, of the leftward maeander). [Philippaki].

NUPTIAL LEBES
(*type 1*)

44 (38). LOUVRE (ex Kalebdjian), fr. On the stand, Eos and Tithonos.

NECK-AMPHORAE
(*no. 45, with twisted handles*)

45 (39). MUNICH 2320 (J. 329), from Vulci. Side, Jacobsthal *O.* pl. 105, d. A, Theseus leaving home (A, Theseus and Ariadne; B, king, and woman running with phialai). See p. 1662.

(no. 46, handles unknown—triple?)

46 (40). Once PARIS, Pourtalès, 134, from Nola. A, Panofka *Pourt.* pl. 1, whence *El.* 1 pl. 20. A, king and woman. B, two youths.

(no. 47, with triple handles)

47 (41). ORVIETO, Faina, 65, from Orvieto? *Boll. Restauro* 23–24, 151, 152 fig. 66, and 162–3; phs. R.I. 38.230–2 and 38.237. A, Polyneikes and Eriphyle. B, two women.

PELIKAI

48 (42). SYRACUSE 22177, from Gela. *ML.* 17 pl. 32 and pp. 443–6; (including the fr. of A which I added) *CV.* pl. 3, 1–3. A, Theseus leaving home (Theseus with Aithra and Ariadne). B, king and woman.

49. LILLE 69. A, Eos and Tithonos. B, youth and woman (both moving to right). [Bothmer]. Much restored.

50 (43). LONDON 95.8–31.1, from Athens. Stackelberg pl. 18, whence *El.* 1 pll. 14 and 30; Cook *Zeus* 3 pl. 59. A, Zeus and Nike; B, Hera and Hebe.

51 (44). SAN SIMEON, Hearst State Monument, 10445 (ex Durham). A, Apollo and goddess. B, two youths (both moving to right).

52. TARTU 107, from Cervetri. A, Malmberg and Felsberg pl. 2, 4. A, Orpheus and a Thracian. B, youth and woman.

53 (45). CORINTH C 34.389, fr., from Corinth. *Hesp.* 6, 261 fig. 2, 3. B, (youth). [Pease].

54 (46). BUDAPEST (ex Hope). A, Tillyard pl. 15, 103. A, athlete and trainer. B, two youths.

55 (47). GOETTINGEN J 36. A, Jacobsthal *Gött. V.* pl. 12, 38; A, *Nachr. Gött.* N.S. 2 pl. 1, 3–4. A, acolytes (youth with oinochoe and youth with incense). B, two youths.

56 (48). BRYN MAWR P 921, fr. B, (male and youth).

HYDRIAI

(nos. 57–69, the picture on the body)

57 (50). MADRID 11023 (L. 162). Alvarez-Ossorio pl. 30, 1; Leroux pl. 20; *CV.* pl. 11, 1 and pl. 12; B.Ap. xvii. 84. Triptolemos with Persephone and Demeter.

58 (51). GELA, Jacona, from Gela. Zeus pursuing a woman (woman in peplos running to left, looking round, Zeus with sceptre and cloak moving to right, woman running to right, looking round).

59 (52). WARSAW 142464 (ex Czartoryski 41), from Nola. De Witte pl. 10; *CV.* pl. 33, 1. Poseidon pursuing a woman.

60 (53). CAPUA 207, from Capua. Philippart *It. ii* pl. 7, 2; *CV.* pl. 8, 2 and pl. 9, 3 and 9. King and two women. Restored.

61 (54). PARIS, Rothschild. Old king and two women (woman standing to right, her hands raised as if holding a wreath, old man standing frontal, head to left, sceptre in left hand, right arm akimbo, woman standing frontal, head to left, left hand raised).

62. NEW HAVEN, Watkins. Unexplained subject: youth and women (woman running to left, looking round, naked youth, cloak over left shoulder, standing to left, stick in left hand, woman standing frontal, head to left, left hand raised). Said to be from Gela, but may be the vase described in *RM*. 8, 340 no. 26, and, if so, probably from Curti or Capua.

63. NEW YORK MARKET. Youth and women (youth in himation standing to right, stick in right hand, woman standing frontal, head to left, holding out a wool-basket with her right hand, woman running to right, looking round).

64 (56). LONDON E 186. Hancarville 4 pl. 96; *CV*. pl. 82, 1. Unexplained subject: three women (1, standing to right, hands raised, on the ground in front of her a hydria, 2, standing frontal, head to left, sceptre in left hand, 3, standing frontal, head to left).

65 (57). EDINBURGH 1872.23.11. Schauenburg *Perseus* pl. 6, 2. Perseus with Hermes and a woman.

66 (58). CAMBRIDGE 12.17. Tischbein 1 pl. 7; Tillyard pl. 15, 109, whence *RM*. 53, 259 fig. 9; Cook *Zeus* 2 pl. 13; *CV*. pl. 35, 1 and pl. 40, 8; Stella 323. The daughters of Pelias. See p. 1662.

67 (59). LENINGRAD (St. 1592). Warrior leaving home.

68 (60). LONDON E 240, from Camiros. *CV*. pl. 100, 1; detail, Anderson *A.G.H.* pl. 23, a. Horseman leaving home. Poor.

69 (61). NEW YORK x. 313.1, from Nola. *Bull. Ital.* 1 pl. 6; *Studies Robinson* 2 pl. 52. Satyr with infant Dionysos, and nymphs. Rather coarse.

(nos. 70–72, the picture on the shoulder, running right round)

70 (62). VATICAN, from Vulci. *Mus. Greg.* 2 pl. 15, 2. Apollo and the Muses.

70 *bis*. VILLA GIULIA, from Vulci. Apollo and the Muses. See p. 1662.

71 (63). BARI, frr. Eos and Tithonos?

72 (64). VATICAN. Millingen *PA*. pl. 35; *Mus. Greg.* 2 pl. 13, 1; *Philologus* 27 pl. 2, 2; *BCH*. 1936 pl. 17 and pl. 18, 1, whence *Bull. Vereen.* 17, 9 fig. 21; Brommer *Satyrspiele*[1] 30–31 = [2]34–35; ph. And. 42070. Satyrs robbing Herakles.

CYLINDROID

73 (65). CAMBRIDGE x 13, fr., from Naucratis. *RM*. 27, Beil. at p. 290, and pp. 291–2; *CV*. pl. 38. Apollo with Artemis and Leto, Ganymede, Hermes, and Dionysos. For the presence of Ganymede compare Syracuse 45911 (p. 1053 no. 32).

OINOCHOE
(shape 1)

74 (66). LENINGRAD 854 (St. 1716). Dionysos and maenad.

LEKYTHOI
(nos. 75–85, red-figured)
(nos. 75–80, standard shape)

75 (67). SYRACUSE 20542, from Gela. *ML.* 17 pl. 26, whence Libertini *Mus. Sir.* 83. Calliope and Mnemosyne.

76 (68). OXFORD 535, from Gela. *JHS.* 25 pl. 2, 1; *CV.* pl. 38, 14 and pl. 35, 1–2. Apollo and Artemis. Slightly restored.

77 (69). CASSEL, Lullies, fr., from Greece. *Jb.* 59–60 pl. 19, 2; ph. A.I. 19411, 3. Danae (part of the carpenter remains). For the subject see p. 1662.

78 (70). OXFORD 1947.25. Nike and woman at altar. ΚΑΛΟΣ ΝΙΚΟΝ.

79 (71). TÜBINGEN E 77, fr. Watzinger 44. Nike.

80 (74). OXFORD 1936.611. Iris (running, with writing-case and caduceus).

(nos. 81–85, secondary shapes)

81 (72). CAB. MÉD. (ex Fröhner), from Greece. Woman spinning. ΦΙΛΕΡΓΟΣ. The earliest instance of the adjective.

82 (73). FERRARA, T. 309, from Spina. Woman with wool-basket.

83. TARANTO 52315, from Taranto. Woman at altar, pouring a libation from a phiale, and praying. A black lekythos, Taranto 52314, found in the same tomb, must be by the same potter.

84. PRAGUE, Nat. Mus., 769, from Greece. *Fasti arch.* 10, 117; *Zprávy* 3, 82 fig. 1. Woman running with torches. Class ATL or near.

85. AEGINA, fr., from Aegina. Woman with mirror (standing to right). The upper part is preserved.

(nos. 86–87: white ground; secondary shape; Class CL or near)

86 (75). LUGANO, Schoen. Neugebauer *ADP.* pl. 71, 165; Lullies *S.G.K.* pl. 33, 74. Woman seated with skein.

87 (76). LUGANO, Schoen. Neugebauer *ADP.* pl. 71, 166; Lullies *S.G.K.* pl. 33, 75. Woman seated holding wreath.

ALABASTRA
(nos. 88–90, red-figured)

88 (77). PROVIDENCE 25.088, from Greece. *AJA.* 1931, 302; *CV.* pl. 22, 3. A, woman with two children. B, youth seated, and woman. See p. 784 no. 2, and *JHS.* 53, 311, right; and above, no. 11 *bis*.

88 *bis*. ATHENS. Woman seated with lyre, girl with flute, woman with lyre.

89 (78). BRUSSELS A 1922. *CV.* pl. 20, 5. Woman seated at wool-basket, and woman.

90 (a). Lost. Tischbein 5 pl. 29. A, Nike at altar. B, woman.

(*nos. 91–94, white ground*)

91 (79). LOUVRE MNC 627, from Greece. Youth and woman; youth and boy.

92 (80). TARANTO 4536 (8284), from Taranto. Youth and woman.

93 (81). GIESSEN. Bieber *Beilage zum Giessener Anzeiger* 18 Aug. 1932, 130; Angermeier pll. 1–4. A, woman spinning; B, woman with mirror.

94 (81 *bis*). ATHENS, Agora, P 5233, from Athens. A, woman; B, woman.

PYXIS
(*type A*)

95 (82). COPENHAGEN inv. 4735, from Greece. *CV.* pl. 162, 4. Peleus and Thetis.

FRAGMENT OF A POT

96 (83). TÜBINGEN E 87, fr. Watzinger pl. 27. (Warrior).

RHYTA
(*no. 97, young ram's head*)

97 (84). ATHENS 15880, from Anavysos. *Soc. Friends Nat. Mus.* 1934–5, 9; *BCH.* 1937 pl. 27, 2 and pl. 28. Youth pursuing a woman.

(*nos. 98–99, fragments, the form of the plastic part unknown*)

98 (85). VILLA GIULIA, two frr. *CV.* Florence pl. 15, B 27. Athletes. See the next.

99. NAPLES, Astarita, 151, fr. (Head, except the face, to left, of a naked youth frontal, with the left shoulder). Belongs to the last?

CUPS
(*no. 100, decorated inside only*)

100 (86). ATHENS Acr. 443, fr., from Athens. Langlotz pl. 37, whence Philippart *C.A.B.* pl. 30, 443. I, (white ground), (foot with part of the chiton).

(*nos. 101–9, decorated outside as well as in*)

101 (87). BERLIN 2522, from Tarquinia. I, Blümel *Sport u. Spiel* pl. 13, 7; *CV.* pl. 97. I, athlete; A–B, athletes.

102 (89). VILLA GIULIA 5993, from Corchiano. *Arch. class.* 2 pl. 7, 1, pl. 6, and pl. A–B. I, victor; A, victor, acontist, and youth; B, jumper, discus-thrower, and man.

103 (88). BOSTON 76.47 (R. 399), from Capua. I, symposion (youth reclining). A, boy with lyre, youth, and man; B, the like.

104. MAPLEWOOD, Noble. *Hesp. Art Bull.* 1 no. 24; I and B, *Man in the Ancient World* 60; I, *AJA.* 1960 pl. 86 fig. 10. I, youth. A–B, komos. Cup type C. See p. 1662.

105 (90). CASSEL T 436. I, komast at altar; A–B, komos.

106. BARCELONA 514 and 520, two frr., from Ampurias. Outside: on one fragment, (komast); on the other, (head of youth). [Shefton]. See pp. 626–7 no. 7.

107 (91). LENINGRAD. I, woman with mirror; A, woman playing ball, and two youths; B, youth seated, woman, and man. The youth on B wears a saccos as well as a himation.

108 (92). WÜRZBURG 486, from Vulci. Langlotz pl. 154. I, woman holding sash; A, youths and woman; B, women and man.

109. BARCELONA 474 and 4315, fr., from Ampurias. A, women (sandals hanging; top of head of a woman seated to right, basket hanging; upper part of a woman standing frontal, head to left; then part of a leaf to left of the handle, above). [Shefton]. See pp. 621–7 no. 7.

NEAR THE VILLA GIULIA PAINTER

ARV.[1] 407.

PELIKE

1 (l 49). ATHENS 1595 (CC. 1279), from Attica. A, two women; B, the like.

WHITE LEKYTHOI
(standard shape)

2 (1). NEW YORK 06.1021.134. Warrior leaving home (warrior and woman).

3. LONDON D 20, from Gela. Murray *WAV.* pl. 22; Riezler 34; Lane pl. 90, a; ph. Ma. Seated woman. Second white used, spoiling the drawing as usual.

WHITE ALABASTRA

4 (2). ATHENS, Vlasto, fr., from Athens. A, woman; B, woman taking wool from a basket. The lower half of the vase remains.

5. TÜBINGEN E 50, fr. A, woman; B, woman.

RHYTON

6. FLORENCE, fr. (Hand of male to right, holding stick).

CUPS

7. BARCELONA 16. ix. 1912, fr., from Ampurias. I, (maeander). A, (lower part of male in himation standing frontal). I do not know if this might

belong either to Barcelona 514 and 520 (p. 626 no. 106) or to Barcelona 474 and 4315 (p. 626 no. 109).

8. ATHENS, Agora, P 17788, fr., from Athens. A, komos (head of a youth playing the flute).

Also related to the Villa Giulia Painter, the

LEKYTHOS
(standard shape)

ATHENS 1342 (CC. 1407), from Tanagra. Woman holding a wreath.

Two fragments recall the Villa Giulia Painter:

BELL-KRATER

1. REGGIO, fr. (two joining), from Locri. (Feet of maenad standing to right, shanks, feet, and tail of satyr moving to right; leftward stopped maeander.)

FRAGMENT OF A POT

2. REGGIO, fr., from Locri. (Breast to buttocks of a satyr moving to right, with the left arm to past the elbow, and the top of the tail). From a bell-krater?

The following bears some resemblance to the cups by the Villa Giulia Painter:

CUP

LAON 37.1059. *CV.* pl. 45, 1, 3 and 5–6. A, youth with lyre; A, youth with flute-case and two youths with lyres; B, youth with lyre and two youths.

The following are stiff and feeble imitations:

LEKYTHOS
(standard shape)

1. OXFORD 322, from Gela. Gardner pl. 18, 1, whence Richter *F.* fig. 132 and Swindler fig. 331; *CV.* pl. 37, 1–2. Herakles, Deianeira, and Hyllos. Restored.

HYDRIA

2. OXFORD 295. Gardner pl. 18, 2, whence Farnell *Cults* 4 pl. 39; *CV.* pl. 32, 10. Apollo with Artemis and Leto. Small.

THE PAINTER OF LONDON E 798

Bad imitations of the Villa Giulia Painter.

RHYTA
(lion's head)

1 (1). LONDON E 798, from Nola. *CV.* pl. 41, 4. Three youths.
2. LONDON E 797, from Nola. *CV.* pl. 41, 3. Three youths.

THE CHICAGO PAINTER

VA. 154–7. *Att. V.* 353–5 and 477. *V.Pol.* 48 and 80. *ARV.*[1] 407–10 and 960.

Named after no. 4.

Follower of the Villa Giulia Painter (p. 618), whose art he continues in a somewhat freer and tenderer form.

VOLUTE-KRATERS

1. FERRARA, T. 19 C VP, from Spina. Alfieri and Arias S. pll. 50–53; A, *St. etr.* 25, suppl., pl. 1; *Mostra* pll. 85–86; Alfieri and Arias *S.G.* pl. 62 and cover. Warrior leaving home. On the neck: A, fight (horse and foot); B, youths with spears pursuing women. See p. 1662.

2 (a). LENINGRAD, frr., from Eltegen. Part, *CR.* 1877 pl. 4, 4–10, whence *WV.* 1890–1 pl. 11, 2; *RM.* 21 pll. 3–4. A, death of Argos. B, (Nike, males). For the subject of A, recognized by Benndorf, see Ducati in *RM.* 21, 98–110.

COLUMN-KRATER
(with framed pictures)

3 (18). VILLA GIULIA 3589, from Falerii. *CV.* pl. 9, 3–4; A, ph. Al. A, satyrs and maenad; B, the like.

STAMNOI

4 (1). CHICAGO 89.22, from Capua. Frickenhaus *Len.* pl. 4; A, Herford pl. 1, d. A–B, Lenaia: A, maenads; B, maenads.

5 (2, +). LOUVRE G 409. A, *Annali* 1862 pl. D, whence Frickenhaus *Len.* 12 no. 24; A, Pottier pl. 142; *CV.* d pl. 15, 3 and 8 and pl. 16, 3; side, ph. Gir., whence Jacobsthal *O.* pl. 102, d. Lenaia: A, maenads; B, maenads. Seven unpublished fragments in the Louvre belong, one of them giving the head and shoulders of the right-hand woman on A; the others, bits of drapery and of floral. Restored.

6. MARKET. A, Lenaia (woman to right, putting a ladle into a stamnos, one of two stamnoi standing on a table in front of the idol of Dionysos, woman seated to left playing the flute); B, three maenads. [Shefton].

7 (3). OXFORD 1929.779. A, maenads; B, maenads.

8 (4). BOSTON 01.8083, from Capua. CB. i pl. 16; the shape, Caskey G. 96. A, maenads; B, maenads.

9. ST. LOUIS 20.15.51. *Bull. City Art Mus.* 40, 17–23. A, maenads; B, maenads. [Diepolder, Bothmer]. See p. 1662.

10 (5). LEIPSIC T 670, fr. (Maenad).

11 (6). CERVETRI, from Cervetri. A, maenads; B, maenads.

12 (7). CERVETRI, frr., from Cervetri. (Women).

13 (8). OXFORD 1914.16, fr., from Greece. *CV.* pl. 50, 11. (Dionysos).

14 (9). CRACOW inv. 1081. *V. Pol.* pl. 21, 2 and pl. 22, whence (detail) Seltman pl. 36, a; side, Jacobsthal O. pl. 103, a; *CV.* pl. 11, 1. A, arming. B, king, woman and youth. Slightly restored.

15 (10). LOUVRE G 418, from near Nola. *CV.* d pl. 20, 7 and 9. A, youth leaving home. B, three women. Restored.

16 (11). OXFORD 1911.619, from Cervetri. *CV.* pl. 27, 3–4 and pl. 30, 7–8, and (augmented by fragments ex Leipsic, Oxford, Heidelberg, and Frankfort) pl. 60, 1–4. A, youth with spears (Theseus?) pursuing a woman. B, king and women.

17 (12). DRESDEN (augmented by fragments ex Leipsic, Oxford, Heidelberg, and Frankfort, see *CV.* Oxford p. 113; a good big fragment in Goettingen, H 39, also belongs), from Cervetri. A, youth with spears (Theseus?) pursuing a woman. B, three women.

18 (13). HEIDELBERG (B 107), fr. (Nose to breast, and left forearm, of woman standing to right). I do not know whether this fragment belongs to the last.

19 (14). BOSTON 01.8082, from Capua. Details, *VA.* 155 and 157, whence (one figure) Seltman pl. 35, a; CB. i pl. 17; side, Jacobsthal O. pl. 104, d; shape, Caskey G. 97. A, komos; B, komos.

19 *bis*. CAPE TOWN 14 (ex Forman 351). A, komos; B, komos. See p. 1662.

BELL-KRATERS

20 (15). BOSTON 10.215, fr. A, (warrior).

21 (16). TÜBINGEN inv. 1569, fr. Woman (standing to right: head and fingers remain). ALKIM[A+OႽ] ΚΑLOႽ.

CALYX-KRATERS OR BELL-KRATERS

22 (17). NEW YORK 17.230.23, fr. Part, Richter *ARVS.* fig. 99, whence LS. fig. 114. (On the right, woman). [Richter].

22 *bis*. REGGIO, fr., from Locri. (Apollo: head, to right, and cithara, remain, with part of the floral border above). ΑΓΟL[LON].

PELIKAI

(nos. 23–28, the pictures not framed)

23 (19). LECCE 570, from Rugge. A, FR. pl. 66, 2, whence Buschor 195, Swindler fig. 339, 2, Schuchhardt and Technau 291; *CV.* pl. 1, 3–4, pl. 2,

3-4, pl. 2, 2-3, and pl. 4, 2-3; A, Buschor *G. Vasen* 189; A, Bielefeld *ZV.* pl. 13 fig. 15; A, Bernardini pl. 38; A, *E.A.A.* ii, 550; A, R. M. Cook pl. 45. A, Polyneikes and Eriphyle. B, youth and woman. See p. 1662.

24 (20). PALERMO 1109, from Agrigento. *Mon.* 2 pl. 17. A, Hermes with the infant Dionysos; B, two women (nymphs of Nysa).

25 (21). LONDON E 383, from Vulci. A, *VA.* 156. A, Apollo and Artemis. B, two women.

26 (22). CAB. MÉD. 394, from Vulci. De Ridder pl. 14 and p. 289. A, youths leaving home: A, youth with phiale and helmet, woman with oinochoe and spear; B, youth with spears and woman with wreath.

27. NAPLES, Astarita, 147. A, goddess and woman (woman standing to right, holding wreath, woman with sprig and sceptre standing frontal). A, male and woman.

28 (23). MARSEILLES, from Saint Mauront. A, Clerc 312, 3 and 1; *R.E.A.* 1940 pl. 1, c. A, two maenads. B, two youths.

(no. 29, the pictures framed; small)

29 (24). LONDON E 361. Hancarville 2 pl. 42 and 4 pl. 88; Kirk pl. 9. A, leaving home (or returning: youth and woman). B, old man and youth.

HYDRIAI

30 (25). NAPLES 3161, from Nola. Gargiulo *Recueil* (1845) 2 pl. 47; *AZ.* 1845 pl. 29; *Mus. Borb.* 2 pl. 29, whence *El.* 2 pl. 28; Angelini pl. 20; ph. So. x, iii, 1. Judgement of Paris (Paris, Athena, and Hermes).

31 (a 1). MUNICH 2432 (J. 340), from Vulci. Inghirami pl. 35, whence *El.* 3 pl. 50, *WV.* 4 pl. 7, 4, and Cook *Zeus* i, 217; FR. pl. 106, 1. Triptolemos with Demeter and Persephone. See p. 1663.

32 (26). NEW YORK 06.1021.192, from Campania (probably Curti or Capua). Sambon *Canessa* pl. 8, 99; Richter and Hall pl. 105 and pl. 172, 103; the shape, Hambidge 103. Youth with spears (Theseus?) pursuing a woman.

33 (27). NEW YORK 06.1021.190, from Campania (probably Curti or Capua). Sambon *Canessa* pl. 8, 100; *Burl. Mag.* 9, pl. at p. 208 fig. 6; Hambidge 100 and plate there; back, Richter *Craft* 22 fig. 29; *N.Y. Shapes* 13, 1–2 = Richter and Milne figs. 83–84; Richter and Hall pl. 104 and pl. 172, 102. Youth with spears (Theseus?) pursuing a woman.

34 (30). LONDON E 199, from Nola. *CV.* pl. 82, 4. Eos and Kephalos.

35 (28). ZURICH, Roš, from Capua or Curti. *Sg Ruesch* pl. 6. Three women.

36 (29). ZURICH, Roš, from Capua or Curti. *Sg Ruesch* pl. 5. Three women.

OINOCHOAI
(shape 4)

37 (31). BOSTON 13.197, from Gela. CB. i pl. 18, 40; the shape, Caskey *G.* 143. Satyr and maenad.

38 (32). BOSTON 13.196, from Gela. CB. i pl. 18, 41, whence Rumpf *MZ.* pl. 31, 4; the shape, Caskey G. 142. Greek and Persian.

39 (33). BOSTON 13.191, from Gela. CB. i pl. 18, 42, whence Buschor G. *Vasen* 188; the shape, Caskey G. 141. Two athletes. ΛΛΚΙΜΑ+ΟΣ ΚΑΛΟΣ.

40 (34). BOSTON 13.192, from Gela. CB. i pl. 18, 43; the shape, Caskey G. 140. Komos (man and youth). +ΑΙΡΙΣ ΚΑΛΟΣ.

LEKYTHOS
(standard shape)

41. HERAKLEION, from Kydonia. Woman with phiale and woman with oinochoe. [Shefton].

PYXIS
(type A)

42. BRAURON, fr., from Brauron. Part, *Prakt.* 1949, 88 fig. 17; part, *BCH.* 1950, 302; part, Ghali-Kahil *H.* pl. 63, 2. Menelaos and Helen. Papadimitriou has added a fragment on the left, giving more of Menelaos.

CUP

43 (35). LONDON E 88, from Nola. *Mém. Ac. Inscr.* 1838 pl. 9, 1, whence Daremberg and Saglio s.v. turibulum fig. 7178; *AJA.* 1939, 250. I, woman at thurible.

A lost vase, shape unknown, may well be by the Chicago Painter:

Once NAPLES, Hamilton. Tischbein 1 pl. 37. Satyr and maenad. ΛΛΚΙ-ΜΑΧΩΣ ΚΑΛΩΣ.

NEAR THE CHICAGO PAINTER
ARV.[1] 410.
STAMNOS

1. MINNEAPOLIS, Walker Art Center, 18. 2 (ex Jekyll). A, maenads; B, maenads. Compare a pelike in Marseilles (p. 630 no. 28).

COLUMN-KRATER
(with framed pictures)

2. LOUVRE C 10769. A, Dionysos and maenads; B, the like.

HYDRIA
(with picture on the shoulder, framed)

3. MONTREAL MARKET (Diniacopoulos). Warriors leaving home, with women and Nike (Nike to right, holding untied wreath, woman in peplos with oinochoe, altar, young warrior with phiale; woman to right with phiale, man in chlamys and petasos, one foot set on a rock).

CUP

4 (3). BOLOGNA 455, from Bologna. Zannoni pl. 29, 11–12; *Mostra* pl. 44; *CV.* pl. 110, 4. I, maenad. May be by the Lyandros Painter (p. 835).

The following is a bad imitation of the Chicago Painter:

PELIKE

LONDON E 382, from Vulci. A, Jahn *Arch. Aufsätze* pl. 2, whence Roscher s.v. Telephos 303 fig. 14; A, Pollak *Zwei* pl. 6, whence (redrawn!) Séchan 126; A, Powell *New Chapters in Gk Lit.* pl. at p. 82; B.Ap. xxii. 5. A, Telephos and Agamemnon. B, satyr and maenad.

Another coarse piece might be described in much the same terms:

PELIKE

NEW YORK 06.1021.191, from Sicily. A, Sambon *Canessa* 64 and pl. 16, 232; A, McClees 78; A, Richter and Milne fig. 37; the shape, Hambidge 95. A, Apollo and Artemis. B, goddess and woman (Hera and Hebe?).

THE PAINTER OF NAPLES 3136

Stiff drawing, imitating, one would say, the Chicago Painter.

OINOCHOAI
(shape 2)

1. CHICAGO 07.12 (ex van Branteghem 93). Komast (youth with lyre).
2. NAPLES 3136, from Nola. Ph. So. 11069, iv, 2. Cup-bearer.

THE METHYSE PAINTER

VA. 160. *Att. V.* 363–4 and 477. *ARV.*[1] 410–11.

Named after a maenad on no. 3. Akin to the Chicago Painter.

LOUTROPHOROI

1. ATHENS, Acropolis Museum, frr., from Athens. Wedding (with chariot) of Admetos and Alcestis. Inscriptions ΑΛΚΕϚΤΙϚ, ΑϚϚΜΕΤΟϚ, ΑΠΟΛΛΩΝ, [ΑΡΤΕ]ΜΙϚ.
2. ATHENS, Acropolis Museum, fr., from Athens. On the neck, two women (one with torches, to right, the other frontal, head to left).

BELL-KRATERS

3 (1). NEW YORK 07.286.85, from Numana. A, Herford pl. 10, g; detail of A, *Hdbk Cl. Coll.* 127; Richter and Hall pll. 109–10 and pl. 171, 109; A, Bieber *HT.* 13 fig. 18; detail, Richter *ARVS.* fig. 78; A, Richter *H.* 228, b; part of A, Buschor *Bilderwelt* 48. Dionysos with satyrs and maenads.

4 (2, +). ATHENS Acr. 751, fr., from Athens. Langlotz pl. 64. A, Pappo-silenos with maenad and satyr. A new Athens fragment added by Mrs. Karouzou gives the middle of Papposilenos, who hugs his knee.

5 (3). SYRACUSE, two frr., from Camarina (P.M. sep. 901). A, (upper part of a woman standing frontal, head to right). B, (upper part of a woman, frontal, head to left).

CALYX-KRATERS

6 (4). BOLOGNA PU 285, from Vulci. Gerhard pl. 158; CV. pl. 77, above, and pl. 78. A, Theseus leaving home. B, three youths. Much restored (and not, as stated in the *Corpus*, 'well preserved'). See p. 1663.

7 (a). LOUVRE G 403. *Annali* 1860 pll. J-K; A, Pottier pl. 141; CV. d pl. 14, 1–2 and pl. 15, 5. A, Neoptolemos leaving Skyros (Neoptolemos, Lykomedes, and Deidameia). B, youth with woman and old man. Much restored.

STAMNOI

8 (5). LOUVRE G 410, from Vulci. CV. d pl. 16, 6 and 9 and pl. 17, 1–3; side, Jacobsthal O. pl. 104, c; A, ph. Gir. 19872. A, maenads; B, maenads.

9 (6). ROME, Torlonia, 78, from Vulci. A, maenads; B, maenads.

DINOS

10 (7). FERRARA, T. 374, fr., from Spina. Aurigemma² 239; one figure, ibid.¹ and ², title-page; Alfieri and Arias S. pll. 45–49; detail, *Mostra*, cover. Maenads. See p. 1663.

OINOCHOE

(*shape 3, chous*)

11 (8). LOUVRE G 440. *Magazin pittoresque* 1865, 148–9; BCH. 1895, 102; detail, Daremberg and Saglio s.v. cathedra, 970 fig. 1249. Three Muses (Kalliope, Melpomene, and Ourania). Restored.

Probably also by him:

BELL-KRATERS

1. ARGOS, from Argos. A, (Dionysos and satyr). B, (youth and woman). Shape and pattern-work are the same as in the bell-krater by Hermonax in Argos (p. 485 no. 23).

2. BASLE, Cahn, 7, two frr. On one, middle of male to right, naked, cloak over left shoulder, then part of a column; on the other, saccos of a seated woman, then head, shoulders, right hand of a king, holding a sceptre, to left.

BELL-KRATERS OR CALYX-KRATERS

3. STRASBURG, Univ., 772, fr., from Boeotia. (Woman).
4. BERLIN, fr., from Athens. *F. Benndorf* 306; *Jb.* 14, 165 fig. 5. (Woman). Trial-piece.

CALYX-KRATER

5. CINCINNATI, Semple, three frr. (ex Curtius). Two, *AJA.* 1950 pl. 21 and p. 120; all, Ghali-Kahil *H.* pl. 10. The third added by Bothmer. White ground. Paris and Helen.

The Eupolis Painter (p. 1072) and the Danae Painter (p. 1074) are connected with the Group of the Villa Giulia Painter.

BOOK VI

EARLY CLASSIC PAINTERS
OF SMALLER POTS

CHAPTER 37

EARLY CLASSIC PAINTERS OF
NOLANS AND LEKYTHOI

THE PROVIDENCE PAINTER

VA. 76–80. *Att. V.* 132–6 and 472. *V.Pol.* 16–17 and 79. *ARV.*[1] 431–7, 960, and 968. CB. ii, 41–45.

The Providence Painter, called after no. 1, is the best of those whose chief work, numerically speaking, was decorating Nolan amphorae and lekythoi: and he is a very good artist.

He must have been a pupil of the Berlin Painter.

In *ARV.*[1] 436–7 I put three small vases under the heading 'Painter of Athens 1806', but added that they were very like the Providence Painter and perhaps from his hand. They are in fact his and are included, with others like them, in the following list.

NECK-AMPHORAE
(nos. 1–2, large, with twisted handles)

1 (1). PROVIDENCE 15.005, from Vulci. Gerhard pl. 24, whence *El.* 2 pl. 13; cleaned, *CV.* pl. 18; *A, Bull. Rhode* 27, 32–33. A, Apollo; B, woman.

2 (2). VATICAN, from Vulci. *Mus. Greg.* 2 pl. 59, 2; A, ph. Al. 35813, whence Bieber *HT.* 2 fig. 2; A, ph. Marb. 29170. A, citharode; B, youth.

(nos. 3–46, Nolan amphorae, with triple handles)

3 (3). BRUNSWICK 257, from Capua. *Anz.* 1890, 8, 1; *CV.* pl. 20. A, Zeus; B, Giant.

4 (4). LONDON E 303, from Gela. A, *VA.* 77; *CV.* pl. 53, 3. A, Dionysos; B, Giant.

5 (5). DRESDEN 172. A, Apollo; B, woman.

6 (6). CAB. MÉD. 367, from Nola. Luynes pl. 24, whence *El.* 2 pl. 17. A, Apollo. B, youth. On A, ΚΑLΟΣ ΚΑLLΙΚLΕΣ.

7 (7). CAB. MÉD. 365, from Nola. Luynes pl. 25, whence *El.* 2 pl. 18. A, Artemis; B, woman with torch. On A, ΚΑLΟΣ ΛLΑVΚΟΝ.

8 (8). OXFORD 1917.59. A, Tillyard pl. 11, 89; cleaned, *CV.* pl. 17, 4 and pl. 18, 1. A, Poseidon; B, woman.

9 (9). FLORENCE PD 454, fr. A, Poseidon.

10 (10). VIENNA 652. A, Sichtermann *Ganymed* pl. 2, 4; A, *Ant. Kunst* 2 pl. 10, 4; *CV.* pl. 58, 1–2 and pl. 59, 1. A, Zeus and Ganymede; B, boy fleeing.

11 (11). AMSTERDAM inv. 1754, from Ruvo. *CV.* Scheurleer pl. 4, 3–4. A, Zeus pursuing a woman; B, man with sceptre. On A, ΚΑLΟΣ ΛLΑV-ΚΟΝ.

12 (12). CAB. MÉD. 368. De Ridder 269 and pl. 12. A, Zeus pursuing, B, a woman.

13 (13). BERLIN MARKET (Graupe: ex Prinz Albrecht, 913). A, Zeus pursuing, B, a woman. Much restored: the lower parts of both figures modern.

14 (14). BOSTON 03.789, fr. CB. ii, suppl. pl. 11, 3. A, Zeus pursuing a woman (Thetis). ΚΑLΟΣ and retr. ΗΙΓΓΟΝΚΑLΟΣ. See CB. ii, 44–45.

15. LONDON MARKET (Spink: ex Leathes). A, Eros pursuing a youth (who holds a lyre); B, youth fleeing. Destroyed by enemy action; some fragments are in Reading.

16 (15). CAB. MÉD. 359. Luynes pl. 41. A, woman with hydria (Amymone?—or rather one of her companions) fleeing to man with sceptre (Danaos?); B, woman fleeing. See CB. ii, 91.

17 (16). WARSAW 142336 (ex Czartoryski 39). De Witte pl. 7; detail, *V.Pol.* pl. 28, 3; *CV.* pl. 22, 1. A, Eos and Kephalos; B, man with sceptre running up.

18 (a 5). CAB. MÉD. 362. Luynes pl. 39. Eos and Tithonos; B, boy fleeing. On A, ΚΑLΟΣ +ΑΡΜΙΔΕΣ.

19 (17). BOLOGNA 158, from Bologna. Zannoni pl. 102, 5–7. A, uncertain subject: Athena and (Hephaistos?); B, man with sceptre. See p. 1663.

20 (18). PHILADELPHIA L. 64.40, from Nola. A, *Bull. Univ. Mus.* 5 pl. 4, 2. A, Athena and youth (Theseus?); B, man with sceptre.

21 (19). LONDON E 305, from Nola. *El.* 1 pl. 86; A, Walters *H.A.P.* pl. 36, 3; *CV.* pl. 54, 2. A, Athena; B, youth.

22 (20). OXFORD 277, from Gela. *CV.* pl. 17, 2 and pl. 18, 7. A, Athena; B, man with sceptre.

23 (a 6). LENINGRAD 698 (St. 1690). A, Athena; B, woman. On A, KΛLOϞ
NIKON.

24 (a 7). VATICAN. A, woman running (to left, looking round); B, woman
with sceptre (goddess?). The chiton-folds on B are unusual for the
painter—as if the drawing had been finished off by someone else.

25. NAPLES, Astarita, 104, fr. A, youth setting out; B, youth. The upper
part remains: on A, frontal, looking back to left, right arm extended,
spears in left hand; on B, in himation, standing to left, right arm extended. On A, KΛLOϞ.

26 (21). Once FRANKFORT, Passavant-Gontard, 38. A, *Sg Passavant-Gontard*
pl. 6, 38. A, Nike and warrior. B, youth.

27 (22). FRANKFORT, Städel Institut. Schaal *F.* pl. 47. Return of youth: A,
Nike and youth; B, woman.

28 (23). LENINGRAD 701 (St. 1732). A, *VA.* 79. A, Nike; B, goddess. On
A, KΛLOϞ HIΓΓO+ϞENOϞ.

29 (24). VIENNA 698. La Borde 2 pl. 37 and pl. 35, 3, whence (A) Panofka
Eigennamen pl. 3, 1, (A) *El.* 1 pl. 98; *CV.* pl. 58, 5 and pl. 59, 2. A, Nike
with cithara; B, youth. On A, TIMONIΔEϞ KΛLOϞ.

30. NAPLES (ex Spinelli 2144), from Suessula. B, Philippart *It.* ii pl. 6, vi,
middle. A, Dionysos; B, satyr. On A, moving to right, looking round,
with oinochoe and thyrsus; B, moving to right with oinochoe.

31 (25). FULDA, Welz. A, Neugebauer *ADP.* pl. 70, 164. A, Dionysos
and satyr; B, maenad. [Neugebauer].

32 (26). NAPLES 3081, from Nola. A, ph. So. 11072, iii, 2. A, satyr and
maenad; B, satyr.

33 (27). VIENNA 740. *CV.* pl. 58, 3–4. A, satyr and maenad; B, satyr.

34 (28). MUNICH 2335 a, from Capua? A, Vorberg *Gloss.* 95, 2 and p. 752;
CV. pl. 53, 1–2 and pl. 56, 1–2. A, satyr assaulting donkey; B, satyr (to
the rescue?).

35 (29). NEW YORK 06.1021.114, from Capua. *Vente 11 mai 1903*, 34 and pl.
1, 17; Sambon *Canessa* 34, 102; B, *VA.* 78; detail of B, Richter *Craft* 37;
Richter and Hall pl. 31 and pl. 169, 32. A, satyr; B, maenad.

36 (30). CERVETRI, from Cervetri. A, satyr; B, maenad. On A, to left; on
B, running to right, looking round, with thyrsus and branch.

37. PARIS, Niarchos. *B. K. Hirsch* pl. 13, 24. A, satyr; B, satyr.

38 (31). LEYDEN PC 86 (xviii h 39), from Vulci. *Oudhed. Mededelingen* 42
pl. 13, a–b. A, youth attacking with sword. B, youth.

39 (32). LOUVRE G 216, from Nola. *CV.* pl. 41, 1–3 and pl. 40, 9. A, youth
attacking with sword; B, man (retreating?) with stone.

40 (33). MUNICH 2339 (J. 259), from South Italy. *CV.* pl. 53, 3–4 and pl.
56, 3–4. Komos (A, man with lyre; B, man).

41 (34). OXFORD 1927.2, from Gela. *CV.* pl. 58, 1–2 and pl. 52, 10–11. Komos (A, man; B, youth). See p. 644.

42 (a 4). BALTIMORE, Walters Art Gallery, 48.54. A, woman running. B, youth.

43. NEW HAVEN, Watkins. A and part of B, *A.A.A.* pl. 84, 277a, and pl. 82, 277b. A, woman seated, and man; B, man. [Bothmer].

44 (a 1). NEW YORK, Gallatin. A, *Cat. Sotheby April 2 1928* pl. 5, 1; *CV.* pl. 53, 2. A, discus-thrower; B, trainer. See p. 1663.

45 (a 2). OXFORD 1914.732. *CV.* pl. 17, 5 and pl. 18, 6. A, man with helmet and spear; B, youth with spear. As the next.

46 (a 3). MUNICH 2335 b and ERLANGEN 244 d. The Munich part, *CV.* pl. 54. A, Zeus; B, Hermes. As the last.

(no. 47: probably a Nolan amphora)

47. BOSTON 03.875, fr. CB. ii, suppl. pl. 11, 1. (God or king). . . . ON-ICALOS.

(no. 48: small, with ridged handles: see CB. ii, 40 no. 4)

48. BRUSSELS R 339. A, *L'Acropole* July–Dec. 1930 pl. 1, 2; *CV.* pl. 15, 1; A, *Bull. Mus. Roy.* 1956, 11. A, boy singing and man seated playing the flute; B, boy.

(no. 49: squat, with convex handles)

49 (35). NAPLES 3176, from Ruvo. A, ph. So. 11009, v, 2. Komos: A, man with lyre; B, man. They are 'Anacreontics' and should be added to the list in CB. ii, 58–60.

AMPHORA OR NECK-AMPHORA (OR PANATHENAIC AMPHORA?)

50. NAPLES, Astarita, 119, and FLORENCE 13 B 61, two frr. The Florence part, *CV.* pl. 13, B 61 (wrongly ascribed to the Triptolemos Painter in *ARV.*[1] 194 no. 22). A, citharode (Apollo?: neck, left arm and breast, cithara, remain); B, Nike (to right, with oinochoe and phiale.) The Florence fragment joins two of the Astarita, one of which gives the upper part of Nike, the other her right heel and part of her chiton. All three Astarita fragments were assigned to the painter by Bothmer. A Florence fragment, with wings, may belong to B.

PANATHENAIC AMPHORAE
(no. 51, large)

51 (36). BOULOGNE 196. Pottier *Mus. prov.* pl. 22. A, Nike; B, man.

(no. 52, small)

52 (37). BARI 1401, from Apulia. A, Nike; B, goddess (Hera?).

PELIKE

53 (38). CAB. MÉD. 392, from Agrigento. Politi *Ill. di un vaso fittile* pll. 1–2; *Annali* 1833 pll. B–C; Luynes pl. 26, whence *El.* 2 pl. 47; phs. Gir. 8083, 29136, and 29265. A, Apollo and Nike; B, Nike.

STAMNOI

54 (39). LOUVRE G 370. *Mon.* 6–7 pl. 58, 2, whence (the Apollo) Overbeck *KM.* pl. 19, 28; Pottier pl. 138; *CV.* d pl. 10, 1, 4, 6, and 8, and pl. 11, 4. A, Zeus and Nike; Apollo and Hera; B, Athena, Poseidon, Hermes; Plouton and goddess (Persephone). Restored. A Louvre fragment joins, adding part of Plouton's breast and cornucopia, with the right arm of the goddess facing him. See p. 1663.

55 (40). BARCELONA 589, from Ampurias. A, Bosch Gimpera *Etn.* 316 fig. 274; A, Bosch Gimpera *L'art grec a Catalunya* fig. 40; A, Bosch Gimpera, Serra-Ràfols, and del Castillo 39, 1; García y Bellido pl. 106; part, Menendez Pidal i, ii, 576. Fight: Achilles and Hector.

56 (41). LENINGRAD 640 (St. 1641), and LOUVRE. *Annali* 1859 pl. G–H, whence (A) Jacobsthal *Theseus* pl. 3, 6. Herakles entering Olympus. Very much restored. The unpublished fragment in the Louvre gives the left elbow of Herakles with part of his bow, quiver, scabbard, the right forearm and hand of Athena with the greater part of her helmet.

57 (42). LONDON, fr., from Gela. (Female head to left, minus the forehead and chin).

58 (43). PARIS, Petit Palais, 316, from Capua. Lenormant *Coll. Dutuit* pl. 17; *CV.* pl. 16, and pl. 17, 1–3. A, Poseidon pursuing a woman (probably Aithra); B, women running to king.

59. NAPLES, Astarita, 111, and FLORENCE 6 B 44, two frr. The Florence part, *CV.* pl. 6, B 44. Peleus and Thetis. One of the two Astarita fragments joins the Florence, adding the right arm of Thetis, the back of Peleus, and, on the left, chin to thigh of a Nereid running to right, then part of the handle-floral. The other Astarita fragment has a foot to right and the lower part of a Nereid running to left.

COLUMN-KRATER
(*with framed pictures*)

60 (44). BOLOGNA 257, from Bologna. A, Hermes pursuing a woman. B, komos.

NUPTIAL LEBES
(*type 1*)

61 (48). ATHENS, Agora, P 4841, fr., from Athens. On the stand, Zeus, Athena, and a god (Hermes?). [Talcott].

HYDRIAI
(*with picture on the body*)
(*nos. 62–63, the picture framed*)

62 (45). WARSAW 142460 (ex Czartoryski inv. 160), from Capua. Fröhner *Gol.* 87; *V.Pol.* pl. 13, 1; *CV.* pl. 21, 1. Zeus with Athena and Nike.

63 (46). WARSAW 142331 (ex Czartoryski inv. 161), from Capua. Fröhner *Gol.* 89; *V.Pol.* pl. 13, 2; *CV.* pl. 21, 2. Apollo and Muses.

(no. 64: not known if the picture framed)

64 (47). ATHENS E 14, fr. (Zeus, seated).

(no. 65: the picture not framed)

65. MYKONOS, fr., from Rheneia (originally from Delos). Dugas *Délos xxi* pl. 26, 65. Two standing at an altar (god—or goddess?—and woman?).

OINOCHOE
(shape 1)

66 (81). MUNICH 2448 (J. 771), from Sicily. *CV.* pl. 84, 2–3, pl. 86, 2–3, and pl. 92, 2. Satyr and maenad.

LEKYTHOI
(nos. 67–111, red-figured)
(nos. 67–99, standard shape)

67 (49). PALERMO V 674, from Gela. *CV.* pl. 21, 5. Warrior leaving home (warrior and woman).

68 (50). Once ROUEN, Bellon, 53. *Gaz. arch.* 1876 pl. 34. Young warrior pursuing a woman. Restored.

69 (51). Once ZURICH, Kleist. Young warrior with sword pursuing a woman. Much restored.

70. HAVANA, Lagunillas. Youth with spear pursuing a woman. Restored.

71 (52). OXFORD 1920.103. *CV.* pl. 38, 8. Youth with sword pursuing a woman (Theseus and Aithra?).

72 (53). GELA (ex Navarra-Jacona), from Gela. Benndorf pl. 49, 5. Woman binding her hair, and maid.

73 (a 8). CATANIA 717. Passeri pl. 204; Libertini pl. 82. Dionysos.

73 *bis.* LONDON MARKET (Hewett). Apollo and Artemis (she hastening to right with oinochoe, he frontal, head to left, with phiale and cithara). [Hecht].

74 (56). BOSTON 95.45, from Thebes. CB. ii pl. 46, 88; shape, Caskey G. 219 no. 173. Apollo. HIΓΓONKALOϞ. See CB. ii, 42.

75 (55). BOSTON 95.43, from Thebes. *VA.* 75 fig. 45; *Class. Studies Capps* 245 fig. 4; CB. ii pl. 46, 89. Athena. HIΓΓONKALOϞ. See CB. ii, 42–43.

76 (54). BOSTON 95.44, from Thebes. *Class. Studies Capps* 245 fig. 5; CB. ii pl. 46, 90; the shape, Caskey G. 215. Wedding of Menelaos and Helen. HIΓ[Γ]ONKALOϞ. See CB. ii, 43–44; and below, p. 1663.

77 (57). NEW YORK 41.162.18. *CV.* Gallatin pl. 58, 4 and pl. 61, 3; *Bull. Metr.* 37, 56; detail, Richter *ARVS.* fig. 54; Richter *H.* 216, a. Artemis. On the shoulder, Nike.

78 (58). OXFORD 1939.73, from Attica. Artemis.

79 (59). NICOSIA M 41.11, from Marion. *S.C.E.* ii pl. 144, 2 and 3 and pl. 53. Goddess (Hera). See *Cypr.* 39–40.

80 (60). PALERMO V 675, from Gela. *CV.* pl. 21, 4.   Nike (or Iris).

81 (61). SYRACUSE, fr.   (Head and shoulders of Nike).

82 (62). LONDON E 572, from Gela. *VA.* 76.   Woman running with spear and helmet.

83 (63). PALERMO V 676, from Gela. *CV.* pl. 21, 6; ph. R.I. 7321.   Woman running with corslet.   IΛSIMΛXOS ΚΛLOS.

84 (64). OXFORD 317, from Gela.   Gardner pl. 25, 3; *CV.* pl. 34, 4.   Woman running with spear and shield.

85 (65). GELA (ex Navarra-Jacona), from Gela.   Benndorf pl. 49, 1.   Woman running with oinochoe and phiale.

86 (66). SYRACUSE 21971, from Gela. *ML.* 17 pl. 12, whence Perrot 10, 651; Matt 88, left; ph. Al. 33388, 1.   Woman laying her himation on a chair.

87 (67). OXFORD 1925.68, from Gela. *Coll. B. et C.* pl. 20, 165; *CV.* pl. 34, 1.   Woman putting lid on basket.

88. LAON 37.954. *CV.* pl. 40, 2 and 4, and pl. 41, 2.   Woman with alabastron and mirror.

89 (68). ATHENS, Agora, P 583, fr., from Athens.   (Head of youth or woman).

90 (69). NEW YORK 07.286.67. *VA.* 75 fig. 44; Norman Gardiner *Athl.* fig. 11; Richter and Hall pl. 30 and pl. 175, 3; details, Richter *ARVS.* 64 fig. 25 and p. 65 fig. 28.   Nike with prize hydria.   HIΓΓONΚΛLOS.

91 (70). GELA (ex Navarra-Jacona), from Gela.   Benndorf pl. 48, 1.   Nike.   HIΓΓON ΚΛLOS.

92 (71). FLORENCE MARKET.   Nike (flying to right, holding her garments with both hands).   NIΚE.

93 (72). ATHENS 12890 (N. 1066), from Eretria. *CV.* pl. 10, 5–6; ph. A.I. NM 1093, whence Bieber *G.K.* pl. 9, 3; Zadoks-Jitta pl. 85, 6.   Woman laying her himation on a chair.

94 (73). OXFORD 1938.313, fr. from Al Mina.   Part, *JHS.* 59, 7, 21.   Woman running.   A fragment added later shows that the thing held is not a basket.

95. SAN SIMEON, Hearst Corporation, 9893.   Woman fleeing (to right, looking round).

96 (74). RIEHEN, Druey (ex Fröhlich).   Schefold *M.* 187, 211 a.   Woman fleeing (to left, looking round, lifting her skirt with both hands).

97 (75). BOSTON 00.341, from Gela. CB. ii pl. 46, 87.   Eros.   See CB. ii, 41.

98. BASLE, Cahn, 11, fr.   Man in chlamys (upper part, head to right: Hermes?).

98 *bis.* LEYDEN 1960.7.2. *Ars Ant. Aukt. II* pl. 60, 154; *Oudhed. Mededelingen* 42 pl. 13, c.   Hunter (or light-armed).   Black shoulder-palmettes as in no. 99.

99 (78). LONDON 67.5-8.1067. Woman running with oinochoe and phiale to altar.

(*nos. 100–11, small; secondary shape*)

100. DUNEDIN 48.223. Woman running, looking round.

100 *bis*. PADULA, from Padula. Maenad (running to left, looking round, right arm extended, thyrsus in left hand).

(*nos. 101–7 form a group, distinguished by the drawing of the maeander above the picture; see also p. 645*)

101 (76). PALERMO, from Selinus. Thracian woman (extract from a Death of Orpheus: see CB. ii, 74 no. 9).

102 (77). ANCONA 5248, from Numana. Nike.

103. NEW YORK MARKET (Hirsch). Nike (moving to right, with phiale and oinochoe).

104 (79). NEW YORK 41.162.117. *CV.* Gallatin pl. 26, 8, whence *Op. ath.* I, 84 fig. 5. Woman running with torches.

105. MUNICH inv. 8734. *Anz.* 1957, 387. Warrior attacking.

106. ATHENS 17200. *CV.* pl. 12, 8–9. Woman holding sash. [Karouzou].

106 *bis*. LENINGRAD B 2640. Woman (Nereid) running with helmet and spear. [Peredolskaya].

107. ROME, Accademia dei Lincei, 2478. Minervini *Barone* pl. 12, 3; *JHS.* 72 pl. 8, 3. Woman feeding dog.

(*nos. 108–111 form another group; very small and late; see also p. 646*)

108. SYRACUSE 14632, from Gela. Woman running.

109. SYRACUSE 14633, from Gela. Woman seated.

110. TÜBINGEN Z 119, from Greece. Woman with phialai at mound-altar.

111. LIPARI, T. 135, from Lipari. Woman running, looking round (in peplos, grasping her wrap with one hand).

(*nos. 112–23, white*)

(*nos. 112–17, standard shape*)

112 (80). OXFORD 548. *JHS.* 25, 76. Woman running with box. Second white used. Restored.

113. ATHENS 1828 (CC. 1020), from Eretria. *Jb.* 2, 163; *CV.* Jb pl. 1, 8. Youth setting out. ΛΛΑVΚΟΝ ΚΑΛΟϟ. Class BL (see p. 675).

114. GREIFSWALD 363, from Athens. Peters pl. 41. Nike. ΛΛΑVΚΟΝ ΚΑΛΟϟ. Second white used. Class BL. Already compared by Peters with Athens 1806 (no. 118).

115 (a). SYRACUSE 21146, from Gela. *ML.* 17 pl. 24, 1, whence *Jb.* 26, 178. Woman running with oinochoe and phiale. ΕΛΑΙΟΝ ΚΑΛΟϟ. Second white used. As Lyons E 413 (no. 116).

116 (a). LYŌNS E 413. Ph. R.I. 7412, 3; ph. Arch. phot. BAA 38. Goddess (Hera) with phiale and sceptre at altar. ΙCΑΛΟϞ ΕΛΑΙΟΝ. Second white used. As Syracuse 21146 (no. 115). The name may be Euaion, although in both vases the second letter of the name is written like a lambda.

117 (a 9). LONDON 1900.7–27.4. Hermes.

(nos. 118–23, secondary shapes, although sometimes close to standard)

118. ATHENS 1806 (CC. 1021), from near Athens. *AM.* 32 Beil. 2, 11, whence *Op. ath.* 1, 84 fig. 4. Nike. ΛΛΑVΙCΟΝ ΙCΑΛΟϞ.

119. ATHENS 15876. *Boll. di storia dell'arte* 2 figs. 82–83 at p. 113. Woman spinning top.

120. ATHENS, Vlasto, from Thorikos. Youth setting out. ΙCΑΛΟϞ ΛΛΑV-ΚΟΝ.

120 *bis*. LONDON MARKET (Hewett). *Cat. Sotheby 5 March 1962* pl. at p. 29. Goddess (Hera) seated (to left, with phiale and upright sceptre; behind her an Ionic column). ΙCΑΛΟϞ and below it ΛΛΑVΙCΟΝ.

121. ATHENS (ex Stathatou). *Op. ath.* 1, 81. Goddess (Hera) seated. ΚΑΛΟϞ ΛΛΑVΚΟΝ. Put by Holmberg with Athens 1806 (no. 118) and other vases.

122. Once LONDON, Rogers, 314, from Athens. Moses *Englefield*, suppl. pl. 7, and pl. 8, 3, whence *Op. ath.* 1, 83. Woman seated at wool-basket. ΙC[ΑΛΟϞ] ΛΛΑVΙC[Ο]Ν. Put by Holmberg with Athens 1806 (no. 118) and other vases.

123. CASTELVETRANO, from Selinus. Woman seated at wool-basket, with wreath. ΛΛΑVΙCΟΝ ΙCΑΛΟϞ.

FRAGMENTS OF POTS

124 (84). BRYN MAWR P 238, fr. *AJA.* 1916, 340, 13. (Herakles, shield).

125 (85). SYRACUSE, fr. (Upper part of a youth's head to right). From a neck-amphora?

126. GREIFSWALD 356, fr. Peters pl. 40. (Woman fleeing). From a pelike according to Peters.

SKYPHOS
(type A)

127 (86). ROMAN MARKET (Pollak: ex Barberini). Passeri pl. 82. A, athlete with haltēres; B, trainer.

CUPS
(no. 128, decorated outside as well as in)

128 (87). ATHENS Acr. 352, from Athens. Langlotz pll. 27–28. I, (Apollo). A–B, Herakles entering Olympus. A new Athens fragment belongs: outside, (part of a sceptre and of one in a himation).

(*nos. 129–35, decorated inside only*)

129 (88). VILLA GIULIA 3590, from Falerii. *CV*. pl. 38, 1. I, youth leaning on his stick.

130 (89) VILLA GIULIA 5238. I, man with lyre.

131. VILLA GIULIA, from Cervetri. I, trainer (man moving to right, wand in right hand, markers in left).

131 *bis*. VILLA GIULIA 50481. I, warrior (youth running to left, helmet in right hand). See p. 1663.

132. HEIDELBERG. I, cup-bearer. See p. 1663.

133. SYDNEY 53.05. I, woman (standing to left, holding a box).

134. BERLIN inv. 4282. Van Hoorn *De vita* 7. I, nurse and little boy.

135. MAYENCE, Univ., 103. Hampe and Simon *G.L.* pl. 27. I, woman at altar. Compare Warsaw 142331 (no. 63).

The following is an imitation of the Providence Painter's Nolans, unless it could be a hasty work by the painter himself:

NECK-AMPHORA
(*Nolan amphora, with triple handles*)

HAVANA, Lagunillas, from Gela. A, Dionysos and satyr; B, maenad. On A, satyr playing the flute, Dionysos with kantharos and thyrsus; on B, with snake and thyrsus.

An ill-preserved vase is probably by the Providence Painter:

NECK-AMPHORA
(*Nolan amphora, with triple handles*)

SAMOTHRACE 57.707, from Samothrace. *Archaeology* 12, 164 fig. 2, right. Komos (A, man with cup and lyre; B, youth with skyphos). Compare Oxford 1927.2 (p. 638 no. 41).

MANNER OF THE PROVIDENCE PAINTER
LEKYTHOI
(*standard shape*)
(*nos. 1–2, rf.*)

1. GELA (ex Navarra-Jacona), from Gela. Benndorf pl. 46, 2. Amazon.

2. LAON 37.963. *CV*. pl. 42, 7 and 13. Hermes running to altar. Compare the white lekythos London 1900.7–27.4 (p. 643 no. 117). Probably by the painter himself.

(*no. 3, white*)

3 (10). LONDON D 19, from Gela. Nike. Restored.

A number of small lekythoi are closely connected with nos. 101–7 in the list of vases by the Providence Painter on p. 642; nos. 1–4, at least, may be by the painter himself:

LEKYTHOI
(secondary shape)
(nos. 1–7, rf.)

1. NAPLES Stg. 253. Nike running with sash. Restored.

2. BASLE MARKET (M.M.). Woman running (to left, looking round, right arm extended; on the right a Doric column).

3. CAMBRIDGE, Museum of Classical Archaeology. Woman seated, twining a wreath.

3 *bis.* ELEUSIS, T. B 8 no. 201, from Eleusis. The like. Compare the last two. [B. F. Cook].

4. LAON 37.969. *CV.* pl. 42, 5 and 9. The like. The lower part modern. Compare the last two.

5. BASLE MARKET (M.M.). *Münzh. Basel 1 Okt. 1935* pl. 41, 1186. Woman (standing to left, arms extended as if holding something; on the right a Doric column).

6. YALE 148. Baur 100. Boreas.

7. ATHENS 17612. *JHS.* 65 pl. 4, a, whence Pickard-Cambridge *D.F.A.* fig. 202. Woman running in after bathing.

(nos. 8–10, white)

8. ATHENS 13260. Man. ΓΛΑΥΙϹΩΝ and below it ΙϹΑΛΟΣ. Shape and palmettes as in Athens 17200 (p. 642 no. 106), maeander as in Athens 1806 (p. 643 no. 118) and Athens 15876 (p. 643 no. 119).

9. LOUVRE N 2586. Nike.

10. COPENHAGEN, Ny Carlsberg, inv. 2781. *From the Coll.* 1, 163 fig. 1. Woman at wool-basket.

Two rough vases go together: they have the same maeander as nos. 1–7, but the style of the figures is different:

LEKYTHOI
(secondary shape)

1. DRESDEN. Naked youth holding helmet and spear.

2. ATHENS 17280. *CV.* Jb pl. 12, 3–4. Youth throwing spear.

The following resemble the group of lekythoi nos. 108–11 in the list on p. 642:

LEKYTHOI

(secondary shape; very small)

1. NAPLES (ex Spinelli), from Suessula. Maenad (in peplos, running to right, looking back; on the right, a thyrsus stuck in the ground).
2. TARANTO. Woman (in peplos) running towards a mound-altar, looking back.

THE OIONOKLES PAINTER

In Tillyard 53–54. *Att. V.* 136–8 and 472. *V.Pol.* 19 and 79. *ARV.*[1] 437–9 and 960.

Called after the kalos-name on nos. 3 and 14–16.

Follower of the Providence Painter.

NECK-AMPHORAE

(nos. 1–31: Nolan amphorae, with triple handles)

1 (1). NEW YORK 41.162.21. *AJA.* 1924 pl. 8; *CV.* Gallatin pl. 15; detail of B, Richter *ARVS.* fig. 76; A, Richter *H.* 225, f. A, satyrs and maenads; B, Dionysos and satyr.

2 (1 *bis*). Once STETTIN. A, satyr pursuing maenad; B, satyr running up. [Luschey].

3 (2). BERNE 12215, from Nola. *RA.* 1910, i, 222–5; Bloesch *AKS.* pll. 32–35 and p. 66; Schefold *M.* 203, 215. A, Dionysos and dancing satyr; B, satyr. On A, OIONOKLEϚ KALOϚ. On B, AKEϚTOPIΔEϚ and retr. KALOϚ.

4 (3). NORTHWICK, Spencer-Churchill. A, maenad; B, satyr. On A, standing with left leg frontal, looking round to right, holding kantharos and thyrsus; on B, moving to left with lyre and wineskin.

5 (4). BERLIN 2334, from Nola. Angelini pl. 8; B.Ap. xviii. 7. A, Dionysos on donkey; B, maenad.

6 (5). NEW YORK 09.221.41, from Capua. Richter and Hall pl. 32, and pl. 169, 33. A, satyr; B, satyr.

7 (6). BERLIN 2331. *Jb.* 26, 282–3; B, *JHS.* 48, 149 fig. 6. Fight: A, Greek; B, Persian.

8 (7). CAPUA 7552 (P. 8), from Capua. *CV.* pl. 2. A, warrior; B, woman holding his sword and shield. On A, ILAPON (= 'Ιλάρων?) and retr. KΛΛΟϚ.

9 (8). CAB. MÉD. 364. Luynes pl. 36. A, Nike; B, jockey.

10 (9). Once GOLUCHOW, Czartoryski, 34. De Witte pll. 4–5; *CV.* pl. 22, 2. A, Nike with cithara; B, citharode.

11 (10). NAPLES Stg. 220. A, Nike; B, old man with sceptre.

12 (11). LONDON E 301, from Capua. Cook *Zeus* ii pl. 5; Albizzati *Due acquisti* 20; *CV*. pl. 53, 1. Death of Orpheus: A, Orpheus and Thracian woman; B, Thracian woman.

13 (12). LONDON E 297, from Nola. Panofka *Eig.* pl. 4, 9; *CV*. pl. 52, 1; A, Greifenhagen *Eroten* 60. A, Eros pursuing a boy; B, old man. On A, ΚΑΛΟΣ, retr. ΚΑΛΟΣ, and ΑΚΕΣΤΟΡΙΔΕΣ. On B, ΑΚΕΣΤΟΡΙΔΕΣ ΚΑΛΟΣ.

14 (13). LONDON E 294, from Nola. Panofka *Eig.* pl. 4, 10; Cecil Smith pl. 11; *CV*. pl. 50, 1; A, Ghali-Kahil *H.* pl. 49, 1. A, Menelaos and Helen; B, old man. On A, ΟΙΟΝΟΚΛΕΣ ΚΑΛΟ[Σ]. On B, ΚΑΛΟΣ ΚΑΛ-ΛΙΑΣ.

15 (14). Once NAPLES, Hamilton. Tischbein 4 pl. 50, whence Ghali-Kahil *H.* pl. 51, 1. A, Menelaos pursuing, B, Helen. On A, ΟΙΟΝΟΚΛΕΣ ΚΑΛΟΣ. On B, ΚΑΛΛΙΑΣ; also an unexplained word, apparently spoken by Helen. I conjecture that the two figures are one on each side of the vase.

16 (15). CAB. MÉD. 358. *Mon.* 1 pl. 5, 3; Luynes pl. 38; phs. Gir. 19301 and 19311. A, Eos and Tithonos; B, old man. On A, ΟΙΟΝΟΚΛΕΣ and retr. ΚΑΛΟΣ. On B, ΟΙΟΝΟΚΛΕΣ ΚΑΛΟΣ.

17. AMHERST (Massachusetts). A, Eos and Kephalos; B, youth.

18 (16). LOUVRE G 210, from Capua. A, Pottier pl. 129; *CV*. pl. 39, 2 and 6–8; phs. Gir. 18799–800, whence *Jb.* 59, 72–73. A, Herakles and Syleus; B, woman (Xenodike).

19 (17, 31, +). CAPUA, fr., from Capua. *CV*. pl. 5, 3. A, Theseus and Skiron. A fragment in Bryn Mawr, P 974, should belong: giving the left arm of Skiron, one calf of Theseus, and, between, part of the cliff and of the tortoise. And so should the fragment Leipsic T 673, no. 31 in *ARV*.[1] 439: giving the head of Skiron, in three-quarter view.

20 (18). LONDON E 304, from Vulci. CB. pl. 54, 1. A, Theseus and Minotaur; B, old man (Minos).

21 (19). NAPLES 3091, from Nola. Foerster *Raub* pl. 2, whence Overbeck *KM.* pl. 18, 11; A, *Jb.* 73, 49; A, ph. So. 11069, iii, 7. A, Plouton pursuing Persephone. B, man. For the subject, Simon O.G. 70 and 75; but this is not the only occurrence in Attic art of the fifth century, since the rape of Persephone is represented on the skyphos in Eleusis, of about 430 B.C., published by Hartwig in *AM.* 21 pl. 12 and p. 379.

22 (20). Once DEEPDENE, Hope, 93. Millin *PVA.* 1 pl. 71, whence *El.* 2 pl. 20. A, Apollo; B, woman running.

23. INGELHEIM, Boehringer. A, Poseidon pursuing, B, a woman. On A, in chitoniskos and wrap, moving to right, right arm raised with trident, dolphin in left hand; on B, running to right, looking round.

24 (21). MYKONOS, from Rheneia (originally from Delos). Dugas *Délos xxi* pl. 21, 54 and pl. 24, 54. A, youth with spears (Theseus?) pursuing a woman; B, woman fleeing.

25 (22). LOUVRE G 209, from Nola. *CV.* pl. 38, 10–12, and pl. 39, 1; phs. Gir. 37889–90, whence (A) *Jb.* 68, 41; A, Villard *GV.* pl. 26, 3; A, Zschietzschmann *H.R.* pl. 18, 2. A, Plouton and Persephone. B, woman.

26 (23). CAB. MÉD. 370, from Nola. *El.* 3 pl. 24. A, Poseidon. B, woman.

27 (24). VIENNA 846. La Borde 2 pl. 29, 4 and 2; *CV.* pl. 60, 1–3. A, youth and seated woman; B, man.

28 (25). CAMBRIDGE 8.1955 (ex Lamb). A, boy singing and man seated playing the flute; B, man.

29 (26). MYKONOS, from Rheneia (originally from Delos). Dugas *Délos xxi* pl. 20, 53 and pl. 46, 53. A, komast; B, komast.

30 (27). MYKONOS, fr., from Rheneia (originally from Delos). Dugas *Délos xxi* pl. 18, 55. Komast.

31 (28). CAB. MÉD. 369. Luynes pl. 35, whence *El.* 1 pl. 77; A, phs. Gir. 8081 and 19998. A, Athena with stylus and tablets; B, man.

(no. 32, small neck-amphora, with triple handles)

32. CHARLECOTE, Fairfax-Lucy, from Nola. A, Eros pursuing a boy; B, old man. On A, ΚΑΛΟΣ. On B, ΚΑΛΟΣ retr., and ΚΑΛΛΙΑΣ. See *AJA.* 1957, 7, xvii. This must be the Crescenzi vase, *Bull.* 1842, 13.

(nos. 33–34, small neck-amphorae with ridged handles: for the shape see CB. ii, 40)

33 (29). CAB. MÉD. 373. A, de Ridder 273 and pl. 12. A, Hermes and Paris; B, king.

34. ATHENS, Kanellopoulos. A, woman running to Poseidon. B, maenad.

(no. 35, neck-amphora, the exact shape unknown)

35 (30). Once ROUEN, Bellon, 609, from Nola. Gargiulo *Recueil* (1845) ii pl. 40, whence Inghirami pl. 169; Fröhner *Coll. Lecuyer* 2 pl. F, 5; *Coll. Camille Lecuyer* 61–62. A, warrior; B, slinger.

LOUTROPHOROS

36. ATHENS, Acr. Mus., fr., from Athens. (Head of woman in saccos).

LEKYTHOI
(standard shape)

37 (32). CLEVELAND 28.660, from Italy. Warrior cutting off a lock of hair. For the subject, *Kl.* 28 and Haspels *ABL.* 73–74.

38 (33). GELA (ex Navarra-Jacona), from Gela. *R.I.* 1859, 75. Youth attacking with sword.

39 (34). NEW YORK 41.162.15, from Sicily. *AJA.* 1924, 282; *CV.* Gallatin pl. 16, 1. Youth attacking with sword.

40. New York 28.57.11. Goddess (Hera).

41. London market (Sotheby) (ex Barberini and Pollak). Passeri pl. 131; *Cat. Sotheby 18 June 1962* pl. at p. 26, 95. Woman with wool-basket.

42 (35). Syracuse 24554, from Gela. *ML.* 17 pl. 55, 1. Maenad.

43 (36). Syracuse 21196, from Gela. *ML.* 17 pl. 33, 1. Tithonos.

44 (37). Los Angeles A 5933.50.16 (ex Hope and Cowdray). Buck pl. 9; Tillyard pl. 15, 107. Uncertain subject: man with sword pursuing a woman).

45 (38). Madrid 11158 (L. 159). Alvarez-Ossorio pl. 36, 1; *CV.* pl. 13, 2 and pl. 14, 2; Simon *G.A.* 89. Eos carrying off Kephalos.

OINOCHOE
(shape 1)

46. Athens, Vlasto, from Anavysos. Nike (standing at altar, holding oino-choe and sacrificial basket).

COLUMN-KRATER
(the pictures not framed)

47 (39). Oxford 1917.60. Millingen *Coghill* pl. 10; A, Tillyard pl. 20, 126; *CV.* pl. 23, 4 and pl. 22, 6. Warrior leaving home: A, warrior and old man; B, youth.

The following might be by the Oionokles Painter:

NECK-AMPHORA
(Nolan amphora, with triple handles)

Tartu 103, from Capua. Malmberg and Felsberg pl. 3, 1–2. A, youth with spear; B, woman bringing his corslet.

NEAR THE OIONOKLES PAINTER
STAMNOS

1. Naples, Astarita, 116, fr. Warriors setting out (the heads of two remain, to left, with the spear of one and the edge of his shield-rim).

NECK-AMPHORA
(Nolan amphora, with triple handles)

2 (1). Berlin 4052, from Locri. *Annali* 1845 pl. C and pl. D, 3; A, Licht iii, 96, 2; A, Brommer *Satyrspiele*[1] 18 = [2]23; B.Ap. xxii. 80. A, shepherd playing the flute and satyr dancing. B, youth and boy. The subject of A recurs on a skyphos, from Padula, in Padula (A, shepherd seated on a rock, playing the flute, and satyr dancing; B, two satyrs dancing).

Also connected with him:

NECK-AMPHORA
(Nolan amphora, with triple handles)

1. CAB. MÉD. 360, from Nola. De Ridder 263 and pl. 12; B.Ap. xxiii. 22, 2. A, Theseus and Sinis; B, woman with sceptre.

STAMNOS

2. LONDON E 457.2, fr. A god pursuing a woman.

THE NIKON PAINTER

VA. 138 note 1. *Att. V.* 131–2 and 472. *ARV.*[1] 441–3 and 960.

Called after the kalos-name on nos. 8, 16, 22, and 26.

NECK-AMPHORAE
(Nolan amphorae, with triple handles)

1 (1). LONDON E 299, from Nola. *El.* 1 pl. 75; *CV.* pl. 52, 2; *JHS.* 53, 100. A, Athena with spear and aphlaston; B, woman running (Asia?). On A, HEPAξ KAΛE. On B, HEPAξ and retr. ICΛΛE. For the subject, *JHS.* 53,100 and Hausmann in *Charites Langlotz* 148.

2 (2). LONDON, Victoria and Albert Museum, 2505.1910, from Italy. Klein *L.* 155. A, Athena; B, woman (priestess). On A, ΛLAVKON and retr. ICAꝶOξ.

3 (3). PROVIDENCE 25.079, from Athens. A, *Bull. Rhode* 16, 45; *CV.* pl. 15, 1 and pl. 16, 1. A, Athena. B, youth. On A, TIMO+ξENOξ KΛLOξ. [Luce].

4 (4). ALTENBURG 274, from Nola. *Annali* 1878 pl. K; A, Bielefeld *G.E.T.A.* pl. 6, 1; *CV.* pl. 44, 1, pl. 45, 4, and pl. 47, 1. A, Nike; B, woman with torch.

5 (5). MADRID 11104 (L. 176). *CV.* pl. 20, 5 and pl. 25, 1; A, R.I. xii. 25. A, Nike with cithara. B, youth with oinochoe at vessel.

6 (6). NAPLES 3384, from Nola. A, ph. So. x, i, 2. A, Nike (with phiale and basket, flying to altar). B, woman.

7 (7). FLORENCE 91804 (d.d. Spranger). A, Nike (with oinochoe and phiale, flying to altar). B, youth.

8 (8). NAPLES 3158, from Nola. A, ph. So. 11069, ii, 5. A, Eos. B, youth with phiale. On A, KΛLOξN[I]KON.

9 (9). NEW YORK 41.162.134. B, *Coll. Arthur Sambon* pl. 18, 164; *CV.* Gallatin pl. 52, 1. A, Demeter; B, woman with phiale. On A, KΛLLI-KLEξ KΛLOξ.

9 *bis.* BUDAPEST 51. 228. A, Szilágyi and Castiglione pl. 12, 1; B, *Sborník* 1959 pl. 1, 1. A, Demeter at altar. B, man at a pillar. The pillar is inscribed ξΓΑΔI/O and is the terma in the stadion (see Frel in *Sborník* 1959, 264–5).

10. GELA V xii, from Vassallaggi. A, woman with torches at altar. B, youth.

11 (10). LOUVRE CA 2243, from Italy. *CV.* pl. 49, 7–9; ph. Gir. 35661, whence (A) *Hist. rel.* 193; A, Simon *G.A.* 77. A, psychostasia (Hermes). B, woman. See CB. iii, text; and below, p. 1663.

12 (a 5). OXFORD 271. Gardner pl. 10, 2 and p. 24 fig. 26; *CV.* pl. 17, 6 and pl. 18, 2. A, Apollo. B, youth. On A, +ΛΡΜΙΔΕ⟩ ΚΑLΟ⟩.

12 *bis* (a 3). ALTENBURG 280, from Nola. *CV.* pl. 43 and pl. 47, 2. A, Dionysos; B, satyr.

13. NAPLES, Astarita, 108, fr. Youth (setting out?: in chlamys, frontal, head to left, right arm extended to left: mouth to waist remain).

14. GELA, from Gela. *Arch. class.* 5 pl. 11; *NSc.* 1956, 215–16. A, youth with spears (Theseus?) pursuing a woman; B, woman fleeing.

15 (11). NAPLES inv. 81475, from Naples. A, ph. So. 11072, i, 5. A, Athena and Nike. B, woman with phiale.

16 (12). CAB. MÉD. 361. Luynes pl. 37. A, Nike, and youth with sceptre, at altar. B, youth holding a cage with a partridge in it. On A, ΝΙΚΟΝ ΙΚΑLΟ⟩.

17 (13). BERLIN 2329, from Nola. B.Ap. xxiii. 34. 1. A, arming (youth and woman). B, youth at pillar. On A, ΚΑLΟ⟩ ΚΑLLΙΛ⟩. On B, +ΛΡ-ΜΙΔΕ⟩ΚΑLΟ⟩ on the pillar.

18 (14). LOUVRE G 217, from Vulci. *CV.* pl. 41, 4–6. A, youth leaving home (rather than arriving: youth and woman); B, youth.

19 (a). LENINGRAD inv. 5577. A, *Anz.* 1930, 34. A, Dionysos and Giant. B, youth. On A, ΚΑLΟ⟩ +⟩ΛΝΟΕ⟩.

20 (15). LOUVRE G 338, from Capua? Pottier pl. 136; *CV.* pl. 50, 8–10. A, youth and boy; B, youth. On A, ΙΚΑLΟ⟩ +ΛΡΜΙΔΕ⟩.

LEKYTHOI

(standard shape)

21 (16). ERLANGEN 261, from Agrigento. Grünhagen pl. 20. Odysseus and Circe.

22 (17). ATHENS 12779 (N. 1024), from Eretria. *CV.* pl. 10, 4. Athena. ΙΚΑ[LΟ]⟩ ΝΙΚΟΝ.

23 (18). OXFORD 316, from Gela. *CV.* pl. 34, 3. Eos.

24 (24). PALERMO (1246). Nike with thurible.

25 (19). OXFORD 1954.245, frr., from Al Mina. *JHS.* 59, 8. Hermes.

26. NEW YORK 53.224. *Bull. Metr.* summer 1962, 8, 8. Apollo.

27. AMIENS 3057.176.37. Nike and boy. [Bothmer].

28 (22). SYRACUSE 19878, from Gela. *Riv. Ist.* 4, 79. Silenos led prisoner.

29 (21). PALERMO V 692. *CV.* pl. 21, 1–2. Warrior. ΙΚΑLLΟ⟩ ΤΗΜΙΝΙ-ΔΕΝ.

29 *bis*. GELA, from Gela. Woman fleeing; on the left, a palm tree. See p. 1663.

30 (20). LOUVRE G 335, from Sicily. Pottier pl. 135. Woman with oinochoe and phiale, and boy.

31 (23). AGRIGENTO (ex Giudice 55), from Gela. Ph. Lo Cascio pl. 95, b. Woman with oinochoe and sacrificial basket approaching altar.

32 (25). AGRIGENTO (ex Giudice 1666), from Gela. Ph. Lo Cascio pl. 93, b. Procession to sacrifice: woman with sprigs, and girl with oinochoe, phiale, and basket. As the last.

33. COPENHAGEN. Woman with phiale and sceptre (goddess) and woman with oinochoe and torch (Demeter and Persephone?).

34. ATHENS 1645 (CC. 1193), from Eretria. Ph. A.I. NM 3030. Mistress and maid. ΛΛΑVΚΟΝ ΚΑΛΟ$ ΛΕΑΛΡΟ. This and the next were wrongly said in *ARV.*[1] 576 nos. 8 and 9 to be in the manner of the Pistoxenos Painter.

35. ATHENS 1496 (CC. 1192). Mistress and maid. ΛΛΑVΚΟΝ ΚΑΛΟ$.

36. TORONTO 961.49, from Greece. Mistress and maid (woman seated to right with mirror and flower, girl standing frontal, head to left, a box in her left hand, her right hand raised).

OINOCHOE
(shape 2)

37 (26). LONDON E 538. Jacobsthal O. pl. 64, a. Eos. ΚΑΛΟ$ ΝΙΚΟΝ.

Probably also by the Nikon Painter:

NECK-AMPHORAE
(Nolan amphorae, with triple handles)

1. LENINGRAD inv. 4305. A, warrior. B, youth with bird. On A, youth, corslet, chitoniskos, wrap, standing frontal, head to right, spear in left hand; on the ground, helmet and shield. The shield-device is a kantharos with the word ΒΟΙΟΤΙΟ$ above it, which, as Waldhauer saw, should refer to the kantharos. See p. 1663.

2 (4). LONDON E 302, from Camiros. *AZ.* 1880 pl. 12, 2; *CV.* pl. 53, 2; detail of A, White *P.* pl. 3, d. A, Phineus and Harpy; B, Harpy.

WHITE LEKYTHOS
(standard shape)

3. BRUSSELS A 1019, from Eretria. *Vente Somzée* pl. 7, 93; Fairbanks ii pl. 33, 2; Buschor *A.L.P.* 32; *CV.* Jb pl. 2, 5; part, Buschor *G. Vasen* 177; Verhoogen *C.G.* pl. 20. Mistress and maid (woman, and maid running with box). ΛΛΑVΚΟΝ ΚΑΛΟ$. Second white used. See p. 1663.

RELATED TO THE NIKON PAINTER

ARV.[1] 443.

NECK-AMPHORAE
(Nolan amphorae, with triple handles)

1 (1). PROVIDENCE 23.323. A, Buck pl. 1; A, Dubois-Maisonneuve pl. 23, 1; Tillyard pl. 9, 88 and pl. 10; *CV.* pl. 15, 2 and pl. 16, 2. A, fight; B, warrior coming to help. On A, ΚΑLLΙΑϟ ΚΑLΟϟ.

2 (2). ABERDEEN 686, from Vulci. A, *Ant. Kunst* 2 pl. 7, 2; B.Ap. xxii. 83, 1. A, Zeus and Ganymede; B, man.

LEKYTHOS
(standard shape)

3 (6). LEIPSIC T 3380, from Gela. Woman with phiale and oinochoe.

THE CHARMIDES PAINTER

VA. 74 and 76. *Att. V.* 129–30. *ARV.*[1] 440–1. CB. ii, 38–39.

Called after the kalos-name on nos. 1, 2, 5–7, and 9–13.

NECK-AMPHORAE
(nos. 1–2: Nolan amphorae, with triple handles)

1 (1). LONDON E 290. A, *JHS.* 4 pl. 30, whence *Philologus* 50 pl. 2, whence Robert *Herm.* 59; *CV.* pl. 48, 2; *Anz.* 1952, 63; A, *Jb. Mainz* 5 pl. 24. A, Herakles and Geras. B, youth. On A, +ΛΡΜΙΔΕϟ ΚΑLΟϟ.

2 (2). Once NAPLES, Cella. *Bull. Nap.* N.S. i pl. 10, 1–3. A, Herakles and the Amazons; B, warrior (Telamon?). On A, +ΛΡΜΙΔΕϟ ΚΑLΟϟ. On B, +ΛΡΜΙΔΕ[ϟ] ΚΑLΟϟ. For the subject, Bothmer *Am.* 142, foot.

3 (3). LONDON E 293, from Nola. Raoul-Rochette pl. 44, 2, whence *El.* 4 pll. 45–46; *CV.* pl. 49, 2. A, Eros pursuing hare; B, Eros. On A, ΤΙΜΟ+ϟΕΝΟϟ ΚΑLΟϟ.

4 (4). LOUVRE G 211. A, *El.* 4 pl. 50; *CV.* pl. 39, 3–5 and 9; B.Ap. xxiii. 36, 2; ph. Gir. 31997. A, Eros; B, youth.

5 (5). LONDON E 292, from Nola. *CV.* pl. 49, 1. A, two satyrs pursuing, B, maenad. On A, +ΛΡΜΙΔΕϟ ΚΑLΟϟ, ΤΙΜΟ+ϟΕΝΟϟ ΚΑLΟϟ.

6 (6). LONDON E 289, from Nola. Gerhard *AB.* 1 pl. 32; *JHS.* 7, 204, 1; *CV.* pl. 48, 1 and pl. 51, 2; A, *E.A.A.* ii, 537; Himmelmann-Wildschütz *Eig.* pl. 15. Judgement of Paris: A, Paris and the goddesses; B, Hermes. On A, +Α[Ρ]Μ[ΙΔ]Εϟ Κ[ΑLΟϟ]. Below B, ghost of another vase.

7. LOUVRE C 10764. A, Nike (flying, picking a plant); B, Nike (flying, legs frontal). On A, ΚΑLΟ complete and +ΛΡΜΙΔΕϟ.

8 (7). Dresden 291. A, Iris (running to right, looking round, caduceus in left hand: cf. B of London E 292, no. 5); B, man (in long chiton and himation, standing to right, stick in right hand: perhaps Zeus?). On A, ΚΛΛΟϞ ΗΙΓΓΟΝ.

9 (8). Dresden 319. A, traveller decking herm. B, warrior. On B, +ΛΡΜΙΔ[Ε]Ϟ ΚΛ[L]ΟϞ.

10 (9). Cab. Méd. 366. A, *El.* 4 pl. 51; B.Ap. xxiii. 36. 1; ph. Gir. 32002, whence (A) Greifenhagen *Eroten* 64. A, Eros (flying with spear and shield). B, woman. On A, ΚΛΛΟϞ +ΛΡΜΙΔΕϞ.

11 (10). Louvre G 337, from Nola. Millingen *AUM.* 1 pl. 31, whence (A) *El.* 4 pl. 47; B, *RA.* 8 (1852) pl. 167; *CV.* pl. 50, 6–7. A, Eros; B, man. On A, +ΛΡΜΙΔΕϞ ΚΛΛΟϞ. On B, ΤΕΙϞΙΛϞ ΙΚΛΛΟϞ.

12 (11). London 96.7–23.1, from South Italy or Sicily. *JHS.* 41 pl. 4, ii, 5; *CV.* pl. 49, 3. A, Eros; B, boy. On A, ΚΛΛΟϞ +ΛΡΜΙΔΕϞ.

(no. 13, small neck-amphora, with ridged handles)

13 (12). Boston 76.46, from Capua. A, Edward Robinson 154; Brommer *Satyrspiele* 50–51; CB. ii pl. 45, 85, and p. 38; the shape, Caskey G. 65. A, satyr carrying his father, and satyr; B, satyr. On A, +ΛΡΜΙΔΕϞ ΚΛΛΟϞ. See CB. ii, 38–39, and for the shape ibid. 40 no. 6.

RELATED TO THE CHARMIDES PAINTER

ARV.[1] 441.

NECK-AMPHORAE

(Nolan amphorae, with triple handles)

1 (2). Sèvres 55. Millin *PVA.* 2 pl. 14, whence Inghirami pl. 113; *CV.* pl. 18, 3–5. A, warrior; B, warrior. On A, ΤΙΜΑ+ϞΕΝΟϞ ΚΛΛΟϞ. Probably by the painter himself.

2 (1). Athens 1690 (CC. 1223), from Corinth. A, CC. pl. 43. A, Nike; B, man. On A, ΚΛΛΟϞ ΚΛΛLΙΛϞ.

3 (4). London E 295. Millingen *AUM.* 1 pl. 19, whence Inghirami pl. 168; *CV.* pl. 50, 2; Bothmer *Am.* pl. 86, 5. A, two Amazons; B, Amazon. On A, ΚΛΛLΙΔΕϞ ΚΛLFϞ. The sixth letter of the name is rather shapeless, and might also be an alpha; see p. 1587. On B, to right of the right leg, ghost of another vase (maeander and cross-square of the same type as on the vase itself).

LEKYTHOI

(standard shape)

4 (l 13). London E 571, from Gela. Eros. +ΛΡΜΙΔΕϞ ΚΛΛΟϞ. Behind, ghost of another vase (maeander with pattern-square, of the same type as on the vase itself).

5 (5). Northwick, Spencer-Churchill. Eos and Tithonos. +ΛΡΜΑΙΟΣ
ΚΛLΟΣ. Much restored. For the inscription, *AJA*. 1927, 350.

Akin to the work of the Charmides Painter, the

NECK-AMPHORA
(Nolan amphora, with triple handles)

London market (Spink). A, man with phiale and woman with oinochoe;
B, woman with torch running up. On A, ΚΑLΕ, ΚΑLΟΣ. On B,
ΚΛLΟΣ.

———————

THE DRESDEN PAINTER

Att. V. 130–1 and 471–2.   *ARV.*[1] 448–9 and 960.

Named after no. 10.

NECK-AMPHORAE
(Nolan amphorae, with triple handles)

1. Copenhagen inv. 13112, from Gela. A, Athena. B, youth.
2 (1). Tübingen E 53, from Nola. Watzinger 41 and pl. 22. A, Nike. B,
   woman at wool-basket. On A, ΚΑLLΙΚLΕΣ ΚΑLΟΣ.
3. Maplewood, Noble, from Gela. A, Nike (flying to altar, with oinochoe
   and phiale); B, youth (standing to left, with phiale). See p. 1664.
4. Stockholm G. 26, from Nola. A, Mazochius 138 fig. 3, whence Lanzi
   pl. 1, 6 and Dubois-Maisonneuve pl. 77, 5. A, Nike; B, youth. On
   A, ΚΑLLΙΚLΕΣ ΚΑΛΟΣ.
5 (2). Naples Stg. 231. A, Artemis. B, woman.
6 (7). Florence 4017. *CV.* pl. 29, 1–2 and pl. 25, 4; A, Stella 263 (with fancy
   caption); A, *E.A.A.* iii, 183; R.I. 7038. A, Eros. B, woman. On A,
   ΚΑLΟΣ ΤΙΜΟ+ΣΕΝΟΣ. Restored.
7. Gela 636, from Gela. A, *Fasti arch.* 10, 150; A, *Ragguaglio* 1, 32; *NSc.*
   1960, fig. 25, 1–2, and fig. 26. A, Eros. B, youth.
8 (5). Dresden 311. A, boy with lyre, fleeing (Tithonos?). B, woman at
   wool-basket.
9 (4). Naples 3046, from Ruvo. A, ph. So. 11069, i, 3. A, boy with lyre,
   fleeing (Tithonos?). B, woman. On A, ΗΙΓΓΟΝ ΚΑLΟΣ.
10 (3). Dresden 312. A, *Jh.* 13, Beibl. p. 248. A, woman seated with wool
   at wool-basket; B, woman.
11 (5). Florence 4018. Inghirami *Mon. etr.* pl. 68; *CV.* pl. 29, 3 and pl. 25,
   5. A, woman with wool at wool-basket; B, youth.
12. Santa Barbara, Brundage. B, Merlo 14, 5. A, woman with mirror at
   wool-basket; B, youth. [H. R. W. Smith].
13. Mariemont G 129. A, Cumont *Coll. Warocqué* i, 48; *Ant. Mariemont* pl.

42. A, woman with mirror at wool-basket, and youth; B, woman. On A, +ΛΡΜΙΔΕΣ ΚΛΛΟΣ.

14 (8). PARIS, Petit Palais, 322. *CV*. pl. 14, 1–4. A, youth and boy; B, woman.

LEKYTHOI
(*standard shape*)

15 (9). ZURICH, Roš, from Sicily. *Vente xi Bâle* pl. 22, 340; Schefold *M.* 207, 223. Poseidon and Amymone. See CB. ii, 89, foot.

16 (14). COLUMBUS (Ohio) (ex Dallay). Woman fleeing.

17. GELA (ex Navarra-Jacona), from Gela. Woman with mirror. ΚΛΛΟΣ [+]ΑΡΜΙΔΕΣ. The forms of the alphas not certain.

18 (16). NAPLES Stg. 351. Man running (in long chiton and himation, looking round, staff or the like in his left hand; restored as Poseidon).

19 (11). VIENNA 747. Women at wool-basket, playing ball.

20 (17). BERLIN 2210, from Nola. *AZ*. 1848 pl. 21, 1–2. Winged goddess——Nike?—pursuing a boy who holds a lyre (Eos and Tithonos, one might have said, but the goddess holds out a sash).

21 (18). PARIS MARKET (Mikas: ex Feuardent). Nike (flying to right, looking round, in chiton and saccos; an altar was indicated in the incised sketch).

22 (12). GELA, Nocera, 16, from Gela. Nike (with phiale, at altar).

23 (13). REGGIO 4104, from Locri. Woman with mirror at wool-basket.

24 (10). SYRACUSE 21857, from Gela. *ML*. 17 pl. 14, 2. Nike.

25 (15). NAPLES Stg. 356. Eros.

ALABASTRA

26 (20). ATHENS, Vlasto, from Koropi. A, mistress and little maid; B, woman.

27 (21). ERLANGEN 289. Part, Grünhagen *Ant. Or.* pl. 19. Woman with wool at wool-basket, woman with alabastron.

28 (22). MAPLEWOOD, Noble (ex Hirsch). A, man (leaning on his stick); B, boy with lyre (running, looking round).

OINOCHOE
(*shape 7*)

29. COLOGNE, Hundsdiecker. *Auktion xviii Basel* pl. 39, 121. Eos and Tithonos. The oinochoe belongs to the same Class, and is by the same potter, as those decorated by the Painter of the Brussels Oinochoai (p. 775).

Near the Dresden Painter, the

LEKYTHOS
(*standard shape*)

SYRACUSE 19868 (or 19368), from Gela. Woman running with spear.

THE PAINTER OF THE YALE LEKYTHOS

VA. 72-74. *Att. V.* 143-5 and 472. *V.Pol.* 18 and 79. *ARV.*[1] 443-7.

Named after no. 30.

STAMNOI

1 (1). ORVIETO 1044, from Orvieto. Mayer *Giganten* pl. 2, whence Vian *R.* pl. 40, 376; *CV.* pll. 9-10; phs. Armoni. Dionysos, satyrs, and giants; satyr driving satyr-biga. See CB. ii, 71-72.

2 (2). WÜRZBURG 518, from Vulci. A and side, Jacobsthal *O.* pl. 93; Langlotz pl. 187. A, Poseidon, Amphitrite, and Nereid; B, Nereus and Nereids.

3 (3). VIENNA 3730 (ex Oest. Mus. 339), from Cervetri. A, Masner pl. 7; B and side, Jacobsthal *O.* pl. 95; *CV.* pl. 67. A, Poseidon and Amphitrite. B, Boreas and Oreithyia.

NECK-AMPHORAE

(Nolan amphorae, with triple handles)

4 (4). NEW YORK 41.162.156. *CV.* Gallatin pl. 13. A, man with sceptre, and woman running; B, woman running. Extract from a pursuit— sisters of the ravished hearing the alarm, leaving their parent, and rushing to her side.

5 (5). LENINGRAD (St. 2072). *CR.* 1862 pl. 1, 8-10. A, winged Artemis caressing a fawn. B, woman (Demeter?) with corn-ears at altar.

6 (6). OXFORD 1937.681. A, Poseidon; B, giant.

7 (7). LONDON E 309, from Gela. *CV.* pl. 55, 3. A, Dionysos; B, satyr.

8. HAVANA, Lagunillas. A, Nike with thurible; B, youth. [Bothmer].

9. KIEL (Berlin 2333 on loan), from Camiros. A, Nike; B, youth. Misattributed in *ARV.*[1] 462 no. 8 and p. 960.

10 (8). CAPUA P. 7, from Capua. *CV.* pl. 1. A, Eos; B, Kephalos.

PELIKE

11 (9). LONDON E 419, from Nola. Warrior leaving home (A, warrior with phiale; B, woman with oinochoe). Small. Restored.

LOUTROPHOROI

12. ATHENS, Acr. Mus., fr., from Athens. Wedding (upper part of the bride, minus the head, arm of the bridegroom).

13. ATHENS, Acr. Mus., fr., from Athens. (Woman with torch).

14. ATHENS, Acr. Mus., fr., from Athens. (Nike).

15. ATHENS, Acr. Mus., fr., from Athens. (Head and hand of a woman, hand of another).

HYDRIAI
(*with picture on the body*)

16 (10). FERRARA, T. 605, from Spina. Triptolemos.

17 (11). ATHENS 1175 (CC. 1252), from Attica. Eos in biga.

18 (12). WARSAW 142348 (ex Czartoryski 45). De Witte pl. 17; *CV*. pl. 20, 3. Dionysos and maenad.

19 (14). OXFORD 297. *CV*. pl. 32, 2. Two women.

20 (13). SYRACUSE 19894, fr., from Camarina. Two women.

PSYKTER

21 (15). BERLIN inv. 3407, from Greece. *Jb. Berl. Mus.* 3, 127 figs. 11–12. A, Eros flying, with hare; B, boy with cock and hoop. Small.

OINOCHOAI
(*no. 22, shape 3, chous*)

22. ATHENS, Agora, P 20076, from Athens. *Hesp.* 19 pl. 107; *JHS.* 70 pl. 2, b; van Hoorn fig. 388 h; *Fasti arch.* 4, 165. Nike.

(*nos. 23–25, shape 2*)

23 (62). ANCONA 3225 (1008), from Numana. Athlete tying up his penis.

24 (63). ROME, Marchesa Isabella Guglielmi, from Vulci. Dionysos (running to right, looking round, with kantharos and stick).

25 (64). BRUSSELS A 2317. *CV*. pl. 21, 4. Warrior.

(*no. 26, shape 1*)

26. FERRARA, T. 225, from Spina. Woman with phiale.

LEKYTHOI
(*nos. 27–69, red-figure*)
(*nos. 27–45, standard shape*)

27 (17). SANTA BARBARA, Brundage (ex Canessa). Merlo 14, 3. Woman tying her girdle, and woman with mirror.

28 (16). PARIS MARKET (Feuardent). Woman at fountain (standing to right, holding hydria with both hands under the panther-head spout).

29 (19). SYRACUSE 21199, from Gela. *ML.* 17, 457. Woman cresting helmet.

30 (20). YALE 146, from Gela. *Coll. B. et C.* pl. 20, 168; Baur 98; Richter *F.* fig. 225. Woman putting clothes away.

31 (21). VILLA GIULIA 50323. *Boll. d'Arte* 7, 320 fig. 22. Woman with sucking-pig and sacrificial basket at altar.

32 (22). SYRACUSE 21162, from Gela. *ML.* 17, 426. Woman with wool-basket and mirror.

33. PARIS MARKET (Segredakis). Zeus and Nike (Zeus standing to right with phiale and sceptre, Nike standing frontal, head to left, oinochoe in right hand, with her left lifting her skirt). Large. Restored.

34 (23). LONDON E 578, from Gela. Nike with cithara, and youth.

35 (29). LONDON E 576, from Gela. Nike and warrior.

36 (26). NAPLES 3047, from Nola. Nike with cithara.

37 (31). PARIS MARKET (Feuardent). *Coll. M.E.* pl. 8, 153. Nike with lyre.

38 (27). WINTERTHUR, Bloesch (ex Giudice). *Vente xi Bâle* pl. 22, 338. Nike feeding thurible.

39 (24). OXFORD 1934.342, from Greece. Woman running to father.

40 (25). BERLIN inv. 30835, from Attica. Ghali-Kahil *H.* pl. 3, 2. Young warrior with drawn sword, and woman.

41 (28). BRUSSELS A 1014. *CV.* pl. 21, 3. Herakles and Athena.

42 (18). NAPLES MARKET (Canessa). Woman with oinochoe and a pair of phialai (to right, looking round).

43 (30). SYRACUSE 21847, from Gela. *ML.* 17 pl. 14, 1. Nike with thurible.

44 (33). KIEL B 369, from Athens. Woman with spear and shield caressing a goose.

45 (32). ATHENS 1303 (CC. 1191), from Eretria. King. ΛLΑ[VΚON] ΚΑΛΟ[ς].

(nos. 46–69, secondary shapes)

46 (34). SYRACUSE 2414. Nike (flying to right).

47 (35). LONDON MARKET (Sotheby, *Cat. July 5 1928 no. 23*: ex Parrish). Nike (flying to right with oinochoe and phiale). Near Class PL (see p. 675).

48 (42). HAMBURG G 34. Nike (flying to right, looking round, with sash).

49 (43). ATHENS E 1288. Eos.

50 (39). OXFORD 1925.84. *CV.* pl. 38, 7. Athena seated. Near Class PL (see p. 675).

51 (44). DITCHINGHAM, C. A. Smith (ex Lembessis). Goddess (probably Aphrodite: seated to right, sceptre in left hand, looking at a goose). Class CL (see p. 676).

52. PRAGUE, Nat. Mus., 1867. Maenad (running to right, looking round, with sprig of ivy). See p. 1664.

53. VIENNA 3209. Maenad (running to right, looking round, with a sprig of ivy in her right hand, and a fawn on her left). Misattributed in *ARV.*[1] 449 no. 19.

54. NAPLES 3353, from Nocera de' Pagani. *Bull. nap.* N.S. 5 pl. 5, 2; ph. So. x, ii, 16. Woman feeding pig. Class PL (p. 676 no. 7).

54 *bis*. PHILADELPHIA MARKET. Woman running with a helmet in her hand. Class PL (p. 676 no. 7 *bis*). See p. 1664.

55 (47). PARIS MARKET (Kalebdjian). Woman with basket (standing to right).

56 (48). ATHENS 1199 (CC. 1433), from Athens. Woman seated with alabastron.

57 (49). ATHENS 1200 (CC. 1452). Woman seated with σπάθη and alabastron.

58 (50). ATHENS MARKET. Woman seated with wreath at wool-basket (in
the field, hanging, on the left, mirror, on the right, lekythos and small
piece of stuff).

59. ATHENS 17640. *BCH.* 1946, 440. Danae and the golden rain (seated at
wool-basket). For the subject, Karouzou ibid.

60 (51). ATHENS MARKET. Woman seated at wool-basket.

61 (36). SYRACUSE 44286, from Gela. Poseidon.

62 (37). MELBOURNE, Univ., V 17 (ex Seltman). Dionysos. Restored.
Class PL (p. 676 no. 8).

63 (38 *bis*). CINCINNATI, Boulter, fr., from Greece. Dionysos (moving to
right, looking round, sprig of ivy in left hand).

64 (38). LEYDEN 1956.6.3 (ex Lembessis). Ph. A.I. Dionysos (moving to
right with branch and thyrsus). Class CL?

65 (45). TARANTO 4589, from Taranto. Hermes.

66 (41). MUNICH inv. 7710, from Greece. Eros.

67 (40). GLASGOW 03.70 l, from Lipari. Eros (flying, holding a piece of
meat).

68 (46). LONDON 1928.1–17.60. Man holding a piece of meat. Class PL or
near.

69 (52). ATHENS 1622 (CC. 1445), from Vari. Youth with spear running.

(*nos. 70–74, white ground*)

(*secondary shapes*)

70 (53). LONDON 1928.1–17.54. Woman with hydria fleeing from snake.
Class PL or near.

71 (54). NEW YORK 07.286.44. Fairbanks ii pl. 32, 1. Warrior doing his
hair with his sword. For the subject, Haspels *ABL.* 73. Class PL or near.

72 (55). CAMBRIDGE 37.32. *CV.* ii RS. pl. 14, 2. Seated goddess (Hera?).
Class PL or near.

73. GELA (ex Navarra-Jacona), from Gela. Dionysos (moving to right,
looking round).

74. BASLE, Cahn, 10. Eros (flying to right with a wreath in each hand).

SQUAT LEKYTHOI

75 (56). BOWDOIN 15.41. Boy with panther-cub, and man.

76. LIMASSOL, Kakoyiannis, from Marion. White ground. Eros (flying to
right, looking round, holding a pomegranate and an alabastron; on the
ground, in silhouette, two cocks fighting). See p. 1664.

ROUND ARYBALLOS

77 (57). ATHENS, Vlasto, from Markopoulo. White ground. A, athlete (moving to right, looking round, with strigil; on the left, pickaxe; on the right, pillar); B, athlete (moving to right, looking round; on the left, pillar with garment on it; and a pair of acontia; on the right, pillar with garment on it).

ALABASTRA

78 (58). BERLIN 4037, from Attica. Furtwängler *Sab.* pl. 54, 2. Women fleeing to old man.

79 (59). ATHENS, from Athens. Women at fountain.

80 (60). EDINBURGH L. 224.417. A, woman seated holding fillet; B, woman holding wool-basket.

81 (61). LONDON E 720, from Camiros. Nike.

ASKOI

82 (65). CAB. MÉD. 856, from Camiros. De Ridder pl. 24. A, Eros; B, Eros.

83 (66). ATHENS 1580 (CC. 1605). A, Eros; B, Eros.

84 (67). LEIPSIC T 2317. A, Eros kneeling, catching a bird; B, the like.

85. ATHENS, Agora, P 23263, from Athens. A, siren; B, siren.

SKYPHOI
(nos. 86–87, type A)

86 (68). BRUSSELS A 10, from Capua. A, Furtwängler *Somzée* pl. 39, i, 1 = *Vente Somzée* pl. 5, 45; *Mededeelingen* 7 pl. 4; detail of B, Buschor *Feldmäuse* 19 fig. 8, 2; *CV.* pl. 18, 1; bottom, H. R. W. Smith *Lewismaler* pl. 30, e. A, Triptolemos; B, initiation of Herakles.

87 (70). VILLA GIULIA 45583, from Cervetri. A, Nike; B, Nike.

(nos. 88–90, type A or type B)

88 (74). ADRIA B 41, fr., from Adria. *CV.* pl. 33, 8. Woman running.

89 (75). ATHENS Acr. 493, fr., from Athens. Youth.

90 (76). ATHENS Acr. (E 94), fr., from Athens. Woman.

(nos. 91–93, type B, glaukes)

91 (71). NAPLES Stg. 241. A, Nike. B, woman running with branch.

92 (72). BERLIN inv. 3140.197, from Marion. Herrmann *Marion* 29; Ohnefalsch-Richter pl. 184, 4. Warrior leaving home? (A, warrior; B, woman).

93 (73). VIENNA 570. *CV.* pl. 40, 1–2. A, man dancing; B, youth.

CUP-SKYPHOS

94 (77). ZURICH, from Capua. *Annali* 1878 pl. C; *Jb.* 59, 75. A, Theseus and Skiron; B, Herakles in Syleus' vineyard.

CUPS

95. SWISS PRIVATE. I, Poseidon and a woman (he standing to right with phiale and trident, she frontal with oinochoe; in the exergue, a pair of dolphins). A–B, return of Hephaistos.

96 (78). LONDON E 90, from Nola. Cecil Smith 115. I, woman at laver.

Probably also:

LEKYTHOS
(standard shape)

SYRACUSE (N.Y.), from Greece. *Alumni News* 12, x (Sept. 1931), 8, ii, 5, and p. 10, 1. Nike (flying with phialai).

NECK-AMPHORA
(Nolan amphora, with triple handles)

LONDON E 291, from Nola. A, *AZ.* 1880 pl. 12, 1; A, *AZ.* 1881, 163; *WV.* C pl. 8, 1; *CV.* pl. 48, 3. A, Phineus praying. B, woman. On A, +ΛΡΜΙ-ΔΕⳡ ΚΛⳂΟⳡ.

In *Sborník* 1959, 243, through a confusion of numbers, I am said to have attibuted the lekythos Prague, Nat. Mus. 770 (ibid. pl. 6, 28) to the Painter of the Yale Lekythos. The Prague lekythos which I attributed to him was 1864 (p. 659 no. 52). For 770 see p. 719 no. 15 *ter*.

NEAR THE PAINTER OF THE YALE LEKYTHOS

LEKYTHOI
(secondary shape)

1. Once AGRIGENTO, Giudice, 78, from Gela. Ph. Lo Cascio pl. 123, c. Poseidon (running to right with trident and fish). Compare the Melbourne lekythos (p. 660 no. 62). Restored.

2 (1). WÜRZBURG 554. Langlotz pl. 205. Woman seated. Class CL (p. 677 no. 8).

3 (2). ATHENS MARKET. Woman with lyre (standing to right, at wool-basket).

OINOCHOAI
(no. 4, shape uncertain)

4. LOUVRE, fr. (Feet and skirt-edge of a woman to right, with the dot-border below).

(no. 5, shape 5B)

5 (3). LOUVRE G 568. Dionysos.

THE PAINTER OF ATHENS 12778

ARV.[1] 334-5.

Near the Kaineus Painter (p. 510).

LEKYTHOI

(secondary shape: the shape, though not the pattern-work, is the same as in the lekythoi by the Flying-Angel Painter and in those associated with them, pp. 282-3—Class ATL, but in a neat version)

1 (1). ATHENS, Vlasto, from Kitsi. Apollo and woman (Artemis?) (he standing to right, with phiale and cithara, she to left, with oinochoe).

2. ANGERS 22, from Vulci. *RA.* 1923, i, 63, above; Henry de Morant pl. 18. Apollo and Artemis?

3 (2). ATHENS 12778 (N. 1073), from Eretria. Ph. A.I. NM 3132. Woman seated spinning, and youth.

Other lekythoi are near those by the Painter of Athens 12778, and stand even closer, perhaps, to the Kaineus Painter than they:

ARV.[1] 335.

LEKYTHOI

(secondary shape)

(nos. 1-3, rf.)

1 (1). PALERMO V 691. *CV.* pl. 22, 7-8. Theseus and Minotaur.

2 (2). LOUVRE CA 1710, from Greece. Ph. Gir. 32820, whence Bothmer *Am.* pl. 73, 7. Amazon taking refuge at altar. Near Class PL (p. 676).

3 (3). PALERMO V 695. *CV.* pl. 22, 6. Woman.

(no. 4, white-ground)

4. FRANKFORT, private. Woman seated (to right, holding out a mirror; behind her a wool-basket; suspended, on the right, an alabastron). KALOS. Near Class PL. Compare Palermo V 695 (no. 3).

MYS

ARV.[1] 459.

Mys stands apart from all the other painters in this chapter.

LEKYTHOS

(standard shape)

ATHENS 1626 (CC. 1362), from Tanagra. Part, CC. pl. 46, 1362; part, Hoppin *Bf.* 468. Apollo with Artemis, Leto, and Hermes. On the shoulder, two Nikai; on the neck, Nike. M[V]ς EΛRAΦ$EN. The mouth of the vase is alien. The painter seems to be imitating compositions by the Altamura Painter.

Compare perhaps the

ASKOS

LONDON E 723, from Rhodes. A, Eros; B, Nike.

CHAPTER 38

PAINTERS OF SLIGHT NOLANS
AND LEKYTHOI

THE ETHIOP PAINTER

VA. 138–9. *Att. V.* 325–6. *ARV.*[1] 464–5.

Called after the negro on no. 1.

PELIKAI

(small)

1 (1). CAB. MÉD. 393, from Nola. *AZ.* 1865 pl. 201, 3–4; A, *E.A.A.* iii, 466. A, Herakles led by one of Busiris' men. B, youth.

2 (2). Once DEEPDENE, Hope, 101. Tischbein 2 pl. 21; A, Tillyard pl. 12. A, Herakles and Athena. B, youth.

3 (3). LOUVRE G 434, from Nola. Millingen *AUM.* pl. 25; *CV.* d pl. 44, 1–4. A, Dionysos and Giant. B, youth.

4 (4). DRESDEN 323. *AZ.* 1865 pl. 194. A, Circe. B, old man (rather than a woman).

5 (5). FLORENCE PD 52, from Populonia. *St. etr.* 12 pl. 63, 1–2. A, Dionysos and maenad. B, youth.

6 (6). OXFORD 1927.3, from Cumae? *CV.* pl. 63, 13–14. A, warrior leaving home (youth and woman at altar). B, youth.

7 (7). LONDON E 413, from Nola. A, warrior leaving home (youth and old man). B, youth.

8 (8). LONDON E 411, from Nola. A, warrior leaving home (youth and woman). B, youth.

9 (9). Once PARIS, de Witte (ex Blacas), from Nola. A, Panofka *Dicht.* pl. 2, 5, whence *Jb.* 31, 133, and (a rude cut) Daremberg and Saglio s.v. Agon, fig. 180. A, Hermes and youth. B, youth. Panofka read the meaningless inscription as *Agon*, and was followed by Saglio (loc. cit.), Schreiber (in Roscher, s.v.), and Weege (*Jb.* 31, 134), but not by Reisch (in P.W., s.v.).

10 (10). COPENHAGEN 148, from Nola. *CV.* pl. 152, 1; A, *Die Antike* 15, 289; A, *Antik-Cab. 1851*, 129. A, Theseus and Minotaur. B, youth.

NECK-AMPHORAE

(no. 11, small, with ridged handles)

11. BALTIMORE, Walters Art Gallery, 48.56. A, youth with spears (Theseus?) pursuing a woman. B, youth.

(nos. 12–16, Nolan amphorae, with ridged handles)

12 (a 1). NEW YORK 56.171.41 (ex Bourguignon and Hearst), from Tarquinia. A, *Vente 18 mars 1901* pl. 2, 33, and p. 13; A, *Bull. Metr.* March
1957, 178, 3. A, Ajax and Cassandra. B, youth.

13 (11). BOSTON 01.18. The shape, Hambidge 80 fig. 6b and Caskey G. 71.
A, warrior leaving home (youth and woman). B, youth.

14 (12). Once Pizzati, from Vulci. B.Ap. xxii. 109. 3. A, fight (youth to
right, in chitoniskos and fur cap, with spear and pelt, youth in chitoniskos and kidaris retreating to right, looking round). B, youth.

15 (13). BOULOGNE 667, from Nola. A, *Mon.* 1 pl. 5, 4 (the man given as B
does not belong). A, Nike and youth. B, youth.

16. GELA (ex Navarra-Jacona), from Gela. A, king with sceptre and woman
with torches. B, youth.

NEAR THE ETHIOP PAINTER

NECK-AMPHORAE
(Nolan amphorae, with ridged handles)

1 (2). Once GOLUCHOW, Czartoryski, F. 28. *V.Pol.* pl. 12, 1; *CV.* pl.
29, 2. A, Athena and Hermes. B, youth. See p. 671 no. 12.

2 (3). LENINGRAD 708 (St. 1458). A, youth with spears. B, youth. See
p. 1664.

3 (4). NAPLES inv. 126052. A, Zeus pursuing a woman. B, youth.

4. ZURICH, Roš. A, *Sg Ruesch* pl. 7. A, Artemis and woman. B, youth.

HYDRIA
5 (5). ATHENS 1483 (CC. 1249). Three women. Small.

OINOCHOE
(shape 3, chous)

6 (6). JENA 423. *Sg Vogell* pl. 3, 12; van Hoorn *Choes* fig. 51. Dionysos and
satyr. The maeander (but nothing else) connects the vase with the Painter
of the Louvre Symposion and the Richmond Painter (pp. 1069–70).

Compare also the

LEKYTHOS
(standard shape)

TARANTO 100567, from Taranto. King and woman.

THE PAINTER OF LONDON E 342

Att. V. 323–5. *ARV.*¹ 459–63 and 960.

Mostly insignificant Nolans, mostly undersized.

NECK-AMPHORAE
(Nolan amphorae, with ridged or convex handles)

1 (1). LONDON E 342, from Nola. *El.* 1 pl. 19; *CV.* pl. 67, 2; A, *E.A.A.* iv, 689 fig. 826. A, seated king. B, youth.

2 (2). MUNICH 2328. *CV.* pl. 68, 3–4 and pl. 69, 6. A, seated king. B, youth.

3 (3). NAPLES Stg. 247. A, seated king. B, youth.

4 (4). LONDON E 325, from Nola. *CV.* pl. 62, 1. A, the Sphinx. B, youth.

5 (5). LENINGRAD 715 (St. 398). *JHS.* 48, 13 fig. 3. A, seated woman. B, youth.

6 (6). LENINGRAD (ex Botkin), from Nola. *JHS.* 48, 13 fig. 2. A, Herakles and Athena. B, youth. [Peredolskaya].

7 (7). LENINGRAD (ex Shuvalov). *JHS.* 48, 15 fig. 4. A, two women. B, youth. [Peredolskaya].

8 (8). VIENNA 1094. *CV.* pl. 61, 3–4. A, Nike. B, youth.

9 (9). DRESDEN 316. A, Apollo. B, youth. Restored.

10 (10). NAPLES 3132, from Ruvo. A, *Annali* 1841 pl. K; A, ph. So. 11072, iii, 4. A, woman with gosling. B, youth.

11 (11). NAPLES 3064, from Ruvo. A, ph. So. 11072, iii, 7. A, seated woman. B, youth.

12 (12). DRESDEN 318. A, woman with thurible at altar. B, woman.

13 (12 *bis*). Once NOLA, Calefatti, from Nola. B.Ap. xxiii. 35. 2. A, Nike with thurible (standing to left). B, youth (moving to left).

14 (13). GOETTINGEN (Berlin 2349 on loan), from Nola. A, Nike; B, youth.

15 (a 4). NEW YORK 06.1021.115. A, *Vente 11–14 mai 1903* pl. 1, 15; A, Sambon *Canessa* pl. 8, 103; Richter and Hall pl. 95, 94 and pl. 169, 94. A, Nike. B, youth.

16. MANCHESTER, Univ., from Capua. A, Nike.

17 (14). TOULOUSE 26.159 (360). Angelini pl. 12. A, Nike; B, youth.

18 (15). CAPUA inv. 215, from Capua. *CV.* pl. 4, 2 and 5–7. A, Nike. B, youth.

19 (16). BOSTON 90.157 (R. 422), from Nola. The shape, Caskey G. 73. A, woman at altar. B, youth.

20. PARIS MARKET (ex Chandon de Briailles: *Vente 11–12 juin 1959* no. 57). Phs. Gir. 31813–14. A, woman (frontal head, to left, right arm akimbo). B, youth (standing to left). [Bothmer]. Restored.

21 (17). GELA (ex Navarra-Jacona), from Gela. Benndorf pl. 55, 5. A, woman with lekythos. B, woman running.

22 (18). Once DEEPDENE, Hope, T. 96. A, woman. B, youth.

23. OXFORD, Walzer. A, *Sg Passavant-Gontard* pl. 5, 36. A, satyr and maenad. B, youth. [Jacobsthal].

24 (19). ALTENBURG 266. *CV.* pl. 46, 3–4 and pl. 47, 8. A, maenad. B, youth.

25 (20). VIENNA 904. *CV.* pl. 61, 5–6. A, man at altar. B, youth.

26. SALONICA inv. 34.51, from Olynthos. Robinson *Olynthus 13* pl. 61. A, youth with lyre, and boy; B, youth or man. [Robinson].

27 (21). LONDON E 327. *CV.* pl. 62, 2. A, two women. B, youth.

28 (22). LONDON E 343, from Nola. *CV.* pl. 67, 3. A, woman seated, and woman; B, youth.

29 (23). LONDON E 341, from Nola. *CV.* pl. 68, 1. A, woman offering lyre to youth; B, youth.

29 *bis.* NAPLES, Museo di Capodimonte, 964. A, youth receiving lyre from woman; B, youth.

30 (24). MUNICH 2341. *CV.* pl. 68, 1–2 and pl. 69, 5. A, seated youth, and woman. B, youth.

31 (25). BRUSSELS R 2511. *CV.* d. pl. 7, 6 and pl. 8, 3. A, youth and woman; B, youth.

32 (26). LONDON E 328, from Nola. *El.* 1 pl. 87; *CV.* pl. 62, 3. A, goddess and youth. B, youth.

33 (27). MANCHESTER, School of Art, from Nola. A, Herford pl. 9, a. A, youth and seated woman; B, youth.

34 (28). LEYDEN K 1894.1.12 (xviii h 40), from Italy. A, king seated, and woman; B, woman. Restored.

35 (29). Once NOLA, Calefatti, from Nola. B.Ap. xxiii. 31. 2; R.I. ix. 81. A, youth with spear seated, and old man. B, male.

36 (30). CAMBRIDGE 7.1955 (ex Lamb). A, arming (youth with spear and woman holding sword). B, youth.

37 (32). VATICAN. A, woman holding spear. B, youth.

38 (33). BRUSSELS R 249. A, Gargiulo *Cenni* pl. 7, 18; *CV.* d pl. 7, 5 and pl. 8, 2. A, Dionysos. B, youth.

39 (34). BRUSSELS R 2510. *CV.* d pl. 7, 4 and pl. 8, 1. A, woman seated, and woman. B, youth.

40 (35). VIENNA 630. *CV.* pl. 61, 1–2. A, woman with basket. B, youth.

LEKYTHOI
(standard shape)

41 (37). PALERMO (37). Two women (1, to right, with sash, 2, in peplos, frontal, head to left, sceptre in left hand).

42 (38). PALERMO (2638). Seated youth.

43 (39). SYRACUSE 21187, from Gela. Nike and seated youth.

44 (40). LONDON E 581, from Sicily. Nike and youth.

45. LUCERNE MARKET (A.A.). Youth and woman (youth in himation to right, holding a pomegranate, woman standing frontal, head to left, holding a sceptre in her left hand and her wrap with her right.

46 (41). Once AGRIGENTO, Giudice, 288, from Gela. Ph. Lo Cascio pl. 109, b. Woman (moving to right, with phiale; on the ground in front of her a goose).

ALABASTRA

47 (42). ATHENS 1240 (CC. 1542). B, Collignon and Couve pl. 46, 1542. A, woman seated; B, woman.

48. BASLE MARKET (M.M.). Mistress and maid (woman seated holding box, and woman holding mirror).

OINOCHOAI

(no. 49, shape 2)

49. GENOA 1159, from Veii. *Le arti* 3 pl. 68, whence *Anz.* 1941, 390; *CV.* pl. 6, 3 and pl. 7, 5. Woman seated, and woman.

(no. 50, shape 5B)

50 (43). VIENNA 383. Gerhard pl. 302–3, 5–6. Woman holding box.

The reverse of the following recalls the Painter of London E 342, but the obverse does not:

NECK-AMPHORA

(Nolan amphora, with ridged handles)

LONDON E 322, from Nola. *El.* 3 pl. 6, whence (A) Overbeck *KM.* pl. 2, 6; *CV.* pl. 6, 1. A, Poseidon. B, youth.

MANNER OF THE PAINTER OF LONDON E 342

Not always easy to separate these from the vases in the preceding list.

NECK-AMPHORAE

(nos. 1–2, Nolan amphorae, with triple handles)

1 (1). PARIS MARKET (Mikas). A, Nike. B, woman. On A, standing to right, with fillet; inscription ⊢NO⅃⊧N downwards. On B, muffled, seated on rock.

2 (2). PARIS MARKET (Feuardent), from Gela. A, woman running (holding tendrils; on the ground, birds). B, youth.

(nos. 3–12, Nolan amphorae, with ridged or convex handles)

3. RUGBY 12. A, youth and seated woman; B, youth. See nos. 11 and 12, and p. 670, foot.

4 (3). BRUSSELS R 255. *CV.* d pl. 7, 1 and pl. 8, 4. A, maenad and fawn. B, youth.

5 (5). MILAN, Scala, 385, from Cumae. A, *Vente 11–14 mai 1903* pl. 2, 7; *Cat. Jules Sambon* pl. 2, 14. A, woman; B, youth.

6 (10). NEW YORK 01.8.9 (GR 592). Richter and Hall pl. 95, 95, and pl. 169, 95. A, man; B, youth.

7 (11). NEW YORK 41.162.131. *CV.* Gallatin pl. 54, 2. A, warrior; B, youth holding scabbard. Compare New York 01.8.9 (no. 6).

8 (12). VATICAN. A, woman holding flower. B, youth.

9 (l 36). Once NAPLES, Vivenzio. Angelini pl. 15, whence Licht ii, 118. A, youth and woman.

10 (a). LONDON E 321. *CV.* pl. 60, 3 and pl. 51, 4. A, Athena and Herakles. B, man.

11 (a). LONDON E 339, from Nola. *Annali* 1841 pl. I; *CV.* pl. 67, 1. A, woman seated playing ball; B, youth. Compare Rugby 12 (no. 3).

12. STUTTGART MARKET. A, *Auktion Kricheldorf 28–29 Mai 1956* pl. 26, 1275. A, woman holding spear and shield; B, youth (leaning on his stick). B recalls Rugby 12 (no. 3).

LEKYTHOI

(*standard shape*)

(*nos. 13–16, red-figure*)

13. MAYENCE, Univ., 119. Hampe and Simon *G.L.* pl. 35, 2. Woman tying her girdle, and girl holding the woman's himation ready.

14 (13). LONDON E 586, from Gela. Nike.

15. CORINTH T 1263, from Corinth. *Art and Arch.* 29, 264 fig. 23. Nike. [Palmer].

16. Once AGRIGENTO, Giudice, 250, from Gela. Ph. Lo Cascio pl. 94, a. Woman seated with flower and mirror.

(*no. 17, white*)

17 (15). BOSTON 95.47 (R. 157), from Athens. Fairbanks i pl. 7. Charon.

The following may be placed in the neighbourhood of the Painter of London E 342:

NECK-AMPHORA

(*Nolan amphora*)

MYKONOS, from Rheneia (originally from Delos). Dugas *Délos xxi* pl. 19, 50. A, maenad running; B, woman running.

The youth on the reverse of another vase is very like those on Rugby 12 (p. 669 no. 3) and London E 339 (p. 670 no. 11):

NECK-AMPHORA
(Nolan amphora, with ridged handles)

OMAHA 1957.6. A, Pollak and Muñoz pl. 43, 1. Youth leaving home (A, youth and old man; B, youth leaning on his stick).

The lekythoi ascribed above to the Painter of London E 342 (pp. 667–9) or said to be in his manner (pp. 669–70) belong to a larger group of limply drawn lekythoi, other members of which are the following: some of them recall the Painter of London E 342; others, the Ethiop Painter.

LEKYTHOI
(standard shape)

1. WINCHESTER 99. Nike (in peplos, with phiale, standing at altar).
2. BALTIMORE, Walters Art Gallery, 48.254. Nike (flying with sash).
3. NAPLES (an old number 132). Nike (standing to left at altar, holding basket and torch).
4. SYRACUSE 19863, from Gela. Woman seated playing ball.
5 (7). SYRACUSE 19864, from Gela. Woman with caduceus running to altar.
6 (a). SYRACUSE 22878, from Camarina. *ML.* 14, 844. Woman with alabastron and perfume-vase, and woman with box. This was found with a white lekythos by the Painter of Athens 1826 (p. 746 no. 7) and may be by the same artist, as Buschor suggested (*ALP.* 16 no. 2).
7 (a). COPENHAGEN 135, from Athens. *CV.* pl. 164, 2. Woman with alabastron and box, and woman with torch. Compare Syracuse 22878 (no. 6).
7 bis. MONTPELLIER, Gallet de Santerre. Youth leaving home (woman to right, youth frontal, head to left).
8 (m 14). TARANTO 5531, from Metapontum. Youth leaving home (youth and woman).
9. SAN SIMEON, Hearst Corporation, 12290. Boy and man (both to right, the man holding stick and lyre: he is the paidagogos, compare the skyphos by the Pistoxenos Painter in Schwerin, p. 861 no. 30).
10 (1). SYRACUSE 21864, from Gela. *ML.* 17 pl. 15, 1. Woman laying (spindles?) on a table.
11 (2). SYRACUSE 21936, from Gela. *ML.* 17, 483. Athena and youth. Compare Syracuse 19861 (p. 672 no. 1).
12 (3). NAPLES 3123, from Nola. Angelini pl. 19; Heydemann *Knöch.* plate; ph. So. 11009, ii, 6; ph. And. 25945, part. Woman playing knucklebones. Compare Warsaw F. 28 (p. 666 no. 1).
13 (4). BERLIN inv. 4982.32, from Kerch. Eos and Tithonos? (so one would have said, but the winged goddess holds out a sash).

14 (6). CRACOW inv. 1252, from Athens. Bieńkowski *O lec.* 17–18, whence *Annuario* 4–5, 134 and van Hoorn *Choes* fig. 40; *CV.* pl. 10, 2. Maenad dancing at idol of Dionysos.

THE PAINTER OF SYRACUSE 19861

ARV.[1] 465.

Recalls the Ethiop Painter.

LEKYTHOI
(standard shape)

1 (1). SYRACUSE 19861. Athena and youth.
2 (2). SYRACUSE 19877, from Gela. Nike with phiale and thurible at altar.

THE PAINTER OF SYRACUSE 22174

ARV.[1] 463, top.

Akin to the Painter of London E 342.

NECK-AMPHORAE
(Nolan amphorae, with ridged handles)

1 (1). SYRACUSE 22174, from Gela. A, *ML.* 17, 439; A, *CV.* pl. 8, 5. A, Zeus and woman (Hebe?). B, maenad.
2 (2). SYRACUSE 22175, from Gela. A, *ML.* 17, 438; A, *CV.* pl. 8, 4. A, two women (Hera and Hebe?). B, youth (moving to right, looking round).

We append the Zannoni Painter to this chapter for want of a more suitable place, although he really belongs to the succeeding period. His slight lekythoi and Nolans are much the same sort of thing as those by the Painter of London E 342 and his fellows.

THE ZANNONI PAINTER

ARV.[1] 716–17.

Named after nos. 1 and 2, published by Zannoni.

COLUMN-KRATERS
(with framed pictures)

1 (1). BOLOGNA 224, from Bologna. Zannoni pl. 60, 1–4. A, youth leaving home. B, komos (man and two women).

2 (2). BOLOGNA 195, from Bologna. Zannoni pl. 124, 2–3; *CV*. pl. 26, 1–2. A, youth with spears (Theseus?) pursuing a woman. B, Poseidon and two goddesses.

3 (3). FERRARA, T. 593, from Spina. A, woman (goddess?) with sceptre and phiale, seated, and two youths. B, youth with sceptre, and two women.

PELIKE

4. MYKONOS, from Rheneia (originally from Delos). Dugas *Délos xxi* pl. 15, 39. A, youth and woman; B, male.

NECK-AMPHORAE
(nos. 5–6, Nolan amphorae, with ridged handles)

5 (4). RANCATE, Züst (ex Giudice), from Gela. A, ph. Lo Cascio pl. 107, a. A, Dionysos and satyr. B, youth.

6. NICOSIA C 767, from Marion. A, woman holding spear and shield. B, male.

(no. 7, small, with triple handles)

7 (5). LONDON E 308, from Nola. A, *El.* 4 pl. 90; *CV*. pl. 55, 2. A, komast ('Anacreontic'); B, youth. See CB. ii, 60 no. 25.

OINOCHOE
(shape 3, chous)

8 (6). ATHENS, Agora, P 5495, frr., from Athens. Van Hoorn *Chees* fig. 22. Sacrifice (man and boy).

LEKYTHOI
(standard shape)

9 (7). BARI 3667. Arming. The picture runs right round the vase.

10 (8). Once St. Audries (*Cat. Sotheby Feb. 23 1920* no. 249). Poseidon and woman (woman standing to right holding sash, Poseidon standing to left, trident in right hand).

11 (9). SYRACUSE 19876, from Gela. Zeus (?) and Nike.

12 (10). SYRACUSE 2412, from Agrigento. *Ant. Kunst* 2 pl. 8, 1–2. Zeus and Ganymede.

13 (11). CHALKIS 560. Dionysos and satyr.

14 (12). ATHENS 1296 (CC. 1424), from Eretria. Apollo and woman (goddess?).

15 (13). Once AGRIGENTO, Giudice, 1677, from Gela. Ph. Lo Cascio pl. 93, a. Woman with mirror, and woman.

16 (14). ATHENS 1297 (CC. 1422), from Eretria. Nike.

16 *bis.* TRACHONES, Geroulanos, from Trachones. Nike (running to an altar, with a basket). See no. 27 *bis.*

17 (15). GELA, Nocera, 7, from Gela. Nike (running to right, holding a helmet, to a pillar).

18 (16). TARANTO, from Pisticci. *NSc.* 1903, 264. Nike.

19 (17). ATHENS 1497 (CC. 1386). Ph. A.I. NM 757, whence *AM.* 32, 105. Nike.

20 (18). ATHENS 1498 (CC. 1390). Woman with phiale at altar.

21 (19). TARANTO 4587, from Taranto. Woman with mirror and alabastron.

22 (20). SYRACUSE 19869. Woman with mirror.

23 (21). LONDON E 600, from Sicily. Woman with mirror.

24 (22). MADRID 11160, from Athens. *CV.* pl. 13, 6. Woman.

25. GELA (ex Navarra-Jacona), from Gela. Woman with perfume-vase (standing to right).

26. NEW YORK, Briskier. Woman with box (standing to right; behind her a column). Restored.

27 (23). LONDON E 602, from Nola. Woman with torch.

27 *bis*. TRACHONES, Geroulanos, from Trachones. Woman seated, holding a wreath or the like. From the same sarcophagus as no. 16 *bis*.

28 (25). ATHENS 1403 (CC. 1373), from Boeotia. Trainer.

29 (26). AGRIGENTO, De Angelis, from Agrigento. Trainer (in himation, standing to right, wand in hand).

Perhaps also the

LEKYTHOS
(standard shape)

ATHENS, Agalopoulou. *Cat. d'une coll. d'ant.* 2, iii, 6. Nike.

Three vases go together and may be by the Zannoni Painter:

WHITE LEKYTHOI
(standard shape; second white used)

1. PARIS MARKET (Segredakis). Woman with oinochoe and basket (standing to right, head bent). [Bothmer].

2. BASLE MARKET (M.M.), from Greece. Woman with (fruit?) and perfume-vase (standing to right; in front of her a heron-like bird). Restored. [Bothmer].

3. BASLE MARKET (M.M.), from Greece. Woman tying her girdle (to right; in front of her a chair with her himation on it). [Bothmer]. Restored.

CHAPTER 39

PAINTERS OF SLIGHT LEKYTHOI
AND ALABASTRA

LEKYTHOI

In point of shape, red-figure and white lekythoi divide into two great classes: Standard Type, and Secondary Types. Standard lekythoi are, in general, larger and more careful.

Within the Standard Type there is the Bowdoin Painter's Type (BL). If his characteristic pattern-work is absent, it is often hard to distinguish the shape from other Standard lekythoi.

The chief Secondary Types are:

(1) the Petit Palais Painter's type (PL): see below;
(2) the type used by the Aischines and Tymbos Painters (ATL): see p. 709. It is derived from the finer shape used by the Diosphos Painter (DL: see below);
(3) the Carlsruhe Painter's favourite type (CL): see p. 676;
(4) the Beldam Painter's type (BEL): see pp. 750-3.

Secondary lekythoi are often rather nondescript in shape. In some of the Aischines Painter's vases the body is broader and more taut than in the rest, so that they approximate to type PL.

In secondary lekythoi, the neck of the vase is nearly always reserved, and the shoulder-decoration consists either of black 'rays' or of small, rough, old-fashioned black palmettes.

Besides these, there is the Diosphos Painter's type (DL), which can hardly be classed as either standard or secondary: see pp. 301 and 676.

CLASS PL

A class of secondary lekythoi named after two in the Petit Palais, 335 and 336 (CV. pl. 33, 1-4: p. 305). Neat make, broad body tapering strongly, shallow echinus mouth. The type shades off, and often all one can say is that 'the shape approximates to PL': the body may taper less, the mouth may be deeper and double-curved: assimilation to, or inter-assimilation with, the commoner Class ATL.

Forerunner, the Sappho and Diosphos Painters' principal type (DL)—but in the *broader* version preferred by the Sappho Painter (e.g. Haspels *ABL*. pl. 32, *CV*. Gallatin pl. 44, 1 and pl. 45, 1; especially New York 41.162.34, *CV*. Gallatin pl. 44, 2): but in PL a simple foot takes the place of the foot in two degrees, and the base is narrower, the mouth more precise. Some of the bf. lekythoi in the Class of Athens 581 (*ABV*. 487), though coarser, approach the shape, and they have the same kind of foot and base.

The following are characteristic specimens of Class PL:

LEKYTHOI
(*nos. 1–17, rf.*)

1. NEW YORK 41.162.27. By the Dutuit Painter (p. 306 no. 1).
2-5. The four rf. vases by the Vlasto Painter (p. 696 nos. 1–4).
6. ATHENS 1508. By the Bowdoin Painter (p. 678 no. 23).
7. NAPLES 3353. By the Painter of the Yale Lekythos (p. 659 no. 54).
7 *bis*. PHILADELPHIA MARKET. By the Painter of the Yale Lekythos (p. 659 no. 54 *bis*).
8. MELBOURNE, Univ. By the Painter of the Yale Lekythos (p. 660 no. 62).
9. HONOLULU 2892. By the Sabouroff Painter (p. 844 no. 153).
10. SAN FRANCISCO, Legion of Honor, 1621. By the Sabouroff Painter (p. 844 no. 156).
11. OXFORD Q. 1939. 3. Related to the Sabouroff Painter (p. 856).
12. BASLE MARKET (M.M.). By the Carlsruhe Painter (p. 733 no. 57).
13. READING 50. x. 4. By the Painter of Reading 50. x. 4 (p. 739 no. 1).
14. LENINGRAD, from Olbia. *Anz*. 1908, 188 fig. 20, 3; *Sov. arkh*. 1941, 318–25; Greifenhagen *Eroten* 52. Eros. Recalls the Dutuit Painter.
15. OXFORD 1946.183, from Attica. Archer.
16. PAESTUM, from Paestum. *Anz*. 1956, 411, a. Athena.
17. PROVIDENCE 25.109. *CV*. pl. 17, 1. Potter?
18. LUND. Woman with phiale at altar.
19. OSLO 11076. Nike (running, with a fruit or the like).

(*nos. 20–22, white*)

20. PARIS, Petit Palais, 336. By the Painter of Petit Palais 336 (p. 305 no. 1).
21. PARIS, Petit Palais, 335. By the Painter of Petit Palais 336 (p. 305 no. 2).
22. OXFORD 1922.18. By the Vlasto Painter (p. 696 no. 5).

CLASS CL

Secondary lekythoi of the Carlsruhe Painter's favourite shape.

Besides those decorated by the Carlsruhe Painter (see p. 730) there are a good many decorated by other hands:

1. ATHENS 17291. By the Bowdoin Painter (p. 679 no. 31).
2. CAMBRIDGE 149. By the Bowdoin Painter (p. 679 no. 32).
3. AMIENS. By the Bowdoin Painter (p. 681 no. 84).
4. STOKE-ON-TRENT. By the Bowdoin Painter (p. 680 no. 61).
5. MUNICH inv. 7689. By the Painter of the Yale Cup (p. 397 no. 51).
6. EUGENE, Moore. By the Painter of the Yale Cup (p. 397 no. 52).
7. PARIS, Seyrig. Related to Douris (p. 452).
8. WÜRZBURG 554. Manner of the Painter of the Yale Lekythos (p. 662 no. 2).
9. BASLE MARKET (M.M.). By the Icarus Painter (p. 698 no. 50).
10. LOUVRE CA. 1728, from Boeotia. Brommer *Satyrspiele*[1] 29 = [2]33; ph. Gir. Satyr as Perseus (running—or flying—with the head of Medusa).
11. CAPE TOWN 18 (ex Torr). *RA*. 1895, i, 221–2; Boardman and Pope pl. 14. Girl dancing pyrrhic. ΙΕΦVΡΙΑ ΚΑLΕ.
12. ATHENS 1752 (CC. 1444), from Athens. Woman with torch at altar. [B. F. Cook].
13. CARLSRUHE 219 (B 1814), from Athens. Welter pl. 14, 33; *CV*. pl. 26, 4. Satyr plunging his head into a pithos.
14. ADELAIDE (ex Sotheby, *Cat. 14 Nov. 1960* no. 126: ex Revelstoke 97, 1). Owl. On the foot of the vase a white line. [B. F. Cook].

Some smaller lekythoi are recognizably of this class:

1. NEW YORK 41.162.197. *CV*. Gallatin pl. 59, 5. Boy walking fast.
2. OXFORD 1927.4460. *CV*. pl. 62, 12. Head of athlete.

For Class ATL see p. 709; for Class BEL, pp. 750–2.

THE BOWDOIN PAINTER

VA. 70–72. *Att. V*. 138–43 and 472. *V.Pol*. 18–19. Haspels *ABL*. 157–60.
ARV.[1] 470–81 and 960.

The pyxis in Bowdoin, after which I named the artist, is not, as I found later, by him (see p. 144 no. 23). I retain the name: thinking not of the pyxis, but of the lekythoi in Bowdoin (nos. 143 and 170).

Miss Haspels has shown that a black-figure artist, the Athena Painter, may be the same as the Bowdoin Painter (*ABL*. 157–60). The potter-work is hardly distinguishable: the workshop is the same; and that the two painters are one seems to me very likely.

On the Athena Painter: Haspels *ABL.* 141–65 and 254–62; *ABV.* 522–33 and 704–5.

The Bowdoin Painter began in the late archaic period, but went on working as late as the third quarter of the fifth century.

The great majority of his lekythoi are of standard shape—of Class BL, named after him: see p. 675. But he sometimes used other shapes: these exceptions are noted; see also p. 692.

LEKYTHOI
(nos. 1–180, rf.)

1 (1). ATHENS 1272 (CC. 1394). Benndorf pl. 36, 8, whence Himmelmann-Wildschütz *Eig.* 25. Artemis (running to altar, with bow).

2 (2). TÜBINGEN E 74, from Gela. Watzinger pl. 25. The like. [Watzinger].

3 (3). TARANTO 2600, from Locri. Artemis (running to altar, with torches).

4 (4). LENINGRAD 673. The like.

5 (7). ATHENS E 1285. The like.

6 (8). NAPLES 3191. The like.

7 (9). ATHENS, Vlasto, from Skopelos. The like.

8 (10). Where?, from near Karabournaki by Salonica. *Albania* 1932, 71. The like.

9 (11). CANTERBURY H 124, from Athens. *JHS.* 57, 82, 2. The like.

10 (6). ATHENS MARKET. Artemis (running to altar, with torch).

11 (5). ATHENS 1313 (CC. 1425), from Eretria. The like.

12 (12). MUNICH inv. 7691, from Greece. Artemis (running to altar, with phialai).

13 (13). PALERMO. Nike (flying to altar, with phialai).

14 (14). FREIBURG S 47. The like.

15 (15). SYRACUSE 2407. The like.

16. BALTIMORE, Walters Art Gallery, 48.257. Nike (flying to altar, with phiale).

17 (16). LEYDEN 1954.12.3 (ex Geladakis). *Coll. E.G.* pl. 5, 117; *Oudheidkundige Mededelingen* N.S. 36 pl. 2. The like.

18. PAESTUM, from Paestum. The like.

19 (17). ATHENS 1621 (CC. 1402), from Velanideza. The like.

20 (18). REGGIO 4106, from Locri. The like.

21. ATHENS 17295. *CV.* pl. 12, 2. The like.

22 (20). LOUVRE, from Elaious. The like. Class ATL.

23 (19). ATHENS 1508 (CC. 1383). Ph. A.I. NM 3122, 1. Nike (flying to altar, with phiale, and fruit or the like). Class PL.

24 (22). ATHENS 1192 (CC. 1376). The like. Normal shape and ornament.

25 (23). PALERMO (571), from Selinus. The like.

26 (24). MADRID 11159, from Nola. *CV.* pl. 13, 3. The like.

27 (21). LONDON E 584, from Sicily. Nike (flying to altar with oinochoe and phiale).

28. TEL AVIV. Nike (flying to altar, with phiale and flower).

29 (25). PARIS MARKET (Socrate). Nike (flying to altar, with phiale and flower). Secondary type (Class PL?).

30 (26). CAMBRIDGE 148. *CV.* pl. 29, 7. Nike (flying to altar, with fruits).

31 (27). ATHENS 17291. *CV.* pl. 12, 1. The like. Class CL.

32 (28). CAMBRIDGE 149, from Athens. *CV.* pl. 29, 4. Nike (flying to altar, with flower and fruit). Class CL.

33 (29). PALERMO V 696, from Selinus. *CV.* pl. 24, 7. Nike (flying to altar).

34 (30). ATHENS MARKET. The like. Above, stopped key; below, key.

35. MYKONOS, fr., from Rheneia (originally from Delos). Dugas *Délos xxi* pl. 45, 101. Nike (flying).

36 (31). LENINGRAD 672. Nike (running to altar, with torches).

37 (32). LONDON E 582, from Gela. Ph. Ma. 3195, right. The like.

38. NEW YORK, New York University. The like.

39 (33). Once AGRIGENTO, Giudice, 252, from Agrigento. Ph. Lo Cascio pl. 96, a. The like.

40. (34). PARIS MARKET (Serrure). Nike (running with torches).

41 (35). PARIS MARKET (Feuardent). Nike (running with torches and phiale).

42. PARIS MARKET (Segredakis). Iris (rather than Nike, as Bothmer points out: running with caduceus; on the left a plant).

43. AMSTERDAM inv. 2567. *Vente xi Bâle* pl. 22, 337. Nike (running, right arm extended). Late.

44 (36). SYRACUSE 26394, from Gela? The like. Late.

45 (37). LENINGRAD 674 (St. 1533). *CR.* 1873, 5. Nike (standing at altar, with phiale and fruit).

46 (38). CANTERBURY H 113, from Athens. *JHS.* 57, 82, 1. Nike (standing at altar, with phiale).

47 (39). BRUSSELS, Errera. Ph. Brussels Museum, Errera ii, 1. The like.

48 (40). Once AGRIGENTO, Giuliana. The like.

49 (41). PRINCETON 28.28 (ex Seltman). The like.

50. GIESSEN. The like.

51 (42). ATHENS 1748 (CC. 1401), from Athens. The like.

52 (43). PARIS, Niarchos (ex Hirsch 149). *Ars Ant. Auktion I* pl. 57, 118. The like. Not early.

53 (44). SYRACUSE 19861. The like.

54 (44 *bis*). LIPARI (ex Syracuse 30957), from Lipari. Libertini *Le isole eolie* pl. 2, 3. The like. Class ATL.

55 (45). COPENHAGEN 134, from Athens. *CV.* pl. 165, 3. The like. Late. Class ATL.

55 *bis*. MAYENCE, Zentralmuseum, O. 29214. Nike (standing at altar, the object in the right hand missing). [B. F. Cook].

56 (47). PALERMO V 683, from Selinus. *CV.* pl. 23, 3. Nike (standing at altar, with oinochoe and phiale).

57 (51). SYRACUSE 21958, from Gela. *ML.* 17, 477. Nike (standing at altar, with fruit).

58 (50). Once AGRIGENTO, Giudice. Nike (standing at altar, with torches).

59. TARANTO 52289, from Taranto. Nike (standing at altar, with caduceus).

60 (48). ATHENS 12846 (N. 1029). For the subject see p. 1665. Late.

61. STOKE-ON-TRENT. Nike (standing at altar). Class CL.

62. Where?, fr., from Al Mina. *JHS.* 59, 7, 20. Female (Nike?) standing at altar.

63 (54). PALERMO (32), from Gela. Nike (standing to right, right arm extended).

64 (58). ATHENS MARKET. Nike (standing to right).

65 (56). OXFORD, Beazley, fr., from Naucratis. Nike (standing to right).

66 (57). ATHENS, Agora, P 5243, fr., from Athens. Nike.

67 (55). JERUSALEM (Jordan), Palestine Museum, P 196, fr., from Tell el Hesy. *Pal. Bull.* 4 pl. 7, 9; *Q. Pal.* 2 pl. 9, a, 3. Nike. Late.

68 (53). LECCE 578, from Egnatia. Nike (standing at altar, bending).

69. GELA, Angelo Jacona, from Randazzo. The like.

70 (52). BIEL, private (ex Hirsch 166), from Gela. Nike (standing at altar, bending, with fruits). Later. See p. 1665.

71. GELA, from Gela. *Boll. d'Arte* 39 (1954), 76; *NSc.* 1956, 370. Nike with hydria, at fountain (bending). [Orlandini].

72 (59). Once AGRIGENTO, Giuliana (ex Giudice). The like.

73. HOBART. Nike bending towards a hydria; she holds a sash.

73 *bis*. REGGIO, fr., from Locri. Woman (Nike?) bending towards a hydria. The lower part of the figure remains.

74 (60). NAPLES Stg. 576. Woman running to altar, with torches.

75 (62). CAMBRIDGE, Museum of Classical Archaeology, 58 (ex Lembessis). Woman running with oinochoe and phiale.

76 (63). LONDON, fr., from Macedonia. Woman running.

77. DUNEDIN, fr. Woman (or Nike) running (the lower part remains).

78 (61). SYRACUSE 19378, from Leontinoi. *RM.* 15, 95 fig. 37. Woman running with torch and phiale (to left, looking round).

79 (64). OXFORD 1914.8, from Greece. *CV.* pl. 38, 4. Woman with skein at wool-basket.

80 (68). BERLIN, Univ., D 438. The like.

81 (65). ATHENS 1343 (CC. 1417), from Tanagra. The like. Late.

82 (71). GENEVA MARKET (Hirsch, 141), from Gela. The like. On the left, garment; on the right, flower-basket. Late.

83 (69). ATHENS 1648 (CC. 1391), from Eretria. Woman with ball of wool at wool-basket.

84. AMIENS. The like. [Bothmer]. Late. Class CL.

85 (66). CORINTH MP 107, from Corinth. *Hesp.* 1, 76 . Woman at wool-basket. [Shoe].

86 (67). GODALMING, Charterhouse. *Greyfriar* March 1921, 88, 2. The like.

87. LUCERNE MARKET (A.A.). The like (standing with both fore-arms extended; behind her a seat; hanging, on the left a piece of stuff, on the right a pair of sandals). Late.

88 (70). ATHENS, Agora, P 9470, fr., from Athens. Dinsmoor *Heph.* 135. Woman at wool-basket.

88 *bis.* REGGIO, from Locri. The like.

89 (72). ATHENS, from Athens (Stables). Woman bending at wool-basket. On the left, a chair.

90 (73). LOUVRE G 334. Ph. Gir. 34054. Woman with balls of wool (or fruits). Restored.

91 (74). BRUSSELS A 3132. *CV.* pl. 21, 1; shoulder, Vian *R.* pl. 31, 245. Woman with mirror. On the shoulder, in black, Gigantomachy. [Haspels]. Compare Brussels A 3131 (no. 107) and see Haspels *ABL.* 159–60.

92 (75). CANTERBURY H 125, from Athens. *JHS.* 57, 82, 3. Woman with mirror.

93 (76). OXFORD 1927.4462, from Vulci. *CV.* pl. 63, 12, whence *E.A.A.* ii, 158 fig. 236. Woman with mirror, bending. Late.

94 (77). GOETTINGEN, fr., from Greece. Woman (standing to right, left arm extended).

94 *bis.* PADULA, fr., from Padula. Woman (the upper part remains, to right).

95. PRAGUE, Univ., E 128, fr., from Greece. *Epit. Haken* pl. 4, 5. Woman.

95 *bis.* REGGIO, fr., from Locri. (Lower half, except the feet, of a woman to right).

96 (81). OXFORD 1954.244, fr., from Al Mina. *JHS.* 59, 7, 16. (Female).

97 (82). Where?, fr., from Al Mina. *JHS.* 59, 7, 17. (Female).

98 (78). BERLIN inv. 3339. Riezler 53 fig. 30. Woman at fountain.

99 (79). SYRACUSE 21856, from Gela. *ML.* 17, 363. The like.

100. BALTIMORE, Walters Art Gallery, 48.256. The like.

101 (80). PARIS MARKET. The like. Above, net-pattern; below, rough egg-pattern.

101 *bis.* CHANIA 1094. Woman at fountain, bending. [Bothmer].

102 (83). NEW YORK 06.1021.90. Sambon *Canessa* 63 and pl. 17, whence *Die Antike* 1, 281; Richter and Hall pl. 33, 34, and pl. 175, 34; back, *AM.* 52, 225; Richter *ARVS.* fig. 56. Woman seated with wool at wool-basket, and Eros. See no. 107 *bis.*

103 (84). ATHENS MARKET. Woman seated at wool-basket (taking wool from it with both hands; hanging, on the left a flower-basket, on the right a piece of stuff).

104 (84 *bis*). BASLE MARKET (M.M.: ex Geladakis). *Coll. E.G.* pl. 5, 121. Woman seated, with skein (behind her a wool-basket; hanging, alabastron and flower-basket).

104 *bis.* GENEVA 18043. Woman seated at wool-basket, holding wreath.

105 (85). Once AGRIGENTO, Giuliana (ex Giudice). Woman seated with mirror at wool-basket.

106 (86). ATHENS 1194 (CC. 1375). Woman seated with mirror.

107 (87). BRUSSELS A 3131. *CV.* pl. 21, 2. Woman seated with wreath. On the shoulder, in black, Theseus and the bull. [Haspels]. Compare Brussels A 3132 (no. 91), and see Haspels *ABL.* 159–60.

107 *bis.* PARIS MARKET (Segredakis). Woman seated, as if holding a wreath. Below the handle and the upper border, as in New York 06.1021.90 (no. 102), a palmette. [Bothmer].

108. PARIS MARKET (Segredakis). Woman seated, holding a sash (hanging, a basket).

109. ATHENS, from Athens. Woman seated, holding a sash (behind her, a chair; hanging, sandals). [Karouzou]. Later.

110 (88). SYRACUSE 22822, from Camarina. *ML.* 14, 824. Woman seated, with lyre.

111 (89). ANCONA (1024), from Numana. Woman seated playing the flute. Ruined and restored.

112. BASLE 1944.2699. *Basel Jahresberichte* 1944, 20 fig. 6. Woman seated playing the flute, and girl dancing.

113 (90). CRACOW 605, from Attica. Bieńkowski *O lec.* 16; *CV.* pl. 10, 5. Naked woman at laver.

114. NEW YORK 46.129.11. Thracian woman (extract from a Death of Orpheus).

115. ATHENS 17877. Maenad. [Karouzou].

116 (91). NAPLES 3209, from Ruvo. Maenad.

117. LAON 37.961. *CV.* pl. 43, 1. Maenad at altar. [Bothmer].

118. MONS 21. Piérard fig. 6. The like. [Piérard].

119 (92). Once Englefield (later London market, Christie). Moses *Englefield* pl. 35, 5; already in Sir Benjamin West's portrait of Adrian Hope and his family (*Museum of Fine Arts, Boston; the Oil Paintings illustrated* s.v. West; Greifenhagen *Gr. Vasen auf Bildnissen* pl. 9). The like.

119 *bis.* REGGIO, two frr., from Locri. Maenad (standing to right, right arm extended). The upper half of the figure remains, except the head.

120 (93). PALERMO V 681, from Gela. *CV.* pl. 23, 2. Maenad running to altar.

121 (94). ATHENS, Vlasto. Maenad on donkey.

122. NICOSIA C 739, from Marion. *Cypr.* pl. 5, 3. Dionysos dancing. See *Cypr.* 40–42.

122 *bis.* BASLE MARKET (M.M.). *Hesp. Art Bull.* 11, 5 no. 191. Satyr (with kantharos and thyrsus). See p. 1665.

123 (95). CAMBRIDGE 37.27. *CV.* ii RS. pl. 13, 1; Greifenhagen *Eroten* 15. Eros (flying, playing the flute).

124 (97). PRAGUE, Nat. Mus., 775 (ex Lembessis). *Časopis Národního Musea* 12 (1938), 183, a; Frel *Ř.V.* fig. 39. The like.

125 (96). CAB. MÉD. 488, from Sicily? De Ridder pl. 20 (the number misprinted 498). Eros (flying to altar, playing the flute).

126. GELA, from Gela. *Boll. d'Arte* 39 (1954), 77; *NSc.* 1956, 296, 1, and 297 fig. 11. The like. [Orlandini].

127 (98). PALERMO V 686, from Selinus. *CV.* pl. 23, 7. Eros (flying with phialai).

127 *bis.* BASLE, Erlenmeyer. Schefold *M.* 207, 222. Eros riding a dolphin and playing the flute.

127 *ter.* LUCERNE MARKET (A.A.). *Ars Ant. Aukt. II* pl. 61, 155. Theseus and the bull.

128 (99). ATHENS 1273 (CC. 1395), from Attica. Flute-player.

128 *bis.* PHILADELPHIA MARKET. *Hesp. Art Bull.* 11, 5 no. 192. The like.

129 (100). FERRARA, T. 172, from Spina. The like.

130 (101). SYRACUSE 21854, from Gela. *ML.* 17, 361. Komast (playing the flute).

131 (102). NAPLES inv. 81576, from Nola. The like.

132 (103). LONDON 1927.4-12.5, from near Lake Copais. The like.

133 (104). GOTHA, from Agrigento. The like.

134 (105). Once AGRIGENTO, Giudice, 708, from Gela. Ph. Lo Cascio pl. 120, a. The like.

135 (106). Once AGRIGENTO, Giuffrida. The like.

136 (107). Once AGRIGENTO, Giudice, 695, from Gela. Ph. Lo Cascio pl. 123, a. The like.

137 (108). PRAGUE, Nat. Mus., 773 (ex Lembessis). *Časopis Národního Musea* 12 (1938), 183, b; Frel *Ř.V.* fig. 37. The like.

138 (109). PALERMO V 685, from Selinus. *CV.* pl. 24, 1. Komast.

139 (110). AGRIGENTO 21, from Agrigento. Cup-bearer (boy with oinochoe and strainer approaching bell-krater). Class PL.

140. ADOLPHSECK, Landgraf Philipp of Hesse, 49. *CV.* pl. 37, 1 and 4 and pl. 39, 2. Acolyte (boy with oinochoe and sacrificial basket approaching altar).

141. LUCERNE MARKET (A.A.). The like (but the key-pattern turned the other way).

142 (111). LIVERPOOL, Univ. Youth seated, playing the flute.

143 (112). BOWDOIN 20.1. The like.

144 (113). FERRARA, T. 790, from Spina. Warrior (in chitoniskos and hat, to right, looking round, with spear and shield).

145 (114). ATHENS 17281. *CV.* pl. 12, 6–7. Jumper.

146 (115). SYRACUSE 22872, from Camarina. *ML.* 14, 843. The like.

147 (116). SYRACUSE 19873, from Gela. The like.

148 (117). PALERMO V 689, from Selinus. *ML.* 32 pl. 95, 11; *CV.* pl. 24, 3–4. The like.

149 (118). MUNICH inv. 7711. The like.

150 (118 *bis*). MILAN, Scala. The like.

151. ATHENS, Agora, P 21284, fr., from Athens. (On the ground, a discus like that in Athens 17281, no. 145). [Yalouris].

152 (119). Once AGRIGENTO, Giudice, 110, from Gela. Ph. Lo Cascio pl. 110, a. Discus-thrower.

153 (120). CAB. MÉD. 487, from Sicily. Ph. Gir. 8129, a, whence *Arch. class.* 2 pl. 12, 3; *BCH.* 1957, 150 fig. 6. Victor.

154 (121). LONDON 1906.12–15.5, from Rhodes. *JHS.* 41, 127. Athlete at laver.

155 (122). BOLOGNA 358, from Bologna. Trainer.

156. LUCERNE MARKET (A.A.). Trainer (youth in himation standing to right, wand in left hand, right arm extended, at a pillar, beside which a discus is half seen on the ground, device an owl within a circle of dots; on the left a sponge, hanging, and a pair of acontia).

157. FERRARA (erratico), from Spina. Trainer (youth to right, wand in left hand, right arm extended).

158. PARIS, Villard. Trainer (youth to right, looking round, wand in right hand, left arm raised).

159 (123). LONDON E 589, from Magna Graecia. Horseman.

160 (124). LONDON MARKET (Spink: ex Giudice). Youth leaning on his stick (in himation, to right, phiale in right hand).

161 (125). FLORENCE 3992. Inghirami pl. 246; *CV.* pl. 72, 1. Youth leaning on his stick at pillar.

162 (126). LONDON E 585, from Nola. Hancarville 2 pl. 72, whence Inghirami pl. 236, *El.* 3 pl. 79, *AJA.* 1942, 65, whence *BCH.* 1952, 606, b. Herm.

163 (127). PALERMO V 687, from Gela. Benndorf, title-page, whence Perrot 9, 238; *CV.* pl. 23, 4. Herm.

164. NOCERA DE' PAGANI, Fienga. Herm (with short garment, to left; altar beside it; on the left, column with hare attached to it; hanging, a plaque representing a satyr).

165 (128). BONN 84, from Athens. *CV.* pl. 25, 1. Head of Athena.

166 (129). ATHENS 1348 (CC. 1406), from Tanagra. Sphinx.

167 (130). YALE 144, from Laurion. Baur 100. Sphinx.

168 (131). MARBURG, from Gela. Siren.

169 (132). PALERMO V 677, from Gela. *CV.* pl. 22, 9. Siren.

170 (133). BOWDOIN 13.5, from Gela. Lion and tree.

171 (134). PROVIDENCE 20.059. *CV.* pl. 19, 4. Lion and tree.

172 (135). WARSAW 199200. Lullies *K.* pl. 14; ph. A.I. varia 397.3. Lion and tree.

173 (136). PALERMO (pencil no. 57), from Selinus. Pegasus.

174 (137). LONDON E 587. Pegasus.

175 (138). SYRACUSE 12760, from Camarina. Pegasus.

176. BLOOMFIELD HILLS, Hall. *Hesp. Art Bull.* 1 no. 25. Pegasus.

177 (139). OXFORD 564. *CV.* pl. 38, 6. Pegasus. Restored.

178 (140). SYRACUSE 19903, from Gela. Bull.

179 (141). LONDON E 588. Owl.

180 (142). FREIBURG. Owl.

(nos. 181–223, white)

181 (143). ATHENS 1827 (CC. 1023), from Eretria. CC. pl. 37, 1023; Fairbanks i pl. 1, 1; *CV.* Jb pl. 1, 6. Nike (flying to altar, with phialai).

182. RICHMOND (Virginia) 56.27.4. *Auction xvi Basle* pl. 27, 115. Nike (flying to altar, with phiale).

183 (144). ERLANGEN 275. Nike (flying to altar, with phiale).

184 (145). CHALKIS 666. The like.

185 (146). ABINGDON, Robertson. Nike (flying to altar, with oinochoe and flower). [Robertson]. Secondary type.

186 (147). BERLIN 2249, from Athens. Nike (flying to altar).

187 (148). OxFORD 265, from Gela. Gardner pl. 25, 2. Nike (flying, with caduceus and fawn). Late.

188 (149). LONDON, Victoria and Albert Museum, C 2494.1910, from Attica. *Burl. 1903* pl. 94, H 35. Nike (standing at altar, with phiale and fruit).

189 (151). VIENNA 192. The like.

190 (150). LENINGRAD. Nike (standing at altar, with phiale).

191 (152). GELA (ex Navarra-Jacona), from Gela. Nike (standing at altar, with oinochoe and phiale).

192 (153). ATHENS MARKET. Nike (standing at altar, with oinochoe and fruit).

193 (154). LUCERNE MARKET (A.A.: ex Hirsch 165), from Gela. *Ars Ant. Aukt. II* pl. 58, 158. Nike (standing at mound-altar with oinochoe and caduceus; black himation). Later.

194 (155). FLORENCE MARKET. Nike (standing at altar, with oinochoe).

195 (156). PARIS MARKET (Mikas). Nike (standing at mound-altar, with oinochoe).

196 (157). LONDON, Russell, fr. Nike (standing to right: wings, head, shoulders, remain; black himation). [Payne].

197 (158). ATHENS MARKET. Nike (bending at altar). Above, key-pattern.

198. PARIS MARKET. Nike (bending: much restored, as pouring wine on altar).

199 (159). ATHENS 1791 (CC. 1026), from Attica. Benndorf pl. 23, 2; Heydemann pl. 5, 2. Nike with hydria at fountain (bending).

200 (160). PARIS MARKET (Segredakis). The like. The neck of the vase is reserved.

201 (162). OxFORD, Beazley. *VA.* 70. Woman with hydria at fountain.

202 (161). BERLIN inv. 2338, from Attica. Riezler 53 fig. 29. The like.

203 (163). PARIS MARKET (Segredakis). The like. Above, net-pattern.

204 (164). WÜRZBURG, from Spata. Ph. in Munich. Woman standing at altar, with phiale and branch (behind her a fawn; on the altar an apple and a bird—dove?). Himation, fawn, bird, are black. See p. 1665.

205 (165). TARANTO 20308, from Taranto. Woman (priestess) running, with oinochoe and sacrificial basket, preceded by a small bull-calf. The shoulder-palmettes are not the painter's. Late.

206 (166). ATHENS 1906 (CC. 1076), from Athens. Woman with phiale at mound-altar. Late.

207 (167). ATHENS 1792 (CC. 1019), from Attica. *AM.* 16 pl. 10, 2. Woman with lyre and dog.

208. BUFFALO, Museum of Science, 26420. Woman standing at wool-basket. Class PL.

209 (168). PALERMO (150), from Gela. Woman bending at wool-basket.

210 (169). RHODES 11902, from Ialysos. *Cl. Rh.* 3, 241; *CV.* III I a pl. 1, 3. Woman seated at wool-basket.

211. ELEUSIS, from Eleusis. *Prakt.* 1950, 134, 2, and p. 135 fig. 31. Woman seated, with wool. [Philippaki].

212 (170). TARANTO 20309, from Taranto. Woman seated, twining a wreath; in front of her a heron. Late.

213. ATHENS, Agora, P 7695, fr., from Athens. (Woman).

214 (171). MISSISSIPPI (ex Robinson). *CV.* i pl. 40, 1. Artemis caressing a fawn. Restored.

215. BRONXVILLE, Bastis. *A.A.A.* pl. 83, 294. Artemis (moving to right, bow and arrows in left hand, right hand raised; behind her a quiver, hanging; in front of her a fawn). Late. See p. 1665.

216 (172). BERLIN inv. 3312. Artemis (standing at altar, with oinochoe and torch; on the left, hanging, bow and quiver). Late.

217 (173). ATHENS 12588 (N. 963: but he gives this number to two vases). *CV.* Jb pl. 1, 7. Maenad.

218 (174). ATHENS 1964 (CC. 1066), from Eretria. Fairbanks i, 49; *CV.* Jb pl. 1, 5; ph. Marb. 154386. Warrior putting on his greaves.

219 (175). LONDON D 22. Hancarville 4 pl. 92, 2; Dubois-Maisonneuve pl. 18; *AZ.* 1885 pl. 12, 2; *Jb.* 30, 87; Kekule *Balustrade* 25; Murray *WAV.* pl. 14. Head of Athena.

220 (176). ATHENS, Vlasto, fr., from Athens. Head of Athena.

221 (177). NORTHWICK, Spencer-Churchill, from Attica. *Burl. 1888* pl. 20, 135; Chittenden and Seltman pl. 24, 102. Head of Athena. Late.

222 (178). LOUVRE L 33, from Greece? *Mon. gr.* 1885–8 pl. 7, 1, whence Rayet and Collignon pl. 10, Perrot 10, 695, and Buschor *Feldmäuse* 11 fig. 4. Head of woman with lyre.

223. ELEUSIS, from Eleusis. *Prakt.* 1950, 134, 3 and p. 135 figs. 11–12. The like. [Philippaki].

SQUAT LEKYTHOI

224 (179). OXFORD, Beazley (ex Feuardent). *Coll. Lambros* pl. 6, 60. Eros flying after a youth, and a dog. Late.

225 (180). MUNICH MARKET. *Aukt. Helbing 19–21 Mai 1913*, 4, no. 600; Jacobsthal *Mel.* 184 fig. 54. Nereid on dolphin (with the helmet and spear of Achilles).

226 (181). SYRACUSE 20100, from Gela. *ML.* 17, 515, 2. Artemis (running to altar, with bow).

227 (183). FERRARA, T. 686, from Spina. Nike (flying to altar, with phiale).

228 (184). FLORENCE 21 B 319, fr. *CV.* pl. 21, B 319. Nike.

229 (182). PALERMO (1190). Nike (standing at altar, with phiale).

230. PARIS MARKET (Mikas).   Woman standing at block-altar, with phiale.

231 (186). BERLIN 2478, from Nola.   Woman playing ball.

232 (187). MUNICH 2505 (J. 217), from South Italy.   Woman standing at wool-basket.

233 (188). NAPLES inv. 86061, from Cumae.   Woman with mirror.

234 (189). ABINGDON, Robertson.   Maid (woman running to left, looking round, right arm extended).   [Robertson].

235. BOSTON 41.911.   Eros flying with lyre.

236 (190). VIENNA 1020.   Youth seated playing the flute.

237 (191). ATHENS, Agora, P 761, fr., from Athens.   Athlete (jumper?) bending.

238 (192). LONDON E 653, from Nola.   Sudhoff i, 32; Anita Klein pl. 24, d. Naked youth at laver.   False interpretation of the unmeaning inscription in *CIG*. 7979.

239 (193). LUGANO, Schoen, 63.   Lullies *SGK*. pl. 24, 63.   Trainer.

240 (194). NAPLES inv. 85955, from Cumae.   Female head.

241 (195). MUNICH 2504 (J. 770), from Sicily.   Pegasus.

OINOCHOAI
(nos. 242–52, shape 1)

242 (196). LOUVRE G 577.   Millingen *Coghill* pl. 32, 6.   Youth in palaestra.

243 (197). WARSAW 140360 (ex Potocki).   *CV*. Potocki pl. 1 (Pologne pl. 129), 3; Michalowski *Sztuka* 109.   Youth seated playing the flute.

244 (198). RHODES 11969, from Ialysos.   Horseman (boy—jockey—riding).

245 (199). VIENNA 394.   Youth and dog.

246. SALONICA, four frr.   Artemis running to altar.

247 (200). NAPLES Stg. 246.   Nike (standing at altar, with phiale).

248 (201). LONDON E 517, from Nola.   Dennis i p. cxv no. 28.   Nike (standing at altar).

249 (202). LONDON E 520, from Nola.   Woman playing the flute.

250 (203). LONDON E 521, from Nola.   The like.

251 (204). NAPLES 3040.   Ph. So. 11069, iv, 3.   Woman with mirror.

252 (205). ATHENS, Vlasto, from Koropi.   Woman seated, with mirror.

(nos. 253–4, shape 2)

253 (206). BOLOGNA 342, from Bologna.   Youth seated playing the flute.

254 (207). BOLOGNA 340, from Bologna.   Woman with mirror.

(nos. 255–7, shape 3, choes)

255 (208). BOLOGNA 354, from Bologna.   Pellegrini 175 fig. 206; *Rend. Lincei* 1922, 326.   Youth running with torch.

256 (209). BOLOGNA 353, from Bologna. Van Hoorn *Choes* fig. 238. Youth folding his himation.

257 (210). CAB. MÉD. 467, from Camiros. De Ridder pl. 19. Youth seated playing the flute, and dog.

(no. 258, special shape: shape 10, but body as in shape 2)

258 (211). NAPLES 3122, from Nola. Ph. So. 11069, iv, 5. Nike (or Iris, running with caduceus).

HYDRIA

259 (212). Once LONDON, Oppenheimer, 71. Moses *Englefield* pl. 34, 5. Woman seated with wreath. Small.

LOUTROPHOROI
(small)

260. ATHENS, Acr. Mus., from Athens. Boreas and Oreithyia.

261. ATHENS, Acr. Mus., two frr., from Athens. (Women running).

262. ATHENS, Acr. Mus., fr., from Athens. (Woman running, flute-player). Belongs to the last?

263. ATHENS, Acr. Mus., fr., from Athens. (Upper part of a woman, head of another).

264. ATHENS, Acr. Mus., fr., from Athens. (Woman holding out wreath, woman with long hair).

SEMI-OUTLINE LEKYTHOI

A group of white lekythoi, black-figure, but with portions in outline, comes from the same workshop as the lekythoi of the Bowdoin Painter: see Haspels *ABL.* 155 and 238, *ARV.*¹ 478 and 960, and *ABV.* 523. These are all near the Bowdoin Painter and the Athena Painter, and again raise the question whether the two artists are not the same.

(For 'semi-outline' lekythoi by other painters see pp. 300–4).

LEKYTHOI
(bf. with white ground)

1 (1). NAPLES 2438, from Ruvo. *Jb.* 7, 188; *BCH.* 1898, 419; ph. So. 11070, iv, 6. Man leaning on his stick, and cock.

2 (2). NICOSIA, G. G. Pierides, from Cyprus. *BCH.* 1898, 417–18. The like.

3 (3). BERLIN 2250, from Athens. Fairbanks i, 24. The like.

4 (4). ATHENS 1809 (CC. 1025), from Aegina. Dumont and Chaplain pl. 11, 1; Rayet and Collignon 215, whence Perrot 10, 690, 377; Fairbanks i, pl. 1, 2. Eros flying with phiale and lyre.

5. SWISS PRIVATE. Eros flying after a hare.

6. BEIRUT 7393, fr., from Byblos. Dunand *Byblos* ii pl. 209. Eros.

7 (5). NEW YORK 08.258.28. *Bull. Metr.* 4, 102 fig. 3; *Charites Langlotz* pl. 26, 2. Dionysos with a small satyr and a goat.

8 (6). NAPLES Stg. 135, from Metapontum. Fairbanks i pl. 2, 1. Apollo (running to altar). Restored. Fairbanks accepts Heydemann's view of the inscription, but the letters are repainted and were doubtless void of meaning.

9 (7). ATHENS 1973 (CC. 964), from Eretria. CV. Jb pl. 1, 2–3. Hunter.

10 (8). ATHENS 12798, from Eretria. CV. Jb pl. 1, 1. Warrior leaning on his spear.

11 (9). CAB. MÉD. 299, from Vulci. Luynes pl. 16, whence *Jb.* 7, 185 and Furtwängler *Mast.* 124; *CV.* pl. 84, 7 and pl. 85, 1; ph. Gir. 8111 a, whence Devambez *L'art au siècle de Périklès* pl. 69. Wounded warrior.

12. BONN 538, from Athens. *Anz.* 1935, 474 fig. 51. Herakles and the bull. Placed by Greifenhagen with Cab. Méd. 299 (no. 11).

13 (10). LONDON 1910.6–15.6, from Thebes. Warrior.

MANNER OF THE BOWDOIN PAINTER

ARV.[1] 478–80 and 960.

LEKYTHOI

(nos. 1–21, rf.)

1 (1). PALERMO V 697, from Selinus. CV. pl. 24, 2. Nike (standing at altar, looking round, with phiale).

2 (l 46). AMSTERDAM 956. Nike (standing at altar, with phiale and flower).

3 (a 4). HEIDELBERG. Nike (with phiale, standing at altar).

4 (2). SYRACUSE 19866, from Gela. Nike (standing at altar, with oinochoe and flower). Late. May be by the painter himself.

5. OLYMPIA, from Olympia. Nike (flying, looking round, with torches). Secondary type.

6 (5). SYRACUSE 6310, from Leontinoi. Woman with drawn sword (moving to right, looking round, in chitoniskos and saccos, sword in right hand, scabbard in left). See *Cypr.* 41; and below, p. 1666.

7 (6). LUCERNE MARKET (A.A.: ex Giudice). Woman with flowers (standing to right, at a wool-basket). Below, billet-border.

8 (7). TORONTO 366. Robinson and Harcum pl. 56. Woman with torch at altar. Imitation by the Painter of Copenhagen 3630 (p. 724 no. 11).

9 (a 2). PALERMO V 684, from Gela. CV. pl. 23, 5–6. Woman at altar, with phiale and fruit. Compare the white lekythos Gela cim. spor. (no. 29).

10 (a 3). SYRACUSE, fr., from Camarina. Woman with sacrificial basket.

11 (a 1). PALERMO V 682, from Gela. *CV.* pl. 23, 1. Woman with spear or sceptre running to altar.

12. MINNEAPOLIS, Walker Art Center, 45.8. Maenad at altar. [Bothmer].

13 (12). ATHENS 1649 (CC. 1199), from Eretria. Athlete folding his himation. Early work by the painter himself? See p. 694, foot.

14. Where?, fr., from Al Mina. (Back of hair, and shoulder, of male standing to right).

15. Where?, fr., from Al Mina. *JHS.* 59, 7, 18. (Altar).

16. Where?, fr., from Al Mina. *JHS.* 59, 7, 19. (Knees of one seated? and flute-case hanging).

17. ATHENS, Agora, P 6158, fr., from Athens. (Forehead, nose, eye, raised right hand—of a discus-thrower or an acontist?)

18 (13). ERBACH. Tischbein 5 pl. 90; Dubois-Maisonneuve pl. 16, 4. Jumper and flute-player. Much restored.

19. LUGANO, Schoen, 62. Lullies *SGK.* pl. 24, 62. Boy chopping up the carcass of a goat.

20 (10). SYRACUSE 6311. Komast (man with stick and skyphos, moving to right).

21 (11). LOUVRE CA 1288 *bis*, from Tanagra. Old man leaning on his stick.

(no. 22, white? or rf.?)

22 (14). Once Cattaneo. B.Ap. xxi. 1. 2. Nike (flying to altar with phialai).

(nos. 23–30, white)

23 (15). ATHENS MARKET. Ph. A.I. varia 387, 1. Nike (standing at altar, with phiale and fruit). The chiton is coloured.

24 (16). ATHENS 1804 (CC. 1627). from Eretria. Nike (standing at altar, with torches). Second white used.

25 (17). CHALKIS 664. Nike.

26 (18). MUNICH inv. 7657. Nike (bending). Secondary shape. See p. 1666.

27 (19). LOUVRE CA 599, from Eretria. Perrot 10, 697; Fairbanks i, 36. Artemis (with phiale, torch, and bull-calf).

28 (20). LONDON D 23, from Gela. Murray, *W.A.V.* pl. 26, a. Woman with phiale (priestess?), and snake. Restored; the inscription alien.

29. GELA (cim. spor. 1948–9), from Gela. Woman standing with alabastron and (ball of wool?). Compare London D 23 (no. 28) and Palermo V 684 (no. 9). See p. 1666.

30. NEW YORK 06.1021.124, from Corinth? Dumont and Chaplain 1 pl. 11, 3. Youth with stick and fruit.

SQUAT LEKYTHOS

31 (21). LONDON E 654, from Nola. Maenad.

NECK-AMPHORAE

(Nolan amphorae, with ridged handles)

32 (23). NEW YORK 41.162.114, from Gela. *CV*. Gallatin pl. 52, 2. A, Apollo pursuing, B, a woman. Late.

33 (24). NEW YORK 41.162.106. *CV*. Gallatin pl. 53, 1. A, king; B, woman fleeing to him. As the last. Late.

Several of the lekythoi in the above lists, although the figure-work is by the Bowdoin Painter or in his manner, are not of standard type and have not his characteristic shoulder decoration: they are 'secondary' lekythoi. Some of them belong to Class PL or are near it; others to Class ATL; others to Class CL. For the terms see p. 875.

Class PL or near:

> Rf.   Athens 1508 (p. 678 no. 23).
> Agrigento 21 (p. 684 no. 139).
> White. Buffalo (p. 686 no. 208).

Perhaps also the rf. lekythos Paris market (Socrate) (p. 679 no. 29).

Class ATL:

> Rf.   Louvre, from Elaious (p. 678 no. 22).
> Lipari (p. 680 no. 54).
> Copenhagen 134 (p. 680 no. 55).

Class CL:

> Rf.   Athens 17291 (p. 679 no. 31).
> Cambridge 149 (p. 679 no. 32).
> Amiens (p. 681 no. 84).
> Stoke-on-Trent p. 680 no. 61).

Also secondary, the class uncertain:

> White. Abingdon, Robertson (p. 685 no. 185).

On the other hand, there are a good many lekythoi which, although the figure-work is by other artists, have the Bowdoin Painter's shape and shoulder-decoration: *ARV*.[1] 480. These shade off, however, into the ordinary standard lekythos. The Bowdoin Painter's shoulder-palmettes long remain common in the lower ranks of the standard lekythos. We mention only one or two lekythoi that look as if they came from the workshop of the Bowdoin Painter:

LEKYTHOI

(*standard shape: Class BL*)

(*rf.*)

1 (β). PALERMO (1194). Trainer (youth in three-quarter view from behind, looking round, wand in right hand). Perhaps not so far from the painter.

2. BERNE 23305. Warrior.

3 (ε). ATHENS 9685, from Eretria. *Festschr. Overbeck* 116; *RA.* 1897, ii, 37. Circe's sty.

4 (γ). SYRACUSE 19822, from Gela. Woman with basket.

5. MAYENCE, Univ., 35. Neugebauer *A.D.P.* pl. 71, 167; Simon *Prokris* figs. 1–3; Hampe and Simon *G.L.* pl. 22. Huntress. Prokris according to Miss Simon.

6. LAON 37. 956. *CV.* pl. 43, 3. Maenad.

BLACK LEKYTHOI FROM THE WORKSHOP OF THE BOWDOIN PAINTER

Haspels *ABL.* 262. *RG.* 65. *ARV.*[1] 481.

Many lekythoi without figure-work came from the workshop of the Bowdoin Painter (and the Athena Painter): black body; his palmettes and tongues, or tongues only, on the shoulder. There is usually a line or a band of pattern at the top of the body. The following are additions to the lists in Haspels *ABL.* 262 and in *RG.* 65.

LEKYTHOI

(*with palmettes and tongues on the shoulder*)

1. LUCERNE MARKET (A.A.). Key-pattern above.

2. TARANTO, from Taranto. Net above.

3. RHODES 11902, from Ialysos. Net-dots above.

4. Once LONDON, Revelstoke, 76, 1. The like.

5. ATHENS 15850. The like.

6. NAPLES inv. 85977, from Cumae. The like.

7. HAVANA, Lagunillas. The like.

8. RHODES 12906, from Camiros. *Cl. Rh.* 4, 112, 4. Above, a reserved band with three red lines on it.

9. LONDON MARKET (Spink). Above, a reserved band with two red lines on it.

10. NICOSIA C 745, from Marion. Above, three reserved lines.

11. SYRACUSE 21851, from Gela. Above, two reserved lines.

12. TARANTO, from Locri?

13. PALERMO, from Selinus (tomba 6).

14. SYRACUSE 2499.
15. SYRACUSE 2498.
16. SYRACUSE 14630, from Gela.
17. PALERMO (580), from Selinus.
18. PALERMO.
19. GELA, from Vassallaggi.
20. PHILADELPHIA L. 64. 187.
21. LYONS.
22. PALERMO (204).
23. CATANIA.
24. NICOSIA C 746, from Marion.
25. PALERMO, from Selinus (tomba 6).
26. SYRACUSE, from Gela.
27. PALERMO (5571), from Selinus.
28. PALERMO (267).
28 *bis*. CAPE TOWN 7. Boardman and Pope pl. 5, 7. [Boardman.]
29. ATHENS 18033.
30. PALERMO (570), from Selinus?

(tongues only)

31. VATICAN G. 79, from Vulci. *RG*. pl. 18, 79.
32. PALERMO.
33. SYRACUSE 21859, from Gela.
34. SYRACUSE, from Gela (Caposoprano, 1902).
35. Once AGRIGENTO, Giuffrida.
36. PAESTUM, from Paestum. *AJA*. 1954 pl. 68 fig. 5, 5. Small.
37. Once AGRIGENTO, Giuffrida.

To all these we append a lekythos in which the shape is the Bowdoin Painter's, but the shoulder-palmettes are red-figure. Miss Haspels (*ABL.* 162 and 262, second list from foot) has grouped this with three lekythoi 'in the manner of the Athena Painter', two of them black-figure, the third black-bodied; and a fourth is added in *ABV*. 524. See also p. 1666.

LEKYTHOS

LONDON E 573. Haspels *ABL*. pl. 22, 2. Pyrrhichist. Early. The figure-work is not remote from the Bowdoin Painter. Compare perhaps Athens 1649 (p. 691 no. 13).

Among the painters who used the Bowdoin Painter's type of lekythos, two inferior ones may find a place here: the Painter of Prague 774 and the Painter of Athens 1308.

THE PAINTER OF PRAGUE 774

Shape and shoulder-decoration of the lekythoi are the Bowdoin Painter's.

LEKYTHOI

(standard shape: Class BL)

1. PRAGUE, Nat. Mus. 774 (ex Lembessis). *Listy fil.* 7 (1959) pl. 1, 6; *Sborník* 1959 pl. 7, 24. Woman running with mirror (to right, looking round).
2. LAON 37.959 *bis. Sborník* 1959 pl. 7, L; *CV.* pl. 43, 2. Woman running with mirror. Replica of the last. This is ζ in the list (*ARV.*¹ 480) of lekythoi that have the Bowdoin Painter's shape and shoulder-decoration, but figure-work by other hands.

ALABASTRON

3. ATHENS, Agora, P 15961, fr., from Athens. Woman standing; woman running.

———————

THE PAINTER OF ATHENS 1308

ARV. 762.

Shape and shoulder-decoration are the Bowdoin Painter's.

LEKYTHOI

(standard shape: Class BL)

1 (1). ATHENS 1308 (CC. 1384), from Eretria. Ph. A.I. NM 3047, 2. Nike (flying).
2 (2). CATANIA. Nike (flying, with tendril).
3 (3). Once AGRIGENTO, Giudice, 90, from Gela. Ph. Lo Cascio pl. 97, b. Nike (flying).
4. LONDON, Hinrichsen (ex Ionides). Nike (flying, holding a wreath, or as if holding one; on the right a plant).
5. Once LONDON, Ionides. Nike (flying, with a flower).
6. MISSISSIPPI (ex Robinson), from Olynthus. Robinson *Olynthus 13* pl. 95. Nike (flying).
7. ATHENS 1747 (CC. 1400), from Athens. Nike (flying). [B. F. Cook].
8. LUCERNE MARKET (A.A.). Nike (flying, arms extended; on the ground in front of her a bowl).

Compare the lekythos (of the same type)

SYRACUSE 19409, from Leontinoi. Woman running with arms outstretched.

———————

THE VLASTO PAINTER

ARV.[1] 481.

LEKYTHOI

(*secondary shape; Class PL, see p. 676 nos. 2–5*)

(*nos. 1–4, rf.*)

1 (1). ATHENS, Vlasto, from Athens.   Youth and woman (woman seated holding wreath, youth leaning on his stick).

2 (2). ATHENS 12428.   Woman seated spinning.

3 (3). ATHENS, Vlasto, from Vouliagmeni.   Woman with perfume-vase and mirror (standing frontal, head to left; on the left a chair, on the right a wool-basket).

4. NEW YORK MARKET.   Nike (in chiton and saccos, flying to right, holding out a wreath; above, a reserved line; below, another).

(*no. 5, white, with glaze outlines*)

5 (4). OXFORD 1922.18.   Woman with perfume-vase. Side-palmette lekythos, see p. 303 no. 6.

With no. 1 compare the damaged white lekythos London D 30.

THE ICARUS-SEIRENISKE GROUP

This consists of vases by the Icarus Painter or in his manner, and by the Seireniske Painter or from his following, in which the Group of Carlsruhe 237 may be included.

THE ICARUS PAINTER

JHS. 47, 233.   Haspels *ABL.* 180 and 270–1.   *ARV.*[1] 482–6 and 961.

Called after no. 1.

Many of these were attributed independently by Miss Haspels.

I have included in the list a good many vases which in *ARV.*[1] I counted as 'in his manner' or 'near him'.   Among them are those there attributed to a 'Painter of Palermo 1191' but said to be perhaps by the Icarus Painter himself: I now think of them as late work by the Icarus Painter.   There may be school-pieces among the less deft members of the list.

The lekythoi are all of secondary type.   Most of them have a broad body and a general shape which approximates to Class PL but tends to be top-heavy.

LEKYTHOI

(*small; secondary shape*)

(*nos. 1–61, rf.*)

1 (1). NEW YORK 24.97.37, from Greece.   *JHS.* 47, 231.   Icarus? See no. 83.

2 (2). ATHENS, Vlasto, from Greece. Eros (flying to altar, playing the flute).

3 (3). BERLIN 2220. Eros (flying to altar, with lyre).

4. CAMBRIDGE 150. Eros (flying to altar, with lyre).

5 (4). SÈVRES 2038, from Nola. *CV.* pl. 18, 7. Boy seated with lyre.

6 (5). PALERMO, from Selinus. Boy seated with lyre.

7 (6). ATHENS E 1291. Boy holding out lyre.

8 (7). ATHENS 12959. Flute-player.

9 (8). ATHENS 11393. Man leaning on his stick, with flower.

10 (9). Once SAN SIMEON, Hearst Corporation, 12328 (ex Lloyd). Man leaning on his stick at altar, with flower.

11 (10). Once AGRIGENTO, Giudice, 706, from Gela. Ph. Lo Cascio pl. 105, a. Man leaning on his stick, with purse.

12. NAUPLIA. Archer.

13 (12). WINCHESTER 64. King (Zeus) enthroned, with phiale and sceptre.

14. MISSISSIPPI. Youth leaning on his stick at herm. [Bothmer.]

15 (a 11). HAMBURG inv. 1934.1, from Gela. *Anz.* 1935, 85 fig. 13; ph. Lo Cascio pl. 115. Man at herm.

16 (11). BERLIN 2213. Gerhard *Ak. Abh.* pl. 63, 1. Herm. Restored.

17. SYDNEY 51.14. Herm. Late.

18 (13). PROVIDENCE 25.084, from Greece. *JHS.* 47, 232; *CV.* pl. 17, 2; Woodward *P.* fig. 20. Danae and Perseus.

19 (14). LOUVRE L 52. Thracian woman running (extract from a Death of Orpheus).

20. AMSTERDAM inv. 2838. *Auction xiv Basle* pl. 19, 76. Nike at fountain.

21 (15). Once ATHENS, Empedokles. The like—or the same vase?

22 (16). BRADFORD, Bradford School, from Greece. Nike at altar (standing to right, her right hand lifting her skirt, her left arm extended).

23 (17). VILLA GIULIA 50582, from Cervetri. Nike at altar (holding torches).

24 (a i 4). PARIS MARKET (Segredakis). Nike (standing to right at a column, holding a basket).

25 (a i 8). WARSAW 142316 (ex Czartoryski 36), from Nola. *V.Pol.* pl. 11, 1; *CV.* pl. 23, 1. Nike (flying to a thurible).

26 (a i 9). LONDON E 616. Nike (flying with a basket). As the last.

27 (a ii a 2). ATHENS 1749 (CC. 1441), from Athens. Nike (flying to altar, with phialai). Late.

28 (a i 7). NAPLES 3216. Ph. So. 11009, ii, 19. Nike, or rather Iris (flying, with writing-tablets and a tendril). Slightly restored.

28 *bis.* REGGIO, fr., from Locri. Nike. Her head remains, and the top of her wings, with the key-pattern above, and part of the shoulder of the vase.

29 (a i 3). PARIS MARKET (Segredakis).   Goddess (Hera?) (standing to right, with phiale and sceptre).

30 (18). Once AGRIGENTO, Giudice, 1748, from Gela.   Ph. Lo Cascio pl. 106, b.   Woman at wool-basket (standing to right; behind her a chair).

31. *Vacat.*

32 (20). COPENHAGEN 137, from Athens.   *CV.* pl. 165, 7.   Woman with flower and mirror.

33 (21). ATHENS 1346 (CC. 1472), from Tanagra.   Woman with flower and mirror.

34 (22). ATHENS 1504 (CC. 1475).   Woman with mirror and flower.

35 (a i 5). SYRACUSE, from Camarina.   Woman at altar (standing frontal, head to left, phiale in right hand).

36 (23). PARIS MARKET (Lembessis).   Woman at altar (standing frontal, head to left, with phiale and sacrificial basket).

37 (25). LOUVRE CA 2567, from Chalkis.   Woman with sacrificial basket at altar.   Slightly restored.

38 (24). BERLIN 2216.   Woman at altar, playing the flute.   The upper part of the figure is modern.

39 (a ii a 1). DRESDEN ZV 2025.   *Anz.* 1925, 122.   Woman at altar.   Late.

40. SALONICA, Univ.   Woman with basket (standing to right, between two columns).

41 (a i 6). HARVARD 1925.30.37.   *CV.* Hoppin pl. 13, 4.   Woman with basket.

42 (26). ATHENS 18572.   *BCH.* 1954, 97 fig. 2.   Woman with flower.

43 (a ii 1). ATHENS 1502 (CC. 1466).   Woman bending with basket.   Late.

44 (a ii 2). BERLIN 2215.   Woman bending with basket.   As the last.   Late.

45 (27). ATHENS 1513 (CC. 1435).   Heydemann pl. 9, 3; *JHS.* 65 pl. 6, b. Woman seated playing ball.

46 (28). LONDON E 606, from Nola.   Woman seated playing ball.   As the last.

47. ATHENS, Agora, P 17601, from Athens.   *Hesp.* 17 pl. 67, 3.   Maenad.

48 (19). WÜRZBURG 549, from Greece.   Langlotz pl. 205.   Maenad.

49 (a). BOWDOIN 13.12.   *Coll. Woodyat* pl. 3, 4.   Maenad (running to left, looking round, with thyrsus and wineskin).   Late.

50. BASLE MARKET (M.M.).   *Vente x Bâle* pl. 20, 417.   Maenad (dancing, with wing-sleeves).   Late.   Class CL (p. 677 no. 9).

51 (29). AGRIGENTO.   Female head (in saccos, to right; in front, a column).

52 (30). BERLIN 2230, from Nola.   Female head.   Restored.

53 (a i 10). PALERMO, from Selinus.   *ML.* 32 pl. 95, 7.   Female head, between columns.   Later.

54 (a i 11). Taranto 2603, from Locri. Head of Athena. Later.

55 (31). Naples, from Cumae. *ML.* 22 pl. 84, 2, whence Buschor *Musen des Jenseits* 56. Siren playing lyre.

56 (32). Copenhagen, Thorvaldsen Museum, 122. Siren.

57 (a ii a 3). Copenhagen 167, from Athens. *CV.* pl. 165, 10. Siren. Late.

58 (33). Boston 01.8090. Owl.

59 (34). Once Agrigento, Giudice (162 or 762). Owl.

60 (35). Frankfort, Liebieghaus. Schaal *F.* pl. 21, c. Owl.

61 (36). London E 613, from Gela. Owl. [Haspels].

(nos. 62–79, white)

62 (37). Athens E 1240. Eros flying with lyre.

63 (38). Athens, Vlasto. Nike (running to right, with thurible).

64. Bryn Mawr, from Greece. Nike (running to right, arms extended).

65 (39). Athens, Vlasto. Haspels *ABL.* pl. 54, 5. Nike.

66 (41). Louvre F 375. Nike (running to altar, with phiale).

67 (40). Copenhagen 133, from Nola. *CV.* pl. 170, 3. Nike at altar. [Haspels].

68. The Hague, private. *Bull. Vereen.* 31, 23. Nike. [Schneider-Herrmann]. As no. 65.

69 (42). Munich inv. 7700. Nike (flying, with sash).

70 (43). Athens market. Nike (flying to right, with wreath; above, a pair of lines).

71 (44). Athens 14647. Woman with baskets of sashes.

72 (46). Tübingen E 57. Watzinger pl. 26. Woman bending to pick up her himation.

73 (47). Athens 1879 (CC. 1036). Female head.

74 (48). Dresden ZV 1824. Female head.

75 (49). Once Goluchow, Czartoryski, 91, from Locri? *CV.* pl. 42, 7. Female head.

76 (50). Vienna 631. Female head between columns.

77. London D 46, from Nola. *AZ.* 1885, 198. Female head between columns.

SQUAT LEKYTHOI
(nos. 78–80, rf.)

78 (a ii 3). Palermo (1191). Woman with basket, between columns. Late.

79 (a ii 4). Naples inv. 86062, from Cumae. Woman with basket. As the last. Late.

80. Cologny, Bodmer. *Aukt. Fischer 21 Mai 1941* pl. 7, 74 e; Schefold *M.* 233, 284. Female head between columns.

(no. 81, white)

81. NAPLES, from Cumae. Female head (in saccos, to left, between flowers).

WHITE ALABASTRON

82. OXFORD 1947.113. Woman and girl (woman with alabastron and sash, girl with perfume-vase and alabastron, a basket on her head).

OINOCHOAI
(shape 3, choes)
(no. 83, rf.)

83 (51). ATHENS, Vlasto, from Vari. *JHS.* 65 pl. 4, b. Icarus? Replica of New York 24.97.37 (no. 1).

(no. 84, white)

84 (52). OXFORD 1927.4467. Van Hoorn *Choes* fig. 150. Nike (flying with sash).

LOUTROPHOROS

85 (53). LOUVAIN, fr., from Athens. *Mél. Holleaux* 136. Prothesis, valediction. His only large-scale work.

MANNER OF THE ICARUS PAINTER
ARV.[1] 484–6 and 961.

LEKYTHOI
(secondary shape)
(nos. 1–8, rf.)

1. LONDON MARKET (Sotheby, *Cat. Feb. 16 1953*, part of no. 125; ex G. C. Croft). Warrior fallen (to left, looking round, with stone and shield; on the right a rock).

2 (i 2). ERLANGEN 172. Nike (running to right, looking round).

3 (iii 5). LONDON E 615. Nike (flying to altar).

4 (iii 4). ATHENS 1516 (CC. 1473). Maenad. Crude, but close.

5 (iii 6). ATHENS, from Athens (Stables). Maenad (to right, with thyrsus and branch). Late.

6 (iv 2). VIENNA 761. Maenad (running to right, wing-sleeves).

7 (iii 1). Once MUNICH, Preyss. Woman with lyre (moving to right, a dog beside her).

8. CRACOW, Univ., inv. 217. Bieńkowski O *lec.* 33; *CV.* pl. 8, 12. Youth leaning on his stick at a pillar.

(nos. 9–11, white)
(Class PL or near)

9. TOULOUSE 26.294, from Eretria. Goddess (Aphrodite?) with flower and sceptre. Close to the painter.

10. LEIPSIC T 429, from Gela. *Jb*. 11, 192, 36. Woman seated at wool-basket playing ball. Close to the painter.
11 (i 12). TÜBINGEN E 59. Sphinx.

LEKYTHOS?

12. ATHENS, Agora, P 16550, fr., from Athens. Maenad.

SQUAT LEKYTHOI

13 (ai 15). LONDON M 125. Hancarville 2 pl. 97, whence Inghirami pl. 237, *El*. 3 pl. 78, Roscher s.v. Hermes, 2393. Herm.
14 (a iv 3). SYRACUSE 14636, from Gela. Nike (flying to altar, with phiale). Late.

OINOCHOE
(shape 3, chous)

15. CAMBRIDGE 29.5. *CV*. ii pl. 26, 5; van Hoorn fig. 92. Swan drawing a cart loaded with two choes.

The following might be by the Icarus Painter:

LEKYTHOS

RANDAZZO, Vagliasindi, from S. Anastasia near Randazzo. *RM*. 15, 240. Eros.

With the Louvain loutrophoros (p. 700 no. 85) compare the

LEKYTHOS
(secondary shape)

OXFORD 1934.294. Seated youth. Near Class CL.

THE PAINTER OF CORINTH T 1256

Akin to the Icarus Painter.

LEKYTHOI
(small; secondary shape)

1. CORINTH T 1256, from Corinth. Nike (flying to left, with oinochoe and phiale). Near Class PL, like some of the lekythoi by the Icarus Painter.
2. PRAGUE, Nat. Mus., 1868. *Sborník* 1959 pl. 8, 32. Woman (with mirror, moving towards a chair).

THE SEIRENISKE PAINTER
ARV.[1] 486–90 and 961.

So called from one of the favourite subjects.

Tiny lekythoi and squat lekythoi from the same workshop as those of the Icarus Painter and very close to them in style.

LEKYTHOI
(small; secondary shape)

1 (1). BERLIN 2229, from Nola. Weicker 164 fig. 84. Siren.

2 (2). LEIPSIC. Siren.

3 (3). NAPLES 3188. Siren.

4 (4). NAPLES Stg. 222. Siren.

5 (5). MUNICH 2487 (J. 248). Siren.

6 (6). MADRID. Siren.

7 (7). PARIS MARKET (Segredakis). Siren.

8 (8). Once MUNICH, Preyss. Siren.

9. NAUPLIA. *BCH.* 1955, 238 fig. 13, 3. Siren.

9 *bis.* LAUSANNE 4325. Siren. [Bothmer].

9 *ter.* MILAN 46.1957. *CV.* pl. 11, 2–3. Siren. [Belloni].

10 (9). TARANTO, from Taranto. Nike (standing to right, with phiale, at altar).

11 (10). CIVITAVECCHIA. The like.

12 (11). ATHENS 1605 (CC. 1449). The like.

13 (12). LONDON E 618. Hancarville 4 pl. 54. The like.

14 (17). BERLIN 2223, from Nola. Nike (standing to right, with mirror, at altar).

15 (13). Once SCICLI, Spadaro, from Camarina. Benndorf pl. 36, 4. Nike running to altar.

16 (14). BERLIN 2225, from Nola. The like.

17 (15). CARLSRUHE 221 (B 220). *CV.* pl. 26, 7. Nike running to altar with torch.

18 (28). PALERMO (26). Nike running to altar with phiale.

19 (16). ATHENS MARKET. The like.

20 (24). AGRIGENTO, from Agrigento. Nike running with torch.

21 (26). GOETTINGEN (Berlin 2227 on loan). The like.

22 (29). PALERMO (1176). Nike running with a phiale to a plant.

23 (25). BERLIN 2226. Nike running. Restored.

24 (18). LONDON E 617. Nike running to column.

24 *bis.* LONDON, Victoria and Albert Museum, 2880.53. The like. [B. F. Cook].

25 (19). LOUVRE G 585. The like.

26 (20). NAPLES Stg. 217. The like.

27. HERAKLEION, Giamalakis. The like.

28. Lost. R.I. xii. 10. 3. The like.

29 (21). BOLOGNA PU. (299?). The like.

30 (22). NAPLES 3187. The like.

31. MANCHESTER, private. Nike running (arms extended). Specially close to the Icarus Painter.

32. ATHENS, Agora, P 25383, fr., from Athens. Woman (or Nike) running.

33 (27). TARANTO, from Taranto. Nike (running to left, looking round, with torch).

34 (23). LOUVRE G 586. Nike (running to left, looking round).

35 (30). Once AGRIGENTO, Giudice, from Agrigento? Ph. Lo Cascio pl. 189, a. Nike (seated to right).

35 bis. LAUSANNE 442. The like. [Bothmer].

36. CAPESTHORNE, Bromley-Davenport. Nike (flying to altar, to right).

37 (31). REGGIO 959. Maenad (standing to right, with thyrsus).

38 (32). TARANTO, from Locri. The like.

39 (33). BERLIN 2217. Woman with phiale at altar.

40 (34). AACHEN 7. The like.

41 (35). PALERMO (728). The like.

42. OLYMPIA, from Olympia. The like.

43 (36). NAPLES 3043, from Nola. Woman with mirror.

44 (37). SYRACUSE, fr., from Camarina. The like. The upper half remains.

45. MYKONOS, fr., from Rheneia (originally from Delos). Dugas *Délos xxi* pl. 45, 100. The like.

46 (39). LONDON 83.11–24.25. Woman running to altar with phiale.

47 (41). NAPLES Stg. 228. Woman running to altar.

48 (42). SYRACUSE 19424, from Leontinoi. The like.

49 (40). VIENNA 637. Woman running with phiale.

50 (43). LOUVRE G 596. Woman running with torch.

51. NAPLES 3041, from Nola. Woman running with torch and basket.

52 (45). BERNE 12346. Woman running (to right).

53 (46). LONDON E 623. The like.

54. PRAGUE, Nat. Mus., 1682, from Greece. *Sborník* 1959 pl. 8, 29. The like.

55 (a 12). LENINGRAD (St. 1570). *CR.* 1863 pl. 2, 18. The like.

56 (47). ATHENS 12484. The like.

57 (48). SYRACUSE 36275, from Gela. The like.

58 (49). PALERMO, from Randazzo. The like.

59 (49 bis). OXFORD 1838–68 p. 11. The like.

60 (51). Once AGRIGENTO, Giuffrida, from Agrigento. Woman running (to right, looking round, between columns).

61. AGRIGENTO. The like.

62 (50). CAIRO 26208. Edgar pl. 12. Woman running (to left, looking round, between columns).

63. MANNHEIM 7, from Campania. *CV.* pl. 32, 8. The like. [Greifenhagen].

64 (52). BOLOGNA (PU 302?). Woman running (to left, looking round).

65 (53). GENEVA I 19. The like.

66 (54). NAPLES 3037. Youth leaning on his stick.

67 (55). VIENNA 767. Female head, and column. Can hardly be separated from the female heads by the Icarus Painter (p. 698 nos. 51–53).

SQUAT LEKYTHOI
(*nos. 68–76, rf.*)

68 (56). NEW YORK 41.162.123. *CV.* Gallatin pl. 60, 2. Siren.

69 (57). BERLIN 2496. Siren.

70 (58). LONDON E 669, from Camiros. Siren.

71 (59). BOLOGNA PU (328?). B.Ap. xxii. 63. 2. Siren.

72 (60). Once AGRIGENTO, Giudice, 217, from Agrigento. Ph. Lo Cascio pl. 188, c. Siren.

73 (61). MUNICH 2503. Woman with mirror.

74 (62). NAPLES. Woman.

75 (63). LONDON E 671, from Nola. Woman running (to left, looking round).

76. PRAGUE, Univ., E 60, from Greece. *Sborník* 1959 pl. 8, 98. Woman running (to right). [Frel]. Barely distinguishable from p. 706 nos. 6 and 7.

(*nos. 77–78, white*)

77 (64). Once AGRIGENTO, Giudice, from Agrigento. Ph. Lo Cascio pl. 192, part. Female head.

78 (a). Once AGRIGENTO, Giudice, from Agrigento. Ph. Lo Cascio pl. 192, part. Female head.

OINOCHOE
(*shape 4*)

79 (65). LONDON E 562, from Nola. Nike flying to altar.

THE FOLLOWING OF THE SEIRENISKE PAINTER

*ARV.*¹ 488–90 and 961.

These small vases continue the lekythoi and squat lekythoi of the Seireniske Painter. The serial numbers in brackets refer to the list in *ARV.*¹, which did not distinguish the various hands, although a beginning was made in the preamble on p. 488.

(i) THE PAINTER OF LONDON E 673

ARV.[1] 488.

LEKYTHOI

(small; secondary shape)

1 (1). BERLIN 2222. Nike (standing to right, with mirror). According to Furtwängler, Berlin 2221, from Nola, which I have not seen (lent to another museum?), is a replica by the same hand.

2 (2). BERLIN 2224. Nike (standing to right, with thyrsus).

3 (3). LONDON (old cat. 776). Nike (standing to right, right arm extended).

4. ATHENS, from the Cabeirion of Thebes. Wolters and Bruns pl. 40, 5. Woman seated.

SQUAT LEKYTHOI

5 (19). ABINGDON, Robertson. Nike (standing to right at wool-basket, with mirror).

6 (20). LONDON E 673, from Nola. Woman seated.

Near these, three that go together:

LEKYTHOI

(small; secondary shape)

1 (13). LENINGRAD (St. 1558), from Nola. *CR.* 1863 pl. 2, 16. Woman seated with mirror. Seems restored.

2 (14). BOLOGNA PU 306. Woman seated with mirror.

3. NAPLES inv. 81598. The like.

Compare with these the

LEKYTHOS

(15). MUNICH 2485 (J. 250), from South Italy. The like. Restored.

Also near the Painter of London E 673:

LEKYTHOS

(4). DRESDEN 339. Nike (standing to right).

―――――――

(ii) THE ANGERS PAINTER

ARV.[1] 488 and 961.

Close to the Painter of London E 673.

LEKYTHOI

(small; secondary shape)

1 (5). ANGERS 23, from Sicily. *RA.* 1923, i, 63, below; H. de Morant pl. 19, b. Nike flying with mirror.

2 (6). COPENHAGEN inv. 1679. *CV*. pl. 165, 9. The like.

3 (7). VIENNA 635. The like.

4 (7 *bis*). SYRACUSE, from Camarina. *ML*. 14, 835. The like.

5. ATHENS, from the Cabeirion of Thebes. Wolters and Bruns pl. 40, 6.
Nike flying.

Near these the

LEKYTHOS

(8). NEW YORK 41.162.149. *CV*. Gallatin pl. 59, 6. Nike.

(iii) THE PAINTER OF SYRACUSE 21975

LEKYTHOI

(small; secondary shape)

1 (11). SYRACUSE 22954, from Camarina. Nike with torch standing at
wool-basket.

2 (17). SYRACUSE 21975, from Gela. *ML*. 17, 339. Woman seated with
torch.

(iv) THE GROUP OF COPENHAGEN 6442

Named after no. 12.

These are probably by one hand.

SQUAT LEKYTHOI

1 (22). ATHENS 1214 (CC. 1507). Woman seated with mirror at wool-
basket.

2 (23). ATHENS E. The like.

3. ATHENS Acr., fr., from Athens. (Head and shoulders of woman seated
to right).

4 (26). ATHENS 1652 (CC. 1533), from Eretria. Woman running to altar.

5. PARIS, Villard. Woman running with phiale to altar.

6. TÜBINGEN Z 194, from Greece. Woman running to wool-basket. As
the next. See p. 704 no. 76.

7. ATHENS, private, 21.3. Woman running to altar (with right arm extended). As the last. See p. 704 no. 76.

8. ATHENS, private, 21.1. Woman running (to right, looking round). As
the last.

9 (28). ATHENS 1745 (CC. 1488), from Athens. Woman with phiale
standing at basket.

10. BOSTON, private. Nike flying to altar (with right arm extended).

11. CORINTH 39.257, fr., from Corinth. Nike.

12 (29). COPENHAGEN inv. 6442, from Rhodes. *CV.* pl. 167, 6. Nike running.

13. ATHENS, from Athens. Nike running. Replica of the last.

14. ATHENS 16256 b. Siren.

Near these:

SQUAT LEKYTHOI

1 (a). CAMBRIDGE 37.40. *Vente 13–14 mars 1911* pl. 5, 11; *CV.* ii RS. pl. 16, 4. Nike flying to altar.

2 (30). HAMBURG 1899.201. Nike flying to altar, with phiale.

3 (31). VIENNA MARKET. Nike flying to altar. Burnt grey.

4 (32). ATHENS 1730 (CC. 1495), from Athens. Youth running to altar.

With Athens, private, 21.1 (above, no. 8) compare the

SQUAT LEKYTHOS

ATHENS, Agora, P 15036, fr., from Athens. Woman fleeing.

(v) VARIOUS

LEKYTHOI

(small; secondary shape)

1 (4 *bis*). Once AGRIGENTO, Giudice. Ph. Lo Cascio pl. 119, part. Nike (flying to column). Restored. See p. 1667.

2 (9). Once AGRIGENTO, Giudice, from Gela. Ph. Lo Cascio pl. 119, part. Nike (standing to right, bending a little, right forearm extended).

3. BRNO 2417. *Epit. Haken* pl. 4, 1. Nike (standing to right, right fore-arm extended). [Frel]. Same pattern above as in Montpellier, S.A., 191 (no. 4).

4 (a). MONTPELLIER, S.A., 191. Nike standing (to right, at wool-basket). Compare Munich inv. 7522 (no. 11). Larger. Restored.

5 (10). BOLOGNA PU (299?). Nike (standing to right, right arm extended).

6 (16). SYRACUSE 2420. Woman standing at wool-basket (behind her a column).

7. BARCELONA, from Ampurias. Woman standing at altar.

8. LONDON E 625, from Nola. Woman standing at altar. Restored.

9. PALERMO (729). Woman squatting at plant.

10. RHODES 12403, from Camiros. *Cl. Rh.* 4, 272, 3, and p. 273 fig. 300. Boy and partridges. Larger.

11. MUNICH inv. 7522. Siren and thyrsus. Compare Montpellier, S.A., 191 (no. 4). Larger.

SQUAT LEKYTHOI

12 (21). LENINGRAD (St. 1575), from Nola. *CR.* 1863 pl. 2, 21. Woman seated with (torch?).

13 (24). SYRACUSE, from S. Anastasia near Randazzo. Woman seated with mirror.

14 (25). LONDON E 670, from Nola. Woman running, looking round.

15 (27). Once AGRIGENTO, Giudice, 17, from Agrigento. Ph. Lo Cascio pl. 188, b. Woman running.

Also related:

LEKYTHOI

(*small; secondary shape*)

1. LONDON E 619. Hancarville 3 pl. 55. Nike (flying to column).
2. LONDON (old cat. 772). Woman at column.

THE GROUP OF CARLSRUHE 237

Two of these were put together by Hafner (*CV.* Carlsruhe i, 33), a third added by Frel (*Epit. Haken* 104; *Sborník* 1959, 244).

The four are probably by one hand.

SQUAT LEKYTHOI

(*small, lowboys*)

(*The subject is a woman standing or moving to left*)

1. CARLSRUHE 237 (B 297). *CV.* pl. 27, 5. [Hafner].
2. NAPLES (ex Spinelli 2430), from Suessula.
3. PRINCETON. *CV.* Matsch pl. 8, 5. [Hafner].
4. PRAGUE, Nat. Mus., 2281. *Epit. Haken* pl. 1, 3. [Frel].

Near these the

SQUAT LEKYTHOS

(*small; lowboy*)

Once AGRIGENTO, Giudice. Ph. Lo Cascio pl. 192, part. Woman (standing to right, right arm extended).

With nos. 1 and 3 Hafner compares the

SQUAT LEKYTHOS

SALONICA inv. 147 (R. 155), from Olynthos. Robinson *Olynthus* 5 pl. 99, 155. Woman.

THE AISCHINES PAINTER

VA. 74. *Att. V.* 320–3. *ARV.*[1] 494–502 and 968.

Called after the kalos-name on no. 222.

The lekythoi are of secondary type, and of the same shape as those by the Tymbos Painter (p. 753): Class ATL (for Aischines—Tymbos—Lekythoi). It is really the same shape as in Class DL, the Diosphos Painter's type (p. 675), and in the better examples the resemblance is fairly close, the chief difference being the shorter mouth; but the work is coarse and the body tends to have a slack outline. In the Tymbos Painter degeneration goes still farther.

The foot is often of two degrees, especially in the larger pieces, but is usually a simple torus.

(A neater version of the ATL shape, and a nearer to DL, appears in the lekythoi by the Flying-angel Painter and the Painter of Munich 2774: see pp. 282–3.)

LEKYTHOI
(nos. 1–180, rf.)

1 (1). ATHENS 1599 (CC. 1410), from Attica. Roscher s.v. Iris, 344; ph. A.I. NM 3127. Nike flying.

2. POMFRET (Connecticut), Howe. Nike flying (with wreath or sash).

3 (2). LONDON MARKET (Spink). *G. R. Spink* 32 no. 62. Nike (standing frontal, head to left, holding sash).

4 (3). LENINGRAD (ex Botkin). *JHS.* 48 pl. 2, a. The like. [Peredolskaya].

5 (4). Once OXFORD, Casson. Nike (standing frontal, head to left, lifting her skirt).

6 (5). ATHENS MARKET. The like.

7 (6). BOLOGNA PU 317, from Athens? Nike (lifting her skirt).

8 (7). SYRACUSE, fr., from Camarina. Nike (in peplos, frontal, head to left).

9 (8). MARBURG 1703, fr., from Greece. Nike (in peplos, frontal, head to left).

10 (9). TÜBINGEN E 75, from Cumae. Watzinger pl. 25. Nike (standing to right, holding wreath).

11 (10). ATHENS 1506 (CC. 1382). The like.

12 (11). ATHENS MARKET. The like.

13 (12). ALTENBURG 302, from Sicily. *CV.* pl. 74, 4–5. The like.

14. LOUVRE C 11030, fr. The like (the hands missing).

15 (13). MARBURG 1749, from Greece. The like (at mound-altar).

16 (14). PARIS MARKET (Mikas). Nike (standing to left, at altar).

17 (15). ATHENS MARKET. Nike (moving to right, with sash, to altar).

18 (16). ATHENS MARKET. Nike (moving to right, looking round, with sash).

19. LONDON MARKET (Spink). The like.

20 (17). DRESDEN ZV 2858, from Attica. *Anz.* 1925, 120. Nike (moving to right, looking round, with oinochoe and phialai).

21 (18). TARANTO 2601, from Locri. Eos.

22 (19). NAPLES. Eos (running to right, arms extended; the mouth of the vase modern—this for identification).

23 (20). CHALKIS?, from Eretria. Papavasileiou pl. 16, 10. Maenad (standing frontal, head to left, thyrsus in left hand).

24 (21). DUNEDIN 48.222 (ex Cook). Anderson pl. 12, 88. The like.

25. STOKE-ON-TRENT. The like. [Webster].

26 (22). TARANTO, from Locri. The like.

27 (23). ATHENS 1354 (CC. 1414), from Tanagra. The like.

28 (25). ERLANGEN 549. The like (at mound-altar).

28 *bis*. PARIS MARKET (Segredakis). Maenad (standing frontal, head to left, with phiale and thyrsus). [Bothmer].

29 (24). ATHENS, from Athens. Maenad (standing frontal, head to left, with oinochoe and thyrsus, at mound-altar).

30 (26). SCHWERIN 1268. Maenad (standing frontal, head to left, with phiale and thyrsus, at mound-altar).

31. CATANIA 732, fr. Libertini pl. 82. Maenad with torch at mound-altar.

32 (27). ATHENS 13752. Maenad (standing to left, with thyrsus).

33 (29). JALGAON, Damry. Woman at altar (standing frontal, head to left, with phiale).

34 (36). ATHENS MARKET. The like.

35. NORTHWICK, Spencer-Churchill. The like (at mound-altar).

36 (30). ATHENS 1277 (CC. 1379). The like.

37 (31). SYRACUSE 24004, from Camarina. The like.

38 (32). Once AGRIGENTO, Giuffrida. The like.

39 (33). LENINGRAD 872. *JHS.* 48 pl. 2, b. The like.

40 (34). Once HALLE, Kern. The like.

41 (35). ATHENS E 1403. The like.

42 (37). ATHENS MARKET. The like.

43 (38). ATHENS MARKET. The like.

44. CORONEIA. The like.

45 (39). ATHENS 1500 (CC. 1389). The like.

46 (40). Once TARPORLEY, Brooks, from Eretria. The like.

47. NEW YORK MARKET (Tozzi). The like.

48 (44). FLORENCE 91805 (ex Spranger). The like.

49 (41). LOUVRE, from Elaious. The like.

50 (41 *bis*). ATHENS MARKET. Woman at altar (standing frontal, head to left, with phiale and sceptre).

51. FERRARA, T. 56 B VP, from Spina. Woman at mound-altar (with phiale and sceptre).

52. ATHENS. Woman with sceptre.

53 (43). Once AGRIGENTO, Giudice, 109, from Gela. Ph. Lo Cascio pl. 110, b. Woman with phiale (standing frontal, head to left).

54 (45). ATHENS E 1844. Woman with mirror (standing frontal, head to left).

55 (46). ATHENS MARKET. The like.

56 (47). JALGAON, Damry, fr. The like.

57. PRAGUE, Nat. Mus., 1865. The like. [Frel].

58. GELA, from Gela. *NSc.* 1960, 146, d. The like.

59. BÉZIERS. The like. [Bothmer].

60 (48). HARVARD 25.30.36, from Tanagra. *CV*. Hoppin pl. 13, 3. The like.

61 (50). ATHENS 1278 (CC. 1381). The like.

62 (51). ATHENS MARKET. The like. On the left, wool-basket.

63. ATHENS MARKET. The like. The face restored.

64 (49). ATHENS, from Athens. The like, but on the left a box.

65. ATHENS, from Peristeri. The like.

66 (52). SYRACUSE 29654, from Gela. Woman with mirror and flower (standing frontal, head to left).

67 (53). TARANTO, from Locri. The like.

68. ROME, Romagnoli. Ph. R.I. 42.316. Woman with distaff (standing frontal, head to left). In some of the preceding vases, too, the thing may be a distaff and not a mirror. [Bothmer].

69 (54). ATHENS Acr. 843, from Athens. Langlotz pl. 75. Woman with flower.

70. OSLO, Dahl. Woman with alabastron and sash (standing frontal, head to left). [Seeberg].

71 (56). NEW YORK 35.54, from Greece. Richter and Hall pl. 95, 93 and pl. 175, 93. Woman. [Richter].

72. ATHENS 17699. Woman (standing to right). Late.

73. GREIFSWALD 354, fr. Peters pl. 40. Woman. [Buschor].

74 (58, 70). ATHENS 14401, from Eretria. Papavasileiou pl. 16, 7. Woman running with sprig (to right, looking round). B. F. Cook points out that my old no. 70 is the same vase as my old no. 58.

75 (59). ATHENS, Vlasto, from Athens. The like.

76 (60). NAPLES 3166. Ph. So. 11009, i, 11. The like.

77 (61). REGGIO 631, from Locri. The like.

78 (62). BASLE 1921.366. The like.

79 (63). KOENIGSBERG 76, from Greece. Ph. A.I. varia 397, 2. The like.

80 (64). Once COPENHAGEN, Wandel (ex Vogell 147). *Sg Vogell* pl. 3, 11. The like.

81 (65). ATHENS MARKET. The like.

82 (66). FERRARA, T. 245, from Spina. The like.

83 (67). *Vacat.*

84 (68). ATHENS 15869. The like.

85 (69). ATHENS 1276 (CC. 1380), from Attica. The like.

86 (70). *Vacat*, see no. 74.

87 (71). ATHENS 1696 (CC. 1423), from Megara. The like.

88 (72). COPENHAGEN inv. 1940, from Attica. *CV*. pl. 165, 2. The like.

89 (73). BRUNSWICK 262, from near Ephesus? *CV*. pl. 28, 11. The like.

90 (74). ATHENS E 1142. The like.

91 (75). ATHENS, Agora, P 10324, from Athens. The like. [Talcott].

92 (76). ATHENS, from Athens (Lenormant Street). The like.

93. BALTIMORE, Walters Art Gallery, 48.255. Woman running with flower (to right, looking round). [Bothmer].

94 (77). SYRACUSE. Woman running with torches (to right, looking round).

95 (78). PARIS MARKET (Lembessis). Woman running with torch.

96. NEW YORK MARKET (Morley). *Coll. Caron* pl. at p. 60, 248. Woman running with torch. [Bothmer].

97 (80). BASLE MARKET (M.M. : ex Elgin). Woman running with phialai (to right, looking round).

98 (82). BOULOGNE 192. Woman running with alabastron (to right, looking round).

99 (83). JERUSALEM (Jordan), Palestine Museum 32.307, from 'Atlīt. *Q.Pal.* 2 pl. 8, b. Woman running (to right, looking round).

100 (84). RHODES 12918, from Camiros. *Cl. Rh.* 4, 117. The like.

101 (85). BASLE MARKET (M.M.: ex Elgin). The like.

102 (86). SYRACUSE, fr. The like.

103 (87). VIENNA 625. The like. Much restored.

104 (88). PARIS MARKET (Feuardent). The like.

105 (89). ATHENS MARKET. The like.

106 (90). ATHENS MARKET. The like.

107 (91). ATHENS MARKET. The like.

108. PRAGUE, Univ., E 96. Frel *Ř.V.* fig. 45. The like. [Frel].

109 (92). LOUVRE G 590. The like.

110 (93). Once OXFORD, Coghlan. The like.

111. HARVARD K 46. The like.

112 (94). PARIS MARKET (Mikas). The like.

113. TEL AVIV. The like.

114 (95). PARIS MARKET (Serrure). The like.

115. NEW YORK 46.91, from Liopesi. The like.

116. NEW YORK 46.132. The like [Bothmer].

117 (96). PALERMO (12), from Gela. The like.

118 (97). PALERMO (13), from Gela. The like.

119 (98). SYRACUSE 19874, from Gela. The like.

120. OBERLIN 42.22, from Greece. The like. [Bothmer].

121 (99). Once AGRIGENTO, Giudice. The like. Restored.

122 (100). ATHENS 1522 (CC. 1438). The like.

123 (101). ATHENS 1600 (CC. 1409), from Athens. The like.

124 (102). LONDON E 609, from Athens. The like.

125 (103). ATHENS E. The like.

126 (104). OXFORD 1954.247, fr., from Al Mina. *JHS.* 59, 7, 27. The like.

127. LAON 37.964. *CV.* pl. 42, 8 and 12. The like. [Bothmer].

128 (105). ATHENS, Agora, P 6504, fr., from Athens. Woman.

129. ATHENS, Agora, P 24834, fr., from Athens. Woman.

130 (106). ATHENS, fr., from Athens. (Head, to left, and breast, of woman).

131. ATHENS, Rabnett, fr., from near Laurion. (Head, to left, and left shoulder, of woman). [Cambitoglou].

132 (107). MELBOURNE, Univ. (ex Seltman). Hermes.

133 (108). ATHENS 1197 (CC. 1413), from Attica. Hermes.

134 (109). ATHENS 1601 (CC. 1412), from Attica. Hermes.

135 (110). SYRACUSE, fr., from Camarina. Hermes.

136 (111). DRESDEN 336. Youth setting out (or Kephalos) (in chlamys, moving to right, looking round).

137 (112). WINCHESTER 65, from Phocis?. The like.

138 (113). CAMBRIDGE 146, from Athens. *CV.* pl. 29, 6 and pl. 40, 7. The like.

139 (114). ATHENS 1198 (CC. 1378), from Attica. The like.

140 (115). ATHENS E 1841. The like.

141 (116). LONDON MARKET (Spink: ex Brooks), from Eretria. The like.

142. STAVANGER. *Anz.* 1941, 62 fig. 4. The like. Much restored.

143. PRAGUE, Univ., E 98, fr. *Listy fil.* 7 (1959) pl. 1, 3. The like. [Frel].

144 (118). ATHENS E 1402. Tithonos.

145 (119). SYRACUSE 18420, from Camarina. Tithonos.

146. TEL AVIV. Tithonos. Much restored.

147 (120). ERLANGEN 245. Youth running (in himation, to right, looking round).

148 (121). VIENNA 676. The like.

149 (122). ATHENS, Agora, P 4940, fr., from Athens. The like.

150 (123). PARIS MARKET (Lembessis). Youth leaving home (in chlamys, standing frontal, head to left, spear in left hand).

151 (124). ATHENS MARKET. The like.

152 (125). LENINGRAD 875 (St. 1481 b). *JHS.* 48, 11. The like.

153 (126). VIENNA 3214. The like.

154 (127). PALERMO (817), from Gela. Youth (in himation, standing frontal, head to left, stick in right hand).

155 (128). LYONS. The like.

156 (129). ATHENS 1517 (CC. 1388). The like.

157 (130). FAYETTEVILLE, Univ. of Arkansas. Youth (in himation, standing with right leg frontal and the left crossed behind it, head to left).

157 bis. LÜBECK, St. Annen-Museum. The like. Replica of the last, but the lekythos is a rather topheavy standard.

158 (131). LECCE 580. Youth (in himation, leaning on his stick to right).

159 (132). Once LONDON, Revelstoke, 97, 2. Youth (in himation, leaning on his stick to left).

160. ATHENS 17595. The like.

161. MONS 22. Piérard fig. 7. The like.

162 (133). ATHENS 1203 (CC. 1453). Naked youth with laurel-staff (moving to left: Apollo?).

163 (134). SYRACUSE, from Camarina. Athlete (standing frontal, head to left, strigil in right hand, cloak on left arm).

164. TEL AVIV. Victor. Class PL. Restored.

165 (135). GOETTINGEN (J. 37). Jacobsthal *Gött.* pl. 12, 39. Eros.

166 (136). PRAGUE, Nat. Mus., 772 (ex Lembessis). *Listy fil.* 7 (1959) pl. 1, 1. Satyr (moving towards a volute-krater).

167 (137). COPENHAGEN 136. *CV.* pl. 165, 1. Satyr dancing.

168. GELA INA casa 1954, fr., from Gela. The like. The legs remain.

169. MAYENCE, Univ., 120. Hampe and Simon *G.L.* pl. 10, 1. The like.

170 (138). OXFORD 536, from Gela. *JHS.* 25 pl. 2, 2; *CV.* pl. 38, 9. Preparations for sacrifice (woman with phiale, and youth with spit and sacrificial-basket).

171 (139). SYRACUSE 22827, from Camarina. *ML.* 14, 826. Nike and maenad.

172. PARIS, Musée Rodin, 213. *CV.* pl. 27, 8. Youth and woman.

173 (140). NAPLES. Youth and woman (he leaning on his stick to right, she standing frontal, head to left, with alabastron).

174 (141). BASLE MARKET (M.M. : ex Preyss), from Greece. Youth and woman.

175 (142). ATHENS MARKET. Youth and (woman?) (he leaning on his stick to right, forearms extended). Neck and shoulder of the vase lost.

176 (143). AGRIGENTO (ex Giudice 1608), from Gela. Ph. Lo Cascio pl. 98, a. Youth and woman (she with mirror, he frontal, head to left, right arm akimbo).

177 (144). ATHENS 1501 (CC. 1420). Two women.

178 (145). LUCERNE MARKET (A.A.: ex Hirsch, 313), from Gela. Two women (one standing to right, with mirror, the other moving to right, looking round, with mirror).

179 (146). SYDNEY 47.06 (ex Brooks). Part, *Hdbk Nich.*[2] 301. Two women.

180 (147). ATHENS 1604 (CC. 1411), from Athens. Hermes and Nike.

(nos. 181–219, white)

181 (148). LONDON 1905.7-11.3. Man and flute-player. Restored.

182 (149). OXFORD 1929.3. Two women.

183 (150). ATHENS MARKET. Two women (one standing to right, holding a wreath, the other standing frontal, with flower and mirror). [Buschor].

184 (151). OXFORD 1928.170, fr., from Greece. Two women.

185 (152). ATHENS 1984 (CC. 1064), from Eretria. Two women. As Athens 1988 (no. 186).

186 (154). ATHENS 1988 (CC. 1063), from Eretria. Two youths (one holding a sash, the other a sash and a purse). As Athens 1984 (no. 185).

187 (153). OXFORD 269, from Gela. Youth and woman.

188 (155). ATHENS 1978 (CC. 1062), from Eretria. Boreas and Oreithyia.

189. PARIS MARKET (Mikas). Eos and Tithonos (Eos to right, arms extended, Tithonos in himation to right, looking round; key-pattern below as well as above).

190 (156). ATHENS 1793 (CC. 1032), from near Athens. Woman with flower and mirror.

191 (157). PARIS MARKET (Segredakis). Woman with flower and mirror (standing frontal, head to left).

192. MUNICH inv. 7655. The like.

193 (158). ATHENS E. The like.

194 (159). ATHENS E. The like.

195 (160). TARANTO 2597, from Locri. The like.

195 *bis*. STOCKHOLM, Galt. Woman (goddess?; in chiton, himation, saccos, standing with right leg frontal, head to left, sceptre upright in left hand).

196 (161). ATHENS E 66, fr. Woman with flower (standing to right).

197 (162). PARIS MARKET (Geladakis). Woman with mirror (standing to right, looking round).

198. SYDNEY 49.06. Woman running (to right, looking round, holding a flower).

199. BLOOMFIELD HILLS 1927.112. Woman running (to right, looking round, holding a sprig). [Bothmer].

200 (164). ATHENS MARKET. The like.

201 (165). NEW YORK 06.1021.126. The like.

202 (166). ATHENS 1787 (CC. 1030), from near Athens. The like.

203 (167). ATHENS, Vlasto, from Athens. The like.

204 (168). PROVIDENCE 25.075, from Sicily. *CV.* pl. 25, 2. Woman running (to right, looking round, with fruit and sprig).

205 (169). Once AGRIGENTO, Politi, from Agrigento. Politi *Esposizione di sette vasi* pl. 2, 4 (reversed). Woman running with sash.

206 (170). ATHENS 1784 (CC. 1027), from Athens. Woman running with alabastron and basket.

207 (171). ATHENS, Vlasto, from Athens. Woman running (to right, looking round; in peplos).

208 (172). ATHENS 1807 (CC. 1038), from Salamis. Woman running (to right, looking round).

209 (173). TÜBINGEN E 58. Watzinger pl. 26. Woman seated, holding wreath.

210 (174). MUNICH inv. 8328, fr. Maenad.

211 (175). TARANTO 20307, from Taranto. Nike (running to right with sash).

212 (176). NAPLES (2440?, from Ruvo). Ph. So. 11070, iv, 3. Nike (standing to right, holding wreath).

213 (177). ATHENS, Vlasto, from Athens. Tithonos (running to right, looking round, lyre in left hand).

214 (178). ATHENS 1857 (CC. 1022), from Salamis. Youth setting out (running to right, looking round, with spears; in chlamys).

215 (179). BASLE. The like.

216. ATHENS, from Peristeri. Youth running with sash (in himation, to right, looking round).

217 (180). GENEVA 5762. Youth leaning on his stick (in himation, to left). Restored.

218 (181). ATHENS, Vlasto, from Taranto. The like.

219 (182). NAPLES 2432, from Ruvo. Ph. So. 11070, iv, 4. Youth leaning on his stick (to right, holding wreath).

SQUAT LEKYTHOI

220 (183). PARIS MARKET (Lembessis). Nike (running to right, a phiale in each hand).

221 (a 24). NAPLES RC 124, from Cumae. Heydemann 1. Girl tying her girdle.

ALABASTRA
(nos. 222–7, rf.)

222 (184). BOSTON 01.8122, from Thebes. Youth and woman. ΛΙΣ+ΙΝΕΣ΅ ΚΑΛΟΣ.

223 (185). EDINBURGH L. 224.416. Woman running and old king.

224. BRUSSELS A 3427. A, woman seated with head-fillet; B, woman with flower and mirror. [Bothmer, Verhoogen].

225 (186). OXFORD 327. *CV.* pl. 41, 7–8; B, *E.A.A.* i, 176. A, woman spinning; B, youth leaning on his stick, with flower.

226 (187). SAN FRANCISCO, Legion of Honor, 1873, from Greece. *CV.* pl. 14, 4. A, woman with alabastron and box; B, woman with alabastron and sash.

227 (188). ADOLPHSECK, Landgraf Philipp of Hesse, 57, from Greece. *CV.* pl. 40, 7–9. A, woman with mirror; B, youth leaning on his stick.

(no. 228, white)

228. ATHENS. A, Nike (to right, with sash). B is lost. [Karouzou].

(no. 229, rf., of special type—with aryballos mouth)

229. SAN SIMEON, Hearst Corporation, (5708). A, Nike (standing at altar, with wreath). B, youth (leaning on his stick to left, with flower).

(no. 230, rf. Columbus alabastron)

230. ROMAN MARKET. Phs. R.I. 57.286–7. Man and youth.

HYDRIA

231 (189). LENINGRAD 750 (St. 1597). Mistress and maids (woman seated and two women). Small.

LOUTROPHOROI

232. ATHENS, Acr. Mus., fr., from Athens. (Under handle, head, to left, and shoulders, of woman).

233. ATHENS, Acr. Mus., fr., from Athens. (Head of Nike to right).

234. ATHENS, Acr. Mus., fr., from Athens. On the neck, A, woman, B, woman.

SKYPHOI
(nos. 235–235 bis, type A)

235 (191). ALTENBURG 287, from Nola. *CV.* pl. 75, 3–4; R.I. xii. 19. A, Nike, holding wreath; B, youth leaning on his stick, with strigil.

235 *bis.* REGGIO, fr., from Locri. (Upper part of a woman in chiton, himation, saccos, earring, moving to right, arms extended; part fired red).

(no. 236, type A ?)

236. LOUVRE C 11142, fr. A, Nike.

(no. 237, type A or B)

237 (a 15). ADRIA B 546, fr., from Adria. *CV.* pl. 33, 9. A, woman running.

(no. 238, type B, glaux)

238. TRONDHJEM (ex Nathan). *Cat. Christie July 14 1959* pl. 6, 1. A, woman seated (holding a mirror, at a wool-basket); B, youth (leaning on his stick, to left). See p. 1667.

CUPS

239 (192). FERRARA, T. 685, from Spina. I, woman (with mirror and alabastron); in a zone round this, youths and women; A, youths and woman; B, three women.

240. FLORENCE 74513, from Falerii. I, woman (with alabastron and flower); A, males and woman; B, (on the right, woman).

241. FERRARA, T. 18 C VP, from Spina. I, woman (with sash and basket); A, youths and woman; B, three women.

242 (a 6). BOLOGNA 390, from Bologna. I, youth with phiale; A, youths and woman; B, youth and women. See p. 823.

243. FERRARA, T. 179 A VP, from Spina. I, youth running to altar; A, youth leaning on his stick, and woman running with a piece of stuff; B, youth and woman running, with sashes.

244 (193). ATHENS Acr. 373, fr., from Athens. I, woman; A, (women).

245 (194). ANCONA 3224 (1045), from Numana. I, woman running (to right, looking round).

CUP OR STEMLESS CUP

246 (195). SYRACUSE (2364 and a final digit), fr., from Camarina. *ML.* 14, 911, 108. A, (woman).

MANNER OF THE AISCHINES PAINTER

ARV.[1] 500–2.

(i)

SUNDRY

ARV.[1] 501–2.

LEKYTHOI
(*nos. 1–21, rf.*)
(*nos. 1–20, secondary shape: Class ATL*)

1 (9). PARIS MARKET (Segredakis). Woman seated at wool-basket, holding

a wreath. As San Simeon 12305 (no. 21); compare also Cambridge 151 (no. 14).

2 (l 67). LONDON E 622. Hancarville 1 pl. 57. Woman running with sprig.

3 (1). ATHENS 1625 (CC. 1447), from Velanideza. Woman with phialai running to altar.

4 (2). BERLIN 2214, from Athens. The like.

5 (3). ATHENS E 1843. Woman running with alabastron. See p. 721.

6 (5). ATHENS. Woman running with flower and mirror (to right, looking round). The face missing.

7. LAON, from Eretria. *Ant. 10 déc. 1904* pl. 2, 4; *CV.* pl. 42, 3–4. Woman running with mirror.

7 *bis.* BASLE MARKET (M.M.). Woman running with a piece of stuff and an alabastron. Compare the last.

8 (a iii 4). ATHENS MARKET. Woman running with phiale and sacrificial basket (to right, looking round). Compare Athens 2025 and 1875 (p. 722, below, nos. 1 and 2).

9 (6). ATHENS (17698?), from Athens. Woman running (to right, looking round).

10 (7). ATHENS (17697?), from Athens. The like (but wearing peplos). Compare the last.

10 *bis.* BONN 1216.234, fr., from Athens. *CV.* pl. 38, 8. Woman.

10 *ter.* REGGIO, fr., from Locri. Woman (standing with right foot frontal, a piece of cloth in the right hand, a distaff or mirror in the left; below, rightward key-pattern).

11 (l 42). LONDON. Woman at altar (standing frontal, head to left, with phiale and sacrificial basket).

12 (4). PARIS MARKET (Lembessis). Woman at wool-basket (standing to right, arms extended; on the left, hanging, a thick sash).

13 (10). GOTHA 25. Nike at mound.

13 *bis.* ATHENS 17296. *CV.* pl. 12, 5. Nike.

14. CAMBRIDGE 151. *CV.* pl. 29, 5. Nike. Compare nos. 1 and 21.

15 (l 28). PARIS MARKET (Platt, ex Feuardent). Stackelberg pl. 24 fig. 6, ii, and fig. 7. Maenad. Compare Bologna PU 355 (p. 723 no. 7).

15 *bis.* TRACHONES, Geroulanos, from Trachones. Maenad (running to right, looking round, arms extended to left and right).

15 *ter.* PRAGUE, Nat. Mus., 770. *Sborník* 1959 pl. 6, 28. Maenad. Compare Bologna PU 355 (p. 723 no. 7) and the Platt lekythos (above, no. 15). In *Sborník* 1959, 243, through a confusion of numbers, I am said to have attributed this to the Painter of the Yale Lekythos. The Prague lekythos which I attributed to him was 1867 (p. 659 no. 52). See p. 1668.

16 (11). BERLIN 2219, from Greece. Athlete with phiale at altar.

17 (13). YALE 145. Baur 100. Athlete.

18 (12). HAMBURG, Hoffmann (ex Giudice), from Gela. Ph. Lo Cascio pl. 118, b. Jumper (moving to right, looking round, with haltēres).

19 (14). ATHENS 1202 (CC. 1457). Man leaning on his stick, holding a sash, at a stele.

20. MAYENCE, Univ., 12. Satyr holding a trap.

(no. 21, standard shape)

21. SAN SIMEON, Hearst Corporation, 12305. Woman seated at wool-basket, holding a wreath. As the Segredakis lekythos no. 1.

(nos. 22–28, white)
(nos. 22–27, secondary shape: Class ATL)

22. BOULOGNE 579. Woman running with sprig (to right, looking round; peplos). Damaged: may be by the painter himself.

23. BASLE MARKET (M.M., 248). Woman with torches running to altar (to right, looking round; peplos).

24. Lost, from Athens. *AM.* 17 pl. 1, 5. Woman running with sash.

25 (21). DRESDEN ZV 1825, from Greece. *Anz.* 1902, 116. Apollo.

26 (22). ATHENS 1918 (CC. 1075), from Vari. Satyr.

27 (23). NAPLES Stg. 111. Satyr.

(no. 28, standard shape)

28. SAN FRANCISCO, Legion of Honor, 1874. *CV.* pl. 14, 1 and pl. 30, 2. Nike. Restored.

(ii)

Three by one hand.

ARV.[1] 500, i.

LEKYTHOI
(*secondary shape: Class ATL*)

1 (1). NEW YORK 41.162.136. *CV.* Gallatin pl. 26, 1. Woman running with torch.

2 (2). MARBURG 1702, fr., from Greece. Maenad (running to right, looking round).

3. NEW YORK 41.162.254. *CV.* Gallatin pl. 26, 3. Woman with alabastron. Restored.

Near these the

LEKYTHOS
(secondary shape: Class ATL)

LONDON MARKET (Augustus Ready).   Woman (standing frontal looking round to left, forearms extended to left and right).

Compare also Athens E 1843 (p. 719 no. 5).

(iii)

Two that go together.

LEKYTHOI
(secondary shape: Class ATL)

1 (l 117). CARLSRUHE 220 (B 50).   Welter pl. 14, 34; *CV.* pl. 26, 5.   Hunter? (youth throwing stone).
2. COPENHAGEN inv. 1989, from Attica.   *CV.* pl. 165, 4.   Nike (running to altar, with phiale).

Compare with these the damaged lekythos, of the same class,

STAVANGER.   *Anz.* 1941, 59 fig. 2 and 61 fig. 3.   Nike (running, with phiale).

ALSO RELATED TO THE AISCHINES PAINTER

LEKYTHOI
(secondary shape)
(nos. 1–5, rf.)

1 (a ii 8). ATHENS, from Athens.   Woman (standing to right, left forearm extended; in front of her a small plant).
2 (2). STUTTGART.   Woman running with mirror (to right, looking round).
3. VICH, from Ampurias.   Bosch Gimpera, Serra-Ràfols, and Del Castillo 37, 5; García y Bellido pl. 79, 51.   Woman running.
4. Lost, from Athens.   *AM.* 17 pl. 1, 3.   Woman running.
5. Lost, from Athens.   *AM.* 17 pl. 1, 4.   Youth running.

(no. 6, white, with black glaze outlines)

6 (3). ATHENS, Vlasto.   Woman with phiale at altar (standing to right, left hand raised).

The following recall the Tymbos Painter as well:

LEKYTHOI
(rf., of the same class)

1. ATHENS 1603 (CC. 1448), from Athens.   Woman with mirror.

3 A

2. STUTTGART MARKET. *Auktion iii Kricheldorf* pl. 6, 122. Woman.

Three alabastra, different one from another, seem all to be connected with the Aischines Painter:

ALABASTRA
(nos. 1–2, rf.)

1. LONDON 1917.12–19.1. *JHS.* 41 pl. 5, iii, 4. A, woman with cock; B, woman with torch and sprigs.
2. SYDNEY 51.13 (ex Liverpool, Univ.). *Ant. class.* 4 pl. 29, 2. Two women and a youth. Better.

(no. 3, white)

3. LOUVRE CA 1856. Perrot 10, 696. A, woman with oinochoe at altar; B, woman with phiale.

A vase attributed to the Aischines Painter in *ARV.*[1] 499 no. 163, though it bears some resemblance to his work, is not from his hand:

WHITE LEKYTHOS
(secondary shape: Class PL)

RHODES, from Ialysos. *Cl. Rh.* 8, 52 fig. 36 and p. 53 fig. 37. Woman seated, holding wreath.

THE GROUP OF ATHENS 2025
ARV.[1] 502.

These stand between the Tymbos Painter and the Aischines Painter. The technique (yellow glaze outlines) is the Tymbos Painter's; the style (although the proportions of the figures are different) is near him; but it also recalls the Aischines, especially in Athens 2025 and 1875.

WHITE LEKYTHOI
(secondary shape: Class ATL)

1. ATHENS 2025 (CC. 1060). Nike seated on a rock. See the next.
2. ATHENS 1875 (CC. 1040). Woman at tomb. By the same hand as the last.
3. ATHENS 1783 (CC. 1047). Woman running with mirror and basket. Compare especially Munich inv. 7661 (no. 8).
4. WARSAW (ex Binental). *CV.* Binental pl. 3 (Pologne pl. 110), 5. Woman running with phiale.
5. BASLE MARKET (M.M.). Woman running with sash and mirror (to right, looking round).

6. ATHENS, Vlasto, from Athens. Woman at altar (standing frontal, head to left, with phiale and wreath).

7. BOLOGNA PU 355, from Athens. Heydemann *Ober* pl. 1, 4. Maenad. Close to the Platt lekythos p. 719 no. 15.

8. MUNICH inv. 7661. Woman moving away from tomb. Compare especially Athens 1783 (no. 3). In *ARV.*[1] 506, nos. 10 and 11, this and the next were put under 'manner of the Tymbos Painter', which is not wrong.

9. GOETTINGEN, fr., from Greece. Woman at tomb (head to left, wreath in left hand). See the last.

10. TOULOUSE 26.123 (331), from Aegina. Woman with sash and mirror.

Compare also the

WHITE LEKYTHOI
(of the same class)

1. WARSAW 142471 (ex Czartoryski 84), from Athens. De Witte pl. 30; *CV.* pl. 43, 3. Two women.

2. BOLOGNA PU 354, from Athens. Pellegrini *VPU.* 61 fig. 53. Youth leaning on his stick.

THE SATYRISKION PAINTER

Related to the Aischines Painter.

LEKYTHOI
(secondary shape)

1. BOSTON 00.351, from Greece. Satyr and midget satyr. The midget jumps over a chair towards the arms of a full-grown satyr; beside the chair a wool-basket.

2. ATHENS, Kanellopoulos. Two satyrs running (one to left, holding drinking-horn and thyrsus, the other to right, holding thyrsus and kantharos).

THE PAINTER OF COPENHAGEN 3830

CV. Oxford 33, text to pl. 41, 5. *ARV.*[1] 447–8.

ALABASTRA
(nos. 1–4, white)

1 (1). COPENHAGEN inv. 3830, from Attica. *CV.* pl. 174, 1. Woman with hen and chaplet; woman with wreath.

2 (2). CAB. MÉD. 507. De Ridder 372. Youth leaning on his stick; woman.

3. ARLESHEIM, Schweizer. Woman with perfume-vase; woman with alabastron. Between them a seat, also a heron like those on Copenhagen inv. 3830 and Cab. Méd. 507 (nos. 1–2). Restored.

4 (3). HEIDELBERG. *Anz*. 1916, 185–6. Youth with dog; woman. Restored; and the incisions seem modern.

(nos. 5–8, rf.)

5 (4). NEW YORK 41.162.71. *CV*. Gallatin pl. 58, 1. Woman spinning; woman with wool-basket.

6. MAYENCE, Univ., 130. Woman; woman. [Hafner].

7 (5). AMSTERDAM inv. 648, from Thebes. Part, Scheurleer *Cat*. pl. 39, 2. Woman with wreath at altar; woman at thurible.

8 (6). OXFORD 1919.36, from Greece. *CV*. pl. 41, 5–6. Woman with bird and dog; youth.

LEKYTHOI
(nos. 9–10, white)
(Class DL, see p. 301)

9 (7). WARSAW 142470 (ex Czartoryski 92). *CV*. pl. 42, 5. Youth with dog. Side-palmette lekythos (see p. 302 no. 14). Restored.

10 (8). ZURICH, Schuh. Youth leaning on his stick, holding a flower. Side-palmette lekythos (see p. 302 no. 15).

(no. 11, rf.)
(Class BL, see p. 675)

11. TORONTO 366. Robinson and Harcum pl. 56. Woman with torch at altar. Imitation of the Bowdoin Painter (see p. 690 no. 8).

With nos. 9 and 10 compare the

WHITE LEKYTHOS
(Class DL ?)

(a). PALERMO. *AM*. 52 Beil. 28, 1. Youth leaning on his stick. Side-palmette lekythos (see p. 302 no. 16).

THE GROUP OF LEYDEN 1957

The two may be by one hand.

Akin to the vases by the Painter of Copenhagen 3830.

LEKYTHOS
(secondary shape)

1. NEW YORK, Love, from Greece. Bothmer *A.N.Y.* pl. 82, 236. Nike (flying to right, holding out a wreath with both hands).

ALABASTRON

2. LEYDEN 1957.1.1. A, woman with mirror; B, youth leaning on his stick.

THE PAINTER OF PALERMO 1162

ARV.[1] 448.

Near the Painter of Copenhagen 3830 and the Dresden Painter.

ALABASTRA
(no. 2, rf.)

1 (1). NEW YORK 41.162.75, from Greece. *CV.* Gallatin pl. 26, 11 and 13. Nike at altar; woman.

(no. 2, white)

2 (2). PALERMO (1162). Maenad (with kantharos and thyrsus); woman with oinochoe.

THE PAINTER OF TARANTO 2602

ARV.[1] 494.

Akin to the Aischines Painter, but the shape of lekythos is not his.

LEKYTHOI
(secondary shape: Class PL)
(no. 1, white)

1 (1). COPENHAGEN 132, from Athens. *CV.* pl. 170, 2. Woman with sceptre (goddess).

(nos. 2–5, rf.)

2 (2). TARANTO 2602, from Locri. Woman at wool-basket.

3 (3). LONDON E 593, from Gela. Woman at wool-basket.

4 (4). OXFORD 1947. 114 (ex Thomson and Macurdy). Woman with mirror at wool-basket. The mouth of the vase is alien.

5 (5). ATHENS MARKET. Woman (standing to right, mirror in right hand; in front of her a box; key-pattern above).

WHITE ALABASTRON

6. WARSAW 142456 (ex Czartoryski 89). *CV.* pl. 42, 8. Woman with mirror, and woman.

The following goes with Copenhagen 132 (no. 1) in shape and pattern-work, and what remains of the picture may be by the same painter:

WHITE LEKYTHOS
(Class PL)

SYRACUSE, from Megara Hyblaea. Woman (holding a tendril?).

THE TWO-ROW PAINTER

ARV.[1] 490–2.

Angermeier (*Das Alabastron* 40) had connected Cambridge 143 (no. 7) with London 1929.7–16.1 and London 1926.4–17.2 (nos. 1 and 8).

So called because the majority of his alabastra have two rows of pictures.

ALABASTRA

(nos. 1–20, white)

(nos. 1–11 have two rows of pictures)

1 (1). LONDON 1929.7–16.1. Above: A, woman with sceptre; B, maenad. Below: A, woman seated at wool-basket; B, Nike. Restored.

2 (2). ATHENS, Vlasto, from Athens. Above: A, woman seated; B, woman with mirror. Below: A, Eos, and B, Tithonos.

3 (3). ATHENS 12806 (N. 978). Above: A, Nike; B, woman spinning. Below: A, woman seated at wool-basket; B, woman.

4. EXETER 80.1931, fr., from Palestine. Above, woman spinning. [Shefton].

5 (4). BERLIN inv. 3322. Above: A, Nike; B, woman. Below: A, woman; B, Nike.

6. LAON 37.929. Above: A, woman with mirror and alabastron; B, woman. Below: A, Nike; B, woman seated.

7 (5). CAMBRIDGE 143, from Athens. A, Ernest Gardner pl. 30, 3; B, *CV.* pl. 29, 10. Above: A, woman; B, woman. Below: A, Nike; B, woman seated.

8 (6). LONDON 1926.4–17.2. Above: A, woman seated; B, woman. Below: A, Nike; B, woman running with torches. Restored.

9 (7). ATHENS 1725 (CC. 1081), from Athens. Above: A, Nike; B, woman. Below, black patterns (palmettes and network). See p. 728.

10 (8). ATHENS 2539 (CC. 1082). Above: A, woman with flower; B, woman. The lower part of the vase is lost.

11 (9). CAB. MÉD. (ex Fröhner), fr. Above, woman with wreath.

(nos. 12–20: a single row of pictures)

12. EXETER 97.1953, fr. A, woman with torches; B, woman with wreath. May have been thought of as extracts from a wedding scene. [Shefton].

13 (10). ATHENS 2189 (CC. 1087), from Eretria. Nike; woman.

14 (11). WÜRZBURG 558, from Athens. Langlotz pl. 207. A, Nike; B, woman.

15 (12). ATHENS, Vlasto, from Athens. A, maenad (woman with flower and thyrsus); B, woman with torches.

16 (13). ATHENS 16457. *CV.* J pl. 19. Woman with mirror, woman with flower, girl with crotala.

17 (14). HEIDELBERG. Part, *Anz.* 1916, 187. Three women. Restored.

18 (15). ATHENS E. Nike (moving to right); woman (moving to right, looking round).

19 (16). ATHENS 479 (CC. 1086), from Athens. A, woman seated; B, woman with mirror.

20 (17). BERLIN 2259, from Athens. Part, *AZ.* 1882, 214; part, Jacobsthal *Mel.* 84. Judgement of Paris.

(nos. 21–22: red-figure)

(no. 21, with two rows)

21 (18). ATHENS, Vlasto, from Athens. Above: A, woman; B, woman with mirror. Below: A, woman with torches; B, Nike.

(no. 22, with one row)

22 (19). ATHENS, Vlasto, from Koropi. Woman (standing frontal, head to left, with wreath and mirror); woman (standing to right, with sceptre).

WHITE LEKYTHOI
(secondary shape)

23 (20). ATHENS, Vlasto, from Athens. Woman running with an apple in each hand (to right, looking round).

24 (a 3). YALE 118. Baur 100. Woman spinning.

25 (21). MUNICH inv. 7658. Nike.

Perhaps also the

LEKYTHOS
(rf.)

(l 22). MUNICH inv. 1750. Nike.

A couple of specially poor vases are very close to the Two-row Painter and probably from his own hand:

ALABASTRA
(rf.)

1 (1). ATHENS, Vlasto, from Attica. A, woman with torch (moving to right, looking round); B, woman with flower (standing to right).

2 (2). CAMBRIDGE 145. Ernest Gardner pl. 29; *CV.* pl. 29, 9. A, woman with torches; B, woman.

Also close to the painter, the

SQUAT LEKYTHOS

(5). COPENHAGEN inv. 3882. *CV.* pl. 174, 4. White ground. Woman.

The palmettes of a better vase resemble those of Copenhagen inv. 3882:

WHITE LEKYTHOS

GREENSBORO (North Carolina), Jastrow. *AM.* 52, Beil. 27 and Beil. 28, 3. Mother and child.

Two vases are no doubt by the painter, but the figure-work has almost entirely disappeared:

WHITE ALABASTRA
(*with two rows*)

1 (1). PALERMO.

2 (2). Once d'Herman. Dubois-Maisonneuve pl. 38, 4.

Miss Haspels has noted (*ABL*. 183) that the following vases are from the same workshop as Athens 1725 (p. 726 no. 9); that the pattern-work which constitutes their decoration is by the same hand as the patterns there; and that the figure-work on Athens 1725 is no doubt by the same hand as the patterns:

WHITE ALABASTRA

1 (1). MUNICH 2295.

2 (2). REGGIO, from Locri. *NSc*. 1913, suppl., 38 fig. 48.

Miss Haspels adds that a black-figure vase goes with these three in shape and decoration:

BF. ALABASTRON

ATHENS 12767 (N. 976), from Eretria. *AM*. 38 pl. 17, 2–3; Jacobsthal *Akt*. 3 fig. 5. White ground. Death of Actaeon.

The following vase resembles the work of the Two-row Painter, but is better:

WHITE LEKYTHOS
(*secondary type*)

ATHENS 1874 (CC. 1037).   Woman running with wreath.

Another white lekythos goes with Athens 1874 in shape and accessory decoration, and the style of the figure is not unlike:

ATHENS 1785 (CC. 1028). Seated youth.

THE BETH PELET PAINTER
ARV.[1] 493.

Named after the provenience of no. 4.

Related to the Tymbos Painter and the Aischines Painter.

LEKYTHOI
(*secondary shape: Class ATL*)

1 (4). DRESDEN 338. Two women with mirrors.

2. GELA (ex Navarra-Jacona), from Gela. Nike and woman.

3 (5). ATHENS 1347 (CC. 1471), from Tanagra. Woman running, looking round.

4 (6). OXFORD 1930.550, fr., from Beth Pelet. Woman.

5. ANCONA 3314. Woman with mirror at chest.

6. ATHENS MARKET. Woman with mirror.

7. ATHENS, École Française. Woman seated.

8. ELEUSIS 621, from Eleusis. Woman seated with mirror.

9. ATHENS, Agora, P 21266, from Athens. *Hesp.* 24 pl. 77, 39. Nike.

10 (7). LONDON CS 1637, from Athens. Nike.

11. READING 49. iv. 1. Nike.

12. ATHENS 17346. Nike.

13. MALMÖ 29263. Nike.

14. MALMÖ 29264. Nike.

15. ATHENS 1505. Nike.

16. PRAGUE, Nat. Mus., 768. *Sborník* 1959 pl. 6, 27. Nike.

17. ATHENS E 1256. Sphinx.

18. LOUVRE G 601. Sphinx.

19. Once BROOMHALL, Elgin. Sphinx.

SQUAT LEKYTHOS

20. LONDON E 655, from Nola. Nike.

ALABASTRA

21 (1). NEW YORK 41.162.110, from Greece. *CV.* Gallatin pl. 26, 5–6. Woman with fillet and wreath; woman with mirror. Compare also the alabastron Cairo 26213 (p. 740 no. 1).

22 (2). ATHENS 12235. Woman with sceptre; woman with mirror.

23 (3). NEW YORK 41.162.67. *CV.* Gallatin pl. 25, 2 and 4, whence (B) *E.A.A.* ii, 71. Above: A, naked woman, and woman; B, woman seated, and woman. Below: A, woman seated, and woman; B, youth pursuing a woman.

THE LETO PAINTER

ARV.[1] 493.

Named after no. 8.

LEKYTHOI

(nos. 1–7, white)

(nos. 1–6, secondary shape)

1 (1). ATHENS 2022 (CC. 1016), from Megara. Youth running with lyre.

2 (2). MUNICH inv. 7702. Eros.

3 (3). BASLE MARKET (M.M.: ex Elgin). Athena (running to right, with spear and shield; the border above is a row of upright strokes).

4 (4). BOLOGNA PU 357, from Greece. Woman with mirror and ala-bastron.

5 (5). BOLOGNA PU 358, from Greece. Pellegrini *VPU.* 61 fig. 54 and 62 fig. 55. Youth leaning on his stick at stele. On the stele, ΚΕΦΙΣΙΟΣ in four lines. Restored.

6 (7). OXFORD 1938.734, from Greece. Woman with torch.

(no. 7, standard shape)

7 (6). BERLIN inv. 3293. Salis *Grabmal des Aristonautes* 6. Warrior approaching tomb.

(nos. 8–9, rf.)

(secondary shape)

8 (8). BERLIN 2212, from Attica. Overbeck *KM.* 3, v (Apollon), 378, whence *Arch. class.* 2 pl. 27, 2; *E.A.A.* iv, 506. Leto with the infant Apollo.

9 (9). PALERMO (66), from Gela. Woman seated, holding a wreath.

Probably also the

LEKYTHOI

(secondary shape)

(white)

1 (1). ATHENS 1883 (CC. 1024). Nike.

(rf.)

2 (2). LEYDEN RO I C 18 (xviii i 47), from Athens. Woman with torch at altar. Compare Athens 1883 (no. 1).

3 (3). LEYDEN RO II 59 (xviii i 46), from Athens. Sphinx.

THE CARLSRUHE PAINTER

VA. 139.   *Att. V.* 326–9 and 477.   *AJA.* 1932, 139–42.   Haspels *ABL.* 180–1. *ARV.*¹ 508–15 and 968.

Named after no. 111.

Several shapes of lekythos are used: for his favourite shape (CL) see p. 676.

LEKYTHOI

(nos. 1–87, rf.)

1 (9). NEW YORK 41.162.140. *CV.* Gallatin pl. 59, 1. Artemis (running with bow). Standard.

2. PRAGUE, Nat. Mus., 767. *Listy fil.* 7 (1959) pl. 1, 4. The like. [Frel]. Class CL.

3 (10). BERLIN, Helfferich. Neugebauer *ADP*. pl. 78, 177. Artemis (running with bow to altar). Near Class PL.

4 (11). DRESDEN ZV. 2969. Athena (running, with spear in right hand and left arm extended in aegis). Secondary (doubtful if neck and shoulder belong).

4 *bis*. DEKELEIA, from Dekeleia. *Ostraka ek Dek.* fig. 33. The like. Class CL.

5. ATHENS E 1284. The like, but looking round. Secondary.

6 (a). HARVARD 2206. *CV*. pl. 17, 1. Athena. Class CL.

7 (12). PALERMO G.E. 3755. Athena. Secondary (Class BEL?).

8 (13). RUVO, Jatta, 1103, from Ruvo. Nike (flying, with sash). Secondary.

9 (14). PRAGUE, Nat. Mus., 764 (ex Lembessis). *Listy fil.* 7 (1959) pl. 1, 5. The like. Class CL.

10 (77). DUNEDIN 48.339 (ex A. B. Cook). The like. Class CL.

11 (15). ATHENS, from Athens. Nike (flying, with basket). Secondary.

12 (16). ATHENS MARKET. Nike (flying to altar with arms extended). Secondary.

13. ATHENS, from Peristeri. The like. Secondary.

14. PARIS MARKET (Feuardent). Nike (running with torches).

15 (20). LONDON E 607, from Athens. Nike (running with phiale and torch). Secondary.

16 (18). DETROIT 24.121 (ex Gotha). Nike (running with sash). Secondary.

17 (19). PARIS MARKET (Lembessis). The like (but line-border above). Secondary.

18 (21). ATHENS 1507 (CC. 1439). Eos. Secondary.

19 (22). NAPLES 3145. Ph. So. 11009, ii, 1. Eos. Class CL.

20 (23). ATHENS 15870. Eos. Secondary.

21 (24). ATHENS MARKET. Eos. Secondary.

22 (25). ATHENS 1510 (CC. 1437). Ph. A.I. NM 3122, b. Eos. Class CL.

23. LOUVRE CA 2022. Eos. Secondary (Class CL?).

24 (26). PARIS MARKET (Lembessis). Maenad (running to right, looking round, with phiale and thyrsus). Secondary.

25. ATHENS 17621. Maenad (running to right, looking round, with thyrsus). Secondary.

25 *bis*. NEW YORK, Love. Woman with lyre (seated to right, looking round, on the left, pillar of a building). [Bothmer]. Class CL.

26 (27). ATHENS MARKET. Woman running with sceptre (to right, looking round). Secondary.

27 (28). CAMBRIDGE 152, from Athens. *CV*. pl. 29, 2. Woman running with mirror (looking round). Class CL.

28 (29). THEBES, from Rhitsona. The like. Secondary.

29 (30). ATHENS E. The like. Secondary.

30 (31). LONDON MARKET (Spink: ex Garabed). The like. Class CL.

31. OMAHA 1952.258. The like. Class CL.

31 *bis.* BERLIN MARKET (Rittershofer). The like. Replica of no. 31, but above the picture a reserved line, and below the picture a pair of red lines.

32 (32). ATHENS MARKET. The like (on the right a wool-basket). Secondary.

33 (33). CATANIA, from Camarina. Benndorf pl. 32, 1. Woman running with mirror. Standard.

34 (34). ATHENS MARKET. Woman running with mirror and basket.

34 *bis.* BASLE MARKET (M.M.) (ex Elgin). Woman running with mirror and basket. Class CL. See p. 1668. [Blatter].

35. ATHENS E 1444. Woman running with flower and torch. Restored. Secondary.

36 (35). ATHENS 1349 (CC. 1470), from Tanagra. *Eph.* 1907, 227, 3. Woman running with torches. Class CL.

37 (35 *bis*). MILAN, Scala. The like.

38 (36). ATHENS 1751 (CC. 1442), from Athens. *Eph.* 1907, 227, 2. Woman running with sash. Class CL.

39 (37). ATHENS, from Athens (Stables). Woman running with lyre (looking round). Class CL.

40 (38). NEW YORK, Bothmer (ex Matsch). *CV.* Matsch pl. 8, 1–2. Woman running. Standard (Class BL or near).

41 (39). SYRACUSE. The like (to right, looking round, arms extended).

42 (40). ATHENS, private. Ph. A.I. varia 398. Woman with sacrificial basket at altar. Secondary.

43 (41). GLASGOW 02.73 au. Woman with sceptre at altar. Secondary.

44 (42). OXFORD 1916.5, from Greece. *CV.* pl. 38, 3. Woman at altar. Class CL.

45 (43). VIENNA, Univ., inv. 526 b, from Greece. *CV.* pl. 11, 8. Woman with phiale and staff. Class CL.

46. CARLSRUHE (B 787). *CV.* pl. 26, 6. Woman with staff. [Hafner]. The upper half of the vase modern. Secondary.

47. ATHENS, Agora, P 15960, from Athens. Woman with phiale and staff (standing to right). Class CL.

48 (44). ATHENS 1275 (CC. 1431). Woman with phiale. Secondary.

49 (45). LOUVRE AM 1066, from Rhodes. Woman with phiale. Secondary.

50 (46). MUNICH inv. 7821. Woman with yarn at wool-basket. Class CL.

51 (47). OXFORD 1927.4461, from Athens. Stackelberg pl. 34, 3, 3, and fig. 4; *CV.* pl. 62, 11. Woman spinning. Class CL.

52 (48). ATHENS. The like. Class CL.

53 (49). ATHENS 1503 (CC. 1465). *Eph.* 1907, 227, 1. Woman with distaff. Class CL or near.

54 (50). ATHENS MARKET. The like. Class CL.

55 (51). ATHENS MARKET. The like. Secondary.

56 (52). CHALKIS 564, from Chalkis. Papavasileiou pl. 19, 2. The like.

57. BASLE MARKET (M.M.). Woman with mirror and distaff. Class PL (p. 676 no. 12).

58 (53). SYRACUSE, from Camarina. Woman with fruit and mirror (standing frontal, head to left). Secondary.

59 (54). ATHENS MARKET. Woman with mirror (?) and wool-basket (standing frontal, head to left). Secondary.

60. ATHENS, Kanellopoulos. Woman with mirror (standing to left, looking round; on the left, wool-basket; on the right, chair half seen). Secondary.

61. MANNHEIM 190. *CV.* pl. 32, 9. Woman standing at wool-basket spinning. [Greifenhagen]. Class CL.

62 (56). NEW YORK 41.162.147. *CV.* Gallatin pl. 26, 9. Woman standing at wool-basket playing ball. Class CL.

63. ROME, Accademia dei Lincei, 2756. *JHS.* 72 pl. 8, 2. The like. [Bulas]. Class CL.

64 (55). OXFORD 1914. 9, from Greece. *CV.* pl. 38, 2. The like. Class CL.

65 (57). ATHENS 1512 (CC. 1468). Woman seated playing ball. Secondary.

66 (58). NEW YORK 41.162.145. *CV.* Gallatin pl. 26, 7. The like. Class CL.

67 (59). BRUSSELS A 2138. *CV.* d pl. 12, 7. Woman standing at woolbasket. Near Class PL (the mouth alien?).

68 (60). PARIS MARKET (Lembessis). The like, but the woman looking round. Secondary.

69 (61). Once OXFORD, Casson. Woman, holding basket, standing at woolbasket. Secondary.

70 (62). NEW YORK 41.162.152. *CV.* Gallatin pl. 18, 3. Dionysos. Class CL.

71 (63). OXFORD 1916.15, from Greece. *CV.* pl. 38, 1. Youth running with drawn sword. Class CL.

72 (64). ATHENS E 1842. The like. Secondary.

73 (65). MUNICH inv. 7521. Man leaning on his stick, with strigil. Secondary.

74 (66). KOENIGSBERG 77, from Greece. Lullies K. pl. 14; ph. A.I. varia 397, 1. The like. Restored. Secondary.

75 (67). ABINGDON, Robertson, from Greece. Man leaning on his stick (on the right, hanging, a flute-case). Class CL.

76 (68). MAYENCE, Brommer (ex Lembessis). Man leaning on his stick, holding a flute-case. Class CL.

77 (69). ATHENS E 1401. Man leaning on his stick (on the left, hanging, a writing-case). Secondary.

78 (70). ATHENS E. Youth leaning on his stick (to right with strigil). Secondary.

79 (71). CAMBRIDGE 154, from Athens. *CV.* pl. 29, 1. Youth leaning on his stick (to left). Class CL.

80. MAYENCE, Univ., 18. The like. Class CL.

81. NEW YORK MARKET (Tozzi). The like. On the left, hanging, sponge and aryballos. Class ATL or near.

82 (72). ATHENS 1279 (CC. 1454). The like.

82 *bis.* ATHENS 17912. The like.

83. TÜBINGEN Z 158, from Greece. Satyr at wool-basket, handling a skein. Class CL. See p. 1668.

84 (73). TÜBINGEN E 80, from Athens. Watzinger pl. 25. Herm. Class CL.

85 (74). LENINGRAD 876. Sphinx. Secondary.

86. ATHENS E 1287. Sphinx. Secondary.

87 (75). ATHENS MARKET. Siren (to right; on the right a sprig of olive). Secondary.

(nos. 88–103, white)
(nos. 88–92, secondary shape)

88 (76). CAB. MÉD. 494. *Gaz. arch.* 1885 pl. 32, 2; ph. Gir. 8116, 2. Artemis. Class CL.

89 (79). CAMBRIDGE 4.17, from Thespiai. *CV.* pl. 30, 2. Nike (flying, with sash). Class CL.

90 (80). LONDON D 76, from Athens. *JHS.* 15 pl. 7; Murray *WAV.* pl. 25, b. Woman with lekythos and basket. Restored. The inscription false. Class BEL. See p. 1668.

91 (82). LONDON D 29. Cecil Smith pl. 24, above. Woman at laver. Class PL or near (mouth and neck lost).

92 (78). Once VIENNA, Trau. Woman spinning (standing frontal, head to left).

(nos. 93–95, standard shape: Class BL or near)

93 (88). NEW YORK 06.1021.129, from Eretria. *Coll. E.G.* pl. 1, 7. Nike (flying, with sash). Second white used.

94 (89). MUNICH inv. 7656, from Greece. Nike (standing, with oinochoe and phiale). Second white used. Restored.

95 (84). ATHENS MARKET. Goddess (Hera?) with phiale and sceptre (standing frontal, head to left; key-pattern above).

(no. 96, shape uncertain)

96 (87). ATHENS, fr. Woman with (ball of wool?) and basket (standing frontal, head to left; on the left, hanging, a basket). Second white used.

(no. 97, standard shape)

97 (81). CORINTH MP 89, from Corinth. *Hesp.* I, 79 fig. 21. Woman with basket.

(nos. 98–102, secondary shape; Class BEL: nos. 99–102 form a group)

98 (86). CAMBRIDGE 138, from Athens. Ernest Gardner pl. 30, 1; *CV.* pl. 30, 1. Woman with basket. Side-palmette lekythos (p. 303 no. 11). Second white used.

99. ATHENS E. Woman at tomb (standing to right, with chaplet and something else; behind, a chair, and, hanging, a basket). Second white used.

100 (85). PARIS MARKET (Platt; ex Feuardent). Woman with basket at tomb (standing to right; mock inscription in two lines). Second white used for the tomb.

101. LAON 37.918. Woman with basket at tomb (standing frontal, head to left). Second white used for the tomb.

102. LAON 37.915. Woman at tomb (standing frontal, head to left, right arm extended, something in the left hand). Second white used for the tomb.

(no. 103, secondary shape: Class BEL)

103 (83). LONDON 1920.7–29.1. Man advancing with drawn sword.

SQUAT LEKYTHOI

104 (94). DRESDEN ZV 2860, from Thebes. *Anz.* 1925, 119 fig. 17. Artemis. Late.

105 (92). NEW YORK 41.162.153. *CV.* Gallatin pl. 60, 3. Nike (running to altar).

106 (93). PARIS MARKET (Lembessis). Woman fleeing (running to right, looking round).

ALABASTRA

107. ATHENS 17917. Athena (running to right, spear in right hand, left arm extended in aegis); woman (running to right, looking round).

108 (96). ATHENS, Vlasto, from Athens. *AJA.* 1932, 140. Youth and woman (youth leaning on his stick; woman with distaff).

109. MYKONOS, fr., from Rheneia (originally from Delos). Dugas *Délos xxi* pl. 46, 108. Woman; (woman?).

PELIKAI
(small)

110 (1). LONDON E 403. A, two women; B, woman.

111 (2). CARLSRUHE 206 (B 10), from Nola. A, Welter pl. 14, 32 a; *CV.* pl. 17 and p. 26. A, mistress and maid (woman and girl); B, woman.

112 (3). LONDON E 386. A, mistress and maid (woman seated, and woman); B, youth.

113 (4). LEIPSIC T 3807. A, man and woman; B, woman. On A, woman running to left, looking round; wool-basket; man leaning on his stick to left; on B, standing to right, with sceptre.

114 (5). Once PARIS, Pourtalès, 148, from Nola. A, Panofka *Pourt*. pl. 6, 2, whence *El*. 1 pl. 68. A, Athena and Nike. B, woman.

115. NEW YORK 57.11.2 (ex van Branteghem 92). A, *Bull. Metr.* summer 1962, 9, 9. A, satyr and maenad. B, woman. [Bothmer].

NECK-AMPHORA
(Nolan amphora)

116 (6). CAPUA, from Capua. *CV*. pl. 5, 1–2. A, woman and girl; B, woman.

OINOCHOAI
(no. 117, shape 1)

117 (7). LONDON E 518, from Nola. Ph. Ma. 3201, left. Eros as acolyte (splanchnoptes, with spit).

(no. 118, shape 3, chous)

118 (8). TÜBINGEN E 124. Watzinger pl. 33; van Hoorn *Choes* fig. 373. Eros (flying).

PYXIS
(special shape)

119 (97). GOTHA 64. Youths and women; on the lid, youth and seated woman, youth and woman. As for the shape, a black pyxis in Athens, 18579, has a very similar body, but the upper part of the lid is different.

FRAGMENT OF A POT

120 (104). TÜBINGEN E 109, fr. Watzinger pl. 28; *Bull. Vereen.* 24–26, 26 figs. 1–2. Danae. For the subject see Luschey ibid. 26–28.

PLASTIC ONE-HANDLED KANTHAROI
(satyr-head)

121 (98). NAPLES 2951, from Apulia. *Mus. Borb.* 4 pl. 35, 1–2; ph. So. 11079, middle, right. King and woman at altar. Late. For the plastic part see p. 1547 no. 3.

122 (99). MUNICH 2740 (J. 862), from South Italy. Lau pl. 44, 1; *Mü. Jb.* 1919 (Buschor *Krok*. 14) fig. 20. King and woman. Late. For the plastic part see p. 1547 no. 1.

123 (100). NEW YORK 23.160.13. *JHS*. 49, 69 fig. 22. Nike, king, and two women (all running). Late. For the plastic part see p. 1547 no. 2.

FRAGMENT
(of a one-handled kantharos or a rhyton)

124. KTIMA 470, fr., from Marion. (King and woman).

RHYTA

(no. 125, pygmy-and-crane)

125 (102). BOSTON 03.799 (ex Magnoncourt 100), from Nola. Jahn *Arch. Beitr.* pl. 2, 1, whence (the shape) Roscher s.v. Pygmaien 3296 no. 10. Women fleeing to kings. Late.

(no. 126, ram's head)

126 (102). WARSAW 198550. Part, Michalowski *Sztuka* 113; phs. R.I. 2960–61. Nike and king, running. Late. See p. 1668.

(no. 127, greyhound's head)

127 (108). PARIS, Petit Palais, 354. *CV.* pl. 29, 1–3. Nike running to king, and king running. Late.

SKYPHOS

(type A)

128 (105). VILLA GIULIA 18098, from Falerii. A, Dionysos; B, maenad.

STEMLESS CUPS

129. LOUVRE C 10922. I, incised patterns (the same as in London E 127, no. 130). A, mistress and maid (woman seated, and woman with box and mirror).

130 (106). LONDON E 127. I and B, *JHS.* 56, 207 fig. 3, and pl. 11, 2. I, incised patterns. A, king and woman, both running; B, king, and running woman.

131 (107). VILLA GIULIA 913, from Falerii. I, maenad at altar. A, youth pursuing a woman; B, woman with sceptre running to king.

132 (118). ADRIA B 329, fr., from Adria. *CV.* pl. 37, 11. I, woman with perfume-vase.

133. ATHENS, Agora, P 22826, fr., from Athens. I, woman.

134 (110). NAPLES 2643, from Nola. B, ph. So. 11006, ii, 3. I, king and Nike. A, youth with sword pursuing a woman (Theseus and Aithra?— and in nos. 135–8); B, woman running to king. Late.

135 (111). Once DEEPDENE, Hope, T. 177. Tischbein 1 pl. 21, whence (A) *Annali* 1844 pl. C, 1. I, king and Nike. A, youth with sword pursuing a woman; B, woman running, and king. Late.

136 (112). WARSAW (ex Binental). I, Pollak *Woodyat* pl. 4, 72; *CV.* Binental pl. 2 (Pologne pl. 109), 6. I, king and Nike. A, youth with sword pursuing a woman; B, woman running, and king. The head of the youth on A perhaps restored? Late.

137 (115). LONDON E 128, from Nola. I, king and Nike. A, youth with sword pursuing a woman; B, woman running, and king. Late.

138. ITALIAN MARKET. I, king, and Nike holding helmet. A, youth with sword pursuing a woman. B, (?). [Shefton]. Late.

139 (114). Villa Giulia 25048 (or 25008). I, king, and Nike holding helmet. A, Nike and king, both running; B, woman running, and king. Late.

140 (113). Roman market (Castellani). R.I. xvii. 13 and 47, and 1886. 25. The like. The same as the last? Late.

141 (109). Carlsruhe 297 (B 122), fr., from Adria. Creuzer *Zur Arch.* iii pl. 2, 3; *CV.* pl. 26, 1; part, Schnellbach fig. 22. I, king, and Nike, holding helmet. Late.

142 (a 7). Barcelona 538, fr., from Ampurias. I, *Anuari* 1911–12, 674 fig. 8. I, king, and Nike. A, (feet—youth pursuing a woman?). Late.

143 (116). Arezzo 1428, 1430, and 1434, frr. I, youth with sword pursuing a woman; A, (on the left, foot of male running—youth pursuing a woman); B, (on the left, woman running to left, looking round—no doubt the same subject). Late.

144 (117). Florence PD 205, fr., from Populonia. B, (on the left, woman running to left, looking round).

145. New York 20.258, fr. A, (on the right, king).

146 (108). Amsterdam inv. 2288, fr. A, (man standing frontal, head to left, and youth in chlamys running to right with lyre).

STEMLESS CUP (or CUP)

147 (119). Leningrad 662, fr. I, woman (standing to right, with mirror or distaff).

CUPS

148 (120). Florence PD 422. *CV.* pl. 104 and pl. 116, 22. I, two youths; A, youths and women; B, youth and boy, youth and woman.

149 (121). Marseilles 1633. I, youth and seated woman; A–B, youths.

150 (122). Paris market (Kalebdjian). *Art antique 26–27 nov. 1934* pl. 2, 143 and 143a. I, king, and Nike holding helmet. A, king and two women; B, the like. The woman in the middle of A holds a sacrificial basket; of B, a box. Late.

151. Louvre C 11955, fr. I, king, and Nike holding helmet. A, king and two women; B, (on the right, king or woman). The middle woman on A holds a sacrificial basket. Late.

152. Louvre C 11956, fr. Outside, (chin, left hand and shoulder of woman standing frontal, staff in hand, then head—to left—, right arm, shoulder, breast, of a woman). Late.

153. Louvre C 11957. I, king and Nike. A, king and two women; B, similar. See the next. Late.

154. Louvre C 11958, fr. Outside, (head, to left, and breast, of woman). Probably belongs to the last—to the right-hand figure on B. Late.

155. Louvre C 11959, fr. A, (on the left, woman standing to right). Late.

156 (123, +). LOUVRE C 11963. I, woman bending, holding a folded garment; A, woman seated, with man and woman; B, woman, man or youth, and man.

157. LOUVRE C 11964, fr. Outside, (upper part of woman standing frontal, head to left, mirror in left hand).

The following is either by the Carlsruhe Painter or in his manner:

LEKYTHOS
(secondary shape)

TRACHONES, Geroulanos, from Trachones. Woman with phiale at block-altar.

_____

MANNER OF THE CARLSRUHE PAINTER

(i)

These fragments should be by the painter himself.

CUPS OR STEMLESS CUPS

1. LOUVRE C 11960, fr. Outside, part of the floral decoration remains.
2. LOUVRE C 11961, two frr. Outside, part of the floral decoration remains.

_____

(ii)

THE PAINTER OF ATHENS 1344

ARV.[1] 514, ii.

Close to the Carlsruhe Painter.

LEKYTHOI
(standard shape)

1 (1). ATHENS 1344 (CC. 1416), from Tanagra. Woman with perfume-vase at wool-basket.

2 (2). ATHENS 1345 (CC. 1415), from Tanagra. Woman with sceptre at altar.

_____

(iii)

THE PAINTER OF READING 50. x. 4

ARV.[1] 514, iii.

LEKYTHOI
(secondary shape: Class PL or near)

1. READING 50. x. 4. Woman running with box (to right, looking round). See p. 676 no. 13.

2 (2). CINCINNATI, Boulter, fr., from Greece. Woman running (to left, looking round; the head missing).

3 (1). ATHENS, Vlasto, from Athens. Woman running (to right, looking round, arms extended left and right; above, billet-border).

4. SYRACUSE. Woman running (to right, looking round, arms extended left and right).

Compare with these the
SQUAT LEKYTHOS
BASLE MARKET (M.M.: ex Elgin). Woman running (to right, looking round, a tendril in the left hand).

Compare also the
LEKYTHOI
(*secondary shape*)

1. MYTILENE 588. Woman running (to right, looking round, her himation over the back of her head).

2. STRASBURG, Amandry. Pan.

(iv)
THE CAIRO GROUP
ARV.[1] 515, iv.
ALABASTRON

1 (1). CAIRO 26213. Edgar pl. 12. Woman with mirror; maenad. Compare also the alabastron New York 41.162.110 (p. 729 no. 21).

SQUAT LEKYTHOS

2 (2). OXFORD, Beazley, fr. Nike running to altar.

Near these the
SQUAT LEKYTHOS

(l 3). MUNICH 2500. Stackelberg pl. 37, 4; *E.A.A.* ii, 256. Youth advancing with drawn sword.

(v)
VARIOUS
ARV.[1] 515, i.
LEKYTHOI
(*nos. 1–2, rf.*)
(*secondary shape*)

1 (2). LONDON E 590, from the Troad. Maenad.

2 (1). SYRACUSE 2417. Woman (standing to right, arms extended).

(nos. 3–5, white)
(standard shape)

3 (l 90). ATHENS, private. Fairbanks i, 167. Woman and man. Second white used. Restored (or the reproduction retouched).

4 (l 91). PALERMO (147), from Gela. *From the Coll.* 1, 175. Woman with flower and mirror (or distaff). Second white used.

SQUAT LEKYTHOS

5. VIENNA 3765 (ex Oest. Mus. 367). Woman holding sacrificial basket, and man, at altar. Late work by the painter himself?

Also related to the Carlsruhe Painter, two that go together and are probably by one hand:

WHITE LEKYTHOI
(standard shape)

1. LEIPSIC. Woman with box and mirror at wool-basket (standing frontal, head to left). Second white used.

2. ATHENS MARKET. Woman with mirror at wool-basket (standing to left; on the right, hanging, a black sash).

In the following the outside resembles the later work of the Carlsruhe Painter. The inside is much finer, but I cannot say that it is not by the same hand as the outside.

COVERED CUP

BOSTON 00.356, from Vari. I and A, *AJA.* 1915 pl. 28 and p. 409; I, Langlotz *GV.* pl. 35; I, Philippart *C.A.B.* pl. 32; CB. i pl. 15 and p. 33, whence (I) Rumpf *MZ.* pl. 31, 5; I, Pfeiff *Apollon* pl. 40; I, Chase *Guide* 82; I, Himmelmann-Wildschütz *Eig.* pl. 19; I, Robertson *G.P.* 132. I, white-ground, Apollo and a Muse (Calliope?). A–B, rf.: A, woman running with tendrils in her hands; B, the like.

Compare the

COVERED CUP

DELPHI, from Cirrha. A–B, *BCH.* 1938 pl. 53, C. I, white-ground, (woman playing the flute: there may have been another figure—a male reclining?); in a zone round this, white ground, symposion. A–B, rf.: A, Dionysos and maenad; B, the like.

THE PAINTER OF AGORA P 7561

ARV.[1] 515.

Placed here because the heads recall the ideal of the Carlsruhe Painter.

SQUAT LEKYTHOI
(small)

1 (1). BASLE MARKET (M.M.): ex Elgin. Female head.

2 (2). ATHENS, Agora, P 7561, fr., from Athens. Female head.

3 (3). PARIS MARKET (Feuardent). Head of maenad (in snood, to right; thyrsus).

4 (4). ATHENS 1532 (CC. 1520). Female head.

5 (5). PARIS MARKET (Lembessis). Female head (in saccos, to right; column).

6 (6). ATHENS MARKET. Female head (in saccos, to right; column).

7 (7). RHODES, from Ialysos. *Cl. Rh.* 8, 181, left, whence *E.A.A.* i, 146. Female head.

8 (8). VIENNA, Univ., 954d. *CV.* pl. 31, 13. Female head.

9 (9). ATHENS MARKET. Head of Hermes (in winged pilos, to right; caduceus).

CHAPTER 40

WHITE LEKYTHOI

THE TIMOKRATES PAINTER

JHS. 54, 90, left. Diepolder *Penth.* 23 note 76. Greifenhagen and Buschor in *CV.* Bonn 49. *ARV.*[1] 578-9.

Called after the kalos-name on no. 3.

The present list includes four vases ('the Group of Athens 1929') of which it was said in *ARV.*[1] (579) that they were close to the Timokrates Painter and might be his.

WHITE LEKYTHOI
(standard shape; second white used)
(nos. 1–7, with rf. shoulder)

1 (1). Athens 12771, from Eretria. *Eph.* 1905 pl. 1; Riezler pl. 3, whence Anita Klein pl. 40, a; *CV.* Jc pl. 3, 3 and 5, whence Buschor G. *Vasen* 190; part, Zervos fig. 283. Mother and maid with baby. ΑΛΚΙΜΑ-ΤΟϹ ΚΑΛΟϹ.

2 (2). Brussels A 1020, from Gela. *Burl. 1888* pl. 12 = Fröhner *Brant.* pl. 43 = *Vente Somzée* pl. 2, 94, whence Farmakovski i, 331 and Buschor *Grab*[1] 48 = [2]60; Furtwängler *Somzée* pl. 39, i, 4 = *Vente Somzée* pl. 5, 94; *CV.* Jb pl. 2, 4. Woman playing the flute and woman with lyre. ΛΚΕϹΤΟΡΙΔΕϹ ΚΑΛΟϹ. See p. 1668.

3 (3). Oxford 267, from Gela. Gardner pl. 21, 1. Youth leaving home (or arriving) (youth in chlamys, with spears, and woman). ΤΙΜΟΚΡΑ-ΤΕϹ Κ[Α]ΛΟϹ. Much restored.

4 (A 1). Harvard 60.335 from Attica. *CV.* Robinson i pl. 39. Two women. ΓΛΑ[ΥΚΟΝ] ΚΑΛ[ΟϹ] ΛΕΑ[ΓΡΟ] in three lines. Restored.

5 (A 2). Athens 1929 (CC. 1642), from Eretria. Ph. A.I. NM 2838, whence *E.A.A.* i, 873 fig. 1095. Two women preparing a basket for a visit to the tomb. [Buschor].

6 (A 3). Athens 1987 (CC. 1645), from Eretria. Ph. A.I. NM 2839. Two women. [Buschor].

7 (A 4). Athens 12770 (N. 980), from Eretria. *AM.* 38 pl. 17, 1; *CV.* Jc pl. 2, 8. Woman holding girdle and girl holding sash.

(nos. 8–9, the shoulder missing)

8. Berne 23316, fr. Warrior and woman (woman standing to right, holding sword, warrior to left). ... ΚΑΛΟϹ.

9. TÜBINGEN E 60, fr. Watzinger pl. 26. (Woman). Watzinger mentions another fragment, which I have not seen, with part of a second woman.

Near these, the

WHITE LEKYTHOS
(standard shape; second white used)
(with white-ground shoulder)

BASLE MARKET (M.M.). *Münzh. Basel 1 Okt. 1935* pl. 41, 1189. Woman with basket and girl with alabastron. The shoulder-palmettes are like those of the Vouni Painter (below).

Compare also the

WHITE LEKYTHOS
(standard shape: second white used)

(A 5). ATHENS 1913 (CC. 1647), from Athens. Part, *AJA.* 1907, 18; Fairbanks i pl. 5, 1. Woman and boy. ΛΙ+Α⸠ ΙⲤΑΛΟ⸠. Compare Athens 1929 (p. 743 no. 5). Shoulder, neck, mouth of the vase alien.

A fragment of a red-figured lekythos brings the Timokrates Painter to mind:

ATHENS 17522, fr. *CV.* d pl. 27, 4. (King seated, and the hand of another person).

THE VOUNI PAINTER
ARV.[1] 580.

Near the Timokrates Painter.

WHITE LEKYTHOI
(standard shape: second white used)
(the shoulder white-ground)

1 (1). NEW YORK 35.11.5. Richter *ARVS.* fig. 83; Richter *H.* 229, a. Woman and boy at tombs.

2 (2). NICOSIA V 453, from Vouni. *S.C.E.* 3 pl. 86, 1–2. Woman with mirror, and woman. ΑΛΚ[ΙΜ]ΑΧΟ . . .

(the shoulder rf.)

3. MEGGEN, Käppeli. Schefold *M.* 209, 227. Amazon, with a goose. [Also Bothmer].

With the Käppeli lekythos compare the

WHITE LEKYTHOS
(standard shape: second white used)
(the shoulder white-ground)

MAYENCE, Univ., 20. Hampe and Simon *G.L.* pl. 35, 1. Woman holding an alabastron, with a goose.

THE LUPOLI PAINTER
ARV.[1] 580.

WHITE LEKYTHOI
(standard shape)

1 (1). TARANTO 4566, from Taranto (contrada Lupoli). Quagliati *Mus. Tar.* pl. 56, 4; ph. Al. 35353, right, whence Philippart *It.* ii pl. 4, 2 and Pareti *Storia di Roma* ii, 2, 3. Oedipus and the Sphinx (or rather, youth at tomb surmounted by the image of a sphinx).

2 (2). TARANTO 4567, from Taranto (contrada Lupoli). Quagliati *Mus. Tar.* pl. 56, 3; ph. Al. 35353, left, whence Philippart *It.* ii pl. 4, 1 and Pareti *Storia di Roma* ii, 2, 1. Girl with perfume-vase and basket. Second white used.

3 (3). BASLE MARKET (M.M.: ex Hirsch). *Ars Ant. Auktion I* pl. 59, 125. Woman with perfume-vase and box. Second white used.

THE PAINTER OF ATHENS 1826
ARV.[1] 465-7.

Most of the vases had been put together by Buschor (*ALP.* 16–17); but he thought of them as early works by the Inscription Painter, in which I cannot follow him. In the list I have counted Buschor's attributions to the Inscription Painter as attributions to the Painter of Athens 1826.

WHITE LEKYTHOI
(standard shape: second white used)
(no. 1: the shoulder reserved, with black palmettes of the Bowdoin Painter's type)

1 (4). ATHENS 1826 (CC. 1641), from Eretria. Riezler pl. 10 and p. 2, 1; ph. Al. 24473, 1, whence *E.A.A.* i, 873 fig. 1094. Woman seated and woman. [Buschor].

(nos. 2–3: the shoulder white, with black palmettes of the Bowdoin Painter's type)

2 (5). ATHENS 1847 (CC. 1634). Fairbanks i, 155; ph. A.I. NM 766. Woman seated holding a stephane. [Buschor].

3 (6). LONDON D 26, from Eretria. Murray *W.A.V.* pl. 21, a, and p. 31, above. Woman seated with fruit and lekythos. [Buschor].

(nos. 4–15: the shoulder white, with black palmettes of special type)

4 (1). LONDON 1928.2–13.1, from Gela. *BMQ.* 3 pl. 2, a. Man and woman at tomb. Early.

5 (2). NAPLES Stg. 122. Fairbanks i, 157. Warrior and old man. Early.

6. LAON 37.930 *bis*. Woman with gosling and woman with basket.

7 (8). SYRACUSE 22789, from Camarina. *ML.* 14, 846. Two women. See p. 747.

8 (9). SYRACUSE 22952, from Camarina. *ML.* 14, 911. Youth and woman.

8 *bis*. PHILADELPHIA MARKET. *Hesp. Art Bull.* 14, 6 no. 7. Man and woman; between them a water-bird.

9 (10). PALERMO, from Selinus (necropoli Galera). Youth and woman (youth in himation to right, with stick, woman frontal, head to left, with alabastron and sash).

10 (11). ATHENS 1846 (CC. 1639), from Eretria. Woman and girl (the woman about to gird herself, the girl holding a girdle). [Buschor].

11 (12). ATHENS 1825 (CC. 1632), from Eretria. *AM.* 15 pl. 1, whence (detail), Riezler 95; Riezler pl. 11. Youth and woman at tomb. [Buschor].

12 (13). ATHENS 1997 (CC. 1644), from Eretria. Woman with sash and woman with sacrificial basket. [Buschor].

13 (15). MUNICH inv. 7703. Two women.

14 (20). BERLIN 2444, from Athens. Fairbanks i, 183; Riezler pl. 15. Warrior, with wife and baby. [Buschor].

15 (22). ATHENS 1763 (CC. 1643). Part, Zervos fig. 277. Woman and girl. [Buschor].

(nos. 16–28, with rf. shoulder)

16 (3). ATHENS 1845 (CC. 1635). Fairbanks i, 144. Woman seated and woman. [Buschor].

17. ATHENS 17279. *Eph.* 1950–1, 150 fig. 1, p. 155 right, p. 158 fig. 6. Woman with girdle, and girl with platter.

18. ATHENS 17493. *Eph.* 1950–1, 150 fig. 2, p. 155 left, p. 158 fig. 7. Woman seated with wreath, and girl with basket.

19. GELA, from Gela. *NSc.* 1956, 363 fig. 8. Two women.

20. GELA, fr., from Gela. Woman and another. Assigned by Orlandini to the same painter as the last.

21 (7). GENEVA MARKET (Hirsch). Two women (one to right, holding a wreath, the other frontal, head to left, holding a sash with both hands).

22 (14). INDIANAPOLIS 47.38. Ph. A.I. varia 418–19. Woman, and woman with box. [Buschor].

22 *bis.* BASLE MARKET (M.M.). Youth and woman at tomb (youth to right, woman frontal, head to left, with oinochoe and phiale).

23 (16). MARBURG 705, fr. (Woman holding a fillet).

24 (17). ATHENS, Vlasto, from Athens. *Eph.* 1950–1, 156 fig. 5. Woman holding a lyre.

25 (18). ATHENS 1912 (CC. 1648), from Athens. Woman running with loaf and basket of loaves. Not certain that the shoulder belongs.

26 (19). ATHENS, Vlasto, from Koropi. *Eph.* 1950–1, 156 fig. 4. Two women.

27 (a 1). OXFORD 549. *JHS.* 25 pl. 3, 1. Woman seated, holding wreath. ΚΑΛΟΣ ΛΙ+ΑΣ. [Buschor].

28 (21). BERLIN inv. 3175, from Athens. Fairbanks i, 146; Riezler pl. 12. Demeter and Persephone. For the subject, Simon *O.G.* 71.

WHITE SQUAT LEKYTHOS
(second white used)

29 (24). CAB. MÉD. 476, from Camiros. Ph. Gir. 8116, 1. Woman holding sash and flower, woman holding girdle.

Probably also:

WHITE LEKYTHOI
(standard shape: second white used)
(no. 1, with rf. shoulder)

1 (1 23). ATHENS 2032 (CC. 1633). Fairbanks i pl. 5, 2. Two women. [Buschor].
(no. 2, the shoulder white, with matt palmettes)

2. ATHENS E 61. Two women (one to right, bending, the other frontal, with head to left). ΛΙ+ΑΣ [Κ]ΑΛΟ[Σ]. The form of the sigma uncertain.

Also near the painter, the

WHITE LEKYTHOS
(standard shape: second white used)
(the shoulder white, with our painter's palmettes)

(2). SYRACUSE 2288. Youth leaving home (youth and woman).

A red-figured vase found with Syracuse 22789 (p. 746 no. 7) may be by the same painter, as Buschor suggested:

LEKYTHOS
(standard shape)

(a). SYRACUSE 22878, from Camarina. *ML.* 14, 844. Two women. [Buschor].

Compare with it the

LEKYTHOS
(standard shape)

COPENHAGEN 135, from Athens. *CV.* pl. 164, 2. Two women.

On these see also p. 671 nos. 6 and 7.

The following bears some resemblance to Athens 1825 (p. 746 no. 11):

WHITE LEKYTHOS
(standard shape: second white used)
(the shoulder white, with Achillean palmettes)

(3). ATHENS 13701. Karouzou *T.W.L.* 7. Man and boy at tomb. The border also is Achillean.

THE GROUP OF ATHENS 1887

Two small vases go together and are not far from the Painter of Athens 1826:

WHITE LEKYTHOI
(secondary shape: Class ATL; second white used)

1. ATHENS 1887 (CC. 1640). Woman playing with a yoyo.
2. ATHENS 17287. *CV.* Jc pl. 20, 2–3. Woman seated, holding a lekythos.

THE INSCRIPTION PAINTER

McMahon in *AJA.* 1907, 21. Buschor *ALP.* (in *Mü. Jb.* N.S. 2), 17. *ARV.*[1] 467–8 and 960.

So called from the rows of short strokes, indicating an inscription, on the stelai in nos. 1 and 3.

WHITE LEKYTHOI
(standard shape)

1 (1). MADRID 19497 (L. 299). Alvarez-Ossorio pl. 43, 2; Leroux pl. 34, 2; Fairbanks i, 194. Two women at tomb. [Buschor].

2 (2). ATHENS 1958 (CC. 1690), from Eretria. *AJA.* 1907, 21; *Jh.* 10, 121; Fairbanks i, 203; Riezler pl. 17; *CV.* Jc pl. 6, 3–5. Two women at tomb. [McMahon]. See p. 1668.

3 (3). ATHENS 1959 (CC. 1691), from Eretria. *AJA.* 1907, 22; Riezler pl. 16, whence Pfuhl fig. 532 (= Pfuhl *Mast.* fig. 86); *CV.* Jc pl. 6, 6–7. Youth (in chlamys) seated at tomb, and woman. [McMahon].

4 (4). ATHENS 1789 (CC. 1681). Benndorf pl. 20, 2; Riezler pl. 18. Youth

(in chlamys) with spear, and woman, at tomb. [McMahon]. As the next.

5 (5). ATHENS 1790 (CC. 1775), from Athens. Youth and woman at tomb. [McMahon]. As the last.

6 (6). BERLIN inv. 3245. *Anz.* 1893, 92, 54; Riezler pl. 19. Warrior running, and girl with a lekythos and on her head a basket, at tomb. [Buschor].

7 (7). ATHENS MARKET. Warrior running, and girl with lekythos and basket at tomb. The shield-device is a club. Free replica of Berlin inv. 3245. According to Bothmer this should be Providence 047.47.1 (on loan).

8 (8). NEW YORK 41.162.102. *CV.* Gallatin pl. 27, 7 and 9. Youth (in chlamys, holding spear and helmet) and woman, at tomb.

9. BESANÇON 957.4.2. Youth and woman at column. [Bothmer]. Mended with alien fragments; doubtful if shoulder, neck, mouth, belong; but according to Bothmer the vent-hole on the shoulder is right for the Inscription Painter.

10. MAPLEWOOD, Noble. *Man in the Ancient World* 61. Youth with lyre, and woman with lekythos and fruit, at tomb. [Also Bothmer].

11. NEW YORK 06.1021.294. Warrior and woman at tomb. See the next.

12. LOUVRE CA 1846, from Attica. Warrior and woman at tomb. As the last. Restored.

13. ATHENS 17277. *CV.* Jc–d pl. 21, 1–2 and 4. Two women at tomb. [Karouzou]. Late.

_____

NEAR THE INSCRIPTION PAINTER

WHITE LEKYTHOI

1. ABINGDON, Robertson, fr., from Greece. Greek and Amazon. See Bothmer *Am.* 195–6 no. 113. Compare New York 06.1021.294 and Louvre CA 1846 (above, nos. 11–12).

2 (a). ATHENS 1968 (CC. 1625), from Eretria. Fairbanks i, 122; Zervos fig. 263. Athena. Second white used.

3. PARIS MARKET (Segredakis). Warrior and woman at tomb (youth in chitoniskos to right holding helmet and spear, woman in sleeveless chiton standing frontal, head to left, holding a casket in her right hand and on her left arm a basket containing an alabastron, an amphoriskos, sashes, and wreaths). Inscription ΚΛΕϛΙΛΛϟ. Late. Compare Athens 17277 (above no. 13).

_____

THE PAINTER OF LONDON 1905

ARV.[1] 506 and 961.

Fairbanks put the two together (ii, 246–9), and Buschor attributed them to the Inscription Painter (*ALP.* 17), whom they certainly recall. They also bring the Tymbos Painter to mind.

WHITE LEKYTHOS
(standard type)

1 (1). LONDON 1905.11–1.1. Fairbanks ii pl. 34, 2; detail, Jacobsthal *Mel.* 190. Youth (in chitoniskos, with spear) and woman at tomb. Now cleaned: the hare and other details were modern.

2 (2). LONDON 1906.5–12.1. Fairbanks ii pl. 34, 1. Youth and woman at tomb. Much restored: the flute, the loutrophoros, the palmette topping the stele, the kalos-inscription, and other details, are modern enrichments.

Somewhere here we may place the

WHITE LEKYTHOS

ATHENS 17294. *CV.* Jc pl. 20, 1 and 4. Thanatos and Hypnos.

THE PAINTER OF ATHENS 12789
*ARV.*¹ 468.

Put together by Riezler (94). Buschor *ALP.* 17 (as 'Inscription Painter nos. 28 and 29').

Related to the Inscription Painter.

WHITE LEKYTHOI
(standard shape)

1 (1). ATHENS 12789, from Eretria. *Eph.* 1906 pl. 1; Riezler pl. 8; Zervos figs. 275 and 269. Woman seated and woman. ΔΙΦΙΛΟ[Σ] ΚΑΛΟΣ.

2 (2). ATHENS 12785. *Eph.* 1906 pl. 2; Riezler pl. 9. Woman seated and woman. ΔΙΦΙΛΟΣ ΚΑΛΟΣ.

Compare the

WHITE LEKYTHOS
(standard shape)

(a). BERLIN inv. 3276. Riezler pl. 13, whence Pfuhl fig. 531 (=Pfuhl *Mast.* fig. 85). Plouton and Persephone. For the subject, Simon *O.G.* 73 and 75.

THE BELDAM CLASS (BEL)
THE BELDAM PAINTER

Haspels *ABL.* 170–91, 266–9, and 367. *ARV.*¹ 469. *ABV.* 586–7 and 709.

He is a painter of black-figured lekythoi, but Miss Haspels perceived (*ABL.* 175) that two white lekythoi with designs in outline, and a red-figured lekythos, were not only made in his workshop, as the potter-work shows, but also decorated by him.

LEKYTHOI
(nos. 1–2, white)

1 (1). ATHENS 1982 (CC. 1067), from Eretria. Haspels *ABL.* pl. 52, 1 and pl. 51, 4. Two women at tomb. [Haspels]. Second white used.

2 (2). ATHENS 1983 (CC. 1065), from Eretria. Haspels *ABL.* pl. 52, 2. Two Amazons. [Haspels]. Second white used.

(no. 3, rf.)

3 (3). COPENHAGEN inv. 1941, from Attica. Ussing *Nye Erhv.* pl. 3; *CV.* pl. 164, 1. Mother, maid, and child. [Haspels].

A third lekythos goes with nos. 1 and 2 in shape and drawing, and the painter is no doubt the same:

WHITE LEKYTHOS

ATHENS MARKET. Woman seated at tomb, and woman (woman to right, one foot on a step of the tomb, holding a basket; woman seated on the steps of the tomb, to right, chin on hand; on the steps, a perfume-vase, a lekythos, a pair of sandals between a pair of aryballoi; the aryballoi show that the seated woman is not the dead, but a mourner for a dead youth). False-bottomed vase (see Haspels *ABL.* 176–7). Second white used.

Rather near nos. 1 and 2, a white-ground lekythos, with patterns only, in the Ceramicus Museum at Athens, no. 6 in Miss Haspels's list of vases by the Beldam Painter (*ABL.* p. 266; Haspels *ABL.* pl. 50, 4 and pl. 51, 3; *Jb.* 61–62 pl. 16–17, 55).

With the Copenhagen vase (no. 3) compare the

ALABASTRON
(rf.)

TÜBINGEN E 140, fr. Watzinger pl. 36. Pyrrhic (girl dancing and woman seated playing the flute); (girl—cup-bearer?—, kottabos-stand).

And with that the
LEKYTHOI
(rf., small, secondary)

1. BOLOGNA PU 304. Drawing Dal Pozzo, whence *P.A.P.S.* 108, 207 fig. 22, above. Woman with lyre at altar. See p. 1668.

2. ATHENS 1499 (CC. 1436). Woman with phiale and sceptre at altar. Later.

A small vase was seen by Miss Haspels to come from the Beldam workshop and perhaps to have been decorated by the Beldam Painter:

WHITE LEKYTHOS

CORINTH MP 90, from Corinth. *Hesp.* 1, 79 fig. 22. Seated woman.

Compare with this the

WHITE LEKYTHOS

ATHENS, from Athens. Woman seated (on platform, to right, looking round).

Other vases of the Beldam Class (BEL) decorated by various painters, are the following:

WHITE LEKYTHOI

The two forming the Group of London D 65 (p. 752). [Haspels].

The two by the Utrecht Painter (p. 753).

Seven of the Carlsruhe Painter's white lekythoi: (pp. 734–5 nos. 90 and 98–103).

LONDON D 31, from Athens. Iris. Much damaged. Not by the Carlsruhe Painter; more like the Beldam Painter, so far as one can tell from the little that remains.

CHICAGO, Univ. See p. 1575.

THE GROUP OF LONDON D 65

Haspels *ABL.* 174. *ARV.*¹ 468.

Miss Haspels put two lekythoi together as 'fashioned by the Beldam *Potter*, but not decorated by the Beldam Painter'. The drawing, however, is quite like the Beldam Painter's. Gross style.

WHITE LEKYTHOI

1 (1). PARIS MARKET (Platt: ex Feuardent). Two women at tomb (one standing to right, with a sash, the other standing frontal, head to left, right hand on head, basket on left arm). Second white for the tomb.

2 (2). LONDON D 65. Murray *WAV.* pl. 27. Two women at tomb.

Near these the

WHITE LEKYTHOS

(a). DRESDEN ZV 2044, fr. (On the left, woman standing to right, holding a rolled-up garment; hanging, on the left, a piece of stuff, on the right, a lyre).

THE UTRECHT PAINTER

Haspels *ABL.* 175. *ARV.*¹ 469.

The two were put together by Miss Haspels as 'smaller works by the Painter of London F 65'. She saw that the shape pointed to the Beldam Potter, and that the drawing imitated the Carlsruhe Painter. The shape is the same as in the Carlsruhe Painter's Beldam lekythoi (pp. 734–5 nos. 90 and 98–103), and the Utrecht vase stands specially close to nos. 99–102.

WHITE LEKYTHOI
(Class BEL)

1 (1). UTRECHT H 16, from Boeotia. *Ned. Jaarboek* 1955, 24, 1. Woman leaving tomb. Second white for the tomb. [Haspels].

2 (2). ATHENS 12750 (N. 1007). Man leaning on his stick at tomb, with hare. Second white for the tomb. [Haspels].

THE TYMBOS GROUP

We give this name to a numerous group of small, coarse white lekythoi which run from the early classic period down to 420 or so. We divide the group into three sections:

(1) vases by the Tymbos Painter;

(2) vases in the manner of the Tymbos Painter, most of them later than those in section (1);

(3) late products of the Tymbos workshop, by various hands: some of these products still echo the style of the Tymbos Painter, but most of them have no connexion with it.

In dealing with these trifling objects, not the most delightful of one's tasks, it is not always easy to distinguish the work of the Tymbos Painter from work that is merely in his manner; and the division is in parts tentative: some of the pieces in section (1) may be only in the manner of the painter, and some of those in section (2) might be from his hand.

The name 'Tymbos Painter' is Buschor's: the representation of the tomb often bulks large in the small picture.

The shape of the lekythos is the same as in the Aischines Painter (p. 709): Class ATL; and the two painters—Tymbos, Aischines—are connected.

The technique is not the same throughout. The outlines are most often in yellow glaze, and in section (1) they are nearly always so; but in some of the later vases the yellow glaze is *mixed* with matt red, and in others matt red is used for the outlines without admixture. Black relief-lines appear on two vases only, both in section (1): New York 75.2.3 (p. 756 no. 55) and Prague, Nat. Mus., 776 (p. 756 no. 50).

The letter C at the end of an item refers to the picture: it means that the figure is shown on this side of the tomb (citra), giving the effect of a stele decorated with a relief.

THE TYMBOS PAINTER

Buschor *ALP.* (in *Mü. Jb.* N.S. 2) 18. *ARV.*[1] 503–8 and 961. Many of the vases by the painter and his followers had been put together by Fairbanks (i. 295–334).

LEKYTHOI
(secondary shape: Class ATL: see p. 709)

(nos. 1–94, white)

1 (1). ATHENS 1876 (CC. 1053). Benndorf pl. 24, 2. Woman (standing to right), tomb (mound). C.

2 (3). ATHENS 1915 (CC. 1072), from Athens. Woman (standing to right), tomb. C.

3. NEW YORK MARKET (ex Matsch). *CV.* Matsch pl. 9, 5 and p. 17. The like. C. Attributed by Miss Kenner to the same hand as our nos. 10, 7, and 11.

4 (2). ATHENS MARKET. Woman (standing to right, holding wreath), tomb. C.

5 (4). MUNICH 2772 (J. 198), from South Italy. Woman seated (to right), tomb. C.

6 (9). ATHENS, private. Fairbanks i, 312 fig. 55. The like. C.

7 (6). TÜBINGEN E 64. Watzinger pl. 26. The like. C.

8 (7). ATHENS 12901. Fairbanks i, 321. The like. C.

9 (8). BASLE MARKET (M.M.: ex Elgin). *Burl. 1903* pl. 93, H 25. The like. C.

10 (9). ATHENS, private. Fairbanks i, 312 fig. 56. The like. C.

11 (10). BERLIN inv. 3324. Benndorf pl. 19, 5. The like. C.

12 (11). PIRAEUS. The like. C.

13. OXFORD 1956.14. *Ashm. Report* 1956 pl. 2, c. Woman seated, with sash, at tomb.

14 (12). LOUVRE MNB 3059. Benndorf pl. 19, 2. Woman standing (to right) at tomb, holding wreath; the tomb is decorated with the figure of a seated woman.

15 (13). LONDON D 36, from Athens. Woman standing (to right) at tomb, holding wreath.

16 (14). LOUVRE CA 2966, from Athens. The like.

17. OMAHA 1954.1. The like . [Bothmer].

18. NEW YORK MARKET (Joseph Brummer). The like.

19. PRAGUE, Univ., E 65, from Greece. *Epit. Haken* pl. 14, 2. Woman standing (to right) at tomb. [Frel.]

19 *bis*. PRAGUE, Univ., E 80, from Greece. *Epit. Haken* pl. 14, 1. The like. [Frel.]

20 (15). COPENHAGEN inv. 1945, from Athens. *CV.* pl. 170, 4. Woman standing (to right) at tomb, with basket.

21 (16). LONDON D 43. The like.

22. SALONICA, Univ. The like.

22 *bis*. NEW YORK MARKET (Sydor Rey). Woman, tomb (on the left, stele crowned with a palmette, then woman in chiton and himation to right, alabastron in right hand, with her left hand supporting a shallow basket on her head). [Bothmer].

23 (17). ATHENS 1904 (CC. 1073), from Athens. Woman standing at tomb.

24 (18). BOULOGNE 172, from Athens. The like.

25 (20). ATHENS 1871 (CC. 1050). Woman standing (to left) at tomb.

26 (21). ATHENS 1872 (CC. 1049). The like.

27 (22). CAMBRIDGE 142, from Athens. *CV.* pl. 31, 1. The like.

28 (a i 1). ATHENS 1803 (CC. 1051). The like, with sash.

29 (23). LONDON D 41. The like.

30 (24). Once ATHENS, private. Benndorf pl. 24, 1. Woman standing (to right) at tomb, mourning.

31 (25). COPENHAGEN ABc 1029, from Greece. *CV.* pl. 170, 5. Woman standing (to left) at tomb, mourning.

32 (a i 2). ATHENS 1986 (CC. 1071), from Eretria. Woman standing (frontal, head to left) at tomb, mourning.

33 (a i 3). Once ATHENS, private. Benndorf pl. 24, 3. Woman kneeling (to left) at tomb, mourning.

34 (19). MUNICH, Lenbachhaus. Woman running to tomb (to right), basket on head.

35. PRAGUE, Nat. Mus., 1706, fr., from Athens. *Epit. Haken* pl. 4, 6. Woman approaching tomb (to right).

36 (26). HEIDELBERG, from Greece. *Anz.* 1916, 179 fig. 11; Pagenstecher *Unt.* pl. 2, a. Woman approaching tomb (to right, looking round).

37 (27). LONDON MARKET (Spink). Woman leaving tomb (to right, looking round).

37 *bis*. RANCATE, Züst. The like.

38 (a i 4). ATHENS 1781 (CC. 1046). Woman with torch leaving tomb (to right, looking round).

39 (28). ERLANGEN. Woman seated at tomb, and youth.

40 (29). ATHENS 1885 (CC. 1039). Benndorf pl. 19, 4, whence *Mü. Jb.* 1906, 3 fig. 7. Sphinx (sepulchral monument).

41 (30). ATHENS, Vlasto, from Spata. Woman standing (to right) at altar, with wreath. As nos. 42 and 49.

42 (31). ATHENS, Vlasto, from Spata. Woman running to altar (to right), with wreath. As nos. 41 and 49.

43 (32). LONDON MARKET (Spink: ex Brooks). Woman standing (to left) at altar, holding an egg or the like.

44 (33). Once TARPORLEY, Brooks. Woman standing (to left) at altar, with wreath.

45 (34). CAB. MÉD. 498. De Ridder pl. 20 (misprinted 488). Woman with wreath, and on her head a basket (to right).

46. OBERLIN 42.14, from Greece. Woman with a basket on her head (moving to right). [Bothmer].

47 (35). ATHENS 2030 (CC. 1059). The like.

48 (36 *bis*). LONDON, frr. Woman with a basket on her head (to right); at her feet a bird.

49 (37). ATHENS, Vlasto, from Spata. Woman standing (to left), holding a saccos. As nos. 41 and 42.

50. PRAGUE, Nat. Mus., 776. Frel Ř.*V.* fig. 61. Woman standing (to left), with mirror.

51 (38). ATHENS, from Athens (Stables). Woman (running, with sacrificial basket and torch, preceded by a small animal).

52 (39). LONDON (old cat. 2901). Woman running (to right).

53. LAON 37.934. Woman (running to right, looking round, holding a wreath).

54 (40). ATHENS 1873 (CC. 1052). Collignon and Couve pl. 37, 1052. Woman (moving to right, looking round, holding a sash).

55 (41). NEW YORK 75.2.3 (GR 603), from near Athens. *AJA.* 1886 pl. 10, 4 and pl. 12–13, 4. Woman seated with mirror.

56 (42). BERLIN 2247, from Athens. Woman seated with phialai.

57 (43). MARSEILLES 1634. Ph. Marb. neg. 1305. Woman seated with wreath.

58. BASLE MARKET (M.M.: ex Elgin). Nike (flying with wreath).

59 (44). ATHENS 2395 (N. 1010). Nike (running with fillet).

60 (45). ATHENS 1884 (CC. 1056). Nike (running).

61. ATHENS 17761. *JHS.* 65 pl. 7, b. Nike (running).

62 (46). BERLIN 2248, from Athens. Benndorf pl. 27, 2. Iris.

63 (47). CARLSRUHE (B 2663). Fairbanks i pl. 14, 4; *CV.* pl. 30, 1. Charon.

64 (48). OXFORD 547, from Greece. *JHS.* 25, 75, below. Charon.

65 (49). BERLIN 2246, from Athens. Youth seated, tomb. C.

66 (50). LONDON D 35, from Athens. Stackelberg pl. 38, 6, whence Panofka *Griechinnen* pl. o, 16. Dead youth, tomb. C.

67 (51). ATHENS 1886 (CC. 1055). The like.

68. CARLSRUHE (B 788). *CV*. pl. 30, 3. Youth leaning on his stick at tomb (to right). Much restored.

69 (54). SAN FRANCISCO, Legion of Honor, 1617. *CV*. pl. 14, 2. Man leaning on his stick at tomb (to right). [H. R. W. Smith].

70 (55). NEW YORK 41.162.118. *CV*. Gallatin pl. 27, 4. Youth leaning on his stick at tomb (to right).

71 (53). LONDON D 38. Cecil Smith pl. 24, 2. Man leaning on his stick at tomb (to right). As Sydney 53.27 (no. 72).

72. SYDNEY 53.27. The like. As London D 38 (no. 71).

73 (62). LONDON (old cat. 2860). Youth leaning on his stick at tomb (to left).

74 (a i 6). MUNICH 2771 (J. 201), from South Italy. The like.

75 (52). MUNICH. Youth at tomb.

76. OXFORD, Somerville College. The like.

77 (56). HEIDELBERG. Pagenstecher *Unt.* pl. 2, b; *Anz.* 1916, 179 fig. 10. Youth standing at tomb (to right), with lyre.

78 (58). PARIS MARKET (Pignatelli). The like.

79 (57). ATHENS MARKET. The like (lyre in left hand, right arm extended holding a small object; on the left, a wreath hanging, as in no. 77).

80 (59). LONDON MARKET (Spink). Youth running to mound (left arm extended).

81 (60). ATHENS MARKET. Youth running to tomb (he wears boots as well as a himation).

82 (61). ATHENS 1780 (CC. 1045). Youth standing (to left) at tomb.

83. NEW YORK MARKET (Joseph Brummer). Youth leaving tomb (to right, looking round).

84 (63). ATHENS 2036 (CC. 1070). Youth leaving tomb (to right, looking round, in chlamys, with spear).

85 (64). ATHENS MARKET. Youth with lyre.

86 (65). BRUSSELS A 1382, from Athens. Furtwängler *Somzée* pl. 38, ii, 3 = *Vente Somzée* pl. 3, 92; Fairbanks ii pl. 32, 2; *CV*. Jb pl. 2, 3. Youth (in chlamys) running with spear.

87 (67). ATHENS 1860 (CC. 1017). Man (in chlamys) running with spear.

88. PARIS MARKET (Hirsch: *Vente 30 juin 1921* no. 184, 1). The like. [Bothmer].

89 (66). LONDON D 34, from Athens. The like.

90 (68). NEW YORK 06.1021.127, from Cervetri? Fairbanks i pl. 10, 2. Youth (in chlamys) running with sword, at tomb.

91 (a ii 20). KOENIGSBERG 88. Lullies *K.* pl. 16, 1. Youth (in chlamys) running with sword. [Lullies].

92 (a i 7). ATHENS 1859 (CC. 1048). Fairbanks i pl. 14, 3. The like.

93. PRAGUE, Nat. Mus., 1675, from Greece. *Obzor Prehistorický* 13 (1946), 36; Frel *Ř.V.* fig. 62. The like. Restored.

94 (a ii 24). CAB. MÉD. 496 *bis*. *Annali* 1847 pl. W, 2; *Gaz. arch.* 1885 pl. 32, 1, whence Farmakovski i, 302. Oriental archer.

(nos. 95–96, rf.)

95 (69). LENINGRAD (St. 1562), from Nola. *CR.* 1863 pl. 2, 27. Woman with mirror.

96 (70). MUNICH inv. 7694. Woman (standing to right, arms extended as holding a wreath).

SQUAT LEKYTHOI
(no. 97, white)

97 (71). LONDON D 18, from Nola. Woman standing at altar, with wreath.

(no. 98, rf.)

98 (73). OXFORD 1925.87, from Greece. *CV.* pl. 40, 18. Woman standing at altar.

NEAR THE TYMBOS PAINTER

LEKYTHOI

(rf.)

1. ATHENS 1196 (CC. 1451). Woman at altar.

2. PRAGUE, Univ., E 130, from Greece. *Sborník* 1959 pl. 6, 85. Woman with mirror. Already connected with the Tymbos Painter by Frel.

Compare also the

WHITE LEKYTHOS

CAMBRIDGE 3.02. *CV.* pl. 31, 2. Woman running with sash. For the subject compare Athens 1873 (p. 756 no. 54).

(ii)

WORKSHOP AND MANNER OF THE TYMBOS PAINTER

ARV.[1] 506–7.

Most of these are later than the lekythoi in the foregoing list. Some of them may be by the painter himself. The later represent the continuation of his production.

WHITE LEKYTHOI
(secondary shape)

1 (1). GOETTINGEN, fr. Woman, tomb. The head remains, to right. C. Near the painter.

2. CORINTH MP 91, from Corinth. *Hesp.* 1, 82. Woman running to tomb (to right, looking round). [Shoe].

3. ATHENS MARKET. Woman with basket (moving to right), tomb. C.

4 (2). MUNICH inv. 7681. Woman kneeling, mourning, tomb. C.

5 (8). CAB. MÉD. 501, from Aegina. Woman mourning at tomb (standing to left).

6 (9). ATHENS. The like.

7 (a iii 12). LONDON D 45, from Rhodes. Woman mourning at tomb (standing frontal, head to left, right arm raised to head, basket on left arm).

8 (4). Once BROOMHALL, Elgin. Woman standing at tomb (to right, right forearm extended).

9 (a iii 2). PROVIDENCE 06.050. *CV.* pl. 25, 4. Woman standing at tomb (to right) with basket. Compare Sèvres inv. 3084. 1 (no. 20).

10 (a iii 3). MUNICH 2781. Woman running to tomb (to right).

11 (a iii 23). MUNICH inv. 1780. Woman standing at tomb (to right). The tomb as in Munich 2781 (no. 10).

12 (5). ATHENS 13036. Woman standing at tomb, with basket.

13 (a iii 5). MUNICH 2770 (J. 224), from South Italy. Woman standing at tomb, with perfume-vase.

14 (6). ATHENS 1808 (CC. 1042), from Salamis. Woman running to tomb with wreath. Near the painter. Compare, perhaps, the rf. lekythos Ghent 15 (*Ant. class.* 22 pl. 5, 9).

15 (7). Once BROOMHALL, Elgin. Woman standing at tomb (to left, holding a fruit or the like).

16 (9). ATHENS 1782 (CC. 1808). Woman standing at tomb (to left).

17. BUCAREST, Kalinderu Museum, 55. Coliu 84 and 85 fig. 64. Woman, tomb. C.

18 (5). ATHENS 13036. Woman seated at altar (to left), with phiale. Near the painter.

19. BASLE MARKET (M.M.: ex Elgin). Woman running with sprigs (to right, looking round; chiton and himation).

20 (a iii 1). SÈVRES inv. 3084.1, from Greece. *CV.* pl. 22, 9–10. Woman running. Compare Providence 06.050 (no. 9).

21 (13). LONDON D 40, from Athens. Woman dancing.

22 (3). CAB. MÉD. Naked child, tomb. C. Near the painter.

23 (12). MUNICH inv. 7662. Athlete, tomb. C.

24 (13). MUNICH (inv. 76547?). Youth leaning on his stick (to right) at tomb.

25 (14). ATHENS 1903 (CC. 1824), from Athens. The like.

26. Boulogne 173.   Youth leaning on his stick (to right); behind him, tomb.

27 (a iii 20).   London (old cat. 2864).   Youth or man leaning on his stick (to left) at tomb.

28 (19).   Athens, Agora, P 6099, fr., from Athens.   Youth, tomb.

29 (a iii 21).   Athens 12251.   Youth at tomb (frontal, head to left, right arm extended).

30.   Athens 14524.   The like.

31.   Dunedin 48.372.   The like.

32.   Dunedin 48.373.   The like.

33.   Syracuse, from Gela.   Youth approaching tomb (moving to left).

34 (16).   Copenhagen, Ny Carlsberg, inv. 2241.   *From the Coll.* 1, 163 fig. 2. Youth (in chlamys) approaching tomb (to left, hand raised to head).

35 (17).   Athens 1861 (CC. 1043).   Youth (in chlamys) leaving tomb (to right, looking round, hand raised to head).   Near the painter.

36 (18).   Heidelberg.   Pagenstecher *Unt.* pl. 2, c; *Anz.* 1916, 180 fig. 12. Youth (in chlamys) leaving tomb (to right, looking round).   Near the painter.

37 (21).   Louvre CA 2967, from Athens.   Youth (in chlamys) running with sword, at tomb.

38 (22).   Bologna PU 356, from Athens.   Heydemann *Ober* pl. 1, 3.   Youth (in chlamys) running with sword; in front of him a rock with a snake on it.   Hardly Kadmos.

39 (23).   Munich inv. 7673.   Youth with spears.   Near the painter.

40 (a iii 4).   London 1928.1–17.55.   Warrior (moving to right, looking round).

41 (25).   Jena 338.   Schadow *Eine attische Grablekythos*, whence *JHS.* 20, 101, whence Roscher s.v. Psyche, 3231; FR. iii, 29, whence Blinkenberg *Hades's Munding* 12; *Jb.* 42, 172; Deubner pl. 8, 2, whence Nilsson *G.R.* i pl. 33, 2.   Hermes at a pithos, charming souls.   Near the painter.

(iii)

Late products of the Tymbos Workshop, by various hands.

*ARV.*¹ 507–8.

WHITE LEKYTHOI
(*small, secondary shape*)

1 (10).   Athens 2031 (CC. 1057).   Woman at tomb (to right, with phormiskos).   Same style as Athens 2029 (no. 20).

2 (6).   Munich 2775.   Woman approaching tomb (to right, with basket).

3 (15). ATHENS 1794 (CC. 1033). The like.

4 (17). LONDON (old cat. 2842). Woman with basket at tomb (to right).

5 (18). ATHENS 1868 (CC. 1725). The like. Same style as Athens 1880 (no. 18).

6 (8). ATHENS 1779 (CC. 1781), from Athens. Woman (?) with basket at tomb (to right).

7 (a iv 1). ATHENS 1866 (CC. 1804). Woman with basket at tomb (frontal, head to right). Same style as Athens 1864 (no. 22).

8. WÜRZBURG 563. Langlotz pl. 207. Woman with basket at tomb (frontal, head to right).

9 (7). ATHENS 2026 (CC. 1015). Benndorf pl. 19, 1. Woman between two tombs.

10. BERKELEY 8.3312, from Athens. *CV*. pl. 59, 2 and pl. 61, 2. Woman with loaf and basket, mound. C.

11. ATHENS 1905 (CC. 1074), from Athens. Woman standing at tomb (to left).

12 (16). ATHENS. Woman at tomb (frontal, looking round to left, forearms extended; tomb on left).

13. WÜRZBURG 562. Langlotz pl. 207. Woman with basket at tomb (frontal, head to left; tomb on left).

14. OXFORD 1927.4463. Woman seated on rock at tomb.

15. NEW YORK 75.2.4 (GR 602). *AJA*. 1886 pl. 10, 1 and pl. 12–13, 1. Woman with lekythos seated at tomb.

16. ATHENS 12250. Woman seated at tomb (to left).

17. BASLE MARKET (M.M.: ex Elgin). Woman seated on rock, head bent. Very late.

18 (19). ATHENS 1880 (CC. 1724). Woman kneeling at tomb. Same style as Athens 1868 (no. 5).

19. GENEVA 8877. Woman (frontal, head to left).

20 (11). ATHENS 2029 (CC. 1058). Youth at tomb (to right). Same style as Athens 2031 (no. 1).

21 (24). ATHENS 1863 (CC. 1774). Youth at tomb (to right).

22 (a iv 2). ATHENS 1864 (CC. 1832). Youth approaching tomb (to right, looking round). Same style as Athens 1866 (no. 7).

23 (28). LONDON (old cat. 2876). Male at tomb.

24. YALE. Youth leaving tomb (to right, looking round, right hand raised to head, in left hand stick and sash). Restored.

25 (25). LONDON D 39. Youth at tomb (leaning on his stick, frontal, looking round to left, right hand raised to head, sash in left).

26. NAPLES Stg. 110. Youth at tomb (right hand raised to head, sash in left).

27 (26). LONDON (old cat. 2894), from Athens. Youth at tomb (frontal, head to left).

28 (a). ATHENS 1862 (CC. 1800). Youth running to mound.

29 (22). LONDON D 44, from Camiros. Youth leaving tomb (to right, looking round).

30. OXFORD 1914.15. Youth at tomb (in chitoniskos, to right, one foot raised, spear in hand).

31. STOKE-ON-TRENT. Man seated at tomb (to left).

32. WINCHESTER 48, from Eretria. Horseman; behind him, tomb.

33 (27). LONDON (67.5–8.1108, but this number crossed out). Youth (to left, looking round).

34. PRAGUE, Nat. Mus., 2474, from Greece. Frel *Ř.V.* figs. 60 and 64. Youth (in chlamys, standing frontal, head to right, with spear) [Frel].

The following are from the Tymbos workshop, and correspond, in red-figure, to some of the late white lekythoi just described:

LEKYTHOI

(rf.)

1. ATHENS 15449. Youth leaning on his stick.

2. LONDON MARKET (Spink: ex Fairfax Murray). *G. R. A. Spink* 25, 50. Youth leaning on his stick.

3. Once ROSTOCK, Witte. *Sg Loebbecke* pl. 7, 527. Youth leaning on his stick.

CHAPTER 41

SOTADES

THE SOTADES PAINTER

Pottier in *C.R. Ac. Inscr.* 1903, 216. Hauser in FR. iii, 92–94. Buschor *Das Krokodil des Sotades* in *Mü. Jb.* 11 (1919), 1–43. Pfuhl 543–9. Curtius *Der Astragal des Sotades. Att. V.* 317–19. *V.Pol.* 27–29 and 80. Peredolskaya in *AM.* 53, 9–16. *ARV.*[1] 450–8 and 960.

For the vases with the signature of the potter Sotades see pp. 772–3. Three of them—two white-ground, one red-figure—were decorated by one artist, the Sotades Painter.

CUPS
(of delicate make, with merrythought handles)

1 (1). LONDON D 6, fragmentary, from Athens. Fröhner *Brant.* pl. 39; Murray *W.A.V.* pl. 17, whence Hoppin ii, 430, Buschor G. *Vasen* 192, Pfuhl fig. 527 (= Pfuhl *Mast.* fig. 82), whence LS. fig. 116; part, Edmonds *Lyra Graeca* i, frontispiece; *Mon. Piot* 29, 109 and 119; A, *N.Y. Shapes* 19, 2 = Richter and Milne fig. 165; part, Robertson *G.P.* 131; ph. Macbeth. White ground. I, Hesperides. Coral red used. [ϹΟΤ]ΑΔΕϹΕΠΟΙΕϹΕΝ. On the inscriptions see *Gnomon* 13, 292 and Daux in *R.A.* 23 (1945), 147–8.

2 (2). LONDON D 5, from Athens. Fröhner *Brant.* pl. 41; Murray *W.A.V.* pl. 16, whence Hoppin ii, 429, Walters *H.A.P.* pl. 40, 2, Swindler fig. 288, Rumpf *MZ.* pl. 29, 3; Pfuhl fig. 526 (= Pfuhl *Mast.* fig. 84); *Mon. Piot* 29, 125; part, Robertson *G.P.* 130; *E.A.A.* iii, 953. White ground. I, Polyidos and Glaukos. [ϹΟΤ]ΑΔΕϹ. On the inscriptions see *AJA.* 1935, 483. Now cleaned.

STEMLESS CUPS
(no. 3, of the same delicate make as nos. 1–2)

3 (3). LONDON D 7, fragmentary, from Athens. Fröhner *Brant.* pl. 40; Murray *W.A.V.* pl. 18, b, whence Rumpf *MZ.* pl. 29, 6; Pfuhl fig. 528 (= Pfuhl *Mast.* fig. 83), whence LS. fig. 117; Robertson *G.P.* 129. White ground. I, unexplained subject: interpreted as the Death of Opheltes, but the man, from dress and face, can hardly be a hero. The handles are modern. [Van Branteghem].

(nos. 4–5, shallow, solid, lipped)

4 (4). BOSTON 03.841, two frr., from Italy. A, (goddess seated, and satyr dancing); B, (satyr striking with a thyrsus). Both satyrs wear the drawers of satyr-drama.

5 (5). NAPLES 2628. A–B, Heydemann *Hum. Vb.* pl. 1, 3; A–B, *AM.* 53 Beil. 6, 1; I, *JHS.* 56, 207 fig. 4; B, *AJA.* 1939, 8 fig. 6; ph. So. 11006, iii, 1. I, impressed. A, satyr and goat; B, satyr and bull.

SKYPHOS
(type B, glaux)

6. NAPLES, Astarita, 101, fragmentary. A, satyr. B, youth. On A, running to right, looking round, his left arm extended in a pelt. B, in himation, bending to right.

KANTHAROS
(type D, Sotadean)

7 (6). Once GOLUCHOW, Czartoryski, 76. De Witte pl. 26, whence *Mü. Jb.* 1919 (Buschor *Krok.*), 21 and Hoppin ii, 432; *V.Pol.* pll. 15–16, whence (B) Seltman pl. 32, a; *CV.* pl. 35. A, satyrs and maenads; B, the like. On A, ΣΟΤΑΔΕΣ ΕΓΟΙΕ complete.

RHYTA
(no. 8, sphinx)

8 (7). LONDON E 788, from Capua. *JHS.* 8 pll. 72–73, whence Perrot 10, 758–9 and pl. 25, FR. iii, 93, (part) *Mü. Jb.* 1919 (Buschor *Krok.*), 20; part, Genick pl. 24, 2; *CV.* pl. 40, 1 and pl. 42, 1; ph. Ma. 3216. Kekrops and Nike, with two women (daughters of Kekrops?) running up; goddess, and seated youth. Below: A, satyr as hunter; B, goddess. Attributed to 'Sotades' by Pottier. For the tomb-group, *AJA.* 1945, 157. See p. 870 no. 89.

(nos. 9–11, crocodile-and-negro-boy)

9 (8). LONDON E 789, fr., from Paphos. *JHS.* 9, 220 fig. 1, and p. 221; *CV.* pl. 37, 4 and pl. 39, 2. Pandora. Below, on one side, man hunting boar (the corresponding picture on the other side lost).

10 (9). PARIS, Petit Palais, 349, from Capua. *JHS.* 9, 220 fig. 2; *Burl. 1888* pl. 15, 78 = Fröhner *Brant.* pl. 48, 1, whence *Mü. Jb.* 1919 (Buschor *Krok.*), 4; *CV.* pll. 26–27, whence (part) Schnitzler pl. 54. Satyrs and maenads; below, on each side, satyr.

11 (10). DRESDEN 364, from Nola. *Mü. Jb.* 1919 (Buschor *Krok.*), 3, and 23 fig. 34. Warrior and youth, woman, and seated woman. [Buschor]. Much restored.

(no. 12, hound's head)

12 (11). ANCONA 3258 (1082), from Numana. Hoffmann *A.R.R.* pl. 12, 2. Satyrs and maenad (A, satyr; B, seated maenad; C, satyr).

(nos. 13–14, ram's head)

13 (12). LENINGRAD inv. 4519 (ex Botkin). *Les trésors d'art en Russie* 50; *Coll. Botkine* 25, below; *AM.* 53 Beil. 4; part, G.P. 64; Hoffmann *A.R.R.* pl. 7, 4. Satyr and maenad; goddess and satyr. [Peredolskaya].

14 (13). BONN 2049, frr. *CV.* pl. 24, 1. Satyr and maenad. [Greifen-hagen].

(no. 15, ram's head dimidiating donkey's head)

15 (a 19). BALTIMORE, Walters Art Gallery, 48.2050, from Athens. Stackelberg pl. 25, 1 and 3–4; *Cat. Christie Dec.* 21 1949, plate; *Bull. Walt.* 4, 1; part, *Archaeology* autumn 1952, 181. Satyrs. [Buschor]. See p. 1669.

(nos. 16–19, fragments, type of rhyton unknown)

16 (14). LENINGRAD inv. 34a, fr., from Kerch. *CR.* 1869 pl. 4, 4; *AM.* 53 Beil. 7, 1. (Woman—Nereid?—running: the inscription ΘΕΤΙϚ may pertain to an adjoining figure rather than to her).

17. REGGIO, fr., from Locri. (Satyr running to right, right arm extended behind; missing, the head and the greater part of the breast, with the left arm).

18. REGGIO, fr., from Locri. Satyr pursuing maenad (both running to left; one leg of the maenad remains, in chiton with kolpos; of the satyr, the middle, with the tail and the greater part of the legs; below, vertical V-pattern).

19 (14 *bis*). LOUVRE SB 4143 and SB 4154, two frr., from Susa. Part, Rostovtzeff *Hellenistic World* pl. 12, 3; Bothmer *Am.* pl. 82, 2. Amazonomachy. See Bothmer *Am.* 195; and here, p. 768 no. 31.

ASTRAGALOS

20 (15). LONDON E 804, from Aegina. Stackelberg pl. 23; HM. pl. 40; *JHS.* 13, 135; FR. pl. 136, 2, whence (part) *Mü. Jb.* 1919 (Buschor *Krok.*), 25 fig. 38, (part) Curtius *Astragalos* pl. 1, (part) Seltman pl. 32, b–c, (part) Richter *ARVS.* fig. 79; *CV.* pll. 26–27; part, *Die Antike* 6, 107–8; part, Lane pl. 76, b; part, Rumpf *MZ.* pl. 29, 1; part, Buschor *Bilderwelt* 43; part, Stella 211; part, *E.A.A.* i, 928. Uncertain subject: women dancing, and a man: the Clouds (Curtius)? [Hauser]. Restored.

MANNER OF THE SOTADES PAINTER

(i)

RHYTA

(nos. 1–2, crocodile-and-negro-boy)

1 (1). MUNICH inv. 6203, from Italy. Part, *Mü. Jb.* 1912, 74, 2; part, *Anz.* 1913, 22 fig. 2; part, *Mü. Jb.* 1919 (Buschor *Krok.*), 2, and 23 fig. 35. Unexplained subject: woman (huntress?), and a woman offering her an alabastron; and two other persons (women?: fragmentary). [Buschor]. 'The chief person has the same Thracian costume as on the Mayence lekythos (p. 693 no. 5): the question of Bendis comes in' (Bothmer). Or Prokris (see p. 607)? The plastic part is restored.

2 (2). BOSTON 98.881, from Capua. *Mü. Jb.* 1919 (Buschor *Krok.*), pll. 1–2 and p. 22. Satyrs and maenads. [Buschor].

(nos. 3–4, pygmy-and-dead-crane)

3 (3). ERLANGEN P1 (ex Preyss), from Italy (Velletri? Numana?). *Mü. Jb.* 1919 (Buschor *Krok.*), 24, and 25 fig. 37. Warrior leaving home (warrior and women). [Buschor]. Restored.

4 (4). BONN 545. Part, *Mü. Jb.* 1919 (Buschor *Krok.*), 18 fig. 28; *CV.* pl. 24, 2–5. Nike; satyr and maenad. Restored.

(no. 4 bis, sphinx)

4 *bis.* REGGIO 148, fr., from Locri. Mounted Amazon (riding to left, holding a pair of horizontal spears). The tiny remains of the plastic part suggest a sejant sphinx (lower edge of the belly, edge of one fore-leg, low down). The Amazon decorates one upright flank of the vase, below the belly. May be by the painter himself. Two other fragments in Reggio no doubt belong. They are from the kantharos part of the vase: on each, forepart of an Amazon riding to right.

(no. 5, grotesque head of an old man, Charun-like, except the nose)

5. FERRARA, T. 18 C VP, from Spina. Maenad. Compare Berlin 2623 (no. 9).

(nos. 6–13, ram's head)

6 (5). BOSTON 95.38, from Campania (probably Curti or Capua). *Mü. Jb.* 1919 (Buschor *Krok.*), 17; part, Richter and Milne fig. 179, whence LS. fig. 18. Seated youth, and woman holding armour (Achilles and Thetis?). [Buschor]. See pp. 769 and 1669.

7 (6). PARIS, Petit Palais, 352. *CV.* pl. 30, 1–3. Satyr and maenad.

8 (8). NAPLES 2956. Satyr and maenad.

9 (7). BERLIN 2623, from Nola. Winnefeld *Bronzebecken* 23; part, *AM.* 53 Beil. 5, 1; Brendel *Schafzucht* pl. 35. Satyr and maenads. [Peredol-skaya]. See p. 1669.

10 (9). ATHENS, fr., from the Cabeirion of Thebes. Wolters and Bruns pl. 39, 2. (Youth attacking with sword). See p. 1669.

11 (10). BERLIN inv. 4982.41. Brendel *Schafzucht* pl. 34. Two maenads running. Compare the Victoria and Albert boar-head (no. 17), and see pp. 769 and 1669.

11 *bis.* REGGIO, three frr., from Locri. Pygmy and crane.

12 (11). LONDON E 800, from Capua. *CV.* pl. 43, 2; ph. Ma. Ivy. Goes with London E 801 (no. 18), as Buschor saw. For the tomb-group see *AJA.* 1945, 156–7 and 1946, 170. See also p. 1669.

13 (11 *bis*). PARIS, Petit Palais, 373. *CV.* pl. 30, 4–5. Ivy. Plaoutine saw that this was from the same workshop as no. 6. See p. 1669.

(nos. 14–15, donkey's head)

14 (12). VIENNA 4401 (ex Trau). *CV.* pl. 100, 3–6. B, satyr attacking maenad; A, satyr; C, satyr.

15 (13). ISTANBUL, fr., from Lindos. Blinkenberg *Lindos* i pl. 130, 2724, and p. 651. Satyr and maenad.

(nos. 16–18, boar's head)

16 (14). COMPIÈGNE 898, from Nola. Jahn *Arch. Beitr.* pl. 12, 1 and a–b, whence (part) Roscher s.v. Pygmaien, 3295 fig. 5; *CV.* pl. 18, 16 and 23, and pl. 20, 10. A, pygmy and crane; B, ivy; C, pygmy and crane. [Peredolskaya].

17 (15). LONDON, Victoria and Albert Museum, 669.1864, from Capua. Part, Chittenden and Seltman pl. 22, 95; part, Hoffmann *A.R.R.* pl. 10, 4. A, satyr and maenad; B, ivy; C, two maenads. Compare the ram-head Berlin inv. 4982.41 (no. 11), and see p. 769 no. 5.

18 (16). LONDON E 801, from Capua. *CV.* pl. 43, 4. A, boar; B, ivy; C, boar. Goes with London E 800 (no. 12). See p. 1669.

(no. 19, ram's head dimidiating boar's head)

19 (17). Once NAPLES, Hamilton. Tischbein 2 pl. 7, whence Panofka *Trinkh.* pl. 1, 12–15. Pygmies and cranes. Compare Compiègne 898 (no. 16). [Peredolskaya].

(no. 20, ram's head dimidiating donkey's head)

20 (18). NEW YORK 06.1099, fragmentary, from Numana? B, (leg—of a satyr?). C, woman (maenad?) running. A is lost. See p. 1669.

RHYTA OR OTHER PLASTIC VASES

21 (20). BOSTON 26.15, fr., from Babylon. *MFA. Bull.* 24, 28; Langlotz *F.B.* pl. 96, d. What remains of the plastic part is a female head in relief; of the picture, bits of a woman, which, so far as they go, might be by the Sotades Painter himself.

22 (21). LENINGRAD inv. 3250, fr. *AM.* 53 Beil. 7, 2. (Satyr and maenad). [Peredolskaya]. Might be by the painter himself.

23. LOUVRE SB 4136, fr., from Susa. De Morgan *Mém. Dél. Perse* i pl. 5, 3. (Maenad). [Bothmer].

24 (22). NEW YORK 58.181, fr., and lost, fr. *AM.* 53 Beil. 7, 3. (Satyr). [Buschor]. The upper fragment of the two components is now missing.

25. NEW YORK, Katz, fr., from Ehnasa (Nile Delta). (Satyr, wearing boots, running to left, looking round, kantharos in left hand). [Bothmer].

25 *bis.* TARANTO, fr., from Locri. (Satyr dancing to right, left arm extended; missing, head, breast, right arm). Rough inside.

26. ATHENS, fr., from the Cabeirion of Thebes. Wolters and Bruns pl. 40, 4. (Satyr).

27. ATHENS 10461, fr., from the Cabeirion of Thebes. Wolters and Bruns pl. 23, 1 and pl. 39, 1. Centaur attacking satyr. For the subject see *EVP*. 100. May be from a ram-head rhyton.

28. VILLA GIULIA 50328, fr. *Boll. d'Arte* 7 (1927), 320 fig. 23. Centauromachy. May be by the painter himself.

29 (23). LOUVRE SB 4135, fr., from Susa. De Morgan *Mém. Dél. Perse* 1 pl. 5, 4. (Hermes, male).

30. LOUVRE SB (no number), fr., from Susa. (On the left of a picture, right hand and foot of an Oriental warrior—Amazon?—moving to right; on the right of a picture—the same?—, shank and foot of a similar warrior moving to left.) [Bothmer]. See the next.

31. LOUVRE SB 4145, fr., from Susa. (Forearm and hand, with sword, of a fallen warrior). [Bothmer]. Bothmer asks whether this may not be from the same vase as the last; whether both may not belong to Louvre SB 4143 and SB 4154 (p. 765 no. 19); and whether all these may not belong to Louvre SB 4138 and SB 4151 (p. 773).

FRAGMENT

(*of an oinochoe shape 8, mug ?*)

32 (24). FLORENCE 18 B 52, fr. *CV*. pl. 18, B 52. (Woman). See p. 769, below, ii, below, no. 4.

SKYPHOS

(*type B, glaux*)

33. LOUVRE G 617, from Capua. A, *Le Musée* 5, 68; A, Pottier pl. 157. A, dwarf running; B, dwarf sitting on the ground.

STEMLESS CUPS

(*nos. 34–37, shallow, solid, lipped*)

34 (25). LEIPSIC T 585, fr. A, *AM*. 53 Beil. 7, 6. I, incised. A, two women.

35 (26). GIESSEN (ex Duisburg), from Capua. *Bull. nap.* N.S. 3 pl. 2, 4–6; Zschietzschmann *Nachr. Giess.* 15 pl. 1, 2–3; A, Brommer *Satyrspiele* 40; phs. R.I. 2984 and 2985, 1. A, satyr pursuing Amymone; B, satyr pursuing maenad. [Peredolskaya]. For the subject of A compare the late-fifth-century cup-skyphos Athens 18763. See p. 1669.

36 (a). SORRENTO, from Vico Equense. A, Philippart *It.* i pl. 6, a; Mingazzini and Pfister *Surrentum* pl. 44, 172–5. A, satyr and maenad; B, the like.

37 (27). NAPLES Stg. 265. A–B, fight (gigantomachy?): A, Ares and Giant; B, maenad (?) and Giant. Unfinished work, by a tyro. Now cleaned.

(*no. 38, shallow; light make; lip inside only*)

38 (28). LENINGRAD inv. 2262, from South Russia. A–B, *AM*. 53 Beil. 5, 2; I, *JHS*. 56, 207 fig. 5. I, incised. A, satyr and maenad; B, the like. [Peredolskaya].

(ii)

THE PAINTER OF FLORENCE 3968

ARV.[1] 454.

Weak imitator of the Sotades Painter.

STEMLESS CUPS

(shallow; light make; lip inside only)

1 (1). FLORENCE 3968. I, *JHS.* 56, 209 fig. 11; A, ph. Al. 45765, 1. I, incised. A, youth and woman; B, the like.

2 (2). FLORENCE 3925. I, *JHS.* 56, 209 fig. 12; A, ph. Al. 45765, 2. I, incised. A, youth and woman; B, the like.

3 (3). NAPLES Stg. 250. I, youth and woman.

4 (4). FLORENCE 3914. I, youth, and woman with thyrsus seated.

Near these, four vases in the manner of the Sotades Painter:

RHYTA

(nos. 1–2, ram's head)

1. BOSTON 95.38. See p. 766 no. 6.

2. BERLIN inv. 4982.41. See p. 766 no. 11.

(no. 3, boar's head)

3. LONDON, Victoria and Albert Museum, 669.1864. See p. 767 no. 17.

FRAGMENT (of a mug?)

4. FLORENCE 18 B 52, fr. See p. 768 no. 32.

(iii)

THE HIPPACONTIST PAINTER

ARV.[1] 455.

Named from the mounted spearmen.

STEMLESS CUPS

(shallow; light make; lip inside only)

1 (1). NAPLES 2625, from Etruria. I, *JHS.* 56, 207 fig. 7; A, ph. So. 11006, i, 1. I, incised. A, horseman; B, the like.

2 (2). BOWDOIN 27.9. I and A, *JHS.* 56, 209 fig. 10 and p. 205. I, incised. A, horseman; B, the like.

3 (3). BASLE 1921.376. I, *JHS.* 56, 207 fig. 6; A–B, Schefold *Basler Ant.* ii pl. 24, b–c. I, incised. A, horseman; B, the like.

4 (4). Boston 13.203. I, *JHS*. 56, 209 fig. 8; the shape, Caskey G. 208. I, incised. A, horseman; B, the like.

A stemless cup of the same type as those by the Hippacontist Painter and those by the Painter of Florence 3968 (p. 769 nos. 1–4) is Sotadean, and is like both artists, especially the former.

Basle market (M.M.). I, incised. A, a woman seated on a rock, and a man leaning on his stick, both talking; B, a woman seated on a rock, talking to a youth.

The fragment Washington 136407, from Orvieto, is from a stemless cup with the same subject as those of the Hippacontist Painter, and contemporary: but the cup is not of the same type, for it has a lip outside as well as in. The drawing is most like that of the Boston stemless, but seems not to be the same.

(iv)

ARV.[1] 455–6.

Other stemlesses are related to those by the Sotades Painter and those in his manner:

STEMLESS CUPS

1 (1). Athens, Agora, P 10410, fr., from Athens. I, incised. Outside, parts of the palmettes remain.

(nos. 2–4, shallow, solid, lipped)

2 (2). Boston 01.8089. The shape, Hambidge 120 fig. 9; the shape, Caskey G. 207, 161. A, fight; B, fight.

3 (5). Syracuse 26612, from Camarina. A, satyr and maenad. B, two youths (or women).

4 (3). Florence 3928. A–B, Farmakovski ii, 281–2; A, *JHS*. 56, 209 fig. 13; A, ph. Al. 45760. I, incised. A, fight; B, fight.

(no. 5, shallow; light make; lip inside only)

5 (4). Louvre G 637. A, Pottier pl. 159; I and B, *JHS*. 56, 207 fig. 2 and pl. 11, 1; A–B, ph. Gir. 17067. I, incised. A, boar-hunt (youth and boar); B, the like. Compared with Florence 3928 (no. 4) by Mrs. Ure.

Another vase resembles some of the Sotadean in shape and interior decoration (see A. D. Ure in *JHS*. 56, 206 no. 9), but the pictures are later in style and cannot be said to bear any real likeness to the work of the Sotades Painter:

STEMLESS CUP

(shallow; light make; lip inside only)

London E 125, from Nola. *JHS*. 56, 209 fig. 9, and pl. 11, 3–4. I, incised. A, satyr resting, and maenad; B, satyr and maenad.

Another is possibly to be compared with the Sotadean stemlesses, but I cannot be sure from the reproduction:

Once NAPLES, Hamilton. Tischbein 3 pl. 14. A, satyr and maenad; B, the like. Restored, or made up in the drawing.

(v)

ARV.[1] 456–7 and 960.

Stemlesses from the same workshop, one would say, as nos 1–3 in the list of vases by the Sotades Painter (p. 763); in drawing, too, they are, in one way or another, somewhat akin to those:

STEMLESS CUPS
(delicate make, with merrythought handles)

1 (1). BRUSSELS A 890, from Athens. Fröhner *Brant.* pl. 38; *CV.* Jb pl. 1, 1; *Mon. Piot* 29 pl. 3 and p. 129; Anita Klein, frontispiece, a; side, Philippart *C.A.B.* pl. 33, a. I, mother and baby. Round this, white.

2 (2). BRUSSELS A 891, from Athens. Fröhner *Brant.* pl. 42, whence FR. ii, 181, Buschor *G.V.* 193, Perrot 10, 728, Hoppin ii, 9, *B.M. Gk and Rom. Life* 193 (whence Rumpf *Rel.* fig. 119, right), *Die Antike* 6, 165 fig. 4, 1; Pfuhl fig. 525 (=Pfuhl *Mast.* fig. 81); *CV.* Jb pl. 1, 2; *Mon. Piot* 29 pl. 2; Anita Klein pl. 18, a; Verhoogen *C.G.* pl. 19. I, white ground: woman spinning top. Coral red used. ΕΓΕSΙΒΟΛΟSΕΓΟΙΕSΕΝ. For the potter Hegesiboulos see also p. 175.

3 (4). LEIPSIC T 954, from Greece. I, seated woman. Coral red used. The picture is by a rude imitator of the Sotades Painter. See the next.

4 (5). BOSTON 03.791, from Greece. I, seated woman. Coral red used. Acquired, I believe, with the last. It is by the same painter.

STEMLESS CUP (OR CUP)

5 (3). AMSTERDAM, Six, fr., from Athens. I, white ground: (feet—of a woman?). Coral red used. Compared by Six with the Sotadean whites: it resembles the Brussels Hegesiboulos (no. 2). The handles are missing.

The following, without pictures, are also from the workshop of Sotades:

CUP
(of delicate make, with merrythought handles)

1 (1). BOSTON 13.4503, from Athens. Fröhner *Tyszk.* pl. 12, 1; Philippart *C.A.B.* pl. 33, c. Coral red used. The picture (Fröhner *Tyszk.* pl. 12, 2, whence Robert *Herm.* 334) was shown by Furtwängler to be modern.

STEMLESS CUP

2 (2). COPENHAGEN inv. 1635, from Athens. *CV.* pl. 175, 2. Coral red used.

Seen by Blinkenberg and Johansen to be from the workshop of Sotades: compare London D 7 (p. 763 no. 3).

Lastly, the make of the following is like the Sotadean (and the lost handles may have been merrythought), but the style of the drawing is quite different and somewhat recalls the Danae Painter:

STEMLESS CUP

BOSTON 00.357, from Vari. Philippart *C.A.B.* pl. 33, b. I, woman with hydria (at fountain). Round this, white. Coral red may have been used outside.

SOTADES, POTTER

ARV.[1] 457-8.

The name of Sotades occurs on eight vases:

CUPS

α. LONDON D 6, from Athens. See p.763 no. 1.

β. LONDON D 5, from Athens. See p. 763 no. 2.

KANTHAROS

γ. Once GOLUCHOW, Czartoryski, 76. See p. 764 no. 7.

PHIALAI

δ. BOSTON 98.886, from Athens. Fröhner *Brant.* pl. 35; Walters *H.A.P.* pl. 40, 1; Hoppin ii, 428; A, *N.Y. Shapes* 22, 1 = Richter and Milne fig. 181, whence LS. fig. 17; the cicada, Richter *Animals* fig. 225. Inside, white, with black lip, and black navel charged with a plastic cicada. Outside, fluted, white, black, and red; the lip black. Incised, ꟅΟ[ΤΑΔΕꟅ] Ε[ΠΟΙΕ].

ε. LONDON D 8, from Athens. Fröhner *Brant.* pl. 36; Hoppin ii, 431; Lane pl. 88, b, 2; Jacobsthal *Gk Pins* fig. 203. As Boston 98.886 (δ) but without the cicada. Incised, ꟅΟΤΑΔΕꟅ ΕΠΟΙΕ complete.

RHYTA

(ζ, *sphinx*)

ζ. VILLA GIULIA, fr., from Vulci. Incised, ꟅΩΤΑΔΗꟅ ΕΠΟΙΗꟅΕΝ.

(η, *horse or horseman*)

η. LOUVRE CA 1526, fr., from Capua. *C.R. Ac. Inscr.* 1903, 2; Hoppin *Bf.* 475. Incised, ꟅΟΤ[ΑΔΕꟅ] ΕΠ[ΟΙΕꟅΕΝ]. See p. 733.

(θ, *mounted Amazon*)

θ. BOSTON 21.2286, from Meroe. *MFA. Bull.* 21, 11, whence Hoppin *Bf.* 474; *Festschr. Loeb* pll. 10-11 and pp. 81-87; Swindler pl. 12; Charbonneaux *Terres cuites* fig. 38; Olmstead *Hist. Pers.* pl. 51, 1; part, Chase *Guide*

72; *Archaeology* summer 1953, 91, below; cleaned, part, Bothmer *Am.* pl. 90, 1. Fight (horse and foot: Greeks and Orientals: the Orientals uppermost). Below: A, lion; B, boar. Incised, ΣΟΤΑΔΗΣ ΕΠΟΙΗΣΕΝ. The pictures cannot be said to have any connexion with the Sotades Painter; for the ductus of the maeander, however, compare such Sotadean vases as London E 788 (p. 764 no. 8), Munich inv. 6203 (p. 765 no. 1), Boston 98.881 (p. 766 no. 2). See p. 1669.

Two vases found together with the phialai δ and ε go with them:

MASTOI

1. LONDON D 9, from Athens. Fröhner *Brant.* pl. 37; *JHS.* 49, 217; Lane pl. 88, b, 1; Jacobsthal *Gk Pins* fig. 202. Inside, white. Outside, fluted: black, red, and white. Restored.
2. LONDON D 10, from Athens. As the last. Restored.

Louvre CA 1526 (p. 772, η) takes with it, as Pottier saw, the

RHYTON
(horse or horseman)

LOUVRE SB 4138 and SB 4151, two frr., from Susa. A, de Morgan *Mém. Dél. Perse* 1 pl. 5, 1–2; *C.R. Ac. Inscr.* 1902, 429–30; A of one fr., Bothmer *Am.* pl. 82, 5. Below, white ground: A, (Amazon); B, (similar). See Bothmer *Am.* 195; and here, p. 768 no. 31.

Two fragments are from the bases of Sotadean plastic vases:

(negro-boy-and-crocodile)

1. REGGIO, fr., from Locri. Of the plastic figures, the negro's left hand remains.

(pygmy-and-crane)

2. REGGIO, fr., from Locri. Of the plastic figures, the pygmy's right foot remains.

CHAPTER 42

SMALL GROUPS OF SMALL VASES

THE HESIOD PAINTER

CB. i, 36–37. *ARV.*[1] 458–9 and 960.

PYXIS
(type A)

1 (1). BOSTON 98.887, from Eretria. Fairbanks *Gk Gods* 21; Hambidge, pl. at p. 48, and p. 49; part, *N.Y. Shapes* 28, 3; details, Richter *F.* figs. 85 and 116; Curtius *Pentheus* 6–7; CB. i pl. 15, 37, whence Schefold *Bildnisse* 57, 1–2 and *Riv. Ist.* N.S. 4, 201 fig. 14; *Eph.* 1952 pll. 1–2 at p. 72; Himmelmann-Wildschütz *Eig.* pl. 20; part, *E.A.A.* iii, 441; the shape, Caskey *G.* 229. White ground. Muses and neatherd (Hesiod?). See CB. i, 34–37 and ii, 101. Hesiod? or rather Archilochus?—see *Eph.* 1952, 57–68 (Kondoleon), *Philologus* 99, 23–26 (Peek), *Philologus* 100, 36–39 (Kondoleon).

STEMLESS CUPS
(of delicate make)

2 (2). LOUVRE CA 482, from Attica? *Mon. Piot* 2 pl. 5, whence Perrot 10 pl. 22 (redrawn!) and Kraiker *M.G.* 96 pl. V; Langlotz *GV.* pl. 36; *Enc. phot.* iii, 42, b, whence Stella 113; part, Wegner *Mus.* pl. 16, b; ph. Arch. phot. MNLA 1329. White ground. I, Muse, tuning her cithara. See p. 1669.

3 (3). LOUVRE CA 483, from Attica? *Mon. Piot* 2 pl. 6; *Enc. phot.* iii, 42, a; ph. Gir. 34160. White ground. I, Muse.

Compare with these an inferior

STEMLESS CUP
(of delicate make)

BERLIN inv. 3408, from Athens. Philippart *C.A.B.* pl. 34; *CV.* pl. 108, 1–2. White ground. I, woman at altar.

THE SOTHEBY PAINTER

ARV.[1] 607.

There the painter was placed in the Penthesilean Group.

PYXIDES
(no. 1, type A)

1 (1). BALTIMORE, Walters Art Gallery, 48.2019 (ex Sotheby), from Greece.

Cat. Sotheby Dec. 7 1920 pl. 1; *Joseph Brummer Collection. Part III,* (*Parke-Bernet no. 1079, June 8–9 1949*), 3, below, right, no. 12; *Journ. Walt.* 1949, 66, right; part, *Fasti arch.* 4, 141; detail, *Archaeology* Summer 1953, 66, left; detail, *Bull. Walt.* 6 no. 7, 1.   White ground.   Maenads.

(no. 2, type C)

2 (2). MISSISSIPPI (ex Robinson), from Greece.   *AJA.* 1930, 178; *CV.* i pl. 47, 2.   White ground.   Fight.

BOBBIN

3. ATHENS 2350 (CC. 853).   *Eph.* 1885 pl. 5, 1; B, CC. pl. 35, 853.   White ground.   A, in the middle, uncertain subject (chariot: of Eos, as Bothmer suggests?). In the zone round this, rape of the daughters of Leukippos. B, in the middle, Europa.   In the zone round this, unexplained subject (two youths about to surprise three women, a chariot waiting).

Perhaps connected with these the

PYXIS
(type A)

LOUVRE MNB 1286, from Athens.   *Mon. gr.* 1878 pl. 2 = Dumont and Chaplain ii pl. A, whence (one figure) Brunn-Bruckmann, text to pl. 727; ph. Gir. 34133.   White ground.   Perseus and Medusa.   See p. 1669.

THE PAINTER OF THE BRUSSELS OINOCHOAI

VA. 133.   *Att. V.* 288–9.   *ARV.*[1] 335.

In my lists previous to *ARV.*[1] these were put together with the vases which I later gave to the Painter of Bologna 228.

OINOCHOAI
(shape 7)

1 (1). LONDON 1912.7–9.1, from Cervetri.   *JHS.* 41 pl. 8, iii, 2.   Two oriental warriors, one of them riding a donkey.

2 (2). BRUSSELS A 719.   *CV.* d pl. 5, 1.   Komos (two men).

3 (3). BRUSSELS A 720.   *CV.* d pl. 5, 2.   Nike and man.

4 (4). LOUVRE G 243, from Nola.   Perrot 9 pl. 17.   Acontist and flute-player.

5 (5). LOUVRE G 439, from Nola.   Pottier pl. 144.   Odysseus and Circe.

6. BASLE MARKET (M.M.).   Youth with sword pursuing a woman (Theseus and Aithra?).

7 (6). ROME, Antiquarium Forense, fr., from Rome.   (Maenad).

See also p. 656 no. 29.

THE GROUP OF BERLIN 2415

Somewhat recalls the Deepdene Painter (p. 498).

OINOCHOAI

(nos. 1–2, shape 3, choes)

1. BERLIN 2415, from Capua. *Annali* 1880 pl. K; FR. pl. 162, 3, and iii, 269; Schuchhardt and Technau 211; Blümel *Gr. Bildhauer an der Arbeit* 41; *Mus. Helv.* 7, 49, below; Zschietzschmann *H.R.* pl. 188, 2; Greifenhagen *A.K.* pl. 46. Athena modelling a horse in clay. See p. 1669.

2. LONDON E 539, from Capua. Heydemann *Hum. Vb.* pl. 1, 1, whence *Jb.* 57, 113; van Hoorn *Choes* fig. 145; Brommer *Satyrspiele²* 36. Satyr as Herakles attacking the serpent of the Hesperides. See p. 1669.

(no. 3, shape 4)

3. NEW YORK 08.258.25, from Sicily. *RM.* 12, 318, whence *R.E.G.* 1907, 408–9 and Rumpf *Rel.* fig. 144; *Bull. Metr.* 4, 104 fig. 7; McClees 5 fig. 3; Richter and Hall pl. 88, 84 and pl. 177, 84; *Jb.* 52, 45. Man at a statue of Athena.

THE PAINTER OF THE OXFORD SIREN-ASKOS

The two askoi have already been compared by Lullies in *CV.* Munich, ii, 31.

ASKOI

1 (1). MUNICH S.L. 478. A, *Sg Vogell* pl. 3, 17; Sieveking *BTV.* 63 and title-page; *CV.* pl. 101, 1 and pl. 100, 4. A, Eros; B, Eros.

2 (2). OXFORD 1925.71. *CV.* pl. 45, 3. A, siren; B, siren.

THE GROUP OF THE BONN ASKOS

The three are probably by one hand.

ASKOI
(type 2)

1. BONN 90. Zimmermann 117, 1; *CV.* pl. 24, 6. Boar-hunt: A, hunter; B, boar.

2. CAB. MÉD. 853. Caylus 1 pl. 30, 1. Replica of the last.

3. BERLIN 2509, from Nola. A, hound; B, fox.

THE GROUP OF AGORA P 5562

ASKOI

1. PRINCETON 55.3245. *Auction xiv Basle* pl. 17, 79. A, lion; B, boar.

2. ATHENS, Agora, P 5562, fr., from Athens. Boar.

The two may be by one hand. Akin to them, the lobster-claw askos in New York (23.160.57) from the Class of the Seven Lobsters (p. 971 no. 6), and the oinochoe Munich 2469, there compared with it.

THE PAINTER OF AGORA P 14384

PYXIS

(type A)

1. LUGANO, Schoen, 65. Lullies *SGK*. pl. 24, 65, and pl. 25. Women (with musical instruments).

LID

2. ATHENS, Agora, P 14384, fr., from Athens. (Woman with box).

THE PAINTER OF OXFORD 1920

CV. Oxford 30. *ARV.*[1] 459.

SQUAT LEKYTHOI

1 (1). OXFORD 1920.55. *CV*. pl. 40, 1–2. Two maenads.
2 (2). BERLIN 2470, from Attica. Two women (one playing kottabos, the other testing a flute).

Compare the

SQUAT LEKYTHOI

LONDON E 647, from Nola. Panofka *Blacas* pl. 11, 2; Overbeck *Gall.* pl. 7, 1. Peleus and Thetis.

NEW YORK 06.1129. Side, *N.Y. Shapes* 25, 4 = Richter and Milne fig. 99. Woman seated with lyre.

THE COW-HEAD GROUP

The two vases are of exactly the same model, and the pictures are close to one another in style, may be by one hand.

RHYTA

(cow's head)

1. PARIS, Petit Palais, 371, from Vulci. *CV*. pl. 29, 7–9; Hoffmann *A.R.R.* pl. 13, 4. Nike and three women, all running.
2. NEW YORK 06.1021.203, from Vulci. Part, Sambon *Canessa* pl. 17, 252; part, *Bull. Metr.* 1, 79 fig. 6; part, Richter *Craft* 30; part, Richter and Milne fig. 180; part, Richter *H.* 229, h; Hoffmann *A.R.R.* pl. 13, 1–2. Woman running to youth; youth and woman.

THE PAINTER OF LONDON E 356

ARV.[1] 593.

Recalls the Penthesilea Painter.

PELIKAI
(small; with framed pictures)

1 (1). LONDON E 356, from Nola. A, old man seated, and woman; B, youth.

2. MANCHESTER, Univ., iii.1.34. *Mem. Manch.* 87 pl. 5, a–b. A, youth and woman; B, youth.

3 (2). VIENNA 692. *CV.* pl. 77, 1–2. A, two women; B, woman.

4 (3). VIENNA 2188. *CV.* pl. 77, 3–4. A, two women; B, youth running.

5. VILLA GIULIA, from Cervetri. A, two women (one of them with her himation over the back of her head); B, woman.

6 (4). CAPUA inv. 209, from Capua. A, woman seated and woman; B, woman running with basket.

7 (5). PERUGIA 125. A, athlete and youth; B, youth at pillar.

8. BRUSSELS A 3097. *CV.* d pl. 17, 2. A, youth and boy; B, youth.

9. ALTENBURG 285, from Nola. A, Bielefeld *G.E.T.A.* pl. 7, 1; *CV.* pl. 51, 1–2 and pl. 47, 6; R.I. ix. 88. A, youth with lyre, and boy; B, youth running with flute-case.

Probably also the

PELIKE
(small; with framed pictures)

NAPLES (3200?). A, two women; B, woman holding a piece of meat. Ess-border below.

THE GROUP OF NAPLES 3208

Two small vases, as Martin Robertson has seen, go together; they are connected by shape and patterns with the Painter of London E 356.

PELIKAI
(small; with framed pictures)

1. NAPLES 3208, from Ruvo. A, ph. So. 11009, iv. 3. A, youth and boy; B, the like.

2. EDINBURGH, Giles Robertson. A, youth and boy; B, the like.

THE GROUP OF PHILADELPHIA 2272

VA. 74.

OINOCHOAI

(shape 8 B, mugs)

1. NEW YORK 41.162.154. *CV.* Gallatin pl. 60, 6. Jumper.
2. PHILADELPHIA 2272. Athlete bending.
3. LONDON E 569. Youth (hunter) throwing stone.
4. NAPLES inv. 85981, from Cumae. Athlete at altar.
5. VATICAN. Boy seated.
6. NICOSIA C 429, from Marion. Satyr dancing up towards a drinking-horn on the ground.
7. NAPLES RC 154, from Cumae. *ML.* 22 pl. 91, 2. Satyr.
8. BASLE MARKET (M.M.). Satyr (moving to right, bending).
9. BOWDOIN 30.2. Satyr (in himation) reclining.
10. HAVERFORD. Comfort no. 26. Herm.

THE GROUP OF ATHENS 10452

These might be by one hand.

OINOCHOE

(shape 8 A, mug)

1. ATHENS 10452, from the Cabeirion of Thebes. Wolters and Bruns pl. 40, 1 and pl. 22, 3. Boy seated with lyre, and dog.

FRAGMENT

(oinochoe of the same shape?)

2. ATHENS, Agora, P 12960, fr., from Athens. Eros flying with lyre.

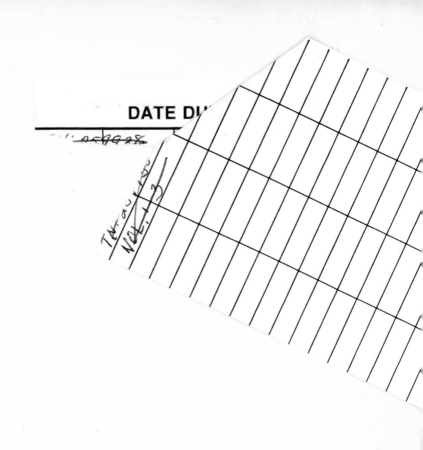

DATE DUE